ECONOMIC
CONCENTRATION

ECONOMIC CONCENTRATION

STRUCTURE, BEHAVIOR AND PUBLIC POLICY

JOHN M. BLAIR

HARCOURT BRACE JOVANOVICH, INC.
New York   Chicago   San Francisco   Atlanta

Cover symbol based on a paper sculpture by Martha Herman

ISBN: 0–15–518781–3

Library of Congress Catalog Card Number: 79–187702

Printed in the United States of America

Copyrights and Acknowledgments

Excerpts from *Merger Movements in American Industry*, by Ralph L. Nelson.
Copyright © 1954 by the National Bureau of Economic Research.
Reprinted by permission of National Bureau of Economic Research.

Excerpts from *Management and Machiavelli*, by Antony Jay.
Copyright © 1970 by Holt, Rinehart and Winston, and Hodder and Stoughton Limited.
Reprinted by permission of the publishers.

Excerpts from *Guidelines: Informal Controls and the Marketplace*,
edited by George P. Schultz and Robert Z. Aliber.
© 1966 by University of Chicago Press.
Reprinted by permission of the publisher.

Excerpts from *Public Policies Toward Business*, by Clair Wilcox.
Reprinted from Wilcox, *Public Policies Toward Business* (Homewood, Illinois:
Richard D. Irwin, Inc.) © 1966.

PREFACE

The action by President Nixon in freezing prices and wages on August 15, 1971, and subsequently establishing an elaborate system of price and wage controls was merely the logical response by government to the problems created by the growth in size and relative importance of the country's largest corporations. Had the economy been composed exclusively of small and medium-size enterprises, the need for the imposition of such controls when more than a quarter of the nation's plant capacity lay idle would never have arisen. It was the power of the large corporations to raise prices in the face of low and falling demand that set the stage for direct governmental intervention in the price-making process. And it was the repeated exercise of that power, whether triggered by an increase in labor (or other) costs or by an effort to widen profit margins, that forced the hand of a reluctant President.

That the continuing rise in economic concentration would make the taking of some such action all but inevitable has long been recognized. Over twenty years ago the House Judiciary Committee, in a report accompanying a bill to strengthen the antitrust laws, said: "The concentration of great economic power in a few corporations necessarily leads to the formation of large nation-wide labor unions. The development of the two necessarily leads to big bureaus in the government to deal with them." [1]

But by and large the executive branch of government has failed to heed the warnings. Although Congress has enacted every strengthening antitrust measure proposed by the executive branch, and although the Supreme Court has handed down favorable antitrust decisions of far-reaching import, actual enforcement has been by fits and starts. As Ben Lewis put it, "It is increasingly evident as we inch tediously and at great expense from one elaborate definitive antitrust case to the next that the headway we are making is pitiful. Sometimes antitrust holds the line, sometimes it even gains a yard; but most of the time it plays in the shadow of its own goal posts." [2] Since the early 1950's the law against existing monopolies has been permitted to lapse into a state of innocuous desuetude. The same is true of the law against sophisticated conspiracies and parallel pricing systems. The law against mergers, while effective against horizontal and vertical acquisitions, was virtually unused against the great wave of conglomerate mergers during the 1960's.

It is little wonder, then, that the 200 largest manufacturing corporations increased their share of manufacturing assets between 1947 and 1968 from 47.1 percent to 60.4 percent and their share of value added by manufacturing between 1947 and 1967 from 30 percent to 41 percent. Nor should it be surprising that of the individual industries for which data are available, the 4 largest companies increased their share of the industry's output in 95, as compared to only 75 in which they suffered a decline.

In view of the increasing importance of the concentrated sector, knowledge of

---

[1] 81st Cong., 1st Sess., House Judiciary Committee, Report to accompany H. R. 2734 (House Report No. 1191), 1949, p. 13.
[2] *Hearings on Administered Prices*, Pt. 9, p. 4716.

v

its structure and behavior is indispensable to an understanding of the economy. But such an understanding is not to be gained from any of the existing theoretical models. The line of reasoning which sees greater size as the inevitable consequence of economies of scale is an explanation for concentration in only a small number of industries. The price behavior expected under classical and neoclassical theory accords nicely with actual behavior where its underlying assumptions (many sellers, ready ease of entry, low concentration) obtain, but not at all where they do not. Even imperfect competition theory, which offered a plausible explanation for the price rigidity of concentrated industries during the Great Depression, provides no explanation for the more recent tendency of their prices to move upward during periods of falling demand. The problem is thus not the incorrectness of existing theory, but its failure to explain either the changes actually occurring in industrial structures or the type of price behavior actually manifested by large concerns. The growth in the size and complexity of the industrial structure and the emergence of new behavior patterns have simply outstripped the body of microeconomic theory. And this in turn has been responsible for the shortcomings of fiscal and monetary policies that have assumed the behavior expected of competitive industries.

Phenomena that cannot be explained by received wisdom are all too often ignored or forced into the mold of existing doctrine. In this way theories can continue to be used as guides for policy and action long after their lack of validity has been clearly established. As the history of medicine attests, a wrong theory can cause far more harm than no theory at all. As an example of "therapeutic mayhem" resulting from the following of an incorrect theory, William B. Bean, professor of internal medicine at Iowa State University, cited the "Brunonian" theory widely followed by physicians up to this century: "It held that life depended on perpetual stimulation, all diseases came from too much or too little; it was sthenic or asthenic (that is, strong or weak). Nothing simpler: purge, vomit and bleed one, and soak the other in alcohol; no other diagnosis or therapy was required. The up-to-date physician . . . was able to add to the physician's havoc, to the disease's handicap, in a dance macabre which is said to have killed more persons than the French Revolution and the Napoleonic Wars taken together." [3]

In the field of economics the recessions of 1957–58 and 1969–70 were engineered by the federal government in the mistaken belief that inflation could be arrested by restrictive fiscal and monetary policies. And, as Keynes emphasized, an incalculable economic loss during the Great Depression resulted from the dedicated adherence by governments everywhere to Say's Law.

Given theoretical models which no longer explain reality, the only recourse is to the empirical approach—the laborious process of developing, organizing, classifying, tabulating, and analyzing countless "bits and pieces" of empirical data, out of which generalizations can hopefully be drawn that may serve in turn as building blocks for a new theory. With respect to economic concentration, the bits and pieces consist of bodies of data and studies of the levels and trend of concentration, its causes, the conduct of business firms, the economic effects on behavior and performance, and the alternative public policy approaches. Part 1 of this book examines the levels and trends of concentration in each of its dimensions—market, vertical, conglomerate, and aggregate. The underlying causes of concentration (and of deconcentration) are the subject of Parts 2 and 3. The

---

[3] 87th Cong., 1st Sess., Senate Subcommittee on Antitrust and Monopoly, *Hearings on S. 1552*, Pt. 1, 1961, p. 269.

manner in which competition may be adversely affected by the competitive conduct of large concerns is examined in both Parts 1 and 3. The economic effects of concentration on price, margins, profits, and resource use are the subject of Part 4. And Part 5 is concerned with the alternative public policies for dealing with concentration—the competitive approach, voluntary suasion, price regulation, and nationalization.[4] Out of a myriad of separate empirical findings relating to each of these aspects of the concentration problem, the effort has been to construct an integrated conceptual whole, in which the relationship of each of the parts to each other and to the whole is clearly delineated.

The principal, though by no means the only, source of empirical material used in examining the various aspects of concentration consists of the 44 volumes of hearings and reports in Economic Concentration and Administered Prices of the Subcommittee on Antitrust and Monopoly of the Judiciary Committee of the U.S. Senate (also referred to for purposes of convenience as the Senate Antitrust Subcommittee).[5] The Hearings on Concentration are made up largely of contributions by economists in specific areas on which they have expert knowledge.[6] This invaluable body of knowledge relating to structural aspects was supplemented by statistical reports on concentration prepared for the Subcommittee by the Bureau of the Census, based on the Census of Manufactures.[7] In the interest of lessening repetition, the term "concentration ratio" will be used here, unless otherwise indicated, to refer to the share of an industry's output accounted for by its 4 largest companies.

With respect to the behavioral aspects, the Hearings on Administered Prices relating to the steel, automobile, bread, and drug industries provided a unique insight into such issues as the nature of pricing standards, price leadership and price followership, cost-price structures, competitive tactics, and the role and costs of nonprice competition. This information was supplemented by special tabulations prepared for the Subcommittee by a number of government agencies, particularly by the Federal Trade Commission on profit rates and the Bureau of Labor Statistics on prices.

While based in good part on the material contained in the hearings and reports, this book, it should be emphasized, does not purport to be a summary of the Subcommittee's investigations. The form of organization, interrelationships of each of the parts, specific findings, and general conclusions are its own. Nonetheless, the work should convey a broad impression of the studies presented by academic economists, of the findings which emerge from Census concentration data, and of the many points developed in the course of the questioning of corporate officials.

[4] For a further brief description of their contents, see the introductions which precede each of the five parts.
[5] Also for purposes of convenience the hearings are referred to throughout the book as the "Hearings on Economic Concentration" and the "Hearings on Administered Prices." Their full citations are given in Appendix 1.
[6] For the volume and page numbers of their testimony, see Appendix 2.
[7] For 1958 and 1963 the Census reports are in two parts, Part 1 consisting of the traditional "Concentration ratios," and Part 2 of a variety of more sophisticated tabulations relating to conglomerate concentration: the relative importance of the largest manufacturing companies in individual industries, the levels of concentration in individual regions, states, and local market areas, etc. Unhappily, neither the Census Bureau nor the Subcommittee has issued (or plans to issue) a report based on the 1967 Census correlative with Part 2 for 1963; thus the latest year for which many of the tabulations used in this work are available is 1963. As a general principle, however, major changes in industrial organization rarely take place in less than a decade.

This work was made possible by the intense personal concern with the monopoly problem of the late Senator Estes Kefauver and his resultant determination to explore in depth the pricing policies and competitive practices of giant corporations. It was also made possible by the patience and understanding of his successor as chairman of the Senate Subcommittee on Antitrust and Monopoly, Senator Philip A. Hart, before whom a procession of economists presented the results of their necessarily technical studies. Indispensable to the hearings, and thus to this volume, were the imaginative and precise contributions of the Subcommittee's economists, E. Wayles Browne, Irene Till Hamilton, and Walter S. Measday. Throughout the hearings and the preparation of the book the research and editorial assistance provided by Emily Zayyani proved to be absolutely invaluable. And Jo Anne Youngblood Lang and Joan Carmichael Cole contributed far more than would be expected from even the best of secretaries.

Everyone interested in the problem of economic concentration is indebted to Gardiner C. Means for his pioneering empirical contributions, which by and large have come to be accepted by most economists only to be ignored in their theoretical models. In the case of this book, an even greater debt is owed to Means for his careful reading of the manuscript and for his many suggestions, all of which were helpful, including the few on which we happen to disagree. Parts of the manuscript were read also by Walter Adams and Alfred E. Kahn, both of whom offered invaluable suggestions. A special debt is owed to two of the other pioneers in Industrial Organization, Philip Sargant Florence of the University of Birmingham (England) and Helmut Arndt of the Free University of Berlin; it was at the latter's *Institut für Konzentrationsforschung* that the actual writing of this work began in the fall of 1966. While the number of works which have been drawn on in the preparation of this book is legion, particularly important to the effort to integrate, where possible, new empirical findings with the existing body of economic theory have been Fritz Machlup's *The Economics of Sellers' Competition* and *The Political Economy of Monopoly,*[8] and Emil Kauder's *A History of Marginal Utility Theory.*[9]

JOHN M. BLAIR
University of South Florida

[8] Johns Hopkins University Press, 1952.
[9] Princeton University Press, 1965.

CONTENTS

PART

2

THE CENTRIFUGAL FORCES   85

PART

3

THE CENTRIPETAL FORCES   255

PART 4

CONCENTRATION AND ECONOMIC BEHAVIOR   403

PART

5

CONCENTRATION AND PUBLIC POLICY   551

ECONOMIC
CONCENTRATION

The Dimensions of Concentration

Since the appearance of Keynes's *General Theory* in 1936 the interest of economists has been centered primarily on macroeconomic issues—the attainment of full employment and rapid economic growth through appropriate policies relating to taxation, government expenditures, the supply of money, interest rates, and the expansion (or contraction) of consumption and capital formation. Up to that time, however, the attention of economists had been focused on what we now refer to as microeconomic issues. A highly developed body of integrated concepts—"classical" and "neoclassical" economic theory—had been developed which had assumed what is generally referred to as a competitive structure of industry. With the passage of time it became increasingly evident that this assumption was irrelevant to much of the industrial economy those industries whose output was concentrated largely in the hands of a few companies. Ignoring this sizable exception to classical theory, the new macroeconomic doctrines have assumed implicitly that industries, generally, would respond to fiscal and monetary policies in the manner expected of competitive industries. The results have been unfortunate; they include an apparent inability to achieve rapid economic growth without a distressingly high rate of inflation (the "Phillips curve" dilemma) and the deliberate creation of unemployment and idle economic resources in a predictably futile effort to arrest the upward movement of prices.

The concentrated sector operates under principles of its own that are not only different from but often the reverse of those applicable to competitive industries. A major purpose of this book will be an empirical exploration of the principles governing the behavior of concentrated industries. Such an exploration should be preceded, however, by an examination of the extent and causes of concentration. This first part of the book will be concerned with the question of extent, the next two parts with causal factors.

The aspect of concentration that has received greatest attention is the horizontal dimension, or "market" concentration—that is, the control of a given industry (or market) by a small number of leading producers who are exclusively, or at least very largely, engaged in that industry. But there are other dimensions of concentration—"vertical," "conglomerate," and "aggregate." Each is of appropriate concern for economic inquiry, since each has its unique effects on market behavior. A true understanding of concentration must therefore embrace the structural and market-behavioral aspects of all four dimensions of concentration.

The term "vertical" has been used commonly to describe a particular type of merger: those in which the acquiring and acquired firms produce different products, but products that are in the same stream of production—that is, the absorption of a supplier by an end-product manufacturer ("backward" vertical) or, conversely, the acquisition of the end-product manufacturer by the supplier ("forward" vertical). There is no reason why the term "vertical integration," as well as being applied to such mergers, cannot be applied to the holding of a share of an industry's output by companies primarily engaged in an earlier or later stage of production. Likewise, the customary usage of the term "conglomerate" has been in relation to a process—i.e., to describe acquisitions that are neither horizontal nor vertical. Again, however, there is no reason why the term cannot also be applied to a type of industry structure in which a share of an industry's output is held by companies primarily engaged in a different and unrelated industry. Finally, there is "aggregate" or "overall" concentration—i.e., the control of much of the industrial economy as a whole by the very largest corporations (e.g., the 200 largest). This dimension of concentration may not be without its own unique effects on market behavior, stemming from "communities of interest" among groups or clusters of the largest firms.

MARKET
CONCENTRATION

The subject of this book, economic concentration, is the obverse of the type of industry structure assumed by classical and neoclassical microeconomic theory (and also by more recent macroeconomic theories) and designated variously as "competitive," "polypolistic," "market determined," "atomistic," and "unconcentrated." The principal structural characteristics of "competitive" or "polypolistic" structures are ready ease of entry, a large number of sellers, and, of most importance, the absence of control over a significant share of the market by any individual seller or small group of sellers.

Market concentration and market behavior

With respect to economic behavior the significance of the "polypolistic" type of industry organization, as contrasted to a concentrated structure, stems from the attitude of mind that sellers have toward their competitors. In Fritz Machlup's words:

> Polypoly is the market position of a seller who is unconcerned about any competitor's reaction to his own actions, ordinarily because he thinks there are so many other sellers in the market, and his own share is relatively so small; that none of the others would feel any effect of what he would do.
>
> *   *   *
>
> . . . polypoly is defined as the market position (or the state of mind) of sellers who know that they have competitors, but, in making up their own minds about changing their selling or production policies, do not ponder over what their competitors' reactions might be. Wherever polypoly exists it will *most likely* be the result of a large number of sellers offering the same or very similar service. For only when the seller can believe that the other sellers will not seriously feel the effects of his actions will he be able to expect that they will not react to them.[1]

In polyopolistic industries the seller's market share is so small that not only is he "too insignificant to affect substantially the business of others," but he can have no "price policy" of his own; raising his price in the face of falling demand cannot even be considered.[2]

Classical theory also recognized the existence of monopoly.

[1] Fritz Machlup, *The Economics of Seller's Competition*, Johns Hopkins Press, 1952, pp. 135, 136. Emphasis in original.
[2] *Ibid.*, p. 138.

Monopoly . . . is defined as the market position of a seller who knows neither any individuals nor any particular groups of other sellers with whom he is in competition.

*   *   *

The monopolist thinks of no other product sold in the market whose price reduction would significantly reduce his sales or whose price increase would significantly increase his sales; nor does he, when he deliberates on the effects of his own price changes, think of any particular sellers to whom he might lose or from whom he might gain any business.[3]

In other words, although their reasons differ, neither the monopolist nor the polypolist is concerned with the reactions of competitors.

But between polypoly on the one hand and the comparatively rare instances of one-company monopoly on the other is a wide compass of industries generally referred to by such terms as "oligopolistic," "imperfectly competitive," "market determining," and "concentrated." Here the critical determinant is control over a substantial share of the market by a small number of producers—usually, a "Big Three," "Big Four," "Big Five," or the like. Their control of the market often stems from difficult conditions of entry—e.g., technology requiring heavy capital outlays, high distribution and advertising costs, governmental restrictions of one kind or another. Fewness of sellers is a frequent but not necessary characteristic, since relatively large numbers of very small firms inhabit the fringes of some of the more concentrated industries. If sellers under both polypoly and monopoly are not concerned with the reactions of competitors, the reverse is true under oligopoly:

The criterion is whether the seller, when he contemplates a decision or action that he might take concerning his selling prices, sales volumes, product qualities, selling efforts, or production capacity is or is not conscious of what his competitors might think or do in reaction.

This rival-consciousness, or self consciousness vis-à-vis competitors, contrasts oligopoly sharply with polypoly and also with monopoly as a type of seller's attitude.

*   *   *

The following circumstances seem essential: the action of the seller must be conspicuous or at least noticeable; its effects upon competitors must be such that they mind; this minding will express itself either in attitudes of disapproval and resentment or in actions affecting the seller in a material way.

*   *   *

The oligopolist usually thinks of certain firms as his rivals; he knows they are watching him or at least will notice his "competitive" actions; he believes he can hurt them or make them angry or cause them to take an action they would not take but for what he has done.[4]

The sensitivity of an oligopolist to his rivals makes him, in Machlup's words, "*very conscious of being in competition* actively or potentially." This being so, he cannot understand how economists can assert that oligopoly involves a *re-*

---

[3] *Ibid.*, pp. 544, 546.
[4] *Ibid.*, pp. 351, 352.

duced degree of competition or that " 'competition is *not so active* among a limited as among an unlimited number.' " [5]

Interest among economists in the effect on market behavior of "competition among the few" dates back to early models of duopoly developed during the last century by Cournot, Bertrand, and Edgeworth. Although serving as important starting points for analysis, these models incorporated assumptions so foreign to actual business behavior as to make them utterly unreal. Through the introduction of more realistic assumptions, better models with greater applicability have been evolved by Joan Robinson and Edward H. Chamberlin, as well as by A. C. Pigou, Roy Harrod, and R. F. Kahn.[6]

The early models had all assumed that in response to his own move, an oligopolist's rivals would make *no countermove*. The need for a more realistic assumption was obvious. As Machlup has observed, "After all, it was somewhat embarrassing for economic theorists to insinuate by implication that in their models the businessmen were dumb, blind, and stubborn, and could never revise their incorrect anticipations about their rival's lack of response." [7] The recognition that oligopolists would indeed react to a move by their rivals and that each oligopolist would be aware of this probability and would act accordingly had important implications for the understanding of market behavior. As Chamberlin has put it:

> If each seeks his maximum profit rationally and intelligently, he will realize that when there are only two or a few sellers his own move has a considerable effect upon his competitors, *and that this makes it idle to suppose that they will accept without retaliation the losses he forces upon them.* Since the result of a cut by anyone is inevitably to decrease his own profits, no one will cut, and although the sellers are independent, the equilibrium result is the same as though there were a monopolistic agreement between them.[8]

The original models had assumed homogeneous products, whereas in the real world products of rival oligopolists are frequently distinguished by trade names, brand names, or other real or imagined differences. What matters, of course, is not product differentiation per se but the importance attached to it by rival oligopolists. Obviously, the greater the protection his products enjoy vis-à-vis those of his rivals, the less an oligopolist has to concern himself with the actions of his rivals—i.e., the greater is his freedom to raise his price or to ignore decreases initiated by others. Conversely, the less his protection, the fewer are the chances that an oligopolist will raise prices unilaterally (or ignore a rival's decrease), and the greater will be his sensitivity to moves and countermoves by others.

In the real world not only are products frequently differentiated but competition in price is often supplemented (or replaced) by the various forms of nonprice competition—competition in quality, service, advertising, and so on. The effect of this economic fact of life is to increase price insensitivity further. In Machlup's words, "The chief significance of nonprice competition in oligopolistic

---

[5] *Ibid.*, p. 353. Emphasis in original. The quotation by Machlup is from John Stuart Mill.
[6] For an incisive analysis of the original duopoly models and the later theoretical developments, see *ibid.*, pp. 368–413.
[7] Machlup, *op. cit.*, p. 404.
[8] Edward H. Chamberlin, *The Theory of Monopolistic Competition,* 5th ed., Harvard University Press, 1946, p. 48. Emphasis added.

positions lies in the fact that variations in quality and selling efforts are commonly used in lieu of variations of price and with a clearly implied message to the competitor that he too should refrain from competing through price." [9]

The analysis can be further complicated by the introduction of variables reflecting differences in costs and demand, implied or express collusion, differences in leadership and followership positions in the industry, and so on. As the number of variables increases, of course, the usual problems of multivariant analysis become more acute: Are usable data available for the different variables, and, if so, how are they to be employed; what weights are to be assigned, implicitly or explicitly; are the variables themselves interdependent, and so on? But more than any other factor it is the difference in the control of the market that gives rise to the theoretical presumption that competition among the few will be distinctly different from competition among the many. In polypolistic industries the fundamental reason why the possible reactions of his competitors are of such little concern to a seller is that his *share of the market is so small that* competitors will be indifferent to his actions. Conversely, in oligopolistic industries, the fact that each oligopolist is very well aware indeed of his rivals' probable reaction to a competitive move stems from the possession by each of a *sufficiently large share of the market* to affect the others adversely.

How do these general principles of oligopolistic behavior apply during the various stages of the business cycle? To answer this question it is necessary to make a distinction between asymmetrical and symmetrical oligopolies—i.e., between those in which one oligopolist is clearly dominant and those in which several have about the same market share. In American industry oligopolies are more frequently asymmetrical than symmetrical.

When demand is below supply (a buyers' market) there is little difference in the price behavior of the two types of oligopoly if what is being considered is a price reduction. For the reasons delineated above, oligopolists in either an asymmetrical or a symmetrical oligopoly will tend to abstain from making price reductions. But if what is being contemplated is a price increase the expectations and reactions will be somewhat different. With no established, recognized, and traditionally followed price leader, each of the major producers in a symmetrical oligopoly should have good reason to fear that any price increase it might make may not be matched by its rivals. In contrast, this type of restraint would be conspicuously lacking in those asymmetrical oligopolies where the leader is the most efficient producer. Operating under the protection of his price "umbrella," the lesser oligopolists will be not only happy to match his increase but fearful that failure to do so will invite retaliation which, because of their higher costs, they cannot meet. Where the established leader is a relatively inefficient, high-cost producer (as is not infrequently the case), the reasons for upward price followership are more obscure. On the surface, it would appear that refusal by a lesser oligopolist to match the leader's increase might be to his advantage, since it would increase his sales and spread his fixed costs over a larger volume, thereby increasing his profit margin. Moreover, it cannot be considered a certainty that the leader would immediately rescind the increase, since by so doing he would forgo the benefits of the higher price on *all* his sales in order to meet the nonconformist's lower price in those particular markets where they both compete. Yet, as is evident from the empirical evidence, a leader's price increases are usually followed by the other oligopolists, even during periods of severely depressed demand

[9] Machlup, *op. cit.,* p. 410.

and even though his higher costs should provide the lesser oligopolists with protection against retaliation. In such cases deductions based on a logical consideration of expectations and reactions of oligopolists operating independently are of only limited value in explaining their behavior.

When demand is in excess of supply (a sellers' market), the leader in an asymmetrical oligopoly will set the price at a level that, in relation to his anticipated volume, will meet the objective of his internal pricing policy.[10] If that price is lower than the price which would maximize his profits in the short run, the result will be what J. Kenneth Galbraith has termed "unliquidated monopoly gains." If his competitors elect to sell at the higher, profit-maximizing price, a "gray market" will develop that will last until the leader raises his price or the pressure of excess demand abates. Since in symmetrical oligopolies there is, by definition, no established leader, the objectives of any internal pricing policy will more readily give way to achieving the profit-maximizing price. In other words, if any of the roughly equal leaders is able to sell at a higher price, the probabilities are that the others will do likewise.

Concentration ratios

The data used in this study to measure the extent of concentration (and also to permit analyses of the causes and effects of concentration) are the so-called Census concentration ratios—the share of the output accounted for by the 4 (or 8) largest firms.[11] Unless otherwise indicated, the term "concentration ratio" will refer to the share of the 4 largest firms. Nonetheless where the 4 leading producers account for as much as half (or possibly even less) of the industry's output they will undoubtedly be acutely conscious of one another's reactions to any competitive moves. And where their share is as small as one-tenth (or perhaps even as large as one-quarter), the chances are that they will be comparatively indifferent to their competitors' reactions. This is the principal theoretical basis for the significance of the concentration ratios.

The concentration ratios are computed in terms of *industries* and *product classes,* which are categories of the Standard Industrial Classification (SIC). This is a system of industrial classification developed over a period of many years by classification experts in government and private industry. It is employed by nearly all government agencies and is the system actually in use in presenting most economic data. Knowledge of its basic characteristic is essential to understanding empirical studies of economic concentration. The system operates in such a manner that the scope of the category becomes progressively narrower with the successive addition of numerical digits. An example of the increasing particularity achieved with the addition of digits is provided by the 3-digit *industry group,* "Meat Products," which is part of one of the 20 two-digit *major industry groups,* "Food and Kindred Products":

[10] See Ch. 18.

[11] Customarily expressed in terms of value of shipments, the ratios are computed for a dozen very large industries in terms of value added by manufacture. This is done to avoid counting the same interplant transfer as both a finished product and a raw material. For industries, but not for the more narrowly defined product classes, ratios are also computed in terms of the 20 and 50 largest companies. Because the use of any lower figure might result in the disclosure of data relating to individual companies, "four" is the lowest number used by the Census Bureau in computing concentration ratios.

Standard Industrial Classification Code	Designation	Name
20	Major Industry Group	Food and Kindred Products
201	Industry Group[12]	Meat Products
2011	Industry[13]	Meat Packing (Slaughtering) Plants
20111	Product Class	Fresh Beef

As will be seen, the term *industry* applies to the 4-digit category (in the example, 2011, "Meat Packing Plants"); there are some 400 four-digit industries. The term *product class* applies to the 5-digit classification (in the example, 20111, "Fresh Beef"); there are slightly more than 1,000 product classes.

In essence, the system seeks to establish spheres of economic activity which are unique and distinguishable from other spheres by a composite of similar characteristics which they have in common. Principal among these characteristics are similarity of processes, products, and materials used, and the bringing together of a group of plants that are economically significant in terms of their number, value added by manufacture, value of shipments, and number of employees. These standards flow very largely from the actual structure into which U.S. businesses have grouped themselves, and it is these characteristics that make the system the best single one for the largest number of uses. In the great majority of instances, an industry comprises producers of similar goods or services. Usually, but not always, the products are made of similar materials and by similar processes, and the producers usually compete with one another.

In the economist's concept the market is made up of buyers and sellers of the same product or substitutable products possessing certain unique characteristics which set them apart from competition by other firms. Substitutability depends not only on physical characteristics but on feasibility—e.g., although for some uses platinum is physically substitutable for steel, the difference in price is so great that they are not, in fact, economically substitutable. How closely do the concentration ratios fit this concept? Since information by which the degree of substitutability, or "cross-elasticity of demand," can be measured is hard to come by, the question is difficult to answer. Where, in terms of the concept of the market, the industry is defined too narrowly—i.e., substitutable products are in different industries—the ratios tend to overstate concentration in the market; for example, because metal cans are classified in one industry and glass containers in another, the concentration ratios for each will overstate the concentration in those markets for which metal cans and glass containers are substitutable.

At the same time, other factors lead the ratios, in some instances, to understate concentration in the market. In general, the production of the individual products comprising an industry is usually more highly concentrated than the industry as a whole. This results from what has been termed "the factor

---

[12] In classifying entire companies according to their principal line of activity, the Census Bureau uses what are known as *enterprise industry categories,* which approximate the 3-digit *industry groups.*

[13] Where shipments of products are aggregated into 4-digit totals, without regard to the industry classification of the plants making such products, the term used is *product group.*

of specialization." Frequently, one large firm will specialize on one or a few products in an industry, and concentration figures for these particular products will tend to be high. At the same time, another large firm may be specializing on other products in the industry, with a similar effect on those products. As a result of this specialization, the degree of concentration will tend to be higher for the individual products than for the industry as a whole.[14]

The effect of the "factor of specialization" can be seen by comparing a number of 4-digit industries with their component 5-digit product classes. The 4 largest producers make 81 percent of a 5-digit product class for which there is absolutely no substitute whatever—salt; yet the concentration ratio for the broader 4-digit industry of which it is a part, "chemical preparations not elsewhere classified," is only 23 percent. The housewife in the supermarket seeking to purchase salad dressing is faced by the fact that 57 percent of the shipments of this 5-digit product class are accounted for by its 4 largest producers; for the broader 4-digit industry "pickles and sauces," of which salad dressing is a part, the 4-company concentration ratio is only 29 percent. The farmer wishing to buy a field tractor is confronted with the reality that 72 percent of the shipments of this product class are made by only 4 companies; for the 4-digit industry "farm machinery and equipment" as a whole the 4 largest companies account for only 44 percent. There is no market for steel, as such, but only markets for its individual products—e.g., structural shapes, tinplate, and rails. In 1958, the 4-company concentration ratio for the 4-digit industry "steelworks and rolling mills" was 53 percent. Yet, according to a study made in 1957 by the American Iron and Steel Institute, the average 4-company concentration ratio for the industry's 39 individual products was 69 percent, while for all but 6 of the products, the 4 largest companies accounted for over 60 percent of the production.[15]

> It is the concentration of the individual product which confronts the
> buyer when he is in the market for steel. The buyer in the market seeks
> a particular steel product or products (with certain specifications as to
> size, quality, etc.). He does not and could not purchase steel as such.
> That the concentration ratio for the industry as a whole is only around
> 55 percent is of little comfort to the contractor needing structural shapes,
> 91.6 percent of which are made by its four largest producers, or to rail-
> roads which have only four producers to turn to for the supplies of each of
> the seven products used principally by their industry.[16]

A further factor causing the national concentration ratios to *understate* concentration in the market is the sale of products primarily in regional or local markets. In any country with a large geographic area, such as the United States, concentration ratios derived for the nation as a whole will frequently understate concentration prevailing in particular geographic markets. This is the case, for example, where the market area is limited inherently by the perishability of the product or by relatively high transportation costs. Thus, for the nation as a whole, the 4-company concentration ratio for bread and other bakery products in 1954 was 20 percent. Yet a special tabulation based on the same data showed that in only three states did the 4 largest companies in the state produce less than 30 percent of the product, while in twenty-three

[14] Federal Trade Commission, *Report on the Concentration of Productive Facilities, 1947,* 1949, pp. 11–12.
[15] *Administered Prices: Report on Steel,* p. 69.
[16] *Ibid.*

Table 1-1

COMPARISON OF AVERAGE MARKET WITH NATIONWIDE CONCENTRATION RATIOS

13 selected industries, 1963

Industry	Average Market Ratio	Nationwide Ratio	Nationwide to Avg. Mkt. Ratio
Set-up paperboard boxes	75%	12%	1.0:6.3
Folding paperboard boxes	58	21	1.0:2.8
Confectionary products	38	15	1.0:2.6
Bread	57	23	1.0:2.5
Cement	73	29	1.0:2.5
Prepared meats	33	16	1.0:2.1
Gray iron castings	57	28	1.0:2.0
Dressed poultry	25	14	1.0:1.8
Ice cream	62	37	1.0:1.7
Corrugated shipping containers	31	20	1.0:1.6
Prepared animal feed	33	22	1.0:1.5
Petroleum products	51	34	1.0:1.5
Fresh meats	40	31	1.0:1.3

Source: *Hearings on Economic Concentration,* Pt. 8, pp. 5384–92 (Average market ratios by Frank J. Kottke)

their proportion was over 50 percent. And in the actual individual market areas represented by large cities the level of concentration tended to be even higher. For a number of industries whose products are conspicuously limited to market areas smaller than the nation as a whole the Census Bureau has computed 4-company concentration ratios in terms of geographic regions and states.[17] In the case of a few industries that are "oriented toward local more than state markets" ratios were also derived for large metropolitan areas. These geographic ratios, it should be emphasized, necessarily were compiled on the basis of the production and not the consumption in the area. That is to say, they show the share of the total value of shipments produced by all plants within a given region, state, or metropolitan area accounted for by those plants that are owned by the 4 companies producing the largest value of shipments within the specified area. For a number of these industries Frank J. Kottke has derived average "market area" concentration ratios. This involved identifying the market area—region, state, or metropolitan area—most appropriate to the way in which the particular industry's products are marketed; computing for such areas weighted average concentration ratios; and, for his purposes, transforming the ratios from an "industry" to a "product" basis.[18] The results of Kottke's computations on an industry basis (rounded here to 2 decimal places) are shown in Table 1-1 for 13 industries. For more than half of the 13 industries Kottke's average market ratios are more than twice the nationwide ratio, and in all but one industry they are at least one and a half times the national figure.

[17] *Concentration Ratios in Manufacturing Industry, 1958,* Pt. 2, Table 36; *Concentration Ratios in Manufacturing Industry, 1963,* Pt. 2, Tables 25, 26.
[18] *Hearings on Economic Concentration,* Pt. 8, Frank J. Kottke, "Estimation of the Weighted Average Market Share of the Leading Four Firms in Markets Important to the Largest Companies in Each Industry Category, Where Any of These Markets Were Regional, 1954, 1958, 1963," pp. 5384–92.

On the other hand again, concentration in the market tends to be overstated because the concentration ratios, based on the Census of Manufactures, relate only to U.S. production. What is sold in domestic markets also includes imports, which in some industries are of considerable importance. The overstatement resulting from the exclusion of imports is reduced, however, to whatever extent the imports are produced in overseas factories owned by the largest domestic companies.

The importance of concentrated industries

There is of course no level of concentration clearly demarking where polypoly ends and oligopoly begins. Moreover, there appears to be a middle area that can be either oligopolistic or polypolistic, depending on the circumstances. After combining the 4-digit industries into what they regarded as more meaningful groups, Carl Kaysen and Donald F. Turner classified the resulting groups into 3 categories according to the share held by the 8 largest companies: a concentrated category, in which the share of the 8 largest was 50 percent or more; an unconcentrated category, in which their share was less than 33 percent; and a middle category, in which the 8-company share was between 33 percent and 49 percent.[19]

In the present study the basis for differentiation is the share held by the 4, rather than the 8, largest companies. This was dictated partly by the fact that 4 is the smallest number for which Census concentration ratios are computed and partly by the happy coincidence that the "4 largest" probably comes closer than any other single figure to representing what economists usually have in mind when they think of oligopoly. No effort has been made to consolidate the 4-digit Census industries into broader groups, since it is by no means clear that for the purpose involved the engineering and economic data and value judgments applied to them would on balance be any better than those underlying the Standard Industrial Classification. As has been noted, it is recognized that concentration tends to be overstated where some substitutable *products* (e.g., beet sugar and cane sugar) are in separate industries, and that concentration tends to be understated where nonsubstitutable products are in the same industry (e.g., salt in chemicals n.e.c.[20]). It is also recognized that *facilities* used in turning out products of one industry are sometimes capable of producing the goods of another. The existence of substitutable facilities currently engaged in another industry would no doubt act as something of a restraint on an industry's pricing policies, and so, perhaps to a somewhat lesser extent, would the possible entrance of any newcomer. But this is hardly a sufficient reason to combine in one category *products* that are nonsubstitutable and are being sold in different and discrete markets.

Like the Kaysen-Turner analysis, the present study employs 3 categories: industries in which the 4 largest firms account for 50 percent or more of the

[19] Carl Kaysen and Donald F. Turner, *Antitrust Policy—an Economic and Legal Analysis,* Harvard University Press, 1959, pp. 295-97. The 400-odd 4-digit industries were combined into 191 broader groups on the basis not only of cross-elasticity of demand (i.e., where the products of 2 or more industries "appear to be close substitutes for the consumer") but also on the basis of cross-elasticity of supply (i.e., "where there is close supply substitution").

[20] Not elsewhere classified.

output (referred to here as the "concentrated" industries), those in which their share is less than 25 percent (the "unconcentrated" industries), and those with 4-company ratios ranging from 25 to 49 percent (the "moderately concentrated" industries). This same trichotomy will be used throughout this work.

In 1963 the value of shipments of all manufacturing industries amounted to $415.7 billion. As can be seen from Figure 1-1 this total was about equally divided among concentrated, moderately concentrated, and unconcentrated industries. Concentrated industries accounted for precisely one-third of the total; the *average* share held by the 4 largest producers in this category was 66 percent. Moderately concentrated industries were responsible for 34.4 percent of the total; the average share held by the 4 largest was 36 percent. And unconcentrated industries made up 32.3 percent of the total; in this category the average share held by the 4 largest was 17 percent.

The third dimension of Figure 1-1 shows the importance of the various industry groups within each of the 3 categories.[21] It should be noted that the same major industry group (e.g., foods) may appear more than once on the chart because the basis of its composition was the 443 individual Census industries. Concentrated food industries, such as biscuits and crackers, are reflected in the 50 percent-and-over category; unconcentrated food industries, such as confectionary products, in the under 25 percent category.

Industries in only 4 of the 20 major industry groups—transportation equipment, primary metals, chemicals, and electrical machinery—accounted for more than 70 percent of the shipments of all concentrated industries. Indeed, about one-third consists of transportation equipment alone, while an additional one-sixth is made up of primary metals. In other words, of the total value of shipments of all industries with concentration ratios in excess of 50 percent, nearly half is composed of industries in just these 2 groups. By comparison, a greater number of industry groups are represented as principal contributors in the other 2 categories. Thus it takes 7 industry groups in the unconcentrated category and 6 in the moderately concentrated category to reach an aggregate output of $100 billion.

How does this distribution compare with the results of the Kaysen-Turner study? The percentage arrived at by Kaysen and Turner for the unconcentrated category is almost identical to that shown here—33.4 percent as opposed to 32.3 percent. Apparently such industry groups as apparel, lumber, and fabricated metal products are so unconcentrated that it makes little difference what standards are used or what industry classification is employed. The effect of combining industries into broader categories, however, is apparent from the somewhat lower proportion shown by Kaysen and Turner for the concentrated category (25.3 percent as opposed to 33.3 percent) and the higher share shown for the middle, or moderately concentrated, category (41.3 percent as opposed to 31.4 percent).

Although most of the sources of over- and understatement in the concentration ratios cannot be quantified, the application of Kottke's market area ratios alone would move 7 industries into the concentrated category—5 from the moderately concentrated and 2 from the unconcentrated category. One of the

---

[21] To simplify graphic exposition, no attempt has been made to show on the chart the segments accounted for by each of the 20 major industry groups; only the groups of greatest importance are shown. For the figures for each industry group in each category, see *Hearings on Economic Concentration*, Pt. 6, pp. 3373 *et seq.*

Figure 1-1

TOTAL MANUFACTURING
DISTRIBUTION OF TOTAL VALUE OF SHIPMENTS
BY CONCENTRATION RATIOS, 1963

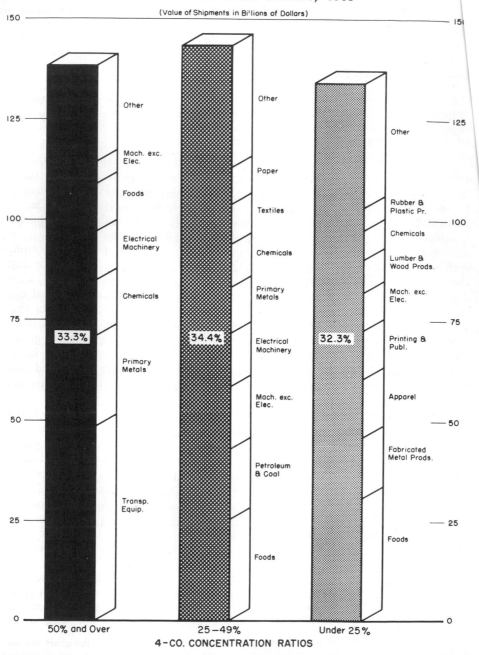

(Value of Shipments in Billions of Dollars)

Source: Bureau of the Census, Department of Commerce, *1963 Census of Manufactures*, 1966, Vol I, Table 2

THE IMPORTANCE OF CONCENTRATED INDUSTRIES

Table 1-2

DISTRIBUTION BY INDUSTRY CONCENTRATION RATIO
OF MANUFACTURING OUTPUT, 1963

Category	Based on National Ratios	Adjusted for Selected Market Area Ratios
Concentrated (50% and over)	33.3%	39.6%
Moderately concentrated (25–49%)	34.4	32.1
Unconcentrated (under 25%)	32.3	28.3
Total	100.0	100.0

Source: Computed from Bureau of the Census, Department of Commerce, *1963 Census of Manufactures*, 1966; *Hearings on Economic Concentration*, Pt. 8, pp. 5384–92

former is petroleum refining, which, in terms of manufacturing activity alone, is the nation's third largest industry. The effect of shifting these industries would be to raise the share accounted for by the concentrated one-third to nearly 40 percent.[22] At the same time 5 additional industries would be shifted from the unconcentrated to the moderately concentrated category.[23] (The last of Kottke's 13 industries would remain in the moderately concentrated category.) The combined effect of the loss of 5 industries to the concentrated category and the gain of an equal number (with lesser output) from the unconcentrated category would be to lower the proportion held by the moderately concentrated category from 34.4 percent to 32.1 percent and the loss of 7 industries (all but 2 to the moderately concentrated category) would lower the unconcentrated category's share from 32.3 percent to 28.3 percent. The effect of the changes is summarized in Table 1-2.

How accurately do these figures reflect control of the *market?* On the one hand, control is understated by the breadth of many Census industry definitions and by the *additional* industries whose products are marketed on a regional or local-market-area basis. On the other hand, control is overstated because of product substitutability and the exclusion of imports. After examining the various sources of over- and understatement in the national ratios, Joe S. Bain expressed the opinion that, on balance, the figures tend to understate concentration in the market: "There is . . . some net average tendency for Census industry concentration measures to understate the degree of seller concentration within the numerous theoretical industries into which existing enterprises should be grouped. We are not in a position to estimate in precise quantitative fashion the average degree of understatement which is involved. It is probably significant but moderate."[24]

[22] The industries shifted and their value of shipments (in millions of dollars) would be petroleum refining ($16,496), bread ($4,506), gray iron castings ($1,984), cement ($1,176), folding paperboard boxes ($1,081), ice cream ($1,076), and set-up paperboard boxes ($226). To be comparable with the data used in making the three-way distribution, these figures are on an industry basis.

[23] Prepared animal feeds ($3,880), dressed poultry ($2,241), corrugated shipping containers ($2,166), confectionary products ($1,934), and prepared meats ($563).

[24] Joe S. Bain, *Industrial Organization*, Wiley, 1959, p. 119.

Concentration within industry groups

While showing the contributions by leading industry groups to the concentrated, moderately concentrated, and unconcentrated categories, Figure 1-1 does not reveal the importance of these 3 categories *within* the various industry groups. This type of distribution is presented in Figure 1-2, which shows for each of the 20 major industry groups the proportions of its shipments made by industries with concentration ratios of 50 percent and over, 25 percent to 49 percent, and under 25 percent. Once again the existence of a fairly well-defined 3-way distribution is apparent. At the top are 3 groups—tobacco products, transportation equipment, and primary metals—in each of which more than three-fifths of the value of shipments is accounted for by concentrated industries. Immediately below are 3 other groups—instruments, chemicals, and electrical machinery—in which concentrated industries make up more than two-fifths of the shipments. Moreover, with the exception of chemicals, the share accounted for by unconcentrated industries in each of these 6 groups is less than 20 percent.[25] At the opposite extreme are 6 unconcentrated groups, shown in the lower part of Figure 1-2—lumber and wood products, furniture and fixtures, leather, printing and publishing, apparel, and fabricated metal products. With the exception of leather, more than three-fifths of the shipments in each group are made by unconcentrated industries; also, with the exception of fabricated metal products, concentrated industries are of negligible importance, making up fewer than 10 percent of the shipments.[26] Between these two extremes are the remaining groups, consisting of rubber and plastic products; stone, clay, and glass; nonelectrical machinery; foods; paper; and textiles. The share of their shipments made by concentrated industries ranges from 35 percent (rubber and plastics; stone, clay, and glass) down to 14 percent (paper and textiles). Obviously, these groups have little in common except that they are neither clearly concentrated nor clearly unconcentrated.

In the above distribution the individual industries are, in effect, "weighted" by the value of their shipments. Such a procedure is appropriate in determining the relative importance of varying levels of concentration in major industry groups as well as in the industrial economy as a whole. At the same time, the results may be influenced strongly by just a few very large industries. This raises the question of whether the distribution of industries among the 3 concentration categories would be altered materially if it were made on an "unweighted" basis—i.e., in terms of numbers of industries. The answer is to be found in Table 1-3, which distributes the 416 industries and the 1,014 product classes in categories similar to those used above.[27]

---

[25] Among these 6 are the 4 groups that appear prominently in the first bar of Figure 1-1—transportation equipment, primary metals, chemicals, and electrical machinery. Though highly concentrated, tobacco products and instruments are of less importance in terms of value of shipments.

[26] In addition, 2 other groups appear near the bottom of the chart—miscellaneous manufacturing and petroleum and coal products. Little significance can be attached to the distribution for the former because of its heterogeneous nature. In petroleum products control over the market derives principally from the exclusion of imports.

[27] There are two slight differences, both occasioned by the fact that the summary tabulations of concentration ratios prepared by the Census Bureau are in terms of intervals of 10 percentage points. Thus, as compared to the range of 25% to 49% used earlier, the interval employed here for "moderately concentrated" industries is 20% to 49%, and as compared to under 25%, the interval for "unconcentrated industries" is under 20%.

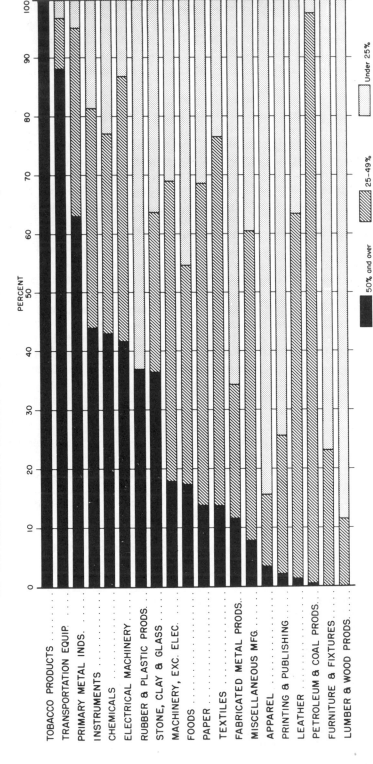

Figure 1-2
DISTRIBUTION OF VALUE OF SHIPMENTS
BY CONCENTRATION RATIOS OF COMPONENT INDUSTRIES, 1963

PERCENT

TOBACCO PRODUCTS
TRANSPORTATION EQUIP.
PRIMARY METAL INDS.
INSTRUMENTS
CHEMICALS
ELECTRICAL MACHINERY
RUBBER & PLASTIC PRODS.
STONE, CLAY & GLASS
MACHINERY, EXC. ELEC.
FOODS
PAPER
TEXTILES
FABRICATED METAL PRODS.
MISCELLANEOUS MFG.
APPAREL
PRINTING & PUBLISHING
LEATHER
PETROLEUM & COAL PRODS.
FURNITURE & FIXTURES
LUMBER & WOOD PRODS.

50% and over   25-49%   Under 25%

Source: Computed from Bureau of the Census, Department of Commerce, 1963 Census of Manufactures, 1966

MARKET CONCENTRATION

Table 1-3

NUMBER OF INDUSTRIES AND PRODUCT CLASSES DISTRIBUTED BY MAJOR INDUSTRY GROUPS AND CONCENTRATION RATIOS, 1958

SIC Code	Major Industry Group	50% and over				20% to 49%				Under 20%				Total			
		Industry		Product Class		Industry		Product Class		Industry		Product Class		Industry		Product Class	
		No.	%	No.	%	No.	%	No.	%	No.	%	No.	%	No.	%	No.	%
20	Food and kindred products	16	12	37	10	20	10	73	15	6	6	7	5	42	9	117	11
28	Chemicals and allied products	23	17	44	12	16	8	37	7	2	2	0	0	41	9	81	8
33	Primary metal products	8	6	35	9	10	5	21	4	1	1	3	2	19	4	59	6
35	Nonelectrical machinery	13	9	42	11	19	9	59	12	9	9	9	6	41	9	110	11
36	Electrical machinery	10	7	53	14	10	5	25	5	1	1	4	3	21	5	82	8
37	Transportation equipment	8	6	22	6	5	2	9	2	1	1	4	3	14	3	35	3
	Total (6 groups)	78	57	233	62	80	39	224	45	20	20	27	19	178	39	484	47
	All others	59	43	137	38	126	61	276	55	80	80	117	81	265	61	530	53
	Total	137	100	370	100	206	100	500	100	100	100	144	100	443	100	1014	100

Source: Concentration Ratios in Manufacturing Industry, 1958, Pt. 1, Tables 2, 4

17

The concentrated industries, it will be recalled, accounted for 33.3 percent of the value of shipments of all manufacturing output. In terms of numbers the proportions are remarkably similar—30.9 percent for industries and 36.5 percent for product classes. In other words, if an industry or product class were picked at random, the chances are about one in three that it would be concentrated. The percentages for the moderately concentrated category, in terms of numbers, are 46.5 percent for industries and 49.3 percent for product classes. These figures are considerably higher than the share held by this category in terms of value of shipments (34.4 percent); part of this difference is due to the use here of a slightly larger class interval. The greatest difference is in the somewhat smaller interval for the unconcentrated category. Such industries accounted for 32.3 percent of all manufacturing shipments; the proportions in terms of numbers were noticeably lower—22.6 percent for industries and 14.2 percent for product classes.

As was also true of the distribution in terms of value, there is here a definite clustering of the concentrated fields in just half a dozen industry groups— foods, chemicals, primary metals, machinery, electrical machinery, and transportation equipment. Industries in these groups made up 57 percent of the number of all highly concentrated industries, while the comparable figure for product classes is 62 percent. Part of this difference, however, arises from the use of a somewhat larger interval for the middle category and a correspondingly smaller interval for the lowest category. When this is taken into account, the shares, whether on a weighted or unweighted basis, are remarkably similar.

Turnover and mobility

A related question concerns the rates of turnover and mobility of the largest companies. Turnover refers to the rate of entry into and exit from the ranks of the largest companies; mobility to the rate of change of position within the ranks of the largest. High rates suggest a condition of ferment—a vigorous striving to break into the largest-size group and a milling around within it. Low rates suggest a distinct cleavage between the top corporations and the remainder of the economy as well as a state of comparative stratification. Indeed, some economists have attached to turnover a special significance of its own—apart from, and indeed more important than, concentration itself. It has remained for present-day economists to express this point of view. Thus Michael Gort has written, "In judging the intensity of competition in an industry, the ability of leading firms to maintain their relative position in the market is probably more significant than the extent of concentration at a single point in time." [28]

Turnover and mobility are of some economic interest, but they are of distinctly secondary importance. The theoretical basis underlying the concern of economists with the problem of oligopoly makes no distinction as to whether the control by the few is in the hands of "new" or "old" oligopolists. By definition, each oligopolist's share of the industry's output is sufficient for his price and output

---

[28] Michael Gort, "Analysis of Stability and Change in Market Shares," *Journal of Political Economy,* Feb., 1963, pp. 51–63. See also S. Hymer and P. Pashigian, "Turnover of Firms as a Measure of Market Behavior," *Review of Economics and Statistics,* Feb., 1962.

decisions to affect the price and output of the other oligopolists. This applies to the "new" as well as the "old" oligopolist. The former, just as much as the latter, assumes that his rivals will be aware of and immediately match any price reduction on his part, with the result that while his price will be lower, his share of the market will be no greater. It is, of course, possible that through longstanding awareness of one another's behavior, "old" oligopolists might be even less inclined to reduce price than is assumed by theory, but this is at best a marginal factor. Indeed, the failure of an "old" oligopolist, Inland Steel, to follow U.S. Steel's 1962 price advance while a "new" oligopolist, McLouth, did go along raises the question of whether independent price behavior might be more frequent under an "old" than a "new" oligopoly. It is not inconceivable that a long-established producer might be more knowledgeable than a newcomer of the lengths to which an independent policy can be pursued before the industry's leader is moved to retaliate.

In a study of the companies which have been the 100 largest in six time periods, beginning with 1909–19 and ending with 1948–58, Norman R. Collins and Lee E. Preston found that turnover and mobility had been declining. An increasing number of the same firms remained in the largest-size group from period to period, while the relative size positions among the giant firms changed less frequently over time. They concluded that "there is considerable reason to believe that firms now at the top of the industrial pyramid are more likely to remain there than were their predecessors. The evidence of mobility is in accord with a general assumption that large-scale corporations enjoy an increasing amount of entrenchment of position by virtue of their size." [29]

According to Census Bureau data, of the 50 largest companies in 1963, 30 had also been numbered among the 50 largest 20 years earlier. Ten came from companies ranked from 51 to 100 and 12 from those ranked 101 to 200. While some shifting took place within the 200 largest, only 4 of the 50 largest came from the ranks of companies outside the 200 largest. Clearly, the evidence indicates the absence, in Marshall's phrase, of any "broad upward movement from below."

Concentration trends within industry groups

What have been the trends of concentration *within* the major industry groups? Has there been a general tendency for concentration to rise in certain areas and to decline in orders? Perhaps the best way of approaching this question is to examine the changes occurring in large individual industries; in most cases the behavior of the group is simply a reflection of the changes taking place in its major industries. What follows is an examination based on census concentration ratios of individual industries with a value of shipments of over $1 billion whose concentration ratios changed between 1947 and 1967 by 3 percentage points or more. Concentration ratios covering this time span were available for 44 such industries, to which were added 4 for which data have been available since 1954.

Based on the behavior of its large industries the food group was clearly an area of increasing concentration; of its 10 large industries increases outnum-

[29] *Hearings on Economic Concentration,* Pt. 1, p. 63.

bered decreases by 7 to 3.[30] The textile and apparel groups were also areas of generally increasing concentration. Included in the groups were 9 large industries, in all but one of which concentration rose.[31]

Two other groups in which increases predominated are lumber and wood products and stone, clay, and glass. While most of these industries were of relatively small size, there were 2 large industries with significant changes, one an increase and the other a decrease.[32]

In the primary-metal products group there were 2 increases against one decrease, but concentration in the group's largest industry, blast furnaces and steel mills, has moved noticeably downward since 1954. Following a sharp increase between 1947 and 1954, its ratio by 1967 had fallen well below the 1954 level—from 55 percent to 48 percent.[33] Although in transportation equip-

[30] Food and Kindred Products	1947	1954	1958	1963	1967
Increasing					
Prepared feeds for animals and fowls	19%	21%	22%	22%	23%
Bread, cake, and related products	16	20	22	23	26
Confectionary products	17	19	18	15	25
Malt liquors	21	27	28	34	40
Bottled and canned soft drinks	10	10	11	12	13
Flavorings, extracts, and syrups	50	53	55	62	67
Soybean oil mills	44	41	40	50	55
Decreasing					
Meat-packing plants	41	39	34	31	26
Ice cream and frozen desserts	40	36	38	37	33
Distilled liquor	75	64	60	58	54

[31] Textiles; Apparel	1947	1954	1958	1963	1967
Increasing					
Weaving mills, cotton	n.a.[a]	18%	25%	30%	30%
Weaving mills, synthetic	31%	30	34	39	46
Knit outerwear mills	8	6	7	11	15
Men's and boys' suits and coats	9	11	11	14	17
Men's dress shirts and nightwear	19	17	16	22	23
Men's and boys' separate trousers	12	12	9	16	20
Women's and misses' suits and coats	n.a.[a]	3	3	8	12
Women's and children's underwear	6	8	8	11	15
Decreasing					
Knit fabric mills	27	17	18	18	15

[a] Not available.

[32] Lumber, Stone, Clay, and Glass	1947	1954	1958	1963	1967
Increasing					
Logging camps and logging contractors	n.a.[a]	8%	13%	11%	14%
Decreasing					
Glass containers	63%	63	58	55	60

[33] Primary Metals	1947	1954	1958	1963	1967
Increasing					
Gray-iron foundries	16%	26%	24%	28%	27%
Iron and steel forgings	24	27	31	30	30
Decreasing					
Steel foundries	23	21	25	23	20

[a] Not available.

ment decreases outnumbered increases, concentration rose sharply in motor vehicles and parts, which alone accounted for more than half of the group's output. At the same time 2 other large industries in the group registered sizable decreases, although the trend has been somewhat irregular.[34]

In instruments and related products as well as in miscellaneous products increases predominated. Although most of these industries are of relatively small size, each group includes one large industry in which concentration has been rising.[35]

Among industry groups characterized by generally declining concentration, the most conspicuous was chemicals and allied products. In the group as a whole decreases well outnumbered increases, and 3 of the chemical industries in which concentration fell had shipments of more than $1 billion.[36] Both the tobacco and petroleum products groups are dominated by a single industry in which concentration declined. Most of the declines in the dominant industries (cigarettes and petroleum refining) took place in the relatively short span of 1947–54.[37] Printing and publishing is another area of generally declining con-

[34] Transportation Equipment	1947	1954	1958	1963	1967
Increasing					
Motor vehicles and parts	56%	75%	75%	79%	78%
Decreasing					
Aircraft engines and parts	72	62	56	57	64
Railroad and street cars	56	64	58	53	53

(The 1967 concentration ratio for motor vehicles and parts, as published by the Census Bureau, is 76%. However, it excludes automotive stamping plants operated by automobile producing companies, which had formerly been included in the motor vehicle and parts industry. For the year 1963 the Bureau has compiled ratios both including and excluding these stamping plants; the figures were 79% and 77%, respectively. Therefore, to retain comparability, the published ratio for 1967 has been increased 2 percentage points to 78%.)

[35] Instruments; Miscellaneous Products	1947	1954	1958	1963	1967
Increasing					
Photographic equipment and supplies	61%	n.a.[a]	65%	63%	69%
Games and toys	20	18	13	15	25
[a] Not available.					

[36] Chemicals and Allied Products	1947	1954	1958	1963	1967
Decreasing					
Industrial organic chemicals	n.a.[a]	59%	55%	51%	45%
Plastics materials and resins	44%	47	40	35	27
Pharmaceutical preparations	28	25	27	22	24
Increasing					
Toilet preparations	24	25	29	38	38
[a] Not available.					

[37] Tobacco; Petroleum Products	1947	1954	1958	1963	1967
Decreasing					
Cigarettes	90%	82%	79%	80%	81%
Tobacco stemming and redrying	88	79	83	70	63
Petroleum refining	37	33	32	34	33

centration, decreases on a national basis occurring in both of its large industries.[38]

The general tendency was also downward in the 2 closely related groups of fabricated metal products and nonelectrical machinery. Included in these groups were 6 large industries, in all of which concentration declined.[39]

Summary of industry concentration changes

Among *all* the industries for which data are available—the medium-size and small as well as the large—what has been the general trend of concentration? Have increases outnumbered decreases, or has the reverse been true? Unhappily, the concentration ratios for about half of the 400-odd industries for which 1963 and 1967 concentration ratios are available cannot be compared with those for 1947, 1954, and 1958, since in the compilation of concentration ratios beginning with 1963, the "new" Standard Industrial Classification was used, involving a general redefinition of industries and reclassification of establishments.

There are, however, 191 industries that remained comparable throughout the entire period. To these can be added 18 other industries that remained comparable beginning in 1954. The changes in concentration in these 209 industries, as reflected in the share of their output accounted for by the 4 largest companies, are distributed in Table 1-4 by the size of the industry. Those whose concentration ratios changed by fewer than 3 percentage points are segregated from those with greater changes in order to focus attention on industries with significant changes. While the degree of the table's representativeness is not known, the industries on which it is based form a very large sample, constituting more than half of the value added by all manufacturing industries.

One of the most widely accepted generalizations concerning concentration has been that since World War II the number of industries with increases in concentration has been roughly matched by the number in which concentration has declined. This has been the basis for the conclusion that, generally speaking, concentration among individual industries has not tended to rise. But, as can be seen from the table, with the appearance of the 1967 ratios, this is no longer true. For the 209 industries the 1947–63 distribution of 85 increases, 81 decreases, and 43 cases of relative stability has, with the appearance of the 1967 concentration ratios, been changed to 95 increases, 75 decreases, and 39 cases

[38] Printing and Publishing

	1947	1954	1958	1963	1967
Decreasing					
Newspapers	21%	18%	17%	15%	16%
Periodicals	34	29	31	28	24

[39] Fabricated Metals; Nonelectrical Machinery

	1947	1954	1958	1963	1967
Decreasing					
Metal cans	78%	80%	80%	74%	73%
Sheet metalwork	21	19	15	11	10
Screw machine products	17	11	9	5	6
Miscellaneous fabricated wire products	20	18	13	13	11
Valves and fittings	24	17	17	13	14
Ball and roller bearings	62	60	57	57	54

Table 1-4

DISTRIBUTION OF CHANGES IN
CONCENTRATION RATIOS

Number of industries

Size of Industry (millions)	1947 (or 1954) to 1963	1947 (or 1954) to 1967
Increases		
$2,500 or over[a]	4	9
$1,000 to $2,500	13	14
$500 to $1,000	14	18
Under $500	54	54
Total	85	95
Less than 3% pts.	43	39
Decreases		
Under $500	44	30
$500 to $1,000	17	21
$1,000 to $2,500	13	15
$2,500 or over	7	9
Total	81	75
Total	209	209

[a]Value of shipments in millions

Source: Bureau of the Census, Department of Commerce, *Concentration Ratios in Manufacturing, 1967, Special Reports*, 1970, Pt. 1, Table 5

of relative stability. The major differences between the two periods were a rise from 4 to 9 in the number of very large industries showing increasing concentration and a drop from 44 to 30 in the number of small industries with decreases in concentration. Because of increases either in their size, their concentration ratios, or both, there were added to the 4 very large industries with increasing concentration 2 in the food group and one each in textile mill products, chemicals and allied products, primary metals, and instruments and related products. The decline in the number of small industries with decreasing concentration was distributed widely among the major groups.

The fact that more industries recorded increases than decreases does not, in itself, mean that the industrial structure became more oligopolistic. Some of the advances took place in industries in which concentration, despite the rise, remained so low that for the leading producers the determining question continued to be the state of the market, not their rivals' reactions. Conversely, where concentration remained high even after a marked decrease, the leading producers probably continued to be preoccupied with their rivals' reactions. For the former, any attempt to raise prices above the market level would continue to be impossible. For the latter, a price increase would continue to be within the realm of the possible, if they could rely on their rivals to match it and adjust their production accordingly.

Although it is thus not possible to equate concentration directly with oligopoly, the fact that increases in concentration have outnumbered decreases is still not without significance. If one takes an industry at random, the odds have become less that the industry's members will behave as polyopolistic sellers, simply accepting what a free market offers, and greater that they will behave as oligopolists. That is to say, even though demand may not be strong enough to support a price advance in a free market, the leading sellers may nonetheless actively consider a price increase. In arriving at their decision they will subordinate the state of the market to their expectations of their rivals' probable willingness to match the increase and make such reductions in output as may be necessary to make the increase effective.

VERTICAL CH 2
CONCENTRATION

Vertical concentration refers to operations by a company in 2 or more industries representing successive stages in the flow of materials or products from an earlier to a later stage of production or vice versa. The degree of an industry's vertical concentration is the share of its output produced by companies primarily engaged in an earlier or later stage in the flow of materials or products. Where a firm is primarily engaged in an earlier stage, its market share of an industry at a later stage may be referred to as "forward vertical concentration"; where it is primarily engaged in a later stage, its share of an industry at an earlier stage may be referred to as "backward vertical concentration." [1]

The term traditionally used in the context of this type of relationship is "vertical integration," which over the years has unfortunately come to be applied to both a process and a state. Moreover, it gives an impression of economies of scale achieved through one gear's articulating nicely with another or a production line moving continuously from a lower to a higher stage of production. From the point of view of economic concentration, such associations are of little relevance, since they occur within the same plant and thus contribute only to market concentration. What does have the potential of causing a further injury to competition is the same ownership of *separate* plants, resources, and enterprises. For these reasons it is appropriate to use the term to refer to a structural state, "vertical concentration."

Vertical concentration and market behavior

The effect of vertical integration on market behavior has been a matter of long-standing interest in the history of economic thought. As Fritz Machlup and Martha Taber have put it:

> What are the effects of vertical integration upon output and prices? If an industry has been "vertically fragmented," that is, if it has consisted of a number of separate firms each operating in only one of the successive stages of production, and if such firms are now combined by "vertical merger," should one expect that, as a result of the integration, the total physical output of the industry will be increased and the price of the ultimate product reduced? [2]

[1] Based on the analogy to the flow of a river, the expansion toward sources of supply (or earlier stages) is often referred to as a movement "upstream," while movement in the opposite direction—i.e., toward the final end product (or later stages)—is referred to as "downstream" expansion.

[2] Fritz Machlup and Martha Taber, "Bilateral Monopoly, Successive Monopoly, and Vertical Integration," *Economica*, May, 1960, pp. 101–19.

The argument has revolved around the effect of vertical concentration on cost and market position. With respect to the former, "There is the possibility of economies of vertical integration, especially where technology is changing and productive establishments, hitherto spatially separated, are brought together; but there is also the possibility of diseconomies through a loss of specialization." With respect to the latter, "There is the possibility that monopolistic positions are extended, strengthened or consolidated by the merger; but there is also the possibility that existing monopolistic restrictions are relaxed and monopoly prices reduced as a result of the merger." [3]

Attempts to derive answers to these questions by theoretical reasoning have been, at best, inconclusive.[4] Unhappily, the dovetailing of theory with empirical evidence that has obtained in the case of horizontal concentration is not present here. This is not to imply, however, that concern over the effects of vertical integration on competition has been wholly lacking. When at the turn of the century U.S. Steel acquired the iron ore deposits of the Mesabi Range, no elaborate analysis was needed to understand how ownership by one company of vast, low-cost resources could injure competition. It is self-evident that vertical integration can affect competition adversely by establishing monopolistic control over scarce natural resources, as a result of which nonintegrated fabricators may be completely cut off from materials or forced by their integrated competitors to operate on an unduly narrow margin. Conversely, through the preemption of critical facilities or buyers, vertical concentration can prevent rival producers from securing access to important markets. Describing the consequences of vertical concentration, Walter Adams has written:

> Vertical power consists of market control in successive stages of production and distribution. It enables a firm or a group of firms to squeeze their non-integrated competitors, through a foreclosure of access to the market, denial of essential raw materials, or manipulation of relative prices so as to effect a simple or double squeeze. . . . It is rooted in the fact that giant companies perform the dual role of supplying raw materials to non-integrated independents, and then competing with these independents in the sale of final products. This dual role gives the integrated giants a leverage that can be exercised with deadly effectiveness.[5]

[3] *Ibid.*

[4] For an account of the development of economic theory on the effects of vertical integration, see *ibid*. The principal shortcoming of theory in this area is described by Machlup and Taber as follows: "Why have economists most of the time assumed . . . that in a situation of bilateral monopoly one party would name a price only and wait for the other party to name the quantity? We may guess that the writers who made this assumption carried over a technique that had proved useful in the analysis of unilateral monopoly, without due examination, to the case of bilateral monopoly. A monopolist selling to many buyers quotes a price and then lets buyers take the quantities they want. A monopsonist, buying from many sellers, names a price and then lets sellers deliver the quantities they choose. This technique is not appropriate when there is only one buyer and one seller, for the two must, of necessity, negotiate and contract for a definite quantity of the intermediate product at a price to which they can agree. Economists are sometimes victims of the habit of using tools that are ready in their kit, especially if these tools are 'elegant.' In this instance, the algebraic and geometric devices, involving offer curves and contract curves (in addition to indifference curves, outlay curves, and reaction curves), had done a neat job in the analysis of simple monopoly and duopoly. It was too tempting to apply them to the analysis of bilateral monopoly, too easy to overlook the fact that this application may imply assumptions concerning the behaviour of bilateral monopolists which are unsuitable in many situations."

[5] 88th Cong., 1st Sess., Subcommittee No. 4, House Select Committee on Small Business, *Hearings,* 1963, Walter Adams, "The Impact upon Small Business of Dual Distribution and Related Vertical Integration," p. 426.

Similarly, Carl Kaysen and Donald F. Turner have stated:

> Finally, vertical integration offers opportunities for the use of market power not available to firms operating in a single-stage market. Both price and nonprice discriminations are made possible by vertical integration, especially partial vertical integration in which a firm is both supplier and competitor of other firms. . . . By narrowing the margin between the price at which it supplies its one-stage rivals and the price at which it sells the product with which their output competes, it can limit their profits, their growth, and even drive them out of business. . . . By rationing the supplies of nonintegrated customers, or by simply refusing to deal with them, the same results can be brought about. . . .[6]

The denial of supplies

In most materials industries, such as steel, aluminum, and petroleum, there are varying numbers of semi- or nonintegrated processors who compete with the large integrated companies in the sale of end products but are dependent upon them for their supply of materials. Not infrequently, these nonintegrated processors are the principal source of price competition encountered by the integrated producers. One of the problems they face is the simple one of securing materials and is to be distinguished from the further problem of the narrowing of their margin. When, during periods of tight supplies, integrated companies absorb an increasing proportion of their production of crude or semifinished materials for their own use, the nonintegrated firms are likely to find their source of supply drying up. They may be limited to amounts determined in relation to their use of these products in some earlier, less prosperous base period, or they may be forced to become dependent upon what are known as "conversion deals"—arrangements whereby the customers of the nonintegrated company procure the raw materials and deliver them to the nonintegrated firm for conversion into finished products. As an alternative, they may be compelled to accept raw materials of a poorer quality than those they normally use.

Moreover, the problem is not a static one. An integrated firm may integrate further, extending itself into stages in which it was formerly not engaged. If these stages are closer to the ultimate consumer, the company comes in competition with a new set of nonintegrated firms that are also its customers at the previous stage. In such a position an integrated company is likely to reserve sufficient supplies produced in its earlier stages for use in its new facilities. In so doing, it may refuse to sell to its former customers, with whom it now competes.

Obviously, the higher the level of general business activity, the less are the chances that nonintegrated firms denied supplies as a result of vertical integration will be able to find alternative sources of supply. Indeed, these other sources are themselves frequently unable to meet the needs of their old customers, to say nothing of taking on a new buyer. If a public or private allocation system is in effect and the nonintegrated producer has no "base period" with one or more suppliers, his plight is likely to be desperate.

Until the past decade the steel industry had been moving almost continuously toward greater integration. Andrew Carnegie stated in an interview in 1899:

> Yes, we have been erecting several new departments, including what I believe will be the largest axle factory in the world. Why, it may be

[6] Carl Kaysen and Donald F. Turner, *Antitrust Policy—an Economic and Legal Analysis,* Harvard University Press, 1959, p. 122.

asked, should steel makers make plates for other firms to work up into boilers when they can manufacture the boilers themselves, or beams and girders for bridges, when they can turn out and build up the completed article, or plates for pipes when they can make the pipes? I think the next step to be taken by steel makers will be to furnish finished articles ready for use. In the future the most successful firms will be those that go the farthest in that direction.[7]

Over the years merchant pig-iron producers acquired or built steel-making facilities; producers of semifinished steel acquired finishing capacity; and producers of finished steel acquired or built facilities for fabricating finished products of which steel is the principal material. The results were a reduction in the amount of open-market pig iron available to semi-integrated steel companies; a reduction in the supply of semifinished steel offered in the open market for purchase by nonintegrated steel companies; and a reduction in the open-market supply of finished steel available for purchase by independent producers of fabricated products made principally of steel. Before the industry became so fully integrated, semi-integrated firms were able to obtain the pig iron needed for their operations, and nonintegrated companies could procure crude and semifinished steel for their own mills. The former could and did buy pig iron from many merchant furnaces, and the latter were able to purchase the excess production of semifinished steel from the integrated and semi-integrated producers. But integration, coupled with the high level of demand, virtually put an end to the sale of steel on the open market. The condition the industry had reached by the end of World War II was described in the annual review issue of *Iron Age,* January, 1946:

> For years, larger steel companies have sold huge quantities of semifinished steel to nonintegrated firms only to face competition from those companies in the sale of finished steel products. . . . Now, with larger steel mills requiring semifinished steel for their own finishing mills, there is a marked disposition to drastically slash the tonnage of semifinished steel being shipped to the small nonintegrated makers. For this reason, it is expected that unless management of the smaller companies can, like a few units in that category, find their own markets in the form of specialties or special services, the going may be so rough as to cause fatalities.[8]

Fatalities did occur, but paradoxically the movement of the major steel companies toward greater integration seems to have slowed down. During the last decade, their acquisitions of steel-using companies have been few and far between. At the same time, the superior profit performance of medium-size steel producers, as well as of small mills smelting scrap in electric furnaces, suggests that the benefits of integration are being outweighed by the economies of specialization.

The price squeeze

In addition to denying them supplies, the integrated producer can impose a "price squeeze" on his nonintegrated rivals by narrowing the margin between the price of the raw material and the price of the finished product. The price squeeze may take the form of an increase in the prices of materials while the

[7] *Iron and Coal Trades Review,* London, May 12, 1899.
[8] *Iron Age,* Jan. 3, 1946.

price of the finished goods is held relatively constant or even reduced, or it may take the form of a reduction in the price of the finished goods while the price of raw materials is held comparatively stable or even increased.

The recurrent use of the price squeeze by the Aluminum Company of America played a major role in the decision against that company in the Department of Justice case decided by the United States District Court for the Southern District of New York. This case, in which the first testimony was heard in 1938, involved actions that occurred at a time when the Aluminum Company of America was the sole U.S. producer of virgin aluminum ingot. The issue of the price squeeze arose because Alcoa had been selling virgin aluminum ingot to independent manufacturers with whom it competed in the sale of fabricated products. While virgin aluminum ingot could also be imported from abroad, such imports never represented more than a small proportion of the total virgin aluminum marketed in the United States.[9] Alcoa was found to have maintained differentials between its selling prices of virgin aluminum ingot and aluminum sheets at such levels as to prevent fabricators from manufacturing sheets at a reasonable profit.[10] The selling prices of these gauges and types of sheet were found to have been "lower than fair prices based on the prices at which it was selling virgin aluminum ingot and the cost of fabricating such sheet." [11] The selling prices for virgin aluminum ingot were found to have been "higher than fair prices based on the cost of production of such virgin aluminum ingot." [12]

> The sheet differentials, determined by subtracting the prices received by Aluminum Co. of America for virgin aluminum ingot from the prices received by it for such aluminum sheet, were less than the cost of fabrication of aluminum ingot into sheet in 31 out of the 112 items. For all five gages of coiled sheet the average profit open to competing fabricators during this period was .84 cents a pound as against 4.7 cents per pound for the five succeeding years, viz, 1933–37; for the four gages of flat sheet the corresponding figures were .59 cents and 4 cents, and for hard alloy sheet 4.9 and 11.8 cents.[13]

Inefficiency and bad judgment on the part of some of the independent fabricators were noted but not regarded as sufficient explanation of the difficulties of the nonintegrated fabricators. The court pointed out that at least as early as 1930, independent fabricators had complained to the Aluminum Company of

[9] According to the decision referred to above, "the virgin aluminum ingot market in the United States consists of, and its aggregate is measured by, (a) the production of virgin aluminum ingot by Aluminum Company of America and (b) the importations of virgin aluminum ingot into the United States, both by Aluminum Company and by others. The percentage of this total which was both produced and imported by Aluminum Company of America during the period from February 2, 1909, to August 14, 1940, varied from a low of 67.90 percent in 1921 to a high of 99.99 percent in 1918. Except for the years 1921 and the years 1910, 1913, and 1922, when its percentage was 74.08 percent, 72.74 percent and 72.09 percent, respectively, its percentage was always over 80 percent, and, from 1934 to 1938, it averaged a trifle over 90 percent." (*United States* v. *Aluminum Company of America, et. al.*, Judgment on Mandate against Aluminum Company of America, *et. al.*, United States District Court, Southern District of New York, April 23, 1946, Amended Finding No. 154, p. 4.)
[10] *United States* v. *Aluminum Company of America, et al.*, Judgment on Mandate against Aluminum Company of America, *et al.*, United States District Court, Southern District of New York, April 23, 1946, Amended Findings Nos. 257, 280, pp. 5–6, 8–9.
[11] *Ibid.*, Amended Finding No. 286, pp. 10–11.
[12] *Ibid.*, Amended Finding No. 260, p. 7.
[13] *Ibid.*, Amended Finding No. 281, p. 9.

America that the differentials maintained by it prevented them from fabricating and selling sheets at a reasonable profit.[14] This price squeeze was found to be in violation of Section 1 of the Sherman Act,[15] and an injunction was issued against its resumption.[16]

Although the denial of supplies and the price squeeze have been treated here conceptually as separate anticompetitive practices, they are both made possible by the same type of industry structure and, indeed, in the real world are employed consecutively or concurrently.

The preemption of markets

Just as backward vertical concentration can restrict competition by impairing the ability of smaller fabricators to secure materials, so also can competition be injured when rival suppliers are blocked off from important markets. This can be illustrated by the du Ponts' long-standing ownership of General Motors stock. The ownership by the du Ponts of 23 percent of GM's stock, from the early 1920's until its termination by court order in 1957, was found by the Supreme Court to have substantially lessened competition in automobile paints, finishes, and fabrics. This was, in fact, the central point on which the celebrated case brought by the Department of Justice turned. In its decision the Supreme Court stated:

> The primary issue is whether du Pont's commanding position as General Motors' supplier of automotive finishes and fabrics was achieved on competitive merit alone, or because its acquisition of the General Motors' stock, and the consequent close intercompany relationship, led to the insulation of most of the General Motors' market from free competition, with the resultant likelihood, at the time of the suit, of the creation of a monopoly of a line of commerce.[17]

The Court cited a number of specific examples of influence exerted by the du Ponts on General Motors. For instance, after the acquisition of General Motors' stock, Du Pont's former sales manager became the vice president in charge of GM's operations committee and actively promoted the use of Du Pont's products. The former principal paint supplier to GM "saw the handwriting on the wall" and asked to be bought out since he "felt he would lose a valuable customer, General Motors"; shortly thereafter his company was bought out by Du Pont and dissolved. Lammont and Pierre S. du Pont both concerned themselves actively with increasing the amount of Du Pont products used by GM; the latter, who at the time was chairman of the board of both Du Pont and General Motors, predicted correctly that as a result of a forthcoming "change in management" the Cadillac, Olds, and Oakland divisions would increase their purchases so that Du Pont "should be able to sell substantially all of the paint, varnish and fabricoid products needed." By 1926 only one of the GM divisions "was obtaining any substantial proportion of its requirements from du Pont's competitors." The exception was the Fisher Body Division, which enjoyed a considerable measure of autonomy under its merger agreement with GM; the

[14] *Ibid.,* Amended Findings No. 262, 285, pp. 7, 10; also Findings of Fact and Conclusions of Law, etc., Finding No. 272, pp. 163–64.
[15] *Ibid.,* Amended Conclusions No. 57, 60, pp. 14, 15; see also para. 8, pp. 21–22.
[16] *Ibid.,* para. 9, pp. 23–24.
[17] *United States* v. *E. I. du Pont de Nemours & Co., et al.,* 353 U.S. 586 (1957), at 588.

Fisher brothers "insisted on running their own show and for years withstood efforts of high-ranking du Pont and General Motors executives to get them to switch to du Pont from their accustomed sources of supply." Summing up the evidence, the Court stated:

> The fact that sticks out in this voluminous record is that the bulk of du Pont's production has always supplied the largest part of the requirements of the one customer in the automobile industry connected to du Pont by a stock interest. The inference is overwhelming that du Pont's commanding position was promoted by its stock interest and was not gained solely on competitive merit.
>
>   *   *   *
>
> . . . du Pont purposely employed its stock to pry open the General Motors market to entrench itself as the primary supplier of General Motors' requirements for automotive finishes and fabrics.[18]

Examples of vertical concentration

In certain industries, although the existence of vertical concentration has long been a matter of common knowledge, its extent has not. Now, through a special tabulation of Census data, this deficiency has been at least partially remedied.[19] The tabulation breaks down the 8-company concentration ratio for 4-digit industries into progressively broader categories: first, the share produced by those among the 8 primarily engaged in the Census enterprise industry category (approximately 3-digit) of which the specified 4-digit industry is a part;[20] second, the share produced by those among the 8 primarily engaged in some other enterprise industry category but within the same major industry group; and, third, the share produced by those among the 8 primarily engaged in an entirely different major industry group. The distribution may be illustrated by the use of the 4-digit industry "tire cord and fabric." In 1963 the 8-company concentration ratio for this industry was 96 percent. Of this proportion those companies among the 8 primarily engaged in the enterprise industry category ("other textile mill products") of which it is a part accounted for only 5 percent of the output of tire cord and fabrics; another 5 percent was produced by those among the 8 principally engaged in other enterprise industry categories but *within* the textile mill products group; the remaining 86 percent was produced by those among the 8 whose principal line of business was completely *outside* the textile mill group. The nation's largest tire manufacturers are known to be integrated backward, producing tire cord for their own use. It is therefore a reasonable inference that most, if not all, of the 86 percent of tire cord produced by leaders outside of the textile mill group was manufactured by tire makers.

This type of distribution is shown in Table 2-1 for tire cord and 7 other cases of vertical concentration. The 4 in the upper grid are examples of integration in a backward direction; those in the lower, of expansion in a forward direction. In addition to tire cord, an example of the former is the cooperage industry, which illustrates the manner in which the preemption of a small but critical

---

[18] *Ibid.*, 605–06.

[19] *Concentration Ratios in Manufacturing Industry, 1963,* Pt. 2, Table 22, pp. 286–94.

[20] The use of the broader *enterprise industry categories,* which approximate the 3-digit categories of the Standard Industrial Classification, was necessary to avoid disclosure of individual companies.

Table 2-1

EXAMPLES OF VERTICAL CONCENTRATION

Shares of output accounted for by companies among 8 leading producers
primarily engaged (a) in the specified industry and (b) in other industries, 1963

| | | | | Percentage Accounted for by 8 Largest Companies | | |
| | | | | | Whose Primary Enterprise Industry Category is in Same— | |
SIC Code	Industry	Number of Companies	Value of Shipments (000)	Total	2-Digit Major Industry Group as Industry	Enterprise Industry Category as Industry[b]
	Backward					
2296	Tire cord and fabric	12	$ 375,689	96%	10^a%	5^a%
2445	Cooperage	71	52,917	71	5^a	5^a
3211	Flat glass	11	549,390	99	40^a	40^a
3694	Engine electrical equipment	163	900,663	79	25^a	25^a
	Forward					
3491	Metal barrels, drums, and pails	95	303,423	56	22	22
3497	Metal foil and leaf	56	180,567	78	29	5
3731	Shipbuilding and repairing	305	1,679,765	63	42	25^a
2895	Carbon black	8	149,122	100	32	25^a

[a]Approximate percentage shown to avoid disclosing figures for individual companies. Actual percentage is within ±5 percentage points of the approximate figure.
[b]The enterprise industry categories of which the 4-digit industries are a part are, respectively, other textile mill products for tire cord and fabric, other wood products for cooperage, glass products for flat glass, other electrical machines for engine electrical equipment, fabricated metal products n.e.c. for metal barrels, drums, pails, and metal foil and leaf, ships and boats for shipbuilding and repairing, and miscellaneous chemical products for carbon black.

Source: *Concentration Ratios in Manufacturing Industry, 1963,* Pt. 2, Table 22, pp. 286–94

"bottleneck" industry can affect competition adversely. As the chart shows, the 8 largest producers turn out 71 percent of the output, of which only 5 percent comes from firms primarily engaged in that enterprise industry category. The remainder, it may be inferred, is produced by plants owned by the major distillers, who immediately after World War II embarked on an ambitious program of buying up not only cooperage facilities but stands of white oak used for aging. In 1948, this acquisition drive was described by the Federal Trade Commission as follows:

> Without whiskey barrels, whiskey cannot be aged, and without aged whiskey to sell, the large distillers would soon have found themselves in an extraordinarily difficult position. It should be noted that the distillers, as owners of the tight cooperage facilities, were able to purchase white oak, the chief raw material used in the manufacture of barrels, at prices which the independent cooperage firms could not meet. This had the dual effect of inducing the independent cooperage firms to sell out and at the

same time making it difficult for any distiller to operate without a captive cooperage plant of its own.[21]

Flat glass and engine electrical equipment appear to be examples of the automobile manufacturers' policy of "tapered integration," under which they produce part of their own requirements, filling out the remainder of their needs with purchases from independent plants. In this way they seek to achieve the twin objectives of avoiding complete dependence on outside sources while securing some of the benefits of the economies of specialization of independent suppliers. Of the 99 percent of the output of flat glass produced by the industry's 8 largest firms, 59 percent came from outside the stone, clay, and glass group; most of this output was probably produced by the automobile manufacturers. Somewhat the same situation probably applies to engine electrical equipment, 79 percent of which is produced by the 8 largest firms. Some 54 percent comes from firms primarily engaged outside the electrical machinery group; it is a reasonable inference that most of this output was produced by the automobile manufacturers.

In an example of forward vertical concentration, some 56 percent of metal barrels and drums was produced by the 8 largest companies, of which 34 percent was produced by companies outside the fabricated metal products group —presumably by the steel producers. Partly to find assured markets for their lower grades of steel sheet, the large steel companies shortly after World War II took over much of this traditionally "small business" industry. At the time the takeover operation was described by *Iron Age* as follows:

> Long, long ago, in 1939, before the words postwar and planning were wedded, the manufacture of heavy steel barrels and drums was a rather volatile business firmly in the hands of a large number of highly individualistic entrepreneurs. Most of these fabricators had started on a precarious shoestring and were justifiably vocal in their pride of success in the classical Horatio Alger Pluck and Luck Tradition.
>
> *   *   *
>
> A few weeks ago, the purchase of Bennett Mfg. Co., Chicago, by the United States Steel Corp. pretty well completed the capture of the entire barrel and drum business by major steel producers. Some 87 percent of the business, representing about 435,500 tons of steel consumption yearly has been corralled by the mills and the remaining 64,500 tons of independent capacity will probably remain so for a variety of reasons.[22]

A more recent case is represented by metal foil and leaf, consisting principally of aluminum foil. Nearly half (49 percent) is produced by companies outside the fabricated metal products group. Presumably, these consist of the principal producers of primary aluminum, each of which promotes its own brand of aluminum foil. Forward vertical integration in the shipbuilding industry is largely the result of the long-established participation in that field by major steel producers—principally Bethlehem Steel. Of the 63 percent produced by the 8 largest firms, 21 percent came from companies primarily engaged outside the transportation equipment group. Before World War II Bethlehem was the nation's largest shipbuilding company. During the war it received $1.246 billion of prime war supply contracts for shipbuilding—an

[21] Federal Trade Commission, *The Merger Movement; A Summary Report,* 1948, p. 64
[22] *Iron Age,* Sept. 21, 1944.

amount exceeded only by the awards to the Henry J. Kaiser Company. And since that time it has continued to be one of the nation's leading shipbuilders.

It is perhaps no coincidence that none of these 8 conspicuous cases of vertical concentration is of recent vintage. Three—cooperage, metal barrels, and metal foil—date from the immediate postwar period, while the remainder can be traced back to much earlier years. This is in keeping with the apparent absence of any current pervasive trend toward greater vertical integration. Although there are important exceptions, most notably in petroleum, materials producers by and large have not been busily engaged in buying up their customers, nor have manufacturers of finished goods been buying up their suppliers. With mergers and acquisitions generally reaching all-time highs in the late 1960's, what is the reason for the relative infrequency of vertical expansion? The most probable explanation is the growing realization among end-product manufacturers that it is frequently more economical "to buy" than "to make" a material, part, or component.

"Make or buy"

On its surface the supplying of one's needs for materials, parts, and components from a "captive" plant would appear, as John M. Clark observed many years ago, "to be a means of getting two profits instead of one or of getting one's materials 'at cost' ":

> But this does not explain why he goes into the particular business of producing his own raw materials and tries to absorb that particular profit instead of doing what men of large property frequently do, invest in wholly unrelated industries. Perhaps he has a special feeling of dislike at having anybody else making a profit out of his own purchase. This is a natural sentiment, perhaps, but hardly an economic argument.[23]

However, while recognizing the possibilities for real economies inherent in integration—assurance of getting "just the kinds of materials which that business needs to use" or in securing greater reliability of delivery—Clark felt that these advantages were outweighed by the advantages of purchasing from specialist suppliers:

> Over against the maxim: "Do it yourself," stands another, sponsored by economists from Adam Smith down. Its modern form is: "If you want a thing cheaply done, hire a specialist. . . ." This is the chief reason why any concern ever buys materials and equipment from other concerns and lets them make profits on the production and sale of these things. If my business takes but a small part of my neighbor's product, he can probably do the thing more cheaply than I could, working as I must on a smaller scale.[24]

Whatever gains in efficiency are secured by the ability to supply one's own materials, parts, and components may well be at the expense of the economies of specialization. Indeed, the achievement of the latter may result in an industrial structure described by Joan Robinson as "vertical disintegration":

[23] John M. Clark, *The Economics of Overhead Costs,* University of Chicago Press, 1923, p. 136.
[24] *Ibid.,* p. 140.

If a motor firm begins to feel the pressure of diminishing returns from entrepreneurship, as it grows in size, it can abandon the manufacture of some part of the car, the radiator or the body for instance, to a specialist firm, and continue to increase its output of cars without increasing its staff. Meanwhile, the specialist firm, as the scale of output increases, will gain from these technical economies which could not be achieved by the car-producing firms because each individually produced too few of this particular part to allow their full development.[25]

Within many large enterprises there is a continuing conflict between integration and specialization—referred to in the business community as the "make or buy" issue. It is the subject of numerous articles in trade journals and has been examined in two significant, though somewhat neglected, economic studies—one by Alfred R. Oxenfeldt and Myron W. Watkins and the other by Robert L. Dixon and William A. Paton. Both reached the same conclusion: manufacturers too frequently make items that they would be better advised to buy from specialist suppliers. In testifying before the Senate Subcommittee on Antitrust and Monopoly, Oxenfeldt attributed this tendency to "very strong pressures [which] in most business firms [are] reinforced by tradition, folklore and prejudices."[26]

A number of explanations are usually advanced for what would appear to be an economically irrational practice. According to Oxenfeldt, managers frequently labor under the illusion that by making a part or component they will be assured of an adequate and reliable supply. But this overlooks the fact that when shortages do appear they are usually of raw materials. Under these circumstances, producing parts or components affords no greater protection than would be provided by reliance upon independent specialist suppliers:

> the firm deciding to make its own requirements will have to look to the same sources of supply of materials as its present suppliers of that part. And since its volume of purchases would very likely be substantially less than theirs, its chances of getting equality of treatment would be less than even. Indeed, its entrance in that market as a competitor of its present suppliers might even stimulate pressure on the materials producers to impose additional handicaps on this upstart customer.[27]

Another argument is that by making a product the manufacturer is utilizing idle capacity. This would obviously have the advantage of spreading fixed overhead costs over a large number of units as well as holding a labor force together. But, as was pointed out by Robert L. Dixon, any company that, ex-

---

[25] Joan Robinson, *The Economics of Imperfect Competition*, Macmillan, 1933, pp. 339–40.
[26] *Hearings on Economic Concentration*, Pt. 4, pp. 1584–88, testimony of Alfred R. Oxenfeldt.
[27] As a specific example, Oxenfeldt cited the case of a refrigerator manufacturer: "The company had been buying its entire requirements of plastic parts from a molded plastics manufacturer who for several years had provided supplies of satisfactory quality at prices the company's purchasing agent regarded as reasonable. However, deliveries were slowed up when a tight market developed in 1951 for the particular type of thermosetting plastic the company used. To meet the steadily increasing demand for its refrigerators the company found it necessary to place special orders with several other plastic suppliers. Not only were the prices on these supplementary supplies higher than it had been (and was still) paying its original supplier, but the proportion of rejections was also higher. The upshot was that the company's average unit cost of plastic parts rose nearly 22 percent within 9 months. And this computation took no account of the time loss of executives in wrestling with production crises and in the vexatious business of securing from the parts suppliers adequate adjustments for defective items."

cept for short periods, can manufacture with its existing facilities an item formerly purchased is "at least temporarily sick—it is suffering from the illness of overcapacity." [28] Dixon went on to add that "something must be out of order" if a company undertakes to produce an additional item on the grounds that it can do so without adding to its fixed costs because of unused capacity: "Fixed costs reflect capacity to operate, and they appear throughout the entire business organization. Evidently if the fixed costs can be ignored in such a calculation, the company is overequipped and overstaffed for its regular work."

But the most frequently expressed justification is that by producing an item the end-product manufacturer will make the supplier's profit. Behind this argument is the manufacturer's assumption that his costs are at least no higher than those of the specialist suppliers. This in turn raises the further question of what he should properly include in his "costs," which in Dixon's words is "the crux of the whole situation":

> For purposes of making the decision to add an activity which may be fairly permanent, the schedule of estimated costs of production should include not only an exhaustive list of the probable added costs, but also a complete assignment of all of the overhead charges (both fixed and variable), even including an allowance for general administration, that are properly prorated against any regular segment of the business.

Failure to include a proper allowance for overhead costs has given many manufacturers the mistaken impression that their costs are lower than those of independent suppliers. A graphic example was presented to the Senate Subcommittee on Antitrust and Monopoly by Clement C. Caditz, president of the Northern Metal Products Company, Franklin Park, Illinois, and formerly national president of the American Metal Stampers Association.[29] As an independent specialist supplier, Caditz described the reaction of a "very large manufacturer" to whom he was trying to sell a part which his company was "uniquely set up to make automatically and which we are selling to all of his competitors":

> The manager of their captive press shop laughed me right out of the building. That part—well, they made it from scrap material—so they didn't have any material cost. They ran it when they had open press time, so they didn't have any machine cost. They used operators only when they had nothing else to do, so they didn't have any labor cost. His foreman arranged for this "in between" so that there wasn't any supervisory cost. And, he, himself, didn't bother much with it, so there wasn't any management cost. Obviously, there was nothing to apply overhead against. This part, as he triumphantly pointed out, the company was getting "for free."
>
> But nothing is free in any business enterprise. It takes storage space to store material, scrap or otherwise; and records to know you have it; and scrap steel itself is a valuable commodity—so there were material costs. The machine depreciated and wore out proportionately as much on that job as on any scheduled job—so there were machine costs. If his operators didn't have anything to do putting them on such a job only hid the fact—it's a labor waste management could otherwise be correcting—so it really turns out to be a very expensive labor cost. His time, and the supervisor's attention, had to be given to accomplish all of this rather

---

[28] *Hearings on Economic Concentration,* Pt. 4, pp. 1671–77, testimony of Robert L. Dixon.
[29] *Ibid.,* pp. 1620–25, testimony of Clement C. Caditz.

complicated synchronization—so there were supervisory and management costs. In addition, he forgot about die setting and die maintenance; and compensation insurance; and taxes; and power and a dozen other costs.

As part of a program of customer education the American Metal Stampers Association prepared an elaborate questionnaire to be used by its members in trying to persuade end-product manufacturers to include in their costs proper allowances for all costs—fixed as well as variable, indirect as well as direct, hidden as well as visible.[30] Caditz observed: "Some experts in the field even suggest adding a 'super-overhead' charge on top of everything else to compensate for the extra burdens imposed on management by the sideline operation."

According to Dixon a manufacturer should not contemplate making a part unless in addition to the full charge for prorated and added costs, "an allowance is added for profit; this allowance should be at least equal to the rate of profit which the company is able to make through its principal operations." In his writings on this subject Dixon has contributed an interesting concept, which he terms "creep": "By creep factors I mean those influences that cause fixed costs to build up in a situation where they were not expected." To put it another way, the manufacturer who, in comparing his costs with those of suppliers, does not make a proper allowance for fixed costs is merely deluding himself, since costs associated with the added activities will sooner or later "creep" into a company's total cost structure: "The added activity will encroach upon the available capacity, and sooner or later this will lead to an actual, though unanticipated, and perhaps unrecognized, increase in fixed costs." The inclusion of profit is no more than an insurance against "creep": "Clearly the relationship between today's costs and today's purchase prices may be only a temporary one, and it is altogether too probable that the nonspecialist producer will lag behind the specialist supplier whom he has discarded in the hope of achieving production economies. Thus the decision can easily turn sour in spite of all the measures which may be taken to avoid mistakes."

Several examples were cited by Oxenfeldt of specific cases in which the end-product manufacturer had in fact lagged behind the specialist suppliers. One involved a manufacturer of vacuum cleaners:

> In the spring of 1953, the R. Co. estimated it could manufacture at a cost of 13.4 cents each the latches used on the housing of its vacuum cleaner, an item for which it was then paying a supplier 15.8 cents. Its estimate turned out to be exceptionally accurate. By the spring of 1954, it was producing its requirement of these latches at an "all in" cost of only 14.2 cents, despite the fact that its current requirements represented only about 80 percent of the daily capacity installed, and the actual rate of output, in mid-1953.
>
> Meanwhile, however, suppliers had adjusted their prices to reflect an improvement in diecasting technique (a device for automatically charging and emptying the molds) which speeded up the process but was economical to use only in very large-scale operations. As a result of this development, along with a shift from a sellers' to a buyers' market, suppliers were in May 1954 furnishing the R. Co.'s competitors comparable latches at a price of 10.8 cents.

[30] Included in the schedule is a long list of questions relating to costs of raw material, working process, maintenance and storage costs, allowances for downtime, and so forth, as well as to the type of allowance a manufacturer should make for general administrating expense, selling expense, depreciation, maintenance, insurance, and general taxes.

With no prospect that its own shop could ever get unit cost down to this level, and a strong likelihood that suppliers' prices on such items would eventually drop even below 10 cents, the R. Co. threw in the sponge and turned again to outside suppliers for its latches.

Another interesting example, cited by Caditz, illustrates the technological expertise available to a specialist by virtue of his production of items that, though somewhat different, are made with the same facilities involving the same processes. When his firm received a contract from one of the world's largest manufacturers of aluminum ladders, "We did not know a thing about making aluminum ladders but the problems were essentially metal-fabricating ones. Because we were able to use the techniques and experiences we had learned in other areas—and because we had nothing to unlearn—we were soon producing ladders at 50% over the highest production rate our customer had ever achieved in his own plant."

Among the other advantages of buying is the fact that most specialist suppliers have a diversity of customers and are thus able to realize the economies resulting from sustained operations. In Caditz's words, "The composite demand from many different companies and areas helps keep the specialist's workload and machine use factors steady. He, therefore, is able to use his direct labor more efficiently and control his indirect labor more effectively. In comparison, the end-product manufacturer who decides to fill an individual need by making a part himself has only one customer—himself. He is faced with less controllable ups and downs of production." As an example he referred to the case of a large end-product manufacturer who found he had "many thousands of dollars" of worthless stampings on hand because in an effort to control the fluctuations in production the manager of his stamping department had produced at one time the total requirements for a year; "and then, as is normal, engineering changes came along and obsoleted the inventory."

By buying, the end-product manufacturer is also able to avail himself of specialists within specialists. Again to quote Caditz, "The range of most manufacturing fields is broad—too broad, generally, for any one specialist to cover and still retain the benefits of specialization. So, subgroups developed to cover special areas within a field." Within a subgroup the individual firms will differ in their machinery, equipment, know-how, and general ability: "It is remarkable how the cost goes down when a part is made on just the right equipment. As his requirements change, a good buyer finds new specialized sources to serve him." In contrast, the end-product manufacturer tends to be limited to what he can produce on his existing machinery and equipment. As an example Caditz cited the case of a manufacturer of automobile radios who produced parts and components on his own equipment. He lost an important contract because his engineers naturally limited themselves in designing their parts to those that could be made on the company's existing equipment, which, in this case, was not the most suitable. This is a danger that the integrating manufacturer can avoid only by adding constantly to his machinery and equipment, thereby increasing the proportion of his capacity that is idle and adding further to his overhead costs. By virtue of the very fact that he has a diversity of customers whose needs are changing and different, the specialist supplier also acquires varied experiences that are not available to an end-product manufacturer who is serving only himself. Knowledge and expertise gained by the specialist in supplying one customer is a transferable asset, available to all who wish to use it.

When the decision "to make" involves acquiring an entire company, the end-product manufacturer incurs a number of additional disadvantages. Thus, according to Oxenfeldt, "When managements undertake to make via acquiring a going business, they always tend to exaggerate the improvement in management that they will bring about." Then too, "they seem to underestimate the danger of accumulating extra management talent that neither by experience nor by temperament and outlook fits smoothly into the parent company's organization."

In a survey of the costs of "independent" versus "captive" tool and die-makers in the Detroit area, Dixon and Paton found that the total unit costs of the independent suppliers were substantially below those of the captive plants (i.e., those owned by the automobile companies). This was despite the unexpected fact that the independents paid higher wages—in Dixon's words, "A survey of hourly wage rates showed a marked difference in rates as between the two classes of shops and, surprisingly at first, it was found that hourly rates in the independent shops were substantially higher." But higher wage rates in the independent shops were more than offset by their lower overhead costs.

> A very important factor in the comparative cost picture is that of overhead costs. Here the independent shops appear to have an overwhelming advantage. Characteristic all-inclusive overhead rates in job [independent] shops range from 70 to 130 percent of direct labor costs. We were not allowed access to the cost data of the automotive plants but by putting together various pieces of evidence it was our conclusion that in the large captive shops the range runs from a minimum of 250 percent to more than 400 percent.

Dixon and Paton expressed their findings in the form of an example that assumed the manufacture of a given set of dies requiring 30,000 labor hours, comparable costs under captive and job shop conditions, and no labor efficiency superiority on the part of the job shop: "With these assumptions . . . a total cost saving ranging from $137,250 to as much as $292,500 is possible on a 30,000-hour set of dies produced under job shop conditions."

The trend of vertical concentration

What has been the net balance of the forces making for greater and for lesser integration? Through vertical integration a large firm may be able to improve its position (a) by curtailing supplies to their nonintegrated competitors, (b) by imposing on them a "price squeeze," and (c) by preempting markets through ownership of important buyers. Vertical integration also creates certain opportunities for the attainment of efficiencies, particularly through achieving a better flow of materials, parts, and components from lower to higher stages of production. At the same time integration can be the source of important diseconomies. Opportunities for savings through specialization and geographic plant dispersal may be forgone, while unnecessary and inflated costs may "creep" into the corporation's accounts.

In earlier years, particularly during the 1920's, many large corporations firmly established vertical structures, which for the most part have endured. But with the growing use of substitute materials it has become increasingly difficult to preempt supplies, while the rapid changes in modern technology have made it increasingly risky to forego the economics of specialization. There are thus *a priori* reasons to believe that the trend toward greater vertical integration, so evident in the past, should have tended to slow down. Confirmation of such a conclusion is provided by recent statistical evidence on the trend of integration. In a study of the ratio of corporate sales to gross corporate product, Arthur B. Laffer found no evidence of any general increase in vertical integration between the late 1920's and the mid-1960's: "The conclusion reached on the basis of this empirical evidence is that there has not been any discernible increase in the degree of vertical integration in the corporate sector. If anything, there might have been a slight decline." [31] Since the available data on gross corporate product are on a plant basis while the figures on corporate sales are on a company basis, the merging of companies that are customers or suppliers of each other would tend to reduce the ratio of sales to product.

> If, for example, firm A has a gross corporate product of 500 and sales to firm B of 1,000 (firm A's purchased materials inputs are 500) and firm B has a gross corporate product of 500 and sales of 1,500, then total corporate sales for both firms equal 2,500 and total gross corporate product equals 1,000. In this instance the ratio of sales to gross corporate product equals 2.5. If these two firms merge, total corporate sales will be 1,500 and gross corporate product will still be 1,000. The new ratio of corporate sales to gross corporate product will be 1.5. Vertical integration has caused a decline in our ratio. As is readily apparent, neither pure horizontal integration nor a pure conglomerate movement will affect our ratio.[32]

For the period 1948–63, and also in comparison with 1929, Laffer found that by his measure, "there is no discernible time trend in the degree of vertical integration." [33]

[31] Arthur B. Laffer, "Vertical Integration by Corporations, 1929–1965," *Review of Economics and Statistics,* Feb., 1969, pp. 91–93.
[32] *Ibid.*
[33] *Ibid.*

CONGLOMERATE
CONCENTRATION

In discussing the state of economic thinking concerning conglomerate expansion, Corwin D. Edwards has observed that the subject "falls outside the limits of our customary analyses of competition and monopoly or of vertical integration. Like those parts of medieval maps of the world that were labeled 'Terra Incognita,' the area covered is one in which our awareness and curiosity have outrun our knowledge." [1] Two theoretical articles on conglomerate activity begin respectively: "The problem of the multiple-product firm has lain in virtual neglect on the threshold of the theory of monopolistic (or imperfect) competition since the pioneering efforts of Chamberlin and Joan Robinson"; [2] and, "It appears that very little has been written about the multi-product firm." [3]

Conglomerate concentration may be defined as the possession of a share of a given industry's resources or activity by companies that are primarily engaged in other industries but are not suppliers or users of the given industry's products. In terms of market concentration, shares become significant when the leaders achieve "substantial monopoly power"—i.e., when they are not required to sell at the price offered by the market but instead are in a position to choose among alternative pricing policies. For reasons that will be delineated later, a leader who is primarily engaged in some other industry may be able to adopt a pricing policy different from that which would be dictated by market forces, even though its share of that industry is less than what is usually conveyed by the concept of oligopoly. In other words, it may be able to choose among alternative pricing policies even though its share of the market is less than what is usually thought of as a necessary condition for such discretionary power.

Conglomerate concentration and market behavior

It is fair to say that the growth of large, multi-industry firms, which during the 1960's proceeded at a feverish tempo, has been greeted by the economic profession with remarkable calm. Although in the past little attention had been devoted to the effect of conglomerates on market behavior, new, and admittedly embryonic, theories have now been developed as to how competition can be affected—and affected very adversely—by the entrance into an industry of

[1] *Hearings on Economic Concentration*, Pt. 1, p. 39.
[2] Eli Clemens, "Price Discrimination and the Multiple-Product Firm," *Review of Economic Studies*, 1950–51, pp. 2950–58.
[3] J. C. Weldon, "The Multi-Product Firm," *Canadian Journal of Economics and Political Science*, May, 1948, p. 176.

a large firm primarily engaged in an unrelated field.[4] In examining these theories, which are summarized below, one must bear in mind that for the most part they rest on the assumption that the conglomerate possesses substantial monopoly power in at least one of the industries in which it is engaged. Without monopoly profits gained somewhere, the conglomerate in all probability will ultimately be a danger only to its own stockholders, regardless of whatever short-run speculative profits are made through the mere act of merging. Even where the conglomerate does possess substantial monopoly power, it will be in a position to injure competition in the long run only if the monopoly profits resulting therefrom exceed the diseconomies of operating unrelated enterprises.

Cross-subsidization

The actual use by a conglomerate of monopoly profits earned in another industry to subsidize sales at a loss or at an abnormally low profit may be referred to as cross-subsidization. Profits can be considered to be abnormally low if over an extended period they remain substantially below what would have been yielded had the enterprise remained a competitive supplier in view of the market's prevailing cost and demand factors.

Cross-subsidization is destructive of competition since it makes the plight of the single-line producer all but impossible. Even though in his own industry the single-line producer is more efficient than the conglomerate, there is little point in pursuing the course of action held out by classical theory—i.e., reducing his price to reflect his greater efficiency—since his price reduction would only be matched or exceeded by a firm that can easily afford to accept losses in his industry. Moreover, any attempt by the single-line producer to diversify into some other field would be hindered by a price level in his own industry that tends to prevent both the retention of earnings and the attraction of capital from the outside.

Our knowledge of cross-subsidization is, to put it mildly, fragmentary. To some observers, this means that the practice is nonexistent.[5] To others it merely signifies the understandable reluctance of corporate officials to provide the antitrust agencies with proof of a possibly unlawful practice[6] or dissident stockholders with evidence of high-level mismanagement. Nonetheless, despite these understandable reasons for nondisclosure, indications of cross-subsidization do on occasion come to the surface.

A detailed case study of cross-subsidization as it is actually practiced in one industry is to be found in a book by Carl Kaysen based on a civil antitrust suit brought by the United States against the United Shoe Machinery Corporation under the Sherman Act.[7] Kaysen had served as assistant to Judge Charles

---

[4] In addition to these theories, cases have been brought against mergers on the grounds that they facilitate and promote reciprocal dealing, i.e., that after a merger, companies which were formerly independent buyers and sellers in competitive markets deal, as divisions or subsidiaries, with each other, thereby abridging markets and sources of supply. Reciprocal-dealing arrangements, however, are not dependent upon merger and under certain circumstances have been proceeded against as constituting, in themselves, an unlawful practice.

[5] See, e.g., Donald F. Turner, "Conglomerate Mergers and Section 7 of the Clayton Act," *Harvard Law Review,* May, 1965.

[6] See *United States* v. *Griffith,* 334 U.S. 100 (1948); *United States* v. *United Shoe Machinery Corp.,* 110 F. Supp. 295 (D. Mass. 1953).

[7] *United States* v. *United Shoe Machinery Corporation,* United States District Court of Massachusetts, Civil No. 7198, filed Dec. 15, 1947 (CCH-912).

Edward Wyzanski, Jr., before whom the case was tried From his detailed study of the case, Kaysen concluded that "the power to engage in extensive and quantitatively large discrimination is an important source of strength to United in maintaining its dominant position in the market." [8] When the suit was instituted in 1947, United was the largest seller of shoe machinery and shoe factory supplies. At the time of its formation in 1899, United had merged 5 shoe machinery manufacturers and from the beginning had dominated the shoe machinery market, with 70 percent or more in each major line.[9] From its initially entrenched market position, United by 1947 had enlarged its share to an estimated 85 percent of the market for shoe machinery.[10] In regard to major machines, Kaysen found that all of United's 22 competitors were small relative to United, all had small shares of the market, and all offered only a few lines of machinery. In the case of minor machines, although United's total share was slightly smaller than for major machines, a similar situation existed, characterized by Kaysen as "United dominant and a number of small and weak rivals in no way of comparable economic magnitude." [11]

United not only offered a full line of shoe machinery but varied the prices of its several kinds of machine in accordance with the degree of competition it encountered. (Since United followed the policy of leasing rather than selling its machines, its charges were in the form of rentals.) Using the broader term "price discrimination" to designate what is here referred to as "cross-subsidization," Kaysen stated:

> The major effect of the full line is the opportunity it gives United to compete against single-line or short-line sellers through price discrimination, an opportunity which exists as long as there are important machines in United's own line which face no competition. By pricing machines facing competition at low markups over cost, and machines facing no competition at high markups over cost, United makes the achievement of success by short-line competitors much more difficult than it would be if United could not discriminate in price. The potentiality of this kind of competition may be as strong a deterrent to the would-be competitor as its existence is a limitation on the ability of actual competitors to thrive and grow. . . . [A] sufficiently wide range of price discrimination exists to justify the inference that it is an important barrier to the development of competition.[12]

As an indication of the variation of United's prices among its different types of machine, Kaysen cited a Terms Committee memorandum to United's president, dated July 26, 1950, showing the variations in the number of years required to return the 10-year investment on the proposed new terms for 66 machines. Since the number of years required to return the 10-year investment is a measure of the price-cost margin (the higher the number of years, the smaller the margin), the spread of these figures shows the extent of the discrimination. At one extreme was a machine with such a high rental that less than 2 years was required to return the 10-year investment; at the other were 4 machines for which the period was 8 years or more: [13]

[8] Carl Kaysen, *United States v. United Shoe Machinery Corporation,* Harvard University Press, 1956, p. 78.
[9] *Ibid.,* p. 7.
[10] *Ibid.,* p. 50.
[11] *Ibid.,* p. 53.
[12] *Ibid.,* pp. 74–75.
[13] *Ibid.,* p. 75.

Number of Years Required to Return 10-Year Investment (Based on Expected Revenues from Proposed New Terms)			Number of Machines
0	to	2	1
2	to	4.5	29
4.5	to	5.5	13
5.5	to	8	19
8	to	10	2
10	to	12	1
12	to	14	1

Examining specific examples of discrimination cited by the Department of Justice, Kaysen found that they fell into certain categories:

> One is the reduction of previously set terms in the face of growing competition. . . . Another is the offer of a new model machine at the same or lower terms as the previous model which it is designed to replace, even though the cost of the new machine is higher than that of the old one. . . . A third is the failure to increase price (and lease terms) on a machine in the face of rapidly rising bulletin costs because of the presence of competition, combined with the appearance of the long since "justified" increase when "competitive conditions" had changed. . . . Finally there is the somewhat extreme example of the development of a new machine . . . to meet the competition of German machines in the slipper trade, and the setting of low terms on the machine; but also an attempt to segregate the market in the slipper trade from the rest of the market and prevent the use of the [new machine] in the shoe trade in general.[14]

On the question of whether there existed on United's part an intent to destroy competition, Kaysen cites an annual report of the Cement Shoe Department that stated: "The writer had confidently expected that after we came out in January 1932 with our USMC Cement Sole Attaching Machine—Model B, and auxiliaries, and the mechanical difficulties had been ironed out, we would enjoy a gradual elimination of our competitors in the cement shoe field." [15] With regard to this question of intent Kaysen went on to state:

> If "intent to exclude" means a specific intent to drive competitors completely out of the market by the adoption of price policies which are explicable only in terms of exclusionary policy—e.g., selling below out-of-pocket costs, no evidentiary basis appears to support a finding of such intent. On the other hand, if the intent in question is displayed by the conscious adoption of price policies which will, in given competitive situations, be relatively advantageous to United and relatively disadvantageous to United's competitors offering machines of one or a few types, and which contribute to a change in the competitive balance in the market in United's favor, it is clear that these examples support the allegation of intent.[16]

Although the court had no difficulty in finding an unlawful intent,[17] Kaysen

[14] *Ibid.*, pp. 130–31.
[15] *Ibid.*, p. 132.
[16] *Ibid.*, p. 134.
[17] *United States* v. *United Shoe Machinery Corp.*, 110 F. Supp. 295, at 346. ". . . Defendant intended to engage in the leasing practices and pricing policies which maintained its market power. This is all the intent which the law requires when both the complaint and the

as l... al;
...ons; he ...nows
... can hurt him
... to fail to initiate

... producers that the
...ition to all the other
...er in trying to determine
...st of a lower price (before
... ability to transform its prob-
...s with which he cannot possibly

...he antitrust action brought by the
...quisition of Clorox by Procter &
...is point, the Supreme Court showed
...nvolved:

...ubstitution of Procter with its huge
... the already dominant Clorox would
...age active competition from the firms
...of retaliation by Procter.

      *   *

...that the smaller firms would become more
...their fear of retaliation by Procter. It is
...become the price leader and that oligopoly

...is not necessary in such cases to establish that
...place. The important consideration was the ex-
...single-line producers "that Procter might under-
... out competition and subsidize the underpricing
...ucts." [21]

...ompetition arising from monopoly power in other

...eneral's National Committee to Study the Antitrust Laws,

... Procter & Gamble Co., 386 U.S. 568 (1967), 575–78.

CONGLOMERATE CONCENTRATION

ina
genera
de mer
ah. Nor wil
just meeting
tion of the d
whatever the "in

Where the single-line r
merely means the confront
power in that industry with
industries. Under those circum
presence of the conglomerate? B
monopoly power themselves and
the actual or potential exercise of
expected that the behavior of the
that of a single-line oligopolist? One
olists might be unable to match the
of rivalry to which oligopolists usually
nonprice competition. In rivalry that tak
model changes, services, and the like, the
the greatest resources, not the lowest costs.
of its operations in other industries, has grea
it could better afford to bear the cost nece
time than could the single-line oligopolists.

Expectations of a reaction

Theories of "monopolistic" or "imperfect" comp
pectation of a reaction—the expectation by each
gopolists will react to a price reduction by imm
same reasoning the pricing behavior of single-li
be affected by their expectations of a conglomer

---

judgment rest on a charge of 'monopolizing,' not merely
fendant having willed the means has willed the end."
[18] Kaysen, *op. cit.*, p. 129.

pursued the matter further, pointing out that the symptoms and consequences are likely to be essentially the same whether the intent is to exclude competitors or simply to earn higher profits. (Kaysen notes, however, an important exception—namely, where exclusionary intent is plainly shown by deliberate sales below out-of-pocket costs.) In either case the results are likely to stem more from the market strength and position of the discriminating company than from its subjective intentions:

> In order that United be able to practice price discrimination, some amount of market power on its part is necessary. Given the market power, the practice of price discrimination will, in general, allow United to achieve higher profits than it could achieve in the absence of discrimination. The essence of such discrimination for profit will consist in the charging of higher margins (over costs) on machines in which there is little competition—either from other machines or from hand labor, and lower margins on machines in which there is much competition. Now this is also precisely the pattern which would be shown if the "intent" behind the discrimination was driving out competitors, rather than increasing profits. In general, a distinction between the two kinds of "intent" cannot be made merely by looking at the actual price structure, if it can be made at all. Nor will a judgment of "intent" rest validly on the distinction between just meeting and undercutting the prices of competitors. The market position of the discriminating seller will do much to determine the results, whatever the "intent." [18]

Where the single-line firms are oligopolists, the entrance by a conglomerate merely means the confrontation of large firms possessing substantial monopoly power in that industry with a large firm that happens to be engaged in other industries. Under those circumstances, how can competition be altered by the presence of the conglomerate? By definition, the oligopolists possess substantial monopoly power themselves and would therefore be relatively impervious to the actual or potential exercise of leverage. And on what grounds could it be expected that the behavior of the conglomerate would be any different from that of a single-line oligopolist? One possibility is that the single-line oligopolists might be unable to match the conglomerate's expenditures in the type of rivalry to which oligopolists usually limit themselves—the various forms of nonprice competition. In rivalry that takes the form of advertising, sales effort, model changes, services, and the like, the advantage tends to go to the firm with the greatest resources, not the lowest costs. Hence, if the conglomerate, because of its operations in other industries, has greater resources and monopoly profits, it could better afford to bear the cost necessary to improve its position over time than could the single line oligopolists.

Expectations of a reaction

Theories of "monopolistic" or "imperfect" competition are based upon the expectation of a reaction—the expectation by each oligopolist that his rival oligopolists will react to a price reduction by immediately matching it. By the same reasoning the pricing behavior of single line producers would logically be affected by their expectations of a conglomerate's probable reaction to a

---

judgment rest on a charge of 'monopolizing,' not merely 'attempting to monopolize.' Defendant having willed the means has willed the end."

[18] Kaysen, *op. cit.*, p. 129.

price cut on their part. The entrance of a conglomerate into an industry consisting of single-line producers in fact introduces a profound change in their price-making calculus. In considering whether to make a price reduction, the single-line firms cannot but be aware of the conglomerate's monopoly power in other industries and of the obvious uses to which that power could be put against any price-cutting rival. Nor can they be expected to be unaware of the fact that whereas their economic life depends on success in one industry, profits from that industry usually constitute a minor portion of the conglomerate's total earnings. They surely are well aware of their consequent vulnerability to the competitive reactions which the conglomerate can take with only a minor effect on its overall earnings. And the single-line firms can be expected to be very well aware indeed of the dangers of a prolonged period of price rivalry against any large firm deriving monopoly profits from other industries that are not scenes of vigorous price rivalry. Thus, just as in the case of oligopoly, it is a subjective attitude that is the important element. To paraphrase Machlup's classic description of the oligopolist's state of mind: the single-line producer will naturally think of a conglomerate operating in his industry as his rival; he believes that the conglomerate will notice his "competitive" actions; he knows that even if he is the more efficient producer the conglomerate can hurt him more than he can hurt the conglomerate, and this will cause him to fail to initiate competitive actions he would otherwise undertake.

It is these considerations in the minds of the single-line producers that the entrance of a conglomerate brings to an industry. In addition to all the other factors which the single-line producer must consider in trying to determine whether the gain of greater business is worth the cost of a lower price (before it is met),[19] he must now add the conglomerate's ability to transform its probable unfavorable reaction into retaliatory actions with which he cannot possibly cope.

This line of reasoning was advanced in the antitrust action brought by the Federal Trade Commission against the acquisition of Clorox by Procter & Gamble. Accepting the FTC's finding on this point, the Supreme Court showed no inability to grasp the conceptual issues involved:

> The Commission found that the substitution of Procter with its huge assets and advertising advantages for the already dominant Clorox would dissuade new entrants and discourage active competition from the firms already in the industry due to fear of retaliation by Procter.
>
>   *   *   *
>
> There is every reason to assume that the smaller firms would become more cautious in competing due to their fear of retaliation by Procter. It is probable that Procter would become the price leader and that oligopoly would become more rigid.[20]

Under the Court's decision, it is not necessary in such cases to establish that retaliation has in fact taken place. The important consideration was the expectation in the minds of the single-line producers "that Procter might underprice Clorox in order to drive out competition and subsidize the underpricing with revenues from other products." [21]

The destructive effect on competition arising from monopoly power in other

[19] See *Report of the Attorney General's National Committee to Study the Antitrust Laws,* 1955, p. 329.
[20] *Federal Trade Commission v. Procter & Gamble Co.,* 386 U.S. 568 (1967), 575–78.
[21] *Ibid.* at 575.

industries is at its greatest where the single-line producers are small firms in competitive or "atomistic" industries. Here, the danger to competition is that what had previously been an actively competitive industry might be transformed into one dominated by a single company and characterized by price leadership and a general absence of price rivalry. This would come about even though the share of the industry in the hands of the conglomerate is no greater than the share held by the firm it replaced.

Potential injury to competition

It is in oligopolistic structures that the "potential injury" doctrine has its greatest applicability. This theory places in juxtaposition internal expansion through new plant construction against external expansion through merger. It holds that if conglomerates are denied the right to enter an industry through the latter route, they will perforce have to make their entrance by building new plants. And whatever adds to an industry's capacity is necessarily a stimulus to competition. Where such a stimulus is particularly needed, of course, is in oligopolistic industries. How a conglomerate makes its entrance into a "competitive" or "atomistic" industry is usually not a matter of serious consequence, since capital entrance requirements tend to be low and other barriers to entry few and unimportant. But where entry is difficult the manner of entrance can be a matter of very real consequence. By their very nature such industries are usually oligopolistic. Hence, freedom to expand by merger kills off one of the few means (expansion of capacity) by which competition can be infused into the very type of industry in which it is most needed.

One of the clearest expositions of this line of reasoning is to be found in the action by Judge Robert Shaw in issuing a permanent injunction barring the acquisition of Potash Company of America by Standard Oil of New Jersey.[22] In his opinion, the judge pointed out, "Production of potash is an industry in which present concentration is substantial," a condition he attributed to the fact that "entry into the potash industry by shaft mining is limited to companies with substantial capital resources." The company Standard sought to acquire was a substantial producer: "It ranks second in North American production. In terms of total current revenues and net profits after taxes *from the sale of potash* it ranks among the most successful companies occupying an enviable position in that field." Moreover, the long-term demand for fertilizers appeared extremely favorable to the acquiring company. According to a report prepared by Esso Chemicals, dated August 14, 1964, "A gradually increasing need for fertilizers is undeniable: the inexorable growth of world population will create in 35 years a need for twice today's food production. . . . Inevitably, lands now lying fallow because of their submarginal fertility will come back into cultivation—but only with heavy applications of fertilizers . . . the fertilizer raw materials seem almost uniquely free of the threat of substitution and of dependence upon industrial growth."

As a supplier of mixed fertilizer Standard enjoyed a "high" net profit return. But an area of even greater profitability appeared to be the production of the materials themselves. In a memorandum of August 11, 1964, Siro Vazquez, head

---

[22] *United States* v. *Standard Oil Company (New Jersey) and Potash Company of America*, United States District Court of New Jersey, Civil No. 954–64, filed March 31, 1966 (CCH–71,736). The quotations in the discussion that follows have been taken from the record of this case.

of Standard's Producing Coordination Department, pointed out that "our studies indicate that the producing function tends to be the most profitable portion of the fertilizer business, which suggests the desirability of integrating backward to raw material production." From Standard's point of view, entrance by acquiring a profitable going concern was preferable to constructing their own facilities: "There is no doubt from the evidence that acquisition of Potash Company of America from the profit aspect was much more attractive than a self-developed potash project." But, in Judge Shaw's view, what is desirable for a private interest must be subordinated in a concentrated industry such as this to the broader interest of stimulating competition by increasing the number of suppliers; if Standard Oil of New Jersey, with its ample resources and its desire to obtain its own source of supply, were to enter this highly concentrated industry, said the judge, it must do so by internal expansion. Summarizing the underlying reasons for his decision, Judge Shaw stated:

> The evidence leaves no doubt as to the fact that Jersey has the available expertise to discover and competently evaluate the potential of profit in new fields of capital investment; that it has embarked upon and emphasized a policy of continued economic growth consistent with maintenance of current percentage of profit return; and that it has the capital resources for acquisition of a profitable enterprise by purchase or for the undertaking of large and long-term capital financing of a self-developed business deemed likely to enhance the ultimate overall profit return to its stockholders.

Like all other approaches to the difficult problem of conglomerate expansion, this "potential injury" theory has its shortcomings. For one thing it accepts implicitly the conclusion that monopoly control is permissible as long as it is achieved by internal expansion, since internal expansion adds to the industry's supply. But the acceptance of any resulting concentration is conceptually in conflict with the doctrine handed down in the *Alcoa* case that possession of a sufficiently high market share, in and of itself, contravenes the antitrust laws, even if the company "had monopoly thrust upon it."

A second limitation has to do with evidentiary requirements. In the *Potash* case the Antitrust Division happened upon engineering reports and market analyses clearly establishing the company's ability and intent to enter the industry one way or the other. In the absence of such documents, how far would the courts go in striking down mergers on these grounds? Would it be enough for the antitrust agencies merely to show that the company had the resources to make its entrance via new plant construction, even though documents were lacking to indicate that such a course of action was ever seriously entertained? On one point the history of antitrust enforcement leaves little room for doubt; whenever a promising new "theory of the case" begins to gain acceptance, the documents to establish it have a way of evaporating.

Mutual forbearance among conglomerates

When a conglomerate confronts not a single-line producer but another conglomerate, its reasons for abstaining from competitive moves are different, though the results will be much the same. Assuming that the conglomerates possess substantial monopoly power in some industry, they should be able to defend themselves against each other. Hence, fear of reprisals in the industry in which they make a competitive move should not be a serious deterrent. But, while they do not labor under the same restraint that inhibits the single-line company from competitive action, a restraint of a somewhat different character would logically be at work. Assume that 2 or more conglomerates confront one another as competitors in a number of different industries. Owing to differences in cost, market shares, and product acceptance, it is only to be expected that the importance of these industries as sources of profits will vary considerably among the different conglomerates. A conglomerate that launches a competitive attack in an industry which is an important source of profits to a rival conglomerate can logically expect a retaliatory attack in an industry which is an important source of profits to it. Realizing this, it will abstain from initiating a competitive move in the first industry. And the greater the number of industries in which given conglomerates confront each other, the stronger the reason for mutual forbearance in each of them. In the words of Corwin Edwards:

> When one large conglomerate enterprise competes with another, the two are likely to encounter each other in a considerable number of markets. The multiplicity of their contacts may blunt the edge of their competition A prospect of advantage from vigorous competition in one market may be weighed against the danger of retaliatory forays by the competitor in other markets. Each conglomerate competitor may adopt a live-and-let-live policy designed to stabilize the whole structure of the competitive relationship. Each may informally recognize the other's primacy of interest in markets important to the other, in the expectation that its own important interests will be similarly respected. Like national states, the great conglomerates may come to have recognized spheres of influence and may hesitate to fight local wars vigorously because the prospect of local gain is not worth the risk of general warfare.[23]

To what extent do conglomerates confront each other as competitors? Some light can be shed on this question by special compilations based on the 1963 Census of Manufactures. One of these tabulations shows the number of the 200 largest manufacturing companies which were *primarily* engaged in each of the various major industry groups.[24] Another shows the number of the 200 largest which *operate plants* classified in each of the major industry groups.[25] Subtracting the latter from the former yields the number among the 200 largest firms which operated plants in a given major industry group but whose principal line of activity was in some other major industry group. To these companies, in other words, their operations in the given industry group constituted a secondary activity. These distributions of the 200 largest are shown in Table 3-1.

Of the 200 largest manufacturing companies 29 were primarily engaged in food and kindred products—i.e., their shipments in this group were greater than their shipments in any other group. But a considerably greater number, 48, had plants classified in this group. Thus, 19 of the 200 largest firms owned plants producing food and kindred products but were primarily engaged in some other industry group. The extremes are tobacco products on the one hand and the combined grouping of paper and lumber products on the other. Tobacco products represented the principal line of business for 6 of the 200 largest, and none of the others had plants in this group. At the opposite extreme, 12 of the largest manufacturers were primarily engaged in paper and lumber products, but no fewer than 71 others had plants producing these products. The latter

[23] *Hearings on Economic Concentration,* Pt. 1, p. 45.
[24] *Concentration Ratios in Manufacturing Industry, 1963,* Pt. 2, Table 24.
[25] *Ibid.,* Table 23.

Table 3-1

200 LARGEST MANUFACTURING COMPANIES

Comparison between companies primarily engaged in and
companies with plants in major industry groups

Major Industry Group	Number of Companies among 200 Largest		Difference (b) – (a)	Ratio (a):(b)
	(a) Primarily Engaged in—	(b) With Plants in—		
Food and kindred products	29	48	19	1.0: 1.6
Tobacco products	6	6	0	1.0: 1.0
Textile and leather products	4	27	23	1.0: 6.7
Apparel and related products	0	12	12	
Furniture and fixtures	0	12	12	
Paper and lumber products	12	83	71	1.0: 6.9
Printing and publishing	6	48	42	1.0: 8.0
Chemicals and allied products	31	101	70	1.0: 3.3
Petroleum and coal products	10	20	10	1.0: 2.0
Rubber and plastics products	4	65	61	1.0:16.2
Stone, clay, and glass products	8	46	38	1.0: 5.7
Primary metals industries	18	62	44	1.0: 3.4
Fabricated metal products	6	70	64	1.0:11.6
Nonelectrical machinery	12	76	64	1.0: 6.3
Electrical machinery	19	59	40	1.0: 3.1
Transportation equipment	30	53	23	1.0: 1.8
Instruments, miscellaneous products	5	63	58	1.0:12.6

Note: To prevent disclosure of the operations of individual companies the Census Bureau in Table 24 combined lumber and allied products with paper and paper products. For the same reason instruments were combined with miscellaneous products.

Source: *Concentration Ratios in Manufacturing Industry, 1963,* Pt. 2, Tables 23, 24

case illustrates that by no means all instances of secondary activity can be regarded as cases of conglomerate confrontation. Many of the 200 largest primarily engaged in some other industry produce paper products used for packaging their own products. Similar cases of vertical integration probably account for some of the differences existing in primary metals, fabricated metal products, and machinery.

But, even allowing for this factor, it seems clear that by 1963 conglomerate confrontation among the nation's largest firms, and the resultant opportunities for mutual forbearance, had become commonplace. In manufacturing as a whole the number of top firms operating in a major group was, on the average, six times the number primarily engaged therein. Clearly, the typical firm among the 200 largest frequently encounters among his competitors other top companies whose primary line of business lies elsewhere.

CONGLOMERATE CONCENTRATION

Theories of the case and conglomerate structure

From the point of view of the antitrust agencies it would be most helpful if there were some body of information to identify the industries in which cross-subsidization is taking place or is threatened, those in which expansion through merger instead of internal growth results in a significant loss of potential competition, and those in which there is mutual forbearance among conglomerates. While there is no such body of data, the form of industry structure that is most susceptible to a given type of injury can be identified. Figure 3-1 illustrates the different ways in which competition may be affected adversely by conglomerate concentration, depending on the structure of the industry. On the vertical axis the chart shows for 124 industries the share of output accounted for by those among the 200 largest manufacturing companies which made shipments in the industry. The horizontal axis depicts the total number of companies in the industry. It will be noted that the axis is constructed in terms of a logarithmic, or ratio, scale; this is the most feasible way by which the extraordinary range in the number of companies—from fewer than 50 to over 10,000—could be shown on one chart. Finally, the chart is divided into 3 grids, according to the level of concentration. At the top are the concentrated industries—those in which the 4 largest companies in 1963 produced 50 percent or more of the output; in the bottom grid are the unconcentrated industries—those with a concentration ratio of under 25 percent; and between are the industries of moderate concentration —those with ratios between 25 and 49 percent.

In the upper left-hand area of the top grid are 12 concentrated industries with 100 or fewer companies; in all but one of these industries companies among the 200 largest accounted for 60 percent or more of the shipments. From the existence of so few companies, the level of the industry's concentration, and the importance of very large companies, it can be inferred that these are industries of formidable barriers to entry. If a company which has the resources to surmount the barriers by entering such an industry through internal expansion is nonetheless permitted to enter by merger, there is a very real loss to potential competition. It is such industries that are particularly in need of the competitive stimulus provided by the construction of new plant and facilities. The same considerations of course apply with progressively lesser force as the level of concentration declines, the share held by the top companies decreases, or the number of companies rises.

The danger to competition posed by cross-subsidization, whether actual or anticipated, is at its maximum in unconcentrated industries populated largely by small single-line firms. In the bottom grid of Figure 3-1 are 38 unconcentrated industries with from 800 to over 10,000 companies. Typically, the bulk of their sales are made by small or medium-size companies that are not engaged in other industries. Yet in 15 of these industries companies among the 200 largest made 20 percent or more of the shipments. To most of their small producers these leading companies of U.S. industry must loom as veritable giants. This is all the more true if the large company derives monopoly profits from some other industry in which it is also engaged. To any one of the hundreds of smaller firms in such industries, making a competitive move which might invite retaliation by a giant competitor could well appear to be an invitation to disaster.

To identify the different forms of industry structure that are most prone to a

Figure 3-1

SHARE OF VALUE ADDED ACCOUNTED FOR BY 200 LARGEST MANUFACTURING COMPANIES IN INDIVIDUAL INDUSTRIES, 1963

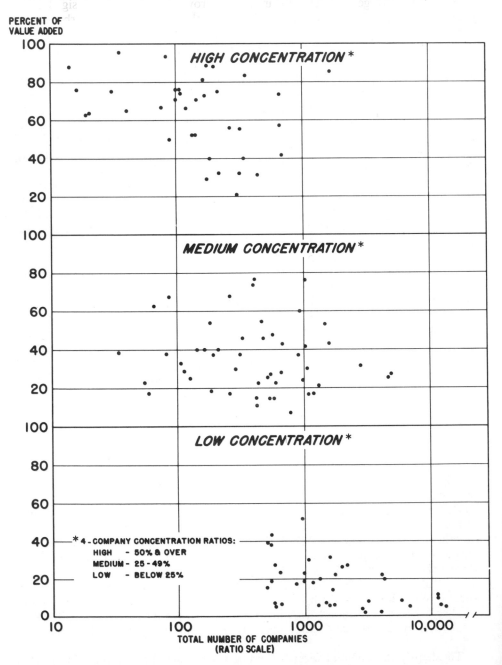

Source: *Concentration Ratios in Manufacturing Industry, 1963*, Pt. 2, Table 23

CONGLOMERATE CONCENTRATION

given type of competitive injury resulting from conglomerate expansion is not to imply that such injury cannot occur elsewhere. Though the effect is generally not as serious, potential competition (as has just been indicated) can be lessened in unconcentrated industries with low capital entrance requirements as well as in concentrated industries with high entrance requirements. Mutual forbearance among conglomerates can take place regardless of the industry structure. And cross-subsidization may appear as a danger to single-line producers in oligopolistic as well as unconcentrated industries, though the behavior of the industry itself is not as likely to be altered.

The conglomerate role of the largest companies

When one of the largest companies in manufacturing as a whole operates in an industry other than the one in which it is primarily engaged, is it usually among the *leading* producers in this field—which to it is a secondary line—or does it tend to be a minor factor? From the point of view of the influence exerted by the conglomerate on behavior in its secondary lines, this is obviously a matter of considerable importance. The participation by a conglomerate as a secondary producer always poses a danger to the single-line firms; the danger becomes very real indeed when the conglomerate is one of the industry's leading producers. What follows is based not on market shares but on the frequency with which the largest companies in manufacturing as a whole appear among the leading producers in the 1,014 individual product classes. Specifically, Figure 3-2 shows for each of the 20 major industry groups the relative frequency with which the 100 largest companies appear among the 4 largest producers of the product classes within the group. For example, at least *one* of the 100 largest companies was represented among the 4 largest producers of *each* of the 5 product classes in the tobacco industry group—cigars, cigarettes, chewing and smoking tobacco, redried tobacco, and stemmed tobacco. This is indicated by the full length of the bar, which in this case extends to 100 percent. In 4 of the 5 product classes in tobacco (indicated by the dark portion of the bar extending to 80 percent), at least 2 of the 4 leading producers came from the ranks of the 100 largest. The extent of the participation by the 100 largest was nearly as high in chemicals and allied products, where at least one of the 4 leading producers was from the 100 largest companies in nine-tenths of the product classes. Moreover, in nearly two-thirds of the group's products at least 2 of the 4 leading producers came from the 100 largest.

At least one of the 4 largest producers came from the 100 largest companies in more than half of the product classes in 12 of the 20 major industry groups. Only in furniture, miscellaneous products, and apparel did their frequency of appearance fall below 25 percent. Moreover, in tobacco, chemicals, rubber products, primary metals, electrical machinery, and transportation products at least 2 of the 100 largest were represented among the 4 largest producers in more than half of the product classes. In addition, at least 2 of the 4 leading producers came from the 100 largest in more than one-fifth of the product classes in fabricated metals, food, instruments, textiles, and machinery.

In more than half of the 1,014 product classes in manufacturing as a whole, at least one of the 100 largest was among the 4 largest producers, and in 31 percent at least 2 came from the 100 largest. It is thus obvious that the 100 largest companies are not limited in their operations to only a few large-scale

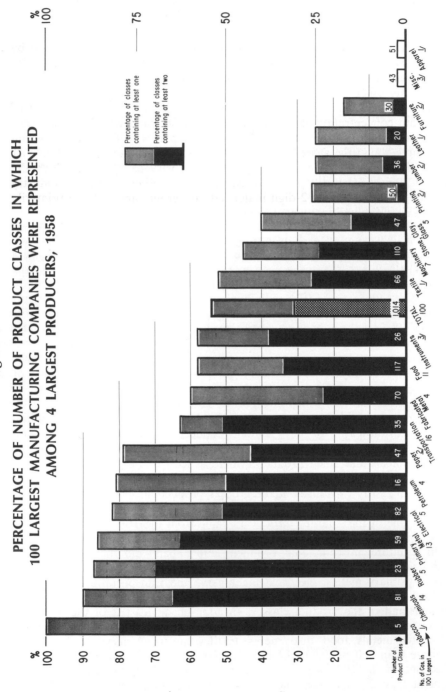

Figure 3-2

PERCENTAGE OF NUMBER OF PRODUCT CLASSES IN WHICH 100 LARGEST MANUFACTURING COMPANIES WERE REPRESENTED AMONG 4 LARGEST PRODUCERS, 1958

Percentage of classes containing at least one

Percentage of classes containing at least two

Number of Product Classes

No. of Cos. in 100 Largest

Tobacco 5 · Chemicals 14 · Rubber 5 · Primary Metal 13 · Electrical 5 · Petroleum 4 · Paper 4 · Transportation 6 · Fabric Metal 4 · Food 11 · Instruments 3 · TOTAL 100 · Textile 7 · Machinery 7 · Stone, Glass 5 · Printing 2 · Lumber 2 · Leather 1 · Furniture 2 · Misc. 3 · Apparel 1

5 · 81 · 23 · 59 · 82 · 16 · 47 · 35 · 70 · 117 · 26 · 1014 · 66 · 110 · 47 · 50 · 36 · 20 · 30 · 43 · 51

1/ 6 Cos. in combined groups of textiles, apparel, leather and tobacco
2/ 6 Cos. in combined groups of lumber, furniture, paper, and printing and publishing
3/ 4 Cos. in combined groups of instruments, miscellaneous manufactures and ordnance

Source: *Concentration Ratios in Manufacturing Industry, 1958*, Pt. 2, Table 29

industries but rather are broadly represented among the largest producers of manufactured products throughout most of the wide spectrum of U.S. industry.

"Outside" leadership

Further information on the extent of conglomerate concentration is provided by a new Census tabulation which shows for individual industries the share of the output accounted for by companies among the 8 leaders that are primarily engaged in some other industry.[26] Already used to provide examples of vertical concentration,[27] the same tabulation can be used to shed light on the extent of conglomerate concentration. Specifically, it shows for each of 244 industries[28] the concentration ratio in terms of the 8 largest companies, which is then broken down in three ways: the shares held by those companies among the 8 that (a) are primarily engaged in the 3-digit enterprise industry category of which the industry is a part, (b) are primarily engaged in another enterprise industry category but within the same 2-digit major industry group, and (c) are primarily engaged in an entirely different major industry group.

In Figure 3-3, the full length of each bar indicates the 8-company concentration ratio; in the case of electric refrigerators it is 91 percent. The share of refrigerator output produced by companies among the 8 leaders primarily engaged in the manufacture of household appliances is 20 percent (the solid area of the

Figure 3-3

EXAMPLES OF CONGLOMERATE CONCENTRATION

Shares of output by companies among 8 leaders primarily engaged in the specified industry and in other industries, 1963

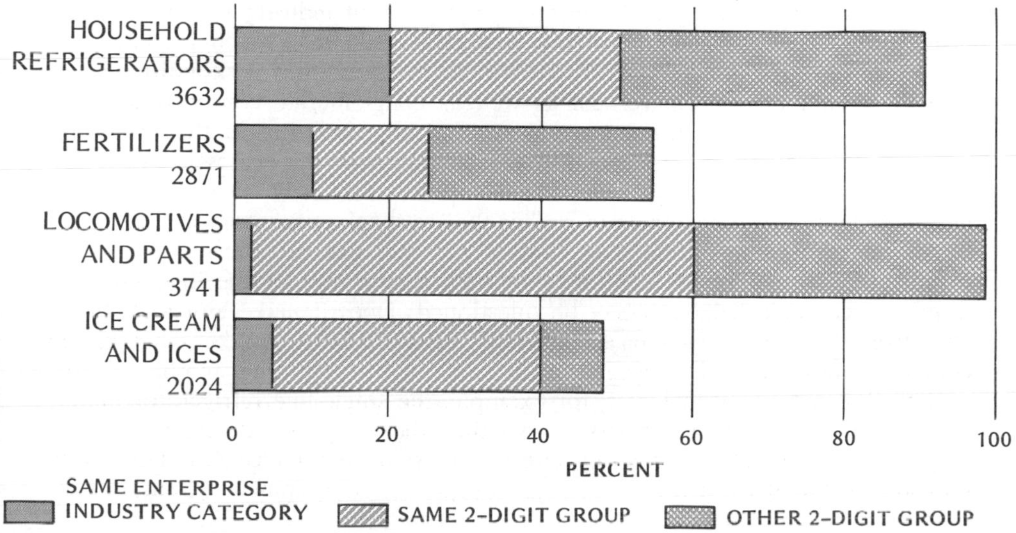

Source: *Concentration Ratios in Manufacturing Industry, 1963*, Pt. 2, Table 22

[26] *Concentration Ratios in Manufacturing Industry, 1963*, Pt. 2, Table 22.
[27] See Ch. 2.
[28] In preparing the tabulation it was necessary, primarily because of disclosure problems, to omit about 40% of the 416 Census industries.

bar); those among the 8 not primarily engaged in appliance production, but whose principal line of business is still within the same major industry group (electrical machinery), accounted for 30 percent of the output (the lined area); and those primarily engaged in an industry entirely outside the electrical machinery group produced 41 percent (the dotted area). For the sake of simplicity, the first figure may be said to refer to the share of the predominantly "single-line" producers—in this case companies such as Maytag and Whirlpool-Seeger; the second to the share of what may be referred to as the "partial" conglomerates —companies such as General Electric and Westinghouse, whose principal line of activity is still within the electrical machinery group; and the third to the share of the "pure" conglomerates—in this case companies such as General Motors (Frigidaire).

In the fertilizer industry the largest share (30 percent) was accounted for by companies outside the chemical group—presumably by large oil companies that have entered the fertilizer industry. The single-line producers have all but disappeared from the production of locomotives and parts: nearly three-fifths (58 percent) came from the "partial" conglomerates—in this case principally General Motors; and 39 percent was produced by companies outside the transportation equipment field—e.g., the manufacture of locomotive engines and parts by electrical machinery manufacturers. In ice cream, again the single-line producers are no longer a significant factor; the largest share (35 percent) is held by the "partial" conglomerates—in this case companies such as National Dairy and Borden, which are principally engaged in some other dairy products industry.[29]

In order to prevent disclosure this tabulation shows, not the share held by those among the 8 primarily engaged in the 4-digit industry itself, but the share held by those in the broader, approximate 3-digit enterprise industry categories. This procedure has the effect of overstating the shares held by the "single-line" producers primarily engaged within the specific 4-digit industry shown.[30] Moreover, it must be remembered that the data relate to 1963, which predated the merger wave of the middle and late 1960's. At the same time it should be noted that the tabulation reflects vertical as well as conglomerate concentration and indeed was used to illustrate cases of vertical concentration in the preceding chapter. Nonetheless, the great majority of instances of the possession of a significant share of an industry's output by companies primarily engaged elsewhere undoubtedly reflects conglomerate, rather than vertical, concentration.

Although the data permit a separation of what has been termed "partial" from "pure" conglomerate concentration, the significance of the distinction in terms of economic behavior may be questioned. Does it make any real difference from the point of view of an industry's behavior in the market whether the conglomerate is primarily engaged in the same or in some other major industry group? Will not the behavior of, for example, the single-line refrigerator manufacturers be the same regardless of whether the conglomerate against which they have to compete is primarily engaged in some other electrical machinery industry (General Electric) or in, say, transportation equipment (General Mo-

[29] For a discussion of the use of cross-subsidization and other practices in the refrigerator and fertilizer industries, see Ch. 14; for a discussion of the role played by government in promoting conglomerate concentration in the locomotive industry, see Ch. 15.
[30] The enterprise industry categories for these 4 industries are, respectively, household appliances, miscellaneous chemical products, other transportation equipment, and other dairy products.

tors)? The reasons for assuming that conglomerate concentration results in particular types of behavior would appear to be the same in either case. The "partial" and the "pure" conglomerate are equally able to engage in cross-subsidization. The single-line producer would have the same reason to expect a reaction to a competitive move regardless of whether the conglomerate was primarily engaged in the same or in some other major industry group. The potential injury to competition resulting from the conglomerate's decision to expand by merger rather than by new plant construction would be the same regardless of where it is primarily engaged. And the same would be true where 2 conglomerates, confronting each other in several industries, abstain from competing in any one of them because of fear of reprisal in others.

If this reasoning is correct, the significant criterion is to be found in the relative shares of an industry's output accounted for by single-line firms on the one hand and conglomerates on the other, regardless of the latters' principal line of activity. On this basis the 244 industries for which information is available may be classified according to the share of their output produced by those companies among the 8 leaders that are primarily engaged in some other enterprise industry category. Table 3-2 separates the industries into 3 groups: (a) those in which the conglomerates accounted for less than one-third of the output, (b) those in which their share ranged from one-third to two-thirds, and (c) those in which their share was two-thirds or more. Industries in which conglomerates, as thus defined, are a minor factor are still in the majority—137, or 56 percent of the total. Nonetheless, in more than two-fifths of the industries (44 percent) at least one-third of the output comes from companies among the 8 leaders primarily engaged in some other enterprise industry category. And in one-sixth of the industries (17 percent) the conglomerates control two-thirds or more of the output. Moreover, significant participation by conglomerates is not limited to

Table 3-2

DISTRIBUTION OF INDUSTRIES ACCORDING TO SHARES
OF OUTPUT
PRODUCED BY CONGLOMERATES, 1963[a]

Industry Group	Number of Industries[a]			Total
	Less than One-third	One-third to Two-thirds	Two-thirds or More	
Food and tobacco	23	7	5	35
Textiles, apparel, leather	14	8	6	28
Lumber, furniture, paper, printing	12	4	6	22
Chemicals, petroleum, rubber	13	10	7	30
Primary metals	10	4	2	16
Fabricated metal products, nonelectrical machinery	18	8	4	30
Electrical machinery	13	8	7	28
Transportation equipment	5	3	1	9
Other	29	14	3	46
Total	137	66	41	244

[a]Share of companies among the 8 largest *not* in same enterprise industry category.

Source: *Concentration Ratios in Manufacturing Industry, 1963*, Pt. 2, Table 22

just a few areas. In electrical machinery and in textiles and related products, conglomerates produced at least one-third of the output in half of the industries. In all but 2 of the remaining groups they produced one-third or more in one industry out of 3.

In the past, statistical data relating to concentration were limited largely to measures of aggregate concentration (e.g., the share of total assets accounted for by the 200 largest firms) and to concentration ratios for individual industries. What was needed was a "bridge" between the two types of data, which would reveal the market share of individual industries held by multi-industry (and presumably large) conglomerates. On only one occasion until now—a special survey in 1950 by the Federal Trade Commission—has this type of information ever been obtained.[31] With the special tabulation of Census data from which the preceding figures were taken, a more current "bridge" has been supplied, and it reveals conglomerate concentration to be of impressive dimensions. If one selects an industry at random, the chances are better than 2 out of 5 that firms primarily engaged in another enterprise industry category will produce at least one-third of that industry's output and better than 1 out of 6 that they will produce two-thirds or more of its output. There is thus a very large segment of the industrial economy in which price making to maximize short-run profits may be subordinated to other considerations more relevant to the long-term interests of the company as a whole—or of its management.

The trend of conglomerate concentration

The mushrooming growth of conglomerate corporations in the 1960's gave rise to the impression that a new form of business organization had been created. What is new, however, is its extent; the multi-industry concern has long been with us. More than 40 years ago the Federal Trade Commission made an investigation of what was in the way of becoming the most massive conglomerate in America's history, before or since. On July 27, 1927, E. I. du Pont de Nemours & Company announced that it had purchased 114,000 shares of the common stock of the U.S. Steel Corporation, for which it paid some $14 million. Coming on the heels of Du Pont's purchase of 22.9 percent of the stock of General Motors, this acquisition would have brought together through stock ownership the nation's largest chemical firm, its largest automobile producer, and its largest steel company. The Commission was concerned primarily with the potential vertical relationships. It is not inconceivable that G. M.'s demand for steel would have been preempted by U.S. Steel in the same way that G. M.'s demand for auto paint was preempted by Du Pont. At the same time, it was not unmindful of other aspects; in its resolution of July 29, 1927, directing that the investigation be made, the Commission indicated its concern over "the establishment of a *community of interests* among these three corporations which are reputed to be the largest industrial corporations in this country." [32] Some 6 months following the initiation of the investigation, the Commission received a letter, dated March 19, 1928, and signed by Irenee du Pont, stating: "E. I. du Pont

---

[31] Federal Trade Commission, *Industrial Concentration and Product Diversification in the 1,000 Largest Manufacturing Companies: 1950*, 1957.
[32] Federal Trade Commission, *Report on du Pont Investments Undertaken by a Resolution of the Commission dated July 20, 1927*, 1929. Emphasis added.

de Nemours & Company had sold its entire holdings of United States Steel Corporation Common Stock." [33]

The earliest general survey shedding light on conglomerate activity is to be found in a remarkable study, *The Integration of Industrial Operations*, published in 1924 by the Census Bureau.[34] Prepared by Willard L. Thorp and based on the 1919 Census of Manufactures, this monograph drew a distinction between "simple" central-office firms (those whose establishments operate in only one industry) and "complex" central offices (those with establishments in 2 or more industries). Even in 1919, 31 percent of the central offices were found to be of the "complex" type,[35] though it should be observed that the latter included vertical as well as conglomerate operations.

Nearly two decades later another study, also prepared under the direction of Thorp, showed that between 1919 and 1937 the complex type had registered noticeable gains, both absolutely and relatively.[36] Speaking of manufacturing as a whole, Thorp said that "there appears to have been at least some decline in the proportion of the simple structure in favor of the complex type." [37]

In 1950 the Federal Trade Commission conducted a special one-time survey covering the operations of the 1,000 largest manufacturing concerns.[38] If only these firms are taken as the possible leading producers, the manufacture of the product was a secondary activity of the leading producer in more than one-fourth of all product classes (254 out of 926).[39] A marked acceleration in the growth of diversification since that time has been shown in a study by Harrison F. Houghton.[40] In 1950 the number of companies among the 1,000 largest that produced as many as 16 to 50 products totaled 128; by 1962 the number of such companies had nearly doubled, rising to 236. Similarly, in 1950 8 companies produced over 50 products; by 1962 the number had risen to 15. At the same time the number of companies within the 1,000 largest that manufactured only one product fell from 78 to 49.[41] If similar data were available following the sharp rise in conglomerate mergers during the middle and late 1960's, they would undoubtedly show a further sharp increase in multiproduct operations.

[33] *Ibid.*, p. 7. The difference in the length of time required to achieve the same result (divestiture) between the judicial process and the focusing of the spotlight of publicity through an economic investigation should not pass unnoticed.

[34] Bureau of the Census, Department of Commerce, Census Monograph No. 3, Willard L. Thorp, *The Integration of Industrial Operations*, 1924.

[35] *Ibid.*, pp. 125–26.

[36] Willard L. Thorp and Walter Crowder, *The Structure of Industry*, Monograph No. 27, Temporary National Economic Committee (TNEC), 1941, pp. 105–226. The industries of both the 1919 and 1937 studies approximate the 4-digit industries of the Standard Industrial Classification.

[37] *Ibid.*, p. 151. Between 1919 and 1937 the definitions of 6 major industry groups remained generally the same. In all but one, central offices of the complex type constituted a greater proportion of all central offices in 1937 than in 1919. They also registered an increase in their share of the total number of plants operated by all central offices.

[38] FTC, 1957, *op. cit.*

[39] *Ibid.*, p. 42. In its analysis of product-class leadership the Commission eliminated from consideration all products where the leading companies made shipments of less than $13 million. The effect was to exclude all but a few instances where a company too small to be included among the 1,000 largest firms made more shipments of a given product class than did any of the 1,000.

[40] *Hearings on Economic Concentration*, Pt. 1, pp. 155 *et seq.*

[41] The study was based on a comparison of the FTC's survey of 1950 with the "Plant and Product Directory" of *Fortune* magazine for 1962. Inasmuch as the former was conducted on a mandatory basis and the latter compiled by voluntary means, the study probably understates the increase in diversification.

CH 4 AGGREGATE CONCENTRATION

By "aggregate" concentration, sometimes referred to as "overall" concentration or the "concentration of economic power," is meant control over a relatively large proportion of the nation's total nonfinancial or industrial resources or activity by a small number of very large enterprises, such as the 100 or 200 largest corporations. Conceptually, aggregate concentration differs from conglomerate concentration in that in the former, each of the top corporations could *conceivably* be engaged in only one industry. For example, the largest 200 could theoretically be made up of, say, 10 companies engaged only in petroleum, 6 engaged only in steel, 3 only in automobiles, and so on. In the real world, of course, most of the largest corporations are engaged in more than one industry, but the conceptual issues raised by aggregate concentration are in addition to those arising from conglomerate concentration.

Aggregate concentration and market behavior

As is true of the other dimensions of concentration, the economic issue arising from aggregate concentration is its effect on market behavior. Is market behavior different because an appreciable part of the output comes from companies which themselves are among the very largest in the country? The principal argument for assuming that aggregate concentration does have a distinct effect on market behavior is based on what have been referred to as "communities of interest." Through such communities, revolving around powerful family and financial groups, clusters of great corporations are said to be related by interlocking directorates, intercorporate stock holdings, historical relationships, and other means. The effect of such communities, it is contended, is to bring about greater cohesiveness and unity of action than would otherwise be the case. Control is sufficient to prevent any member of a community from undertaking a course of action which, though beneficial to itself, would be harmful to other members of the community. The inevitable result is a lessening of the potential for independent, competitive behavior.

Indeed, it can be argued that even without any overt activities, intercorporate stock holdings by family owning groups, investment and commercial banks, or institutional investors will in and of itself be injurious to competition. Thus, if a large corporation whose stock is so held takes an action that seriously injures other firms in which an owning group also has substantial stock interests, the latter will discreetly make known its displeasure to the offending management. If it comes to a showdown, the owning group usually has the votes to discipline or remove the offending management; and corporate managers, being well aware of this fact, abstain from making the competitive moves they would otherwise undertake. Whether the company which would be injured is in the same or a different industry is irrelevant; what is important is an awareness by the management of a given company that the owning interests holding effective control over it are also important stockholders in the companies which would be injured by its action.

On the other hand it can be argued that stock ownership in the large corporation is too widely diffused to permit control over management; that through stock options, management itself has come to be a not insignificant ownership group; that even where a large institutional investor holds sufficient stock to exercise control, it abstains from so doing because of legal and institutional restraints; that since large corporations have been able to meet most of their financial requirements through internal savings, they have become immune from any possible influence financial interests might seek to exert; that commercial and investment banks are more dependent for their income on the goodwill of corporate management than vice versa; and that for all practical purposes management is thus independent and self-perpetuating.

There is also the view that it really makes little difference in terms of market behavior whether ultimate control is vested in management or in some powerful family, financial, or investment group. Through long association, managers and owning interests customarily have come to see eye-to-eye on issues that otherwise might provoke conflict. They agree that the corporation should achieve its "target" profit rate, meet the interest on its fixed obligations, retain or improve its share of the market, display a satisfactory "growth" rate, finance its operations from earnings and thus avoid diluting the stockholders' interest, enjoy a steady appreciation of stock values, avoid the "disruption" of price competition, and in other ways conform to the established standards of successful business enterprise. Even in those cases where the owners (or some influential groups thereof) are in a position to do otherwise, they are generally content to sit on the sidelines as long as management follows policies that at least do not appear to run counter to their own interests. Only in rare instances does a conflict arise between the interests of management and those of ownership in the normal course of business, and only in a small proportion of these does a real contest develop over who will be controlling.

The trend of aggregate concentration

Whatever the reason, the concern with aggregate concentration seems to be a function of its trend. If the biggest corporations are not occupying an increasingly large segment of the economy—or at least cannot be shown to be doing so— aggregate concentration, regardless of its level, is usually greeted with relative indifference. But when the trend is upward, aggregate concentration becomes a matter of concern, which may stem from purely economic fears of injury to competition or from such darker specters as the possible establishment of a collective state and the loss of individual freedoms.

The long-term trend

Determining the long-term trend of concentration is a matter of considerable difficulty because the data become rarer and poorer as one moves backward in time. The longer the time span covered, therefore, the more tentative must be any conclusion. At best, only a rough impression can be gained from the separate statistical series that are available, compiled from time to time by different authorities using different sources and methods and covering different intervals of time. The trends shown by seven of these series are illustrated in Figure 4-1 and Table 4-1.

As will be observed, there are 2 figures for the earliest year shown, 1909, both of which have been put forward by their proponents as "cautious estimates." According to Gardiner C. Means, the 200 largest "non-financial" corporations then held 33 percent of the total assets (less taxable investments) of all nonfinancial corporations (Series 1).[1] Norman R. Collins and Lee E. Preston have estimated that in 1909 the 100 largest firms accounted for 17.7 percent of the total assets of all firms in manufacturing, mining, and distribution (Series 2).[2] When allowance is made for the difference in the number of companies (200 by Means and 100 by Collins and Preston) and the inclusion by Means of two concentrated segments of the economy not included by Collins and Preston (railroads and utilities), these two estimates do not appear to be too far apart. If they are only approximately correct, the subsequent movements of the two series would indicate a pronounced long-term increase in overall concentration.

Such a conclusion has been challenged by G. Warren Nutter, who held that between 1901 and 1937 overall concentration in fact declined.[3] His study was not based on the share of overall resources accounted for by the largest companies; rather he sought to determine the relative importance within total manufacturing (and the major industry groups) of "monopolistic" industries—i.e., those in which the 4 leading producers accounted for more than half the output. Described by Stanley Lebergott as a proposition "contrary to virtually the whole body of received opinion—right, left and center," [4] Nutter's conclusion rests fundamentally on the validity of his estimates for the turn of the century; obviously the higher the level of concentration indicated for 1901, the less likely the chances of any subsequent increase. In Lebergott's words:

> Briefly put, Dr. Nutter's estimate of the extent to which enterprise monopoly changed from 1899 to 1937 rests on a single, arbitrary assumption. Change that one assumption and you reverse his conclusion that monopoly declined or, at most, rose insignificantly. His detailed estimates for the trend of monopoly in manufacturing rely on some informed guesses made about 1905 by John Moody on the percent of each industry controlled by trusts.
>
> *   *   *
>
> The heart of Dr. Nutter's discussion of trends in monopoly 1899–1937 is the accuracy with which industries as of 1899 are separated between the monopolized goats and the competitive sheep; any undue generosity for 1899 will minimize the growth of monopoly.[5]

Lebergott then found that for a number of industries Moody's estimates were in

[1] National Resources Committee, *The Structure of the American Economy,* 1939, Pt. 1, p. 107, prepared under the direction of Gardiner C. Means.
[2] *Hearings on Economic Concentration,* Pt. 1, p. 62.
[3] G. Warren Nutter, *The Extent of Enterprise Monopoly in the United States, 1899–1939,* University of Chicago Press, 1951.
[4] Stanley Lebergott, "Has Monopoly Increased?" *Review of Economics and Statistics,* Nov., 1953, pp. 349–351.
[5] *Ibid.*

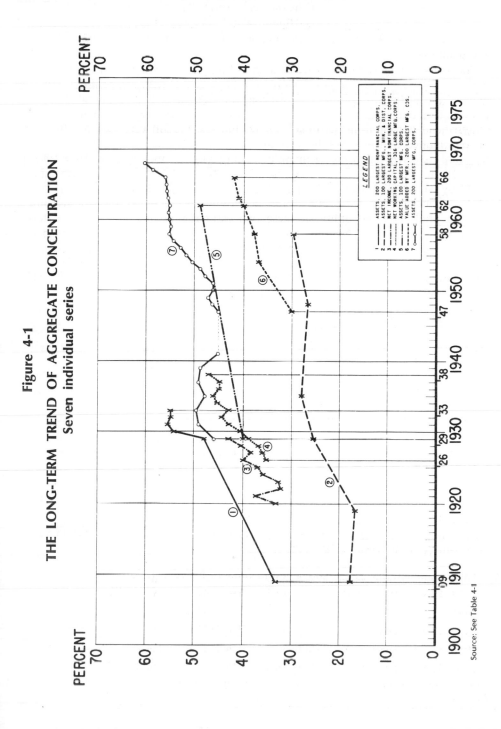

Figure 4-1

THE LONG-TERM TREND OF AGGREGATE CONCENTRATION
Seven individual series

LEGEND

1 ASSETS, 200 LARGEST NONFINANCIAL CORPS.
2 ASSETS, 100 LARGEST MFG., MIN. & DIST. CORPS.
3 NET INCOME, 200 LARGEST NONFINANCIAL CORPS.
4 NET WORKING CAPITAL, 316 LARGE LARGE MFG. CORPS.
5 ASSETS, 100 LARGEST MFG. CORPS.
6 VALUE ADDED BY MFR., 200 LARGEST MFG. C3S.
7 ASSETS, 200 LARGEST MFG. CORPS.

Source: See Table 4-1

Table 4-1
THE LONG-TERM TREND OF AGGREGATE CONCENTRATION
(Percentages of total)
Seven individual series

1. Total assets of all nonfinancial corporations (less taxable investments): 200 largest corporations

1909 33.3   1929 47.9   1930 54.3   1931 55.5   1932 54.8   1933 54.8

Source: National Resources Committee, *The Structure of the American Economy*, 1939, Pt. 1, p. 107, prepared under the direction of Gardiner C. Means

2. Total assets of all manufacturing, mining, and distribution corporations: 100 largest corporations

1909 17.7   1919 16.6   1929 25.5   1935 28.0   1948 26.7   1958 29.8

Source: Norman R. Collins and Lee E. Preston, "The Size Structure of the Largest Industrial Firms," *American Economic Review*, Dec., 1961

3. Total net income of all nonfinancial corporations: 200 largest corporations

1920 33.4   1921 37.6   1922 32.2   1923 32.8   1924 36.0   1925 37.1

1926 40.0   1927 38.4   1928 40.4   1929 43.2

Source: Adolf A. Berle and Gardiner C. Means, *The Modern Corporation and Private Property*, Macmillan, 1933

4. Total net working capital of all manufacturing corporations: 316 largest corporations

1926 35.3   1927 36.0   1928 37.0   1929 39.0   1930 40.5   1931 43.2

1932 44.4   1933 43.2   1934 45.4   1935 46.2   1936 44.9   1937 44.8

1938 47.0

Source: Donald Woodward, Moody's Investors Service

5. Total assets of all manufacturing corporations: 100 largest corporations

1929 40   1962 49

Source: *Hearings on Economic Concentration*, Pt. 1, p. 18, testimony of Gardiner C. Means

6. Value added by manufacture: 200 largest manufacturing corporations

1947 30   1954 37   1958 38   1962 40   1963 41   1966 42

1967 42

Source: Bureau of the Census, Department of Commerce, Concentration Ratios in Manufacturing, 1967, *Special Reports*, 1970, Pt. 1, Table 1

7. Total manufacturing assets: 200 largest manufacturing corporations

1929 45.8   1931 49.0   1933 49.5   1935 47.7   1937 49.1   1939 48.7

1941 45.1   1947 45.0   1948 46.3   1949 47.1   1950 46.1   1951 46.1

1952 47.7   1953 48.7   1954 50.4   1955 51.6   1956 52.8   1957 54.3

1958 55.2   1959 54.8   1960 55.2   1961 55.4   1962 55.1   1963 55.5

1964 55.8   1965 55.9   1966 56.1   1967 58.7   1968 60.4

Source: Federal Trade Commission Staff, Economic Report on Corporate Mergers, 1969, p. 173

AGGREGATE CONCENTRATION

fact substantially higher than the market share figures he was able to construct from Census data.[6] Lebergott also asked why Nutter failed to make use of Moody's *qualitative* information when he did not hesitate to use similar material for 1937:

> The monograph very properly makes good use of Clair Wilcox's evaluations for 1937—for example, tires and tubes are considered to be non-monopolized despite concentration of their production. This approach yields one of Nutter's two monopoly measures. However, very similar judgments by Moody for 1900 are not used. If we were to use them, a great increase in monopoly 1899–1937 would be indicated. Moody defines monopoly in terms of "restraint of competition, power over production and prices"—a surprisingly realistic and contemporary approach. . . . Based on this definition he states that the element of monopoly in industries which Nutter classified as monopolized (using Moody's data) is in fact "small" (rubber shoes), "small" (gum), "unimportant" (rubber goods), or even "none" (canned goods). . . . Surely Moody's qualitative evaluations deserve some attention. More than that, they suggest—when compared with Clair Wilcox's judgments for 1937—the kind of increase in monopoly which has been generally assumed.[7]

Moreover, there appears to have been a systematic bias toward overstatement in the concentration figures for those early years. In his authoritative study of mergers at the turn of the century, Ralph L. Nelson points out that the reports for the largest companies were likely to be exaggerated by the then common practice of stock watering: "Often an asset value for a business greatly in excess of its true value was suggested by the amount of authorized (and issued) capital. Stock watering was commonplace at the turn of the century, and the popularity of such financial chicanery may have varied with the intensity of stock speculation."[8] The concentration figures were further inflated by the use of 1901 as the base year. That particular year was toward the end of the greatest consolidation movement in history—a movement termed "explosive" by George W. Stocking and "episodic" and "huge" by Nelson. A significant number of the early consolidations did not long remain among the nation's industrial leaders.[9] What the lure of quick profits from stock manipulation had joined together was often quickly put asunder by the cold realities of the marketplace. Hence, Nutter's conclusions would in all probability be reversed by any measure of concentration extending back beyond the great consolidation movement or beginning a few years after its end. And such indeed are the showings of the long-term series beginning in 1909—those of Means and Collins and Preston.

[6] Some of the comparisons are as follows:

	Moody		Lebergott	
Shipbuilding	50%	(2 companies)	15%	
Woolen and worsted	60	(1 company)	30	
Leather	51+	(2 companies)	25	(5 companies)
Confectionary products	51+		20	

[7] Lebergott, *op. cit.*

[8] Ralph L. Nelson, *Merger Movements in American Industry*, Princeton University Press, 1959, p. 19.

[9] Nineteen companies—mostly consolidations formed at the turn of the century—that had been among the top 100 industrial firms in 1909 were no longer among the top 100 just 10 years later (*Hearings on Economic Concentration*, Pt. 1, pp. 244–45).

While little is known about the trend of concentration during World War I, a report of the Ordnance Department revealed that even then the federal government followed what has become its customary procedure of having its own facilities operated by a very few large enterprises. More than two-thirds (67.8 percent measured in terms of value) of the land and facilities owned by the Ordnance Department, but privately operated, was run by only 10 companies. E. I. du Pont de Nemours & Company and its subsidiaries accounted for 37.5 percent of the total, and 2 other companies, Hercules Powder Company and Atlas Powder Company—which had been separated from Du Pont in 1912 by an antitrust action—accounted for another 14.2 percent.[10]

But, as was to be the case in World War II, the important effect was not so much on industry structure during the conflict as in imparting a powerful impetus to further concentration after the war. As a consequence of lucrative war contracts and soaring prices, vast amounts of profits had accumulated and were pressing for profitable investment. In his now famous and prophetic "Report of the Treasurer of du Pont Company to the Finance Committee recommending investment in General Motors-Chevrolet Motor Stock, December 19, 1917," John J. Raskob, under the heading "Necessity for Finding Investments," stated:

> The total amount we have succeeded in investing in new industries to date, counting $12,500,000 for the dye business ($7,500,000 for plant investment and $5,000,000 for working capital investment) is $40,000,000 leaving a balance of $50,000,000 still seeking employment and it is imperative that this amount be employed, otherwise the earnings of our Company after the war will be insufficient to support the dividend policy and the matter of properly employing this money in a way that will result in proper return to our company is one of most serious consequence.[11]

It was this pressure of surplus funds for employment that led to the highly profitable purchase by Du Pont of 22.9 percent of the stock of General Motors and an abortive stock acquisition of U.S. Steel. Of even greater importance, however, was the speculative temper of the times. The making of mergers had become a handy instrument for the enhancement of stock values—and vice versa. As the stock market continued to reach new highs, so also did the ability of merger-minded companies to acquire other properties through the exchange of stock. By 1929 merger activity had reached an all-time high.[12] The movement was particularly active in the iron and steel and machinery industries, which during the years 1919–28 accounted for about one-fifth of all mergers in manufacturing and mining. Among other industries prominently involved in mergers during this period were oil, chemicals, and textiles. Food producers, such as independent dairies, cheese factories, and bakeries, were absorbed in large numbers by leading companies.

It is therefore not surprising to find that overall concentration during the 1920's moved noticeably upward. As can be seen in Figure 4-1, the share of total net income accounted for by the 200 largest nonfinancial corporations reg-

---

[10] National Archives, *Report of Land in the United States in which the Ordnance Department Has a Pecuniary Interest,* Records of the War Department, Office of Chief of Ordnance, May 12, 1919. The study covered the value of facilities in the production of explosives, artillery, communication, metal components, small arms and tanks, tractors, and trailers, of which explosives was by far the most important.

[11] Quoted in Federal Trade Commission, *Report on du Pont Investments Undertaken by a Resolution of the Commission dated July 20, 1927,* 1929, p. 15.

[12] See Willard L. Thorp, "The Changing Structure of Industry," in *Recent Economic Changes in the United States,* McGraw-Hill, 1929, Vol. I, p. 186.

istered an advance from 32.2 percent in 1922 to 43.2 percent in 1929 (Series 3).[13] And a series prepared by Donald Woodward of Moody's Investors Service showed that 316 large manufacturing companies increased their share of the net working capital of all manufacturing corporations from 35.3 percent in 1926 to 39.0 percent in 1929 (Series 4).[14]

These same series also showed a further and rather sharp increase during the 1930's.[15] The cause, however, was certainly not to be found in the pressure of accumulated funds or in mergers, which all but vanished from the industrial scene. Rather, the overriding cause was undoubtedly the higher rate of attrition among smaller firms, which had smaller financial reserves than their larger rivals and were less able to withstand the rigors of a prolonged depression.

During World War II overall concentration appeared to register a decline.[16] On the face of it this seems inexplicable in view of the extreme concentration of resources for war production, with no fewer than two-thirds of the prime contracts going to the top 100 contractors.[17] Only 68 top corporations received two-thirds of the value of federal contracts for research and development, while the top 10 received nearly two-fifths of the total.[18] And the top 100 corporations operated 75 percent of publicly financed facilities.[19] One explanation was the severe curtailment of the production of normal peacetime products by the petroleum and automobile industries—two areas long dominated by very large enterprises. Six of the 10, and 11 of the 20, largest manufacturing companies were in these 2 industry groups. Although the oil and automobile companies converted some of their facilities to wartime use and operated some publicly financed facilities, the total magnitude of their facilities expansion was relatively limited.[20]

[13] Adolf A. Berle and Gardiner C. Means, *The Modern Corporation and Private Property*, rev. ed., Harcourt Brace Jovanovich, 1967.

[14] Also by 1929 the 200 largest nonfinancial corporations had increased their share of total assets to 47.9% from 33% in 1909. During the same period the 100 largest industrial firms had increased their proportion of total assets to 22.5% from 17.7%.

[15] According to the Means series the 200 largest nonfinancial corporations increased their share of total assets from 47.9% in 1929 to 54.3% in 1933. The 100 largest of Collins and Preston's series increased their proportion of the total industrial assets from 25.5% in 1929 to 28.0% in 1935. And the Woodward series shows a rise by the 316 large manufacturing corporations from 39.0% of net working capital in 1929 to 43.2% in 1933 and a further advance to 47.0% in 1938.

[16] See 79th Cong., 2nd Sess., S. Doc. 206, Smaller War Plants Corp., Report for the Senate Select Committee on Small Business, *Economic Concentration and World War II*, 1946. That overall concentration did decline during the war is the logical conclusion to be drawn from an analysis of data put forward by Gardiner C. Means. Comparing 1929 with 1962, Means estimated that in the former year the 100 largest corporations accounted for 40% of the total assets of all manufacturing corporations (*Hearings on Economic Concentration*, Pt. 1, p. 15). The use of the same methods yields almost an identical figure for 1947—41.3% (*ibid.*, p. 206). Yet the evidence seems conclusive that during the Depression overall concentration moved upward. It therefore follows that to have arrived in 1947 at approximately the same level as prevailed in 1929, overall concentration must have declined during World War II from the higher levels reached during the Depression.

[17] 79th Cong., 2nd Sess., S. Doc. 206, Smaller War Plants Corp., Report for the Senate Select Committee on Small Business, *Economic Concentration and World War II*, 1946, p. 29.

[18] *Ibid.*, p. 53.

[19] *Ibid.*, p. 54.

[20] For the automobile group (which also included combat vehicles, trucks, and related items) the total expansion of both publicly and privately financed facilities between July, 1940, and June, 1945, amounted to less than half of the group's capital assets in 1939. By comparison the wartime expansion of facilities in aircraft and shipbuilding was more than twenty times the value of their prewar facilities. Similarly, the wartime expansion of facili-

But, as in the case of World War I, what is significant here is not so much the change in industry structure during the war but the resources, placed in the hands of the largest corporations, that could be used to further strengthen their position after the war:

> economic concentration will probably be higher in the postwar years than before the war as a result of: the production improvements and scientific research which big business gained during the war; the increase in the liquid funds and general financial strength of big business; the ability of big business to keep its name and trademarks before the public eye during the war; and finally the fact that big business will probably acquire a greater share of the war-built facilities which it operated than will small business, regardless of whether economic conditions are prosperous or depressed.[21]

It cannot be demonstrated that it was precisely these factors which were responsible for the early postwar increase in overall concentration. But whatever the cause it is a fact that the rise in aggregate concentration during the Depression, its fall during World War II, and its subsequent rise in the immediate postwar years has brought about a level of aggregate concentration which is substantially higher than the 1929 level. According to a new series compiled by Gardiner C. Means, the 100 largest manufacturing corporations increased their share of the total assets of all manufacturing corporations from 40 percent in 1929 to 49 percent in 1962 (Series 5).

The trend since World War II

Since World War II there has been a marked improvement in the quality of the data used to measure aggregate concentration and thus in our knowledge concerning its trend. Measures have been constructed in terms of both activity (value added) and resources (assets). The share of the total value added by manufacture that is accounted for by the 200 largest manufacturing companies is now compiled regularly by the Census Bureau. The term "value added by manufacture" is the value of shipments minus, principally, the cost of materials.[22] The purpose of deducting the cost of materials is to eliminate the duplication that would arise if the same transaction was counted twice, once as the sale (or interplant transfer) of a product by a supplier and then again as the cost of material by its recipient. It is in terms of this measure that the Census Bureau's figures on concentration for manufacturing as a whole (as well as for 15 broadly defined industries[23]) have regularly been compiled (Series 6). In the words of

---

ties in petroleum was less than one-fifth the value of the group's 1939 capital assets; in contrast, the wartime expansion in chemicals was more than one and one-half times the value of the prewar plant. (*Ibid.*, p. 38.)

[21] *Ibid.*, p. 61.

[22] Also deducted are a number of related and less important expenditures—the cost of supplies and containers, fuel, purchased electrical energy, and contract work.

[23] Industries in which 1958 concentration figures are based on value added:

2011 Meat Packing Plants	3585 Refrigeration Machinery
2013 Prepared Meats	3661 Radios and Related Products
2084 Wines and Liquors	3664 Telephone and Telegraph Equipment
2251 Full Fashioned Hosiery Mills	3717 Motor Vehicles and Parts
2271 Wool Carpets and Rugs	3721 Aircraft
3312 Blast Furnaces and Steel Mills	3722 Aircraft Propellers
3331 Primary Copper	3731 Shipbuilding and Repairing
3332 Primary Lead	

the Census Bureau, "Value added avoids the duplication in the value of shipments figures which results from the use of products of some establishments as materials by others. Consequently, it is considered to be the best value measure available for comparing the relative economic importance of manufacturing among industries and geographic areas." [24]

A sharp increase in the share of total value added accounted for by the 200 largest companies (and by each subgroup thereof) occurred between 1947 and 1954, followed by relative stability between 1954 and 1958 and then by a slow but steady upward tendency. Over the entire period 1947–66, the gain for the 200 largest was from 30 percent to 42 percent, an increase of 12 percentage points. For the 50 largest the increase was from 17 percent to 25 percent, a rise of 8 percentage points.[25] In 1958 a total of 269,834 companies were classified in manufacturing.[26] Thus, less than one-tenth of one percent of the total *number* of companies accounted in that year for more than two-fifths of the total value added by all manufacturing companies. The concentration data in terms of value added for the 200 largest and for subgroups thereof are shown in Figure 4-2.

There are no known sources of overstatement in these figures, but there are several possible sources of understatement. In determining which plants should be tied in to which companies, the Census Bureau asks the owning company to identify the plants it "owns or controls"; the plants are also required to identify the company that "owns or controls" them. Where the relationship takes the form of majority stock ownership, the Bureau feels that the plants are properly tied in to the owning company. But, in addition to those cases in which a parent company actually exercises "control" over another while owning less than 50 percent of its stock, there are other sources of understatement. For one thing, the majority of the major integrated oil companies are not included among the Census Bureau's 200 largest manufacturers, even though, year in and year out, about half of the 20 largest industrial firms in terms of assets are oil companies. These corporations are engaged extensively, not only in manufacturing, transportation, and distribution, but as mining enterprises in the extraction of petroleum from the ground.[27] Because of tax savings that can be secured through percentage depletion of mineral reserves and the treatment of intangible drilling costs, the major oil companies maximize after-tax profits by allocating the greater part of the value of their operations to mining instead of manufacturing. As a consequence, the Census Bureau has not classified 10 major oil companies, all within the 50 largest industrials, as manufacturing enterprises.[28]

[24] Bureau of the Census, Department of Commerce, *1958 Census of Manufactures,* 1961, Vol. II, p. 13.

[25] In 1967 the shares of value added accounted for by the 200 largest manufacturers and the subgroups thereof were the same as in 1966 (Bureau of the Census, Department of Commerce, *Concentration Ratios in Manufacturing,* 1967, 1970, Pt. 1).

[26] Bureau of the Census, Department of Commerce, General Report, *Enterprise Statistics: 1958,* Series ES 3, No. 1, Pt. 1, p. 22.

[27] "The list [of the 50 largest companies in terms of value added] was compared to the *Fortune* list of the 500 largest 1954 corporations (supplement to the July 1955 issue), which ranked companies by sales. Of the 50 largest *Fortune* companies, 13 were not among the Census' top 50. Ten of the 13 were oil companies. Apparently much of the value added in petroleum is recorded at the well-heads, which represent establishments classified in mining and thus out of the scope of the present analysis." (Ralph L. Nelson, *Concentration in the Manufacturing Industries of the United States,* Yale University Press, 1963, p. 92.)

[28] All the major oil companies are classified as manufacturing enterprises by the FTC-SEC in their Quarterly Financial Report program as well as by *Fortune* magazine in its annual "Directory of the 500 Largest U.S. Industrial Corporations."

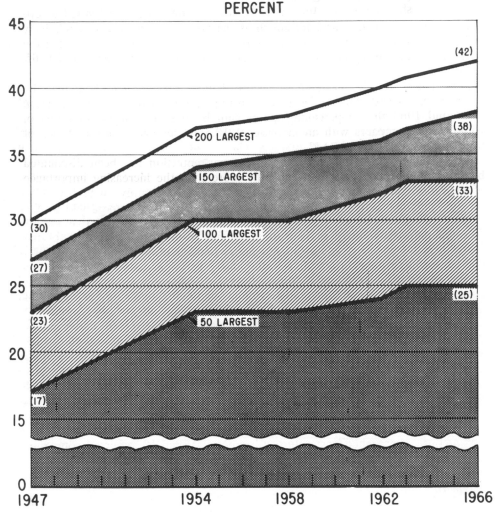

Figure 4-2
SHARE OF VALUE ADDED BY MANUFACTURE
ACCOUNTED FOR BY 200 LARGEST MANUFACTURING COMPANIES
1947–66
PERCENT

Source: *Concentration Ratios in Manufacturing Industry, 1963*, Pt. 1, Table 1

Another questionable statistical procedure followed by the Census Bureau is its treatment of enterprises owned by 2 or more other firms as independent, separate companies. Where a majority of the stock is owned by firms that are themselves within the 200 largest, the effect is to exclude enterprises actually under the ownership and control of companies among the 200 largest.[29]

[29] For example, the shipments of Owens-Corning Fiberglas Corp. would not have been included in the Census figure for the 200 largest, although 31% of its stock was owned by Owens-Illinois Glass Co. and 31% by Corning Glass Co., both of which were among the

AGGREGATE CONCENTRATION

Even in the absence of these downward biases, concentration in terms of activity would still be lower than concentration in terms of resources owing to inherent differences in what is being measured. Thus, the available figures on resources include mineral reserves held for future use, whereas the data on activity relate to operations in a given year. In addition, figures on resources include assets owned in foreign countries, whereas the latter are limited to operations in the United States. Inasmuch as the largest companies own relatively more reserves for future use and are more extensively engaged abroad than the average manufacturing company, these factors alone explain much of the difference.

Nonetheless, insofar as *trend* is concerned, it is interesting to note that the series on assets and value added tended to reinforce each other. Thus, between 1947 and 1963 the 11-percentage point gain by the 200 largest in terms of value added compares with an increase of 10.5 percentage points in terms of total assets (Series 6 and 7).[30]

The significance of the rise in aggregate concentration has been discounted by some authorities as representing little more than the increasing importance of the more concentrated industries in the economy. Certainly, in as broad an area of economic activity as total manufacturing, the relative share held by the largest companies can and does fluctuate with changes in the relative importance of different industries. The argument has been made that much of the sharp increase between 1947 and 1954 in the share held by the 200 largest was due to this factor, since the industries in which the largest companies were primarily engaged experienced an unusually rapid expansion. But the argument loses most of its force in the face of the fact that in the recession year of 1958 these same industries, such as steel and automobiles, suffered a greater-than-average curtailment in output. On the basis of the "changing weights" argument, a decrease in overall concentration should have occurred. Instead, the share held by the 200 largest actually showed a slight advance, rising from 37 percent in 1954 to 38 percent in 1958.

Aggregate concentration and individual industries

A long-term increase in aggregate concentration can be of interest, in itself, to historians, political scientists, and sociologists. Its interest to economists lies in its effect on competition in individual markets. And for it to have any such effect the largest companies in the economy as a whole must hold significant shares of individual industries. It is one thing if the largest companies derive their importance as producers in a few very large industries; it is something else again if, as a group, they hold significant shares in a considerable number of industries.

Light on this question is shed by Figure 4-3, which shows the share of employment held by the 200 largest manufacturers, as a group, in the "company industry groups" used in the Census of Business, which approximate the 3-digit

---

200 largest (for other examples, see *Hearings on Economic Concentration*, Pt. 1, pp. 82–83).

[30] Another measure registered a similar increase. Willard Mueller, Director of the Bureau of Economics of the Federal Trade Commission, estimated that "between 1947 and 1962 the share of all manufacturing assets held by the 113 largest manufacturing corporations probably increased by about 10 percentage points. . . ." (*Hearings on Economic Concentration*, Pt. 1, p. 122.)

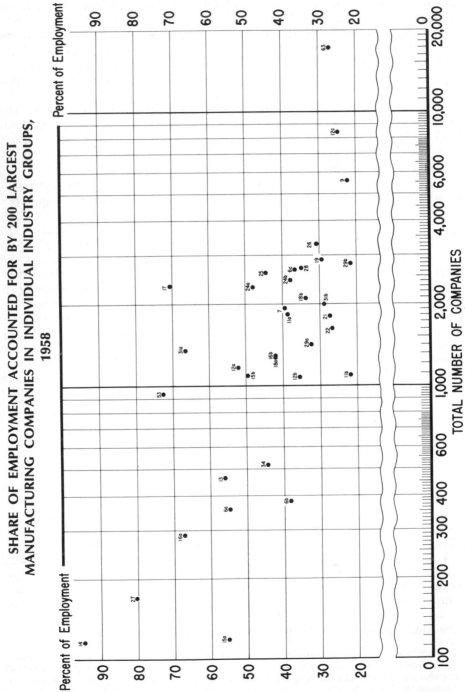

Figure 4-3

SHARE OF EMPLOYMENT ACCOUNTED FOR BY 200 LARGEST
MANUFACTURING COMPANIES IN INDIVIDUAL INDUSTRY GROUPS,
1958

Source: *Concentration Ratios in Manufacturing Industry, 1958*, Pt. 1, Table 1; Pt. 2, Table 2; Pt. 2, Table 33

AGGREGATE CONCENTRATION

KEY TO INDUSTRY GROUPS AND NUMBER
OF COMPANIES AMONG 200 LARGEST

Key	Industry Group	Total Number of Companies	Percent of Employment by 200 Largest
6a	Tobacco manufactures	355	54.7%
6b	Other transportation equipment	381	38.2
6c	Meat-packing plants	2,645	36.6
7	Ships and boats	1,912	39.3
9	Bakery products	5,573	22.2
11a	Soap and related products	1,807	38.6
11b	Heating and plumbing equipment	1,086	21.7
12a	Glass products	1,156	52.0
12b	Other electrical machinery	1,067	35.4
12c	Dairy products	8,433	24.7
13	Office and store machines	461	55.8
14	Aircraft	114	94.6
15a	Engines and turbines	117	55.2
15b	Rubber products	1,079	49.5
16a	Petroleum refining	288	67.2
16b	Drugs and medicines	1,273	42.0
17	Motor vehicles and equipment	2,306	70.6
18a	Service and household machines	1,255	41.9
18b	Tin cans, cutlery, hardware	2,083	33.7
19	Grainmill products	2,883	29.3
21	Paints, etc.	1,777	27.2
22	Paperboard containers	1,606	26.6
24a	Communication equipment	2,280	47.9
24b	Tractors, farm and construction machinery	2,414	37.8
25	Nonferrous metals	2,572	44.4
26	Instruments, optical, etc.	3,292	30.7
27	Steel mills	167	80.4
28	Electrical industrial apparatus	2,678	34.8
29a	Primary metals n.e.c.	1,400	32.3
29b	General industrial machinery	2,781	21.6
31a	Aircraft parts	1,333	66.5
31b	Other pulp, paper and products	2,000	28.8
34	Pulp, paper and board	514	44.3
53	Chemicals, inorganic and organic	938	72.6
63	Miscellaneous manufacture and ordnance	16,976	26.9

industries of the Standard Industrial Classification.[31] As measures of concentration in the market, these figures suffer from two major sources of understatement. Most, if not all, the company industry groups are of such breadth as to contain products that are not substitutable for each other.[32] Moreover, concen-

[31] Since these are combined groupings and often had the effect of making the resulting industry designation rather lengthy, a number of the latter have been abbreviated here. Except for several further compressions made to provide additional safeguards against disclosure, these are the industry groups used by the Census Bureau in its publication *Enterprise Statistics, 1958,* Pt. 1.

[32] Thus, the 2-digit major industry group "electrical machinery," which has 21 4-digit industries, is broken down here into only 3 broad categories—"electrical industrial apparatus," "communications equipment," and "other electrical machinery"—each of which contains numerous nonsubstitutable products serving different purposes and meeting different needs (see Ch. 1, pp. 10–12).

tration figures based on employment tend to understate concentration in the market because the larger enterprises tend to be more mechanized and thus to have a lower ratio of employment to shipments than smaller firms.[33]

Two unusual features should be noted in the design of the chart. While the vertical axis depicting the proportion of each industry group held by the 200 largest is constructed in terms of the usual arithmetic scale, the horizontal axis depicting the number of companies is constructed in terms of a semilogarithmic scale in order to encompass the wide range in the number of firms—from 114 to 16,976. In the second place, the number of companies *within* the 200 engaged in an industry is used as the identifying symbol of the industry. For example, reference to the accompanying key will show that the figure of 14 marking the observation near the upper left-hand corner of the chart identifies the observation as the aircraft industry; it also means that 14 of the 200 largest companies were engaged in this industry. Similarly, the figure 9 near the lower right-hand part of the chart identifies the group as bakery products; it also means that 9 of the 200 largest were engaged in that industry.

With the previously noted sources of understatement in mind, one can derive a few general conclusions concerning the importance of the largest 200 manufacturers in individual industries. Of 62 company industry groups, the 200 largest accounted for more than 20 percent of the employment in the 35 shown in the chart; these 35 company industry groups made up 53 percent of total manufacturing employment. In these industry groups, excluding instances of employment of fewer than 500 workers, the 200 largest manufacturers accounted, on the average, for 45.7 percent of the employment. Or, to put it another way, in some three-fifths of all industries, comprising more than half of all manufacturing employment, the 200 largest firms employed, on the average, nearly half of the workers.

Not surprisingly, the 200 largest held impressive proportions in such long-established bastions of big enterprise as aircraft (94.1 percent), steel mills (80.4 percent), petroleum refining (67.2 percent), and engines and turbines (55.2 percent). In each, capital entrance requirements are high, and the companies are large in size and few in number. The total number of firms in these industries was only 114 in aircraft, 117 in engines and turbines, 167 in steel mills, and 288 in petroleum refining. The 200 largest also employed more than half of the workers in 6 other industry groups—chemicals (72.6 percent), motor vehicles and parts (70.6 percent), aircraft parts (66.5 percent), office and store machines (55.8 percent), tobacco manufactures (54.7 percent), and glass products (52.0 percent). Despite the relatively high market shares of the major companies, these industries tended to have a considerably greater number of companies. Aside from motor vehicles and equipment and aircraft parts, whose numbers are swelled by numerous small-parts makers, the number of firms ranged from 355 in tobacco manufactures up to 1,156 in glass products.

Between 40 and 50 percent of the employment was held by the 200 largest in 5 additional industries, each of which numbered more than 1,000 companies— rubber products (49.5 percent), communication equipment (47.9 percent),

[33] In 270 (or 61%) of the 443 industries the concentration ratios in terms of the 4 largest companies were higher on a shipments than on an employment basis by 2 percentage points or more, while the reverse was true in only 52 industries (or 12%); in the remaining 121 industries the difference between the shipments and employment ratios was one percentage point or less (*Concentration Ratios in Manufacturing Industry, 1958*, Pt. 2, p. 464).

nonferrous metals (44.4 percent), drugs and medicines (42.0 percent), and service and household machines (41.9 percent).

One of the most surprising findings is the presence of the largest manufacturers in traditional "small business" industries, areas of low capital entrance requirements and numerous enterprises. Companies among the 200 largest accounted for 29.3 percent of the employment in grainmill products, which numbered 2,883 firms; 22.2 percent in bakery products, which had 5,573 concerns; and 24.7 percent in dairy products, with 8,433 companies.

These findings make it clear that the largest companies in the industrial economy as a whole are by no means confined to a few large-scale industries but hold significant market shares throughout most of the range of U.S. industry.

Control of the large corporation

With control over so much of the industrial economy in the hands of so few corporations, the question of who controls the corporation has quite understandably been of continuing interest. On this issue two schools of thought have emerged. One sees control lodged firmly in the hands of a self-perpetuating group of corporate managers. To the other, control over at least many of the largest corporations is seen as residing in some powerful family such as the Rockefellers, Mellons, or du Ponts, in a leading financial institution such as the House of Morgan, or more recently in large institutional investors. To the former, each of the corporations appears as an autonomous unit, run by managers whose best interests are served by promoting the interests of the corporation itself. To the latter, ultimate power is regarded as being even more centralized than is indicated by the figures on aggregate concentration.

The former school of thought can be traced back to the pioneering work 40 years ago of Adolf A. Berle and Gardiner C. Means, who held that control over the large corporation has been effectively divorced from ownership.[34] Responsibility for the direction of corporate affairs is seen as having shifted to management, which is largely insulated from any danger of challenge from the great body of stockholders. Such a shift in the locus of power is regarded as the inevitable consequence of the widespread dispersion of stock ownership among countless small stockholders, no one of whom holds more than a fractional share. With such a small amount of stock, the average stockholder understandably takes little interest in the affairs of the corporation of which he is technically part owner. By and large he is content to receive his dividends, clip his coupons, and leave the managing of the corporation to those who are well paid to manage it. Moreover, legal devices such as nonvoting stock, voting trusts, and pyramided holding companies have often been used to divest stockholders of effective control over corporate affairs. In the words of Berle and Means:

> over the enterprise and over the physical property—the instrument of production—in which he has an interest, the owner has little control. At the same time, he bears no responsibility with respect to the enterprise or its physical property. . . . The spiritual values that formerly went with ownership have been separated from it. . . . Finally, in the corporate sys-

[34] Berle and Means, op. cit. See also James Burnham, *The Managerial Revolution,* Day, 1941; J. Kenneth Galbraith, *The New Industrial State,* Houghton Mifflin, 1967; R. J. Larner, "Ownership and Control in the 200 Largest Nonfinancial Corporations, 1929 and 1963," *American Economic Review,* Sept., 1966.

tem, the ownership of industrial wealth is left with a mere symbol of ownership, while the power, the responsibility, and the substance which have been an integral part of ownership in the past are being transferred to a separate group in whose hands lies control.[35]

The role of management has also been strengthened by legislation intended to limit the influence of financial groups. The Banking Act of 1933 was designed to separate commercial from investment banking; the Banking Act of 1935 was designed to eliminate interlocking bank directorates; the Securities Act of 1933 increased the responsibility of underwriters and in other ways restricted their freedom of action in the sale of new issues; the Securities and Exchange Act of 1934, among other things, limited the ways in which bankers could profit from security dealings and corporate connections. Moreover, as large corporations have tended to rely more and more on "internal" financing, the need for the services of underwriters has diminished.

On the other hand, those who lean toward a "financial control" thesis have stressed the importance of interlocking directorates, investment houses, owning families, and, more recently, institutional investors and commercial banks.[36] With respect to the first, many of the largest corporations have been and continue to be interconnected through the instrument of interlocking directorates. For the year 1965 Peter C. Dooley examined the interlocking directorates among the 200 largest nonfinancial corporations (115 industrial, 10 merchandising, 25 transportation, and 50 public utility corporations) plus the 50 largest financial corporations (32 banks and 18 life insurance companies).[37] On the boards of these 250 corporations sat 3,165 directors holding a total of 4,007 directorships. More than one-sixth of these men (562) sat on the boards of 2 or more of these companies; 5 men held 6 directorships each. This pattern was remarkably similar to the distribution of 30 years earlier disclosed by the National Resources Committee. In 1935, 2,722 men sat on the boards of the 250 largest corporations, holding among them a total of 3,544 directorships.[38]

---

[35] *Ibid.,* pp. 64–65.

[36] See C. Wright Mills, *The Power Elite,* Oxford University Press, 1959; Jean-Marie Chevalier, "The Problem of Control in Large American Corporations," *Antitrust Bulletin,* Spring, 1969.

An earlier study prepared by Paul Sweezy and published as an appendix in National Resources Committee, *op. cit.,* identified what it regarded as 8 more or less clearly defined financial interest groups. Corporations were linked to those groups on the basis of a *combination* of intercorporate ties, such as interlocking directorates, intercorporate stock ownership, common affiliations with investment banks, and intangible personal interrelationships. One hundred sixty of the 250 largest corporations were said to be controlled by the 8 interest groups, accounting for 29% of the total assets of all nonfinancial and banking corporations. Three of the 8 interest groups, the Rockefeller, Mellon, and du Pont groups, rested on the relatively firm foundation of substantial minority stock ownership. Two, Morgan-First National and Kuhn-Loeb, centered around leading financial institutions deriving their influence from interlocking directorates, their historic role in forming corporations within their respective spheres, their continuing position as the investment and banking houses for the corporations in their group, and their own preeminence in the world of high finance. Each of the remaining 3 groups had as its nexus a city—Boston, Chicago, Cleveland. Corporations in these areas were said to be linked through prominent regional banking and financial institutions, through interlocking directorates, and through family connections and other historical ties.

[37] Peter C. Dooley, "The Interlocking Directorate," *American Economic Review,* June, 1969, pp. 314–23.

[38] National Resources Committee, *op. cit.,* p. 158.

Clearly, the institution of the interlocking directorate has not only survived but prospered.

In Dooley's words, "The critical question is what purpose (or purposes) does it serve?" [39] One purpose it obviously does *not* serve to any significant extent is the suppression of competition through the holding by a given person of directorships in 2 or more *directly competing* corporations. Of the 1,049 interlocks held by directors of the industrial corporations, only 133 were classified as with competitors;[40] of the 97 interlocks by directors of merchandising corporations, none was with a direct competitor. Thus, taken together, less than 12 percent of the interlocks in these two areas were with competitors. And when allowance is made for nonparticipation in the same local or regional geographic market and the occasional excessive breadth of the Census product classes used in the analysis, the proportion becomes even smaller. This is not too surprising since "direct" interlocks between competitors are prohibited per se by the antitrust laws.[41]

But the antitrust laws do not prohibit what are known as indirect interlocks— i.e., the coming together of directors of competing firms on the board of a third concern. The third concern is usually a bank or other financial institution. Thus, meeting together as directors of a bank, the directors of competing companies can engage in the very activities that the prohibition of direct interlocks was intended to prevent. An example is provided by the indirect interlocks in the steel industry. The relationship of the Morgan financial interests to the U.S. Steel Corporation has long been a matter of record, as was revealed in the hearings of the "Money Trust" investigation:

UNTERMYER: At the time of the organization of the United States Steel Corporation did you name the entire board of directors?

MORGAN: No. I think I passed on it.

UNTERMYER: Did you not, as a matter of fact, name the board and pass out a slip of paper containing the names of the board?

MORGAN: I cannot say that no one else helped me in it.

* * *

UNTERMYER: Did you not only pass on it and approve it, but did you not further select the board and determine who should go on and who should stay off?

MORGAN: No, I probably did the latter.

UNTERMYER: Yes; and having determined who should stay off, you necessarily determined who should go on?

MORGAN: I am quite willing to assume the whole responsibility.

UNTERMYER: I only want the fact.

MORGAN: . . . Whoever went on that board went with my approval.

[39] Dooley, *op. cit.*

[40] The designation of whether corporations were competitors was based on whether they were engaged in the same 5-digit SIC product class, as compiled by the Federal Trade Commission for the House Antitrust Subcommittee.

[41] Section 8 of the Clayton Act provides that "no person at the same time shall be a director in any two or more corporations, any one of which has capital, surplus and undivided profits aggregating more than $1,000,000, engaged in whole or in part in commerce, other than banks, banking associations, trust companies, and common carriers . . . if such corporations are or shall have been . . . competitors, so that the elimination of competition by agreement between them would constitute a violation of any of the provisions of any of the antitrust laws."

UNTERMYER: And from time to time . . . whoever has gone on the board has gone on with your approval, has he not?

MORGAN: Not always:

UNTERMYER: Has he gone against your protest?

MORGAN: No, sir.[42]

Four decades later the Federal Trade Commission found that directors of U.S. Steel met together with directors of 2 other major steel companies on the boards of major financial institutions. U.S. Steel was interlocked with Armco through the Equitable Life Assurance Society and with Inland through the Northern Trust Company. In addition, U.S. Steel's directors came together with directors of other steel companies on the boards of 2 important customers, both, like U.S. Steel itself, creations of J. P. Morgan. Thus, it was interlocked with Jones & Laughlin and Crucible Steel through New York Central and with Youngstown Sheet & Tube and Superior Steel through General Electric.[43]

But whether in fact schemes to suppress competition are hatched and carried out by directors of competing firms when they meet together as directors of a bank, or, indeed, any type of third concern, is not known. To the argument that directors of competing firms should not be allowed to meet on the boards of third concerns the rebuttal has been advanced that such a prohibition could not prevent competitors from meeting together if they are determined to do so; there are always resorts, hotels, social clubs, and golf courses. Quite apart from what value they may have as "escape hatches" from the antitrust laws, there are understandable reasons for interlocks between banks and industrials. The former have funds to lend, and the latter have need for credit. Moreover, as important stockholders through their trust departments, banks have more than a passing interest in knowing how a company is being run. Whatever the reason, interlocks between industrials and financial institutions are commonplace; of the 1,049 interlocks held by directors of industrials, 36 percent (378) were found by Dooley to be with banks and insurance companies.

It also must be recognized that from the point of view of the industrial concern there is much to be said for having on its board at least some "outside" directors, including members of the financial community. They bring to a company fresh points of view, new thinking, and broader horizons. There is a very real danger that "management-controlled" companies (i.e., those whose directors are managers of the company itself) will tend to become insulated and provincial. And, indeed, Dooley found, "The frequency of interlocks with other corporations declines as the proportion of active company officers, president, vice-president, treasurer, etc., on the board increases."

More binding than interlocking directorates, and also more difficult to uncover, are intercorporate stock holdings. Just as the Berle and Means work is the fountainhead of the "divorce between ownership and control" thesis, the basic empirical foundation for the argument that large corporations are interconnected through stock ownership with powerful owning and financial interests is TNEC Monograph No. 29, prepared by the Securities and Exchange Commission. For the first and only time this has been done, the SEC went

[42] 62nd Cong., 3rd Sess., Subcommittee of the House Committee on Banking and Currency. *Investigation of Financial and Monetary Conditions in the United States,* Pt. 15, 1913, p. 1025.

[43] Federal Trade Commission, *Report on Interlocking Directorates,* 1950, pp. 118–23.

behind book shareholdings (owners of record) to determine actual ownership (beneficial owners):

> Book shareholdings, as reflected in the books of the corporations, are in many respects an inadequate measure of the distribution of the ultimate beneficial ownership of stock. A small proportion of the names appearing in the books of the corporation are not those of the beneficial owners but those of nominees, such as brokers, banks and trustees. Thus what appears to be a large concentrated block may in reality represent the property of numerous owners, each of whom holds but a small number of shares. On the other hand, the beneficial owner of a large amount of stock may have distributed his holdings among several nominees.[44]

Summarizing the TNEC data, Robert Aaron Gordon classified 176 of the 200 nonfinancial corporations as to whether they were under "family control" or "management control." [45] Some 44 percent of the assets of the 176 nonfinancial corporations as a whole were found to be under "management control." Yet no less than 31 percent were found to be under "family ownership control." The remaining 25 percent were controlled by other corporations. While in this last group ultimate control is not known, it is more likely to rest with management than with ownership groups.[46] There were, however, important differences among various major branches of the economy. Surprisingly, among the manufacturing corporations, family control predominated. Nearly 57 percent of the assets of all the manufacturing corporations included among the 176 were found to be under family ownership control. Those under management control represented somewhat more than one-third (36 percent) of the group's total assets. In addition to the du Ponts, Rockefellers, and Mellons, other important family groups were found to be Ford (automobiles), McCormick (farm implements), Hartford (chain groceries), Harkness (oil), Duke (power and tobacco), Pew (oil), Pitcairn (glass), Clark (sewing machines), Reynolds (tobacco), and Kress (retail stores).

The Berle-Means thesis received impressive support in a study by R. J. Larner published in 1966, which attempted to update the earlier findings on the extent of management control.[47] Since in only a very few large corporations does any group of stockholding interests hold a majority of the stock, the ques-

---

[44] Securities and Exchange Commission, *The Ownership of the 200 Largest Non-Financial Corporations,* Monograph No. 29, Temporary National Economic Committee (TNEC), 1941, p. 5. The data, it must be emphasized, are more than 30 years old. As time has passed and new stock issues have been floated, the holdings of the family groups have undoubtedly become diluted. Moreover, the du Ponts' stock ownership in GM has been terminated by court order.

[45] Robert Aaron Gordon, *Business Leadership in the Large Corporation,* Brookings Institution, 1945. Twenty-four of the 200 proved to be subsidiaries (by virtue of ownership of 50% or more of the stock) of companies among the 176.

[46] Condensed from *ibid.,* pp. 40–41. The "family ownership" group includes single and multiple groups and also family-corporate groups. The latter represent instances where control is divided between families and corporations, although in most such cases the families appeared to be the controlling factor (see SEC, *op. cit.,* pp. 1486–87). "Management control" refers to cases where no dominant stockholding group is apparent. "Ownership" refers in all cases to possession of either (a) 10% or more of the stock or (b) stockholding interests of less than 10% associated with a considerable degree of control as evidenced by representation of the stockholding group in management.

[47] R. J. Larner, "Ownership and Control in the 200 Largest Nonfinancial Corporations, 1929 and 1963," *American Economic Review,* Sept., 1966.

tion of whether the corporation is subject to stockholder or management control turns largely on the standard used to establish minority stockholder control. The "control threshold" used by Berle and Means was 20 percent of the stock. Because of the great increase since 1929 in corporate size and also in the dispersion of stock ownership, Larner regarded a corporation as subject to minority stockholder control if a stockholder group owned, directly or indirectly, only 10 percent of the stock. Of the 200 largest financial corporations, 104 were manufacturing enterprises, of which Larner found that 4 were subject to majority control, 17 to minority control, and the remaining 83 to management control. With control over four-fifths of the largest industrial corporations thus resting in the hands of management, the Berle-Means thesis of a divorce between ownership and control would appear to have been affirmed.

A more recent study, however, questions whether even the 10 percent standard may not be too high. In a study of the largest manufacturing corporations, Jean-Marie Chevalier contends that corporations can be subjected to meaningful minority stockholder control if the group owns as little as 5 percent of the stock and is represented on the board of directors. As examples of corporations where an owning group holds control although holding less than 10 percent of the stock, Chevalier cites Chrysler, "controlled by Consolidated Coal, which holds 7.3 percent of the stock," Whirlpool, "controlled by Sears Roebuck, holding 7 percent of the stock," and Armour, controlled "by the Prince family, which retains 6.2 percent of the stock." [48]

The difference that the use of a 5 percent as compared to a 10 percent standard makes in the distribution of the locus of control can be seen below:

	Larner 1963	Chevalier 1965–66
Majority control	4	4
Minority control	17	40
Dominant influence	0	9
Management control	83	51
Total	104	104

The use of the lower standard, it can be seen, reduces the proportion of leading industrials under management control from four-fifths to approximately half. Whether under today's conditions the proper "control threshold" is 10 percent, 5 percent, or any other figure will remain a matter of dispute. Just as examples can be cited of effective control by stockholder groups possessing very small proportions of the stock, other examples can be cited of relatively high proportions of stock held by ownership groups, particularly by commercial banks, that apparently have exercised little influence over the corporations. But Chevalier raises the interesting question of whether, as their ownership role increases, commercial banks will continue to abstain from seeking to influence management:

> According to the figures cited, it will be noted that the commercial banks (or rather *some* commercial banks, because of concentration and specialization in pension trusts) hold an important fraction of the total common

[48] Jean-Marie Chevalier, "The Problem of Control in Large American Corporations," *Antitrust Bulletin,* Spring, 1969, p. 165.

stock outstanding, and that this fraction tends to increase, notably because of the augmentation of pension fund assets.

One may well ask whether the banks will use these shares in order to intervene in the administration of the industrial corporations. Up to now, they have not seemed desirous of so doing, but will they be in a position to *not* make use of the formidable power lawfully conferred on them when, in 1980, they are responsible for close to $225 billion of assets? It is a legitimate question.[49]

It has been estimated that institutional investors in this country hold more than $1 trillion in assets, of which 60 percent is in the hands of commercial banks. The most dramatic growth has taken place in pension and other employee benefit funds, over 70 percent of which are managed by commercial banks. In a two-volume, 2,000-page report issued in 1968 the House Banking and Currency Committee showed the percentage of the stock of leading industrial enterprises held in trust accounts managed by commercial banks.[50] In making the report public, Chairman Wright Patman pointed to the danger to competition inherent in banks' stock holdings in competing companies:

> To take an important example the Morgan Guaranty Trust Company, the nation's largest bank trust operation, with $16.8 billion in trust assets, holds 7.5% of the common stock of American Airlines and has a director interlock with the airline. At the same time, Morgan holds 8.2% of the common stock of United Airlines and 7.4% of the common stock of Trans World Airlines. . . . No one can question that these major domestic air carriers are in direct competition and yet each has as its largest stockholder a single banking institution.[51]

Other examples cited were the ownership by Morgan Guaranty of common stock in 4 competing cosmetic manufacturers and of 11.9 percent and 16.5 percent, respectively, of the common stock of the Trane Company and the Carrier Corporation, 2 major competitors in central air conditioning. The Cleveland Trust Company was shown to have significant shareholdings in leading manufacturers of machine tools,[52] as well as in 3 large, competing iron ore corporations. Commercial banks may not actually have used their stock ownership in rival firms to suppress competition, but the opportunity and temptation to do so will certainly become greater as commercial banks increase their stock holdings in industrial corporations.

The Japanese experience

The contrasting behavior of Japanese industry before and after World War II provides one of the few opportunities to examine empirically whether communities of interest can affect market behavior. Before and during the war a large proportion of Japanese industry was under the control of the "Zaibatsu."

[49] *Ibid.*, p. 179.
[50] 90th Cong., 2nd Sess., House Committee on Banking and Currency, Staff Report for the Subcommittee on Domestic Finance, *Commercial Banks and Their Trust Activities: Emerging Influence on the American Economy*, 1968, Vols. I, II.
[51] *Ibid.*, press release, p. 2.
[52] Cleveland Twist Drill Co. (52.4%), Parker Hannifin Corp. (14.5%), Timken Roller Bearing (11.4%), Warner & Swasey Co. (9.1%), Osburn Manufacturing Co. (42.6%).

Derived from the Japanese terms for wealth (*zai*) and a clique or estate (*batsu*), the term has been used to designate a few huge, family-based combines. Through separately incorporated companies operating under the unified direction of top holding companies, the Zaibatsu held substantial market positions in coal, shipbuilding, shipping, chemicals, trading, steel fabrication, electrical equipment, banking, and other fields. Some idea of the breadth of their operations can be gathered from the number of their subsidiaries—Mitsui, 300; Mitsubishi, 250; Sumitomo, 160; and Yasuda, 60.[53]

After the war the principal focus of the Occupation's deconcentration efforts under General MacArthur was on breaking the links which had bound one subsidiary of a Zaibatsu to another and on severing the ties which had enabled each top holding company to subject its whole complex to unified direction. The top holding companies were dissolved, family ownership ties were severed, and horizontal connections among the major subsidiaries were cut. Testifying before the Senate Subcommittee on Antitrust and Monopoly,[54] Eleanor Hadley stated: "The major consequence of the deconcentration program has been that the groupings have been without their control centers. One still has (or through consolidations regained) Mitsubishi Heavy Industries, Mitsui & Co. (formerly Mitsui Trading), and Sumitomo Metal Industries, but notwithstanding the identicalness of corporate names, the meaning behind these names is very different. The groupings are 'headless.' They do not move with singleness of purpose." With the power and influence of the "control centers" sharply curtailed, their operating subsidiaries have suffered from a loss of discriminatory advantages and government favoritism.

> DR. BLAIR: You mentioned the fact that the old zaibatsu exercised various forms of discriminatory advantages.
>
> DR. HADLEY: Right.
>
> DR. BLAIR: That they had advantages with respect to obtaining capital and credit, that they were able to influence the Government and obtain favored treatment for their firms and that through these and similar discriminatory advantages the reestablishment of the old holding companies over the operating companies would, in itself, result in a marked diminution of competitive rivalry among the operating companies.
>
> DR. HADLEY: Right. Exactly. This is the thesis of my paper really, that market positions are not essentially different today than they were under the combine system. What is different is that the command center at the top was removed and in consequence, one had a sharply more rivalrous sort of relationship. . . .

Although market shares have remained much the same, competition in the postwar years has been intense, whereas in the earlier period it had been quiescent. With greater competition have come higher levels of investment and a fantastic growth rate of the Japanese economy. In contrast, according to Hadley, "Japan began war against the United States when its national income had been stagnant for 4 whole years." In commenting on this difference, she observed, "In the case of private investment the evidence suggests to me that 'noncordial oligopoly' is more stimulating, more rivalrous than 'cordial.'" If

---

[53] *Hearings on Economic Concentration*, Pt. 7, p. 3512, testimony of Eleanor Hadley. For further indicia of the extent of the Zaibatsu's operations see *ibid.*, pp. 3512–13.

[54] *Ibid.*, pp. 3512–31.

the power and influence of the "command centers" were to be restored, the result would be a pronounced reduction of competition in the market:

DR. BLAIR: I would like to get your opinion on this question. Suppose that the market shares were the same but the old zaibatsu had reestablished the same control as they had in the past, would competition today be less by virtue of their ownership and influence?

DR. HADLEY: Yes. Normally, we economists think of a market where there are only a few producers as frequently being moderately cordial. Sometimes we talk about price leadership, the major firm being the price leader and everybody following the pattern of the major firm. Sometimes one has cutthroat competition in an oligopolistic market, but usually oligopolistic markets are moderately "live and let live" sorts of affairs. What I was suggesting in the Japan case was that one had a most exceptional sort of oligopoly because not only was there this relationship within one market but this relationship spread across the whole economy and that what had made conditions more rivalrous in the postoccupation period is that one removed the command centers making the oligopolists the same across the whole economy. The economy is more rivalrous today because the linkages tying the oligopolists in one market to oligopolists in other markets were cut.

DR. BLAIR: To put it another way, if the same control over the operating companies were to be reestablished as existed under the old zaibatsu, there would be less competition within the individual industries even though the market share remained the same?

DR. HADLEY: This, I do funamentally believe would be true, that market positions could be exactly the same and one would definitely reduce the degree of rivalry in such a circumstance.

DR. BLAIR: And, that would come about by means of the various types of influences that the top owning groups could exert in addition to their reciprocal fear of reprisals for stepping on each other's toes?

DR. HADLEY: Right.

The Centrifugal Forces TWO

For over two centuries greater concentration of output was the inevitable result in good part of the drive for greater efficiency. New technilogies were constantly being introduced, requiring progressively larger amounts of capital, which in turn continuously raised the barriers to entry. A further source of efficiency was the application of managerial economies to the operation of many separate plants brought under common ownership and control. Again the essential requirement (and result) was greater size and thus concentration.

Since World War II, however, these forces appear to have lost their thrust. Most of the increases in concentration since 1947 have taken place in industries with relatively simple technologies and low capital intensities —food, textiles, apparel, lumber, clay building materials, toiletries, foundries, and the like. At the same time, concentration has been going down not only in steel but in such other highly mechanized, capital-intensive industry groups as machinery and chemicals. Likewise, the postwar trends provide little support to the thesis that rising concentration is the inevitable product of the superior skills of centralized management. In point of fact, most of the industries in which concentration has risen have a relatively low incidence of multiplant operations. At the same time there has been no pervasive upward movement in industries in which multiplant operations are important; for example, in the electrical machinery group increases in concentration have been offset by an equal number of decreases.

More recently, concentration has been explained on the grounds that under the conditions of modern science and technology new products and processes can be expected to come mainly from the laboratories of large corporations. Yet, here again, the argument gains scant support from recent evidence. The industries in which most of the increases have occurred are generally notorious for their small expenditures on research in relation to sales. Conversely, in chemicals, which has long been noted for its emphasis on research, the trend in concentration has been distinctly downward.

Indeed, evidence is accumulating that these forces are now making for lesser rather than greater concentration; in effect, they appear to have reversed their course. As compared to the previous methods of production, today's new technologies make possible economical production with far lesser capital outlays. Increasing difficulties are apparently being encountered in achieving efficiency in the management of giant multiplant, multi-industry corporations. And, despite the vast resources at its disposal for research and development, the large concern does not appear to be a particularly fertile source of creativity; significant new inventions continue to come from smaller firms and individuals, particularly the new "technological entrepreneur." In short, the very forces that have been responsible for much of the past trend toward centralization now appear to be exerting a decentralizing effect; they have been transformed from centripetal to centrifugal forces.

TECHNOLOGY AND
CONCENTRATION

From the late eighteenth century through the first third of the twentieth century, technological change exerted a powerful impetus toward greater concentration. But before World War II there began to appear new technologies that reduced the size of plant and amount of capital outlay required for optimal efficiency. Except in a few primarily defense industries, the relative importance of the largest plants has tended to decline in recent years. Concentration has increasingly become a function of multiplant operations rather than plant size. Today more of the output of the concentrated sector comes from industries with a wide divergence between company concentration and plant concentration.

The trend toward a larger scale of operations

The essential foundations of any economy are its sources of power, types of materials, methods of fabrication, and means of transportation. In each the technological explosion touched off by the Industrial Revolution required increases in plant and company size on a scale never before imagined. Up to the invention of the steam engine, industry had relied on water wheels as its major source of power. The slow movement of the big wheels and the small amount of power they generated imposed severe limitations upon the size of plants. With the introduction of steam, however, power in infinitely greater quantities could be created and transmitted by pulleys and belt lines over a much larger floor space. Moreover, the use of steam greatly increased the speed with which industrial machinery could be operated, which in turn made possible the use of new types of cutting and drilling machinery that could not be operated except at high speeds. As Lewis Mumford, with his customary prescience, noted many years ago:

> The steam engine tended toward monopoly and concentration. . . .
> Since the steam engine requires constant care on the part of the stoker and
> engineer, steam power was more efficient in large units than in small ones:
> Instead of a score of small units, working when required, one large engine was kept in constant motion. Thus, steam power fostered the tendency toward large industrial plants already present in the subdivision of the manufacturing process. Great size, forced by the nature of the steam engine, became in turn a symbol of efficiency. The industrial leaders not only accepted concentration and magnitude as a fact of operation, conditioned by the steam engine: They came to believe in it by itself, as a

mark of progress. With the big steam engine, the big factory, the big bonanza farm, the big blast furnace, efficiency was supposed to exist in direct ratio to size. Bigger was another way of saying better.[1]

Just as the substitution of steam for water gave a powerful impetus to centralization, so the substitution of steel for wood provided a new material that could be fabricated most efficiently in relatively large plants. In almost every way, wood had been undesirable for mass production: it is not malleable; it cannot be melted and poured into a designed shape; it is bulky and breakable; it defies complete standardization; and it requires a relatively high degree of skill in fabrication.

With steam turning the wheels of industry and steel providing a uniform, consistent, and durable material, highly specialized machines and processes were developed to take advantage of the opportunities for mass production. Existing machine tools such as the lathe became high speed and automatic, and entirely new forms of cutting, milling, forming, and shaping machines were developed. The capacity and size of that modern-day battering ram, the stamping machine, were steadily enlarged, requiring the use of increasingly costly dies and presses. The "continuous process," involving enormous capital outlays, was introduced as the means of production in steel, glass, paper, and other materials industries. These and similar mechanical improvements raised the number of stages of production that could be conducted in a single plant, requiring greater capital outlays and contributing in one way or another to the trend toward large-scale operations.

Since steam provided sufficient power for the performance of a series of consecutive functions and steel offered a homogeneous material to which they could be applied, it now became possible to apply to a far greater extent than heretofore the principle of the division of labor. Workers could be assembled in consecutive groups, each performing a simple repetitive function, which in sequence transformed a raw material into a finished product. The day of the master craftsman and artisan who himself performed all the functions was over. His place was taken by unskilled or semiskilled workers, brought together in larger plants and producing en masse what had formerly been made by one individual on a custom basis.

While the Industrial Revolution was transforming the industrial process, a similar revolution was taking place in transportation, as the railroad replaced the canal, the wagon, and the oxcart. Materials taken from a few large deposits moved along inflexible routes to the increasingly congested terminal centers, drawing with them population and manufacturing enterprise. The world's important markets, if not there already, necessarily came to be located along the railroad routes. Similarly, the advent of the steamship greatly increased the quantities of raw materials that could be brought economically into a manufacturing center as well as the finished goods that could be distributed to the far corners of the world.

Although concentration in terms of ownership was often well beyond what was required by technology, the fact that control over the market was moving in the same general direction as technology gave the trend toward greater concentration an aura of inevitability. Hardly any field of enterprise failed to provide striking examples of the achievement of greater efficiency through the use of larger plants and more costly machinery and equipment. Examples cited by

[1] Lewis Mumford, *Technics and Civilization,* Harcourt Brace Jovanovich, 1934, pp. 161–62.

Harry Jerome in his classic study of mechanization are more or less typical.[2] In the cement industry the major development was the introduction of the rotary kiln and its subsequent enlargement; between 1909 and 1929 the average annual capacity of cement kilns increased threefold—from 93,000 to 283,000 barrels.[3] In paper making, capacity was enlarged in each of the processes of production; the daily capacity of Fourdrinier paper machines, for example, rose from 11.4 tons in 1904 to 23.6 tons in 1929. Jerome observed, "Changes in mechanical equipment frequently occur in this way. The general principles of the paper machine were well established . . . and much of the improvement in equipment has been by means of augmenting the capacity of the machine units. . . ."[4] In the plate glass industry a revolutionary development was the introduction in 1921 of a machine that replaced the individual stages of production with a continuous flow from raw material to finished product. Some idea of its capacity can be gathered from the fact that in 1927, although there were only 4 plate glass plants in the country using this process, the 1929 Census reported that the capacity of the continuous-flow machines was about half the total of the entire industry.[5] In tire making a "chief development" was the introduction of larger rolls, with the result that "one operator handled probably 300 pounds where formerly he had tended only a 100-pound batch."[6] Speaking of industry as a whole during the first two decades of this century, Jerome remarked, "One generally observable trend in the character of mechanized equipment is the enlargement of the capacity of the machine unit, either by increasing the physical size of the machine or the speed at which its parts function."[7]

The pervasive increase in size was, in the view of P. Sargant Florence, the natural consequence of the operation of three principles that explain how "large scale production . . . results in maximum efficiency. . . ." Under the first, which he termed the principle of bulk transactions, "the total monetary, physical or psychological cost of dealing in large quantities is sometimes no greater (and in any case less than proportionately greater) than those of dealing in small quantities. . . ." The second, referred to as the principle of massed reserves, is "the statistical theory of probable error that the greater the number of items involved the more likely are deviations in their amounts to cancel out and leave the actual result nearer to the expected result. The probable deviation in orders for similar items that a reserve guards against is thus proportionately less when orders are many, and the cost of reserves per unit of output falls correspondingly." Finally, under the principle of multiples, "The smaller the scale of operation and the fewer the total number of persons dividing and diffusing their labor, the less chance there is of all of them being fully made use of as specialists. . . ."[8]

It was in the steel industry that the trend toward bigness in plant and equipment reached some sort of apotheosis. According to Jerome, "The essential principles of operation have remained the same since the early furnaces of the

---

[2] Harry Jerome, *Mechanization in Industry*, National Bureau of Economic Research, 1934.
[3] *Ibid.*, pp. 80, 245.
[4] *Ibid.*, pp. 89–90.
[5] *Ibid.*, p. 103.
[6] *Ibid.*, p. 113.
[7] *Ibid.*, p. 244. Jerome also noted, "The increase in the physical size of factory machinery has been furthered by the development of mechanical handling devices capable of lifting and moving materials or products in larger units than could be readily handled by manual methods." (*Ibid.*, p. 248.)
[8] P. Sargant Florence, *The Logic of Industrial Organization*, Kegan Paul, 1933, pp. 11–20.

Middle Ages, but in scale and method of operation, design, auxiliary equipment, and effective utilization of materials the changes of the past four decades are among the most spectacular in the annals of technology." [9] It is steel which has most frequently been cited as proof positive of the greater efficiency of large-scale operations. Gains in efficiency have been achieved through increases in size in each of the three stages of steel production: the making of raw steel in the form of ingots, the breakdown of the ingots into smaller semifinished forms, and the rolling of the latter into finished steel products. Until the recent advent of the oxygen conversion process, raw steel was produced mainly in the open hearth, which is essentially a great brick oven with refractory lining and with means to employ the outgoing fumes to heat the incoming air. The liquid metal is poured from the open hearth into large ingot molds. The next step is the inferno of the blooming mill, which breaks down the 5-ton ingot into semifinished forms—blooms, billets, and slabs—suitable for use in the final stage, the rolling mill. The blooming mill must be a large, costly, and rugged facility, since up to 20 "passes" may be required to reduce an 18 x 21-inch ingot to a 4 x 6-inch bloom.

Increases in size and capacity in the first two stages took place gradually over half a century. Since its introduction in 1870 the efficiency of the open hearth has been increased simply by enlarging its size. In contrast, the increase in the scale of operations in the third stage occurred almost overnight with the introduction in 1927 of the continuous-strip rolling mill. In a typical continuous-strip mill the hot slab, which comes from the blooming mill, travels along on rolls, passing first through a number of huge "roughing" stands, elongating the slab into a continuous strip. It is then carried into a series of finishing stands, which reduce its size so dramatically that a single strip may be going through the rollers of 6 stands simultaneously.[10] Over 1,000 of the traditional, hand-operated rolling mills were quickly put out of existence by these mechanical marvels, each of which had an output of at least fifty times that of the old-style mill. The combination of large open hearths, giant blooming mills, and continuous-strip mills created a barrier to entry that few could surmount. Even if the industry had not already been highly concentrated through merger, these technologies would have produced a concentrated structure—which is only now slowly giving way to new capital-saving techniques being introduced, albeit belatedly, in each of the industry's three stages of production.

While raising the barrier to entry and thus leading to higher concentration, the increasingly costly techniques just mentioned yielded substantial—often sensational—savings in unit costs, particularly in labor costs. In some industries, however, the nature of technological advance was less dramatic, neither requiring any great increase in capital outlays nor resulting in any sharp reduction in labor requirements. The hypothesis is thus suggested that the new technologies, when heavily capital intensive, had a dual effect, tending to lessen greatly the need for labor and at the same time to promote concentration. One can test this hypothesis by comparing for 20 large industries the 4-company concentration ratios in 1935 [11] with the change in wages as a percentage of the

[9] Jerome, *op. cit.*, p. 60.
[10] John M. Blair, *Technology in Our Economy*, Monograph No. 22, Temporary National Economic Committee (TNEC), 1941, Pt. 2, p. 111.
[11] National Resources Committee, *The Structure of the American Economy*, 1939, App. 7, Table 1.

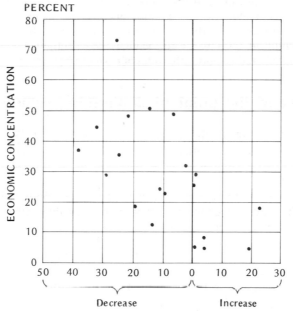

Figure 5-1

RELATIONSHIP BETWEEN ECONOMIC CONCENTRATION[a] AND CHANGE
IN WAGES AS PERCENTAGE OF VALUE ADDED BY MANUFACTURE[b]

20 manufacturing industries

[a]Value of products of 4 largest companies as percentage of industry total.

[b]From 1914 to 1935

Source: National Resources Committee, *The Structure of the American Economy*,
1939, App. 7, Table 1; Bureau of the Census, Department of Commerce,
1914 Census of Manufactures, 1917; *1935 Census of Manufactures*, 1937

value added by manufacture between 1914 and 1935.[12] Since wage rates were
rising during this period, the comparison, illustrated in Figure 5-1, understates
the actual reduction in unit labor requirements, which of course is the reciprocal
of labor productivity. Clearly, the scatter shown in the chart provides some
support for the hypothesis. Substantial decreases in labor's share of value added
were clustered among the more concentrated industries and actual increases
(or limited decreases) among the less concentrated fields. At one extreme, the
industries with concentration ratios of 50 percent or more showed an average
decrease of 15.7 percent in labor's share; at the other, those with ratios of
under 10 percent had an average *increase* of 5.1 percent. For the industries
with concentration ratios of more than 40 percent, the average change in labor's
share was a decrease of 20.1 percent; for those with ratios of less than 20 percent, the average change was an increase of 1.4 percent.

[12] In the well-known chart of "American Business Activity" prepared by the Cleveland
Trust Company, most of 1914 is shown as being near the level of "normalcy." The reaction to the outbreak of World War I—principally a decline in certain security values—
occurred late in the year.

Too much significance, however, should not be attached to these showings. For one thing, a decrease in labor requirements is not the only possible cause of a decline in the proportion of value added made up by wages; even if wages were to remain constant, the proportion would also fall if prices rose. For another, it is known that during this period concentration was often the product of factors other than technology—e.g., mergers and acquisitions. Nonetheless, the showings are consistent with the hypothesis that heavily capital-intensive technologies, introduced because of the savings they achieved in unit production costs, also contributed importantly to higher concentration.

Beyond the point of diminishing returns

The push toward larger plants, more costly equipment, and bigger aggregations of men and material began eventually to encounter formidable economic barriers. Despite the striking potential of the new technologies there were limits to the size of facilities in which they could be employed economically; the law of diminishing returns had not been repealed. Moreover, there began to appear even newer capital-saving technologies that made possible efficient operations with smaller, rather than larger, capital investments.

Perhaps the most dramatic example of the effort to push size beyond the point of diminishing returns occurred in the automobile industry. During the early and middle 1920's more than half the U.S. output of automobiles was produced by one company, which in turn had only 2 plants, both located in Detroit. The company was Ford, and the plants were its older facility at Highland Park, the original site of the moving assembly line, and its new "industrial colossus" at River Rouge. The product of the elder Henry Ford's restless imagination, River Rouge was intended to centralize at one site not only the assembly and manufacture of parts and components but the production of basic materials and supplies as well. Brought together at one site were facilities to produce iron, fabricate wood, consume coal, generate power, manufacture automotive parts, components and supplies, assemble vehicles, and in so doing be able to handle vast quantities of incoming materials and countless thousands of outgoing automobiles: "As elements of production all were in a large sense one, and he believed the company could relate and control them, forging a new and superior type of industry." [13]

By the mid-1920's River Rouge employed 75,000 workers producing coke, pig iron, steel, castings, forgings, and parts and components for cars and tractors, as well as carrying on the final assembly. Occupying over 1,000 acres were 93 separate structures, 23 of which were "main buildings." Railroad trackage covered 93 miles, conveyers 27. A force of 5,000 did nothing but keep it clean, wearing out 5,000 mops and 3,000 brooms a month, using 86 tons of soap on the floors, walls, and 330 acres of windows: "The Rouge was an industrial city, immense, concentrated, packed with power." But it soon became evident that size had been pushed well beyond the optimal point: "By its very massiveness and complexity it denied men at the top contact with and understanding of those beneath, and gave those beneath a sense of being lost in inexorable immensity and power." [14] The constant and unremitting tempo of the huge quan-

[13] Allan Nevins and Ernest Hill, *Ford, Expansion and Challenge: 1915–1933,* Scribner's, 1957, p. 201.
[14] *Ibid.,* pp. 293, 295.

tities of the materials coming in and automobiles going out took its toll not only of workers but of management itself. According to a former Ford official, Philip E. Haglund:

> Everybody was on edge. They ran around in circles and didn't know what they were doing. Physically everybody was going like a steam engine but not so much mentally. As long as their feet were on the go they were working hard. The more a man ran around the better he was. . . . Officials had no offices—only desks in the open factory at which they stood. They couldn't keep records, and lower officials could not discuss their problems together.[15]

Partly because of these diseconomies it became increasingly evident that manufacturing complete cars at one site and shipping them all over the country was more expensive than shipping parts and components for final assembly to scattered, decentralized plants. Even while River Rouge was under construction the elder Ford was establishing branch assembly plants; by 1928, 35 were being erected in the United States and others abroad.[16] That this has been the subsequent trend of production is indicated by the fact that in 1963 General Motors and Ford shared between them over 130 separate manufacturing plants in motor vehicles and parts.[17] For years most of the mighty industrial complex at River Rouge has been shut down; in recent years only the foundry has been in use. Although impressed by its size and ability to operate, Nevins and Hill acknowledged that in its subsequent decline and fall "sheer bigness was a factor . . . the coming and going of a still larger army of workers and the shipping of a greater volume of raw materials and finished products to and from a single site both threatened to create problems of congestion." [18]

More recently it has been asked whether the point of diminishing returns may not also have been exceeded in industries, such as petroleum refining and chemical manufacture, in which the raw material itself is homogeneous and readily lends itself, as a liquid or gas, to a continuous-flow operation in which the successive stages of processing are performed and controlled automatically. New and improved petrochemical plant designs have dwarfed anything known only a few years ago. Ethylene, one of the building blocks in petrochemicals, is now being produced in plants with thruputs of over half a billion pounds a year. Synthetic ammonia plants have tripled in capacity. H. S. Robinson, chief engineer of the Oil Insurance Association, has raised the question of whether, in the decision to build such giant facilities, adequate thought has been given to economic considerations other than their costs operating under ideal conditions.[19] Losses for equipment failures, he has pointed out, may run more than $50,000 *a day*. For the very large plants the equipment is specially designed and tailor-made; "off-the-shelf" items or even semicommon items are rarely used.

---

[15] *Ibid.*, p. 296.

[16] *Ibid.*, p. 298.

[17] According to the Census of Manufactures the 4 largest producers had 138 plants classified in this industry.

[18] Nevins and Hill, *op. cit.*, pp. 295, 298.

[19] H. S. Robinson, "Loss Risks in Large, Integrated Chemical Plants," Speech given before American Institute of Chemical Engineers, Houston, Texas, Feb. 20, 1967, and "Is Operating Process Safety Keeping Pace with Changing Technology," Speech given before 32nd Midyear Meeting of the American Petroleum Institute, Los Angeles, California, May 16, 1967. The quotations that follow have been taken from a mimeograph of the text of these speeches.

"Everything is 'jumbo' in size and the only one of its kind that will do the job. . . . If anything goes wrong, the plant is usually idled until that unit can be repaired." As the size and complexity of the equipment increases, so does the period of idleness: "Lead time for ordering equipment, if anything, is getting longer. Not only is this true of the large, expensive items, but often minor parts can hold up the entire plant for weeks. Replacing an ammonia convertor may take 12 to 18 months for delivery." Speaking from the point of view of the insurance companies who have to cover the losses incurred during breakdowns, Robinson said: "These are 'go or no go' plants in that if any link in the rather simple chain of operations is impaired, the entire plant is shut down. Our recent experience tells us that many of these plants are almost as much 'no go' as 'go.' "

The losses from equipment failures are greatest in plants that conduct a series of operations formerly carried on by separate plants. When there is a breakdown or failure anywhere in an integrated plant, the entire plant shuts down. As contrasted to nonintegrated units the integrated plant, by its very design, offers little flexibility with which to by-pass and store intermediate products for later processing: "If the catalytic cracker goes down, you are out of the refining business until it can be repaired. . . . Delays of from 3 to 6 months and longer are common for many, many items. In the meantime the plant sits there producing nothing or, at least, very little which can become very expensive."

Noting that there are such things as "weld failures," "piping failures," and "metal fatigue," Robinson also called attention to a number of recent explosions that completely destroyed catalytic crackers and other costly facilities. The risk factor is compounded by the storage problem. As the output of the plant increases, so does the amount of space required to store the product. Using ammonium nitrate as an example, Robinson stated that as much as 20,000 tons are stored, "not a mile or two from the plant, but right within the operating areas. . . . Just last fall there was an explosion in a fertilizer mixing plant which involved some 25 to 40 tons of bagged ammonia nitrate. All that remained of the plant was a good size hole in the ground. If 40 tons can do this, imagine what 10,000 tons could do."

For the insurance companies Robinson represents, the possibility of excessive size is no theoretical abstraction. Observing, "General design concepts today emphasize larger and larger plants able to produce at lower and lower unit costs," Robinson challenged the petroleum and chemical companies, as well as their design and contracting engineering firms, to ask themselves some difficult questions:

> Isn't it possible to build a plant too large or too integrated? Isn't it possible to be faced with operational and loss potential problems too big to be solved by the best operations or protected by all the insurance capacity in the world? Have the days of the "white elephants" been completely eliminated? . . . Shouldn't the law of diminishing returns be given some thought? Can't a plant be too big, or too congested, or too integrated for its own good?

To these questions should be added two further queries: Would plants not be smaller if the protection provided by the insurance companies were unavailable? And why should the risk of building plants of excessive size be lessened by contributions to insurance reserves on the part of companies that tend to avoid the danger? As compared to major producers, according to Robinson, "independents with only one or two refineries have been much more aware of the problem. . . ."

In the type of situation exemplified by the chemical and petroleum plants, a company can take the chance of incurring what might otherwise be intolerable costs of breakdowns and damage because the risk is shared with other firms. Even without the protection of insurance a firm can also gain the economies of large size without incurring such diseconomies if they are borne by society as a whole. In the case of oil tankers the capital investment, the propulsion costs, and the size of crew rise less rapidly than the quantity of oil carried, thereby yielding important economies of scale. It is worthwhile for an oil or shipping company to avail itself of these economies as long as the cost of such diseconomies as oil spills are borne by governments and the public generally. Hence the dramatic increase in the size of large tankers from 100,000 tons of only a few years ago (e.g. the Torrey Canyon) to the 500,000 ton supertankers of today and to the megatankers planned for the future. Similarly, it is worthwhile for utility companies to build power plants, such as the huge installation at Farmington, New Mexico which puts into the air 350 tons of soot and fly ash a day (more than twice that of New York City's daily discharge), as long as the cost of these emissions are borne by the public in the form of the impairment of health. It is also worthwhile for coal companies to use enormous power shovels which strip away more than 200 cubic yards of earth at a bite, as long as the cost represented by the irreparable loss of top soil and the permanent damage to the land is borne by society at large.

The early decentralizing technologies

Although from the dawn of the Industrial Revolution through the first third of this century the general direction of technological change was toward a larger scale of operations, technology, like a great river, is always in motion; its only constant is change. And, like a river, technology can completely reverse its course. When an easier and simpler route presents itself, it can move in a direction opposite to what had been true of the past and would be logically expected for the future. Up to the 1930's, observers of the industrial scene could be forgiven for having failed to foresee that what had been true of the past would not be true of the future. There was little warning that the effect on size of the emerging new technologies would be quite different from the technologies of the past. By making possible economic production with a smaller capital outlay, these new technologies have lowered the barriers to entry, thus creating a potential stimulus to competition. By enabling small plants to match, or even exceed, the productive efficiency of large plants, they have brought about a radical geographic decentralization of production.

The early "capital-saving" or "decentralizing" technologies have occurred in much the same areas as the improvements that underlay the Industrial Revolution—power, machines, and transportation. Just as steam had replaced water wheels as the primary source of industrial power, so was steam replaced by electricity; as single-purpose, highly specialized machines operating in sequence had replaced skilled craftsmen, so were they replaced by newer, more flexible and adaptable multipurpose machines; and as railroads had replaced the canal, the wagon, and the oxcart, so have railroads suffered from the inroads of truck and automobile.

Electrification has been the essential prerequisite to industrial decentralization. While steam had a centripetal effect by drawing industrial plants in around the source of power, electricity has had a centrifugal effect by diffusing power to the plants, thereby making possible their location in terms of markets and other economic factors. As compared to direct steam power, the difference in cost according to the quantity used is negligible with electricity. Electricity can be turned on and off and used in such quantities as desired. And because it can be transmitted over great distances industrial use of electric power is feasible in areas that do not have access to adequate supplies of low-cost fuels.

The importance of electricity as a decentralizing factor was noted as early as 1921 by the British Standing Committee on Prices, which, in commenting on the increasing importance of small plants in the furnishing industry, stated: "Certain economic factors aid this development, as for instance, the availability of electric power in the small workshop." [20] Similarly, Jerome, writing in the early 1930's, observed that electric motors appeared to be something of an exception to the general trend toward "increasing physical size of machine units." Noting that between 1909 and 1919 there had been relatively little change in the horsepower of electric motors, he concluded, "Apparently the increasing use of individual electric motors for small machine units has more than offset the tendency of the increasing size of many types of power-driven equipment to require larger electric motors." [21]

The decentralizing effects of electricity extend to the individual machine, which can be located wherever it can be most advantageously operated. This mobility of equipment is in striking contrast to the inflexible and centralizing effects of steam, which tended to crowd together as many machines as possible along great line shafts hung from the ceilings and carrying pulleys to which the individual machines were belted.[22]

By greatly widening the area in which plants can be located, by freeing the individual machines from the long line shafts, by making possible the introduction of the individual, independently operated, multipurpose machine, and by permitting the use of industrial measuring, recording, and controlling instruments and controls, electricity set in motion a profound transformation of the whole structure of industry. In Mumford's words:

> With electricity, the advantages of size from any point of view, except in possible special operations like the production of iron, becomes questionable . . . the efficiency of small units worked by electric motors utilizing curent either from local turbines or from a central power plant has given small-scale industry a new lease on life; on a purely technical basis it can, for the first time since the introduction of the steam engine, compete on even terms with the larger unit. . . . Bigger no longer automatically means better: flexibility of the power unit, closer adaptation of

[20] I. F. Grant, "The Survival of the Small Unit in Industry," *Economic Journal,* Dec., 1922, pp. 489–505.

[21] Jerome, *op. cit.,* p. 247.

[22] Among the resulting inefficiencies were: loss of much of the applied power through friction and slippage in the belt system; location of machines, not in accordance with the flow of work or other desirable economic arrangements, but rather where power could be secured with the least possible loss in transmission; breakdowns in the main shaft or in important belt lines, which brought the entire plant to a standstill; inability to use traveling cranes or similar means of internal transport because of the shafting and belting, and so on.

means to ends, nicer timing of operation, are the new marks of efficient industry. So far as concentration may remain, it is largely a phenomenon of the market, rather than of technics: promoted by astute financiers who see in the large organization an easier mechanism for their manipulations of credit, for their inflation of capital values, for their monopolistic controls.[23]

Decentralizing technologies also began to appear in the areas of machinery and processes. The most important mechanical capital-saving technique is the independently operated, multipurpose machine. Powered by electricity and practically independent of its surroundings, the multipurpose machine can operate intermittently and quickly change the nature of its product, thereby enabling the small plant to adapt its output to changes in demand. Moreover, with the addition of a few appurtenances, the general-purpose machine is capable of high-speed output; thus, the ordinary lathe can be transformed readily into a high-speed mechanism, capable of producing thousands or millions of the same product at a rate approaching that of the most expensive specialized machine. But, whereas the specialized machine is forever wedded to the same type of product, the multipurpose machine can pick and choose among an almost unlimited range of products. With one set of fixtures, jigs, chucks, and the like, it can make one product; with a slight adjustment of these fixtures, it can turn out an entirely different product; the permutations and combinations of its possible output are endless. As measured by the three basic criteria of machine operations—speed, precision, and versatility—one multipurpose machine with automatic adjustments may represent the equivalent of a whole series of specialized machines; a few multipurpose machines may replace whole factories.

The world of chemistry also gave rise to a number of processes that speeded operations, reduced waste, and improved the value of products with only a relatively small capital expenditure. An early example of the capital-saving potential of chemical processes was cited by the British Standing Committee on Prices: the substitution of "wood," "unbrewed," or "artificial" vinegar for the regular or "brewed" vinegar. The production of the latter "requires an expensive plant, the maintenance of a brewery, and, before the brewed vinegar is passed out for sale, the whole process, including maturing, requires many months and a considerable expenditure in labor and fuel." In contrast, the production of "unbrewed" vinegar involves only the simple dilution of acetic acid with water and the addition of caramel; only experts can taste the difference. "Unbrewed vinegar is easily made on a small scale in domestic fashion, without any works maintenance or appreciable outlay of capital. . . . So long as any small trader can, on his own premises, produce unbrewed vinegar at a cost not appreciably higher than that at which the larger makers can produce, there is obviously little or no possibility of makers selling such vinegar in a district which necessitates any considerable expenditure in distributive costs." [24]

The decentralizing technologies received a tremendous impetus from a revolution in transportation which made it possible for the small plant to obtain supplies and get its products to the market. With the advent of the motor truck it was no longer necessary to channel raw materials over great distances from a relatively small number of rich sources into a few giant clusters of industrial facilities located along railroad routes. And no longer was the mass distribution

[23] Mumford, *op. cit.*, pp. 225–26.
[24] Grant, *op. cit.*, p. 492.

of the finished products limited to those markets which could economically be served only by the railroads. In essence, the truck tended to transform the inflow of materials and the outflow of finished products from a giant national pattern into smaller regional and local patterns. Within these smaller market areas, the decentralized plant, obtaining its materials and distributing its finished products by truck, frequently gained important advantages over the distant, larger plants, harnessed to the inflexible railroad lines. The truck-serviced, decentralized plants tapped nearby sources of low-cost raw materials that had never been exploited merely because they did not exist in sufficient quantities to justify the expense of a railroad line. But of even greater importance was the decentralized plant's ability to service nearby markets and to share in their growth and expansion.

Quite apart from the truck, the automobile had its own decentralizing effects. No longer was it necessary for a plant to be located within a large industrial center in order to be assured of an adequate supply of labor. Rather, the workers, using their automobiles, could commute over long distances between their homes and the plant. By means of the automobile, workers have been enabled to come to the plant, wherever it is, instead of the plant's being brought to the workers. Indeed, because of the growing problem of traffic congestion the location of large plants within a major city has become a rarity.

The relative efficiency of large plants

The impression that efficiency rises with increasing size of plant stems not only from the nature of the earlier technologies but from the apparent showings of employee productivity for manufacturing as a whole, as well as the trend in the relative importance of large plants. It is true that among *all* manufacturing plants, shipments per employee rise with the size of plant. But this merely reflects the fact that industries with high ratios of shipments per employee tend to have larger plants than industries with low ratios. When examined on an industry-by-industry basis, which means that all plants are operating on the basis of a more or less common technology, the highest productivity levels are generally found in plants in the middle size range. According to the 1967 Census of Manufactures this was true of three-quarters of the 420 (4-digit) industries. It was true, for example, of 32 of the 44 food processing industries.[25]

While very small plants obviously cannot enjoy the economies of scale available to large plants, it is also clear that beyond a medium size of plant the economies of scale are outweighed by the diseconomies, apparently because the large plants are encumbered by administrative, supervisory and clerical personnel whose contributions to operating efficiency are not commensurate with their number.

There can be little question but that larger plants came to play an increasingly important role throughout the nineteenth century and the early part of this century. Unhappily, the early Census data on plant size are available only in terms of employment—i.e., number of wage earners—a measure that is particularly susceptible to the bias resulting from the more rapid pace of mechanization of the larger plants. Moreover, the largest size class for which data were shown consisted of plants with more than 1,000 workers, which embraced many plants that would now be regarded as of medium size.

[25] Based on size distributions of shipments per employee, by industry, compiled by Jay M. Gould, Economic Information Systems, New York City.

Stimulated no doubt by the expansion and centralization of output in World War I, plants with over 1,000 wage earners sharply increased their share of manufacturing employment from 18.0 percent in 1914 to 26.5 percent in 1919. After World War I their share fell back to 23.3 percent in 1923 and then rose at a moderate rate through the remainder of the decade, reaching a level of 24.4 percent in 1929. Nonetheless, it is interesting to note, there were 25 *fewer* such plants in 1929 than in 1919. Between 1929 and 1939 there was a further decline of 106 in the number of such plants, and their share of the total number of workers fell again—from 24.0 to 22.3 percent. For this period figures are available in terms of a larger, and more meaningful, class interval—plants with more than 2,500 workers. Again the trend is in the same direction. There were 19 fewer such plants in 1939 than in 1929, and their share of the total number of workers was down slightly—from 10.9 to 10.5 percent.

It is a little-known fact that during the long-term period between 1914 and 1937, when the large plant was capturing the imagination of observers everywhere, average plant size was actually decreasing in a significant number of industries. Out of 204 industries for which comparable data are available, average plant size (as measured by wage earners per establishment) decreased in no fewer than 63, or in roughly one-third of the total.

The type of information on plant size currently available from the Census Bureau dates from 1947. During a period of great expansion, such as the economy has enjoyed since that date, the logical expectation would be that smaller plants would grow to medium-size units, medium-size plants would become large establishments, and the scale of operations would increase all along the line. And it would appear at first that this is what has happened. The number of plants with 2,500 or more employees rose from 504 in 1947 to 544 in 1963, while their share of total value added by manufacture increased from 17.3 percent to 21.8 percent. But as an indication of what took place in industry generally this is an illusion, resulting largely from an abnormally rapid expansion in 5 defense industries plus motor vehicles. Four of the 5 industries—ordnance, aircraft, aircraft engines, and aircraft equipment—are direct defense industries, while defense orders figure prominently in the demand for radio, TV, and communications equipment. Because most defense activity is based on "negotiated" rather than "competitive" bids, the free play of market forces is of distinctly secondary importance in determining the size of the optimal plant. Inasmuch as a Defense Department contract covers all costs plus a profit, the plant involved in the award may be significantly larger—or smaller—than the optimal size. By its very nature, automobile production, which also enjoyed a vast expansion during this period, is an industry of large plants. As can be seen in Table 5-1, if these 6 industries are excluded, the number of manufacturing plants with 2,500 or more employees actually fell during this period of great economic expansion, from 398 in 1947 to 345 in 1963, while their share of total value added by manufacture declined from 13.0 to 12.2 percent.

Has this downward trend in the role of large plants also been true of *individual industries?* Using as his basis of measurement the change in value added accounted for by the largest employment size classes, William G. Shepherd found that between 1947 and 1958 the share of the largest plants decreased in 78 of 133 industries: "Apparently there are strong pressures in many industries toward smaller employment-size of plants including changes in transportation and information handling, both of which encourage greater decentralization." [26]

[26] William G. Shepherd, "What Does the Survivor Technique Show About Economies of Scale?" *Southern Economic Journal,* July, 1967, pp. 113–22.

Table 5-1

PROPORTION OF OUTPUT ACCOUNTED FOR
BY PLANTS WITH 2,500 OR MORE EMPLOYEES

| | | 1947 | | | 1963 | | |
| | | | Value Added by Manufacture | | | Value Added by Manufacture | |
SIC Code	Industry	Number of Plants	(mils.)	Percent of Mfg.	Number of Plants	(mils.)	Percent of Mfg.
19	Ordnance	2	$ 41		26	$ 2,316	
3721	Aircraft	17	538		21	3,343	
3722	Aircraft engines	6	170		17	1,665	
3729	Aircraft equipment				10	863	
3662	Radio, TV, and communication equipment	12	218		43	2,676	
3717	Motor vehicles and parts	69	2,190		82	7,546	
	Total (6 industries)	106	$ 3,157		199	$18,409	
	Total manufacturing	504	$12,835	17.3%	544	$41,819	21.8%
	Total manufacturing less 6 industries	398	$ 9,678	13.0%	345	$23,410	12.2%

Source: Bureau of the Census, Department of Commerce, *1947 Census of Manufactures*, 1950, Vol. I, Ch. 3, Table 1; *1963 Census of Manufactures*, 1966, Vol. I, Ch. 2, Table 3.

He found that with the elimination of 10 of the 133 industries, "the share of the largest-size plants in all other industries declined from 14.2 to 13.2 percent of value-added." As a group these 10 "grew much more rapidly (183%) during 1947–1958 than did the rest of the industries (81%)." Six of the 10 were heavily involved with defense procurement. Summarizing his findings he states: "Altogether one concludes that there has been no widespread shift at all toward larger plants (as measured by number of employees). The relatively few upward shifts have been focused in a few industries, and most of these are involved in defense production." [27]

As has been noted, conclusions concerning the role of large plants based on published Census statistics are open to criticism on the grounds that employment is not a satisfactory basis for size distributions, since large plants tend to be more mechanized than smaller establishments and hence use fewer employees per unit of output.[28] This problem has been obviated, however, by the preparation of special Census tabulations showing for individual industries the proportions of the value added by manufacture accounted for by their 4, 8, 20, and

[27] *Ibid.* The defense industries were aircraft, aircraft engines, scientific instruments, photographic equipment, guided missiles, and sighting and fire-control equipment. The other 4 were cigarettes, pharmaceutical preparations, petroleum refining, and blast furnaces and steel mills.

[28] The measure "total employees," which includes salaried workers as well as production workers, is less affected by this bias than the measure "number of wage-earners."

Table 5-2

CHANGES IN PLANT CONCENTRATION, 1947-1958[a]

Change (% Pts.)	Number of Industries[b] with	
	Increases	Decreases
10 and over	9	31
7 to 9	9	5
4 to 6	8	15
Total	26	51

[a]Share of 8 largest plants based on value of shipments
[b]Exclusive of industries with value of shipments in 1958 of less than $100 million and industries with change of 3 percentage points or less.

Source: *Hearings on Economic Concentration*, Pt. 4, p. 1730

50 largest plants, ranked by *value of shipments*.[29] Apart from 120 small indus-tries with a value of shipments of less than $100 million, plant concentration ratios for 1947 and 1958 were available for 125 industries. Using the share accounted for by the 8 largest plants as the basis of measurement one finds that the industries with decreases in plant concentration outnumbered those with increases by 67 to 48, or by nearly 40 percent. When industries with only a minor change in plant concentration—3 percentage points or less—are omitted, the decreases outnumbered the increases by 51 to 26 (see Table 5-2). Not only did the decreases outnumber the increases by nearly two to one, but most of the decreases were quite substantial. In 31 of the 51 industries with decreases in plant concentration, the decline in the share accounted for by the 8 largest plants was 10 percentage points or more. Moreover, substantial decreases in plant concentration were not confined to a few sectors of the economy but were scattered throughout a broad diversity of industry groups, including tobacco products, textiles, furniture, rubber products, chemicals, stone, clay, and glass, primary metals, machinery, electrical machinery, transportation equipment, and miscellaneous products. The declining importance of large plants would there-fore appear to stem not from the unique nature of particular industries but from a pervasive characteristic of modern technology.

Single-plant versus multiplant operations

The general tendency for the share of the largest plants to decline since World War II has *not* been accompanied by any similar tendency on the part of the larg-est companies.[30] Today, the position of the leading companies is based only in-frequently on their operation of one or a few large plants; rather, it rests on their ownership of many—sometimes even hundreds of—separate plants. This has been established in an unusual study by Ralph L. Nelson, who had been granted access by the Census Bureau to individual plant and company reports.[31] The

[29] *Hearings on Economic Concentration*, Pt. 4, pp. 1549–51, 1720–29.
[30] See Ch. 3.
[31] This was the result of an arrangement, including certain restrictions, between the Census Bureau and the Social Science Research Foundation, under which Nelson was sworn in as a Census Bureau employee.

relative importance of single plants was compared with what Nelson termed "sister" plants—i.e., those owned by the same company and operating in the same industry. In only 4 of 83 industries did the 4 leading companies in 1954 operate only one plant each; in 47 industries they operated more than 3 plants each. It was in general the companies other than the 4 largest which were single-plant producers. These firms operated on the average only 1.08 plants per company; for the 4 leading companies the average was 5.22. And this pattern was pervasive, companies other than the 4 largest being essentially single-plant producers in industries of high as well as low concentration. Yet even in the industries of lowest concentration (i.e., those with a concentration ratio of less than 30 percent), the 4 leaders averaged more than 4 plants per company, while in industries with ratios of over 70 percent the 4 leaders averaged more than 7 plants per company.

Noting that the leading companies usually operated both multiple and large plants, Nelson found that "the variance in the proportion of an industry's plants owned by its leading companies contributed more than the variance in the size of leading company plants relative to the whole industry." He concluded:

> The inference to be drawn from these findings is that, with few exceptions, the concentration of an industry is only indirectly related to the operation of large plants. In most industries of high concentration not only is the operation of large plants a common practice in leading firms, but so also is the operation of many large plants. The operation of only one or two plants by leading companies is found mainly in the smaller industries. Efficient plant operation would appear to require high concentration in only a small minority of industries, industries that are most often small and of lesser economic importance.[32]

The divergence between plant and company concentration

It is one thing to know that, in general, concentration in terms of ownership is based on multiplant operations. It is something else to know the extent to which this is true among the various industries. That information can be found by comparing concentration on a plant basis with concentration on a company basis. Where concentration in the largest companies is high but is closely approached by the concentration in the largest plants, oligopoly is obviously the inescapable consequence of the requirements of technology and must be accepted as an inevitable fact of economic life. But if concentration in terms of companies is substantially higher than concentration in terms of plants, the explanation for oligopoly must be sought in factors other than technology.

On the basis of the 1963 Census of Manufactures it has been possible to measure the levels of both plant and company concentration and to determine the difference, or "divergence," between the two for industries representing 78 percent of total manufacturing output.[33] The divergence between technology

[32] *Hearings on Economic Concentration*, Pt. 1, p. 271.
[33] *Concentration Ratios in Manufacturing Industry, 1963*, Pt. 1, Table 2, pp. 6–41. The data for company concentration are the concentration ratios for the 4, 8, 20, and 50 largest producers, as published in the report of the Census Bureau prepared for the Senate Subcommittee on Antitrust and Monopoly. The data on plant concentration were obtained partly from a special tabulation made by the Census Bureau for the Subcommittee and partly by derivation from information contained in the Census Bureau's publication "Size of Establishments."

and ownership concentration was measured in terms of the percentage point difference between the shares held by the 8 largest plants and those held by the 8 largest companies.[34]

In order to facilitate comparisons among the varying degrees of divergence, four categories have been established: (a) industries with "extreme" divergences (i.e., the share held by the 8 largest companies exceeds that of the 8 largest plants by 40 percentage points or more); (b) those with "wide" divergences (company concentration exceeds plant concentration by 20 to 39 percentage points); (c) those with "moderate" divergences (between 10 and 19 percentage points), and (d) those with "narrow" divergences (under 10 percentage points). In the first two categories concentration of ownership and control has very little to do with technology; these are industries in which company concentration could be lowered substantially without impairing technological efficiency. This is less true of the industries in the third class and hardly true at all of those in the fourth. Two examples of each of these four divergence patterns are shown in Figure 5-2.

"Extreme" divergence is illustrated by the 2 industries at the top of the chart, gypsum products and soybean oil mills. In the former the 8 largest companies account for 97 percent of the value of shipments, the 8 largest plants for only 22 percent. The divergence is thus 75 percentage points. The difference between plant and company concentration can also be seen in the fact that the proportion accounted for by the 50 largest plants is about the same as that of the 4 largest companies. The other example of extreme divergence, soybean oil mills, is illustrative of those industries in which company concentration is somewhat lower but still far above the level of plant concentration: here the share of the 8 largest companies, 70 percent, contrasts to a proportion for the 8 largest plants of only 30 percent.

Immediately below are examples of "wide" divergence, biscuits and crackers and computing machines. Although concentration in terms of the technological unit is somewhat higher than in the first category, it is still well below the level of company concentration. In both, the share held by the 8 largest companies is about twice that of the 8 largest plants. The share held by the 20 largest plants is about the same as that of the 4 largest firms.

The next 2 industries, steam engines and turbines and photographic equipment, are illustrative of "moderate" divergence—not so narrow as to completely preclude deconcentration, but still so limited as to seriously restrict its extent. In the former a reduction in company concentration to the level of plant concen-

---

[34] Because of the Census disclosure rule, the use of any figure less than 8 for plant concentration would have necessitated omitting a considerable number of industries. Among the types of information published by the Census Bureau in terms of size classes is the value of shipments, which is the basis on which the company concentration ratios are compiled. The selection of companies constituting the leading producers is in terms of value of shipments, whereas the published distributions by size of plant are in terms of employment. However, a comparison of those industries for which figures were available for the 8 largest plants selected on both bases revealed only negligible differences between the two. Where the number of plants in the largest size class of the published distribution was fewer than 8, a value for 8 could readily be obtained by interpolation since data were almost invariably shown for at least one other size class. Where the number in the largest size class was in excess of 8, a value for 8 was derived by extrapolation, but only if the number of plants in the largest size class was 9 or 10 and the number of plants in the next largest size class was fewer than 30. Extrapolating from a line drawn from two observations, one 10 or fewer and the other 30 or fewer, should provide reasonably accurate values for the 8 largest.

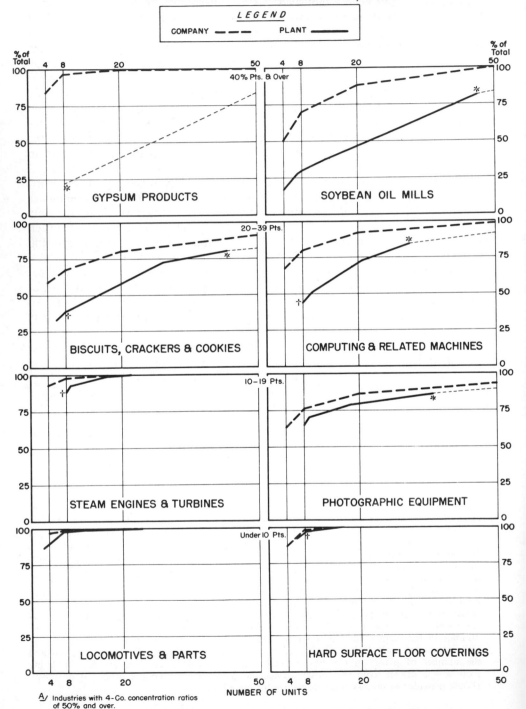

Figure 5-2
HIGHLY CONCENTRATED INDUSTRIES ᴬ/
WITH VARYING DIVERGENCES BETWEEN PLANT
AND COMPANY CONCENTRATION, 1963

LEGEND

COMPANY — — —   PLANT ———

GYPSUM PRODUCTS

40% Pts. & Over

SOYBEAN OIL MILLS

BISCUITS, CRACKERS & COOKIES

20–39 Pts.

COMPUTING & RELATED MACHINES

STEAM ENGINES & TURBINES

10–19 Pts.

PHOTOGRAPHIC EQUIPMENT

LOCOMOTIVES & PARTS

Under 10 Pts.

HARD SURFACE FLOOR COVERINGS

NUMBER OF UNITS

ᴬ/ Industries with 4-Co. concentration ratios
of 50% and over.

✳ Dashed line from this observation to 50 based on next known observation.   † Interpolated or extrapolated.

Source: Computed from Bureau of the Census, Department of Commerce, *1963 Census of Manufactures*, 1966

tration would still leave the 8 largest companies with 88 percent of the value of shipments; in the latter they would still account for 65 percent.

In locomotives and parts and hard surface floor coverings, shown at the bottom of the chart, the limit to deconcentration set by the level of plant concentration is so high as to make deconcentration impossible. The plant and company concentration curves are virtually identical, yielding a divergence that is "narrow" by any standard. In both, a reduction of company concentration to the level of plant concentration would still leave the 4 largest companies with nearly 90 percent of the output.

Which of these divergence patterns is of greatest importance in our industrial structure? For total manufacturing[35] the distribution is as follows:

Pattern		Percentage of Value of Shipments
"Extreme"	(40% Pts. and over)	22.3%
"Wide"	(20–39% Pts.)	34.1
"Moderate"	(10–19% Pts.)	22.4
"Narrow"	(Under 10% Pts.)	21.3

But from the point of view of public policy the important area is not total manufacturing but the concentrated industries. It should occasion little surprise to note that where company concentration is low, it is not—and indeed cannot be—substantially above the level of plant concentration; deconcentration is manifestly impossible in an industry such as sawmills and planing mills in which the 8 largest firms account for only 6 percent of the output.[36] The accompanying chart, Figure 5-3, shows the relative importance of the four patterns of divergence within the concentrated, moderately concentrated, and unconcentrated categories of industries.[37]

In the concentrated industries—i.e., those in which the 4 largest firms account for 50 percent or more of the output—the most arresting showing is the comparative unimportance of the "narrow divergence" industries; in the aggregate they account for only 7.3 percent of the output of all concentrated industries. Of even less importance are the industries with "moderate" divergence, which make up only 6.3 percent of the total. In other words, in the concentrated segment of our industrial economy as a whole, less than one-seventh of the output comes from industries in which high company concentration can be seen to be the direct and inevitable consequence of the "imperatives of technology." More than four-fifths of the output of the concentrated industries comes from fields in which the share of the 8 largest companies exceeds that of the 8 largest plants by at least 20 percentage points, while in more than half (54.7 percent) the divergence is at least 40 percentage points. To put it another way, the output of concentrated industries with "extreme" divergence, alone, is more than four

---

[35] These industries represent 78% of the value of shipments in all manufacturing.

[36] The same consideration would be expected to apply, but with less force, to the moderately concentrated industries. It therefore is a matter of some surprise to note that over half the output of the moderately concentrated group comes from industries with a divergence of 20 percentage points or more.

[37] As was explained in Ch. 1, the "concentrated" industries are those in which the 4 largest firms account for 50% or more of the output; the "moderately concentrated" industries are those in which the share of the 4 largest is from 25 to 49%; and the "unconcentrated" are those in which the share is under 25%.

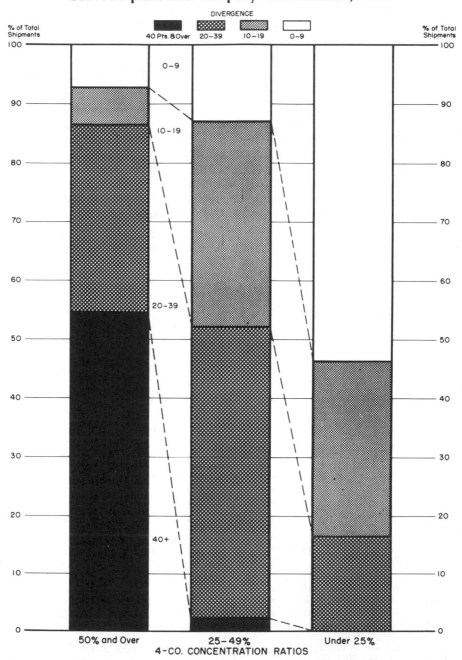

Figure 5-3

DISTRIBUTION OF TOTAL VALUE OF SHIPMENTS
By concentration ratio and divergence
between plant and company concentration, 1963

% of Total Shipments

DIVERGENCE

40 Pts. & Over   20–39   10–19   0–9

% of Total Shipments

50% and Over   25–49%   Under 25%
4-CO. CONCENTRATION RATIOS

Source: Computed from Bureau of the Census, Department of Commerce, *1963 Census of Manufactures,* 1966

times that of "narrow-" and "moderate-divergence" concentrated industries combined. For all but a minor segment of the industrial economy the explanation for concentration is clearly to be found in multiplant operations, not in the requirements of technology to achieve economies of scale.

The dimensions of the problem area can be narrowed still further by an examination of divergence in a few specific, concentrated industries with "extreme divergence." Because of their size the restructuring of these industries would lessen significantly the importance of concentration in the economy as a whole —and because each is dominated by one or 2 companies, these industries would lend themselves readily to restructuring. Figure 5-4 shows the divergence for 8 such industries. All but 2 had shipments in 1963 of more than $1 billion,[38] and all had divergences of at least 40 percentage points. These 8 accounted for 49 percent of the value of shipments of all concentrated industries and for 89 percent of the output of all such industries with "extreme" divergence. Dissolution down to the level of plant concentration in just these 8 industries would reduce the magnitude of the concentrated sector (on a national basis) from one-third to only one-sixth of the total industrial economy.[39]

A long-standing argument against deconcentration has been that any conceivable reduction in the size of the leading companies would still leave substantial control in the hands of a few large producers; oligopoly would not be as "tight," but substantial monopoly power would remain. That argument, it should be clear, has little relevance to these industries. With 2 exceptions, the reduction in the share of the 4 largest companies to that held by the 4 largest plants would shift the industry all the way from the concentrated to the unconcentrated category. In 2 of these industries (motor vehicles and parts and metal cans) the share accounted for by the 4 largest plants is less than 15 percent; in 4 others (blast furnaces and steel mills, soap and other detergents, primary copper, and asbestos products) it is less than 25 percent. Only in the case of tires and electric lamps would the shift be merely from concentrated to moderately concentrated.

The impact on economic thinking

Since the Industrial Revolution the steady increase in plant size has seemed to convey the inevitable prospect of monopoly. The question plaguing economists has been, in D. H. Robertson's phrase, whether the process could "be played upon by the mind" without abandoning the theory of competition. The noted German economist Walter Eucken commented on the long-prevailing point of view:

> According to the old widely spread and influential view, modern technical progress demands giant units, destroys small and medium-sized

[38] In the other 2, electric lamps and asbestos products, shipments were in excess of $500 million.

[39] In 1963 shipments by industries with 4-company concentration ratios of at least 50% constituted 33% of the shipments of all manufacturing industries. Of this, 49% was accounted for by the 8 industries shown in Figure 5-4, which thus made up 16.3% of total manufacturing output. This estimate excludes the industries, representing 22% of the total value of shipments, for which divergence could not be measured. The assumption is that the distribution of these industries among the different divergence categories is similar to the distribution of those industries for which such information is available.

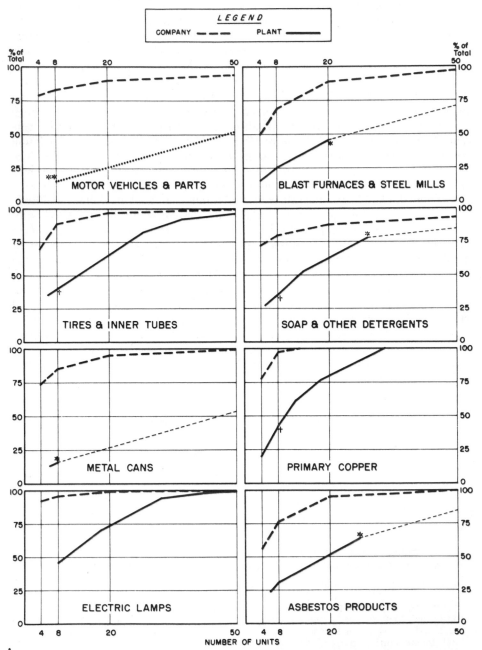

Figure 5-4

LARGE, A/ HIGHLY CONCENTRATED B/ INDUSTRIES WITH DIVERGENCES OF 40 PERCENTAGE POINTS OR MORE, 1963

LEGEND

COMPANY ▬ ▬ ▬   PLANT ▬▬▬▬

MOTOR VEHICLES & PARTS

BLAST FURNACES & STEEL MILLS

TIRES & INNER TUBES

SOAP & OTHER DETERGENTS

METAL CANS

PRIMARY COPPER

ELECTRIC LAMPS

ASBESTOS PRODUCTS

NUMBER OF UNITS

A/ Each with 1963 shipments of over $500 million.
B/ Industries with 4-Co. concentration ratios of 50% and over.

* Dashed line from this observation to 50 based on next known observation.
† Interpolated or extrapolated.
** Dotted line from this observation to next observation at 50.

Source: Computed from Bureau of the Census, Department of Commerce, *1963 Census of Manufactures*, 1966

enterprises, and it gives rise to an imminent conflict between the size of the plant, the rigidity of supply and the changing requirements to which production cannot be adapted any longer. To maintain economic order it would be necessary to have holding companies, trusts, cartels and other monopolies, state intervention, public corporations. . . . This is the picture most people hold.[40]

The effect of these new technologies on the mind of man has, if anything, proved to be greater than their impact on industry structure itself. To "the early Victorian economists, marvelling over the mechanical efficiency of the monster textile mills," [41] size came to be equated with efficiency. But they were also strong believers in competition, so the attribution of efficiency to size gave rise to a conceptual dilemma that moved even the most reserved of British economists to describe it as "vexatious" and as the "dilemma which has given rise to all this pother." [42] On several occasions the dilemma was "resolved" by recourse to theoretical assumptions, only to reappear again when the assumptions were challenged and discarded. Except for the minority of industries in which costs remained unchanged or rose with greater output ("constant returns" and "decreasing returns" industries), the question was how competition could be reconciled with greater efficiency resulting from larger size. What was there to prevent a given company from increasing its size (at the expense of the remainder of the industry) and thereby achieving greater economies, increasing its size again and thus achieving still greater economies, and so on *ad infinitum* until it had monopolized the industry? [43] In D. H. Robertson's words:

> The root difficulty about increasing returns has always been to understand how, where they prevail, equilibrium can exist without the whole supply of the commodity in question becoming concentrated in the hands of one producer. . . . If we take an increasing return industry which is out of equilibrium, with demand price in excess of supply price, and watch its progress toward equilibrium, we must surely conclude that frequently the main factor in this process is the scramble by individual firms, regardless of the actions of their neighbors, to reap the direct advantages of large-scale organization and plant—advantages which have always been obvious and are in no sense being brought into existence, either through the medium of increased specialization or in any other way, by the growth in the output of the industry as a whole. The question is whether this

[40] Walter Eucken, "Technical Evolution, Concentration and Economic Order," *Ordo*, Vol. 3, 1950, pp. 3–17. The author is indebted to Professor and Mrs. Ernst Mestmacker for calling his attention to Professor Eucken's article and translating it for him.

[41] Mumford, *op. cit.*, p. 226.

[42] Different aspects of this theoretical problem are discussed in the following articles: J. H. Clapham, "On Empty Economic Boxes," *Economic Journal*, Sept., 1922; A. C. Pigou, "Empty Economic Boxes, a Reply," *Economic Journal*, Dec., 1922; D. H. Robertson, "Those Empty Boxes," *Economic Journal*, Jan., 1924; Piero Sraffa, "The Laws of Returns under Competitive Conditions," *Economic Journal*, Dec., 1926; A. C. Pigou, "The Laws of Diminishing and Increasing Cost," *Economic Journal*, June, 1927; G. F. Shove, "Varying Costs and Marginal Net Products," *Economic Journal*, June, 1928; Lionel Robbins, "The Representative Firm," *Economic Journal*, Sept., 1928; Allyn Young, "Increasing Returns and Economic Progress," *Economic Journal*, Dec., 1928; D. H. Robertson, Piero Sraffa, G. F. Shove, "Increasing Returns and the Representative Firm: A Symposium," *Economic Journal*, March, 1930.

[43] This problem was not raised by the operation of external economies, since any expansion of an industry as a whole would, presumably, result in an expansion of each of its members, thus involving no major change in the relative size distribution of the industry.

process, which admittedly does not always end in the abandonment of competition, *can or cannot be played upon by the mind with any success without abandoning the theory of competition.*[44]

The answer considered adequate for many years was that supplied by Alfred Marshall in his theory of the "representative" firm.[45] Marshall held that the growth of a firm cannot continue indefinitely because the abilities and energies of the enterpreneur (or of his heirs) are likely to decay after a certain time (a sort of sociological law with Marshall); because in many industries large-scale economies are counteracted by the difficulty of enlarging the firm's market; and because there is, "on the whole, a broad movement from below upward" (i.e., ability would always find the capital necessary to enter industry, and so on). Between the economies of large-scale operations on the one hand and the difficulty of expanding the firm's market on the other was Marshall's "representative" firm—one that has not reached the age or size that is susceptible to the "decay of faculties" but is able to use large-scale economies up to that point where they begin to diminish in intensity owing to the increasing difficulty in marketing.[46]

The virtues of competition, so obvious to the early British economists, were of course utterly lost upon Marx, who regarded competition as merely an evolutionary stage in the development of capitalism—a particularly exploitive stage at that. To one who had little use for competition, the greater efficiency of the larger plants posed no dilemma whatever: competition was in conflict with the requirements of technology and would therefore have to pass from the scene. Along with the labor theory of value—which he had adopted from the British economists—belief in the superiority of size became a *sine qua non* of Marx's thinking. Buttressing his argument with examples from early British industrial history, he sought to prove that new machines would lead to concentration and the destruction of competition. As Eucken has pointed out, Marx

> gave these thoughts their decisive power when he, believing in his discovery of the law of concentration as an inherent part of historical development, effectively worded this thought. He says in his "Concentration of Workers and Machines in Big Factories": the very big spinning-mills would supplant the small ones, the medium ones, and finally even the big spinning-mills. The present condition of technical development or—in Marx's own words—"the stage of evolution of the materialistic powers of production" would require the concentration of all production within

[44] D. H. Robertson, Piero Sraffa, G. F. Shove, "Increasing Returns and the Representative Firm: A Symposium," *Economic Journal*, March, 1930, pp. 84, 87. Emphasis added.

[45] For a summary and criticism of Marshall's position see Joseph Steindl, *Small and Big Business*, Blackwell, 1947, pp. 1–12.

[46] Unfortunately, but perhaps with his customary acute foresight, Marshall was exceedingly vague in presenting any further descriptive details concerning the representative firm. We learn merely that it is neither a young, growing firm nor a decaying firm; it is not a firm of unusually large size or with unusual advantages; the "normal" economies which can be obtained in an industry are open to firms which are of representative size; and the representative firm tends to increase in size as the industry as a whole expands. Somewhere between these different sets of polar extremities the representative firm is to be found. Many years later A. C. Pigou, in trying to make clear what Marshall had in mind, delivered himself of the not-too-helpful generalization that Marshall's representative firm is meant to be "a firm of, in some sense, average size . . . a typical firm, built on a scale to which actual firms tend to approximate . . ." and that there is good evidence that "this conception is appropriate to actual conditions." (A. C. Pigou, *Economics of Welfare*, 3rd ed., Macmillan, 1929, p. 788.)

one or a very few large enterprises: this would necessarily lead to a monopoly.[47]

The greater efficiency of their plants will enable the larger producers to undersell their smaller rivals and thus gain a greater share of the market: "One capitalist lays a number of his fellow capitalists low." As a result capital becomes "centralized" in the hands of fewer producers, and production becomes concentrated in ever larger industrial establishments.[48] The process will continue until the few monopolies that are left drop "like ripe plums" into the hands of the workers.

The lasting impact of Marx's argument derives from his persuasive ability to transform a commonplace observation into an eternal "law." Had he contented himself with observing that the new technologies of the early nineteenth century brought with them a larger scale of operation, he would merely have been repeating the obvious. But by purporting to discover a "law of concentration" he transformed the transient into the transcendental. Increasing concentration was the inescapable result of "the action of the immanent laws of capitalistic production, itself, the centralization of capital." These immanent laws would result in a "constantly diminishing number of the magnates of capital, who usurp and monopolize all advantages of this process of transformation. . . ." The argument thus lent an aura of inevitability, or "scientific determinism," to his political doctrines. As Leon Herman has put it, "Marx, of course, was not a mere disinterested observer of economic trends. He was at all times scanning the economic horizon for evidence to support his own grim prophecy that the capitalist system of production was doomed to create the very conditions required for its own destruction." [49] The monopolies resulting from technological progress could be expected, like monopolies everywhere, to exploit the people, whose misery ultimately would be such as to drive them to revolution. In a famous passage Marx wrote: "Capitalist monopoly becomes a fetter upon the method of production which has flourished with it and under it. The centralization of the means of production and the socialization of labor reach a point where they prove incompatible with their capitalist husk. This bursts asunder. The knell of capitalist private property sounds. The expropriators are expropriated." [50]

In word and deed Lenin carried Marx's argument to its logical conclusion: "We base our faith entirely on Marx's theory. . . . It has shown how the whole development of modern capitalism is advancing towards the large producer ousting the smaller one, and is creating the prerequisites which make a socialist order of society possible and necessary." [51] Following Marx's precept the trend toward increasing concentration assumed the character of an historical "law." Lenin simply took it to be an incontestable fact that these "huge enterprises, trusts, and syndicates have brought the mass production technique to its highest level of development." In addition to their superiority at the technological level, they were able to secure further advantages through "planning": "Having brought under their domination entire branches of industry, the capitalist monopolistic corporations are regulating in a planned way the production of com-

[47] Eucken, *op. cit.*
[48] *Hearings on Economic Concentration*, Pt. 7A, Leon M. Herman, "The Cult of Bigness in Soviet Economic Planning."
[49] *Ibid.*, p. 4346.
[50] Karl Marx, *Capital*, Dent, 1934, Vol. II, p. 846.
[51] V. I. Lenin, "Our Programme," in E. Burns, ed., *Handbook of Marxism*, Random House, 1935, p. 571. Cited by Herman in *Hearings on Economic Concentration*, Pt. 7A, p. 4347.

modities upon which millions of people depend." The monopolistic corporations were both the last stage of capitalist development and the instrument for the achievement of a socialist political order: "Socialism is nothing more than capitalist monopoly applied for the benefit of the whole nation." [52]

Belief in the superiority of size has by no means been the exclusive prerogative of Marxists. A typical statement of the case was set forth some 35 years ago by Arthur R. Burns, in his well-known work, *The Decline of Competition*.[53] Literature on concentration, he wrote, "is founded upon naive conceptions of 'competition' and 'monopoly' and unreal assumptions concerning the possibility of reviving the competitive market." Rather the transformation of the industrial system has been brought about by "underlying forces," notably technological changes requiring large plants for their efficient utilization: "The reduction of the number of firms and their increasing size over the past half century are clearly due, in part, to the use of methods of production which are economical only if large quantities are produced under a single organization." The antitrust approach of breaking up large corporations would necessarily impair productive efficiency, resulting in higher production costs and thus higher prices. In Burns's words: "Much of the recently acquired knowledge of methods of production involves mass production; if firms are reduced in size, some of the benefits of mass production must be abandoned." [54] More recently the same general point of view has been set forth by J. Kenneth Galbraith. In his most recent work, he finds justification for bigness as the type of "organization required by modern technology and planning." Emphasizing the latter, he draws examples from the large automobile companies, which have been models of successful corporate planning. The success of their planning has been achieved by their central offices—their "massive and complex business organization." [55]

The rationales for size are, if anything, held more strongly abroad than in the United States.[56] The much publicized "indicative planning" of the French government rests directly upon a belief in the superior efficiency of large organizations. Within the European Economic Community, a conflict is seen between its original objective of bringing to Western Europe the benefits of wider competition and the necessity of recognizing the superior efficiency of large—and noncompeting—enterprises. In France, belief in the superior efficiency of bigness has assumed the character of an *idée fixe*. As William James Adams has observed,

> The specter now haunting Europe is technology. American technology. And that specter assumes its most lurid incarnation in France. Obsessed with current speculation on the year 2,000, the French government fears that the French economy will lose its advanced standing unless it cultivates technological independence of the United States. Accordingly, in the belief that absolute and relative firm size are essential ingredients of research activity on an effective scale, the French government has actively promoted the concentration of French industry.[57]

[52] See Herman in *Hearings on Economic Concentration*, Pt. 7A, p. 4347.
[53] Arthur R. Burns, *The Decline of Competition*, McGraw-Hill, 1936.
[54] *Ibid.*, pp. v, 8, 525.
[55] J. Kenneth Galbraith, *The New Industrial State*, Houghton Mifflin, 1967, pp. 6, 16.
[56] For an analysis of the effects of the veneration of size in Communist countries, see Ch. 25.
[57] William James Adams, "Firm Size and Research Activity," *Quarterly Journal of Economics*, Aug., 1970, pp. 387, 394–95. From Adams's findings it would appear that the policy of deliberately promoting concentration will only widen further the technological

In Japan each step toward the restoration of the power of the old family money-cliques, or "Zaibatsu," and toward the further weakening of its Fair Trade Commission is taken in the interests of "greater efficiency." A belief in the superiority of size has also induced many of the underdeveloped countries of the world, such as India, to squander their limited capital resources on large plants which, even before they were on the drawing boards, had been rendered obsolete by newer and less costly technologies. In Great Britain belief in the benefits of size has been shared equally by right-wing businessmen and left-wing socialists, providing the conceptual justification for government intervention in the economic process, forced mergers, and a relatively quiescent antitrust policy. In the words of A. S. J. Baster:

> It seems at first sight odd that proposals which, in principle at least, constitute a standing threat to the democratic way of life should make such a strong appeal to democratic parties of the Left as well as of the Right. The conclusion is perhaps inescapable that in the political principles of the Corporate State, tired businessmen with no fundamental belief in their own position in society, and tired radicals who have but their early vision of the equalitarian millennium can safely and easily unite. The former hope, with considerable historical justification, that in practice they will be able to reach a compromise with the politicians favorable to their interests; the latter, with more logic on their side, hope that in practice it will be easy to squeeze out the businessmen by constitutional means and restore Paradise by stealth. It is only the discredited but unrepentant minority who think they see in this unnatural union between two opposing interests at the same time the most striking and most threatening phenomenon of modern democratic politics.[58]

Beginning with the new technologies of the Industrial Revolution, the veneration of size has come to take on the character of a mystique, and, like most mystiques, it has come to enjoy an independent life of its own. The danger is that the size mystique will continue to grip men's minds long after the circumstances that originally gave rise to it have disappeared. In this case the circumstances have not only disappeared but are being replaced by forces operating in the opposite direction—the new decentralizing technologies discussed at greater length in the following chapter.

---

gap between France and the United States. For example, in 4 of 5 industry sectors (electrical equipment, chemicals, machinery and metals, and other manufacturing) French firms with fewer than 1,000 employees accounted for a higher share of employment in research and development (R&D) than of the sector's total employment; in each of the 4 sectors (the aerospace sector being the exception) the reverse was true of firms with 10,000 or more employees. In French industry the ratio of R&D expenditures to sales was higher for firms with 500 to 999 persons (5.0%) than for those with 5,000 or more employees (3.3%); in only one of 8 industries did firms in the larger size group have a distinctly higher R&D ratio.

[58] A. S. J. Baster, *The Little Less,* Methuen, 1947, p. 104.

CH 6 NEW DECENTRALIZING TECHNOLOGIES

Electricity, the multipurpose machine, and the truck, introduced during the first third of this century, initially arrested and then reversed the trend toward a larger scale of operations. And it is now evident that they were merely the precursors of a whole host of new technologies whose effect on industry structures appears to be in the same direction. These new technologies are to be found principally in new forms of materials, new ways of creating power, and the new methods of employing electricity that go by the name of electronics. Some of these new technologies have already become a familiar part of the industrial scene, while others await only a critical technological breakthrough. But, whether they are a present-day reality or a potentiality for the future, these new technologies have one common characteristic differentiating them from the older technologies: they make possible economic production with smaller capital outlays, thereby reducing the barriers to entry, stimulating the entrance of newcomers, and lending a strong impetus to the restoration of competition.

Materials

Just as steel had replaced lumber, so steel is now being replaced by newer materials, which, unlike lumber, provide complete standardization for production but resemble the older material by permitting fabrication with simpler and less costly equipment in smaller establishments. Not only are these materials equal to steel in uniformity; they are superior in other important respects, such as strength and stiffness in relation to weight, resistance to corrosion, and insulation properties. All are essentially families of materials, to which new variants are continually being added. The most important of the ongoing developments in the field of materials are plastics, fiberglass-reinforced plastics, "high performance" composites, and new forms of concrete such as prestressed concrete.

Plastics

While their use dates back to the nineteenth century, it was not until the years following World War II that plastics came to occupy an important role in the American economy. As can be seen from Figure 6-1, the growth of plastic production has been little short of astonishing, output having doubled every 5 years. From a level of only a billion pounds in 1945 the production of plastics and resins rose to some 4 billion pounds in 1955, to nearly 15 billion pounds in 1965, and to slightly below 20 billion pounds in 1970: "The minimum forecast

Figure 6-1
PRODUCTION OF PLASTICS AND RESINS

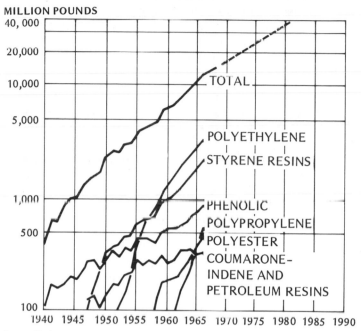

Source: *Hearings on Economic Concentration*, Pt. 3, p. 1196

for plastic materials production is 40 billion pounds in 1980," according to Ralph L. Harding, Jr., executive vice president of the Society of the Plastics Industries (SPI), "and I'm hearing numbers of up to 60 billion pounds for shortly after 1980. . . . On a volume basis, plastics will catch steel between the mid-1980's and 2000."

No other industry begins to compare with plastics in projected growth rates. One study, for example, has predicted a growth rate for plastics roughly *ten times* that of any other materials industry. Between 1965 and 1980 McGraw-Hill anticipates a growth for nonferrous metals of 80 percent, for stone, clay, and glass of 75 percent, for iron and steel of 56 percent, for lumber of 20 percent and for leather of 16 percent. But for the plastics industry the predicted growth is 722 percent.[1] Noting these differences, the plastics industry's trade association has observed, "The statement that we are moving toward a 'plastic age' is not so far wrong. Students of the subject believe, in fact, that twenty years hence *more products will be made of plastics than of all other materials combined*."[2]

In appraising the effects of plastics on size of operations, it is necessary to distinguish between the production of plastic materials and the fabrication of finished and semifinished products from such materials. For the most part the materials themselves are manufactured by a few large chemical and oil companies. The decentralizing effects come in the later stages of fabrication into semi-

[1] "The American Economy, Prospects for Growth Through 1980," McGraw-Hill (Department of Economics), Sept., 1965. Mimeograph.
[2] Brochure of the Society of the Plastics Industries for the Plastics Exhibition, Oct. 5–12, 1967. Emphasis added.

finished and finished products—a remarkably unconcentrated area. Since most of the fabricating industries that are feeling the inroads of plastics are themselves concentrated, the process of substitution exerts a decentralizing influence on individual markets as well as on the economy as a whole. These decentralizing effects can be demonstrated by a pair of examples that could be multiplied many times over. Despite antitrust suits, the manufacture of glass bottles has long persisted as a conspicuous example of concentration. But today more than 500 dairies in some 40 states are using plastic bottles. Interest is particularly marked in multitrip containers, which have an average service life of 100 trips as compared to an average of only 25 for glass bottles. Similarly, the plumbing fixtures industry, long a highly concentrated area, is now feeling the competition of such plastic products as unitized built-in bathroom fixtures, one-piece molded reinforced shower stalls, and plastic pipe and tube.

A major component in the growth of the plastics industry has been the independent custom molders, the overwhelming majority of whom are "small producers" by any definition of the term. According to William T. Cruse, former executive vice president of the Society of the Plastics Industries, the emergence of these custom molders grew from the need of ultimate users for expertise in selecting and processing the best available material for a specific application: "The expanding choice of materials and production methods put an increasing value on the services of a competent guide to the numerous end-results obtainable. The responsible, independent plastics custom molder filled this guiding role. He had the up-to-date knowledge and accumulated background to advise on the plastic material that would give a product the desired end-use properties, yet permit an attractive selling price." [3] Because of his specialized knowledge the custom molder has come to serve as "innovator, engineer and production specialist."

As acceptance of plastics grew, custom molders proliferated, but so did the number of end-user captive plants. A detailed survey in 1969 by *Plastics Technology* magazine showed 14,197 plastics-processing plants in the United States with materials purchases of $100,000 or more.[4] Of this number, 5,511 were independent custom plants, 7,653 end-user captive plants, and 1,033 supplier-owned plants. Certainly many of the captive operations belong to industrial giants—Ford and General Motors, Western Electric and RCA—using plastics in making product components much as they do other materials. But this does not seem to have inhibited the continuing growth in numbers and prosperity of smaller molders, both custom and proprietary. To quote Harding again: "We believe that many smaller independent operators will continue to grow and prosper through their unique talents and their unique ability to specialize by market, process or material."

According to a study by Alan Greenspan, the average plastics fabrication establishment is "a very small operation" with average employment of little more than 50 workers per plant:

> The major reason the industry is made up of relatively small plants is the absence of any substantial economies of size. A cursory glance shows that average profit as a percent of sales or net worth does tend to increase as plant size gets larger. However, this is almost all accounted for by the large number of unsuccessful small companies whose losses ob-

[3] *Hearings on Economic Concentration*, Pt. 6, pp. 2627–56, testimony of William T. Cruse.
[4] Unpublished; privately circulated.

scure the profitability of the other small companies. When the analysis is limited to profit-generating plants, rate of return on sales or against net worth shows no evidence of being markedly higher with increasing plant size.

There is no doubt that ease of entry, low capital requirements and relatively small plant size have made both the plastics materials and the fabrication industries highly price competitive. Margins and rates of return have become decidedly subnormal compared with other industries as prices have deteriorated beyond normal "equilibrium" levels. There are some offsets, however. The extraordinary price competition has been a key factor in the growth in volume. One can argue that the major inroads of plastics as a competitive material displacing rubber, aluminum, paper and textiles could not have proceeded in so rapid a manner if prices had been higher.[5]

The unconcentrated structure of plastics fabrication derives from the simplicity and low cost of the machinery and equipment involved. Capital entrance requirements are low, making possible ready ease of entry. This is true of each of the principal methods of production—compression molding, transfer molding, injection molding, blow molding, and extrusion and thermoforming. In contrast, a metal such as steel can be formed into desired shapes only by machining, which involves high labor and machinery costs, or by stamping, which requires expensive dies and presses. According to Forbes Howard of Borg-Warner's Marbon Division, "a thermo-forming mold made of epoxy . . . costs approximately *one to two percent* of an equivalent steel stamping die and we have yet to find out how many pieces can be run from such a mold before the mold needs replacement." [6] In contrast to the multimillion dollar outlays required for steel-stamping presses and dies, Howard cited the cost of a large injection-molding machine—a highly automated type of plastics-fabricating equipment—as only $200,000 and that of "the biggest and best vacuum forming machine available" as only $100,000. As a general proposition, "large capital outlays are no longer necessary to produce major products in volume at low cost. . . ."

The history of the plastics industry goes back to the year 1868, when John Wesley Hyatt, a printer in Albany, New York, created celluloid. Hyatt's invention had been in response to an offer of $10,000 by what is now the Brunswick Corporation for a substitute for natural ivory in the manufacture of billiard balls. Other products soon came to be made from celluloid—collars and cuffs, combs, brushes, mirrors, false teeth, and the like. The next important development was the invention in 1909 by Leo Hendrick Baekland of the thermosetting plastic Bakelite, a phenolic material that is superior to celluloid in strength and electrical characteristics. But the plastics industry as it exists today is largely a post-World War II development. It is the product of a number of remarkable new materials, which as often as not had been discovered before the war but had remained laboratory curiosities until some wartime need called forth their production. Their subsequent history has been based on the discovery of new peacetime uses, new methods of processing, and new properties. A typical case in point is polyethylene, one of today's large-volume plastics. Originally discovered in Great Britain during the mid-1930's, it met a critical wartime need for a tough and easily processed material that would provide insulation for high-fre-

[5] Alan Greenspan, "The Financial Profile of Plastics," *Proceedings of the First Annual Meeting of SPI Voting Representatives, New Orleans, Louisiana, April 29–May 1, 1970.*
[6] *Hearings on Economic Concentration,* Pt. 6, pp. 2982 3002, testimony of Forbes Howard.

quency radar cables. The U.S. Navy signed contracts with Union Carbide and Du Pont to manufacture the product. At the end of the war, demand for radar cable virtually disappeared, and, in the words of Cruse, "Union Carbide found itself with a fine plant and no markets." The search for civilian uses led first to the replacement of lead sheathing for the jacketing of telephone cables. Other important uses came one upon the other—tumblers, waste baskets, garment bags, garbage bags, and many types of packaging, including plastic squeeze bottles.

Polystyrene, used for such diverse items as toys, battery cases, wall tile, and portable-radio housings, was also invented in the 1930's. Polyurethane, although introduced in 1954, had been known for some 20 years. Again, its first uses were of a military nature, as in aircraft and radar. Today it is used to make such diverse products as gears, gaskets, and other mechanical devices, foam latex, crash pads, arm rests, and the like. In Cruse's words, "Perhaps the keynote and underlying source for opportunity, and the expression of novel and good ideas that is associated with urethane plastics is derived from the extreme versatility of the materials, which permits their use or consideration for almost any fabricated item."

The history of fluorocarbons follows much the same pattern. Traceable back to 1938, these products were used in proximity fuses for bombs and artillery shells. Their best-known peacetime use—Teflon coating—is in cookware. In addition, the tough fluorocarbons are employed in such divergent uses as bearings, piston rings, insulators, switches, linings for pipes, and tubes. Also well known are the epoxy resins, or "miracle glues," introduced commercially in the late 1940's and employed widely not only as bonding agents but in paints, protective coatings, and molded products.

Being man-made, synthetic materials can constantly be improved through minor molecular modifications and combinations. In contrast, the spectrum of changes that can be made in natural materials without impairing their quality and properties is quite limited. While its strength (and also its cost) can be raised by the addition of further alloying elements, steel remains essentially steel.

Some idea of the rapidity with which innovation can proceed in creating synthetics can be gained from the fact that during the 23-year period 1942–65 no fewer than 21 new plastic materials made their appearance in commercial products—a rate of nearly one a year. In addition to those described earlier, these include such materials as polypropylene, from which safety helmets are made; polycarbonate, which goes into appliance parts; polyallomer, which is used to make typewriter cases; the ABS plastics (combinations of acrylonitrile, butadiene, and styrene), from which most luggage is now produced; polyphenylene oxide, which is used for battery cases; and many others.

Almost all plastics can be reinforced by other synthetics as well as by natural materials, providing a class of materials called reinforced plastics, which divide into reinforced thermosets and reinforced thermoplastics.[7] The Reinforced Plastics/Composites Division of the Society of the Plastics Industries forecasts a growth in shipments in this class of products from 948 million pounds in 1970 to 3.158 billion pounds in 1976, or 233 percent. Anthony T. Di Benedetto, professor of chemical engineering at Washington University in St. Louis, has estimated that in the 4-year span 1968–72 this class would record a three- to four-

[7] Thermoplastics are plastics that may be reversibly formed and reformed by heat and pressure any number of times; examples are polyethylene, vinyl chloride, and polystyrene.

fold increase in tonnage.[8] As an example he cited the case of reinforced nylon: "Nylon reinforced with up to about 40 percent . . . glass fibers, possesses heat distortion temperatures up to 490°F compared with 150°F unreinforced, and stiffness up to four times greater than the unreinforced materials." While part of their usage will be as replacement for other plastics, "a significant fraction of the growth, however, should occur at the expense of die cast zinc, aluminum and steel." In Di Benedetto's opinion, "this group of composites may well become the most widely used of the reinforced plastics." [9]

An important technological breakthrough has been the perfection of methods making it possible to form certain plastics into large structures and products. Most of the industry's past progress was based on the manufacture of relatively small products. But through the development of a process variously called "thermoforming" (because heat is applied to a plastic sheet) or "vacuum forming" (because the plastic sheet is sucked into the contour of the mold), it is now possible to produce in one or a few forms such large products as refrigerators, boats, and even automobile bodies. In the words of Forbes Howard, "In fact it is difficult to find a product line normally made from sheet steel that cannot be made by this process using one or another of the modern thermoplastic materials." He went on to describe a 14-cubic-foot refrigerator that can be produced from ABS plastics in only 4 basic formings. Weighing only slightly more than half as much as a standard refrigerator, it "has appearance and functionalism equal to the steel case units now requiring millions of dollars for capital equipment and tooling." The potential of this process for use by smaller firms is illustrated dramatically by the case of automobile bodies:

> An example of this tool cost variation is found in a small 4-door sedan auto body that cost the manufacturer 12 million dollars in steel. We have quoted this same body tooling in water-cooled epoxy thermoforming molds at $210,000.
>
>   *   *   *
>
> A very small company in Detroit is now starting production of a 400 pound, 6-wheel amphibious vehicle that we designed and tooled for $20,000. The two-piece body can be made at the rate of 12 per hour on a $40,000 forming machine. This body is more involved than golf carts where as much as $200,000 has been spent to tool for the same productive rate using steel stampings.

According to Howard, thermoforming will "relieve the smaller companies from heavy initial investment to get their product off the ground in the marketplace. Competition in vehicles and refrigerators, for example, is far from dead because plastics has really come of age." Machinery builders are moving toward larger, high-output equipment that combines several operations into an integrated process. This requires a greater capital outlay (though not comparable to outlays for steel fabrication equipment), but it has the effect of permitting smaller manufacturers, without large engineering staffs, to set up plants and mold plastics products successfully. At the same time, other new and simple processing methods are lowering even further the entrance requirements for custom and proprietary molders. For example, a combination of vacuum-forming and spray-up techniques being licensed by Federal-Huber Corporation has put more

---

[8] 91st Cong., 1st Sess., Senate Subcommittee on Antitrust and Monopoly, Senate Committee on the Judiciary, *Hearings on Governmental Intervention in the Market Mechanism: The Petroleum Industry*, 1969, Pt. 3, p. 1195.
[9] *Ibid.*

than 30 small companies into plastics fabricating. In one of its own plants, a simple $13,000 vacuum former to shape thermoplastic skins and a $2,000 gun to spray chopped glass fiber, glass spheres, and thermosetting resin to rigidify the skin permit production of 39 bathtubs an hour.

There are additional advantages to the use of certain plastics for large consumer products. Painting is unnecessary since the plastic material can be impregnated with nearly any desired color pigment, and "scratches and scrapes make little or no difference in appearance since the color goes all the way through the sheet." Since the specific gravity and thus the weight of steel is several times that of plastics, the manufacturer using plastics enjoys a substantial advantage in terms of freight costs, "So obviously, the light ABS [plastic] products will give a small manufacturer a foothold in a high dollar market and will have a tendency of keeping consumer prices extremely competitive. . . ." Then there is the advantage of ease of repair, which has contributed so greatly to the popularity of fiberglass boats. Minor repairs can usually be made simply with a repair kit containing materials to be applied to the damaged area.

The future of plastics is also brightened by an economic consideration—differential price behavior. Prices of plastic materials have tended to decline, whereas prices of metals have generally been moving upward. In 1957 ABS and polypropylene were in excess of 50 cents per pound, while polyethylene was just below 40 cents. By 1967 ABS had fallen to 30 cents per pound, polypropylene to less than 20 cents, and polyethylene to only 15 cents. In contrast, the prices for both steel and brass have moved steadily upward, and that of aluminum has remained virtually unchanged. As a consequence, brass and aluminum, which 10 years earlier had enjoyed a substantial cost advantage, had by 1966 become more expensive than the plastic materials, while the advantage of steel had been considerably narrowed. It is probable that these differential price trends will persist, since the cost of extracting metals from depleting reserves will continue to rise, while the supply of petroleum, the raw material of plastics production, is so abundant that, were it not for artificial restraints, its cost would decline. Wages, which will undoubtedly continue their long-term advance, are a much more important element in the cost structure of metals than of plastics. Finally, plastic materials are frequently substitutable for one another, which has resulted in a considerable degree of interproduct price competition.

Fiberglass

Like many plastics, fiberglass—plastic reinforced with glass fibers—was introduced during World War II, which provided the first real impetus for its use— as radomes for aircraft, electronic components, body armor, and protective clothing. Since the war its growth rate has roughly paralleled that of plastics generally, output doubling about every 5 years (see Figure 6-2 and Table 6-1). As can be seen, this expansion, again like that of plastics, has been helped along by price reductions that have taken place in the face of rising prices for competitive materials.

Because glass, an inorganic material, is created at temperatures that no organic material can withstand, it is remarkably stable. As John M. Briley, vice president of Owens-Corning Fiberglas Corporation, put it, "in the very act of its composition and formation, glass has made peace with its environment. Heat, cold, moisture, dryness—all environmental conditions—have little or no effect

Figure 6-2

FIBERGLASS[a]

PRODUCTION, 1940-1966   PRICE COMPARISON, 1954-1966

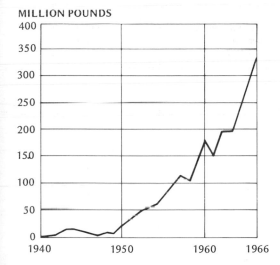

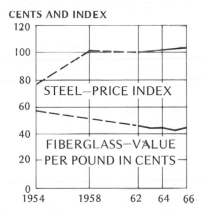

[a]Excluding insulation type.

Source: See Table 6-1

on glass." [10] And the advantages of combining plastics and fiberglass (also referred to as fiberglass-reinforced plastic, or FRP) were summarized by Robert Morrison, president of Molded Fiber Glass Companies, Ashtabula, Ohio, as: "higher strength-to-weight ratio; greater resistance to damage without permanent deformation; one-fifth the specific gravity of steel; freedom from rust and corrosion; excellent heat and electrical insulation properties; ability to be molded in large, complex shapes impossible to draw in one piece of metal; production tooling costs about one-eighth of tooling costs of similar metal parts; and translucency, opacity, or colored as desired when molded." [11]

Although it is generally because of a combination of its attributes that fiberglass has come to be widely used, there is usually present a particular utility which is of paramount importance for a given product. For example, while lower maintenance and repair costs have been contributing factors, the revolution in boat building would never have occurred had it not been for the great economies in production that fiberglass made possible. Building boats by applying resin-saturated fiberglass mat, cloth, or chopped fiber to an open mold is a far cheaper operation than putting a boat together in the traditional manner of nailing and joining wooden or plywood planks to a frame. The lower capital costs of this new technology and the ability to use unskilled or semiskilled labor resulted in the entrance of numerous small firms and thus in vigorous competition, drastic reductions in prices, a great increase in demand, and a growth in employment, not only in boat production itself, but in numerous ancillary activities—outboard engines, marinas, and the like. The contribution by large firms to this remarkable growth pattern has been negligible. According to Morrison, "With a small investment, a small plant, and a few key people, a regional FRP maker can make just as good boats at a somewhat lower cost than a large maker trying to cover a national market."

[10] *Hearings on Economic Concentration*, Pt. 6, pp. 2827–40, testimony of John M. Briley.
[11] *Ibid.*, pp. 2840–63, testimony of Robert Morrison.

Table 6-1

FIBERGLASS[a]

Production and price comparisons, 1940–66

Year	Production (Million Pounds)	Value of Shipments per Pound (Cents)	Finished Steel Products (1957–59 = 100)
1940	1.4		
1941	3.1		
1942	8.0		
1943	14.7		
1944	16.0		
1945	14.5		
1946	9.9		
1947	4.1		
1948	8.6		
1949	8.2		
1950	23.5		
1951	34.5		
1952	45.0		
1953	50.3		
1954	59.2	57.9	78.2
1955	75.8		
1956	96.5		
1957	110.5		
1958	103.8	52.6	100.6
1959	147.4		
1960	177.0		
1961	149.3		
1962	190.3	47.6	101.4
1963	191.9	47.4	102.0
1964	239.5	46.8	102.8
1965	282.3	44.6	103.3
1966	332.4	46.3	104.7

[a]Excluding insulation type.

Source: Production: Textile Economics Bureau, Inc.; value: Bureau of the Census, Department of Commerce, *1963 Census of Manufactures*, 1966; Bureau of the Census, Department of Commerce, Annual Surveys, 1962, 1964–66; steel price index: Bureau of Labor Statistics, Department of Labor, Wholesale Price Index

For another group of uses the overriding advantage of fiberglass is that it lends itself to prefabrication. One-piece tub-shower units have become commonplace, while unitized bathrooms and kitchens molded on a production-line basis are now making their appearance. Throughout the world imaginative architects are incorporating fiberglass in their designs because of its potential for lower costs through prefabrication. A leading Mexican architect, for example, has designed a fiberglass cottage complete with bath, closets, built-in sofa beds and shelf space, which, when sold in units of a thousand, should cost only $640. It is just a question of time until the pressure of the expanding population, both here and abroad, will force the acceptance of prefabrication with new composite materials in the construction of homes, apartments, and other buildings.

Other users have been attracted to fiberglass primarily because of its light weight in relation to its strength. The use of fiberglass in truck cabs, hoods, and fender assemblies has resulted in weight savings of up to 300 pounds, which have made possible corresponding increases in payload. In the new and rapidly expanding containerization market, containers made of fiberglass, alone or combined with plywood, provide minimum weight with maximum strength. Here the saving in weight is particularly important since airlines, using the new jumbo jets, expect to handle an increasing amount of containerized freight. The birth of a whole new industry, the manufacture of snowmobiles, has been made possible by the light weight, strength, and resistance to cold of fiberglass.

Because fiberglass cloth does not burn at any temperature, it is used for protective suits worn by firefighters, racing-car drivers, and astronauts. But the important markets opened up by this property are in such uses as tire cord. As compared to nylon or rayon, the heat resistance of fiberglass results in cooler-riding and thus longer-wearing tires. At the other end of the temperature scale, the material's resistance to cold has led to its use in refrigerated store cases and household refrigerators.

Still another property of fiberglass is its ability to withstand corrosion, which has led to its widespread adoption for such uses as fertilizer hoppers, supplanting metal hoppers, which are rapidly corroded by the chemical action of fertilizer materials. Resistance to corrosion plus light weight in relation to strength resulted in one of the first commercial uses of fiberglass—in fishing rods, introduced in 1948 by the Shakespeare Company of Kalamazoo, Michigan. A combination of properties—insulation, resistance to rust, and conductivity—has led to its increasing use in electrical products such as switch gear and circuit breakers.

These applications represent only a few of the uses that have been found for this remarkable material, which less than two decades ago was all but unknown. Others include automotive parts, chemical and gasoline storage tanks, pipes, golf clubs, vaulting poles, bows and arrows, surfboards, seating of all types, playground equipment, and, of course, draperies, curtains, and insulation material.

Where a greater degree of mechanization is sought than is provided by hand layups, capital costs are higher in fabricating products from fiberglass than from plastics, though still far below the costs involved in using steel. As a general rule, the capital costs for plastics are about one to 2 percent, and for fiberglass about 8 to 10 percent, of the costs of fabrication from steel. Essentially, the higher capital costs for fiberglass arise from the fact that, being impervious to heat, it cannot be injected into a mold in liquid form. Unlike the giant stamping presses for steel, which achieve their effect by the application of tremendous force against expensive stainless-steel dies, the presses for fiberglass apply only moderate pressure and heat, which unites a plastic resin such as polyethylene with the glass fiber and forms the combined material into the shape of the dies. In the words of Briley, "Fiber glass reinforced plastics [FRP] are ideal for small and medium-sized businesses, because of the relatively low investment required to start up operations. As little as $50,000 can make a company an FRP fabricator." Briley cited the example of a manufacturer of refrigerating equipment: "From the refrigerator fabricator's standpoint, FRP is an ideal way to expand production facilities because of its lower tooling cost. For its new FRP store cases, for example, Nolin required a much lower investment in stamping dies and allied equipment than would have been required with metal."

Just as the disappearance of many individual automobile manufacturers 30 years ago was due in part to the shift from wood to all-steel bodies, Morrison felt that fiberglass would also exert a profound influence on concentration in the automobile industry—but in the opposite direction:

> Until the advent of the all-steel body in the middle 1930's, the small volume car manufacturer was able to stay in business in competition with much larger companies, but the tremendous tooling costs involved in producing steel-bodied cars made it impossible for them to produce cars with steel bodies, so they dropped out. Over the past 32 years several larger car makers have closed up, Graham, Auburn, Hudson, Willys, Kaiser, Packard, and Studebaker. Costs of tooling for frequent body and front end sheet metal restyling were a major factor in their decision to quit.

Morrison then went on to speak of his own efforts to persuade automobile manufacturers to use fiberglass for their bodies, referring to the fact that almost 200,000 Corvettes and Avantis are on the road with fiberglass bodies, while tens of thousands of trucks have cabs or hood and fender assemblies made of the new material. He placed the cost of dies, drilling and punching fixtures, and assembly jigs required to produce a car body from fiberglass at around $1 million as compared to $10 million for steel. In addition to the savings in capital costs, the use of the new material would, he held, bring other advantages: "lighter weight, better performance, greater safety, absolute freedom from rusting and corrosion which now puts most cars into the scrap heap before their chassis wear out, higher resale value and better operating economy."

That capital entrance requirements in fiberglass fabrication are low has facilitated the entrance of smaller firms; that the industry consists almost entirely of small producers appears to be due to the inability of large firms to master the technological and marketing intricacies of this new and rapidly growing field. According to Morrison, the failure of large companies to take over the industry has not been for want of trying:

> Over the years there have been many large, well-known companies which are quite successful in their main line of business who have gone into matched metal die molding of fiber glass-reinforced plastic. Most of them have dropped out, but I believe all of those large companies who are still involved in producing FRP parts in matched metal dies have not yet earned a profit over the years, after deducting all the losses they have incurred.

He went on to speak of these "weird rapidly-expanding conglomerates" that have attempted to buy their way into the industry "by underbidding or out-promoting existing producers like ourselves who have spent years developing demand for FRP products." Drawing a contrast between the resources available on the one hand to the single-line firm and on the other to the conglomerate, he stated:

> Our companies have to exist and make a profit on the production of fiber glass plastic products alone, while these large companies have very profitable, well-established businesses in entirely different fields, and can subsidize their losses in the fiber glass plastic field for several years. In custom molding, they underprice existing producers. In the boat field, they put on a tremendous sales force, a big advertising campaign, and extend credit and other special considerations to dealers which the existing manufacturers cannot match. Fortunately, most of these companies have dropped out of the boat business after huge losses. . . .

Subsequently, Morrison submitted to the Subcommittee a list of large firms that had entered and then withdrawn from the fiberglass industry. In molding they include Goodyear Aircraft, Minnesota Mining and Manufacturing, General American Transportation Company, American Hard Rubber Company, Dow Chemical Company, General Electric Company, and the Fisher Body Division of General Motors Corporation; in boats Brunswick, Textron, Hupp, Bigelow-Sanford, and Goodyear.

One explanation for these failures is that the large conglomerate encounters serious difficulties in hiring engineers and technicians skilled in the new technology, who, because it is new, are in short supply. But of more importance is the fact that, in Morrison's words, a new field of technology "just has too many problems that must be solved promptly at a high point in the organization." A technological breakthrough today may make it possible to satisfy the needs of a customer whose requirements could not have been met yesterday. Someone who has intimate and detailed knowledge of production, engineering, the characteristics of the product, and its costs must be able to give a prospective customer a firm idea as to whether an entirely new use of the material is feasible and at approximately what price. The rapidity of change does not permit the luxury of time-consuming intracompany memoranda and reports, staff meetings, conferences, or the other nonessential behavioral activities of bigness. According to Morrison:

> the top manager-owner of the business must be practically on the molding line on a daily basis and should be his top technical expert, his top salesman, and a hard-working experienced businessman. He must be very familiar with molding problems and techniques, with equipment, with die and part design, with customers' and prospects' problems, and with the advantages, and particularly the disadvantages and shortcomings, of the material with which he works.

In the opinion of Briley of Owens-Corning, the leading materials supplier, the fabricating stage of the industry will continue to remain largely in the hands of the smaller firms: "The key to this progress will continue to be the small and medium size fabricator—who produces quality FRP products that will compete with metals, wood, non-reinforced plastic and other conventional materials."

High-performance composites

The most exciting of the new materials are the "high-performance" composites—filaments of extremely high stiffness and strength bonded together by a soft plastic matrix. The idea of achieving superior properties by combining different materials is not new; in the *Iliad* Homer describes shields made of wood, hide, and bronze. The oriental war bow is a composite of wood, sinew, silk, and horn. High-grade armor was made in the Middle Ages by combining soft iron and hard steel, which, it was found, was superior to either constituent by itself. In the words of Albert G. H. Dietz, "We are not talking about something new; we are talking about something very old, indeed. But it is only within the last few years that the great interest in composites has developed and composite materials are undergoing intensive study today." [12]

[12] *Transactions of a Symposium on High-Performance Composites Sponsored by Monsanto Co. and Washington University,* Nov. 10, 1965, p. 51.

Figure 6-3

STRENGTH AND STIFFNESS PROPERTIES OF
GLASS, BORON, AND CARBON COMPOSITES

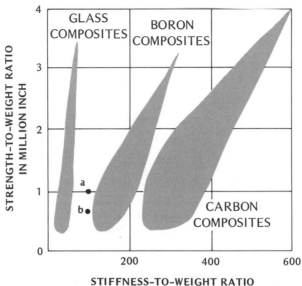

STIFFNESS–TO–WEIGHT RATIO
IN MILLION INCH

ᵃSteel.   ᵇAluminum.

Source: *Hearings on Economic Concentration*, Pt. 6, p. 2614

This research is directed toward achieving materials with the highest possible rigidity or hardness combined with the highest possible strength and toughness, the lightest possible weight, and a minimum variation with changes in temperature.[13] In general, the most important structural properties of a material are stiffness and strength: stiffness governs the deformation or deflection of the structural member; strength governs the ultimate load that the member can carry. And it is in these qualities that the new composites are far superior to natural materials such as steel and aluminum. In testimony before the Senate Antitrust Subcommittee, Stephen Tsai, professor of engineering at Washington University and formerly director of its Materials Research Laboratory,[14] presented a chart comparing the structural properties of carbon and boron composites with steel and aluminum, shown here as Figure 6-3. Increasing performance would be represented by a line from the lower left-hand to the upper right-hand corner of the chart.

It will be observed that the representations for steel and aluminum are limited, specific observations, each shown by a dot. This is because their properties, reflected in their stiffness and strength-to-weight ratios, are invariant, fixed by nature itself. In contrast, the carbon and boron composites are represented by shaded areas covering a considerable range of properties, since, being synthetics, they display variable stiffness and strength-to-weight ratios depending

[13] *Ibid.*, Paper by Rolf Buchdahl, Director of Basic Research, Chemstrand Research Center, Inc., p. 95.
[14] *Hearings on Economic Concentration*, Pt. 6, pp. 2611–27, testimony of Stephen Tsai.

on the specific type of fiber used, the plastic material with which it is combined, the general construction of the composite, and so on. As can be seen, the upper limits of the carbon composites far exceed the traditional materials in terms of both strength and stiffness. The advantage of the boron composites is less marked, although in terms of strength-to-weight ratios the upper limit of its range approaches that of carbon. Carbon composites have strength-to-weight ratios ranging up to four times those of steel and aluminum. In terms of stiffness, both the upper and lower limits are well in excess of those of both steel and aluminum, the advantage ranging from two to five times over the traditional materials. To put it another way, carbon composites can provide the same strength as steel with as little as one-fourth the weight, the same stiffness with as little as one-fifth the weight.

Their potential for the future was summarized by Tsai in the following words:

> Boron composites are under intensive development and are being experimented [sic] in many military systems. Carbon composites will be an even better composite system in the very near future. Other filaments and fibers are being developed. The cost of materials is being reduced. All of these factors contribute to the keen interest in composite materials during recent years. In military systems, composite materials have already made important contributions. It is anticipated that nonmilitary applications will increase in the future.

Some idea of their potential can be gained from a few examples. The use of high-performance composites in place of aluminum would reduce the structural weight of an aircraft from 30 percent of the gross weight to 20 percent, permitting an increase in payload, a lengthening of flight range, or a reduction in fuel consumption. Their use in high-speed trains would reduce gross weight by 50 percent as compared to conventional steel construction, making possible not only an increase in speed but lighter suspension systems, smaller engines, less fuel consumption, and greater safety resulting from better braking. Automobiles, in Tsai's view, also appear to be a promising field: "For the same performance, we can use smaller engines and less fuel, both of which will reduce air pollution. . . . Safety can increase because cars made of composite materials can be made more maneuverable and more energy-absorbing." An example of this latter use is the Ford GT-40 racing car, which won the 1968 Le Mans 24-hour road race: "The weight of the Ford body, made in England by Glass Fiber Engineering Ltd., was reduced from 140 pounds for the glass-fibre-cloth-reinforced polyester to 70–80 pounds. The same body in steel weighs about 500 pounds." [15]

The new composite that appears to hold the greatest promise is carbon fiber, and the country in which most of the progress has been made is Great Britain. Described as threads of "pure carbon having enormous strength and looking like fine strands of shiny dark grey hair," it is regarded by *The Economist* as "a material that could form the basis for a whole new engineering industry and where Britain has, for once, a head and shoulders lead over the rest of the field." [16] It starts as a man-made fiber, polyacrylonitrile, whose basic molecular structure is then rearranged by heat treatments in very-high-temperature furnaces and set in epoxy resins, which results in a material "four times stronger than steel." [17] Although still in the development stages, the new material is

[15] *Aviation Week & Space Technology,* Nov. 18, 1968.
[16] *Economist,* Dec. 7, 1968.
[17] *Ibid.*

beginning to find commercial uses. Among the first are in jet engines, spacecraft structures, launch vehicles, guided missiles, vertical-takeoff aircraft, helicopter tail booms, pressure bottles, high-speed radar reflectors, aircraft structural members, and similar uses requiring high ratios of strength and stiffness to weight.[18]

That potential uses thus far are limited largely to the aircraft and space field is traceable mostly to the material's stratospheric price—$400 to $500 a pound. Only buyers to whom costs are a matter of relative indifference, such as defense agencies and subsidized airlines, can even think of using the material. In the words of an engineer of the Royal Aircraft Establishment, "the crunch comes after we have sold them on the uses, and they ask the price." An analyst for a large aircraft company stated, "We would like to see it a good deal cheaper—one thinks it would be very cheap indeed since the basic material . . . is cheap." And, from a senior researcher of a helicopter manufacturer: "The cost of carbon fibers is purely, as I see it, a fictitious cost, though one is prepared to pay it for experimental exercises." [19]

Stemming from original research at the Hartwell facility of the Royal Aircraft Establishment, the patents are owned by the British government, which has licensed them to only 2 British firms, Morgan Crucible and Courtalds. Only one American firm, the Whittaker Corporation of Los Angeles, has received a sublicense. An observer "close to the development" has been quoted as saying: "There has been a steady stream of the top U.S. companies, all of whom are extremely anxious to do a deal, but the patent belongs to the National Research Development Corp. [the patent agency for goverment laboratories]. What conditions the NRDC wants, I can't say, but I get the feeling that the Americans are unhappy with them." [20]

Here again is the endless cycle of a high price restricting consumption, which limits output and thus makes for a high price. But in this case, because of the capital-saving nature of the new technology, only a relatively small volume of output would be needed to recapture the capital costs required to build a continuous carbon fiber production plant. In the words of an official of one of the British licensees: "It [mass production] would involve a substantial plant but *not* any vast amount of heavy equipment." [21] Once the costs of producing the fibers are brought down to commercially feasible levels, the same presses, dies, and other equipment that have already been developed by fiberglass fabricators can be used in fabricating plastics reinforced with the high-performance composites. In Tsai's words, "As different types of filaments and plastics become available, the processing equipment does not change. Carbon fibers can be processed essentially the same way as glass fibers." In the making of the carbon fiber body of the car that won the 1968 Le Mans race, "the manufacturing process is said to have been quite similar to that used by molding bodies entirely of glass cloth reinforced plastic." [22] Receiving his materials in the form of rovings, chopped strands, and containers of plastics, the fabricator of high-performance composites will put the constituents together in the process of making the finished product. According to Tsai, "The entrance barrier of

[18] For a survey of the state of the art in late 1968 see *Aviation Week & Space Technology,* Nov. 18, 1968.
[19] *Aviation Week & Space Technology,* Nov. 25, 1968.
[20] *Ibid.*
[21] *Ibid.* Emphasis added.
[22] *Ibid.*

this type of enterprise should be considerably lower than that of a steel mill or refinery. Small parts made of composite materials can be handled by garage-type operations. Mixers, extruders, presses, and ovens will be needed. This type of equipment is relatively inexpensive."

Although adoption of the new composite materials can be accelerated by public policy, their ultimate replacement of the older materials seems inescapable. Referring to the new era as "the age of chemical synthesis," Robert E. Van Geuns of the Industrial Development Division of the Georgia Institute of Technology described the replacement of natural products by synthetics as "a general phenomenon, which is repeated over and over":

> The picture is always the same. A few synthetic products begin to invade the market of a natural product. At first the manufacturers of the natural product do not pay any attention to the insignificant newcomer, claiming that those synthetic products are very inferior to the natural ones. Then gradually the synthetics begin to make headway and increase in volume. Now, the natural product manufacturers begin to worry. They intensify their efforts to convince the public that the natural product is superior. But, the synthetics keep on increasing their market share. Finally, the natural product producers start to improve the quality of their product, which, of course, is a tacit admission that their product actually is not superior to the synthetics. Those efforts might stem the tide for a while but after a shorter or longer period the inevitable happens, the synthetics take over completely.[23]

Prestressed concrete

Like plastics and fiberglass, prestressed concrete has enjoyed a spectacular expansion since World War II and, like them, it is manufactured largely by small producers. Although concrete has little strength in tension, it has great strength in compression. Prestressing is a method of putting this strength to work. The manner in which this is done can be illustrated by the act of lifting books from a shelf: the exertion of pressure between the hands, forcing the books together, gives them the unity necessary for lifting. In prestressing, concrete is similarly compressed or forced together by the application of artificial stresses. In the most commonly used method of production, a mold conforming to the desired shape of the structural member is laid out; within the mold are placed one or more high-tension steel cables, which are then stretched by a hydraulic jack beyond their normal length; concrete is poured into the mold and allowed to harden, forming a bond around the cable; when the cable is released, it is prevented by the binding action of the hardened concrete from contracting to its original length. In this way the great compression strength of concrete is brought into play, as it is, in effect, being constantly pushed together by the artificial stresses imparted by the cables.

As might be expected from the simplicity of the technique, capital costs are quite low. According to R. J. Lyman, executive secretary of the Prestressed Concrete Institute, "It is possible to construct a minimum plant in our industry for approximately $250,000 today, but an average figure of $500,000 is considerably more realistic and a number of new plant facilities costing well over $1,000,000 have been constructed in the past two years. An average sized plant in our industry will employ 50 to 75 workers." [24] He went on to com-

[23] Senate Subcommittee on Antitrust and Monopoly, 1969, *op. cit.*, p. 1377.
[24] *Hearings on Economic Concentration*, Pt. 6, pp. 2677–87, testimony of R. J. Lyman.

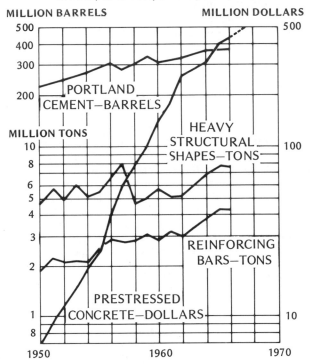

Figure 6-4

PRESTRESSED CONCRETE

Growth, with comparisons, 1950–1967

Source: See Table 6-2

pare these costs with the capital costs of the competitive products—concrete reinforcing bars and structural steel shapes. "In contrast with these limited capital costs, it has been estimated that the cost of establishing a small steel mill equipped with an electric furnace to produce merchant bar and angle is in the range of 8 to 10 million dollars, while a basic steel mill able to produce large and heavy structural shapes perhaps would require upward of $50 million." The structural-steel industry is one of the most highly concentrated in the American economy. Only 2 mills produce most of the heavy structural shapes in the country; one is owned by the Bethlehem Steel Company at Bethlehem, Pennsylvania, and the other by U.S. Steel at Gary, Indiana.

The growth rate for the prestressed-concrete industry is compared in Figure 6-4 and Table 6-2 with the rates for reinforcing bars and heavy structural shapes. As can be seen, during each of the 4-year intervals 1950–54, 1955–59, and 1960–64, the output of prestressed concrete more than tripled.[25] By 1967 it had attained a volume of a half-billion dollars—most of which was at the expense of the steel industry. In contrast, the output of heavy structural shapes remained relatively stable, the production in 1965–66 being actually below the level achieved 10 years earlier. Similarly, the use of concrete reinforcing

[25] The only available figures indicating output of prestressed concrete are in terms of value of shipments; however, as prices for these products were declining during this period, these figures tend to understate the industry's growth rate.

Table 6-2

PRESTRESSED CONCRETE

Growth, with comparisons, 1950–67

| Year | Prestressed Concrete Sales Volume (Mils.)[a] | Portland Cement Shipments (Million Barrels) | Steel (Million Tons)[b] | |
			Heavy Shapes	Concrete Reinforcing Bars
1950	$ 7	228	4.8	1.9
1951	10	241	5.9	2.2
1952	13	251	5.0	2.1
1953	17	261	6.1	2.2
1954	21	274	5.2	2.1
1955	25	296	5.5	2.6
1956	43	312	6.7	3.0
1957	61	292	8.1	2.8
1958	77	310	4.7	2.9
1959	96	338	5.0	3.1
1960	140	314	5.8	2.9
1961	177	323	5.1	3.2
1962	265	334	5.2	3.0
1963	290	352	6.0	3.4
1964	310	368	7.0	3.8
1965	400	374	7.8	4.3
1966	444	381	7.8	4.4
1967	495			

[a] Includes some precast concrete in prestressed-concrete plants.
[b] Domestic production plus imports.

Source: Prestressed concrete: Prestressed Concrete Institute; portland cement: Bureau of Mines, Department of the Interior, *Minerals Yearbook*, 1967; structural steel: American Iron and Steel Institute, *Statistical Reports*; Department of Commerce, *Business Statistics, 1967*

bars remained relatively constant at around 3.0–3.4 million tons a year from the mid-1950's to the mid-1960's; only in 1965 did it surpass 4 million tons a year.[26]

The idea of prestressing dates back to 1886, when a California engineer, P. H. Jackson, obtained patents on a system of tightening steel rods through artificial stone to form floor slabs. Work continued both here and abroad, but these early efforts proved to be largely unsuccessful. It is now known that the types of steel then utilized were subject to creep and shrinkage, causing the material to become "unstressed." It was not until the period between the two World Wars that this problem was overcome by the use of high-strength steel and higher-strength concrete.

The industry received its greatest impetus in the rebuilding of devasted European cities following World War II. The necessity for building new apartments, industrial and commercial structures, and homes, coupled with the inability to obtain structural steel, directed attention to prestressed products. Although

[26] The figures for concrete reinforcing bars as well as heavy structural shapes include imports as well as domestic production; imports constitute an important proportion of consumption, however, only for the former.

acceptance in this country was somewhat slower, the industry received a sharp impetus from the shortage of structural steel here during the Korean conflict. Also an important factor was the influence of one individual, William Dean, former chief highway engineer of the state of Florida, who pioneered the use of prestressed concrete in highway construction for bridges and overpasses. When building was stimulated by the federal highway program, other states came to accept what had been proven to be successful in Florida. Some idea of the rapidity of this acceptance can be gained from the fact that in less than a decade prestressed concrete structures came to account for approximately one-fifth of the $1.1 billion authorized for new bridge construction with participation of federal funds.

Availability has come to be one of the principal advantages of prestressed products. With more than 200 producers located in or near most major metropolitan centers, the shortages of supply and extended delivery dates that from time to time have plagued structural shapes are not a serious problem. Another advantage is that the decentralized nature of the industry gives it an important advantage in freight costs. Prestressed products are readily available in nearly any area of the United States, eliminating the need for long-distance shipping. In terms of production costs alone, prestressed concrete is competitive for most uses with other materials. Although the high-strength cable used for prestressing costs about three times as much as ordinary mild steel used in reinforcing bars, it is up to six times as strong. Likewise, although the high-strength concrete used for prestressing costs one-fifth more than regular concrete, it has twice the strength. "Thus," according to Lyman, "the cost of a structural member in dollars per ton of load resistance is lower in prestressed concrete, other factors being equal."

Quite apart from considerations of availability and cost, certain characteristics of the product itself have contributed to its rapid acceptance. Because of its resistance to fire, it earns high fire ratings with insurance companies. Corrosion is not a serious problem since prestressed structures are comparatively crack-free. Framing members can be left exposed, and surfaces of slabs and wall panels require no further treatment. The use of high-strength concrete in building contributes to long life and low maintenance costs. Finally, the use of prestressed structural members gives architects a flexibility in design that they have never enjoyed before by making possible long spans with minimum depth and large interior areas free from supporting columns. Moreover, the mold in which the concrete is poured can be laid out in the form of curves and other shapes that cannot be duplicated by steel.

The future expansion of the industry will come not only from architects' increasing familiarity with the properties of the material but also from the development of new techniques. Among the innovations with the greatest potential is the use of chemical action to impart the necessary stresses. According to Lyman:

> Recent laboratory and field experiments have been conducted on chemical prestressing of concrete elements. In this technique the high-strength steel is placed under tension by action of an expansive cement used in the concrete. Although the art and techniques involved are yet to be fully developed, the use of expansive concrete holds great promise in the prestressing field for economical production of pressure pipe, precast thin shell elements, wall panels and pavements.

From this review of recent developments in the field of materials it can be seen that the problem of the manufacturer increasingly will be to select from a wide array of materials and their combinations the particular one that is best suited for a given use. For each of the materials, he must possess or have access to expert knowledge on costs, applicable methods of fabrication, properties, applications, characteristics, strengths, weaknesses, and so on. And, in contrast to what is needed for natural materials, whose properties are more or less fixed, this knowledge must include an awareness of how the properties of synthetic materials can be altered by changing their chemical composition. It is partly because of this premium on specialized knowledge that most of the fabrication of plastics products is done by custom molders who are experts in that one particular field; it is for the same reason that the large conglomerate corporations have done so poorly in fiberglass. As Tsai put it:

> Composite materials are highly sophisticated materials and require sophisticated understanding for their proper design and utilization. The traditional method for materials selection of ordinary metals is no longer adequate. Substitution of aluminum for steel or titanium for aluminum no longer applies in the case of composite materials. A given composite system, e.g., boron-plastic composites, covers a range of properties depending on the particular design of fiber orientation, fiber volume fractions, methods of laminations, and processing. Thus the utilization of a composite material requires a higher level of technology than that of ordinary materials.

Given the materials and the knowledge of how to use them, relatively little is required in the way of either labor or capital. These new materials are neither labor intensive nor capital intensive; they are knowledge intensive. In Tsai's words, "The emerging technology in composite materials will require ingenuity which comes primarily from brain power rather than horse power."

Energy

For centuries the production process has been powered by fossil fuels—repositories of the energy of the sun. Originally employed to yield light and heat, coal and oil became sources of power through a long history of mechanical inventions beginning in the early days of the Industrial Revolution. These inventions were founded on the principle of the "Carnot," or heat cycle, in which chemical energy residing in the fossil fuels is converted into heat, which is then converted into mechanical energy by engines and motors. In stationary electric generating plants an additional step is required, since the mechanical energy must be converted by turbines and generators into electrical energy. The conversion of chemical energy into heat and then into mechanical energy is by its very nature complex, wasteful, and costly.

Because it brings improved efficiency, less waste, simpler operations, and less maintenance and repair, the achievement of greater simplicity is an inherent objective of scientific and engineering progress. Just as the essential character of the new materials is simplicity in use, so also is simplicity the common characteristic of new power-creating technologies. In the case of some of the new power sources, such as batteries and fuel cells, simplicity is achieved by converting chemical energy directly into electrical energy, by-passing the heat stage. In others, principally those suitable for electric power plants, the objective is the elimination of the mechanical stage. In still others, notably gas turbines and rotary-piston engines, greater simplicity is achieved by substituting continuous rotary motion for up-and-down reciprocating action. From the point of view of industrial structure, the significance of the new technologies lies in the fact that their greater simplicity means savings in capital costs and thus a greater potential for decentralization of output.

Invented in the latter part of the nineteenth century by the German engineer Nikolaus August Otto, the gasoline-powered reciprocating engine has remained, in principle, basically unchanged: stored energy in the form of fossil fuel (gasoline) is mixed with air in a carburetor and forced into the cylinders, where it is ignited; the combustion forces pistons downward, which causes a connecting rod to turn a crankshaft. To make this mechanism work a whole series of remarkable mechanical feats must be accomplished with split-second timing. The gasoline and air must be combined in precisely the right mixture and fed into the cylinders; valves must open to receive the mixture, close during ignition, and open again to discharge the unburned gases; the fuel must be ignited properly in the cylinders; the pistons must move upward to compress the fuel and downward to impart power; the moving parts must be lubricated by oil, which must not reach the combustion chamber. And each of these and other separate episodic events must be repeated hundreds of times a minute. It is little wonder that an engineer, Yura Arkus-Duntov, testifying before the Senate Subcommittee on Antitrust and Monopoly, said of the internal combustion engine, "It appears almost miraculous that it works so well in spite of its complexity. This certainly is a tribute to engineering ingenuity if not to engineering intelligence." [27] It is this same complexity that led an economist, Lloyd Orr, to remark, "Despite immense refinement the reciprocating, internal combustion engine is still an inefficient machine with design characteristics and supporting components which create maintenance problems while it progressively deteriorates." [28]

Interest in propelling a vehicle by the direct conversion of chemical energy developed soon after La Plante's invention of the storage battery in 1860. On the basis of work by independent inventors dating back to 1888, electric vehicles were introduced commercially shortly after the turn of the century. Between 1900 and 1915 some 100 manufacturers put electric cars on the market. By 1912 production of electric vehicles had reached a level of 6,000 passenger cars and 4,000 commercial vehicles a year. Powered by a lead-acid battery, these vehicles had a range of about 20 miles and a speed of 25 miles per hour. Recharging could be done overnight, and maintenance problems were minimal. Numerous innovations later incorporated into the gasoline-powered car had their origins in electric cars, including completely enclosed bodies, steering wheels, and a drive shaft instead of a chain drive.[29] In the early 1920's, how-

[27] *Hearings on Economic Concentration*, Pt. 6, pp. 2775–85, testimony of Yura Arkus-Duntov.

[28] *Ibid.*, pp. 2786–2800, testimony of Lloyd Orr.

[29] "A gearing system was introduced which allowed both halves of the axle to travel in the same direction but at different speeds. The entire weight of the 2-horsepower motor and axle was under 100 pounds, which was less than the weight of the usual rear axle with its differential gearing. The motor was designed to act as a generator to help recharge the battery when certain speeds were exceeded going down hill.

"Also during that period ideas were introduced for electric 'plug-in' charging stations, and stations for the exchange of a set of discharged batteries for a recharged set. One

ever, the battery-powered electric automobile engine gave way to the gasoline engine, which did not have to be recharged and was superior in speed and performance.

Today, the electric vehicle has again become a subject of interest for both economic and ecological reasons. The economic argument is based on the vehicle's impressive efficiency for short trips, which in the aggregate make up a large proportion of the total miles traveled. According to information placed in the record by Orr, trips of fewer than 10 miles accounted in 1967 for more than three-fourths of the number of trips and made up nearly 30 percent of the miles traveled; trips of fewer than 20 miles accounted for more than 90 percent of the number of trips and nearly half (48 percent) of the miles. Electric cars with a range of 40 miles, which could make 4 trips a day of fewer than 10 miles or 2 trips of fewer than 20 miles, could thus take over about half the total passenger car usage.[30]

Obviously the ability of battery-powered vehicles to serve this very large, short-trip market would be increased to the extent that the weight of the vehicle was reduced. Savings in weight are inherent in the simplicity of the mechanism itself; through the use of an electric power plant over half of the weight of the present internal-combustion engine could be made available for batteries. Additional savings could also be achieved by using a plastic or fiberglass body; Alastair Carter, president of Carter Engineering Company Ltd., has plans to introduce an electric-powered vehicle weighing less than 900 pounds.[31] This is to be accomplished partly by the use of a plastic body and partly by lightweight electric motors mounted directly on the wheels.

The question, though, remains: Why should anyone who is free to choose between the gasoline-powered car and a battery-powered car willingly choose the latter, since he would be selecting a car suitable only for short trips in preference to one that can be used for both short and long trips? One reason is economy; operating costs of one cent or less a mile are claimed for the electric car as compared to 3 to 4 cents for the gasoline-powered automobile. Other selling points are simplicity of operation and an absence of maintenance problems, which are particularly important where the principal use would be as a second car for the housewife to take the children to and from school, make visits to the supermarket, and perform similar functions.

But the most compelling reason may well turn out to be a compulsory governmental requirement necessitated by the growing menace of air pollution, over half of which stems directly from the fumes emitted by the gasoline-powered reciprocating engine. If it proves impossible to bring the emissions of the reciprocating engine down to acceptable levels, as is not at all unlikely, action will have to be taken to force the use of alternatives. The ultimate form such action could take cannot be anticipated. Legislation prohibiting the sale of new automobiles whose emissions exceed certain minimum standards suffers from two shortcomings: it would not apply to the millions of cars already on the roads, and, unless dramatic improvements are made, the effectiveness of present equipment designed to cut down on emissions declines rapidly with in-

---

car, the 1916 Wood Dual Power, included both an internal combustion engine and a battery-powered electric motor." (Federal Power Commission, *Development of Electrical Vehicles,* Feb., 1967, pp. 2–3.)

[30] Derived from data contained in Automobile Manufacturers Association, *Automobile Facts & Figures,* 1967, pp. 65, 67.

[31] *Hearings on Economic Concentration,* Pt. 6, pp. 2583–98, testimony of Alastair Carter.

creasing usage. Among the alternatives are the granting of government subsidies to manufacturers of low-pollutant vehicles, the imposition of a stiff tax on a family's second (or third) car unless it is powered by batteries or some other low-pollution device, making the federal tax on the type of fuel used by the reciprocating engine almost prohibitive, and so on. As the air pollution problem worsens, steps that today might seem unthinkable will probably prove to be inescapable.

Batteries

The most immediate way of making an electric car once again a commercial reality is through the use of batteries. The process by which batteries yield electrical energy is the liberation at a negative electrode by one type of chemical (the fuel) of electrons which, after traversing an external circuit, are consumed at the positive plate by another type of chemical (the oxidant), the circuit being completed by the transfer of ions across the electrolyte space. Instead of gasoline, the chemicals used are such materials as lead or zinc for the fuel and lead dioxide, magnesium dioxide, or air (oxygen) for the oxidant.

The oldest form of storage battery is the lead-acid battery: "It works well, it is durable and it is cheap." [32] Inasmuch as passenger cars powered by this battery had a range of 20 miles 40 years ago, it should not be surprising that today ranges of over 60 miles have been reported. Referring to criticism of the battery on the grounds that it has an energy density of only 8 to 12 watt hours per pound, Raymond Jasinski, author of *High Voltage Batteries,* noted in testimony before the Senate Antitrust Subcommittee that this represents its use in turning over and starting an internal combustion engine, not its full potential capability.[33] A British manufacturer, Alastair Carter, testified that in an improved form a lead-acid battery had already yielded 19.1 watt hours per pound and that further advances seemed likely.

A lead-cobalt battery developed by Robert Aronson, founder and president of Electric Fuel Propulsion, achieves 18 watt hours per pound, which has given his vehicle a range of over 60 miles and a speed of over 60 miles per hour.[34] The battery is of tri-polar construction—i.e., the grids are connected with each other in three places instead of one—and cobalt had been plated onto the positive plate, which is ordinarily subject to oxidation and corrosion.

Not yet available but on the horizon is the zinc-air battery. With a specific energy of 60 to 80 watt hours per pound, it would multiply by several times the range of the lead battery. The English manufacturer Carter expressed the view that in a few years "there will be available commercially a zinc-air battery which will give my vehicle a range of nearly 200 miles." Many of the traditional problems of the zinc electrode have been solved.[35] In addition, work is going forward on a number of other types of batteries, each of which has its own

---

[32] *Ibid.,* Pt. 6, pp. 2598–2609, testimony of Raymond Jasinski.
[33] An agency of the federal government was party to this erroneous criticism of the lead-acid battery: see Federal Power Commission, *Development of Electrical Vehicles,* Feb., 1967, p. 8.
[34] *Hearings on Economic Concentration,* Pt. 6, pp. 2877–89, testimony of Robert Aronson.
[35] The only remaining problem Jasinski foresaw was that of developing an inexpensive catalyst for the air electrode: "Air is very particular on what catalysts it reacts." And obtaining materials that will also resist physical and chemical deterioration on recharge has proved to be a formidable problem.

promise and problems. Among these are the nickel-cadmium battery, which dates back to the turn of the century and has long been used in Europe,[36] as well as silver-cadmium and silver-zinc batteries, which have high energy densities but whose use would be held back by the scarcity and high price of silver.[37]

Fuel cells

Like the battery, the fuel cell converts chemical energy directly into electrical energy, but it does so without recharging. Operating on a fuel which, like gasoline, can be externally stored and replenished, the device will function as long as the fuel supply lasts. The constituents of interest in a fuel cell, in its present stage of development, are hydrogen (the fuel) and oxygen (the oxidant). It is relatively simple in construction, the main physical components being the negative electrode (cathode), the positive electrode (anode), the electrolyte, inlets for the reactants, and outlets for the products. After moving from a tank to a negative electrode, hydrogen molecules split into individual hydrogen atoms absorbed on the electrolyte's surface; the atoms release free electrons to the electrode, forming hydrogen ions, which pass into the electrolyte. The voltage difference between negative and positive electrodes results in a flow of electrons—and electric current.

From a theoretical point of view the advantages of a fuel cell are overwhelming. Testifying before the Subcommittee, Donald J. Looft, Chief of the Electrotechnology Laboratory of the U.S. Army Mobility Equipment Command, stated that

> the fuel cell is the only device that directly converts chemical energy in a fuel to electrical energy, consequently it is a highly efficient device not limited by the heat cycle barrier. Further, there is no combustion process, there is no combustion exhaust, only reaction products which are in almost all systems an inert gas and water. Still further, the conversion process in fuel cells is a chemical reaction not accompanied by controlled explosions such as those in a combustion chamber so that except for pumps and blowers to bring the fuel and oxidant to the reaction site, remove reaction products and provide cooling and conditioning as required, the process is silent and static. All these characteristics make fuel cells potentially an ideal power source.[38]

The development of the fuel cell, whose efficiency far surpasses that of any other energy-producing device, has passed well beyond the theoretical stage. In 1959 an Allis-Chalmers farm tractor was powered successfully by a fuel cell. In 1965 power was furnished for the Gemini V space capsule by a hydrogen-oxygen fuel cell. A year later the Army successfully powered an M-37 truck with a hydrazine fuel cell: "Fuel cell engineering has advanced to the point where systems large enough to power automobiles and trucks can be purchased on a special-order basis." [39] In Jasinski's words, "fuel cells have passed into

---

[36] According to Jasinski, "The battery is durable and capable of many thousands of cycles. The problems are ones of improving reproducibility, reliability and capacity while decreasing cell weight."

[37] Recently, attempts have been made to substitute nickel oxide for silver oxide in order to solve the economic problem, and some success has been achieved in obtaining improved charge-discharge cycles.

[38] *Hearings on Economic Concentration*, Pt. 6, pp. 2553–82, testimony of Donald J. Looft.

[39] Department of Commerce, Report to the Commerce Technical Advisory Board, *The Automobile and Air Pollution*, 1967, p. 66.

a second generation R & D stage; prototype hardware has been built, resulting in the solution of some engineering problems and the definition of others."

That the fuel cell is not in more widespread use is due simply to the lack of fuels that are both chemically suitable and inexpensive. Pure hydrogen must be stored at extremely low temperatures in pressurized containers, which cannot be done practically in a moving vehicle. It is therefore necessary to use some other fuel from which hydrogen can be extracted. But here a dilemma presents itself. Those fuels that are most reactive electrochemically—e.g., hydrazine—are regarded as too expensive for commercial use, whereas those whose costs are low enough to permit commercial use—e.g., gasoline—are not highly reactive electrochemically. The task of improving the reactive qualities of the latter group has been approached in two ways. The direct approach has been to make the inexpensive fuels reactive by raising the cell temperatures. But the use of high temperatures (e.g., 1300°C) may harm the cell itself and result in corrosion and other unwanted side reactions. The indirect approach has involved changing the fuel into a form more acceptable to the cell. But this adds a considerable measure of complexity, equipment, and cost to the process.

Among the fuels that *are* reactive electrochemically, hydrazine, a colorless liquid with an odor like ammonia, most closely meets the requirements of an operational fuel cell. The hydrazine fuel cell can start up from room temperature and yet operate below 100°C. With about the density of water, hydrazine can be handled like gasoline. Such cells are the lightest that can use air. For tactical purposes the Defense Department in its research and development program is giving "primary emphasis" to fuel cells and regards the hydrazine-air system as the "most advanced" of the special fuel approaches. Testifying before the Subcommittee, Looft stated, "Hydrazine fuel cells are clearly superior to any other available silent power source."

The use of hydrazine fuel cells is held back not so much by any technical shortcoming as by an economic barrier. According to Jasinski, "At present the only limitation to this application is the high cost of hydrazine." [40] Similarly the Defense Department cited "cost and availability" as the reason hydrazine fuel cells are "not compatible" with the Department's program. But the agency's spokesman went on to add, "This could change drastically with a breakthrough (costwise) in the production of hydrazine." [41]

What are the dimensions of this cost barrier? According to Jasinski, "Today hydrazine runs between $1.00 and $1.25 per pound. Various estimates indicate that a cost of 25 to 35 cents per pound would be necessary to develop a commercial system." That such a reduction is not beyond the area of the possible was suggested by a noted chemical engineer, Ju Chin Chu, who has developed and received a patent[42] on a new process of producing hydrazine involving the use of a fuel cell.[43] Although recognizing the difficulty of cal-

---

[40] In addition, hydrazine presents a potential toxicity hazard; it was suggested that this problem could be met using the fuel in the form of a gel instead of a liquid (see *Hearings on Economic Concentration,* Pt. 6, p. 2872, testimony of Ju Chin Chu). The only other problem appears to be the use in the air electrode of platinum—a rare and costly element; the quantity involved is small and a less expensive material may be developed.

[41] See U.S. Army Engineer Research and Development Laboratories, "Research on Unconventional Vehicular Propulsion," Feb. 18, 1967.

[42] U.S. Patent 3,280,015 (Oct. 18, 1966).

[43] In this new process, the traditional chemical reactor would be replaced by a fuel cell,

culating cost savings, Chu estimated that his process would make possible a reduction of up to 40 to 45 percent in the cost of producing hydrazine.[44] Such a saving would bring the price down to within sight of the 25- to 35-cent target level regarded by Jasinski as necessary for commercial use.[45]

But hydrazine is not the only candidate. Pratt and Whitney has built a hydrocarbon-air fuel-cell system; Shell Research Ltd. has constructed a methanol-air system; and, in the words of N. A. Cook of Allis-Chalmers, "The list could be continued, but it is apparent that there is a considerable amount of technology available with respect to fuel cells for terrestrial applications and yet there are no practical devices for sale."[46] The principal reason seems to be a pervasive consensus that costs would be excessive. Addressing himself to the use of an ammonia-air fuel cell for a small vehicle of the Volkswagen size, Cook concluded that "there does seem to be an excellent possibility that alkaline fuel cell technology can be developed to a cost in the order of $150/kw." This would mean that a Volkswagen-type vehicle "could be built with a fuel cell system whose cost would be about $1,200." If such an automobile were beefed up with a battery to give greater power for peak loads, the result would be "a very frisky town car with nominal performance for extended trips."[47]

Another form of hybrid, of which prototypes are now being developed, would be part electrical and part combustion engine. The engine would provide the cruising power (at which pollution emissions are lowest); the electrical system would supply the acceleration power (at which emissions are highest).

When, as, and if the electric car becomes widely used, the effects on the highly concentrated structure of the automobile industry should be far-reaching. Whether powered by batteries or fuel cells, the electric car is such a simple mechanism that not only medium-size but small manufacturers should be able to enter the ranks of automobile producers. Referring to the potential entrant, Orr stated, "The outside availability of power train components and the use of plastic bodies should reduce his capital costs markedly below what is currently required to enter the industry at any given level of output." Two further factors contribute to the potential thrust toward decentralization. Neither the battery nor the fuel cell is subject to scaling limitations: their efficiency is virtually independent of size. Moreover, the close tolerances required of a piston engine are not necessary for an electric unit, which makes for reductions in

---

thereby reducing the amount of power required, which "is the main reason why hydrazine still commands a high price today." The fuel cell reactor would serve the dual function of producing hydrazine solution and furnishing power for the concentration of hydrazine in the later stages after the fuel cell reaction.

[44] *Hearings on Economic Concentration,* Pt. 6, pp. 2863–76, testimony of Ju Chin Chu.

[45] There is a further route to cost reduction. In the United States, hydrazine is produced by only 2 plants, one of which is owned by the U.S. Air Force and operated by the Olin Chemical Co. Located at Saltville, Virginia, this plant was originally built to supply fuel for rocket engines. With the shift from liquid to solid propellants, however, the plant's principal source of demand disappeared, and since that time it has been operating far below capacity. Spread over a relatively small number of units, its unit overhead costs and thus its average unit costs are high. Referring to the high cost of hydrazine, Donald Looft testified: "Cost is largely a function of the quantity of fuel produced. Fuel manufacturers estimate that nearly an order of magnitude (10 fold) cost reduction is possible if production is correspondingly increased."

[46] N. A. Cook, "Analysis of Fuel Cells for Vehicular Applications," Paper presented at Automotive Engineering Congress and Exposition, Jan. 8–12, 1968.

[47] *Ibid.*

both capital and labor costs. Underlining his belief that the small producer of electric cars has "a fair chance of survival," Aronson cited the fact that "no industry as yet dominates or controls the production of electric propulsion system components, nor the production of plastic or fiberglass bodies and . . . these components can be purchased economically in relatively small quantities."

In response to a question concerning capital requirements, the British manufacturer Carter pointed out that the electric car "is a far less complex vehicle than the existing motor car, and contains about one-fifth of the parts that are in present-day cars." He could produce his bodies from ABS plastic either by thermoforming, which would require an outlay for a vacuum-forming press of about $3,000, or by injection molding, which would require a capital outlay of approximately $1.5 million for 2 large machines. The former would produce bodies at the rate of about one every 15 minutes whereas the latter would turn out bodies at the rate of one every 15 seconds. In either case, however, the capital entrance requirements are only a small fraction of the $500 million required to enter into the production of the conventional steel body, piston engine car. Because of what he referred to as "the difficulties and upsets of sociology," Carter stated that he would not like to see production concentrated in "one large industrial complex making the cars, with thousands of employees," indicating his preference for "small units in many large cities producing the cars locally, purchasing their components from different centralized manufacturing sources."

Rotary engines

Simplicity can be achieved, even in a heat engine, by substituting rotary motion for up-and-down reciprocating action. Rotary engines have the inherent advantage of continuous movement in the same direction. In contrast, reciprocating action is of a stop-and-go character, with the piston coming to a complete, though momentary, stop before beginning its downward thrust and then again before returning to its original position. Two types of engine embodying the principal of rotary motion have been developed for vehicular use—the turbine engine and the rotary-piston (Wankel) engine. Reflecting their greater simplicity, both can be produced economically with a substantially smaller capital outlay than is required for the piston engine. Moreover, air pollution would be reduced very definitely by the turbine and possibly by the rotary-piston engine.

A turbine engine operates by forcing a mixture of fuel and air, compressed at high temperatures, through the angled blades of a wheel, which, by turning, creates mechanical energy. Consisting mainly of a series of rotating wheels plus devices for taking in and compressing air and reusing and emitting used gases, the engine is simpler to make and service than the piston engine, since it has only one-fifth as many moving parts. For this reason an official of one of the Big Three auto makers acknowledged that "with the materials and parts suppliers now in existence and with the production and distribution systems which they have organized, turbines could be built and finally assembled by both *large and small* manufacturers." [48]

The turbine is also inherently clean, with much lower exhaust emissions than the piston engine. Indeed, in its present form it emits fewer pollutants than the

[48] *Hearings on Economic Concentration,* Pt. 6, pp. 2757–74, testimony of George J. Huebner, Jr. Emphasis added.

ideal of the piston engine several years hence, when the latter presumably will be equipped with afterburners, reactors, catalytic agents, and other pollution-reducing devices. Use of the turbine would greatly reduce emissions of carbon monoxide (indeed, it is impossible to commit suicide by running a turbine in a closed garage) and completely eliminate the use of leaded gasolines, which contribute 200,000 tons of pollutants annually to the atmosphere.[49] Although it can run on a variety of fuels, what will probably be used is diesel fuel, which is already dispensed by about 30 percent of the filling stations. Moreover, this shift in the type of fuel should result in a saving in operating costs, since diesel fuel is considerably cheaper than gasoline.

For years the major problem in adapting it to motor vehicles was reducing the cost of the turbine from the atmospheric heights tolerated by aircraft buyers to the levels required for the commercial sale of automobiles. For example, the rotating wheels used in aircraft turbines cost from $5 to $7 per pound; the production process involves making the feathered blades at the rim by expensive machining. By making a one-piece iron alloy casting of which the blades are an integral part, Chrysler's engineers, under the direction of George J. Huebner, Jr., have been able to reduce the cost to around 30 cents per pound. So successful is this process that aircraft engine manufacturers are now using it under license from Chrysler.

Other major problems that had to be overcome included high exhaust temperatures and excessive fuel consumption at low speeds. Here, also, the experience of the aircraft turbine was of little value. Testifying before the Senate Antitrust Subcommittee, Huebner revealed that the solution had been found in a regenerator that takes the hot exhaust fumes and recycles them back to the engine: "A rotating regenerator reduced high exhaust temperature and brought low-speed fuel consumption to within shooting distance of the piston engine." He went on to add, "In the 1950's the general opinion of those skilled in the turbine and powerplant fields was that this problem could never be successfully solved. Even after we had cars running on the public streets, the successful solution was sometimes disputed by experts as being impossible." Beginning in late 1963 the engine was road tested in 50 experimental handbuilt cars, which were lent to 203 qualified drivers selected at random from more than 30,000 persons who had written Chrysler about its turbine work: "The public trial of these 50 experimental cars was highly successful," Huebner reported.

If the major technical problems have been overcome and the road testing was "highly successful," how does it happen that the car is still not on the market? Huebner's response was, "Low-speed fuel consumption was not *quite* good enough; noise, while *acceptable* to most of the drivers, needed further reduction; greater engine braking was *desirable;* and a *slight* lag in acceleration from a standing start had to be eliminated." [50] Such a reply raises more questions than it answers. Obviously, by their very nature as well as by the way in which they are described, these problems are of a *de minimis* nature. And it is certainly not clear by whose standards fuel consumption is not "quite" good enough, or noise still excessive (though not to "most" drivers), or the "slight" lag in acceleration not acceptable. In view of its enthusiastic reception by the 203 drivers, it is hard to understand why Chrysler has not given the market an opportunity to decide.

---

[49] At the high temperature at which the turbine operates, lead in the gasoline turns to lead oxide, which is harmful to the engine itself.

[50] Emphasis added.

Perhaps, if given the chance, a substantial number of buyers would decide that these shortcomings were more than offset by the car's remarkable attributes, including savings of nearly 50 percent on fuel costs. And from the point of view of the public interest, these shortcomings would appear to be a small price to pay for an engine that can approach the piston engine in performance but at the same time reduce drastically the emission of pollutants.[51]

Another rotating mechanism, the rotary-piston engine, is now a commercial reality, owing to the pioneering efforts of NSU, a small German automobile manufacturer, and more recently by Toyo Nogyo, the third largest Japanese automobile producer. It is the product of research and development work going back to 1926, when the German engineer Felix Wankel became interested in rotating engines and established an institute for their study because he "considered the shaking and pounding of the reciprocating piston engine unesthetic as compared with the running of a turbine or electric motor." [52]

Perhaps the simplest way to envisage the engine is to imagine a horizontally placed cylinder within which the piston rotates instead of moving back and forth. It has also been described as "consisting of a three-corner rotor that swirls in a combustion engine shaped like a fat-waisted figure eight." [53] The problems of developing a workable configuration between the rotating piston, or rotor, and its housing had long been considered all but impossible of solution. A major difficulty was to devise a workable design that would perform the functions carried out by valves in a piston engine. Another problem was that of sealing the chambers; what was involved here was the more complex task of sealing clearances in several planes, including corners. As described before the Subcommittee by Yura Arkus-Duntov,[54] who as an engineer had participated in the engine's development, the solution was Wankel's design of the engine in the shape of an epitrochoid, "a plane curve traced by a point on the radius of a circle rolling on the outside of a fixed circle . . . the outer surface of the inner rotor approximates the inner envelope of this epitrochoid during their relative rotation. The apexes of the inner rotor are in contact with the epitrochoid at all times which simplifies their sealing."

In Arkus-Duntov's words, this replacement of reciprocating with rotary motion results in "a major saving in weight, size and complexity." Eliminated are "valves and valve mechanisms, connecting rods, unbalanced inertial forces, various orders of vibration, limitation on rpm's, problems of hot exhaust valves and a resulting limitation on compression ratio." Other advantages are the use of less expensive, low-octane gasoline; less vibration; and fewer parts and compo-

---

[51] Aside from the performance of the engine itself, there is the problem of educating mechanics in servicing this new type of engine. But when the industry introduced automatic transmissions, mechanics throughout the country were brought into service centers and given training in servicing the new mechanisms. As Huebner acknowledged, "The introduction of automatic transmissions and all of the steps leading to and following their introduction were accomplished with a minimum of dislocation throughout the industries involved." And, because of its simplicity, the turbine should be easier to service than the automatic transmission. It will, of course, be necessary to design new machine tools, provide training of production engineers and workers, and so on, but these are the normal complements of technological advance and certainly should not prove to be insurmountable to an industry that changes its models every year.

[52] Quoted in John Jewkes, David Sawers, Richard Stillerman, *The Sources of Invention,* rev. ed., Macmillan, 1969, p. 355.

[53] *Time,* Sept. 8, 1967.

[54] *Hearings on Economic Concentration,* Pt. 6, pp. 2775–85.

nents requiring lubrication, care, and maintenance. The saving of about one-third in the weight of the engine makes possible reductions in the size of the car, suspension, brakes, and tires. And, what is of principal interest here, the fundamental simplicity of the mechanism also makes possible economical production in smaller plants. According to a report in the trade press, "NSU says it will soon be possible to build a twin-rotor engine for about 60 percent of the costs of an equivalent six-cylinder conventional engine, even in the volume its relatively *small factory* works in." [55] A further potential saving in capital costs arises from the fact that the power of the engine can be increased simply by adding additional rotors.

In 1964 the first Wankel engine was introduced by NSU in a sports car. Three years later a two-rotor version was introduced in a sedan comparable in size and appointments to a Mercedes 250SL. The engine produced 113 brake horse-power, roughly the same as a normal reciprocating engine. Leading firms, including the Curtiss-Wright Corporation and the Outboard Marine Corporation in the United States, Rolls-Royce in England, Alfa Romeo in Italy, and Mazda in Japan, have paid NSU for licenses; Citroen and NSU set up a joint corporation to produce a Wankel-powered small car in France. Mercedes has unveiled an experimental sports car using the engine. Most recently, General Motors has agreed to pay $50 million for nonexclusive rights to the engine.

In its original form the engine was a notorious contributor to air pollution, emitting large quantities of hydrocarbons and carbon dioxide. Ironically, the worldwide concern over air pollution is the cause for increasing interest in the Wankel engine. According to an article in a trade journal:

> Emerging from this first phase and looking at the tougher emissions standards coming up in 1974 and '75, engineers suddenly spotted new merit in the Wankel rotary. Its combustion takes place at a relatively cool temperature, which helps reduce its output of oxides of nitrogen. Yet its exhaust gases are relatively hot, which helps hold a higher temperature level in a thermal reactor or catalytic converter. In addition, the gases come out only two or three holes instead of the six or eight of a comparable piston engine, so they're easier to handle. And, being inherently smaller than reciprocating engines of the same output, the Wankel leaves more room under the hood for emissions-reduction equipment. Should developments lead in the direction of very lean mixtures, the rotary is known for its tolerance of these . . . Felix Wankel's engine is also very happy with fuels of relatively low octane rating, which could be an aid to keeping power up as the lead content of gasoline goes down. Suddenly, for all these reasons, the Wankel is back in the big ball game. [56]

Moreover, the design of the engine makes it peculiarly well suited to the reduction of pollution through stratified charging—i.e., the injection of fuel directly into the cylinders. The principal cause of air pollution from internal-combustion engines is the discharge of unburnt gases resulting from an excessively rich mixture of fuel and air by the carburetor. In Arkus-Duntov's words, "the physical configuration of the Wankel engine is more suitable for stratified charge design than the conventional reciprocating engine. In such a design, the amount of fuel supplied does not exceed the amount of air available to burn it.

[55] *Automotive News,* Sept. 4, 1967. Emphasis added.
[56] *Car and Driver,* Nov., 1970.

Near-complete combustion would substantially reduce the amount of unburned fuel in the exhaust."

Electronics

Since World War II enormous advances have taken place in the development of a wide range of devices for commercial use which utilize the flow of electrons in a vacuum, in gaseous media, or in semiconductors. As a general principle the improvement in speed, range, and flexibility of operations made possible by these devices has far outweighed their cost. For some uses—e.g., miniaturization —they have improved performance while at the same time dramatically reducing the size and cost of capital equipment. In other applications—e.g., computers— the increase in capital costs has been far less than the utilities yielded.

Records of transactions are essential to the exchange of goods in even the most rudimentary form. Among the earliest known inscriptions are records of sales, debts, and credits. Whether inscribed on papyrus, clay tablets, or parchment, "paperwork" has always been with us; the only change has been an increase in its ratio to the actual volume of transactions. The necessity for record keeping has, in itself, led to important advances in civilization. The Roman numeral system was replaced by the Arabic primarily because the latter lent itself more readily to record keeping. Similarly, double-entry bookkeeping was a response to the urgent need during the Industrial Revolution for better knowledge of profitability.

The use of records for business purposes involves the posting of information, its retrieval, and, finally, its organization into meaningful aggregates. In this century the carrying out of these functions has passed through three stages. In the not-too-distant past bookkeepers and clerks, wearing green visors and garters on their sleeves, posted figures by hand on ruled yellow ledgers, usually with exquisite penmanship. Although today the image seems archaic, their performance of one of the three functions—the initial screening—has never been surpassed. If a report did not "look right" when compared to his knowledge of previous or similar reports, the clerk would instinctively subject it to further examination. Moreover, owing to the fantastic memory of the human mind, retrieval was conducted far more efficiently than might be assumed. The great weakness was in organizing the data into aggregates. Even with the aid of adding machines, comptometers, and calculating machines the number of aggregates into which the data could be compiled was limited and the time involved inordinate.

The next stage was the punch card and related tabulating machinery. Entries were no longer recorded by hand but punched on cards, which could then be retrieved by sorting machines and aggregated into totals by tabulating machines. The new method far outstripped hand work in retrieval and tabulation; in the initial posting of the data, however, what was gained in speed was lost in accuracy, for even with the most careful screening the semiskilled keypunch operator never approached the skilled clerk in determining instinctively whether a given entry "made sense" before it was posted.

The third stage, of course, has been the computer, or electronic-digital-computer system (EDP, "electronic data processing"), which combines the binary form of mathematics (a one and a zero) with the incredible power and switching capabilities of electronics. The computer has increased fantastically both the range of possible aggregates and the speed of compilation.

Since their introduction in the early 1950's computers have been widely regarded as constituting a powerful force toward a further concentration of industry. This impression has been based partly on cost; only the largest firms, it was thought, could afford them. And partly it has been based on the assumption that their principal use would be within the *plant;* the larger the plant and the more functions it performs, the greater the opportunities for cost savings through computers. The image of the computer-controlled, unstaffed, fully automated plant has bemused businessmen and intellectual apostles of cybernetics alike. That it has not come to pass, except in special circumstances, has certainly not been for want of effort. Immeasurable amounts of energy, time, brainpower, and money have gone down the drain in trying to "computerize" productive operations. But even before the computer made its appearance routine functions within the plant had already been automated with simpler and less costly devices — the electrical and electronic devices that indicate, measure, record, and control temperature, speed, pressure, flow, dimension, viscosity, chemical composition, and other physical conditions of production. Contrary to general impression, these devices have applicability to plants of all sizes.

Shortly after the introduction of the computer, Henry Dever, an official of one of the principal manufacturers (Honeywell), told a group of businessmen:

> You see, for every multi-million dollar electro-mechanical machine, for every new, man-made "brain" development that threatens to obsolete even push-button devices, there are literally hundreds of more prosaic, less expensive, off-the-shelf automatic instruments which daily function as the "sinews" of this trend toward factory or process automation. My own firm has been involved in this field since 1859. . . . Because of the tendency of many commentators to superlatives on automation—to say nothing of the more glamorous equipment's stiff price tags—there is a persistent inclination to consider automation the "privileged pasture" of today's industrial giants.[57]

After citing a number of ways in which automation was able to increase production and otherwise improve operations in relatively small enterprises, Dever stated: "You don't need two or three million dollars for plant purchases to get your feet wet in automation. Much automation can be bought at conventional equipment costs." [58] Admittedly, the large company may have the advantage in high-volume products with limited design or style variation. But, he added, "The highly specialized and integrated automatic tooling equipment needed means that the larger firm requires longer runs but more or less standardized design and set-up times. The smaller company, with lower overhead, greater flexibility, more direct supervision, can capitalize on these initial production-restricting factors affecting its larger contemporaries and protect—and even expand—its own business right under the gun, so to speak." [59] By enabling the small plant to speed up its output, industrial instruments, particularly the controlling devices, have made it possible for a small plant to serve a larger market with only a small increase in its capital outlays. By automatically assuring uniformity of product, they have helped the smaller company to compete on a front on which the large firms have long asserted their superiority—quality of

[57] Speech given on October 11, 1956. Mimeograph.
[58] *Ibid.*
[59] *Ibid.*

product. And by eliminating or reducing sudden changes in the speed of operation, temperatures, pressures, and the like, these devices have extended the life and usefulness of existing equipment, thereby reducing capital costs.

Unlike industrial instruments, the computer has found its home not so much in the plant as in the front office, providing management with an extremely efficient and versatile tool to carry out that great variety of functions subsumed under "indirect" costs—from simple record keeping to the most sophisticated forms of sales inventory control.

In hearings before the Senate Subcommittee on Antitrust and Monopoly, John R. Opel of the Data Processing Division of the IBM Corporation referred to fears "that only large corporations can afford to install and use computers and related equipment." [60] But, he went on to say, "An examination of the record of the data-processing industry will show just the opposite to be the case." Similarly, Walter W. Finke, president of the Electronics Data Processing Division of Honeywell, the second largest computer producer, referring to the view that "only large firms can avail themselves of the usefulness of these instruments," emphasized, "I have an opposite point of view." [61]

The history of the computer industry has been brief but explosive. It was only in 1951 that the first computer, installed by the Census Bureau, was put into use for processing commercial information. In their first stage, computers utilized vacuum tubes; in their second, transistors; and most recently, microminiature circuits. Describing the nature and effects of these rapid technological changes, Opel stated:

> These new technologies have made computers much more compact, and for a very good reason—to increase computational speed. An electronic impulse travels about one foot in one billionth of a second. While a delay this brief may sound insignificant, in the world of the computer, this can quickly add up to processing delays of minutes or even hours.
>
> *   *   *
>
> Designers, therefore, have used these new technologies to bring computer components closer together. The growing compactness of computers is evident from the fact that in vacuum tube days a computer had about 320 components per cubic foot, whereas today there are about 30,000 components per cubic foot.

These and other changes have brought about dramatic improvements in the size, speed, cost, modularity, and languages of computers. And these improvements in turn have greatly broadened the functions that the computer can perform. When first introduced in the business world, the computer was used simply for the routine tasks of billing, payrolls, and general accounting. "Then," in Opel's words,

> the power and flexibility of the computer began to make itself felt. Modern EDP methods were developed and extended to the functional and decision making areas of business in such applications as preparing sales analyses and maintaining control of stock and inventory. This, in turn, led to better understanding of the type of current information the management level of a company needed to operate efficiently.
>
> As management gets faster and more complete operating information, it is able to reduce inventories, control its in-stock position and increase its overall effectiveness.

[60] *Hearings on Economic Concentration,* Pt. 4, pp. 1651–67, testimony of John R. Opel.
[61] *Ibid.,* pp. 1571–80, testimony of Walter W. Finke.

At their inception, computers were indeed expensive devices, costing upward of $2 million each. Unfortunately, the view that they were definitely not for smaller firms has persisted despite the fact that the price has gone steadily downward. At the same time an even more impressive improvement has taken place in performance. On an early vacuum tube computer the cost to the customer of performing 100,000 multiplications was $1.38; in the second or "transistorized" stage, the cost was 25 cents; and in the current microminiature-circuit stage, the cost is down to 3½ cents or less. From the vacuum tube computers to the current models, the improvement in the price-performance ratio was held by Walter W. Finke to be of a "magnitude of 125 to one."

Also helping to bring the computer within the reach of smaller firms has been the introduction of small "desk-size" models, which can be purchased for a few thousand dollars and are capable of performing thousands of calculations per second. Models with comparable performance would have been classed a few years ago as large-scale computers, renting for "many thousands" a month; in Finke's words, "These machines are now so versatile and capable that for businesses of even the corner drugstore variety, a new computing capability has been made available." [62]

But the development that has brought the computer within the financial reach of even the smallest concerns is the data-processing center—a service organization which operates electronic computer equipment and provides processing services for a fee. There are now thousands of such centers in the United States, with hundreds in every major city in the country. Pointing out that the availability of such centers "puts the computer within reach of the smallest manufacturer, retail store, bank or professional office," Byron S. Carter of the National Cash Register Company listed their advantages as follows:

> 1. The small businessman obtains the efficiencies of electronic data processing without having to buy or lease a computer.
> 2. Startup costs are minimum.
> 3. The business that uses the services of a data center receives specialized "programming" aid without having to employ specialized personnel and without having to develop or provide training courses for its own employees.
> 4. Flexibility of services enables the smaller business to experiment with new systems in a way that its larger, more rigid competitor often cannot. Since he makes no capital outlay, the small businessman can abandon with impunity a system that proves unsatisfactory.
> 5. Data processing services are available on relatively short notice. Where the time factor is dominant in a system, this advantage becomes crucial.
> 6. Most computer installations are relatively immobile. Once prepared, a computer site can be moved only with considerable expense and inconvenience. The businessman who deals with a data processing center avoids this possible cost.
> 7. Objective analysis of his specific data processing problems by a disinterested agency gives the small businessman a way to help meet the competition presented by larger businesses.
> 8. Using the services of a data processing center provides protection against obsolescence of purchased computer equipment. [63]

[62] *Ibid.*, p. 1785.
[63] *Ibid.*, pp. 1601–09, testimony of Byron S. Carter.

Many of these centers are able to introduce and operate even the most sophisticated approach to data processing, that of the "total system." In such systems the basic data are obtained as part of the original transaction. Such data can be "captured" from a simple adding machine, ordinary cash register, or conventional accounting machine equipped with a punch-paper tape recorder or optical type font (specially shaped numerals that can be "read" electronically). Once the data are thus captured as a routine part of normal business operations, they can be read automatically into the computer, which can be programmed to print out, again automatically, the reports desired by management. According to Carter, "The presence of the modern data processing center makes a 'total system' . . . available to virtually any business, regardless of size."

The reduction in price, the improvement in performance, the appearance of low-cost, desk-size models, and the emergence of numerous data-processing centers have all contributed to making the computer available to small firms. But availability is not the whole story. There are at least two reasons for believing that the computer may be of even greater importance to the small and medium-size firm than to the very large corporation.

For one thing, the computer enables the smaller firms to perform functions whose costs under previous methods of data processing—hand tabulation, punch-card systems, and so on—were prohibitive to all but the largest firms. In other words, in the past the smaller firm was barred by its lack of resources from securing types of information that could be obtained by the larger company. Commenting on this point, Opel stated that there is now available to the smaller user a "methodology which he formerly could not afford." As an example, he pointed to the ability of the small consulting firms to compete on jobs that under past methodologies were beyond their "in-house" capability:

> if you are an engineer or mathematician, the mathematical problems are the same for you as they are for your large competitor. Solving or evaluating solutions to typical engineering or scientific problems such as linear equations on a bridge design can involve many thousands of calculations. In the past, the small consultant did not have the in-house capability to perform this work.
>
> With these small, low-cost machines, which began to appear in the marketplace about two years ago, this is no longer the case. The small consulting firm can be and is competing effectively today.

Finke emphasized that for the large company the computer's principal benefit is in bringing about savings in money and time as compared to older methodologies, whereas for the smaller firm it adds an entirely new capability:

> Big companies have always been able to afford detailed analyses of their problems and opportunities. Even before computers, they had the staff and the size to make this possible. For them, the addition of a computer made it easier and perhaps cheaper to do these analyses.
>
> Small businesses rarely could afford detailed analyses, in the same sense that they could not afford a large staff, simply because they did not have sufficient volume to spread the expense over. But powerful, new low-cost computers now make this analysis possible for small business.
>
> Therefore, while both large and small companies will benefit from computer analysis, for large companies it is only a matter of degree. For small companies it is a matter of kind.[64]

[64] *Ibid.,* p. 1788.

In assessing the strengths and weaknesses of smaller firms, Finke emphasized that this new capability would strengthen small firms precisely in those areas where they have traditionally been weakest—e.g., it would enable them through closer control of inventories to reduce their needs for credit, which is always more costly for smaller than for larger businesses:

> In my view, the great strengths of a small business cannot be undermined by someone else's use of a computer. Those strengths are the ability to develop sound products, to provide good or better service than the competition, to respond quickly to changing trends, to keep overhead to a minimum, and to be able to communicate and adjust quickly as the situation may demand.
>
> The weaknesses of a small business are first, limited financial muscle, if you want to describe it as such, limited product line development and most important, limited staffs. Now in every one of those instances, the availability of this computer system is going to enable these small businesses to overcome these weaknesses in a way relatively more significant to them than is the case in a situation involving a large business. These systems can be used to reduce inventory, improve receivables—obviously, they cannot borrow money for a small business, but they can make the operation of the business more efficient within the confines of the sums available.
>
> They can do analyses on product lines. They can substitute for large staffs and give better results.

An even greater advantage to smaller firms lies in the computer's potential for use in day-to-day decision making. Properly programmed into a company's operations, the computer can provide almost instantaneous information on key factors needed for intelligent decisions. It can tell management which products, and even which models, designs, colors, and so on, are selling best and in which geographic areas; it can show the inventory status of the rapidly selling versus the lagging items, thus enabling management to make prompt adjustments in factory production; it can enable management to keep on top of the progress of a new or experimental model, permitting the prompt discontinuance of an unsuccessful item before heavy losses are incurred; it can show which is the most successful of different advertising programs, sales approaches, or advertising media; it can reveal which dealers and which types of distributorship have the best—and the poorest—performance records in moving the company's products.

Since the computer makes such information available to any firm, this, in itself, constitutes no advantage for small companies over larger ones. The potential for a differential advantage lies in the ability and willingness of the decision makers, themselves, to become expert in the use of the computer, an expertise that is essential to taking full advantage of this versatile tool. Those who make the business decisions must know what the computer can and cannot do. They must learn to think in its language—to frame questions, instinctively, in such a way that the computer can provide answers. Under the hierarchical system of big business, there is an almost inherent separation between the making of business decisions and the supplying of information—a separation that is usually less formidable in the smaller firm. Although, like their counterparts in the large enterprise, smaller businessmen chronically "do not have the time" to take on anything new, they are more likely to find the time if it is necessary to make effective use of a new piece of equipment which is costing their company money.

This difference in effective utilization became evident in an informal special survey of its own regional offices conducted by IBM in preparation for its presentation to the Senate Antitrust Subcommittee. In response to an inquiry from their head office, their regional managers reported that the most sophisticated users of the computer were generally firms of a medium size. The possible reasons were discussed in the hearings. Thus, Finke of Honeywell referred to "the basic weakness of clogged and inefficient communications within a highly structured business" and to the "enormous" task for the larger companies of refining "literally mountains of data." [65] The following exchange took place between Finke and the Subcommittee's chief economist:

> DR. BLAIR: . . . the tendency in more recent years has been toward a greater utilization of the computer in the decision-making process—sales analysis, cost analysis, inventory control, inventory-sales analysis, and so forth, in which the function of a computer is to provide to management data on the basis of which management can more intelligently and more quickly make a decision concerning some vital aspect of the company's operations. Is that a correct understanding?

> MR. FINKE: Yes, that is correct. . . .

> DR. BLAIR: And therefore, it would follow that the company that will make the best use of the computer as an aid to decision-making would be the company whose decision-making management becomes intimately acquainted with the language and the uses and the limitations of the computer and begins to think and frame its questions in terms of the computer's language—of what the computer can and cannot do. Is that correct?

> MR. FINKE: That is correct. That is one of the requirements of this new age in which we live. I happen to feel so strongly about it that I think that any advanced degree in business should carry as a prerequisite a complete and understandable course in the role of the computer before the student graduates.

> DR. BLAIR: And there is no reason, therefore, why the management of the smaller company cannot become just as versed in this language and the capability of using the computer as an aid to decision-making as the management of a large company?

> MR. FINKE: That is right.

> DR. BLAIR: And might indeed be able to translate the knowledge provided by the computer into decision-making more rapidly than could management in the larger enterprise where there is greater separation between this knowledge and ultimate decision-making which is subject to more remote control?

> MR. FINKE: Well, I think that the difference in density between a large business and a small business may cause that result.

Similarly, Opel of IBM pointed out that the small businessman who "does not have staff departments at his disposal . . . has greater reason to become personally involved in the data processing function." Although noting that large companies could closely integrate the computer into decision making, Opel stressed the importance of the absence of "levels of management":

> The second point is that, again, it is related to whether or not the general manager of a small firm has a greater potential involvement in the system than the general manager of a large firm, and here, again, I think he has a greater potential to become involved, because he lacks levels of

[65] *Ibid.*, p. 1786.

management between himself and the computer operation, and to that extent there are examples where this is clearly true. Again that is not to exclude the possibility that it can occur in a large firm. It is a question of difficulty and necessity perhaps.

*   *   *

With plastics, fiberglass, and high-performance composites providing high-strength and easily processed materials suitable for an infinite variety of applications; with energy provided by such simple and efficient devices as high-energy batteries, fuel cells, turbine engines, and rotary piston engines; with computers providing a means of instantaneously retrieving, sorting, and aggregating vast bodies of information; and with other new electronic devices harnessing the flow of electrons for other uses, there appears to be aborning a second industrial revolution, which, among its other features, contains within itself the seeds of destruction for concentrated industrial structures.

THE RATIONALES OF MANAGERIAL ECONOMIES

Gains in efficiency can be secured not only from within the individual plant but by bringing several, indeed many, plants under common ownership and control. Through multiplant operations efficiency can be improved in a number of ways —by rationalizing output among the different plants, by bulk purchasing, by broadening product lines, by securing easier access to capital and credit, and by better financial controls and staff services. That such economies are potentially available through multiplant operations is not disputed; the question is whether or not they are more than offset by the resultant diseconomies. The diseconomies of multiplant operations include the waste inherent in hierarchical structures, the impediments of "proper procedures," the inescapable conflicts between line and staff, the diseconomies arising from advancement, the resistance to change, and others. The heart of the matter was put succinctly by Austin Robinson over 35 years ago:

> for every type of product there is in a given state of technique some size at which the rational and other economies of larger scale production are outweighed by the increasing costs of the coordination of the larger unit, or by a reduced efficiency of control due to the growth of the unit to be coordinated. . . . The limitation to the scale that can be managed arises . . . from the limitations of human abilities, from the fact that they can only crowd so much work into twenty-four hours, that persons take time to convince and so on.[1]

This chapter will be concerned with the conceptual arguments relating to both economies and diseconomies, while the ensuing chapter will summarize the available empirical evidence.

Managerial economies

During the nineteenth century the interest of economists in the relationship between size and efficiency was focused almost exclusively on the plant and on the single-plant firm. When serious attention came to be paid to multiplant operations, the principal ways in which they could bring about further economies were soon identified. To these traditional arguments have recently been added a number of additional rationalizations advanced on behalf of conglomerate corporations, of which the most persuasive are those relating to financial controls and staff services.

[1] Austin Robinson, "The Problem of Management and the Size of Firms," *Economic Journal,* June, 1934, pp. 247–56.

Rationalization of operations

Originally put forward as a justification for cartels, the rationalization argument holds forth the prospects of economies resulting from greater specialization plus easier transfer of knowledge, skill, and know-how. Referring to the "ownership of manufactories of the same general kind at various points," Charles R. Van Hise noted over half a century ago:

> Under these considerations it is possible to make the same product at the different plants, or to specialize the different manufactories under the same organization so that one shall handle one line of work, and another another. Further, the work of any one branch may become standardized and require comparatively little shifting or changing of machines. Thus the shapes, forms and sizes of the manufactured iron which comes from a given plant may remain the same month after month, or even year after year; and this very greatly promotes efficiency.[2]

A company that operates a number of plants can "rationalize" its operations by centralizing production in its more efficient establishments and shutting down the higher-cost plants. Purchase orders can be sent from the central office to the particular plant that can best fill them. By pooling the orders calling for a particular set of specifications as to grade, shape, dimension, model, size, and so on, the individual plants can achieve more fully the economies of specialization. Moreover, the processes, techniques, and know-how gained in the efficient plants can be transmitted to the poorer units, thus bringing the latter up to the level of the best.

But if the industry had been competitive in the first place, would there have been any need for efforts to achieve economies through rationalization imposed by central-office management? If one assumes that bringing together separate plants under common ownership and control results in savings, the question is: savings as compared to what? It is not at all unlikely that inefficiencies could have developed in an industry which, because of oligopoly or collusion, had been relatively immune from the rigors of price competition. And it is also conceivable that these inefficiencies could be eliminated through rationalization made possible by multiplant operations. But if the industry had been competitive in the first instance, such inefficiencies presumably would not have existed. As Austin Robinson noted: "Where firms which were previously engaged in imperfect competition are amalgamated and the conditions of the market are thereby changed, it may be possible through increased specialization to secure greater technical economies without greater total costs of coordination. *But in conditions of perfect competition the optimum degree of specialization will already have been achieved.*" [3]

Quite apart from this theoretical consideration the gains from rationalization must always be weighed against certain inherent disadvantages. For one thing it is impossible to gain the economies of scale resulting from large scale operations without incurring the diseconomies of greater control and coordination. As Robinson put it: "If, in an attempt to diminish the degree of centralization and coordination, the unit of production is kept small, the economics of technical scale must be forfeited. If it is sought to secure the economies of large-scale technical production, the diseconomies of coordination must be incurred. It is

[2] Charles R. Van Hise, *Concentration and Control,* Macmillan, 1914, p. 10.
[3] Robinson, *op. cit.* Emphasis added.

impossible to enjoy simultaneously both the technical gains of large scale and the managerial economies of decentralization." [4]

A similar incongruity arises if one attempts to claim both the economies of specialization and savings in transportation costs. An example of the former, cited by John M. Clark, was the action by the American Steel Hoop Company in dividing up its 90 sizes and varieties so that each plant specialized in one type of product. As a result the company was able to save from $1.00 to $1.50 per ton simply by avoiding the need for frequent changes of rolls.[5] But what if a customer wanting a particular size and variety was located at a great distance from the only plant making that particular size? As Clark observed, "The savings of cross-freight and the specializing of plants are always mentioned, though generally without calling attention to the fact that the same combination cannot get both savings at once, and that to the extent that it gets one it must sacrifice the other." [6]

The existence of opportunities for rationalization is one thing; their realization is another. The production site from which U.S. Steel would logically have been expected to supply the growing southern and western markets was its integrated plant at Birmingham, Alabama. Acquired many years ago from Tennessee Coal & Iron, the Birmingham works had the twin advantages of geographic proximity to these markets and its own nearby, low-cost deposits of iron ore and coking coal. Since the steel companies, under their basing-point pricing system, sold only on a delivered basis, the shorter the distance, the higher their realized mill net price. Yet a prominent management consultant firm, Ford, Bacon & Davis, which had been retained by the company to study its operations, found that U.S. Steel had persisted over many years in supplying markets closer freightwise to Birmingham from their higher-cost, more distant northern mills. In so doing they not only incurred greater freight expenses but failed to take advantage of Birmingham's nearby, low-cost materials. In dollar terms the study found that U.S. Steel's failure to supply its southwestern and Pacific Coast markets from Birmingham was costing the corporation $1 million a year.[7] On some products the Birmingham mill even had an advantage in eastern markets. Thus the engineers found that the corporation could produce tin plate at Birmingham, ship it to the eastern seaboard, and warehouse it for $2.48 per ton less than its Pittsburgh mills could deliver it to this market, which accounted for over 50 percent of total U.S. domestic consumption. Yet despite this advantage, the Birmingham mill had not produced a pound of tin plate.[8] After analyzing the results of the study, which had been described unhappily to the House Antitrust Subcommittee by U.S. Steel officials, George W. Stocking concluded:

> Ford, Bacon & Davis . . . pictured the corporation as a big, sprawling, inert giant, whose production operations were improperly coordinated; suffering from the lack of a long-run planning agency; relying on an antiquated system of cost accounting; with an inadequate knowledge

[4] *Ibid.*
[5] John M. Clark, *The Economics of Overhead Costs,* University of Chicago Press, 1923, p. 96.
[6] *Ibid.*, p. 142.
[7] See 81st Cong., 2nd Sess., House Subcommittee on the Study of Monopoly Power, House Committee on the Judiciary, *Hearings,* 1950, Pt. 4A, "Steel."
[8] George W. Stocking, *Basing Point Pricing and Regional Development,* University of North Carolina Press, 1954, pp. 106–08.

of the cost or of the relative profitability of the many thousands of items it sold; with production and cost standards generally below those considered everyday practice in other industries; with inadequate knowledge of its domestic markets and no clear appreciation of its opportunities in foreign markets; with less efficient production facilities than those of its rivals; slow in introducing new processes and new products.[9]

The case of U.S. Steel illustrates the further question of incentives. What motivation is there for large producers in an oligopolistic industry to adopt the available opportunities for rationalization? Except on rare occasions U.S. Steel has long been immunized from the discipline of price competition and thus from the unsettling, continuous ferment which is the normal condition of competition. While such ferment is good for a company's efficiency, it is hard on its personnel. Shifting output from one plant to another, closing down some facilities while expanding others, increasing the output of high-profit products and curtailing that of low-profit items are highly disruptive to an orderly life for both management and labor. If the oligopolist is able to avoid the discipline of competition and if through the monopolistic control of price he is able to earn a profit rate that keeps the stockholders tolerably satisfied, he will naturally tend to avoid making those disruptive and disagreeable changes which a controlled and quiescent market does not force upon him.

Bulk purchasing

By pooling the demands of separate plants for goods and services, the multiplant firm is frequently able to achieve savings in purchases. These savings may come as quantity discounts, special concessions off the list price, or a variety of hidden forms, including reciprocal arrangements under which the supplier agrees to make *his* purchases from the company that has agreed to buy its supplies from him. The few available unit cost studies invariably reveal the largest companies to have a significant advantage in materials cost.[10] As an example, George Romney, then president of American Motors Corporation, referred to price advantages enjoyed by the large automobile manufacturers in their purchases: "Senator, in the procurement area there is not any question that some of the car companies that bit the dust in the past resulted from better prices extended to the large companies by the major sources of raw materials and parts." [11]

It is of course impossible to determine the extent to which such advantages have been due to real economies as contrasted to the exercise of monopsonistic power. By virtue of their buying power, large firms may be able to secure concessions that have nothing to do with their efficiency as buyers. That such is often the case is suggested by the infrequency with which companies accused of violating the Robinson-Patman Act avail themselves of its "cost defense," which, if demonstrated, is a complete defense against a charge of price discrimination. The law exempts "differentials which make only due allowance for differences in the cost of manufacture, sale or delivery resulting from the differing methods or quantities in which such commodities are to such purchasers sold or delivered. . . ." [12] As explained by the House Judiciary Committee, the provision

[9] *Ibid.,* p. 141.
[10] See Ch. 8.
[11] *Hearings on Administered Prices,* Pt. 6, p. 2854.
[12] Robinson-Patman Act (1936), Sec. 13(2)(a).

"leaves trade and industry free from any restriction or impediment to the adoption and use of more economic processes of manufacture, methods of sale and modes of delivery." The Committee emphasized that because of this provision the bill contained nothing to discourage efficiency or reward inefficiency. That despite its clear intent so little use has been made of the cost defense has been attributed by some observers to the difficulty of segregating the relevant cost data, the burden of computing costs adequate to show the savings, and the frequent absence of the underlying cost information itself.[13] Such arguments imply that companies making price discriminations do not know what they are doing. It may well be true that concessions are granted without knowledge of the relationship of the resultant net price to costs, but this is hardly a testament to efficiency. It is at least equally possible that the cost defense is ignored simply because the concessions transcend any economies that could conceivably be associated with purchasing in larger quantities.

The broadening of product lines

If the different plants of a multiproduct corporation produce different and unrelated products, the opportunities to achieve economies of scale in production are virtually nonexistent. There are few, if any, opportunities to rationalize production among the different plants, to achieve economies of specialization by concentrating production of given styles, sizes, or models in separate plants, to reduce cross-freight, and so on. But in the area of distribution the multiproduct firm does have some opportunities to secure real economies. From a theoretical point of view, however, any attempt to justify conglomerate operations on the basis of savings in selling costs concedes the existence of at least some monopoly power. The seller of a nondifferentiated product in a free market has neither any selling costs nor any occasion to incur them. As Edward H. Chamberlin has observed, "Selling costs are very naturally passed over in competitive theory since they are at odds with the assumptions of pure competition. . . ."[14] The addition of a further product to a company's line makes it at least theoretically possible to save the supply price of one salesman. A favorite example cited by proponents of this argument is the combining of the distribution of glass and paint: "The production of these [paint] items on a large scale has been logical because paint stores generally feature glass as well. . . ."[15]

But how, in a truly competitive industry, could a firm afford the incremental selling costs of handling additional and unrelated products? Of course, if the industry is oligopolistic and competition in price has been replaced by rivalry in selling effort and advertising, the company's existing sales expense might well provide a "cushion" permitting the handling of additional products without impairing sales of the original product. But what this amounts to is a subsidy out of monopoly profits, not a cost saving. If the firm is an oligopolist in glass, its monopoly profits from that industry may enable it to subsidize its sales in the highly competitive paint industry, the cost of which, however, can only depress

[13] See Corwin D. Edwards, *The Price Discrimination Law,* Brookings Institution, 1959, pp. 612–13.
[14] Edward H. Chamberlin, *The Theory of Monopolistic Competition,* 4th ed., Harvard University Press, 1942, pp. 126–27.
[15] G. E. Hale, "Diversification: Impact of Monopoly Policy Upon Multi-Product Firms," *University of Pennsylvania Law Review,* Feb., 1950, p. 320.

the company's overall earnings. And in point of fact this appears to be exactly what has happened. According to a business magazine:

> Sometimes management concentrates so much on its traditional, successful operations that it overlooks other problems. Initially, it made sense for PPG salesmen to sell both glass and paint. But the market changed. In glass PPG's one major competitor was Libbey-Owens-Ford. In paint it faced hundreds of small suppliers. PPG salesmen naturally pushed glass because it was easier to sell. As a result PPG didn't score the gains in paint that it was capable of.[16]

Access to capital

Multiplant companies also find justification as suppliers of capital. The essence of the argument is that they are able to supply financing to divisions and subsidiaries which, as independent companies, would wither on the vine for lack of funds. It has long been recognized that smaller firms are either completely unable to obtain equity capital and long-term credit or, if successful, must bear far higher financing costs than their larger rivals. The logical solution would be to establish financial machinery closing up this "institutional gap" (referred to in Great Britain as the "MacMillan gap" because of the former prime minister's long concern with the problem). Certainly, the dimensions of the gap in the United States have narrowed with the growth of over-the-counter securities trading and the formation of the small business investment companies. But as long as it remains, an argument can be made for multiplant companies as suppliers of capital to business organizations that would be unable to secure it as independent companies.

To advance the argument, however, is to raise the question of what *are* the sources of capital. If a large multiplant company is supporting a division engaged in one industry with monopoly profits made in another, it is the consumers of the latter who are providing the financing. And whether the funds are supplied by consumers or investors, it is the managers of multi-industry companies who are deciding on their disposition. When industries are made up of competitive, single-line companies, thousands of individual investors can make their selection among the different industries and, further, among the different firms in each industry. Their decisions are based upon their own expectations of the future prospects of the various industries and the performance records of their producers. Thus, the chances are maximized that the optimal allocation of capital will be attained, since the possibilities of error are minimized by the diffusion of the decision-making. In contrast, the investment decisions of corporate managers may be based on considerations that will make little if any contribution toward bringing about an optimal allocation of resources. They may wish to shore up an ailing division in which they have already sunk an inordinate investment, or to subsidize losses in the hope of driving out competitors, or to continue through simple inertia an activity which should long since have been discontinued. The making of decisions is further impeded by the imperfect nature of the data on which they are based. The cost records on which the managers must base their decisions are substitutes for the profit and loss statements of single-line enterprises. Even the best of accounting systems will of necessity reflect some arbitrary method of allocating the indirect costs of a

[16] *Forbes,* Jan. 1, 1969.

multi-industry concern. Indeed, the managers may even ignore costs as long as the company's total return is satisfactory. As Willard L. Thorp and Walter Crowder noted, "even if costs were known, the flow of supply might not follow accordingly. The company managers are interested in the profitability of the entire unit . . . as long as there are several products with different profit ratios, total profit may be maximized . . . by selling some lines below accounting cost." [17]

Other sources of economies

Some of the fashionable rationalizations for conglomerates are more in the nature of metaphors than appeals to reason. For example, it is said that conglomerates, like a few medications, have a "synergistic" action—i.e., that the effect of the component elements when combined is greater than the sum of their effects as separate elements. Exactly how the corporate whole becomes greater than the sum of its parts remains obscure. Likewise, officials of conglomerates have likened their organizations to symphony orchestras, with the head office functioning as the conductor, "orchestrating" the ensemble into a balanced, coordinated performance. If the different plants of a conglomerate were making their own separate and distinctive contributions to the production of a given product, as do the various instrumentalists in the performance of a symphony, the analogy would possess at least surface plausibility. But since the products are different, the appropriate analogy would call for the different instrumentalists to be playing different tunes.

In the area of financial controls and staff services the arguments are more persuasive. Conglomerates have been in the forefront in using the computer to implement the simulation models, decision rules, and discounted-cash flow (DCF) analyses of managerial economics. The poor profit performance of conglomerates, however, suggests that even the most sophisticated techniques of managerial economics are no substitute for operating experience in the industry. Similarly, conglomerates have been among the leaders in the use of corporate staff services—programming, national advertising, financial staff services, and the like. But, as Joel Dean has pointed out, it is not necessary that a company be a conglomerate or even large to secure the benefit of these services: "Most of these services can be obtained at the market place by small-scale users at costs that are competitive with large-scale self-supply. Even big companies hire Battelle to do research, use time-shared computers, buy software from outsiders, partner with strangers on national TV, and hire economic and financial consultants. The make-or-buy choice is ever present and often close." [18]

As a general proposition, conglomerate acquisitions have the least claim, of all the forms of merger activity, to promoting economic efficiency:

> The lower costs that might result in a horizontal acquisition from the pooling of skills and know-how gained in the production of the same product from different facilities are absent. Likewise the conglomerate acquisition affords little opportunity for the closing down of the less efficient facilities and the centralization of production in the more efficient.

[17] Willard L. Thorp and Walter Crowder, *The Structure of Industry,* Monograph No. 27, Temporary National Economic Committee (TNEC), 1941, p. 667.
[18] *Hearings on Economic Concentration,* Pt. 8, pp. 5253–67, testimony of Joel Dean. Dean's testimony includes a listing of other claims to efficiency made on behalf of conglomerates (*ibid.,* p. 5258).

Similarly, the gains in a vertical acquisition which might result from the more logical and orderly arrangement of facilities employed in the successive stages of a continuous production process are not present. Because what is involved is the production of unrelated products, the conglomerate acquisition provides few opportunities for the securing of economic efficiency in such matters as specialization as between plants, exchange of cost information between plants, savings in handling and reheating, operating with smaller inventories, reductions in the number of styles and sizes, savings in cross-freight, etc.[19]

Managerial diseconomies

Beginning with Alfred Marshall British economists have long recognized important sources of managerial diseconomies. In Marshall's view the growth of a firm cannot continue indefinitely because the abilities and energies of the entrepreneur (or of his heirs) are likely to decay after a certain time, management becoming less energetic, slower to adopt new methods, and less able to cope with misfortune. The opportunity is thus presented for younger and smaller firms to make gains at the expense of the older, established enterprises, even where the latter, had they been able to continue their growth, would have achieved a further reduction in costs.

In the early 1930's further sources of managerial diseconomies were identified by Austin Robinson and P. Sargant Florence. A noteworthy contribution was C. Northcote Parkinson's well-known 1955 article, "Parkinson's Law," which has been followed more recently by the works of Jay, Peter, and Townsend. Although couched in the form of irony (perhaps because of the nature of the subject matter), the form of these recent critiques is not a valid reason for ignoring their substance.

Organizational structures are generally of the hierarchical (or pyramidal) type, although there is recurrent interest in the cellular (or functional) structure. A movement toward the latter occurs as organizations occasionally seek to free themselves from the diseconomies of the pyramidal form of organization. But since the cellular structure has its own sources of diseconomies, experience with it often induces the organization to move back toward the hierarchical form. For reasons that will be discussed later,[20] the demands for *correct* decision making at the top are greater under the cellular structure; it takes only a few wrong decisions to breed a spirit of disenchantment with the looser form of organization. Because of this factor, and also because of inertia, the structure of the typical large organization will tend to be more hierarchical than cellular.

Traceable back to the earliest days of society and brought to its fullest fruition in religious and military organizations, the form of the hierarchical structure is a pyramid: "One or more persons are placed under a superior, that superior under a 'supersuperior', and each of these superiors exercise a rule over their subordinates that extends to all types of work. There is, in fact, a regular chain of authority covering all subjects and extending all the way down the line." [21]

---

[19] John M. Blair, "The Conglomerate Merger in Economics and Law," *Georgetown Law Journal,* Summer, 1958, pp. 679–80.

[20] See pp. 169–72.

[21] P. Sargant Florence, *The Logic of Industrial Organization,* Kegan Paul, 1933, p. 119.

They may not put it down on paper, they may not even mention it in discussion, but a great many administrators and managers carry in their heads a pattern of the "ideal" organization. That pattern is the classic hierarchy, the family tree; one man at the top, with three below him, each of whom has three below him, and so on with fearful symmetry unto the seventh generation, by which stage there is a row of 729 junior managers and an urgent need for a very large triangular piece of paper.

This mental picture is probably less clear about the exact function of the managers at each level, but it generally carries the assumption that each is supervising the work of those below him, passing down policy guidance from above, and passing up requests and queries from below, ensuring that those below carry out their duties and that those above have the right information for their decisions and that responsibility is carefully graded so that at each promotion a manager takes a little more of it, until finally one of the original 729 contemporaries gets to the very top and takes it all.[22]

The ascending steps in any hierarchical system customarily are differentiated by recognizable insignia. The corporate counterparts of robes, vestments, and "bishops' gaiters," of epaulettes, shoulderboards, and officers' insignia, are the size and location of the office, the quality and dimensions of the desk and other office furnishings, the thickness of the rug, the number of secretaries, entrée to the executive dining room and washroom, access to such tax-deductible corporate facilities as limousines, the company plane, intown apartments, hunting lodges, and so on.

But beneath the superficial appearance of modern-day perquisites are the same assumptions on which organizational structures have been founded since the beginnings of civilization. Based on his own business experience culminating in his highly successful tenure as president of the Avis Company, Robert Townsend questions the appropriateness of these assumptions—that "people hate work," that they "have to be driven and threatened with punishment," and that they "like security, aren't ambitious, want to be told what to do, dislike responsibility": according to Townsend, "we're in this mess because for the last two hundred years we've been using the Catholic Church and Caesar's legions as our patterns for creating organizations. And until the last forty or fifty years it made sense. The average churchgoer, soldier and factory worker was uneducated and dependent on orders from above. And authority carried considerable weight because disobedience brought the death penalty or its equivalent." [23]

By its very nature a hierarchical structure is the source of a variety of diseconomies. Although in this work the emphasis is on the large, multiplant private corporation, these diseconomies are common to hierarchies of any kind—military, governmental, religious, labor, educational, charitable, and so on. They are also common to any type of economic system—capitalist, socialist, or Communist. Indeed, they are probably most pronounced in those economies that have eliminated the last restraint upon egregious inefficiency—bankruptcy.

The waste inherent in hierarchies

Inherent in hierarchical structures is a constant tendency to expand, resulting from tendencies toward the multiplication of both subordinates and superiors.

[22] Antony Jay, *Management and Machiavelli,* Holt, Rinehart & Winston, 1970, p. 68.
[23] Robert Townsend, *Up the Organization,* Knopf, 1970, p. 137.

THE RATIONALES OF MANAGERIAL ECONOMIES

As set forth by Parkinson in his original article, the tendency toward the multiplication of subordinates has its genesis in the desire of a superior to enlarge his own organizational unit.[24] Although Parkinson attributes this desire to the superior's feeling (either real or imagined) that he is overworked, other motivations are commonly present. Officials in all hierarchies know that elevation tends to be a function of the number of one's subordinates. They also know that the best protection against budgetary cutbacks is a request for expansion, which means that the effect of a cutback will fall on subordinates yet to be added rather than on the existing staff. Moreover, a desire to expand is generally looked on favorably by one's superiors as evidence of industry, energy, and drive. But whatever the motivation, with superiors at all levels constantly seeking expansion, a certain proportion will inevitably succeed. This sets in motion a cumulative process, since the effect of granting the superior, A, two assistants, C and D, will be to create two further sources of expansion. In Parkinson's words:

> When C complains in turn of being overworked (as he certainly will) A will, with the concurrence of C, advise the appointment of two assistants to help C. But he can then avert internal friction only by advising the appointment of two or more assistants to help D, whose position is much the same. With this recruitment of E, F, G and H, the promotion of A is now practically certain.
> Seven officials are now doing what one did before.[25]

Some observers may leap hastily to the conclusion that this multiplication of subordinates will leave some of them idle or able to work shorter hours. But such a conclusion merely reveals a failure to understand the workings of a bureaucracy. As Parkinson observes, "The fact is that the number of officials and the quantity of work to be done are not related to each other at all." [26] The officials are busily engaged in creating paperwork for each other. While to outsiders Parkinson's illustration may seem extreme, to those who have been caught in the meshes of hierarchical structures it has about it the ring of truth:

> For these seven make so much work for each other that all are fully occupied and A is actually working harder than ever. An incoming document may well come before each of them in turn. Official E decides that it falls within the province of F, who places a draft reply before C, who amends it drastically before consulting D, who asks G to deal with it. But G goes on leave at this point, handing the file over to H, who drafts a minute, which is signed by D and returned to C who revises his draft accordingly and lays the new version before A. . . . He corrects the English—none of these young men can write gramatically—and finally produces the same reply he would have written if officials C to H had never been born.[27]

Performance thus comes to be measured in terms of the ability to turn out for higher officials memoranda, reports, analyses, and other documentary material to be read, noted, filed, or used as the basis for still further memoranda, reports, and the like, to *their* superiors, and so on *ad infinitum*. This form of activity and the staff needed to perform it can expand while the functions actu-

[24] C. Northcote Parkinson, "Parkinson's Law," *Economist,* Nov. 19, 1955, pp. 635–37.
[25] *Ibid.*
[26] *Ibid.*
[27] *Ibid.*

ally performed by the organization diminish. As Parkinson observed in two pointed illustrations, the number of officials in the British Admiralty increased between 1914 and 1928 by 78 percent, while the size of the Royal Navy decreased by one-third in men and two-thirds in ships; similarly, the number of officials of the British Colonial Office increased from 372 in 1935 to 1,661 in 1954, while the sun was setting on ever larger areas of what had once been the British Empire.

Not only do the internal dynamics of any hierarchical structure inherently make for constant growth and expansion; they also serve to frustrate the periodic efforts of a zealous incoming superior to "eliminate waste," "cut off the fat," and thereby save the taxpayer's (or stockholder's) dollar. It takes him a while to discover (usually to his surprise) that everyone *is* busy, and by the time he learns who is doing necessary and who unnecessary work it is his turn to be replaced. Because of growth in the organization itself and because of the multiplication of subordinates, the number of superiors also tends to increase. Efforts in the name of economy to hold down the number of superiors by widening the area of their responsibility are generally self-defeating. As Florence puts it, "There is a limit to the number of subordinates that can be directly commanded by one man." [28] Failure to observe this principle results in overloading the superior with administrative trivia. Matters requiring decision pile up in logjams as the harried executive goes from subject to subject, on none of which he can spend sufficient time to acquire anything like an adequate understanding. The resultant diseconomies are aggravated by a normal human frailty: confronted with an excessive number of issues on which decisions must be taken within a given period of time, the tendency of the overworked executive will be to give attention to those issues that are least demanding, least complex, and least controversial. And the greater his exhaustion, the greater is the attraction of whatever is relatively mundane, simple, and uncontroversial. The result of course is the constant putting off until tomorrow of precisely those issues most urgently needing action today.

The impediments of proper procedures

If anything of other than a routine nature gets accomplished in a hierarchical organization, it is despite the impediments of red tape, of going only through "regular channels," and of generally observing "proper" procedures: "Red tape and bureaucracy are words often flung in the teeth of hierarchical organizations but seldom actually defined. When these words are used they seem to refer to such a rigid adherence to formalities that rules become masters rather than servants. The result is an exceedingly roundabout method of reaching decisions, and a certain imperviousness to changing circumstance and technique." [29]

Red tape, or at least a major element of it, consists of those documents prescribing and implementing the procedures and channels to be observed. The larger the organization, the greater will be the number and complexity of its procedures and channels and thus the greater the danger of becoming "strangled in red tape." It is customary to set forth procedures and regulations in policy manuals, which in the view of one successful businessman are one of the first things that should be dispensed with: "The only people who read policy manuals

[28] Florence, *op. cit.*, p. 121.
[29] *Ibid.*, p. 125.

are goldbricks and martinets. The goldbricks memorize them so they can say: (1) 'That's not in this department' or (2) 'It's against company policy.' The martinets use policy manuals to confine, frustrate, punish and eventually drive out of the organization every imaginative, creative adventuresome woman and man." [30] Then there are forms to be filled out—requisition forms, travel forms, leave forms (sick and annual), telephone forms, and so on. In addition are the reports, monthly, annual, and intermittent—activities reports, progress reports, budget and financial reports, reports on meetings and conferences, performance reports, planning reports, and the like. Anything that is not covered by a form or report must of course be set down in a memorandum. And all these forms, reports, memoranda, and other documents must move upstream to be noted, recorded, filed, and occasionally acted upon, and appropriate instructions and directions, again in written form, must then move down the line. But this usually does not take place without due deliberation at one or a series of meetings and conferences, which is itself one of the most expensive, time-consuming forms of activity known to man:

> Apart from the relatively insignificant clerical costs, there are the far more important costs which arise from the time spent by valuable executives in conferences, discussions and committees, in the composition of memoranda and the persuasion of others where the author is already persuaded. In addition to all these are the costs which arise from the loss of initiative and the opportunity to secure without reference to higher authority that the right thing is done at the right moment, or from the relative stagnation which tends to emerge where executives lose hope of convincing higher authority of the necessity for change.[31]

Destructive as it is to a corporation's performance, red tape can be invaluable to the artful bureaucrat who wishes to combine an appearance of vigorous activity with a minimum outlay of effort. The truly accomplished official will never make a contribution himself but will always have passed a project down to a lower level for further work or up to a higher level for review or approval. In this way he not only can avoid being criticized for holding things up but can display one of the hallmarks of managerial efficiency—a perpetually clean desk.

In addition to the impediments of red tape, proper procedures require that contacts and communication be conducted through "regular" channels: "Hierarchic corporations are often riddled with prohibitions and inhibitions about who can write or talk to whom without long bureaucratic journeys of permission up one side of the hierarchy, across one of the great divides, and down the other side." [32] Behind these prohibitions and inhibitions is the desire to keep work moving up and instructions moving down a continuing line of command. And the requirement of moving through channels is reinforced by the natural rivalry between rival lines of command for greater recognition, a larger share of the company's budget, and the like. Whatever the cause, permission must be sought and approval granted "through channels" before any joint or cooperative effort can be undertaken. By the time the request has wended its weary way up, over, and down and the approval has come back via the same tortuous route, the official who initiated the idea may well have lost interest in the whole project.

[30] Townsend, *op. cit.,* p. 147.
[31] Robinson, *op. cit.*
[32] Jay, *op. cit.,* p. 77.

Moreover, the observance of proper procedures inevitably imposes a barrier to the upward flow of information and ideas. A hierarchy has been described by Thomas Burns of the University of Edinburgh as "a system where information goes up through a series of filters, and commands and prohibitions come down through a series of loudspeakers." [33] The information that comes up from below is ignored or neglected "for the very reason that it comes from a subordinate." [34] It does not take long for this fact of life to dawn on even the most ambitious of subordinates, with the result that before long the upward flow of meaningful information tends to dry up. As an example, Florence cites the prophetic warnings in World War I by subordinate French army officers that the military defenses of Verdun were inadequate. Rebutting these warnings, Marshall Joffre told the Ministry of War, "I cannot be a party to soldiers under my command bringing before the Government, by channels other than the hierarchic channel, complaints or protests concerning the execution of my orders. . . . It is calculated to disturb profoundly the spirit of discipline in the Army." The officers were rebuked and dismissed.[35]

The inescapable conflict between line and staff

In the life of any organization there come times when incorrect decisions can no longer be tolerated. Thus, necessity has been the mother of a supplement to the pyramidal structure. Any hierarchical organization "must in almost every case be supplemented by a staff organization, whether the staff be formally recognized as such or not." [36] Historically, the idea of a "staff" to supplement the "line" originated in the army, where the consequences of incorrect decisions are most immediately and dismayingly apparent: "We have already seen how information, if it comes from the lower ranks, is inclined to be neglected. To remedy this source of inefficiency military commanders gradually delegated power to certain persons to specialize in giving information." [37] But the establishment of the staff, no matter how necessary, has also created a built-in conflict. In Florence's words, "There is always a tendency inherent in the staff system for the creation of a superior highbrow set who are pictured as sitting at headquarters devising paper forms and questionnaires to annoy the executive line officers and men doing the 'donkey work' at the real front." [38]

What began as relatively simple adjuncts have today become sizable components of every large organization, embracing in the business world such diverse activities as personnel, budget control, accounting, administrative management, planning and programming, research and development, advertising, public relations, legal counseling, and numerous variants or components thereof. To line officials it often seems that the staff exists only for the purpose of impeding their ability to get on with the job of making and selling the company's products by continually making demands on their time for irrelevant or useless

[33] Quoted in *ibid.*, p. 76.
[34] Florence, *op. cit.*, p. 124.
[35] Liddell Hart, *The Real War,* quoted in *ibid.*, p. 125. This action, taken by the French army, directly contravened one of Napoleon's own military maxims: "A commander-in-chief cannot take as excuse for his mistakes in warfare an order given by his minister or his sovereign, when the person giving the order is absent from the field of operation and is imperfectly aware or wholly unaware of the latest state of affairs."
[36] Robinson, *op. cit.*
[37] Florence, *op. cit.*, p. 133.
[38] *Ibid.*, p. 137.

chores. Before an employee can be hired to perform a new function the personnel office requires the operating departments to provide it with a precisely worded job description. In order to expand or even stand still, each operating division must submit and justify ambitious work programs, at least annually, to the budget office. Financial data, often of considerable complexity, must be prepared for the accounting division. The experts in administrative management must be told continuously why a given function cannot be performed with fewer persons. Information must be submitted to the experts in planning and programming describing how the work of the operating divisions fits into the "overall" objectives of the corporation. For their part the advertising men keep coming up with new promotional gimmicks requiring changes in production and sales approaches. The public-relations men have their own, often bizarre, demands on time and personnel. And the lawyers are particularly fertile in coming up with ideas as to why something the line wants to do cannot be done.

Likening those in the line, such as production and sales managers, to medieval barons and those in the staff to courtiers, Antony Jay writes:

> The medieval baron, busy keeping invaders from the borders of the realm, doubtless felt the same emotion when at the height of the trouble he heard of some new land tax which would take all of the hard-built morale out of his peasant-soldiers when they heard about it. And the same goes for the regional manager, short of salesmen in a tough competitive situation when he gets a document from head office demanding six pages of statistical returns, notifying him of a new invoicing procedure, and telling him to cut back on expense claims and use of company cars by his salesmen. The baron thinks the courtiers are remote, airy-fairy smart-alecks who ought to spend a few weeks at the sharp end just to learn what it is all really about, the courtier thinks the barons are dim, out of date, unsystematic, unimaginative cowboys who cannot see beyond their noses. All too often they can both prove it.[39]

In this conflict the line suffers from an inherent disadvantage in that its success or failure can be determined objectively; either the production manager turns out the goods and the sales manager meets his quota or they do not. But there is no way of measuring empirically the performance of the staff:

> How do you set a quota for the public relations officer? Or the personnel manager? The firm may have an appalling press reputation and a disastrously high staff turnover, but you just try pinning that on the courtier responsible. He can prove conclusively that it has happened despite all his vigilance and effort, and that without his brilliance, his imagination, and his unflagging labors the situation would be far worse. His success or failure are not objective like the baron's, they are in the eye of the beholder. He is as successful as the chief executive believes he is. For this reason his standing at court becomes all important to him; he is one of those wretched men that hang on princes' favors.[40]

In Robert Townsend's view the conflict can be resolved simply by getting rid of staff—an acceptable solution if one assumes that its *essential* functions can be performed by the line. He advocates firing outright the personnel department, the public-relations department, and the purchasing department. With

[39] Jay, *op. cit.*, p. 148.
[40] *Ibid.*, p. 149.

regard to the first he observes, "The trouble with personnel experts is that they use gimmicks borrowed from manufacturing: inventories, replacement charts, recruiting, selecting, indoctrinating and training, job rotation and appraisal programs. And this manufacturing of men is about as effective as Dr. Frankenstein's was." [41] His proscription of public-relations activities includes not only a company's own department but outside P.R. firms as well: "Most businesses have a normal P.R. operation: press releases, clipping services, attempts to get interviewed; all being handled, as usual, by people who are embarassingly uninformed about the company's plans and objectives." [42] In their place he recommends centering contacts with the press in the company's top ten or so operating officials. The trouble with purchasing departments is that "they cost ten dollars in zeal for every dollar they save through purchasing acumen. . . . 'They'd hire Einstein and then turn down his requisition for a blackboard.' " Again, the solution is to turn over the function to line officals: "The company will benefit from having each department dealing in the free market outside instead of being victimized by internal socialism." [43] Also to be eliminated are the "assistants-to," who in the large corporation operate under a variety of titles: "Some are called V.P. or Senior V.P. or Executive V.P. or even Chairman of the Executive Committee." Whatever the title the "assistant-to" can be identified by his method of operation: "He moves back and forth between the boss and his people with oral or written messages on real or apparent problems —overlapping and duplicating efforts and make-working." He exemplifies the divisive role of staff, "getting between the boss and the people who report to him, usurping power, crossing wires and draining the organization's strength and zeal." [44]

Townsend would also eliminate a number of activities imposed by staff that contribute little to the company's efficiency but are a constant drain on the time and energy of line officials. High on the list are reports—reports on long-distance calls, on interviews, on progress and activities, and so on and on. Particularly to be banned is the "manager's monthly [report] or any other time-consuming report imposed on the troops by 'top' management. It's a joke because it consumes ten pounds of energy to produce each ounce of misunderstanding." [45] Certain types of research can do little for a company except cost it money: "Ad agencies love to spend your money on market research, and lawyers on legal research. CPA firms all have systems departments and it doesn't take much to start them doing systems work. With all three groups it is well to set up some kind of general alarm that goes off before you accidentally discover they've spent a lot of your money doing work you don't want done." [46]

The diseconomies arising from advancement

If there can be such a thing as an ideal condition for a hierarchy, it is a static state. All positions are filled with persons reasonably competent to perform their assigned tasks, movement within the structure is at a minimum, and the work to be done is of a known, repetitive character. The most ominous

[41] Townsend, *op. cit.*, p. 144.
[42] *Ibid.*, p. 148.
[43] *Ibid.*, p. 159.
[44] *Ibid.*, p. 23.
[45] *Ibid.*, p. 125.
[46] *Ibid.*, pp. 157–58.

threat to a hierarchy is change—from within or without. Since human beings are mortal, change from within is inescapable. The short-run effect on the organization's efficiency of replacing those who leave, whether because of death, retirement, or other causes, will always be adverse, as time is required for subordinates to get used to the new incumbent's way of doing things, to become acquainted with his likes and dislikes, to learn where they stand with the new boss. And time will be taken for the new superior to get the "hang of the job" and learn something about his new subordinates—who can and does produce the work, who can but does not produce, and who neither can nor does.

In the long run the hierarchy's efficiency may be increased by the advancement of a more vigorous and usually younger official into a position formerly occupied by one who had outlived his usefulness and was merely marking time until retirement. At the same time there will always be an adverse effect, stemming from the disappointment of those who have been passed over. The mere structure of a hierarchy in which, at any given level, there are several competing aspirants for a superior's position makes this, mathematically, an important source of diseconomies. If there are three officials at each rung on the ladder, the odds against promotion are two to one; if four, they are three to one. As in a game of musical chairs the mere arithmetic of it means that fewer and fewer will be chosen. And what of those who are not?

> In human terms, a man strives for promotion and reward and success up to a certain point, but, earlier or later, almost all realize that whatever they do they are not going to get much further. Some will leave; a great many of the rest reach a switch-off point, when they say to themselves, "The difference between going on bursting my guts and taking it easy is about $1,000 a year before tax. So I'm not going to try." They then change from aiming at the maximum possible to the minimum excusable; their ingenuity and energy are converted from the task of getting more power and money to that of giving less time and effort. They try to pass the rest of their time with the corporation in a spiritual recess.[47]

If the official who is passed over leaves, the corporation loses its investment in his training, which will have been considerable by the time he has reached the middle ranks. Ironically, companies that would never think of scrapping a usable machine hardly give a second thought to the loss of a manager in whom they have a far greater investment. But if he stays, the loss to the firm may be even greater. There is not only the decline in his output, as he goes from "the maximum possible to the minimum excusable"; there is the further effect on the work of his subordinates. If they think that their boss is an up-and-coming man, one who is "going places" in the company, they will be eager beavers, working above and beyond the call of duty. Not only will they be stimulated by his drive and ability, but they will hope to share in his success. At the very least they will be competing vigorously for his position in the expectation that he will soon be promoted. But what of the subordinates whose superior has been passed over and is quite obviously not going anywhere? As he serves out his time before retirement, he will hardly be a source of inspiration to anyone. No one is going upward in the wake of his success, and even his own spot is not likely to become vacant until his actual retirement. At any given time and at any given level, the arithmetic of the hierarchical system means that more subordinates are going to be working for "passed over"

[47] Jay, *op. cit.*, p. 70.

than for "promoted" superiors. This factor is undoubtedly a leading cause of today's remarkably high turnover in the ranks of lower and middle management.

Frustration in the hierarchical organization, however, extends to all ranks of management. The higher the strata, the greater the rewards for elevation and thus the bitterer the pill for those who were in the running but didn't make it. At best the corporation suffers the loss in efficiency inherent in their disappointment. At worst, it suffers the loss of a high official, privy to all its strategies and secrets, *to a competitor*. Since much of the success the competitor may have will probably be at the expense of his former—and ungrateful—employer, he can be expected to enter into his new position with enthusiasm.

What of the official who *did* receive the promotion? A clue to whether his performance in the new position will be better than that of his predecessor is provided by the manner in which his advancement was achieved. If it was attained by seniority, as is all too often the case even in the private sector, there will probably be little change. The mere fact that he labored under the departed superior a greater length of time than any of his rivals means that he had a greater opportunity to learn his predecessor's *modus operandi* and absorb it as his own. If the advancement was secured by intrigue and influence, the odds are greater for a definite change in performance—but whether for better or worse depends on the circumstances. In some cases the mere fact that the aspirant was able to have pull exerted on his behalf means that he possesses imagination, resourcefulness, and knowledge of the organization's structure that he can put to use in carrying out the responsibilities of his new position. But in others it means merely that he has a special gift for internal politicking, which is of absolutely no value to the performance of his official duties. Of course, there is always the chance that the advancement was due solely to a clear and manifest display of outstanding ability. This eventuality, however, is somewhat remote, not because of the absence of able men but because of the premium placed by hierarchical structures on conformity. As Laurence J. Peter has observed, "in most hierarchies *super-competence is more objectionable than incompetence*. . . . Super-competence often leads to dismissal, *because it disrupts the hierarchy,* and thereby violates *the first commandment* of hierarchical life: *the hierarchy must be preserved.*" [48] Or, put another way, nothing fails like success.

In Peter's view every employee in a hierarchy tends "to rise to the level of his incompetence," where he remains: "In time, every post tends to be occupied by an employee who is incompetent to carry out its duties." [49] The organization is able to function because of the activities of those who have not attained this state: "Work is accomplished by those employees who have not yet reached their level of incompetence." [50] The factory worker who is good at his job will tend to become the foreman. If he is competent in his new position, he stands a good chance of becoming plant superintendent; but if he proves to be an incompetent foreman, it is there that he will stay. The woman who is a good schoolteacher and because of that fact is promoted to principal will remain in that position if, as a principal, she proves to be incompetent. In a hierarchy an employee is seldom demoted from a position in which he is incompetent to a lower grade in which his competence has been demonstrated.

[48] Laurence J. Peter and Raymond Hull, *The Peter Principle,* Morrow, 1969, p. 45. Emphasis in original.
[49] *Ibid.*, p. 27.
[50] *Ibid.*

Therefore, the question of whether an organization's performance is improved by the replacement of a departed superior will be determined by whether the new incumbent has the competence to perform the functions of the office to which he has been promoted. If not, he will remain in this new position, and because he is incompetent to carry out its duties, the performance of the organization will suffer.

Peter emphasizes that the principle "The cream rises until it sours" applies to every form of society: "The Marxists have proved as wrong in their analysis as have the capitalist theoreticians. My studies in comparative hierarchiology have shown that capitalistic, socialistic, and communistic systems are characterized by the same accumulation of redundant and incompetent personnel." [51] The real threat to any society is the progressive accumulation of deadwood: "Any government, whether it is a democracy, a dictatorship, a communistic or free enterpise bureaucracy, will fall when its hierarchy reaches an intolerable state of maturity." [52]

In appraising the "Peter Principle" one must distinguish official from non-official duties of a position and recognize that at progressively higher levels the importance of the nonofficial tends to increase. Thus, the official duties of a sales manager will include seeing to it that his sales quota is met, maintaining good relationships with the principal buyers, keeping his salesmen alert and aggressive, noting changes that should be made in the company's product, recommending improvements in its advertising and promotional campaigns, and the like. In addition, his unofficial duties will include informal contacts with the higher-ups (lunches, cocktails, dinners, parties, golf matches); attempts to create a favorable impression for himself and his division with his superiors, including the comptroller, budget officer, or other official controlling the allocation of funds; arranging political alliances with other divisions to promote some mutually beneficial project; and so on. Whatever competence he might have in performing his official duties is largely irrelevant to the conduct of these nonofficial functions. Here what is called for is skill in intrigue, influence, and office politics. Hence, contrary to the Peter Principle, the mere fact that he is incompetent in carrying out the official duties of sales manager does not mean that he will remain in that position. If he is sufficiently skillful in performing the unofficial functions, he will rise, regardless of any other consideration. The ultimate in organizational inefficiency is achieved when the skills of those at the highest levels relate only to the conduct of nonofficial functions.

The resistance to change

If the workings of a hierarchy can be impeded by the normal processes of internal attrition and advancement, they can be utterly disrupted by a radical change from without. A hierarchy can work with tolerable efficiency in dealing with a comparatively stable subject matter—an unquestioning acceptance of the faith, wars fought with conventional weapons, a constant technology, a known and unchanging pattern of consumer demand. But it works badly, if at all, when confronted with change. The natural tendency is to resist that which cannot be readily assimilated—hence the tendency of established religious

[51] *Ibid.*, p. 70.
[52] *Ibid.*, p. 75.

bodies to reject departures from established canons, of armies and navies to ignore and even oppose new weapons, of long-established corporate giants to lag in invention and innovation, and of leading producers in rapidly expanding industries to suffer losses in their share of the market.

The tendency to reject anything that might upset a hierarchy's well-ordered and usually comfortable way of life is common to all economic systems. For example, the fact that of all industrialized countries the Soviet Union has been the slowest to shift from coal to oil has been attributed in the petroleum trade press to a long-standing close relationship between the ministry of fuels and the coal industry. Over the years the ministry had become intimately familiar with the coal industry and its problems; a shift to oil not only made this accumulated knowledge redundant but confronted the ministry with a whole range of new problems on which it had absolutely no expertise.

Not only does the proponent of change have a difficult row to hoe; he labors under the virtual certainty that the full responsibility for failure will be his and his alone, while credit for success will attach to his superiors. On this point Richard Walton, one of the nation's leading independent inventors, testified:

> A few years ago I was having lunch in the executive dining room of a large company. Alone at a small table sat a distinguished-looking man. No one spoke to him or even appeared to glance in his direction. I was informed that he was a company official responsible for taking a license on an invention from outside the company. It had failed and cost the company a million dollars. His relationship to the president had saved his job, but his lonesomeness served as a constant reminder to younger executives of the dangers of being associated with a development from outside the company.
>
>   *   *   *
>
> There is little individual reward for success, because the success is diffused by the numerous people ultimately involved; it is the company which receives credit. There is seldom any doubt where the burden of failure falls. It falls on the individual who has taken responsibility of pushing that product.[53]

Or, as Townsend has put it, "the world seems to be divided into those who produce the results and those who get the credit." [54]

The special problems of the cellular structures

In dialectical terms the cellular structure is the antithesis of the hierarchical. Instead of a pyramid, its form is a group of circles radiating outward from a "central office," or "control center." Instead of progressive centralization of authority, its objective is maximum possible decentralization. Instead of neatly packaging in one organizational unit all functions relating to a given activity, it tolerates and sometimes even encourages the carrying on of the same function in different organizational units. Instead of regarding duplication as one of the cardinal sins, it promotes rivalry among its different cells. Instead of preoccupying itself with proper procedures and regular channels, it seeks to minimize organizational checks and restraints of any kind. Instead of centering all meaningful decision making at or near the top, it seeks to diffuse authority

---

[53] *Hearings on Economic Concentration,* Pt. 6, pp. 2702–03.
[54] Townsend, *op. cit.,* p. 61.

and responsibility to lower levels. Above all its character is revealed in a state of mind:

> The hierarchic attitude is revealed in phrases like, "This memo must go through me," "I must be notified before one of your staff comes here," "If you want to talk to my subordinate then I must be present"; the cell attitude, in phrases like, "Why don't you go and put it to him yourself?" . . . "Come back to me if you need some more ammunition," "Perhaps you'd better drop over and have a word with the marketing boys." [55]

Not surprisingly, the cellular structure has a great attraction for the ambitious who have been mired down in a hierarchy. Its virtues seem endless.[56] Preoccupation with form is replaced by concern with substance. Officials with the power to say no are greatly reduced in number. The route of a new idea to implementation is foreshortened. Individual performance is recognized and rewarded. Out of the rivalry among the different units come new ideas that would never have been thought of in a hierarchy. The dull cast of uniformity is replaced by the sparkle of diversity. The human spirit is liberated. The millennium in organizational structures would appear to be at hand.

With all these attributes of cellular structure, it may seem surprising that the hierarchical structure is not only still with us but continues to be the dominant form of business organization. One reason, of course, is resistance to change by those who have found in the hierarchy a comfortable way of life. The prospect of changing to the hurly-burly of the decentralized structure would be particularly terrifying to the incompetent who, through seniority, intrigue, or the operation of the Peter Principle, have risen to relatively high positions. At the same time it must be recognized that the cellular structure suffers from serious shortcomings of its own. For one thing, the line of command is at best uncertain. In a hierarchical structure the constant complaint is, "You can't get anything done"; in a cellular system it is, "Nobody seems to be in charge." For another, a greater number of managers capable of intelligent decision making are required. By increasing the number of positions with authority, the cellular system spreads the already scarce supply of competent managers even thinner.[57] In Robinson's words, "If wise men are scarce it may be better to have decisions made on insufficient evidence by wise men than on sufficient evidence by fools." [58]

The cellular structure also presents something of a paradox. While the number of units with meaningful authority is greater, so also is the need for *correct* decision making at the top. With all these semiautonomous cells vying with each other, someone has to decide which are to grow, which are to be held back, and which are to be eliminated. An incorrect decision by top management can work havoc on a company for years to come. General Electric, which has long made a veritable religion of decentralization, provides a striking example of this type of error: "Ex-G.E. Chairman Ralph Cordiner concedes that he didn't put enough top management into computers; and today's computer losses are a big reason why G.E.'s earnings growth is only 4.2 percent yearly, 371st in the Forbes 500." [59] A year after this admission General Elec-

---

[55] Jay, *op. cit.*, p. 79.
[56] For an enthusiastic exposition of its attributes, see *ibid.*, pp. 75–80.
[57] See Edith Penrose, *The Theory of the Growth of the Firm,* Blackwell, 1959.
[58] Robinson, *op. cit.*
[59] *Forbes,* Jan. 1, 1969.

tric removed itself from the computer industry by disposing of its computer business to a new joint venture, the majority stockholder of which is its competitor, Honeywell.

Perhaps the most serious liability of cellular structures is the difficulty of securing coordination: "Apart from the friction, jealousy and rancor that are apt to spring up between departments, there is an inevitable getting out of touch." [60] In the absence of some effective form of coordination, a decentralized corporation is likely to give an appearance of verging on chaos, with

> production schedules being drawn up without consulting a sales forecast, two representatives—one from the region and one from the product division—trying to sell the same product to the same customer while telling him conflicting facts about it, sales drives aimed at a volume of orders which the factories cannot in fact meet . . . and the general state of affairs where the planning department is an expensive joke and the firm has as many policies as managers.[61]

Although a fundamental purpose of decentralization is to stimulate intracorporate rivalry, there remains the need for a minimum degree of coordination. But recognizing the need and actually implementing it are two different things:

> The larger the field in which coordination is being attempted the greater must be the knowledge which ought to be in the minds of the coordinators. But man's mind and man's memory is essentially a limited factor. It cannot absorb, understand and retain material without end. One of the problems of the high official, both in politics and in industry, is to find time for the necessary minimum of reading. No perfection of staff organization can enable a given unit of coordination to coordinate an infinitely large unit of operation . . .[62]

Moreover, the task of coordination is not without its costs, of which the most important is the time lost by managers in the process of being coordinated, which is usually attempted through conferences and committee meetings. As a source of inefficiency the committee meeting has achieved a status of its own. Since the objective of a committee meeting is to arrive at a consensus, the natural tendency is to paper over the real differences. The accomplished committee chairman is thus an artist in generalized phraseology, skilled in translating the reality of conflict into the illusion of harmony. During the process interminable periods of time are consumed in debating minute differences in semantics. And the larger the committee, the greater the consumption of time, since each participant must get into the discussion the position of his own division. Like an amoeba splitting, each meeting is the occasion for others. There is need to go over suggested drafts, to "clarify" positions, and to bring new considerations to the attention of the group. It is not without reason that committee meetings have been defined as "slightly organized wastes of time." For the truly slothful the committee meeting is an ideal way of combining participation in a prestigious form of activity with a minimum expenditure of mental and nervous energy. Where no amount of artful language can camouflage the existence of real differences the majority will usually prevail, which may be in keeping with democratic principles but bad for the organization.

Some large corporations, particularly conglomerates, have moved toward the

[60] Florence, *op. cit.*, p. 132.
[61] Jay, *op. cit.*, p. 59.
[62] Robinson, *op. cit.*

cellular structure by establishing within the company decentralized "profit centers." Those of the corporation's divisions that are in similar or related industries (or have some apparent connection with one another) are established as separate "profit centers." Through stock ownership or options on the stock of the parent company, their officials are rewarded in accordance with the center's performance. Commenting on their record, Joel Dean has concluded, "Experience over the past 25 years indicates . . . that profit-center structuring of management has not eliminated but only somewhat reduced the managerial disadvantages of diversity and size." [63] The fundamental problem is a conflict between the measure of the center's performance, customarily profits in the short run, and the need for investments in the development of products, markets, and the like, which determine profits in the long run. By retaining control over most of the investment decisions, the central office is largely determining today what the performance of the profit center will be tomorrow. Yet in Dean's view, "the High Command does not have enough intimate experience with each diverse industry to guide (or reverse) decisions of profit-center managements on intangible investments where short-run profits must be sacrificed for long." [64]

It is manifestly inequitable to grant rewards to one center that has been favored with adequate investment while withholding them from another that has had to make do with its old facilities and limited resources. Similarly, it is inequitable to grant rewards to a center that happens to enjoy the benefit of an established monopoly position while withholding them from another that is engaged in a fiercely competitive industry. Such inequities obviously have a debilitating effect upon the very managerial incentives that the profit-center approach is designed to promote. And even under the best of circumstances these incentives fall far short of providing the equivalent of ownership in the profit center as a separate company. In Dean's words, "Stock ownership or options *in the mother company* don't even approximate the narrow ownership incentives that are needed for [the] profit center." [65]

The special problems of mergers

While mergers can yield both economies and diseconomies in the long run, the latter will almost invariably outweigh the former in the short run. The uncertainties resulting from a company's acquisition inevitably impair the ability of its managers to direct its affairs. A state of uneasiness begins to set in when rumors first circulate that the company might be acquired. By the time the acquisition actually takes place some of the best officials have probably left. Few are comforted by the routine notice contained in most acquisition announcements: "Present plans call for the new subsidiary to be operated under existing management. No personnel changes are contemplated."

Managers of acquired companies are only too well aware that aggressive conglomerates frequently dispose of at least part of what they have recently

---

[63] *Hearings on Economic Concentration*, Pt. 8, pp. 5253–67.
[64] It is interesting to note that this same conflict between short-run profits and long-run investments is the most serious problem confronting enterprises in Yugoslavia that are owned directly by their own workers (see, e.g., *Hearings on Economic Concentration*, Pt. 7, pp. 3758–84, testimony of Joel B. Dirlam; *ibid.*, Pt. 7A, pp. 4495–4506, Stevan Kuboleca, "Review of Movements in Yugoslav Economy Toward Decentralization").
[65] Emphasis added.

bought up. What looked so promising as an independent firm may turn sour when it is made into a division. Part or all of the acquired company may be found not to "fit into" the conglomerate's overall expansion plan. Or perhaps the conglomerate simply needs cash. In any event sell-offs of recently acquired properties have become an increasingly familiar part of the industrial scene.[66] In some cases what is sold off consists only of used plant and machinery: the cash and other liquid resources have been preempted; the employees have been let go; and the conglomerate is seeking to get whatever it can from what remains in the way of physical facilities. For the managers of a formerly independent company this is the end of the road. The process may be illustrated by Teledyne's acquisition in 1967 of Firth-Sterling, a producer of specialty steels and tungsten carbide cutting materials. Prior to its acquisition Firth-Sterling had been making remarkable progress. Its sales had mounted from $23 million in 1964 to what would have been over $30 million in 1968, while earnings had risen from 8 cents to an anticipated $1 per share in 1968. It had secured a market share of around 9 percent for tungsten carbide, 6 percent in high-temperature alloys, and 4 percent of the cutting-tool and die business. But after the acquisition its steel division, which made about half of its sales, was abolished. In all, 800 persons, or 50 percent of its employees, were displaced; these included the top executives, the sales force, the metallurgists, and middle management officials.[67]

Even without a subsequent sell-off an acquisition can be unsettling. Do the new owners plan to let the enterprise operate more or less as it has in the past or do they plan some sweeping new reorganization? What are the lines of communication to the central office? Among their new bosses, who has the real power? What products are they going to want pushed? How much freedom will the old management retain? How frequently, and on what issues, must they report to their new bosses? Indeed, will they be retained at all? Commenting on the disruptive effects of corporate takeover, a trade journal has observed: "What of the father with school age children forced to move on short notice to keep a job with a new parent company, the corner blocked suddenly by executives of the parent company; the job-losses created by the purchase of a competitor and the talented people crammed into odd little corners to preserve their income, if not their dignity?"[68] Uncertainties reach some sort of peak when the new heads know little or nothing about the business of the acquired company. After the acquisition by Norton Simon of a sizable portion of Crucible Steel's stock a new head was brought in to take over as president. Radical shifts in assignments were made with little or no notice. An "atmosphere of purge" was created; of the nine officers listed in Crucible's 1966 annual report only three remained 2 years later.[69]

Not only do conglomerate mergers fail to hold forth the promise of efficiency gains, which are at least theoretically attainable through horizontal or vertical mergers, but the mere fact that the product mix is disparate means that it tends to be noneconomic. Noting that the product lines of the typical conglomerate have been achieved "accidentally," Joel Dean observes, "Rarely do the diverse products and activities that result from opportunism actually sup-

[66] One publication, *Mergers & Acquisitions,* devotes several pages of fine print each quarter to simply listing sell-offs.
[67] *Metalworking News,* Dec. 20, 1968.
[68] *Ibid.* See I. Barmash, *Welcome to Our Conglomerate—You're Fired,* Delacorte, 1971.
[69] *Ibid.*

port one another (as is often claimed). Rarely do the product lines have significant managerial similarities that obviate the need for managerial specialization by industry and consequently produce *net* economization of management." [70] Plausible but unproved is the new doctrine of "free-form management," which holds that managerial ability, having achieved the status of a profession, is readily transferable across industry lines. The analogy ignores the high degree of specialization that has developed within most professions and the difficulty of applying to other fields ability and knowledge which are the product of years of experience in a particular specialty. The unimpressive profit showings of conglomerates constitute persuasive evidence that, except for certain specialized services, managerial skills are in fact not transferable.[71] In Dean's words, "Managerial efficiency is usually tied quite closely to the particular industry or setting in which the manager develops and operates. The reason is that a good manager's intuitions grow out of long experience with the special markets, competitive structure, and technology of a given industry."

To the extent that their product mix is noneconomic and managerial skills are nontransferable, the drive on the part of conglomerates for greater size will increase the opportunities for efficiency losses. Efforts to direct the affairs of more and more unrelated businesses by managers untrained and unskilled in the particular industries in which they must operate can lead only to a progressive decline in a company's efficiency. In economic terms the question is the shape of the managerial cost curve. As Dean puts it:

> At what size do the scale economies of central management of a diversified empire run out? Management is just another factor of production. Like other kinds of labor, managers find it efficient to specialize by function and by industry. Additional economies in the division of managerial labor within the firm provide an incentive to grow to the size that permits full use of an efficient managerial group. Beyond some point, the managerial cost curve turns upward, with the exhaustion of managerial economies of scale and the ever present rising costs of coordination. Larger firms exist but they owe their size to the continued pull of scale economies of some sort (or to lag in the market place correction of human error or to impregnable monopoly position). For every very large firm, that is not a sheltered monopoly, a plausible and important source of scale economies can be found that is entirely consistent with a rising managerial cost curve. . . . For most companies, justification for larger size must come from some scale advantage other than an alleged increase in the efficiency with which the enlarged company can use managerial resources.
>
> After it attains some size, which is far below Fortune's 500, the conglomerate experiences rising costs of coordination and control.

[70] Emphasis in original.
[71] See Ch. 8.

THE EVIDENCE OF MANAGERIAL ECONOMIES

How do the economies of multiplant operations balance out against the diseconomies? Are the gains in efficiency that can be realized by centralizing different plants under common ownership and control greater than the resultant efficiency losses, or does the reverse tend to be true?

This question can be examined through the use of a number of types of empirical information. Unhappily, the best data for the purpose of measuring the amount of resources required to produce a given output, unit costs, are fragmentary and out of date. Because they are usually regarded by producers as "trade secrets" and are seldom made available for any purpose, unit-cost data are conspicuous by their rarity. The most recent studies relating size to unit costs are based on reports filed during World War II with government agencies and are thus a quarter of a century old. Yet it may be of passing interest to note that in none of the 3 industries for which such data are available—bread, rubber tires, and fertilizer—were the largest companies, all with extensive multiplant operations, the lowest-cost group of producers.

In a study of bread-baking plants the lowest unit costs were recorded by 10 medium-size regional producers. They were followed by the nation's 4 largest bakers and then by other groups 'in descending order of size.[1] Similarly, in a comparison between the 4 largest tire manufacturers and 10 smaller producers, the latter recorded lower total unit costs.[2] The smaller companies had the advantage in the indirect items, particularly in selling, general, and administrative expenses. As was also the case in the bread industry, the largest firms had lower labor and materials costs, the latter possibly resulting not only from superior efficiency in purchasing but from monopsonistic buying power. In mixed fertilizers, which involves a relatively simple production process of combining active fertilizer ingredients with inert materials, the lowest costs were found in the second smallest size group. And in the production of bulk superphosphate, which involves a much larger scale of operations, the lowest costs were found not in the largest but in the second largest group of companies.

Another type of empirical evidence consists of "engineering estimates" of optimal size. In addition to comparing existing concentration with the concentration that would be required by the optimal plant, Joe S. Bain examined the importance of multiplant economies in 12 industries for which such information could be obtained. In 6 of these, multiplant economies appeared to

[1] 79th Cong., 2nd Sess., H. Doc. 535, Federal Trade Commission, *Report on the Wholesale Baking Industry,* 1946, Pt. 11.

[2] Office of Temporary Controls, Office of Price Administration (Economic Data Analysis Branch), *Survey of Rubber Tire & Tube Manufacturers,* OPA Economic Data Series, 1947, No. 10.

be simply nonexistent. In 4 of the remaining 6, multiplant economies were "small" or "slight," ranging up to only 3 percent of total costs. In only 2 of 12 industries, shoes and steel, did the upper limit of the range exceed 3 percent —and then only slightly (2 to 4 percent in the former and 2 to 5 percent in the latter). Speaking of all the industries in his study, Bain concluded: "In the sample as a whole the existing degree of concentration by multiplant firms lacks a clear cost justification in perhaps 13 of 21 cases, although in seven of these we have a simple lack of any definite estimates. In two more cases the multiplant phenomenon is not very important." [3] Although the data are in the nature of estimates that are over 20 years old, they also, like the available cost studies, suggest that multiplant economies are not of overriding importance.

The question may also be examined in a number of other ways that permit the use of more recent information covering a wider range of industries. For one thing, attention can be directed toward the relationship of size to profitability. If multiplant operations do, on balance, contribute to efficiency, it would follow, *ceteris paribus,* that multiplant firms would have higher profit rates than their single-plant competitors and, correlatively, that the very large firms operating many plants would be more profitable than those of smaller size operating only one or a few plants. A second approach is to make comparative examinations of the profit performance of actively merging companies, which, by the very process of merger, are extending their multiplant operations. A company's efficiency is also reflected by its responsiveness to a substantial increase in the industry's output resulting from an expansion in demand, new technologies, and so on; if the large, multiplant firms are more responsive than their smaller competitors, sharp increases in output should be accompanied by increases in concentration.

Size and profitability

The usefulness of profitability comparisons in evaluating efficiency is heightened by an inherent bias operating against the appearance of higher profit rates in smaller companies. Higher profit rates may be the result not merely of greater efficiency but of monopoly power. The greater the monopoly power, the greater the resources with which a firm can differentiate its product from those of competitors, mount lavish advertising, promotional, and selling campaigns, make annual model changes, and indulge in other forms of nonprice competition, all of which should tend to enhance its share of the market and thus yield above-average prices and profits. If one assumes that their plants are at least as efficient as those of their lesser rivals, any failure on the part of the largest multiplant firms, which tend to have the greatest monopoly power, to earn the highest profit rates must therefore reflect adversely on the efficiency of multiplant operations.

However, even apart from possible misstatements or distortions in the published profit figures themselves, there are difficulties in using profit data to analyze the relationship of size to efficiency. But these effects can be minimized by limiting the analysis in a number of specific ways. One problem is the fact

[3] Joe S. Bain, "Economies of Scale, Concentration, and the Condition of Entry in Twenty Manufacturing Industries," *American Economic Review,* March, 1954, p. 35.

that profit rates are available only on a "consolidated" basis—i.e., for the corporation as a whole. There would, of course, be little difficulty in classifying the various corporations according to the SIC 2-digit major industry groups (e.g., food and kindred products). But these categories are so broadly defined, encompassing so many different industries producing unrelated and nonsubstitutable products, as to make their use for this purpose almost meaningless. The categories that come closest to representing a generally acceptable compromise between the breadth of the industry definition on the one hand and the diversity of the company's products on the other are the 3-digit industry groups (e.g., meat products, dairy products). Even so, companies classified in one industry group will not infrequently derive profits from operations in other industry groups. This problem can at least be held within tolerable limits simply by excluding from the analysis those industry groups in which the leading producers are engaged most extensively and conspicuously in other industry groups.

A second problem is that in tabulations ranging from the smallest to the largest size of companies, profit rates for the former tend to be understated, since the entrepreneurs of very small concerns frequently take a substantial part of their real profits in the form of salaries. In the absence of adjustment, statistical tabulations tend to show lower profit rates in the smallest size classes; but when adjustment is made, the showings can be just the opposite.[4] Inasmuch as the adjustment is necessarily arbitrary, the conclusion thus becomes simply a function of the nature of the adjustment. Again, the problem can partly be met by limiting the analysis—in this case by excluding the distinctly small concerns.

Finally, exception can be taken to measuring profitability in terms of investment on the grounds that plant and equipment built in earlier years when the price level was lower are undervalued relative to newer plant and equipment. The objection loses much of its force, however, in view of the fact that a very large proportion of our present industrial plant is of fairly recent vintage. Moreover, the higher cost of current facilities is offset to a large degree by their greater productivity. Hence, the incomparability in the cost of facilities resulting from a rising price level should not make investment unusable as a basis for measuring profitability.

What follows is based on a report issued annually by the Federal Trade Commission, *Rates of Return for Selected Manufacturing Industries,* which shows the profit rate, after taxes, as a percentage of net worth for individual medium-size and large manufacturing firms classified by 3-digit industry groups. For the most part the companies are large enough to be "listed" with the Securities and Exchange Commission, and in all cases their financial statements are published in the standard financial manuals. The report itself thus excludes the distinctly small companies in which earnings may be camouflaged as salaries, and an effort has been made in this analysis to exclude as well those industry groups whose leading producers appear to derive a substantial share of their income from other fields.

Inasmuch as the report appears annually, a selection had to be made of the year to be studied. Obviously, other factors being equal, the more recent the

[4] In an important study, J. L. McConnell showed that when compensation of officers is included in profits, profit rates tend to decline with increasing size of corporations. McConnell endeavored to make a proper allocation of officers' compensation between profits and the "market value" of the officers' services (Department of Commerce, *Survey of Current Business,* May, 1945).

year the better, but other factors have not remained the same. In recent years many large corporations that had long followed conservative accounting principles tending to understate income changed their methods in such a way as to show considerably higher earnings.[5] Since these changes, if adopted at all, were made at different times by different companies, they could be a source of serious distortion in interfirm profit comparisons. A defensive maneuver against conglomerate takeovers, such changes were particularly noticeable during the late 1960's. Among the more recent years for which the FTC report has been issued, 1966—a year of relatively high economic activity—would appear to be less affected by the practices than later years.

Scatter diagrams were prepared for each of 30 industries, with the size of each of the companies (in terms of total assets) being expressed as a percentage of the size of the industry's largest company; the profit rate is the rate of return on stockholders' investment after taxes.[6] On the basis of free-hand regression lines drawn on these scatters, the industries were classified according to the relationship existing between profit rate and company size (see Figure 8-1).

In 6 of the 30 industries increasing size was accompanied by increasing profitability. A clearly discernible direct relationship was evident in the motor vehicle industry. At one extreme was General Motors, with a profit rate of 21 percent; at the other extreme were American Motors and Checker (with less than 5 percent and one percent respectively of GM's assets), both operating at a loss. The leading automobile manufacturer is generally regarded as a highly efficient operator in all phases of the industry. It also possesses substantial monopoly power, stemming from its ability to exploit its differentiated products through expensive model changes and advertising, its control of a vast distribution organization, the tendency for trade-in values to be highest for the company with the greatest volume of sales, and the securing of monopoly profits from other fields, notably automobile finance.[7]

In the business machines industry the overwhelming predominance of the largest producer, which is eight times the size of the second largest firm, makes it difficult to discern any systematic relationship between size and profitability. At one end of the scale is International Business Machines; at the other are all other producers. Nonetheless, although the profit rates of the latter varied widely in 1966, they are, with one exception, below IBM's. Like those of General Motors, IBM's superior profit showings stemmed not only from its efficiency but from its monopolistic position in the market (computers, punch cards and tabulating machines, electric typewriters, and other types of business machines).

In malt liquors the superior profit performance of the industry's largest and third largest firms (Anheuser-Busch and Pabst Brewing) was probably the result of both superior efficiency and monopoly power. Efficiency has been improved by rationalization as older breweries have been shut down and by savings

---

[5] Many large companies changed the method of determining depreciation for accounting purposes from an accelerated to a straight-line basis. Another change involved the investment credit; companies that had formerly deferred the credit and amortized it over the lives of the properties acquired changed to flowing the full investment credit to income as realized. In the case of U.S. Steel the effect of these two changes was to increase reported income for the year 1968 by $94.0 million, or $1.74 (out of $4.69) per share of common stock (see *Hearings on Economic Concentration*, Pt. 8A, p. 132).

[6] The FTC follows the procedure of using as the figure for stockholders' investment (or net worth) for a given year the average of the figures at the beginning and end of the year.

[7] See *Administered Prices: Report on Automobiles.*

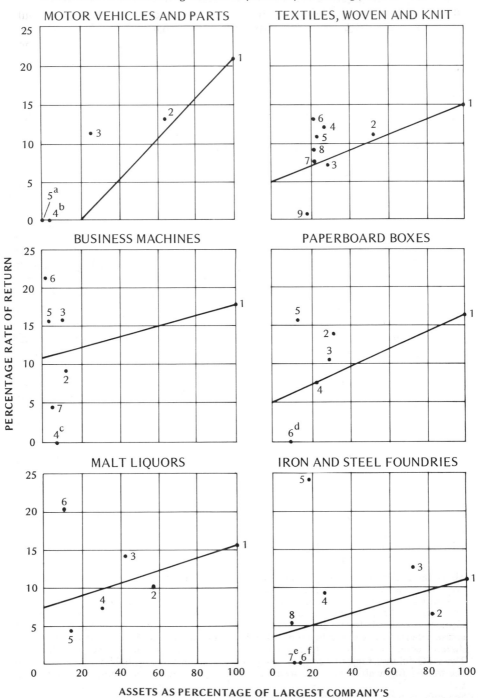

Figure 8-1

RELATIONSHIP OF RATE OF RETURN
TO ASSET SIZE OF LEADING CORPORATIONS

6 industries with increasing size accompanied by increasing profitability, 1966

MOTOR VEHICLES AND PARTS

TEXTILES, WOVEN AND KNIT

BUSINESS MACHINES

PAPERBOARD BOXES

MALT LIQUORS

IRON AND STEEL FOUNDRIES

PERCENTAGE RATE OF RETURN

ASSETS AS PERCENTAGE OF LARGEST COMPANY'S

[a]−4.1. [b]−5.9. [c]−2.0. [d]−9.0. [e]−.7. [f]−2.9.

Source: Computed from Federal Trade Commission, *Rates of Return for Selected Manufacturing Industries*, 1966

in transportation costs as new breweries have been located near consuming centers. At the same time the leaders have sought to improve their market shares by buying up numerous regional and local concerns and by greatly intensifying their efforts to promote their differentiated products, particularly through TV advertising.

The largest producer of textiles (Burlington) was also the most profitable. Although it has expanded vertically into a number of consumer goods industries (e.g., hosiery) in which it is able to differentiate its product, the bulk of Burlington's output is in unfinished and semifinished products, where it encounters vigorous competition from many rivals. In paperboard boxes the superior profit position of the industry's leader, the Container Corporation, appears to be due in good part to greater efficiency in view of the industry's low level of concentration and its many sellers. This would also seem to be the case in iron and steel foundries, whose products are sold almost exclusively to other manufacturers. The 2 most profitable firms are the largest producers, Abex (formerly American Brake Shoe) and the third largest firm, U.S. Pipe & Foundry.

In contrast to the 6 industries in which profitability clearly tended to rise with increasing size, there were 8 in which the reverse was true (see Figure 8-2). Since it hardly can be contended that the largest firms possess less monopoly power than their smaller rivals, the only possible explanation for their poorer profit performance is poorer efficiency.

Four of these industries are producers of important basic materials—steel, nonferrous metals, aluminum, and pulp and paper. The first 3 constitute the industrial underpinnings of any metal-based economy. The leading firms have been dominant in their industries for over a half-century and, as such, have long enjoyed all the perquisites of power. If superior ability could be attracted by immense wealth, they should have obtained it. If they were not among the first to experiment with new technologies and new managerial methods, it could not be for want of resources. Moreover, their share of the industry was such as to give them a very substantial degree of monopoly power. In the late 1950's U.S. Steel had the largest capacity for 22 of 33 steel products, in 13 of which its share of the industry's capacity was not only over 33 percent but at least 10 percentage points above its nearest rival.[8] Until the late 1940's the Aluminum Company of America enjoyed a virtual monopoly in its industry. In nonferrous metals the industry's largest producer, Anaconda, long held over one-third the refining capacity for copper and over two-thirds that of zinc. Their dominance over other leading producers in their respective industries is evident from Figure 8-2. In steel the second largest producer, Bethlehem, is less than half and the third largest, Republic, is less than a quarter the size of U.S. Steel. In nonferrous metals the second, third, and fourth largest firms, American Metal Climax, Phelps Dodge, and American Smelting & Refining, are each only two-fifths the size of Anaconda. Yet with all their advantages Alcoa and Anaconda were in 1966 the least profitable of the companies in their industries, while U.S. Steel was able to outperform only chronically depressed Wheeling.

In the pulp, paper, and paperboard industry the leader, International Paper, fared somewhat better, but there is still a downward slope of the regression line. It, too, has been the industry's leader for over a half-century.

Among the 4 additional industries exhibiting an inverse relationship between size and profitability were 2 in the food group, in both of which the largest firms

[8] *Administered Prices: Report on Steel,* p. 71.

Figure 8-2

RELATIONSHIP OF RATE OF RETURN TO ASSET SIZE OF LEADING CORPORATIONS

8 industries with increasing size accompanied by decreasing profitability, 1966

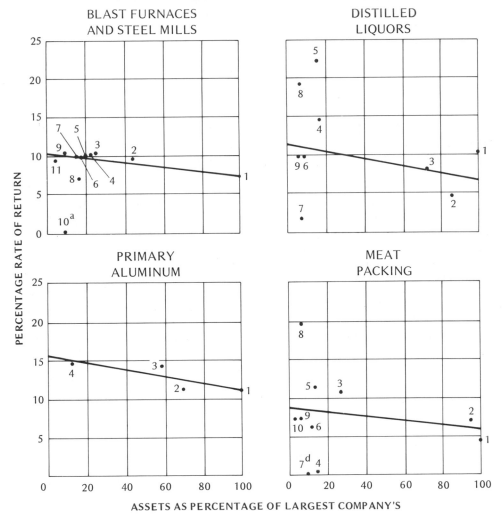

ASSETS AS PERCENTAGE OF LARGEST COMPANY'S

have long been the industry leaders. The 3 largest makers of distilled liquors—National Distillers, Seagram, and Schenley—have dominated their industry since the repeal of Prohibition. Possessing a majority of the leading name brands, they have promoted their use vigorously through expensive advertising and promotional programs. Although there is little difference in size among the Big Three, they are in a class by themselves when compared to the rest of the industry; the fourth largest firm, Brown Forman, has less than one-fifth the assets of National Distillers. But in terms of profitability the performance of the Big Three is easily surpassed not only by Brown Forman but by 2 even smaller concerns.

Meat packing is an industry dominated by a Big Two, Swift and Armour,

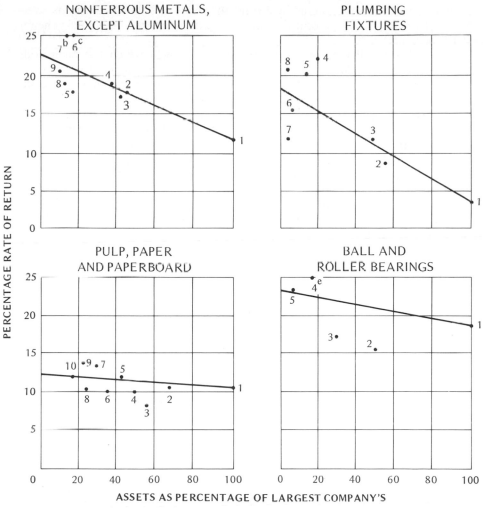

NONFERROUS METALS, EXCEPT ALUMINUM

PLUMBING FIXTURES

PULP, PAPER AND PAPERBOARD

BALL AND ROLLER BEARINGS

PERCENTAGE RATE OF RETURN

ASSETS AS PERCENTAGE OF LARGEST COMPANY'S

[a]−7.5.   [b]30.6.   [c]25.4.   [d]−26.0   [e]28.6.

Source: Computed from Federal Trade Commission, *Rates of Return for Selected Manufacturing Industries*, 1966

which achieved their ascendency shortly after the turn of the century, largely as a result of the application of mass-production methods to meat processing and the development of artificial refrigeration. Again, little difference in size exists between the leaders, but they far transcend the other producers; the third largest firm, Wilson, is only slightly more than one-fourth the size of Swift. But in terms of profitability the leaders were far surpassed not only by Wilson but by firms ranked fifth (Oscar Mayer) and eighth (Iowa Beef Packers).

One of the clearest inverse relationships between size and profitability is exhibited by the plumbing fixtures industry. With a long history as the industry's leader, American Radiator & Standard Sanitary is nearly twice the size of the second largest firm. It also recorded by far the lowest profit rate of any of the 8 principal producers. Not only was its rate of return, 3.5 percent, less than half that of the 2 next largest firms (Crane and Grinnell), but it was far surpassed by profit rates registered by 3 firms that were less than one-fifth its size—Parker Hannifin (22.3 percent), Walworth (20.6 percent), and Luckenheimer (21.9 percent).

The ball and roller bearing industry is another field which has been dominated for many decades by one company. Before World War II, Timken Roller Bearing was responsible for 80 percent of the production of tapered bearings alone; the second largest firm, Federal-Mogul Corporation, is only half its size. Perhaps reflecting the highly concentrated nature of the industry, profit rates tend to be relatively high. With a rate of return of 18.6 percent, Timken outperformed the second and third largest companies. However, it was surpassed by Hoover Ball and Bearing and by Borden; the former, only one-sixth the size of Timken, showed a rate of return of 28.6 percent and the latter, less than one-tenth its size, a rate of 23.6 percent.

There remain 16 industries in which no clear relationship, either direct or inverse, between size and profitability was discernible. In most cases the absence of a relationship stemmed from widespread variations in the profit rates of the smaller companies, particularly those less than one-fifth the size of the industry leader.

A similar analysis, using the same source and including the same number of industries, had been made for an earlier period, the only difference being that the profit rates were the average for the 5 years 1959–63.[9] As can be seen below, the results were generally similar to the findings for the year 1966:

Relationship	Number of Industry Groups	
	1959–63	1966
Direct	7	6
Inverse	8	8
None	15	16
Total	30	30

Of the 6 industries with a direct relationship in 1966, 4 displayed a similar relationship in 1959–63; these were motor vehicles, business machines, textiles, and paperboard boxes.[10] Similarly, of the 8 industries with an inverse relationship in 1966, 4 had evidenced the same type of relationship in the earlier period; these were blast furnaces and steel mills, pulp and paper, distilled liquors, and meat products.[11]

To summarize: in less than a quarter of the 30 industries studied was increasing size accompanied by rising profit rates; in about half of these industries the higher profit rates of the leaders were due at least in part to substantial monopoly power. In the other three-quarters either the tendency was in the opposite direction or there appeared to be no relationship whatever. In nearly all 30 industries, the leading firms are extensively engaged in multiplant operations. If it is assumed that their individual plants are no less efficient than those of the smaller companies shown, the logical conclusion must be that the dis-

[9] *Hearings on Economic Concentration,* Pt. 4, pp. 1551–54.
[10] The 3 other industries that displayed a direct relationship in 1959–63 (but not in 1966) were candy and confectionary products, machine tools, and shipbuilding.
[11] The 4 other industries that displayed an inverse relationship in 1959–63 (but not in 1966) were sugar, malt liquors, textile machinery, and aircraft.

economies of multiplant operations either outweigh or at least offset the economies. If the plants of the leading firms are, in themselves, less efficient than those of their competitors, the explanation for their failure to show a better profit performance is technological backwardness. In either event their profit showings suggest that in only a minority of industries is great size a contributor to efficiency.

Mergers and profitability

In addition to comparing the profitability of companies of different size, it is possible to shed light on the efficiency of multiplant operations by examining the performance of actively merging companies. How does their profitability compare with the profitability of nonmerging companies, or with that of the industry of which they are a part, or with the profitability of their component enterprises before consolidation? Since mergers result in an addition to the number of facilities operated under common ownership, showings of improved profitability associated with mergers would constitute indirect evidence of the efficiency of multiplant operations, and vice versa.

The first statistical analysis of the profitability of mergers was made in 1922 by Arthur S. Dewing, who compared the earnings of 35 consolidations with the previous earnings of the constituent firms making up the consolidation.[12] Dewing limited himself for the most part to combinations that had been organized before 1903, had been in existence for at least 10 years before 1914, were formed as a combination of at least 5 separate and independent competing plants, and had a national rather than a mere sectional or local significance. In 20 of the 35 cases the 10-year period began in 1900 and therefore, in Dewing's words, included "quite as many years of marked business activity as of marked business depression." [13] Briefly, Dewing found that the aggregate earnings of the separate competing establishments prior to consolidation were nearly one-fifth greater than their average for the 10 years following the consolidation. In 22 of the 35 cases, the earnings prior to the consolidation were greater than the average for the forthcoming years: "In brief, the earnings of the separate plants before consolidation were greater than the earnings of the same plants after consolidation." [14]

The profitability of mergers has again become a subject of interest. Although based on better data and more sophisticated techniques than were available a half century ago, newer studies leave Dewing's essential conclusions unchanged: mergers appear to be a singularly poor way of achieving greater efficiency.

In a cross-sectional study Samuel Richardson Reid analyzed the growth and profit performance of 478 of the 500 largest industrial corporations, classified

---

[12] Arthur S. Dewing, "A Statistical Test of the Success of Consolidations," *Quarterly Journal of Economics*, Nov., 1921, pp. 84–101. As a general rule, attempts to determine the relationship between size and efficiency by measuring the profitability of different sizes of companies do not yield meaningful results, since higher profitability may be the result not merely of greater efficiency but of the possession of monopoly power. Dewing, however, avoided this problem by comparing the profit rates of the same enterprises before and after consolidation. Since the extent of profitability owing to monopoly power was obviously greater after consolidation, the study had, if anything, a bias against the pre-consolidation, independent companies.
[13] *Ibid.*
[14] *Ibid.*

according to their merger intensity.[15] The measure of merger intensity was the number of firms acquired during the period 1951–61. The companies were classified into four groups: "pure internal growth" firms (those with no reported mergers during the period), "occasional acquirers" (one to 5 mergers), "moderate acquirers" (6 to 10), and "active acquirers" (11 or more). Not surprisingly, Reid found that companies which have grown by external as well as internal expansion have expanded more rapidly than those which have grown by internal expansion alone: "The more actively firms have merged during the period, the larger their relative increases in sales, assets and number of employees tend to be." [16]

Profitability was examined by measuring the increase in earnings for the original stockholders; the equivalent of the number of shares outstanding in 1951 was multiplied by the increase in earnings per share (adjusted for stock splits and stock dividends). The increase in share earnings was related, or "scaled," to the size of company by assets in one test and by sales in another. On the basis of these tests, Reid found that as the merger intensity of the companies increased, there was a tendency for the relative increase in "profits attributable to the original stockholders to be smaller." [17] His findings led Reid to conclude that there is not merely a "divorce" between ownership and control, as postulated by Adolf A. Berle and Gardiner C. Means many years ago, but an actual conflict: "Managers' personal and group goals of security, power, prestige, increased personal income and advancement within the firm may well be identified more with firm growth . . . than with classical profit maximization." [18] As Reid notes, it is size, not profitability, that has been found in several studies to be correlated directly with executive compensation.

Reid's study does have one serious weakness—the use of the *number* of acquired companies as a proxy for their importance. It is true that for this broad, cross-sectional type of analysis, numbers were the only available measure. And it is also true that for some purposes, such as the determination of trend, numbers based on a consistent source can be a useful measure. But even casual inspection of Reid's source[19] reveals frequent and extensive differences in the size of the acquired firms. Were it possible to classify the 3,300 acquired firms according to their size, the grouping of many of the acquiring companies would undoubtedly be changed.

To a considerable extent this problem can be by-passed by focusing attention on the extremes—companies with no recorded mergers and those with 11 or more. The probabilities are that the contribution of mergers to growth is significantly greater for a company which made as many as 11 acquisitions than for a firm which made none. There is in fact a sharp difference in the showings between the "pure internal growth" firms and the "active acquirers." The growth in earnings for the original stockholders, whether related to assets or sales, was

[15] Samuel Richardson Reid, *Mergers, Managers and the Economy*, McGraw-Hill, 1968. See also *Hearings on Economic Concentration*, Pt. 5, pp. 1914–39; *ibid.*, Pt. 8, pp. 4603–17. The statistical data were originally derived from a study, "Mergers for Whom—Managers or Stockholders?" made at Carnegie Institute of Technology by John Bossons, Kalman J. Cohen, and Samuel Richardson Reid.
[16] *Ibid.*, p. 156.
[17] *Ibid.*
[18] *Ibid.*, pp. 133–34.
[19] 87th Cong., 2nd Sess., House Select Committee on Small Business, Report: *Mergers and Superconcentration, Acquisitions of 500 Largest Industrial and 50 Largest Merchandising Firms*, 1962.

more than six times greater for companies relying exclusively on internal expansion than for the "active acquirers."

Reid also endeavored to ascertain whether this relationship obtained within broad industry groups. His conclusions, which he regards as only "slightly less favorable to the underlying hypothesis," are that:

> In seventeen of the total of twenty combinations of stockholders' interest variable and industry for which mergers mattered, the effects of merger activity were in the negative direction, as hypothesized. The only exceptions are (1) mergers fail to be negatively associated with profits for original stockholders scaled by assets for both the electrical equipment and the miscellaneous industries, and (2) mergers fail to be negatively associated with profits for original stockholders scaled by sales for the electrical equipment industry.[20]

With comparison again limited to the extremes, the "pure internal growth" firms outperformed the "active acquirers" in 4 groups—food, chemicals, machinery, and transportation equipment. The reverse was clearly true of only 2 —paper and printing and miscellaneous products. The apparent superiority of the actively acquiring firms in petroleum is undoubtedly traceable to the highly profitable operations of the major oil companies in the Middle East. And a similar showing in electrical machinery unquestionably reflects the high earnings of the leading manufacturers, which at the time were enjoying the fruits of their celebrated price-fixing conspiracies. In the remaining groups there were no firms or only one firm in either the "pure internal growth" or "active acquirer" groups.

What are the reasons for the generally superior earning performances of the nonmerging companies? Reid suggests three possibilities. A rapid expansion resulting from the acquisitions of sizable enterprises "may be less profitable than a step-by-step expansion that is subject to repetitive reexamination of the costs and benefits for each additional increment of growth." [21] Moreover, substantial premiums over the market value of the acquired firm are often paid; according to one survey acquiring companies paid an average of 113 percent of the price-earnings ratio at which the acquired firms' shares were selling just before the merger announcement. Contributing further to the cost of acquisition is the practice (which, as Reid notes, "is seldom given adequate attention") of giving side payments to the managements of the acquired firms: "There is a growing body of evidence supporting the fact that the managers of acquired firms receive payoffs or side payments in return for permitting the firms they are managing to be acquired." [22]

In a later study Reid compared the profit performance in 1968 of various groups of conglomerates (i.e., those cited in *Forbes, Fortune,* and elsewhere) with the performance of companies that had grown only by internal expansion. Specifically, he compared the percentages of firms of each type that were above their industry medians in terms of several measures of profitability. Summarizing his results he states: "Perhaps the most striking finding was the superior performance of the firms following a pure 'internal-growth' strategy, a result that suggests investments in new plant and equipment add specially significant productivity advantages and that firms aggressively using this method of growth can benefit not only the economy but their stockholders as well." [23]

[20] *Hearings on Economic Concentration,* Pt. 5, p. 1924.
[21] *Ibid.*
[22] Reid, *op. cit.,* p. 165.
[23] Samuel Richardson Reid, "A Reply to 'Tests of the Efficiency Performance of Conglomerate Firms,' " article to be published.

Just as Reid studied the relationship of profitability to frequency of mergers among the 500 largest industrial corporations, Donald F. Eslick examined, for the same group, the relationship of profitability to degree of diversification.[24] Whether measured in terms of numbers or assets, most of the merger activity of the last decade has brought together companies in different industries. Accordingly, the logical expectation would be that if profitability is related inversely to merger activity, it would also be related inversely to diversification. Had Eslick found that profitability rises with increasing diversification, it could be inferred that diversification enhances "the possibility of achieving economies of scale in research, production, administration or marketing." Increasing profitability would be indicative "of a significant difference in efficiency due, in most instances, to the integration of the common activities of the various products produced by each diversified firm." The converse would point to "managerial diseconomies of scale," suggesting "(1) the increased difficulty of simultaneously managing products whose technologies, production methods and markets differ widely, and (2) the reduced likelihood of integrating many of the activities required to produce and distribute the firm's products when those products are quite dissimilar."

The measures of profitability used were the average rates of return on stockholders' equity (net worth) for two periods, 1956–65 and 1959–61, as well as the rate of change in earnings per share during 1955–65. Two measures of diversification were employed: (a) the number of SIC products that the firm produced and sold in 1960 as indicated by *Fortune's* "Plant and Product Directory" and (b) the *ratio* of the number of industries (4-digit) *outside* the company's primary industry group (2-digit) to the number of industries *within* its primary industry group. The basis of the former consisted of differences in a firm's operations sufficient to place them in different Census industries. The latter took into account a firm's participation in industries outside the major industry group in which it is primarily engaged.

Regardless of which measure of profitability was used the results were the same: "the average profitability of large industrial firms becomes lower the more diversified the firm. . . . In summary, the overall results indicated a tendency for more diversified firms to be less profitable than more specialized firms." [25] The findings are illustrated in the following table, which is based on the average rate of return for 1959–61.[26]

Number of Industries in which the Firm Is Engaged	Average Rate of Return, 1959–61
1	10.9%
10	9.6
20	8.8
30	8.4
40	8.2

[24] *Hearings on Economic Concentration,* Pt. 8, pp. 4702–11, testimony of Donald F. Eslick.
[25] This conclusion was based on the results of seven equations, three using the 1959–61 average return on equity, three using the 1956–65 average return, and one using the 1955–65 rate of change in earnings per share.
[26] The number of firms engaged in more than 40 industries (8) was considered too small a sample to yield reliable results.

While the profit rate continues to decline throughout the range of observations, the decrease becomes quite gradual after a point of 20 industries is reached: "the rate of profit decline diminishes as the level of firm diversification rises." In fact, nearly all of the decline takes place between the single-line firms and those engaged in 20 industries. In this respect, as well as in the finding of a general decrease, Eslick's conclusions are in harmony with Reid's findings. Among firms of sufficient size to be among the 500 largest, it is the firm that is engaged in only one industry and makes no acquisitions which displays superior earnings as compared to firms that are either moderately or extensively diversified or are moderate or active acquirers.

Eslick made similar comparisons for 7 industry groups, also using firms among the 500 largest.[27] Again, it was found that increasing diversification was associated with declining profitability. Among the 7 groups the one exception was petroleum, in which, as has been noted, the after-tax profitability of foreign oil production is undoubtedly more than sufficient to offset any diseconomies associated with diversification. On the basis of this analysis of major industry groups Eslick concluded, "No matter which of these preferred measures is utilized, the strong impression is created that the level of firm profitability is adversely affected by high levels of product diversification in all industry groups except petroleum." [28]

By studying the ratio of the number of industries in which a company is engaged to the number outside the firm's primary industry group, Eslick also found that "most highly diversified firms typically have products which are spread throughout the industry groups. It is positive evidence that the number of firms with large numbers of closely related products is less significant than might commonly be supposed." [29] Thus, only a very few of the multi-industry firms enjoy the economies of scale that arise by virtue of the fact that their products "are related to one another through having a common technology, similar or identical production methods, a common material and/or similar or identical markets. . . ." [30]

In a study of 43 "actively acquiring" corporations, Thomas F. Hogarty addressed himself to two questions: (a) Do active acquirers have a better performance record than their respective industries? And (b) has the combined firm resulting from a merger been more profitable than the component firms would have been, in the aggregate, had no merger occurred? [31] To have been included in his sample a firm must have experienced at least a 20-percent growth in sales and assets due to the merger and completed most of its acquisitions by 1962. An additional standard was that the sample not be concentrated in a few industries. The companies selected ranged in size from $7 million to $700 mil-

---

[27] Food and kindred products, chemical and allied products, petroleum refining and related industries, primary metals, nonelectrical machinery, electrical machinery, and transportation equipment.

[28] A total of 63 equations were employed for the 7 industry groups, consisting for each group of the 3 profitability measures and 3 equations: "Of the 63 diversification coefficients, 49 were negative." Of the 14 positive coefficients, 8 were based on the rate of change in earnings per share, "the most poorly specified of the three that were used." Only 6 of the 14 involved the use of the rate of return measures. And all 6 were in the petroleum group.

[29] Hearings on Economic Concentration, Pt. 8, p. 5012.

[30] Ibid., p. 5004.

[31] Ibid., pp. 4647–53, testimony of Thomas F. Hogarty.

lion in assets and were distributed among 29 3-digit industry groups. Moreover, two-thirds of the companies had a pre-merger growth in sales, exclusive of merger, that was at least as rapid as the general growth in sales of their respective industry groups, while fewer than one-sixth had experienced losses in any of the 5 years preceding merger. The last considerations are particularly important since Hogarty was comparing the performance of each of the 43 against that of their respective industry groups.

To answer the first question he calculated for each of his 43 firms an "investment performance index" representing the value of capital gains and cash dividends received. This was then compared to a similar index for the industry group of which the company was a part: "If mergers had a neutral impact on investment performance, then one would expect to find that approximately one-half of the firms in the sample had index values greater than that for their respective industries." But only 14 of the 43, or fewer than one-third of the active acquirers, had an investment performance superior to that of their respective industry groups: "Clearly, active acquirers are less profitable than ordinary firms, at least in the long run. This result implies that stockholders do not generally benefit from active acquisition programs; in fact, relative to similar opportunities, they lose on the average."

To answer the second question it was necessary to compare the profits of the combined firm, after merger, with some measure of what the profits of the component firms would have been had the merger not taken place. As his basis for predicting what these profits would have been Hogarty used the net income before taxes for the various 3-digit industry groups, as shown in the Internal Revenue Service's *Sourcebook for Statistics of Income.* The assumption in this comparison was that "if *predicted* profits exceeded *actual* profits, then the merger (series of acquisitions) was unsuccessful."

The results were about evenly distributed; in 20 of the 43 firms the predicted profits exceeded the actual profits. But this showing is more adverse to mergers than would be indicated by the figures alone. The net income for the various industry groups includes, of course, returns from companies that were losing money or making minimal profits, whereas, before merger, the 43 companies were "healthy, growing and profitable." They had thus a better than average chance in their merger programs of achieving economies of scale through "synergy"—making the whole greater than the sum of its parts. But on the basis of his findings Hogarty states that "it seems fair to conclude that synergy through merger is beyond the reach of the ordinary industrial firm."

Hogarty also addressed himself to the question of whether success in achieving economies through merger is predictable. The argument has been advanced that a "tradeoff" must be made between increased efficiency and a lessening of competition, assuming a given merger is likely to produce both.[32] To be made operational, any policy regarding such a tradeoff requires that the antitrust agencies be able to forecast not only whether a given merger will yield economies but whether such economies will be sufficient to offset the cost of a lessening of competition. Hogarty's method consisted of comparing, for 26 of his companies, the premium paid to the stockholders of the acquired firm with his measures of merger success:[33] "Thus, one might expect a tendency for acquisitions effected

[32] See Oliver E. Williamson, "Economies as an Antitrust Defense: The Welfare Tradeoffs," *American Economic Review,* March, 1968.

[33] The premium consisted of the ratio of the consideration paid to the owner of the ac-

Table 8-1

MERGING vs. NONMERGING COMPANIES:
PERCENTAGE OF SUCCESSES

Companies	Stock Price	Price-Earnings Ratio	Capital Turnover	Profit Margin
Basic data				
Merging companies	50%	60%	67%	43%
Nonmerging companies	50	40	33	57
Differential of 10% or more				
Merging companies	47	62	75	40
Nonmerging companies	53	38	25	60

Source: Eamon Kelly, *The Profitability of Growth Through Mergers,* Center for Research of the College of Business Administration, Pennsylvania State University, 1967, p. 50

at higher than average premiums to also demonstrate a higher than average incidence of success. In brief, acquisitions made at 'premium prices' should produce synergy." He found, however, that the correlation between merger success and premiums paid was close to zero: "Accordingly, it would appear that even those most intimately associated with the given merger are unable to predict the amount of synergy which will result."

Focusing his attention on specific companies Eamon Kelly sought to determine whether firms which have pursued an active policy of securing growth by merger have had a better profit performance than companies with roughly comparable product lines whose growth has been largely through internal expansion.[34] He defined a merging company as one with an increase of at least 20 percent in sales as a result of merger activity; the upper limit for nonmerging companies was 5 percent. On the basis of an extensive examination of several hundred firms, he selected 40 companies comprising 20 pairs with roughly comparable product lines distributed in 18 industries. Within the overall time span between the end of World War II and 1960, calculations were made for 5-year averages before and after merger activity on the part of the merging members; the measures used were changes in (a) market price, (b) the price-earnings ratio, (c) capital turnover (net sales per common share), (d) cash earnings per common share, and (e) the profit margin (operating income before depreciation as percentage of net sales). Kelly's results are summarized in Table 8-1.

Of the measures Kelly employed, only the profit margin provides an indication of efficiency. Capital turnover, while contributing to a firm's profits, is not a measure of profitability but a function of growth. It should hardly occasion any surprise to learn that companies which have grown by both internal and external expansion have shown a greater increase in net sales per common share than those that have grown only by internal expansion. Changes in stock prices and in price-earnings ratios suffer from a different drawback: they are influenced strongly by a subjective consideration—the evaluations of investors, which in the case of conglomerates have been subject in recent years to tremendous fluc-

quired firms relative to the pre-merger market value of the acquired firms' common stock.

[34] *Hearings on Economic Concentration,* Pt. 8, pp. 4632–47, testimony of Eamon Kelly. See also his *The Profitability of Growth Through Mergers,* Center for Research of the College of Business Administration, Pennsylvania State University, 1967.

tuations.[35] It would appear that from 1966 to 1968 too many investors regarded mergers as the "open sesame" to higher profits. And as long as this view was widely shared in the investing community the stocks of conglomerates continued to rise. But, beginning with the divulgence of disappointing earnings reports early in 1968, declines began to set in, accelerating in 1969. By the latter part of 1969 most of the fabulous gains recorded in the previous 2 years had been lost. Although changes in stock prices and in price-earnings ratios are too greatly affected by "a caprice of human psychology" to be used as measures of efficiency, in terms of profit margin, the nonmerging companies outperformed their merging counterparts in 57 percent of the cases. If those cases with a difference in results of less than 10 percent are ignored, the nonmerging companies were superior in 60 percent of the cases.

A closer examination of Kelly's data on profit margins suggests an even greater superiority on the part of the nonmerging firms. Of the 20 pairs, the nonmerging firms registered a greater increase in 12.[36] Two of the 9 instances in which the merging firms excelled would appear to be special cases. The comparison of National Tea (merging) with A&P (nonmerging) pits an aggressive, rapidly growing medium-size chain against one that has been operating under two handicaps: (a) restraints on its behavior stemming directly or indirectly from a major antitrust action and (b) apparent diseconomies of excessive size that have been manifested not only in profit showings but in a declining share of the market. Also, although Revlon (a merging firm) displayed a greater increase in profit margin than its nonmerging counterpart, Avon, the use of averages for two 5-year periods failed to reveal a significant difference in trend. According to Kelly, ". . . Revlon demonstrated a steady, downward trend in the profit margin, while Avon's trend was upward. While Revlon's initial merger significantly improved its profit margin, the company was not able to maintain this improvement concomitant with its follow-up mergers. These further mergers brought the company into a variety of diversified products." [37]

If because of these special factors the two cases are eliminated, the nonmerging companies outperformed their merging counterparts in terms of profit margin by almost two to one, or more precisely by 11 to 7. Once again evidence is provided of an inverse relationship between profitability and merger activity. Of special interest here is the poor performance of each of the conglomerate merging companies, which was the subject of the following colloquy:

> DR. BLAIR: Dr. Kelly, the results of your research were expressed in greater detail in your booklet published by the Pennsylvania State University, "The Profitability of Growth Through Mergers." In that volume you refer on page 60 to: "The poor profit margin performance of every one of the conglomerate merging companies in our sample." Would you care to elaborate on that observation?
>
> DR. KELLY: Yes. It is difficult to deal with conglomerate merging firms because you have to get similarity of data. It is hard to identify any period in which conglomerate firms had an accounting system which was

[35] For a depiction of the extraordinary fluctuations in stock prices of 7 leading conglomerates between 1966 and 1969, see *Hearings on Economic Concentration,* Pt. 8, pp. 4618–24.

[36] In all but one of these cases the nonmerging firms also showed a greater gain in cash earnings per common share (adjusted for stock splits and stock dividends). Incidentally, this itself is a remarkable showing in view of the ways in which an aggressive, merger-minded company can manipulate earnings per share upward.

[37] Eamon Kelly, *The Profitability of Growth Through Mergers,* Center for Research of the College of Business Administration, Pennsylvania State University, 1967, p. 33.

comparable with nonmerging firms. But in going through the 500 largest firms and 50 largest firms, I was able to isolate four such major merging companies: the Philip Morris Company, the National Distillers and Chemical Corporation, McCrory Corporation, and Revlon. In each case the nonmerging company did substantially better than the conglomerate merging company in maintaining the profit margin. So Philip Morris, which expanded from just the cigarette industry into adhesives, textile chemicals, razors and razor blades, toiletries and gum, experienced a one percent increase in their profit margin compared with a 21 percent increase by American Tobacco. This is despite the fact that in the tobacco component of their business Philip Morris moved into filter tips where the tobacco is a great deal less expensive. Most firms in the industry were experiencing substantial improvements in the profit margin with the filter tip business, but Philip Morris did not.

National Distillers and Chemicals moved into chemical plastics and fertilizers and their profit margin declined by 44 percent between the pre-merger and post-merger period as opposed to an 18 percent increase by Seagrams. Once again, it was not the whiskey business that caused the decline in the profit margin: It was moving into the chemicals, plastics and fertilizers.

The McCrory Corporation, a variety and general merchandising firm, moved into auto parts and supplies. Its profit margin declined by 39 percent. . . .

In the Revlon case (Revlon being a merging company and Avon being a nonmerging company) Revlon moved from cosmetics and toiletries into pharmaceuticals, shoe polishes and brushes, electric razors, medicines and artificial plastic flowers; its profit margin, however, increased by 49 percent. The increase in the profit margin occurred with its first merger which was a complementary merger. When it moved into the diversified acquisitions and became a real conglomerate, the decline in the profit margin became fairly obvious. Because of this downward trend in the profit margin, the price-earnings ratio, the multiplier of earnings resulting in the level of stock prices, declined by 74 percent, the result of this downward trend in the profit margin.

So you have a poor profit margin performance and also poor stock price performance in each of the conglomerate merging companies.

The performance of the other merging companies in Kelly's sample, although not uniformly unsuccessful as was the case of the conglomerates, is certainly no testament to the success of horizontal mergers. Of the pairs in which the merging member was *not* a conglomerate, superiority in improving the profit margin was about equally divided between the nonmerging and the merging members. The wide variety of circumstances in which mergers proved to be of doubtful value to the acquiring company is illustrated by those instances in which the profit performance of the merging company proved to be inferior to that of the nonmerging firm.

In the oil and chemical groups Kelly compared Sunoco, a nonmerging company, with Pure Oil, a merging firm. Sunoco maintained its profit margin while increasing its capital turnover ratio. In contrast, Pure Oil suffered a substantial drop in profit margin. Also in the oil industry, Richfield, a nonmerging company, turned in a better profit margin performance than Sunray, a merging firm. In chemicals Kelly compared Wyandotte, which concentrated on internal expansion, with Hooker, which emphasized growth through merger. The "decisive factor" in their comparative performance was Wyandotte's substantial improvement in its profit margin in an industry plagued by cost problems and overcapacity.

In the machinery area Kelly compared Caterpillar Tractor, a nonmerging company, with Allis-Chalmers, a merging firm. Caterpillar's performance was "dramatically superior" whether measured by market valuation or rate of return. In an industry troubled by increasing competition, union problems, cyclical swings, and rising wages, Caterpillar was able to improve its rate of return by increasing both capital turnover and profit margin. In contrast, Allis-Chalmers' attempts to solve some of its problems by expansion via merger "aggravated rather than aided" its profit margin problems. The results were similar in a comparison of 2 manufacturers of bearings, Timken Roller Bearing, a nonmerging firm, and Federal-Mogul-Bower Bearings, a merging company. Timken's performance was superior in both market valuation and profit margin, and the company enjoyed greater price appreciation as the result of its improved earning power.

In building materials U.S. Gypsum, which during most of the period surveyed relied on internal expansion, was compared with National Gypsum, which achieved growth by merger. The performance of U.S. Gypsum was superior with regard to rate of return. National Gypsum paid "too high a price" in trying to attain volume and efficiency through merger. Similarly, in the cement industry Lehigh, which had relied on internal expansion, did a "much better job" than Ideal, a merging company, in maintaining efficiency, showing a substantial improvement in profit margin.

In basic materials a dramatic contrast was provided by a comparison of 2 medium-size steel producers, McLouth, a nonmerging company, and Detroit Steel, a merging firm. The McLouth management displayed a "definitely superior performance" in every category except price-earnings ratio. McLouth recorded a huge increase of 321 percent in its capital turnover while simultaneously improving both its profit margin and its price-earnings ratio. Also in steel, Granite City, a nonmerging company, was contrasted with Acme, a merging firm. Both companies increased their market valuation and rates of return, but Granite City's performance was "definitely superior."

As a general proposition, the idea that mergers are a means of achieving greater efficiency has yet to be substantiated empirically.[38] The evidence suggests that, if anything, the reverse is more likely to be true. This is the case regardless of whether profitability is being related to a process—i.e., mergers—or to what in the past two decades has been their usual result—i.e., greater diversification. This is the conclusion to be drawn from Reid's finding that the most active acquirers recorded a much lower growth in profitability than com-

[38] A study by Shaw Livermore has occasionally been cited as evidence of the profitability of mergers. (See his "The Success of Industrial Mergers," *Quarterly Journal of Economics,* Nov., 1935, pp. 68–96.) However, Livermore did not follow Arthur Dewing's procedure of comparing the profitability of identical enterprises before and after consolidation, and therefore his study provides no direct evidence on the question of whether or not the act of consolidation promotes efficiency. Livermore merely traced the profit record of a large number of consolidations after the original merger had taken place. He found that their profit showing was somewhat better than commonly had been assumed, and he attributed this to the capabilities of management. However, it might just as well be attributed to monopoly power, a possibility Livermore dismissed: "Nor was monopoly power, after the first decade, the means by which earnings were obtained." Or, "monopoly power was largely lost after 1910, except for a handful of companies (e.g., United Shoe Machinery) by the growth of new competition or because of legal interference." (*Ibid.*)

panics making no mergers. Also in point are Eslick's finding of an inverse relationship between profitability and diversification,[39] as well as the comparatively poor profit performance of Hogarty's 43 active acquirers. Further corroboration is provided by the uniformly poor showings of Kelly's conglomerates, as well as by the lack of success of at least half of his horizontally merging companies. In the face of this evidence belief that greater efficiency is achieved by the extension of multiplant operations through merger must be regarded as simply an article of faith.

The inverse relationship between growth and concentration

Profitability is one, but by no means the only, measure of business performance. Another is the ability of companies of different size to exploit changes in demand or technology that make possible rapid increases in an industry's output. The ability to capitalize on an opportunity for growth is certainly an important aspect of efficiency. And it is an aspect in which large firms would presumably enjoy a number of important advantages. Their research staffs should be able to apprise themselves quickly of the scientific and technical knowledge relating to any invention or innovation. Through test market studies and other methods of ascertaining consumer response, their market analysts should be able to determine its salability. As volume producers of many different items, their plants should be able to cope with any production problems involved. And, perhaps of most importance, large companies, either from their own internal sources or from new financing, should be better able to provide the funds required to develop, produce, and sell a new or improved product. Because of these and related advantages, the logical expectation would be that in industries undergoing a rapid increase in output, the large companies would tend to improve their share of the market. In point of fact just the opposite generally takes place.

The discovery that changes in real output are related inversely to changes in concentration was first made by the Federal Trade Commission in 1954. In the case of 75 of 114 industries for which concentration ratios were available, the Commission was able, through the use of a variety of price indexes, to deflate the change in the value of shipments between 1935 and 1947. Reporting on its findings the Commission stated: "Among those industries in which real output increased one and a half times or more in the 12-year period, . . . 11 industries had declines in the concentration ratio of more than 5 percentage points, while only 3 had equivalent increases. Conversely, among those industries where output increased, but by less than 1½ times, increases in the concentration ratios exceeding 5 percentage points outnumbered such decreases 14 to 4." [40]

[39] A finding that diversification is more or less neutral in its effect on efficiency was reached by Richard F. Arnould in a study limited to 104 companies primarily engaged in food processing. Their rate of return was compared to their degree of diversification in 1966, with diversification measured on two bases: the share of the company's employment in industries outside food and kindred products and that share multiplied by the number of 4-digit industries in which the firm operates. Regardless of which measure was used he found "no discernible relationship between . . . the level of diversification and profitability." (*Hearings on Economic Concentration,* Pt. 8, pp. 4679–4702.)

[40] Federal Trade Commission, *Changes in Concentration in Manufacturing,* 1954, pp. 54–56. This conclusion was based on a scatter diagram presented in terms of 4-company concentration ratios; a similar conclusion was indicated by a scatter in terms of the 8 largest companies.

Table 8-2

RELATIONSHIP BETWEEN CHANGES IN CONCENTRATION
RATIOS AND REAL OUTPUT, 1935–1947

Change in Real Output	Number of Industries with Changes in Concentration Ratio of						Total
	−10.1% and Over	−5.1% to 10.0%	−2.1% to 5.0%	2.1% to 5.0%	5.1% to 10.0%	10.1% and Over	
.0 to 49.9%		1	1	2	1	2	7
50.0 to 99.9	1	1	2	3	2	5	14
100.0 to 149.9	2	2	1	1	2	1	9
150.0 and over	6	4	3	1	4	2	20
Total	9	8	7	7	9	10	50

Source: Computed from Federal Trade Commission, *Changes in Concentration in Manufacturing*, 1954

Omitting industries with a change in concentration of 2 percentage points or less, the FTC study included 50 industries, the data for which are summarized in Table 8-2. There it can be seen that of the 20 industries with an increase in real output of 150 percent or more, 13 were characterized by decreases in concentration and only 7 by increases. Conversely, of the 7 industries in which real output rose by less than 50 percent, concentration increased in all but 2. And of the 21 industries in which production stopped short of doubling, concentration rose in more than two-thirds (15).

An even more impressive showing is yielded by data on the relationship between changes in concentration and changes in the number of plants. The latter can be taken as a rough indication of change in real output, since for some time the more usual method of enlarging capacity in the United States has been, not by expanding an existing older plant, but by constructing new and typically decentralized plants. Again omitting industries with a change in concentration of 2 percentage points or less, Table 8-3 summarizes, for 82 industries for which data are available, changes in concentration and in number of plants between

Table 8-3

RELATIONSHIP BETWEEN CHANGES IN CONCENTRATION
RATIOS AND NUMBER OF PLANTS, 1935–1954

Change in Number of Plants	Number of Industries with Changes in Concentration Ratio of						Total
	−10.1% and Over	−5.1% to 10.0%	−2.1% to 5.0%	2.1% to 5.0%	5.1% to 10.0%	10.1% and Over	
.0 to 49.9%	2	7	3	9	11	11	43
50.0 to 99.9	2	2	5	1	8	1	19
100.0 to 149.9	8	1	3	1	1	0	14
150.0 and over	3	3	0	0	0	0	6
Total	15	13	11	11	20	12	82

Source: Computed from Federal Trade Commission, *Changes in Concentration in Manufacturing*, 1954

1935 and 1954. Of the 6 industries that recorded increases of 150 percent or more in number of plants, all showed decreases in concentration; of the 20 in which the number of plants at least doubled, 18 were characterized by decreases in concentration. Conversely, concentration rose in nearly three-fourths (31) of the 43 industries with increases of less than 50 percent in the number of plants.

In a study of changes in concentration and growth rates during 1947–54, Ralph L. Nelson found similarly that "declines in concentration were more common among the most rapidly growing industries. Conversely, increases in concentration were more common among the declining or slowly growing industries." [41] Moreover, an examination was made of the relationship in 13 major industry groups: "By confining the comparison to industries of similar technologies and marketing apparatus the basic relationship might be revealed more clearly. The findings for individual industry groups confirmed the overall relationship just described. A negative relationship between industry growth and concentration change was found for industries within 10 of the 13 manufacturing sectors that I examined." Finally, Nelson made a similar analysis for 101 industries that survived changes in industrial classification between 1935 and 1954: "The findings are consistent with the 1947 to 1954 findings. The greater the relative growth of an industry, the more likely it was to show a decline in concentration. The greater the relative decline of an industry, the more likely it was to show an increase in concentration."

In a study of 426 industries covering the period 1947–58, William G. Shepherd found the same type of relationship.[42] Summarizing these studies, Nelson noted that "the evidence is accumulating that one of the factors that determine the direction in which concentration will go in an industry is how fast the industry is growing. If it is declining, chances are concentration will not decline. It will probably do no better than stay the same and probably increase. If the industry is rapidly growing we may expect by and large, that concentration may go down."

In view of its prevalence and persistence, this inverse relationship gives rise to a number of significant, and not incompatible, implications. It suggests that where rapid growth is not present and large firms are not preoccupied with the problems occasioned by industry expansion, they are able to devote their full attention, with successful results, to enhancing their position within the existing scope of their industry. It suggests a higher rate of attrition among smaller firms, which apparently are less able than their larger rivals to survive a condition of depressed demand—an implication that is suggested also by the tendency of aggregate concentration to rise during depressions. And, further, it suggests that the advantages of large firms in the form of research laboratories, market analyses, production know-how, and easier access to credit and capital are more than offset by the disadvantages of delays in decision making, problems of communication, inertia, inflexibility, and a general inability to adapt to change. Insofar as the ability to take advantage of growth situations is concerned, it is clear that the managerial economies of size are more than offset by the diseconomies.

[41] *Hearings on Economic Concentration*, Pt. 1, pp. 266, 379, testimony of Ralph L. Nelson. Nelson's data are based on his *Concentration in the Manufacturing Industries of the United States*, Yale University Press, 1963.

[42] William G. Shepherd, "Trends of Concentration in American Manufacturing Industries, 1947–58," *Review of Economics and Statistics*, May, 1964, pp. 200–12.

Relevance to economic thinking

How do these empirical findings on managerial economies and diseconomies relate to major issues which have long been of interest to economists concerning the relationship of size to efficiency? For one thing, it may be noted that two-thirds of the industries in which the rate of return tended to rise with increasing size were among the less concentrated sectors of the economy. In these generally competitive areas the better showings of the larger firms may well be, in D. H. Robertson's words, the result of "the scramble by individual firms . . . to reap the direct advantages of large-scale organization and plant—advantages which have always been obvious." [43]

Conversely, all the industries in which the tendency was toward decreasing profitability are among the more concentrated sectors. Whether because of high capital entrance requirements, their control of scarce raw materials, their use of predatory practices to suppress competition, or other factors, they have enjoyed long periods of relative immunity from the rigors of price competition and thus from the competitive necessity of constantly lowering their costs. Moreover, in each industry the leader is a long-established firm which has been in business for over half a century. And the older a company grows, the more susceptible it becomes to the various forms of managerial diseconomies—rigid and wasteful hierarchical structures, the impediments of red tape, "regular" channels and "proper" procedures, conflicts between line and staff, internal struggles over advancement, status and budget, resistance to change, and so on. In the modern world of large corporate organization, these sources of diseconomies have the same effect as Marshall's "decay of entrepreneurial faculties." But unlike the firms in Marshall's "forest and trees" analogy, these leaders have not given way to any "broad upward movement from below." The very factors which have made for a concentrated industry structure have enabled them not only to continue to exist but to retain their position as their industry's dominant, though not particularly profitable, enterprise. Lower profit rates, however, are not the only symptom of what might be referred to as "corporate arteriosclerosis." The same ailment would explain the manifest inability of leading firms, generally, to keep pace with their smaller (and usually younger) rivals in exploiting new developments in either supply or demand that bring about a rapid expansion of the industry's output.

The empirical findings also tend to confirm the view that mergers are not, per se, a source of efficiency and that expansion by merger is not as effective as internal expansion in achieving economic benefits, and that, in particular, the effect of conglomerate mergers (and even diversification per se) is a loss in economic efficiency.

[43] D. H. Robertson, Piero Sraffa, G. F. Shove, "Increasing Returns and the Representative Firm: A Symposium," *Economic Journal,* March, 1930, p. 84.

INVENTION AND
INNOVATION

As large corporations have continued to grow and diversify, coming to own scores and even hundreds of separate plants not only in their original industry but in a variety of different and unrelated industries, it has become almost self-evident that their enormous size cannot possibly be explained merely in terms of plant economies. And with evidence lacking that efficiency is promoted by bringing many plants under common ownership and operation, something of a vacuum has developed in the intellectual defense of bigness. Like nature, any well-established status quo abhors a vacuum. It is therefore hardly surprising that, to fill the void, a new and more persuasive rationale has made a timely appearance. Stemming originally from the writings of Joseph Schumpeter,[1] its combination of surface plausibility and a few case examples has proved irresistible even to critical minds; thus J. Kenneth Galbraith writes: "A benign Providence . . . has made the modern industry of a few large firms an almost perfect instrument for inducing technical change. . . . There is no more pleasant fiction than that technical change is the product of the matchless ingenuity of the small man forced by competition to employ his wits to better his neighbor. Unhappily, it is a fiction. Technical development has long since become the preserve of the scientist and the engineer." [2]

A typical expression of the rationale is to be found in a paean of praise to big business by David E. Lilienthal, in which he equates bigness with scientific progress:

> Most significant research and development require large resources and often a long period of time during which no results are forthcoming. . . . Only large enterprises are able to sink the formidable sums of money required to develop basic new departures; a small corporation is rarely able to risk those large sums, perhaps enough to wreck the company if the gamble fails, on the success or failure of a major new project in such areas as electronics or chemicals, for example. . . . Bigness and research activity are largely synonymous whether in big business or in government. The greatest single factor in competition today is indeed research and development. This fact alone makes obsolete and inadequate many of our "horse-and-buggy" ideas about how competition can be maintained.[3]

The body of scientific research itself has reached such dimensions, it is held, that further contributions can come only from teams of specialists working in

[1] Joseph Schumpeter, *Capitalism, Socialism and Democracy,* Harper, 1942.
[2] J. Kenneth Galbraith, *American Capitalism, the Concept of Countervailing Power,* Houghton Mifflin, 1952, p. 91.
[3] David E. Lilienthal, *Big Business: A New Era,* Harper, 1952, pp. 69–72.

large, well-equipped laboratories; only the large corporations can afford to buy the expensive equipment and facilities, to hire the specialists, and to pay the other costs of conducting research in the world of modern science. The change in the nature of the inventive process, it is concluded, has made concentration a prerequisite to progress. The day of the independent inventor and innovative small enterprise is over.

Like the efficiency justification this "research rationale" has been transformed into a mystique—a product not of objective inquiry but of images—the white-robed scientists in the gleaming laboratories peering into microscopes, holding up test tubes, working with computers, and in other ways comporting themselves as advertising and public-relations men expect scientists to behave. There are two methods of evaluating the contribution of large companies to the invention-innovation process: the statistical and the historical. Studies of the former type have been based primarily on two bodies of data: statistics on expenditures for "research and development" and statistics on patents. Studies of the latter type consist of historical accounts of the origins, development, and progress of individual inventions. Taken together, the studies based on these different approaches constitute an impressive body of empirical evidence with which the validity of the research rationale can be appraised.

Statistical studies

The Census Bureau regularly collects for the National Science Foundation statistics on expenditures for research and development (or "R&D," as it is termed) broken down by size of company. At first glance the data would appear to lend support to the research rationale, since they regularly show a relatively high degree of concentration in research and development expenditures. But when related to other measures of economic activity, concentration of R&D becomes considerably less impressive. Moreover, pointed criticisms have been advanced concerning the appropriateness of using this body of data for *any* purpose. The criticisms are, first, that expenditures on research and development are measures of *input* rather than of output and, second, that the term R&D has come to embrace a great variety of activities that have little relationship to the traditional meaning. The other body of statistical data—figures on patents—suffers from shortcomings of its own, of which the most important, of course, is the great variation in the significance and use of individual patents.

Studies based on R&D expenditures

It is true that most of the expenditures for research and development are made by a relatively small number of firms. But it is also true that this concentration of R&D outlays is *less* than the concentration of economic activity, as represented by sales or employment. Among 352 of the 500 largest manufacturing corporations, the 4 largest firms accounted in 1955 for only 9.7 percent of their employment in research and development while enjoying 19.9 percent of their sales. The 8 largest accounted for only 16.4 percent of the R&D employment of these companies while accounting for 27.5 percent of their sales. The figures for the 30 largest (corresponding roughly to firms with 1955 sales in excess of $1 billion) were 44.7 and 49.0 percent.[4]

When these companies are distributed by size among 4 broad groups of industries, there is a clear tendency in 3 groups for R&D employment (per billion dollars of sales) to *decline* after a company size of $200 million in sales is reached. The exception is basic chemicals and drugs, in which the R&D employment-sales ratio is highest in the largest size shown—companies with sales of over $1 billion. Similarly, another study found no tendency among firms with more than 5,000 employees for R&D employment in relation to total employment to rise with increasing company size.[5] In this study, based on 340 firms, the relative amount of R&D employment increased with firm size in only 2 of 19 industry groups. A point to be stressed here is that both the size of $200 million in sales (after which in the former study the ratio tended to fall) and the minimal size of 5,000 employees (used in the latter study) are well below any size that might give rise to concern over concentration, either in manufacturing as a whole or in most of the major industries.

The meaning of "research and development"

In addition to the fact that statistics on research and development, when related to sales or employment, provide little support for the "research rationale," the point has been made that even such figures exaggerate greatly the extent of what has been traditionally thought of as "research" or "inventive" activity. The leading exponent of this criticism has been David Novick, whose position as head of the Cost Analysis Department of the Rand Corporation makes him singularly well qualified to comment on the subject.

According to Novick most of the frequently cited increase in expenditures on research and development—from $1 billion at the end of World War I to $10 billion in 1959 and to $20 billion in 1966—is illusory, since the term has been stretched to embrace such a variety of activities as to be rendered almost meaningless.[6] In a paper before the American Association for the Advancement of Science, Dale Wolfie observed, "If words could talk, research would surely complain of being overworked. The word is used to describe the scholarly activities of a Nobel laureate and to give prestige to such immediately useful records as counting the customers of a chain store." At the same meeting Merle A. Tuve stated, "We have lumped under 'research and development' so many huge technological activities in the national budget, and correspondingly in corporation budgets and elsewhere, that the figures have become practically meaningless." [7] In this connection Novick cited a description of research by Bergen and Cornelia Evans in their *Dictionary of Contemporary English Usage*:

> Research has become very popular in the United States since the outbreak of World War II. As Henry D. Smyth has observed, the idea that the

[4] *Hearings on Economic Concentration*, Pt. 3, pp. 1194–98, testimony of Frederic M. Scherer. The 352 represented those among the 500 largest for which Scherer could obtain figures on employment in research and development.
[5] *Ibid.*, pp. 1284–85, testimony of Daniel Hamberg.
[6] Novick testified before the Subcommittee on Antitrust and Monopoly on two occasions. See *Hearings on Administered Prices*, Pt. 18, pp. 10510–23; *Hearings on Economic Concentration*, Pt. 3, pp. 1241–56.
[7] Quoted by Novick in *Hearings on Administered Prices*, Pt. 18, p. 10513.

object of research is new knowledge does not seem to be widely understood and "a schoolboy looking up the meaning of a word in the dictionary is now said to be doing research." Indeed, it has been debased even further. Research is frequently used to describe reading by those to whom reading, apparently, is a recherché activity, and for many a graduate student it is a euphemism for wholesale plagiarism. The word needs a rest or at least less promiscuous handling.[8]

In addition to a certain status conveyed by the term itself, a number of more mundane consideratons have governed the vast expansion in its usage. For one thing, the investment community came to look with favor upon corporations that were said to be "research oriented." [9] Testifying in 1960 Novick stated, "That the investing public has bought the thesis that research pays off can be illustrated by the spectacular rise in the price of the securities of Texas Instruments, Thiokol, Minnesota Mining & Manufacturing, International Business Machines, and others of the so-called science stocks. This indicates the investors believe that research does pay." [10]

Probably an even more important inducement is the result of a change in the treatment of research expenditures for tax purposes. Prior to 1954 research expenditures could be capitalized and amortized only over their useful life. If their useful life could not be determined, no deduction at all was available except for losses due to abandonment. But, since the 1954 revision in the Internal Revenue Code, research expenditures can be either capitalized or treated as ordinary business expenses deductible in the year incurred. Moreover, firms wishing to do so can treat research expenditures as "deferred expenses" to be amortized in 5 years or more, but with the amortization period beginning only *after* income resulting from the research is realized. In other words, the use of the research expenditures to reduce a corporation's taxes can be held off until the firm is receiving income from the research. Whatever their merits for tax purposes, these new methods of treating research expenditures have obviously had the effect of inducing companies to classify as "research and experimental" many activities formerly carried on under other accounts.

A further consideration of perhaps more than passing importance derives from the lofty status research now enjoys in the public mind. To the extent that its growth can be said to be the result of research, a company secures respectability from the community and immunity from criticism. Institutional advertising campaigns stressing research have become *de rigueur* for leading companics, including many to whom it has in fact been something of a *recherché* activity. During an investigation of the drug industry carried out by the Subcommittee on Antitrust and Monopoly, the industry's constant and continuous reiteration of the research argument reflected a keen awareness that it constituted a complete defense; the only problem is that, at best, it left unexplained over 93 percent of the price.

[8] Quoted by Novick in *ibid.*, p. 10512.
[9] In his testimony in 1965 Novick qualified this observation in the light of the more recent performance of the "research stocks." In response to the question of whether "the wise investor will tend to put his money on the corporation that appears to spend more on research and development," Novick replied, "Yes. However, I am not sure that that is going to continue, because the science companies that were booming so nicely in 1959–60, some of them have come very much a cropper in 1965–66." (*Hearings on Economic Concentration*, Pt. 3.)
[10] *Hearings on Administered Prices*, Pt. 18.

Discussing the more mundane reasons behind the apparent great increase in research and development expenditures, Novick stated:

I think the first major increase in R & D can be directly attributable to that enactment [the 1954 change in tax treatment], because if you plot the figures, you suddenly get a jump in 1955–56 that just does not have any explanation other than the change in tax treatment. You then get another jump in 1957–58 as a result of the launching of sputnik, meaning that the military should do R & D. Prior to 1957–58 it was the practice of the military departments to play down research and development, and as a consequence the budgets for R & D or code 600 money ran well under a billion. In other words, for all three services as of 1956 the total was probably just about $1 billion of 600 money.

Suddenly after sputnik when they decided that it was fashionable or proper to be in the R & D business, this number jumped to something like $6 or $7 billion. Now, this did not mean that anything had changed. The activities in the development of missiles and aircraft and related components were going forward in the same way in 1954, 1956, and 1958. But in 1954 and 1956, the 600 money was kept down, and the production and procurement money was kept up. Starting in 1958 after sputnik production money was reduced and the R & D money was increased.

This again introduced a major statistical change in the series that no one ever pays much attention to. I mean there was no change in the basic activity of R & D. It was just a reclassification of figures. With sputnik, and the result of this change, everybody decided that they wanted to be in the R & D business. . . .[11]

It is Novick's position that the process of what is referred to as research and development must, for any meaningful purposes, be broken down into four stages. Step 1 is what is usually thought of as *basic research*—explorations into the "brave new world"—whose promise may be great but is not identified with specific uses and purposes. Of the $10 billion said to have been spent by this country on research and development in 1959, only one percent, according to Novick, went to support this most fundamental form of inquiry. Step 2, or *applied research,* consists of identifying the applications of the fundamental discoveries resulting from Step 1. Here the expenditure was in the neighborhood of 3 percent of the total. Step 3 consists of the *development, evaluation, and testing* of products devised from what was regarded in Step 2 as potential. At this stage "do-ability" has been established. About 25 percent, Novick estimated, was spent at this stage. Step 4, *applied research and testing,* consists of finding new uses, applications, or modifications of *existing* products and methods. In Novick's words, "some success is reasonably assured since it is evolutionary rather than revolutionary." [12] It is here that the great bulk—70 percent —of the research and development expenditure is made.

Stressing that each of the subsequent steps is dependent ultimately on basic research itself, Novick questioned whether there has in fact been *any* increase in truly creative activity:

The bulge in our scientific discoveries in the last twenty-five years is probably more the result of European scientists coming to this country to escape Fascism, Communism, and Naziism than any real expansion in

[11] *Hearings on Economic Concentration*, Pt. 3.
[12] *Hearings on Administered Prices*, Pt. 18.

our indigenous capability. Einstein, Fermi, von Neumann, and Teller are a few of the scientists whose U.S. contributions are transplants from Europe. There is no assurance that we have yet developed the essential "climate" for basic research in this country.[13]

Novick also regarded as "useful" (although less meaningful than his four-part classification) the widely employed distinction between "invention" and "innovation"—the former being the creation of new ideas and principles, the making and verifying of discoveries, and their transformation into a *conceptual* design of a new product or process; the latter being the translation of the concept into marketable goods.[14] In terms of this classification Novick would assign only about 5 percent of the R&D expenditures to invention:

> In terms of the problem this committee is addressing, I reject the idea that technological advance under present day conditions requires the resources of bigness. Let me repeat, for the most part basic research and invention are essentially thinking processes, which commonly means one man. Let us recognize this and at the same time stop saying $20 billion for research and development for 1965. It is more appropriate to say $19-plus billion for development and something less than $1 billion for the basic research and invention where the great new discoveries will be made.[15]

That so little goes to invention is due partly to the nature of the activity itself, which, as Novick says, is essentially a thinking process. It is also due partly to the pressure on scientists from the business community to come up with something of commercial value. The closer a research project comes to the "developmental" or "innovative" stages, the more understandable it appears to corporate managers, and thus the better are its chances for approval. Also at work is a perverse attitude on the part of those who control the funds for research in business, government, and foundations. Because basic research is an exploration into the unknown with only a slight chance of yielding anything of tangible value, requests for financial assistance have to be expressed in the vaguest of terms—the purpose of the project can be described only generally, and no promise nor even much hope can be entertained for a result of tangible value. Also, because the equipment is usually simple, consisting of paper and pencil or blackboard and chalk, secretary, file cabinet, small office, and at most a small laboratory, a request for funds to conduct basic research may amount to only $25,000. Not infrequently, such requests strike the grantors of funds as too small to warrant serious consideration. In Novick's words:

> You have to have a big project to interest the administrators. This means that it is not easy to get support for what one might do for $25,000. So we blow it up into something like $250,000, or more probably $2.5 million, and then we can get somebody interested in it. At this juncture, the scientist who had the idea ceases to be a scientist and instead becomes an administrator. Instead of being a scientist he is a big wheeler and dealer. As a consequence . . . we are getting a lot less for $250,000 or $2.5 million than we could have gotten for $25,000 ten years ago.[16]

[13] *Ibid.*
[14] *Hearings on Economic Concentration,* Pt. 3.
[15] *Ibid.*
[16] *Hearings on Administered Prices,* Pt. 18.

Studies based on patents

In the late 1950's the share of U.S. inventive patents held by 448 firms among the 500 largest industrial corporations was found by Frederic M. Scherer to have been *smaller* than their share of total sales.[17] (This finding, it will be noted, parallels the results based on a comparison of concentration in R&D employment with that in sales.) While the 4 largest firms made 18.2 percent of the sales of these firms, they held only 9.9 percent of their patents. The 8 largest made 25.2 percent of the sales of these companies but held only 15.9 percent of their patents; the corresponding figures for the 30 largest were 44.9 and 40.7 percent.

When the figures on patents are distributed by firm size among 4 broad groups of industries, the number of patents in relation to sales does not tend to rise with increasing company size. Indeed, in 3 of the 4 groups the ratio of patents to sales was lower in the largest size group (companies with sales of over $1 billion) than for any of the other size classes except the smallest.[18] The same was found to be true of employment in research and development in relation to sales. In Scherer's words:

> Altogether in six classes out of eight, the highest average rates of patenting and R & D employment per billion dollars of sales are found for firms with 1955 sales of less than $200 million. These patterns persist when two-digit industries are analyzed one-by-one. The results clearly do not support the hypothesis that bigness per se is especially conducive to technological inventions and innovations. If anything, they imply that giant firms are somewhat less progressive relative to size than their smaller brethren.

Statistics on patents can be related also to the funds spent on research and development to provide an indication of the productivity of R&D expenditures. Such an analysis, prepared by Jacob Schmookler, is presented in Table 9-1, which shows the amounts spent per patent pending in 6 broad industry groups, broken down into 3 size classes.[19]

As will be seen, the largest firm spent more in every industry group on R&D per patent pending than firms in the smallest size class. Except for chemicals, they also spent more than firms in the medium-size group. For the combined industry groups, firms in the largest size class spent about twice as much on research and development per patent pending as did firms in the 2 smaller size classes. Thus, in terms of this standard, the larger the firm, the lower was the productivity of its research and development effort.

Moreover, despite their greater expenditures per patent, the patents secured by the larger corporations appear to be less significant than those of smaller firms. Based upon a 2-percent random sample of inventions patented in 1938, 1948, and 1952, a study by the Patent Foundation of George Washington University found that large firms used only 51 percent of their inventions commercially

---

[17] *Hearings on Economic Concentration*, Pt. 3, pp. 1194–98. To allow for the customary 4-year time lag between the application for and the issuance of a patent, the comparison was between sales in 1955 and patents assigned to firms in 1959.

[18] The exception is petroleum products, in which patents per sales in the second largest size class were slightly lower than in the largest.

[19] *Hearings on Economic Concentration*, Pt. 3, pp. 1258–65, testimony of Jacob Schmookler. The data relate to 1953, which was the last year for which the National Science Foundation collected this type of data on patents.

Table 9-1
RESEARCH AND DEVELOPMENT OUTLAYS PER PATENT PENDING, 1953
($ Thousands)

Industry	Size of Firm			Industry Average (Unweighted)
	Under 1,000 Employees	1,000 to 4,999 Employees	5,000 or More Employees	
Machinery	$ 8.5	$14.2	$24.2	$15.6
Chemicals	11.2	24.4	23.6	19.7
Electrical equipment	15.7	12.6	25.6	18.0
Petroleum products and extraction	10.0	8.4	15.6	11.3
Instruments	15.8	14.4	37.5	22.6
All other industries	15.4	7.1	27.8	16.8
Average, all industries (unweighted)	$12.8	$13.4	$25.6	

Source: *Hearings on Economic Concentration*, Pt. 3, p. 1258

as compared to 71 percent for small firms.[20] Similarly, a study of large firms by the Harvard Business School revealed that corporations with sales in 1956 of over a half-billion dollars used only 51 percent of their potential inventions as compared to 56 percent for firms with smaller sales.[21] What is perhaps the most surprising finding is that the rate of use by the large companies, 51 percent, was found in the latter study to be virtually the same as that for patents obtained by independent inventors—49 percent.[22] In view of the difficulties encountered by independent inventors in getting their inventions used, the logical inference is that on the average the quality of their patents must be superior to those of the large companies.

The meaning of patent statistics

Statistics on patents have an important advantage over figures based on R&D expenditures in that they are a measure of *output*. Moreover, they appear to represent an "objective" or "independent" measure. Yet what they measure is the willingness of the Patent Office—and the courts—to issue a monopoly grant. Over the years the standards of patentability have tended, through interpretation, to move away from the original concept of a "creative burst of genius" toward minor changes in novelty and utility. Patents on drugs, for example, have been issued regularly because of a slight difference in molecular structure, even though the compound has no greater utility or therapeutic value than its predecessors.[23] As a result, the securing of a patent has come increasingly to be merely a function of the resources needed to achieve the requisite minor

[20] Barkev S. Sanders, "Patterns of Commercial Exploitation of Patented Inventions by Large and Small Companies," *Patent Copyright and Trademark Journal*, Spring, 1964, pp. 51–92. Large companies were defined as those holding over 100 patents or with some patents and over $100 million in assets; small firms were defined as the remainder.

[21] Frederic M. Scherer, *Patents and the Corporation*, Galvin, 1958, p. 112.

[22] Sanders, *op. cit.*

[23] See 87th Cong., 1st Sess., Senate Subcommittee on Antitrust and Monopoly, Senate Committee on the Judiciary, *Hearings on S. 1552*, "To Amend and Supplement the Antitrust Laws, with Respect to the Manufacture and Distribution of Drugs," 1962, Pt. 3.

modification, thereby imparting a strong bias in patent statistics in favor of large enterprises.

Another source of bias operating in the same direction stems from the deliberate practice by large companies of obtaining a succession of minor "improvement" process patents as well as "blocking" patents—i.e., patents covering alternate processes or products.[24] Other distortions were cited in a colloquy during the Antitrust Subcommittee's hearings:

> DR. BLAIR: A final source of bias would stem from the fact that the smaller firm and the independent inventor who have discovered a patentable invention may not patent it, for the reason that they do not want to make the disclosure which is required by the Patent Office. They may be apprehensive that if they do make the disclosure, the large firm will in effect pirate their invention, and that, being small, they are without the resources required to successfully mount a case involving infringement of patents. As you know, those cases are frequently quite expensive.
>
> DR. SCHMOOKLER: Yes; I am sure you are right.
>
> DR. BLAIR: In the Subcommittee's drug hearings an official of a medium-size firm, one with fairly considerable resources, testified that when they made discoveries, as they had, they no longer even bothered to try to market them as patented specialties, but rather just licensed them to all firms, since the cost of bringing a patent infringement suit was simply prohibitive. So would this not be a further source of bias?
>
> DR. SCHMOOKLER: I am sure that that source also exists.

The existence of these biases obviously lends greater force to the following summary of the evidence by Schmookler: "Evidently, as the size of firm increases, there is a decrease per dollar of R&D in (a) the number of patented inventions, (b) the percentage of patents used commercially and (c) the number of significant inventions."

Historical studies

Historical research into the origins and development of individual inventions is slow, laborious "donkey work." Even the simplest of inventions usually has a tangled history, moving from the first conception through successive stages of development and improvement, failure and rejection, reformulation and more improvement, to final success. By the very nature of the subject matter, this type of inquiry does not lend itself readily to compression. Nor, like many other areas of knowledge, does it lend itself to mathematical treatment. As David Novick has observed:

> No one is going to provide a verifiable, analytic summation of the role of the large firm in the advance of technology. It is not possible to state, for example, that large firms account for x percent of technical progress, either in a single industry or in the overall economy. We know of no way to assign values to individual discoveries of new applications of technical knowledge, especially when the effect of discovery or application is to provide goods or services not previously available. In general,

---

[24] The latter might constitute one of the explanations for the relatively low use rate of the largest companies, cited above.

it is not possible even to rank individual technical advances. We cannot compare the values of advances in different fields in any meaningful way—for example, compare an advance in medical knowledge with one that provides a new hair spray. The possibility of valuing contributions to science or to basic technical knowledge that have not yet resulted in commercial or social applications is even more remote.[25]

The "Jewkes study"

The most comprehensive study of the history of invention is the important work *The Sources of Invention,* by John Jewkes, David Sawers, and Richard Stillerman (referred to for convenience here as the "Jewkes study").[26] Originally published in 1958, it traced the history of 61 important inventions made during the twentieth century. About two-thirds were made after 1930 and over two-fifths after 1940. Each has been a commercial success or an effective weapon of war. Some have transformed ways of living: radio, television, jet engines, nylon, quick freezing, plastics, stainless steel. Some rank among the great medical discoveries: penicillin and insulin. Some represent new techniques, new tools of production, new instruments for research, and new materials: the continuous hot-strip rolling mill, continuous casting of steel, shell molding, tungsten carbide tools, catalytic cracking of petroleum, the cyclotron, the electron microscope, neoprene, the cotton picker. Also included are important consumer goods such as the safety razor, the zip fastener, the self-winding wrist watch, the long-playing record, and the ball-point pen. As the authors observe, the inventions chosen—with such exceptions as atomic energy and the electronic devices employed in automation—seem to constitute a cross-section of the technical progress of the twentieth century.

Far from having vanished during the nineteenth century, the individual inventor was found still to be very much with us. For example, the gyrocompass was invented by a young man who was neither a scientist nor a sailor; the manufacturers of navigational equipment played no part whatever in its invention. A chemist working in the oil industry discovered the process of transforming liquid fats by hardening them for use in soap and, single-handed, pursued his research and efforts to get the process adopted. An independent worker was responsible for the crucial invention in magnetic recording as well as for a number of important improvements; the interest of the companies arose much later. An independent engineer invented the catalytic cracking of petroleum, and it was his efforts that finally forced the industry to adopt the process. Two groups of individual inventors, each working with limited resources, were able to bring their ideas concerning a mechanical cotton picker to the point where large firms were prepared to buy or license their product for subsequent development.

Despite the considerable sums spent on research by the large chemical companies, it was an individual inventor who produced Bakelite, the first of the thermosetting plastics. A metallurgist working in his own laboratory developed

---

[25] *Hearings on Economic Concentration,* Pt. 3.
[26] John Jewkes, David Sawers, Richard Stillerman, *The Sources of Invention,* Macmillan, 1958, rev. ed., 1969. Unless otherwise noted the page citations are to the first edition. For a study of inventions between 1946 and 1955 see Daniel Hamberg, *Research and Development,* Random House, 1966 (summarized in *Hearings on Economic Concentration,* Pt. 3, pp. 1281–92).

INVENTION AND INNOVATION

the first and still the most important commercially practical method of producing ductile titanium; the process was neglected for years by the leading metallurgical and chemical corporations. The helicopter was the result of the enthusiasm of individual inventors; up to 1938 only one large aircraft manufacturer had taken much interest in it, and even that only as the result of the personal interest of the head of the firm. The groundwork for the successful Kodachrome process was laid by two young musicians whose ideas were later taken up by a large photographic firm. The safety razor came from two individuals, one a salesman in crown corks, who struggled through financial and technical doldrums before finally meeting with success. Two engineers are responsible for the zip fastener, which was not taken up for large-scale production until many years later. A British watch repairer invented the self-winding wrist watch, and Swiss watch manufacturers were slow to see its importance. A patent attorney invented xerography, which was ignored for years by the large photographic firms.

Small and medium-size companies have continued to be another important source of invention. A one-man effort in a then small American firm was responsible for the development of cellophane. A medium-size firm in the English cotton industry invented the crease-resisting process. The continuous hot-strip rolling of steel was conceived by a company official who might be considered an individual inventor and was perfected in a medium-size American steel company. A firm that had no direct interest in the production of new fibers was responsible for the invention of the synthetic fiber Terylene.

A third group of inventions, including the cyclotron, penicillin, streptomycin, insulin, electric precipitation, and chromium plating, came from university laboratories. Still another group consists of cases that, in Jewkes's words, "seem to defy classification." Among these he cites the long-playing record, which was invented by an engineer of the Columbia Broadcasting System in charge of a completely different line of activity, color television experiments. Important discoveries relating to stainless steel were made almost simultaneously by an individual inventor and one working in a company's research laboratory. Radar emerged from the combined work of government research stations, radio companies, and scientists in the universities.

Of the 61 inventions on Jewkes's original list, only 16 can be attributed directly to organized research by large corporations. These are acrylic fibers (such as orlon), DDT, the diesel-electric locomotive, Duco lacquers, fluorescent lighting, Freon refrigerants, Krilium, methyl methacrylate polymers, neoprene, nylon, polyethylene, silicones, synthetic detergents, television, tetraethyl lead, and transistors. Even some of these contributions were built upon the prior work of independent scientists and inventors.[27] Summing up the evidence the study concludes:

> More than half of the cases can be ranked as individual invention in the sense that much of the pioneering work was carried through by men

[27] About half of this group of 16 are in the general field of chemicals. Commenting on this "intriguing" phenomenon, Jewkes observes: "Individual chemical invention was not unknown in the 19th century—Goodyear, Perkin, Mercer and Cross are famous in that connection. It is still to be found in industries which may be regarded as peripheral to the chemical industry such as photography, metallurgy, textile finishing and chemotherapeutics. And at least some of the great chemical inventions of recent years, such as those of Carothers, Whinfield and Midgley, although made in industrial research laboratories, were produced by small groups operating with relatively inexpensive equipment." (*Ibid.*, p. 89.)

who were working on their own behalf without the backing of research institutions and usually with limited resources and assistance or, where the inventors were employed in institutions, these institutions were, as in the case of Universities, of such a kind that the individuals were autonomous—free to follow their own ideas without hindrance.[28]

The costs of R&D

The invention-innovation rationale rests in no small part upon the assumption that because of today's complex and costly technologies, the ability to carry on research and development work tends to be a function of a company's size and resources. And from this assumption it would logically follow that those concerns best able to carry the financial burden would have the best records in making scientific and technological advances. The empirical knowledge gained through the historical studies of the history of inventions permits an examination of both propositions.

It is true that a few extremely costly types of equipment, such as giant atom smashers and huge radio telescopes, are far beyond the resources of independent inventors, and small firms. But such items are also beyond the resources of large firms and therefore are necessarily financed directly or indirectly by the government. Moreover, in analyzing the cost of research, the customary distinction between invention and innovation must again be made. Since the former, as Novick pointed out, is a thinking process, its costs are usually modest; a number of typical case examples were cited before the Senate Antitrust Subcommittee by Richard Stillerman, co-author of the Jewkes study:

> in this century, scores of inventions have been conceived with simple equipment and advanced with modest expenditures. Chester Carlson used crude equipment to prove out his ideas for xerography. Farnsworth, in his television experiments, expressed a preference for simple tools. The newness of the field forced him to improvise his own research and measuring instruments. Julius Hyman and his group, working on a small scale, discovered the insecticides chlordane, aldrin, and dieldrin. Not only did the Wright brothers build their own wind tunnel for testing wing shapes, but also their historic airplane. Nicholas Christofilos, the self-trained nuclear physicist, formulated mathematically his idea for strong-focusing, which simplified the construction of large accelerators; and Ernest O. Lawrence's first cyclotron was a combination of window glass, sealing wax, brass, and wire. The basis for Kodachrome blossomed from experiments in a kitchen sink. When John Bardeen and Walter Brattain invented the transistor, their most costly piece of equipment was an oscilloscope. Charles H. Townes' prepared mind received the inspiration for the maser while he sat on a park bench; experimental verification of the idea did not involve high costs. Robert Goddard made fundamental progress in rocketry with his own handmade rockets; parallel work by the early German rocket enthusiasts proceeded with limited funds and primitive tools. The record of modern invention demonstrates that it is the quality of the researcher not the elaborateness of his equipment that determines success. Inventors who place increased reliance on specialized tools and less on thinking power and personal observation may get caught up in the machines and miss solutions lying near the surface of things.[29]

[28] Jewkes, Sawyers, Stillerman, *op. cit.*, p. 82.
[29] *Hearings on Economic Concentration,* Pt. 3, pp. 1081–83, testimony of Richard Stillerman.

In contrast to the cost of inventing, the cost of development may on occasion be quite large. It is perfectly evident that no small company—and few large ones for that matter—could match the expenditures by Du Pont of $27 million for the development of nylon, $25 million for Corfam synthetic leather, and $50 million for Delrin plastic. But these are extreme cases. For most innovations the development costs are not beyond the reach of medium-size and even many small firms. This is particularly true if, as there is reason to believe, the small firm can make its development dollar go farther than the large company.

In testimony before the Subcommittee on Antitrust and Monopoly, Arnold C. Cooper presented the results of a study of the development costs of large and small companies, from which he concluded that "a large company typically spends from 3 to 10 times as much as a small one to develop a particular product." [30] This remarkable conclusion was based partly upon 25 interviews in the New England area, principally with men who had managed development in *both* large and small companies, and partly upon cost comparisons of "parallel development projects" in which both a large and a small company had independently developed the *same* product. With respect to the former, Cooper stated:

> Those men I have talked to who have managed development in both large and small companies are, on the whole, extremely outspoken in their belief that substantial differences exist in the efficiency of development activities between large and small companies. (The typical man in this category had been a section head or department head in the development organizations of one or more large companies, usually with at least several thousand employees, before leaving to go with a newly founded small firm, often in the same field.)

Moreover, this inverse relationship was held to be true not only in a comparason of large versus small companies but *within* any company as it grew in size:

> Most of these men believed their development organizations to have become less efficient as their companies grew. . . .
> Some of these men were most vivid as they spoke of the problems of inspiring and controlling their growing research organizations. The president of a firm which does contract development and which has grown from a few founders to over 400 personnel said, "We're less efficient now than when we had only 50 employees, but I'm afraid we're not as inefficient as we're going to be when we grow even larger."
> The director of research of a firm in the semiconductor industry spoke of the changes in the atmosphere he had observed as the firm grew from total personnel of about 20 to over 4,000.
> He said, "I wish I knew what to do to create the same kind of atmosphere we had when we were small. No one really cares as much anymore."

Interviews were also held with officials who had worked only for large companies: "Most of these men considered their own companies to be less efficient than smaller competitors in developing new products." The same conclusion was reached in studies of parallel product development projects, particularly one involving the independent development of a new protective coating by a

[30] *Ibid.*, pp. 1296–1304, testimony of Arnold C. Cooper.

small and a large company.[31] The former was one of the smallest firms in its segment of the chemical industry, with about 50 employees and a research department consisting of 2 chemists. The large company had over 20,000 employees, with over 500 (including some 50 chemists and technicians) in its protective-coating division alone. For the small company the total direct cost was estimated at $1,400 and the time involved at less than 12 months. For the large company, which, incidentally, started its project after the small firm had put its product on the market, total direct costs were nearly 8 times as much ($11,000), and the time consumed was 38 months.

Cooper attributed the better showings of the smaller firms primarily to their ability to attract people who were technically competent and creative, who had the ability to see "the core of a problem," and who were motivated by an intense personal drive to achieve solutions:

> In many small companies, the technical staff consists of only a handful of engineers, all of whom might be described as "highly visible." The president of one small research-based firm said, "we're so close to each other, it's hard not to know what each individual engineer is doing." In addition, the managers of many small companies, particularly if the situation is a bit precarious, often feel they cannot afford to have people on the payroll who are poor or barely average. Thus, in the interviews held with many small company R & D managers, instances came to light of technical people having been fired simply because they were not quite good enough.

A second and related factor is that the technical employees in a small company tend to be more "cost-anxious." The company is not some vast amorphous organization whose earnings are not affected significantly by the cost of its R&D organization. Excessive expenditures on technical development in the small company can mean the end not only of its R&D effort but of the company itself. Neither the resources nor the opportunities are available for the ostentatious display of status. As Cooper observed,

> The small company is less likely than the large company to suffer from the propensity of engineers to order laboratory equipment they really could get along without and from the effort of individuals to obtain laboratory assistants or secretaries, more to demonstrate their status than because of a real need. An executive of one large electronics firm ruefully remarked, "People often have the attitude, 'there's more where that came from,' so that every engineer wants his own oscilloscope, and every section head wants two filing cabinets."

Finally, problems of communication and coordination tend to be more serious in the large company. In the field of product development the competent technical man must be sensitive simultaneously to the needs of the market for which the product is being developed and to the production facilities available to manufacture it. The difficulties of trying to secure such awareness within the large company were described by one R&D director as "monumental." The differences between large and small companies were illustrated in Cooper's testimony by the example of protective coatings:

> In the small firm, the chief chemist worked about 10 feet from the door to the plant and usually had samples made up by production personnel who would use temporarily idle production facilities. If there were produc-

[31] In order to protect the companies, the product was described only in general terms.

tion problems, he often worked with the plant superintendent to help solve them. In the sales area, he was in frequent contact both with company salesmen and with customers, inasmuch as a great deal of his time was spent in devising special formulations to meet the needs of particular customers. He also spent a great deal of time in customers' plants, helping them to use these formulations.

In the large company, the project chemist had his samples made up by laboratory technicians on special laboratory equipment. Although he had been in the company's and in customers' plants, his principal duties centered on the development of new products in the company's research center.

The difference in familiarity with sales and production problems was an important factor in the great disparity in development costs incurred by the two companies. In the small company, there were absolutely no problems in "transferring the new product to production," since even the earliest samples had been made by production personnel on production equipment. The chief chemist, with his great sensitivity to market preferences, developed only a limited number of formulations (each of which could be modified). He actually turned down requests to develop certain special formulations for which he thought the market would be inadequate.

In the large firm, the transfer of the product to production was extremely difficult, inasmuch as the chemist had utilized processing methods which were unrealistic under factory conditions; many months had to be devoted to solving this problem. In addition, the project chemist had developed a large number of formulations, each in response to a request from some prospective customer. Management later simplified the line (to about the same number of formulations as had been developed by the smaller firm) because of lack of potential for the other formulations.

Invention in the most concentrated industries

If smaller companies are barred from conducting research and development by its expense, the leaders in conceiving and adopting new processes and products should logically be the large corporations in the most concentrated industries. To quote Richard Stillerman, "If monopoly power gives a firm the stability, financial resources and ability to retain the benefits of its research, then we should find that the more concentrated industries are the most research oriented and technically progressive." There is little in the evidence, however, to support such a presumption. As Stillerman noted,

> In the United States, the most concentrated industries are aircraft propellers, primary aluminum, locomotives and parts, cyclic (coal tar) crudes, flat glass, electric lamps (bulbs), telephone and telegraph equipment, safes and vaults, soap and glycerin, gypsum products, chewing gum, carbon and graphite products, reclaimed rubber, primary copper and steam engines and turbines. Not all of these industries are regarded commonly as pacemakers in technology; some spend little on research. If we rank certain major industry groups from highest to lowest concentration, it is difficult to argue that they retain the same ranking in terms of their interest and accomplishments in research. Clearly particular industries of low concentration such as apparel and furniture are not research conscious, but neither are such concentrated industries as tobacco and dairy products. Some industries of relatively low concentration, notably scien-

tific instruments, insecticides and fungicides, and plastics materials are technically active.

Citing reports of the Monopolies and Restrictive Practices Commission, Stillerman pointed to the laggard's pace set by the more concentrated industries in Great Britain. For example, although the British Oxygen Company Ltd. long held a near monopoly on oxygen and acetylene, it had no research department until 1945 and pioneered none of the major inventions in its field.[32] Among the most concentrated of the British industries is matchmaking, which still uses the conventional process adopted in the nineteenth century and whose leading firm, British Match Corps Ltd., not only does not conduct research but has discouraged it among other machinery makers.[33]

In the United States the performance of our single most concentrated major industry—primary aluminum—also constitutes a striking refutation of the argument. Although a few producers were added after World War II, primarily through the disposition of government-built surplus plants, the industry now numbers only 7 producers, and its 4 largest firms account for over 95 percent of its value of shipments.[34] Many new processes and products involving aluminum have been developed, but according to a study by Merton J. Peck, few have come from the primary-aluminum producers.[35] Of 52 inventions that he recorded relating to the joining, or welding, of aluminum, only 6 came from the aluminum producers. The largest source was equipment manufacturers—a far less concentrated area—which were responsible for 26. When the analysis is limited to "major" inventions, the conclusion remains the same: "The origin of these apparently more major inventions corresponds roughly with the results obtained from the counting of the inventions, with one each coming from a British equipment maker, a domestic equipment maker, an end-product manufacturer and one jointly from an end-product manufacturer and a primary producer."

The idea for the "most significant" invention in this area, the Koldweld process, came from a Royal Air Force officer who, upon observing that a weld sometimes occurs between two sheets of copper cut with dull sheers, sought to establish the conditions under which such a weld would regularly take place. Peck recorded 76 inventions in the conversion of the aluminum ingot into semifinished forms for use by the end-product manufacturers; only 10 of these came from the primary-aluminum producers. Again the equipment makers were the most important source, with 37 of the inventions, followed by independent fabricators with 13. The 3 major inventions in fabricating technique originated abroad during World War II. Johannes Croning, a German engineer, was responsible for the most important, shell molding, which utilizes a plastic shell rather than the more expensive metal die or mold. Also during the war, German aircraft firms built 4 extremely large forging presses, which could form entire aircraft subassemblies, thereby reducing the number of parts while simplifying and increasing structural strength. An Italian engineer invented a continuous casting process for aluminum, which permits a single machine to convert aluminum ingot directly into redrawn rod, eliminating a number of inter-

[32] London, Monopolies and Restrictive Practices Commission, *Report on the Supply of Certain Industrial and Medical Gases,* 1956.

[33] London, Monopolies and Restrictive Practices Commission, *Report on the Supply and Export of Matches and the Supply of Matchmaking Machinery,* 1958.

[34] *Concentration Ratios in Manufacturing Industry, 1963,* p. 25.

[35] *Hearings on Economic Concentration,* Pt. 3, pp. 1438–50, testimony of Merton J. Peck.

mediate steps (and the equipment for them): "None of these inventions were introduced in the United States by the primary producers, which is consistent with the relatively limited role of these firms in the invention of fabricating techniques." [36]

Finally, Peck examined inventions relating to new product uses for aluminum, which "are too numerous for listing" but include such items as low-tension electrical wire, store fronts, lighting fixtures, window frames, wall panels, shelving, refrigerator shelves, and irrigation pipe. While important in expanding the use of aluminum and occasionally calling for the solution of difficult technical problems, these developments represent "less of an advance in the state of the arts." And, although the primary producers have been "important contributors to this kind of technical change," nonetheless "the end-product manufacturers are the major sources of these inventions."

Recent inventions

As a depiction of the present-day inventive process, the Jewkes study has been criticized on the grounds that by including inventions made in the early years in this century, it gives undue weight to the era predating organized scientific research. C. Freeman has contended that if the study had been confined to a more recent era, the discoveries made by the large corporations would form a larger proportion of the total.[37] After surveying more recent studies and adding 10 additional case histories of new discoveries, Jewkes, in the second edition of his study, rejects the argument:

> the most recent evidence does not support Freeman's suggestions. Hamberg, in his study of inventions emanating between 1946 and 1955, finds that of a total of twenty-seven, twelve originated in the work of independent inventors. Among the case histories which we have added to this volume there are a number of the more important—oxygen steel-making, the Hovercraft, Computers, the Wankel engine, the prevention of Rhesus Halmalytic Disease, chlordane and associated chemicals, Photo-typesetting —which cannot be attributed mainly to large institutions. We think this is also the correct interpretation with other recent innovations: the Maser and Laser, the Tunnel Diode, the Fuel Cell, certain of the tranquilizer drugs and the Auto-Analyses.[38]

In addition to Jewkes's new case histories, Hamberg's study for the 1946–55 period,[39] and studies for individual industries, the record of the Senate Antitrust

[36] In addition Peck recorded inventions in the finishing of aluminum and in aluminum alloys. The primary producers played an even less important role in the former but were responsible for most of the new alloys. Both, however, were special cases. Finishing is of importance primarily to the aircraft industry and is therefore "a less valid test for the relative role of different classes of invention," while in the development of new alloys, firms other than the primary producers "do not have access to the technology and cannot realize direct and immediate gains from such inventions."

[37] Thus Freeman's argument is that if the line of 61 inventions studied in the original Jewkes study are divided into two groups—those before and those after 1928—the very large organizations show a better performance record in the later than in the earlier period (see C. Freeman, "Research and Development in Electronic Capital Goods," *National Institute Economic Review,* Nov., 1965).

[38] Jewkes, Sawers, Stillerman, *op. cit.* (rev. ed.), pp. 208–09.

[39] See footnote 26.

Subcommittee contains a considerable body of information relating to the sources of invention and innovation. Included in this material are case histories of important inventions of fairly recent origin—the "wonder drugs," aircraft, the turbojet engine, rocketry, xerography, the mercury dry-cell battery, and the "continuous mix" baking process. In these cases, which are summarized below, the role of the large corporation was, at best, that of providing financial assistance to university-based scientists and aiding in the later stages of development work; at worst, it was a record of indifference and even hostility.

"Wonder drugs"

A voluminous body of information relating to the discovery of new products was secured in the investigation of the drug industry conducted by the Subcommittee. It is a little-recognized fact that most of the truly original breakthroughs in drugs—discoveries that have led to the creation of whole classes of new drugs—have come from the work of individual scientists who were *not* staff employees of any private company. In the three classes of so-called wonder drugs that were examined by the Subcommittee (corticosteroids, tranquilizers, and antibiotics), the original breakthroughs came from creative individuals and not from organized or group research.[40] This is true even in those cases where the research was conducted in universities or clinics but financed by major drug companies, which, in addition, often provided other forms of assistance.

Corticosteroids, used in the treatment of rheumatoid arthritis and many other ailments, stem from the discovery of the use of cortisone by Philip S. Hench of the Mayo Clinic, who was aided by financial and other assistance from Merck & Company. As is usually the case in drugs, once the original discovery had been made, modifications were soon made by a number of manufacturers. Eminent medical authorities appearing before the Subcommittee agreed that some of the early modifications, notably prednisone, were distinct therapeutic improvements over the original product, but they were skeptical as to whether the later variants represented any further advance.[41]

The Subcommittee examined the origins of both the potent and the mild tranquilizers, as well as the closely related product reserpine. A French anesthetist, Laborit, had the original idea that led to the development of the potent tranquilizers. He had observed that certain antihistamines (which are drugs used in the treatment of hay fever, hives, and other allergic diseases) had the undesirable side effect of inducing drowsiness. Acting on the idea that what was undesirable in an antihistamine could be useful in an anesthetic, he commissioned the French drug manufacturing company Rhone-Poulenc to develop a phenothiazine compound in which the antihistaminic properties would be reduced to a minimum and the sedative properties maximized. The product Rhone-Poulenc came up with was chlorpromazine, sold in this country as Thorazine. Laborit used it in anesthetizing, and a short while later two French psychiatrists, Delay and Denicker, at the University of Paris, as well as Heinz Lehmann at the Verdun Protestant Hospital in Montreal, used it to calm or "tranquilize" the mentally ill. Although many modifications were subsequently

[40] With respect to the fourth category, oral antidiabetics, not enough is known concerning the sources of discovery of the most important product in this group, tolbutamide, which was first marketed and patented by the Hoechst Co. of Germany.

[41] *Hearings on Administered Prices,* Pt. 16, pp. 9024–34, 9049–89, testimony of Heinz Lehmann; *ibid.,* pp. 9034–38, 9049–89, testimony of Fritz Freyhan.

introduced, both here and abroad, Lehmann, author of the first publication in the English language on tranquilizers, testified: "There hasn't been a very much better one than the very first ones that came out in the six or seven years of frantic research since then."

The widely used mild tranquilizer meprobamate (sold principally under the trade names of Miltown and Equanil) is the discovery of Frank M. Berger, who became vice president of Carter Products. Born in Czechoslovakia, Berger found refuge during World War II in Great Britain. While searching for a preservative for penicillin, he noted that a mouse injected with one of the compounds would, if placed on its back, be unable to right itself for over an hour. Either the mouse was too relaxed to care, or its muscles were too relaxed to move. He then began an intensive examination of muscle relaxants and hit upon mephenesin in 1946. Coming to the United States after the war, he joined the staff of Wallace Laboratories Division of Carter Products and continued his work on muscle relaxants, the result of which was meprobamate, a derivative of mephenesin. Berger held it to be superior to mephenesin in that it had a more intense effect, induced effects of longer duration, and had fewer side effects.

The discovery of reserpine, used as a tranquilizer and in the treatment of hypertension, represents an amalgam of long usage, independent research by Indian scientists, and organized research in an international drug company. Reserpine is a derivative of the rauwolfia root, which has been used for centuries in India for ailments ranging from insomnia and headaches to fevers and snakebite. In the early 1930's the active ingredients were isolated by two Indian chemists, and evidence was published in 1933 by an Indian physician demonstrating that crude rauwolfia had remarkable abilities to produce sedation and lower blood pressure. As a result of work they had been conducting off and on for several years, the laboratory staff of the Swiss drug firm CIBA isolated serpentine in 1950, something the Indians had already achieved, and a year later succeeded in extracting reserpine from the brown muddy fraction that remained.

The discovery, early development, and initial testing of penicillin represent the very antithesis of purposeful, directed, organized research.[42] Modern antibiotics had their origin in a classic example of serendipity—a chance and perspicacious observation in September, 1928, by Alexander Fleming in St. Mary's Hospital of London. In Fleming's own words:

> While working with staphylococcus variants a number of culture plates were set aside on the laboratory bench and examined from time to time. In the examinations these plates were necessarily exposed to the air and they became contaminated with various micro-organisms. It was noticed that around a large colony of a contaminating mould the staphylococcus colonies became transparent. . . . It was found that broth in which the mold had been grown at room temperature for 1 or 2 weeks had acquired marked inhibitory, bactericidal and bacteriolytic properties to many of the more common pathogenic bacteria.[43]

For the next decade little was done to develop the implications of the original observation. In the 1930's H. W. Florey, professor of pathology at Oxford University, became interested in another Fleming discovery, known as

[42] See Federal Trade Commission, *Economic Report on Antibiotics Manufacture*, 1958, App. 2, "Discovery and Development of Penicillin," pp. 302–54.
[43] Quoted in *ibid.*, p. 303.

lysozyme, but soon concentrated his research on penicillin. Aided by a grant of $5,000 from the Natural Science Division of the Rockefeller Foundation, Florey and Chain were successful in establishing in 1940 the remarkable therapeutic properties of penicillin in mice and other animals. They were able to show that penicillin was not toxic, that the white blood cells were unaffected, that the activity of penicillin was not affected by pus, blood, or the number of bacteria present, and that it was absorbed after injection. In later writings Florey has emphasized that this early scientific work antedated any thought of large-scale usage:

> Although in the application [to the Rockefeller Foundation] the possible practical results were brought forward, the research was conceived of as an academic study with possibilities of wide theoretical interest, both chemical and biological. Statements have appeared from time to time that the work on penicillin was started as an attempt to contribute to the treatment of septic wounds in World War II. This is quite erroneous, as the work was planned well before the outbreak of war, and in any case there was then no idea that penicillin could play the important part which it has done in the treatment of war injuries.[44]

Despite the promising results of their animal testing, Florey and his associates continued to be beset with difficulties. With their own resources and existing methods they were unable to produce enough penicillin to make possible adequate clinical testing in man, and without the results of such clinical tests they were unable to obtain the assistance of drug companies. Referring to further animal tests carried out in May and June, 1940, Florey stated, "The enthusiasm of the Oxford workers was believed by many to be premature and though an approach was made to a commercial firm, this firm and others who might otherwise have helped in the project were overburdened with war work." [45] Armed with the results of a few tests on humans as well as their animal investigations and aided by a second grant of $5,000 from the Rockefeller Foundation, Florey came to the United States to secure assistance in finding ways and means of increasing production:

> Florey . . . visited a number of drug firms in the United States and Canada with a request which now looks modest but at the time seemed formidable—to brew 10,000 liters of culture fluid and extract the penicillin, so that more clinical trials might be made at Oxford. None of the information which had been accumulated at Oxford was withheld. Though certain of the firms thought the matter worth attention, a number of them showed little interest, and some none at all. Amongst the first to tackle the problem seriously were Merck & Co., Inc., E. R. Squibb & Sons, and Chas. Pfizer & Co., Inc.[46]

But the greatest assistance came from experts with long experience in mold fermentation stationed at the Northern Regional Research Laboratory of the U.S. Department of Agriculture at Peoria, Illinois. These experts contributed the ideas that made possible the subsequent great expansion in penicillin output,

[44] Quoted in *ibid.,* p. 308.
[45] Quoted in *ibid.,* p. 310. Some idea of the straits to which they were reduced in their efforts to increase production is provided by their reliance for fermentation vessels upon old-style bed pans. But even here their efforts to obtain 600 of these vessels were frustrated when it was found that they had been replaced by a more modern streamlined structure without the lid that was necessary for fermentation.
[46] Quoted in *ibid.,* pp. 314–15.

principally the idea of using cornsteep liquor as the medium of fermentation and the idea of producing penicillin in deep culture in the revolving drums used for gluconic acid and other fermentations. From this point on, most of the work on penicillin consisted of refining and improving the application of these methods of production and of accumulating additional information concerning the drug's behavior in man. In this developmental stage important contributions were made not only by the Northern Regional Research Laboratory but by drug companies in both the United States and Great Britain. By May, 1944, production of penicillin in the United States was sufficiently great not only to meet the needs of the armed forces of the Allies but to permit limited sale through hospitals. For a few years following the war the discoveries of new antibiotics came thick and fast as the recognition grew that nature provided a multitude of molds. Following penicillin came the discovery of streptomycin by Selman Waksman at Rutgers University, with the assistance of Merck & Company, and of chloramphenicol (Chloromycetin) by Paul Burkholder at Yale University, with the aid of Parke, Davis. These were followed by the tetracycline family—chlortetracycline (Aureomycin), oxytetracycline (Terramycin) and tetracycline, each of which came from the laboratories of the large U.S. drug companies. Although their importance cannot be minimized, the discovery of new molds in nature, while undoubtedly time consuming and costly to the companies in terms of laboratory and clinical testing, hardly falls in the same creative category as the pioneering work of the Oxford scientists and the Peoria Laboratory.

Aircraft

In their recent book Ronald Miller and David Sawers, after surveying the history of invention in aircraft, conclude:

> Invention *within* the aircraft industry is most noticeable for its absence. Of all the major inventions made in the past half-century, only those of two types of flap can wholly be credited to the employees of aircraft manufacturers. The institutions that have been most productive of inventions are the universities and government-financed research institutes —especially in Germany—while about a quarter of the inventions have come from inventors with no institutional backing.[47]

In view of the vast sums that reportedly are spent on aircraft research and development, such a conclusion seems startling. But, in the view of Miller and Sawers, these amounts are spent mostly on development and production, while very little goes to research. Moreover, much of what is spent on development comes from government agencies, such as the National Advisory Committee for Aeronautics, whose primary function since World War II appears to have been pursuing development work on ideas originated before and during the war by German scientists. As Sawers testified,

> The result was by the end of the war in 1945 German designers had built or were testing nearly all the ideas that have been incorporated in American aircraft in the past 20 years; these included the swept-back wing, the delta wing, the wing with variable sweepback, the area rule

[47] Ronald Miller and David Sawers, *The Technical Development of Modern Aviation*, Routledge and Kegan Paul, 1968, p. 246. Emphasis added. For a summary of their work see the statement by David Sawers in *Hearings on Economic Concentration*, Pt. 3, pp. 1505–08.

and forged wing spars. The contribution of the National Advisory Committee for Aeronautics was to develop many of these ideas, notably the area rule and variable sweepback until they could easily be applied by manufacturers.[48]

The fountainhead of German aerodynamics knowledge was the research center at Göttingen University, long headed by Ludwig Prandtl. This center "provided a unifying influence as well as scientific inspiration, for most [German] designers had studied there." [49] Its purpose was to achieve an understanding of the laws of aerodynamics and to create aircraft designs that were in accord with this developing body of scientific knowledge. Speaking of the accomplishments that flowed out of Göttingen, Miller and Sawers observe:

> later in the decade [of the 1930's] a new generation of designers came to the fore in Germany, products of Gottingen and the gliding movement. These men better appreciated the lessons they could learn from science than their predecessors or designers in Britain and the United States, who remained practical men in the tradition of the industry. So Germany quickly attained a lead in design when understanding of recent aerodynamic research—mostly done in Germany—became essential to the designer, as it did in the development of transonic and supersonic airplanes during the war. Only the military defeat of Germany in 1945 prevented the German industry from becoming as dominant as the American industry is today.[50]

In their listing of important aircraft inventions, the two most recent are the swept-back wing and the variable-sweepback wing. At an international conference on aircraft design in 1935, Adolph Busemann of Göttingen suggested that sweeping back the wing would ease the problem of drag encountered at speeds near or above the speed of sound. A further contribution was made in 1939 by Albert Betz, also of Göttingen, who pointed out that the really significant reduction in drag comes when the wing is swept back enough to maintain subsonic flow over the leading edge.[51]

In endeavoring to develop designs for supersonic speeds the Germans were not inhibited, as were British and American scientists, by wind tunnel tests which seemed to indicate that drag would increase so sharply with rising speed as to prevent an airplane from reaching the speed of sound. In a wind tunnel the model of an airplane must of course be mounted on a support; it was the manner in which the model was mounted that gave rise to the rapid increase in drag. As the Germans had learned, the problem disappears when the model and its support are properly mounted.[52]

The most recent invention listed by Miller and Sawers, the variable-sweep-back wing, is also of German origin. Alexander Lippisch received a secret German patent in 1941 for a swept-back wing that could be moved forward for lower speeds and backward for supersonic speeds. Such a wing would gain the advantages of a swept-back wing at high speeds, while overcoming its poor handling qualities at low speeds. Because of its obvious conceptual advantages such a wing was incorporated in Boeing's winning design for the American

[48] *Hearings on Economic Concentration,* Pt. 3, p. 1505.
[49] Miller and Sawers, *op. cit.,* p. 169.
[50] *Ibid.,* p. 247.
[51] *Ibid.,* pp. 24, 167.
[52] *Ibid.,* p. 168.

supersonic transport plane, but because of mechanical problems it subsequently had to be abandoned in favor of a fixed wing.

Regardless of how far back one goes in the listing of aircraft inventions, the contributions of the large enterprises remain conspicuous by their infrequency. In the words of Miller and Sawers, "For a science-based industry the aircraft manufacturers—especially in Europe—show surprisingly little interest in research." [53]

The turbojet engine

Although not the first to conceive of a turbojet engine, Frank Whittle of Great Britain supplied much of the scientific knowledge and engineering skill required to transpose the idea into a working mechanism.[54] The idea first appeared to Whittle in 1930, when he was a junior officer in the Royal Air Force. But his initial efforts to interest the large manufacturers of aircraft engines and industrial steam turbines were completely unsuccessful. Their reasons for rejection were the absence of sufficient knowledge in the underlying sciences of metallurgy and engine design plus the inability of existing airframes to use such a high-speed mechanism. Whittle dropped his idea and even let his basic patent lapse.

It was not until 5 years later, when Whittle was studying engineering at Cambridge University, that an old acquaintance heard of the turbojet and became convinced of its merits. Through this friend limited financing was obtained, and a new company, Power Jets Ltd., was founded in 1935 with about $10,000 in cash. In his study of the history of the turbojet, Robert Schlaifer credits Whittle with having been largely responsible "for setting the sound general management policies in regard to development which were followed by Power Jets Ltd. and without which no amount of scientific ability could have brought success."

Despite the growing menace of Hitler's Germany during the late 1930's, the British government gave the project only the most nominal assistance.[55] During this period the total amount raised by Power Jets was only some $83,000 from private sources, supplemented by about $16,000 from the government. It was not until the middle of 1939 that, on the basis of the work done by Power Jets, the government became convinced of the practicality of the turbojet and only then did the project begin to receive adequate financial assistance. Summarizing the history of this development Schlaifer states:

> There can be no question but that, if the new firm of Power Jets had not been formed and financed with funds no part of which came from the aircraft industry, the development of turbojets in Great Britain would have been delayed by at least five years. The same delay would have occurred in the United States, both because the first flyable turbojets produced in this country were almost exact duplicates of an imported

[53] *Ibid.*, p. 249.
[54] *Hearings on Economic Concentration*, Pt. 3, pp. 1230–39, testimony of Robert Schlaifer. See also his "Big Business and Small Business," *Harvard Business Review,* July, 1950.
[55] During this same period the German government was seeking to promote work on the jet engine. According to Schlaifer, "In Germany the earliest development was begun in 1936, just about the date at which development began in Britain, and was due to two manufacturers of airframes. At least one of the regular producers of engines had considered jet propulsion as early as 1930 but had rejected it for the same reason that the British engine producer mentioned above rejected it in that same year. As late as 1938–39 it required considerable pressure from the German Government to persuade the engine manufacturers to enter the new field."

Power Jets engine and even more because the spark which set off the intensive development of powerjets of native American design was the knowledge that such engines had actually flown in Britain.

Interestingly, the frustrations encountered by Whittle had their historical parallel a quarter of a century earlier in the difficulties faced by the developer of the air-cooled aircraft engine—a small American firm, Lawrence Aero Engine Corporation. Founded in 1917 with a capitalization of only $50,000, it had neither production experience nor manufacturing facilities. What it did have was vision, ability, and persistence in the person of its founder, president, and chief engineer, Charles L. Lawrance. Only 2 years after its formation, the firm had brought out a design for a 3-cylinder engine of about 60 horsepower and obtained backing from the Navy Department to finance the development of a 9-cyclinder engine of around 200 horsepower. Only 3 years later the Navy, which had become convinced of the superiority of air cooling over liquid cooling, began putting the larger engine into actual service.

As is generally true of procurement agencies, the Navy preferred to deal with one of the large established companies, which in this industry consisted only of the Curtiss Aeroplane & Motor Company and the Wright Aeronautical Corporation. However, to quote Robert Schlaifer, "From 1919 to 1922 the Navy's efforts to interest these two companies in the project failed completely." Preoccupied with its efforts to build a high-powered version of the old liquid-cooled engine, Curtiss's management "flatly refused to divert any time to a side issue which might delay the attainment of the major goal." In Schlaifer's words, "There can be no doubt that if the Navy had been forced to rely on the two large firms in the industry, the development of this type of engine would have been delayed by 5 years at least."

Rocketry

The space ships of today and their military counterpart, guided missiles, can be traced directly to the work of one man, Robert H. Goddard. In 1935, a 22-foot rocket he had designed, engineered, and personally built reached a height of 7,500 feet. What is remarkable is not so much the height attained as the nature of the vehicle that reached it. In the words of Goddard's biographer, Milton Lehman, the discoveries incorporated in this rocket "led the way to virtually every modern rocket—from V-2 to sputnik to Gemini to the ionized and nuclear and solar propelled rockets of tomorrow." [56]

It is well recognized that today's space ships and guided missiles represent refinements, elaborations, and improvements of the German V-2 rocket of World War II. What is not so well known is the extent to which the German missile was itself a product of Goddard's earlier work. On this point Lehman testified:

> In Germany Goddard's work stimulated Herman Oberth, and led us directly as an arrow to the technological accomplishments of Dr. Wernher von Braun at Peenemunde and years later at Huntsville, Alabama. It led far more directly to Dr. von Braun's work than Americans—almost all of us have been informed or are likely to be informed by the German expatriates. For Goddard's work did underlie the German's rocket development in World War II—entirely and fully.

[56] *Hearings on Economic Concentration*, Pt. 3, pp. 1311–33, testimony of Milton Lehman. See also his *This High Man, The Life of Robert H. Goddard*, Farrar, Straus, 1963.

Remarkably similar to the smaller German V-1 rocket was a Goddard patent that had been published in the German aviation journal *Flugsport* on January 4, 1939—5 years before the first buzz bomb fell on London.[57] A diagrammatic comparison between the 46-foot German V-2 of 1943 and the 22-foot Goddard rocket of 1939 also reveals striking similarities.[58] On inspecting a captured V-2 in March, 1945, one of Goddard's crew was quoted by Lehman as saying, "Of course it was more elaborate and much larger than the rockets we'd worked on, but it seemed extremely familiar—the injection feeding system, the pump assembly, the general layout. The only thing that looked at all new to me was the German design of their turbine."

For over 30 years Goddard had been making public his work through patents and scientific papers. He was awarded over 200 patents on rockets, each of which contained a description of the invention. Among his scientific writings one of the most interesting is a monograph, *A Method of Reaching Extreme Altitudes,* published in 1919 by the Smithsonian Institution. Here he asserted in a footnote that it was mathematically possible for a rocket, light in weight and heavy in fuel, to reach the moon. Two of his patents, issued in 1914, introduced features basic to all future rocket development: the use of a combustion chamber with a nozzle; the feeding of propellants, liquid or solid, into the combustion chamber; and the principle of the multiple-stage or step rocket. With respect to the last, he asserted in his patent: "What I do claim is . . . in a rocket apparatus, in combination, a primary rocket, comprising a combustion chamber and a firing tube, a secondary rocket mounted in said firing tube, and means for firing said secondary rocket when the explosive in the primary rocket is substantially consumed." [59]

Goddard combined in one person research scientist, inventor, and innovator. He conceived the ideas of the essentials of rocket flight, invented the necessary items of hardware, and put them together in a workable vehicle. In addition to the design of the combustion chamber, the method of feeding propellants, and the principle of the multiple-stage rocket, other essential features of modern rocketry that originated with Goddard include the use of liquid fuel in the form of hydrogen or oxygen, movable vanes worked by gyroscope to control the flight, the cooling of the combustion chamber by the circulation of a liquid around the inside of the chamber (curtain cooling), and the design of a pump to force-feed the liquid fuel and oxygen into the combustion chamber. Where he could not purchase a necessary item, Goddard made it in his own workshop. Over a 40-year period the total amount available to him was only $250,000, out of which had to come the salary of his crew, the cost of his hardware, and the fees for his patents, as well as the maintenance of his household. The sources of these funds were his salary as a professor plus small grants from the Smithsonian Institution and the Guggenheim Foundation. Not only did the armed services fail to provide any financial assistance; they repeatedly rejected Goddard's efforts to interest them in rockets as an instrument of warfare.

The record of support by industry was no better. Although the Linde Air Products Company had a plant in Goddard's home town of Worcester, Massachusetts, it refused to sell him the small quantities of liquid oxygen he needed at a price he could afford to pay. His requests to Ingersoll-Rand and Worthington Pump for a powerful miniature pump were turned down on the grounds

[57] *Ibid.,* p. 1519, exhibit by Milton Lehman.
[58] *Ibid.,* p. 1523, exhibit by Milton Lehman.
[59] Quoted by Lehman in *ibid.,* p. 1316.

that the cost was too great and that there was no ready market for such a device. At a conference of Du Pont engineers arranged by Goddard's supporter Charles A. Lindbergh, the idea of a rocket was dismissed as impractical: "A rocket, however used, would generate such enormous heat and pressure that its combustion chamber would require a heavy lining of fire brick. To elevate a load of fire brick into the atmosphere—this, of course, was impossible." As Lehman commented, "While U.S. industry gave Goddard few assists, the inventor assuredly gave many to industry. His creative vision, reduced to sound and workable patents, became the basic foundation of every corporate and missile manufacturer in the country today, who tend to pay their respects to the inventor through stuffy industrial rocket banquets from time to time."

Xerography[60]

The inventor of electrophotography, or "xerography," was a patent attorney, Chester Carlson. His interest in better methods of copying was aroused by the very nature of his work; patent attorneys are in constant need of copies of documents and drawings. In his words, "There was no convenient method for obtaining them. It involved completely retyping a manuscript, or sending a drawing out to a photocopy firm. I thought how fine it would be if one could feed an original into a small machine, just push a button, and get out a copy." [61]

Like many other inventors, he made a deliberate decision to ignore existing technology—as he put it himself, "Who was I to compete with Eastman Kodak?" In a relatively short period of time he hit upon the approach of using electrostatics and photoconductive materials. The idea, as he perfected it, called for a plate consisting of a conductive base covered by a layer of photoconductive insulation. Upon the insulation, he would first place an electrostatic charge. Then the positive image of whatever was to be reproduced would be projected on the charged plate. Wherever the light impinged, the charge would drain off. Next, the plate would be dusted with a special powder and gently blown so that the only dust remaining was that which adhered to those areas of the plate that still retained the electrostatic charge. This dust would then be affixed to paper and the paper heated, resulting in a permanent copy of the original. On October 22, 1938, in a room behind a beauty parlor in Astoria, Long Island, he transferred the words "10-22-38 Astoria" from one piece of paper onto another.

Seeking aid to develop his invention, Carlson went to more than 20 companies and, as he puts it, "was met with an enthusiastic lack of interest." He was turned down by IBM, among others, who felt that the idea was not worth the risks. In 1944 the Battelle Memorial Institute agreed to take on the development work, for which they were to receive 60 percent of the proceeds from the invention. Battelle in turn located a businessman who manifested real interest in the invention—Joseph C. Wilson, who had just become president of the Haloid Company, a small concern with a yearly net income of only $100,000. In Wilson's words, "We were able to convince Battelle that we would run with it and not put it on the back burner. They were soured on big companies and had about decided to give it to a small company, even if it looked like the wrong choice on paper." [62]

[60] *Hearings on Economic Concentration,* Pt. 3, pp. 1108–11, testimony of Daniel V. De-Simone.
[61] Quoted by Daniel V. DeSimone in *ibid.,* p. 1109.
[62] Quoted by Daniel V. DeSimone in *ibid.,* p. 1110. ⁻

Wilson brought to the project that indispensable ingredient of entrepreneurial enthusiasm without which many inventions might still be languishing. As is the case with most radical new departures, the road from success in the laboratory to profits in the market was long and arduous. On more than one occasion Haloid came close to the abyss. It was not until 1960 that the first xerographic copier was marketed for office use, 25 years after Carlson had "reduced his idea to practice." It has been estimated that by mid-1966 Battelle had received some $60 million (in cash and stock) under its agreements with the Xerox Corporation. Carlson's share of Battelle's receipts had accumulated to roughly $24 million.

The mercury dry-cell battery[63]

The importance of the mercury dry cell lies in the small but numerous changes it has brought about in lifestyles. It is the source of power for portable radios and similar devices, for hearing aids, for electronic watches and cameras, for synchronizing devices that pulse the heart, and for numerous other items. It was the creation of an independent inventor, Samuel Ruben, who has also been responsible for many other inventions, including the solid-state rectifier and the dry electrolytic capacitator—both items of widespread use.

Its predecessor, the zinc-carbon dry battery, suffered from a number of serious disadvantages—most notably, a relatively short "shelf life," particularly in hot, humid weather. What was needed to power portable radio receivers, transmitters, and the like was a long-life cell, capable of discharging high currents. During World War II the military demand for portable communications and mine-detecting equipment accentuated the need. Two weeks after Pearl Harbor, Ruben informed the Army Signal Corps through the National Inventors Council —which had made known the need for a cold-resistant dry cell—that he had the answer in the form of a low-ambient-temperature cell, which obviated the low-temperature problem.

But there remained the need for a high-current battery with a long shelf life that would operate in conditions of high as well as low temperature and humidity. The relatively rapid deterioration of the dry cells then available was the result of chemical reaction; gas would expand with rising temperature, quickly destroying the cells in hot climates. Opening the cells would let in moisture, corroding the electrodes. On the other hand, hermetically sealing them would cause the rising gas pressure to rupture the container.

Ruben's mercury dry cell solved the gas and other problems. Among its features were long shelf life over a wide temperature range, very low internal gas pressure, and a very high ratio of output capacity to cell volume, which is essential to the miniaturization of batteries (e.g., in hearing aids and electronic watches). The invention has had the effect of broadening greatly the range and uses of battery-powered products.

The "continuous mix" process

Since time immemorial the process of bread making has defied substantial change.[64] It was only with the introduction of the "continuous mix" process

---

[63] *Hearings on Economic Concentration,* Pt. 3, pp. 1106–08, testimony of Daniel V. De-Simone.
[64] The historical method of bread making involves several separate and distinct stages. First

that the long-embedded methods of the past gave way to technological progress. The history of this new process was described before the Subcommittee by Joseph P. Duchaine, president of Quality Bakers of America (QBA) and one of the nation's largest independent, single-plant bakers:

> For many years, Dr. John C. Baker, of Wallace & Tiernan, a noted cereal chemist, dreamed of a way to revolutionize this process. For many years he sought a way of accomplishing all of this which required from 5 to 6 hours or more, in a matter of minutes. He dreamed of a "continuous" mix process in which the ingredients would flow in a steady even stream into a mechanism which would properly and quickly blend and develop them into dough in small continuous amounts and result, therefore, in a continuous flow of dough ready for the pans.[65]

By the early 1950's Wallace & Tiernan had made sufficient progress in developing the process to announce that it planned to build a number of field models for experimental purposes. Among the large bakery corporations, Continental, General, American, and National each contracted for a unit. In addition, one was contracted for by the management cooperative of the independent bakers (QBA) and installed in Duchaine's plant in Massachusetts. As is usually the case with a new process, numerous "bugs" developed between the pilot-plant stage and commercial production. Although the large companies soon lost patience with the process and discontinued their experimental work, Duchaine persisted. In recounting his experience, he revealed that quality of dogged, stubborn persistence which seems to be unique to the small enterpriser and the individual inventor:

> It became a matter of personal pride with me and while my agreement with QBA covered only the cost of the equipment if unsuccessful, I spent a small fortune on my own in literally hundreds of experiments, wasted and destroyed dough, and upsets of my working force.
>
> By fall of 1953, we really began to make progress and in the spring of 1954 we converted all of our white bread production to the new process.
>
>   * * *
>
> Despite the initial investment which today represents some $150,000 plus an equal amount for advertising, some 30 QBA members have installed the equipment, plus others who have the equipment on order, and it is my opinion that QBA members alone have risked a total of $8 or $10 million in the process.
>
> I feel that this is an excellent illustration of the fact that smaller corporations are neither unwilling, incapable, nor undesirous of venturing into research and taking the risks involved.

The new process not only reduced the cost and time of manufacture but, according to Duchaine, produced a superior product: "Its uniformity and fine grain is noticeable and we advertise: 'Compare. No holes, no streaks, no poor end slices in Sunbeam Bread.' "

Today the continuous-mix process is widely used throughout the United States in the production of white bread. In addition to the Wallace & Tiernan

---

a "sponge" is made containing the primary ingredients—flour, yeast, water, etc. This is allowed to ferment for several hours and then remixed with the balance of the ingredients. It is then passed through a series of machines to be divided and rounded. From there it goes to a complicated apparatus known as a "proofer," then to a molder, then to the steam proofer and finally to the oven.

[65] *Hearings on Administered Prices,* Pt. 12, pp. 6527–31, testimony of Joseph P. Duchaine.

process, a somewhat comparable method, the Amflow process, has been developed more recently by American Machine & Foundry and adopted extensively by chain-store and other bakeries. According to George Graf, general manager of OBA, the reduction of costs and uniformity of product made possible by these continuous processes have enabled many independent bakers to survive, and in some cases to expand their operations.

Mr. Duchaine went on to offer a few general observations concerning the contributions of large versus small bakeries to technological progress:

> ". . . I can honestly say I know of no major or revolutionary research contributions to the industry by the large corporations. I am aware of the fact that Continental Baking Co. [the industry's largest producer] has a sizable research budget . . . I understand it averages over a half million dollars annually. I must presume, however, that the output of this department is devoted primarily to research on cutting costs and strengthening themselves in competition, for I know of no important direct industry contribution which has come from their research.

Instead, he held, it is the smaller firms, sometimes with the help of machinery manufacturers, who have been primarily responsible for innovations. For example, he cited the "brown 'n serve" process of baking, which has added new markets and increased the industry's sales; the process, according to Duchaine, "was developed by a very small bakery and promoted by General Mills." The slicing of bread was "first developed and exploited by smaller bakers before the big corporations took over." Other examples he cited were "the process known as hot sponges for better bread flavor"; the process known as "loose molding," which made possible the achievement of better grain and texture; new methods of truck loading; and new processes of packaging, registration, and wrapping.

CH 10 THE CREATIVE BACKWARDNESS OF BIGNESS

Aside from some notable exceptions, particularly in the field of chemicals, the contribution of large corporations to technical progress has fallen far short of what would have been expected in view of their resources, their facilities, and their shares of the market. This is evidenced not only by the statistical and historical material presented in the preceding chapter but by the typically lengthy interval between the making of an invention and its introduction as an innovation.

In a study of 35 processes and products John L. Enos found that for the group as a whole the arithmetic mean between invention and innovation was 13.6 years (see Table 10-1).[1] Excluding the extreme case of fluorescent lights (for which the interval was 79 years), the average was 11.6 years. In other words, by the time an invention has been introduced, over two-thirds of its patent life has expired. What is perhaps of most interest is the failure of the interval to decrease with the passage of time. Again excluding fluorescent lamps, the group includes 6 inventions with a date of innovation between 1930 and 1940; the arithmetic mean between their invention and innovation was 8 years. For 10 products with a date of innovation between 1940 and 1950 the average was 12.6 years, and for the 2 introduced in the 1950's it was 12.5 years (12 years for dacron and 13 for xerography). In other words, the great expansion of large corporations during the period covered by this study was not accompanied by any acceleration in the time required to develop an invention and introduce it on the market. Indeed, Enos observes, "The interval appears shorter when the inventor himself attempts to innovate than when he is content merely to reveal the general concept."[2]

The explanation for the poor performance of large corporations is to be found not in any single cause but in the combined effect of a matrix of factors. The relative importance of these causes will vary from company to company and from time to time, but they include the desire to protect the investment in an older technology, indifference to technological advance, underestimation of the demand for new products, neglect of the inventor, misdirection of research, incompatibility between organization and creativity, and the military's built-in resistance to change.

[1] *Hearings on Economic Concentration*, Pt. 3, p. 1489.
[2] *Ibid.*

The protection of an older technology

A classic example of outright opposition to a new technology is provided by the attitude of the major communication firms toward radio in its early days. When, as a result of the creative contributions of three independent inventors, Guglielmo Marconi, Reginald Fessenden, and Lee De Forest, the practicality of radio transmission had been demonstrated, attempts were undertaken to interest Western Union, Postal Telegraph, and American Telephone & Telegraph. In the words of W. Rupert Maclaurin: "The managements of both Western Union and Postal were apparently more interested in buying up competitors and making protective agreements than in the fundamental development of communications. Western Union had been willing to withdraw from the telephone field in 1879 in exchange for Bell's promise to keep out of the telegraph business." [3] As for the American Telephone & Telegraph Company, "Its scientific energies were absorbed in developing central switchboards and increasing distances which might be covered by its long-lines division." Maclaurin went on to point out, "For these various reasons, the established electrical companies played no part in earlier developmental phases of the American radio industry. This advance was to come from new concerns and new capital."

An interesting example of the particularly negative attitude toward new technologies often exhibited by financial interests was cited by Maclaurin:

> On December 11, 1906, Fessenden gave a demonstration of radio telephone from Brant Rock to Plymouth, Mass., a distance of 11 miles. Following these tests, Walker and Given [Fessenden's backers] tried hard to sell out to some existing firm. American Telephone and Telegraph, Western Union and Postal were approached. The Telephone executives showed considerable interest and an engineering investigation was ordered. The original report was favorable and optimistic. Chief engineer Hayes in transmitting it to President Fish concluded: "I feel that there is such a reasonable probability of wireless telegraphy and telephony being of commercial value to our company that I would advise taking steps to associate ourselves with Mr. Fessenden if some satisfactory arrangement can be made."
>
> But in 1907 a change in the Baker banking control of the Telephone company from Boston to the Morgan-Baker banking interests of New York, led to the replacement of President Fish by Theodore N. Vail. The study of the Fessenden wireless matter was continued now under the new regime with much greater scepticism, and the final decision was negative.

Not only did the established companies make no contributions to the industry: they endeavored to block its development. According to Maclaurin, "The telegraph and cable companies did their best to prevent Marconi from getting a franchise in Newfoundland. Somewhat later the Postmaster General of Great Britain saw the Marconi Company primarily as a potential competitor of the government-controlled telegraph industry and instantly refused to connect the Marconi overseas service with the post office telegraph lines."

Overt opposition to new technologies is also to be seen in antitrust cases directed against conspiracies to restrain their introduction. Because other and often

[3] W. Rupert Maclaurin, "The Process of Technological Innovation; the Launching of a New Scientific Industry," *American Economic Review*, March, 1950, pp. 90–112.

Table 10-1

TIME INTERVAL BETWEEN INVENTION AND INNOVATION FOR 35 DIFFERENT PRODUCTS AND PROCESSES

Invention			Innovation		Interval Between Invention and Innovation (Years)
Product	Inventor	Date	Firm	Date	
Safety razor	Gillette	1895	Gillette Safety Razor Company	1904	9
Fluorescent lamp	Bacquerel	1859	General Electric, Westinghouse	1938	79
Television	Zworykin	1919	Westinghouse	1941	22
Wireless telegraph	Hertz	1889	Marconi	1897	8
Wireless telephone	Fessenden	1900	National Electric Signaling Company	1908	8
Triode vacuum tube	de Forest	1907	The Radio Telephone and Telegraph Company	1914	7
Radio (oscillator)	de Forest	1912	Westinghouse	1920	8
Spinning jenny	Hargreaves	1765	Hargreaves'	1770	5
Spinning machine (water frame)	Highs	1767	Arkwright's	1773	6
Spinning mule	Crompton	1779	Textile machine manufacturers	1783	4
Steam engine	Newcommen	1705	English firm	1711	6
Steam engine	Watt	1764	Boulton and Watt	1775	11
Ball-point pen	I. J. Biro	1938	Argentine firm	1944	6
Cotton picker	A. Campbell	1889	International Harvester	1942	53
Crease-resistant fabrics	Company scientists	1918	Tootal Broadhurst Lee Company Ltd.	1932	14
DDT	Company chemists	1939	J. R. Geigy Co.	1942	3
Electric precipitation	Sir O. Lodge	1884	Cottrell's	1909	25
Freon refrigerants	T. Midgley, Jr. and A. L. Henne	1930	Kinetic Chemicals, Inc. (General Motors and Du Pont)	1931	1
Gyro-compass	Foucault	1852	Anschütz-Kaempfe	1908	56
Hardening of fats	W. Normann	1901	Crosfield's of Warrington	1909	8
Jet engine	Sir F. Whittle	1929	Rolls Royce	1943	14
Turbo-jet engine	H. von Ohain	1934	Junkers	1944	10
Long playing record	P. Goldmark	1945	Columbia Records	1948	3
Magnetic recording	V. Poulsen	1898	American Telegraphone Co.	1903	5
Plexiglas, lucite	W. Chalmers	1929	Imperial Chemical Industries	1932	3
Nylon	W. H. Carothers	1928	Du Pont	1939	11
Power steering	H. Vickers	1925	Vickers, Inc.	1931	6
Radar	Marconi; A. H. Taylor and L. Young	1922	Société Francaise Radio Electrique	1935	13
Self-winding watch	J. Harwood	1922	Harwood Self-Winding Watch Co.	1928	6

THE CREATIVE BACKWARDNESS OF BIGNESS

Shell moulding	J. Croning	1941	Hamburg foundry	1944	3
Streptomycin	S. A. Waksman	1939	Merck and Co.	1944	5
Terylene, dacron	J. R. Whinfield, J. T. Dickson	1941	Imperial Chemical Industries, Du Pont	1953	12
Titanium reduction	W. J. Kroll	1937	U.S. Government Bureau of Mines	1944	7
Xerography	C. Carlson	1937	Haloid Corp.	1950	13
Zipper	W. L. Judson	1891	Automatic Hook and Eye Company	1918	27

Source: *Hearings on Economic Concentration,* Pt. 3, p. 1489 (Table by John Enos)

persuasive explanations of the failure to introduce a new product or process are usually present, evidence of such conspiracy is hard to come by. Nonetheless, it has been developed in a sufficient number of cases to make it clear that the practice is by no means unknown. In perhaps the most famous case of this kind, Standard Oil of New Jersey and several leading foreign competitors (notably the German firm I. G. Farben) were found to have used their combined patents to suppress the development of a synthetic-rubber industry in the United States, seriously impairing the U.S. war effort.[4] Elsewhere, Hartford-Empire was found to have acted to prevent the development of new and different automatic glass machinery outside the scope of Hartford's patents and also to have discouraged its licensees from making improvements in machinery by requiring that such improvement become the property of Hartford-Empire.[5] In another type of machinery, United Shoe Machinery Corporation was found to have engaged in practices retarding the development and introduction of mass production techniques in shoe manufacturing, restricting labor productivity in shoe factories, and preventing reductions in shoe-manufacturing costs.[6] Through patent pooling, the purchasing of patent rights, and cartel arrangements with leading foreign competitors, the General Cable Corporation was found to have suppressed the commercial exploitation of a superior and more economical type of cable.[7] Bendix Aviation Corporation, a leading manufacturer of braking systems, was found to have acted with its competitors to suppress inventions and improvements in braking systems that might compete seriously with their products.[8] The Diamond Match Company was found to have suppressed inventions and improvements in the match art.[9] The True Temper Corporation, which in 1957 accounted for 90 percent of the sales of golf club shafts, was found to have agreed not to make specially designed steel shafts to the order of any customer except with the approval of the 4 leading manufacturers of golf clubs (Wilson, Spaulding, McGregor, and Hillerich & Bradsley), and these 4 manufacturers, which made 80 percent of the sales of golf clubs, agreed not to introduce glass shafts for golf clubs unless the others adopted such shafts simultaneously.[10]

[4] *United States* v. *Standard Oil Company (New Jersey), et al.,* United States District Court of New Jersey, Civil No. 2091, filed March 25, 1942 (CCH-56, 198).

[5] *United States* v. *Hartford-Empire Co., et al.,* 46 F. Supp. 541 (N.D. Ohio 1942).

[6] *United States* v. *United Shoe Machinery Corporation,* United States District Court of Massachusetts, Civil No. 7198, filed Dec. 15, 1947 (CCH-67,436).

[7] *United States* v. *General Cable Corporation, et al.,* United States District Court, Southern District of New York, Civil No. 40-76, filed Jan. 30, 1947 (CCH-62,300).

[8] *United States* v. *Bendix Aviation Corporation, et al.,* United States District Court, Southern District of New York, Civil No. 44284, filed Dec. 9, 1947 (CCH-62,349).

[9] *United States* v. *Diamond Match Company, et al.,* United States District Court, Southern District of New York, Civil No. 25-397, filed May 1, 1944 (CCH-57,456).

[10] *United States* v. *True Temper Corporation, et al.,* United States District Court, Northern District of Illinois, Civil No. 58C1159, filed June 30, 1958 (CCH-69,441).

On occasion a new technology that would make obsolete a corporation's existing line of business is discovered within the corporation itself. The company is thus confronted with a most difficult decision: adopting the new technology means not only losing its investment in the older technique but risking its commercial future on an uncertain quantity. On the other hand, sticking with what is tried and true means not only sacrificing an opportunity to cut costs or increase demand but risking the adoption of the new technique by a competitor. The danger of the latter becomes very real indeed if the unhappy inventor of the suppressed technique leaves the company. Such a case was cited before the Senate Subcommittee on Antitrust and Monopoly by Donald Schon:

> DR. BLAIR: One last question, Dr. Schon. You state that we have seen the continuing significant role of technically trained, sophisticated, independent inventors who have broken off either from universities, government laboratories, or industrial firms. If they were with industrial firms, why have they broken off? What is the motivation?
>
> DR. SCHON: Well, I can think of several cases which would suggest why they may have done that. A large company making appliances, with which I used to consult, had a laboratory in which a man developed a new method of preserving food, not refrigeration. He was encouraged by the top man in the company to do so and produced a model that showed feasibility of doing this.
>
> But then when they went after the question of actually commercializing it, they discovered that this company already had 25 percent of the refrigerator business. The sales department was not interested in upsetting its marketing system, its distribution outlets, by introducing this new development.
>
> The existing production plants were committed to refrigerators and technology of refrigerators, and were very good at it and they had no interest in experimenting with a new device of this kind.
>
> Moreover, market research showed that consumer response was likely to be negative to this new development.
>
>   *   *   *
>
> The legitimate reasonable interest of the established division of a given company formed on the basis of the existing technology and existing market structure will always oppose the introduction of any radical technological change which can't help but be upsetting to the whole base of the ongoing profitable current organization. That is why established firms always encounter a major internal problem, the means by which they will commercialize any new, radically significant technological change.[11]

Indifference to technological advance

Even though existing investments are not threatened, a new technique may be resisted merely because corporate management is well satisfied with things as they are. If buyers are content with the product as it is, if the present production process is operating smoothly, and if the result of the whole operation is a satisfactory profit rate, what is the purpose of change? This source of resistance will be particularly strong in an oligopolistic industry because of the desire of each producer to avoid price reductions. If the reduction in costs made possible by the new technique permits only a limited price reduction that can be matched

[11] *Hearings on Economic Concentration,* Pt. 6, pp. 2725–56, testimony of Donald Schon.

by the existing technology, a producer considering its adoption cannot look forward to enlarging his share of the market. If it can bring about a cost reduction so dramatic as to permit a price reduction that cannot be matched, the innovator will be able to enlarge his market share, but only until the new technique has been adopted by his rivals, at which time price will again be stabilized—at a lower level. Therefore, in an oligopolistic industry a new cost-reducing technique can expect a favorable reception only if it permits an unmatchable price reduction that brings about an increase in the profits of the innovating oligopolist (until adopted by the other oligopolists) more than sufficient to offset the combined effect of the cost of its introduction and the lower revenues resulting from the price reduction.

Whether for these or other reasons leading producers in oligopolistic industries have frequently displayed an attitude of indifference to technological advance. For over 50 years the major steel companies of the U.S. have been noted for their unresponsiveness, if not hostility, to new technologies. The entrenched backwardness of U.S. Steel in particular has been outlined by George W. Stocking:

> It was slow in introducing the continuous rolling mill; slow in getting into production of cold-rolled steel products; slow in recognizing the potentials of the wire business; slow to adopt the heat-treating process for the production of sheets; slow in getting into stainless steel products; slow in producing cold-rolled sheets; slow in tin-plate developments; slow in utilizing waste gases; slow in utilizing low-cost water transportation because of its consideration for the railroads; in short, slow to grasp the remarkable business opportunities that a dynamic America offered it. The Corporation was apparently a follower, not a leader, in industrial efficiency. American Rolling Mills perfected and patented the continuous sheet rolling process and made it available to its rivals on a royalty basis. National Steel was the first outsider to use it. National was the first integrated company to acquire a steel plant in the Detroit area. With its cheap water transportation, well-planned integration, modern equipment, and flexible pricing, National was the only major steel company to show a profit throughout the depression. According to Ford, Bacon and Davis, the steel corporation ranked last among the 10 leading steel makers in its rate of earnings on investment during the 10 years 1927–36. Clearly the steel corporation has lagged, not led. It was neither big because it was efficient, nor efficient because it was big.[12]

A further commentary on the steel industry's resistance to innovation was introduced into the hearings of the Senate Antitrust Subcommittee in a letter from H. H. Brassert & Company, consulting engineers for the iron and steel industry. Herman Brassert is an internationally recognized authority on iron ores, ore reduction, blast furnaces, and related aspects of steel making. In this letter the president of the company, J. E. Brassert, states:

> I do believe the true reason for the lack of initiative in this field, in the steel industry is the fact that in the United States the proportion of technically trained men at the heads of steel corporations is one of the lowest in the world. Specifically, this proportion is far lower than in most European countries and in the U.S.S.R. . . . The relative absence of such training at the highest executive level appears to be borne out by the

[12] 81st Cong., 2nd Sess., House Subcommittee on the Study of Monopoly Power, House Committee on the Judiciary, *Hearings*, 1950, Pt. 4A, "Steel," pp. 967, 969.

pattern followed in the commercialization of new processes in the United States steel industry. With monotonous regularity the majority of steel producers quickly retrace the steps of the one company which has dared to take the lead in advertising or financing a new process. Rarely does the procession wait long enough for the accumulation of technical information. Carefully engineered proposals, on the other hand, gather dust for years, because executives have not the interest or initiative to base their decisions on the products of scientific evaluation alone. There are, accordingly, few tasks as difficult as to break the ground for new processes in the United States steel industry.[13]

Since World War II two major innovations in steel making have made their appearance. In the first, the oxygen conversion or "L-D" process, large quantities of oxygen, instead of air, are injected into a Bessemer-type converter. In this way a "heat" of molten steel can be produced in about 45 minutes compared to the 8 to 10 hours required in an open-hearth furnace. As described before the Subcommittee by John V. Groner of the McLouth Steel Corporation—the first firm to introduce it in the United States—the process is the essence of simplicity:

> In brief, the process comprises filling a vessel to about one-fifth its total depth with molten pig iron, scrap and limestone. A long pipe, known as a lance, connected with the oxygen supply, and having at its end a water-cooled nozzle . . . is positioned over and may protrude into the open top of the converter.
> Through this lance, oxygen is jetted on this charge, under great pressure and at a very high velocity, so that, in effect, it tunnels a hole of some depth into the charge. This results in the generation of great heat and the formation of gases and of various chemical reactions which cause the undesired constituents in the molten charge to pass either into the slag or as a gas into the air, thus refining the metal into steel.[14]

That oxygen would be preferable to air had long been recognized, since nitrogen, which makes up 80 percent of the air, tends to make steel brittle and less malleable. But two practical problems stood in the way: the absence of low-cost supplies of oxygen and the tendency of oxygen, when injected into a converter, to destroy its lining. Based on the Linde-Frankle process perfected in Germany in 1929, oxygen production capacity was increased tremendously during World War II. One of the sites for this expanded capacity was a small town in Austria where it was employed to cut armor plate used in the production of tanks. With the end of the war a new use was sought for the oxygen-producing facility. The second problem was solved by the successive work of three inventors, C. V. Schwarz of Germany and John Miles and Robert Duerrer of Switzerland, and a small Austrian steel firm, Voert. As Walter Adams and Joel B. Dirlam have put it: "The oxygen process was developed in continental Europe and perfected by the employees of a nationalized enterprise, in a war-ravaged country, with a total steel ingot capacity of about 1 million tons—by a *firm* that was less than one-third the size of a single *plant* of the U.S. Steel Corporation." [15]

The date of the first large-scale commercial use of oxygen conversion by the Austrian firm was 1952; the date of its first use in the United States—by McLouth Steel—was 1954. By 1963, 12.9 million tons of oxygen capacity had been in-

---

[13] *Hearings on Administered Prices,* Pt. 4, p. 1371.

[14] *Ibid.,* Pt. 3, p. 782.

[15] Walter Adams and Joel B. Dirlam, "Big Steel, Invention and Innovation," *Quarterly Journal of Economics,* May, 1966, pp. 167–89.

stalled in the United States, but none by the 3 leading producers. The compelling reasons for its adoption by the other steel makers were a reduction in capital costs of around $15 per ton and a saving in operating costs of $3 to $5 per ton. Republic installed no oxygen capacity until 1965; U.S. Steel and Bethlehem installed none until 1964—12 years after its first successful use in Austria and 10 years after it had been adopted in the United States.[16] Referring to this lag by the industry's leaders, Adams and Dirlam commented:

> Their indifference is explicable either on the grounds of ignorance or delinquency, and the first of these alternatives must be rejected almost summarily. In view of the wide publicity given to the Leoben conference of 1951, the thousands of articles on oxygen and steelmaking in technical and trade journals, and U.S. Steel's assertion that it is aware of every new development in the industry, it is incredible that the engineers of Big Steel were unaware of the Austrian breakthrough.[17]

The largest steel companies also remained indifferent to the second of the recent technological advances in steel making, continuous casting. After the production of the steel ingot, it is reduced in the giant blooming or "breakdown" mills into semifinished forms—blooms, billets, or slabs—which are then fed into the rolling and finishing mills. Continuous casting greatly reduces the amount of capital equipment required to transform the molten metal into semifinished forms, by eliminating not only the blooming mill itself but the large molds in which the ingots are cast, the deep soaking pits used for reheating the ingots, the enormous cranes used to move the ingots, and other large-scale equipment required in the conventional process. The reduction is accomplished by a relatively small "continuous casting" machine into which molten steel is poured, coming out as a slab or billet ready for the rolling mills.

As in oxygen conversion, the process was conceived by European inventors, aided by a relatively small American steel producer, Allegheny-Ludlum Steel Corporation. Experimental work was also carried out by an equipment manufacturer, Babcock & Wilcox, in cooperation with Republic Steel Corporation. Continuous casting was first used to produce steel in 1949 in Germany by Siegfried Junghans, who had previously developed the process for use with nonferrous metals. Using the Junghans machine, Allegheny-Ludlum began experimenting with continuous casting in 1950. Four years later the process was put into commercial operation by another small firm, the Atlas Steel Company of Welland, Ontario. Nearly a decade elapsed before it was introduced by the major U.S. steel producers.

The glass industry, also a concentrated field, provides another striking example of indifference to invention. In 1959 Pilkington Bros. Ltd., the leading British manufacturer of glass, put into commercial operation the radical new "float glass" process.[18] Conceived in 1952 by Alastair Pilkington, a member of the family, and developed under his personal direction, the new process was a great improvement over traditional methods. Hitherto, flat glass had been made either by stretching a lump of molten glass by blowing or pulling, which tended to cause distortion, or by casting a plate of glass and then making it transparent by grinding and polishing, which was expensive, time-consuming, and wasteful.

[16] *Ibid.*
[17] *Ibid.*
[18] John Jewkes, David Sawers, Richard Stillerman, *The Sources of Invention*, rev. ed., Macmillan, 1969, pp. 334–36.

Under the new process a continuous ribbon of glass floats along a bath of molten tin, yielding, when cooled and annealed, a flat product with a bright surface requiring no grinding or polishing.

What is relevant here is the fact that a patent for a virtually identical process had been issued by the U.S. Patent Office to an American inventor over half a century earlier. After Pilkington's attorneys had filed for a U.S. patent, they were surprised to learn that in September, 1902, a patent had been issued to Willam E. Heal of Marion, Indiana, for a method of

> flowing the molten glass . . . into an adjacent receptacle, containing melted material of greater specific gravity than glass [preferably of tin or alloys of tin and copper] and causing the molten glass to float upon and spread into, a continuous sheet, and then drawing the sheet of glass therefrom, and causing it to pass into their lehr for annealing and by one continuous operation . . . to simplify, facilitate and cheapen the manufacture of plate glass to improve its quality.[19]

It is, of course, one thing to outline a process in a patent application; it is something else to transform it into a commercial reality. It took Pilkington 7 years of intensive effort to get the process into actual operation—a success that is a tribute to both their persistence and their ingenuity. "Nevertheless," in John Jewkes's words, "it is intriguing that the idea was not taken up much earlier by one or other of the large glass manufacturers in the world." [20] Among the firms that failed to do so were the 2 U.S. giants, Libbey-Owens-Ford and Pittsburgh Plate Glass. The most charitable explanations are ignorance of the U.S. patents, which would hardly be a tribute to their technical awareness, or satisfaction with the existing technology and a consequent disinclination to embark on the development work ultimately and successfully pursued by a smaller British firm.

Underestimation of demand

Still another source of resistance to change consists of management's underestimating the magnitude of demand. The history of invention is replete with examples of new products that were withheld for this reason. The prolonged delay by General Motors in introducing power steering is a case in point. The invention of power steering stemmed from the interest on the part of an independent consulting engineer, Francis Davis, in the factors limiting the size of motor trucks.[21] During the 1920's increasing the size of a truck beyond a capacity of 5 or 6 tons made the vehicle unmanageable for two very good reasons: it could not be stopped or steered. The braking problem was soon solved, but the steering problem remained. Although Davis developed a power-steering mechanism in 1926, a quarter of a century passed before it was put on the market.

Davis's first device was workable but cumbersome, requiring the use of a number of accessories—a pump, a pressure tank, hose lines, an unloader valve, and several other devices to maintain the hydraulic fluid at a high pressure. The design, although unsatisfactory, led ultimately to the so-called open-center-valve

---

[19] Quoted in *ibid.,* p. 336. A patent for a somewhat similar process was issued to H. K. Hitchcock of Walten, Pennsylvania, in 1905.

[20] Jewkes, Sawers, Stillerman, *op. cit.,* p. 337.

[21] *Hearings on Economic Concentration,* Pt. 3, pp. 1103–06, testimony of Daniel V. De-Simone.

principle, which enabled Davis to do away with most of the accessories and the requirement that the oil be at a continuous high pressure. The open-center valve, covered in Davis's first U.S. patent in the power-steering field, was the big break-through.

In a Pierce Arrow fitted with the new power-steering gear, Davis drove to Detroit from his small shop in Waltham, Massachusetts. Fully expecting the automotive world to beat a path to his car, he called on 10 different companies in 10 days, and the car was driven by 26 individuals. After many negotiations and tests, General Motors signed a one-year option agreement, which gave them the first opportunity at a license and the right to make further studies and tests. This was followed in 1928 by a license agreement with General Motors, giving Davis a very fair yearly minimum royalty. In 1932 Cadillac had a 12-cylinder car equipped with power steering ready for manufacture, but when the steering-gear division of General Motors submitted the tooling cost, it was decided that the value of the invention did not justify the tooling expense. Moreover, although General Motors wanted to continue the license, it was no longer willing to pay the guaranteed minimum royalty.

Not surprisingly, Davis severed his connections with General Motors in 1935 and signed an agreement with the Bendix Corporation. Two experimental cars equipped with power steering were built in 1941, and plans were made to introduce power-steered Buicks to the public. But 1941 saw the entrance of the United States into World War II and the closing down of automobile production. During the war, however, Davis's power steering was widely and successfully used in English and U.S. armored cars, trucks, and other ordnance vehicles. On the basis of their performance Davis again expected widespread and early adoption of his invention, but once again he was destined to be frustrated. Since in the immediate postwar years the automobile companies were enjoying a seller's market, they felt little need to introduce an innovation that would increase their costs but not their sales. Not until after the first postwar downswing, 1948–49, did the automobile manufacturers again become seriously interested in his invention. In 1951, power steering was finally made available to the public—by Chrysler Corporation. Then, because public acceptance proved to be far greater than had been anticipated, General Motors and the other auto makers at last equipped their cars with power steering.

Demand for an innovation can be understimated owing to the mistaken idea that buyers are satisfied with the product as it is. This was the attitude of watch and clock makers, backed by hundreds of years of experience, when the inventor of the automatic regulator sought to interest them in his innovation.[22] The regulator, which is now part of every clock and many watches, was the product of the inventive mind of Jacob Rabinow, a professional inventor holding 130 issued patents. Among his pioneering achievements are the magnetic fluid clutch, automatic controls for guided missiles, and inventions in the field of optical character recognition.

Like many inventions Rabinow's clock regulator originated with a chance observation. As he tells it, "I had just finished setting my watch, when it occurred to me what an awful lot of trouble it was to take the back off whenever I wanted to reset the speed regulator."[23] Not very many people would set their own watches even if they knew they could. Obviously what was needed was an

[22] *Ibid.*, pp. 1097–1100, testimony of Daniel V. DeSimone.
[23] Quoted by Daniel V. DeSimone in *ibid.*, p. 1098.

automatic regulator. Automatic regulation could be achieved by tying the hand-setting knob to the speed regulator. The coupling could be proportioned so that the movement of the knob would exactly compensate for the error in speed, but this exactitude was not necessary. It could be accomplished, again automatically, but step by step, after so many settings. One by one Rabinow solved a succession of technical problems and finally achieved a workable mechanism.

Next, he approached various watch manufacturers, hoping they would take licenses for the use of his invention. Although conceding the merit of his invention, they saw no future for it in their own watches. "Why," said one leading manufacturer, "you know we advertise a *perfect* watch." Rabinow replied that no watch was perfect. "It's not important what the watch is," countered the manufacturer. "What counts is what the customer thinks it is. They think it's perfect. Who needs an automatic regulator to make a perfect watch more perfect?" [24] Rabinow had run into an obstacle all too familiar to the independent inventor. As Daniel V. DeSimone, head of the Bureau of Standards' Office of Inventions and Innovations, observed:

> Innovation is an arduous and risky process, and the reluctance of companies to take what they perceive to be unnecessary risks is understandable. But, in addition, there are psychological barriers. Not the least of these is the psychological impact on the corporate manager or his technical staff of an outsider (the independent inventor) saying, "Here is an opportunity or a solution to one of your problems," and implying, "how come you (or the geniuses you hired) didn't think of it?" The not uncommon answer is, "who needs it?"

Rabinow suffered a series of discouraging episodes. One company asked him to make a large number of models for use in sales promotion. The company went bankrupt. Another company began selling a self-regulating watch that infringed one of Rabinow's patents. A settlement was reached; the infringement was discontinued, but so also was production of the watches. Finally, in one of those quirks of fate. Rabinow had a meeting with the president of General Time Corporation to discuss an unrelated matter, and out of this encounter came a license agreement for the regulator. General Time Corporation became Rabinow's exclusive licensee, worldwide, for all nonjeweled watches and clocks.

The neglect of the inventor

Corporate management can easily become so absorbed, indeed overburdened, with day-to-day work on productions, sales, advertising, and other operating details that it can devote little attention to the critical question of future profits. As a result, whether he is employed by the corporation itself or is an independent, the inventor is all too often neglected.

Although the "inside" inventor gains a measure of financial security and access to research facilities, he forfeits his right to share in the income resulting from his discovery. When corporations profit from new products and processes developed within their own organizations, the rewards go not to those who gave them birth but to stockholders and management. This was demonstrated in a survey of 21 major drug companies conducted by the Senate Antitrust Subcommittee. (On this matter the drug companies do not appear to constitute any particular exception to the general practice of large firms.) It was found that 18

[24] Quoted by Daniel V. DeSimone in *ibid.*, p. 1099.

of the 21 firms customarily required a scientist entering their employment to sign a waiver of any patent rights to inventions he might make while in the company's employ. For signing such a waiver the scientist received either nothing or a token payment of around $10 (see Table 10-2).[25]

While companies provide research facilities and pay scientists' salaries, private enterprises have never been the exclusive provider of laboratories and income for research and are becoming less so. In years past, particularly during the depressed 1930's, the corporate laboratory offered security and salaries well above those available from any other source. But those days are gone, perhaps forever. Today private corporations must compete vigorously for the services of trained scientists not only with one another but with universities and with a new competitor—the tax-exempt foundation. In terms of security the universities and foundations can match anything that private corporations have to offer. Moreover, the scientist in a university or foundation is usually free to market his invention as a property, paying on the proceeds only a capital-gains tax. When

Table 10-2

SPECIAL COMPENSATION PAID TO RESEARCH PERSONNEL BY PHARMACEUTICAL COMPANIES, 1960[a]

Company	Amount Paid	Number of Recipients				
		Total	Receiving less than $2000	Receiving $2000 to $5000	Receiving $5001 to $25,000	Receiving over $25,000
American Cyanamid	$ 106,209	23	9	5	9	0
Carter	80,000[b]	1	0	0	0	1
CIBA	29,250	23	19	4	0	0
Hoffmann-La Roche	112,634	39	6	29	4	0
Mead Johnson	44,395	97	92	4	1	0
Merck	34,500[c]	9	1	5	3	0
Norwich	79,732	15	5	5	5	0
Pfizer[d]	526,047	290	253	18	16	3
Richardson-Merrell	17,866	13	9	4	0	0
U.S. Vitamin	20,000[e]	9	7	1	1	0
Warner-Lambert	65,650	27	18	7	2	0
Total	$1,116,283	546	419	82	41	4

[a]Includes both awards for inventions or other research accomplishments and participation in profit-sharing plans.
[b]Estimated.
[c]Payments for 1961 to October; no such payments in 1960.
[d]Does not include subsidiaries.
[e]Payments made in February, 1961, for 1960.

Source: Special compensation reported by companies to Senate Subcommittee on Antitrust and Monopoly

[25] 87th Cong., 1st Sess., Senate Subcommittee on Antitrust and Monopoly, Senate Committee on the Judiciary, *Hearings on S. 1552*, "To Amend and Supplement the Antitrust Laws, with Respect to the Manufacture and Distribution of Drugs," 1962, Pt. 5, p. 2812. The exceptions were Abbott Laboratories, Carter Products, and Hoffman-La Roche.

the income from a successful invention can be so treated, the resultant after-tax income can be matched by a corporation only with a salary of truly astronomic proportions.

The outside inventor, on the other hand, while he participates in income resulting from his discovery, must find ways and means of financing his own research and of overcoming seemingly insurmountable barriers in marketing his inventions. The nature of these obstacles was described in testimony before the Subcommittee by Richard Walton, one of the nation's leading independent inventors and holder of 30 U.S. patents and over 400 foreign patents in the mechanical fields of textile and paper processing, washing machines, materials handling, and other areas.[26]

In seeking to interest a large company in his invention the independent inventor must overcome the almost inevitable objections of the firm's patent attorney. In Walton's words, "if he is doing a good job . . . [he] must point out the weaknesses in the inventor's patent and possible ways of getting around it." Indeed, one of the problems frequently encountered by the independent is that no corporate official will talk to him at all unless he already has a patent and then will do so only if the patent and the accompanying technical know-how are made freely available to the company for any experimental and development work it might wish to pursue. The corporation regards this as necessary to protect it from infringement suits brought by "disgruntled inventors." Corporate attorneys are quick to cite examples of inventors who came to their firm with a new idea, which was tested and found wanting, but who nonetheless felt that some later innovation introduced by the company was based on their ideas. From the inventor's point of view, however, this requirement means that he must turn over everything he has or knows, trusting in the firm's good faith to grant him a satisfactory settlement if it decides to use his ideas. If, by accident or design, the company does pirate his invention, it is the rare inventor who has the financial resources to mount a successful infringement suit. In this way resistance to outsiders becomes institutionalized. Often the steps to be followed are set forth conveniently in a printed brochure so that the outside inventor who wishes to bother the company with a money-making idea will know in advance what he is up against.

Even if he has a strong patent and will let the company experiment with his "know-how," the independent must overcome the predictably hostile attitude of the firm's director of research. In Walton's words:

> Probably the one executive in any corporation, who must do the most soul-searching when faced with an outside-invention of direct interest to his company, is the research director. Not only does he have a number of products developed by his own engineering staff, which he is trying to get his company to accept, but his problems are compounded by the difficulties of lessening frustrations, as well as rewarding individual engineers who have created these products which he cannot get accepted by the company.

This negative, if not hostile, attitude is shared fully by the company's individual scientists and engineers:

> Imagine how the engineers must feel, when asked to develop an invention coming from the outside, lacking even the satisfaction of having their own previously developed inventions accepted. Not only are they

[26] *Hearings on Economic Concentration*, Pt. 6, pp. 2702–15, testimony of Richard Walton.

resentful of the imagined implication that they themselves should have come up with this invention; but the thought that some lucky person . . . should have made the invention is anathema to them. Further, that they should help assure him a continuing royalty without any further labor on his part rubs salt in the wound.

Resistance is even encountered at lower levels: "Often a mechanic will tell me that a part cannot be machined. After demonstrating how it can be done—I can run most machine tools—I gain his respect. A mechanic's negative decision can be passed along through the engineers to the research director. The difficulty may be so magnified by this time that the invention is labeled unworkable."

Another barrier is the market research survey. The more the new product differs from what consumers are familiar with, the greater are the chances of a negative reaction. Truly radical innovations require elaborate explanations of their nature and their advantages over what is currently available, and market research firms are seldom able to provide such explanations to the many buyers who would have to be interviewed in any adequate survey. For example, even after the first Xerox commercial copier had at last been perfected, IBM, which was offered a license (for the second time), turned it down; a prominent market research firm that had been retained by IBM to survey the potential market reported that sales prospects were unpromising.[27] In Walton's view market research surveys "are excellent for deciding the size of a toothpaste tube or the kind of print or color that should be on it. . . ." Their limitation lies in their inability to portray consumers' probable reaction to genuine novelty. In Walton's words, "they do not dare to do creative market research. Where there are two or three variables involved, they do not dare to say that the market exists. It takes key officers in the company after they have studied the negative market research report, to say they still think the market is there."

To overcome these and other barriers the independent inventor must be a man of many parts. As Walton put it, "We really demand a great deal of one person when we expect him to reach out and grasp ideas, which are floating by to eternity, and at the same time expect him to be engineer, lawyer, marketer, gambler, and banker."

The misdirection of research

Because the results flowing from research are unpredictable and cannot be programmed into the general operations and objectives of the corporation and because administrators have an inherent distaste for what is seemingly unproductive, research does not lend itself readily to the accepted principles of proper organization and management. In the words of C. E. K. Mees of Eastman Kodak:

> The best person to decide what research work shall be done is the man who is doing the research. The next best is the head of the department. After that you leave the field of best persons and meet increasingly worse groups. The first of these is the research director, who is probably wrong more than half the time. Then comes a committee, which is wrong most of the time. Finally there is a committee of company vice-presidents, which is wrong all of the time.[28]

[27] See *ibid.*, Pt. 3, pp. 1108–11.
[28] Quoted in Jewkes, Sawers, Stillerman, *op. cit.*, p. 138.

With reference to his work on the Jewkes study as well as to later research, Richard Stillerman testified, "More often than not, they [modern inventions] originate with inventors having a persistence amounting almost to an obsession." [29] Such men seldom take kindly to direction of any kind from above, and when it is obvious to them that the research project is ill conceived and unlikely to be of any significance, impatience can quickly be transformed into stronger forms of hostility. During the Subcommittee's investigation of the drug industry, physicians who had formerly been medical directors of major drug companies testified that instead of permitting their scientists to pursue basic research leading to entirely new chemical compounds, the major drug companies have been devoting their research efforts primarily toward developing variants of existing drugs sufficiently different to ensure the receipt of a patent but not so different as to jeopardize participation in a proven financial success.

On this issue Haskell Weinstein, former acting medical director of the J. B. Roerig Division of Pfizer, recommended that the drug companies "be required to clearly identify expenditures for research as those which are devoted to basic studies," adding that "this should markedly decrease the justification for some of the very high prices paid." He went on to deplore what he regarded as a waste of scientific talent: "A great many extremely fine scientists are employed by those manufacturers. Their talents should not be expended on patent-bypassing chemical manipulations, on ridiculous mixtures of drugs, or inconsequential additives to established drugs. Since the number of well-trained capable scientists is severely limited, their potential should not be wasted." [30] As specific examples of products with limited usefulness whose development absorbed the talents of drug company scientists, Weinstein cited the corticosteroids following prednisone, the potent tranquilizers following Thorazine and Compazine, the new reserpine derivatives following reserpine, and the additions of various ingredients to the antibiotic tetracycline for the purpose of achieving higher blood levels—a result that can be obtained by a slightly higher dosage of tetracycline itself.

The former medical director of Squibb, A. Dale Console, offered an analogy between the discoveries of the potent tranquilizer chlorpromazine (Thorazine) and of the heart stimulant digitalis. He likened the discovery that one of the millions of possible chemical compounds, chlorpromazine, had a beneficial effect in schizophrenia to the discovery that one of the millions of plants, foxglove, contained digitalis, which is effective in heart failure. Each advanced immeasurably our knowledge of the unknown and our ability to cope with these diseases. Pursuing his analogy a step further, he described as a new and useful improvement the discovery that chlorpromazine's activity could be increased significantly by the introduction of a piperazine ring into the side chain of the molecule. This, he said, would be analogous to discovering that a rare species of foxglove contained a higher concentration of digitalis. But, he went on,

if the new species of foxglove happened to have 12 leaves, no one would be impressed if new "inventors" demonstrated that 10- and 13-leaved plants of the same species were also active. This is not invention. . . . Yet 10-, 12- and 13-leaved examples of the piperazine derivative of chlorpromazine are inventions and each is patented. . . . The logical conse-

[29] *Hearings on Economic Concentration,* Pt. 3, p. 1077.
[30] *Hearings on Administered Prices,* Pt. 18, p. 10254.

quence of the process is the devising and patenting of apparently different drugs which are in fact virtually identical in their therapeutic effect.[31]

Console emphasized that once a drug company decides to put on the market a compound that has no significant therapeutic advantage over products already available, it sets in motion a cumulative process resulting in wastes of scientific personnel in the subsequent stages of animal pharmacology and clinical evaluation:

> This may take one or two years, or more, requiring many man-hours of time contributed by experts in various disciplines. Most if not all of this research is wasted as is the time of scientists who might be better engaged in producing something worthwhile.
>
> All along the line of this misdirected effort the pressure is on to make the compound appear better than it is. This is not conducive to integrity in research. The distortion reaches its peak in the phase of clinical evaluation. Here the criteria are least rigid and there is wide latitude for poor research. To the medical director these mediocre compounds always pose problems, and the diversion of the efforts of his staff is not the greatest. Because they are unimaginative, uninteresting compounds, it is virtually impossible to interest reliable investigators in their study. They are not motivated to confirm the obvious. Since they are deficient it is safer to subject them to superficial studies rather than critical examination. Claims rather than scientific evidence are the primary objective. And so, poor research breeds more poor research.[32]

The incompatibility of organization and creativity

Even if they were adequately compensated and not subjected to misdirection, could "the awkward, lonely, enquiring, critical men—the men of 'wide-ranging, sniffing, snuffling, undignified, unself-dramatising curiosity' "[33] ever be successfully harnessed to pull together in a large organizational structure of any kind? Because what the inventor is doing is different—different from anything that has gone before, different from accepted concepts, and different from what is authoritatively held to be possible—skepticism and resistance must be his accepted lot. To persevere in his journey off the beaten path, to continue to push ahead in the face of seemingly insurmountable obstacles, and to meet repeated failures with a renewal of creative effort requires resourcefulness, determination, and self-confidence in very large measure indeed. The essential dilemma is that those who are creative, the "disinterested fools," seldom conform well to the restraints inherent in organizational life, whereas those who conform well are not noted for creativity. In the words of the Jewkes study, "There can be no final resolution of this problem, for the inventor and the scientists will go on expecting to enjoy the benefits of organization without its restrictions, whilst the administrator of research will constantly be striving to infuse predetermination into results essentially unforeseeable. A group of workers devoted to innovation cannot, in fact, be organized by the methods normally subsumed under the idea of administration."[34]

---

[31] Senate Subcommittee on Antitrust and Monopoly, op. cit., Pt. 3, pp. 1539 et seq.
[32] Ibid., p. 1542.
[33] Jewkes, Sawers, Stillerman, op. cit., p. 142. The quotation by the authors is from Sinclair Lewis.
[34] Ibid., p. 136.

Quite apart from the misdirection of research from above, there are other features of organizational life that are out of harmony with the creative temperament. The environment itself is bound to be unhappy

> where the allocation of functions is determined in such a way that voluntary and ephemeral groupings among the research workers are impossible or are frowned upon; where men are asked to report at regular intervals upon ideas around which their minds are still anxiously groping; where achievements are constantly being recorded and assessed; where spurious cooperation is enforced by time-wasting committees and paper work and where painstaking efforts to "avoid over-lapping" frequently quench originality.[35]

No proof has ever been advanced that it should be possible to organize creativity in the industrial arts while it is manifestly impossible in other areas of creative effort—painting, sculpture, literary composition, and the like. Few who have had experience with the genre will not agree that collective efforts at writing (as in reports by committees) range from the mediocre to the disastrous. Speaking to the graduating class of 1957, A. Whitney Griswold, president of Yale University, asked:

> Could Hamlet have been written by a committee, or the Mona Lisa painted by a club? Could the New Testament have been composed as a conference report? Creative ideas do not spring from groups. They spring from individuals. The divine spark leaps from the finger of God to the finger of Adam, whether it takes ultimate shape in a law of physics or a law of the land, a poem or a policy, a sonata or a mechanical computer.[36]

As a general principle, the larger the organization, the greater is the number of bureaucratic layers between the research division and the decision makers, and thus the less are the chances that any proposal embodying a new idea will ever reach for consideration those who have the power to implement it. Indeed, it can be postulated that as an organization grows at an arithmetic rate, the difficulty of "getting things done" tends to increase at a geometric rate—and so, incidentally, does the opportunity of surviving without doing anything at all. Theoretically, the resistance of bureaucracy should reach some sort of apex in a Communist state. Support for this hypothesis is provided by that remarkable Russian novel *Not By Bread Alone,* which recounts the endless frustrations encountered by a Russian engineer in trying to obtain consideration for his new pipe-making invention.[37]

Recognizing the inherent conflict between creativity and organization, some of the more prescient corporations have adopted the practice of deploying their research workers in small teams. A team of 90 qualified men developed the TH system of microwave transmission of telephone and television messages for Bell Telephone. The spectacular successes of the French firm Dassault in designing military aircraft have been achieved by a design team numbering "in tens rather than in hundreds." [38]

In research the main problem of large numbers is the difficulty of providing them with meaningful direction and coordination. In the opinion of Midgley of General Motors, the controlling factor is "the capacity of the research director

[35] *Ibid.,* p. 138.
[36] Quoted by Milton Lehman in *Hearings on Economic Concentration,* Pt. 3, p. 1327.
[37] Vladimir Dudintsev, *Not By Bread Alone,* trans. by E. Bone, Dutton, 1957.
[38] Jewkes, Sawers, Stillerman, *op. cit.,* p. 218.

to maintain an efficient understanding of the various problems for which he is responsible." [39] Implicit in Midgley's observations is the assumption that the director himself is a scientist or inventor deeply and personally involved in the project and intellectually as well as administratively in charge. He must at all times have "a total picture" of the project in all its phases. The responsibility for altering or modifying its course must be his. If specialists are to be used, he must decide what contributions they are to make. And the task of evaluating their contributions and of fitting them properly into the project as a whole must also be his. The ability of the research director to perform these complex functions successfully will decline rapidly as their number (and the number of scientists whom he must supervise) increases. It is for this reason that successful inventors in industrial research laboratories are inclined to stress the virtues of small groups. Insofar as the efficiency of research is concerned, the optimal size would therefore be that of a company sufficiently large to support one or a few of these small groups, which in most industries would be far below the size of the largest companies.

Resistance by the military

From ancient times to the present the natural tendency of military organizations has been to resist radical innovations until they are thrust upon them. According to Arnold Toynbee, changes in warfare move in long-term cycles: an existing, highly developed method of warfare is replaced by a new technique against which it is powerless to defend itself; over a period that may encompass centuries the new technique is brought to a high state of perfection, becoming in turn the established method; but in the process it becomes highly structured, rigid, and inflexible, and therefore incapable of adjusting to the unexpected challenge of a still newer technique, and so on *ad infinitum*.[40]

The first stage in this cycle was the perfection of the individual combatant, or hoplite. The fortunes of war turned upon the prowess of mighty heroes—Hector, Achilles, Goliath—as individual combatants or as leaders of their compatriots who also fought as individuals: "Before the fatal day on which he challenges the armies of Israel, Goliath has won such triumphant victories with his spear whose staff is like a weaver's beam and whose head weighs six hundred shekels of iron, and he has found himself so completely proof against hostile weapons in his panoply of casque and corselet and target and greaves, that he can no longer conceive of any alternative armament; and he believes that in this armament he is invincible." [41] But against the radical new technique of a slingshot Goliath was powerless to defend himself.

In this case David's victory did not lead to the general adoption of the slingshot as the new method of warfare; rather its significance lay in dramatizing the vulnerability of the individual. Individual combat was replaced by a new technique, the phalanx, which represented the antithesis of combat by individuals; "the essence of the phalanx lay in the military discipline which had transformed a rabble of individual warriors into a military formation whose orderly evolutions could accomplish ten times as much as the uncoordinated efforts of an equal number of equally well-armed individual champions." [42] But after the

[39] Quoted in *ibid.*, p. 159.
[40] Arnold J. Toynbee, *A Study of History*, Oxford University Press, 1947, pp. 332 *et seq.* (Abridgement of Vols. I–VI by D. C. Somervell.)
[41] *Ibid.*, p. 332.
[42] *Ibid.*, p. 333.

perfection of the phalanx, which enabled the Spartans to sweep all before them, they "rested on their oars," with the result that the phalanx in turn gave way, first to the "Athenian swarm of peltasts," then to the "tactical innovation of the Theban column," and finally to the Macedonian formation that integrated the phalanx with heavy cavalry into a single fighting force.

But the Macedonian formation in turn went down to defeat before the Roman legion. This formation utilized a new type of armament, which made it possible for any soldier, and any unit, to fight as a member of a phalanx or as an individual and to change from one to another at a moment's notice: "under a series of great captains from Marius to Caesar, the legion attained the greatest efficiency possible for infantry before the invention of firearms." [43]

Although the victory of the horse-archer over the legion at the battle of Carrhae in 53 B.C. should have been a warning, the Romans persisted in using the legion until they were decimated at Adrianople in 378 A.D. by the cataphract, a mailed cavalryman armed with a lance: "For at least the last four of the six centuries between these two battles the Romans had rested on their oars. . . . [44] Although changes took place in armament and tactical use, the heavily armed lancer reigned supreme for more than a thousand years. The cataphract was brought to its highest perfection as a disciplined fighting force by the Mamluks of Egypt: "By the close of the thirteenth century the Mamluks, having established their superiority over both the French and the Mongols, stood in the same position of unchallenged military supremacy within their own horizon as the Roman legionaires after Pydna. In this eminent but enervating situation the Mamluk, like the legionaire, rested on his oars." [45]

The day of the heavily armed warrior on horseback finally was brought to an end by a revived infantry, armed first with the longbow and crossbow and later with firearms. Infantry armed with firearms progressed rapidly from the relatively small, mobile, and well-drilled armies of Napoleon and Frederick the Great to the troops deployed in the trench warfare and economic blockade of World War I. It was almost predictable that the French, having achieved with their allies a victory through siege tactics in World War I, would place their reliance on the same method 20 years later. During the interim, however, the Germans had perfected the blitzkreig, centering around the use of a mechanical cataphract. First used by the British in World War I and greatly improved by the invention of an American, George Christie, the tank made the Maginot Line a supreme example of the folly of relying on an antiquated technique.

In summing up this history, Toynbee writes:

> Each link has been a cycle of invention, triumph, lethargy, and disaster; and, on the precedents thus set by three thousand years of military history, from Goliath's encounter with David to the piercing of a Maginot Line and a West Wall by the thrust of mechanical cataphracts and the pinpoint marksmanship of archers on winged steeds, we may expect fresh illustrations of our theme to be provided with monotonous consistency as long as mankind is so perverse as to go on cultivating the art of war.[46]

Throughout these 3,000 years each radical new technique came from "the outside"—i.e., from an adversary of the state that had perfected the existing

[43] *Ibid.*, p. 334.
[44] *Ibid.*
[45] *Ibid.*, p. 336.
[46] *Ibid.*, p. 337.

THE CREATIVE BACKWARDNESS OF BIGNESS

method. The very fact that it was employed by a new and usually less powerful state meant that it could also have been employed by the existing power. That it was not is due primarily to the impossibility of reconciling a radical technique with either the existing methods of warfare or their accompanying organizational structures.

Convinced of the superiority of the method of warfare that ultimately had proved successful in World War I, the armed forces of France, Great Britain, and the United States all but ignored the new weapons that were to prevail in World War II. During the years between the great wars the tank was neglected by the French army, not because of any ignorance of its existence, but because the army itself was organized to conduct the type of warfare that had prevailed in World War I. The tactics of blitzkrieg had no place in such an organizational structure, as the young Col. Charles de Gaulle learned to his dismay. The record of the United States was no better. George Christie, an American, invented the torsion-bar-suspension tank, whose low silhouette gave it a great advantage over its towering predecessors mounted on huge springs. Although adopted before World War II by both Germany and Russia, it was neglected by the U.S. Army, and as a consequence, the United States entered the war still equipped with the hopelessly obsolete spring-suspension tank.

During the same years the armed services grudgingly accepted the other great weapon of World War II, the airplane, but only at the insistence of "non-expert" members of Congress. Public opinion in support of the airplane was aroused by champions who were "outsiders" to the armed services, notably Captain Billy Mitchell and Alexander de Seversky. Frank Whittle's difficulties in trying to interest the British government in the turbojet engine have already been recounted (see Chapter 9).

But just as the tank and the airplane were rejected by proponents of massed infantry and trench warfare, so was the newest and most fearsome weapon, the rocket, rejected by the military strategists whose conduct of World War II finally came to be based on the tank and the airplane. Robert Goddard's efforts to interest the U.S. military in rocketry went back as far as 1914.[47] Its response was a rather perfunctory request for "actual samples of your rockets for a test"; at that early stage Goddard of course had no "samples." But on November 7, 1918, he successfully demonstrated at Aberdeen Proving Grounds a new solid-propellant rocket for warfare—the predecessor of the "bazooka" of World War II. Four days later Germany surrendered, and the rocket was forgotten by the military. The rebirth of interest was associated not with the terrifying purpose for which rockets were used by the Germans just a few years later but with the limited purposes of antitank warfare. To hurl a shaped charge at a tank the Army had tried specially built rifles, whose recoil knocked the soldiers down or broke their shoulders, and specially built mortars, which collapsed on firing. At last a test of the rocket was permitted; it performed perfectly, hitting a moving tank nine out of ten times. Observing that it looked like "Bob Burns' bazooka," a visiting major gave it the name by which it has subsequently been known. But this was the only use made of rockets by the U.S. armed forces in World War II.

Although Goddard continued to make trips to Washington to talk with military authorities, his efforts "met with cool rebuff, even at the highest level."

[47] *Hearings on Economic Concentration,* Pt. 3, pp. 1311–33, testimony of Milton Lehman. The discussion of rocketry in this chapter is concerned only with the resistance of the military; the history of rocketry is summarized in Ch. 9.

His particular *bête noir* was Vannevar Bush, then chairman of the National Defense Research Committee of the National Advisory Committee for Aeronautics. Refusing even to appoint Goddard to any major committee, Bush opposed rocketry throughout the war. As late as 1945 he testified before the Special Senate Committee on Atomic Energy; this testimony, incidentally, has been cited as proof of the maxim that when an eminent elderly scientist says something is possible, he is probably right, but when he says it is not possible, he is probably wrong:

> There has been a great deal said about a 3,000 mile, high-angle rocket. In my opinion such a thing is impossible and will be impossible for many years. The people who have been writing these things that annoy me have been talking about a . . . rocket shot from one continent to another carrying an atomic bomb, and so directed as to be a precise weapon . . . I say technically I don't think anybody in the world knows how to do such a thing and I feel confident it will not be done for a long period of time to come. I think we can leave that out of our thinking.[48]

The attitude of the top military officers was, if anything, more explicit; they simply wanted no part of it. As Goddard's biographer, Milton Lehman, tells it: "Throughout World War II . . . Goddard had persisted in seeking a place with the military. On one of his trips to this Capital City from his test center near Roswell, New Mexico, the professor was not merely shunted aside but assured by Army and Navy brass that there was no need for 'Buck Rogers stuff' in World War II."

The consequences of this resistance in terms of the unnecessary prolongation of the war are incalculable. It is Lehman's view that with any reasonable assistance, "we could have fired Goddard rockets from England against Germany in such strength and number as to make the sacrifice of D-Day in Normandy unnecessary." By 1940 Goddard already had a tested, workable first-stage rocket and "with some help beyond his own crew and resources could have stepped up the size and range of his great first-stage rocket, and started to add to it the other stages he had planned."

From this historical survey it can be seen that at any given point in time the military of a dominant power will be perfecting a method of warfare that has proved successful in the past and that they believe will prevail in the future. But a preference for the tried and true is not the only explanation for their resistance to radical new weapons. Also at work is their natural instinct to protect their organization, the value of their training, their expertise, and their very reason for being. This motivation was described by Elting Morison in his study of continuous-aim firing (a new and better method, which had been rejected by the Navy until President Theodore Roosevelt intervened):

> The Navy is not only an armed force. It is a society. In the 40 years following the Civil War, this society had been forced to accommodate itself to a series of technological changes. . . . These changes wrought extraordinary changes in ship design, and therefore in the concepts of how ships were to be used; that is, in fleet tactics and even naval strategy. . . . To these numerous innovations, producing as they did a spreading disorder throughout a service with heavy commitments to formal organization, the Navy responded with grudging pain. It is wrong to assume, as civilians frequently do, that this blind reaction to technological change

[48] Quoted by Lehman in *ibid.*, p. 1324.

springs exclusively from some causeless Bourbon distemper that invades
the military mind. There is a sounder and more attractive base. The opposi
tion, where it occurs, of the soldier and the sailor to such change springs
from the normal human instinct to protect oneself and more especially
one's way of life. Military organizations are societies built around and
upon the prevailing weapon systems. Intuitively and quite correctly the
military man feels that a change in weapons portends a change in the
arrangements of his society.[49]

Since World War II, it may be objected, all this has changed. To an extent
undreamed of before, science has become the handmaiden of the military. It
is the scientific community that has created and perfected the instruments of
modern weaponry—nuclear bombs, guided missiles, supersonic planes, deadly
bacteriological and chemical agents, and others too numerous to mention. Far
from opposing new weapons, the military has become their most enthusiastic
supporter—except perhaps for the companies that manufacture them. But it
is not, in fact, the self-protective instincts of the military that have changed;
rather, there has been a broadening of the organizational structure with which
the higher officers identify.

In earlier days the young man entering the armed services as a junior officer
was regarded as having embarked on a life-long career; he entered, he served
to an advanced age, and he retired. Throughout this period the organizational
structure with which he identified was his service. A change in weapons did
portend, in Morison's words, "a change in the arrangement of his society."
Today the "society" of many higher officers is no longer simply their service;
it is their service plus the larger contractors—in President Eisenhower's celebrated phrase, the "military-industrial complex." In recent years there has
been a virtual exodus of high-ranking military officers into the higher-salaried
upper echelon of aerospace companies and other large contractors.

By February, 1969, some 2,072 retired military officers of the rank of colonel
or Navy captain and above were employed by the 100 companies with the
largest volume of military prime contracts (or an average of 22 per firm);
these 100 companies held 67.4 percent of the $38.8 billion of prime military
contracts. Ten years earlier the total number employed by the 100 top prime
contractors was only 721, or an average of 8 per company.[50] In 1969 the 10
companies with the largest number of high-ranking officers on their payrolls
employed 1,065 retired officers, or an average of 106 per firm; 10 years earlier
the top 10 contractors had employed only 372, or an average of 37 per company.

In placing these figures in the *Congressional Record* Senator Proxmire commented on "the significance of this situation":

> Whether sought or unsought there is today unwarranted influence
> by the military-industrial complex which results in excessive costs, bur-
> geoning military budgets, and scandalous performances.
>
>   *   *   *
>
> This is a most dangerous and shocking situation. It indicates the in-
> creasing influence of the big contractors with the military and the military

---

[49] Elting Morison, "A Case Study of Innovation," *Engineering & Science,* April, 1950. Quoted
by Schon in *Hearings on Economic Concentration,* Pt. 3, p. 1213.
[50] 91st Cong., 1st Sess., *Congressional Record,* March 24, 1969, Vol. 115, No. 50, p. 7207,
    remarks by Senator Proxmire. The number of the 100 top prime contractors reporting
    on their employment of high-ranking officers was 95 in 1969 and 88 in 1959.

with the big contractors. It shows an intensification of the problem and the growing community of interest which exists between the two. It makes it imperative that new weapon systems receive the most critical review and that defense contracts be examined in microscopic detail.

* * *

This matter is particularly dangerous in a situation where only 11.5 percent of military contracts are awarded on a formally advertised competitive bid basis. It lends itself to major abuse when almost 90 percent of all military contracts are negotiated, and where a very high proportion of them are negotiated with only one, or one or two, contractors.

Formerly high-ranking military officers have an entree to the Pentagon that others do not have. I am not charging that is necessarily wrong. I am saying that it is true.[51]

To the officers who have moved into the corporate life, and to those who are planning to do so, the upsetting effect of an innovation upon the service itself has become a secondary consideration. It is a price that must be paid if the corporations are to have something new and different to sell the government, without which they cannot grow and give employment to, among others, former high-ranking military officers.

Also helping to change the military's attitude toward science has been the introduction of the so-called weapons systems approach. A military service, together with one or more large prime contractors (often aided by a consulting "think tank"), decides on a new weapons system that will meet a real or conceivable military need and appears to be technologically feasible. Burton Klein of the Rand Corporation has described the procedure: "Before any major project is begun, the planners painstakingly figure out what performance characteristics the weapons system is supposed to have *and the technological innovations it will contain.* The development program is spelled out stage by stage, and then reviewed by numerous agencies within the armed services, by special committees, and by the staff of the Assistant Secretary of Defense for Research and Engineering."[52] If all goes according to plan, the nation benefits from a new and possibly better weapons system, the appropriations of the military services are increased, and the prime contractor profits from its manufacture.

Implicit in the whole procedure, however, is the assumption that science can be programmed. From its very inception the weapons system assumes the use of technologies which are either in existence or which, it is anticipated, can be made to be forthcoming. To the extent that it is based on the former, there will be little really new in the new weapons system; to the extent that it is based on the latter, it rests upon the dubious belief that creativity can be forced. Where, as is not infrequently the case, science defies all attempts to make it produce to order, the result is a failure of the system, or its reformulation on less ambitious lines to permit the use of older technologies. It is this conflict between design and performance which is the principal source of the major "cost overruns."

What of the truly important discoveries that happen to lie outside the scope of any ongoing weapons system? In the words of Donald Schon, "A military technical administrator operating within such a system cannot easily shift his attention to radical technical ideas not obviously related to his requirements, and so he finds it even more difficult to invest in risky individuals who will not be able to carry their innovations into production later on."

[51] *Ibid.*
[52] *Fortune,* May, 1958. Emphasis added.

Assuming a systems approach in World War II similar to that employed today, rocketry would have enjoyed a better fate only if it could have been integrated into an existing or projected system—a most unlikely possibility as long as it was regarded by those at the top as "impossible" and "Buck Rogers stuff." By the very nature of things, the more revolutionary and far-reaching the discovery, the less likely are the chances that it can be fitted into what usually turn out to be either extremely expensive failures or planned "voyages into the known."

Alternatives to corporate research

The causes of the creative backwardness of bigness are endemic to the large corporations themselves. There should be nothing particularly surprising about their unreceptivity to new technologies that would destroy their existing capital investment; about their indifference to new ideas when their existing technology is operating satisfactorily; about their tendency to underestimate the demand for that which is unproved and untried; about their neglect of inventors whose contributions to the corporation's profits are at best infrequent; about the natural bent of corporate officials to direct research into channels which, to them, appear promising; about the difficulties inherent in trying to fit the creative temperament into a hierarchical organization; or about their cooperation with the military in manufacturing weapons systems that seek to combine the appearance of novelty with the use of proven technologies.

The conclusion seems inescapable: if inventiveness and innovation are to be accelerated, the need is for less emphasis on the large corporation and more on its alternatives—traditionally the individual inventor and the small manufacturing enterprise. To these can now be added a comparatively new source of creativity —the science or technological entrepreneurs. Like most inventors in today's world of complex technologies, they are technically well trained, usually holding advanced degrees in some branch of science or engineering. Also like most inventors, they are imaginative and creative. What distinguishes them is that they have broken away from the research divisions of established organizations— large corporations, government agencies, or private foundations—and set up their own research laboratories or small manufacturing enterprises. Not infrequently they also keep one foot in the academic world by becoming professors in science or engineering at nearby universities. This provides them with a regular salary, access to costly research facilities, academic prestige, and various fringe benefits such as the free use of graduate students. As the owners of much of their own companies' stock, they stand to profit handsomely (on a capital-gains basis) if their endeavors prove successful; they are all aware of cases in which colleagues, under similar circumstances, have become millionaires almost overnight.

But it is not just the promise of financial rewards far greater than would be theirs as salaried employees that spurs them on. In a study of this new breed of inventor undertaken for the Senate Antitrust Subcommittee, Donald Schon, formerly Director of the Institute for Applied Technology of the National Bureau of Standards, found that they had personality traits in common: "They are imaginative, stubborn, rebellious in spirit, dedicated to their ideas to the point of fanaticism, and motivated by an overwhelming desire to 'show them'—to prove to the establishment, scientific or industrial, that something that others felt to be impossible can, in fact, be done." [53] A similar description of the technological entrepreneur has been given by David Allison:

> They like to think about Polaroid, High Voltage Engineering, Bolt Beranek & Newman, and the scores of others who once were small, struggling enterprises of scientists and engineers. The dream of achievement is vivid among them. They possess an unyielding conviction of eventual success, for confidence and belief-in-self is the stuff of the science entrepreneur.
>
> Over the past several months, I have talked with many of them, men who have quit the industrial laboratories, the not-for-profit research institutes, or the great universities to establish themselves in the technical "business." They work in small buildings, usually new. (I found none who worked out of the romantic garage.) They are seldom more than ten miles from a university. They carry short, telegraphic names—like those found in second-rate business novels: Invac, Aero Vac, Bytrex, Rotek. Their lights burn late.
>
> They eat at their desks instead of Kiwanis and sleep the sleep of men with problems. It is a good, hard life, they say, and they are glad to have put behind them the security of the large organization.
>
> Is it the promise of wealth that makes them go? In part, I believe it is, but there is always another reason too, for talk of money does not arouse in them the same intensity of interest as does talk of new ideas. These are men who must burn off extraordinary quantities of energy—a compulsion. It is impossible to talk with one of them for more than ten consecutive minutes, for their doors are swinging and their telephones jangling from eight until six.[54]

Clusters of small research organizations and manufacturing enterprises are to be found around major universities in various parts of the country, such as the Cambridge-Boston-Route 128 area, in association with the Cambridge university community. During the last three decades approximately 300 new technology-based firms are estimated to have emerged from work going on at the Massachusetts Institute of Technology alone. At the other end of the country is another large innovative community, the Berkeley-Stanford-Bay area in association with the University of California at Berkeley and Stanford University at Palo Alto. More recently, Dallas, Cleveland, and Pittsburgh, and to a lesser extent Purdue, Ann Arbor, and Baltimore, have also moved toward the formation of such communities.

Facilitating the establishment of these independent, science-based enterprises have been their low capital entrance requirements. On the basis of a detailed examination of a half-dozen specific case examples, supplemented by numerous interviews, Schon found that in undertaking the first technological and commercial development of a new technology, the capital requirements "are apt to be small." The Stroboscopic Lighting Development was started by Harold Edgerton on a "moonlighting" basis with small funds. When Information International (a developer of film-reading equipment that can be programmed to operate with other automatic data-processing equipment) received its first order, it had only $20,000 in operating capital. Only limited funds were used by Jordan Baruch in

---

[53] *Hearings on Economic Concentration,* Pt. 6, pp. 2725–56.
[54] David Allison, "The Science Entrepreneur," *International Science & Technology,* Jan., 1963, p. 40.

developing Soundstream's product, a small-scale perforated technique replacing costly long sound tunnels. From an investment of a little over $2 million came the prototype demonstrating the workability of such an important advancement as the inertial-guidance system. In the words of one of the entrepreneurs, "It does not take a great deal of capital to invent or to develop in the electronics business. One can carry an invention a good way toward the market without incurring heavy financial costs." [55]

Contrary to general belief, important contributions at the development stage can be made by small technology-based companies. If sales of the new product are sufficiently large, the small firms may undergo a rapid expansion, becoming themselves companies of respectable size. As an example of this process, a report of Arthur D. Little, Inc., cites the case of the semiconductor industry, which was founded on the discovery of the transistor by scientists of a large organization, Bell Laboratories:

> Quite a number of the non-Bell discoveries in the U.S. were made by the so-called small companies. However, one must remember that in the early stages of the semiconductor industry, all the companies or at least their solid state divisions were small. Gordon Peale joined Texas Instruments in 1952 and brought with him from Bell his considerable skill in growing germanium crystals to the then relatively small electronics company engaged in making electronic equipment for geophysical exploration. After considerable time and effort, his group found ways of applying these same principles to silicone materials, and in 1954 announced the first commercially grown junction silicone transistor which had relatively good characteristics for the time. These soon found application in many pieces of electronic equipment for the military and helped to project Texas Instruments into its subsequent growth.
>
> Fairchild Semiconductor was founded in 1958 by eight men who had previously been employed by the Shockley Laboratory, another small semiconductor firm headed then by William Shockley. They first started to build the then conventional silicone mesa diffused transistor, but very soon they brought innovations of the masking oxide protection schemes which have provided a much more stable transistor and has led to the technology now commonly used in the silicone field. Based, certainly, upon Bell Labs' discoveries of the oxide masking, the group at Fairchild proliferated upon this and used the innovation of keeping the oxide on the transistor throughout all the subsequent fabrications, thereby simplifying fabrication and providing a permanent inner protection over the surface.
>
> At Transitron, the gold bonded diode was brought to a considerable degree of perfection, far beyond the initial experiments described by Bell Laboratories. Likewise, in the silicone rectifiers group they used aluminum sheets for doping N type materials to form a junction. After difficulties in making good contacts to the aluminum metal, they used, in desperation, sheets of heavily doped P type silicone to which contacts could be made in a more conventional method. These two products, diode and rectifier, launched that rather small company into its early explosive growth.[56]

[55] Quoted by Schon in *Hearings on Economic Concentration*, Pt. 6, p. 2746.
[56] Arthur D. Little, Inc., "Patterns and Problems of Technical Innovation in American Industry," *Report to the National Science Foundation*, Sept., 1963. Quoted by Schon in *Hearings on Economic Concentration*, Pt. 6, pp. 2742–43.

The case histories of Texas Instruments, Fairchild, and Transition Electronics, which are among the semiconductor industry's largest firms, demonstrate that selling out to a large company is not the only way a new technology-based enterprise can solve its growth problems. Even when it is taken over, the spinning off of creative personnel continues. As Schon has put it, "The process may come full circle when the large-scale business based on the new technology, spins off new individuals who leave the business (as they now occasionally leave firms such as North American, Raytheon, General Electric and the like) to undertake new technology-based ventures of their own." The sources of dissatisfaction within a large organization remain, regardless of whether it is in a traditional industry or a new, rapidly expanding field.

The
Centripetal
Forces

T H R E E

During the past two decades decreases in concentration have been matched—indeed exceeded—by increases. Necessarily, therefore, if one set of forces has been operating to reduce concentration, other forces have been operating in the opposite direction—i.e., with a centripetal effect. Both the centrifugal and the centripetal forces can be at work at the same time, producing increasing concentration in some industries and decreasing concentration in others. They can also be at work simultaneously within a given industry—e.g., new decentralizing technologies may be reducing the capital entrance requirements while the leading firms are engaged in a vigorous program of mergers and acquisitions. The absence of change in an industry's concentration ratio thus may result merely from the fact that the two opposing sets of forces have offset each other.

As was the case during previous eras of rising concentration, mergers and acquisitions have probably been the strongest of all of the centripetal forces. Their effect on market concentration can be illustrated by developments in textiles and apparel, which, it will be recalled, have been areas of rapidly rising concentration. Between 1951 and 1968 more than 1,000 acquisitions of textile firms were recorded by the Federal Trade Commission. While many were of small mills, 70 were classified as "large" mergers, with assets totaling $2.1 billion. In terms of direction the movement in textiles has been predominantly horizontal, with over two-thirds of the large acquisition being made by other textile companies. By 1968, 8 of the 23 largest textile firms of 17 years earlier had been acquired by other top textile producers.[1] A similar merger movement,

---

[1] Federal Trade Commission, *Enforcement Policy with Respect to Mergers in the Textile Mill Products Industry,* Nov. 22, 1968, pp. 5–7.

though on a somewhat smaller scale, took place in the apparel industry. Through forward vertical acquisitions several of the largest textile firms became leading producers of apparel as well.

From the continuing analysis of concentration ratios it has become more and more evident that increases in concentration tend to be found in consumer goods and decreases in producer goods industries; that increases are particularly prevalent among those consumer goods where products are differentiated by brand or trade names; and that the significant determinant is not differentiation per se but whether the product is heavily promoted by TV advertising. For reasons peculiar to it, TV advertising appears to be remarkably successful in achieving its objective—the promotion of the sponsor's product at the expense of his rivals. Since only large firms can afford the cost of extensive TV promotion, the almost inescapable result is an increase in concentration in industries relying heavily on TV.

In the past a widely recognized cause of increasing concentration was price discrimination and other predatory practices—the "strong-arm tactics of monopoly." Although all but dismissed in recent years by many academicians, in-depth studies continue to reveal that predatory practices are still very much with us. Thus, on the basis of an investigation of the bread industry,[2] the Senate Sub-committee on Antitrust and Monopoly found that in waging competitive warfare against smaller bakeries, the leading bread manufacturers frequently charged lower prices in outlying communities than in the city where the bread was baked, used "fighting brands" made from a leaner formula and expanded with air to resemble a standard-weight loaf, and granted discounts and allowances to selected retailers in order to meet or beat the prices of local bakeries—a practice referred to by one smaller baker as paying money "over, under and through" the table. These and similar practices have made a trend toward greater concentration in the industry all but inevitable. The share of the 4 largest companies, which had risen from 16 percent in 1947 to 22 percent in 1958, advanced further to 26 percent by 1967.

A further force making for higher concentration is the power of the government. In the United States the government's policy toward concentration is ambivalent. On the one hand, through antitrust laws and positive assistance to smaller firms it seeks to bring about reductions in concentration—or at least to hold further increases in check. On the other hand, it engages in a variety of activities that tend to produce exactly the opposite result. The very purpose of such time-honored restraints as tariffs and patents is to keep outsiders out. In recent years there has been a growing tendency to invoke governmental assistance in controlling the market by industries whose ability to do so by private methods has been eroding. As a result of the discovery of new sources of supply, the introduction of new technologies, and changes in consumer demand, established firms are seeking increasingly to induce the government to do by public means that which they can no longer accomplish privately. The result is a growing recourse to such publicly conferred monopolistic privileges as commodity agreements, import quotas, and actions by regulatory bodies to exclude newcomers. In addition, the bulk of defense contracts, awards for research and development, and other forms of government largesse regularly go to a handful of the largest corporations.

[2] *Administered Prices: Report on Bread.*

CONSOLIDATIONS, MERGERS, AND ACQUISITIONS

Of the centripetal forces, probably the most important in the twentieth century has been the bringing together of formerly independent companies under one corporate roof through consolidation, merger, or acquisition. The term "consolidation" generally has been used to denote the more or less simultaneous bringing together of a number of firms into one company. In contrast, the terms "merger" and "acquisition" refer to the taking over of one firm by another, either as an isolated action or as one of an extended series. The technical distinction between mergers and acquisitions relates to the manner in which the combining is effected, the former referring to the fusion of assets and the latter to the acquisition of stock. Since any company that holds controlling stock ownership in another can at any time merge the assets of the two, the distinction is more of form than of substance. Except in a technical context, the two have come to be used interchangeably. Taken together, consolidations, mergers, and acquisitions constitute external expansion (as distinguished from internal expansion—the building of new plant and facilities financed by sales of stock, loans, or internal savings). The terms "the merger movement," "growth by merger," and "merger activity" have come to be used as synonyms for external expansion.

There have been in our industrial history three great waves of merger activity—1897–1905, 1925–29, and 1960–69. These upsurges in the rate of external expansion are readily apparent in Figure 11-1, which shows the number of manufacturing and mining firms disappearing by merger from 1895 to 1968.

The turn-of-the-century movement

The importance of the initial era of merger activity in shaping our present-day industrial structures can hardly be exaggerated. Not only did the consolidations put together during a short span of about 10 years transform competitive industries into oligopolistic structures, they determined the form of the oligopoly itself. Typically this form was asymmetrical, with one (and in some cases 2) oligopolists dominant and the others of distinctly secondary importance. Except where the consolidation proved unsuccessful, usually because of an inability to control the market, the asymmetrical oligopolists created during the "great consolidation movement" have endured for nearly three-quarters of a century. Referring to the period 1895–1904 Ralph L. Nelson has observed:

Figure 11-1

ANNUAL FIRM DISAPPEARANCE BY MERGER, 1895–1968

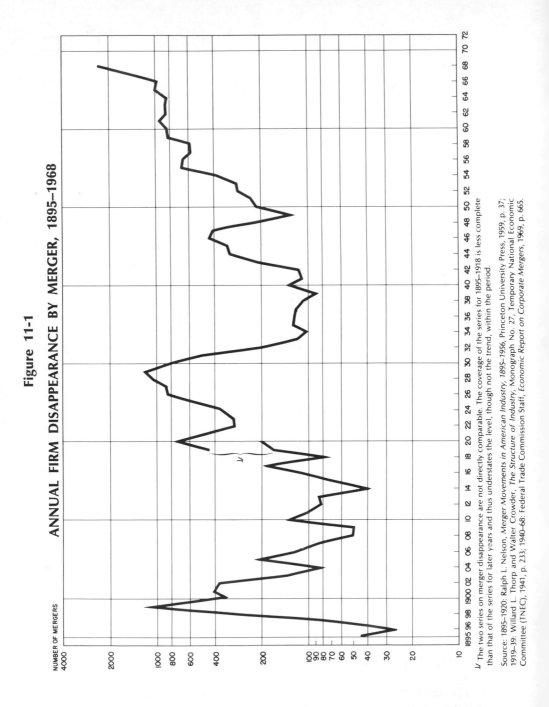

Source: 1895–1920: Ralph L. Nelson, *Merger Movements in American Industry, 1895–1956,* Princeton University Press, 1959, p. 37; 1919–39: Willard L. Thorp and Walter Crowder, *The Structure of Industry,* Monograph No. 27, Temporary National Economic Committee (TNEC), 1941, p. 233; 1940–68: Federal Trade Commission Staff, *Economic Report on Corporate Mergers,* 1969, p. 665.

1/ The two series on merger disappearance are not directly comparable. The coverage of the series for 1895–1918 is less complete than that of the series for later years and thus understates the level, though not the trend, within the period.

In this ten-year period the average number of firms disappearing annually was 301. Five of these years, 1898–1902, saw a burst of merger activity never exceeded in importance in our history, with 1028 firms disappearing into mergers in 1899 alone. The huge turn-of-the-century merger wave produced U. S. Steel, American Tobacco, International Har-

CONSOLIDATIONS, MERGERS, AND ACQUISITIONS

vester, Du Pont, Corn Products, Anaconda Copper, American Smelting & Refining, to name only a few. Its effect on American industry was widespread and enduring.[1]

Some impression of its general effect can be gained from a comparison made by Nelson of the capitalization of the companies involved in mergers (as reflected by their gross assets) to the total capitalization of their industry group (as reflected by the value of land, plant, equipment, and working capital reported to the 1904 Census of Manufactures). During this particular period, Nelson cautions, the comparison provides only a rough indication because of "the incompleteness of reporting acknowledged in the census report and the varying amounts of 'watered assets' and 'watered stock' in both the census and the present compilations. . . ." [2] The data are shown in Table 11-1. An extreme example is primary metals, in which the capitalization of the merged companies is shown to be more than twice the capital of the entire industry.[3] Nonetheless, even after making every allowance for the over-capitalization of assets and the other difficulties in the data, there can be little doubt that in these important fields the early consolidations brought together firms representing substantial proportions of the industries' total resources. The capitalization of the merged companies was more than half the industry's reported capital in transportation equipment, machinery, paper, and chemicals, not to mention primary

Table 11-1

ABSOLUTE AND RELATIVE MERGER ACTIVITY, 1895–1907

SIC Code	Industry	Absolute Merger Activity (Adjusted Merger Capitalizations) (Mils.)	Relative Merger Activity (Percent)
33	Primary metals	$3,168.4	210.0%
20	Food and kindred products	937.8	39.4
35	Nonelectrical machinery	404.0	71.9
37	Transportation equipment	391.0	75.1
21	Tobacco products	314.3	47.6
28	Chemicals	245.3	50.6
22	Textiles	213.5	14.5
32	Stone, clay, and glass products	160.5	40.5
26	Paper and allied products	157.4	56.7
36	Electrical machinery, etc.	78.8	43.8
29	Petroleum products	74.0	1.5
31	Leather and products	45.2	18.6
24, 25	Lumber and wood products, and furniture and fixtures	42.3	8.2
27	Printing and publishing	18.9	4.9

Source: Ralph L. Nelson, *Merger Movement in American Industry, 1895–1956,* Princeton University Press, 1959, p. 172

[1] Ralph L. Nelson, *Merger Movements in American Industry, 1895–1956,* Princeton University Press, 1959, p. 34.
[2] *Ibid.,* pp. 170–71.
[3] See Charles R. Van Hise, *Concentration and Control,* Macmillan, 1914, p. 115.

metals, and between one-third and one-half in tobacco products, electrical machinery, food and kindred products, and stone, clay, and glass.

Few events in history have contributed more to concentration in U.S. industry than the formation in 1901 of U.S. Steel, referred to at the time as the "giant of giants." All in all, its creation brought together some 170 subsidiary concerns consisting of over 80 mining companies, 40 manufacturing companies, over 30 transportation companies, and several gas and miscellaneous enterprises. When formed, U.S. Steel had steel works with an annual capacity of 9.4 million tons, 1,000 miles of railway, 112 lake ore vessels, iron ore deposits estimated to contain from 500 to 700 million tons of ore, more than 50,000 acres of high-grade coal lands, and numerous related properties. The total number of plants under the control of the corporation exceeded 200.[4]

In the copper industry the first and third largest producers—Anaconda and American Smelting & Refining—were put together during this period. The same was true of the first and third largest producers of farm machinery—International Harvester and Allis-Chalmers. Also formed during the period were the 2 leading producers of tobacco products—American Tobacco and R. J. Reynolds. Other industries in which the leading company of today can be traced back to mergers during the great consolidation movement are chemicals (Du Pont), electrical machinery (General Electric), paper (International Paper), metal cans (American Can), photographic equipment (Eastman Kodak), meat packing (Swift), nickel (International Nickel), shoe machines (United Shoe Machinery), corn products (Corn Products Refining), and silver (International Silver). In addition, the second largest producers of today in glass (Pittsburgh Plate Glass) and dairy products (Borden) were put together during this period.

By 1904 the so-called trusts had in their hands an estimated 40 percent of all the manufacturing capital in the United States.[5] John Moody estimated that before this wave of industrial amalgamation subsided, 78 corporations had gained control of more than half of the total production in their respective industries.[6]

In addition to its astonishing rapidity, the movement had other characteristics. Most of the amalgamations were of the horizontal type, involving producers in the same industry. Typically, most of the leading producers would be combined in one action, with the consolidation then being "rounded out" by the acquisition of smaller producers. Most of the consolidations were effected through the purchase of stock rather than assets. It is this characteristic of the movement that explains the seemingly anomalous action by Congress in 1914 of granting the Federal Trade Commission, under Section 7 of the Clayton Act, the authority to prevent acquisitions of stock but of failing to grant it the power to prevent the merging of assets, an omission that later made the law a dead letter.[7]

There can be little doubt that one of the driving forces behind the formation of many of these consolidations was the desire to eliminate competition. In his examination of the degree of market control achieved by individual consolida-

---

[4] *Ibid.*, pp. 114–15.
[5] Henry R. Seagar and Charles A. Gulick, Jr., *Trust and Corporation Problems,* Harper, 1929, p. 61.
[6] John Moody, *The Truth About the Trusts,* Moody, 1904, p. 487. In retrospect, Moody's estimates appear to be unduly high, owing probably to the difficulty of obtaining adequate data for the universe totals, i.e., the figures for the industry as a whole. (See Ch. 4.)
[7] See Ch. 22.

tions, Nelson discovered, "Almost one-half of firm disappearances, and seven-tenths of merger capitalizations were accounted for by mergers that gained a leading position in the market." [8] In his words, these findings "tend to demonstrate the existence of a fairly strong desire to avoid rigorous competition." [9] A vivid example was the case of U.S. Steel, as was brought out in congressional hearings. Among the witnesses was an official of the corporation, John W. Gates:

> MR. GATES: . . . Mr. Carnegie took it into his head that he would build a railroad from Lake Erie points—from some point on Lake Erie to his various works around Pittsburgh—and that he would also build a tube works; and he proposed to build this tube works, if my memory serves me aright, at Ashtabula, Ohio, where a great deal of the ore is unloaded. Mr. Hill and Mr. Morgan had dined together—James J. Hill —and Mr. Morgan had expressed to Mr. Hill the fear that if Carnegie went into the building of railroads he would demoralize the entire railroad situation as he had demoralized the steel situation, and that if he built a tube works at Ashtabula it would result in a demoralization of the prices of tubes.
>
> *　　*　　*
>
> MR. GATES: The trouble was that Carnegie had threatened to build the tube mill at Ashtabula and a railroad to haul his own ore down.
>
> THE CHAIRMAN: He was going to build a railroad to come into competition with the existing railroads?
>
> MR. GATES: Yes; and a tube plant to tear the National Tube, that Morgan had just put together, all to pieces.
>
> THE CHAIRMAN: He was going to give Morgan trouble, both in his manufacturing industry and with his common carrier?
>
> MR. GATES: It looked that way.
>
> THE CHAIRMAN: And it was to obviate this anticipated competition that this tentative plan was drawn up that afterwards became the United States Steel Corporation?
>
> MR. GATES: Yes, sir.
>
> *　　*　　*
>
> THE CHAIRMAN: Mr. Carnegie was also threatening to go into the tin-plate business, was he not, at that time?
>
> MR. GATES: I guess he was threatening the whole line.
>
> *　　*　　*
>
> MR. BEALL: The real cause of complaint against Mr. Carnegie was that he would not abide by the agreement, but would insist on cutting the price?
>
> MR. GATES: He was like a bull in a china shop. He would get a thing into his head once in a while and go and do absurd things, that I really think he did not think much about . . . I can not state it any plainer than Mr. Morgan stated to Mr. Schwab and me—that if Mr. Carnegie should build this tube works at Ashtabula and a railroad from Ashtabula to his works in the Pittsburgh district it would demoralize the whole situation. That was Mr. Morgan's statement and not mine. [10]

---

[8] Nelson, *op. cit.*, p. 102. Nelson also explored other factors that have been suggested as possible causes of the turn-of-the-century movement.

[9] *Ibid.*, p. 103.

[10] 62nd Cong., 2nd Sess., Committee on Investigation of the United States Steel Corporation, *Hearings,* 1911–1912. Quoted in W. H. Stevens, *Industrial Combinations and Trusts,* Macmillan, 1922, pp. 82, 84–85. For confirmatory material see *ibid.*, pp. 11, 98–99, 112–17.

In a deterministic interpretation of history, the recurrent periods of intense merger activity would be attributed to broad, underlying economic forces, beyond the control or influence of any man or small group of men. But to ignore the pivotal role played by particular individuals who are in positions of power is to do violence to historical accuracy. A recognition that the course of economic events can be influenced by individuals who have the imagination and the power to take advantage of prevailing conditions does not constitute acceptance of a "conspiracy" theory of history.

Had it not been for the ability, energy, and drive for power of John Pierpont Morgan, the initial merger wave would never have reached the heights it did. Although best known for his role in organizing the first billion-dollar combine in history—U.S. Steel—other industrial giants were created by Morgan more than three-quarters of a century ago. Indeed, the very process of combining and centralizing formerly competing firms into great consolidations came to be known as "Morganizing" industry.[11] General Electric was organized by Morgan in 1892 as a consolidation of Edison General Electric Company and the Thomson-Houston Electric Company. At its formation, it had two Morgan representatives, while Morgan and Company served as a depository, was a stockholder, and marketed its securities. The nation's largest manufacturer of plumbing and heating equipment is the product of consolidations engineered by Morgan: American Radiator was a consolidation in 1899 of nearly every heating apparatus concern in the United States, controlling about three-fourths of the business; it expanded greatly during the next 30 years and in 1929 merged with the Standard Sanitary Manufacturing Company, itself the product of numerous previous mergers. Through early associations with its founder, George M. Pullman, the House of Morgan played an important role in the forming of the Pullman Company. After the merger of Pullman with Standard Steel Car, the new board numbered six Morgan and three Mellon directors.[12] By 1912, when Morgan testified before the Pujo Committee investigating the "Money Trust," Morgan partners were found to hold 341 interlocking directorates. Discussing the significance of Morgan's power, Louis D. Brandeis wrote:

> If the bankers' power were commensurate only with their wealth, they would have relatively little influence on American business. Vast fortunes

[11] In 1895, upon the death of Anthony J. Drexel, the firm became J. P. Morgan & Co. At this time the Paris branch became Morgan, Harjes & Co. Later it became Morgan & Cie, while the London branch became Morgan, Grenfell & Co. Further changes took place when, a half-century later, the Banking Act of 1933 required the divorce of deposit banking from underwriting. J. P. Morgan & Co. elected to continue in business as a deposit bank, and a new firm, Morgan, Stanley & Co., Inc., was formed by a number of the partners of J. P. Morgan & Co. and Drexel & Co. (the Philadelphia branch of J. P. Morgan & Co.) to take over the investment-banking business. In March, 1940, the partnership form was dropped, and the deposit banking firm was incorporated as J. P. Morgan & Co., Inc.

[12] The Pullman Corporation's exclusive position as the only company both producing and operating sleeping cars was attacked in 1940 by the Department of Justice. The Supreme Court found that the company had, by preclusive contracts with the railroads, so fortified its monopoly position as to eliminate any possibility of competition and held that a monopoly so maintained violated the Sherman Act. Pullman was directed to sell its interests in the operation of sleeping cars but, over the opposition of the Department of Justice, was permitted to dispose of these interests to the railroads (*United States* v. *Pullman Co., et al.,* 330 U.S. 806; 50 F. Supp. 123 [E.D. Pa. 1943]; 53 F. Supp. 908 [E.D. Pa. 1944]; 64 F. Supp. 108 [E.D. Pa. 1945]).

like those of the Astors are no doubt regrettable. They are inconsistent with democracy. They are unsocial. And they seem peculiarly unjust when they represent largely unearned increment. But the wealth of the Astors does not endanger political or industrial liberty. It is insignificant in amount as compared with the aggregate wealth of America, or even of New York City. It lacks significance largely because its owners have only the income from their own wealth. The Astor wealth is static. The wealth of the Morgan associates is dynamic. The power and the growth of power of our financial oligarchs comes from wielding the savings and quick capital of others.[13]

Under the guidance of J. P. Morgan, Jr., the firm continued its activities in promoting mergers and acquisitions, though in a somewhat more sophisticated manner. During the merger movement of the 1920's it helped (along with General Electric) to organize the Radio Corporation of America, assisted the du Ponts in taking over General Motors, put together a conglomeration of food brands into Standard Brands, and organized the United Corporation to control a vast utility and power network.

After examining a variety of possible causes of the 1895–1905 movement, including the rate of industrial growth and the development of interregional transportation, Ralph Nelson concluded by observing, "The leading factors of immediate importance appeared to be the newly achieved development of a broad and strong capital market and the existence of institutions that enabled the organizers of mergers to utilize this market." [14] The timing of peaks in merger activity was found to be related more closely to stock prices than to indices of general economic activity or of business expansion, with mergers being "more positively correlated to stock-price changes than to changes in industrial production in the three periods of high merger activity—1895–1904, 1919–31 and 1943–54." [15] Within the initial period the relationship was clearly demonstrated during 1901 and 1902, when both merger activity and stock prices showed downward trends while industrial production continued to rise: "This suggests that the large merger wave ended not so much in response to an adverse turn in the underlying level of production as to an adverse turn in the condition of the stock market." [16]

Mergers have invariably represented a way of capitalizing on the rise in the stock market; only the method of capitalization has changed. In the initial merger wave it was the essence of simplicity: stock issued vastly in excess of the true value of the merged properties provided both the reward to the merger promoters and the compensation for the owners of the acquired companies. With remarkable understatement, Willard L. Thorp observed, "The new enterprise would be formed, with extensive capitalization of the alleged benefits of consolidation. . . . It was regularly true that the whole was greater than the sum of its parts." [17] The Commissioner of Corporations was somewhat more explicit, pointing out that in the case of the formation of the U.S. Steel Corpora-

[13] Louis D. Brandeis, *Other People's Money*, Stokes, 1932, p. 18.
[14] Nelson, *op. cit.*, p. 6.
[15] *Ibid.*, p. 119.
[16] *Ibid.*, p. 120.
[17] Willard L. Thorp and Walter Crowder, *The Structure of Industry*, Monograph No. 27, Temporary National Economic Committee (TNEC), 1941, p. 231.

tion, "actual market value of the Steel Corporation's entire tangible properties at its formation, omitting all factors of merger, integration, and concentration was not over $700,000,000, just about one-half its capitalization." [18] A popular saying had it that the water in U.S. Steel would float the combined navies of the United States and Great Britain. Many of the new combinations were foredoomed to an early death by weaknesses in their capital structure, the result of an overemphasis by their banker-promoters on issuing enormous amounts of watered stock rather than on creating sound and efficient organizations. As Andrew Carnegie once said, "They throw cats and dogs together and call them elephants." But the monopoly power of many others was sufficient to enable them to carry their excessive capitalizations.

The merger wave of the 1920's

The second wave of mergers, beginning in the mid-1920's, had been preceded by a sharp upturn, which began immediately following World War I and extended through 1919, 1920, and the early part of 1921, until it was interrupted by the postwar depression. Merger activity then turned upward, reaching new heights in 1928 and 1929. The greatest merger activity took place in iron and steel and machinery, with 18 percent of the recorded disappearances. The next most active field was food and liquor, which accounted for 14 percent, followed by petroleum and nonferrous metals with 11 percent each. Like the turn-of-the-century movement, the merger wave of the 1920's contributed to, and was facilitated by, a rapidly rising stock market. According to Nelson, "From 1924 through 1929 stock prices increased greatly while industrial production increased only moderately. The merger series more closely followed stock prices." [19]

In other respects, however, the characteristics of this movement were somewhat different from those of the earlier one. On the whole, the mergers involved less capital and resulted in the formation of somewhat smaller units, but there were many more of them. Furthermore, they included not only horizontal acquisitions of direct competitors producing similar goods but vertical acquisitions involving the purchase either of suppliers on the one hand or of further fabricating facilities on the other. Many manufacturing firms carried their operations forward into the distribution field as well. Finally, the conglomerate acquisitions, which involved the purchase of firms in distant and often completely unrelated lines, made their first real headway during this period. Compared to the earlier consolidations, a larger proportion of the acquisitions now took the form of the absorption of assets rather than the purchase of stock, primarily because of Section 7 of the Clayton Act.

Typical examples of horizontal expansion during this period are the purchases that were made by National Dairy Products. Beginning in 1924 this corporation acquired more than 360 concerns. As an ice cream company, it acquired 150 direct competitors, and as a fluid-milk concern, 119 direct competitors. In addition, its expansion took it into other dairy products industries—cheese, butter, and condensed and evaporated milk. As a result of its vigorous drive, the cor-

[18] *Report of the Commissioner of Corporations on the Steel Industry*, Pt. 1, July 1, 1911, p. xxii.
[19] Nelson, *op. cit.*, p. 121.

poration before World War II had acquired 20 to 30 percent of the commercial ice cream business in Florida, Alabama, South Carolina, Rhode Island, and New York; from 30 to 40 percent in Massachusetts, Pennsylvania, Tennessee, and New Hampshire; and over 40 percent in Maine, Virginia, the District of Columbia, North Carolina, New Jersey, Vermont, and Connecticut. In addition, it distributed from 20 to 30 percent of the fluid milk consumed in such metropolitan centers as Boston, New York, and Hartford; from 30 to 50 percent in Philadelphia and Pittsburgh; and over 50 percent in Baltimore and Washington, D.C.[20]

The purchase by the major copper-mining companies of brass- and copper-fabricating firms represents a typical example of the forward vertical acquisitions of the period. Early in 1922 the Anaconda Copper Company purchased 99 percent of the outstanding capital stock of the American Brass Company, the nation's largest brass manufacturer, and followed this action with the purchase of additional fabricators. A similar policy of expanding into the fabricating field was put into effect by the Kennecott Copper Corporation and the Phelps-Dodge Corporation. Each of these 3 major copper producers became so heavily engaged in the fabricating field that it was able to absorb the entire copper output of its domestic mines and refineries.[21]

At the same time that mining companies and other basic-material producers were extending themselves forward into fabricating fields, finished-goods producers expanded backward into the materials industries. Thus, the major tire companies acquired cotton tire cord plants—for example, Martha Mills was acquired in 1929 by the B. F. Goodrich Company.

The early conglomerates formed during this period were exemplified by the General Foods Company, which acquired firms in practically every line of the food industry. Its acquisitions included concerns in the fields of gelatin, tapioca, cocoa, salad dressing, coffee, baking powder, salt, margarine, shell fish, fresh fish, oysters, shrimp, poultry, citrus fruit juice, canned fruits and vegetables, breakfast cereals, cake flour, shredded coconut, syrups, laundry aids, pectin, baking powder, flavoring, dog food, and coffee—both with and without caffein.

Among the other important industrial mergers of the 1920's were: in petroleum, the acquisition of Associated Oil by Pacific Oil (1920), of Midwest Refining by Standard Oil of Indiana (1921), of Magnolia Petroleum by Socony Mobil (1925), of Pan American Petroleum & Transportation by Standard Oil of Indiana (1925), of Pacific Oil by Standard Oil of California (1926), of General Petroleum by Socony Mobil (1926), of Pacific Petroleum by Standard Oil of California (1926), and of California Petroleum by the Texas Corporation (1928); in copper, the acquisitions of Chile Copper by Anaconda Copper (1923) and of Greene Cananea Copper by Anaconda (1929); in steel, the purchases of Lackawanna Steel by Bethlehem Steel (1922), of Midvale Steel & Ordnance by Bethlehem Steel (1923), and of Steel & Tube of America by Youngstown Sheet & Tube (1923); in meat packing, the absorption of Morris & Company by Armour & Company (1923); and in automobiles, the acquisition of Dodge Bros. by Chrysler (1928).[22]

---

[20] 79th Cong., 1st Sess., House Committee on the Judiciary, *Hearings on H.R. 2357*, "To Amend Sections 7 and 11 of the Clayton Act," 1945, pp. 250–60.

[21] Federal Trade Commission, *Report on the Copper Industry, Summary*, March, 1947.

[22] Adolf A. Berle and Gardiner C. Means, *The Modern Corporation and Private Property*, rev. ed., Harcourt Brace Jovanovich, 1967, pp. 320–21.

Just as the movement at the turn of the century had been brought to an end by the stock market crash of 1907, so the movement of the 1920's was ended by the crash of 1929. Yet, as in the earlier period, many of the most active firms in the merger movement survived the ensuing depression as leading factors in their industries.

Writing at the height of the second wave of mergers Willard L. Thorp compared it to the turn-of-the-century movement:

> The present mergers are unlike those of the great combination period at the end of the 19th century. In the earlier instances, the incentives were usually either the formation of a monopoly or profits of some promoter. The present mergers often appear to be quickly followed by new financing, thus implying that the desire for additional capital is an important motive. A further incentive, in certain industries, has come from modern marketing methods, in which the concern which is large enough to undertake national advertising has a definite advantage over its smaller rivals.[23]

As a general proposition, direct control of the market was more difficult to achieve during the 1920's than during the great consolidation movement. Consolidations had already been formed in those industries that lent themselves most readily to concentrated control; it had become increasingly difficult to monopolize rapidly expanding industries. At the same time other methods of stabilizing markets were being perfected with greater emphasis coming to be placed on creating a unique demand for a firm's products through product differentiation. Long-existing companies, such as Borden, were invested with homey symbols (Elsie the Cow), while comforting homemakers (Betty Crocker) were conjured up to attest to the quality of General Foods' products. National Dairy Products vigorously exploited such trade names as Sealtest and Kraft. Although its leading position stemmed partly from patent controls, Radio Corporation of America owed much of its preeminence to advertising and promotional programs built around its trade names, RCA and Victor. Similar programs figured in the success of General Motors in automobiles and the "Standard" companies in petroleum. Even before the Great Depression the American public had been conditioned "to rely" on the products of well-known "name" companies.

As to the movement's general effect on concentration, the FTC staff has found that between 1925 and 1929 mergers accounted for "nearly all" of the increase in the 100 largest companies' share of total manufacturing assets: "The share of total manufacturing assets held by the 100 largest corporations of 1931 rose from 35.6 percent in 1925 to 43.9 percent. . . . Of this increase, 3.5 percentage points occurred between 1925 and 1929. Significantly, the assets acquired during this period were equal to 3.2 percent of all corporate manufacturing assets."[24] The logical expectation would be that any pronounced acceleration in the rate of merger activity, such as that of the 1920's, would be accompanied by an increase in aggregate concentration. That a noticeable increase did occur is evident from the available series on the long-term trend:

---

[23] Willard L. Thorp, "The Changing Structure of Industry," in *Recent Economic Changes in the United States,* McGraw-Hill, 1929, Vol. I, p. 217.

[24] Federal Trade Commission Staff, *Economic Report on Corporate Mergers,* 1969, pp. 180–81. Reprinted as Pt. 8A of *Hearings on Economic Concentration.* Acquired-assets data in the report were compiled by Carl Eis.

	200 Largest Corporations Percentage of Nonfinancial Net Income[25]	316 Large Corporations Percentage of Manufacturing Net Working Capital [20]
1929	43.2%	39.0%
1926		35.3
1925	37.1	
Increase (% Pts.)	6.1	3.7

Although there were no J. P. Morgans putting together U.S. Steels overnight the investment bankers brought merger promotion during the 1920's to a high art, developing many of the methods and techniques still employed today. By the early 1920's most of the leading investment-banking houses had come to have "new business" or "industrial" departments whose function was to keep their respective firms posted on prospects for refinancing, new financing, and merger financing. As the leading industrial corporations came to rely increasingly on internal savings for their new financing, the investment banks placed greater emphasis on merger financing as a source of income. Although their primary interest was, and continues to be, in the new securities that may be required to effect a merger—common stock, preferred stock, debentures, and warrants—they also gave attention to the technological, managerial, and marketing aspects of mergers, as well as to the type and degree of competition to be encountered (or eliminated).

To appraise the desirability of particular mergers, investment banks began to retain management-engineering or industrial-consulting firms to advise them. It has been the function of these firms to analyze the properties of the companies involved in relation to the availability of raw materials, accessibility to consuming markets, transportation costs, technology, efficiency of producing facilities, competence of management, marketing methods, financial structure, research capabilities, and so on. Not overlooked is the intensity of competition in the industry and the market share to be achieved by the acquisition.

To aid and abet the investment banks in their merger work, there emerged a group of individuals specializing in bringing companies together. Known as "finders," they typically have been small financial houses, brokers, dealers, or individuals. The more prominent finders usually develop a long-standing association with a particular investment bank. With no more than a copy of Moody's Industrials, a telephone, and some contacts a finder might suggest 20 to 30 pieces of prospective merger business a year to an investment bank or active acquiring firm. If only one comes to fruition, his finder's fee will put him in the upper income brackets. His compensation will be based either on a fixed fee or on a percentage, the latter usually consisting of 2 percent of the acquired company's sales up to $2 million, with a downward-sliding scale thereafter. His actual functions may be legion: arranging introductions, serving as intermediary, ironing out points of conflict, suggesting an appropriate basis for the exchange of stock, and arranging with investment banks for financing.

[25] Adolf A. Berle and Gardiner C. Means, *The Modern Corporation and Private Property,* Macmillan, 1933.
[26] Donald Woodward, Moody's Investors Service.

Investment banks, management engineers, and finders have usually gone about their business in a discreet and quiet manner. Meetings have been informal, discussions exploratory, and agreements tentative. Even reports prepared by management engineers are confidential, intended for use only by their clients. It is therefore not surprising that data with which to appraise their role in merger promotion are virtually nonexistent. Only rarely does information of any kind relating to their activities reach the public record. One such occasion, however, was in the antitrust suit brought by the Department of Justice in 1946 against most of the leading investment bankers.[27] The thrust of the case was against an alleged conspiracy among the investment bankers to divide up the market. It was alleged that once a banking firm undertakes to float the securities of an individual firm, that concern "belongs" to the investment bank; for any other investment bank to solicit its business is considered unethical. Although the decision in the lower court went against the government (and was not appealed to the Supreme Court), specific instances of investment-banker participation in mergers were cited by the Department of Justice in its "Answers to Interrogatories." Although couched in formalistic legal prose, these "answers" give a unique, behind-the-scenes insight into what really goes on in the making of mergers.

The desirability of eliminating competition, together with an awareness of the way to circumvent the antitrust laws, was displayed by

> the occasion in August 1931 when Ralph E. Nollard of Dillon, Read & Co. and a director of Commercial Investment Trust Corp. in connection with the prospective merger of Commercial Investment Trust Corporation and Commercial Credit Corporation wrote: "It seems evident that the two Companies combined into one, with no other independent competitor approaching in magnitude and importance, should be able to do much more satisfactorily and profitably the business for which they now compete so sharply." Nollard also wrote that he thought, "A way around any such difficulty [as the Clayton Act] could probably be found possibly by one company acquiring the assets of the other."

The effect of mergers upon employment was manifested by "the occasion in July 1940 when Consolidated Cigar Corp. acquired the good will, plants, machinery and equipment of Congress Cigar Co., in the financing of which merger Dillon, Read & Co., bankers for Consolidated Cigar Corp. took an active part; the plants of Congress were closed upon acquisition."

An example of the manner in which negotiations for merger are frequently initiated is provided by "the occasion in August of 1943 when Col. Deeds and Chick Allyn of National Cash Register Company, met Charles McCain and Karl H. Behr of Dillon, Read & Co. at 'lunch in a private room of the Recess Club' to discuss the merger of Addressograph-Multigraph Corporation with National Cash Register Co."

An illustration of the awareness by investment banks of where control ultimately resides is provided by "the occasion in 1945 when Dillon, Read & Co., suggested to one of its partners in the west that it call on the controlling stockholders of Friden Calculating Machine Co., Inc. with a view to interesting them in selling control, as they felt quite certain that National Cash Register might be interested in considering the purchase of this company."

The way in which mergers can serve as the basis for the issuance of securities

[27] *United States* v. *Henry S. Morgan, et al.,* 118 F. Supp. 621 (S.D.N.Y. 1946).

is illustrated by "the occasion in and before January 1943 when Dillon, Read & Co. sought to promote the merger of Colorado Milling Co. with Commander-Larabee Milling Company and proposed underwriting a $6,000,000 12-year privately placed debenture issue of the merged companies." Further examples of the tie-in between merger promotion and the issuance of securities are provided by "the occasions in 1944, when Dillon, Read took steps to increase its security merchandising business by instigating and promoting the acquisition of certain companies for the purpose of merging or consolidation with Superior Oil Co."; by "the occasion in 1942 when Dillon, Read & Co. approached National Oil Products Company with a proposition to acquire Chemical Products Inc. of Miami, Florida, and told Mr. Fullick of National Oil Products Company that 'if further capital was acquired (sic) to develop this situation, we would be interested in talking to him about it' "; by "the occasions in 1944, when Dillon, Read took steps to increase its security merchandising business by instigating and promoting the acquisition of certain companies for the purpose of consolidation with Corn Products Refining Co."; by "the occasion in March 1946 when Dillon, Read & Co. in connection with current security issue of Colonial Mills, Inc. financed the acquisition by Colonial Mills of several textile mills including Robbins Mill, Red Springs Mill and Hannah Pickett Mill"; and by "the occasions in 1944, when Dillon, Read took steps to increase its security merchandising business by instigating and promoting the acquisition of certain companies for the purpose of consolidation with Standard Brands."

That the mergers with which investment bankers concern themselves can be of considerable moment is illustrated by "the occasion in the spring of 1935 when Kuhn, Loeb & Co., J. P. Morgan & Co., and Edward B. Smith & Co. (by reason of John Cutler's position as director and a member on the executive committee of International Telephone Company) were conferring concerning an attempt to merge the Postal Telegraph Co., the International Telephone Co. and the Western Union Co." This proposal, incidentally, was blocked by President Roosevelt. But in this case the financial interests persisted, as the Department of Justice cited "the occasion in early 1939 when Lehman Brothers conferred with Kuhn, Loeb & Co., who had interest in Western Union, for the purpose of suggesting a merger between the Western Union Telegraph Co. and the Postal Telegraph Co., and endeavoring to obtain permission of Western Union to join with Lehman Bros. in a study and promotion of some plan of consolidation."

That investment bankers can be instrumental in the taking over of much of an entire industry (in this case metal barrels and drums) is illustrated by "the occasions in 1937 through April 1944 when Blyth & Co. underwrote at least seven issues for Rheem Manufacturing Company and Dillon, Read & Co. deferred to Blyth's right to head this business. During this period said issuer acquired the businesses of various competitors including Muerer Steel Barrel Company, Inc., of Newark, New Jersey, National Steel Barrel Company of Cleveland, Ohio, Wackman Welded Ware Co., Texas & Southern Steel Barrel Co., Inc., New Orleans, La., among others." Bethlehem Steel then acquired 29 percent of Rheem's common stock.

The continuing absorption process

The merger movement since World War II has been made up of three components: (a) a more-or-less *ad seriatim,* continuing absorption of medium-size and small firms by larger companies, (b) acquisitions by major oil companies, and (c) the dramatic, almost overnight creation of huge new holding companies ranking among the largest companies in the nation—the so-called new conglomerates. The difference between the first and third is a matter of timing and degree. As part of the continuing absorption process new conglomerates were created—e.g., Textron, Martin Marietta, Food Machinery Corporation—but the process was slower in tempo and more moderate in extent. As to the major petroleum companies, the magnitude of their cash flows and the range of their diversification make their mergers a case apart. The first two components will be examined in this chapter; the following chapter will be devoted to the new conglomerates.

Specific sizable acquisitions 1950-1963

Some impression of the nature of the ongoing absorption process can be gathered from an analysis of sizable acquisitions by large companies between 1950 and 1963—specifically, acquisitions of firms with assets of at least $1 million by companies among the 200 largest manufacturers. Among the large food processors, the Borden Corporation was one of the most active, acquiring one seafood company, 5 producers of canned fruits and vegetables, one each of dehydrated fruits and vegetables and pickles and sauces, 2 manufacturers of confectionary products and, outside the food field, one maker of coated fabrics, 2 producers of plastics materials, 2 of printing ink, one of toilet preparations, one of glue and gelatin, and one of surgical appliances and supplies.

Another food processor with a conspicuous record of conglomerate expansion is National Distilleries, which has moved into such dissimilar industries as fertilizers, plastics products, plumbing fixtures, electrical apparatus, and aircraft equipment. But its most important expansions were into chemicals, with the purchase of U.S. Industrial Chemicals, and into copper rolling and drawing, with the acquisition of Bridgeport Brass; at the time of acquisition the former had assets of $50 million and the latter of $88 million. Particularly prominent in the food area have been the disappearances of sizable independent firms with well-established trade names. For example, Van Camp Sea Food Company (Chicken of the Sea and White Star), which accounted for about one-third of the tuna market, was acquired by Ralston-Purina while Star Kist Foods was absorbed by H. J. Heinz. The Planters Company (Mr. Peanut) became the property of Standard Brands, and Hills Brothers went to National Biscuit. The Snow Crop line of frozen citrus juices was absorbed by its leading competitor, Minute Maid, which in turn was acquired by Coca-Cola.

Numerous horizontal acquisitions were made by the leading textile producers. Burlington Industries made 18 significant acquisitions, all of which were of textile producers. It purchased Pacific Mills (with assets of $80.5 million), Ely & Walker ($55 million), and 6 other cotton textile mills with combined assets of $134.5 million, plus 6 manufacturers of synthetic fabrics with combined assets of $59 million, as well as 2 manufacturers of woolen carpets with assets of $107 million, including the important producer James Lees & Sons. Another leading textile manufacturer, J. P. Stevens, moved to the forefront of the industry through a 1946 consolidation with 9 other textile companies. From 1950 to 1963 the company enhanced its position in the woolens industry through 4 large acquisitions with combined assets of over $40 million and in broad-woven cotton textiles through 3 acquisitions with assets totaling $34 million; included among the latter was the well-known manufacturer of bed linens Utica-Mohawk.[28]

Another industry of predominantly direct horizontal acquisitions has been sawmills and planing mills—long one of the nation's least concentrated industries. Between 1950 and 1963 it witnessed no fewer than 19 significant acquisitions, 13 of which had been companies engaged in the same industry. Confining most of its merger activity to the industry in which it had long been engaged, Georgia Pacific acquired no fewer than 9 sawmills and planing mills, with aggregate assets of $268 million. In addition it purchased 2 millwork plants with combined assets of $41 million. Moreover, in a move toward the consumer it acquired 3 paper and paperboard mills with total assets of $99 million.

One of the clearest cases of forward vertical expansion is provided by the nation's largest lumber company, Weyerhaeuser, which acquired a plywood plant and a pulp mill, the former with $34 million of assets and the latter with $26 million. By purchasing the Eddy Paper and Hamilton Paper companies (with combined assets of $62 million), it extended its operations into the paper industry. It moved even farther toward the consumer with its largest acquisition, Kieckhefer Containers (with assets of $104 million), which had been one of the nation's leading producers of paper boxes and other containers.

At the same time, the large paper manufacturers have been moving backward into logging and lumbering. Four leading paper firms made 5 important acquisitions in the sawmill industry (with associated logging activities). The largest was the acquisition by International Paper of Long-Bell Lumber Corporation, the nation's second largest lumber producer. Moving in the same direction, St. Regis Paper Company purchased 2 lumber companies, while Kimberly-Clark and Scott Paper Company acquired one each. But among the leading paper manufacturers horizontal mergers have been more conspicuous. Most active of the paper companies has been St. Regis, which made no fewer than 27 significant acquisitions, 21 of which were in paper and allied products. Its principal areas of activity were paper boxes, in which it made 12 acquisitions with combined assets of $74 million, and paper and paperboard mills, in which it made 4 acquisitions with total assets of $81 million.

Monsanto Chemical Company became the sole owner of one of the nation's largest producers of synthetic fibers, Chemstrand (of which it had formerly been joint owner with American Viscose); in addition, it made both backward and forward vertical acquisitions. By acquiring Lion Oil (with $148 million in assets), it secured a source of hydrocarbon feedstock for its fertilizer and plastic-resin production. In the opposite direction, Monsanto's forward vertical acquisition of Plax Corporation, formerly a jointly held company, provided the company with major facilities for the manufacture of plastics materials, polystyrene and polyethylene. Among other active acquirers in the chemicals group, Procter & Gamble went far afield in purchasing a prominent coffee roaster, J. H. Folger. American Cyanamid, one of the country's leading manufacturers

[28] In the case of the 3 major textile industries, horizontal acquisitions appear to have been an important cause of changes in the industry structure. Between 1947 and 1958 the number of companies in the woolen-textile industry fell from 427 to 263, while the share of the industry's value of shipments accounted for by the 4 largest firms rose from 28% to 36%. In the synthetic broad-woven fabric industry, the number of firms dropped from 432 to 328, while the share of the 4 largest rose from 31% to 34%. Data relating to 1947 for the cotton broad-woven fabric industry do not exist. In only 4 years, however, the number of firms declined from 413 in 1954 to 321 in 1958, while the 4 largest producers increased their share from 18 to 25 percent.

of drugs and chemicals, extended itself into hair preparations by absorbing the John H. Breck Company, and became a leading producer of composition materials by purchasing Formica. Another drug company with an impressive record of acquisitions is Pfizer, which absorbed another drug manufacturer, J. B. Roerig, as well as a leading cosmetic firm, Coty. The largest acquisition in the drug field was the merger of Squibb, with assets of $107 million, into Olin Mathieson; subsequently Squibb was spun off as a separate operating company, merging with Beech-Nut.

Since World War II the container field has been the scene of a series of technological improvements that have broadened the uses of the different types of containers and thereby increased the competition among them. Glass container manufacturers responded to the threat of lined cans for beverages, fruits, and the like with the development of inexpensive "throwaway" bottles and jars. Through new or improved coated- and laminated-paperboard products, the paper container industry began to enter the established markets of the metal-can firms. The plastics industry developed containers and packaging films that competed with all three of the older materials.[29] Mergers have occurred in line with such changes. After acquiring producers of collapsible metal tubes and plastic containers, American Can absorbed Dixie Cup Company, one of the largest producers of paper cups and containers, as well as Marathon Corporation, a leading integrated paper company; the 2 acquisitions provided American Can with $225 million in paper industry assets.

In the broad area of machinery, limited-line manufacturers have long been important as producers of specialized types of machinery. One of these firms, Buda Company, a leading manufacturer of gasoline and diesel engines for heavy equipment, was acquired by Allis-Chalmers, while Kiekhafer Corporation, manufacturer of Mercury outboard motors, was acquired by Brunswick. In construction machinery, La Plante-Choate was acquired by Allis-Chalmers and Shepherd-Niles Crane & Hoist by Ingersoll-Rand. In oil-field machinery and tools such well-known firms as National Supply Company, Lane-Wells Company, and Parkersburg-Aetna Company have disappeared. The absorption of the successful limited-line manufacturer is also evident in computing machines. For years a fixture of most offices was a Monroe, a Friden, or a Marchant calculating machine. The first has been absorbed by Litton Industries, the second by Singer, and the third by Smith-Corona (now SCM Corporation).

As elsewhere, many independent manufacturers in the electrical-machinery group with well-known trade names have disappeared through acquisition. To cite but a few examples: Bendix, the pioneer in home washing machines, was sold to Avco, then to Philco, which in turn was acquired by Ford. Speed Queen, with a well-established line of washers, dryers, and ironers, was absorbed by McGraw-Edison. RCA's stove and air-conditioning lines were taken over by Whirlpool Corporation, as were Seeger and Servel, long-time manufacturers of refrigerators. Sylvania, long the only sizable competitor of General Electric and Westinghouse in light bulbs and other electrical goods, is now a division of General Telephone & Electronics. Stromberg-Carlson, best known for its sound systems and radio and TV sets, was absorbed into General Dynamics. The York

[29] The speed with which these changes took place is suggested by the observation in Continental Can's annual report for 1963: "It is a rare motorist, for instance, who is aware that the motor oil he buys has shifted in four years from tin cans to aluminum cans to paperfoil cans and soon will appear in test-packed plastic cans."

line of air conditioners disappeared into Borg-Warner Corporation. Indeed, acquisitions have literally decimated the ranks of single-line appliance firms.

In addition to the assets of $210 million acquired in its purchase of Philco, Ford absorbed $28 million in assets from one of the nation's leading independent producers of automotive batteries, spark plugs, and other automotive electric equipment, Electric Autolite. Through a series of direct horizontal acquisitions, the White Motor Company has brought together in one enterprise most of the nation's independent manufacturers of motor trucks. In 1951 it acquired Sterling Motor Truck (with $5 million in assets), which was followed 2 years later by Autocar ($22 million), then in 1957 by Reo Motors ($52 million) and a year thereafter by Diamond-T Trucks ($17 million).[30] In addition, it has expanded into agricultural implements by acquiring in 1963 2 of the limited number of full-line farm machinery manufacturers—Oliver Corporation (with $41 million in assets) and Minneapolis-Moline ($20 million).

General Dynamics, an early conglomerate, is in good part the product of the bringing together of 3 firms—Consolidated Vultee (with $147 million in assets), Stromberg-Carlson ($44 million), and Materials Service ($93 million). The first was a leading aircraft manufacturer, the second a producer of radios, TV sets, and sound systems, and the third a supplier of concrete and other materials used in construction.

In the sporting-goods field Brunswick (primarily a manufacturer of bowling equipment) is now engaged in manufacturing a diversified line ranging from golf clubs to yachts, the former through the acquisition of McGregor Sporting Products and the latter through the purchase of the Owens Yacht Company. Another producer of golf clubs, the Ben Hogan Company, has been acquired by American Machine & Foundry, which, in addition, absorbed 3 manufacturers of specialized types of machinery. Three acquisitions by two camera manufacturers were recorded in photographic equipment: Argus was acquired by General Telephone, Revere Camera by Minnesota Mining & Manufacturing, and Dynacolor, a film processor, by Minnesota Mining.

Finally, a number of today's conglomerates are companies that were put together gradually during the 1950's and early 1960's. Textron leads all other manufacturing enterprises in the number of its acquisitions—more than 70 manufacturing enterprises (exclusive of those it has subsequently disposed of).[31] It is engaged in more than two dozen industries ranging from animal feed to boat building and from plastics materials to aircraft. Its largest acquisitions have been Spencer Kellogg (with assets of $52 million), Bell Aircraft ($32 million), and Benada Aluminum ($20 million).

Martin Marietta is to a considerable extent the product of the merger of Glenn L. Martin and American Marietta. In addition to this consolidation, which added $246 million to American Marietta, the firm absorbed 4 cement producers with combined assets of $110 million, 10 manufacturers of concrete products ($22 million), and 3 of ground and treated minerals ($38 million).

One of the largest mergers made by any company during the period 1950–63 was the absorption by the Food Machinery Corporation (FMC) of the complete manufacturing facilities of American Viscose (with assets of $335 million). Other acquisitions have taken FMC far afield from its original area of

[30] Had it not been for opposition by the Department of Justice, these absorptions would have been followed in 1964 by the absorption of the last of the independents, Mack, into Chrysler.

[31] *Hearings on Economic Concentration*, Pt. 1, p. 176, testimony of Harrison F. Houghton.

manufacturing specialized machinery for the food industry into such unrelated fields as insecticides, water treatment equipment, high-speed centrifugal pumps, and oil-field machinery.

Quantitative importance of the continuing merger process

While a general impression of the continuing absorption process can be gained from these specific examples, they do not of course provide any quantitative measure of its extent. For at least part of the period the need for such a measure has been met by a special report of the Census Bureau, *Acquisitions and Disposals of Manufacturing Facilities, 1959–62,* which presents data on mergers in terms of the size of the companies involved, as measured by employment.[32] Since the report is limited to 1959–62, it precedes the development of most of the "new conglomerates" and thus provides a means of analyzing the first component of the postwar merger movement—the continuing, *ad seriatim* acquisition process.

During the 4-year period covered by the survey 3,322 acquisitions of manufacturing facilities were recorded, four-fifths of which meant the disappearance of complete manufacturing companies. At the time of their purchase these 3,322 acquired companies employed 819,700 workers, or 5.3 percent of total manufacturing employment in 1958. The average annual rate of merger activity (in terms of the employment of acquired companies as a percentage of total manufacturing employment) was thus 1.3 percent. At a rate of 1.3 percent a year, 10 percent of all manufacturing workers, other factors being equal, would be absorbed by acquisitions in only 8 years, while one-fifth would be absorbed in less than 16 years. The 820,000 workers involved in mergers during this period increased the 1958 employment of the acquiring companies by 16 percent, or about one-sixth.

Most of these workers had been employed in facilities bought by large companies. Acquiring companies with 5,000 or more employees absorbed 39.9 percent of all employees involved in acquisitions; companies with 1,000 to 5,000 workers absorbed 37.1 percent of the total. Thereafter, as the size of acquiring companies fell, there occurred a precipitous decline in merger activity. Obviously the combining of smaller firms has not been a very significant element in the overall rate of merger activity.

In terms of size of acquired facilities the great bulk of affected employees had been engaged in medium-size facilities. Only 6 large facilities with over 5,000 workers were acquired during this period; they employed 58,000 workers, which represented only 7 percent of the total. At the other extreme, 3 percent had been employed in small companies with fewer than 50 workers. In contrast, nearly 60 percent of the employees had been engaged in medium-size companies with 250 to 1,000 workers.

Although it was not possible to follow the traditional classification—horizontal, vertical, and conglomerate—the Census Bureau was able to distribute merger activity in a manner which sheds some light on the direction of external expansion. One category consists of those acquisitions in which both the acquiring and acquired companies were in the same industry. Except for substitutable prod-

---

[32] The source of the Census report is its *Annual Survey of Manufactures,* which is based on reports from about 60,000 plants, including all plants with 100 or more employees.

ucts, this group probably encompasses all horizontal acquisitions, although owing to the breadth of the industry definitions the converse is not true. A second category consists of those in which the companies involved, though not within the same industry, were nonetheless within the same two-digit major industry group. This group is made up predominantly of vertical as well as "product-extension" conglomerate acquisitions. And the third consists of those in which the acquiring and acquired companies were in entirely different major industry groups. Such acquisitions consist largely of "pure" conglomerate mergers plus some vertical acquisitions.

Of the 820,000 workers involved in acquisitions during 1959–62, 37 percent were engaged in facilities classified in the same industry as the acquiring company. One-sixth of the total were in other industries but within the same major industry group. But the biggest segment, or almost half of the total, had been engaged in facilities that were not within the same major industry group as the acquiring firm. It is thus clear that the "pure" conglomerate acquisition has been the most important form of merger activity.

As to aggregate concentration, 461 establishments employing 220,000 workers, or 27 percent of the total employment of all acquired facilities, were absorbed by the 200 largest manufacturing companies. In other words, less than one-half of one percent of the total number of manufacturing companies accounted for more than one-fourth of the employment involved in industrial mergers. In addition, the size of the 100 largest in terms of employment was increased through merger by 5.3 percent, or 1.1 percent a year.

The oil company mergers

The petroleum industry is of such overwhelming size that any major oil company is, by definition, one of the nation's very largest companies; in 1968 6 of the 10 largest and 9 of the 20 largest industrial firms were oil companies. But the oil companies are leaders in merger activity not just because of their size but because of the pressure of their immense internally generated funds for effective utilization. Reflecting the tax advantages enjoyed by the industry, particularly the foreign tax credit and the depletion allowance, the cash flow of oil companies in 1968 totaled $9.6 billion, consisting of $5.8 billion in net income after taxes and $3.8 billion in depletion and depreciation reserves. This is equal to the assets of more than 60 percent of the total number of all manufacturing corporations. *cash flow*

The accompanying matrix chart, Figure 11-2, distributes by industry the number of companies acquired between 1956 and 1968 by each of the 20 major oil companies. Each of the 20 had assets in 1967 of over a half-billion dollars, and each is extensively engaged in the retail distribution of gasoline under its own brand name. In addition the figure shows the number of gasoline service stations acquired—a minimum of 18,737, as reported in *Moody's Industrial Manual*.

In terms of size by far the most important actions were the absorptions of other petroleum refiners. During the 12-year period the 20 major firms absorbed 20 others primarily engaged in petroleum refining, of which about one-third were of substantial importance. These were mergers that brought together fully integrated enterprises operating in different regions of the country. Thus the acquisition of a refining company shown on the chart for Standard Oil of

Figure 11-2

ACQUISITIONS BY 20 PETROLEUM COMPANIES,[a] 1956–1968

COMPANY	HORIZONTAL			VERTICAL											CONGLOMERATE											
	Direct	Substitute Fuel		Backward	Forward																					
					MANUFACTURING				DISTRIBUTION																	
	Petroleum refining	Bituminous coal	Nuclear power	Crude petroleum and natural gas	Fertilizers	Plastics materials and resins	Plastics products	Other chemicals	Highway and street construction	Fuel oil and bottled gas dealers	Crude petroleum pipelines	Petroleum bulk stations	Chemical wholesalers	Wholesalers n.e.c. (fertil.)	Crushed and broken stone	Sand and gravel	Foods, miscellaneous	Sawmills and planing mills	Paper and allied products	Tires and inner tubes	Refrigeration machinery	Brooms and brushes	Automatic merchandising	Tire, battery dealers	Total	Gasoline service stations[b]
Standard Oil (New Jersey)	1			5		2		1		3		2													14	1,669
Mobil Oil				5	1		1					2													9	20
Standard Oil (California)	1			2								1													4	8,874
Standard Oil (Indiana)	1			2		1				2		3		1											10	86

20 major oil firms each w > $.5 bill/1967 assets

Standard Oil (Ohio)		1		3			4	1	2	1												2	2		16	
Texaco				2	1					2															5	
Gulf Oil	2		1	2				1																	6	2,300
Shell Oil	1			2						1				1											5	
Phillips Petroleum				1			1			1									3						6	11
Continental Oil	2	1		7	2		1	4		1	2	1													21	497
Union Oil of California	1			2					1			2									1				7	44
Atlantic Richfield	1		1	2				1	4			1											1		11	4,600
Cities Service				2	1	1	1	1				2													8	
Sinclair Oil	1			4				1																	6	
Getty Oil				4				1		8		8													21	350
Sun Oil	2			4	1					3	1	1													12	184
Signal Companies	3			1													2				2		1		9	
Marathon Oil	2			1							1	1													5	102
Kerr-McGee	1		5		5			1				2						2							16	
Ashland Oil and Refining	1			1		2	1	4	5			3	6		3	4				2				3	35	
	20	2	7	52	11	6	9	16	12	22	4	29	6	2	3	4	2	2	3	2	3	2	4	3	226	18,737

[a]Companies with 1967 assets of over $500 million and with retail distribution of own brand of gasoline; includes acquisitions made by acquired firms prior to mergers with companies shown.

[b]Number as reported in Moody's; if number of service stations was not specified the acquisition was counted as 1.

Source: 91st Cong., 1st Sess., Senate Subcommittee on Antitrust and Monopoly, Senate Committee on the Judiciary, *Hearings on Governmental Intervention in, the Market Mechanism: The Petroleum Industry*, 1969, Pt. 3, p. 1179

California represented its absorption of Standard Oil of Kentucky, whose assets at the time totaled $142 million, including over 8,000 filling stations. With this acquisition Standard of California, which was the leading seller in its home state, also became the leading marketer in Florida, the second largest in Georgia, and a leading seller in Alabama, Kentucky, and Mississippi. Similarly, by absorbing Pure Oil (with assets of $766 million), Union Oil improved its ranking among the 500 largest industrials from fifty-sixth in 1960 to thirtieth in 1968. Union was the third largest gasoline marketer in California, while Pure was the fifth largest in Ohio and the sixth largest in Virgina, Georgia, and Minnesota and in addition was an important seller in Florida, North Carolina, and Michigan. Of similar importance was the acquisition of Sunray DX Oil, with assets of $749 million, by Sun Oil, which moved the latter's ranking among the industrials from fifty-fourth to twenty-eighth. Sun was the second largest gasoline marketer in Ohio, third in New Jersey, fourth in Washington, D.C., and fifth in Michigan and also was an important factor in New York and Virginia. Sunray ranked ninth in both Indiana and Missouri.

But the oil company that has been involved most actively in recent merger activity has been Atlantic Refining Company. In 1966 Atlantic, with $994 million in assets, merged with Richfield, with some $500 million, becoming Atlantic Richfield. Again the merger was of the market-extension variety, as Atlantic's market area had been in the East and Richfield's in the West. Atlantic was the largest gasoline marketer in Pennsylvania and the eighth largest in New Jersey and New York. Richfield was the fourth largest seller in California. In 1969, Atlantic Richfield acquired Sinclair, but to meet objections of the Antitrust Division, it then sold $400 million in assets, including 9,700 filling stations, to British Petroleum. Atlantic was left with $1.41 billion of Sinclair's $1.81 billion in assets and 1,800 of its 10,500 service stations. Later in the year British Petroleum entered into a complicated contract under which it agreed over a period of years to acquire Standard Oil of Ohio.

The matrix chart also reveals that 52 of the 226 acquisitions made by the 20 majors took the form of backward vertical expansion into the production of crude oil and natural gas. Although most of the majors hold concessions to foreign reserves, the import quota severely limits their right to bring foreign oil into this country. Thus, their acquisition of crude producers contributed to assuring themselves of adequate domestic supplies.

In addition to acquisitions within the oil industry itself, the companies acquired several producers of substitute fuels. Continental Oil purchased the nation's largest coal company, Consolidated Coal, with assets of $249 million, while Standard Oil of Ohio acquired Old Ben Coal Company, with assets of $54 million. Occidental Petroleum, not shown on the preceding chart, acquired the third largest coal producer, Island Creek Coal Company, with assets of $113 million. Much smaller in size but of potentially far greater significance were the acquisitions by 7 companies in the nuclear-power field—one by Gulf, one by Atlantic Richfield, and no fewer than 5 by Kerr-McGee.

Just as the oil companies have moved backward to acquire sources of supply, so have they expanded forward into industries that use petroleum products as their raw materials. The 20 major oil companies acquired 11 manufacturers of fertilizers, 25 of plastics materials and products, and 16 of other chemicals. As a result of this forward vertical expansion no fewer than 11 of the 30 top sellers of chemicals in 1968 were petroleum companies; the leaders were Standard Oil of New Jersey, which ranked sixth in chemical sales, Occidental (eleventh), Shell (thirteenth), Phillips (seventeenth), and Mobil (nineteenth).[33]

The forward vertical movement extended into distribution as the 20 majors absorbed 29 petroleum bulk stations, 6 dealers of fuel oil and bottled gas, 8 firms engaged in highway and street construction, 6 chemical wholesalers, and a number of other distributors and wholesalers. In addition, they bought up 4 crude-oil pipelines.

Finally their expansion programs took them into a variety of different industries that have little, if any, relationship to petroleum. By acquiring 2 of the few available tire manufacturers and 3 tire and battery dealers, they strengthened their hold over the supply of accessories for their filling stations. Even this tenuous connection with their primary field is absent in their acquisitions of companies producing crushed stone, sand and gravel, foods, paper, refrigeration machinery, brooms and brushes, and automatic vending machines. But their most sweeping conglomerate expansion consisted of their acquisitions in the fertilizer materials industries. This expansion has its vertical aspects, since nitrogen is produced from natural gas, and the major oil companies have long been important suppliers of natural gas, formerly a waste product and now an essential and increasingly expensive fuel. The absorption of the fertilizer companies took place virtually at one fell swoop in 1963. The most important actions were the acquisitions by Cities Service of the Tennessee Corporation (with assets of $99 million), Socony Mobil's purchase of Virginia-Carolina Chemical Company ($92 million), Continental Oil's absorption of American Agricultural Chemical ($79 million) and Gulf's purchase of Spencer Chemical ($126 million). With the acquisition in later years of Smith Douglas by Borden, of International Ore & Fertilizer and Best Fertilizer by Occidental, and of American Potash & Chemical by Kerr-McGee, there remains only one major independent fertilizer company, International Minerals & Chemicals.

The mergers and acquisitions by major oil companies can be used to illustrate how competition may be lessened as a result of greater market concentration, vertical integration, conglomerate expansion, and the strengthening of communities of interest. The simplest to visualize is the impact on competition resulting from the combining of firms selling in the same market. The merger of Sun with Sunray, for example, eliminated a direct competitor in Kentucky, Indiana, and Michigan. Phillips's acquisition of the Western Division of Tidewater eliminated a direct competitor in Idaho, Nevada, Oregon, Washington, and Arizona. In another instance, the Antitrust Division's objection to the elimination of a direct competitor in states where they both operated led Atlantic Richfield to dispose of Sinclair's service stations and other facilities serving 11 northeastern states.

On a somewhat higher plane of analysis, competition can also be affected adversely by the change in an industry's structure from competitive to oligopolistic or from loosely to tightly oligopolistic. Competition in price is replaced by rivalry in advertising, service, promotional activities, and claims of product superiority. According to the Federal Trade Commission, precisely this change has been taking place within the petroleum industry. In its *Report on Anticompetitive Practices in the Marketing of Gasoline*, the Commission stated:

> The major prefers not to engage in price competition . . . Price reductions would be followed by sellers of equal size and would not be accompanied by compensating increases in total demand. Accordingly,

[33] *Chemical & Engineering News*, June 16, 1969.

THE CONTINUING ABSORPTION PROCESS

the major favors various forms of non-price competition, the basic forms being competition for the purchase or lease of preferred service station locations and claims of superior service and product quality. . . . Market share is protected or increased on the basis of product differentiation through national advertising and other forms of non-price competition, such as credit cards and promotions. Superior product quality and service, rather than price, are stressed through massive expenditures for advertising.[34]

The effect of the large market-extension mergers has thus been to increase the number of national giants who tend to limit their rivalry to nonprice competition and to decrease the number of regional firms large enough to be troublesome rivals when they elect to engage in price competition.

The change in the petroleum industry's structure had a further adverse effect on competition. This was in weakening the constraint placed on the leaders by the threat of entry. As the FTC staff report observes, "The threat of this entry tends to restrain the members of the market from exacting too high a price, lest the potential entrant be lured in." It is the medium-size firms with important positions in one region who exercise the most effective restraint against unusually large price increases elsewhere: "The most likely potential entrants are those already in the same line of business and serving other geographical markets. They have the experience, the capital resources and the incentive to expand their territorial operation in order to gain additional revenues and profits." [35] But once the medium-size regional firms join the ranks of the national leaders the constraint is lost. No longer do the majors have to fear the entrance into a given region by sizable firms struggling for a position in a new market. The newcomers have become national majors themselves, and they would suffer as much as the older majors from the outbreak of competition in any given market.

Owing to the unpredictability of the weather, unexpected transportation problems, breakdowns in production and distribution facilities, and similar unexpected eventualities, what is produced by an integrated oil company may be greater than what it can get into consumption through its own outlets. When this happens to a medium-size company operating in one region, the natural market for its excess supply consists of the small, independent refiners, distributors, and marketers in a nearby market. Whatever happens to prices there is obviously a matter of little concern to a company not operating in that region. But when through merger the regional firm becomes a national major, what happens to price in any market becomes a matter of real moment to it. The surpluses available to independents tend to dry up not only for this reason but because of the ability of the new national major to absorb in one region the surpluses that have developed in another. Even if the distance and transportation problems are such that the surplus cannot be physically moved, the company will probably be able to work out an exchange agreement with another major, under which the latter will absorb the former's surplus, providing the equivalent amount elsewhere. Thus, by increasing the firms' ability to accommodate their own surpluses, the transformation of integrated regional oil firms into national

[34] Federal Trade Commission, *Report on Anticompetitive Practices in the Marketing of Gasoline*, Manuscript, 1969, pp. 11–12.
[35] Federal Trade Commission Staff, *Economic Report on Corporate Mergers*, 1969, p. 294.

majors has severely reduced what had been an important component of the "free-market" supply.

Competition among suppliers to a market is lessened also through mergers of companies offering substitutable products. It is axiomatic that common ownership of substitutable products will tend to destroy the natural rivalry between them. The absorption of over a half-billion dollars in coal-company assets obviously reduced actual competition in the supply of fuel to electric generating plants, which are usually equipped to use oil or coal. And it could lessen potential competition in the supply of motor fuel in the event of a technological breakthrough making coal competitive costwise with petroleum as a source of gasoline. The same of course would apply to the acquisition of the 7 nuclear energy companies.[36] Allowing them to be taken over by the oil companies is indeed a case of "turning the child over for nurture to those who have the greatest interest in its demise."

The oil company mergers also illustrate how competition may be adversely affected by vertical integration. The majors' purchase of 52 producers of crude oil and natural gas obviously reduced the supply of raw materials available to independent refiners. Of possibly greater importance was their expansion in' the opposite direction, notably their taking over of 29 bulk terminal operators. Purchasing and storing petroleum products in large quantities, the terminal operator is an indispensable source of supply for the independent fuel oil dealer and gasoline marketer. Without him the latter must depend for supplies on the major oil companies with whom they are in competition in retail markets. And, by acquiring independent marketers of gasoline or fuel oil, the majors have diminished directly the number of competitors at the retail level. In a study of gasoline marketing Fred C. Allvine and James M. Patterson note that "several major companies have invaded each other's territories by purchasing private branders which had been weakened by price wars." [37] Little time is wasted, they go on, in converting "their newly acquired stations from the private branders' marketing strategy to the higher priced approach used by most majors." [38] The change in structure tends to be permanent:

> The net effect of these mergers has been a systematic reduction in the number of independents and the important intertype competition that they represent. Nor can we expect the independents to reappear in many of these markets, since such mergers often result in the drying up of supply sources. Typically, the majors that purchase outlets in a new market cease to supply the remaining independents in that area since they now have a retail stake in the market which makes "dumping" unattractive.[39]

The taking over of most of the fertilizer industry by the oil companies has been followed by what would appear to be a clear example of cross-subsidization. The acquisitions of American Agricultural Chemical by Continental Oil, Virginia-Carolina Chemical Company by Socony Mobil Oil, Tennessee Corporation by Cities Service, and Spencer Chemical by Gulf Oil have, alone, brought nearly $400 million worth of fertilizer industry assets under oil company ownership.

[36] See *Hearings on Economic Concentration,* Pt. 8, Walter S. Measday, "Oil Companies' Entry into Nuclear Energy Field," pp. 5267–69.
[37] 91st Cong., 1st Sess., Senate Subcommittee on Antitrust and Monopoly, Senate Committee on the Judiciary, *Hearings on Governmental Intervention in the Market Mechanism: The Petroleum Industry,* 1969, Pt. 3, p. 1294.
[38] *Ibid.*
[39] *Ibid.*

As a result of their acquisitions, plus new plant construction, major oil companies by March 1, 1969, held 40 percent of the country's ammonia capacity, 29 percent of the phosphate-rock-mining capacity, and 24 percent of the phosphoric-acid capacity.[40]

What have been the reasons for this wholesale invasion of a largely unrelated industry? One factor is certainly the role of the oil companies as important suppliers of natural gas. But natural gas is only one of the three elements used to make only one of the three fertilizer ingredients. Moreover, in view of the developing shortage of natural gas, the oil companies certainly did not have to build their own ammonia plants in order to find profitable outlets. Another explanation derives from concern over the population explosion. In the race against famine the underdeveloped countries of the world must make use of rapidly increasing quantities of fertilizers. The view was widely shared that, through some form of aid program, the U.S. government would surely come to their assistance. Finally, and not necessarily of least importance, was the pressure for profitable investment of the immense financial reserves of the major oil companies.

But something went wrong. The entry by the oil companies has transformed fertilizer from an industry of long-run moderate profitability to one of extremely low profits or actual losses. According to a trade periodical:

> Oil's romance with fertilizer has unmistakably cooled.
> Bluntly, 1968 was a very sorry profits year for the $3 billion U.S. Fertilizer business.
> This year [1969] will be better but still a far cry from the high return oil firms anticipated when they plunged into the business.
> One of the 16 major oil companies in fertilizers thinks it unlikely that there'll be any significant upturn until 1971. And another doubts the business will ever be as profitable as participants originally hoped.[41]

One explanation is to be found in the lower-than-anticipated rise in demand. Purchases of fertilizer by the U.S. government have not materialized in the magnitudes expected. At the same time the industry has been plagued by the enormous capacity of the new single-train centrifugal ammonia plants. While easily the lowest-cost producing units, they suffer from a serious economic shortcoming: they are "go" or "no go" facilities, which either have to be operated at or near full capacity or shut down completely. The former contributes to excessive supplies; the latter provides no return to set against their expensive capital costs. But the oil companies' share of the new centrifugal plants is not greater than their share of all forms of ammonia-producing capacity, old and new—40 percent.[42] Thus, the troubles of the fertilizer industry cannot be traced simply to the introduction of a superior technology by the new entrants. Moreover, market distress has extended to other fertilizer elements whose production has not been revolutionized by new technologies.

Finally, there is the profit experience of International Minerals & Chemical, long the industry's largest single-line producer. This experience is particularly noteworthy in view of the fact that the company is *not* extensively engaged in the area of greatest distress, ammonia. Moreover, it is perhaps the most efficient fertilizer producer in North America, having successfully introduced new tech-

[40] *Oil and Gas Journal,* March 17, 1969.
[41] *Ibid.*
[42] *Ibid.*

nologies in both potash mining and the handling of phosphate.[43] As can be seen in Table 11-2, the decline in its earnings has transformed its rate of return from an acceptable level of 13.8 percent in 1966 to a loss, − 10.1 percent, in 1969. This downward trend is in sharp contrast to the record of steady profitability registered by the oil companies.

As long as profits in petroleum give them an almost infinite survival capability, the oil companies can well afford to absorb losses in fertilizers, or in any other industry into which they have expanded. In contrast, a number of single-line fertilizer manufacturers, such as First Mississippi Corporation and Farmland Industries, have already shut down their plants.

Finally, the oil company mergers illustrate the potentiality of injury to competition through "communities of interest." As a condition of permitting the acquisition of Sinclair by Atlantic Richfield, the Department of Justice required that Sinclair's stations and facilities in the area served by both be disposed of to a third party, which turned out to be British Petroleum. In so doing the Department permitted the replacement of one of the last of the sizable independents by one of the original and long-standing members of the petroleum industry's most important community of interests—the international petroleum cartel. Through a perfect maze of restrictive production and marketing agreements, British Petroleum was found to be inextricably intertwined with the 6 other international majors—Standard Oil of New Jersey, Socony Mobil, Standard Oil of California, Gulf, Texaco, and Royal Dutch Shell. Under one of the agreements, the other companies producing in Iraq—American, Dutch and French—agreed to pay British Petroleum's predecessor company a 10 percent overriding royalty on all oil obtained from the area originally reserved to British Petroleum.[44] Outside the United States, British Petroleum is a major producer in most of the oil-producing areas of the world, holding 25 percent of the world's known reserves; in this capacity it has entered into production exchange agreements

Table 11-2

RATES OF RETURN OF
INTERNATIONAL MINERALS & CHEMICALS CORPORATION
AND PETROLEUM-REFINING COMPANIES

Year	Net Income (Mils.)		Stockholders' Equity (Mils.)		Rate of Return	
	IMC	Petroleum	IMC	Petroleum	IMC	Petroleum
1969	$-20.6[a]	$5,884.0	$197.7	$51,393.0	-10.4%	11.5%
1968	9.4	5,794.0	229.5	48,083.0	4.1	12.0
1967	14.7	5,497.0	207.6	45,119.0	7.1	12.2
1966	24.6	5,055.0	177.8	41,733.0	13.8	12.1
1965	20.3	4,442.0	160.1	38,881.0	12.7	11.4
1964	15.8	4,095.0	144.7	36,459.0	10.9	11.2

[a]Although most of this deficit stemmed from plant closings and losses on investment, an operating deficit would have remained even without the nonrecurring losses.

Source: *Moody's Investors' Manual*; FTC SEC *Quarterly Financial Reports for Manufacturing Corporations*, 1964–69, Table 8

[43] *Fortune*, June 1, 1968.
[44] 82nd Cong., 2nd Sess., Federal Trade Commission Staff, Report for the Senate Select Committee on Small Business, *The International Petroleum Cartel*, 1952, p. 64.

with the American international majors.[45] It also markets petroleum products in most of the world's consuming countries; in this role it has entered into marketing agreements with the U.S. majors.[46] Were British Petroleum to become a source of active price competition in the U.S. market it would not only invite retaliation elsewhere from the American companies but would be acting contrary to the objective which all the agreements are intended to accomplish—the stabilization of the market.

[45] See *ibid.*, Chs. 3–6.
[46] See *ibid.*, Chs. 8, 9.

THE NEW CONGLOMERATES

Superimposed on the continuous absorption process and the oil company mergers has been the explosive emergence of the "new conglomerates" of the 1960's. By piling merger in one industry on merger in another, they entered within a few years into the ranks of America's largest corporations. Some did not even exist prior to the start of the decade, but even those that had been rather large companies owe most of their present size to mergers made during this period.

The growth of the new conglomerates

The expansion movement was dominated by 8 companies, each of which made acquisitions during the decade totaling more than a half-billion dollars; for 6 the asset value was over a billion dollars. Table 12-1 shows the number and

Table 12-1

ASSETS ACQUIRED BY 8 "NEW CONGLOMERATES," 1961-1968

(\$ Millions)

| Company | Acquisitions 1961–68 Inclusive | | Change in Assets of Company | | | Acquired Assets as Percent of Total Assets | Rank among Largest Industrial Corporations[c] | |
	Number	Total Assets of Acquired Companies	1960	1968	Change		1960	1968
ITT	50	\$3,705[a]	\$ 924	\$6,240[a]	\$5,316	59%	35	9
Gulf & Western	67	2,882	12	3,455	3,443	83		17
Ling-Temco-Vought	23	1,901	94	2,648	2,554	72	335	22
Tenneco	31	1,196	1,734	3,888	2,154	31		16
White Consolidated	29	1,080[b]	19	1,257[b]	1,238	86		66
Teledyne	125	1,026	0	1,146	1,146	90		74
Occidental Petroleum	15	767	7	1,788	1,781	43		41
Litton	79	609	119	1,421	1,302	43	275	55

[a]Includes acquisition of Hartford-Empire, Grinnell, and Canteen.
[b]Includes acquisition of Allis-Chalmers.
[c]*Fortune*; adjusted to include assets of nonconsolidated subsidiaries.

Source: Computed from Federal Trade Commission Staff, *Economic Report on Corporate Mergers*, 1969, pp. 260–61, 542, 594–98

asset value of their acquisitions, their growth in size, the proportion of their growth contributed by acquisitions, and their rank among the nation's largest industrials.

The lowest ranking of the companies among the 500 largest was seventy-fourth (Teledyne); International Telephone & Telegraph ranked ninth. Yet in 1960 4 had not even been among the 500 largest, while only one, ITT, had ranked among the first 100. The importance of merger in their growth is evident from the fact that the assets they acquired between 1961 and 1968 ranged from 31 to 90 percent of their 1968 assets. All told, during the 1960's these 8 companies acquired companies with $13.166 billion in assets. This can be compared to $9.916 billion of assets acquired by the 17 other most active acquirers during this period. In view of the magnitude and centralization of this external expansion, it is not surprising that measures of aggregate concentration moved sharply upward during the period.

While there can be little doubt concerning the general importance of recent merger activity, the question remains as to the incidence of its importance. For this purpose the accompanying matrix chart, Table 12-2, has been constructed, distributing by 3-digit enterprise industry categories the number and asset size of the acquisitions made by these 8 "new conglomerates." The chart is limited to "large" acquisitions—i.e., those with assets of more than $10 million—and thereby understates, though not greatly, the extent of their conglomerate merger activity.

Alone among the rapidly expanding conglomerates, International Telephone & Telegraph had been one of the nation's largest companies before embarking upon its diversification program. Added to its pre-merger base, its acquisitions and other expansions through 1970 made it by 1971 the ninth largest industrial firm in the nation. From 1961 to 1969, the asset value of its acquisitions totaled $3.583 billion, *not* including the American Broadcasting Company, the attempted acquisition of which was dropped in the face of opposition by the Department of Justice. During the later 1960's ITT's acquisition drive has concentrated on leading suppliers of important consumer goods and services. It absorbed the nation's largest bakery (Continental), the largest hotel chain (Sheraton), the second largest car rental service (Avis), the leading housing builder and developer (Levitt), one of the largest property and casualty insurance companies (Hartford), a leading vending-machine company (Canteen), as well as 2 important consumer finance companies (Aetna and Thorp Finance). The acquisition of Hartford Insurance Company, with assets of $1.892 billion, is the largest recorded during this decade. Thus the average citizen can buy his home from ITT, live in one of its "planned communities," have the house insured by another of ITT's divisions, take a trip in one of ITT's rental cars, stay at one of ITT's hotels or motels, purchase his bread and other bakery products from another of its divisions, buy his cigarettes and coffee from one of its vending machines, obtain a loan from one of its finance companies, and could, had it not been for antitrust objections, watch TV on an ITT-owned network. Outside the consumer area ITT's important acquisitions have been of a major producer of automatic fire protection systems and equipment (Grinnell Corporation) and of suppliers of raw materials, which, however, have little in common: Rayonier, a leading forest products firm and the world's largest supplier of chemical cellulose from wood pulp; and Pennsylvania Glass Sand, a leading producer of silica used in glass manufacture.

In terms of assets, the next most active acquirer was Gulf & Western, whose

13 acquisitions had combined assets of $2.815 billion. More than half this total was represented by its purchase of Associates Investment Company, a firm primarily engaged in financing business and insurance. In manufacturing, its largest acquisition was Brown Company, an integrated manufacturer of paper products. Gulf & Western acquired 5 other large manufacturers, all but one of which were sizable enterprises with assets of more than $100 million. As is the case with most of the other new conglomerates, what most distinguishes this pattern of acquisitions is the utter dissimilarity of the industries involved: sugar (South Puerto Rico Sugar), tobacco products (Consolidated Cigar), nonferrous metals (New Jersey Zinc), and rolling mills and metal work presses (E. W. Bliss). In addition, Gulf & Western's sizable acquisitions included 2 motion picture companies (Paramount Pictures and Desilu Productions) and 2 insurance companies (Capitol Life Insurance and Provident Washington Insurance).

The 9 largest acquisitions by Ling-Temco-Vought totaled $1.902 billion. Again, approximately half the total was accounted for by one purchase—that of the nation's fourth largest steel producer, Jones & Laughlin. Next in importance was LTV's acquisition of a conglomerate holding company, Greatamerica. Although divesting itself of Greatamerica's banking, insurance, and car rental interests (National), LTV retained Braniff Airways. With its acquisition of the $200-million Wilson & Company, it became the nation's third largest meat packer, a leading seller of golf clubs and other sporting goods, and a manufacturer of animal-derived chemicals and pharmaceuticals. None of these important acquisitions had anything in common with LTV's early field of activity as an electronics and aerospace manufacturer. Its first major acquisition had been its purchase of Chance Vought, an important aircraft and missile supplier with assets of $102 million. Its subsequent acquisitions included 3 electronics manufacturers with combined assets of $103 million (Okonite, Allied Radio, and Escon).

The fourth company whose acquisitions during the 1960's passed the $1-billion mark is Tenneco, which began its existence as the Tennessee Gas & Transmission Company and whose early growth was in the petroleum industry. Two-thirds of the asset value of its acquisitions proceeded from its absorption of the Kern County Land Company, a holding company that had previously purchased the nation's third largest producer of agricultural machinery, J. I. Case. At the time of the takeover by Tenneco, over 70 percent of Kern County's assets consisted of its holdings of Case and of the latter's associated credit company. Tenneco's other sizable acquisitions were of companies in widely disparate industries: Newport News Shipbuilding (with assets of $139 million) and Packaging Corporation of America ($126 million). The former was the nation's largest privately owned shipyard, the latter a large manufacturer of paperboard and containers. Tenneco, like other petroleum-based firms, expanded into chemicals by acquiring 4 chemical manufacturers with combined assets of $127 million, about half of which consisted of the properties of Heyden Newport Chemical Company.

Originally a sewing-machine manufacturer, White Consolidated Industries has concentrated in its expansion program on the metals, machinery, and household appliance industries. Potentially its largest acquisition by far is Allis-Chalmers; the merger is currently being opposed under Section 7 of the Clayton Act by the latter's stockholders as well as by the Federal Trade Commission. With assets of $637 million, Allis-Chalmers is among the nation's 4 largest

Table 12-2

8 ACTIVELY-ACQUIRING CONGLOMERATES

Number and asset value (in millions) of large companies acquired, 1961–69a

Industry	ITT	Gulf & Western	Ling-Temco-Vought	Tenneco	White Consolidated	Teledyne	Occidental Petroleum	Litton	Total
Manufacturing									
Meat packing			1/ $196						1/ $196
Other canned and frozen food								1/ $35	1/ 35
Bread and related bakery products	1/ $187								1/ 187
Sugar		1/ $122							1/ 122
Tobacco products		1/ 129							1/ 129
Floor-covering mills			1/ 50						1/ 50
Furniture and fixtures n.e.c.								1/ 13	1/ 13
Pulp, paper, and board	1/ 292								1/ 292
Paperboard containers and boxes				1/ $127					1/ 127
Other paper and allied products		1/ 196						1/ 14	2/ 210
Books	1/ 20							2/ 39	3/ 59
Commercial printing and business forms								1/ 11	1/ 11
Basic chemicals, plastics, synthetics				4/ 121			1/$367		5/ 488
Miscellaneous chemical products				1/ 11			1/ 11		2/ 22
Other nonmetal mineral products	1/ 46								1/ 46
Blast furnaces and steel mills			1/ 1,093			1/ $20			2/ 1,113
Malleable iron and steel foundries		2/ 59							2/ 59
Primary steel products n.e.c.						3/ 80			3/ 80
Nonferrous primary metals		1/ 143				1/ 30			2/ 173
Farm machinery and equipment				1/ 706	1/ $637				2/ 1,343
Construction machinery				1/ 10					1/ 10
Mining and materials-handling machinery								1/ 49	1/ 49
Metal-cutting machine tools					1/ 28			3/ 140	4/ 168
Other metalworking machinery	1/ 112					1/ 17			2/ 129

Industry									Total
Special industry machinery					3/ 202				3/ 202
Pumps and compressors	1/ 27								1/ 27
Other general industry machinery	2/ 200								2/ 200
Office machines								2/ 109	2/ 109
Service industry machinery	1/ 141								1/ 141
Radio, TV, and communication equipment	1/ 14		1/ 13			1/ 34			3/ 61
Electronic components and accessories	1/ 32		3/ 103						4/ 135
Household appliances					3/ 196				3/ 196
Lighting and wiring	1/ 32					2/ 25		1/ 10	4/ 67
Other electrical machinery	1/ 11					1/ 12		2/ 47	4/ 70
Aircraft and guided missiles			1/ 102						1/ 102
Aircraft engines and parts						1/ 143			1/ 143
Ships and boats				1/ 139				1/ 15	2/ 155
Ordnance (except guided missiles)	1/ 128	1/ 128							1/ 128
Total manufacturing	12/ 1,002	8/ 889	8/ 1,557	9/ 1,114	8/ 1,063	11/ 361	2/ 378	16/ 483	74/ 6,847
Nonmanufacturing									
Mining	2/ 374						2/ 148		2/ 148
Pipeline transportation							2/ 102		2/ 102
Real estate, hotels, motels		2/ 183					1/ 67		3/ 441
Moving pictures									2/ 183
Insurance	1/ 1,892	2/ 161				2/ 472			5/ 2,525
Finance	2/ 210	1/ 1,582				1/ 56			4/ 1,848
Other nonmanufacturing	2/ 105		1/ 345	2/ 66		1/ 17	2/ 70	2/ 49	10/ 652
Total nonmanufacturing	7/ 2,581	5/ 1,926	1/ 345	2/ 66		4/ 545	7/ 387	2/ 49	28/ 5,899
Total manufacturing and nonmanufacturing	19/$3,583	13/$2,815	9/$1,902	11/$1,180	8/$1,063	15/$906	9/$765	18/$532	102/$12,746

aCompanies with assets of more than $10 million.

Source: Federal Trade Commission Staff, Economic Report on Corporate Mergers, 1969, pp. 459-654

manufacturers of wheeled tractors, harvesting machinery, crawler tractors and loaders, electric transformers, motors and generators, diesel engines, and many other types of machinery. Earlier White had absorbed 3 producers of industrial machinery with combined assets of $202 million: Blaw-Knox, a leading producer of rolling mills, construction equipment and food-processing equipment, plus Whitten Machine Works and Scott & Williams, both leading producers of textile machinery. In addition, by acquiring the Bullard Company it entered the machine tool industry. In the field of household appliances White has made 3 acquisitions with combined assets of $196 million. As a result of its purchase of the Kelvinator Division of American Motors, the Hupp Corporation, and the Franklin Appliance Division of Studebaker, White now produces refrigerators, freezers, washers, dryers, air conditioners, dishwashers, and ranges sold under such well-known names as Kelvinator, Gibson, Easy, and Hamilton, as well as under many private labels.

Created in 1960 by two former Litton executives, Teledyne, like Litton, emphasized in its formative years the acquisition of relatively small, defense-oriented, high-technology firms. Up to 1968 its major activities had been in electronic control systems and components and specialized metals. Its role as a leading conglomerate stems largely from three 1968 acquisitions of nonmanufacturing companies. These consisted of 2 insurance companies (United Insurance of America, with assets of $361 million, and Argonaut Insurance with $111 million) plus a California investment company (Fireside Thrift, with $56 million). Teledyne's only other sizable acquisition, also in 1968, was of Ryan Aeronautical. With assets of $143 million, Ryan in 1967 ranked twenty-fifth among the leading military prime contractors and in addition controlled Continental Motors. In the metals field Teledyne acquired a semi-integrated steel company, Firth-Sterling with assets of $20 million, plus 3 producers of specialty metals, Vasco Metals, Wah Chang, and Rodney Metals, whose combined assets totaled $80 million. Returning to its original field of electronics, it absorbed Packard Bell, a leading West Coast manufacturer of television sets with assets of $34 million.

Although Occidental Petroleum's principal source of sales and income—oil production in Libya—was not obtained through merger, some $765 million of its total 1968 assets of $1.2 billion is made up of companies it has acquired. Like other petroleum-based companies, Occidental has expanded into the chemicals industry by acquiring Hooker Chemical (with $367 million in assets); Hooker is a large manufacturer of plastics, farm chemicals, and chemicals used for a variety of industrial purposes. The other major fields of expansion have been in coal mining, pipelines, and real estate. In Island Creek Coal Company, Occidental obtained the nation's third largest coal producer (with assets of $113 million). In acquiring Island Creek, Occidental stressed the future potential of coal as a substitute for oil in the face of declining domestic oil reserves. At the same time, it became an important pipeline operator by acquiring the Permian Corporation (with assets of $62 million) and McWood Corporation ($40 million); both purchase crude oil from producers in the mid-continent marketing area and resell it to refiners and other users. Occidental's acquisitions can thus be said to have at least a distant relationship to its original field of activity: it transports oil for others, manufactures chemicals out of oil, and is an important producer of a competitive source of energy.

Among the best-known of the conglomerates, Litton Industries has absorbed 18 large firms with combined assets of $632 million. Unlike ITT, Gulf &

Western, and LTV, Litton owes none of its growth to the absorption of insurance firms, finance companies, and holding companies. From its original field of defense-related electronics, Litton's expansion program took it into office machines. Its acquisition in 1958 of the long-established Monroe Calculating Machine Company with assets of $25 million, was followed by its absorption of Royal McBee, the second largest typewriter manufacturer, with $70 million in assets, and of the German firm Triumph-Adler, which ranked second in the international typwriter market with $39 million in assets. The industry in which it has been most active, in terms of assets, has been machine tools; the 3 firms it acquired in this field, New Britain Machine Company, Landis Tool, and UTD Company, had combined assets of $140 million. Other industries in which Litton has made notable acquisitions are in such widely different industries as frozen foods (Stouffer, with $35 million in assets), and materials-handling machinery (Hewitt-Robins, with $49 million). In moving away from dependence on defense contracts Litton's expansion has been only partly through the acquisition of firms in rapidly expanding industries—electronics, frozen foods, professional services. Of greater importance has been its purchase of well-known companies in established industries—typewriters, machine tools, materials-handling equipment, and shipbuilding.

Questionable accounting methods

The growth of the new conglomerates has been facilitated by the employment of questionable accounting techniques whose use has been approved by the accounting profession but whose effect, if not purpose, has been to mislead investors by maximizing apparent earnings resulting from an acquisition while minimizing apparent cost. Among the more widely used techniques has been the pooling of interests under which the conglomerate adds to its own assets only the *book* value of the acquired company, which is invariably far less than the price actually paid. As described by the FTC staff:

> Many devices, of varying degrees of subtlety, enable merger-active companies to report substantial increases in earnings per share without improving operating efficiency. Among the most notable is the pooling of interests method of accounting for business combinations. Despite two accounting studies recommending its abolition, pooling remains the most common method of accounting for merger effected by an exchange of voting stock. Under a pooling of interests, the book values of both businesses are simply added together. In this circumstance, the values prevailing at the time of acquisition need have no relation to the actual market value of the transaction. Through acquisition, an acquiring company can do what it cannot do through internal growth; that is, list the value of assets at less than real cost.[1]

The report notes that the effect of pooling is to introduce a continuing bias in favor of the acquiring company, which is reflected in its subsequent financial statements:

> . . . Litton Industries suppressed $80 million in costs when it pooled with American Book and Jefferson Electric Company during its fiscal

[1] Federal Trade Commission Staff, *Economic Report on Corporate Mergers*, 1969, pp. 122–24. Reprinted as Pt. 8A of *Hearings on Economic Concentration*.

year ending July 31, 1967. These values, "which presumably have produced or will produce revenues for Litton over the years, have not entered into such statements. As a result the corporation's earnings will be exaggerated over the years by the amount thus suppressed." With pooling and other devices for cost suppression in widespread use, it is surprising that merger-active companies as a class do not inevitably indicate superior profitability by whatever measure used.[2]

As an alternative to pooling but with a similar effect, the acquiring company can enter as the cost of the acquisition only the book value of the acquired company, while charging the difference between book value and purchase price to goodwill, which remains static, neither amortized nor charged to year-to-year operations. For example, when AMK acquired 80 percent of United Fruit, it paid a total of over $630 million, mostly in bonds and stock, but charged only $286 million to the net assets taken over from United Fruit. The remainder, nearly one-third of a billion dollars, was charged to goodwill. As Abraham J. Briloff put it, "it [AMK] is issuing quarterly statements picking up United Fruit profits at the rate of more than $3 million monthly as part of the AMK consolidation. AMK must know this to be specious coin since the sprinkling of the $344,215,000 to United's underlying assets would have added very appreciable amounts to the interim cost data with a corresponding suppression to the reported income." [3]

By such techniques the earnings of an acquiring company can be overstated in relation to the cost of securing them. By the use of "leverage"—i.e., the financing of acquisitions with preferred stock or debt instruments—the earnings of an acquiring company can be added to those of the acquirer without increasing the latter's number of shares of common stock. The result is of course an increase in the acquirer's earnings per share. The only reservation is that allowance must be made for dividends on the preferred stock or interest payments on debt before the figuring of the net addition to earnings that remains.

> LTV's acquisition of Wilson & Co., the meatpacker, illustrates the use of leverage. LTV paid so large a premium for this acquisition that it made Wilson's price-earnings ratio higher than LTV's. Yet, LTV realized an immediate earnings gain. The acquisition increased LTV's earnings per share by 31 percent, from $4.32 to $5.68. Before the announcement of the acquisition, Wilson's price-earnings ratio was 9.0, substantially less than LTV's ratio of 17.2; however, LTV paid a 108 percent premium for Wilson, thereby raising Wilson's price-earnings ratio to 18.5. By issuing no new shares of common stock, LTV utilized the maximum possible amount of leverage by paying for this acquisition with about $144 million in cumulative preferred stock and $81.5 million in cash, $80 million of which was financed with debt instruments.[4]

The appearance of an improvement in earnings can also be achieved by a variety of other accounting techniques, such as extending depreciation charges over a longer period of time, combining extraordinary income arising from the sale of property with unused operating income, capitalizing research and development expense, and changing the method of handling inventory: "AMK, after acquiring John Morrell & Co., shifted from conservative to liberal accounting methods for depreciation and inventories and thereby converted what

[2] *Ibid.*, p. 124.
[3] *Hearings on Economic Concentration*, Pt. 8, pp. 5155–58, testimony of Abraham J. Briloff.
[4] FTC Staff, *op. cit.*, p. 135.

would have been a decline in earnings to a reported increase of $.74. . . .
After acquiring New Jersey Zinc Co. in 1965, Gulf & Western switched the
treatment of Zinc's exploration and development account and showed an increase in earnings of $1.6 million." [5]

From the viewpoint of a conglomerate's management it matters little whether
the gain in earnings is illusionary or real as long as it is accepted by investors.
According to one study, *traceable* changes in accounting practice converted
an average 2.5 percent decline in 1964 earnings into a reported 11 percent increase.[6] Had these changes not been made, the stock prices for these companies
would probably have declined or at best registered only a slight advance. Yet
the average for the sample rose 17.6 percent, compared to 14 percent for the
Standard & Poor index. In the words of the FTC staff report: "This experience
substantiates the conclusion that profit growth, whether real or apparent, became the standard by which investors judged companies in the 1960's." [7]

The three stages of conglomerate expansion

Like the corporations formed in the previous merger movements, the new conglomerates of the 1960's, to use Willard L. Thorp's phrase, have also been "excited products of speculative enthusiasm." [8] But the methods of using mergers
to capitalize on a rising securities market have become far more intricate. Most
of the rapidly expanding conglomerates, it would appear, have passed through
three distinct stages in their life span.

The securing of high P/E ratios

In the first stage, as they are making their initial acquisitions, the conglomerates,
either by accident or design, are able to secure high P/E ratios. A high multiple
of market price times earnings is a *sine qua non* for the investor approval needed
for future expansion: To quote Abraham Briloff:

> As is generally known, the securities market place has been much af-
> fected by the so-called "P/E syndrome," by which is meant that securities
> are valued by applying to the company's earnings a certain multiple (the

[5] *Ibid.*, pp. 129–30.

[6] See Dean E. Graber, "Real and Illusory Earnings Growth," *Financial Analysts Journal*,
March–April, 1969.

[7] FTC Staff, *op. cit.*, p. 82.

[8] "The same basic forces were present in the twenties as in the earlier period of merger
activity. Promoters were extremely active, new issues were frequently floated where the
sum exceeded the parts. High hopes were entertained that the new enterprises had extraordinary economic strength.

"If the above analysis is correct, it indicates that these periods of merger activity were
not solely the result of necessary economic evolution, but rather were brought about to
a large extent by promotional activity during periods favorable to new security issues.
The control therefore lies in considerable degree in control over the money markets.
The basic problem shifts from the field of business structure and corporate entities to
the financial world. If the Securities and Exchange Commission, by exposing new issues
to cold, objective scrutiny, can prevent the run-away excitement of these two earlier
periods, then corporate expansion will have to come by plowing back earnings or by
making a convincing, positive case. This seems like a more promising path for our economic evolution than the excited products of speculative enthusiasm." (Willard L. Thorp
and Walter Crowder, *The Structure of Industry*, Monograph No. 27, Temporary National
Economic Committee (TNEC), 1941, Pt. 3, p. 234.)

"P/E" ratio). The mystique of this P/E determination is something beyond the comprehension of most mortals. While one recognizes that the factor varies from industry-to-industry and from time-to-time, one cannot identify by whom and how the determinations are effected.[9]

To a considerable extent high P/E ratios are a product of imagery. Companies have become invested with the mystique by creating in the minds of investors the impression of pioneering in exciting new "growth" industries—computers, electronics, aerospace, new communication techniques, and the like; of developing sophisticated new products; of becoming important defense contractors; of applying to their operations the new "systems approach"; of staffing their central office with bright, youthful management engineers able to focus their combined skills on any problem area; of obtaining instant knowledge through computers of all phases of the company's operations; and above all of being "synergistic," capable of making the corporation as a whole more profitable than the sum of its parts.

The securing of a high P/E ratio through the creation of such an image has represented the first stage in the life history of most of the new conglomerates. Gulf & Western's initial acquisitions took it from automotive parts into aerospace and electronics. Starting in electronics and aerospace, LTV soon became an important defense contractor; by 1968 it had become the tenth largest recipient of military prime contracts. Teledyne owed almost all of its early growth to the acquisition of high-technology companies, becoming an important producer of electronic and aviation control systems and components and of high-performance specialized metals used principally in nuclear, aerospace, and aviation applications. In the early stage of ITT's merger program it absorbed a series of companies in such rapid-growth fields as electronic components, electromagnetic-vibration equipment, vacuum tubes and components, wire and tubing for electrical conductors, and electronics hardware. At its inception as the Electro Dynamics Corporation, Litton's field was microwave tube technology and other branches of advanced electronics; its early acquisitions took it into such other growth industries as business machines and professional services and equipment.

It was not only their participation in expanding growth industries that caused the Wall Street community to look favorably upon the new conglomerates; it was also their ability to convey the impression of imparting a fresh, imaginative approach to traditional business problems. The image conveyed by Litton was copied, almost as successfully, by the other leading conglomerates. In the words of the FTC staff report:

> Two attributes often linked to Litton's expansion-through-merger program are its technological capability and its propensity to combine different technologies into a "systems" approach that provides a unique solution to a problem. Litton's first wave of acquisitions was composed of small electronics firms which specialized in particular segments of this greatly expanding industry. Probably the greatest contribution that these companies made to Litton's success was to bring creative personnel together. Lately, however, the company's acquisitions have been in office furniture, textbooks and frozen foods—areas in which technology hardly

[9] See Abraham J. Briloff, "Distortions Arising from Pooling-of-Interests Accounting," *Financial Analysts Journal,* March–April, 1968; "Out of Focus," *Barron's,* July 28, 1969; "Much Abused Goodwill," *Barron's,* April 28, 1969; "That Funny Money Game," *Financial Analysts Journal,* May–June, 1969.

plays a role. Still, the company continues to emphasize its ability to use a systems approach. In its 1967 Annual Report, the word "systems" is used in 35 of 195 indexed items.[10]

Also contributing to high P/E ratios has been the method of financing favored by the burgeoning conglomerates. The policy was the reverse of that employed by the early "trusts" formed during the great consolidation movement at the turn of the century. Instead of issuing vast quantities of "watered" stock, they tended to restrict the issuance of common stock, relying more on "leverage" through senior securities and debt. As the increment to their income consisting of the earnings of their acquired firms increased more rapidly than their shares outstanding, the inevitable consequence was an increase in their earnings per share.

Whatever the reasons, the new conglomerates early in their careers were able to secure the blessings of high P/E ratios. In Briloff's words, the " 'gnome of Zurich' might be the arbiter; it may also be that the P/E is a determinate rather than the determinant. In any event it's there. . . ." And because it was there the conglomerates came to be well regarded by investment banks, who would underwrite their new security offerings, and by commercial banks, who would grant them loans for new acquisitions.

The attraction of low P/E ratios

But of most importance, because of their high P/E ratios, the new conglomerates achieved the ability to make instant "merger profits" by taking over firms with low ratios. It was this type of activity that occupied the second stage of their history. Simply through the operation of the principle of comparative advantage a company with a high P/E ratio can secure an immediate improvement in its *earnings per share* by acquiring a firm with a lower ratio.[11] The greater the differential between the P/E ratios of the acquiring versus the ac-

---

[10] FTC Staff, *op. cit.*, pp. 575–76.

[11] The operation of the principle can be illustrated with the following hypothetical example, which assumes 3 firms—the acquirer (A) and 2 acquired firms (B and C). Each has an income of $1,000, 2 shares, and earnings per share of $500; the only difference is in the P/E ratios: A has a ratio of 14 to 1, B a ratio of 7 to 1, and C a ratio of 21 to 1.

	Before Acquisition			Co. A After Acquisition of	
	Co. A	Co. B	Co. C	Co. B	Co. C
Income	$1,000	$1,000	$1,000	$2,000	$2,000
Number of shares	2	2	2	3	5
Earnings per share	$ 500	$ 500	$ 500	$ 667	$ 400
P/E ratio	14 to 1	7 to 1	21 to 1		
Price per share	$7,000	$3,500	$10,500		

A can acquire B by issuing just one additional share, the owners of the latter agreeing to exchange their 2 shares worth $3,500 each for one share of A's stock worth $7,000. A's income will double as a result of absorbing B but its number of shares will increase only from 2 to 3. Hence its earnings per share will rise from $500 to $667. To acquire C, however, A will have to issue 3 new shares of stock, the owners of C exchanging their 2 shares worth $10,500 each for 3 shares of A worth $7,000 each. Added to its original 2 shares A will have 5 shares outstanding, giving it an earnings per share of $400 as compared to its pre-acquisition figure of $500.

quired firms, the fewer the shares of the former required to absorb the latter and thus the greater the increase in the acquirer's earnings per share.[12]

The logical expectation, therefore, would be that, having secured high P/E ratios, the conglomerates would then proceed to acquire long-established, "unexciting" companies in mature industries. From the matrix chart presented earlier it can be seen that this is precisely what has happened. Nearly three-fourths of the manufacturing assets acquired by the 8 rapidly expanding conglomerates have been made up of companies primarily engaged in just 4 major industry groups:

Industry Group	Percentage of Manufacturing Assets Acquired
Machinery	34.7%
Primary metals	20.8
Paper	9.2
Food and kindred products	7.9
Total	72.6

None of these 4 areas can by any stretch of the imagination be regarded as a dynamic growth industry with exciting prospects for the future. The one common characteristic they have is maturity; their leading producers for the most part are long-established, well-known firms—with low P/E ratios. In the machinery group by far the largest component is farm machinery, long one of the nation's most depressed industries. Speaking of the steel industry, *Forbes* observes, "Their profitability is to put it mildly substandard. And their earnings growth is more often than not an earnings *decline*. Most investors have tired of waiting for the corner to be turned, for the payoff to come from the huge investments of recent years . . . [and] steel continues to lose sales to aluminum, plastics, reinforced concrete and other substitutes." [13] Most of the assets acquired in the food group were in meat packing and bakeries, in both of which leading firms have not infrequently been recording actual losses. Only an unexpectedly large increase in foreign demand saved the paper industries from a glut of excess capacity.

The explanation for the locus of these acquisitions is thus to be found in the converse of the conglomerates' image. The expansion has taken place where it has *because* the companies acquired have been engaged in industries not of rapid but of slow growth, not of exciting but of unexciting (though not necessarily alarming) prospects for the future. It is the long-established companies in mature industries which possess the characteristics that attract the energetic conglomerate—a low price-earnings ratio, usually coupled with large depreciation reserves, and undervalued assets—the products of conservative accounting methods stressing liquidity and low indebtedness. Commenting on the reason long-established machinery manufacturers have been such a prime target for takeover, *Forbes* states:

[12] For a fuller exposition see Walter J. Mead, "Instantaneous Merger Profit as a Conglomerate Merger Motive," *Western Economic Journal,* Dec., 1969.
[13] *Forbes,* Jan. 1, 1970.

Things like steel-making furnaces, machine tools, pumps, rail equipment, abrasives, boilers, materials handling gear and all the rest are as necessary to American industry as autos and appliances are to American consumers.

It follows, then, that there will always be industrial-equipment companies around to supply these necessities. But it does *not* follow that the same industrial-equipment companies that exist today will still be in business five or ten years from now. Or even next year. The fact is, quite a few of these companies, including some big enough to qualify for listing in the Forbes Yardstick rankings, are disappearing.[14]

In *Forbes's* view, "The industrial-equipment company's nightmare is that it will become a corporate ghost by fading away into a company with a higher P/E ratio." The article goes on to say: "The problem is the stock market, not the basic business of many of these companies. They are not glamour stocks in today's market. They make the go-go types yawn. They sell, the best of them, for ten times earnings and even less. And so they are very vulnerable. Basically good companies but with depressed prices, they are tempting targets for glamour companies with high price earnings ratios." [15]

Because of their low P/E ratios the industrial-equipment companies are hard put to defend themselves by making acquisitions on their own: "The obvious problem is that their low stock multiples put them at a serious disadvantage in coming to anything like favorable terms with another company in a recognized growth field. . . . Blocked from making good acquisitions themselves, vulnerable to take-over, the industrial-equipment companies present quite a paradox in days when glamour seems to be worth more than value." [16]

During this second stage the attitude of Wall Street, in the words of Joel Dean, "perpetuated the high multiple of the conglomerate acquirer (e.g., Litton, Gulf & Western) and made each acquisition fuel a further one." He went on to observe:

> The high-multiple myth is the belief that a company whose stock sells at a high earnings-multiple, because its gradient of growth in earnings per share has been steady and steep, can keep its multiple high and its price kiting indefinitely by a succession of slow growth acquisitions that trade its own high-multiple stock (usually via convertible preferred) for the low multiple stock of the pedestrian growth companies it buys. This myth has made possible the formation and growth of many conglomerates.[17]

Statistical corroboration has been provided by Walter J. Mead, who compared the P/E ratios of acquiring conglomerates with those of their acquired companies.[18] The body of data consisted of all manufacturing and mining mergers, as recorded by the Federal Trade Commission in 1967 and the first half of 1968, in which the acquired firms had assets of more than $10 million. Of the 122 mergers recorded, 104 were conglomerate mergers. Comparing the P/E ratios of the companies involved, Mead found, "For the 104 conglomerate

---

[14] *Ibid.*
[15] *Ibid.*
[16] *Ibid.*
[17] *Hearings on Economic Concentration*, Pt. 8, p. 5255.
[18] Walter J. Mead, *op. cit.*, pp. 295–306. Included in *Hearings on Economic Concentration*, Pt. 8, pp. 5237–48.

mergers, the geometric mean of that ratio was 1.40. In the absence of the hypothesized relationship, we would expect a random distribution of the ratio of price-earnings ratios to have a geometric mean of 1.00." On the basis of statistical tests of significance he concluded that "the geometric mean of the ratio of P/E ratios for conglomerate mergers is significantly greater than unity." As might be anticipated, he also found that the mean for conglomerate mergers (1.40) was higher than the mean of the relative price-earnings ratios for horizontal or vertical measures. He concluded that "conglomerate mergers are characterized as cases in which there is a price-earnings differential favorable to the acquiring firm. . . ."

The search for liquidity

The first merger wave was brought to an end by the "panic" of 1907, the second by the crash of 1929. The explanation for the ending—or possibly only abatement—of the third wave must be sought elsewhere, since merger activity had crested nearly a year before the stock market began to decline. The turning point in merger activity appears to have been in early 1968, when Litton reported for the first time a decline in quarterly earnings.[19] The 1967 year-end P/E ratio for Litton had been 43, while its common stock was selling at 108. This was the climax of the steadily improving record which had led Joel B. Dirlam to observe that Litton seemed to be "watched over by a good fairy." But in the first quarter of 1968 actual earnings fell far short of expectations.[20] Earnings were lower for the entire year, which, according to the FTC staff, "appeared to result from losses in their shipbuilding, office furniture and business machines divisions." [21] By mid-1969 Litton's P/E ratio had fallen to 18, while its market price was down to 43.

The early part of 1968, when it absorbed Jones & Laughlin, also appears to have been the turning point for LTV. In an article entitled "J & L Steel Acquisition Yields Little But Grief for Ling Conglomerate," the *Wall Street Journal* stated that since the acquisition "earnings have plunged, failing to cover the J & L dividend in three of the last five quarters and dropping the company's profitability to the lowest among the major steelmakers." The principal reasons cited were labor strife, a lack of cash to undertake needed modernization, and management uncertainties associated with the takeover: "One factor . . . was that 'when Ling came in, there were morale problems at J & L. A lot of people were sitting around gossiping about what he would do, instead of turning out steel.' " [22]

Although launched more than a year after the conglomerates' stock prices had started to decline, the filing of antitrust suits in 1969 against a series of conglomerate acquisitions certainly contributed to the rapid decline of their security prices. Also contributing to the downward trend were efforts to trim defense spending—in which most of the leading conglomerates are heavily involved—by cutting back military programs, reducing "cost overruns," and eliminating "waste." As a result of all these factors, between early 1969 and early 1970 the market price of all 8 conglomerates suffered serious declines.

[19] *Fortune,* April, 1968.
[20] *Ibid.*
[21] FTC Staff, *op. cit.,* p. 108.
[22] *Wall Street Journal,* Jan. 5, 1970.

Ironically, the very practices that facilitated the growth of conglomerates on the upswing became an albatross around their necks during a downswing. As total sales and earnings fall, the payments on fixed obligations incurred through leverage—interest on debt and dividends on preferred stock—absorb progressively larger shares of gross income, leading to even further declines in net earnings. The intensification of competitive rivalry inherent in buyers' markets requires cost-reducing improvements in facilities; if they are financed through new stock issues, the result is a "dilution" of the value of existing shares; if they are financed through credit, the result is a further increase in payments on fixed obligations.

In a study of 24 leading conglomerates Mead found that in 1968 common stock and surplus represented 53.3 percent of their total capitalization—"significantly below" the 74.6 percent average equity base for other industrial firms. He also found that the use of leverage by the conglomerates has been increasing; as compared to the figure of 53.3 percent in 1968, 8 years earlier 60.2 percent of their capitalization had been made up of common stock and surplus. Commenting on these findings, he observed, "Debt must be serviced on penalty of possible bankruptcy proceedings. In the event of a widespread decline in business activity, heavily leveraged firms are vulnerable. The experience of the 1930's with heavily leveraged public utility firms in particular demonstrated the spillover social cost due to extensive leverage in individual firms." [23] As compared to an advance of just under 50 percent registered by Standard & Poor's index of 500 common stocks, the increases in the conglomerates' market prices between the fall of 1966 and their peak in 1967–68 were over 400 percent in the case of Ling-Temco-Vought, over 200 for Gulf & Western and Norton Simon, 175 for Textron, and 100 for Litton. By the end of 1969 all these gains had been erased.[24]

Under these circumstances it could be expected that the conglomerates would become attracted to firms possessing large reserves of liquid funds that could be used to shore up their worsening financial structures. In Briloff's words, "It is more than coincidence that the conglomerates directed their acquisitive bent towards these insurance companies. They coveted their huge pools of liquidity, their cash flow, and . . . their latent pools of suppressed profits represented by the unrealized appreciation in the portfolios accumulated by the insurance companies over the century or more of their respective security accumulations. There was, then, a symbiotic relationship formed between the conglomerates and insurance companies."

From Table 12-2 it can be seen that the 8 conglomerates acquired 5 insurance companies with total assets of $2.525 million. Gulf & Western acquired Capitol Life Insurance and Providence Washington Insurance; Teledyne purchased United Insurance Company of America and Argonaut Insurance; and ITT acquired Hartford Insurance Company. What is most significant about these acquisitions is their timing; all took place in 1968 except the purchase of Hartford, which occurred in 1969. Other conglomerates have also taken over insurance companies. In the few cases that have come to light thus far they have lost little time in having the acquired insurance firms declare "extraordinary dividends" to their new parent companies. For example, National General,

---

[23] Mead, *op. cit.*
[24] See charts in *Hearings on Economic Concentration,* Pt. 8, pp. 4618–24.

after taking over Great American Insurance, made a withdrawal of $175 million; Leasco, after taking over Reliance Insurance, took out $39 million.[25]

Another type of highly liquid enterprise is finance companies, 4 of which with combined assets of $1.848 billion were acquired by the 8 conglomerates: Aetna Finance and Thorp Finance were absorbed by ITT, Associates Investment by Gulf & Western, and Fireside Thrift by Teledyne. Again all of these acquisitions took place in 1968. All told, insurance and finance companies have accounted for 33 percent of the assets of all companies acquired by the 8 conglomerates between 1960 and 1969.

Whether these and similar withdrawals will be sufficient to stem the recent downward trend in the market prices, P/E ratios, and earnings per share of the acquiring conglomerates remains to be seen. But just as the second stage was the logical consequence of the first stage, so the third stage has been the logical consequence of the end of the second stage.

Gulf & Western: a case example

This three-stage history of conglomerate expansion is illustrated by a series of key acquisitions in the growth of Gulf & Western. From its original field of automobile parts, the company's initial expansion drive took it into such growth industries as aerospace and electronics. Partly as a consequence, it secured a comparatively high P/E ratio.

In the second stage its acquisitions could be expected to consist mainly of large, well-established companies with low P/E ratios and substantial undervalued assets. Such a company was New Jersey Zinc, which, according to Gulf & Western's listing statement, "ranks among the first four domestic producers of slab zinc and supplied in 1966 something more than 13% of the estimated zinc metal consumption in the United States. It is the largest domestic producer of zinc pigments, accounting for approximately 33% of 1966 shipments of lead-free zinc oxide." [26] While not exactly an example of "the minnow swallowing the whale," the acquisition was clearly a case of a smaller fish swallowing a larger one. At the time of acquisition Gulf & Western's assets were $104 million as compared to New Jersey Zinc's $135 million; its annual net income was $5.5 million as compared to New Jersey Zinc's $12.8 million.[27] The acquisition was made possible partly by the differential advantage of a higher versus a lower P/E ratio, partly by the issuance of preferred stock, and partly by a large, unsecured loan from one of the nation's largest commercial banks—Chase Manhattan. The effect of the acquisition on Gulf & Western's stock price was instantaneous and dramatic, as was brought out by Kenneth R. Harkins, chief counsel of the House Antitrust Subcommittee, in an exchange with Gulf & Western's chairman and chief executive officer, Charles G. Bluhdorn:

> MR. HARKINS: On August 18, 1965, the date Mr. Zerbe first came to you, Mr. Bluhdorn, to talk about the New Jersey Zinc acquisition, the price of Gulf & Western's common stock at the market closing was $41.25.

[25] *National Underwriter,* Dec. 27, 1969. This article also lists other "upstream transfers of funds made by an insurer to its holding company."
[26] Gulf & Western, *Listing Application to the New York Stock Exchange,* A-24501, June 9, 1967, p. 40.
[27] 91st Cong., 1st Sess., Subcommittee No. 5, House Committee on the Judiciary, *Hearings on Conglomerate Investigations,* 1969, p. 88.

On September 10, 1965, the date the stock purchase agreement was signed and announced, the price of Gulf & Western's common stock merger was finally consummated, the price of Gulf & Western's common stock closed at $110.75. During this time period, Gulf & Western's price-earnings ratio remained at about 16 times, and any inflated earnings per share figure, or the earnings per share figure in your proxy statement, would result in a higher price for Gulf & Western's stock if it were inflated; would it not?

MR. BLUHDORN: We don't acknowledge that it was inflated, but I would say, Counsel, that if, in fact, the price of G. & W. did go up, which it did, then the New Jersey Zince shareholders benefited to the same extent.[28]

By the first half of 1969 Gulf & Western's use of leverage to effect acquisitions had brought it to a point where nearly half of its net income was absorbed in servicing fixed charges:

MR. HARKINS: During this period [from 1964 through the first half of 1969] the total long term debt of Gulf & Western has increased from $11.5 million to $931 million. This is an increase of, according to our figures, approximately 7,800 percent. The interest and preferred stock dividend coverage has declined from 7.3 to 1 to 2.6 to 1 as of January 31, 1969. . . .

This means, does it not, that nearly half of all your net earnings at this time must be devoted to fixed charges for interest and preferred stock dividends?

* * *

MR. GASTON: Yes, I would say that by and large the 2.6 to 1 at the present time is approximately correct.[29]

Of key importance to the acquisition of New Jersey Zinc—and thus to Gulf & Western's subsequent growth—was an unsecured 6 percent loan from Chase Manhattan, entered into on September 10, 1965. Up to that time all Chase had made available to the company was a "lending arrangement" of $20 million, only $5 million of which could be outstanding at any one time. The circumstances under which this crucial loan was made are of more than passing interest. It was signed on behalf of Gulf & Western by Bluhdorn and for Chase by one of its vice presidents, Roy T. Abbott, Jr. Six months later, on February 21, 1966, the same Abbott became a senior vice president of Gulf & Western. In the course of the hearings it was developed that during the summer months preceding the granting of the loan in September Bluhdorn had mentioned to Abbott the possibility of moving to Gulf & Western:

MR. BLUHDORN: I have a summer home in Connecticut. Mr. Abbott was staying at his summer home up in Candlewood Lake, which was very close by. In fact, driving down to New York he passed within about 30 seconds of my home. I used to take a ride with him once in a while downtown, and that has been recollected to me, and I have no doubt that it is so.

I may have said to him at that time, "Roy, you know, you would be the sort of fellow that we would like to have on the Gulf & Western team some day," something of that sort.[30]

* * *

[28] *Ibid.*, pp. 93–94.
[29] *Ibid.*, p. 97.
[30] *Ibid.*, p. 23.

CHAIRMAN CELLER: In any event, you had a line of credit of $20 million. Very likely you didn't use that full line of credit, and now in September, you were given an unsecured loan of $80 million.

Do you want this committee to believe that the loan of $80 million on top of this line of credit of $20 million had nothing whatsoever to do with the hiring of Mr. Abbott?

MR. BLUHDORN: Mr. Chairman, I can state unequivocally that this was 100 percent the case.[31]

While still with Chase, however, Abbott had recommended the granting of credit to Gulf & Western:

MR. HARKINS: In June 1964, you authorized a revolving credit agreement and a term loan agreement with Gulf & Western, did you not?

MR. ABBOTT: That really is what I was going to add to the last sentence that I just made. The $20 million, as well, was beyond my lending limit authority at the Chase Manhattan Bank, so, the answer to your second question is, no, I did not authorize it. I simply relayed it to the company, as an officer of the bank.

MR. HARKINS: You recommended such a loan at that time as an officer of the bank?

MR. ABBOTT: Oh, yes, I did.[32]

It should not be thought that the granting of credit to Gulf & Western was without its advantages to Chase. In any large industrial corporation there are certain more-or-less routine activities—depositing savings accounts, payroll withholding taxes, social-security taxes, and the like—that are customarily performed for a fee by a bank. These services had in the past been performed by local banks in the communities in which the companies acquired by Gulf & Western had been located. When the "lending agreement" was entered into, however, these service activities were transferred to Chase:

MR. HARKINS: I will read the first paragraph of the January 8, 1965 letter, to Mr. Roy T. Abbott from T. H. Neyland, of Gulf & Western:

"I have now corresponded with all of the subsidiaries of Gulf & Western that will be moving their account to the Chase Manhattan Bank. I am enclosing a copy of the instruction furnished, for your information."

Then it lists accounts that were to be transferred, I hand you the letter and request that you also show it to Mr. Judelson.

Mr. Judelson, were these companies, subsidiaries, or other divisions of Gulf & Western that had been acquired by acquisition?

MR. JUDELSON: Yes, they were, sir.[33]

Gulf & Western's home office took pains to see to it that the transfers to Chase did in fact take place. Referring to a letter of March 9, 1965, from Neyland of Gulf & Western to the heads of its subsidiaries, the chief counsel of the Subcommittee stated:

MR. HARKINS: The letter gives instructions to these people for depositing savings accounts, payroll withholding taxes, and social security taxes, and it says:

[31] *Ibid.*, p. 25.
[32] *Ibid.*, p. 32.
[33] *Ibid.*, p. 39.

"You are also requested to see that the system is perpetuated each month so that our good friends at The Chase will not be constantly calling some 'malingerer' to my attention."

Mr. Abbott, were you the good friend at Chase calling malingerers to their attention?

MR. ABBOTT: I don't know that I was, but I would hope anybody in my group that was following these, if we hadn't been getting these, that we would have called it to their attention.

MR. HARKINS: Would you have called them a malingerer? Is this an instance where Chase is policing an arrangement with Gulf & Western?

MR. ABBOTT: This would be an instance in which apparently the company had set these arrangements up, and had x number of companies or operations that were sending their taxes in, and I am sure, as Herb pointed out in his letter, if they were not coming in we would want to know about it, and we would have called it to their attention.[34]

As might be expected, some of the local banks that were losing this business were not happy about the transfer. An example was the reaction of the Bank of the Southwest, which, according to an internal Chase memorandum of January 26, 1965, from J. M. Lindberg to Pension Trust files, put up "quite a howl":

Roy Abbott was told today by Herb Neyland, financial vice president, that everything still pointed to CMB [Chase Manhattan Bank] as the prospective trustee for the company's pension arrangements. However, Herb said that the Bank of the Southwest has put up quite a howl about the company's decision to give this business to us. The company has told the Bank of Southwest that CMB would be well known to all of their scattered subsidiaries as a leader in this field whereas the Bank of Southwest would be completely unknown to them. Accordingly they have told the Bank of Southwest that, unless there is some overriding reason that they can come up with, the trusteeships will be given to CMB. The only thing the local bank has come up with so far is their prowess with oil royalties.[35]

The absorption of New Jersey Zinc is typical of a conglomerate's acquisitions in the second stage not only because it was effected largely by leverage and the company acquired was a large, long-established enterprise with a lower P/E ratio; it is also typical because, as a result of its conservative financial management, the acquired firm itself had substantial "hidden assets" that could be used to buy up still other firms. At the time of its acquisition New Jersey Zinc held in its portfolio $35 million in negotiable securities. Although part of this amount was used to pay off outstanding loans, there remained $8 million, which was then used by Gulf & Western to acquire Paramount Pictures:

MR. HARKINS: Mr. Gaston, on April 15, 1966, there was a memorandum from you to the board of directors. In paragraph 2 of this memorandum, it states:

"G. & W. had about $8,000,000 of marketable securities (Ford, General Motors, General Electric, and Kennecott common stocks) remaining from the New Jersey Zinc Securities Portfolio. These stocks

[34] *Ibid.*, pp. 42–43.
[35] *Ibid.*, p. 47.

will be sold and the proceeds used in part payment of the approximately $12,000,000 required for this Paramount stock purchase."

*   *   *

MR. GASTON: . . . We obviously had a portfolio in New Jersey Zinc which over a period of time was sold. A substantial portion of the proceeds were used directly in paying off the $13 million-some-odd loan that New Jersey Zinc had that had to be paid off at the time of the merger. The balance of the proceeds were combined with the other resources of Gulf & Western and either used in debt retirement or for other corporate purposes.

CHAIRMAN CELLER: Doesn't the memorandum speak for itself? "These stocks will be sold and the proceeds used in part payment of approximately $12 million required for this Paramount stock purchase"!

MR. GASTON: I think that speaks for itself.[36]

The sequence, however, did not stop here, for Paramount too was a storehouse of "hidden assets." The form the acquisition took is itself something of a classic example of leverage. The amount paid, mostly in the form of preferred stock, was worth about $185 million at the time of issue. Yet it was entered in at $100 million—the value of film properties, real estate, and other assets appearing on Paramount's books. Thus, $85 million of the actual cost incurred by Gulf & Western in making the acquisition never showed up in its accounts. At the same time that it was thus minimizing the cost of the acquisition, Gulf & Western proceeded to generate "instant earnings" by selling to television Paramount's feature films (severely written down on its books). Although payment was to be made over time in installments, Gulf & Western took the total income to be received in one fell swoop:

> And the G & W management was able to assert . . . that while tired old Paramount had earned less than $3 million the year before the takeover, in the less than a year immediately following its getting into the pool with G & W, it was able to earn more than 7 times that sum—over $22 million. . . . Overlooked was the fact that G & W was doing nothing more than stripping the top soil which was so carefully nurtured by the traditional Paramount management and proceeding to sell this fertile soil.[37]

Paramount's "hidden assets" in the form of its film library were an important consideration in the decision to make the acquisition. Referring to the acquisition of Paramount Pictures, an internal Chase memorandum dated August 17, 1965, states:

> The logic behind this deal involves the issuance of junior securities in order to acquire: (a) hidden assets far in excess of book value, which provides a source of future cash flow; (b) gain an entrance to a leisure time industry which is expected to yield profitable operations with the financially oriented management; and (c) add strength to the total G. & W. balance sheet due to the creation of junior securities. This latter point opens the door for more borrowing room in the present debt agreement.

> *   *   *

> This asset [the film library] represents hidden value in the Paramount balance sheet. Gulf & Western estimates the rental value approximates some $165 million. The timing of the realization of this revenue stream

[36] *Ibid.*, pp. 95–96.

[37] *Hearings on Economic Concentration*, Pt. 8, p. 5157, testimony of Abraham J. Briloff.

can only be assumed to be according to their policy of (1) optimizing the return of each film package, while (2) filling cash flow needs and meeting the stock market's anticipation of earnings per share. Running against this policy is the factor whereby today's dollars become larger tomorrow when invested profitably, that is; the concept of discounted cash flow.[38]

To the head of Gulf & Western acquiring Paramount was like "buying a bank." An internal Chase document of February 10, 1967, refers to a luncheon meeting of Gulf & Western and Chase officials:

> Bluhdorn discussed the purchase of Paramount which he felt was equivalent to buying a "bank." He emphasized: (a) the hidden asset values and cash flow generating abilities of the film library, and very confidentially, he mentioned that he had completed negotiations with one of the three major networks for another film lease package of 32 pictures for $23,375,000 to run for 2 years. This contract is in addition to their deal with ABC for $20 million, which was announced last fall.[39]

During the second stage a further source of financial strength to a rapidly expanding conglomerate consists of the profits it makes from mergers that do *not* take place. When it becomes known that a widely publicized merger-minded conglomerate is buying up the stock of a given company, investors scramble to acquire its stock, anticipating further rises, particularly if a real takeover struggle ensues. Not infrequently, however, the conglomerate abandons the effort: the antitrust agencies may have objected, the cost appears prohibitive, key stockholders refuse to sell, the firm was bought up by some other acquirer. The difference in the stock price between the time the conglomerate makes its purchases (or in the words of the trade "takes a position") and the time it abandons the effort and disposes of the stock may yield a very substantial profit.

Using short-term credit from Chase, Gulf & Western bought minority interests in 4 well-known firms that, for one reason or another, it subsequently sold. Referring to a table prepared by the House Subcommittee staff, the chief counsel noted: "This table sets forth profits in four of the transactions that Gulf & Western did not ultimately acquire, Armour Co., Allis-Chalmers, Pan American World Airways, and Sinclair Oil. The total profits in abandoned transactions from securities where you took a position amounts to $51,882,578 in the period between January 1, 1968 through April 17, 1969." [40]

---

[38] House Subcommittee No. 5, *op. cit.,* pp. 148–49.
[39] *Ibid.,* p. 149.
[40] *Ibid.,* p. 105. The table referred to is as follows (*ibid,* p. 110):

Gulf & Western Abandoned Transactions and Profits

	Cost	Value Received	Profit	Date of Transaction
Armour & Co.	$ 28,149,915	$ 44,400,000	$16,250,085	Jan. 16, 1968 to Oct. 15, 1968
Allis-Chalmers Manu-facturing Co.	117,074,000	122,080,000	5,006,000	May 7, 1968 to Dec. 6, 1968
Sinclair Oil Corp.	88,774,283	112,953,620	24,179,337	Oct. 24, 1968 to Mar. 4, 1969
Pan American World Airways, Inc.	10,802,844	17,250,000	6,447,156	Jan. 1, 1968 to Apr. 17, 1969
Total profit			$51,882,578	

GULF & WESTERN: A CASE EXAMPLE

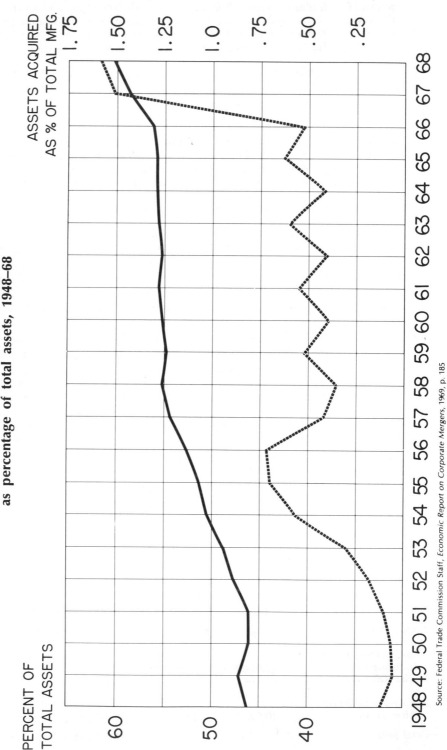

Figure 12-1

200 LARGEST MANUFACTURING CORPORATIONS
Share of total assets and assets acquired
as percentage of total assets, 1948–68

PERCENT OF
TOTAL ASSETS

ASSETS ACQUIRED
AS % OF TOTAL MFG.

1948 49 50 51 52 53 54 55 56 57 58 59 60 61 62 63 64 65 66 67 68

Source: Federal Trade Commission Staff, *Economic Report on Corporate Mergers*, 1969, p. 185

THE NEW CONGLOMERATES

Finally, the history of Gulf & Western also illustrates the behavior of conglomerates during the third stage of declining stock prices and increasing financial stringency. As has already been noted, Gulf & Western, like the other major conglomerates, moved in 1968 into the insurance field, acquiring Capitol Life Insurance and Providence Washington Insurance, with combined assets of $344 million. In addition, in 1969 it found another potentially liquid firm, Resorts International, a land development and gambling enterprise on Grand Bahama Island; a principal source of its revenue was the $10,000–$12,000 a year to be yielded by each of 350 slot machines.

> MR. HARKINS: Would you agree that the primary source of income for Resorts International is now its gambling operation?
>
> MR. LANE: At the present time that is true.
>
> MR. HARKINS: And in connection with its gambling operation, Resorts has an exclusive gambling license on Paradise Island?
>
> MR. LANE: Yes, sir.
>
> MR. HARKINS: And no casino can be built within a radius of 10 miles for 10 years; is that correct?
>
> MR. LANE: That is correct.[41]

The effect on concentration

What has been the effect of the conglomerate merger movement—as well as the continuing absorption process and the oil company mergers—on aggregate concentration? According to the FTC staff report, had they made no mergers, the 200 largest companies of 1968 would have increased their share of total manufacturing assets from 42.4 percent in 1947 to only 45.3 percent in 1968, instead of to their actual share of 60.9 percent. Mergers alone thus accounted for 15.6 of the 18.5-percentage-point increase in the share of total manufacturing assets recorded by the 200 largest companies of 1968.[42]

Another way of ascertaining the effect of mergers on concentration is through a comparison of merger activity with aggregate concentration. Figure 12-1 contrasts for the postwar period the share of total manufacturing assets held by the 200 largest companies with the asset value of their acquisitions, expressed as a percentage of the assets of all manufacturing firms. As can be seen, between 1948 and 1952 neither measure showed any significant change. The assets acquired by the 200 largest constituted in each of these years less than two-tenths of one percent of all manufacturing assets, while the share held by the 200 largest fluctuated within a narrow range. But in the next 4 years the relative importance of merger activity by the 200 largest moved sharply upward. So did their share of manufacturing assets. Although during the next 2 years the former measure fell off while the latter was rising, merger activity still remained well above the 1947–52 level. From 1958 to 1966 little change took place in either measure. But between 1966 and 1968 both measures rose precipitously; the assets acquired by the 200 largest increased from .5 to 1.5 percent of all manufacturing assets, while their share of total assets rose from 56.1 percent to 60.4 percent.

[41] *Ibid.*, p. 155.
[42] FTC Staff, *op. cit.*, p. 191.

CH 13 NONPRICE COMPETITION

Nonprice competition is both a result and a cause of concentration. It is a result because as an industry becomes concentrated, oligopolists will tend to abstain from competing in price and will increasingly confine their rivalry to the various forms of nonprice competition—advertising and other types of sales promotion, quality, service, and the like. In Fritz Machlup's words, "A firm maintaining its old prices but offering 'better values' may try to demonstrate to its rivals that it continues to believe in the 'ethics of the industry' which interdicts price competition but permits nonprice competition. Every act of nonprice competition may be used as a 'sign' directed toward the competitors, telling them, as it were: 'You see, I will not cut prices; I confine myself to these more civilized ways of competing! I trust you will do likewise.' "[1] In addition to depriving the economy of the benefits of price competition, nonprice competition results in economic waste, often on an extraordinary scale. For example, in a study of the cost of model changes in the automobile industry, Franklin M. Fischer, Zvi Griliches, and Carl Kaysen found, "The total costs of model change [in the automobile industry] as estimated so far came to about $700 per car (more than 25% of the purchase price) or about $3.9 billion per year over the 1956–60 period."[2]

This chapter, however, will be concerned with nonprice competition not as a result of concentration nor as a source of economic waste but as a causal factor. On the basis of the behavior of concentration ratios it would appear that one form of nonprice competition, TV advertising, is among the most important causes of concentration and that, under certain circumstances, another of its forms, design and model changes, may contribute significantly to higher concentration.

It is fair to say that the various forms of nonprice competition, particularly advertising, generally have not been well regarded by the economics profession. The long-prevailing attitude has been stated succinctly by Lester G. Telser:

> Hardly any business practice causes economists greater uneasiness than advertising. Among the many reasons for this feeling is the opinion held by some economists that competition and advertising are incompatible. Henry Simon, perhaps one of the most outspoken critics of advertising, summed it up neatly when he wrote that "a major barrier to really competitive enterprise and efficient service to consumers is to be found in advertising—in national advertising especially and in sales organizations which cover great national or regional areas."[3]

[1] Fritz Machlup, *The Economics of Seller's Competition,* Johns Hopkins Press, 1952, p. 459.
[2] Franklin M. Fischer, Zvi Griliches, Carl Kaysen, "The Cost of Automobile Model Changes Since 1949," *American Economic Review,* May, 1962, p. 260.
[3] Lester G. Telser, "Advertising and Competition," *Journal of Political Economy,* Dec., 1964, p. 537.

The economic pros and cons of advertising

Telser, Stigler, and others have held this attitude to be unwarranted. From an economic point of view advertising, it is claimed, is actually beneficial. Although many secondary and tertiary claims have been made, this position rests essentially on three arguments: (a) that advertising widens the market for, and hastens the acceptance of, new products; (b) that certain types of advertising provide buyers with helpful and useful information, and (c) that advertising helps manufacturers to achieve economies of scale in both production and distribution.

Summarizing the first argument Nicholas Kaldor wrote, "In the case of . . . some new commodity, such as the vacuum cleaner, the wireless or the refrigerator, advertising might clearly help in securing the more rapid adoption of the commodity for general use by spreading knowledge about it more quickly than would have been done otherwise." But, he went on to point out, "This . . . is an initial effect, whereas the important question is whether *continued* advertising exerts a steady influence on the demand for a commodity already in general use." [4] This same point of view has been expressed by the Senate Antitrust Subcommittee in its report (p. 92) on the automobile industry:

> In its early days advertising undoubtedly performed for this industry its socially desirable function of expanding the market. Through advertising buyers were made aware of the existence and usefulness of this new form of transportation. As the quality of the car was improved and the services which it could perform were enlarged, advertising became the principal means of communicating knowledge of these improvements to the mass market.
>
> But after the automobile had become an established, accepted and well-known reality, it is doubtful whether advertising contributed significantly to the further expansion of the market. The basis for this conclusion lies implicitly in the findings of studies of elasticity of demand for automobiles. In these studies . . . it has been found possible to explain most of the fluctuations in automobile sales over long-term periods in terms of just two variables, price and income. In other words, it has not been found necessary to introduce advertising as a separate variable to explain changes in automobile sales.

With reference to the second argument, Kenneth E. Boulding notes, "There is a case for a certain amount of advertising, such as the purely informative advertising which is descriptive of the qualities and prices of commodities. This is a form of consumer education which is necessary if consumers are to make intelligent choices; in fact it makes competition more nearly perfect." The trouble, however, is that the dissemination of such helpful information represents a very minor part of modern advertising: "Most advertising, unfortunately, is devoted to an attempt to build up in the mind of the consumer irrational preferences for certain brands of goods." [5] Stigler has argued that advertisements

[4] Nicholas Kaldor, "The Economic Aspects of Advertising," *Review of Economic Studies,* 1949–50, pp. 1–27. Among the other arguments on behalf of advertising, as cited by Kaldor, are: "that it makes for better labour relations in industry; that it increases consumer satisfaction because of the pleasure derived from advertisements and because (by promoting the sale of branded goods) it makes for greater convenience of shopping; and, finally, that by the subsidy it pays to the newspaper industry it promotes a free and independent press." (*Ibid.,* p. 8.)
[5] Kenneth E. Boulding, *Economic Analysis,* Harper, 1941, p. 621.

containing information on prices assist the buyer in ascertaining the most favorable price and thereby lessen the dispersion of prices. How much, though, of today's advertising contains information on prices? Stigler acknowledges, "These remarks seem most appropriate to newspaper advertisements of the 'classified' variety." But he avoids commenting on the usefulness of "the spectacular television show or the weekly comedian" by observing, "We are not equipped to discuss advertising in general because the problem of quality has been (and will continue to be) evaded by the assumption of homogeneous goods." [6]

The argument that advertising assists a manufacturer in achieving greater efficiency rests on the assumption that through its use he can increase his output of a specific type of goods, thus reducing his unit costs more than the cost of advertising. As compared to the irregular and often dissimilar orders passed on to him by wholesalers, advertising provides the manufacturer with the means of building up a sustained demand for a particular product, enabling him to obtain economies of scale and of specialization. This argument can be objected to, however, on the grounds that under competition such economies would have been achieved anyway. In Kaldor's words,

> if the concentration is economically justified owing to economies of large-scale production, it does not necessarily follow that it would not have come about without advertising; for in the absence of advertising, firms would have been driven to compete on the basis of price, and price competition would have brought about the same result, in a more beneficial way to the consumer. If, on the other hand, the concentration is not justified by the existence of economies of large-scale production . . . concentration brought about by advertising is definitely harmful; for quite apart from the rise in costs caused by advertising, there is a rise in the margin of profit, and hence in the prices paid by the consumer, due to the reduction in the degree of freedom of entry to newcomers, and the consequent increase in the degree of monopoly power enjoyed by those inside the trade.[7]

Foremost among the economic arguments against nonprice competition, and advertising in particular, is that it results in social waste. A better use could be found for resources devoted to creating and disseminating advertisements that neither enlighten consumers concerning a truly new product (as distinct from a new brand or model) nor provide useful information on the price, quality, and related properties of an existing product. These advertisements, in Boulding's words, "seek to associate the commodity in question with something else which the consumer likes or with the avoidance of something which the consumer seeks to avoid. Drinks are portrayed with beautiful flowers; cigarettes with beautiful girls; soaps are associated with love and marriage and so on. There is very little place in the technique of advertising for the sober, truthful presentations of the qualities and prices of commodities." For this type of advertising, "clear social waste," he finds little economic justification: "The only possible case for it is that it may increase the velocity of circulation of money and thus avoid some unemployment. There are, however, cheaper and more dignified ways of increasing employment." [8]

[6] George J. Stigler, "The Economics of Information," *Journal of Political Economy,* June, 1961, p. 222.
[7] Kaldor, *op. cit.*
[8] Boulding, *op. cit.*, pp. 620–21.

A second argument is that the responsiveness of buyers, or "elasticity of demand," is probably less with respect to the various forms of nonprice competition than with respect to price. On *a priori* grounds this would certainly appear to be the case for services, style changes, and advertising. A true improvement in quality confers added utilities on the buyer and thus could be regarded as the equivalent of a reduction in price. But even here there is a point beyond which demand elasticities might well begin to differ. If, for instance, instead of steadily reducing the price of the Model T, the elder Henry Ford had made correlative improvements in its quality, it is unlikely that the resultant increase in demand would have been as great as that which resulted from the price reductions that "put America on wheels." On the basis of this argument a change in an industry's structure from polypolistic to oligopolistic, with its accompanying greater emphasis on nonprice as compared to price competition, would tend to have a depressing effect on the industry's sales, production, and employment.

Finally, nonprice competition has been criticized on the grounds that it constitutes a barrier to entry and thereby impairs competition. Kaldor advances the hypothesis that the process of concentration "might go on indefinitely (or until complete monopoly is established) so long as the basic assumption that a larger expenditure on advertising exercises a greater 'pulling power' than a smaller expenditure, and that the sums which particular firms can devote to advertising are more or less proportionate to their sales, remains valid." [9] But even in the absence of this "basic assumption," nonprice competition can still operate as a barrier to entry if one of its forms (i.e., advertising) is simply not available to smaller firms through a particular medium or, if available, costs them substantially more than it does large concerns. The result of such a situation, as has been pointed out by Donald F. Turner, is an adverse effect on competition, both present and potential:

> If heavy advertising expenditures . . . serve to raise the barriers to entry, the adverse competitive consequences are important not only because new firms are kept out, but also because frequently it is the prospect of new entry which serves as a major competitive restraint upon the action of existing firms. Moreover, where the number of firms in an industry are few, this potentiality may be the most significant competitive factor that inhibits firms from setting high prices and achieving extensive monopoly rewards.[10]

It is not the purpose of this work to weigh these opposing arguments to arrive at some overall value judgment concerning the economic desirability of advertising. Attention is focused on one particular form of advertising as it affects concentration. The question at issue, in other words, is whether TV advertising makes for higher levels of concentration than would otherwise exist.

Monopolistic characteristics of TV advertising

Inherent in TV advertising is a combination of characteristics that inevitably makes for higher concentration: a finite limit on the available time and a greater effectiveness, or "pulling power," as compared to other media whose supply is

---

[9] Kaldor, *op. cit.*
[10] Donald F. Turner, "Advertising and Competition," *Federal Bar Journal,* Spring, 1966, p. 94.

readily expandable. Unlike advertising space in newspapers and magazines, the supply of TV time available for advertising cannot be varied with the demand. The supply is fixed, first, by the amount of time that the station is on the air; second, by the operation of the law of diminishing returns after an optimal point is reached in the frequency and duration of commercials; and, third, by the limitations imposed by public authority. This unique characteristic of advertising on TV (and to a much lesser extent on radio) was described in hearings before the Senate Antitrust Subcommittee by Gerald T. Arthur, president of the advertising firm of Mercury Media: "It isn't the same as in newspapers where they can print so many pages and fix their costs or with a magazine that knows that they are going to have a 48- or 52- or 68-page issue. If the broadcaster's minute is not sold today it is gone forever. . . . There is just so much time in the TV spectrum of prime-nighttime time. That is what it comes down to." [11]

A central objective of most TV commercials involves another finite limit— the physical amount of shelf space available in the retail store. For most consumer goods a place on the shelf is an indispensable prerequisite for survival. Its importance was outlined to the Subcommittee by Jess Nicks, president of General Brewing Corporation:

> Supermarkets depend naturally on volume sales. A beer that does not sell in sufficient volume may be denied shelf space.
>
> "Display space" might be a better term than "shelf space." The relationship of advertising to supermarket display space is the key relationship.
>
> Strong, successful advertising programs can influence supermarket managers to grant expanded display space—including shelf space and floor display space—to a given brand of beer. For example, supermarket managers may permit large floor displays, which can greatly boost sales, during a specific brand promotion.
>
> In general, a retail merchant will allocate the most advantageous display space on the basis of product sales. To the extent that advertising is effective in motivating the consumer, it affects display space.[12]

Rivalry for display space has induced leading advertisers to promote not only different products but different brands of the same product. The result has been the preemption of both the fixed supply of TV advertising time and the fixed supply of shelf space. The greater the preemption of TV time, the less are the chances that the smaller manufacturers will be able to obtain shelf space; the greater the preemption of shelf space, the less are the chances that the smaller sellers will be able to secure the revenues needed to purchase TV time. There do not appear to exist any natural market forces to break this vicious circle.

A fixed supply for any medium will of course tend to promote higher concentration. But the effect will be compounded if, as compared to other forms of advertising, the medium with the fixed supply is the most effective, or, in Kaldor's term, has the greatest "pulling power." The question of the relative cost-effectiveness of the various media—TV, radio, magazines, newspapers, direct mail, and so on—is of course a highly controversial issue, with each medium having its own partisans and proponents. Fortunately, this is one of the issues that need not be resolved here. Suffice it to say, as compared to the trends for the

---

[11] 89th Cong., 2nd Sess., Senate Subcommittee on Antitrust and Monopoly, Senate Committee on the Judiciary, *Hearings on Possible Anticompetitive Effects of Sale of Network TV Advertising*, 1966, Pt. 1, pp. 117, 119.
[12] *Ibid.*, pp. 140–41.

other media, the upward movement in the use and costs of TV advertising makes it clear that it has come to be regarded by manufacturers of branded and trademarked consumer products as the preferred form of advertising. The preemption by large firms of the medium whose supply is fixed and which, in addition, has the greatest pulling power should make higher concentration almost a certainty.

As the demand for TV advertising has increased, the segments into which the available time is broken up and merchandised have been steadily compressed. In the words of Albert T. Hyde, president of the Mentholatum Company, "it used to be that you bought an hour or half-hour show. Then they got down to participation, and now they are down to minutes." [13] Such a trend would appear to promise smaller advertisers easier access to the medium. But again the principle of diminishing returns imposes a limitation. Apparently there is an interval of time beyond which commercials cannot be further compressed without serious impairment of their effectiveness. In the words of Gaylord La Mond, president of Chock Full O'Nuts Coffee, "the selling effectiveness of a 10- and 20-second commercial is substantially less than a 60-second commercial." [14] Similarly, Jeno F. Paulucci, president of the Chun King Corporation, testified, "We knew that 20-second spots would be a waste of money, at that time." [15] Moreover, the cost of these shorter commercials is not lowered in proportion to the reduction in time. The result, in La Mond's words, is that, "The only prime time advertising possibilities for regional advertisers are 10- and 20-second commercials, which are ridiculously overpriced. . . . If anything, a 10-second commercial should cost one-sixth rather than 50 percent of a 60-second commercial. Likewise, a 20-second commercial should cost one-third of a 60-second commercial rather than the 90 percent cost of a 60-second. It should even be lower when we consider the diminishing selling effectiveness of the shorter commercial." [16]

Increasingly the trend has been toward merchandising the minimum effective time interval in "packages" of "spot" commercials scattered over a number of different and unrelated programs appearing at different times. As described before the Subcommittee by Robert Boslet, advertising manager of the Norwich Pharmacal Company:

> By "package" we mean an assortment of commercial minutes dispersed over a variety of programs and distributed throughout the calendar quarter. These "packages" are custom built by the networks to meet our particular specifications and needs. They must be assembled so that no competitive product commercial is positioned near to ours and most importantly so that they will deliver our selling messages to the type of viewer who we believe will be most interested in our products.
>
> The "packages" that we have been buying are referred to in the trade as "scatter plans" because they provide an advertiser only a few minutes of commercial participation in each of many programs as opposed to sponsorship, either sole or partial, in one or two programs.[17]

The nonavailability of prime time

Regardless of how it is segmented and merchandised the great bulk of the available prime time is used by a small number of very large advertisers. As Arthur

[13] *Ibid.*, p. 149.
[14] *Ibid.*, p. 199.
[15] *Ibid.*, p. 40.
[16] *Ibid.*, p. 199.
[17] *Ibid.*, pp. 66–67.

of Mercury Media put it, "As a matter of fact, in most advertising circles, certain blocks of time have nicknames: the General Foods time, the P & G segment or P & G block, and so on." [18] According to a study of commercial units during prime time on the three TV networks, there were 1,697 commercial announcements in March, 1966, of which just under one-fifth (19.86 percent) were placed by only 5 companies—Bristol-Myers (5.72 percent), Procter & Gamble (4.82 percent), General Foods (3.89 percent), American Home Products (2.71 percent) and Colgate-Palmolive (2.71 percent).[19] For the same period the study also measured the frequency of commercials in 75 markets on the "nonnetwork or spot side." It is through spot commercials placed directly with the individual station that smaller firms have their greatest access to the medium, but even here the bulk of the commercials, 68.53 percent, were placed by national advertisers and only 31.47 percent by local advertisers.[20]

The emergence of "scatter" or "participation" plans has not altered the basic nature of the problem. In the words of Hyde of the Mentholatum Company: "About this time of year [June] we go down to buy our fall advertising and they bring out a checkerboard like this, as Mr. Arthur pointed out, and every show is in there and there is a line across it for half hour or 15 minutes, and they show you what is taken. Now, you try to buy something in what is left. But, just as he said, General Foods is in there, General Motors, Procter & Gamble. These things are gone when you see them." [21]

Terming what becomes available to the regional advertiser as "distress merchandise," La Mond of Chock Full O'Nuts stated:

> The packages that are made available . . . are either distressed or low-rated packages or there are availabilities offered because of the budget or sales problem of a national advertiser. Maybe he does not have distribution and he is willing to give up a few spots. But you just cannot jump in and take it if you are going to have a well-coordinated advertising program.
>
>   *   *   *
>
> Distress merchandise or low-rated packages do become available. But they are offered to everybody in the marketplace and you either have to make a snap decision, yes or no, or by the time you check them out, maybe the availabilities are gone if you are interested in buying them.[22]

Coming up against the reality of preemption can be an unsettling experience for even the well-established, medium-size manufacturer, as was recounted by Paulucci of the Chun King Corporation, who emphasized that "advertising is essential for us, just as it is for everybody who makes consumer products. You can't live without it." [23] Recounting his effort to buy some spots on the daytime Garry Moore TV program, he testified that "the advertising agency got back to us with word that the show was all booked up. No room for us." He then changed advertising agencies: "Our new agency was a large one with a famous name, and we were told they felt they could buy the time for us." But the result was the same: "Again we spread the word to our customers, and again the agency came back to tell us the spots were not available after all." [24] Refusing

[18] *Ibid.*, p. 119.
[19] *Ibid.*, p. 209. The study was made by Broadcast Advertisers Reports.
[20] *Ibid.*
[21] *Ibid.*, p. 147.
[22] *Ibid.*, pp. 200–01.
[23] *Ibid.*, p. 39.
[24] *Ibid.*

to take "no" for an answer, he then came to New York to talk to the CBS Television Network national sales manager:

> So I was there, in short, to plead our case, hat in hand, like you did in the early days when you went to the bank to borrow money. . . . I said, "Please sell me some of that publicly owned air time."
>
> He said, "No." He was polite but firm. I told him it was hard to believe there wasn't room for us somewhere on the year's schedule. I even asked him if he wanted to be paid in advance. If so, I was ready to write out a check. To tell you the truth, I felt I was in a kind of Alice in Wonderland world where the buyer has to plead with the seller, and I really began to get angry.
>
> Finally, I was told they would give my entreaty every consideration. They would get in touch with me, the old story of "don't call us; we'll call you." Where would I be? I pointed in his outer office to his couch and said "right there." And believe me a few minutes later I was all but escorted to the elevator.
>
> We did finally get those 1-minute commercials, but this incident taught me one thing—that my dollars were not as good, in the eyes of the network, as the dollars of the larger companies. The giants are given the red carpet treatment when they want to buy time, whereas I was practically escorted to the elevator.[25]

Based on his experience in trying to secure TV time on a regional basis, La Mond testified: "We are unable to purchase 60-second announcements during prime time on the major networks because the networks obviously want to sell as easily as possible, and, therefore, they make these prime time sponsorships or participations available to the more likely national buyers." He went on to add, "The large national multiproduct advertisers control the best TV spots. They have accomplished this by hanging on to the best spots on a year-round basis."[26]

The problems encountered by Chock Full O'Nuts in the East were paralleled by the difficulties experienced by Hills Bros. Coffee in the West. According to its president, Reuben W. Hills III, "We make little use of 60-second spot television announcements in prime viewing periods because we find these spots difficult to obtain. Generally speaking, it has been our experience that prime-time 60-second commercial locations exist only in programs and are sold as part of network program purchases." Commenting on the current availabilities, he stated, "No acceptable network packages or program buys were offered to us for the 1965–66 season and, to date, nothing has been brought to our attention by our advertising agency as being worth our consideration for the 1966 67 season."[27]

Emphasizing the competitive aspect of the problem, W. K. Rivers, president of Creomulsion Company, a proprietary drug firm, stated: "We find prime time generally preempted by network programs under contracts with the giants. A number of these giants are in our field and are our competitors. Prime minute spots are simply not made available to the individual stations for spot sale to us. Whatever we are able to obtain in the way of prime time is limited to 20-second chain breaks. This is a major competitive disadvantage."[28]

[25] *Ibid.*, p. 40.
[26] *Ibid.*, pp. 198, 199.
[27] *Ibid.*, p. 58.
[28] *Ibid.*, p. 135.

After noting that the disappearance of most of the smaller local and regional breweries had coincided with the emergence of TV as the principal advertising medium, Jess Nicks, president of General Brewing Corporation, testified: "General Brewing does not purchase network television advertising because it is not normally available to us. The opportunities to buy regional portions of network time are few." In his market area the problem applied even to spots on local stations: "In San Francisco, as in most markets, it is extremely difficult to buy 1-minute spots in prime time, due to the lack of availability and the large number of 60-second advertisers. Even the independent stations are tight on efficient 60-second commercials in prime time." [29]

The preemption also extends to the more effective advertising agencies. As described to the Subcommittee by Arthur of Mercury Media:

> One of the main attractions that agencies have for many clients is the leverage they can exercise in the TV network arena. Many times accounts will shift to a new agency, not for a creative new look but rather for that agency's adroitness in negotiating with TV and other broadcast media. Naturally the agency who actively is placing large advertising dollars in the networks has the competitive edge. It brings to the negotiating table the combined weight of all its clients' dollars. The use of this leverage is somewhat limited by counterpressure from the networks. A network can kill an agency by suggesting that it doesn't know how to negotiate.
>
> Because many large advertisers have a diverse list of products—sometimes including all three brands in one category—and since in most cases they do not allow any agency to handle conflicting products, the smaller advertiser finds most of the agencies with the necessary bargaining weight for TV and radio negotiation foreclosed to him." [30]

Restrictive practices

The preemption of the desirable time by the giants has been facilitated by a number of restrictive practices on the part of the networks, among which are proscriptions against joint buying and against subcontracting of time.

The TV networks have refused to give 2 or more companies, who wish to act as a joint buyer of time, the same treatment they accord to a large multidivision corporation. From the point of view of maximizing their own profits, this policy appears to be irrational, since it restricts the number of potential buyers. From the point of view of competition, it confers an indefensible advantage on size and diversification per se. The nature of the problem was described by the head of Creomulsion:

> The sales volume and multiple products of the giants enable them to tie up year-round programs with substantial discounts based on number of announcements. In an effort to compete with such discounts we have approached stations in cooperation with other small companies requesting that we be permitted to join with such other small companies whose products required seasonal advertising adjacent to ours in order to purchase programs on a longer term basis and thus equalize to some extent the numerical advantage. We have been advised that this is not permissible since such companies do not have single ownership. This appears to us totally illogical when we and others like us are each no larger than many separate divisions, or even subdivisions of the giants. . . .[31]

[29] *Ibid.*, p. 141.
[30] *Ibid.*, p. 118.
[31] *Ibid.*, pp. 135–36.

NONPRICE COMPETITION

He went on to cite a specific example:

> We and another company in Atlanta, also small, undertook to buy 26 weeks of a particular set of availabilities in a number of stations. Their product happens to be a spring season sale product, ours happens to be winter. We were not permitted to do that. We were not permitted to be given the discount rate that somebody would be given at a 26-week rate even though we agreed to put the money in escrow. It wasn't a question of financial responsibility.[32]

Another example, cited by Hyde of the Mentholatum Company, involved a joint effort on the part of his company and the manufacturers of Clearasil (Combe Chemical): "So we would have had a television-radio budget of approximately a million and a quarter. . . . We were told we could not do it . . . because of the National Association of Broadcasters' rules, or whether it is a real law, I don't know, but I know you can't do it." To Hyde the restriction seemed utterly illogical:

> I don't see how the networks can justify—not just the networks but print media—can justify this stand. When it comes to merger, what we were told, if we owned a parent company that owned 51 percent of the controlling interest of each company, then that company, being the parent company, can go ahead and place the advertising, but none of the little ones at that time wanted to give up their right to run their own business.[33]

Because of this restriction the potential economies inherent in complementarity, whether on a seasonal or regional basis, are denied to the small firms but can be realized by the large multiproduct companies. The resultant preferential advantage to the latter was described by La Mond of Chock Full O'Nuts Coffee as follows:

> For example, in our case, much more coffee is consumed during cold weather, and we therefore cannot afford to advertise during the summer months. General Foods is "in the same boat" as far as their coffee is concerned, but they substitute an item like Jello or Kool-Aid which are warm weather items. Similarly the Coca-Cola Co. substitutes their cold drinks when it does not pay for them to advertise their coffee, and Procter & Gamble changes from coffee to one of their many other products. The fact that the large national multiple-product advertisers control the best spots by working their products in and out should be alleviated possibly by allowing control only on a one-product basis and making the spots available immediately to other advertisers when a specific product relinquishes that particular time.[34]

A second restrictive practice followed by the networks is a ban on subcontracting. If an advertiser who has entered into a contract with a network calling for commercials to be shown at specified times wishes, for any reason, to discontinue the use of the time for his products, he is not allowed to subcontract the remaining time out to some other firm. Instead, he must work out a cancellation on terms that are satisfactory to the network, which will itself find another advertiser for the unused time. Again, the question of how the practice works to the best interest of the networks is unclear. The payments for the time called for under the original contract will continue to be received, but from a

[32] *Ibid.*, p. 137.
[33] *Ibid.*, p. 148.
[34] *Ibid.*, p. 199.

second party. And if subcontracting were permitted, the networks would be relieved of the time, trouble, and expense at a late date of negotiating a cancellation with the first advertiser and of finding and working out an acceptable new contract with his replacement. If the networks were apprehensive that the subcontractor's products, as in the case of distilled liquors, should not be promoted on TV, suitable limitations as to products to be excluded from subcontracting could be incorporated in the original contract. Concern with the subcontractor's ability to pay should not be a factor, since the responsibility would still rest with the original advertiser. The only apparent purpose of this restraint is to keep control over TV advertising firmly in the hands of the networks.

Rate discrimination

When the smaller manufacturer does succeed in obtaining access to the medium, the rates he pays are apparently considerably higher than those charged his giant competitor. Up to the time of the Subcommittee's hearings in 1966 the networks set forth their charges in "rate cards" that were highly discriminatory and also extraordinarily confusing. As described by Paulucci of Chun King:

> A close reading of network rate cards in all their complexity showed that giant advertisers could, by taking advantage of all possible discounts, get up to 70% off the price of the time. I don't say they usually got that much. But I understand that 50 percent was not an unusual or uncommon figure.
> Those rate cards were incredible. There were discounts for buying shows "back to back," discounts for buying an entire 52-week schedule, discounts for this and discounts for that. What it amounted to was that anybody with lots of money to spend could buy time far cheaper than the small advertiser who didn't have that kind of money.[35]

A similar description was presented by Paul DeDomenico, vice president of Golden Grain Macaroni Company, the manufacturers of Rice-a-Roni and Noodle-Roni:

> As best we can interpret, a manufacturer could combine the purchase of nighttime programs with the purchase of daytime programs and spots and thus earn major discounts in both areas. Other discounts not available to us are frequency discounts, "continuity discounts," and to quote one network's card, "overall discounts"; "BMP" discounts, "station hour discounts"; and so forth. I have only a hazy knowledge of what they mean, but I do know that it means we are not large enough to enjoy any of them.[36]

In an interesting coincidence the networks at the time of the Subcommittee's hearings revised their rate cards, eliminating the more egregious cases of discrimination. For its daytime programs NBC issued a single rate card, showing no discrimination for the large network advertiser and making no distinction whether the advertiser bought one or 260 spots. CBS also revised its card to eliminate daytime discounts and give a maximum discount of $1,000 per minute for its nighttime programs. But according to witnesses before the Subcommittee

[35] *Ibid.*, p. 41.
[36] *Ibid.*, p. 163.

this was a change more of form than of substance. For one thing rate cards were simply irrelevant to the rates charged under the increasingly popular "scatter plans." In the words of Hyde of the Mentholatum Company, "The prices paid by competitors for advertising, that is pretty much his business, between him and the network. You do your best and he does his best. . . . But if you are buying a package which calls for 10 or 15 spots in a bunch of shows, that is not on the card and how in the world do you know what he pays for it?" [37] The same point was made in a colloquy between the Subcommittee's chief counsel and Boslet of Norwich Pharmacal, one of the early users of "scatter plans":

> MR. COHEN: What you are really saying, then is that unless you have a program you want to sell to the network, the rate card is relatively meaningless. That getting these commercial minutes and putting these scatter plans and these packages together; determining which show you are going to get it on; . . . what time you are going to get, is largely a matter of continuous negotiation between the advertiser and the network, is that correct?
>
> MR. BOSLET: In scatter plans, yes.[38]

Moreover, speaking from his past experience as vice president of advertising agencies handling the accounts of widely advertised products, Arthur testified that for the large advertiser rate cards always had been simply a "beginning point" for bargaining: "Sometimes with weaker bargaining factors, such as small, low-budget advertisers, they are adhered to and at other times they are brushed aside. Occasionally, stations and networks deliberately inflate their rate cards. If they do, almost every sale is made only after prolonged negotiation." [39] In Arthur's opinion the results of the negotiations would be rates for the very large advertisers of approximately 30 percent under the *average* of the nighttime advertisers. Referring to the cost per thousand viewers he stated that "the average of the nighttime advertiser is somewhere between $3.50 and $4.00, maybe $3.70, in that range, whereas the General Foods would pay closer to $2.50, if you would actually see what they are paying." [40]

Citing examples taken from the records of FTC cases (which, incidentally, were based on actual prices paid) and from testimony by network officials, William W. Leonard expressed considerable skepticism with the industry's claims of reform, observing that

> in the year before merger Clorox had obtained 592,020 seconds of television time, and after merger with Procter & Gamble, 803,060 seconds of television time with no change in advertising expenditures. This represented an increase of 35.6 per cent and fully justified the Commission's finding that "at least 33⅓ per cent more network television advertising" could be obtained for the same amount of money when Clorox became part of the Procter line.

> * * *
>
> Late in 1963, at about the time of the Federal Trade Commission's decision in the Procter & Gamble case, a complaint was issued against the General Foods Corporation for its acquisition of S.O.S., maker of half the steel-wool pads in the country. . . . The Commission's decision noted:

[37] *Ibid.*, p. 146.
[38] *Ibid.*, p. 69.
[39] *Ibid.*, p. 117.
[40] *Ibid.*, p. 125.

"The costs of advertising S.O.S. products were substantially reduced by reason of the discounts which were available as a result of the over-all General Foods' advertising budget, estimated to amount to a net saving of 23 per cent, or a net increase in TV time of 28 per cent in the case of network TV advertising, a 15 per cent decrease in the cost of spot-TV advertising and a range of 5–15 per cent discount in magazine advertising."

. . . A.B.C. reported a sharp contrast between prices of daytime packages purchased by Bristol Myers. Armour, and Colgate—listed among its top ten advertisers—and those bought by Helene Curtis industries, Ralston, and Charles Pfizer, all among its ten smallest advertisers. Prices per minute for these packages ranged from $1,731 to $2,390 for the large advertisers and from $2,517 to $2,919 for the small advertisers. The dates of each of the A.B.C. packages show price unrelated to the proximity to broadcast. The highest price package among those listed ($2,949 per minute) was purchased by Helene Curtis Industries five days before Colgate bought its package at $2,390 per minute.

Evidence was also presented to show that American Motors bought a package on N.B.C. costing $3.41 per 1,000 homes, while General Motors bought a package at $2.30. The General Motors figure was corrected by Don Durgin, President of N.B.C. network television, to $2.89 per 1,000 on the basis that some of the shows bought by General Motors had lesser audiences than estimated.[41]

In their testimony, officials of smaller companies were in general agreement concerning the nature and extent of the discrimination and its adverse effect on their competitive position. In the words of Ivan Combe, president of Combe Chemical Company:

Clearasil was the first of its kind, let us say, a specific over-the-counter remedy for acne. Some of these large companies, then, and very large television advertisers, did come into the field in competition with Clearasil. When they came in I recognized that whereas I was a small buyer of television, and never have bought more than $500,000 worth in a year, I was up against people who were buying multimillion dollars of television time, and were getting discounts, as is well known, which are very substantial—perhaps as much as 40 percent. This is a field, as you know, in which advertising is an important element of expense. Thirty percent of sales for consumer advertising is not unusual in this field. So it is obvious that if one is against a competitor who in making this expenditure gets a 40-percent discount, this is indeed quite a handicap and it is something to contemplate. . . .[42]

The testimony of Hyde of the Mentholatum Company was to the same effect:

We purchase on TV, radio and other advertising to run generally from October through March. Thus, in TV we earn a 26-week discount. Our two largest competitors are products of companies which have large advertising budgets, usually running 12 months a year, and, as a result, earning a 52-week discount, which generally speaking, is twice the dis-

[41] William N. Leonard, "Network Television Pricing: A Comment," *Journal of Business*, Jan., 1969, pp. 93–103. This article is a criticism of an earlier article by David M. Blank, vice president for economics and research, Columbia Broadcasting System, "Television Advertising: The Great Discount Illusion, or Tonypandy Revisited," *Journal of Business*, Jan., 1968.

[42] Senate Subcommittee on Antitrust and Monopoly, *op. cit.*, p. 105.

count that our company earns. This is certainly a competitive advantage that is extremely difficult, if not impossible, to overcome.[43]

He went on to point out that the existence of the discrimination provides a strong incentive for merger:

> I have been approached several times in the past few years by management of some of these large firms who have suggested to me that it would be to our advantage to merge our company with theirs in order to have the additional leverage that these larger advertising budgets obtain.
>
> It also was pointed out to me that our advertising buys would have more muscle, and that the additional discount that would evolve could save as much as 20 to 30 percent of our advertising dollars.[44]

The incentive to merge arising from the ability of the large firms "to tie up year-round programs with substantial discounts" was also stressed by Rivers of Creomulsion, who pointed out, "As a relatively successful small company we have been approached by large companies as to any interest in being acquired." Emphasizing their lack of any such interest, he stated, "However in such preliminary discussions it is made abundantly clear that the competitive advantages in large-scale advertising immediately would have a favorable effect on our profits either by reducing considerably our advertising expenses to do exactly what we are now doing or by enabling the purchase of many more spots for the same expenditure of dollars. This is a constant and difficult situation for our stockholders and directors to face." [45]

Summarizing the available evidence of rate discrimination Leonard concludes:

> In the conventional market, large firms occupy prime time and other parts of the schedule as a matter of priority and as a result of the high costs of the choice times and programs. In the larger participations market negotiated sales offer opportunities to the large advertisers to use their market power vis-a-vis the network, and there is ample proof (not rebutted by the networks) that this results in discriminatorily lower prices for these advertisers. Only evidence of greater access of small and regional advertisers to the network market and proof that advertisers of all sizes pay the same prices for equivalent packages of time purchased contemporaneously in the market can rebut the presumption that network pricing discriminates in favor of large advertisers.[46]

TV network advertising and concentration

In order to determine whether extensive outlays on TV advertising have in fact been accompanied by increasing concentration, a study was made of consumer goods industries before and after the medium had achieved anything like its present importance. Concentration in 1963 was compared, where possible, with 1947, when TV was in its infancy or, alternatively, with 1954, when its use was still far below the 1963 level. Specifically, the study was limited to those fields (a) in which network TV expenditures in 1963 totaled more than a quarter of a million dollars, (b) which were characterized by a significant change in con-

---

[43] *Ibid.*, p. 144.
[44] *Ibid.*, pp. 144–45.
[45] *Ibid.*, p. 136.
[46] Leonard, *op. cit.*

centration (i.e., of more than 3 percentage points), and (c) for which it was possible to obtain reasonable comparability between the Census definitions and the categories in which TV expenditures were published. The study was also limited to expenditures on the sponsorship of network programs, which had not yet been widely replaced by "scatter" or "participation" plans. The unique feature of the study is that both variables were on an unconsolidated basis, the advertising expenditures as well as the concentration ratios relating only to the specified industry. It should also be emphasized that the cutoff point ($250,000) was a minimal figure, since it covered only network TV gross time billings and excluded the very substantial additional amounts that must be spent on talent and production costs. As a further standard, the analysis was limited to fields in which a substantial share of the expenditures were made *in that industry* by what appeared to be at least one of *its* 4 leading firms. Also, whenever it appeared that the industry, as defined by the Census, encompassed several discrete product markets and comparable data were available, the narrower 5-digit product classes were utilized in place of the 4-digit industries. For example, the product class, dog and cat food, has been used instead of the more broadly defined industry, prepared feeds for animals and fowls, which also includes feed for commercial growers of livestock and poultry. Since concentration ratios were first compiled for the narrower categories in 1954, the comparisons involving product classes are from 1954 to 1963; those involving industries are from 1947 to 1963.[47]

All told, information was available for 33 industries (or product classes) meeting these standards, of which 25, or three-fourths, recorded significant in-

[47] This study was presented in a somewhat shorter form as part of the author's testimony before the Senate Subcommittee on Antitrust and Monopoly (*Hearings on Economic Concentration*, Pt. 5, pp. 1902–12). It has subsequently been critized by Jules Backman on a number of grounds (see his *Advertising and Competition*, New York University Press, 1967, pp. 96–101). His first criticism is to the effect that the study should have been limited to concentration ratios compiled on a "commodity" basis on the grounds that ratios on an "industry" basis include shipments of secondary products—i.e., products classified in other industries. Since 1954 was the first year for which concentration ratios on a commodity basis were compiled, the time span of the analysis would have been shortened to 1954–63. Such a limitation would have been inappropriate in a study whose central purpose was to compare concentration levels before and after the advent of TV; for this purpose ratios for 1947, where usable, were obviously preferable to those for 1954. Moreover, Backman did not attempt to show through the available "primary product" or "specialization" ratios that the change in any of the 33 industries' ratios of secondary products to total shipments was sufficiently important to affect significantly the change in its concentration.

Backman's second criticism is to the effect that the figure of $250,000 in gross time billings used as the cutoff point was too low. But nowhere does he acknowledge that billings for time were merely one component of total TV cost, to which must be added the very sizable outlays required for talent and production costs (see *Hearings on Economic Concentration*, Pt. 5, p. 1913). Further, Backman did not argue that TV had not become an important form of advertising in any of the industries (or product classes) included.

Finally, he holds that the selection of the fields should have been based on advertising-to-sales ratios rather than on a minimum dollar figure. But such ratios, as prepared by the Internal Revenue Service, are available only in terms of 3-digit industry groups, which are even broader than the 4-digit industries, many of which were, themselves, found to be too broadly defined for this type of study. Moreover, the use of these ratios would have had the effect of excluding certain large-scale industries in which advertising expenditures would appear to constitute an important barrier to entry. For example, the expenditures on advertising by the major automobile companies, though large in an absolute sense, are comparatively small in relation to their total sales.

NONPRICE COMPETITION

creases in concentration, while only 8 registered declines. The 25 fields of rising —and usually rapidly rising—concentration covered an exceedingly broad spectrum of consumer goods fields, embracing specific industries in such disparate major groups as foods, tobacco products, textiles, apparel, paper, publishing and printing, chemicals and allied products, fabricated-metal products, electrical machinery, transportation equipment and miscellaneous products. Moreover, the increases were impressive in magnitude. Of the 25, 17 had increases of more than 10 percentage points. With the advent of TV advertising, even fields with relatively high concentration levels in 1947 (or 1954) showed further increases by 1963. Thus, the 4 largest manufacturers in cereal preparations increased their share from 79 to 86 percent, in chewing gum from 70 to 90 percent, and in hard-surface floor coverings from 80 to 87 percent.

It will be recalled that during this period in manufacturing as a whole, increases in industry concentration were roughly matched by decreases.[48] But among these TV-advertised fields increases outweighed decreases by more than three to one.

Eight of the industries (or product classes) in which concentration rose are in food and allied products. The changes in their concentration were as follows:

4-Company Concentration Ratios

	Flour Mills	Dog and Cat Food	Cereal Preparations	Chewing Gum
1963	35%	42%	86%	90%
1954	—	32	—	—
1947	29	—	79	70
Change (% Pts.)	6	10	7	20

	Malt Liquor	Flavorings[49]	Roasted Coffee	Margarine
1963	34%	62%	54%	50%
1954	—	—	45	39
1947	21	50	—	—
Change (% Pts.)	13	12	9	11

For most of these food industries a critical bottleneck is the availability of shelf space in retail grocery stores. As has been noted, a few large multiproduct companies, each offering a number of brands of the same or closely related products, can create a demand for each, thereby literally crowding their smaller competitors off the shelves. An example is cereal preparations, in which the 4 largest producers accounted for 86 percent of the output in 1963 in comparison

---

[48] See Ch. 1.

[49] Flavorings has been included in the food group, since it includes beverage basic and soft-drink syrup. Coca-Cola Co., for example, has traditionally been a supplier of syrups to a large number of franchised local bottlers. The company's advertising is directed toward consumers in the expectation that by thereby increasing sales of the bottling companies, Coca-Cola's own sales of syrup will rise.

to 79 percent in 1947. Nearly all of the sixty-odd brands of breakfast cereals were produced by only 5 companies. Kellogg used TV network time on no fewer than twelve cereal brands, the most heavily advertised of which were Special K, Rice Krispies, and Kellogg's Corn Flakes. General Mills also offered a dozen brands, with especially heavy outlays for Cheerios, Wheaties, and Total. Among other leading advertisers were General Foods (Post Toasties, Alpha Bits, Sugar Crisp, and five other brands), Quaker Oats (Quaker and Mother Oats, Puffed Rice, Puffed Wheat, and Life), and Ralston (Ralston hot cereals, Wheat Chex, and Rice Chex). Another industry that had been highly concentrated but achieved an even higher level was chewing gum, in which the share held by the largest producers rose from 70 to 90 percent. Although there were 20 companies in the industry in 1963, only 3 were network TV advertisers: Beech-Nut, Wrigley, and Warner-Lambert (Chiclets and Dentyne).

In coffee roasting the share of the top 4 rose from 45 percent in 1954 to 54 percent in 1963 as smaller roasters disappeared from consumer markets or were acquired by larger companies primarily engaged in other industries—for example, Folger by Procter & Gamble, Martinson's by Beech-Nut, and Duncan by Coca-Cola. Moreover, the advent of instant coffee lessened the importance of conducting the roasting operation near the marketing area. Because of these and other factors the promotion of national brands has tended to supplant consumer loyalty to local and regional varieties.

The same conclusion emerges from a comparison of industries that are similar in most respects but differ greatly in their use of TV advertising. The malt liquor industry is among the nation's heaviest users of TV advertising, but through an informal agreement among TV broadcasters the use of the medium is denied to sellers of distilled liquor. The trends in concentration have been uninterruptedly in opposing directions:

4-Company Concentration Ratios

	Malt Liquors	Distilled Liquors
1963	34%	58%
1958	28	60
1954	27	64
1947	21	75
Change (% Pts.)	13	−17

Although the quantities needed to yield the desired effect differ, the nature of the demand for the products of both industries is essentially the same. In addition, both have enjoyed sizable increases in consumption; neither can be described accurately as a declining industry. In both, concentration on a company basis is well in excess of concentration on a plant basis, indicating that differences in economies of scale in production are not a determining factor. But during the period under investigation 3 of the 4 largest brewing companies were among the nation's largest users of network TV. At the time Falstaff was the industry's leading advertiser and its most rapidly growing company, followed by Schlitz and Pabst. In contrast the reports by *Advertising Age* show *no* expenditures on network TV by any of the leading companies in distilled liquors—Distillers Corporation-Seagrams, National Distillers, Schenley Industries, or Hiram Walker.

NONPRICE COMPETITION

Another example of interesting behavior in the food group is the meat-pack-ing industry. As a result of governmental inspection and grading, most of its out-put consists of undifferentiated products, which cannot be promoted effectively by TV advertising. Like distilled liquors, meat packing constitutes an exception to the general tendency toward increasing concentration among the food indus-tries.[50] And as in the case of distilled liquors, the major producers were unable to make effective use of TV advertising to combat the competitive inroads being made by smaller companies.

4-Company Concentration Ratios

	Meat Packing
1963	31%
1958	34
1954	39
1947	41
Change (% Pts.)	−10

Cigars represents an example of an industry whose structure was transformed during this period from moderately concentrated to oligopolistic. Between 1947 and 1963 the number of producers fell from 765 to 164, while the 4 largest in-creased their share of shipments from 41 to 59 percent. The 2 largest companies were large-scale users of network TV advertising in 1963. Consolidated Cigar Corporation used network TV to promote Dutch Masters, El Producto, and Muriel, three of the company's nine brands. Out of its total of eight brands, General Cigar Company also used network TV to promote three—Robert Burns, White Owl, and William Penn.

Another interesting line of comparison involves specific industries that were the *only* users of TV advertising in their respective industry groups. Such cases are represented by synthetic fabrics in textile mill products, corsets and allied garments in apparel, sanitary paper products in paper and allied products, greet-ing cards in printing and publishing, and cutlery (including razor blades) in fabricated metal products. All showed increases in concentration—and in most cases very substantial increases, as can be seen below:

4-Company Concentration Ratios

	Synthetic Fabrics	Corsets and Allied Garments	Sanitary Paper Products	Greeting Cards	Cutlery (Including Razor Blades)
1963	39%	29%	61%	57%	66%
1954	—	—	37	—	—
1947	31	16	—	39	41
Change (% Pts.)	8	13	24	18	25

[50] Of 26 food industries which remained comparable between 1947 and 1963, the con-centration ratio rose by 3 percentage points or more in 13 and declined in 7.

Manufacturers of synthetic fabrics do not supply consumers directly; nevertheless, they use TV advertising for the purpose of persuading consumers to buy apparel made of their respective fibers. With the acceptance by the TV networks of advertisements for their products, 2 manufacturers of·corsets and allied garments had by 1963 become important users of TV network time. Each was a relative newcomer to this industry—both by acquisition. Stanley Warner (Playtex) was originally in the entertainment field, while I. Rokeach (Exquisite Form) had been a kosher food manufacturer.

With respect to sanitary paper products, Kimberly-Clark (Kleenex and Delsey products) and Scott Paper, in particular, have extensively promoted by TV the sale of facial tissues, paper towels, and napkins. In the greeting-card industry two-thirds of the increase in concentration occurred between 1958 and 1963, the period in which Hallmark became one of the leading national TV advertisers, sponsoring one 60-minute and four 90-minute special programs. Hallmark's position as the only national TV advertiser in the greeting-card industry may help to explain the industry's sharp rise in concentration, despite an increase of nearly 50 percent in the number of greeting-card manufacturers.

More than three-fifths of the cutlery industry's shipments consist of razor blades and nonelectric razors. Each of the 3 leading manufacturers made extensive use of TV commercials, although Gillette's expenditures on this product were more than three times those of Philip Morris (Pal and Personna) and more than ten times those of Eversharp (Schick blades).

The toilet preparations industry is a field of intense TV-advertising rivalry; it is also an industry of rapidly rising concentration, the 4 largest firms having increased their share between 1947 and 1963 by 14 percentage points. The leading advertiser in this industry was Procter & Gamble (Crest and Gleem toothpastes, Prell and Head & Shoulders shampoos, Lilt home permanents, and Secret deodorants). In second place was Bristol-Myers (Clairol, Lady Clairol, and Miss Clairol hair products for women, Score and Vitalis hair dressings for men, Ban deodorants, Softique bath oils, and Ipana toothpaste). The third leading advertiser was Colgate-Palmolive (Colgate dental cream, Halo and Lustre Creme shampoos, Palmolive shaving cream, Wildroot hair dressing, and Soaky, a bubble bath for children). The leading razor blade manufacturer, Gillette, was also an important advertiser in toiletries (Tame Creme rinses and dandruff shampoo, Adorn hair spray, White Rain hair spray and shampoo, Sun Up after-shave lotion, Right Guard deodorants, Deep Magic skin cream, and no fewer than four home permanent brands—Bobbi, Silver Curl, Toni, and Tonette).

Unusually sharp increases in concentration took place in electrical appliances, in most of which the leading firms, though advertising appliances heavily, were primarily engaged in other industries. Later evidence is presented suggesting that during this period major appliances were being sold by large conglomerate corporations at little or no profit.[51] If so, the combination of such cross-subsidization plus extensive TV promotion should have been sufficient to ensure the result that did occur—the disappearance of most of the medium-size and small producers.

The leading TV advertisers of household refrigerators were General Motors (Frigidaire), and General Electric (GE), with small expenditures being made by Borg-Warner, Whirlpool, and Amana (acquired by Raytheon in 1965). In home and farm freezers, the leading advertisers were General Motors and Gen-

---

[51] See Ch. 14.

4-Company Concentration Ratios

	Household Refrigerators	Home and Farm Freezers	Household TV Receivers	Household Laundry Equipment
1963	76%	82%	58%	78%
1954	62	63	45	—
1947	—	—	—	40
Change (% Pts.)	14	19	13	38

eral Electric, with Amana and Whirlpool well behind. The pattern was somewhat different in home TV sets, which were not produced by General Motors. Here the leading advertisers in 1963 were RCA and Ford (Philco), with lesser outlays by General Electric and Zenith; the last is the only one of the 4 primarily engaged in this industry. Advertising of household laundry equipment, which recorded an extraordinary increase in concentration of 38 percentage points between 1947 and 1963, was dominated by General Motors and General Electric (GE and Hotpoint), with much smaller expenditures by Borg-Warner (Norge) and Ford (Philco). Only 2 companies that were primarily appliance manufacturers were among the leading network advertisers: Whirlpool (which supplies Sears) and Maytag.

General Electric's combined outlays in 1963 on network advertising for all four of the above areas were considerably less than its use of network time for "corporate image" promotion ("At General Electric Progress Is Our Most Important Product"), no doubt reflecting the company's conviction that the GE label alone is enough to sell appliances. Over the whole range of heavy appliances, General Electric spent less on behalf of GE-label products than it did for its other brand, Hotpoint, which is less closely identified with the company's image.

That changes in concentration are seldom the result of a single cause is nowhere more evident than in motor vehicles and parts. The 4 largest producers increased their share from 56 percent in 1947 to 79 percent in 1963, despite an evident growth in the number of parts manufacturers. This increase in concentration is the product of a complex of factors, including the need for large plants to secure economies of scale, the necessity of maintaining a nationwide system of distribution and repair, the tendency of trade-in values to vary directly with the company's sales, the sizable capital outlays required for frequent design and model changes, and so on.[52] Although there is no way of determining its relative importance among these multiple causes, one of the important factors would certainly appear to be advertising, both because of its entry-limiting costs and its interaction with design and model changes. Through widespread advertising the stylistic changes adopted by the leader tend to become the standard to which, regardless of utility or cost, the lesser manufacturers must conform. The promotional problems faced by a smaller car manufacturer are dramatized by the fact that in 1963 the total expenditures on network TV by American Motors were less than a quarter of General Motors' outlay on one program alone (*Bonanza*).

The remainder of the 25 fields are remarkable in their diversity, having no characteristic in common except the extensive use by their leaders of TV advertising:

[52] See *Administered Prices: Report on Automobiles.*

	Household Insecticides	Polishing Compounds	Watches and Clocks	Sporting and Other Athletic Equipment	Hard-Surface Floor Coverings
1963	36%	49%	46%	37%	87%
1954	31	37	—	—	—
1947	—	—	41	24	80
Change (% Pts.)	5	12	5	13	7

The same company appears as the leading advertiser of both household insecticides and polishing compounds. More than two-thirds of the network time used to advertise household insecticides was accounted for by S. C. Johnson (Raid), and the remainder by American Home Products (Black Flag). S. C. Johnson also accounted for the lion's share of the network time used for polishing compounds; excluding shoe polishes, Johnson's expenditures on behalf of its various brands (Carnu, Glo-Coat, J Wax, Jubilee, Klear Wax, Pledge, and Pride) were approximately three times those by American Home Products (Aerowax) and more than four times those by Simoniz (Simoniz and Vista products). With regard to shoe polish, Johnson's purchases of network time were somewhat below those of American Home Products (Griffin) but more than twice those of the other 2 substantial advertisers, Revlon (Esquire), and Kiwi Polish Company.

Watch and clock advertising on network TV has been dominated by U.S. Time Corporation (Timex watches), which in 1963 purchased more than three times as much network coverage as its closest competitor, General Time Corporation (Westclox clocks and La Salle watches). The only other network advertisers were General Electric (GE electric clocks) and Hamilton (jeweled watches), each with relatively minor outlays. The declining fortunes of the long-established American manufacturers of jeweled watches are undoubtedly due in part to the success of U.S. Time in improving the styling and quality of its products, backed up by the heaviest advertising program in the industry.

Network-advertising expenditures for sporting and athletic equipment were made by only 2 companies, Wilson and AMF. Similarly, the largest manufacturer of hard-surface floor coverings, Armstrong Cork Company, was the industry's only network TV advertiser.

In summary, these 25 fields of increasing concentration included a majority of the industries (or product classes) in foods and related products; the only industries in which such expenditures were made in textiles, apparel, paper, printing and fabricated metals; all the major household appliances; motor vehicles and parts; and a miscellany of other fields. While dissimilar in nearly every other respect, these diverse areas have in common one characteristic: the ability of their leading producers to exploit their differentiated products in a manner and on a scale simply not available to their smaller competitors.

As contrasted to the 25 with increasing concentrations, there were 8 industries meeting the standards of this study in which concentration registered significant declines. Five of these 8 were in the food group:

	Canned Milk	Dehydrated Food Products	Frozen Fruit Juices and Ades	Frozen Vegetables	Shortening and Cooking Oils
1963	66%	37%	28%	39%	51%
1954	79	—	40	52	55
1947	—	56	—	—	—
Change (% Pts.)	−13	−19	−12	−13	−4

A possible explanation for at least some of these decreases is to be found in the promotion by grocery chains of their own private-label or store-brand merchandise sold in competition with nationally advertised brands. Often given prominent display space within the store, featured as weekend "specials," and usually sold at lower prices, private brands have come to be particularly important in frozen foods. According to a survey of 113 retail chains conducted for the National Commission on Food Marketing, private-label products accounted for 50 percent of the 1964 sales of frozen fruit juices and 49 percent of frozen vegetables. In addition, private brands for these and similar products are also promoted by group wholesalers for sale through independent retail stores.[53]

While private-brand sales may also have accounted for part of the decline in canned milk (shipped by consumer-type containers), a contributing factor was a change in the Census treatment of milk-based liquid weight-control products and infant dietary suppliments (such as Mead Johnson's Metrecal and Gerber's Modilac), which had the effect of increasing the size of the universe. Largely manufactured by companies outside the concentrated-milk industry, these products were included for the first time in 1963 in the canned-milk product class, accounting for 20 percent of its total shipments.

Another conspicuous case of falling concentration was the cigarette industry, in which the share of the top 4 producers fell from 90 percent in 1947 to 80 percent in 1963. But this loss was more than compensated for by the gains of the second tier of 4, which increased their proportion from 9 to 20 percent. This second group had been especially aggressive in promoting filter-tip cigarettes under new brands—a practice that later came to be emulated by the top 4.

The other 2 heavily advertised industries in which concentration declined were pharmaceutical preparations (from 28 percent in 1947 to 22 percent in 1963) and games and toys (from 20 percent to 15 percent). The former is a classic example of an industry whose definition is so broad as to be of little use for any purpose; within "pharmaceutical preparations" are to be found a variety of classes of both prescription and over-the-counter drugs that are unusually highly concentrated and are not substitutable for one another.

On balance, it can thus be seen that not only were the decreases far outweighed by the increases but that in most cases the declines appear to have been due to unusual or explainable factors—the rise in private-brand sales of retail food products, the relative slowness of the top 4 cigarette makers in

[53] National Commission on Food Marketing, Special Studies in Food Marketing, Technical Study No. 10, *Private Label Products in Food Retailing*, 1966, pp. 20–21.

introducing the filter tip, and changes in, or the excessive breadth of, Census definitions.

What has been the trend since 1963, the terminal years of the study? Has concentration continued to rise among industries that are heavy users of TV advertising, or did the widespread increases recorded during the earlier years of TV represent an episodic occurrence that came to an end after the medium had achieved maturity? Although the same type of analysis presented for 1947–63 cannot be applied here to more recent years, some light on the issue can be shed through a "consolidated" approach in which a company's total TV-advertising outlays are not distributed among the various industries in which they are made. Specifically, *Advertising Age* publishes annual figures for more than 100 leading advertisers showing their total "media expenditures," broken down by type of medium, among which are "Net TV" and "Spot TV." From this information the specific 4-digit industries on which TV expenditures by these companies have been in excess of some minimum figure can fairly well be identified. For this purpose a minimum total figure for both "net" and "spot" TV of $5 million is used.

This approach is not without its limitations. For example, it is known that a substantial, but unknown, proportion of Gillette's advertising outlays are in toiletries. Nonetheless, its total annual TV expenditures are so large (30–40 million) that its outlays in cutlery (including razor blades) must be well in excess of $5 million. The same reasoning applies to such other industries as roasted coffee and the major household appliances. Also, it is known that the great bulk of advertising outlays of many of the other leading companies are confined to one industry—e.g., Armstrong Cork in hard-surface floor coverings, Wrigley in chewing gum, Mars in chocolate and cocoa products, Hallmark in greeting cards, RCA in radio and TV receivers, Eastman Kodak and Polaroid in photographic equipment, Kellogg and Quaker Oats in cereal preparations, National Biscuit in biscuits and crackers, General Cigar and Consolidated Cigar in cigars, Stanley Warner in corsets and allied products. And of course there is no question but that the TV outlays by their leading firms far exceeded $5 million in such industries as cigarettes, tires and inner tubes, toilet preparations, and motor vehicles and parts.

It would appear that there are some 21 industries in which annual expenditures on TV by leading advertisers, as reported in *Advertising Age,* have averaged in excess of $5 million. The industries are listed in Table 13-1, which also shows, where available, the concentration ratio for 1947. Of the 21 industries the share held by the 4 largest companies increased between 1963 and 1967 in 13, remained unchanged in 4, and declined in 4. During this short span of 4 years, increases of 2 percentage points or more were recorded in 9 of the industries, while decreases of this magnitude took place in only 2— soaps and detergents and chewing gum. There can thus be little doubt about the continuation of the upward trend in concentration among industries with high TV-advertising intensities.

Of the 12 industries for which comparable 1947 ratios are available, the 4 largest companies increased their shares in all but one—cigarettes. But what is of particular interest is the extraordinary extent of the increases. All but 2 were in excess of 10 percentage points, embracing such diverse and unrelated industries as cutlery, malt liquors, greeting-card manufacture, cigars, chewing gum, corsets and allied products, toilet preparations, and chocolate and cocoa

NONPRICE COMPETITION

Table 13-1

CHANGES IN CONCENTRATION RATIOS, 1963-1967

Industries with annual TV expenditures by leading advertisers
of more than $5 million

Industry	Concentration Ratio			Change (% Pts.)	
	1947	1963	1967	1947–67	1963–67
Greeting cards	39%	57%	67%	18	10
Radio and TV receivers	–	41	49		8
Photographic equipment	61	63	69	8	6
Malt liquors	21	34	40	19	6
Household cooking equipment	n.a.[a]	51	56		5
Cutlery (including razor blades)	41	66	69	28	3
Hard-surface floor coverings	80	87	89	9	2
Cereal preparations	79	86	88	9	2
Chocolate and cocoa products	68	75	77	9	2
Cigarettes	90	80	81	–9	1
Sanitary paper products	n.a.[a]	62	63		1
Roasted coffee	n.a.[a]	52	53		1
Corsets and allied products	16	29	30	14	1
Tires and inner tubes	n.a.[a]	70	70		—
Cookies and crackers	n.a.[a]	59	59		—
Cigars	41	59	59	18	—
Toilet preparations	24	38	38	14	—
Motor vehicles and parts	n.a.[a]	77	76		–1
Household refrigerators and freezers	n.a.[a]	74	73		–1
Soaps and detergents	n.a.[a]	72	70		–2
Chewing gum	70	90	86	16	–4

[a]Not available.
Source: Concentration ratios: Bureau of the Census, Department of Commerce, *Concentration Ratios in Manufacturing, 1967,* 1970, Pt. 1, Table 5; advertising expenditures: *Advertising Age,* Aug. 19, 1968

products. Moreover, in the remaining 2, hard-surface floor coverings and cereal preparations, the increases amounted to 9 percentage points.

Other studies

The nature of the relationship between advertising and concentration has been the subject of a number of other studies, which differ from the analysis presented above in that their concern has been with advertising in all its forms. Using questionnaires and interviews, Joe S. Bain examined the barrier to entry in 20 industries, finding that "the most important barrier to entry is probably product differentiation." This factor, he found, constituted a substantial entry barrier in 5 consumer goods industries—fountain pens, soap, liquor, cigarettes, and automobiles. And in all but automobiles, product differentiation was accompanied by a high ratio of advertising to sales. On the other hand, the ratio was low in the other 5 consumer goods industries in which Bain rated the product differentiation barriers as "negligible," "slight," or "moderate." [54] Since the study was conducted in the early 1950's, when TV was in its early days as an important advertising medium, it tends to understate the importance of advertising in creating preferences for given branded or trade-marked products.

Bain's work was followed by three other studies, all of which reported negative findings. On the basis of an analysis of advertising in 48 industries, George Stigler found that "there is no significant relationship between firm size and advertising expenditures. . . . The average ratio of advertising expenditures to sales was 1.97 percent in consumer goods and 0.57 percent in producer goods industries, but in neither group was there a significant relationship between the ratio and firm size." [55] It should be noted that the subject of his study was the relationship of advertising expenditures not to concentration but to the size of firms, which often bears little relationship to the control of output.

In a study of some 80 products Lawrence C. Murdock found "no significant correlation" between advertising-to-sales ratios and concentration ratios. He did, however, point out that, "This does not mean that advertising may not move a product along the scale toward monopoly." [56]

In a study covering three periods, 1947–48, 1954, and 1957–58, Lester Telser also found no relationship between advertising-to-sales and concentration ratios, observing that "a 1 percent increase in ratio of advertising to sales is associated with only a 0.08 percent increase in concentration. Thus, for the forty-two broadly defined consumer product industries at the three-digit level, the correlation between concentration and advertising is unimpressive." [57] But if the question at issue is defined, not as the degree to which the advertising-to-sales ratio will rise with a given increase in concentration, but whether consumer goods industries that are concentrated tend to have a higher advertising-to-sales ratio than those that are unconcentrated, Telser's data for his most recent period yield a somewhat different conclusion, as can be seen below:

4-Company Concentration Ratio, 1958	Advertising-to-Sales Ratio, 1957		
	Under .2	.2 to .4	.4 and Over
50% and over	4	4	3
25% to 50%	8	9	5
Under 25%	6	2	—

All but 2 of the 8 unconcentrated industries—i.e., those with concentration ratios of under 25 percent—had advertising-to-sales ratios of under .2; none

[54] Joe S. Bain, *Barriers to New Competition,* Harvard University Press, 1956, p. 216. He qualified his conclusion, however, by stating that "only the roughest sort of judgments can be made concerning the relation of actual sales promotion costs to the height of the product differentiation barrier to entry." (*Ibid.,* p. 202.)

[55] George J. Stigler, "The Economies of Scale," *Journal of Law and Economics,* Oct., 1958, p. 66. The rank correlation coefficients were −.187 for consumer goods and −.059 for producer goods.

[56] Lawrence C. Murdock, "Advertising and Charlie Brown," *Business Review,* Federal Reserve Bank of Philadelphia, June, 1962, pp. 3–16.

[57] Telser, *op. cit.,* p. 544. The coefficients of correlation were .16 for each of the 3 years.

had ratios of as high as .4. In contrast, 3 of the 11 industries with concentration ratios of 50 percent and over had advertising-to-sales ratios of .4 and over, while 4 had ratios of .2 to .4. If, as has been suggested by some authorities, .2 is regarded as the differentiating point between "high" and "low" advertising-to-sales ratios, three-fourths of Telser's unconcentrated industries had "low" ratios, while nearly two-thirds of his concentrated industries had "high" ratios.

Telser's study has also been criticized on the grounds that in seeking to determine the influence of advertising on concentration it is inappropriate to include in the analysis industries in which advertising expenditures are relatively unimportant. Thus, Charles Ynew Yang has pointed out,

> One of the shortcomings of Telser's test lies in his indiscriminate treatment of all consumer goods industries without due regard to possible differences in the effect advertising may have in different market structures. Apparently, this heterogeneity of market characteristics within a universe has obscured the true effect of advertising for those markets in which advertising is significant as a concentration determinant. In fact, a substantial improvement in the coefficient of the correlation between the change in advertising intensity and the change in concentration ratio is achieved when industries with a low advertising-sales ratio are excluded.[58]

The significant determinant in Yang's view is not the level of advertising but the *change* in the share of advertising expenditures made by the largest firms: "The hypothesis states that the extent to which advertising affects industrial concentration depends to a large extent on the change in the advertising of the dominant firms relative to the remaining firms in the industry." The hypothesis was tested by comparing for 20 "product-differentiated" consumer goods industries the change in the concentration of sales with the change in the concentration of advertising expenditures.[59] The period was 1948 to 1958; the measure of concentration was the share accounted for by the 4 largest companies; and the data were derived from the *Source Book* of the Internal Revenue Service, which assured comparability between the two variables—a rare feature of this type of study. The result was a "very high" correlation coefficient of .84 and a finding that a 10 percent increase in the advertising share of the 4 companies would produce approximately a 3 percent increase in their market share. Summarizing the results of his study Yang states:

> Advertising can affect concentration by creating barriers to entry and promoting intra-industry concentration. Previous statistical tests, which repudiated the significance of the relationship between advertising and concentration, have generally ignored the importance of intra-industry competition. This study points out the overwhelming strength of this factor in linking advertising and industrial concentration.

*   *   *

[58] Charles Ynew Yang, "Industrial Concentration and Advertising," Paper presented at Annual Conference of American Academy of Advertising, June, 1966 (included in *Hearings on Economic Concentration*, Pt. 5, pp. 2153–63). Using Telser's data and limiting his analysis to industries with an advertising-to-sales ratio of .2 or higher and a concentration ration of less than 50%, Yang found that the coefficents of correlation were .441 for the 1947–54 period and .468 for the 1954–58 period (*Hearings on Economic Concentration*, Pt. 5, p. 2156n).

[59] The finding was not significantly altered in a multiple-correlation analysis introducing, along with advertising intensity, variables representing industry growth and differences in market structure.

Hence, any change in the advertising share of the leading companies will produce a subsequent change in their market share and therefore in the concentration ratio. It was found that this factor is highly significant.

Since the relative advertising position of the leading companies could rise or fall, the effect of advertising on concentration through intra-industry competition could run in both directions. That is, advertising can *promote* as well as *reduce* concentration, depending on the extent and the direction of a change in the advertising intensity of the dominant firms relative to the rest of the industry. In fact, there were as many as six industries in the group where the concentration ratio declined as a result of an improvement in the advertising position of the smaller companies relative to the four leading companies.[60]

An increase in the share of advertising expenditures made by the largest firms can logically be expected to be accompanied by an increase in the concentration of sales, as Yang has demonstrated, unless one assumes that larger expenditures have *lesser* "pulling" power than smaller expenditures—the converse of the Kaldor thesis noted earlier. Even if there is no increase in the concentration of *total advertising* expenditures, the concentration of sales can be expected to rise if access to a particular advertising medium, which per dollar of expenditure has a greater "pulling power" than other media, is substantially preempted by larger firms. If the supply of such a medium is essentially fixed and cannot, as with other media, be readily expanded with an increase in demand, the greater the likelihood of its preemption by the larger firms and thus the greater the probability of an increase in the concentration of sales.

Design and model changes

Unlike TV advertising, the form of nonprice competition consisting of changes in appearance does not appear to be, in itself, a significant cause of concentration. Changes in appearance may represent quality improvements, in which case they tend to be the equivalent of price reductions. Often, they represent only changes in style designed to appeal to consumers' changing tastes and preferences. In the words of an industrial designer, Richard S. Latham, "there is nothing, to our mind, inherently wrong with the idea of style changes per se, provided it is applied where it belongs. It works quite successfully on soft goods and women's clothing, for instance, where it is recognized that people like change when it is optional, inexpensive, or just plain fun." [61] But appearance changes can become an important contributor to concentration where (a) the capital costs of making them are so formidable as to constitute a formidable barrier to entry and (b) incurring such costs is a requisite to survival. In testifying before the Senate Antitrust Subcommittee George Romney, then head of American Motors, cited the automobile industry as a field where both conditions obtain:

> The automobile business really has some aspects about it that make it similar to three businesses. One is the millinery business where fashion is such a big part of it, and the other is the perishable product business, because you have got to move the cars pretty fast or they lose their value, you see, and the other is the hard goods business where you are really building metal objects that require heavy investments in tooling and so on.

[60] *Hearings on Economic Concentration,* Pt. 5, pp. 2160–62. Emphasis in original.
[61] *Hearings on Administered Prices,* Pt. 6, p. 2791.

Now, Senator, in this millinery aspect, in the fashion aspect, a company doing 45 to 50 percent of the business can make an aspect of car appearance a necessary earmark of product acceptance by the public just as a hat manufacturer—a women's hat manufacturer—who sold 50 percent of the hats would have a much easier time of making all other hat manufacturers put cherries on their hats if the cherries were decided by it to be the fashion note for the year.

Now we have had that sort of thing in the automotive industry, and I called attention to it in my testimony. I pointed out that if one of the smaller companies had put a wraparound windshield on its car, it probably would have been a flop, but the fact that it was put on cars by a company doing as much business as the company that put it on helped to make the thing a success, because in this field of fashion, Senator, familiarity brings acceptance. Familiarity brings acceptance.[62]

In its early days the automobile industry was a ferment of technological change resulting in real quality improvement. In explaining the industry's heavy mortality, which reached 26 percent in 1910, Ralph C. Epstein pointed out that "extensive redesigning of models meant incurring heavy expenses for new dies, jigs, templates, or even new machinery." [63] The most important innovation was the change from one- and two-cylinder to four-cylinder automobiles, which involved redesigning not only the motor but other components, such as axles and transmissions. Those manufacturers who could not or would not make the necessary changes fell by the wayside.

The next stage in the industry's history saw the dominance of Henry Ford's Model T, in which change was held to an absolute minimum. In the words of Allan Nevins and Ernest Hill, "The nimble sturdy little Ford, even after the concessions of 1917–1920 to grace in design, and a further restyling in 1923, stood squarely on its reputation for utility. Nobody ever called the Model T handsome, much less beautiful; nobody ever rhapsodized over its silhouette; nobody ever praised its comfort. It could plow through bogs, surmount hills, skitter along slopes, and take stumps and rocks in its stride." [64] As such, it reflected the elder Henry Ford's impatience with the idea of "conspicuous consumption," which he strongly condemned in his own book, *My Life and Work:*

> It is considered good manufacturing practice, and not bad ethics, occasionally to change designs so that old models will become obsolete and new ones will have to be bought either because repair parts for the old cannot be had, or because the new model offers a new sales argument which can be used to persuade a customer to scrap what he has and buy something new. We have been told that this is good business, and that the object of business ought to be to get people to buy frequently, and that it is bad business to try to make anything that will last forever, because when once a man is sold he will not buy again.
>
> Our principle of business is precisely to the contrary. We cannot conceive how to serve the customer unless we make him something that, as far as we can provide, will last forever. . . . It does not please us to have the buyer's car wear out or become obsolete. We want the man who buys one of our products never to have to buy another. We never make an improvement that renders any previous model obsolete.[65]

[62] *Ibid.,* p. 2983.
[63] Ralph C. Epstein, *The Automobile Industry,* Shaw, 1928, p. 181.
[64] Allan Nevins and Ernest Hill, *Ford, Expansion and Challenge; 1915–1933,* Scribner's, 1957, p. 394.
[65] Quoted in *ibid.,* p. 412.

But Ford was virtually alone in resisting change. By the late 1920's General Motors had become the industry's style leader, principally by incorporating in its cars the improvements pioneered by others:

> Of the great recent improvements in cars it [General Motors] had produced none. An electric vaporizer in the carburetor (1919) was a contribution from the Franklin. The use of hydraulic brakes and the fitting of four-wheel brakes on stock cars (1921) was credited to the Duesenberg, a leader also in fine body design. It was the Wills-Sainte Claire which first used molybdenum steel in construction (1921). Other companies led . . . in introducing balloon tires, high pressure chassis lubrication (Alemite), and lacquer finish for bodies. Packard brought in the hypoid gear drive in 1926, and that same year Stutz introduced the use of safety glass in body construction. Henry Ford regarded the Model T (to a great extent correctly) as a marvel of utility; yet by 1926 other cars not much more expensive were so much better equipped with improved devices that they were really more useful.[66]

The effect of these and similar technological advances, including particularly the all-steel body, was to improve the quality of the vehicle; the cost of making them also contributed to the disappearance of automobile manufacturers. Of the 181 companies that actually did manufacture and sell automobiles between 1903 and 1926, 137, or over three-fourths, had retired by 1927.[67] By 1930, even before the Depression had taken its toll, such well-known companies as Stearns Knight, Locomobile, Peerless, Chandler, and Moon had disappeared.

Beginning in the late 1940's, after the Depression and the pause in automobile production during World War II, changes in the nature of the product again became an important sales factor. These changes consisted in part of true quality improvements and in part of what Ruby Turner Morris has termed "fancification," which in automobiles has been achieved through the annual model change.[68] In testifying before the Senate Antitrust Subcommittee, she stressed the unsuitability of the automobile as a "vehicle for fashion":

> The automobile is ill adjusted to be a style guide, to be subject to an annual change . . . the automotive engineers themselves must regret when perfectly good dies, capable of putting out millions of more excellent cars, have to be thrown in the dust heap as a sacrifice to the great god of fashion and change for change's sake, regardless of the importance of the new inventions that may have come along.
>
> Many a year we change models only and solely in order to have something new to promote. This is wasteful of our natural resources. I insist it is a big waste, not a little waste. . . .
>
> It is the industry which, in the active competition for sales between the oligopolistic producers, has advertised itself into a position in which each firm must, or thinks he must, make an annual model change in order to hold its position.

A similar distinction between true and apparant improvement was drawn by Richard Latham:

> Slowly techniques were refined to promote maximum customer acceptance—and to induce customers to pay money for a given product. This was called merchandising. It was bordered on the left by pricing, packaging, and promoting, and on the right with display, advertising, and com-

[66] Nevins and Hill, *op. cit.,* p. 416.
[67] Epstein, *op. cit.,* pp. 164–168.
[68] *Hearings on Administered Prices,* Pt. 6, pp. 2434–2470, testimony of Ruby Turner Morris.

NONPRICE COMPETITION

munication of all kinds. Eventually the cart began to drag the horse: merchandising ceased to be an aid to acceptance, and became an aggressive sales weapon with "newness" as its chief ammunition. Lately, to this collection of merchandising techniques has been added styling—*the introduction of some new visual element to make a whole product appear new, usually without the kind of basic change that requires major adjustments by the consumer.*[69]

To an industry leader in the position of General Motors the annual model change has been an immensely valuable competitive weapon. Accounting for more than half of the industry's sales, GM enjoys a much greater probability of acceptance and runs a far smaller risk of rejection. If more than a majority of the new cars have a new appearance characteristic, the chances are overwhelming that it will be accepted by new car purchasers as the latest and most desirable style. Moreover, the costs of making model changes are "optional fixed" costs, which, per unit of output, tend to vary inversely with volume. It is for these reasons that model changes were warmly endorsed by GM officials as merely responsive to consumers' wishes but criticized by Ford and Chrysler spokesmen as a necessary evil. Thus Theodore Yntema, vice president of Ford, testified, "When the competition comes out with a changed model, we find ourselves in trouble." He went on to say,

> In our experience we find when the model is not changed substantially, the customers do not buy it. Not only we, but our competitors, have had the same experience, and this is a very, very unfortunate thing, from our point of view.
>
> We would like to have lower tooling costs; we would like to have people buy our models, but we find we have to make these changes if we are going to get an increasing share of the business.[70]

The testimony of L. L. Colbert, president of Chrysler, was to the same effect: "if you go into the same car year after year when General Motors or Ford or both of them are changing to new cars each year, you'd pretty soon be out of business; they'd get the business." [71]

Obviously, the greater the cost of model changes, the stronger is the position of the leader and the greater the competitive disadvantage of the lesser oligopolists. A substantial part of these costs is included in the "special commercial tool accounts" regularly reported by the automobile companies. They include the cost of tools and dies ordered for the production of a particular model line. With a change in model they become useless except in providing replacement parts. Since their useful life is deliberately limited, they are amortized as production costs over the model run for which they are acquired. They do not of course include other costs involved in making model changes, such as the actual expenses of installation or of styling and engineering, which are carried in general overhead. As can be seen from Table 13–2, the amortization of special tools and equipment for General Motors, Ford, and Chrysler combined rose from $104.6 million in 1947 to $584.2 million in 1956 and to $1,359 million in 1966. Between 1950–52 and 1964–66 it increased sixfold—from an annual average of approximately $200 million to $1.2 billion. It would be instructive to ascertain the extent to which the lower profit rates of Ford and Chrysler (as compared to General Motors) and the recurrent financial difficulties of Chrysler are traceable to the costs of style followership.

[69] *Ibid.*, p. 2791. Emphasis added.
[70] *Hearings on Administered Prices*, Pt. 6, p. 2657.
[71] *Ibid.*, p. 2828.

Table 13-2

GENERAL MOTORS, FORD, AND CHRYSLER
Combined amortization of special tools and equipment, 1950–66,
in millions of dollars

Amount		Amount		Amount	
1947	104.6	1954	421.0	1961	739.8
1948	147.3	1955	644.6	1962	764.1
1949	210.1	1956	584.2	1963	988.1
1950	182.3	1957	763.0	1964	921.7
1951	246.6	1958	729.1	1965	1,169.5
1952	260.1	1959	694.2	1966	1,359.0
1953	476.8	1960	867.4		

Source: Hearings on Economic Concentration, Pt. 6, Table 2

That model changes have been a formidable barrier to entry and have worked to the advantage of the leader in the automobile industry seems a virtual certainty; that they have had anything like a comparable effect in other industries is far less sure. Certainly, the skilled purchasing agents of the large buyers who place most of the orders for producer goods are not likely to be diverted from their preoccupation with price and quality by considerations of style and appearance. And in consumer nondurable goods the cost of making appearance changes is minimal and the barrier to entry that it represents unimportant. Even in consumer durable goods the cost may be moderate or consumers resistant. An example of the latter situation was cited by Latham, who contrasted style changes in automobiles and refrigerators. Despite the most intensive promotion of new models, efforts by refrigerator manufacturers to shorten the time span between style changes had run up against an impenetrable wall of consumer resistance: "statistics show that people want a new one every 12 years." [72] Leonard W. Weiss found that although 48 of a sample of 83 industries showed decreases in their concentration ratios between 1947 and 1958, 7 of the 9 consumer durables included in the sample recorded increases.[73] But in most of the 7, other centripetal forces were also at work—e.g., mergers, cross-subsidization, and TV advertising. If these other factors were restrained, it is quite possible that the pervasive upward trend of concentration in consumer durable goods (excluding automobiles) would come to an end.

[72] *Ibid.*, p. 3146.
[73] *Hearings on Economic Concentration*, Pt. 2, p. 734.

NONPRICE COMPETITION

PREDATION

In this work the question at issue concerning "predation" also referred to as "predatory" practices, "discriminatory" practices, or "monopolistic" practices, is whether it contributes to economic concentration—i.e., whether it operates as a centripetal force. This relates to, but is not the same as, the question of whether predatory practices tend to lessen or promote competition and are thus injurious or beneficial to consumers. As will be evident later, such practices can conceivably promote concentration and at the same time stimulate competition; they can work against the interests of smaller firms and at the same time serve to benefit consumers. During the last quarter of a century the net effect of predation on competition has become the subject of a voluminous and intense economic and legal controversy. Even if one were to reach the conclusion that, on balance, competition tends to be benefited, it would still be possible to conclude that any benefits to competition are short-term and would be outweighed by long-run injury resulting from the promotion of concentration.

Before getting to the questions of effects on competition and on concentration, there is a prior question that must be examined: whether predatory practices exist at all—at least above a *de minimis* level.

The existence of predatory practices

The idea that predatory practices are something of a rarity is of fairly recent vintage, traceable only to readings of the *A&P* case by M. A. Adelman and of the "old" *Standard Oil* case by John S. McGee. It is these readings that constitute the "impressive body of literature" cited in a report prepared for President Nixon under the direction of George J. Stigler as evidence in support of "the improbability that a profit-maximizing seller, even one with monopoly power, would or could use below-cost selling to monopolize additional markets." [1] These readings also serve as a basis for the assertion by Donald F. Turner that "few or no verifiable examples" of predatory pricing have come to light.[2] Those who cite these readings frequently overlook the fact that completely contrary conclusions were drawn by Joel B. Dirlam and Alfred E. Kahn from their reading of the *A&P* case[3] and by Samuel M. Loescher from his reading of the old *Standard Oil* case. With respect to the latter Loescher writes:

[1] *American Trade Regulation Review*, June 10, 1969.
[2] Donald F. Turner, "Conglomerate Mergers and Section 7 of the Clayton Act," *Harvard Law Review*, May, 1965, p. 1344.
[3] Joel B. Dirlam and Alfred E. Kahn, *Fair Competition; the Law and Economics of Antitrust Policy*, Cornell University Press, 1954, pp. 211–41; "Antitrust Law and the Big Buyer: Another Look at the A & P Case," *Journal of Political Economy*, April, 1952.

Combination-by-merger was the central issue (especially the ultimate conglomerate-type mergers of 1899), not unfair competition. To the extent that "unfair competition" was an issue (designed both to bolster the inferences of intent to restrain trade and to perpetuate the effectiveness of this restraint), possession and application of power to generate differential transportation cost advantages constituted the principal forces of the exclusionary charges. The charges of localized sharpshooting discrimination constituted but a subsidiary, though non-trivial, element in the charge of unfair competition.

A reinterpretation of conglomerate-type "deep pocket" power suggests that Standard Oil possessed an incentive to employ such tactics—not to bankrupt rivals—but to contain the expansion of rival sales, by limiting access to local markets—characterized by relatively substantial economies of scale for bulk station and tank distribution. Both the record and later-undertaken historical studies show that the Standard Oil Combination did employ (and sometimes dramatically) some discriminatory sharpshooting practices. That the record is not loaded substantially more heavily with a compilation of such practices (not to mention Standard documents explaining purpose and intention) may be attributed primarily to: (1) the major thrust of charge—combination into a holding company to restrain potential competition, (2) the aged character of many incidents, and (3) an inability of government to make an unrestricted file search, and to make more than modestly successful use of its subpoena powers, in a civil action conducted before a Special Examiner.[4]

In testimony before the Senate Subcommittee on Antitrust and Monopoly, Robert C. Brooks questioned the propriety of accepting as proof of the non-existence of a general practice the reading of a particular case by one authority, particularly when other authorities on reading the case have reached the opposite conclusion:

Now, my general statement includes a consideration of a theory that I feel is too easily accepted by many who have not investigated the facts themselves. This arises when someone who does not really believe that predatory price cutting exists decides that he will go through the records of a case where it was charged, and he can generally find another explanation for everything that happens according to that record.

Then, having found "no evidence" of such price discrimination, he makes the statement that again predatory price discrimination does not exist and "the record of the case shows no evidence of such price discrimination."

Now, it bothers me that this is accepted as conclusive by some people who have similar biases in that direction and it is not challenged by others.

In judging evidence and records of cases, an unprejudiced viewpoint would be desirable, but if the investigator thinks that a policy of predation does not even make sense, he is hardly likely to find any evidence of it in the record of a case. But those, on the other hand, who think that predatory price discrimination is possible would be equally biased if they thought that such price discrimination always occurred, but I have not run across anybody that thinks this type of price discrimination is

[4] Samuel M. Loescher, "A Sherman Act Precedent for the Application of Antitrust Legislation to Conglomerate Mergers," *Essays in Honor of Edward S. Mason*, Houghton Mifflin, 1970.

the order of the day, and so, on the extremes, we have only this one viewpoint represented—that it could not possibly exist.[5]

Even if the authorities were in agreement, deriving conclusions from a few Sherman Act cases is a singularly inappropriate methodology. It is inappropriate because the principal legislative bases for acting against predatory practices are the Clayton Act and the Federal Trade Commission Act, not the Sherman Act. Whereas the sole responsibility for proceeding against monopoly and the primary responsibility for proceeding against conspiracy and collusion have come to rest with the Department of Justice, the primary responsibility for proceeding against predatory practices resides by law and custom with the Federal Trade Commission. Between the time of its establishment in 1914 and mid-1970, the Federal Trade Commission had issued over thirteen hundred cease and desist orders against unfair methods of competition, price discrimination, and other predatory practices. This is exclusive of its orders against mergers and interlocking directorates. It is also exclusive of nearly a hundred orders against collusion, many of which have involved the concerted use of predatory practices. Any attempt to determine the incidence of predatory practices should begin with this vast repository of case work, which in turn represents, at most, only the visible part of the iceberg. To this evidence can be added a considerable body of references in academic literature.[6] This, not a few readings of a differ-

---

[5] 91st Cong., 1st Sess., Senate Subcommittee on Antitrust and Monopoly, Senate Committee on the Judiciary, *Hearings on S. 1494,* "Price Discrimination Legislation—1969," 1970, pp. 140–41.

[6] References in academic literature to predatory practices in specific industries, compiled by Brooks (Senate Subcommittee on Antitrust and Monopoly, *op. cit.,* pp. 157–58), include: Gunpowder: William S. Stevens, "The Powder Trust, 1872–1912," *Quarterly Journal of Economics,* 26, 1912, pp. 444–81; also his *Industrial Combinations and Trusts,* 1922, pp. 333–39; George W. Stocking, *Workable Competition and Antitrust Policy,* 1961, extended note, pp. 320–21, from an article originally appearing in the *Virginia Law Review,* 44, 1958, pp. 1–40. Tobacco: William H. Nicholls, *Price Policies in the Cigarette Industry,* 1951, p. 26. Building products: Corwin D. Edwards, *Maintaining Competition,* 1949, pp. 169–70. Pectin: Almarin Phillips, "Price Discrimination and the Large Firm," *Virginia Law Review,* 43, 1957, pp. 685–96, especially regarding the dissent of Commissioner Mead. Bakery products: cited by Jerrold G. Van Cise, *The Federal Antitrust Laws,* 1965, p. 50. Chicory (*E. B. Muller* v. *Federal Trade Commission*): Robert C. Brooks, Jr., "Businessmen's Concepts of Injury to Competition," *California Management Review,* 3, 1961, pp. 89–101; *Antitrust Bulletin,* 6, 1961, pp. 569–90; Lee E. Preston, ed., *Social Issues in Marketing,* 1968, pp. 168–79. The *Muller* case, as well as other examples of predatory pricing, is cited by the *Attorney General's National Committee to Study the Antitrust Laws,* 1955, pp. 165–66. Examples of predatory pricing subsequent to this 1955 report appear in a supplement to the report prepared by the Section on Antitrust Law of the American Bar Association. These recent examples include woodenware (*Forster Manufacturing Co.* v. *Federal Trade Commission*), roofing materials (*Voluseo Products Co.* v. *Lloyd A. Fry Roofing Co.*), and other cases cited in *Antitrust Developments, 1955–1968,* 1968, pp. 128–31.

For testimony by economists on price discrimination before congressional committees, see: 84th Cong., 1st Sess., House Select Committee on Small Business, *Hearings on Price Discrimination,* 1955, Walter Adams, Vol. II, p. 615; Joel B. Dirlam, Vol. II, p. 785; Corwin D. Edwards, Vol. I, pp. 111, 124; Leo Fishman, Vol. II, p. 667; Horace M. Gray, Vol. II, p. 657; Vernon A. Mund, Vol. II, p. 639; Almarin Phillips, Vol. II, p. 692; Irwin M. Stelzer, Vol. II, p. 937; Holbrook Working, Vol. II, p. 630. 84th Cong., 1st Sess., Senate Subcommittee on Antitrust and Monopoly, Senate Committee on the Judiciary, *Hearings on Distribution Practices,* 1955, Walter Adams, p. 1003; Joel B. Dirlam, p. 955; Richard B. Heflebower, p. 980; Jesse W. Markham, p. 929. 84th Cong., 1st Sess., House Antitrust Subcommittee, House Committee on the Judiciary, *Hearings on Current Antitrust Problems,* 1955, Walter Adams, p. 290. 84th Cong., 2nd Sess., Senate Subcommittee on Antitrust and Monopoly, Senate Committee on the Judiciary, *Hearings on S. 11,* "To Amend Section 2 of the Clayton Act," 1956, John S. McGee, p. 567.

ent type of case brought under a different statute by a different agency, should constitute the basis for the proper evaluation of the importance of predatory practices.

Price discrimination

The controversy over the effect of predatory practices on competition has revolved largely around price discrimination. In its defense the argument has been made that objections to price discrimination derived from economic theory have little relevance to the real world since theory itself is an artificial construct based on arbitrary and unreal assumptions. Carried to its logical conclusion this argument would simply reject as irrelevant the whole body of economic theory, something few economists would be prepared to do. That economic theory has little relevance to industries in which its underlying assumptions are simply not present almost goes without saying. But where its assumptions are present, behavior in the real world has been found to be remarkably similar to the behavior expected from theory. And in the intermediate area—i.e., where the underlying assumptions are neither wholly absent nor wholly present—theory can still provide a useful clue to expected behavior. As Holbrook Working has pointed out:

> Consider why the theory of perfect competition was constructed. Its purpose was to analyze the effects of competition under conditions which are somewhat artificially simplified for purposes of analysis, but which were supposed to fairly well approximate actual or attainable conditions in a considerable part of the economy. The results of this analysis were to show that competition of the sort considered had desirable results. Among those results that were considered desirable are some that depend directly on the absence of price discrimination. The belief that price discrimination tends to be objectionable runs as a thread through all the history of economic thought on the effects of competition. Any implication that economists have held only that price discrimination was objectionable under the peculiar and special conditions of perfect competition, and under those conditions only, is untrue.
>
> If long-standing beliefs regarding the effects of price discrimination deserve to carry weight, then there is a burden of proof on those who would argue that price discrimination is harmless under particular conditions.[7]

It has also been contended that price discriminations tend to "erode" into general price cuts. Control over markets by oligopolists, it is held, can be and frequently is broken by the power of oligopsonists, such as chain stores, mail order houses, and other large buyers. The imperfections in the market on the selling side are said to be thus offset by imperfections on the buying side—a case of "countervailing power," to use J. Kenneth Galbraith's term. The big buyer demands of the big seller a special price concession, letting it be known that unless the discount is forthcoming he will give his business to someone else, put his own private brand on the market, or even construct his own facilities and make the product himself. Confronted with these alternatives and wishing to secure the large market represented by the big buyers' operations,

---

[7] 84th Cong., 1st Sess., House Select Committee on Small Business, *Hearings,* 1955, Pt. 2, p. 631.

PREDATION

the big seller accedes and grants the concession. In order not to offend his other customers who are in competition with the big buyer, he makes the concession secretly. But secrecy in matters of this kind is hard to maintain. Word of the concession, it is held, gets out to the other buyers, who one by one come to demand equal treatment. Soon the seller finds that he is making the concession to so many of his customers that he ends all pretense of secrecy and transforms his selective price concession into a general price reduction. Thus, it is argued, what had begun as a discriminatory price available to one buyer gradually "erodes" into a general price reduction available to all. Had it not been for the right of the big seller to make that initial price discrimination, the general price reduction would never have taken place, and the consumer would have been deprived of the benefit of the lower price. In this way the right to secure price discriminations helps to break down rigid price structures.

For all its plausibility, which is considerable, the erosion theory has not yet found support in any organized body of data. Indeed its proponents appear to have difficulty even in citing case examples in its support. Appearing before the Senate Antitrust Subcommittee to present the results of his research into the *Standard Oil of Indiana* case,[8] John S. McGee was interrogated by the Subcommittee counsel, Joseph Seeley:

> MR. SEELEY: First, I must say at the outset I understood your thesis with respect to price discrimination is that it is a good thing, that it results in general price cuts; is that correct. . . . You think that is oversimplified, but that is the gist of your position?
>
> MR. MC GEE: I think that is right.
>
> MR. SEELEY: Do you favor aggressive price discrimination?
>
> MR. MC GEE: As an economist I think it would contribute more to an effective competitive society than it would detract.
>
> MR. SEELEY: Well, Mr. Chaffetz [Counsel for Standard] made the statement that the prices were fluctuating frequently and continuously, and I asked Mr. Ross [official of Standard] if he could give us any instance, and he could not give any instance off-hand of a single price reduction since 1951.
>
> Now, they have promised to submit some information on that for the record. But I ask you what you know about this, what you can tell us.
>
> MR. MC GEE: Well, I cannot really tell you very much about it.
>
> MR. SEELEY: Mr. McGee, can you, as an economist, cite a case where the result of obtaining one or more price concessions by favored buyers has been a general price cut?
>
> MR. MC GEE: Well, put it this way: I think the apparatus or the structure of a market which produces a price cut.
>
> MR. SEELEY: I would like to have you answer that question specifically. You surely should be able to give us one case.
>
> MR. MC GEE: I am not sure that I should.[9]

The erosion argument has been questioned by Joel B. Dirlam and Alfred E. Kahn in their analysis of the *A&P* case:

[8] John S. McGee, "Price Discrimination and Competitive Effects: Standard Oil of Indiana Case," *University of Chicago Law Review,* Spring, 1956.

[9] 84th Cong., 2nd Sess., Senate Subcommittee on Antitrust and Monopoly, Senate Committee on the Judiciary, *Hearings on S. 11,* "To Amend Section 2 of the Clayton Act," 1956, pp. 608, 609, 614.

It was A & P's systematic attempt to force suppliers to discriminate in its favor which constituted the essential element in the government's case. Setting aside the possible cost justifications of such discounts, what support does the evidence provide for the theory that coercive bargaining of this sort may force suppliers' prices down closer to the purely competitive level?

The record of the case discloses few significant examples of A & P's buying policy exerting any influence on prices of groceries supplied under seriously monopolistic conditions. The soap companies apparently refused to grant special concessions, no matter how much pressure was applied. From Quaker Oats and Ralston, two large cereal manufacturers, A & P received concessions not available to its competitors, but these were on trading items only, list prices of branded products were probably not affected by these discounts or by the private-brand competition which they made possible. A & P apparently never bothered to bargain for special concessions on evaporated milk. Patent control on processed cheese for a long period deprived it of a vital bargaining weapon—the threat to manufacture itself.[10]

Data gathered by the Senate Antitrust Subcommittee relating to purchases of meat by chain stores provide a further basis for questioning the erosion theory and thus tend to support the negative findings of Dirlam and Kahn. The meat-packing industry is made up of a few large firms, principally Swift, Armour, and Wilson, a number of medium-size firms, especially in pork packing, and a large number of small firms. In retailing, the national chain stores with annual sales of hundreds of millions of dollars compete with smaller regional chains and independently owned grocery stores for the consumer's meat dollar. The question at issue here is what proportion of their requirements the large chain stores, as contrasted to smaller chains, obtain from the large meat packers.[11] In analyzing the data, the sample was divided into two parts, chains with sales in excess of $100 million annually and chains with sales below that amount. Six firms fell in each size class. For each firm, purchases of beef, veal, lamb, and pork were analyzed to determine the proportion of chain store purchases made in the aggregate from Swift, Armour, and Wilson. A simple average of the six chain store percentages was then taken.

**Proportion of Chain Store Meat
Purchased from Swift, Armour, and Wilson, 1956**
(U.S. Average)

Annual Sales of Chain Stores	Beef	Veal	Lamb	Pork
Greater than $100 million	43.5%	29.4%	63.7%	29.6%
Less than $100 million	52.5	54.1	70.7	30.3

[10] Joel B. Dirlam and Alfred E. Kahn, "Antitrust Law and the Big Buyer: Another Look at the A & P Case," *Journal of Political Economy,* April, 1952, pp. 127, 128.

[11] A questionnaire was sent to a sample number of food chain stores concerning their meat-buying practices. The chains chosen represented a fairly adequate cross-section of the industry by size and geographical distribution. An attempt was made to secure a large and a small chain food store in each geographic area. The questionnaire consisted of two parts, A and B. Part A referred to the overall operations of the firm and its meat-packing operations if any. Part B was to be filed for each meat-buying unit of the organization. Thus, where buying was decentralized, separate reports were to be submitted. Of the reports received by the Subcommittee, a limited number were answered satisfactorily. Twelve firms, with sales ranging from $20 million to almost $2 billion annually, supplied data concerning firms from which meat was purchased. In the case of the larger firms, more than one meat-buying report was supplied in some instances.

In each case the large chain group purchased relatively *less* from the major packers than their smaller counterparts. Only in pork (which is characterized by a much larger number of small packers than the other types of meat) were the proportions about the same.

On the basis of the limited data available, it was possible to make several geographic comparisons. Meat buying by the largest chain in the sample (one of the nation's largest chains) is decentralized, and it was therefore possible to make area comparisons between this firm and its smaller competitors. Again the general showing, as can be seen in Table 14-1, is that the large chain store and the large meat packer tend to bypass each other. In the Missouri-Iowa-Illinois area the large chain purchased relatively less than the small chain from the major meat packers for 3 of the 4 products. The relatively large number of packers dealing in pork, which were available as sources of supply to the small chain, may account for the exception. Of the 3 products for which comparable data are available in Texas, the large chain purchased relatively less from the large meat packer than the small chain in 2. In the Washington-Maryland-Virginia area the pattern was consistent; the large chain secured a lesser proportion of its requirements from the major packers on each product. In Los Angeles, among the products for which comparisons can be made, only pork is an exception.

In the Pennsylvania-New Jersey area, no small chain supplied data. However, one medium-size chain can be compared with another chain that was excluded from the sample because of failure to provide a breakdown of its purchases. This latter firm, more than three times the size of the medium-size chain in annual sales, purchased only 11 percent of its total meat supplies from the major packers, whereas the smaller firm in this same area purchased 36 per-

Table 14-1

PROPORTION OF CHAIN STORE MEAT
PURCHASED FROM SWIFT, ARMOUR, AND WILSON, 1956

Selected areas

Missouri, Iowa, Illinois	Beef	Veal	Lamb	Pork
Large chain	18%	29%	57%	64%
Small chain	80	90	92	7
Texas				
Large chain	15	50	60	9
Small chain	50	40	n.a.[a]	34
District of Columbia, Maryland, Virginia				
Large chain	3	12	48	6
Small chain	98	91	80	27
Los Angeles				
Large chain	6	n.a.[a]	28	46
Small chain	24	—	97	38

[a]Not available.

Source: 85th Cong., 1st Sess., Senate Subcommittee on Antitrust and Monopoly, Senate Committee on the Judiciary, *Hearings on S. 11*, "To Amend Section 2 of the Clayton Act," 1957, Pt. 2, pp. 1179 80

cent of its entire meat requirements from these same large packers. New England represents the consistent exception to the rule. There the one small chain in the sample purchased relatively less from the major packers than did the competing large chains.

These showings, plus the findings of Dirlam and Kahn, give rise to a hypothesis somewhat different from the erosion theory but with plausible elements of its own—i.e., that the large buyer, instead of locking horns with the large seller and thus immobolizing his monopsonistic power, will seek to avoid the large seller and fulfill his requirements from smaller sellers who lack the monopoly power with which to resist him. Similarly, the large seller will, if possible, seek to dispose of his output through small buyers who are not in as good a position to extract price concessions from him. To be sure, in the real world large sellers and large buyers do encounter each other, but they will seek if possible to bypass each other, using their monopoly power where it will be of greatest strategic value.[12]

For the sake of argument, however, let it be assumed that the large buyer and the large seller do "butt heads," as it were, and that the large buyer is able to secure a special price concession. Does this concession actually spread to other buyers? To what extent does the erosion proceed? Does it invariably, or even usually, reach the point of a general price cut? Or does it stop after only a few buyers have been granted the advantages of discrimination? Or, perhaps, does it fail to spread at all? These are pivotal elements in the erosion theory on which its proponents have provided little enlightenment.

If the large producer is permitted to make selected concessions even below the small firm's price, or if it is permitted to meet a "general competitive situation" rather than a specific price, the efficient small producer will have little opportunity indeed to inject price competition into an oligopolistic industry. His opportunity will be only slightly greater if, as is currently true under the *Standard Oil of Indiana* decision, the large firm is permitted to meet, though not beat, the small firm's price.[13] Let it be assumed that a smaller producer endeavors to pry away a customer from a large firm by offering a lower price, which, as is generally the case with small enterprises, is assumed to be a nondiscriminatory or "lawful" price. Under the *Standard Oil of Indiana* decision, that competitive move by the smaller producer can be met by a defensive discriminatory action on the part of the large concern. It can be met because under that decision price discriminations can be made in good faith to meet the "lawful" price of a competitor. Ironically the very act of the small producer in offering the lower nondiscriminatory (lawful) price thus legitimizes a discriminatory attack upon him which, assuming the other tests of the law could be met, would otherwise be unlawful. The large producer can maintain his price to all other customers while lowering it only to the customers sought by the small producer. And there is no limit on the extent to which the large producer can continue to cut his price to those particular customers as long as he keeps meeting the lower price offers of the smaller producer. The *Standard Oil of Indiana* decision must therefore appear to the large producer as a heaven-sent instrument for putting out competitive fires touched off by his smaller rivals.

Since the smaller producer must realize that no matter how low a price he

---

[12] Dirlam and Kahn, *op. cit.,* pp. 127–28.
[13] For a discussion of the *Standard Oil of Indiana* decision see Ch. 22.

may offer the large producer is permitted to match it with a discriminatory price, the question then arises as to what incentive there is for the small producer to offer the lower price in the first place. The small producer must realize that his large rival generally has an advantage in such matters as advertising, sales effort, brand names, trademarks, and other forms of nonprice competition. He must therefore realize also that if prices are equal, the buyer will generally be predisposed to give his business to the large firm. Consequently, being unable to offer the nonprice advantages of the large producer, and realizing that under the present interpretation of the law any price offer that he makes can be matched through price discrimination, why should the small seller bother about trying to be competitive in the first place? Will not his inclination be simply to give up any ideas of independent price action, charge the oligopoly price, and take whatever portion of the industry's business happens to come his way? How many times does a small producer in his struggle to obtain customers have to lose out to a discriminatory counteroffer by a large producer before he realizes the futility of it all? And if these considerations operate against the established small producer, will they not operate with even greater force against the potential newcomer—the enterpriser who is merely contemplating entrance? To the extent that this analysis of the small producer's reaction is correct, the present state of the law, which permits a considerable measure of price discrimination, may be seen to make for greater, not less, price rigidity. It has the effect of drying up the principal wellspring of price competition in oligopolistic industries and of making prices in such industries more rigid than they would otherwise be.

Primary-line discrimination

Price discrimination can take place at either the primary line or the secondary line of the seller. It is "primary-line discrimination" if the injury resulting from the discrimination is to *competitors* of the firm making the discrimination. It is "secondary-line discrimination" if the injury resulting from the discrimination is to certain *customers* of the firm making the discrimination. Discrimination at the primary line can in turn be broken down between those that do and those that do not involve geographic differentials—i.e., sales by a producer at prices higher in some market areas than in others. While the former appear to be more prevalent, competition among rival sellers may still be injured even though no geographic differentials are involved—e.g., where a leading firm sells the same product at a high price under a well-known trademark and at a lower price under a private brand.

When the prices paid by buyers at different locations vary from the sum of the price at the plant plus transportation charges, the result is geographic (or "spatial") price discrimination. It may take a variety of forms, principal among which are the charging of lower prices to distant buyers on routes served out of a given plant and the discriminations inherent in the operation of a basing-point or similar delivered-price system. The former can be illustrated by the pricing policies of the major bread-baking companies, the latter by the operation of the basing-point system in the steel industry.

On the basis of price information obtained by the Senate Antitrust Subcommittee from the bread industry's 3 leading producers as of September 1, 1958, it was possible to construct a series of charts showing the differences

Figure 14-1

PRIMARY-LINE PRICE DISCRIMINATION IN THE BREAD INDUSTRY

Continental Baking Company, Columbus, Ohio

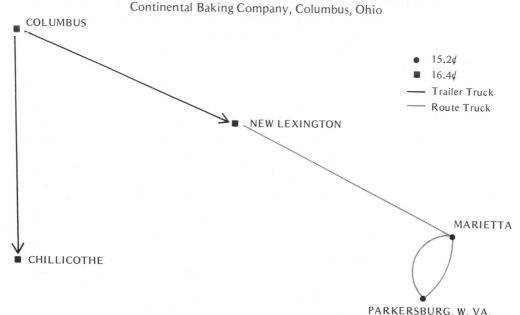

Source: *Hearings on Administered Prices*, Pt. 12, Chart 5

between prices at the plant where the bread was baked and prices in areas served by trucks operating out of such plants.[14] As a rule, bread is transported to outlying areas in large truck trailers and deposited at loading stations, where it is transferred to smaller trucks, which in turn deliver it to local communities. In the movement from baking plant to loading station to retail outlet, price discrimination may be practiced at one or more points of delivery. A local baker in a given community is being discriminated against if the sum of the large baker's plant price plus transportation cost to the community is greater than the price charged there by the large baker. But the discrimination assumes its most striking form when the price charged in a distant local community is *lower* than that charged at the plant. As was brought out in the Subcommittee's hearings, this pricing practice is engaged in widely by the leading wholesale bakers. What follows are examples of the practice as described before the Subcommittee by its chief economist; the first concerns prices charged out of the Columbus, Ohio, plant by the nation's largest bread manufacturer, Continental Baking Company (see Figure 14-1; the solid line represents transportation to loading stations, the dashed, from loading stations to retailers).[15] In appraising these illustrations, one should bear in mind that at the time of the survey the added transportation cost of transporting bread into outlying areas amounted to .5 cents per 50 miles.

> MR. BLAIR: A simple example . . . is provided by the . . . distribution of bread by Continental Baking Co. out of its Columbus, Ohio, plant. At Columbus, Continental sells the bread at 16.4 cents a pound.

[14] See *Administered Prices: Report on Bread*, pp. 38–63.
[15] *Hearings on Administered Prices*, Pt. 12, pp. 6159–69.

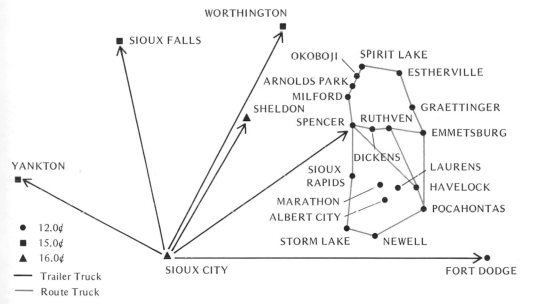

Figure 14-2

PRIMARY-LINE PRICE DISCRIMINATION IN THE BREAD INDUSTRY
Continental Baking Company, Sioux City, Iowa

Source: *Hearings on Administered Prices*, Pt. 12, Chart 7

The big truck trailer then carries the bread to New Lexington, which is a distance of 55 miles. There the bread is then transferred into route trucks.

At New Lexington the price is also 16.4 cents. One of those route trucks goes all the way into West Virginia. It goes to Marietta from New Lexington, a distance of 59 miles, and then from Marietta down to Parkersburg, a distance of 14 miles, making a distance of over 120 miles from where it is baked.

The interesting fact about the showing is that at Parkersburg the bread is sold at a lower price than where it is made in Columbus. It is sold at 15.2 cents, as contrasted to 16.4 cents at Columbus.

MR. DIXON:[16] And handled twice?

MR. BLAIR: Yes, sir, and handled twice. And of course, both the delivery truck and the truck trailer then have to deadhead it back to their respective destinations empty. The costs of such distribution of course are probably not insignificant.

Similar discriminatory pricing practices were engaged in by Continental in its Iowa plants, as Figure 14-2 and the following account bring out:

MR. BLAIR: At Sioux City Continental bakes bread in its plant there and sells at 16 cents a pound.

It then distributes that bread to several points where it is sold at 1 cent below the price at Sioux City. . . . Bread is also transported 125 miles to Fort Dodge where it is sold at 12 cents, or no less than 4 cents less than where it is produced in Sioux City.

[16] Paul Rand Dixon, chief counsel of the Subcommittee on Antitrust and Monopoly.

Figure 14-3

PRIMARY-LINE PRICE DISCRIMINATION IN THE BREAD INDUSTRY
General Baking Company, Philadelphia

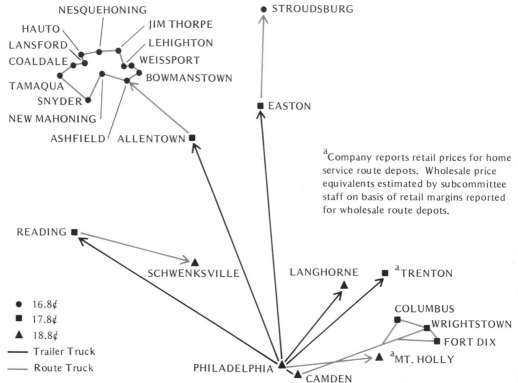

Source: *Hearings on Administered Prices*, Pt. 12, Chart 4

In addition, one truck carries bread to a loading station at Spencer, where it is transferred to delivery trucks which then distribute into a number of communities in the general Spencer area. . . . In all of these communities served out of Spencer which is 96 miles away from Sioux City, the price is only 12 cents a loaf.

The same situation obtains out of the Waterloo plant. There the price is 16.4 cents a loaf. The bread is distributed at that same price at Decorah and Mason City . . . a delivery truck moving out of Mason City distributes the bread to the communities of Robinson, Iowa Falls, Bradford, and Geneva where it is sold at 12.3 cents, again 4 cents below the price at the city where the bread is baked.

One of the most striking examples of route price discrimination revealed at the hearings involved the plant of General Baking Company at Philadelphia, which was explained as follows (see Figure 14-3):[17]

> MR. BLAIR: General Baking Co. is by far the leading producer in Philadelphia, Pa. It will be noted here that the price at Philadelphia is 18.8 cents . . . the bread is carried by the truck trailers to certain loading stations—one at Reading, one at Allentown, one at Easton, one at

[17] *Hearings on Administered Prices*, Pt. 12, pp. 6229–30.

Trenton, and a few others, at each of which the price is not 18.8 cents, but 17.8 cents.

The distance to Reading from Philadelphia is 54 miles. The distance to Allentown is 55 miles. The distance to Easton is 56 miles. In each case the price is a cent lower than it is in Philadelphia. . . . A delivery route is served from Easton and one from Allentown. The delivery truck moving out of Easton transports the bread to Stroudsburg where the bread is sold at a further reduction of a cent below the Philadelphia price, or at 16.8 cents.

Similarly, a route truck distributes the bread to Ashfield, Snyder, Tamaqua, and interestingly enough, to a community called Jim Thorpe, in each of which the price is 16.8 cents, or 1 cent below the loading station price at Allentown and 2 cents below the price in Philadelphia.

Ward Baking Company also engaged in route price discrimination, which was illustrated by the pricing pattern out of its Pittsburgh, Pennsylvania, plant:[18]

> MR. BLAIR. Now, perhaps of most interest . . . is the pricing pattern prevailing out of the loading station at Uniontown. The Uniontown price is the same as the price of Pittsburgh—17.4—but in routes served out of Uniontown the price drops sharply when the delivery trucks cross over the West Virginia line. Thus, the price goes down to 14.1 cents at Morgantown, W. Va., then rises to 16.5 at Kingwood, then drops to 14.1 cents at Fairmont, Prentice, and Blacksville. The distance to Uniontown is 49 miles. The distance from Uniontown to Fairmont is an additional 43 miles, making a total of 92 miles, and at Fairmont the price is, as noted, 3.3 cents below the price at Pittsburgh where the bread is made. I think it is particularly important to call attention to the fact that in previous testimony, in previous hearings before Congressional committees, witnesses have appeared and testified as to the injurious effects upon their ability to remain in business and operate efficiently, effectively, at this lower price prevailing in the Morgantown-Fairmont area.
>
> These witnesses were smaller bakers located in this area.

Ward's pricing practices out of its Cleveland, Ohio, plant were also described:

> MR. BLAIR: The pattern here is relatively simple. The bread is baked at Cleveland, where it is sold at a price of 17.2 cents. At each of the loading stations shown on the chart the price is lower than at Cleveland where the bread is baked. The bread is transported west from Cleveland to a loading station at Tiffin where the price is 16.4 cents. Another loading station is at Willard, a distance of 75 miles from Cleveland. There the price is 16.4. It is also transported to Mansfield, a distance of 74 miles, where it is again priced at 16.4 cents. It is shipped last to Ashtabula, where the price is even lower 16 cents. It is shipped to a loading station at Erie, Pa., which is 100 miles from Cleveland. There the price is 15.2 cents, or 2 cents below the price prevailing at Cleveland.

That such price discriminations will tend to result in higher concentration is almost self-evident. There remains the question of their ultimate effect on competition and the welfare of the consumer. The consumer is often grateful for the opportunity to be the short-run beneficiary of price discrimination. The basic argument over price discrimination hinges on the question of whether

[18] *Ibid.*, pp. 6258–66.

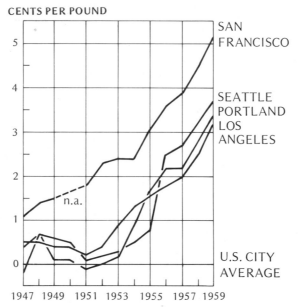

Figure 14-4

DEVIATIONS OF WEST COAST RETAIL BREAD
PRICES FROM U.S. CITY AVERAGES, 1947–1959

CENTS PER POUND

SAN FRANCISCO

SEATTLE
PORTLAND
LOS ANGELES

U.S. CITY AVERAGE

1947 1949 1951 1953 1955 1957 1959

Source: Bureau of Labor Statistics, Department of Commerce,
Consumer Price Index and special tabulation

in the long run, once the smaller sellers have been eliminated or economically bludgeoned into quiescent acceptance of a large firm's price policy, the consumer will continue to enjoy the benefit of low prices or whether he then will pay higher prices than would have prevailed had there been no price discrimination in the first place. Since this question requires the examination of given markets involving a specific group of sellers over a lengthy time period, it is exceptionally difficult to answer through empirical analysis. Nonetheless, some light might be shed on it by developments in the bread industry on the West Coast during the late 1950's.

In 1959 prices in West Coast cities ranged from 3.2 cents per pound (Los Angeles) to 5.2 cents per pound (San Francisco) above the U.S. average. As Figure 14-4 shows, a truly sizable deviation of West Coast prices from the national average began around 1953. And from 1953 to 1959 the rate of increase in West Coast bread prices was much sharper than in the nation as a whole. During this period, the national average retail price rose by 3.3 cents per pound, while the average price in Los Angeles rose by 5.6 cents, in San Francisco by 6.1 cents, in Portland by 6.5 cents, and in Seattle by 6.7 cents. In short, between 1953 and 1959 West Coast prices increased nearly twice as much as the national average.[19]

[19] The argument might be made that higher costs of production and distribution on the West Coast may explain the differential between West Coast prices and those in the rest of the country. Yet according to data covering more than 100 member plants of the Quality Bakers of America Cooperative, costs per pound, including both production cost and selling expense, in western plants during 1958 were only .5 cents per pound above the national average. In that year the West Coast prices ranged from 2.5 cents to 4.5 cents above the national average.

This unusually sharp increase in price was accompanied by an extensive merger movement on the West Coast. Between 1947 and 1959 no fewer than 17 independent companies were absorbed by 6 of the nation's largest baking firms; 14 of these independent companies, with 20 plants, had been important producers in various West Coast bread markets. In addition to those that were acquired, other independent bakers disappeared from the market. This high mortality rate both through absorption by major companies and through simple extinction is especially startling in view of the fact that no other region of the nation during this period showed a more rapid or sustained expansion of its economy and population—an expansion that theoretically would have brought with it greater opportunities for the formation of new firms.

The increase in price was accompanied by a striking identity—both as to timing and magnitude—of price changes among the various baking companies: "With few exceptions, the major companies in each market have moved either simultaneously or within a day or two of each other; the fact that substantial price increases have not been rescinded or shaded on any occasion shows an absence of unwillingness on the part of important independents to closely follow the major companies." [20]

Another important form of primary-line discrimination arises from the operation of a basing-point or similar delivered-price system. The result of any delivered-price system, such as basing-point pricing, is identity of delivered prices at any *given* point of destination from all sellers regardless of their location. Under the basing-point system this result is achieved by (a) the observance by all sellers of the base price at the "governing" basing point (usually the one nearest the buyer); (b) the addition thereto of the same freight charges (usually based on—though not always identical to—rail freight) from the governing basing point to the buyer's destination; (c) the use of common "extra" charges for deviations from standard specifications; and (d) a refusal to sell except on a delivered-price basis. If followed by all members of an industry, such a system yields delivered prices at any given point of destination that are identical, even to four decimal places. But because of differences in the sellers' location, the system produces variations in the realized price at the plant (mill net realization). Under the basing-point system, freight is concealed in the delivered price, the amount of the freight varying with the location of the supplier. The supplier located at a governing basing point, that is, the basing point nearest the buyer, absorbs no freight. The supplier located farther from the buyer will absorb freight from his location to the governing basing point. Obviously, the greater the distance between his location and the governing basing point, the greater is the amount of freight he absorbs. Thus, although the delivered price to a given buyer is the same from all plants, the amount of freight contained in the delivered price varies greatly among the supplying plants. The more distant the supplier from the governing basing point, the greater is the amount of freight and the lower the mill net realization. This consequence can be illustrated by an examination of the effect on potential competition of the basing-point system in the steel industry in Birmingham, Alabama, and Pueblo, Colorado. Birmingham was a basing point for most steel products; Pueblo, Colorado, was a nonbase mill (the nearest basing point for most products was Chicago). Regardless of the difference in form, the effect was the same in each area—a stultification of the growth of the local steel mills and of their nearby steel-consuming industries.

Any failure on the part of the Birmingham mills to expand and prosper

[20] *Administered Prices: Report on Bread*, p. 178.

cannot be attributed to inefficiency or high costs, since the Birmingham mills have long been the lowest-cost mills in the country.[21] On the basis of their advantage in efficiency, it logically follows that the Birmingham mills should have secured a reasonably large share of at least their own home market—the South. Here, they would have had the advantage not only of their greater productive efficiency but also of lower freight costs. What share of the southern market did the Birmingham mills actually obtain? Data relating to this issue have been secured on only one occasion.[22] It was found that the nine Alabama counties *immediately surrounding Birmingham* obtained no less than 37 percent of their structural shapes from distant sources, most of the material (28 percent) coming from Chicago. The same situation holds true with respect to the southern states generally; their purchases of structural shapes from northern mills ranged from 33 percent of their total purchases in the case of Georgia to 82 percent in the case of Texas.

If the basing-point system had been eliminated, the buyers of structural shapes in the nine Alabama counties surrounding Birmingham would have incurred freight charges of only $.94 per ton by buying from the Birmingham mills, as compared to around $15.00 per ton by buying from the northern mills. By purchasing from Birmingham, Mississippi buyers would have saved about $11 per ton, Georgia buyers about $7 per ton, Tennessee buyers about $3 to $5 per ton, and so on. To most buyers in the metal-fabricating industries such savings would have represented a substantial gain. Had the southern metalworking plants thus been able to obtain the advantages of the lower transportation costs to which their natural location entitled them, the savings they would have made in their purchases of steel would have enabled them to expand their markets. And with the expansion of their markets would have come lower production costs and thus the opportunity for an even greater market expansion.

The experience of the Birmingham mills with reference to structural shapes was by no means unique. For example, Georgia obtained 29 percent of its requirements of steel plates from Pennsylvania. In the case of plain drawn wire, although the Birmingham mills had a sharp freight advantage in Tennessee, they supplied only 26 percent of Tennessee's requirements. Birmingham supplied none of the Texas market for plain drawn wire, although under the basing-point system most Texas shipments were priced on a Birmingham base, that is, Birmingham was the nearest basing point (freightwise) to Texas. Nor did

[21] "No other region in the United States is so favorably situated with regard to the essential raw materials. Here deposits of iron ore, coal for coking, and lime for fluxing are found close together. Frequently the lime and ore are intermixed and hence the ore is self-fluxing. The ore is not so high in iron content as that of the Mesabi range—35 per cent as compared with 50 per cent—and it is high in phosphorous content. But technology solved the phosphorous problem and the low ore content is more than compensated for by low assembly costs." (George W. Stocking, *Basing Point Pricing and the South,* Institute on Anti-Trust Laws and Price Regulations, Southwestern Legal Foundation, 1950, pp. 263–64.) The Board of Investigation and Research compared the cost of producing a ton of pig iron in 1939 in the six principal producing states. Again the Alabama mills were shown to have the lowest costs. The sum of wages, costs of materials and supplies, and fuel and power costs per ton of pig iron amounted to $10.39 in Alabama, as compared to an average of $13.44 for the six states combined and to $15.23 for Pennsylvania, $14.47 for Ohio, and $14.56 for Illinois (79th Cong., 1st Sess., S. Doc. 80, Board of Investigation and Research, *Economics of Iron and Steel Transportation,* 1945, p. 127).

[22] A special survey conducted by the Temporary National Economic Committee covering shipments in the month of February, 1939.

South Carolina buy any of this product from Birmingham, although it also was nearer freightwise to Birmingham than to the northern mills that supplied it. The nine counties surrounding Birmingham secured no less than 81 percent of their shipments of hot-rolled strip from the distant northern steel center of Youngstown, Ohio. Shipments from Youngstown accounted for 31 percent of the total shipments of this product into Georgia and 66 percent of the shipments into Tennessee.

Under the basing-point system the preemption of southern markets by northern mills set in motion an endless circle working against the southern producer. Northern mills dumped their surplus steel output into the southern area, thus depriving the southern mills of their natural market. The southern mills, unable to sell their output at home, had to look elsewhere for markets and shipped a considerable proportion of their output into remote areas. The shipments into these remote areas involved heavy freight absorption and lower mill net prices on the part of the southern mills, thus further retarding their natural expansion and development.

Hot-rolled sheets provide an illustration of this pattern. The demand from southern buyers for this product, as for other steel products, was substantially greater than the productive capacity of the Birmingham mills. The demand from only six southern states (Alabama, Georgia, Tennessee, Mississippi, Louisiana, and portions of Texas) in which Birmingham had a distinct freight advantage was greater than Birmingham's output. Yet the Birmingham mills were able to dispose of so little of their tonnage to southern buyers that they had to ship hot-rolled sheets into no fewer than nineteen different states, including North Atlantic coast states and Pacific coast states. On most of these distant shipments, the Birmingham mills were forced to absorb large amounts of freight.[23]

The Colorado Fuel & Iron Corporation's mill at Pueblo, Colorado, illustrates the injury to potential competition of what is known as the nonbase mill. For most steel products the nearest basing point to Pueblo was Chicago. Under the basing-point system Colorado Fuel & Iron sold its steel at a delivered price that was the sum of (a) the base price *at Chicago* plus (b) rail freight *from Chicago*. Thus a buyer located in Pueblo purchasing steel produced in the Pueblo mill paid "phantom freight" for an imaginary shipment from Chicago to Pueblo. On deliveries to eastern points the Pueblo mill reduced this phantom freight by the amount of freight it actually paid to move the steel from Pueblo to the point of delivery. In March, 1943, the phantom freight from Chicago to Pueblo amounted to $19.80 per ton—or about 40 percent of the average price of steel.[24] If the Pueblo mill delivered steel at, say, Colorado Springs, it paid the actual freight from Pueblo to Colorado Springs, which would reduce the phantom freight to $15.40, and so on.

From the point of view of the Colorado Fuel & Iron Corporation itself, this form of pricing had one advantage and two disadvantages. The advantage, of course, was the high net price obtained on local sales incorporating phantom

---

[23] It is recognized that the inability of the Birmingham mills to obtain a greater share of their natural market might be due not only to the operation of the basing point system but to artificial restrictions that may have been imposed on Tennessee Coal & Iron by U.S. Steel. While these restrictions may have prevented Tennessee Coal & Iron from extending its sales into more distant areas in which it still had a freight advantage—e.g., the Southwest—it is unlikely that the restrictions would have been of such a nature as to explain the failure of Tennessee Coal & Iron to obtain a greater share of its own immediate market, the Southeast.

[24] American Iron and Steel Institute, Freight Tariff No. 4-13.

freight. The disadvantages were (a) that its natural market had to be shared with distant mills, and (b) that the growth potential of local steel-consuming industries was restricted by the high price of steel.

Since the delivered price to any given buyer in Colorado was the same from all mills, there was of course no economic incentive for the Colorado buyer to purchase from the Pueblo mill. Distant mills, it could be assumed, would therefore secure a large share of the Colorado market. Aside from rails, the demand for which is highly specialized, Colorado Fuel & Iron's most important product was structural shapes. Approximately half of the heavy structural shapes delivered in the state of Colorado came from distant mills—principally Chicago-Gary, Pittsburgh, and even Buffalo, New York! Moreover, the necessity of paying a delivered price for steel, which included up to $20 of phantom freight, obviously tended to limit the activities of the local steel-consuming firms. The restrictive effects of phantom freight on local Colorado industry were described before a subcommittee of the Senate Committee on Interstate and Foreign Commerce by the secretary-treasurer of the Wire Specialties & Manufacturers Corporation of Denver, Colorado:

> Under the old basing-point system with its ghost freight, we had a serious handicap whereby we paid as much as 25 percent more for our raw materials than did our competitors in Chicago because of this ghost freight but we had to sell our finished products at the same price as Chicago.
>
> *　　　*　　　*
>
> This system made the manufacturer in our territory pay a price for steel equal to his competitors' price in Chicago, plus the freight from Chicago, even though the steel only traveled 118 miles and not approximately 1,000 miles.
>
> *　　　*　　　*
>
> It is almost impossible for a manufacturer in our region—operating under this "ghost" freight handicap—to compete for his own market much less compete in the territory half way to Chicago. It is utterly impossible for a manufacturer in our region to compete with a Chicago manufacturer and sell in Chicago; while a Chicago manufacturer can compete very nicely in Denver, due again, and only, to the basing-point system with "ghost" freight.[25]

In view of the necessity of sharing its natural market with distant mills and the debilitating effects of phantom freight on local steel consumers, it is not surprising to find that Colorado Fuel & Iron's operating rate was traditionally well below the average for the industry, as was its profit rate.

The final adverse effect of basing-point pricing on potential competition lies in the way the system lends itself to disciplinary action against nonconformist producers, particularly those located in outlying areas. Under the system other companies can establish at the location of a price cutter a "punitive" basing point which can then be gradually reduced until the recalcitrant producer capitulates. The manner in which this method of disciplinary action operates was described by the Supreme Court in the *Cement Institute* decision as follows:

> During the depression in the 1930's, slow business prompted some producers to deviate from the prices fixed by the delivered price system. Meetings were held by other producers; an effective plan was devised to punish the recalcitrants and bring them into line. The plan was simple but successful. Other producers made the recalcitrant's plant an involun-

---

[25] 80th Cong., 2nd Sess., Hearings before a subcommittee of the Senate Committee on Interstate and Foreign Commerce, *Study of Pricing Methods*, 1948, p. 786.

tary base point. The base price was driven down with relatively insignificant losses to the producers who imposed the punitive basing point, but with heavy losses to the recalcitrant who had to make all its sales on this basis. In one instance, where a producer had made a low public bid, a punitive base point price was put on its plant and cement was reduced 10¢ per barrel; further reductions quickly followed until the base price at which this recalcitrant had to sell its cement dropped to 75¢ a barrel, scarcely one-half its former base price of $1.45. Within six weeks after the base price hit 75¢ capitulation occurred and the recalcitrant joined a portland cement association. Cement in that locality then bounced back to $1.15, later to $1.35, and finally to $1.75.[26]

Secondary-line discrimination

What is involved in secondary-line discrimination is the ability of large buyers to secure price concessions, which usually take the form of special deals—discounts for volume purchases, cash discounts, allowances for advertising and promotional services, variations in guarantees and replacement arrangements, and so on. The injured parties are the buyers to whom such concessions are *not* given, and the injury to competition arises from their subsequent inability to compete. What is involved in secondary-line discrimination can best be understood from a few typical examples. In each of the cases cited below, the company making the discrimination had the opportunity to justify the difference in prices by showing that it reflected savings in costs associated with a larger volume. Either the companies elected not to invoke the cost defense, or, if it was advanced, their showings were not accepted. Tires

A striking example of secondary-line discrimination is provided by the tire industry. On the basis of a survey the Federal Trade Commission found that during 1947, 48,000 dealers and other distributors purchased replacement tires and tubes from 21 manufacturers. At one extreme were small dealers, purchasing less than $100,000 annually, who represented more than 98 percent of the buyers and supplied about 52 percent of the replacement market. At the other extreme were 63 large buyers, with annual purchases of from $600,000 to $50 million, who constituted thirteen hundredths of a percent of the buyers but accounted for 30 percent of the replacement market. As compared to the small dealers, these 63 buyers paid, on the average, 26 to 30 percent less for passenger tires and 32 to 40 percent less for truck tires. The FTC found that a 30-percent differential would enable the largest buyers to resell at prices about equal to the smallest purchasers' cost. Although other factors were certainly at work, the discounts obtained must have contributed to the increase in concentration in tire distribution; the small dealers who accounted for 52 percent of the replacement business in 1947 had done about 90 percent in 1926, the year in which large discounts began to be made available to a few large buyers.

Purchasers of salt from the Morton Salt Company who bought 50,000 cases in any consecutive 12-month period paid a price of only $1.35 a case, a discount of over 15 percent as compared to $1.60 paid by small-buyers making less than carload purchases. Only 4 or 5 large buyers were found to be able to utilize this discount. In this case the argument was made that the price discrimination could not result in any substantial lessening of competition, since salt was such a small item in most wholesale and retail businesses and in the consumer's budget. In rejecting this contention the Supreme Court stated:

[26] *Federal Trade Commission* v. *Cement Institute, et al.,* 333 U.S. 683 (1948), at 714.

There are many articles in a grocery store that, considered separately, are comparatively small parts of a merchant's stock. Congress intended to protect a merchant from competitive injury attributable to discriminatory prices on any or all goods sold in interstate commerce, whether the particular goods constituted a major or minor portion of his stock. Since a grocery store consists of many comparatively small articles, there is no possible way effectively to protect a grocer from discriminatory prices except by applying the prohibitions of the act to each individual article in the store.[27]

In an action against Standard Brands, the FTC found the price of bakers yeast to range from 14 to 25 cents per pound, depending on volume. To get the 14-cent price a buyer was supposed to purchase 50,000 pounds per month. Of approximately 35,000 customers, fewer than a dozen purchased their yeast at 14 cents per pound. Actually, on the basis of the company's own discount schedule, none of these large buyers was entitled to the 14-cent price since an examination of the company's records revealed that no single delivery of 50,-000 pounds in one month was made to any buyer. The savings associated with this discount were substantial; for example, had one large buyer paid the going price for the quantity of yeast actually delivered to its various branches, it would have paid $116,000 more than it did.[28]

In another case it was found that Automatic Canteen Company, a large buyer of candy and other confectionary products which it dispenses through vending machines, purchased chewing gum from the Wrigley Company at a price of 38 cents per hundred sticks, which it resold to its distributors at 56 cents per hundred, a markup of approximately 46 percent. Other customers competing with Automatic Canteen paid Wrigley a price of 55 cents. For the same amount of gum for which Automatic Canteen paid Wrigley $8,823,728, competing customers paid Wrigley $12,771,240. Of Automatic Canteen's gross profit in the sale of gum, approximately 96 percent consisted of the difference between what its competitors paid and the preferential price it received from the Wrigley Company.[29]

Large food chains have frequently received preferential prices substantially below the prices at which the same supplier sells to wholesalers who in turn sell to smaller chains and independent retailers. Not infrequently, large retail chains have been able to purchase at prices so low that they have been able to resell products to customers at lower prices than those at which the wholesaler could buy them. Where the chains did not pass on these savings to customers the effect of the discounts was simply to enlarge their margin, thus strengthening their ability to compete in other ways.[30]

Cross-subsidization

Cross-subsidization is the term that has come to be most widely used to designate the use of profits obtained by a conglomerate corporation in industries in which it possesses substantial monopoly power to subsidize sales made at a

---

[27] *Federal Trade Commission* v. *Morton Salt Co.*, 334 U.S. 37 (1948), at 49.
[28] Docket 2986, *Standard Brands, Inc.*, 30 F.T.C. 1117.
[29] Docket 4933, *Automatic Canteen Co. of America*, 46 F.T.C. 861.
[30] Typical of this type of discrimination was the *C. F. Sauer Company* case (Docket 3646, 33 F.T.C. 812).

loss in competitive industries.[31] Cross-subsidization is thus a form of discriminatory pricing, except that it differs from the usual meaning of the term in that what is involved is the sale by a given company of different products at varying profit rates rather than the sale of the same product to different buyers at varying prices.

Such a practice can make the plight of the single-line producer all but impossible. Even if in his own industry he is more efficient than the conglomerate, he can find little point in pursuing the course of action held out by classical theory—i.e., reducing his price to reflect his greater efficiency—since his price reduction will only be matched or exceeded by a firm that can readily accept losses in any of the industries in which it is engaged. Moreover, any attempt by the single-line producer to diversify into some other field will be hindered by a price level in his own industry that prevents both the retention of earnings and the attraction of capital from the outside.

The dangers of cross-subsidization have long been recognized. Referring to it as a form of price discrimination Arthur R. Burns observed over three decades ago:

> it gives rise to opportunities for price discrimination in the sense of selling individual products at prices exceeding or falling short of the total costs of producing and selling. . . . The inducement to discriminate is most likely to be present when the integrated firm enjoys advantages in one market; it may exploit these advantages and divert part of the monopoly profits thus obtained to subsidize sales at less than apparent cost in other markets . . .[32]

The manner in which competition can be injured by this practice was also described by A. D. H. Kaplan: "The manufacturer of a full line enjoys an advantage somewhat analogous to that of the seller operating in a number of markets. He can theoretically manipulate his margins to take lower profits on products that require forcing or for which demand is more elastic and compensating higher profit on those in which his position is more stable." [33]

In this chapter cross-subsidization is illustrated by developments that have taken place in the electrical-appliance and automotive-radio industries. Among the 400-odd manufacturing industries few have experienced a more rapid increase in concentration since World War II than electrical appliances. A widely defined area, the electrical-appliance industry embraces numerous different products that have different uses and are in no way substitutable for each other. Ranging from $2 fans to $500 freezers, its products have in common only the characteristics of being durable goods powered by electricity and customarily used in the home. Although the industry is defined so broadly as to have little meaning, concentration ratios are available for most of its individual product classes. Shown in Table 14-2, for the years 1954, 1958, and 1963, are the shares of the 4 leading producers for 7 different types of electrical appliance, which account for more than three-fifths of the total shipments of all electrical appliances.

---

[31] Cross-subsidization could also be said to exist if sales in competitive industries were made not at a loss but at an unduly low profit. Profits could be considered to be unduly low if they were substantially below what would have been yielded if the firm had behaved as a competitive supplier in view of the market's prevailing cost and demand factors.

[32] Arthur R. Burns, *The Decline of Competition*, McGraw-Hill, 1936, p. 451.

[33] A. D. H. Kaplan, *Big Enterprise in a Competitive System*, Brookings Institution, 1954, p. 214.

Table 14-2

CONCENTRATION IN SELECTED ELECTRICAL APPLIANCES

SIC Code	Product	4-Company Concentration Ratios			Change (% Pts.)	
		1954	1958	1963	1954–58	1954–63
36322	Home and farm freezers	44%	58%	63%	14	19
36321	Household refrigerators	62	73	76	11	14
3633	Household laundry equipment	58	67	71	9	13
36341	Electric fans, except industrial	46	54	44	8	−2
36350, 35840ª	Vacuum cleaners	55	59	n.a.ᶜ	4	—
36360	Sewing machines	76	ᵇ 82		—	6
36391	Electric household water heaters	39	37	40	−2	1

ª Household vacuum cleaners (36350) and commercial and industrial vacuum cleaners (35840) combined for 1958 to provide a comparable figure with the 1954 product class 3584.

ᵇ Withheld to avoid disclosure of individual company figures; concentration ratios for 8 largest companies: 89 in 1954; 92 in 1958.

ᶜ Not available.

Source: "Concentration Ratios in Manufacturing Industry, 1958," Pt. 1, Table 4; "Concentration Ratios in Manufacturing Industry, 1963," Pt. 1, Table 4

Most of the increases, as can be seen, took place during the mid-1950's. The share held by the 4 largest producers of home and farm freezers registered a precipitous advance—from 44 percent in 1954 to 58 percent in 1958. Almost as large was the increase in household refrigerators—from 62 percent to 73 percent. During these 4 years the concentration ratio rose by 9 percentage points in household laundry equipment, while an increase of 8 percentage points was registered by electric fans. The share of the 4 largest companies in sewing machines could not be revealed because of the Census disclosure rule, but the share held by the 8 largest rose from 89 percent in 1954 to 92 percent in 1958.

According to the trade press the mid-1950's was a period of recurring weaknesses in the market. The major appliance manufacturers apparently did not limit supplies, as a result of which inventories accumulated and prices weakened. Paradoxically, at the same time that the market was reported to be glutted by "overcapacity," the largest and most diversified producers were making substantial expansions in their capacity. In January, 1956, General Electric, the industry's largest producer, was reported to be lowering the prices of its small appliances "up to 30%," featuring a reduction in the price of vacuum cleaners from $69.95 to $49.95. The purpose of the price change, it was stated, was to allow GE to promote new products "at more realistic prices." [34] A month later it was reported that 4 firms, including Westinghouse, would reduce their prices for these appliances "to stabilize the appliance industry." [35] Several

[34] *Appliance Manufacturer,* Jan., 1956.
[35] *Ibid.,* Feb., 1956.

PREDATION

months later an official of a substantial but smaller company, Norge, reacted critically to these price reductions, stating, "In an effort to buy an out-of-proportionate share of the market, a few selfish manufacturers have set off a whole chain of wheeling and dealing price merchandising tactics. A price—any price —below price of competition is their price to dealers." [36]

Between the fourth quarter of 1954 and the fourth quarter of 1960 the Wholesale Price Index rose 9.1 percent, the price index for consumer durable goods increased 8.7 percent, and the index for metals and metal products advanced 17.3 percent. In contrast, the prices of GE major appliances registered pronounced decreases, ranging from 9 percent for free-standing ranges to 27 percent for standard 10-cubic-foot freezers. Built-in ranges, deluxe refrigerators, and 13-foot freezers were reduced by 19 percent. Prices of refrigerators, freezers, and washers were reduced between 1954 and 1957 and again between 1957 and 1960. Substantial reductions were made in the price of GE ranges between 1954 and 1957.

This was also a period of a wholesale exodus of single-line manufacturers— large and small—from the industry. Articles in the trade press reflected a premonition that the future of the industry lay only with the large multiproduct firms, for whom appliance manufacturing constituted only a small part of their business. Thus, in late 1956, *Retailing Daily* proclaimed, "The ever-changing profile of the major appliance industry suffered its most radical alteration in many a day" with the shutdown of one firm and the sale of another, which climaxed "24 months of shuffling, shifting, buying and selling. . . ." The article continued, "the result of all the shifting within the industry is one of reducing the number of competitive brands on the market. Like a poker game, apparently, the more players that can be knocked out of a hand, the greater is the possibility of winning." [37] Whirlpool-Seeger's president was quoted as saying that of the 26 independent home laundry manufacturers in 1940, 10 had merged into full-line companies, 8 had been liquidated or gone into bankruptcy, leaving only 8 still in business. He stated that among the advantages of the full-line company is its ability *"to subsidize a line of appliances in a given market or at a given season."* [38]

Between 1954 and 1961, 60 formerly independent appliance manufacturers disappeared through mergers and acquisitions. More than half the casualties occurred in 1955 and 1956, during which period 7 home laundry manufacturers and 7 refrigerator or freezer manufacturers, as well as 3 electric range manufacturers, were eliminated through merger. A good number of these firms were sizable enterprises that could reasonably be expected to have attained the available economies of scale and had long-established and well-known trade names. Among the disappearances were firms with such well-known names—which either vanished entirely or have been used for prestige purposes by an acquiring company—as Deepfreeze, York, Welbilt, Bendix, Speed Queen, Easy, Eureka, Jordan, Dormeyer, Servel, Universal, Ever Bright, and Philco.

The result of this period of industrial turmoil was that a few large conglomerate corporations—notably General Electric and, to a lesser extent, General Motors and Westinghouse—were left with substantial control over most of the industry's product lines. According to a market survey conducted by *Look* mag-

[36] *Ibid.*, July, 1956.
[37] *Retailing Daily,* Nov. 15, 1956.
[38] *Ibid.* Emphasis added.

azine in 1961 as a service to advertisers, General Electric had the largest market share in no fewer than 5 of 8 major appliances surveyed—ranges, refrigerators, clothes dryers, water heaters, and dishwashers.[39] In 2 of the remaining products —freezers and automatic clothes washers—it had the second largest share, while in the remaining product it was the third leading producer. In the 5 products of which it was the leading producer, GE's share ranged from 24 percent (refrigerators) to 40 percent (electric ranges), while in the 3 remaining products it held from 9 to 21 percent. General Motors was the second largest producer of refrigerators (17 percent) and of ranges (15 percent), the third largest producer of washing machines (11 percent) and of freezers (9 percent), and in addition the fourth largest in dryers (13 percent), dishwashers (11 percent), and electric water heaters (2 percent). Westinghouse appears as the third largest producer of ranges (10 percent), clothes dryers (13 percent), and electric water heaters (2 percent) and the fourth largest of freezers (6 percent).

That the increases in concentration were the result of cross-subsidization by the largest producers has been suggested by T. K. Quinn, former chairman of GE's sales committee, vice chairman of the General Electric Supply Corporation, and operating head of its appliance business. Holding that the company had long followed a policy of using profits from its "monopoly lines" to drive out competition in other lines, Quinn wrote that the "secret" of GE's predominance and growth rested upon two foundations:

> 1. As a J. P. Morgan combine originally (like General Motors and U.S. Steel) it had abundant capital, including access, through Morgan, to life insurance funds.
> 2. It had high-profit, monopoly lines which enabled it to finance other lines until they, too, could reach volumes that would assure their continuance on a self-supporting and profitable basis.

Referring to the latter point he went on to state:

> Notable among these lines was the incandescent electric lamp bulb monopoly. G. E.'s net profit in its lamp department at times approximated 50% on investment. . . .
> It was from its lamp profits that General Electric financed its entry into the home appliance field. There was no purpose or advantage of efficiency involved.[40]

[39] For the *Look National Survey,* Audits & Surveys Co. used a multistage area probability sampling technique, with interviews conducted in 4,808 households for the 1959 survey and in 5,292 households for the 1961 survey. The results compare closely with the Census data, as can be seen below:

	4 Largest Companies	
Product	Census 1958	*Look* Survey 1959–60
Electric household ranges	67%	74%
Household mechanical washing machines, dryers and washer-dryer combinations	68	73 [a] 71 [b]
Vacuum cleaners	64	60
Water heaters	37	42
Electric household refrigerators	73	64

[a] Automatic clothes washers
[b] Electric clothes dryers

[40] T. K. Quinn, *Unconscious Public Enemies,* Citadel Press, 1962, pp. 112–14.

PREDATION

In this connection it should be observed that the manufacture of electric lamps is one of the most highly concentrated industries in the nation, with the 4 largest producers regularly accounting for more than 90 percent of the output. According to data put into the court record in a 1953 antitrust case, General Electric alone accounted for approximately 55 percent and Westinghouse for 25 percent of lamp sales.[41] Another probable source of monopoly profits was heavy electrical machinery. It was during the mid-1950's that General Electric, Westinghouse, and most of the other producers were engaged in an overt conspiracy to fix the prices of electrical machinery.[42]

Another possible indication of the importance of cross-subsidization lies in the vigor with which GE, following its conviction in the 1960 "Philadelphia" conspiracy case, opposed an attempt by the Department of Justice to enjoin the use of the practice. The Department was apprehensive that GE and the other large companies would use their conviction for failing to compete as a pretext for competing by sales below costs against smaller rivals. To prevent this, the Department attempted to write a prohibition against "unreasonably low" prices into the consent orders. This clause was actually signed by one defendant company,[43] while 4 others, including Westinghouse, initially gave assurances of their acceptance. But, preferring the possibility of a court battle, General Electric refused to sign, contending that the language was vague and would tend to stifle rather than encourage competition. For a company which during its lifetime had run afoul of the antitrust laws on so many occasions, this concern with the cause of competition was rather unexpected. Moreover, GE had just been convicted for engaging in the most egregious price-fixing conspiracy of modern times, resulting in the imprisonment of several of its top officials. Hence, one would not have expected GE to have been eager to precipitate still another court battle— unless the practice involved was of key importance to its corporate strategy. For reasons that have never been clear the Justice Department quietly dropped the provision from the final decree.

Another example of cross-subsidization appears to be provided by the fertilizer industry. Although more than half (55 percent) of the nation's output of fertilizer was produced in 1963 by its 8 leading producers, only 10 percent came from companies whose principal line of business was the manufacture of fertilizers. Another 15 percent was accounted for by companies that were primarily engaged in some other chemical industry. However, the largest proportion (30 percent) came from companies whose principal line of products was completely outside the chemicals and allied products group. Presumably, these were oil companies.

[41] *United States* v. *General Electric Co., et al.,* 115 F. Supp. 835 (D.N.J. 1953), 882–83, App. Tables 1, 2.

[42] See Ch. 21.

[43] C. H. Wheeler Manufacturing Co. (*United States* v. *Foster-Wheeler Corp.,* United States District Court, Eastern District of Pennsylvania, Civil No. 28,229, filed May 22, 1961 [CCH-70,035]). The provision that was so obnoxious to GE appeared as follows: "V. Defendant . . . is enjoined and restrained from, directly or indirectly:

"(F) Selling condensers at unreasonably low prices with the purpose of intent, or where the effect is, or where there is a reasonable probability that the effect will be, substantially to injure, suppress or stifle competition or tend to create a monopoly; provided, however, that in any proceeding for civil contempt based upon an alleged violation of this subsection (F) in which the plantiff shall have sustained its burden of proving that the defendant in such proceeding has made sales which would violate this subsection (F) if such sales were at unreasonably low prices, the burden of proof shall be upon such defendant to establish that it did not sell such condensers at unreasonably low prices."

In the late 1950's and early 1960's several of the nation's largest fertilizer manufacturers were acquired by oil companies. Although this movement had forward vertical aspects in that ammonia is synthesized from hydrocarbons produced by the oil companies, ammonia contributes to only one of the three fertilizer ingredients—nitrogen; it has nothing to do with the production of phosphates or potash and of course is completely removed from fertilizer mixing and

Another example of cross-subsidization concerns automobile accessories, specifically the price to be charged by the Ford Motor Company for "service radios" —i.e., automobile radios sold as optional equipment. As a result of private litigation a series of intracompany memoranda by various officials of the Ford Motor Company has become part of the public record.[44] Like the other major automobile manufacturers Ford sells automobile radios both as original and as optional equipment. The problem to which the documents were addressed was the disappointing sales of the latter—a development that was attributable largely to the aggressive sales efforts of an independent manufacturer, the Automatic Radio Manufacturing Company.[45] These sales efforts were directed at Ford dealers, who install the "service" radios. The problem was summarized by a Ford official as follows:

> In the past few years there has been a marked increase in the market activity of independent automotive radio manufacturers. Because there is a substantial profit margin in car radios, these independents have been able to obtain a significant amount of business from authorized Ford dealers by selling car radios for dealer installation for prices which are as much as $15 below our prices. While minor design differences exist, these radios are essentially of Ford quality and are remarkably close in appearance.[46]

Automatic's principal selling point was its lower prices: "The Automatic push-button radio is generally offered to Ford dealers for about $40, or for $20 less than the Ford push-button 6-button tube radio. . . . Because of its appearance similarity to the Ford radio, our dealers frequently merchandise the Automatic as a Ford radio, thereby making $15 additional profit on the radio sale." [47] On the basis of price quotations to a group of Detroit Ford dealers it was found that ". . . Automatic undersells the Ford service-installed radio by a minimum $16, by a probable average of $20, and by more than $20 when orders exceed 25 radios." [48] Among the automobile manufacturers Ford had made itself particularly vulnerable to competitive inroads by failing to make price reductions on its service radio. To combat "the independent's infiltration of the car radio market" General Motors, Chrysler, and American Motors had reduced their service radio price as much as $10 below their production-installed prices: "In contrast . . . Ford has kept the price of its service radio above the production installed price since 1955 to encourage dealers to order through production." [49]

[44] The documents are to be found in the Plaintiff's Motion for Production of Documents and Things under Rule 34, *Automatic Radio Manufacturing Company* v. *Ford Motor Company,* United States District Court of Massachusetts, Civil No. 63-387-C, filed Jan. 30, 1970.

[45] S. N. Karyla, memorandum to A. R. Miller, Aug. 1, 1958.

[46] L. A. Iacocca, memorandum to J. E. Lundy and J. O. Wright, Sept. 27, 1962.

[47] Karyla, *op. cit.*

[48] S. M. Vass, memorandum to M. S. McLaughlin, March 26, 1963, App. B.

[49] Planning and Research, memorandum on the 1963 Radio Marketing Program of Parts and Service, Aug. 13, 1963.

In addition to the price advantage Automatic operated a unique "exchange radio" system: "When a radio chassis is defective the dealer is permitted to install another radio, placing the defective radio in a carton, and, by calling Distributing Sales, this company will discharge one of their own trucks to pick up the defective radio. The distributor makes the necessary repairs and places the repaired radio back in their stock." [50] This procedure not only removes from the dealer the burden of making radio repairs but provides the buyer with quick and efficient service: "In the case of defective radios, immediate exchange of the radio is made creating a wonderful impression with the customer." [51]

On examination Automatic's product was found to be of acceptable quality. A Ford engineering staff evaluation on March 10, 1958, concluded, "In general, the Automatic radio receiver compares favorably to the Ford receiver." While Automatic's product was found to be "susceptible to distortion when exposed to extremely strong signals," this quality deficiency was not considered to be important enough "to dissuade dealers from representing the Automatic as a genuine Ford radio." [52]

The loss of revenue resulting from the competitive inroads by Automatic, and to a lesser extent Stromberg-Carlson, was of substantial proportions: "In the case of Ford . . . the average radio revenue loss per average car accounted for about half of the net decline in Ford average unit revenue from all factory-installed extra equipment." [53] Confronted with this problem Ford management officials gave considerable attention over a period of years to seeking a solution. Quickly ruled out, however, was a simple across-the-board reduction in price:

> A major reduction in the price of production installed radios has been discussed as a means of solving the radio problem. However, this approach does not appear prudent *since it would apply action on a national basis to correct a regional problem.* More importantly, establishment of a fully competitive price on both production and service radios would reduce revenues by about $12 million annually at present installation rates. Recovery of this revenue loss through increased radio sales is impossible since it would require installation rates in excess of 200%.[54]

Consideration was also given to a variety of "package deals" in which a radio would be combined with other types of optional equipment at a combined price substantially below the aggregate price of the items taken separately. But the approach that received the most favorable attention was the simple one of price cutting to be financed by increases in profits elsewhere:

> Accordingly, the most reliable counter-measure would be to cut the price of the radios—possibly by ⅔ of the gap that now exists between our radios and competitive radios—and make up the resulting revenue loss by an increase in the price of the car or the price of other extra equipment. . . . As mentioned above none of these measures would be as effective as a price reduction—*provided we are willing to offset the radio price reduction with increases in other areas.*[55]

[50] S. E. Aubuchon, memorandum to C. T. Doman, Nov. 11, 1960.
[51] R. L. Ziegler, Parts and Service Sales Representative, memorandum to Assistant Products Manager, Feb. 7, 1958.
[52] Vass, *op. cit.,* App. B.
[53] *Ibid.,* App. A.
[54] *Ibid.* Emphasis added.
[55] Karyla, *op. cit.* Emphasis in original.

This general approach was later modified to one limiting the price reduction to those particular geographic areas in which competition was most intense: "To meet the problem of intense local jobber competition which now exists in the major metropolitan markets in the northeastern quarter of the country, it seems essential that we also provide for the possibility of localized price reductions. . . ." [56] Recognizing the ineffectiveness of alternative courses of action such as appeals to loyalty and "package deals," the final recommendation in the available documents was for selective price cutting:

> The character of this problem is regional rather than national and is limited primarily to high-volume dealers. In order to regain the business that has already been lost therefore, we suggest that Ford service radios be priced to meet competitive conditions in local markets.
>
> *   *   *
>
> In summary we recommend that supplementary price action at this time be selective and limited to high-volume dealers in those large metropolitan areas where we have incurred the greatest losses to independent suppliers.[57]

Cross-subsidization may be practiced not only on a product or industry basis but also on a geographic basis. That is, a company may finance losses in some geographic areas in which it has a small share of the market with profits made in other areas in which it has a relatively large market share. As part of its investigation of the *National Tea* case, the Federal Trade Commission obtained figures for each of the company's regional branches on its average market share in 1958 and its average net taxable income for the three years 1957–1959. In the words of the Commission's chief economist, Willard Mueller, "The association between these two factors is extremely close and much too close to be explained by chance." [58] As can be seen in Figure 14-5, net income was high in such branches as Indianapolis, Denver, and Chicago, where National Tea enjoyed a relatively large market share; in three branches in which its market share was small, Davenport, Detroit, and Memphis, it suffered actual losses. These negative profits appear to have resulted from National Tea's efforts to achieve a larger market position in these branches. As can be seen by the regression line 1, net taxable income in these three branches appears to be far below expected values. Regression line 2, which shows the trend line with these three branches excluded, yields an even closer statistical relationship between market share and net income.[59] In Mueller's words, "In sum, [this large chain] enjoyed substantially higher profits in cities and branches in which it held relatively large market shares."

Obviously no multi-industry concern can be expected to make the same profit rate in each of the industries in which it is engaged; even losses in some divisions are to be expected from time to time. The danger to competition arises when there is a *combination* of factors:

1. The conglomerate is in possession of substantial monopoly power in one or more of the industries in which it is engaged.

2. Any losses it incurs in one or more of such industries are *not* an episodic occurrence, beyond the control of management, but continue over a period of time.

[56] Planning and Research, *op. cit.*
[57] Vass, *op. cit.*
[58] *Hearings on Economic Concentration,* Pt. 6, pp. 1868–70, testimony of Willard Mueller. The simple correlation coefficient was .891, which is statistically significant at the 1% level.
[59] Excluding Davenport, Detroit, and Memphis, the simple correlation coefficient is .969.

Figure 14-5

AVERAGE MARKET SHARE IN 1958 AND
AVERAGE NET TAXABLE INCOME, 1957–1959
Eleven branches of the National Tea Company

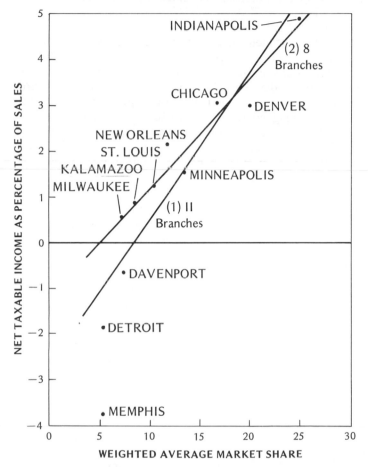

Source: *Hearings on Economic Concentration*, Pt. 5, p. 1869.

3. Such losses have only a minor effect on the corporation's overall earnings.

4. The losses are not merely the result of the conglomerate's inability to achieve reasonable and customary levels of efficiency prevailing in the industry.

5. The losses are not merely the product of decreases in demand or increases in costs affecting the industry as a whole.

Obviously most losses by conglomerates in particular industries would fall far short of meeting this combination of factors. But where they are met, the evidence should be regarded as indicative of a serious danger to competition.

Exclusive dealing and tie-in contracts

Where their effect "may be to substantially lessen competition or tend to create a monopoly," exclusive dealing arrangements and tie-in contracts are prohibited under Section 3 of the Clayton Act: "The former involves the condition that the purchaser or lessee of goods shall deal only in the goods of the seller or lessor and refrain from dealing in the goods of competitors; the latter involves a condition that the goods sold or leased shall be used only with other goods of the seller or lessor, the purchaser or lessee agreeing not to deal in such other goods of competitors. . . ." [60]

Meeting the substantial-competitive-injury test is not unduly burdensome, since it is almost self-evident that exclusive-dealing contracts, when imposed by large suppliers, will injure competition by preventing the smaller manufacturers from getting their goods on the market and by depriving distributors and dealers of their freedom to handle lines of competitive producers. There are few, if any, circumstances under which exclusive dealing imposed by large concerns can be envisaged as promoting competition. As Judge Medina pointed out, the presumptive illegality of exclusive dealing was so obvious to Congress that the early versions of what is now Section 3 contained an outright prohibition of all exclusive-dealing contracts; the "effect on competition" reservation was added only for the purpose of keeping this competitive weapon available to small companies:

> At the time of its initial approval by the House of Representatives, that portion of the Clayton bill relating to exclusive-dealing contracts contained an unqualified proscription of agreements of such a nature. . . . However, the Senate Judiciary Committee, apparently in the belief that the Federal Trade Commission bill then pending would adequately cover this matter, struck the section entirely. Upon a reconsideration of the Committee's action on the floor of the Senate, issue was taken with the unqualified nature of the House version only insofar as it declared these contracts unlawful even when engaged in by newcomers or small business enterprises in a particular line of commerce who, perhaps, could effectively compete with established interests only if these devices were available to them. . . . It may be inferred, therefore, that the Conference Committee's compromise provision, which included this qualification in the exclusive-dealing contract section for the first time, was designed to accomplish no more than the protection of the "newcomer" or "small" business organization.[61]

An illustration of exclusive dealing arrangements is represented by the sales tactics of the country's largest manufacturer of carburetors, Carter Carburetor Corporation. The company adopted a policy of entering into sales contracts and granting preferential discounts only to dealers who sold exclusively carburetors manufactured by it. In addition to notifying all of its distributors and service stations to this effect, Carter terminated contracts with a number of dealers who had persisted in selling the products of competitive manufacturers. By ordering the company to discontinue the practice, the Federal Trade Commission opened up a large potential market to smaller competitive manufacturers of carburetors and of related parts and accessories.[62]

Perhaps the most important decision concerning exclusive dealing arrangements was the *Standard Oil of California* case.[63] Standard Oil of California re-

[60] *Judson L. Thomson Manufacturing Co.* v. *Federal Trade Commission,* 150 F. 2d 952 (C.C.A. 1, 1945), at 955.

[61] *Dictograph Products, Inc.* v. *Federal Trade Commission,* 217 F. 2d 821 (C.C.A. 2, 1954), at 827.

[62] *Carter Carburetor Corp.* v. *Federal Trade Commission,* 112 F. 2d 722 (C.C.A. 8, 1940).

[63] *Standard Oil of California* v. *United States,* 337 U.S. 293 (1949), 305, 306.

quired its gasoline dealers to purchase and sell only those tires, tubes, batteries, and accessories, as well as petroleum products, handled by the company. The principal issue in the case was whether the amount of commerce involved was "substantial." The exclusive contracts covered 16 percent of the retail outlets in the western area, while Standard's sales of gasoline to independent service stations amounted to 6.7 percent of the total volume of gasoline sold in the area. In the opinion of the Court this was sufficient to be "substantial": "Where such conditions are successfully exacted, competition on the merits with respect to the tied product is inevitably curbed." [64]

Tie-in arrangements are often utilized by owners of patented machines, who lease them on condition that only their unpatented products will be used in the machines. The effect, of course, is to extend a legitimate patent monopoly to cover unpatented supplies and to deprive competitive suppliers of their market. Examples of such tie-in arrangements have been provided by FTC cases involving wire and strapping and automatic rivets. In the former the FTC ordered the respondent to cease from incorporating in contracts for its equipment any condition that the licensee or purchaser shall not use any wire or strapping acquired from others.[65] The Commission's order had the effect of opening the channels of distribution to a large number of small competing manufacturers of wire and strapping. In the latter the Commission ordered manufacturers of automatic rivet-setting machines to stop selling their machines on the condition that the purchaser not use in their machines any rivets acquired from others.[66]

Other predatory practices

When Congress in 1914 passed the Clayton Act, it was acting against those specific types of business activity leading to "trusts, conspiracies and monopolies" with which it had become familar—price discrimination, exclusive dealing, mergers, and interlocking directorates. Recognizing, however, that in this area there is no limit to the "inventiveness of the mind of man," Congress also enacted a general, or open-ended, prohibition of "unfair methods of competition." A new agency, the Federal Trade Commission, was established, equipped not only with broad investigatory powers but with the power in Section 5 to order business enterprises to "cease and desist" from engaging in practices regarded by the Commission as "unfair methods of competition." In the ensuing half-century the orders issued by the Commission under this section have been of three general types: those against collusive activity, those against false and misleading advertising, and those against predatory practices.

Any sampling of the Section 5 orders against predatory practices establishes beyond any question the correctness of the original congressional assumption concerning human inventiveness. Even to develop a classification for these actions would be a major—and incidentally much needed—research undertaking. What is important, however, is that over a period of 50 years a body of case law has developed under which a wide variety of specific types of business practice have come to be regarded as unlawful. Their illegality is recognized

[64] *Ibid.* at 305.
[65] *Signode Steel Strapping Co.* v. *Federal Trade Commission,* 132 F. 2d 48 (C.C.A. 4, 1942).
[66] *Judson L. Thomson Manufacturing Co.* v. *Federal Trade Commission.*

not merely by the FTC itself, but by private law firms specializing in FTC matters, by much of the business community, and by the final authority, the courts. Among the practices whose illegality has become well established are boycotts to destroy competition. Those who find merit in predation as a form of "hard" competition would be hard put to explain how the competitive effect of boycotts and similar practices on competition can be anything other than injurious.

The usual purpose of boycotts is to force an "unduly" aggressive competitor back into line by threatening him with a loss of supply or markets. Typically, some degree of collusion is involved, but the burden of proof would be considerably greater if, in addition to establishing the existence of the practice, the FTC had to show that it was engaged in pursuant to a conspiracy. An important case in the development of the law involved a boycott against firms supplying rubber heels and soles to 5-and-10-cent stores. The boycott was engineered by the ITS Company, a large wholesaler obtaining its supplies principally from B. F. Goodrich, in cooperation with the National Federation of Master Shoe Rebuilders. The Commission found that the ITS Company and the association had entered into an agreement to induce shoe manufacturers, jobbers, repairers, and hardware stores to boycott and refuse to deal with manufacturers and wholesalers who sold to 5-and-10-cent stores. Literature was circulated that was falsely derogatory to those who sold to 5-and-10-cent stores. Also circulated were "white lists" and "black lists" containing the names of manufacturers and wholesalers who did and did not sell to the 5-and-10-cent stores. Further, such information was disseminated in person by "missionary men" and sales forces. The effect was to deprive manufacturers competing with ITS of their outlets, to protect shoe repairers from their principal source of competition, and to deny consumers the opportunity to purchase from lower-price outlets.

A similar effort to cut off from their regular market manufacturers who supplied low-price outlets involved warm-air furnaces. A boycott was organized against the manufacturers who were selling to the mail order houses at prices that enabled them to undersell the independent dealers. The boycott was put into effect by the New York State Sheet Metal Roofing and Air Conditioning Contractors Association along with one of the larger manufacturers. Bulletins containing the names of the manufacturers selling to mail order houses were distributed to dealers and their associations throughout the country. Dealers were urged not to do business with the blacklisted companies and to confine their orders to manufacturers who did not sell to mail order houses. Again, the effect was to injure competition and deprive consumers of supplies at lower-price outlets.

*　　*　　*

Predation has come to be welcomed by many—if not most—economists as a sign of "hard competition," signifying the breaking down of rigid price structures. But there is also the very real possibility that in oligopolistic industries predatory practices can be a handy instrument to snuff out competition at its most likely source. Since oligopolists tend to avoid competing with one another in price, the question arises as to where price competition in such industries is to come from. In the past, thinking on this issue has often gone off on a tangent because of the assumption that the oligopolists are more efficient than the industry's smaller firms. Where this is so, the latter of course live by sufferance under the "price umbrella" held up by the oligopolists. But what of the reverse situation, where the advantage in efficiency lies with the smaller firm? In any competitive struggle based simply on differences in costs, the oligopolists will lose. But they need not lose if they can take predatory actions against the particular smaller firm responsible for the outbreak of price competition.

Even before the advent of the new decentralizing technologies, the existence in considerable numbers of smaller firms with distinctly lower costs than their larger rivals was not as rare a phenomenon as has generally been assumed. The one impression of lasting value to be drawn from the TNEC study of size and efficiency is of the wide range of costs and the surprisingly large number of smaller companies with relatively low unit costs.[67] Although the average for the smaller enterprises was seldom below the average of the large firms, there were in nearly all the industries studied a large number of small concerns with costs significantly lower than the costs of most of the large concerns. If this was true during the 1920's and 1930's, when most of the cost surveys examined in the TNEC study were undertaken, it should be even more true today owing to the growing importance of decentralizing, capital-saving technologies. To the extent that smaller firms do have lower costs, the freedom to engage in predation becomes essential to the survival of high-cost oligopolists. Without the right to offer concessions to individual customers of a particular low-cost smaller firm, to cut prices in its specific geographic area, and to subsidize sales of the particular product with profits made elsewhere, the inefficient large firm will almost inevitably suffer a slow but steady loss in its share of the market.

[67] *The Relative Efficiency of Large, Medium and Small Business,* Monograph No. 13, Temporary National Economic Committee (TNEC), 1941, pp. 12–14.

CH 15 THE ROLE OF GOVERNMENT

In its effect on competition the role of government is ambivalent. On the one hand, the function of the antitrust agencies is to preserve and strengthen competition, while loans and other forms of assistance are provided to smaller firms by the Small Business Administration. On the other hand, government is a powerful contributor to higher concentration and the suppression of competition. It contributes directly to concentration by the manner in which it procures what it needs, disposes of what it no longer needs, and leases to others what it owns. It directly suppresses competition through quotas, patents, tariffs, and a wide variety of other restraints imposed by different agencies. As new decentralizing technologies make their appearance, as new sources of supply continue to be discovered, and as changing consumer tastes render old products and processes obsolete, the private methods of market control that worked in the past are found to be increasingly ineffective. Confronted with the unpleasant reality of uncooperative newcomers, interproduct competition, and unstabilized prices, established industry tends increasingly to enlist the power of government to do that which it is no longer able to do itself. The result is a steady and pervasive increase in the use of the powers of government to shore up weakening private controls of the market. The effect on competition is far more serious since voluntary cooperation, on which all private methods ultimately depend, is being fortified or replaced by the compulsory power of the state. The price cutter no longer suffers merely the opprobrium of his business rivals; he is now a violator of the law, subject to civil and criminal penalties. Once the state is committed to the preservation of the old, obsolete, and obsolescent, there is virtually no end to the means by which it can act to accomplish this objective. And once committed, governmental intervention tends to become institutionalized, invulnerable to criticism or attack; nothing is so permanent as a law or regulation that is clearly out of date.

Governmental intervention can also creep in through the back door, so to speak. Large corporations which, because of their managerial incompetence or technological backwardness, are in straitened financial circumstances come, hat in hand, to government seeking direct subsidies, guaranteed loans, and other forms of financial assistance. Once having made the grant, government will naturally be concerned with protecting its investment. And this may well lead directly to intervention into the affairs of the company or the industry itself. There will be a strong temptation for government to seek to suppress competition if the recipient of its financial largesse is unable to meet it.

The role of government in promoting concentration has been repeatedly deplored by economists appearing before the Senate Antitrust Subcommittee. Referring to the principal causes of concentration, Walter Adams testified:

> Some [corporations] are big because the Government itself has frequently promoted the very concentration which the antitrust laws are designed to prevent.
> Industrial concentration, as Professor Gray and I have pointed out in our recent book, is not inevitable. It is not the result of spontaneous generation or natural selection.
> It is not the outgrowth of modern technology or, as Karl Marx believed, the end product of an inexorable dialectic.
> On the contrary, it is often the result of unwise, discriminatory privilege-creating governmental measures which throttle competition and restrict opportunity.[1]

In his recommendation concerning public policies to deal with the problem of economic concentration, Adams placed first on his list the cessation of governmental intervention in the free market:

> First and foremost, the Government, through its legislative, executive and regulatory actions should refrain from promoting concentration, whether this be in the disposal of Government property, the award of defense contracts, the distribution of the tax burden, the allocation of subsidies, et cetera.
> *   *   *
> I have made an intensive study of the trucking industry, for example, and I found that the Interstate Commerce Commission does not protect the public against the industry but protects the industry against the bargaining power of the public.

Fritz Machlup testified to the same effect:

> It happens that our Government has done much more to create monopoly than to destroy monopoly. I need refer only to the tariff laws, to the corporation laws, to the patent laws, to the large number of franchises and licensing laws in the States and municipalities. There are features in our tax law which foster concentration.
> *   *   *
> On the one hand we go ahead and eliminate a little monopoly here, or a little there, but on the other hand we create monopolistic restraints all the time through restricting imports, through raising tariffs, through reducing quotas, through enforcing support prices, through making it more difficult for newcomers to enter industries, and so on and so forth.[2]

Alfred E. Kahn deplored the tendency of government to intervene whenever price competition begins to hurt:

> Even if the Government were to refrain from embarking on a positive program of breaking up existing concentrations of market power, it could do a great deal of good if it were merely to resolve to refrain henceforth from protecting such power centers against competitive attack and from conferring new monopoly privileges, as it is all too prone to do. The government must stop its all-too-prevalent practice of reso-

---

[1] *Hearings on Administered Prices,* Pt. 9, p. 4785. The study of trucking referred to is the report of the Senate Select Committee on Small Business entitled *Competition, Regulation and the Public Interest in the Motor Carrier Industry* (84th Cong., 2nd Sess., Senate Report No. 1693, 1956).
[2] *Ibid.,* Pt. 10, pp. 4955–56.

lutely stepping in to prevent competition every time a price threatens to decline, a profit margin to be squeezed, a job to be lost.[3]

Inasmuch as some prices are bound to rise, Kahn noted, others must be permitted to fall if the general price level is not to advance continually:

> I do not suggest that the problems with which these various policies attempt to deal are susceptible of easy solution. But I do suggest that they are far too often resolved in the easy way from the standpoint of the interests directly involved—by protection and insulation—and the wrong way if the Government is to give adequate heed to the broader public interest in economic growth and general price-level stability. It is no less true of governmental than of private efforts that if the general price level is to be held stable, individual prices must be permitted to fall; and that if constantly new and better ways of doing things are to be introduced, then there must be permitted some injury to, or at least discommoding of, private parties who have an interest in the older and less efficient ways of doing things.[4]

According to Horace M. Gray, restraint on competition stemming from the exercise of governmental authority has been on the increase, as

> year after year aspirants to monopoly power exerted unrelenting pressure on government for grants of privilege; and year after year government yielded to this pressure, slowly and grudgingly at first, out of deference to the tradition and public hostility, then at an accelerated pace as new and more sophisticated rationalizations were perfected . . . all monopolies of major significance today rest squarely on some special privilege granted by government. This is the "new mercantilism" of the late 20th century.[5]

Edwin G. Nourse emphasized the ambivalence of government: "There is a glaring inconsistency when a government pledged to free-competitive enterprise, harbors within itself a great variety of structures and programs which grant immunities or extend disproportionate privileges to special classes or groups. And yet the roster of such discrepancies in our economy is long." [6] In his view, business enterprise today is free in its competitive discretion in "only a highly Pickwickian sense"; in one industrial area after another the government has moved in to frustrate the forces of the free market. Nourse remarked: "Every one of these restrictive expedients has been designed to cope with some special problem of the times out of which it grew. But each was engineered by some special group, working through the political process. Many a 'joker' or ex parte provision was slipped into the original legislation or subsequent administrative rulings. Likewise, many features of our tax system are inimical to fair and effective competition." [7]

[3] 88th Cong., 1st Sess., Senate Subcommittee on Antitrust and Monopoly, Senate Committee on the Judiciary, *Administered Prices: A Compendium on Public Policy,* 1963, p. 172.
[4] *Ibid.*
[5] *Ibid.,* p. 142.
[6] *Ibid.,* p. 249.
[7] *Ibid.*

Procurement

Year in and year out the federal government is the largest buyer of goods and services in the world. When, as in World War II, defense outlays become the principal component of our gross national product, the manner in which the government procures supplies and later disposes of assets can have a profound and lasting effect on both aggregate and market concentration. These effects can also be significant when military spending, though well below the peak of total war, is sustained at relatively high levels over a continuing period of years. During World War II nearly $200 billion of prime supply contracts were entered into between the suppliers of products and the Army, Navy, and other government procurement agencies:

> Companies obtaining prime contracts secured thereby the instruments of economic power. They received money in the form of substantial profits for the production of goods, the sale of which was assured. They obtained materials and supplies, since naturally, they were granted priorities and allotments for needed materials, parts, components, etc. And, further than this, they were granted the power of determining how much of these priorities and allotments should be passed down to subcontractors, who and how many the subcontractors should be, and how much of the allocations each should receive.
>
> In addition, the receipt of a substantial prime contract generally gave to a company the right, if it desired to use it, of expanding its own facilities under the extremely favorable amortization and carry-back provisions provided by the tax laws. Companies holding large prime contracts experienced little difficulty in obtaining "certificates of necessity" which allowed them to take advantage of the special amortization tax provisions.
>
> Also, it was the companies that were the principal recipients of prime contracts which operated most of the Government-owned facilities built during the war, and these companies generally obtained options to buy the plants after the war.[8]

Fully 30 percent of the value of prime contracts awarded between June, 1940, and September, 1944, went to the 10 leading contractors, 49 percent to the top 30, and two-thirds to the top 100. The extent of concentration was even higher when measured in terms of the active contracts outstanding at a given date instead of in terms of the total amount issued over an extended period of time. The top 100 recipients held 75 percent of the prime contracts outstanding on September 30, 1944, as compared to 67 percent of the awards issued during the entire 4-year period. Contrasting this degree of concentration with the level prevailing before the war, the War Production Board noted, "The 100 leading corporations, ranked by value of product shipped in 1935 accounted for almost *one-third* of the total value of products, while the 100 highest in terms of active supply contracts held *three-fourths* of all the value." [9]

[8] 79th Cong., 2nd Sess., S. Doc. 206, Smaller War Plants Corp., Report for the Senate Select Committee on Small Business, *Economic Concentration and World War II*, 1946, p. 27.

[9] War Production Board, Bureau of Program Statistics, *Corporate Distribution of Prime War Supply Contracts Awarded June 1940 to September 1944*, March 8, 1945, p. 8. Emphasis added.

Although the list of the largest prime contractors was dominated, not unexpectedly, by aircraft manufacturers, it also included many long-established firms in traditional industries. Seven of the 15 leading contractors were not aircraft companies. At the top was General Motors, which received 8 percent of the prime contracts. The third and seventh leading contractors were the other 2 leading automobile producers, Ford Motor Company and Chrysler Corporation, which received 3 percent and 1.9 percent respectively. Also among the 15 top recipients were the nation's largest companies in electrical machinery (General Electric), communications (American Telephone & Telegraph), and chemicals (Du Pont), as well as the second largest steel producer (Bethlehem), which was also a leading shipbuilder. Among the top 100 were other companies that before the war had been primarily engaged in such disparate fields as foods, textiles, rubber products, chemicals, petroleum, machinery, electrical machinery, and railway equipment.

The extreme concentration of prime-contract awards was due partly to the fact that it is always easier for the procurement agencies to deal with a few large concerns than with numerous medium-size and small companies. Moreover, it must be recognized that leading wartime products, such as aircraft, ships, tanks, and other heavy ordnance, could be manufactured and assembled only in huge plants, owned almost of necessity by large companies. Nonetheless, there remained a considerable list of military end-items that could have been produced readily in small plants, while a greater volume of the subcontracting of parts and components could have gone to small enterprises.

Subcontracting to small plants was in reality never as great as has been commonly assumed. The Smaller War Plants Corporation in 1943 made a study of the prime and subcontracting records of 252 of the largest corporations, which received the bulk of the prime-contract awards. Large companies employing more than 500 wage earners and receiving 78 percent of the prime contracts subcontracted 34 percent of their contracts. Three-fourths of these subcontracts went to other large companies, with the remaining one-fourth allocated to small companies. The large-company subcontractors, in turn, passed along 13 percent of their subcontract business to further subcontractors, with other large companies receiving 44 percent. Thus the small companies' share of total war production consisted of (a) 22 percent of the prime contracts, (b) 6 percent in subcontracts at the first tier of subcontracting, and (c) one percent of subcontracting at lower levels. The share of military output produced by firms other than the 252 largest was therefore approximately only 30 percent of the total.[10]

The World War II experience established a pattern of military procurement that appears to have changed very little in the subsequent 25 years, despite the disappearance of emergency conditions which made reliance on the available large enterprises more understandable. In fiscal 1968 the share of defense prime contracts received by "small business" was 18.8 percent; in 1943 the share received by companies other than the 252 largest corporations had been

---

[10] The estimate of 30% accords closely with figures on the share of manufacturing employment held by small firms derived from data of the Bureau of Old Age Survivors Insurance. Omitting industries not covered by the SWPC 1943 survey of subcontracting—tobacco, printing and publishing, leather, food, stone, clay, and glass, furniture, apparel, lumber and furniture—the BOASI data showed that in 1944 firms with fewer than 500 workers in the remaining industries employed 26% of the manufacturing workers (Smaller War Plants Corp., op. cit., p. 33).

22 percent.[11] In 1968, 42.6 percent of the value of the prime contracts was subcontracted; in 1943 it had been 34.4 percent. In 1968 the addition of their subcontracts to their proportion of prime contracts raised small business' share of defense procurement to 35 percent; in 1943 it had been 30 percent.[12] Although the definition of what constitutes the small-business share was not identical in both periods, the centralization of prime contracts remained so extreme within the first 50 companies that definitional differences would occasion little difference in results.[13]

The small-business share undoubtedly would have been considerably smaller in both periods had it not been for the creation by Congress of the Smaller War Plants Corporation and its successor, the Small Business Administration. Each was given the responsibility of "mobilizing" the facilities of small business for military production. The SBA's ability to carry out this function has been strengthened by the power to require that shares of designated defense contracts be "set aside" for small firms. While the establishment of these agencies may have been due in part to sociological and political motivations, they have also performed a purely economic function by restricting the waste of overly centralized procurement. This waste results from the building of new plant and equipment when adequate facilities are already available or from the accumulation of extensive order backlogs in large enterprises when available capacity of small firms lies idle.

During World War II order backlogs in metal products industries at the end of 1943 amounted to more than 12 months for large plants, as compared to 3 months for small plants.[14] Long backlogs in big plants and short backlogs in small plants existed not only for items that could be produced only in large plants, such as tanks or ships, but for products that could just as easily have been manufactured in small plants, such as metal pails, metal office and store fixtures, water purification equipment, airplane landing mats, commercial cooking equipment, bedsprings, or innerspring mattresses. This overconcentration of orders led to a disruption of scheduling, planning, and controlling of war production. When large order backlogs developed, all the services wanted their orders produced immediately, which brought the intervention of expediters, special directives, uncertainty, and confusion on a scale which had to be experienced to be believed.

The Medium Shell Program of November, 1944, affords an example of how small plants in noncritical labor areas had been neglected in favor of large

[11] The figures for fiscal 1968 are taken from the *Nineteenth Annual Report* of the Senate Select Committee on Small Business (91st Cong., 1st Sess., Senate Report No. 91-627, 1969, pp. 12–13).

[12] Logically, if what one is interested in is the share of defense production accounted for by small business exclusive of contributions by large firms, the purchases by small prime and subcontractors of materials and supplies from large firms should be deleted. Deletions for such purchases were *not* made in either the 1943 or the 1968 surveys.

[13] In this comparison the small-business segment in 1943 consisted of all corporations other than the 252 largest. For recent years, the small-business share has been derived on an industry-by-industry basis, consisting in general of the share accounted for by companies with fewer than 500 employees. For some capital-intensive industries, however, firms of larger absolute size are regarded as "small"; e.g., for aircraft the cutoff point is 1,000 workers, and for motor vehicles it is 1,500.

[14] Smaller War Plants Corp., *Thirteenth Bimonthly Report to Congress,* June–July, 1944, as set forth in 78th Cong., 2nd Sess., S. Doc. 234, pp. 3, 15–25. Before adjustment for noncoverage the figure for small plants was 8 months.

plants in tight labor areas.[15] In November, 1944, the Army was confronted by a critical shortage of medium shells. At that time the known production facilities, 71 small and 156 large plants, were already producing at capacity. The Smaller War Plants Corporation undertook a rapid field survey to determine available capacity among other small plants, submitting 237 screened nominations. The Ordnance Department accepted for consideration 120 of these small firms. Actual contracts were awarded to 52 small plants, including 26 of those recommended by the Smaller War Plants Corporation. This constitutes only one of many examples of the way economic waste was reduced and war production accelerated by securing a greater participation by small firms.

During periods of emergency the government not only determines which companies shall produce the items it purchases; it decides which companies shall provide essential services such as transportation and the equipment needed therefor. At each stage in the economic process the intervention by government creates the opportunity for the promotion of concentration. An example is the way in which, through government priority and allocation orders, General Motors was enabled to monopolize the locomotive industry.

Before the introduction of diesels General Motors had not been a producer of locomotives. For many years the production of steam locomotives had been largely in the hands of American Locomotive, Baldwin, and Lima. Contrary to a widespread impression, the diesel locomotive was not introduced by General Motors; the first diesel, a switcher, was built by American Locomotive in 1924 and operated on the Jersey Central Railroad for 30 years. In testimony before the Senate Antitrust Subcommittee, William F. Lewis of Alco Products (formerly American Locomotive) recounted the history of the diesel:

> As early as 1927, Alco was engaged in designing a diesel engine which would be lightweight and compact in size, and we produced the first experimental diesel locomotive developed for passenger service in 1929. It was not until the mid-thirties, however, that sufficiently light and compact diesel engines were developed for passenger service, and it was not until 1940 that the freight diesel locomotive, as we know it today, was produced. This is a significant point—for freight locomotives at that time comprised about 75 percent of the total market potential for diesels. This meant that at the threshold of World War II, the diesel era, as such, still lay ahead for the locomotive industry. For a full appreciation of this fact, let us quickly examine the composition of the motive-power industry of United States class I railroads[16] as of December 31, 1941. At that particular bench-mark, there were 41,771 locomotives in service on United States class I railroads. Of this total, 39,624 were steam locomotives and 1,267 diesel. Of the diesel group, slightly over 1,000 were switchers, with Alco the manufacturer of a substantial share. That brings us to the conclusion of what might be termed the pioneering era of the diesel.[17]

Another common misconception is that while General Motors was producing diesel locomotives on a mass-production basis, the other manufacturers were turning them out "by hand." In point of fact, American Locomotive in-

[15] Smaller War Plants Corp., *Sixteenth Bimonthly Report to Congress,* Dec., 1944–Jan. 1945, pp. 4–5.
[16] Railroads earning more than $1 million gross a year, which account for more than 90% of rail traffic—J. M. B.
[17] 84th Cong., 1st Sess., Senate Subcommittee on Antitrust and Monopoly, Senate Committee on the Judiciary, *Hearings on General Motors,* 1955, Pt. 6, pp. 2382–83.

vested approximately $20 million in converting its Schenectady, New York, plant, producing between 1946 and 1953 some 5,000 diesel locomotives. In the words of its spokesman, "In many of those years we produced at capacity level, at times reaching a peak of 5½ diesel locomotive units a working day, or more than 100 locomotives a month. Production of this capacity requires an obviously high level of efficiency. . . ." [18]

It was an action by the government, plus an inherent reciprocal relationship with the railroads, which largely explains General Motors' success in capturing the market. At the outset of World War II GM was the only company that had built *freight* diesel locomotives—the type for which there would inevitably be the greatest market. It had turned out *two* such engines in 1940! Yet American Locomotive "at the end of 1941 had virtually completed the engineering on what would have been the first fully complete line of diesel locomotives of an entirely new design." [19] Under limitation orders the War Production Board froze this "historical" pattern of the industry, "restricting" GM to the production of freight engines and the other producers largely to switchers. As might have been anticipated, production of freight engines was steadily and sharply increased, while during most of the war the output of switchers and passenger engines remained relatively stable.

Deliveries of Diesel-electric Locomotive
Units Built in the United States[20]

	Freight		Switchers and Passengers	
	GM	Other Companies	GM	Other Companies
1940	2	0	217	108
1941	47	0	233	209
1942	96	0	146	214
1943	184	0	15	290
1944	500	0	0	489

In the words of one of GM's competitors, the effect of allocating the fast-growing segment of the market to one company and confining the others to the remainder was to give GM a "tremendous headstart" from a "protected position." Trying to catch up proved an impossible undertaking since railroads, which had already equipped themselves with GM locomotives, understandably did not want to be using two different makes of engines requiring dissimilar repair and maintenance parts. Only 10 years after the end of the war, GM had 83 percent of the market for freight locomotives, 100 percent for passenger diesels, and 53 percent for switchers.

Contributing also to GM's monopolization of the industry was the natural tendency of railroads to place their locomotive orders with the nation's largest user of their services—namely, General Motors. While uncertain of its importance, officials of rival locomotive producers acknowledged that it was undoubtedly a factor. The following colloquy took place between an official of American Locomotive and the Subcommittee's chief counsel, Joseph Burns:

[18] *Ibid.,* pp. 2383–84.
[19] *Ibid.,* p. 2383.
[20] Compiled from *ibid.,* Pt. 8, pp. 3963–64.

MR. BURNS: Have you encountered in any way the problem of meeting the situation which has been referred to of General Motors being the largest single shipper by rail in the United States, and thus being a customer of the railroads to whom it is trying to sell its products?

MR. LEWIS: Well, I think with the size of General Motors, I think it is recognized that they must have a tremendous amount of traffic.

* * *

SENATOR O'MAHONEY: Mr. Lewis, will you make a little more clear . . . this principle of helping one another that you say exists in the business world today?

MR. LEWIS: Well, I think that, Senator, it is recognized we like to do business with our friends, particularly if our friends are responsible and reliable.

I think business in any field—I do not mean to refer to the railroad industry or the railroad-manufacturing industry—but you might take it in any industry that is in existence, I think it is only—you do business through friends.

SENATOR O'MAHONEY: And through customers?

MR. LEWIS: And through customers; that is right.

SENATOR O'MAHONEY: And the bigger the customer the better the friendship?

MR. LEWIS: That might be true in many cases; it might be true.[21]

Mr. O. DeGray Vanderbilt III, vice president of Baldwin-Lima-Hamilton Company, was of the same opinion:

MR. BURNS: In addition to the advantage which resulted from the ability to produce these on a mass-production basis was the fact that the diesels were being made by General Motors, a company which ships itself over the railroad tremendous quantities of freight. I believe it has been stated that it is the largest shipper of freight in the United States. Do you feel that that in any way gave it advantages in selling its locomotives over a company like yours, which did not have so much freight being shipped over the railroads?

MR. VANDERBILT: Oh, I think that is true. I think we would be naive to assume that General Motors' tremendous volume of traffic over the railroads does not have a profound influence on railroad purchasing. If the railroads didn't take it into consideration, I am sure they wouldn't be doing their job.[22]

Disposals

The government not only procures; it disposes. And the most lasting effect of World War II on industry structure lay in the manner in which government-financed facilities were disposed of. Their disposal is significant also in that it illustrates dramatically the pattern still generally followed in the sale of facilities built for defense purposes. The new facilities built during World War II increased by more than *half* again the nation's entire existing productive capacity. In 1939 our manufacturing facilities carried a gross valuation of $40 billion. To this was added by June, 1945, about $26 billion of new plant and

[21] *Ibid.,* Pt. 6, p. 2391.
[22] *Ibid.,* pp. 2369–70.

equipment. Roughly two-thirds of this expansion was provided directly from federal funds, the remainder coming from private sources. In general, most of the plant expansion took the form of high-quality, high-cost construction; for example, most of the new machine tools were designed to use the highly productive tungsten carbide cutting tools. Unfortunately it is impossible to obtain anything approaching a complete record of what happened to this enormous expansion of productive capacity. Part of the increase, notably facilities for shipbuilding and repair, ordnance, specialized aircraft equipment, explosives, artillery, ammunition loading, and the like, could not in any case have been feasibly converted to civilian production. Although estimates vary, probably about one-third of the total was unusable for peacetime purposes. Records are not available concerning the disposition of that portion of new facilities which consisted of machinery and equipment. Of the $26-billion outlay, $14 billion was for new plants, $4.2 billion for expansion of prewar plants, and $7.8 billion for conversion of prewar plants to war production and for replacement of old equipment. There is practically no information available on the disposal of government-owned plant equipment sold after the war by both the owning agencies and the disposal agencies.

By the end of 1946 corporations among the 250 largest had received 70.1 percent of the plants disposed of, based on reported costs; in 1939 these 250 giants had held 65.4 percent of usable facilities; 6 of the 250 obtained 48 percent of the war plants, based on original cost; in 1939 these 6 had accounted for less than 10 percent of the gross capital assets of all manufacturing corporations. In all, 87 large corporations purchased or leased some 209 plants representing no less than 65 percent of the reported cost of all disposals. In terms of sales alone these large buyers purchased 157 plants representing 69 percent of the reported cost of all plants sold. No less than 54 percent of the plant disposals went to just 16 firms, only one of which (Tucker) was not among the nation's 250 largest.[23]

The effect of disposal policy on concentration could have been minimized through sales of smaller facilities to small companies. Yet in the case of plants costing from $1 to $5 million, which were within the range of many small and medium-size companies, no fewer than 40, representing 52.6 percent of their value, went to the 250 giants. Similarly, they obtained 33 distinctly small plants costing less than $1 million each.

What is most meaningful from an economic point of view, of course, is the effect of the disposal on concentration in individual industries. In the steel industry the 3 leading producers—U.S. Steel, Bethlehem, and Republic—acquired plants with an aggregate reported cost of $422 million, nearly half of which was represented by one plant alone, the giant Geneva, Utah, plant purchased by U.S. Steel. The sale of this plant illustrates the focus of primary criticism of the disposal agencies—the overemphasis on price as the guiding principle in plant disposal. There were six bids for the purchase or lease of the $200-million plant, including bids by 2 well-established western steel producers, but none was able to match the bid of United States Steel. The purchase of this mill raised U.S. Steel's proportion of steel-making capacity from 33.8 to 35.1 percent on a national basis and from 17.3 to 52.7 percent in the Far West. This completely integrated basic steel-producing operation at Geneva was the single most elaborate and costly of the plants financed by the

[23] See War Assets Administration, "Relations Between Plant Disposal and Industrial Concentration," Dec. 31, 1946. Mimeograph.

government during the war. It was located in easy range of plentiful raw materials and was strategically situated with respect to western markets.

For a generation efforts had been made to create an iron and steel industry on the Pacific coast. Western steel-fabricating industries had been paying premium prices for steel even when it was produced on the Pacific coast. According to a brief submitted by the Western States Council:

> The Pacific coast price has in general been from $10 to $15 more per ton than in the eastern steel production centers. In fact their prices have been paid by western buyers of steel for steel produced in and delivered by eastern mills and also for steel fabricated in western plants. As a consequence, western manufacturers and fabricators have paid prices for steel that limited their ability to market products made from steel to definitely restricted market areas.[24]

At the same time, these extra charges enabled eastern fabricators to compete at a decided advantage in western markets and served as a constant spur to the efforts to obtain an independent western steel industry. The outcome of these efforts was described by a small western steel producer in testimony before the Truman committee: "There never has been a question of the feasibility of an iron and steel industry in the area, but on each occasion when the efforts have been made to establish an industry, the planning and work of those engaged in the project has been frustrated through connivance and intervention on the part of existing steel corporations and existing financial combinations." [25]

To guide the disposal of this property, as required under the War Mobilization and Reconversion Act of 1944, Attorney General Biddle submitted a report to Congress on June 29, 1945, entitled "Western Steel Plants and the Tin Plate Industry," in which he stressed the monopolistic practices of the United States Steel Corporation and other leading eastern steel producers and emphasized the importance to the development of western industry of the independent operation and control by western interests of the Geneva plant.[26] Biddle observed that

> the western steel industry [should] be free from monopolistic control so that it can adopt pricing policies which will permit it to compete aggressively with the eastern mills. Up to the present time, tin plate has not been sold on a competitive basis in the West. A concentration of producers and of consumers has resulted in high and rigid prices. The future owners of the newly developed western steel plants should have the opportunity to enter into this market on a competitive basis.
>
> The future disposition of this plant with its 1,280,000 tons of ingots is crucial to the reconversion program in the West. The policies and purposes of those who buy this government plant may well be the determining factor in the future of the western steel industry. Everything possible should be done to assist potential purchasers of the Geneva steel plant to draw plans for its operation.
>
> Disposal to eastern steel interests, especially those with water access to western parts, would substantially lessen competition and could retard development of western facilities.[27]

[24] 79th Cong., 1st Sess., Senate Subcommittee on Surplus Property, Senate Committee on Military Affairs, *Hearings,* 1945, p. 147.

[25] 77th Cong., 2nd Sess., Special Senate Committee Investigating the National Defense Program, *Hearings,* 1942, Pt. 14, p. 5839.

[26] Reports to Congress under the following statutes: War Mobilization and Reconversion Act (1944), Sec. 205; Surplus Property Act (1944), Sec. 19(a).

[27] *Ibid.*

The considerations described by the Department of Justice were ignored by the War Assets Administration, which based its award on the single determinant of price. By so doing it all but guaranteed disposal to U.S. Steel, since no other bidder was able to match its $40-million cash bid. After reviewing the bid for lease by the Colorado Fuel & Iron Corporation, War Assets stated in a press release, "This bid does not provide an adequate return to Government and is not as favorable as the United States Steel bid." And, in rejecting the bid of the Pacific-American Steel and Iron Corporation of Seattle, Washington, War Assets said, "This bid is not as favorable as the United States Steel bid." [28]

Republic Steel Corporation, the third largest steel producer, obtained the second largest steel plant built by the government—the South Chicago plant. This facility, which was the largest electric steel mill in the world, was built at a cost of $91 million and sold to Republic for $35 million, payable over a period of 20 years. By obtaining this plant, which occupied 55 buildings on a site of approximately 180 acres, Republic improved its position from the fourth to the largest electric steel producer and its percentage of the nation's electric furnace capacity from 9 percent to 28 percent. As in the case of the Geneva plant, there were other bidders for this giant mill. A bid of Philip D. Fitzgerald of Chicago was rejected because, in the words of a War Assets Administration press release, "financial guaranties were not forthcoming following its submission." In addition, a bid of C. A. Dupue of Clinton, Iowa, proposing to buy the property for $20 million, guarantee $10.77 million in working capital, and spend $10 million on additional machinery and equipment, was rejected because, according to War Assets, "it was considerably under the Republic bid." Again the emphasis by War Assets on the price factor was the decisive consideration.

Bethlehem Steel is one of the few large corporations that purchased the plants they operated at option or cost price. Bethlehem exercised its option on 6 steel plants, located in Pennsylvania, New York, and Maryland, paying the full reported cost of $20.2 million.

Just as the 3 largest steel corporations acquired the great bulk of the government's surplus steel facilities, so also did General Electric and Westinghouse account for most of the disposals of electrical-machinery facilities. In terms of number of plants acquired, General Electric led all other corporations, having bought 14 and leased 2, with a total cost value of $35.8 million. Westinghouse, with $23.6 million of surplus plants, was not far behind, again illustrating the old adage that Westinghouse "keeps General Electric out of jail."

An interesting feature of GE's expansion was its deliberate emphasis on smaller plants. "With fewer people," said Charles E. Wilson, president of General Electric, "we find that management can do a better job of organizing facilities and personnel. This results in lower manufacturing costs and better production control." [29] The average cost of the 14 plants purchased by General Electric amounted to only $2.4 million each, as compared with $10.7 million for the 2 plants purchased by Westinghouse and $80 million for the 4 plants purchased by U.S. Steel. Seven of the plants acquired by General Electric

[28] In addition to Geneva, U.S. Steel also purchased for $44 million the third largest government-owned steel mill, the Homestead works, whose reported cost was $86 million. This plant represented a substantial addition to U.S. Steel's flat-rolled capacity, with slab and plate mills, two new blast furnaces, a new open-hearth unit, electric furnaces, and facilities for armor forging and heat treating and alloy heat treatment.

[29] *Wall Street Journal,* April 14, 1947.

cost less than $1 million each. Just as the sale of the steel mills is an example of one defect of disposal policies—the overemphasis on price—so does the sale of these plants illustrate another deficiency—the sale of small plants to large corporations. On the customary terms of payment of 10 or 20 percent down and the remainder in 10 years, there were thousands of small and medium-size companies in the machinery industries with sufficient capital to acquire the $1- and $2-million plants that went to the world's largest maker of electrical products.

Disposals in the agricultural-machinery industry were dominated completely by the leading producer, International Harvester, which before World War II accounted for 37 percent of the industry's sales. With an outlay of $28 million, International purchased 5 surplus plants that had cost the government $41.9 million. The prize package obtained by International was the enormous Melrose Park, Illinois, engine plant. This huge facility, occupying 135 acres and 1.2 million square feet of manufacturing floor space, was one of the largest plants built by the government. Two other large facilities purchased by International were the aircraft plants at Louisville, Kentucky, and Evansville, Indiana. These 2 plants were both about the same size—around a million square feet; both cost the government slightly over $9 million, and both were sold to International Harvester at about 60 percent of their reported cost. There can be little doubt that the effect of these disposals was to improve International's position relative to its competitors. In comparison with International's purchases of $42 million, the surplus acquisitions by the other farm machinery producers were inconsequential.

But disposals need not necessarily promote concentration. An example of what could be accomplished in the opposite direction was the Aluminum Plant Disposal Program, which substantially reduced economic concentration in a monopolized industry and infused new competition into a basic field of industrial activity. Prior to World War II, the Aluminum Company of America had been the sole domestic producer of primary aluminum and its source material, alumina. In addition, it owned more than 80 percent of the U.S. fabricating capacity for all aluminum products, with the sole exceptions of foil, cooking utensils, and castings. The enormous wartime demand for aluminum required a nearly sixfold increase in capacity, most of which was government-built but operated by Alcoa. Following the mandate of the courts and recommendations of the Department of Justice, the War Assets Administration gave first choice to competitors of Alcoa. In addition, it took steps to assist new producers by providing engineering and other assistance in developing suitable policies to control the disposal of surplus secondary metal, and aid in obtaining supplies.[30] Thus Reynolds was enabled to improve its position materially, and Permanente Metals Corporation (Kaiser interests) gained a position in the industry as a new producer by acquiring alumina, primary-aluminum, and fabricating plants.

What was accomplished in aluminum could to a greater or lesser extent have been achieved in other areas as well. Congress had declared the objectives of the Surplus Property Act to be "to facilitate and regulate the orderly disposal" of surplus property so as to accomplish such economic and social results as the following:

[30] See War Assets Administration, First Supplementary Report, *Aluminum Plants and Facilities,* Feb. 12, 1947, p. 2.

> To effect broad, equitable and wide distribution at fair prices; to discourage monopolistic practices . . . to aid in the establishment and development of free, independent operators in trade, industry and agriculture; to afford returning veterans an opportunity to establish themselves as proprietors of agricultural, business and professional enterprises; to strengthen the competitive position of small business concerns . . . to render more secure family type farming as the traditional and desirable pattern of American agriculture; to dispose of surplus as promptly as feasible without fostering monopoly or restraint of trade. . . .[31]

The congressional mandate, however, was largely ignored by the officials of the disposal agencies. In describing their approach to the job at hand Myron L. Hoch commented:

> Although the objectives read like a New Deal testament, the administrative officials who were "practical" men with a double entry bookkeeping approach, viewed the task in the narrow terms of a "business" problem (i.e. turnover of inventory). They appeared to be obsessed with the "burden" of the tremendous inventory of capital and consumer goods. They expected that their performance would be judged in terms of volume and rate of sales rather than in terms of vague "dreamy" intangibles like "equitable" distribution. They plunged into the job with the zest with which they would meet a payroll.[32]

Leases

Since 1954 the federal government through the Department of the Interior has granted leases in the amount of $4 billion for the right to drill for and extract oil from federal lands on the outer continental shelf off Louisiana and Texas. Despite the impressive magnitude of the outlay, what has thus far been leased represents only a small proportion of the potential oil-bearing area on these federal lands.

The great bulk of these leases have gone to fewer than a dozen major oil companies. This concentration of awards, it is widely believed, is the inescapable result of the high cost of expensive drilling rigs, which are thought to be beyond the financial resources of anyone but the majors. This, however, is a misapprehension; there are any number of small and medium-size oil companies, and even individuals, who are able to command the financial resources required to own and operate their own offshore rigs. Rather, the cause is to be found in the bidding procedure followed by the Interior Department, a procedure that incidentally is *not* required by any act of Congress. Under this procedure, known as "bonus bidding," a low royalty (one-sixth of the revenue) is required of all bidders, with the award going to the bidder who makes the highest cash bid (above a $30 per-acre minimum figure). One bid in the Gulf of Mexico ran as high as $27,000 per acre on a tract of some 3,500 acres— a total bid of $94 million. It is hard to conceive of a bidding procedure more favorable to the largest firms and more disadvantageous to smaller enterprises. If by chance a small firm, or even a group of them, could manage to outbid the majors, the cost of the bid itself would absorb financial resources that should better be devoted to undertaking an adequate drilling program.

[31] Surplus Property Act (1944).
[32] Myron L. Hoch, "Some Economic Implications of Government Surplus Disposal," *City College Business Review*, Fall, 1948, p. 2.

E. Wayles Browne has proposed reversing the bidding procedure, fixing a flat dollar amount per acre and varying the royalty percentage, with the award going to the bidder who offered the government the greatest share. Under this procedure any company equipped to drill or able to contract for an offshore well could enter the bidding with some possibility of emerging as the successful bidder. Substantially all its working capital would be available for use in geological and geophysical work and drilling, with no significant bleed-off for lease bonus. Since the initial investment would result in more drilling, more oil on the average should be found. Since more bidders could afford to participate, the return to the government should over the long run be greater. The only disadvantage to the government of substituting percentages for dollar bonuses lies in the deferral of returns. According to former Secretary of the Interior Udall, the Budget Bureau has urged the cash bonus sale of more offshore leases in order to bring in quick cash revenues to the Treasury. Hurrying national assets to market to keep the Treasury in pocket money hardly seems a proper basis for a major national policy.

Patents

In endowing Congress with the power "To promote the progress of science and useful arts, by securing for limited times to authors and inventors the exclusive right to their respective writings and discoveries," the framers of the Constitution were reflecting the prevailing point of view of the early British economists.[33] Although to Adam Smith monopoly was "necessarily hurtful to society," he saw a temporary monopoly granted to an inventor as a good way of rewarding his risk and expense. The attitude of the classical school was summarized by John Stuart Mill, who urged that "the condemnation of monopolies ought not to extend to patents" and that the inventor "ought to be both compensated and rewarded."

In support of patents it has been argued that man has a natural property right in his own ideas; that patents are a way of securing justice for the inventor by rewarding his services in proportion to their usefulness to society; and that patents are a way of striking a bargain between inventors and society, with the inventor surrendering the possession of secret knowledge in exchange for a temporarily exclusive right to its industrial use. But these arguments, which played important roles in the past, have largely given way to the contention that the patent monopoly, by stimulating inventive effort, will yield a greater flow of new discoveries and that this gain outweighs the cost in the form of higher prices charged during the patent's life. Also heard is the argument that without a patent the individual inventor, who continues to be an important source of new discoveries, has nothing to use in bargaining with a large corporation for a license to his invention and that therefore, unless he is prepared to set himself up as a producing and marketing enterprise, he is deprived of his only significant inducement to invent.

On the other hand, the arguments against patents have been legion. It has been contended that patents are an unnecessary inducement to the truly cre-

[33] The following summary of the history of economic thought on the patent issue is based largely on *An Economic Review of the Patent System* by Fritz Machlup (85th Cong., 2nd Sess., Senate Subcommittee on Patents, Trademarks and Copyrights, Senate Committee on the Judiciary, Study No. 15, 1958).

ative individual ("Geniuses, just as stars, must shine without pay"); that patents have led to an undesirable degree of bigness (in the words of Alfred Marshall, "Many giant businesses have owed their first successes to the possession of important patents. . . ."); that, in the words of John Bates Clark, the patentee is able to enjoy his monopoly "beyond the period covered by his patent" and that a patent "builds up a great corporation which afterward, by virtue of its size is able to club off competitors that would like to enter its field"; that the monopoly control founded on patents extends far beyond the patent monopoly itself, permitting, in the words of Lionel Robbins, "the creation of a whole network of tying contracts, forced joint supply, resale price maintenance and other trade practices . . . cumulatively highly conducive to the consolidation of monopolistic conditions"; that by enabling the holder to destroy his competitors in a variety of other ways, patents restrict competition to a much greater extent than is inherent in the principle of patent protection; that it is unrealistic to carve out slices of the continuing expansion of knowledge, particularly when the rewards tend to go not to the scientists who make the fundamental discoveries but to firms which merely adapt them to some commercial use; that there is no relation between the earnings under a patent and the "social usefulness" of the invention; that patent monopolies may actually impede economic progress since, in the words of Arnold Plant, "competitors, instead of helping to improve the best, are compelled in self preservation to apply themselves to the devising of alternatives which, though possibly inferior, will circumvent the patent"; that patents are frequently obtained on only minor changes in the art, which is a principal reason why those patents whose validity has been tested in litigation have in general fared badly; and that the mere existence of a patent, even one of dubious validity, has an economic value in that an infringement suit is a costly undertaking from which small firms may emerge victorious in the legal fray but be vanquished financially. In addition to these objections to patents themselves, there is the further argument that in practice protection may be longer than the life of the patent. This may be accomplished, in Machlup's words,

> (a) through procedural devices, especially through delays in the pendency of the patent between application and issuance; (b) through secret use of the invention prior to the application for a patent, or through incomplete disclosure . . . (c) through the successive patenting of strategic improvements of the invention which make the unimproved invention commercially unusable after expiration of the original patent; (d) through creation of a monopolistic market position based on the goodwill of a trademark associated with the patented product or process, where the mark and the consumer loyalty continue after expiration of the patent; and (e) through licensing agreements which survive the original patent because they license a series of existing improvement patents and a possibly endless succession of future patents.[34]

After his characteristically careful review of the literature Machlup reached a "Scotch verdict":

> No economist on the basis of present knowledge could possibly state with certainty that the patent system, as it now operates, confers a net benefit

[34] 85th Cong., 2nd Sess., Senate Subcommittee on Patents, Trademarks and Copyrights, Senate Committee on the Judiciary, Study No. 15, Fritz Machlup, *An Economic Review of the Patent System*, pp. 10–11.

or a net loss upon society. The best he can do is to state assumptions and make guesses about the extent to which reality corresponds to these assumptions.

If one does not know whether a system "as a whole" (in contrast to certain features of it) is good or bad, the safest "policy conclusion" is to "muddle through"—either with it, if one has long lived with it, or without it, if one has lived without it. If we did not have a patent system, it would be irresponsible, on the basis of our present knowledge of its economic consequences, to recommend instituting one. But since we have had a patent system for a long time, it would be irresponsible, on the basis of our present knowledge, to recommend abolishing it.[35]

For an empirical evaluation of the issue what is needed is a comparison for given industries of price levels and rates of inventiveness where patent protection exists and where it does not exist. If it were found that under patents prices are higher but that this burden to the public is not offset by a greater frequency of discovery, the case for patent protection would be seriously undermined. Such a comparison has in fact been made for one field—the drug industry. It happens that most countries of the world do not award patents on pharmaceutical *products*. The basis for exempting drugs from patent protection is the philosophical concept, going back to the eighteenth century, that no person should have the right to withhold from another human being products essential to the prevention of suffering and the preservation of life itself. Patents are granted on *processes* of making drugs, but, as in most chemical industries, process patents are a relatively weak form of protection. Probably more than any other industry, chemical products lend themselves to manufacture by several alternative processes; as a result process patents in drugs are commonly referred to in the trade as constituting only "a basis for litigation."

> The limitation of protection for chemical products in general as well as pharmaceutical products in particular, to process claims, is essentially a continental European conception, and is tied up with social thinking in the 19th century during the industrial revolution. It became a matter of practically unassailable dogma that if the public is to receive the benefit of new chemical or pharmaceutical products at a reasonable price and in amounts sufficient to meet the demand, that this could only be accomplished by restricting the inventor to his process, so that others will be encouraged to invent new and improved processes which will make the product cheaper and available in greater quantity.[36]

In its investigation of drug prices the Senate Antitrust Subcommittee requested the State Department to obtain price information on selected drugs from foreign countries, including most of the highly industrialized countries in the free world. Of 17 foreign countries for which usable price information was obtained product patents on pharmaceuticals are granted in 6 (Australia, Belgium, Canada, Great Britain, India, and Panama plus, of course, the United States), while they are not granted in 11 (Argentina, Austria, Brazil, France, Germany, Holland, Iran, Italy, Japan, Mexico, and Venezuela).[37] The average prices of countries without product patents are compared with the corresponding figures of countries with product patents for 12 major drug products in Table

---

[35] *Ibid.*, pp. 79–80.
[36] Leonard J. Robbins, "Pharmaceutical Patents in Foreign Countries," *Journal of the Patent Office Society*, April, 1955, p. 276.
[37] *Administered Prices: Report on Drugs*, pp. 105–14.

THE ROLE OF GOVERNMENT

15-1, which shows both the generic and the leading brand name of the product, the latter in parentheses. For the 12 products the average price was nearly 40 percent higher in countries with product patents than in those without them.

The greatest difference was registered by the tranquilizer prochlorperazine (Compazine), with an average price for countries with drug patents of 255 percent above that of countries without such protection. In 4 of the 12 products, the average price was more than 50 percent higher in countries with product patents and in all products except the antibiotics it was more than 25 percent higher. The fact that the difference was more limited in the case of the antibiotics is not to be unexpected in view of the restrictive cartel agreements entered into between U.S. patent holders and firms in countries that do not have patent protection.

The extent of the difference is understated in the table because of the inclusion of underdeveloped countries, most of which do not grant product patents. Since the drugs themselves are usually imported into such countries, the state of competition within the country has little or no effect on the laid down price. This problem can be avoided if one limits the comparison to the industrialized countries. There are 7 such countries for which information on drug prices and patents was available; product patents are not granted by 3 (Italy, France, and West Germany) and are granted in 4 (the United States, Canada, Great Britain, and Belgium). The average prices for 10 major drug

Table 15-1

COMPARISON OF AVERAGE PRICES IN 17 COUNTRIES WITHOUT AND WITH PATENT PROTECTION ON DRUG PRODUCTS, SPRING, 1959

| Product | Average Price in Countries | | |
	Without Product Patents (a)	With Product Patents (b)	Percentage $\left(\dfrac{b}{a}\right)$
Prednisone (Meticorten)	$14.75	$22.36	151.6
Chlorpromazine (Thorazine)	1.24	1.89	152.4
Prochlorperazine (Compazine)	.80	2.84	355.0
Promazine (Sparine)	1.57	1.98	126.1
Meprobamate (Miltown)	2.53	3.31	130.8
Reserpine (Serpasil)	1.73	2.79	161.3
Tolbutamide (Orinase)	2.03	3.02	148.8
Chlorpropamide (Diabinese)	3.81	4.87	127.8
Penicillin V	10.87	13.19	121.3
Chloramphenicol (Chloromycetin)	3.17	3.77	118.9
Chlortetracycline (Aureomycin)	4.68	5.53	118.2
Tetracycline (Achromycin)	4.63	5.68	122.7
Average: 12 products	$ 4.32	$ 5.97	138.1

Source: Administered Prices: Report on Drugs, Table 34

products in both types of countries is shown in Table 15-2. With the elimination of the underdeveloped countries the average price in countries with product patents was 60 percent higher than in those without product patents; excluding antibiotics it was 106 percent higher.

There do not appear to be any factors other than the difference in patent policy that could explain price differences of this magnitude. Wage rates of course differ, but wage costs in drug manufacture are of minimal importance. Another possible explanation is the existence in some countries of price controls. But as the Senate report notes, prices among countries without product patents were about the same regardless of whether price controls were in effect. In the one country in which they appeared to have a noticeable restraining effect—Great Britain—the result was to *lower* the average price for countries with product patents.

Is the existence of prices averaging nearly two-thirds above the competitive level "justified" by a higher rate of inventiveness? This question can be approached by a comparison of discoveries of new drugs in countries that grant patent protection with discoveries in those that do not. If the former have recorded a superior performance, a value judgment must be made in weighing a liability measured in terms of price against an asset measured in terms of inventions. But if the discovery performance of the patent-granting countries was not superior, no value judgment is required; there is no credit to offset the debit.

As part of its investigation of the drug industry, the staff of the Senate Anti-

Table 15-2

COMPARISON OF AVERAGE PRICES IN 7 DEVELOPED COUNTRIES WITHOUT AND WITH PATENT PROTECTION ON DRUG PRODUCTS, SPRING, 1959

Product	Average Price in Countries		
	Without Product Patents (a)	With Product Patents (b)	Percentage $\left(\dfrac{b}{a}\right)$
Chlorpromazine (Thorazine)	$ .90	$2.23	247.8
Prochlorperazine (Compazine)	.80	2.84	355.0
Promazine (Sparine)	1.07	2.33	217.8
Reserpine (Serpasil)	1.24	2.54	204.8
Meprobamate (Miltown-Equanil)	1.93	2.89	149.7
Tolbutamide (Orinase)	2.10	3.06	145.7
Chlorpropamide (Diabinese)	1.81	4.49	248.1
Chloramphenicol (Chloromycetin)	3.31	4.18	126.3
Chlortetracycline (Aureomycin)	4.48	5.09	113.6
Tetracycline (Achromycin)	4.37	5.55	127.0
Average: 10 products	$2.20	$3.52	160.0

Source: Administered Prices: Report on Drugs, Table 36

THE ROLE OF GOVERNMENT

Table 15-3

LISTING OF DRUGS ACCORDING TO PLACE OF DISCOVERY

Classes of Drugs	Countries Without Product Patents	Countries with Product Patents		
		Foreign	United States	
			Commercial	Noncommercial
Hormones	13	1	7	1
Antidiabetic drugs	3	1	2	1
Antibiotics	5	2	13	8
Tranquilizers	19	3	6	—
Polio vaccines	—	—	—	2
General drugs	42	8	32	7
Total	82	15	60	19

Source: Administered Prices: Report on Drugs, Table 38

trust Subcommittee classified 176 important drug discoveries according to place of discovery.[38] The listing was broken down between countries that do grant product patents and those that do not. Among the latter, discoveries within the United States were further distributed according to whether they were made in commercial or noncommercial laboratories. The results are shown in Table 15-3. The inducement of patent protection played no role whatever in the discovery of such products as bacitracin, found by Frank Meleney of Columbia University Hospital under a grant from the U.S. Army, or the Salk polio vaccine which came from research financed by public subscription. It may, however, have helped induce drug companies to assist Phillip S. Hench of the Mayo Clinic in his work on cortisone, Selman Waksman of Rutgers University in his work on streptomycin, and Paul Burkholder of Yale University in his work on chloramphenicol. But methods far less costly than the toll taken by a monopolized product could be used to finance research in university laboratories.

Insofar as foreign countries are concerned, the performance of those that do not grant product patents was far superior (82 to 15). When the contributions of the United States are added, the advantage shifts slightly to the countries that do grant patent protection (94 to 82). But if the discoveries made in noncommercial U.S. laboratories are deleted, the countries without product patents have the advantage (82 to 75). The performance of the nonpatent countries would undoubtedly have appeared even more impressive had it not been for the two world wars. Of the drugs discovered abroad, more than one-fourth came from Germany. Following both wars the scientific staffs of its drug firms were dispersed and the fruits of their research preempted by the victorious Allied powers.

On balance, it does not appear on the basis of the experience of the drug industry that new discoveries are dependent upon the granting of a patent monopoly over a product. At least in this industry the cost of patents in the form of higher prices does not appear to be offset by any compensating benefit in the form of greater inventiveness.

[38] *Ibid.*, pp. 114–120.

Tariffs and quotas

Long referred to as the "Mother of Trusts," the tariff and its even more restrictive offspring, the import quota, have been inveighed against regularly by economists since the days of Adam Smith. Under the principle of comparative advantage one of 2 countries is richly endowed with resource A and is deficient in resource B, while the reverse is true of the second country, a failure of each country to specialize on the resource peculiar to it increases the total costs of supplying the needs of both. The result is a misallocation of resources, economic waste, a lowering of living standards, and a lessening of the wealth of nations. By keeping lower-cost supplies out of home markets, tariffs and quotas not only make it possible for the high-cost producer to remain in business but yield inordinate profits to low-cost producers. The former do not shift to some other line of production where their resources could be more efficiently employed, while the latter, protected from competition from abroad, tend to become lethargic and unresponsive to technological progress, with the result that in time they too become high-cost producers with obsolete equipment and antiquated ideas.

After centuries of throttling their own growth the nations of western Europe, through the European Economic Community, are struggling to dismantle a maze of tariffs, quotas, tolls, duties, and other barriers to trade with one another. In so doing they are following—by nearly 200 years—the example set by the United States. In the short span between the end of the Revolutionary War and the ratification of the Constitution the United States had the good fortune of experiencing the baleful effects of internal tariffs erected against each other by the newly independent states. Because of this experience trade among the states has not been impeded by such artificial restraints; the remarkable economic growth of the United States during the last two centuries was made possible by their absence.

> When the war was legally over, the British merchants unloaded their over-stocked inventories on the free colonies and the home manufacturers set up the same howl the colonial merchants had when the British tried to undersell smuggled tea.
>
> This time, however, the manufacturers could not, as the tea merchants had, dump the imports overboard, since there was no national grievance to give "cause" to protection of local commercial interests. Immediately the manufacturing colonies began erecting tariff barriers, against England, against each other, against anybody who might undersell them. To Benjamin Harrison, governor of an agricultural state [Virginia], it of course became obvious that tariffs to protect manufacturers would merely substitute Northern economic discrimination for British, and Virginia was experiencing enough difficulty as it was in regaining solvency.[39]

[39] Clifford Dowdey, *The Great Plantation, A Profile of Berkeley Hundred and Plantation Virginia from Jamestown to Appomattox,* Rinehart, 1957, p. 275. The two features of the new Constitution that were strongly resisted by the Virginia delegation were the commerce provision and the extension of the slave trade. With respect to the former, "what Harrison and [Patrick] Henry gagged at was the provision over protective tariff for manufacturers. This, the most significant of the compromises, gave Congress the regulation of commerce on a majority vote . . . Benjamin Harrison and a majority of the Virginians

THE ROLE OF GOVERNMENT

Most of the arguments on behalf of tariffs, if they can be dignified as such, are merely assertions that the expected benefits accruing to the protected industry will in some way extend to other segments of the economy as well. Nearly one hundred years ago they were the subject of a satire, "The Petition of the Candle-Makers of Paris," by the French writer Frédéric Bastiat. The candle makers, it seemed, were seeking a ban on the free importation of their major source of competition:

> We are subjected to the intolerable competition of a foreign rival, who enjoys, it would seem, such superior facilities for the production of light, that he is enabled to inundate our market at so exceedingly reduced a price, that, the moment he makes his appearance, he draws off all custom from us; and thus an important branch of French industry, with all its innumerable ramifications, is suddenly reduced to a state of complete stagnation. This rival, who is no other than the sun, carries on so bitter a war against us, that we have every reason to believe that he has been excited to this course by our perfidious neighbor England. In this belief we are confirmed by the fact that in all his transactions with this proud island, he is much more moderate and careful than with us.
>
> Our petition is, that it would please your honorable body to pass a law whereby shall be directed the shutting up of all windows, dormers, sky-lights, shutters, curtains, vasistas, oeil-de-boeufs, in a word, all openings, holes, chinks and fissures through which the light of the sun is used to penetrate into our dwellings, to the prejudice of the profitable manufac-tures which we flatter ourselves we have been enabled to bestow upon the country; which country, cannot, therefore, without ingratitude, leave us now to struggle unprotected through so unequal a contest.
>
> We pray your honorable body not to mistake our petition for a satire, nor to repulse us without at least hearing the reasons which we have to advance in its favor.
>
> And first, if, by shutting out as much as possible all access to natural light, you thus create the necessity for artificial light, is there in France an industrial pursuit which will not, through some connection with this important object, be benefited by it? [40]

The petition pointed out that the shutting out of natural light would increase the demand for tallow and hence for cattle and sheep. More oil would be re-quired, which would swell the demand for olive trees and for vessels to be employed in whale fisheries. A great stimulus would be given to the manufacture of all types of lighting fixtures—crystal chandeliers, lamps, reflectors, and candelabras: "There is none, not even the poor manufacturer of resin in the midst of his pine forests, nor the miserable miner in his dark dwelling but who would enjoy an increase of salary and of comforts." The petition went on to admonish the government in terms that still have a certain currency: "You have no longer any right to cite the interest of the consumer. For when-

---

at home thought their delegation had yielded too much, and trusting tariff to a majority in Congress became the point where they stopped." With respect to the latter, the Virginia delegation "agreed on a twenty-year extension of the slave trade, to please the other Southern states and the New England slave traders, when Virginians wanted to abolish slave trade then and there." One of the leaders of the Virginia delegation, George Mason, "refused to sign even the Constitution because it legalized the continu-ance of the slave trade." (*Ibid.*, pp. 282–84.)

[40] Frédéric Bastiat, *Sophisms of Protection,* Putnam's, 1963. Quoted in *Hearings on Ad-ministered Prices,* Pt. 10, p. 5169.

ever this has been found to compete with that of the producer, you have invariably sacrificed the first." [41]

For many years the only rationale for protectionism was the "infant industry" argument. Because unit costs at a low level of output tend to be high, an industry which would be able to hold its own against foreign competition, once it had attained volume production, needs protection in its formative years. The problem, of course, is getting rid of the trade barrier once the infant industry has grown up. As Machlup has noted:

> Although the infant industry argument has been fully exploited by the advocates of tariff protection, the fact that it is an argument for *temporary* protection has been ignored in practice. Many industries thus protected have, even after decades, failed to "grow up" and tariff protection has been continued and often increased long after it became abundantly clear that the industry never would be suited to the country. In other cases industries have reached a stage where they could stand on their own feet, but have refused to step out from behind the shelter of the tariff and face the rigors of foreign competition. [42]

After nearly a century of reiteration the "infant industry" argument has lost most of its persuasiveness. The case for protectionism in the United States has come to turn largely on the need for preserving industries that are anything but "infant." Since World War II mature industries, it is argued, have lost their former commanding superiority of capital resources, as the Western European nations and Japan have been busily engaged in modernizing their own facilities. Hence the United States is no longer able to offset the lower costs of such countries by the greater productivity of better plant and equipment. But if the argument is true, the proper economic response would be for the United States to shift its resources to other fields, particularly to those based on technologies in which it has a decided lead over other countries. Denying the right of foreign countries to sell oil, steel, and textiles in the United States will not only force American consumers to pay higher prices for those products but will inevitably foreclose to U.S. firms the right to sell in foreign markets products in which it has a cost or quality advantage, such as chemicals, plastics, synthetic fabrics, electronic devices, computers, aircraft, machinery, instruments, and farm products. When the United States increased its tariff on lead and zinc, Germany retaliated with a ban on coal imports; the price of protection for U.S. lead and zinc miners was thus the destruction of jobs in the U.S. coal-mining industry.

Even apart from this argument there is a question of the extent of the cost disadvantage of U.S. industries. While wage rates in even the most industrialized foreign countries are substantially lower than U.S. rates, part of this difference is offset by (a) higher fringe benefits and (b) less freedom by management to hire and fire and exercise other managerial prerogatives over the labor force. In some industries it is also offset by lower materials costs. In the steel industry, for example, direct costs are made up of three roughly equal elements—labor costs, coking coal, and iron ore. Even with their higher fringe benefits European steel mills enjoy a substantial advantage in terms of unit labor costs, which, however, is offset in large part by much higher costs for coking coal. Because of the great depths

---

[41] *Ibid.*
[42] Fritz Machlup, *The Political Economy of Monopoly,* Johns Hopkins Press, 1952, pp. 269–70. Emphasis in original.

of the European mines and the leanness of their seams, coking coal from America can be laid down at European steel mills more cheaply than coal from their own mines.[43]

Regulatory actions

Actions by the state giving preferential advantage to larger firms are of two types: those required by law and those granted at the discretion of government agencies. Regardless of their merits, the former, such as patents and tariffs, are the outcome of due deliberation and debate in which Congress, in order to promote some objective, has chosen to create exceptions from the underlying principle of competition governing the economy. If a new product meets the requisite tests of invention, a patent must under the law be issued; if a product is of a certain type and character, a specified import duty must under the law be paid.

In addition to these and other privileges required by law, however, actions taken at their discretion by government agencies often work powerfully to the advantage of the larger companies against their smaller rivals. Efforts to secure a modification of regulations that are unnecessarily destructive to competition tend to be exercises in frustration. The agency's position will usually be that the regulation is necessary to carry out the general purpose or intent of the law and that if there is any fault, it lies not in the regulation but in the law. Yet, because the law is a set of generalized principles, any attempt to modify it might well have consequences above and beyond those involved in the particular regulation itself; consequently, Congress is usually reluctant to change the law in order to rectify a specific regulation. Moreover, with the passage of time, the regulations increasingly come to be looked on not as the application of the law but as the law itself. A regulation may no longer be necessary either because the problem to which it was originally directed has disappeared or because new powers have been conferred making the old regulation unnecessary. But there are few undertakings more difficult of accomplishment than trying to get an edict of a regulatory body eliminated once it has been issued and published in the Federal Register.

Although not initially conceived as such, the theory of the regulatory agency, as it has developed, represents a compromise between the common law approach of Great Britain and the Napoleonic Code. It reflects, in part, the underlying assumption of the British tradition that the law, to be effective in the real world of constantly changing conditions, must consist of a generalized set of principles. At the same time it represents an effort to emulate the French

[43] "The average (delivered) value of coal carbonized in U.S. oven-coke plants in 1960 was $9.89 per short ton, with substantial variations from State to State depending upon transportation distances. For purposes of comparison, a good example is Pennsylvania; with coke ovens located relatively close to coal supplies, the average delivered value of coal was $8.45 in 1960. This may be contrasted with an average 1961 price of $14.33 a short ton for Ruhr coal delivered to Ruhr coke ovens. . . .

"Aside from coking coal used for steelmaking in the Ruhr and mined in the Ruhr or the Netherlands and that used for steelmaking in one Belgian steel center (Seraing) and mined in the Netherlands, U.S. coal was delivered at lower prices at each of the [European] steelmaking centers than coal from any of the European coal mining basins. Even in the Ruhr itself, U.S. coal at $15.93 a metric ton is approximately competitive with Ruhr coal at $15.67 a ton." (87th Cong., 2nd Sess., Senate Judiciary Committee, *Hearings on Refusal of Certain Steel Companies to Respond to Subpoenas*, 1962, p. 124.)

approach of expressing the law in clear, logical, and specific terms by delineating through detailed regulations its applicability to particular conditions and circumstances. It departs from the British tradition in that the initial application of the principles is placed not in the courts but in a regulatory body, equipped with an expert staff. It departs from the French tradition in that the governing principles are the generalized statutes enacted by the legislature rather than the regulations themselves and that the regulations can be modified from time to time in accord with changing circumstances.

What makes an analysis of special privilege granted by government so difficult is not only that each agency develops its own rationalizations, which usually have about them a certain ring of plausibility, but that these rationalizations, as well as the operations of the agency itself, are couched in a form of semantics, "governmentalese," peculiar to each agency and all but incomprehensible to anyone except employees of the agency and attorneys practicing before it. Moreover, the actual facts underlying a particular action can usually be ascertained only after painstaking analysis of the agencies' files. Yet access to the files is generally denied to the public and particularly to a firm which feels that a regulation unduly impedes its ability to compete.

Trucking affords a classic example of the way government regulation can throttle competition arising from an industry that by its very nature is highly competitive. With low capital entrance requirements, optimal efficiency attainable at a relatively small scale of operations, and potential entry easy, the trucking industry conforms almost ideally to the competitive model. Yet in trucking the allocation of resources, the protection of consumers from unduly high prices or poor service, and the attainment of economic progress are presumably assured not by the "unseen hand of competition" but by a regulatory body, the Interstate Commerce Commission. Originally established in 1880 to protect the public interest from the railroads, the ICC has over the years become increasingly preoccupied in protecting the railroads from the competition of the trucks and more recently in protecting the large, established motor carriers from the competition of smaller trucking companies. The process has involved the extension of controls from an industry that is a natural monopoly to one that is its very antithesis:

> A natural monopoly is an industry in which there are marked economies of scale, i.e., as successively larger firms develop, the average unit costs of production at an efficient rate of utilization decrease. The typical public utility industry generally requires a large minimum investment and much fixed investment with the additional result that economies of utilization can be obtained by allowing additional business to go to existing firms up to the point when least cost utilization is achieved. Such industries must be regulated because the firms in it can exert too much power over prices and output in markets with many areas of inelastic demand. But . . . the trucking industry does not fit this description. On the contrary, its economic characteristics are such as to make competition both feasible and desirable.[44]

Under the Motor Carrier Act of 1935, as interpreted by the Interstate Commerce Commission, the right of a trucking firm to engage in business is determined not by its success in competing with other carriers but by its ability

[44] 84th Cong., 2nd Sess., Senate Select Committee on Small Business, Senate Report No. 1693, *Competition, Regulation and the Public Interest in the Motor Carrier Industry,* 1956, p. 23.

to demonstrate to the ICC that there is a public need for the service, that existing service is inadequate, or that the carrier already serving the field will be unable to adequately supply an expanding market. The applicant must also meet a number of other requirements, which have been described by Dudley Pegrum as follows:

> In addition, the new applicant will have to defend his operating financial plans, prospective profits, schedules, and so forth in the face of opposition of existing carriers, both of his agency and others that may be affected, or think that they may be affected, at some future date. The traffic to be developed, the possibilities of such traffic, the economic development of the area, and the future prospects of the area will all have to be portrayed for the tender scrutiny of those carriers already occupying the field. Moreover, even the descriptions of the equipment which is to be used will be examined by intervenors who wish to see the application denied.
>
> The foregoing is not a caricature of proceedings. It is a summary statement of what is taking place every day all across the country before examiners of the Interstate Commerce Commission. Hearings are prolonged into years and the money spent on endeavoring to secure operating authority on occasion runs into hundreds of thousands of dollars. This does not cover the expense arising from the array of talent alined against the applicant.[45]

Not only is the process wasteful, but the severity of its restrictive effect tends to increase as the size of the applicant diminishes. In Pegrum's words, "it is hardest on the small operator who cannot afford the expense involved and who cannot match the resources marshaled by his opponents to keep him out of competition. . . . In other words, current procedures are stacked against the small carrier, not deliberately by the ICC but by the false premises upon which current regulatory practices are erected." [46]

Based on an in-depth investigation conducted under the direction of Walter Adams, the Senate Select Committee on Small Business cited a number of critical requirements imposed by the ICC that appear to have little purpose except the restriction of competition. Thus, before they can serve a new area carriers must secure ICC approval of route extension applications. A small trucking firm operating between Chattanooga, Tennessee, and Birmingham, Alabama, wished to extend service to 2 small Alabama towns not then directly served by any large motor carrier. After 4½ years of proceedings, the ICC granted the applicant limited approval to serve one of the towns but not the other. In its report the Committee stated, "According to the Commission, these towns had only 'limited transportation needs' and the service, despite shipper testimony to the contrary, was not 'so inadequate as to justify a grant of additional authority.' " [47]

A carrier must stay on the route authorized by the ICC even though it can render the service more rapidly and economically on some alternate route. The approved certificate of a trucking firm operating between Philadelphia and Montreal required that all traffic go by way of Reading, Pennsylvania. The company petitioned the ICC for permission to use an alternate route that would

[45] 84th Cong., 1st Sess., Senate Select Committee on Small Business, *Hearings on ICC Administration of the Motor Carrier Act*, 1955, p. 469.
[46] *Ibid.*
[47] Senate Select Committee on Small Business, 1956, *op. cit.*, p. 6.

make Philadelphia 62 miles closer to Montreal and New York City 202 miles closer. The application was rejected on the basis of tests the Commission has developed to govern applications for alternate routes; the effect of these tests has been described by Commissioner Elliott in these words:

> In short, this formula assures the large carriers that they will be granted alternate routes, and it just as surely assures the small carrier that he will not be granted alternate routes. I am, of course, opposed to any such test, even though it may have been used since 1935. Instead of preventing a monopoly, it helps to establish one, and once created, it becomes a case for the perpetuation of the monopoly. It encourages the large competitors to seek more equal and more convenient routes consistent with the national transportation policy, but in the same breath, it tells the small operator he must continue to operate, if he can, over his present route, no matter how wasteful and inconvenient that may be.[48]

In addition to being limited to carrying specified commodities between specified points on specified routes at specified times, truckers are frequently also limited by ICC certification to a one-way haul. The denial of the right to haul payloads on the return results in unbalanced route structures, higher transportation charges, and pure economic waste. A firm that each day shipped 70 semivans and 80 tanks of dairy products from Goshen, New York, to New York City sought permission to carry return loads of liquid sugar for milk tanks. Except on about 15 percent of the tanks involved, permission was denied. Confronted with inadequate service from established common carriers, a small manufacturer in Mississippi established its own trucking operation to haul turpentine, rosin, and pine oil to its customers in the Southeast and the Midwest. On about 80 percent of their loads its trucks were forced to return empty:

> When we started into the delivery part of our business, we made a few inquiries and found, for example, that a local electric blanket manufacturer uses about a truckload of blanket shells out of Ohio every week. We in turn have a truckload going into Ohio every week. We fail completely to understand the reasoning which necessitates our trucks coming back empty and letting the other man pay common carrier transportation on this material which would provide us an excellent backhaul.[49]

Some small truckers have found a partial solution to the problem of empty returns through "trip leasing"—i.e., leasing their trucks to another firm that does have the authority to haul commodities on the return route. But trip leasing itself has been in a constant state of jeopardy at the ICC. A small trucker hauling meat products to cities on the eastern seaboard had tried without success "to get return ICC certificates. . . . Therefore it is necessary that we be able to lease our equipment to other carriers who have authority to get return hauls for our trucks. We frequently haul loads from the Indiana area to Boston, Mass., New York City, and Miami, Fla., and you could imagine having to bring a truck home from such a distant point empty. On this basis our operations would be broke overnight." [50]

The animus of the ICC against competition is nowhere more evident than in its constant and unremitting opposition to the "agricultural exemption."

[48] Senate Select Committee on Small Business, 1955, *op. cit.*, p. 22.
[49] *Ibid.*, p. 461.
[50] *Ibid.*, p. 459.

Under Section 203(b)(6) of the Motor Carrier Act, as amended, motor vehicles used in carrying property consisting of livestock, fish, or agricultural products are exempt from economic regulation by the ICC. According to the Senate Small Business Committee: "Here is an unregulated segment of the trucking industry which, according to witnesses most intimately familiar with its operations, has admirably served the interest of farmers, consumers and the general public." [51] In a series of administrative actions, the ICC has sought to narrow the scope of the exception. It endeavored to establish the doctrine that the exemption was not applicable to any vehicle which hauled *both* exempt and nonexempt commodities, even though they were not hauled on the same load. It endeavored to limit the exemption to cover farm products only to the point where they first enter the ordinary channels of business. Both interpretations were struck down by the courts. It has sought to narrow the exemption by narrowly defining what constitutes agricultural products, holding, for example, "that redried tobacco stems are an agricultural commodity, but that redried tobacco leaf is not; that a live chicken is an agricultural commodity but that a chicken with its head cut off is not; that nuts in the shell are agricultural commodities, but shelled nuts are not; that lint cotton is an agricultural commodity, but cotton linters are not; etc." [52] Noting that "every amendment that Congress has made to it has broadened and liberalized its provision in favor of exemption and . . . that although often importuned to do so Congress has uniformly and steadfastly refused or rejected [narrowing] amendments" Judge Gavin held that dressed or eviscerated poultry is an agricultural product: "It is the feeling of the court that an opposite holding would in reality constitute an attempt to accomplish by judicial construction that which Congress has steadfastly refused to allow to be accomplished by legislation." [53]

Another example of the promotion of monopoly by government regulation is provided by the drug industry; what is involved are the requirements imposed on *successive* applicants for a New Drug Application to market a drug *already on the market*. The requirements in question are not to be found in the law but in rulings issued by a regulatory body—the Food and Drug Administration. Most drugs prescribed today by physicians come within the regulatory orbit of the FDA as technically "new drugs." Under the Federal Food, Drug and Cosmetic Act of 1938, Congress gave the FDA power to prevent the sale of "unsafe" drugs by prohibiting the sale in interstate commerce of "any *new* drug unless an application filed . . . is effective with respect to such drug." [54] A "new drug" was defined as (a) a drug that is not generally recognized by qualified experts as safe for use under the conditions prescribed or suggested in the labeling or (b) one that has become recognized as safe as a result of investigative studies but has not been "used to a material extent or for a material time" as recommended in its labeling. [55]

Among other things the 1938 Act specified that applicants shall submit "full reports of investigations which have been made to show whether or not such drug is safe for use." [56] The Kefauver-Harris amendment of 1962 added

[51] Senate Select Committee on Small Business, 1956, *op. cit.*, p. 15.
[52] *Ibid.*, pp. 16–17.
[53] *Interstate Commerce Commission* v. *Kroblin, Inc., Allen E., et al.*, 113 F. Supp. 599 (N.D. Iowa 1953), 630–31. Included in Senate Select Committee on Small Business, 1955, *op. cit.*, pp. 377–404.
[54] Sec. 355(a). Emphasis added.
[55] Sec. 321(p)(2).
[56] Sec. 355(b)(1).

the requirement that the applicant shall support with "substantial evidence" the claims he proposes to make concerning the efficacy of the drug. By regulation the FDA broadened the scope of the statutes to require that the safety and efficacy of a drug already on the market must be shown by clinical studies submitted by *each successive applicant*. Approximately $50,000 to $100,000 is required at a minimum for sufficient animal and human testing work upon which to construct a report showing a drug's safety and efficacy. Since few of the smaller firms can meet such requirements, the effect on competition is to bar from the market for "new" drugs the companies that are the sources of the intense price competition prevailing in "old" drugs, i.e., drugs not subject to the FDA's requirements of a New Drug Application clearance. Most of the latter are sold by the smaller companies under their generic names at prices considerably lower than the same compound marketed by the major manufacturers under private brand names. Apart from the financial barrier, the supply of experienced medical investigators available to conduct the clinical studies is limited; not unnaturally their interest is in genuinely new compounds that have promise and that excite their curiosity. Pharmacological testing of a product already on the market to satisfy the requirements of the FDA's procedures is merely an administrative chore.

The need to duplicate the clinical testing on drugs already on the market serves as a very effective supplement to patents in restricting competition. For one thing, the requirement keeps newcomers off the market while the Patent Office delays the issuance of a patent, sometimes over a period of several years, because of a dispute over which company first made the invention. In drugs as in other fields invention occasionally takes place almost simultaneously in a number of separate laboratories; all file for a patent and an "interference" is declared by the Patent Office, during which time it seeks to determine which company first made the discovery. Control of the market through patents may also be impossible because the drug is declared a product of nature and therefore unpatentable. Or the patent may be weak and vulnerable to attack. But whether the product is unpatentable, or the patent is weak, or the product is tied up in an interference fight, an effective NDA for any "new drug" is essential. And if its cost is prohibitive to all but the largest companies, the inevitable result is to promote monopoly control by the few.

The problem has been compounded by an exemption permitting the company that first obtains an NDA to select other companies for which, at its request, the requirement will be waived by the FDA. When he so desires, the initial NDA holder may, by a "letter of authorization" to the FDA, permit a second company—or as many others as he wishes—to use *his* original clinical data in support of *their* applications, thereby relieving the latter of the need to conduct clinical testing on their own. This practice was apparently first initiated when the recipient of a letter of authorization purchased all of his finished drug, usually in bulk powder form, from a company already holding an effective NDA. The FDA apparently took the practical view that there was no need for repetition of clinical testing where the second company merely purchased the drug in bulk from the first. Eventually the letter of authorization procedure was extended from situations in which the second company bought the drug in bulk to those in which it was produced independently by the second firm.

It is impossible to reconcile the existence of the letter of authorization with the FDA's basic position that the protection of the public health requires an evaluation of clinical tests resulting from use of *each* applicant's product. For a firm receiving the benefit of a "letter of authorization," the FDA in effect considers the public health to be adequately protected by the clinical data submitted in the original application, plus a showing that the second company's product is the same as that in the original application. If duplicate clinical testing can be foregone by those secondary applicants fortunate enough to obtain a letter of authorization, all secondary applicants producing the same drug should be accorded the same treatment. Through the letter of authorization, the initial holder of the NDA can give ready access to the market to only those whom it elects, barring all others who cannot afford to incur the heavy expense of engaging in duplicatory clinical testing. And, conversely, it can use the letter of authorization as a bargaining lever in its negotiations with other companies on this or other drug products.

The function of rewarding the innovator is lodged with the Patent Office, not with the Food and Drug Administration, whose jurisdiction is limited to matters affecting health. For the FDA to operate as a secondary patent office is for it to assume a function not granted to it by Congress and for which it has neither expertise nor jurisdiction.

It should not be thought that, in seeking to protect from competition the large firms they are supposed to regulate, the ICC and the FDA are in any way unique. The problems of the small truckers before the Interstate Commerce Commission or the small drug manufacturers before the Food and Drug Administration are no different, substantively, from those of the smaller airlines before the Civil Aeronautics Board, or of small oil users before the Oil Import Administration, or of new, competing applicants for a radio or TV license before the Federal Communications Commission. Through a process termed "clientism" by Senator Paul Douglas, the attitude of a regulatory agency toward the industry under its jurisdiction undergoes a metamorphosis, changing gradually from initial hostility to a spirit of accommodation and finally to protective concern with the industry's well-being. It would be a mistake to attribute this process solely to the incompetence of government officials or to their constant departure for high-salaried positions in the companies they formerly regulated. Of at least equal importance is the constant day-to-day preoccupation with the industry and its problems. And looked at from government's point of view, nothing can cause more problems than competition. On their side companies in the regulated industries go through a similar metamorphosis. The initial anger at being placed under regulation slowly gives way to a recognition of mutuality of interests and a desire "to work things out together." The final stage is reached when the companies come to realize the value of regulation in suppressing competition, providing insurance against charges of profiteering, and virtually assuring the comforts of a sheltered life. What had been bitterly fought becomes accepted and then indispensable:

> Vice is a monster of so frightful mien,
> As, to be hated, needs but to be seen;
> Yet seen too oft, familiar with her face,
> We first endure, then pity, then embrace.[57]

[57] Alexander Pope, *Essay on Man,* Epistle 2, ll. 217–20.

Concentration and Economic Behavior

FOUR

The preceding parts of this work have been concerned primarily with the "structural" aspects of concentration: its extent, trend, and dimensions (Part I) and the causal factors at work—those making for lesser concentration (Part II) and those making for greater concentration (Part III). Parts I and II were also concerned with what has been referred to as the "conduct" aspects of concentration—i.e., the ways in which competition could be adversely affected by each of the dimensions of concentration—market concentration (or oligopoly), vertical concentration, conglomerate concentration, and aggregate concentration. In this part attention is focused on what have been termed the "behavioral" and "performance" aspects of concentration. Conceptually, the difference between behavior and performance originally was conceived to turn on whether comparative analysis was employed. But with the passage of time this distinction has become blurred, since the examination of economic effects has little meaning without reference (at least implicitly) to standards of some kind.

Although the evidence is fragmentary, there is some basis for the view that, by and large, control over the market (principally through local monopolies) tended to diminish during the nineteenth century and that this weakening market control was accompanied by greater price flexibility and a general tendency toward lower prices. And there is also empirical support for the view that during the first third of the twentieth century, prices became less flexible in those particular industries which, it is known, had become highly concentrated. But it was not until the "administered price" controversy, beginning in the mid-1930's, that the effects of differing industry structures on price behavior became a matter of general economic interest. The fundamental issues of that debate, which raged around the writings of Gardiner C. Means, remain as relevant to the formulation of public policy today as they were 35 years ago.

After World War II little attention was paid to the effects of industry structures on price behavior, as the interest of economists shifted to macroeconomics, model building, and econometrics. Yet a new and significant form of price behavior began to manifest itself; no longer were prices of concentrated industries merely remaining relatively rigid in the face of declining demand; they were actually tending to rise. Although attention was called to this "perverse flexibility" when it appeared in the 1957–58 recession[1] and again in the 1970–71 recession,[2] it received little attention by economists or policy makers. Yet it constitutes the root cause of the inability of fiscal and monetary restraints to arrest, or even retard, the inflation of prices.

The tendency of large firms in concentrated industries to raise their prices in the face of falling demand does not spring, to paraphrase Elting Morison, from "some causeless Bourbon distemper that invades the corporate mind." Rather, it is the logical result of the application in the short run of a variant of full-cost pricing referred to as "target return" pricing. This is the form of pricing most widely used by industry leaders in asymmetrical oligopolies.

Even though the lesser oligopolists may follow the leader's prices, no corporation, regardless of its size and market share, is entirely free from constraints upon its pricing power. In addition to occasional noncompliance by smaller competitors, any industry leader in setting its prices must take into consideration the effect of those prices upon demand, the potential ability of large buyers to supply their own needs, and the stimulus that price increases impart to the use of substitute products.

Despite the presence of these constraints, a clearly discernible difference exists in both the long-run and short-run price behavior of concentrated, as against unconcentrated, industries. Through its consequences on margins and profitability, concentration thus has an *income* effect; through the limitation of output it has a *production* effect. And, when its signals are read as if they represented the behavior of competitive industries, concentration has a *policy* effect.

[1] See *Hearings on Administered Prices,* Pt. 10, John M. Blair, "Price Behavior of Administered versus Market Price Products in the Current Inflation," pp. 4997–5013.
[2] See 91st Cong., 2nd Sess., Joint Economic Committee, *Hearings on Problems of Inflation and Recession,* 1970, testimony of Gardiner C. Means and John M. Blair.

THE HISTORY OF
OLIGOPOLISTIC PRICING

The history of price behavior in this country is *not* a continuum. Over a period of nearly two centuries, 1790–1970, the most prominent feature displayed by the general price index consists of episodic and precipitous rises in the price level associated with wars, followed by equally precipitous collapses.

During the nineteenth century the trend of price was predominantly downward. Prices became increasingly flexible and responsive to changes in supply and demand as handicrafts and local monopolies gave way to the expansion of industry and transportation. In the twentieth century the sharp rise during World War I had been preceded by a slow upward movement but was followed by a gradual decline in the 1920's and then by a pronounced decrease during the 1930's. By comparison with previous conflicts the decline following World War II was relatively limited. Thereafter, the trend has generally been either upward or comparatively stable.

The long-term trend of prices

The long-term trend of the Wholesale Price Index is shown in Figure 16-1.[1] Immediately apparent are the peaks associated with the War of 1812, the Civil War, World War I, World War II, and the Korean War. Aside from these war-induced rises, the general tendency during the nineteenth century was moderately downward, as can be seen by comparing 1820–40 with 1880–1900. Up to 1897 the Wholesale Price Index was lower than in the previous year for 56 of the years and higher in only 41.[2] But from 1897 through 1969, the index was higher than in the previous year for 62 of the years and lower for only 18. If the nineteenth and twentieth centuries are each divided into three periods the difference becomes even more apparent:

---

[1] For a summary of the factors customarily considered responsible for wartime price inflation, see Charles O. Hardy, *Wartime Control of Prices*, Brookings Institution, 1940, pp. 5–9.

[2] Based on a tabulation prepared by Julius Allen, Chief, Division of Economics, Legislative Reference Service, Library of Congress. For the years 1931–58 the source was Department of Labor Bulletin No. 1257, *Wholesale Prices and Price Indexes, 1958;* figures for subsequent years are the annual averages published by the Bureau of Labor Statistics, converted to a 1947–49 base. For years prior to 1913, the index used is that compiled by George Taylor and Ethel Hoover, using as a base 1850–59 converted to 1947–49 (86th Cong., 1st Sess., Joint Economic Committee, *Hearings on Employment, Growth and Price Levels*, 1959, Pt. 2, "Historical and Comparative Rates of Production, Productivity and Prices," pp. 394–97).

Period	Total number of years in period	Number of years in which Wholesale Price Index was higher than in previous year	Number of years in which Wholesale Price Index was lower than in previous year
1800–1830	31	10	21
1831–1864	34	22	12
1865–1896	32	9	23
1897–1920	24	20	4
1921–1932	12	3	9
1933–1969	30	25	5

In two of the three intervals of the nineteenth century decreases outnumbered increases; the exception was 1831–64, which embraced not only the Civil War but widespread land speculation, credit expansion, the California gold discoveries, vast spending accompanying the rapid expansion of the railroads, and unprecedented capital outlays by state and local governments. But in the twentieth century increases predominated during both 1897–1920 and 1933–69. The exception was the period 1921–32, in which decreases outnumbered increases by 9 to 3. This was due partly to the price reductions of the Depression and to the fact that, surprisingly, prices trended downward during the "New Prosperity" of the 1920's.

Historical changes in concentration and price behavior

Is there any connection between the changing direction of the price level between the nineteenth and twentieth centuries and changes in control over the market?

Figure 16-1

WHOLESALE PRICES

Bureau of Labor Statistics index (1947-49 =100)

ANNUAL AVERAGES

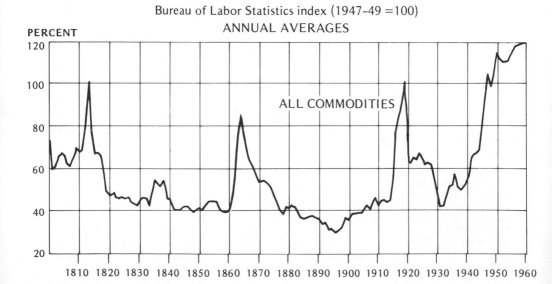

Source: Board of Governors of the Federal Reserve System, *Historical Chart Book* (using BLS figures)

This question can be explored in terms of both general analyses relating to the economy as a whole and specific comparisons for individual products. While any inferences to be drawn from the former must be regarded as only suggestive, they are consistent with the findings derived from an examination of individual products.

General changes

Although other factors were unquestionably at work, the general tendency of prices to move downward during the nineteenth century was certainly in keeping with the increasingly competitive character of the times. During the early part of the century economic conditions were anything but favorable to competition. As F. D. Jones has pointed out, rival producers of competing goods were few and far between: "New York, the chief city of the nation, had only a population of about 33,000 in 1790. Manufacturing was negligible, most of the necessities being produced by the versatile pioneers in their own homes." [3] Local monopolies tended to be the rule, as the barriers to transportation restricted sales to an extremely limited area:

> Miserable roads and sectional jealousies at that time made interstate trade negligible except between the larger cities. Trade consisted basically of two great branches: (1) the extraction of raw materials and production of foodstuffs, and their collection for exportation, (2) the distribution of manufactured articles from abroad. The great agency of trade was the country store which bartered the manufactured goods of Europe for the export products of its community. In the small communities these stores often possessed a monopoly of trade, sometimes forcing groups of neighbors to organize market trips to larger towns to exchange their products for the commodities needed by them.[4]

Manufactured output consisted largely of handicraft items of distinctive quality, which by their very nature had no identical counterparts to compete with. The standardization of products that came with the factory system was only beginning to make its appearance. The guild system, transplanted from Europe, exerted its usual depressing effects on rivalry and innovation. A further restrictive influence was the granting of state monopolies in the old tradition of mercantilism—e.g., the granting by the state of New York to Robert R. Livingston and Robert Fulton of a monopoly of the navigation of all waters within the jurisdiction of the state with boats "moved by fire or steam."

But with the passage of time the economic conditions that had made for monopoly in the early part of the century gave way to conditions more favorable to competition. Rival producers began to spring up en masse. Railroads, ships, and barges broke down the transportation barriers, broadening the area in which the individual producer could compete. The individualized product of the craftsman was replaced by the standardized product of mass production. Against the onslaught of the factory system, guilds gradually crumbled away. As a result of new state laws and judicial decisions, mercantilism all but vanished as an active

---

[3] F. D. Jones, "Historical Development of the Law of Business Competition," *Yale Law Journal*, Dec., 1926, pp. 207–34. The article appeared in four installments (June, Nov., Dec., 1926; Jan., 1927).
[4] Jones, Dec., 1926, *op. cit.*

economic doctrine. In Jones's words, the nation had entered "a great new era of unrestricted individualism and free competition." [5]

Not only did the overall price level move generally downward, but individual prices became more responsive to changes in supply and demand. Basing his findings on a study of wholesale prices in Philadelphia, Rufus Tucker distributed prices of 135 items according to frequency of change during 20-year periods, beginning in 1791 and ending in 1860.[6] With each 20-year period the proportion of the price structure that could be described as "inflexible" became progressively smaller. Of the 135 items 92 had fewer than 4 changes a year during the earliest period, 1791–1810. The figure then fell to 84 items in 1811–30, to 81 in 1831–40, and to only 66 in 1841–60. Similarly, the number of items with fewer than 6 changes a year dropped from 124 in the first period to 111 in the second, to 103 in the third, and to only 89 in the last.[7] The same inference is to be drawn from a consideration of price behavior during the depressions following 1837 and 1873. Distributing commodities by number of price changes,[8] Tucker found that in the earlier depression over 50 percent of the products were inflexible—i.e., they had fewer than 30 out of 95 possible changes. In the latter downswing, however, the proportion had fallen to 29 percent. At the opposite extreme, the most flexible items—those with more than 11 changes a year—represented less than 5 percent of the products in the earlier depression but 23 percent in the latter. In Tucker's words, "Here we see a great increase in the number of extremely flexible items." [9]

During the first third of the twentieth century consolidations, mergers, acquisitions, the use of increasingly costly technologies, and other factors radically transformed the structure of many industries. Generally speaking, these changes in structure appear to have been associated with a change in price behavior. In a study extending back to 1890, Edward S. Mason concluded, on the basis of three statistical tests (two of frequency and one of amplitude), that there had been no general long-term increase in the inflexibility of prices.[10] But on the basis of the more significant measure, amplitude, this negative finding did not hold for certain important commodity groups. Thus, Mason showed the long-term flexibility of each of the 10 BLS commodity groups on the basis of amplitude of change during several periods beginning with the depression of 1890–97

---

[5] Jones, June, 1926, *op. cit.,* p. 938.

[6] Rufus Tucker, "The Reasons for Price Rigidity," *American Economic Review,* March, 1938, pp. 41–54.

[7] Since the figures were not shown in the article, they have been estimated by inspection of the charts.

[8] Tucker presented a more complete chart for the period 1840–47, including 251 commodities taken mainly from the Philadelphia study, which shows an ever greater degree of rigidity in the earlier period. His chart for the depression following 1873 included a substantially greater number of items (317).

[9] Tucker, *op. cit.*

[10] Edward S. Mason, "Price Inflexibility," *Review of Economic Statistics,* May, 1938, pp. 53–64. In the first frequency test he compared the actual number to the possible number of changes of all prices quoted in the BLS index from 1890 to 1936, finding that the ratio of the actual to the possible number remained fairly stable throughout the entire period, with of course the exception of the years during World War I. In the second he examined the frequency of price change of all items in the BLS index by 8-year periods from 1890–1933. In each of those 8-year intervals, again excepting the war years, the distributions present the familiar U-shaped pattern. Similar negative findings in terms of frequency of change were reached by Don H. Humphrey ("The Nature and Meaning of Rigid Prices," *Journal of Political Economy,* Oct., 1937, p. 651).

and ending with that of 1929–33.[11] Although this measure revealed no increase in rigidity for all commodities or for the majority of the commodity groups, it did reveal a striking increase in the rigidity of two very important groups, metals and metal products and chemicals and drugs—the two areas in which concentration had shown the greatest increase during this 40-year period. Whether expressed in absolute or relative terms, Mason's measure revealed that the flexibility of these two fields declined by about one-third over the entire period. Noting this change Mason observed that "metal and chemical and drug prices . . . particularly if attention is focused on the last period (1926–33)—seem to exhibit relatively less flexibility."[12] The data on amplitude presented by Mason would suggest that from the latter part of the nineteenth century through at least the early 1930's, the price structure became more and more "mixed," with prices remaining flexible in most fields but tending to become rigid in certain important areas which were being transformed from an unconcentrated to a concentrated structure.

Individual product changes

Concentration of industry on a widespread scale made its first appearance on the American scene as a result of the great consolidation movement of 1897–1905. Immediately prior to this era the nation had experienced a pronounced economic decline beginning in 1890 and ending in 1897. This downswing, coming as it did just before any sizable segment of industry had become concentrated, provides an opportunity to compare price behavior during a period when production was largely unconcentrated with that during the later downswing of 1929–33, by which time leading firms had come to hold significant market shares in many industries. Although concentration ratios are of course not available for the earlier depression, it is still possible to identify those products that showed markedly less flexibility during the 1929–33 downswing and then seek to ascertain from a variety of sources whether this change in behavior had been accompanied by a noticeable increase in concentration. Although 1890–97 was, in the words of the Commissioner of Corporations, a period of "depressed" conditions,"[13] no downswing in history has approached in severity the 1929–33 depression. Thus, other factors being equal, a showing of equal flexibility is not to be anticipated since prices would be expected to decline more in the later

[11] Mason used as his measure of amplitude the percentage ratio of the difference between the highest and lowest monthly quotations for a period and the arithmetical average of the monthly prices for that commodity.

[12] Mason, *op. cit.*

[13] According to the long-term index of "American business activity" prepared by the Cleveland Trust Co., the general period was one of depressed economic conditions, with a downswing in 1893 and 1894 ("Panic of 1893"), followed by a very brief upturn ("Recovery of 1895"), which was followed in turn by another downswing of about equal severity in 1896 and 1897 ("Silver Campaign Depression"). Warren and Pearson's long-term index of physical production shows a decided dip ending in 1895, followed by a lesser downturn in the next 2 years. To the extent that price trends can be assumed to mirror the general state of economic conditions, the available information would suggest that the low point was not reached until 1896 or 1897. The all-commodity Wholesale Price Index of the Bureau of Labor Statistics (with 1913 as the base) declined from a level of 80.5 in 1890 to 66.7 in 1896, rising by only a tenth of a percentage point to 66.8 in 1897. The majority of the individual commodity groups did not reach their low point until 1897. In describing the period, the Commissioner of Corporations used such terms as "depressed conditions," "commercial depression," "slack demand," "acute depression." (*Report of the Commissioner of Corporations on the Steel Industry*, July 1, 1911, Pt. 1, pp. 63, 72, 75.)

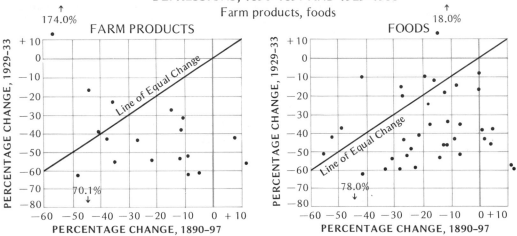

Figure 16-2
COMPARISON OF PRICE FLEXIBILITY IN TWO
DEPRESSIONS, 1890–1897 AND 1929–1933
Farm products, foods

Source: Bureau of Labor Statistics, Department of Labor, Wholesale Price Index

depression; a showing of lesser flexibility in the 1929–33 period would indeed be contrary to the general expectation.

An analysis of the behavior of *identical* products also has the advantage that it tends to limit (though it cannot entirely remove) the effect on price of other variables. Moreover, the validity of the price series could be questioned only if it were assumed that the index for a given product, despite the improvements in reporting and collection, becomes increasingly inadequate with the passage of time.[14] Price series covering both depressions are available from the Bureau of Labor Statistics for 168 commodities, of which 122 are used in this analysis.[15] In most cases the description of the product is virtually the same in both periods.[16] The study compares the price changes during both depressions in the following major product groups: farm products (19 items); foods (38 items);

[14] It can of course be argued that the price information deteriorated significantly on the grounds that secret discounts became more important. But such concessions were by no means unknown in earlier depressions, as is illustrated in the following typical quotations from the *Engineering and Mining Journal*; these quotations relate to the steel industry, in which concentration was then relatively low: "in some quarters it is only by concessions from quoted rates that buyers can be induced to consider business which is in excess of their current wants." (Jan. 19, 1895.) And "concessions have been made in prices of Bessemer pig and billets and some kinds of finished materials. There are prices on paper which until recently were prices that buyers had to pay, but at present, there are special prices varying according to quality, delivery, terms of payment, conditions of the order books, etc." (Nov. 23, 1895.)

[15] The 46 products for which price series were available but which were not included were: fabricated metal products, which were omitted because of the absence of information on concentration in the earlier depression; chemicals and drugs, omitted because of the apparent unreliability of their BLS price series; stone, clay, and glass products, omitted because they generally are sold on a regional or local basis for which concentration information was not available; and petroleum products, omitted because price series were available for only 2 relatively unimportant items—Pennsylvania crude oil and kerosene.

[16] This is not an essential requirement. What is essential is that the product's definition not be changed in such a way as to result in a significant understatement or overstatement of its price change within a given downswing.

textiles and related products (30 items); lumber and wood products (13 items); iron and steel (9 items); copper, lead, and zinc (7 items); glass (4 items); and anthracite (2 items). Obviously, the 122 commodities do not constitute a representative sample of the economy as it is today. The effect of the exclusion of products introduced after 1890 is to understate the more concentrated sectors. The 122 products fall into three categories:

1. Those whose prices were flexible in both depressions (the majority). Included in this grouping were most farm products, foods, textiles, and lumber. These products were unconcentrated in both depressions.

2. Those products that exhibited less flexibility in the later depression, despite its greater severity (a sizable minority). By and large such commodities were found to have undergone a marked rise in concentration.

3. Those that showed greater flexibility in the later depression (a small minority). These products were found to have been characterized by a decrease in concentration and a general weakening in the control of the market.

Figure 16-2 compares the depression price behavior of 1890–97 with that of 1929–33 for farm products in the upper grid and foods in the lower. Each grid is bisected by a line of equal change. Products falling below and to the right of the line had greater price declines in the later than in the earlier depression, the reverse being true of products falling above and to the left of the line. As will be noted, most of the farm products fall below and to the right of the line—i.e., they showed greater flexibility in the 1929–33 depression than in the earlier period, as would be expected in view of the greater severity of the later depression. This was true of all but 4 of the 19 farm products for which price data are available. The exceptions consisted of potatoes, oats, barley, and hops. During economic declines the demand for potatoes customarily shows little decline—or even increases as families shift to this low-cost source of nutrition. The change in flexibility of barley and hops is explained by the unusual circumstances of the imminent repeal of Prohibition; thus, the price of hops, which declined by 56 percent during 1890–97, rose by 174 percent during 1929–33.[17]

Food products present much the same pattern. Of the 38 items for which price series are available, all but 9 showed greater flexibility in the later depression. The exceptions include three types of dried fruit—apples, prunes, and raisins. As in the case of potatoes, these deviations from the general behavior may have been due to the shift in demand to lower-cost foods. But the deviations also included 5 pressed food products which were transformed from unconcentrated to concentrated areas of production   canned Salmon, salt, soda crackers, molasses, and granulated sugar.[18]

In the case of salmon, only 2 of the half-dozen leaders were in existence at the time of the 1890–97 depression. Pacific American Fisheries, long the world's largest fisher and canner of salmon, did not come into existence until 1902, when, under the name of Pacific Packing & Navigation Company, it was

[17] The increase in the price of oats is probably traceable to the same factor, as oats could be substituted for many of the other uses of barley.

[18] That the price of the other exception, coffee, showed a greater decline in the earlier depression is traceable to the fact that 1897 marked the end of one of Brazil's 7-year coffee cycles. Because of increased plantings made earlier in the cycle, production in the seventh year tends to be high and prices low. The cycle of 1890 to 1897 was no exception, the coffee tree population of Sao Paulo—the principal producing state—rising from an estimated 220 million in 1889 to 660 million in 1900 (see Federal Trade Commission, *Report on the Investigation of Coffee Prices*, 1954, pp. 22–25.)

organized "as a consolidation of some sixteen concerns located in Puget Sound and the coast of Alaska engaged in the business of catching and canning salmon." [19] Three of the other principal enterprises were not organized until the 1920's. By the time of the later depression, the industry was fairly well centralized, with 8 companies in 1934 producing more than half, and 2 companies more than one-fourth, of the output. Moreover, the industry appears to have developed leadership and a high degree of price uniformity.[20]

In salt the 2 leading companies, i.e., International Salt Company and the Morton Salt Company, were not formed until after 1897. The former, which produces about 25 percent of the industry's output,[21] was organized in 1901, acquiring in the next 4 years the capital stock of 11 independent firms. Similarly, the latter was not formed until 1922, when it was organized as a successor to a line of companies originating in Chicago during the mid-nineteenth century.[22]

Neither of the 2 leading producers of soda crackers, i.e., the National Biscuit Company and the Loose-Wiles Company, was in existence at the time of the earlier depression, the former having been organized in 1898 and the latter in 1912.[23] By 1935 National Biscuit and Loose-Wiles sold over 60 percent of the biscuits and crackers produced by the more than 330 American bakers, with National Biscuit accounting for approximately 42 percent and Loose-Wiles for about 20 percent.[24] According to the Federal Trade Commission, "In the cracker industry it is stated that manufacturers must and do follow the lead set by the National Biscuit Co. and Loose-Wiles." [25]

Likewise, the 2 principal producers of molasses, i.e., the American Molasses Company and Pennick & Ford Ltd., were not organized until after 1897. The American Molasses Company was incorporated in 1905 as a consolidation of formerly independent firms. Pennick & Ford was not organized until 1898, and its principal acquisition, the Douglas Company, was not organized until 1903.

[19] *Moody's Manual,* 1904, p. 1516.
[20] "Although no cooperation or agreement has been proved to exist among the canners, there has been great uniformity in the opening prices (at which about 90 percent of the pack is sold) since 1905; nearly all canners follow the prices of one or two large companies, and refuse to quote prices until those of the large firms have been announced. The Alaska Packers Association has taken the lead in declaring the prices of all grades except one and its prices have been followed by nearly all the other canners in declaring their prices . . . . Both the uniformity of the prices declared and the uniformity of time of declaration suggest that the prices of one or two leading firms are used as a guide." (Arthur R. Burns, *The Decline of Competition,* McGraw-Hill, 1936, p. 139.)
[21] *Standard and Poor's Corporation Records,* Dec. 8, 1949, p. C-2-5.
[22] Pools in the salt industry, of which the principal organization was the Michigan Salt Association, had existed for some time prior to the 1890–97 depression. The stock of Michigan Salt was held by manufacturers of salt in proportion to their production capacity. The members agreed to deliver to the association all the salt produced or to lease their plants to the association, with, however, the important exception that by paying the sum of 10 cents per barrel the members were entitled to market their own salt. Since the penalty was thus relatively moderate and no restriction was placed upon the output of the members, the association, while successful for a number of years, finally collapsed in 1882. (Arthur R. Burns, *op. cit.,* p. 151n.)
[23] According to *Moody's Manual* of 1901, "National Biscuit Co. was incorporated under the laws of New Jersey, Feb. 3, 1898, for the purpose of carrying out a plan to purchase the principal cracker manufactories in the United States . . . . The Company owns many baking plants and controls the greater part of the trade in this line east of the Rocky Mountains" (p. 985).
[24] Federal Trade Commission, *Agricultural Income Inquiry,* 1938, Pt. 3, p. 41.
[25] Federal Trade Commission, *Report on Open Price Trade Associations,* 1929, p. 78.

Figure 16-3
COMPARISON OF PRICE FLEXIBILITY IN TWO
DEPRESSIONS, 1890–1897 AND 1929–1933
Textiles and related products, lumber and wood products

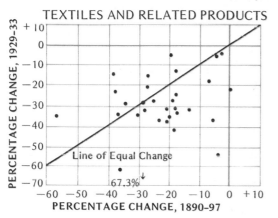

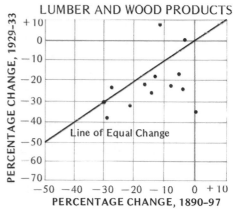

Source: Bureau of Labor Statistics, Department of Labor, Wholesale Price Index

In both depressions the price movements of two other unconcentrated areas, textiles and lumber, resemble those of farm products and foods (see Figure 16-3). Two-thirds of the 30 textile products showed greater flexibility in the later depression. Half of the exceptions consisted of one type of commodity: wool products. Similarly, in all but 2 of the 13 lumber and wood products, price decreases were greater in the 1929–33 period; the exceptions were bedroom chairs and matches, the latter registering an actual 10-percent increase in its price.

While the Diamond Match Company was formed 10 years before the beginning of the 1890–97 depression, it was not until 1901 that it entered into an agreement with the British firm, Bryant & May Ltd., under which the latter agreed "to refrain from manufacturing or selling matches in North America." And it was not until 1903 that it entered into a similar agreement with the Swedish Match Company, under which the latter "agreed not to manufacture matches in the United States except by arrangements with Diamond Match Co." [26] Inasmuch as the safety match had been a foreign development and sales by foreign companies had been important in the U.S. market, it was not until these cartel agreements were entered into that the domestic market could be said to have been controlled. By the time of the 1929–33 depression, the Diamond Match Company exercised unquestioned control over the domestic markets, not only through its position as the leading producer but also through its holdings in other match companies. In 1939 its stockholders owned the shares of the Ohio, Lion, Universal, Federal, and West Virginia match companies. Diamond's president held 51 percent, and Diamond itself held the other 49 percent, of the stock of the Berst-Forster-Dixfield Company. These 7 concerns together produced nine-tenths of the nation's output of matches.[27]

[26] Ottawa, Report of the Commissioner, Combines Investigation Act, Department of Justice, *Investigation into an Alleged Combine in the Manufacture, Distribution and Sale of Matches*, Dec. 27, 1949, p. 7.
[27] Clair Wilcox, *Competition and Monopoly in American Industry*, Monograph No. 21, Temporary National Economic Committee [TNEC], 1941, p. 191.

Figure 16-4

COMPARISON OF PRICE FLEXIBILITY IN TWO
DEPRESSIONS, 1890–1897 AND 1929–1933
Iron and steel; copper, lead, and zinc

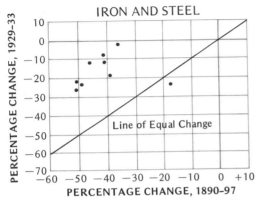

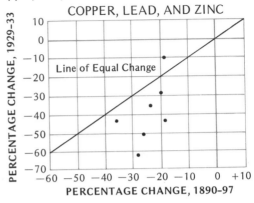

Source: Bureau of Labor Statistics, Department of Labor, Wholesale Price Index

Among the commodities whose behavior changed from flexible in the earlier depression to rigid in the later downswing, the most prominent were iron and steel products—an industry whose structure had been transformed dramatically. In Figure 16-4 the observations for steel products, with one exception,[28] fall above and to the left of the line of equal change—i.e., prices dropped less in 1929–33 than in 1890–97. For example, steel rails declined by more than 33 percent in the earlier depression but by less than 2 percent in the later downswing. Earlier findings also pointing to increasing rigidity had been made by Abraham Berglund in his study of price behavior before and after the formation of the U.S. Steel Corporation (specifically, in 1898 as compared to 1902–14)[29] and by George J. Stigler in his comparison of the actual to the total possible number of price changes during 1898–99 as contrasted to 1939–40.[30]

In 1935 the 4 largest companies in steelworks and rolling mills accounted for 49.3 percent of the industry's value of product and 45.5 percent of its value added by manufacture. And the level of concentration for the individual steel

[28] The exception, hot-rolled sheets (7), had the lowest concentration ratio of any of the major steel products (see Willard L. Thorp and Walter Crowder, *The Structure of Industry*, Monograph No. 27, Temporary National Economic Committee [TNEC], 1941, p. 463). In the early 1930's a considerable proportion of the product's capacity was held by relatively small semi-integrated producers.

[29] Abraham Berglund, "The United States Steel Corporation and Price Stabilization," *Quarterly Journal of Economics*, Nov., 1933. Although the earlier period used in Berglund's analysis is subsequent to the depression period under study here, there is every reason to believe that steel prices were at least as flexible in the period 1890–97 as in the period 1898–1901. Berglund concludes that "the percentages of greatest annual and monthly fluctuations from the mean of the periods considered, are much less for the years 1902 to 1914 than for the four years before and during the formation of the U.S. Steel Corporation." (*Ibid.*, p. 14.)

[30] George J. Stigler, "A Theory of Delivered Price Systems," *American Economic Review*, Dec., 1949, p. 1152. Stigler found that in Pittsburgh there were 27 actual changes out of 51 possible changes in the earlier period but only one out of 103 possible changes in the later period, with similar results for the other major market areas.

THE HISTORY OF OLIGOPOLISTIC PRICING

products tended to be considerably higher.[31] In contrast, the Commissioner of Corporations states, "In 1890 there were scarcely any consolidations of the modern type in the steel industry." The industry "was characterized by the competition of a large number of independent concerns." [32] "The larger companies were distinct entities with respect to ownership. . . ." [33] Not only was the industry composed of a "large number of independent concerns," but vertical integration was generally conspicuous by its absence. According to Charles R. Van Hise, "Before the consolidations of the companies producing highly finished products, the constituent companies bought their steel billets from the primary companies." [34] The Commissioner of Corporations stated that "the production of ore, broadly speaking, was a business by itself, and comparatively few iron and steel companies had extensive holdings of ore lands." There were also separations between iron and steel and between semifinished and finished steel. "Moreover, a substantial proportion of the country's pig iron was produced by 'merchant' furnaces, which sold their product instead of manufacturing it into more finished articles. Even the larger manufacturers of steel bought considerable quantities of pig iron. . . . Most manufacturers of finished articles purchased their supply of semi-finished steel, instead of producing it." [35]

Although repeated attempts were made by the steel companies between 1890 and 1897 to control the market, pools and gentlemen's agreements proved to be ineffective, tending to disintegrate in the face of declining demand:[36] "During the recession of 1896–97, all of the variously reported pools and price associations appear to have collapsed and the demoralization of trade became acute." [37] According to the Commissioner of Corporations:

> With the exception of the steel-rail pool, most of these organizations [pools and gentlemen's agreements] had a precarious existence, the agreements being subject to frequent violation. In the latter part of 1896, and the early part of 1897 in particular, there was a rather general abandonment of such combinations. Thus, the collapse of the wire-nail and billet pools was soon followed by the disruption of the steel-rail pool itself; a number of other similar agreements were also abandoned, at least temporarily, about this time.[38]

On the general state of the industry before the formation of U.S. Steel the authorities are in agreement. Myron W. Watkins described it as "a competitive

[31] National Resources Committee, *The Structure of the American Economy*, 1939, Pt. 1, p. 240. For measures of iron and steel capacity on a product-by-product basis, see 80th Cong., 2nd Sess., House Select Committee on Small Business, *Hearings on the Matter of Problems of Small Business Resulting from Monopolistic and Unfair Trade Practices*, 1948, pp. 1268–84.

[32] *Report of the Commissioner of Corporations on the Steel Industry*, July 1, 1911, Pt. 1, p. 63 (hereafter referred to as the *Report of the Commissioner*). It should be noted that the period under examination here ends before the last 2 years of the century, which saw the formation of a number of important consolidations, most of which were, in turn, absorbed by the U.S. Steel Corporation in 1901 (see *ibid.*, p. 79).

[33] *Report of the Commissioner*, p. 65.

[34] Charles R. Van Hise, *Concentration and Control*, Macmillan, 1914, p. 113.

[35] *Report of the Commissioner*, p. 66.

[36] Pools for a number of the industry's most important products were not formed until after the 1890–97 depression had run its course. For example, the structural-steel pool and the steel plate pool were not formed until 1897 and 1900, respectively.

[37] Vernon A. Mund, *Open Markets*, Harper, 1948, p. 163.

[38] *Report of the Commissioner*, p. 75.

trade." [39] Van Hise concluded, "During the period before consolidation, competition had been severe and prices alternately high and low, depending upon the trade conditions and the extent of cooperation." [40] The Commissioner of Corporations was explicit, stating that "as a rule the ownership of iron properties was widely scattered and, in this, as in the manufacturing branch of the industry, *competition rather than concentration* was the distinguishing characteristic. . . ." [41]

That differences in price behavior do not stem from differences in the nature of demand is suggested by the contrasting behavior of steel products and that of other primary metals, which were more responsive to competitive forces. As may be seen in the lower part of Figure 16-4 the distribution of copper, lead, and zinc is in sharp contrast to the scatter of iron and steel. With only one exception—i.e., zinc sheets—the nonferrous metals were characterized by greater flexibility in the later depression. While the domestic concentration ratios of manufacturing production for the nonferrous metals are relatively high, they substantially overstate the control of the market. Since nonferrous metals had long been sold on a world market, their prices were immediately responsive to international developments. Referring to the copper industry in a report issued in 1934, the National Resources Board stated: "International movements in a commodity selling at several cents a pound are extraordinarily fluid, and except for freight and tariff differentials the price of copper is a world price. Competition from foreign sources is keen, so keen, in fact, that American copper producers have found it impossible to realize the full advantage of the import duty adopted in 1932." [42] Since these metals are produced in scattered areas of the world under widely differing conditions, there have been conflicts between high-cost and low-cost producers, between producers in surplus countries and producers in deficiency countries, between producers in established areas who wish to reduce output and those in new areas with great potential for expansion, between producers with small stocks who favor only a moderate reduction of production and those with large stocks who want to see output severely limited and stocks disposed of. In both depressions these sources of conflict were of sufficient importance to prevent the carrying out of effective international cartel arrangements. [43]

[39] Myron W. Watkins, *Industrial Combinations and Public Policy*, Houghton Mifflin, 1927, p. 123.
[40] Van Hise, *op. cit.*, p. 113.
[41] *Report of the Commissioner*, pp. 66, 68, 75. Emphasis added. Of interest is the use of the term "concentration" in contradistinction to "competition."
[42] National Resources Board, *A Report on National Planning and Public Works in Relation to National Resources and Including Land Use and Water Resources with Findings and Recommendations*, 1934, p. 409. Speaking of the lead industry, the National Resources Board in its 1934 report stated, "Return of predepression prices cannot be expected, as the domestic price is controlled by the London price, plus a tariff differential, and recent expansion of capacity by low-cost producers abroad makes it probable that world prices will be lower than those formerly prevailing." (*Ibid.*, p. 412.) And of the zinc industry, the Board stated, "A return to predepression prices probably cannot be expected, for the domestic price is controlled by the London price, plus a differential of about 1¼ cents, owing to the tariff, and excess productive capacity abroad makes low world prices probable for some years to come." (*Ibid.*, p. 414.)
[43] For a discussion of the attempts to establish effective cartels for these products in the later depression, see Alex Skelton and Elizabeth S. May in W. Y. Elliott, ed., *International Control in the Nonferrous Metals*, Macmillan, 1937. Chs. 8, 10, and 12 are by Skelton; Chs. 9, 11, and 13 by May. Similar attempts during the earlier depression are described in U.S. Industrial Commission, *Report of the Industrial Commission*, 1900, Vol. I, p. 93, and *Engineering and Mining Journal*, Jan. 5, 1895; May 18, 1895.

The nonferrous metals are relatively immune to corrosion and are practically indestructible. Each year's output thus adds to the supply of scrap that can be processed by secondary smelters and refiners, who contribute an important competitive element in their markets. In 1930 scrap dealers and secondary refiners supplied 35.9 percent of the nation's copper requirements. In the lead industry the automobile storage battery reservoir forms "a huge circulating fund"; by 1933 the proportion of secondary to domestic primary lead was 86 percent, while in zinc the proportion in 1932 was 23 percent.[44] Finally, much of the output of the independent lead and zinc mines has long found its way to the market through the medium of custom smelters. Inasmuch as these smelters operate on the basis of a fixed margin between the ore price and the refined-metal price, it is to their interest "to operate at a high level of capacity, regardless of price." The resulting conflict with the interests of the integrated companies "became apparent from the commencement of efforts to agree on a united policy." [45]

If increasing concentration has been accompanied by increasing price rigidity, the converse should also be true. In point of fact, there are 2 industries—window glass and anthracite—in which increasing price flexibility appears to be explained

Percentage change in price

	Window Glass		Anthracite	
	Single "A"	Single "B"	Chestnut	Egg
1890–97	−1.3%	−9.9%	+11.4%	+5.1%
1929–33	−28.7	−32.7	−12.6	−13.9

primarily by a weakening control over the market.[46]

By the time of the 1890–97 depression the window glass industry in the United States "was ruled by the joint power of the combination of workers and the combination of employers." [47] Or, as another authority put it: "In no branch of the [glass] industry during the period 1880–1920 did organizations of laborers, employers, and wholesale dealers wield as much monopolistic power for as long a time as did those involved in the production of window glass." [48] Through Local Assembly 300, Knights of Labor of the Window Glass Workers of America, rigid limitations were imposed on the amount of output to be "blown" per hour, per week, per month; on the number of months worked per year, which by 1885 had been reduced to 9; and on the size of the labor supply. "It is thus clear from the beginning of its national history, L. A. assumed rigid control of window-glass production." [49] On their part, employers were organized into the American Window Glass Manufacturers Association, which "decided how many and what works should be closed, what wages should be paid (in negotiation

[44] Alex Skelton in W. Y. Elliott, ed., *International Control in the Nonferrous Metals*, Macmillan, 1937, pp. 625, 772.
[45] *Ibid.*, pp. 711, 727.
[46] The lesser severity of the earlier depression would hardly be an explanation for the price *increases* of anthracite and the extreme rigidity of Single "A" window glass.
[47] Pearce Davis, *The Development of the American Glass Industry*, Harvard University Press, 1949, p. 131.
[48] Warren Scoville, *Revolution in Glassmaking*, Harvard University Press, 1948, p. 217.
[49] Davis, *op. cit.*, p. 130.

with the national union) and what prices charged." [50] In 1895 a selling pool known as the American Glass Company was founded, handling the business of 85 percent of the window glass factories then in existence. The effect of this new organization upon the price level was almost immediate: "The formation in 1895 of the selling pool . . . permitted the price of windowpanes to be pushed upward, not only absolutely, but also relatively to other commodities." [51]

By the time of the later depression the control over the market by the selling pool and the bilateral cooperation of workers and employers had disappeared. The skilled workers and the use that could be made of their union to restrict output had been eliminated by the introduction of mechanized processes, and the industry-wide selling organization was a thing of the past.

A similar loss of effective control occurred in the anthracite industry. During the earlier depression the industry was under the close control of a few railroad companies, which owned most of the anthracite-bearing lands. Concentration of control was facilitated by the fact that deposits were highly centralized in a small area comprising less than 500 square miles in five counties of northeastern Pennsylvania. By 1890 the so-called line companies (those owned by the railroads) had obtained possession of more than 95 percent of the anthracite reserves.[52] The industry had also experienced nearly two decades of attempts to control the market involving at least 5 separate agreements, or "combinations," as they were termed.[53] Although, like that of most such arrangements, the history of these agreements was typically one of temporary success, followed by recurrent noncompliance and breakdown, and then by reconstitution, a new allotment plan was adopted in 1895. On this occasion the producers did abide by their allotted shares of the market: "In every case the deviation of shipments from the percentage allotted was less than one-half of one percent." [54] The success of the plan is attested by the fact that prices rose during a period of declining economic activity, the average price of stove coal rising from $3.13 per ton in 1895 to $3.79 in 1896 and to $4.01 in 1897.[55]

In 1906 Congress passed the Hepburn Act, prohibiting railroads generally from transporting in interstate commerce goods they produced or sold. After a number of efforts, in 1920 the Department of Justice finally secured a favorable decision under this Act,[56] as a result of which several of the major railroads divested themselves of their mining properties. Although the railroads set up a perfect maze of interlocking directorates with the anthracite properties, the control of the market established by these indirect methods appears to have been more than offset by other developments affecting the industry's structure.[57] For one thing, the market was demoralized by the rise of "bootlegging." By 1936–37, the bootleg industry produced and sold anthracite coal at the rate of 2.4 million bags a year. In the words of the Anthracite Coal Industry Commission, "By 1932, it had become a problem of grave consequence for the whole anthracite industry." [58]

[50] *Ibid.*
[51] Scoville, *op. cit.*, pp. 230–31.
[52] Wilcox, *op. cit.*, p. 179.
[53] Eliot Jones, *The Anthracite Coal Combination in the United States,* Harvard University Press, 1914, p. 229.
[54] *Ibid.*, p. 56.
[55] *Ibid.*
[56] See *United States* v. *Reading Co.,* 253 U.S. 26 (1920).
[57] Commonwealth of Pennsylvania, *Report of the Anthracite Coal Industry Commission,* 1938, Chart 3, after p. 361.
[58] *Ibid.*, pp. 43–44.

But even more important was the loss of position of the line companies to new large independent firms "who could not be controlled." [59] With the coming of the Depression, the line companies, reappraising the value of their large-scale holdings, increasingly leased their holdings to independents. Visions of ever-increasing demand associated with the expected rise in population had come to be replaced by the hard realities of increased costs, reduced prices, and the prospects of a long-term decline in demand: "The practice of leasing mines to independent operators, large and small, in the years after 1929 indicates the speed with which the line companies hastened to take account of the revisions in expectations." [60] Between 1929 and 1933 large independents increased their share of the industry's production from 24.8 to 37.7 percent. For the most part the important independents were new entrants: "The development of these new large independent producers is the most important element of the internal change of the industry." [61] As compared to earlier periods the control held by the line companies had declined substantially.[62]

The administered-price controversy

Although the systematic analysis of the relationship of industry structure to price behavior dates from the work of Gardiner C. Means in 1935, the comparative infrequency of price change in concentrated industries had been noted in earlier studies. For example, in a study of price behavior in England, Germany, and the United States, Gerhard Tintner had observed, "The frequency of monthly price changes is especially small in monopolized goods, in comparison with goods produced under conditions of free competition." [63] But it was the work of Means that touched off what has proved to be one of history's major economic controversies. Following the appearance of his initial study, it progressed to theoretical arguments in the economic journals—criticisms, replies, and rejoinders—and from there to elaborate statistical investigations with, apparently, conflicting findings. In the 49 years from 1886 to 1935 the *Index of Economic Journals* listed three articles on rigid prices; in the next 4 years it listed fourteen.[64] The fundamental issues around which the debate has revolved are just as relevant to an understanding of economic behavior—and to the formation of public policy—today as they were during the Depression, and they will remain so as long as an important segment of the price structure behaves in a manner inexplicable under classical theory.

[59] William R. Pabst, Jr., "Monopolistic Expectations and Shifting Control in the Anthracite Industry," *Review of Economic Statistics,* Feb., 1940, pp. 45–52.
[60] *Ibid.*
[61] *Ibid.*
[62] Pabst argued that "the hypothesis that the shifting control in the industry results from differences between the adjustments of competitive and monopolistic producers, in respect to prices and costs, cannot be maintained." The reason is, "The individual independent operators did not step up production, but generally, from the largest to the smallest, lost in about the same degree as the line operators." (*Ibid.*) What he was referring to was the behavior of those independents who were in business throughout the period. His observation does not hold true, as he recognized, for the "new" independents, who accounted for most of the gains shown for the independent group. These firms greatly increased their output and in general followed the norms of competitive behavior.
[63] Gerhard Tintner, *Prices in the Trade Cycle,* Springer, Vienna, 1935, p. 79.
[64] George J. Stigler and James K. Kindahl, *The Behavior of Industrial Prices,* National Bureau of Economic Research, 1970, p. 13.

When on January 17, 1935, Senate Document 13, *Industrial Prices and Their Relative Inflexibility,* by Gardiner C. Means was issued, the Administration of Franklin D. Roosevelt was provided with its first intellectual basis for ignoring the received wisdom of Say's law (production creates its own demand), which for years had paralyzed the will of governments to combat continuing massive unemployment.[65] Although it was of course John Maynard Keynes who delivered the mortal blow, his *General Theory of Employment, Interest and Money* was not published in London until 1936, and it was not until the following year that it had become well known in Washington economic circles, by which time most of the New Deal reforms had been adopted.

For Means the root cause of the continuing economic distress was the failure of a sizable segment of the price structure to exhibit the sensitivity to falling demand assumed by classical theory. If prices did not fall, real incomes would not rise, and the increase in demand expected to result from lower prices would not be forthcoming. Under classical theory the role of government was simply to permit prices and wages to fall until, in accordance with "natural laws," production and employment began to rise. Direct governmental actions to arrest this deflationary process could only make a bad situation worse. Viewed from this perspective it can be seen that Means's argument went to the very heart of the proper role of government in the economic process. Obviously, if any substantial proportion of the price structure remains inflexible during a period of falling demand, a policy of simply waiting for the natural laws to automatically bring about recovery is worse than useless, and the case for direct governmental action is made.

When Means was writing his critique in 1934 the natural laws had had 4 years to bring the country out of the Depression and were manifestly working very poorly. Although his intent had been to provide a rationale for direct government intervention in the area of macroeconomic policy, some saw in Means's arguments a powerful microeconomic attack on concentrated industries. The result was the administered-price controversy of the 1930's, since which time Means's concepts regularly have been interred, only to rise, phoenix-like, when prices begin to behave in a manner inexplicable under competitive theory.

The report that set off the controversy was written by Means in his capacity as economic consultant to the Secretary of Agriculture and was, in Means's word, "commandeered" by the Senate. At the heart of his analysis was a distinction between "market" prices and what he termed "administered" prices. Means introduced the concept of administered prices with the following definition: "An administered price is . . . a price which is set by administrative action and held constant for a period of time. We have an administered price when a company maintains a posted price at which it will make sales or simply has its own prices at which buyers may purchase or not as they wish." [66]

As Means has emphasized, under his definition the great bulk of all prices are "administered," since they are set by "administrative action" and "held constant for a period of time." Not long after Means had introduced the general concept,

[65] Jean-Baptiste Say, Traité d' Economique Politique, Antoine-August Renouard, Paris, 1814; Paul H. Douglas and Aaron Director, *The Problem of Unemployment,* Macmillan, 1931, pp. 121–38.

[66] 74th Cong., 1st Sess., S. Doc. 13, Gardiner C. Means, *Industrial Prices and Their Relative Inflexibility,* 1935, p. 1 (hereafter referred to as *Industrial Prices*). See also Gardiner C. Means, "Price Inflexibility and Requirements of a Stabilizing Monetary Policy," *Journal of the American Statistical Association,* June, 1935, pp. 401–13.

some economists began to focus their attention on one particular type of administered price. These are prices which, in Edwin G. Nourse's words,

> depart from the theory of automatic price-making in that producers are differentiated as to product, location, or other significant factors and in that the individual concern makes a sufficiently large percentage of its distinctive articles (with attached services) so that it can exercise a price policy and give the policy some degree of force through its *control of the volume of output*. This ability to administer a block of resources of significant size under an integrated production and price policy gives many large industrial executives a power of control akin to that of a public agency engaged in authoritarian price-making.[67]

In testifying before the Senate Antitrust Subcommittee Nourse emphasized that his concern was with those prices that, when demand falls off, are maintained through a decrease in production: "The essential point is that they can maintain a predetermined price by restricting production. . . . That is the essential point." [68]

Similarly, in the first report issued during the course of its inquiry into "administered prices," the Senate Antitrust Subcommittee in a section entitled "Definitions and Concepts" stated, "Prices which are 'administratively set,' 'administratively maintained' and are insensitive to changes in the market, e.g., they are maintained when demand falls off through a curtailment in output, are the 'administered prices' . . . with the potential for inducing economic distress; and these are the prices which are of concern to this subcommittee in its inquiry into 'administered prices.' " [69]

The fact that Nourse and other economists, as well as the Subcommittee, chose to emphasize the importance of this particular type of administered price does not detract from the value of Means's empirical findings, which may be summarized briefly as follows:

1. There is, in point of fact, a tendency for most prices to change either relatively frequently or infrequently: "We are dealing with two quite different types of prices." [70]

2. There is a direct relationship between frequency of change and amplitude of change: "The items which changed frequently in price showed a large drop during the depression while those having a low frequency of change tended to drop little in price." [71]

3. There is an inverse relationship between price and production declines: "for industries in which prices dropped most during the depression, production tended to drop least, while for those in which prices were maintained, the change in production was usually greatest." [72]

[67] Edwin G. Nourse, *Price Making in a Democracy*, Brookings Institution, 1944, p. 17. Emphasis added. Nourse used the term "administered prices" to refer to these prices, but it is clear that they constitute only one class of "administered prices" as defined by Means, since there are products whose prices are "set by administrative action" and are "held constant for a period of time" but whose output is not reduced when demand falls off.

[68] *Hearing on Administered Prices*, Pt. 1, p. 20.

[69] *Administered Prices: Report on Steel*, p. 6.

[70] Means, *op. cit.* This characteristic of the price structure had been observed earlier by Frederick C. Mills, who had found a clustering of prices at the extremes of frequent and infrequent changes (see his *The Behavior of Prices*, National Bureau of Economic Research, 1927).

[71] *Ibid.*

[72] *Ibid.*

4. Price rigidity is due principally to concentration in the market.[73]

The statistical basis of the first point was a chart in which 447 commodities, which then made up the BLS Wholesale Price Index (except railroads and utility rates and a few composite items), were distributed by frequency of change between 1926 and 1933; the result was the unusual statistical phenomenon—a U-shaped distribution:

> In the right-hand column of the chart are 125 items which changed practically every month in the 8 years. In the left-hand column are 95 items which changed price less than five times in 8 years. . . . The U-shaped character of the distribution curve carries the usual suggestion that *there are two quite different types of prices.* It is clear that the highly flexible prices of the right-hand group of items are for the most part made in the market, and are the type of prices around which traditional economics analysis has been built. . . . More than half the items covered in the chart averaged less than three changes a year. These items represent a type of price essentially different in its effect from the flexible market price on which the policy of laissez faire has been founded.[74]

The significance of Means's second finding—i.e., that a direct relationship exists between frequency and amplitude of change—derives from the importance of amplitude to economic theory. The original empirical basis was a relationship between frequency of change during 1926–32 and percentage change during 1929–32: ". . . frequency of price change and magnitude of price change in the depression have gone together. . . . The items which changed frequently in price show a large drop during the depression while those having a low frequency of change tended to drop only a little in price." [75] Four years later Means presented a more detailed statistical analysis, establishing beyond question that those products represented by the BLS index which changed most frequently in price tended to show the greatest declines during economic downturns, while those which changed least frequently tended to have the smallest decreases. In this analysis Means grouped the various products of the Wholesale Price Index into five classes according to the number of occasions in which price changes were recorded and then plotted, by months, the movement of each of the five groups from 1926 through 1938 (see Figure 16-5).[76] Describing the chart in hearings before a congressional committee some 30 years later, Means stated:

> This was done on the assumption that market prices which were determined by supply and demand would change practically every month with identical prices in successive months a matter of pure chance. Thus market prices would show a high frequency of price change. On the other hand, in concentrated industries where prices like those of steel or automobiles were administered and kept constant for considerable periods of time, the frequency of price change would be low. Where industries were less concentrated but not made up of a forest of enterprises or where changes in raw material prices dominated the

[73] National Resources Committee, *The Structure of the American Economy,* 1939, Pt. 1, p. 143, prepared under the direction of Gardiner C. Means.
[74] *Industrial Prices,* p. 2. Emphasis added.
[75] *Ibid.,* pp. 3–4. As to the importance of amplitude, see Tibor Scitovsky, "Prices Under Monopoly and Competition," *Journal of Political Economy,* Oct., 1941, p. 679. Five other authorities who made statistical studies of price inflexibility (Willard L. Thorp, Alfred C. Neal, Edward S. Mason, Don H. Humphrey, and Gerhard Tintner) used amplitude of change; some did not use frequency even as an auxiliary measure; and none based his findings principally on frequency.
[76] National Resources Committee, *op. cit.,* p. 147.

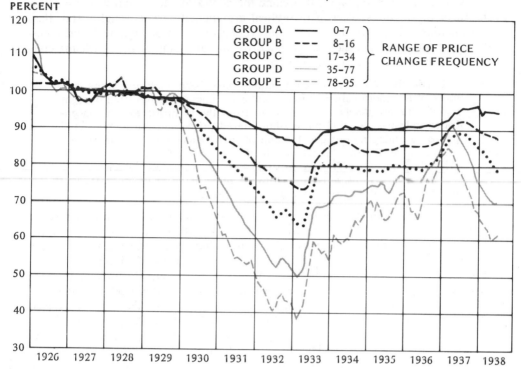

Figure 16-5

MONTHLY WHOLESALE PRICES FOR FIVE FREQUENCY GROUPS,
1926-1938 (1926-29 = 100)

GROUP A —— 0-7
GROUP B --- 8-16   RANGE OF PRICE
GROUP C —— 17-34   CHANGE FREQUENCY
GROUP D ····· 35-77
GROUP E --- 78-95

Source: National Resources Committee, *The Structure of the American Economy*, 1939, Pt. 1, Chart 26,
prepared under the direction of Gardiner C. Means

prices of finished products the way cattle prices dominate the price of
beef, prices would tend to show an intermediate frequency of change.
Frequency of price change is, of course, a very crude index of the
market power exercised in concentrated markets but the clear cut
pattern it shows suggests its validity and other investigations . . . confirm this.[77]

Emphasizing that the five series tend to diverge from one another during
downswings and come together during recovery, Means observed:

As you can see, the five indexes are almost on top of each other in
the four years of relatively high employment from 1926 to 1929. Then
with deepening depression, the index for market prices, represented by
the lowest line, dropped 60 percent while the index for administered
prices in the more concentrated industries dropped only 15 percent. The
intermediate indexes behaved in an intermediate fashion.

In the recovery period, the five indexes all rose with those that had
dropped most recovering most until they were fairly close together in
1937. With the recession in 1937–38 they splayed out again as in 1930
to 1932.[78]

[77] 91st Cong., 2nd Sess., Joint Economic Committee, *Hearings: 1970 Mid-Year Review,* 1970,
Pt. 2, p. 232.
[78] *Ibid.,* pp. 232–33.

Concentration and price inflexibility

Of all the issues in the administered-price discussion, by far the most controversial was the question of cause. It became the central point around which most of the furor raged, the subject of theoretical argumentation and weighty statistical investigations. To begin the task of unraveling the lines of argument and counter-argument, it is necessary to go back to an early statement by Means concerning concentration as a causal factor:

> Gradually as our great corporations have been built up, more and more of the coordination of individual economic action has been brought about administratively . . . as we go from the atomistic to the concentrated industries we find more administered prices and the administered prices becoming more rigid. In spite of many exceptions, the more concentrated the industry in relation to its market, the more inflexible do prices become. . . . Though no study has yet been made which conclusively establishes this correlation between price rigidity and concentration, preliminary studies clearly indicate its existence.[79]

The fullest development of the concentration thesis is to be found in a study by the National Resources Committee directed by Means. Price and concentration data were compiled for all of the Census industries, the former from the Bureau of Labor Statistics and the latter from the Census of Manufactures. Industries were then screened out (a) which are not "relatively homogeneous in product," (b) where less than "one-third of the value of the product is believed to come from manufacturing activity," (c) where the product is not produced "for a national or international market," and (d) where "reasonably reliable data" are not available as to the price of the product.[80] Only one-fifth of the then 282 manufacturing industries met these standards.

The need for the first and last tests is self-evident. The second is required in order to exclude industries whose prices are affected unduly by fluctuations in the prices of their raw materials: "Thus the price of beef is dominated by the price of cattle so that the depression sensitivity of the price of cattle is transferred in large part to the price of meat, and a comparison between the sensitivity of meat prices and concentration in the meat-packing industry is misleading."[81] The third standard is needed to exclude industries whose available concentration ratios—which are on a national basis—are conspicuously inappropriate with respect to their actual regional or local markets: "Fresh bread, for example, is necessarily produced for a relatively local market, while the weight of cement prevents plants at one end of the country from supplying markets at the other end in an economical fashion. In these industries, figures on concentration for the country as a whole cannot throw light on the actual degree of concentration existing in particular markets."[82]

[79] Means, *op. cit.*
[80] National Resources Committee, *op. cit.*, p. 142.
[81] *Ibid.*
[82] *Ibid.*, Ernest Doblin observed that when examination is made of all the 282 industries from which Means drew his 37, the result is a quite different picture. Although the results of his analysis are not presented in chart form, Doblin states: "If these price decreases and concentration ratios are plotted together, the items are scattered in a rather irregular fashion. . . ." ("Some Aspects of Price Flexibility," *Review of Economic Statistics,* Nov., 1940, pp. 185–86.) What Doblin did, of course, was to ignore the standards for the selection of products which Means had followed. The assumption is that more meaningful results are produced by ignoring reasonable standards and substituting none in their place.

Figure 16-6

RELATIONSHIP BETWEEN CONCENTRATION
AND DEPRESSION DROP IN PRICES

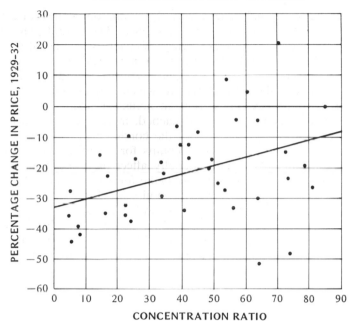

Source: National Resources Committee, *The Structure of the American Economy*, 1939, Pt. 1, Chart 2, prepared under the direction of Gardiner C. Means

The relationship found by Means is shown in Figure 16-6, a reproduction of his original scatter of 37 industries to which have been added 3 industries (represented by open circles) that should have been included.[83] Commenting on the scatter Means concluded, "When the depression drop of prices in these industries is compared with the proportion of value of product which in each was produced by the four largest enterprises, a rough relation is apparent between concentration and price insensitivity." [84] The "rough relation" would have been even more apparent had the scatter included farm products, for which price sensitivity is extremely high and concentration extremely low (though no concentration ratios are available).

It will be observed that there are 5 conspicuous deviations from the central tendency, all of which are among the concentrated industries. Three are above the regression line, and in each the deviation results from the fact that the price was *increased* between 1929 and 1932—hardly an exception to Means's argument. In the other 2, rayon and zinc, the price decreased about 50 percent. At least part of the price decline of rayon may be attributed to the normal and

[83] Means inadvertently omitted 3 industries—agricultural implements, sewing machines, and washing machines—that meet all of his standards. Their omission appears to have been the result of a typographical or clerical error. Since 2 of these industries fall close to his regression line, their omission had the effect of *weakening* his case. (See John M. Blair, "Means, Thorpe, and Neal on Price Inflexibility," *Review of Economics and Statistics*, Nov. 1958, pp. 427–35.)

[84] National Resources Committee, *op. cit.*, p. 142.

expected behavior of a new industry. And the price of zinc, as was explained earlier, is influenced strongly by its price on the world market, as a result of which the concentration ratio in the United States overstates the level of control.[85]

In view of the conceptual issues involved, the appropriateness of using regression analysis for this purpose may be questioned. The central point at issue, it should be remembered, is whether price behavior is significantly different in oligopolistic industries from behavior in those approaching a state of pure competition, *not* whether there are differences in the price behavior of oligopolistic industries that differ only in the degree to which they are oligopolistic. The focusing of attention on deviations from an actual or inferred central tendency, once the point of oligopoly has been reached, merely tends to direct attention away from the essential question. Once the condition has been established that each of a small group of producers accounts for a sufficient proportion of the total output that his actions can materially affect the price, the argument that further increases in concentration would make for even less price flexibility must rest upon the assumption that each oligopolist will become *progressively* more aware of, and concerned with, his rivals' probable reaction to a price cut and thus be *progressively* more reluctant to make one. Instead, there are reasons to assume that prices will tend to be more flexible under monopoly than under oligopoly. Eliminated is the communication problem faced by members of an oligopoly in reaching a consensus, either directly or indirectly, as to what a proper and appropriate price reduction would be. A monopolist is free to make a moderate price reduction without having to concern himself with the possibility that it might get out of hand, developing into a price war and a complete breakdown of the price structure. Nor need he concern himself with the question of whether a price decrease, which might be in his own best interest, would be less advantageous or even harmful to other oligopolists who have different cost-price relationships. And, being a monopolist, he is bound to be more sensitive than any oligopolist to public and governmental censure.[86] At the other end of the scale it can be argued that in unconcentrated industries, it matters little whether the leading producers have an aggregate market share of 1 percent, 10 percent, or even more, so long as none is sufficiently large to affect the price and each is therefore oblivious to his rival's probable reaction to his actions.

To avoid these problems, Means's original scatter (after the addition of the 3 inadvertently omitted products and the deletion of zinc and rayon) can be distributed in accordance with the three concentration classes used earlier.[87] It happens, as shown in Table 16-1, that the 38 industries are distributed almost equally among the three intervals: 50 percent and over (14 industries); 25–49 percent (12 industries) and under 25 percent (12 industries). At the extremes 7 of the concentrated industries had price decreases of less than 15 percent, while only one showed a decrease of over 30 percent. Conversely, only one of the unconcentrated industries had a price decrease of less than 15 percent, while 8 showed decreases of over 30 percent. The price changes of more than

---

[85] Omitting zinc and rayon, the regression line would run from -37.5% price change at 0 concentration to $+25\%$ at 100% concentration, with 3 observations on the line, 16 above, and 16 below.

[86] For an argument that prices can well be higher under oligopoly than under monopoly, see A. J. Nichol, "Professor Chamberlin's Theory of Limited Competition," *Quarterly Journal of Economics,* Feb., 1934.

[87] See Ch. 1.

Table 16-1

CONCENTRATION RATIOS AND PRICE DECREASES, 1929-1932

38 manufacturing industries

Concentration Ratio[a]	Decrease in Price			Total
	Under 15%	15% to 30%	Over 30%	
50% and over	7[b]	6	1	14
25% to 49%	4	7	1	12
Under 25%	1	3	8	12
Total	12	16	10	38

[a]1935.
[b]Includes 3 price increases.

Source: National Resources Committee, *The Structure of the American Economy*, 1939, Pt. 1, Chart 22, prepared under the direction of Gardiner C. Means

half of the industries in the intermediate concentration group fell in the intermediate price change interval.

In his early writings Means had said that "we are indeed faced with a serious problem. . . . Unless we would accept a poorly functioning economy, one that gets worse with further concentration, the conflict between inflexible prices and a smoothly functioning economy must be resolved." [88] Arguments that public policy was not involved because concentration was not the cause were not long in forthcoming. The criticism of Means took the form of theoretical refutations, empirical studies, and criticisms of the validity of his price data.

Theoretical refutations

On the demand side the theoretical refutations centered around the question of postponability. The argument ran that where buyers are able to withhold their purchases, the adjustment to a downswing will naturally take the form of a reduction of output rather than price. As Rufus Tucker put it, "Obviously if an article like an automobile has in good times a normal life of three years in the hands of one owner, that life can be increased to four or five years without much difficulty if the owner wants to economize." [89] In contrast, it is to be expected that the production of nonpostponable items will be maintained, since "most articles of food will last for one meal only in good times or bad." Hence, on such items the adjustment to the downswing will necessarily occur in price. For this reason the adjustment through the curtailment of output and the maintenance of price can be expected to be more pronounced in durable than in nondurable items, in luxuries than in necessities, and in producer than in consumer goods. Although some of these commodity characteristics, such as durability and use as producer goods, are sometimes cited as constituting reasons, in themselves, for price rigidity,[90] they are only different manifestations of

[88] Means, *op. cit.*, p. 408.
[89] Tucker, *op. cit.*
[90] See, e.g., the listing of "Factors and Conditions which May Affect Price Inflexibility" in Jules Backman, "Price Flexibility and Changes in Production," *Conference Board Bulletin*, Feb. 20, 1939, pp. 474–75.

the same underlying factor—a high inelasticity of demand during depressions owing to postponability.

It is one thing, however, to cite postponability as an explanation for differential changes in demand. It is something else to offer it as a refutation of the argument that price rigidity results from concentration. In the words of Ralph C. Wood:

> Two very different points are involved in this argument. To assert—with much injustice—that durable goods frequently attain high inelasticities of demand in times of depression is not to explain why the individual producer has to concern himself with what the market as a whole, or any appreciable portion of it, will take. Dr. Tucker's primary argument, it is well to recall, is that size of enterprise (and, impliedly, fewness of sellers), has nothing to do with rigid prices. Essentially, he is arguing that competition as it exists in the industries with rigid prices is as pure as competition in the agricultural staples. But if this were true, of what direct concern would it be to the individual seller of automobiles whether demand in the market as a whole were elastic or inelastic? The demand for farm products is at all times comparatively inelastic; but the individual farmer does not have to consider the effect of his own output on price under such conditions. Under pure competition the individual seller is not directly concerned with the inelasticity of demand of the whole market; at the market price, which he views as given and as something over which he has no control, demand for his product is perfectly elastic.
>
> Dr. Tucker's "conditions of demand" provide a very useful suggestion as to why price policies in certain industries are what they are; *but they do not show how it comes about that an individual seller is able to have a price "policy."* The explanation lies in the fact that in many industries he is confronted by a sloping demand curve instead of the horizontal demand curve of pure competition. Whether the slope of the curve results from fewness of sellers or product differentiation or both, the individual seller is in possession of a partial monopoly. His freedom to choose a price "policy" is explicable on no other basis.[91]

On his part, Means sought to meet the criticism by showing that *within* commodity groups possessing the same general characteristics the more concentrated items are less sensitive and vice versa. This analysis was in the form of listings of the BLS products within *given* commodity groups, ranked by degree of price sensitivity. Means could not apply his four standards of relevance, since to do so would have left him with an inadequate number of observations within any given group.

Within the area of durable goods, the sensitivity of atomistic cast-iron pipe and lumber contrasted with the insensitivity of concentrated galvanized pipe and roofing tile—all building materials; the sensitivity of atomistic steel scrap contrasted with the insensitivity of concentrated Mesabi ore—raw materials for the same industry; the sensitivity of atomistic yellow-pine flooring contrasted with the insensitivity of a concentrated type of flooring, felt base, part carpet. Within nondurable goods, the more interesting contrasts include the sensitivity of all but one of the farm products listed (onions) versus the insensitivity of such concentrated food products as salt, sweet crackers, molasses, bananas, and canned soup: the sensitivity of the atomistic raw material lum-

---

[91] Ralph C. Wood, "Dr. Tucker's 'Reasons' for Price Rigidity," *American Economic Review*, Dec., 1938, pp. 663–73. Emphasis added.

ber versus the insensitivity of the concentrated finished products newsprint and wrapping paper. A striking affirmation of Means's argument is provided by the least sensitive products in his list of raw materials—phosphate rock, aluminum, barites, crude sulphur, and Mesabi ore—each of which is concentrated. Most of the remaining raw materials are of one and the same type—highly sensitive farm products—which constitute most of the raw materials included in the BLS index.

On the supply side Tucker contended that in agriculture output tends to be sustained because of (a) the perishability of agricultural products and (b) the length of time of the period of production. Because of their perishability, agricultural products must be placed on the market, sold, and consumed within a fairly short period of time. Because of the length of the crop year, it is impossible for the farmer to make sharp and immediate curtailments in output to reflect changing market conditions, even if he were so inclined. The lack of control by the farmer over his output is aggravated by weather conditions, which, if they prove to be favorable, can result in an even greater supply than had been anticipated. Agricultural goods "in any given crop period (one to three years) are practically fixed in supply, irrespective of the wishes of the producers, consequently, the adjustment of demand to supply within the crop period must be entirely by means of price." [92] In addition to the farmer's lack of control over output, Tucker maintained, there are other reasons why prices of agricultural commodities tend to be more flexible than those of manufactured products: (a) the greater relative importance of overhead costs[93] and (b) the greater flexibility of both overhead and direct costs.[94]

In reply, Wood pointed out, first, that a large proportion of agricultural output consists of staples which are "scarcely" perishable and, second, that the length of the period of production could not be regarded as an adequate explanation since it was well exceeded by the duration of the 1929–33 depression:

> The magnitude of the decline in this period in the general level of prices for agricultural staples certainly finds no explanation in the "perishability" of farm products; the fact is, of course, that the great staples are scarcely perishable in the ordinary sense of the word. The duration of the lengthy downward movement of farm prices far exceeds all crop periods, so the length of time required to change the supply cannot be offered in explanation of the trend in prices. Nor did weather conditions provide any explanation.[95]

---

[92] Tucker, op. cit.

[93] "The proportion (of costs) that can be reduced is usually greater in agriculture than in manufacturing because the overhead is proportionately greater and because a larger proportion of the costs are not out-of-pocket costs but can be deferred or even dispensed with. The farmer will ignore or defer his depreciation to a greater extent than the manufacturer, either because he is less careful about such matters or because he feels he has no choice since his farm is also his home." (Ibid.)

[94] ". . . although the laborers employed in factories are paid in cash and their rates of wages are very rigid, partly because of custom and partly because of union regulation, the wages of farm laborers are partly paid in food and lodging and even the part paid in cash can be more easily reduced in bad seasons. . . . As long as hired workers in industry refuse to accept wage reductions while farmers on their own farm continue to work with practically no current returns for their own services, there must be a big difference between farm products and factory products in the extent of the downward readjustment of their prices to changes in demand." (Tucker, op. cit.)

[95] Wood, op. cit.

Wood objected to Tucker's cost arguments on the grounds that they exaggerated the difference between agriculture and manufacturing. Instead of "a rigid dichotomy of cost conditions," Wood held, the difference between agriculture and manufacturing is one only of degree. "Clearly overhead costs in certain manufacturing industries are proportionately as great as, or greater than, they are in agriculture; in other manufacturing industries the proportion is only slightly smaller. . . ." [96] If the various agricultural and manufacturing industries were ranked according to the relative importance of their overhead cost they would form, in Wood's words, "a hierarchy, not a dichotomy."

On the question of cost flexibility, Wood's reply was, again, that no sharp distinction exists between agriculture and manufacturing. Thus, in regard to depreciation charges, "industrialists on occasion treat them quite as cavalierly as farmers are said to do." [97] And direct costs were flexible in both agriculture and manufacturing: "In manufacturing industries wages have been reduced, material costs have been reduced. . . . In the light of those facts it is clear that the striking flexibility of agriculture prices, in contrast with prices for many manufactured goods, is not to be explained in terms of the characteristics of agricultural costs, because there is no sharp distinction between cost conditions in agriculture, on the one hand, and in manufacturing industries, on the other." [98]

A number of additional—and less important—explanations for price rigidity were also advanced. Backman cited the influence of putting "suggested prices" on packages, building advertising campaigns around standard prices, and price lining as additional factors making for rigidity, but, he carefully observed, "Where changes in quality or size are made, it is evident that the price inflexibility is more apparent than real." [99] Tucker emphasized the practice followed by many manufacturers of publishing their market prices, which involves announcing prices in advance; informing salesmen, dealers, and consumers; printing price lists and advertisements; and so on—all of which make it cumbersome and even costly for the manufacturer to change his price. But, while this factor might contribute to rigidity in terms of frequency of change, it would have no bearing on the more important question of amplitude: "The relative infrequency of change among some groups of manufacturing prices does not explain why the changes that do occur, besides being the most infrequent, are relatively the smallest." [1] To repeat Wood's basic reply: these factors may help explain why price policies are what they are, but they do not explain how in a competitive industry a seller can have a price policy.

Empirical studies

The major statistical assault on Means's findings was a study prepared (ironically enough) for the Temporary National Economic Committee by Willard L. Thorp.[2] This analysis differed from Means's study in two important respects: (a) standards were not employed to eliminate products that are not meaningful for this type of analysis, and (b) the price data consisted of Census realization

[96] *Ibid.*
[97] *Ibid.*
[98] *Ibid.*
[99] Jules Backman, "Price Flexibility and Changes in Production," *Conference Board Bulletin,* Feb. 20, 1939, p. 485.
[1] Wood, *op. cit.*
[2] Willard L. Thorp and Walter Crowder, *The Structure of Industry,* Monograph No. 27, Temporary National Economic Committee (TNEC), 1941.

figures derived by dividing the total number of physical units shipped into the value of shipments.[3] From the distribution of the observations Thorp concluded, "The changes in the average realized prices of products with high concentration ratios were neither significantly more nor less than the changes of products with low concentration."[4] He then proceeded to a study of product groups, seeking to determine whether a relationship existed *within* such groups of roughly comparable products as consumer goods, producer goods, nondurable goods, durable goods, semimanufactured goods, and finished goods. In each case the answer was in the negative.

The absence of any discernible relationship between concentration and price rigidity, coupled with the varying behavior of the different product groups, led Thorp to conclude that differences in depression price flexibility are the result, not of concentration, but of the characteristics of the product:

> A logical explanation of price and quantity behavior of manufactured products would . . . of necessity appear to run in terms of the product characteristics such as durability, use to which the products are put, and the nature of the raw materials from which they are fabricated. For some products, the concentration in the control of their production is undoubtedly an important factor, but for manufactured products in general there is no close relationship between control and any particular price and quantity behavior.[5]

In view of the number of products included in his scatter (407) and the use of a type of price data that reflects secret discounts, it is not difficult to understand why Thorp's study received widespread acceptance. At the same time it is open to criticism on several grounds, principal among which is his use of *national* concentration ratios for products sold predominantly in local or regional markets, his inclusion of products whose costs are made up largely of raw materials and whose prices may therefore be expected to fluctuate more or less in accordance with changes in the prices of their raw materials, and his inclusion of products whose Census realized price is distorted by changes in the absorption of freight. During the Depression, mills in many concentrated industries such as steel, chemicals, and nonferrous metals followed some sort of delivered-price method. Regardless of the exact method—whether a basing-point system, zone pricing, or other—the effect during a period of declining demand is a reduction in mill net realizations (and thus in Census prices) as orders from nearby customers fall off and mills increase their shipments to distant areas. Such reductions merely reflect the offering of the same delivered price by a greater number of sellers. Here again, the effect was the appearance of high concentration accompanying flexible prices.

Perhaps Thorp assumed that if enough products were included, any biases which might arise from his failure to apply standards of relevance would tend to offset each other. But all of the biases would seem to operate against the appearance of a relationship; there is none that operates clearly in the opposite direction. Flexibility in the less concentrated products is not overstated nor is rigidity in the more concentrated items.

In an endeavor to determine the locus of the biases Jules Backman deleted from Thorp's scatter (a) a list of "raw-materials affected" products, (b)

[3] *Ibid.*, p. 346.
[4] *Ibid.*, p. 360.
[5] *Ibid.*, p. 406.

iron and steel and chemicals as the "freight absorption" products, and (c) unconcentrated stone, clay, and glass products as the "geographically isolated" products.[6] Aside from the fact that this is a most incomplete list of deletions, nearly half of the remaining products were in only 2 major industry groups: textiles and their products and stone, clay, and glass.[7] As Backman was forced to recognize, this "would not be a very representative sample of the entire economy." [8]

The validity of the BLS prices series

The most enduring attack on the administered-price thesis has been the argument that its empirical foundations, the BLS Wholesale Price Indexes, understate the true flexibility of prices since they fail to reflect hidden discounts and concessions. The lasting effect of this criticism is traceable to the fact that few have been interested in following the tedious argumentation over such an arcane matter as the technical features of price indexes. The criticism was plausible; it was voiced by high authority; and refutations, if printed at all, were buried in "replies" in academic journals and then ignored by the critics.

The criticism was first made in 1936 by Willard Thorp and is invariably brought forth again—often as an original discovery—whenever the issue of price policy becomes a matter of public concern. In the words of its original exponent: "Frequently a commodity will be quoted at an unchanged price over a period of years and thus to the extent that indexes include this type of quotation they will remain relatively unchanged. Actually, the manufacturers of the product may have shaved or cut the price of the item drastically, in periods when business was slow and boosted it as economic conditions improved without the change being recorded in the quoted price." [9] To illustrate the importance of hidden concessions, Thorp cited the case of a manufacturer of flexible cord who drastically changed his discount structure between 1933 and 1934. But, as so frequently occurs, after the discount structure had finished its gyrations, the base price itself was lowered, and the discount structure returned to practically its original form. Hence, the illustration itself suggests only a lag rather than a failure of the base price to reflect the actual price change. If the price reduction were made before the end of the time period under survey, only frequency and not amplitude of price change would be affected. A more recent case in point concerned sheet steel, which during the latter part of 1968 became the subject of a price war waged with secret discounts and concessions. But, apparently growing weary of trying to keep track of which deals had been granted to which customers and of endeavoring to keep their nonfavored buyers in ignorance, the steel companies finally announced a reduction in their list price. Speaking of this episode the *Wall Street Journal* observed: "That situation prompted Bethlehem to formally cut book prices on hot-rolled steel by 22%, a sort of shock therapy that soon ended the price war as steelmakers realized such deep cuts would have disastrous results." [10]

[6] Jules Backman, "Economic Concentration and Price Inflexibility," *Review of Economics and Statistics,* Nov., 1958.

[7] These consist of those stone, clay, and glass products with concentration ratios in excess of 50%.

[8] Quoted in John M. Blair, "Economic Concentration and Price Inflexibility: Rejoinder," *Review of Economics and Statistics,* Nov., 1958, pp. 405–06.

[9] Thorp and Crowder, *op. cit.,* p. 339; see also Willard L. Thorp, "Price Theories and Market Realities," *American Economic Review,* March, 1936.

[10] *Wall Street Journal,* June 19, 1970.

For the purpose of analyzing the relationship between concentration and price rigidity the BLS series are invalidated only if it is assumed that during a downswing secret discounts become relatively more important in products of high than in products of low concentration. Neither Thorp, Stigler, nor the other critics of Means ever explicitly made this assumption, nor, incidentally, did Means ever call upon them to do so. From common observation concerning, say, the apparel and lumber industries, it is obvious that hidden discounts are not unknown in industries of low concentration, and it is equally obvious that they do not remain unchanged in periods of declining demand.

Nor is it sufficient to dismiss the BLS series with a casual reference to a few horrendous examples, among which the favorites have been sulfuric acid, ammonia, and men's shirts. For every such illustration, other examples could be cited of indexes that move in close conformity with what would appear to be the behavior of the actual prices. What is important, of course, are the results of multiproduct comparisons. In examining the relationship between concentration and price change, Means had attempted to evaluate the series for the various Census industries and eliminate those for which the data appeared to be inadequate. One of the bases used in making this evaluation was a comparison of BLS prices with Census (or Bureau of Mines) realized prices.[11] As shown in Figure 16-7, for products falling above and to the left of the "line of equal flexibility," the 1929–33 price decline reflected by the BLS series was less than that of the Census figure, with the reverse being true of the items falling below and to the right of the line.

The most conspicuous deviations are to be found in the field of chemicals, an area in which the BLS series have long been regarded as notoriously unreliable; the BLS prices for sulfuric acid and carbon black, which recorded no change, are obviously out of line with the more flexible realization prices. A number of the remaining deviations, however, are more apparent than real. Thus, in the case of products sold under delivered-price systems, such as cement, hydrated lime, and crushed stone, the realization figures (which were on a plant basis) fell more than the BLS series (which at the time were on a delivered-price basis), a disparity to be expected since the former reflected the increased absorption of freight and the latter did not. The greater decline in the realized price for men's dress shirts obviously reflected the relatively greater sales during the Depression of lower-priced shirts. On the other hand remarkable similarity between the two series was shown by such diverse products as asphalt, steel rails, mixed fertilizer, fire brick, window glass, structural steel, sand-lime brick, salt coke, and denims. In general, the Census figures declined on the average by only about 7 percent more than the BLS prices. Moreover, there was no relationship between the deviation between the two series and the level of concentration: In about half of the 13 products in which the deviation between the two series exceeded 5 percentage points, concentration was relatively low.

A similar and more comprehensive comparison of BLS with Census prices has been made by Howard Norman Ross.[12] In a study of 44 industries, divided into 16 "unconcentrated" and 28 "concentrated" groups, Ross contrasted the

[11] National Resources Committee, *op. cit.*, App. 1, Saul Nelson, "A Consideration of the Validity of Bureau of Labor Statistics Price Indexes."
[12] Howard Norman Ross, *The Theory and Evidence of Price Flexibility*, doctoral dissertation, Columbia University, 1964.

Figure 16-7

RELATIONSHIP OF PRICE DECLINES SHOWN BY
BLS PRICE SERIES AND CENSUS "REALIZATION" PRICES

19 selected products, 1929–33

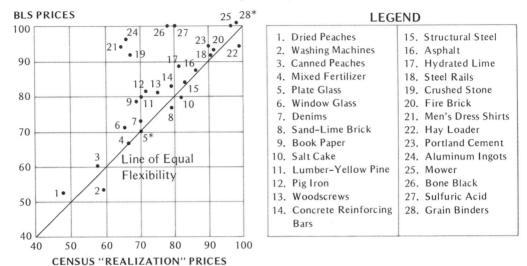

Source: National Resources Committee, *The Structure of the American Economy*, App. 1, p. 183
prepared under the direction of Gardiner C. Means

BLS with the Census price changes for 1929–31.[13] Significant deviations were conspicuous by their infrequency, and this was true of both the concentrated and unconcentrated groups. For the unconcentrated group the BLS price fell on the average almost as much as the Census price, the average difference being only 1.4 percent. For the concentrated industries the difference was not much greater, averaging only 5.3 percent. That the Census figures will tend to show a greater decline during downswings is to be expected owing to a shift to lower-priced items *within* a Census product. Other sources of error in the Census realization prices were pointed out by Ross: "derived as ratios of indexes of Value of Product to indexes of production (the most accessible form of the data), they are average annual values at the industry level of a conglomerate and changing output. . . . Reporting errors, changes in establishment coverage and arbitrary intra-company transfer values in vertically integrated firms impede the estimation of a true value." [14]

With the re-emergence of interest in oligopolistic prices during the late 1950's, and particularly with Means's contention that most of the rise in the Wholesale Price Index between 1953 and 1958 had resulted from increases in the "administered price" industries,[15] this well-known "defect" in the BLS series was once again discovered. Studies by John Flueck and Harry E. McAllister, com-

---

[13] Ross's unconcentrated industries were those in which the 8 largest producers accounted in 1935 for less than 50% of the value of product and the 4 largest for less than 40% (*ibid.*, p. 83). His comparisons were necessarily limited to the Census years, 1931 and 1933; he regarded the former as preferable because during most of 1933 recovery had already set in, and prices had begun to rise following the low point in 1932.

[14] Ross, *op. cit.*, p. 80.

[15] See *Hearings on Economic Concentration*, Pt. 9, pp. 4746–80; Pt. 10, pp. 4897–4923.

434   THE HISTORY OF OLIGOPOLISTIC PRICING

paring BLS with "real" prices, were cited by George J. Stigler as constituting further evidence of the unreliability of the BLS indexes.[16]

Flueck's study was based on the premise that BLS prices can properly be compared with government bid prices.[17] Yet sales to the government have certain characteristics distinguishing them from ordinary commercial sales, and it is the latter that the BLS series are designed to reflect. Orders by the government tend to be in larger quantities, thus permitting larger production runs and the attainment of economies of scale. Selling and advertising expenses are largely dispensed with. In view of these differences, it is somewhat surprising to note that in 9 of Flueck's 32 products the BLS prices showed the same (or a greater) number of changes than the bid prices and that in 9 others the BLS recorded at least two-thirds of the changes reflected by the bid prices.

McAllister pointed out that an index combining the reports of several reporting companies would tend to change more frequently than an average of the separate companies. Commenting on McAllister's study, Stigler observed caustically:

> We emerge, then, with the finding that Means' tabulations of frequency of price change are unknown mixtures of the actual behavior of quoted prices and the number of firms reporting such prices. By increasing the number of price reporters, the B.L.S. can reduce price inflexibility by the same order of magnitude as the increase in the number of reports. The major development which Means believes to have outmoded neoclassical economic theory is the "development" of collecting a number of price quotations inappropriate to the measurement of short-run flexibility.[18]

Stigler had erroneously assumed that in arriving at his frequency distributions Means had simply counted the number of times the published price indexes changed. Actually, Means had been granted access to the reports *to the BLS* and had taken either the average of the number of changes reported by each of the reporters or, where the number of reporters was more than 3, the number of changes by a single reporter who appeared to be typical of the group.[19]

The attack on the BLS prices has its greatest plausibility when the official series remain relatively unchanged in the face of sharply declining demand. At such times discounts off list prices would be expected to be at their maximum as sellers offer special deals of one kind or another to retain business. But, as will be brought out in the next chapter, the typical recession behavior of concentrated industries has increasingly come to be one, not of price stability, but of price increases. In such a context the criticism of the BLS series loses much of its plausibility, for it makes little sense to assume that businessmen would be offering *greater* discounts at the very time they are *raising* their list

[16] 87th Cong., 1st Sess., Subcommittee on Economic Statistics, Joint Economic Committee, *Hearings on Government Price Statistics*, 1961, pp. 373 et seq.
[17] *Ibid.*, pp. 419–58.
[18] George J. Stigler, "Administered Prices and Oligopolistic Inflation," *Journal of Business*, Jan., 1962, p. 5.
[19] In 1939 Means had described (albeit cryptically) his procedure (National Resources Committee, *op. cit.*, p. 187). Stigler first misstated Means's procedure in 1962 (Stigler, *op. cit.*). In 1964 the fact that it was a misstatement was pointed out in the same journal (John M. Blair, "Administered Prices and Oligopolistic Inflation: A Reply," *Journal of Business*, Jan., 1964). In 1970 in a book co-authored by Stigler the misstatement was repeated (Stigler and Kindahl, *op. cit.*, p. 20). In a letter dated March 30, 1971, addressed to the editor of the *Journal of Economic Literature*, Stigler acknowledged that his criticism of Means was "based upon a misunderstanding of his procedures, and I apologize for the error (which I had previously committed in the *Journal of Business*, Jan., 1962, p. 5)."

prices. It also makes little sense to assume that corporate officials, whose price policies are a matter of public concern, would needlessly invite censure by making meaningless increases in their list prices. As Walter Adams and Robert F. Lanzillotti have pointed out,

> if Stigler is correct about the illusion of quoted prices, why in the spring of 1962 did United States Steel not simply raise its transaction prices to the level of its quoted prices? Why did Roger Blough, who is certainly conversant with the facts of life in the steel industry, insist on raising a fictitious price? Did he not know that a simple revision of transaction prices would have served his purpose and also saved him from detection by the B.L.S. (and its henchmen)? In short, given Stigler's model, Mr. Blough was either a fool or a provocateur, hankering for a joust with the President of the United States. Both these interpretations of Mr. Blough's behavior tax credulity.[20]

Neither the theoretical criticisms nor the attempts at empirical refutation have cast any serious cloud over Means's original observations. Clearly, the price structure is made up in good part of prices whose behavior makes impossible the operation of classical theory—the constant gravitation toward an optimal use of resources through the flexibility of factor prices and the mobility of labor. Where prices are nonresponsive, such maxims as John Stuart Mill's "law of value" are simply irrelevant: "Demand and supply, the quantity demanded and the quantity supplied, will be made equal. If unequal at any moment, competition equalizes them, and the manner in which this is done is by an adjustment of the value. If the demand increases, the value rises; if the demand diminishes, the value falls; again if the supply falls off, the value rises; and falls, if the supply is increased. . . . This then is the Law of Value."[21]

Also left standing is the original explanation of the phenomenon, as set forth by J. Kenneth Galbraith shortly after the appearance of Means's initial work:

> Only where monopoly power is present could it be possible for industries to show the price and product behavior which we are considering. Under anything approaching pure competition (i.e. the absence of monopoly elements or monopoly power) it would be impossible for the prices of the products of an industry to remain constant while production found its own level. Where numerous producers compete freely in the sale of an undifferentiated product, the inevitable sequence of reduced demand is lower prices and a new adjustment of output. There is no way under such circumstances that the reduced demand could be attended by constant prices and curtailed output, save perhaps where all costs were prime costs and all production carried on to order. Should one producer attempt to maintain his prices, his production would not drop in the proportion that the new demand stands to the old but to zero.[22]

For fiscal and monetary policy the implications of the type of price first identified by Means are far-reaching and only partly explored. Although not too much attention has been paid to these implications by Keynes's successors (who

[20] 88th Cong., 1st Sess., Senate Subcommittee on Antitrust and Monopoly, Senate Committee on the Judiciary, *Administered Prices: A Compendium on Public Policy,* 1963, pp. 6–7.

[21] John Stuart Mill, *Principles of Political Economy,* 1848, Book III, Ch. 2, Sec. 4.

[22] J. Kenneth Galbraith, "Monopoly Power and Price Rigidities," *Quarterly Journal of Economics,* May, 1936.

for the most part have simply assumed a competitive model), Keynes himself went to some lengths to make it clear that "administered" prices were outside his theoretical structure:

> If money-wages are inflexible, such changes in prices as occur (i.e., *apart from "administered" or monopoly prices which are determined by other considerations besides marginal cost*) will mainly correspond to the diminishing marginal productivity of the existing equipment as the output from it is increased.
>
> *   *   *
>
> *Apart from "administered" or monopoly prices* the price level will only change in the short period in response to the extent that changes in the volume of employment affect marginal prime cost; whilst in the long period they will only change in response to changes in the cost of production due to new technique and new or increased equipment.[23]

[23] John Maynard Keynes, *The General Theory of Employment, Interest and Money*, Harcourt Brace Jovanovich, 1936, pp. 268, 270–271. Emphasis added.

CH 17 OLIGOPOLISTIC PRICE BEHAVIOR

Interest in oligopolistic price behavior was cut off abruptly by World War II and has remained more or less in limbo since that time. The prevailing assumptions have been that concentration is a *de minimis* problem; or, if not *de minimis* structurally, that the price behavior of concentrated industries does not differ significantly from that of competitive industries, especially if account is taken of secret discounts and concessions; or that in the long run oligopolistic price behavior is actually beneficial since it contributes to price stability. Yet during this quarter of a century evidence has been accumulating that concentration is very definitely not a problem of minor importance; that the difference between oligopolistic and competitive price behavior, which so concerned economists during the 1930's, has continued and indeed taken on a new form; and that over the long run oligopolistic price behavior has contributed more to inflation than to stability in the price structure. These conclusions rest partly on intensive investigations of particular industries (notably steel, automobiles, drugs, electrical machinery, and petroleum) and partly on cross-section studies covering a number of different industries. In this chapter the question of differential price behavior will be examined on the basis of four types of cross-section studies: (a) the BLS "Quintile" study—i.e., the movements of BLS wholesale prices classified into five classes according to frequency of change; (b) a "pairs of products" comparison—i.e., the movements of sets of products with much the same demand factors but with widely differing concentration ratios and frequencies of price change; (c) correlation analyses—i.e., studies for particular periods of the relationship of concentration to the change in price; and (d) the new National Bureau price data—i.e., an analysis of the difference in price behavior of concentrated versus unconcentrated industries, as shown by the new "transaction" prices of the National Bureau of Economic Research.

The BLS "quintile" study

Information on the price trends of groups of products classified according to frequency of price change is available in a special report prepared by the Bureau of Labor Statistics.[1] In a special study the 1,789 products in the Wholesale Price Index were classified according to the frequency of price change during the

---

[1] Bureau of Labor Statistics, Department of Labor, Report No. 142, Herschel Ernest Riley, *Frequency of Change in Wholesale Prices: A Study of Price Inflexibility*, 1958. Originally the series covered the period 1947–56. The BLS has extended them through 1966.

3-year period 1954–56; these represented all of the products then in the Index with the exception of certain items whose prices are secured on a confidential basis, certain seasonal products, and a few items for which the price series was not suitable for the purpose of the study. Table 17-1 shows the distribution of the products into five categories, or quintiles, according to the frequency of change, together with the number of products in each quintile and its percentage of the weight of the total index. For each group the median number of changes per year was similar to that used by Means in his distribution for 1926–33.

There is much to be said against using one of the characteristics of concentration, infrequent price change, as a proxy for concentration. No direct relationship has been established between the number of price changes and the level of concentration. Moreover, this particular distribution of the BLS series *is* subject to the McAllister-Stigler criticism, since it is based on the number of changes in the published indexes themselves, not on the average number of changes by companies reporting to the BLS.

On the other hand, it can be argued that at least an indirect relationship exists on the grounds that concentration has been shown to be related inversely to amplitude and amplitude directly to frequency. But of more importance are the economic realities involved. In most of the major concentrated industries (e.g., steel, automobiles, aluminum, petroleum), it is a known fact that price changes are usually made once a year and seldom followed during the year by more than one "revision." Where the structure of an oligopoly is asymmetrical, the other oligopolists and the smaller producers usually change their prices within a very short period after the dominant producer has announced his change. Where the structure is symmetrical, the frequency of change may be somewhat greater, as the roughly equal leaders test the market and one another's responses. But, as is evidenced by such symmetrical oligopolies as tires and cigarettes, this testing (when it occurs) also takes place usually only once a year and lasts for only a limited period. Thus the typical oligopoly, whether asymmetrical or symmetrical, is not likely to have more than 2 changes a year, which would encompass quintiles I, II, and III. Rarely would it have as many as 4 changes a year—the median of quintile IV—and virtually never would it average 8 changes a year—the median of quintile V. There are thus good *economic* grounds to assume the price behavior of oligopolistic industries to be reflected

Table 17-1

DISTRIBUTION OF BLS PRODUCTS AMONG QUINTILES BY FREQUENCY OF PRICE CHANGE

Price Flexibility Group	Number of Price Changes		Products	
	1954–56	Median per Year	Number	Percent of Weight
Quintile I	0 to 2	0.3	370	13.3%
Quintile II	3 to 4	1.2	308	14.3
Quintile III	5 to 7	2.0	405	19.2
Quintile IV	8 to 14	3.7	355	16.4
Quintile V	15 to 36	8.5	350	36.8
Total			1,788	100.0

Source: Computed from Bureau of Labor Statistics, Department of Labor, Report No. 142, Herschel Ernest Riley, *Frequency of Change in Wholesale Prices: A Study of Price Inflexibility*, 1958, pp. 33–82

by the movements of the first three quintiles. And in view of their weight and known infrequency of change, it is probable that the movements of these three groups are determined largely by the price changes of the major oligopolistic industries. In contrast, the behavior of quintile V can be taken to represent the movement of competitive industries, while that of quintile IV reflects the movements of an intermediate grouping, which is partly oligopolistic and partly competitive.[2]

The behavior of the quintiles can be analyzed in terms of both their secular and cyclical changes. The movements of each of the classes over the long-term period 1947–66 are shown in Figure 17-1 for all commodities and in Figure 17-2 for durable manufactured products. The significance of the latter derives from the exclusion from quintile V of farm products and foods, whose prices are strongly influenced by weather conditions and crop cycles.

Secular changes

Between 1947–49 and 1966 two of the three groupings that averaged 2 or fewer changes a year, quintiles II and III, had registered increases of 40 percent and 45 percent respectively. In contrast, the group averaging 8 or more changes a year, quintile V, increased by only 16 percent. The increase of the intermediate grouping, quintile IV, was between these extremes. Hence, a basis exists for the conclusion that, except for the most rigid products, the less the frequency of change, the greater is the long-term increase. The exception, quintile I, registered an advance of 25 percent. Part of the explanation may be found in its composition, since nearly one-fourth of its weight is composed of chemicals and allied products. As has been noted, the BLS series for chemicals have long been known for their extreme stability, attributed by some observers to a failure to reflect hidden discounts and concessions. Another important component of the quintile consists of apparel items, many of which are sold on a "price-lined" basis, with competitive rivalry taking the form of changes in quality rather than price.

For durable manufactures the general pattern was the same, again with the exception of quintile I. On the one hand, quintiles II and III registered advances of more than 50 percent. On the other, quintile V showed an increase of 33 percent, much of which came during the economic expansion of 1965–66.[3]

Over the two decades other prominent features revealed by both all-commodities and durable manufactures were the sharp increases during the Korean War (1950–51), the pronounced rises during the mid- and late 1950's (except in quintile V), the remarkable stability in the price structure during the

---

[2] Incidentally, the infrequency with which oligopolists actually change their prices, which is not only a matter of common observation but can be expected on theoretical grounds, also weakens the force of the McAllister-Stigler criticism. After the lesser oligopolists have met the leader's change in asymmetrical oligopolies, calling for reports from a larger number of producers will only increase the number of responses containing the same information.

[3] If 1952 is taken as the base, the pattern is the same, though the extent of the change is of course smaller:

Percentage Increases in Quintiles II, III, and V

	All Commodities			Durable Manufactures		
	II	III	V	II	III	V
1947–49 to 1966	40	45	16	51	52	33
1953 to 1966	19	30	9	30	28	15

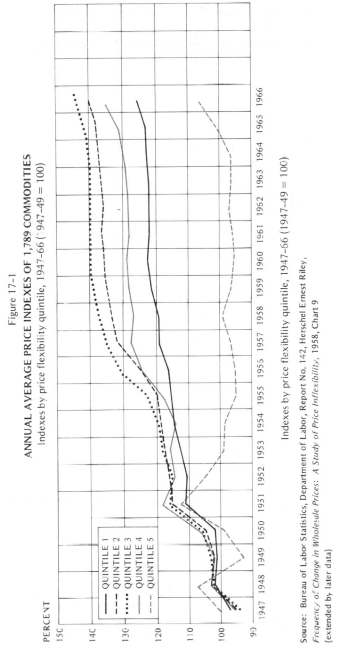

Figure 17-1

ANNUAL AVERAGE PRICE INDEXES OF 1,789 COMMODITIES

Indexes by price flexibility quintile, 1947-66 (1947-49 = 100)

Indexes by price flexibility quintile, 1947-66 (1947-49 = 100)

Source: Bureau of Labor Statistics, Department of Labor, Report No. 142, Herschel Ernest Riley, *Frequency of Change in Wholesale Prices: A Study of Price Inflexibility*, 1958, Chart 9 (extended by later data)

early 1960's (1959–64), and the noticeable increases in the mid-1960's (1965–66), presumably reflecting the Vietnam buildup. The war-induced rises represent a familiar phenomenon, but the remarkable stability during the early 1960's and the sharp upward movement immediately before it warrant further discussion.

In neither all-commodities nor in durable manufactures did any of the quintiles exhibit a pronounced change between 1959 and 1964. Although the downswing of 1960–61 was so limited in both extent and duration that its effect is

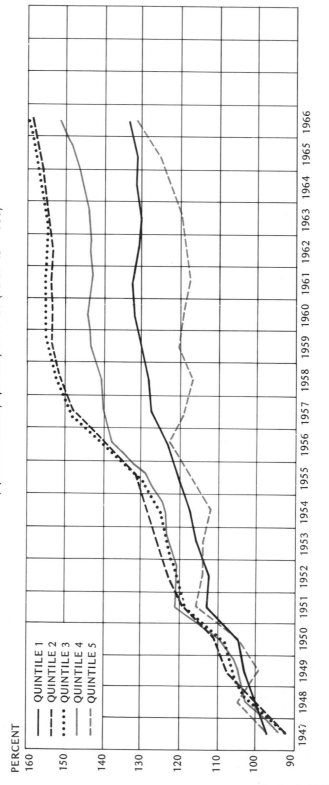

Figure 17-2

ANNUAL AVERAGE PRICE INDEXES OF DURABLE MANUFACTURED COMMODITIES

Indexes by price flexibility quintile, 1947–66 (1947–49 = 100)

Indexes by price flexibility quintile, 1947–66 (1947–49 = 100)

Source: Bureau of Labor Statistics, Department of Labor, Report No. 142, Herschel Ernest Riley, *Frequency of Change in Wholesale Prices: A Study of Price Inflexibility*, 1958, Chart 10 (extended by later data)

OLIGOPOLISTIC PRICE BEHAVIOR

hardly apparent in yearly figures, the most flexible category within durable goods did show a noticeable decline. Nonetheless, for the 5-year period as a whole the stability of quintile V suggests the existence of a balance between expansionistic and deflationary forces in the economy. This would also explain much of the stability displayed by the inflexible groups, though here other factors were also at work.[4]

This protracted period of stability, it should be noted, represents something of an exception to traditional economic thinking, which assumes the different stages of economic activity to be a dichotomy. Whether formalized into a recurring pattern of business cycles or simply recognized as an economic fact of life, it has come to be expected that "upswings" will be followed by "downswings," "upturns" by "downturns," periods of "rising" by periods of "falling" economic activity. An inspection of economic history, however, reveals the interruption of this cyclical behavior, often for protracted intervals, by periods of relatively stable economic activity that come at varying times, last for no set interval, and are without any apparent common cause. The first half of the 1960's appears to have been such a period.

Contrasting sharply with this price stability was the steep upward movement of the mid- and late 1950's, which was particularly pronounced in two of the three inflexible-price groupings. In contrast the flexible-price category showed virtually no net change. This behavior of quintiles II and III (which contain most of the major steel products) tends to confirm an earlier finding by Gardiner C. Means that the price inflation of that period had been largely steel-induced. Appearing before the Senate Antitrust Subcommittee, Means had presented a chart (see Figure 17-3) that showed for each of the broad BLS commodity groups (a) the extent of its 1953–58 price rise; (b) its weight in the overall index (reflected by the width of the bar); and (c) whether, in Means's judgment, it was largely an "administered-price" (black), a market-price (white), or a "mixed" (gray) sector.[5] Describing the chart, Means stated:

> I have divided metals and metal products into three categories—steel, steel products, and other metal products. Each of these is plotted separately and only the first two are given the black color to represent domination by administered prices. The other group is given a dark grey to indicate a mixture of administered prices such as aluminum and nickel and such market prices as iron and steel scrap and those of tin and other metals whose prices are made in world markets.

Commenting on the chart's showings, he said:

> Not only have steel prices risen most but the steel-using machinery and motive products and other steel products have risen more than any other groups. In fact, these steel and steel-using groups account for two-thirds of the gross increase in prices shown in the chart, that is, two-thirds of the area above the base line. . . . If the prices of steel, steel products, and the products of steel-using industries had remained constant, the wholesale price index would have gone up less than 2%.

Cyclical changes

That in periods of rising demand prices of concentrated industries tend to rise more slowly than prices in competitive industries has frequently been noted.[6]

[4] For a discussion of these other factors see Ch. 23.
[5] *Hearings on Administered Prices*, Pt. 9, pp. 4754–60, testimony of Gardiner C. Means.
[6] See, e.g., Edward S. Mason, *Economic Concentration and the Monopoly Problem*, Harvard University Press, 1957, p. 170.

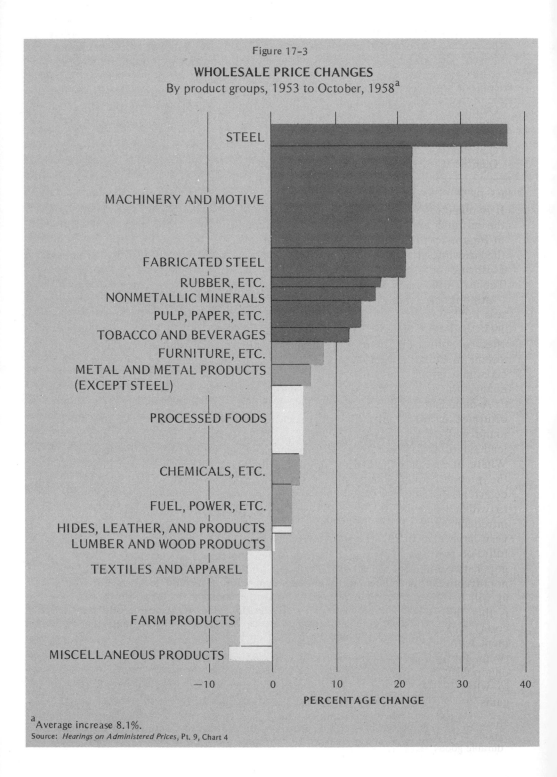

Figure 17–3

WHOLESALE PRICE CHANGES
By product groups, 1953 to October, 1958[a]

[a]Average increase 8.1%.

Source: *Hearings on Administered Prices*, Pt. 9, Chart 4

Table 17-2

CHANGES IN PRICE DURING
ECONOMIC UPTURNS

Price Flexibility Group	All Commodities		Durable Manufactures	
	1958–59	1964–66	1958–59	1964–66
Quintile I	1.2% pts.	2.7% pts.	2.5% pts.	1.8% pts.
Quintile II	1.2	3.3	2.9	3.6
Quintile III	1.7	4.7	2.7	4.6
Quintile IV	2.3	6.0	3.4	6.3
Quintile V	−2.4	10.9	4.7	10.5

Source: Bureau of Labor Statistics, Department of Labor, special tabulation

It is reflected, for example, in the behavior of the less flexible as compared to the more flexible product groups during the late 1930's, as has been shown in Figure 16-5. It can be seen also in the behavior of the BLS quintiles during the upswing, or "reflation," immediately following the 1958 recession, as well as during the marked acceleration in economic activity in 1965 and 1966 (see Table 17-2).[7]

Among all-commodities the only exception to a consistent direct relationship was a price decline between 1958 and 1959 in quintile V; a poor crop year in 1958 had been followed by a good year in 1959, with a resultant depressing effect on farm prices. Among durable manufactures the relationship was consistent in both periods. In general it can thus be seen that during periods of economic expansion, the more flexible the group, in terms of frequency of change, the greater the increase in price.

A number of reasons have been put forward to explain the tendency of concentrated industries to content themselves during periods of rapidly rising demand with relatively limited increases in price. Where there is a tradition of leadership, the lesser oligopolists may wait for the dominant concern to act. Where there is no such tradition, uncertainty by each of the oligopolists as to the probable extent of the upward adjustment by the others may act as a deterrent. As has been noted, there is in most oligopolistic industries a practice, to which buyers have become accustomed, of making price changes only at infrequent intervals. On occasion it may be deemed wise by the management of very large enterprises, in the interest of good public relations, to weigh carefully, or even condition, the public reaction to a price increase. Moreover, oligopolists cannot be presumed to be oblivious to the attraction that a full monopoly price has for potential entrants or producers of substitute products. But, as will be brought out in the next chapter, perhaps the most important reason is that the expansion of output (and the consequent reduction of unit fixed costs) makes it possible for the price leader to meet his target return on investment without raising prices. Whatever the reason, there is generally a lag between the increase in demand and the price adjustment thereto made by the oligopolists. Except for anticipatory price increases, this time lag gives rise to what J. Kenneth Galbraith has characterized as "unliquidated monopoly gains":

[7] Between 1958 and 1959 industrial production rose in manufacturing 13%, in durable goods 17%. Between 1964 and 1966 the increase for manufacturing output was 19%, for durable goods 28%.

With inflation, the demand curves of the firm and industry are moving persistently to the right. Under these circumstances there will normally be an incomplete adaptation of oligopoly prices. Prices will not be at profit-maximizing levels in any given situation, for the situation is continually changing while the adaptation is by deliberate and discrete steps. This means that at any given time there will ordinarily be a quantum of what may be called unliquidated monopoly gains in the inflationary context. The shift in demand calls for a price increase for maximization; since the adaptation is currently incomplete, prices can at any time be raised and profits thereby enhanced.[8]

What distinguishes the behavior of inflexible from flexible products during periods of expanding demand is a difference in their rates of price increase; during periods of declining demand the distinguishing characteristic is a difference in the *direction* of change. The period covered by Figures 17-1 and 17-2 encompasses three economic downturns—those of 1948–49, 1953–54, and 1957–58. During the first the Federal Reserve Board's index of industrial production for manufacturing dropped by 6 percent; during the latter two it fell by 7 percent. Under virtually any standard, including those used by the National Bureau of Economic Research, all three qualify as recessions.

Insofar as the all-commodities index is concerned, the difference in direction first became evident in the 1953–54 recession. In the first downturn the movements were more or less in accord with what would have been expected on the basis of past experience—i.e., relative stability in the infrequently changing prices accompanied by a decrease in the flexible prices. But in 1953–54 all of the quintiles averaging 2 or fewer changes per year moved upward, while the flexible-price grouping registered a decline. It is true that these upward movements were of limited magnitude, but it is also true that *any* increase in price during a recession is unusual. During the 1957–58 recession the inflexible-price groupings repeated their anomalous behavior, but on this occasion quintile V also moved upward. It would appear, however, that the increase by the flexible-price grouping was the result of unusual factors affecting farm production. (Nearly two-thirds of the weight of quintile V was made up of farm products, 35.6 percent, and processed foods, 28.8 percent.)

Farm prices moved upward in 1958 partly because of bad weather; according to the Department of Agriculture, "freeze damage brought smaller supplies and higher prices for vegetables in the first half of the year and for citrus fruits." [9] Whether botanical, as in tree crops, or economic, as in corn and hogs, cycles constitute another factor over which the individual farmer has little control. Thus, 1958 was a year of reduced supplies of both hogs and cattle: "Prices of hogs and cattle are substantially higher this year [1958] than last, reflecting reduced marketings of meat animals." [10]

The influence of farm products on quintile V is apparent from Figure 17-4, which compares the movements of farm products with those of two components of quintile V—products with 13 to 29 changes between 1954 and 1956 and those with 30 to 36 changes. The extremely close parallelism between the latter component and farm products confirms what is a matter of common knowledge—i.e., that most farm products are extremely flexible. The poor weather and re-

[8] J. Kenneth Galbraith, "Market Structure and Stabilization Policy," *Review of Economics and Statistics,* May, 1957, p. 127.
[9] U.S. Department of Agriculture, "The Agricultural Outlook for 1959," Nov. 17, 1958.
[10] *Ibid.*

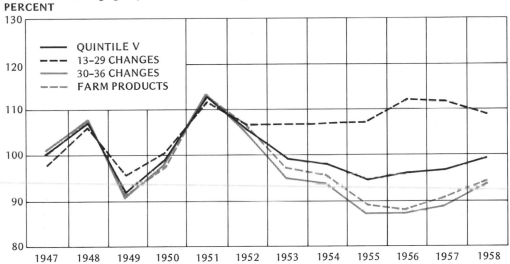

Figure 17-4

ANNUAL AVERAGE PRICE INDEXES FOR QUINTILE V,

Price change groups 13–29 and 30–36, and farm products, 1947-58 (1947–49 = 100)

Source: Bureau of Labor Statistics, Department of Labor, Report No. 142, Herschel Ernest Riley,
Frequency of Change in Wholesale Prices: A Study of Price Inflexibility,
1958, Supplement, p. 2 (extended by later data)

duced marketings of livestock which in 1958 caused farm products to depart from their behavior of past recessions thus had a parallel effect on the more flexible component and, to a somewhat lesser extent, on quintile V itself. What is of most interest, however, is the behavior of the less flexible component—products with 13 to 29 changes. As can be seen from the chart, the movement of this component in 1958 did not parallel the behavior of farm products but instead registered a noticeable decline. Thus the logical inference would be that apart from the unusual factors affecting farm production, the reaction of flexible prices to the contraction in demand was in accord with the expectations of classical theory.

The contrasting behavior of inflexible and flexible prices is also borne out by a comparison of quintile II with quintile IV. Although not at the extremes, the difference in frequency of change was significant; products in the former registered an average of only slightly more than one change a year, while those in the latter group averaged 4. What makes this comparison particularly interesting is the similarity in the two groups' composition. Of quintile II's total weight 41.8 percent was made up of 2 commodity groups: metals and metal products and machinery and motive products; in quintile IV the proportion represented by these same groups was 43.8 percent. In both, the remainder was widely dispersed among other commodity groups. As can be seen from Figures 17-1 and 17-2, the relative stability of both quintiles in 1948–49 had by 1953–54 given way to a divergence in behavior. An upward movement in the less flexible group was accompanied by a clearly discernible decline in the more flexible quintile. Again, during the 1957–58 downturn quintile II moved upward, while quintile IV registered a decline.

As is invariably the case, the brunt of each of the three downswings fell on the durable-goods sector. The output of durable goods fell 10 percent in 1948–49, 11 percent in 1953–54, and 14 percent in 1956–58. Because of the greater reduction in demand and also because of the exclusion of farm products, the recession behavior of the different quintiles within durable goods is of particular interest. The behavior of the most flexible group in durable goods was consistent. In each of the three recessions quintile V registered a noticeable decline. Thus, within the sector of the economy most severely affected by recessions the price behavior of the most flexible grouping, in terms of frequency of change, accorded perfectly with the expectation of classical theory. In contrast, each of the three inflexible-price quintiles moved upward in each of the recessions. For durable goods as a group, what may be referred to as "perverse flexibility" during recessions has become the usual form of price behavior.

Pairs of products

The strength of the quintile analysis is that it is based on virtually all of the BLS price series; its weakness is that the relationship of differing price movements to differing levels of concentration, while based on plausible economic grounds, must nonetheless be inferred. It therefore needs to be supplemented by a different type of analysis in which the levels of concentration are established. Such an analysis is presented here in the form of comparisons of the price movements of 16 pairs of products, the members of which are subject to similar expansions or contractions in demand but differ greatly in both the level of concentration and the frequency of price change. Specifically, one member of each pair is a concentrated, inflexible-price price product; the other is an unconcentrated, flexible-price product. The strength and weakness of this approach are the reverse of those of quintile analysis; it is based on only a selective sample of commodities but the level of concentration (as well as the frequency of price change) is known.

For most of the products the concentration data consist of the Census Bureau's 4-company concentration ratios; for steel products, however, the ratios used were those compiled by the American Iron and Steel Institute, which more closely matched the BLS product definitions. In order to make a comparison between products that differed in terms not only of concentration but of frequency of change, the products were drawn from the BLS quintile study. Since the only really flexible group in that study is quintile V, the starting point in drawing the comparisons consisted of products in that group. The fact that nearly half of its products (accounting for nearly two-thirds of its value) are farm products and foods, and that there are few such products in the other quintiles imposed a severe limitation on the numbers of comparisons which could be developed. To this initial limitation certain other restrictions were added in order to make the analysis more meaningful: (a) comparisons were made only in those cases where the concentrated product had 4 or fewer changes (an average of one or fewer a year) during the 1954–56 base period [11]; (b) because of their presumed inadequacies, no use was made of BLS price series for chemi-

[11] Some steel products were reported by the BLS to have had 5 or 6 changes during the 36-month period, falling just outside the standard. During this period there were only 4 changes in the base prices of most steel products. The additional changes represented changes in the so-called extras, some of which are incorporated as price changes by the BLS. Since other products have analogous changes, modifications of which are not treated by the BLS as price changes, changes in extras should properly be ignored in comparing the flexibility of different products.

cal products; and (c) no comparisons were made involving products typically sold on a "price-lined" basis; the principal effect was the exclusion of apparel items.

The one further step was the determination of which products are subject to reasonably comparable demand forces. Here the test was not whether one product was an exact substitute for another, although in several instances (e.g., the comparison between pig iron and steel scrap) such was the case.[12] Rather, the standard employed was whether the products used in a given comparison are subject to the same general expansions or contractions in demand.

For a few of the flexible-price products concentration ratios were not available, but it is known that their level is relatively low and in each case far below the inflexible products with which they are compared. The use of copper and brass as unconcentrated products is based on a number of circumstances, which have previously been described—viz., the irrelevance of domestic concentration ratios to the relevant (world) market, the importance of secondary smelters, and the influence on price of custom smelters operating on the basis of a fixed margin between the ore price and the refined-metal price.[13]

copper as non-concentd [handwritten margin note]

The concentration and price data for the 32 products involved in the analysis are shown in Table 17-3. Taking the first pair as an example, the 4 largest firms can be seen to have produced 65 percent of the nation's output of pig iron, while between 1954 and 1956 only 3 price changes were reported by the BLS, all of which were increases. In contrast, while no precise concentration ratio is available, the collection and handling of steel scrap is known to be extremely unconcentrated, the 4 largest firms probably accounting for less than 5 percent of the collections. Of 36 opportunities, a change in price was reported in 31, of which 12 were decreases and 19 increases.

For the concentrated products the 4 largest companies produced, on the average, 72 percent of the output; for those unconcentrated products for which figures are available the average was 27 percent, and had figures been available for the other unconcentrated products, the average would have been even lower. During the 3-year base period the concentrated products averaged 3.3 price changes, or a little over one a year. These consisted of 2.8 increases and only .5 decreases. In contrast, the unconcentrated products averaged 27 changes, or three-fourths of the opportunities. Increases and decreases were more evenly distributed, the unconcentrated products averaging 11.6 increases and 15.4 decreases. These differences between the two sets of products are pervasive. In 14 of the concentrated products the share held by the 4 largest companies was 60 percent or higher; in 7 of the 11 unconcentrated products for which ratios are available the share of the 4 leaders was 30 percent or less, the 3 exceptions being the copper and brass products, which have been included in the unconcentrated products for the reasons cited above. Among the concentrated products the maximum number of price changes was 7; among the unconcentrated the minimum number was 15.

---

[12] Where substitutability does exist, the expectation would be that if changes in demand were the determinant of price changes, the price of a flexible product would decline less during a downswing than that of its inflexible-price counterpart. At the outset of a downswing buyers would attempt to shift to the sensitive declining product from the insensitive stable product, thus tending to shore up demand for the former and weaken it for the latter. If, despite this, the price of the flexible product throughout the downswing declines more than that of the inflexible item, changes in demand become even less persuasive as the explanation for changes in price.

[13] See Ch. 16.

Table 17-3

16 PAIRS OF PRODUCTS WITH COMPARABLE DEMAND

Concentration ratio and frequency and magnitude of price change, 1953–1958

Concentration Ratio	Commodity	Frequency of Change, 1954–56			Indexes (1947–49 = 100)					
		Total	Negative	Positive	1953	1954	1955	1956	1957	1958
65%	Pig iron, basic	3	0	3	136.5	138.3	141.4	149.9	160.0	163.0
5%	Steel scrap	31	12	19	115.1	83.6	113.6	149.9	133.5	101.1
75%	Steel billets, rerolling, carbon	3	0	3	148.6	160.6	167.7	177.7	198.7	205.7
n.a.[a]	Red-brass ingot	23	8	15	136.8	141.6	196.6	205.4	158.6	140.9
72%	Steel bars, hot rolled, carbon	5	1	4	136.7	145.3	152.1	166.9	183.4	191.9
47%	Yellow-brass rod	16	7	9	n.a.	143.2	159.2	177.0	140.4	123.2
60%	Steel sheets, hot rolled, carbon	6	2	4	133.7	139.4	144.8	158.3	175.6	181.0
89%	Aluminum sheets	5	0	5	130.0	134.2	142.2	153.1	162.0	163.4
46%	Copper sheets	16	5	11	n.a.	151.0	174.7	193.2	164.4	156.9
82%	Aluminum ingot, primary	6	0	6	131.2	136.9	148.6	163.5	172.9	169.0
28%	Aluminum ingot, secondary	32	14	18	123.6	114.2	158.4	149.7	125.5	122.0
65%	Steel pipe, black	5	0	5	134.7	141.4	150.7	168.7	185.4	191.6
46%	Copper tubing	15	4	11	n.a.	144.6	163.9	179.7	158.1	153.6
92%	Structural steel shapes	4	1	3	138.2	143.8	151.9	162.9	187.5	195.3
20%[b]	Douglas fir timbers (construction)	34	12	22	119.9	123.0	142.9	153.5	135.4	125.7
69%	Steel bars, concrete reinforcing	7	2	5	141.0	153.7	158.8	169.7	184.1	190.8
20%[b]	Douglas fir dimension (construction)	34	14	20	120.7	121.7	134.0	133.3	122.3	119.4
87%	Gypsum wallboard	1	0	1	120.2	121.1	121.1	124.9	124.9	129.4
18%	Plywood, Douglas fir, interior	17	9	8	107.1	103.0	106.1	97.4	88.7	89.6
73%	Roofing shingles, asbestos	3	0	3	130.3	133.5	133.5	140.0	150.4	151.9
17%	Oak, red, flooring, select	24	8	16	113.5	114.2	128.0	132.2	118.5	118.0
30%	Crude petroleum, Okla.-Kans.[c]	0	0	0	115.7	120.2	120.2	120.2	130.0	130.8
	Lubricating oil, cylinder stock, Pa.	15	4	11	67.8	40.9	44.1	70.8	76.6	59.4
54%	Synthetic rubber, neoprene	0	0	0	128.5	131.7	131.7	131.7	131.7	131.7
n.a.[a]	Natural rubber[d]	35	12	23	117.8	122.0	202.7	178.3	161.7	141.0

Table 17-3 (continued)

16 PAIRS OF PRODUCTS WITH COMPARABLE DEMAND

Concentration ratio and frequency and magnitude of price change, 1953–1958

Concentration Ratio	Commodity	Frequency of Change, 1954–56			Indexes (1947–49 = 100)					
		Total	Negative	Positive	1953	1954	1955	1956	1957	1958
37%	Container board, test liner, Cent.	1	0	1	117.8	120.9	120.9	124.8	126.1	125.1
n.a.[a]	Ponderosa pine box board[e]	36	16	20	128.1	114.0	125.3	125.1	114.3	113.2
79%	Viscose staple	2	2	0	99.7	96.8	96.3	92.7	88.3	91.0
n.a.[a]	Wool tops	36	15	21	114.7	112.5	99.9	95.9	108.8	83.5
78%	Viscose filament yarn	4	1	3	104.4	104.3	104.7	107.4	113.0	103.4
19%	Wool yarn, Bradford, weaving	31	18	13	114.0	111.3	100.5	100.9	109.5	95.1
81%	Salt	4	1	3	123.2	145.6	143.4	152.1	157.1	160.1
n.a.[a]	Pepper, whole black	36	27	9	179.9	103.4	63.3	44.5	38.2	35.7

[a] Not available.
[b] Holdings of privately owned timberlands on the West Coast in the hands of the 4 largest owners are estimated to be less than 20% of the amount held by all private ownership.
[c] Supply limited by government controls.
[d] The producers of natural rubber are numbered in the thousands. The small holdings produce roughly half the world's supply of natural rubber, the balance coming from independently owned estates.
[e] Ponderosa pine #3 board used as reasonably equivalent in price movement to box board.

Source: Price data: Bureau of Labor Statistics, Department of Labor, Report No. 142, Herschel Ernest Riley, *Frequency of Change in Wholesale Prices: A Study of Price Inflexibility,* 1958; concentration ratios (steel products): *Administered Prices: Report on Steel,* p. 70; concentration ratios (others): *Concentration Ratios in Manufacturing Industry,* 1958, Pt. 1, Table 4

The question at issue here is whether there was any significant difference in the price behavior of these two types of products. The answer can be seen in Figure 17-5, which shows the price movements from 1953 to 1958 for 16 pairs of commodities.

The first comparison is between the price of pig iron and that of steel scrap (Grid 1). Since both are used as raw materials in the production of steel, the demand for both is governed by the rate of steel production. The behavior of steel scrap is illustrative of the type of price movement typically displayed by unconcentrated products. A decline in price during the 1953–54 downswing was followed by an increase during the 1954–56 recovery and then by a further decline in the recession that, insofar as producer goods are concerned, actually began around the middle of 1956. In sharp contrast, the price of pig iron moved slowly upward during the 1953–54 downturn, rose at a more rapid rate during the 1954–56 recovery, and continued to advance during the 1957–58 recession.

The next comparison (Grid 2) involves 2 semifinished products, steel billets and brass ingots, both of which are used as materials by semi-integrated producers. As compared to the other steel products, which are purchased by the customers of the integrated steel producers rather than by their smaller semi-integrated competitors, steel billets showed a price increase during the 1953–54 downswing that was unusually pronounced, averaging 8 percent. The price continued to rise during the subsequent recovery as well as in the 1958 recession. Reflecting weakness in world copper markets, however, the price of red-brass ingots, after peaking in 1956, fell sharply during the next 2 years.

The contrast (Grid 3) between steel bars and yellow-brass rod, the demand for which is determined by the general level of metalworking activity, is a reptition of the pattern displayed by steel billets and brass ingots. The price behavior of the concentrated products, steel sheets and aluminum sheets (Grid 4), contrasts strongly with that of a similar but flexible-price product, copper sheets. Except for the fact that aluminum sheets advanced at a slower rate during the 1958 recession, the trends of the former 2 products displayed a remarkable symmetry. In contrast, the price of copper sheets fell sharply. The similarity in behavior between steel and aluminum reveals that, whatever the reason, the producers of the latter certainly did not take advantage of the opportunities presented by steel price increases to promote the use of their product as a substitute material. Demand for the products shown on Grids 5 and 6 also is determined largely by changes in metalworking activity. Both of the unconcentrated products, secondary aluminum ingot and copper tubing, exhibited marked declines during both recessions, whereas, with one exception, their concentrated counterparts moved upward. This exception was a slight price decline in primary-aluminum ingot between 1957 and 1958, which can be attributed in part to the competitive pressure of lower-priced foreign supplies.

Demand for the products shown on Grids 7 and 8 is largely a function of construction activity. In both cases the concentrated products, structural steel shapes and concrete reinforcing bars, moved steadily upward throughout the entire period. During the 1958 recession this was in sharp contrast to the marked declines manifested by their unconcentrated counterparts—Douglas fir timbers and Douglas fir dimension. The level of construction activity is also the principal determinant of demand for the products shown on Grids 9 and 10. Douglas fir plywood declined noticeably in both downswings; red-oak flooring, although remaining virtually unchanged during the earlier decline, dropped significantly during the latter. Their concentrated counterparts, gypsum wallboard and asbestos roofing shingles, moved irregularly upward throughout the period. Particularly striking is the contrasting behavior of asbestos shingles and oak flooring beginning in 1956.

Insofar as market behavior is concerned, concentration ratios for either the production or refining of crude petroleum (Grid 11) are largely irrelevant; the controlling factor is a system of government controls over supply. Through market demand proration, particularly in Texas and Louisiana, and through a quota on imports, supply is limited to anticipated demand. No such controls exist in the Pennsylvania lubricating-oil industry, which is composed of a substantial number of small producers. The effect of government controls over supply is dramatized by the difference in price behavior. Pennsylvania lubricating oil suffered price decreases during both recessions, while in each crude petroleum moved upward. The price of synthetic rubber (Grid 12) is the most inflexible of any of the commodities included in this analysis, remaining unchanged throughout the entire period, with the exception of a slight increase of 2.5 percent occurring during the recession of 1953–54. This stability is in striking contrast to the precipitous rise in the price of natural rubber in 1955 and the ensuing steady decline.

The comparison on Grid 13 involves packaging materials—container board versus ponderosa pine box board. Although their movements were not as pronounced as in most of the other pairs, the unconcentrated product declined in both recessions, while the concentrated product rose. The two comparisons involving textile products (Grids 14 and 15) present a number of exceptions to the general pattern displayed by the other commodities. Thus, the price of the concentrated product, viscose staple, suffered a slight decline in the first downswing and the ensuing upturn. However, part of the loss was recovered by a price increase in 1957–58, which was accompanied by a decrease in the price of its unconcentrated counterpart, wool tops. The concentrated product, viscose yarn, remained unchanged during the earlier downswing, while wool yarn declined. But between 1957 and 1958 both the concentrated and unconcentrated products declined. In the final comparison (Grid 16) a precipitous and sustained decline in the price of pepper was accompanied by a substantial and, except for 1954–55, uninterrupted increase in the price of its concentrated counterpart, salt.

As can be seen from the accompanying table, the general pattern during the two recessions was one of price increases in the concentrated, inflexible-price products and of decreases in their unconcentrated, flexible-price counterparts. Thus during the 1953–54 downturn 15 of the 17 concentrated products registered increases in price, of which 5 amounted to 5 percent or more. In contrast, in 8 of the 13 unconcentrated products[14] decreases were recorded, of which half were 10 percent or more.

During the later recession the directions of change were the same but their extent varies depending upon whether the point of comparison for 1958 is 1956 or 1957. The index of industrial production for manufacturing was virtually the same in 1956 and 1957.[15] Most of the 33 products are producer goods, the demand

[14] For 3 products price data for 1953–54 were unavailable.
[15] The FRB indexes are as follows (1967 = 100):

	Manufacturing	Durable	Nondurable
1956	62.7	63.5	61.7
1957	63.1	63.5	62.5
1958	58.4	55.2	62.6

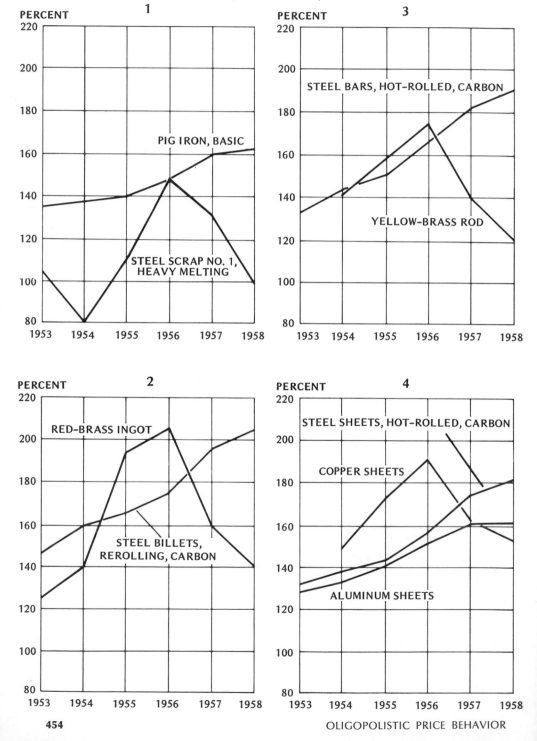

Figure 17–5

**PRICE MOVEMENTS OF INFLEXIBLE[a]-VERSUS
FLEXIBLE[b]-PRICE PRODUCTS, 1953–1958**

(1947–49 = 100)

OLIGOPOLISTIC PRICE BEHAVIOR

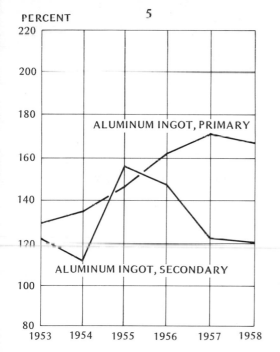

PERCENT 5

ALUMINUM INGOT, PRIMARY

ALUMINUM INGOT, SECONDARY

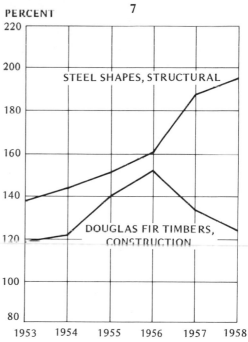

PERCENT 7

STEEL SHAPES, STRUCTURAL

DOUGLAS FIR TIMBERS, CONSTRUCTION

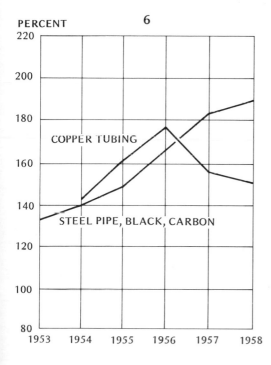

PERCENT 6

COPPER TUBING

STEEL PIPE, BLACK, CARBON

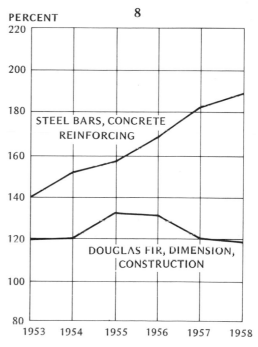

PERCENT 8

STEEL BARS, CONCRETE REINFORCING

DOUGLAS FIR, DIMENSION, CONSTRUCTION

PAIRS OF PRODUCTS

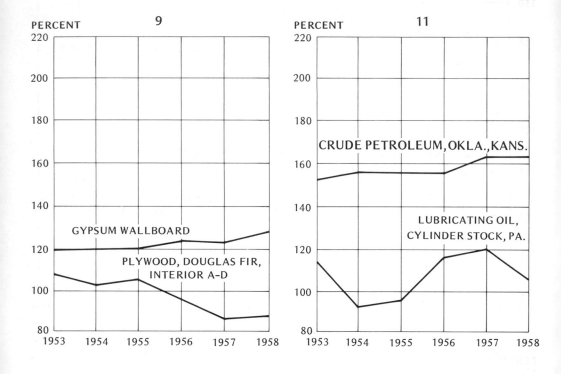

9

PERCENT

GYPSUM WALLBOARD

PLYWOOD, DOUGLAS FIR, INTERIOR A-D

1953 1954 1955 1956 1957 1958

11

PERCENT

CRUDE PETROLEUM, OKLA., KANS.

LUBRICATING OIL, CYLINDER STOCK, PA.

1953 1954 1955 1956 1957 1958

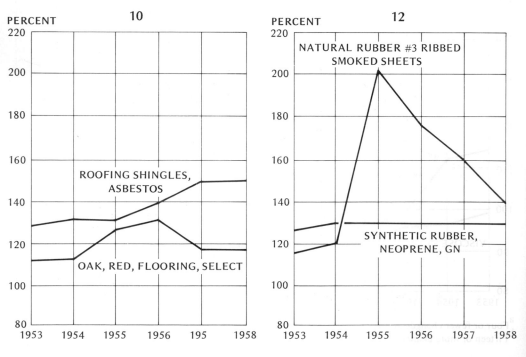

10

PERCENT

ROOFING SHINGLES, ASBESTOS

OAK, RED, FLOORING, SELECT

1953 1954 1955 1956 195 1958

12

PERCENT

NATURAL RUBBER #3 RIBBED SMOKED SHEETS

SYNTHETIC RUBBER, NEOPRENE, GN

1953 1954 1955 1956 1957 1958

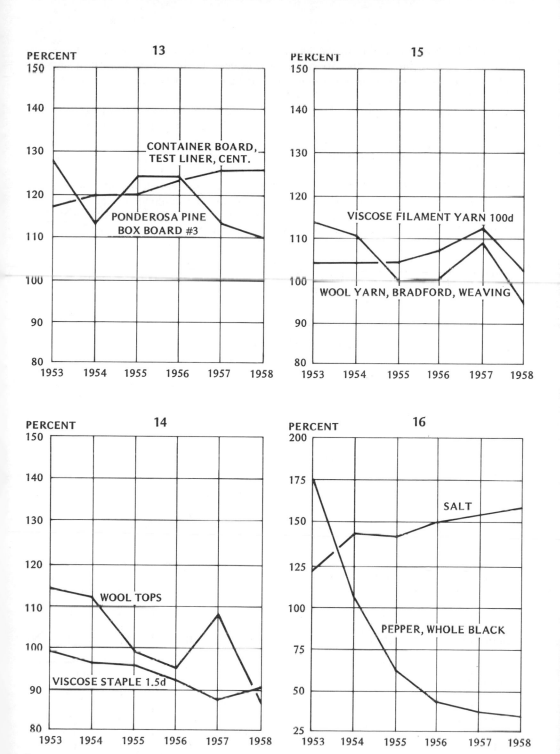

PERCENT 13

CONTAINER BOARD, TEST LINER, CENT.

PONDEROSA PINE BOX BOARD #3

PERCENT 15

VISCOSE FILAMENT YARN 100d

WOOL YARN, BRADFORD, WEAVING

PERCENT 14

WOOL TOPS

VISCOSE STAPLE 1.5d

PERCENT 16

SALT

PEPPER, WHOLE BLACK

[a]Four or fewer changes in price between 1954 and 1956.
[b]Fifteen or more changes in price between 1954 and 1956.

Source: *Hearings on Administered Prices*, Pt. 10, p. 5009–12

for which began to decline in the latter half of 1956. Reflecting this slowdown, the prices of all but 2 of the 16 sensitive products declined between 1956 and 1957. For the particular products included in this analysis, the more meaningful comparison would therefore be 1956–1958.

During this interval prices of 13 of the 17 concentrated products moved upward. Most of these increases were substantial, 11 amounting to 5 percent or more. The behavior of the unconcentrated products was consistent; all 16 registered price declines, and in all but 3 the decreases were 10 percent or more. For the 1957–58 interval the number of concentrated products registering increases (12) was nearly as great as for 1956–58, but the extent of increase was smaller, 11 amounting to less than 5 percent. Again, the behavior of the unconcentrated product was consistent, or nearly so. All but one registered decreases, 8 of which were 10 percent or more. Thus in the recessions both of 1954 and of 1958 (regardless of the interval used), the behavior of the concentrated and the unconcentrated products alike confirmed the conclusion suggested by the quintile analysis. The concentrated products tended to move perversely; the unconcentrated products in the manner expected under classical theory (see Table 17-4).

Correlation analyses

A number of statistical studies have approached the concentration-price issue by seeking to determine whether a linear relationship exists between the degree of price change and the level of concentration (either by itself or in conjunction

Table 17-4

DISTRIBUTION OF PRODUCTS BY PERCENTAGE CHANGE IN PRICE

Recessions of 1954 and 1958

Number of Products by Percentage Change	1954 Recession		1958 Recession			
			1956–58		1957–58	
	Concen-trated	Unconcen-trated	Concen-trated	Unconcen-trated	Concen-trated	Unconcen-trated
Increases						
+10 or over	2	0	6	0	0	0
+5 to +9	3	0	5	0	1	0
Under +5	10	5	2	0	11	1
No change	0	0	1	0	3	0
Decreases						
Under –5	2	3	3	0	1	6
–5 to –9	0	1	0	3	1	1
–10 or over	0	4	0	13	0	8
Total	17	13[a]	17	16	17	16

[a]Price information not available for 3 additional products.

Source: Computed from Bureau of Labor Statistics, Department of Labor, Report No. 142, *op. cit.,* and special tabulation

why large scale statistical studies are inadequate

with other variables). Against the background of the conceptual issue involved, this approach suffers from several inherent limitations. Implicit in its use is the assumption that the issue has been whether successive increments to concentration result in successively smaller decreases in price (as during the 1930's) or in successively larger increases in price (as during the 1950's). Yet, as was emphasized earlier, the point at issue has never been whether differences exist in the price behavior of oligopolistic industries that differ only in the degree to which they are oligopolistic; rather, it is whether price behavior differs distinctly and significantly between oligopolistic and polypolistic industries. As has been noted, the focusing of attention on deviations from an actual or inferred central tendency, once the point of oligopoly has been reached, tends merely to direct attention away from the essential question of whether, in general, there is a significant difference in price behavior between the two different types of industry. Similarly, there is no conceptual reason why price behavior should differ significantly among unconcentrated industries that differ only in the degree to which they are unconcentrated. On theoretical grounds there is no reason to expect any difference in price behavior as long as the leading producers cannot affect the price significantly by varying their level of output and therefore have no reason to be concerned over the reactions of their competitors. In a review of the recent literature, William G. Shepherd correctly stated the issue:

> Means, Blair, and other critics of administered prices focused their criticism on certain major concentrated industries whose prices persisted in rising even during the two recessions of the 1950's. In the surprisingly nettlesome debate which ensued, some counter-critics (incorrectly) reinterpreted the administered price "thesis" into a straw-man claim that there is a positive *general* association of secular price rises and industry *concentration*. This argument would lift the burden of proof from the major industries (to justify their price rises at times of idle capacity), placing it instead upon the "administered price" critics to demonstrate that such an omni-industry relationship exists. A study failing to find such a relationship could then be construed as rebutting the entire "administered price" thesis—indeed the whole price-output flexibility problem.[16]

Principal among the studies to which Shepherd refers is one by Horace J. DePodwin and Richard P. Selden purportedly demonstrating through low correlations the absence of any relationship between 1953 and 1959 between the level of concentration and the degree of price increase.[17] Aside from the absence of standards to eliminate industries that manifestly should not be included in this type of analysis, the interval examined is from a year of reasonably normal economic activity to a year of recovery from a recession; and, as has been long established, prices during economic expansion tend to rise less rapidly in concentrated than in unconcentrated industries. Even so, the study fell well short of demolishing the administered-price thesis. As Shepherd observes,

> in their haste to reach their conclusion, DePodwin and Selden overlooked the embarrassing fact that their own data actually tend to contradict their conclusion more than to support it. As Means has already noted, the regression slopes for at least two of their equations imply no price rise for

[16] William G. Shepherd, *Market Power and Economic Welfare*, Random House, 1970, pp. 199–200. Emphasis in original.
[17] Horace J. DePodwin and Richard P. Selden, "Business Pricing Policies and Inflation," *Journal of Political Economy*, April, 1963.

unconcentrated industries during 1953–59, and about a 20 percent price rise for industries with maximum concentration. This would support even the misconstrued administered price thesis! [18]

A study by Richard Ruggles also emphasizes the importance of selecting for study a time period which is meaningful for this type of analysis. Ruggles claims to have found that changes in price were explained largely by changes in input costs.[19] In this case the period examined was from a recession year (1954) to a year of recovery (1959). It would have been most unlikely to have found that prices in concentrated industries rose at an above-average rate between a year in which they were relatively high and one in which they were relatively low.[20] In point of fact, prices in concentrated industries, as has been shown, did rise during the 1953–54 recession but advanced less rapidly than those in unconcentrated industries during the 1958–59 recovery.

Relating concentration to price change between 1947–49 and 1958 for 224 industries, Shepherd found a "statistically faint" relationship. "Low concentration goes with a 6 percent price rise while maximum concentration goes with a 36 percent rise. This holds despite the presence of other variables which might be expected to be influential but which were not; growth, large-firm share, and imports." [21]

The relationship of concentration to price changes during recessions, periods of stability, and economic expansions has also been studied by Leonard W. Weiss, with results similar to those suggested by the quintile and "pairs of products" analyses.[22] Summarizing his findings for the 1958 downturn Weiss states: "Reexamination of the 'administered inflation' of 1953–58 seemed at first to show no significant relationship between price change and concentration, but when changes in direct costs were allowed for there turned out to be a significant tendency for prices to rise more, the greater the degree of industrial concentration." [23] For the period of economic stability during the early and mid-1960's he found that "concentration has a negative but statistically insignificant effect on price changes." [24] And during the economic upturn of the late 1960's the concentrated industries displayed their familiar behavioral pattern of a relatively slow rate of increase; "for periods after 1967, concentration has a statistically significant negative effect, whether or not unit costs and demand change are taken into account." Although at the time data were not yet at hand, Weiss emphasized that the "positive relationship" might again appear during the 1970 downturn: "In light of the experience of the 1950's, the result may be another 'administered inflation' in the early 1970's." [25]

[18] Shepherd, *op. cit.,* p. 200. The analysis by Means referred to is to be found in *Hearings on Economic Concentration,* Pt. 1, pp. 496–97.
[19] *Hearings on Administered Prices,* Pt. 1, pp. 128–62.
[20] Shepherd also notes that since the input price indexes used by Ruggles "explain" only 40% of the price changes, "the 'unexplained' 60 percent residual variation of output price changes is larger than might be expected." (Shepherd, *op. cit.,* p. 201.)
[21] Shepherd, *op. cit.,* p. 201.
[22] Leonard W. Weiss, "Business Pricing Policies and Inflation Reconsidered," *Journal of Political Economy,* April, 1966, pp. 180–81.
[23] 91st Cong., 2nd Sess., Joint Economic Committee, *Hearings: 1970 Mid-Year Review,* 1970, Pt. 1, Leonard W. Weiss, "The Role of Concentration in Recent Inflation," p. 115.
[24] *Ibid.,* p. 116.
[25] *Ibid.*

Concentration and transaction prices

A new source of price data that can be used to examine the influence of concentration on price behavior is a study issued by the National Bureau of Economic Research—*The Behavior of Industrial Prices,* by George J. Stigler and James K. Kindahl.[26] Unlike the price series of the BLS, which are obtained from sellers, it is based on information reported by buyers. Its central purpose is to examine the administered-price doctrine of Gardiner C. Means; its method is to test the validity of the doctrine's empirical basis by comparing the BLS wholesale price series against the new National Bureau (NB) indexes of buyers' prices. Price information was secured for 64 products, representing 18.9 percent of the value of all commodities in the BLS index, excluding farm and food products. In selecting their products, the authors gave "special attention to the areas in which the charge of inflexible prices has been heard most frequently"; they also excluded "almost all" commodities subject to rapid change in their product characteristics. The study is thus "heavily biased toward widely used staple individual materials" because they are less subject to "elaborate product changes." The period covered is 1957–66. The buyers from whom prices were obtained consisted of 33 government and governmental agencies—federal, state, and local; 137 industrial, utility, and transportation companies; and, in the case of drugs, 9 hospitals. Since there was an "overwhelming reliance . . . on large companies and institutions" as sources, the study is biased in the direction of those buyers who are most likely to be the recipients of secret deals and concessions.

If a cloud can be cast on its empirical basis, one can ignore as an amusing bit of folklore Means's "celebrated" doctrine of administered prices, with its "startling" statistics of prices and its "sweeping inferences . . . about the role of price rigidity in the economic malaise of the 1930's. . . ." Citing a sharp increase in the number of articles on rigid prices appearing in economic journals, the authors remark that Means "had in fact created a new subject":

> The proposition that in many important industrial markets prices do not respond quickly or fully to changing supply and demand conditions in the way a competitive market had became generally accepted by the late 1930's. It was accepted first by the economists and then increasingly by the general public. Public acceptance is illustrated by the congressional hearings to which changes in the price of steel products have been subjected since 1948.[27]

The same would apply to Means's "widely publicized testimony" attributing the inflation of the mid- and late 1950's primarily to increases in administered-price industries. From this view, which "was endorsed in substantial measure by economists as eminent as Abba Lerner and J. K. Galbraith," there was a "natural evolution to the 'guidelines' of price and wage policy announced by the Council of Economic Advisers in 1962 and applied to steel, aluminum and other products in a series of highly dramatic confrontations of the Presidential office and the industries in question." [28] Public policy had thus come to be predicated upon

[26] George J. Stigler and James K. Kindahl, *The Behavior of Industrial Prices,* National Bureau of Economic Research, 1970.
[27] *Ibid.,* p. 13.
[28] *Ibid.,* p. 14.

the uncritical acceptance of an unproved doctrine: "The existence of inflexible industrial prices is accepted because it is believed to be an implacable empirical fact. One large purpose of our study is to determine whether it is indeed a fact." [29] The reader can be forgiven for anticipating a demolition of the empirical foundation of a doctrine that Stigler holds in such ill-disguised contempt.

The demolition, however, never comes off. What is implied in the introduction to the study is one thing; what is set forth in the body of the work is quite another. At no point do the authors make any general condemnation, or even criticism, of the BLS series as indicative of the movement of prices in individual industry groups. Indeed, instead of providing a basis for the refutation of the BLS prices, the two types of price exhibit a remarkable parallelism in most of the industry groups. This parallelism is most clearly evident from the charts presented for each of the industry categories examined.[30] Usually, the close correspondence is acknowledged. Thus, in the case of steel, which is of particular importance in view of the responsibility attributed to it by Means, as well as by Otto Eckstein and Gary Fromm,[31] for the inflation of the 1950's, Stigler and Kindahl state:

> The B.L.S. and N.B. prices of steel products *move together so closely* that a description of one is a description of the other . . . this finding, it must be confessed, comes as a surprise to us. . . . With the exception of three steel products [reinforcing bars, pipe and stainless steel], however, we were unable to learn of any important and continuous departures from quoted prices . . . the general picture was one of close adherence to quoted prices even for very large buyers of steel.[32]

In contrast to the pattern shown for steel—stability interrupted occasionally by stair-step increases—both indexes for nonferrous metals fluctuate widely with changes in demand but in the same direction and to about the same extent. Both series show a steep drop in 1957–58, a sharp recovery in 1959–60, a more gradual decline in 1961–63, and a sustained rise thereafter. During the last stage the NB index does show a sharper increase, which, however, is explained as follows: "The greater rise in the N.B. index in 1964–66 reflects the more rapid rise in transaction prices than in quoted prices, which were under 'guideline' control." [33]

[29] *Ibid.,* p. 15.

[30] See *ibid.,* Ch. 5.

[31] 86th Cong., 1st Sess., Joint Economic Committee, Otto Eckstein and Gary Fromm, *Steel and the Postwar Inflation,* 1959.

[32] Stigler and Kindahl, *op. cit.,* pp. 73–74. Emphasis added. The authors do not explain just why the parallelism of the BLS steel prices with their own transaction prices should come as a surprise. In a special survey conducted in the early days of World War II, the BLS compared their own published series with the delivered prices actually paid by buyers (see *Iron Age,* April 25, 1946). Of particular interest in this context would be a period of relatively free supply when discounts and concessions would presumably be at their greatest—e.g., the third quarter of 1939, at which time the operating rate was 63%. For the 8 steel products examined the deviations averaged only −5.9%, ranging from a low of −2.0% for merchant bars to a high for cold-rolled strip of −11.0%. Similarly, a comparison of the changes of the BLS between 1954 and 1958 with the Census realized prices revealed an average increase of 28.8% according to the former and 25.1% according to the latter. As would be anticipated, the deviations were greatest for the products with the widest Census definitions—structural shapes, hot-rolled sheets—and smallest for those whose definitions most closely approximated the BLS specifications—rails and electrolytic tin plate (see John M. Blair, "Administered Prices and Oligopolistic Inflation: A Reply," *Journal of Business,* Jan., 1964, pp. 72–74).

[33] Stigler and Kindahl, *op. cit.,* p. 75.

Except for a greater volatility of the BLS series, which is attributed partly to the fact that it represents essentially "spot" prices and partly to the stability of transaction prices paid by railroads for diesel oil, "the two indexes [for petroleum and products] show *fairly similar cyclical patterns.*" Noting a sharper increase by the BLS series for 1965–66, the authors observe, "The more rapid secular fall of the N.B. index is due exclusively to this difference in the last two years." [34] Suggesting an improvement during recent years in the quality of the BLS series for this group, "The N.B. composite index for all chemical falls more rapidly than the B.L.S. index, but in other respects the series *agree fairly well.*" [35] Moreover, "The agreement betwten the B.L.S. and N.B. price indexes for paper and pulp products is *broadly satisfactory.* . . . Neither price index has a strong trend. . . ." [36]

Relatively close correspondence between the two series is also apparent from the charts for 3 other industry groups for which no textual comment is offered—nonmetallic mineral products, electrical machinery, and lumber and wood products.[37] Only in the case of rubber and products do the two series differ significantly in trend and cyclical behavior. But even here the authors observe, "On average the B.L.S. and N.B. indexes *agree tolerably.*" [38]

That there is such a close correspondence between the NB and the BLS price indexes is not surprising in view of the improvements made in the latter over the years. Improvements have been made in the nature, completeness, and accuracy of prices reported by cooperating sources: field trips are undertaken regularly by commodity analysts, and conferences are held with trade and industry associations;[39] the product samples and specifications are frequently reviewed; commodity analysts automatically check price changes beyond a specified limit; and systems have been developed to make adjustments for quality changes in products based on physical characteristics—e.g., in automobiles.[40]

In view of the parallelism between the two series, it is difficult to see how the administered-price doctrine could find support in the BLS indexes but be disproved by the new transaction prices. In a recent article Means has endeavored to ascertain whether the new buyers' prices actually do refute his concepts. The issue is focused most sharply during periods of falling demand; in the words of Stigler and Kindahl:

> Classical theory leads one to expect prices to fall in competitive industries during a business contraction, because both demand and marginal production costs fell, and that reverse movements will occur in expansions. This expectation was not subject to elaborate analysis perhaps because a similar pattern was expected under monopoly. Here too, marginal costs would fall and there was no strong reason to expect marginal revenues to rise, although a price reduction was no longer a *necessary* result of a leftward shift in demand and cost functions. The great impact of

[34] *Ibid.,* p. 76. Emphasis added.
[35] *Ibid.,* p. 80. Emphasis added.
[36] *Ibid.,* p. 77. Emphasis added.
[37] *Ibid.,* pp. 83, 84, 86.
[38] *Ibid.,* p. 77. Emphasis added.
[39] In fiscal 1970, for example, such conferences were held with associations in 10 different industries.
[40] See Bureau of Labor Statistics, Department of Labor, *Guidelines for Adjustment of New Automobile Prices for Changes in Quality of Product,* Aug. 29, 1968.

Table 17-5

BEHAVIOR OF ADMINISTRATION-DOMINATED PRICES IN TWO CONTRACTIONS[a]

Price Behavior	Number of Products	
	As Reported	As corrected for Averaging
Decreasing	25	11
Neutral	0	23
Not decreasing	28	19
Total	53	53

[a]July, 1957, to April, 1958, and April, 1960, to July, 1961.

Source: George J. Stigler and James K. Kindahl, *The Behavior of Industrial Prices*, National Bureau of Economic Research, 1970; Gardiner C. Means, "The Administered Price Thesis Re-confirmed," *American Economic Review*, June, 1972

Means's writings on administered prices is attributable to the contradiction of this expectation by the price statistics.[41]

Since market prices are not at issue, the critical question is the behavior of what Means refers to as "administration-dominated" prices. Table 17-5 compares the Stigler-Kindahl findings as reported with the same findings after an adjustment made by Means. The adjustment consisted of placing in a "neutral" category products with differing behavior in the two contractions but which Stigler and Kindahl had classified on the basis of their *average* movement in both periods. Describing the need for the adjustment, Means stated that

a price which showed "no change" in one contraction and declined in the other was classed as decreasing. If the issue were one of the *average* behavior of individual prices this procedure would be appropriate. But the basic issue is one of *tendency*. An item which goes up in one contraction and down in another cannot be said to have a *tendency* to go down and an item which does not change in one contraction and decreases in the other shows just as much of a tendency to stay constant as a tendency to go down.[42]

Even as reported, 53 percent of the "administration-dominated" prices did not conform to the expectations of classical theory. With the elimination of the "neutral" products the proportion rises to 63 percent. It would rise even farther if there were also eliminated those products whose behavior was *relatively* inflexible—i.e., those with relatively limited decreases as compared to market-price products.[43] Thus, the same general conclusion Means had arrived at more than 35 years ago based on the BLS data is reconfirmed by the new NB data. In Means's words, "The actual behavior of administration-dominated prices in the [Stigler-Kindahl] sample tends to differ so sharply from the behavior to be expected from classical theory as to challenge the basic conclusion of classical theory that, in the short run, price tends to equal marginal cost and marginal revenue. How-

[41] Stigler and Kindahl, *op. cit.*, pp. 60–61. Emphasis in original. While contrary to the expectations under competition, Means's findings were not contrary to the expectations under oligopoly (see Ch. 1).

[42] Gardiner C. Means, "The Administered Price Thesis Re-confirmed," *American Economic Review*, June, 1972.

[43] By making the question at issue whether administered-price products showed *any* decline, not whether (as Means had repeatedly emphasized) their decrease was *relatively* limited as compared to market-price products, Stigler and Kindahl set up a straw man, which, ironically, their own data did not permit them to knock down.

Table 17-6

DISTRIBUTION OF CHANGES IN NATIONAL BUREAU ("TRANSACTION") PRICES

January, 1957, to April, 1958

Products	Changes in Price		
	Increases	No Change[a]	Decreases
Concentrated (50% and over)			
Steel	9	—	—
Aluminum	—	—	3
Rubber products	2	—	—
Paper products	—	1	—
Chemicals and drugs	4	1	2
Stone, clay, and glass	—	—	2
Total	15	2	7
Moderately concentrated (25–49%)			
Paper products	1	1	2
Petroleum products	—	—	3
Chemicals and drugs	3	3	—
Stone, clay, and glass	1	—	—
Total	5	4	5
Unconcentrated (under 25%)			
Paper products	—	—	1
Chemicals and drugs	1	—	—
Lumber products	—	—	2
Total	1	—	3
Total	21	6	15

[a]Plus or minus .05%.

Source: George J. Stigler and James K. Kindahl, *The Behavior of Industrial Prices,* National Bureau of Economic Research, 1970, pp. 108–71; *Concentration Ratios in Manufacturing Industry,* 1958, Pt. 1, Table 2

ever well it may apply to market-dominated products, it would not seem to apply to the bulk of administration-dominated prices in the sample."[44]

A showing that the majority of the NB prices did not decline with a contraction of business activity casts a very large cloud on classical theory; it does not establish, in itself, that this failure to behave in accordance with competitive expectations was the consequence of concentration.[45] To shed light on this question a distribution of price changes by concentration ratios was constructed from the data presented in their appendices for the 1957–58 recession (see Table 17-6).[46] It was possible to match the product data, as shown in the appendices,

[44] Means, *op. cit.*

[45] Stigler and Kindahl present in a footnote a distribution by concentration ratios, but it is based on the *average* change in two contractions, 1957–58 and 1960–61 (Stigler and Kindahl, *op. cit.,* p. 61n). As noted, Means has pointed out the inappropriateness of using such averages to measure a *tendency.*

[46] According to the National Bureau the peak of the downturn was July, 1957, and the trough April, 1958. But, as has been pointed out, demand for producer goods had begun

with concentration ratios for 49 products[47] from which 7 nonferrous-metal products were deleted. As has been set forth earlier, the available (domestic) concentration ratios for these products substantially overstate concentration in the relevant (world) market.

Of the 24 concentrated products, fewer than one-third (7) behaved in the manner expected under classical theory. More than three-fifths (15) exhibited "perverse flexibility," while 2 remained unchanged. Among the concentrated products the increases were centered in steel, rubber products, and chemicals. Decreases in aluminum appear to have been the result of a short-lived invasion of the U.S. market by French and Norwegian producers.[48] Both of the declines recorded by chemicals were extremely limited, -1.3 percent for caustic soda and $-.8$ percent for glycerine. But the decreases for the glass products were substantial, -4.6 percent for plate glass and -6.6 percent for safety and window glass. Although the coverage of unconcentrated products was quite small, it is still of interest to note that 3 of the 4 unconcentrated products declined. The one exception, paint, registered an increase of 1.6 percent. Once again the intermediate concentration group was about equally divided among the different price-change intervals, with 5 increases, 5 decreases, and 4 cases of no change.

The NB prices thus provide further evidence that where the structural conditions of classical theory are present the recession behavior of price will be in accord with theoretical expectations, but where such conditions are not present, the behavior tends to be not merely different from, but opposite to, the expectations.

---

to decline in the latter part of 1956, and most of the products included in the Stigler-Kindahl study are producer goods. Industrial production for manufacturing had begun to fall off in the last quarter of 1956 but then stabilized in the first half of 1957, the seasonally adjusted index of industrial production being the same in January as in July. For these reasons this analysis uses as its starting point January, 1957, the earliest month for which the NB prices are available.

[47] For most of the products the Census concentration ratios (1958) were used; because of their closer conformity to the product descriptions the ratios used for carbon steel products were those of the American Iron and Steel Institute.

[48] See Ch. 18.

OLIGOPOLISTIC PRICE
DETERMINATION

Economists have long regarded it as inconceivable that a leading firm, with substantial discretionary authority over price, should not have developed over the years rational standards to determine the level of price. Without standards price changes would be capricious and episodic, explainable after the fact by any number of convenient rationales. But if standards are employed and can be ascertained, what has happened in the past becomes logical, and what may happen in the future becomes, within limits, predictable. A number of intriguing and plausible hypotheses of oligopolistic price determination have been put forward, all of which imply a type of price behavior quite different from that of the competitive model.

Taking a leaf from Clausewitz's *Principles of War,* K. W. Rothschild likened the avoidance of price change in an oligopoly to a strategy of entrenchment in military warfare. Such a course of action will be followed as a result of deliberate choice; that is, "the quoted price is not the mechanic result of impersonal market forces nor the essential adjustment to a constantly changing environment, but the expression of a strategic policy." [1] This policy will be one of "rigid" maintenance—of declaring a position as a stronghold:

> The existence of a stable price instead of a fluctuating price will deter rivals from starting panicky price-reduction campaigns, and it will not induce newcomers to enter a booming market; consumers, too, are often supposed to prefer fixed prices. Thus the desire for building of a strategic stronghold will—within certain limits—neutralize the profit maximizing principle of changing price with every change in demand or costs. Even a price change of one's rivals may be ignored as long as one's relative position in the industry is not affected. It follows: Price rigidity is an essential aspect of "normal" oligopolistic price strategy. [2]

The rigidity in the price will be accompanied by a plethora of changes in the various forms of nonprice competition—"quality, credit and discount arrangements, salesmanship, etc." In addition to enabling the firm to make some adjustment to changes in demand and costs, such "minor weapons" also serve as "tools for tactical maneuver in the enemy's territory, testing his strength without provoking a major conflict; or to provide a 'defense in depth' against inroads from the rivals. . . ." [3] But changes in the price itself will be made rarely. Increases will be avoided because of the apprehension that they will not be

---

[1] K. W. Rothschild, "Price Theory and Oligopoly," in G. Stigler and K. Boulding, eds., *Readings in Price Theory,* Irwin, 1952, p. 455.
[2] *Ibid.,* p. 455.
[3] *Ibid.,* pp. 455–56.

matched by the other oligopolists; decreases will be shunned because of the frightful possibility of a price war, the result of which may be the "annihilation" of a leader's independence "or the reduction of his status to that of a price follower." [4] The real significance of Rothschild's line of thought has been well put by Howard Norman Ross: "The implications of war psychology, however close the parallel may be, at least remind us that special psychological forces are at work which do not nicely fit the traditional assumptions of rational behavior tailored to competition and monopoly." [5]

Another hypothesis, advanced independently by Joe S. Bain[6] and Paolo Sylos-Labini,[7] is that price will be set at a level which maximizes earnings while at the same time discouraging entry. Behind the hypothesis is the assumption that in the long run earnings will be greater under a price low enough to discourage entry than under a higher price that induces entry. Where entry does take place, the established oligopolists will probably maintain their production, as a result of which the price will fall, thereby reducing earnings. The entry-limiting price will be higher, the greater the barriers to entry, regardless of whether they consist of economies of scale, emphasized by Sylos-Labini, or of such barriers, stressed by Bain, as patents, preferential access to raw materials, and the costs of nonprice competition associated with product differentiation. For these reasons "oligopoly prices subject to the *prospect* of entry will not behave like competitive prices subject always to the *reality* of entry. What is more, it suggests that those prices will be inflexible. . . ." [8]

Paul M. Sweezy advanced the notion that there is a "kink" in the demand curve—i.e., that the curve is inelastic downward and elastic upward.[9] Rival oligopolists will match price cuts but not price increases, which to any producer would constitute good and sufficient reasons for avoiding both. This means in effect that the downward elasticity of demand is lower than the upward elasticity and the demand curve has a kink at the current price. While this concept may have appeared plausible as an explanation for price rigidity during the early 1930's, it is of little relevance where upward price followership has become a customary form of industry behavior. As Machlup has observed, "The theory of the kinky oligopoly demand curve does not apply to a seller who believes that his competitors would follow his price increases as well as his price reductions." [10]

As an explanation for the infrequency of price change in "administered price" industries, Gardiner C. Means advanced the hypothesis that sellers with monopoly power are confronted with a "zone of relative indifference." [11] Both above and below the price which maximizes their returns are prices which will yield them virtually the same return. Since they seldom know with any exactitude what their profit-maximizing price is, their tendency will be to leave the price unchanged as long as it remains in the zone of indifference. Citing as an example

[4] *Ibid.,* p. 461.
[5] Howard Norman Ross, *The Theory and Evidence of Price Flexibility,* doctoral dissertation, Columbia University, 1964, p. 34.
[6] Joe S. Bain, *Barriers to New Competition,* Harvard University Press, 1956.
[7] Paolo Sylos-Labini, *Oligopoly and Technical Progress,* Harvard University Press, 1962.
[8] Ross, *op. cit.,* p. 65. Emphasis added.
[9] Paul M. Sweezy, "Demand Under Conditions of Oligopoly," in G. Stigler and K. Boulding, eds., *Readings in Price Theory,* Irwin, 1952, pp. 404–09.
[10] Fritz Machlup, *The Economics of Seller's Competition,* Johns Hopkins Press, 1952, pp. 442–73.
[11] *Hearings on Administered Prices,* Pt. 1, pp. 77–90, testimony of Gardiner C. Means.

his own business experience as the seller of a specialty product, Means testified that "within limits I was free to make my own choice. The question was what price should I set." In Means's view, "no producer can draw a line showing precisely what his demand and what his revenue will be. All he knows is a fuzzy band within which this line would be likely to lie":

> There is a fairly broad zone. In the case of any of our big corporations I am willing to believe that it is quite wide. The combination of (1) the fact that a price a little higher or a little lower brings practically the same total profit, and (2) the fact that you do not know where this revenue line really lies means that there is quite a range of prices where it really does not make very much difference and you therefore finally come to be relatively indifferent as to which price you choose.
>
>   *   *   *
>
> I believe this zone of relative indifference is to a considerable extent responsible for the infrequency of changes in administered prices. Once I had set my price, there had to be a considerable change in demand or cost before it was worth my making a change.

As explanations for present-day price behavior, each of these hypotheses suffers from the same deficiency. In general, they were developed against the background of the Great Depression, in which the general presumption, based on both theoretical and empirical grounds, was that prices in oligopolistic industries tend to be "rigid." But since World War II prices in oligopolistic industries have been "rigid" in terms only of frequency and not of amplitude. While rising somewhat less than prices in polypolistic industries during rapid economic expansions, they have actually increased during recessions.[12] In addition, they have shown a greater long-term increase than have prices of unconcentrated industries; and this is true both with and without the inclusion of farm products. These differences in behavior are what make economic concentration a matter of such far-reaching importance from the point of view of public policy.

Full-cost pricing

In an empirical effort to find an explanation of both the movement and the level of oligopolistic prices, R. L. Hall and C. J. Hitch published a study in 1939 based on interviews with 38 British businesses.[13] This was followed 3 years later by a study by C. C. Saxton based on a questionnaire of 50 firms.[14] In these works, as well as in later studies by Dean[15] and Oxenfeldt,[16] the thesis was advanced that businessmen arrive at their prices as the sum of "full costs" plus an allowance for profit at some assumed volume of output. Strongly supported by Richard A. Lester,[17] the concept seemed to provide an explanation for the anomaly of rigid prices during the 1930's. As Richard B. Heflebower has pointed

[12] See Ch. 17.

[13] R. L. Hall and C. J. Hitch, "Price Theory and Business Behavior," *Oxford Economic Papers,* May, 1939.

[14] C. C. Saxton, *The Economics of Price Determination,* Oxford University Press, 1942.

[15] Joel Dean, *Managerial Economics,* Prentice-Hall, 1951.

[16] Alfred R. Oxenfeldt, *Industrial Pricing and Market Practices,* Prentice-Hall, 1951.

[17] Richard A. Lester, "Shortcomings of Marginal Analysis for Wage-Employment Problems," *American Economic Review,* March, 1946. For an opposing point of view see Fritz Machlup, "Marginal Analysis and Empirical Research," *American Economic Review,* Sept., 1946.

out in his admirable survey of the literature, "in the 1930's economists were in a more receptive mood for such heresy as the full-cost pricing idea. During those years of declining demand the flexibility of prices in the markets where sellers were numerous compared to the rigidity of those in concentrated industries called for explanation." [18]

Since "full costs" are made up partly of fixed costs, which per unit of output tend to vary inversely with volume, the derivation of price assumes some "normal" or "standard" volume of production. Variable costs (principally labor and materials) are simply assumed to remain constant per unit of output. With both unit fixed costs and unit variable costs held constant, it is necessary only to add some margin for profit, which is usually the amount needed to yield some desired return on investment. The result is what has been referred to as a "benchmark" price.

Obviously, when prices are determined in this manner costs (or what businessmen think of as costs) become dominant, and demand is assumed to be inelastic; excluded from consideration is the possibility that as a result of a high price, demand (and thus output) might be so reduced as to result in an increase in unit costs. In Heflebower's words, "The theory is a direct challenge to two tenets of generally accepted economic theory, i.e. (1) that demand as well as supply conditions, or costs, enter into price determination (for which Marshall used the 'two blades of the scissors analogy'); and (2) that the rational solution of all price problems requires the equating of *marginal* revenue and *marginal* costs." [19] Full-cost pricing becomes an explanation for price rigidity, as price is seldom varied because of changes in demand: "Once the price exists, all proponents of the cost-to-price theories agree that price will not be changed because volume rises or falls moderately, except when a rival decreases a price first." [20]

The nature of target return pricing

Nearly 15 years before the appearance of the Hall-Hitch survey, full-cost pricing had been described in considerable detail by a vice president of General Motors. In a series of articles appearing in a business publication, Donaldson Brown outlined in 1924 most of the essential elements of the pricing method used to this day by General Motors and widely copied by other industry leaders. [21] As it has come to be actually applied, this method, known as "target return pricing," is a variant of full-cost pricing. Thirty years later, Albert Bradley, who with Brown had formulated and implemented the method during the 1920's, informed the Senate Antitrust Subcommittee that "the principles we established at that time still govern." [22] The "principles" to which he was referring involve setting a desired target rate of return, classifying costs as "fixed" or "variable," and establishing a volume of production at which the target return is to be met.

[18] Richard B. Heflebower, "Full Costs, Cost Changes and Prices," in *Business Concentration and Price Policy,* National Bureau of Economic Research, 1955, p. 361.
[19] *Ibid.,* p. 363. Emphasis in original.
[20] *Ibid.,* p. 366.
[21] Donaldson Brown, "Pricing Policy in Relation to Financial Control," *Management and Administration,* Feb., March, April, 1924; pp. 195–98, 283–86, 417–22.
[22] 84th Cong., 1st Sess., Senate Subcommittee on Antitrust and Monopoly, Senate Committee on the Judiciary, *Hearings on General Motors,* 1955, Pt. 7, p. 3593.

The target rate

Under target return pricing, price is set in relation to costs (or what are assumed to be costs) at such a level as to provide a profit margin *on the product* that will yield a predetermined, or "target," rate of return *on the investment*. In Brown's words,

> An acceptable theory of pricing must be to gain over a protracted period of time a margin of profit which represents the highest attainable return commensurate with capital turnover and the enjoyment of wholesome expansion, with adequate regard to the economic consequences of fluctuating volume. *Thus the profit margin, translated into its salient characteristic rate of return on capital employed, is the logical yardstick by which to gauge the price of a commodity with regard to collateral circumstances affecting supply and demand.*[23]

What should this "rate of return" be? While Brown stopped short of handing down any iron-clad requirement, he did suggest a figure of 20 percent: "Thus prices might be maintained to yield 20% average return on capital on the assumption of plants operating at an average of 80 per cent of practical annual capacity"; and again, "Assuming 20% economic return attainable as the expression of policy. . . ." [24]

In later testimony before congressional committees officials of GM have used a figure of 15 percent on "capital employed," embracing items that include most of the company's assets. The rate of return on manufacturing investment, which Brown used to derive the profit component of price, was based on gross working capital (cash, receivables, and inventories) and net fixed assets (real estate, plant, and equipment). If related to the total of these items (including short-term government securities and cash) plus investments in unconsolidated subsidiaries and miscellaneous investments, a return of 15 per cent on "capital employed" will appear as 20 percent on stockholders' investment. In other words GM arrives at its prices by adding to "full costs" a margin sufficient to yield a 15-percent net return on capital employed, in the expectation that this will yield in the neighborhood of 20 percent a year on stockholders' investment—i.e., net worth.

Fixed costs versus variable costs

A second feature of Brown's articles, and indeed of all writings on full-cost pricing, is the emphasis placed on the distinction between fixed costs and variable costs. The emphasis derives from the fact that whereas total outlays for variable costs (principally materials and labor) vary with output (in Brown's term they are "controllable"), the aggregate amount expended for most other costs ("indirect" or "overhead" costs) remains "fixed" regardless of output (i.e., they are "uncontrollable"). The result, of course, is that while *unit* variable costs are largely independent of output, *unit* fixed costs vary inversely with volume. And the greater the importance of costs other than materials and labor, the greater the variation. In Brown's words, "Ordinarily, raw materials and productive labor may be referred to as 100 per cent variable, as the aggregate will vary with volume, and remain uniform per unit of product except for price changes.

[23] Brown, Feb., 1924, *op. cit.,* p. 197. Emphasis in original.
[24] Brown, March, 1924, *op. cit.,* pp. 283–86.

Among the uncontrollable items are such expenses as depreciation, taxes, etc., which may be referred to as 100 per cent fixed, since within limits of capacity the aggregate will not change, but, per unit of product, will vary indirectly with volume." [25]

Brown recognized a third category—expenses that are "partially controllable" and for which there is no precise means of determining the degree of variation. These include such items as light, heat, power, salesmen's and other salaries, traveling expenses, and so on. But in order to make this pricing method operable each of these cost items has to be rated according to its "variability" and then classified as either "100 percent variable" or "100 percent fixed."

In all subsequent discussions of target return pricing, officials of General Motors have continued to emphasize that costs are either fixed or variable. Thus, according to Harlow Curtice, chairman of the board:

> In addition to direct costs of labor, materials and services, the manufacturer must give consideration to his overhead costs, a large proportion of which are fixed.
> These so-called fixed costs include supervision, maintenance expenses, and depreciation; tooling styling and engineering costs; administration expenses and insurance and local taxes.
> The total amount of such fixed costs is relatively constant whether the volume be 500,000 or 1 million units This means that on a unit basis, overhead costs vary inversely with volume. . . .
> The higher the volume, the lower the percentage of fixed costs that must be borne by each unit. The lower the volume, the higher the percentage that each unit must bear. [26]

Depreciation is charged regardless of whether the plant operates or stands idle. Building and equipment also require maintenance, even if the facilities are not used. Property taxes, interest on borrowed capital, and other similar charges against income must be met from year to year regardless of output. Curtice did not discuss the treatment accorded those expenses referred to by Brown as "partially controllable" and also known as "fixed optional outlays." In addition to the items cited by Brown, they include such currently important categories as supervisory and clerical expenses, adertising and promotional expenses, executive salaries, bonuses and other remuneration. If, as Brown had recommended, they are classified in either one category or the other, the probabilities are that the greater portion is treated as fixed costs on the grounds that once such commitments have been made for a given production period—say, a year—the firm can only hope that they will be justified by the sales volume. And if they are so treated, the result will be to inflate fixed costs, thereby exaggerating the apparent increase in total unit costs during a recession.

The extent to which unit fixed costs will vary with changes in output depends of course on their importance in the total cost structure. In most concentrated industries these costs will tend to be relatively high. Where the oligopolistic position arises from economies of scale resulting from large plants and expensive equipment, depreciation charges, property taxes, and maintenance expenses will be high. Where it arises from expensive forms of nonprice competition, advertising outlays, selling expenses, and styling costs will be high. Some impression of the extent of the variation of unit fixed costs with output can be gathered on the basis of data for General Motors. Figure 18-1 breaks down the average sales

[25] *Ibid.*
[26] *Hearings on Administered Prices,* Pt. 6, pp. 2519–20, testimony of Harlow Curtice.

price into four components: hourly-rated labor costs, materials and other direct costs, overhead expenses, and profits.[27] In addition to figures for actual 1957 output, the chart also presents estimates of what overhead expenses and profit would have been had output been 25 percent under and 25 percent over the 1957 level. Had GM sold 25 percent fewer vehicles than it did in 1957, the spreading of overhead expense over the smaller output would have raised unit overhead costs from $550 to $733 per car and reduced profit correspondingly from $313 to $130. Had it sold 25 percent more cars, its unit overhead costs would have fallen from $550 to $440 and its unit profit risen from $313 to $423.

The "standard volume"

Full-cost pricing can become operational only if an arbitrary assumption is made as to the volume of output over which the estimated outlays for fixed costs are to be spread. This volume of production should, in Brown's words, represent "the average condition," the "normal average rate of plant operation." This average rate of output, which he termed the "standard volume," is "the basis on which costs will be measured, and upon which the margin of profit is determined as necessary to afford a given average rate of return upon capital employed." [28] The figure he suggested in 1924 and used since that time is 80 percent of what

[27] *Administered Prices: Report on Automobiles*, p. 129.
[28] Brown, March, 1924, *op. cit.*

Figure 18-1

GENERAL MOTORS CORPORATION
Actual sale price, actual profit, and estimated components of cost per vehicle in 1957, with examples to show effects of volume fluctuations*

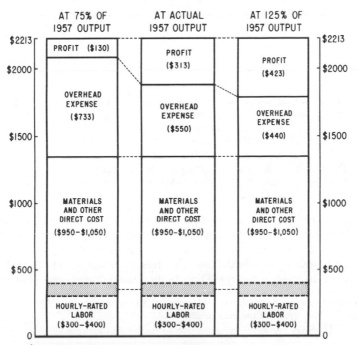

* Assuming identical unit labor and material costs, and same amount of total overhead costs at each volume.

Source: *Administered Prices: Report on Automobiles*, Chart 10

GM refers to as "rated" plant capacity. The manner in which the company arrives at "standard volume" was explicitly described by Bradley:

> We endeavor in planning for capacity to—we take the number of days there are in the year, and then take out the Sundays and holidays, and then we take out the minimum number of days . . . to turn around— I mean to bring out new models.
> From that, we find there are 225, taking out all the Sundays, holidays, and Saturdays, and 15 full days, or 30 half days, for turning around, giving 225 days which we would like to run the plants year in and year out.
> But we don't use 225, we use 80 percent of that as a standard volume, because ours is a business that you might call cyclical. . . . So, to allow for that cyclical factor and other conditions beyond our control, we take 80 percent of that 225 days. . . . So that gives us 180 days. And that, multiplied by our daily capacity, gives us a standard volume, which we work up by divisions, and which we hope to average.[29]

Since the lower the "standard volume," the greater must be the profit margin to yield the target return on investment, it is interesting to note that GM plans to make a net profit of 20 percent on its investment by operating slightly less than half the days of the year.

The profit margin

There is one critical difference between the pricing method formulated by Donaldson Brown and target return pricing as it has actually come to be employed by General Motors and other industry leaders. This difference concerns the profit margin. Obviously, the inevitable increase in unit fixed costs accompanying a decline in volume would necessitate an increase in price if the profit margin were to be maintained. But Brown explicitly warned against such a policy: "As unit costs are affected by fluctuations in volume, *it is not practical nor desirable to alter selling prices so as to maintain a uniform profit margin.*"[30] Indeed, among the "special considerations" that would justify a deviation of the "actual" price from the "base price equivalent" (or benchmark price) were the following:

> High prices in periods of high volume with correspondingly low prices in periods of low volume will tend to flatten the production curve, and consequently increase the productivity of capital employed.
> Low prices are desirable in periods of reduced volume to stimulate demand; but a price cannot be fixed below the *base price equivalent* unless the resulting decrease in profits can be recouped during periods of high volume through the establishment of prices correspondingly higher.[31]

As will be shown later, it has not been necessary to follow a policy of charging high prices during periods of high volume to recoup low profits resulting from low prices during periods of reduced volume, since during the latter prices have not been reduced but raised. That this has been the policy of GM was implied by Curtice in his testimony: "The higher the volume, the lower the per-

[29] Senate Subcommittee on Antitrust and Monopoly, 1955, *op. cit.,* p. 3584.
[30] Brown, March, 1924, *op. cit.* Emphasis added.
[31] Brown, April, 1924, *op. cit.,* p. 417.

centage of fixed costs that must be borne by each unit. The lower the volume, the higher the percentage that each unit must bear." An official of the Aluminum Company of America was even more explicit. "If fixed costs were applied on the basis of *anticipated* or *actual* level of operations, we would be faced with increasing fixed costs per unit of production during a prolonged period of abnormally low-volume level." But, he went on, a policy of raising prices during a recession to cover the increase in unit fixed costs obviously has its problems: "When volume is low, it is usually a poor time to inform your sales department that prices should be increased." [32]

The extent of target return pricing

A pioneering Brookings study of the pricing methods actually employed by large corporations found that "target return on investment was probably the most commonly stressed of company pricing goals." [33] Summarizing information developed in the study, one of its authors, Robert F. Lanzillotti, wrote that the "principal pricing goal" of oligopolists who were dominant in their industries—the leaders—was the securing of a target return on investment: "in most cases the target was regarded as a long-run objective . . . the average of the targets mentioned was about 10 percent to 15 percent (after taxes); only one was below 10 percent; and the highest was 20 percent." [34] Essential to this pricing method was the possession of substantial monopoly power and a position of leadership: "Firms that were conscious of shooting for a particular target return on investment in their price policies were those that sold products in a market or markets more or less protected and in which the companies were leaders in their respective industries . . . they assumed that they would have some chance of being able to reach the target return." [35]

The target returns of leading firms in 5 major industries—General Motors, U.S. Steel, Aluminum Company of America, Standard Oil of New Jersey, and E. I. du Pont de Nemours—are shown in Table 18-1. As can be seen, the targets range from a low of 8 percent (U.S. Steel) to a high of 20 percent (General Motors and Du Pont).

It should be emphasized that the target objectives of General Motors and the other price leaders are after taxes; on a before-tax basis the figures would be roughly double those shown. To the extent that the leaders attain their target rates, the corporation income tax is effectively transferred to the consumer. In terms of the time required to pay off their investment, General Motors and Du Pont seek to price their products in relation to costs in such a way as to yield an amount that would enable them to pay their corporate income taxes *and* recapture the stockholders' investment in only 5 years. In the case of Standard Oil the tax could be paid and the investment recaptured in slightly over 8 years; for the other 2 companies the required period would be some-

---

[32] T. W. Kerry, Speech given before the South Florida National Association of Cost Accountants, March, 1956. Emphasis in original. Quoted in A. D. H. Kaplan, Joel B. Dirlam, Robert F. Lanzillotti, *Pricing in Big Business,* Brookings Institution, 1955, p. 27. In this speech Kerry was describing a method, used by his company, of charging fixed costs in direct proportion to machine use to meet this very problem.

[33] A. D. H. Kaplan, Joel B. Dirlam, Robert F. Lanzillotti, *Pricing in Big Business,* Brookings Institution, 1955, p. 130.

[34] Robert F. Lanzillotti, "Pricing Objectives in Large Companies," *American Economic Review,* Dec., 1958, pp. 921–40.

[35] *Ibid.*

Table 18-1

PRICING GOALS OF LARGE INDUSTRIAL CORPORATIONS

Company	Principal Pricing Goal (Return on Investment after Taxes)	Collateral Pricing Goals
General Motors	20%	Maintaining market share
U.S. Steel	8	Target market share Stable price Stable margin
Alcoa	10	"Promotive" policy on new products Price stablization
Standard Oil	12	Maintaining market share Price stabilization
Du Pont	20	Charging what traffic will bear over long run Maximum return for new products—"life-cycle" pricing

Source: Robert F. Lanzillotti, "Pricing Objectives in Large Companies," *American Economic Review,* Dec., 1958 (specific target rates for Standard Oil of New Jersey and Du Pont based on interviews by author; rate for General Motors based on testimony by company officials in *Hearings on Administered Prices,* Pt. 6)

what longer—10 years for Alcoa and 12 years for U.S. Steel. To earn profits sufficient to meet such objectives is a formidable undertaking in view of the immense amounts invested. As of 1968 the stockholders' average investment was $9.5 billion in General Motors, $3.3 billion in U.S. Steel, $1.1 billion in Alcoa, $10.0 billion in Standard Oil of New Jersey, and $2.5 billion in Du Pont—a total of $26.4 billion. If in 1968 the companies had matched their target returns, their combined income would have been nearly $4 billion after taxes or $8 billion before taxes. Actually they fell short, but by only 5 percent.

The implementation of target return pricing

The manner in which this pricing formula is actually applied was described in some detail to the Antitrust Subcommittee by GM chairman Harlow Curtice:

> First, labor and material costs that are directly applicable to each unit produced are calculated on the basis of current wage rates and material prices. Indirect or overhead costs are then determined on a cost per unit basis by distributing them over the determined standard volume. Fixed unit costs so measured are not affected by short-term fluctuations in volume. . . . This method of estimating unit costs on the basis of standard volume gives us a benchmark against which to evaluate our cost-price relationship.

In applying this formula management has fairly exact knowledge of some of the variables. Allowances can be made for probable changes, if any, in the company's wage rates and fringe benefits for the coming year. The present costs of materials, components, and other supplies can be projected with reasonable exactitude. And, per unit of output, there should be little variation in these cost elements regardless of the volume of production. Since forecasting demand is far from an exact science, the problem arises with respect to those cost factors that do vary widely with changes in demand. Consequently, the actual price will be higher if it is felt that demand will be less than is implicitly assumed in the calculation of the "standard volume," since unit costs will be higher not only because of the spreading of overhead costs over a smaller number of units but because of a slower gain, or actual decline, in labor productivity.

The influence of productivity

In virtually all of the literature on full-cost pricing, the assumption is made that unit labor costs are unaffected by changes in output. But the evidence indicates that this is not true of one of the key determinants of unit costs; productivity tends to vary directly with output. As a consequence, productivity gains, which could help offset higher fixed costs, will be minimal or nonexistent during a recession. But during a period of rapidly expanding demand, they will be at their maximum and, in combination with declining unit fixed costs, may yield a veritable bonanza.

The relationship between year-to-year changes in output and productivity[36] between 1953 and 1968 is shown in Figure 18-2 for motor vehicles and parts, steel mill products, and primary aluminum. For the other 2 industries examined in this chapter—petroleum refining and industrial chemicals—labor costs constitute a very small proportion of total costs and are therefore of only marginal significance in price determination. In both motor vehicles and steel the relationship is direct and close: substantial increases in output are accompanied by sharp gains in productivity, substantial decreases by acutal declines in productivity.

In motor vehicles output rose by more than 20 percent during 1958–59, 1964–65 and 1967–68; in two of these intervals productivity shot up by more than 9 percent and in the third by nearly 7 percent. And when output fell by 25 percent during the recession of 1957–58, productivity registered a decline of 2.8 percent. Similarly when production fell off (though to a lesser extent) in 1960–61 and 1966–67, virtually no gains took place in productivity. The only significant difference between motor vehicles and steel is that in the latter a given decline in output was accompanied by a greater decrease in productivity and a given rise in output by a greater increase in productivity. During the 1958 recession the drop in steel production (−25.3 percent) was almost identical to that in motor vehicles, but the decline in productivity (−7.5 percent) was more than twice as great (−2.8 percent). Likewise, similar decreases in output during the "minirecession" of 1966–67 were accompanied in motor vehicles by virtually no change in productivity but in steel by a noticeable decline (−3.1 percent). Yet the rise in steel productivity (12.3 percent) between 1958 and 1959 was greater than any yearly productivity gain registered in motor vehicles, even though the increases in output were frequently greater. Apparently, when production is being reduced it is more difficult to make corresponding reductions in the work force in steel than in motor vehicles, whereas when production is being expanded smaller increments in the work force are required.

---

[36] The measure of productivity used is output per employee man-hour. Since price must include the cost of nonproduction workers, this is a more significant measure for price determination purposes than is output per production worker man-hour.

Figure 18–2

YEAR-TO-YEAR CHANGES IN PRODUCTION AND OUTPUT PER EMPLOYEE HOUR

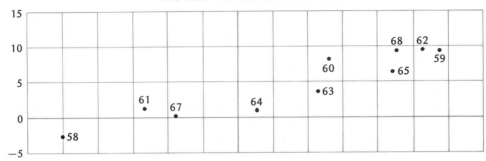

MOTOR VEHICLES AND PARTS

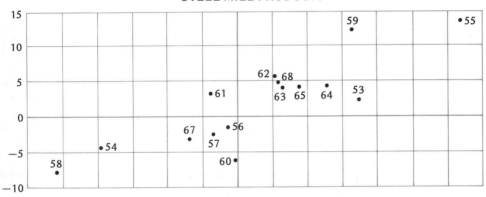

STEEL MILL PRODUCTS

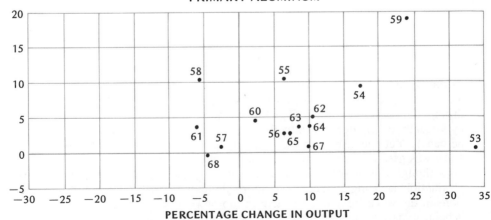

PRIMARY ALUMINUM

Source: Bureau of Labor Statistics, Department of Labor, special tabulation

Although the relationship is less close in the aluminum industry, the influence of output is still discernible. On the one hand decreases in output during 1960–61 and 1967–68 were accompanied by only a limited productivity gain in the former (3.9 percent) and an actual decrease in the latter (−0.4 percent), whereas sharp increases in output during 1953–54 and 1958–59 were accompanied by productivity gains of 9.7 percent in the former and of no less than 19.0 percent in the latter.

The differences among the 3 industries are only of degree. Essentially, they all confront the price makers with much the same problem. Because of lesser gains, or actual decreases in productivity, as well as higher unit overhead costs, their ability to meet their target returns will be imperiled if demand proves to be less than had been anticipated when prices were set.

The influence of wage advances

By increasing labor productivity, technological progress tends to widen profit margins, thereby making it easier for a price leader to secure its target return. By increasing wage rates (and fringe benefits), labor unions tend to narrow profit margins, thereby making the attainment of the target return more difficult.

It is inherent in their nature that labor organizations will exert continuing pressure for higher compensation for their members. For one thing, to the extent that price increases are due to factors other than increases in wage costs, labor unions can be expected to press for higher wage rates merely to maintain their existing share of the sales dollar. The same will be true when they are confronted, as will continually be the case, with increased mechanization and a consequent decrease in unit labor requirements. Then, too, rivalry among labor leaders is one of those forms of competition which have very definitely not disappeared from the economy; the head of a labor union can ignore superior gains obtained by a rival union leader only at his own peril. In striving continually to secure benefits for their members, labor organizations are no different from organizations of management, farmers, physicians, or indeed teachers.

Awareness that labor unions will always be seeking more is of course of little value to a price leader. To make target return pricing operational what management needs above all else is knowledge of the extent to which wages will have to be raised in the future. Hence, the growing practice of entering into contracts calling for stipulated wage increases over a period of years; the 3-year contract seems to be the most popular.

Another procedural step taken to lessen variability is the substitution of joint bargaining for individual negotiations with separate companies. If the terms granted by the price leader are more favorable to the union than those granted by its rival oligopolists, its profit rate will suffer by comparison, as will also the esteem in which its management is held by stockholder interests. If the terms are less favorable, it can expect demands for immediate revisions and will certainly be the prime target in the next round of wage negotiations.

Moreover, there are other advantages to joint negotiations. An important incentive for an oligopolist to resist a wage advance is his apprehension that his rivals might be able to make a less costly bargain with the union. To the extent that this happens, the more successful bargainers would have an incentive not to join in the next price advance. But as rival firms come to bargain in concert with the union, the uncertainty tends to disappear. In addition to eliminating uncertainties, the very act by rival firms of collectively negotiating a wage agreement provides a unique opportunity for a common appraisal of the effect of wage advances on costs and thus implicitly on price. Even though the wage negotiation is not used as a fortuitous occasion to fix prices, each oligopolist necessarily gains knowledge of his rivals' probable reaction to a given wage increase. The range of uncertainty as to the probable price change each oligopolist may anticipate from the others is accordingly narrowed. To a price leader such knowledge should be particularly valuable in setting a price high enough to meet general approval from the other producers but not so high as to needlessly invite undercutting.

Armed with a contract extending several years into the future and secure in the knowledge that they do not have to concern themselves with the possible consequences of a lesser wage advance granted by a competitor, the management of a price leader is in a position to determine the effect on unit costs (at the standard volume) of the wage advance. If unit costs are increased less by the wage advance than they are reduced by productivity gains, the target return could be met with a lower price; alternatively, management could preempt the difference simply by keeping price constant. If the increases in wages and in productivity balance each other, no change in price would be required. If the effect of the wage increase is to raise unit costs more than they are reduced by the increase in productivity, the attainment of the target return would require a price advance. For the price leader the moment of truth arrives when the cost of a wage increase can no longer be passed on in the form of a higher price without a loss in volume. Even if its price increase is matched (as is customarily the case), it may suffer a loss in volume by virtue of constraints which exist on price-making discretion. The price increase may have the effect of stimulating the flow of imports or the use of substitute materials. It may induce large buyers to integrate backward, becoming suppliers of their own needs. And, depending on the elasticity of demand, it may result in a sales decrease of a magnitude more than sufficient to offset the increase in revenues arising from the price advance. It is not wage increases themselves but the loss in volume resulting from compensatory (or other) price increases that is the real cause of what is widely referred to as the "profits squeeze."

Wage increases which have been contracted for become an even more serious problem to management if, in a given year, it appears that output will fall below the standard volume. Not only will unit fixed costs rise, but the increase in productivity, which had been assumed to offset all or most of the wage increase, will be less than anticipated or even nonexistent. Under these circumstances an increase in price will appear to be the only way of meeting the target return. And attaining this objective in the short run will usually outweigh any consideration given to adverse consequences in the long run.

Target or maximized returns

The actual behavior of oligopolistic prices and profits during periods of strong and rising demand raises the question of whether a target return is only a minimum objective or one that it is essential to meet but not particularly important to exceed. If the latter is the case, the managers would obviously not be behaving in accordance with the precepts of classical theory since they would not be maximizing profits in the short run. In point of fact there are good reasons to assume that during an upswing management has little to gain, and possibly something to lose, by raising prices to yield profits well in excess of the target. By attracting competitors or merger-minded "raiders," unduly high profits could lead to such unfortunate developments as price wars or takeover attempts. Substitute products would receive a powerful stimulus. Demand might fall off more in response to price increases than had been anticipated. Large buyers might establish their own sources of supply. And charges of profiteering might be levied by the executive or legislative branches of government.

Above and beyond these possible dangers is the overriding fact that in the large corporation the rewards to management are not determined by the ability of the company to maximize profits in the short run. Nowhere was this more dramatically demonstrated than by Robert Aaron Gordon's analysis of executive compensation during the Depression. Between 1929 and 1932 executive compensation of 51 large industrial corporations fell only 30 percent in comparison to declines of 68 percent in dividends paid, 64 percent in factory payrolls, and 105 percent in income available for dividends (other than executive compensation). Moreover, management of the large firms was relatively insulated from the ravages of unemployment that afflicted virtually all other sectors of the economy: "Executive employment in these firms was phenomenally stable during the years 1928–36. The 51 companies reported 696 executives in 1929 and *exactly the same number in 1932*." [37] But just as these executives suffered only a modest loss in income and no loss in employment at a time when their corporations were recording catastrophic declines in profits, so also is there less than a proportionate rise in their compensation with an improvement in economic conditions. And this of course dampens the incentives to pursue policies that would enable the corporation to maximize its earnings on the upswing.

The rewards to management are both financial and nonfinancial. Largely unrelated to short-term changes in the corporation's profit performance are the principal component of the former and all of the latter. Salary scales are not expected to rise and fall with changes in the corporation's profitability. The personal power, prestige, and other nonfinancial rewards of management are about the same in recessions as in upswings. Bonuses and stock options do have some relationship to the corporation's earnings, but it is at best tenuous. The granting of bonuses is usually capricious and seldom geared in any systematic way to the corporation's profit performance; the value of stock options is the product of the collective judgment of investors, whose opinions are influenced less by profits earned on investment than by the general condition of the economy, the current behavior of the stock market, and such irrelevant variables as the increase in earnings per share.[38] This is not to suggest that management can or should regard profits as irrelevant. In Gordon's words, "The profits criterion can never be disregarded by salaried executives. As a minimum, it is necessary to keep director and stockholders passive. Beyond this, however, the executive group may or may not seek, with every decision to be made, to enlarge profits still further. There is considerable opportunity to follow other

[37] Robert Aaron Gordon, *Business Leadership in the Large Corporation*, Brookings Institute, 1945, pp. 281–83. Emphasis added.
[38] See Ch. 12.

goals."[39] And preeminent among those "other goals" are the maintenance of the company's competitive position and the attainment of long-term profit objectives.

More recent studies confirm the secondary importance for management of profit maximization for the firm. William J. Bannock advanced the thesis that the primary motivation is sales growth, not profit maximization.[40] In a study of 420 companies between 1953 and 1964 it was found that 60 percent of the variance in top executive pay was explained by difference in company sales: "For every doubling of company size, experience shows that the compensation tends to increase about 20%." In contrast, "the profit increases between 1953 and 1964 of the companies with the highest paid chief executives (relative to company size) in 1953 were no better than the profit gains turned in by their lowest paid competitors."[41]

The attainment of target returns

How successful have the leading firms been in meeting their target objectives? This question should be examined in terms of both long-range performance and year-to-year changes.

Long-term performance

In Table 18-2, the target returns of 5 industry leaders are compared for a 16-year period with their actual profit rates in terms of rate of return (after taxes) on net worth—i.e., stockholders' investment. The period surveyed begins with 1953, thus avoiding the inflation in profit rates resulting from the release of pent-up demand following World War II. The interval includes two recessions (1953–54 and 1957–58), a period of comparative economic stability (1959–64), and one of rapid economic expansion (1965–68).

Over the 16-year period the success of the 5 leaders in meeting their profit objectives is little short of remarkable. As compared to its target return of 20 percent, the weighted average of General Motors' actual rate of return on net worth was 20.2 percent. As compared to its target of 8 percent, U.S. Steel averaged 8.4 percent. Of all the firms, Alcoa's profit rate experienced the widest year-to-year fluctuations, but its average of 9.5 percent compared closely to its objective of 10.0 percent. The company with the steadiest performance was Standard Oil of New Jersey, which matched its target of 12.0 percent with an average performance of 12.6 percent. The highest average return was recorded by Du Pont, whose earnings for the entire period averaged 22.2 percent as against its objective of 20.0 percent. Aside from Alcoa, the average actual rate of return exceeded the target rate; the deviations above target outweighed, though slightly, those below target.[42]

[39] Gordon, *op. cit.*, p. 327.

[40] William J. Bannock, "On the Theory of the Expansion of the Firm," *American Economic Review,* Dec., 1962.

[41] Arch Patton, "Deterioration in Top Executive Pay," *Harvard Business Review,* Nov.–Dec., 1965. See also Samuel Richardson Reid, *Mergers, Managers and the Economy,* McGraw-Hill, 1968.

[42] In terms of percentages rather than percentage points, Alcoa fell below its target by 5%; Du Pont surpassed its objective by 11%; U.S. Steel and Standard Oil exceeded their targets by 5%; while General Motors was almost exactly on target, surpassing its objective by 1%. For the group as a whole, the performance exceeded the objective by 3%.

Table 18-2

COMPARISON OF TARGET WITH ACTUAL RETURNS, 1953–1968

Rate of Return	General Motors	U.S. Steel	Alcoa	Standard Oil	Du Pont	Average
Target	20.0%	8.0%	10.0%	12.0%	20.0%	14.6%
Actual	20.2	8.4	9.5	12.6	22.2	15.1
Deviation (% Pts.)	.2	.4	−.5	.6	2.2	.5

Source: Actual rate of return Federal Trade Commission, special tabulation

The same was true of the 5 companies as a group. Multiplying the target rate of each of the companies times its net worth yields the net income that would be required to meet the profit objective; the resulting figures can then be totaled and divided by their combined net worth, yielding an average target return for the 5 companies combined. This in turn can be compared to their combined actual return. Primarily because General Motors, with its relatively high target, has grown more rapidly than firms with lower objectives, the combined average target has tended to increase, rising from 14.2 percent in 1953 to 15.1 percent in 1968. As can be seen from Table 18-3, the average target return for the 5 leaders combined over the 16-year period was 14.6 percent; their actual combined return was slightly better, averaging 15.1 percent.

The success of the leaders in meeting and indeed, except for Alcoa, slightly exceeding their target objectives parallels the performance during an earlier period by the leaders examined in the Brookings study. According to Lanzillotti, "for the nine-year period 1947–55 the target-return companies earned on the average slightly more to substantially more than the indicated profit objective." [43]

Year-to-year changes

The close relationship of actual to target returns for the period as a whole is not simply a statistical happenstance—the product of offsetting above- and below-target performances. Considering the uncertainties and the number of variables involved, some deviations both above and below target are to be expected. Nonetheless, for these 5 leaders the targets were exceeded, matched, or closely approached in most of the individual years. In 14 of the 16 years General Motors achieved at least three-fourths of its target—i.e., its profit rate was 15 percent or better. In 12 years U.S. Steel's actual performance was within three-fourths of its objective. The comparatively erratic behavior of Alcoa is attested by the fact that in 7 of the 16 years its profit rate fell below three-fourths of its objective. On the other hand, Standard Oil of New Jersey met the three-fourths test in every year. Like General Motors, Du Pont failed to meet it in only 2 years. Out of 80 individual occasions the leaders came within at least three-fourths of their objectives on 65, a performance record of 81 percent. For the 5 companies as a group the actual average return came within at least three-fourths of the average target rate in each of the 16 years.

Although more frequent revisions are sometimes made, most leaders that price on a target-return basis set their prices to cover a considerable period in

[43] Lanzillotti, op. cit.

Table 18-3

RATES OF RETURN (AFTER TAXES) ON STOCKHOLDERS' INVESTMENT FOR 5 LEADING MANUFACTURING CORPORATIONS, 1953-1968

Year	GENERAL MOTORS Stockholders' Investment (000)	Net Income (After Taxes) Target (000)	Reported (000)	Rate of Return	U.S. STEEL Stockholders' Investment (000)	Net Income (After Taxes) Target (000)	Reported (000)	Rate of Return	ALCOA Stockholders' Investment (000)	Net Income (After Taxes) Target (000)	Reported (000)	Rate of Return
1968	$ 9,503,519	$ 1,900,704	$ 1,731,915	18.2%	$ 3,282,599	$ 262,608	$ 253,676	7.7%	$ 1,081,031	$ 108,103	$ 104,677	9.7%
1967	8,986,920	1,797,384	1,627,276	18.1	3,235,011	258,801	172,480	5.3	1,017,783	101,778	107,366	10.5
1966	8,477,825	1,695,565	1,793,392	21.2	3,459,835	276,787	249,239	7.2	947,821	94,782	106,071	11.2
1965	7,925,354	1,585,071	2,125,606	26.8	3,612,105	288,968	275,476	7.6	889,392	88,939	75,587	8.5
1964	7,381,524	1,476,305	1,734,782	23.5	3,488,922	279,114	236,785	6.8	851,251	85,125	60,764	7.1
1963	6,915,867	1,383,173	1,591,823	23.0	3,401,838	272,147	203,549	6.0	823,378	82,338	51,078	6.2
1962	6,385,753	1,277,151	1,357,616	21.3	3,365,180	269,214	163,680	4.9	793,329	79,333	56,447	7.1
1961	5,978,564	1,195,713	892,821	14.9	3,360,226	268,818	190,122	5.7	843,265	84,327	37,984	4.5
1960	5,660,511	1,132,102	959,042	16.9	3,296,935	263,755	304,171	9.2	826,438	82,644	36,895	4.5
1959	5,269,871	1,053,974	873,100	16.6	3,199,997	256,000	254,563	7.0	792,906	79,291	53,715	6.8
1958	5,031,417	1,006,283	633,628	12.6	3,103,810	248,305	301,558	9.7	763,188	76,319	45,485	6.0
1957	4,806,650	961,330	823,791	17.1	2,927,104	234,168	419,407	14.3	724,195	72,420	87,218	12.0
1956	4,492,887	898,577	847,396	18.9	2,718,203	217,456	348,099	12.8	649,641	64,964	106,871	16.5
1955	3,897,360	779,472	1,189,477	30.5	2,508,959	200,717	370,099	14.8	563,211	56,321	105,151	18.7
1954	3,290,489	658,098	805,974	24.5	2,342,179	187,374	195,418	8.3	486,290	48,629	78,413	16.1
1953	2,978,672	595,734	586,122	19.7	2,244,314	179,585	222,088	9.9	424,301	42,430	72,980	17.2
Total (1953-68)	$96,983,183	$19,396,636	$19,573,761		$49,547,717	$3,963,817	$4,160,470		$12,477,420	$1,247,743	$1,126,703	
Target Return		20.0				8.0				10.0		
Return on stockholders' investment after taxes			20.2				8.4				9.5	

Source: Federal Trade Commission, special tabulation

484

Table 18-3 (Continued)

	STANDARD OIL (NEW JERSEY)				DU PONT				Total (5 Leading Manufacturing Companies)				
	Stockholders' Investment (000)	Net Income (After Taxes) Target (000)	Net Income (After Taxes) Reported (000)	Rate of Return	Stockholders' Investment (000)	Net Income (After Taxes) Target (000)	Net Income (After Taxes) Reported (000)	Rate of Return	Stockholders' Investment (000)	Target Net Income (After Taxes) (000)	Target Rate of Return	Reported Net Income (After Taxes) (000)	Reported Rate of Return
Year													
1968	10,042,741	1,205,129	1,323,802	13.2%	2,474,609	494,922	371,871	15.0%	26,384,499	3,971,466	15.1%	3,785,941	14.3%
1967	9,612,102	1,154,172	1,233,370	12.8	2,363,162	472,632	313,860	13.3	25,220,978	3,784,767	15.0	3,454,352	13.7
1966	9,177,595	1,101,311	1,134,948	12.4	2,254,255	450,251	389,118	17.3	24,317,331	3,619,296	14.9	3,672,768	15.1
1965	8,891,787	1,067,014	1,077,272	12.1	2,128,163	425,633	407,229	19.1	23,446,801	3,455,625	14.7	3,961,170	16.9
1964	8,507,648	1,020,918	1,092,064	12.8	2,011,888	402,378	471,426	23.4	22,224,233	3,263,840	14.7	3,595,821	16.2
1963	8,715,743	973,889	1,066,375	13.1	1,942,664	388,533	472,262	24.3	21,199,490	3,100,080	14.6	3,385,086	16.0
1962	7,666,247	919,950	879,825	11.5	1,888,267	377,653	451,601	23.9	20,098,776	2,923,301	14.5	2,909,169	14.5
1961	7,257,594	870,911	794,142	10.9	1,808,167	361,633	418,163	23.1	19,247,816	2,781,402	14.5	2,333,292	12.1
1960	7,048,419	845,810	720,435	10.2	1,729,069	345,814	381,403	22.1	18,561,372	2,670,125	14.4	2,401,947	12.9
1959	6,874,217	874,906	663,483	9.7	1,635,637	327,127	418,696	25.6	17,772,628	2,541,298	14.3	2,263,557	12.7
1958	6,505,892	770,707	609,562	9.4	1,543,732	308,746	341,249	22.1	16,948,039	2,420,360	14.3	1,931,482	11.4
1957	5,907,185	708,862	879,445	14.9	1,447,121	289,424	396,610	27.4	15,812,255	2,266,204	14.3	2,606,471	16.5
1956	5,331,955	639,835	883,517	16.6	1,352,990	270,598	383,401	28.3	14,545,676	2,091,430	14.4	2,569,284	17.7
1955	4,898,409	587,809	776,003	15.8	1,266,211	253,242	431,556	34.1	13,154,150	1,877,561	14.3	2,872,286	21.9
1954	4,397,247	527,670	667,345	15.2	1,197,827	239,565	344,386	28.8	11,714,032	1,661,336	14.2	2,091,536	17.9
1953	3,833,676	460,041	628,806	16.4	1,142,338	228,468	251,371	22.0	10,623,801	1,506,258	14.2	1,761,367	16.6
Total (1953-68)	$114,074,457	$13,678,934	$14,430,394		$28,186,100	$5,637,219	$6,244,202		301,268,877	$43,934,349		$45,595,530	
Target return		12.0				20.0					14.6		
Return on stockholders' investment taxes)			12.6				22.2						15.1

advance, usually a year. Of particular interest, therefore, is the ability of the leaders to meet their target objectives during a year in which demand, and thus production, is well below, or above, the level of the preceding year. And during such years what is their price behavior? The answer may be found in Figure 18-3 (see also Table 18-4), which for each of the 5 leaders shows on the horizontal axis the percentage change from the preceding year in its industry's index of production and on the vertical axis the deviation from the company's target objective; the percentage change in price is shown in parentheses.[44]

As will be observed, General Motors experienced two pronounced decreases in output, motor vehicle production falling 17.3 percent in 1955–56 and 17.6 percent in 1957–58. Nonetheless, in the former GM almost attained its target rate, falling below by only 1.1 percentage points. Although the 1958 decrease in output was no larger, the company missed its target by a wide margin (7.4 percentage points)—its most conspicuous failure during the 16-year period. The difference in profit performance is attributable in good part to a difference in price behavior. In the former period the price of motor vehicles was raised by 5.7 percent, in the latter by 3.2 percent. That the 1958 increase was not greater is probably traceable to an error in planning. In 1955 automobile production had reached a then all-time high, and a subsequent contraction was almost inevitable. But there is reason to believe that the extent of the 1958 decline caught the automakers by surprise. By the time they appreciated its full magnitude, the model year was nearly over, and it was too late for a further upward revision. It is interesting to note that with but one exception, all of the years with price increases of more than one percent were also years of below-target performance. The exception was 1955, when a production increase of nearly 40 percent plus a 3-percent price advance combined to give GM the highest profit rate during the 16-year period—30.5 percent.

The performance of U.S. Steel in slightly exceeding its target rate during the recessions of 1953–54 and 1957–58 represents a spectacular example of successful corporate planning. Although steel production fell by more than one-fifth, the effects of the resultant cost increases were almost exactly offset by price increases of 4.7 percent in the former downturn and 3.5 percent in the latter. By way of contrast, the corporation in 1962 fell more than 3 percentage points below its target despite a 6.6 percent increase in steel production. A price increase had been instituted but was rescinded at the insistence of President Kennedy. The three conspicuous above-target performances of 1955, 1956, and 1957 were apparently the result of an abortive effort on the part of the company to raise its target objective.[45] Except in 1967, when steel output dropped 8.2 percent and U.S. Steel's earnings fell 2.7 percentage points below target, the mid- and late 1960's were characterized by moderate increases in output, slightly below-target profit performances, and small increases in price; the largest price increase during these years, a 2.4 percent advance in 1968, brought the corporation within .3 percentage points of its target return.

In the 1954 recession the behavior of the Aluminum Company of America closely paralleled that of U.S. Steel. Confronted with a decline in output, it raised its price, thereby surpassing its target objective. And, like the leading

[44] The figures on industrial production are from the Federal Reserve Board; actual returns on net worth are from the Federal Trade Commission; the target rates are as shown in Table 18-4; the price series are from the Bureau of Labor Statistics.
[45] For a further discussion of the above-target performances of 1955–57 and of the below-target performance of 1962 see Ch. 23.

Table 18-4

5 INDUSTRY LEADERS

Year-to-year changes in industry production and in Wholesale Price Index, and deviations from leaders' target returns, 1953–1969

Year	GENERAL MOTORS			U.S. STEEL			STANDARD OIL (NEW JERSEY)			ALCOA			DU PONT		
	Change in Production	Change in Wholesale Price Index	Deviation from Target (% Pts.)	Change in Production	Change in Wholesale Price Index	Deviation from Target (% Pts.)	Change in Production	Change in Wholesale Price Index	Deviation from Target (% Pts.)	Change in Production	Change in Wholesale Price Index	Deviation from Target (% pts.)	Change in Production	Change in Wholesale Price Index	Deviation from Target (% Pts.)
1969	16.9%	1.5%	-1.8	5.9%	4.8%	-0.3	4.2%	1.5%	1.2	9.9%	5.8%	-0.3	11.0%	-0.7%	-5.0
1968	-8.5	2.2	-1.9	-8.2	2.4	-2.7	4.0	-1.9	0.8	-3.6	2.5	0.5	6.8	1.0	-6.7
1967	-2.5	1.0	1.2	-0.2	1.1	-0.8	3.9	2.7	0.4	12.7	1.8	1.2	12.6	1.8	-2.7
1966	15.2	-0.4	6.8	4.8	1.4	-0.4	2.1	3.8	0.1	18.3	0.0	-1.5	10.0	0.7	-0.9
1965	2.8	-0.4	5.5	16.0	0.5	-1.2	3.3	3.4	0.8	12.9	3.3	-2.9	9.6	0.8	3.4
1964	7.7	-0.2	5.0	6.9	0.8	-2.0	3.7	-4.6	1.1	12.4	4.9	-3.8	10.2	-0.6	4.3
1963	17.3	-0.8	1.3	6.6	0.6	-3.1	3.9	-1.0	-0.5	13.5	-5.3	-2.9	13.8	-1.6	3.9
1962	-9.3	-0.8	-5.1	-6.8	-0.3	-2.3	2.1	-1.1	-1.1	0.2	-6.4	-5.5	8.0	-2.1	3.1
1961	14.0	-0.4	-3.1	2.7	-0.4	1.2	2.5	1.7	-1.8	-0.0	-2.0	-5.5	7.0	-2.1	2.1
1960	24.7	-1.5	-3.4	16.1	-0.1	-1.0	6.7	1.1	-2.3	29.9	4.8	-3.2	20.5	0.3	5.6
1959	-17.6	2.2	-7.4	-25.2	1.6	1.7	-1.2	-0.5	-2.6	-2.5	-0.3	-4.0	-1.8	0.3	2.1
1958	7.6	3.2	-2.9	-4.0	3.5	6.3	-0.1	-8.8	2.9	-7.6	-2.3	2.0	5.3	0.0	7.4
1957	-17.3	4.3	-1.1	-1.6	9.6	4.8	5.0	7.2	4.6	3.2	5.7	6.5	6.5	1.7	8.3
1956	39.2	5.7	10.5	34.1	8.4	6.8	7.4	5.6	3.8	35.7	10.0	8.7	22.1	2.7	14.1
1955	-6.9	3.0	4.5	-21.2	4.6	0.3	-0.8	2.0	3.2	-8.9	8.6	6.1	-0.6	0.5	8.8
1954		0.2	-0.3		4.7	1.9		-2.5	4.4		4.4	7.2		0.0	2.0
1953															

Source: Production: Federal Reserve Board, Indexes of Industrial Production; price: Bureau of Labor Statistics, Department of Labor, Wholesale Price Index; target deviation: Federal Trade Commission, special tabulation

steel producer, Alcoa apparently endeavored during the mid-1950's to raise its target return. The result was conspicuous above-target performances between 1954 and 1957, made possible by substantial price increases. Indeed, there was a striking similarity during this period in the price increases of steel and aluminum (see Table 18-5). At the very least it can be said that the aluminum producers studiously abstained from making inroads in the market for the older material. In the 1958 recession, however, Alcoa was unable to raise its prices; indeed, price fell by 2.3 percent, and Alcoa's earnings dropped 4

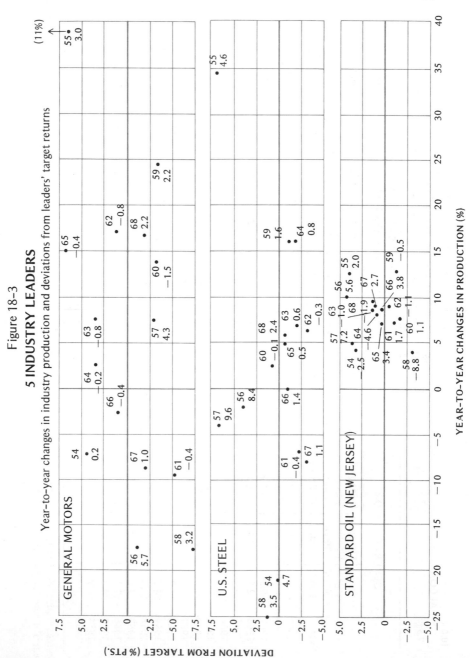

Figure 18-3

5 INDUSTRY LEADERS

Year-to-year changes in industry production and deviations from leaders' target returns

made by European producers selling at discount prices and thereby depressing Alcoa's earnings until the mid-1960's.[46] After the source of market disturbance was removed, Alcoa's profit performance moved up to its target objective; between 1965 and 1968 its profit rate averaged 10.7 percent as compared to its target of 10.0 percent.

Changes in petroleum-refining activity are kept within narrow limits through a combination of market demand proration and import quotas limiting supply to demand. And so also have changes in Standard Oil's profit rates been kept

[46] For a further discussion of the role of the foreign aluminum producers, see pp. 492–93.

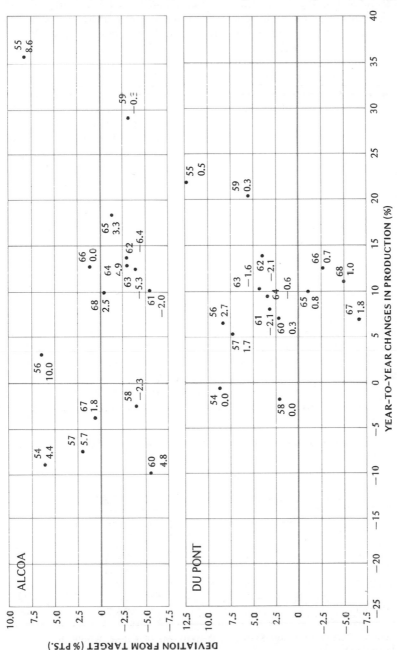

Note: The figures opposite each observation refer to the year and the year-to-year percentage change in the industry's B.L.S. Wholesale Price Index

Source: Production: Federal Reserve Board, Indexes of Industrial Production; target deviation: Federal Trade Commission, special tabulation

within narrow limits. The only two conspicuous deviations were above-target performance in 1956, which is traceable to a 5.6-percent price increase during the first Suez crisis, and a below-target performance in 1958, which was the product of an 8.8-percent price decline resulting from the breakdown of the "voluntary" import program.[47] With the subsequent imposition of the mandatory quota the profit rate moved upward during the next 2 years. In the ensuing 8 years the profit rate displayed a remarkable degree of stability, moving between 1.1 percentage points below and 1.2 percentage points above the target return.

Like petroleum refining, industrial chemicals has been an industry of almost constantly increasing production. The recessions of 1954 and 1958 occasioned only slight reductions in chemical output. And until the late 1960's, Du Pont's profits were consistently well above target, even though prices were usually stable or even reduced. It was not until 1965 that Du Pont failed to meet its target return of 20 percent. But thereafter its profit rate moved downward—to 17.3 percent in 1966 and 13.3 percent in 1967, recovering slightly to 15.0 percent in 1968. This deterioration in Du Pont's earnings, which was common to all of the major chemical companies, resulted from a weakening control over the market and growing competition in most branches of the chemical industry.

Like any gyroscopic guidance system the function of price in an asymmetrical oligopoly can thus be seen to keep the leader on target. Confronted with a decline in demand, the only step oligopolists can readily take to meet their target return is to raise prices by an amount sufficient to cover the increase in costs resulting from the smaller output. Where necessary, and possible, this has been the course of action followed by these 5 oligopolists. It was followed by General Motors in both 1956 and 1958, except that in the latter year the price increase was insufficient to meet the objective. In the face of a more than 20-percent drop in output, it was the course followed by U.S. Steel in the downswings of 1954 and 1958, enabling it to exceed slightly its target during both recessions. It was the course followed by Alcoa in the former downswing, although import competition prevented its use in the latter. As a result of a series of price rises following World War II, Standard Oil was able to exceed its target in 1954 even with a decrease in price. But 4 years later it fell well short of its target because rising uncontrolled imports resulted in a decrease in price. And in the case of Du Pont, price increases to meet its target were never necessary until very recent years, by which time they had become impossible.

During periods of relatively stable economic activity, the target return can usually be met without price increases. This appeared to be the case during the

[47] For a further discussion of the breakdown of the voluntary import control program, see p. 493.

Table 18-5

PRICE INCREASES OVER PREVIOUS YEAR

Year	Steel Mill Products	Aluminum Ingot
1954	4.7%	4.4%
1955	4.6	8.6
1956	8.4	10.0
1957	9.6	5.7
Total	24.3	26.7

Source: Bureau of Labor Statistics, Department of Labor, Wholesale Price Index

first half of the 1960's, a period of comparative price stability. Between 1959 and 1964 prices actually moved downward slightly in 3 of the 5 industries examined, remaining virtually unchanged in the other 2. Nonetheless, with the exception of Alcoa, the leaders succeeded in surpassing or coming very close to their respective target returns. The same was true during the rapid expansion of 1965–68. With the exception of Du Pont the leaders were generally able to meet their targets with limited or no advances in price. The absence of pronounced price increases during periods of rapidly rising demand is proof positive that the objective of corporate leaders is to meet, or perhaps slightly exceed, their target returns and not to maximize profits in the short run.

For the 5 companies, individually and as a group, there is no general tendency for profit rates to rise (or fall) as production increases. If there is any tendency at all, it is the surprising one of constant returns. Classical economic theory had been concerned largely with increasing returns, since it simply was assumed that up to a very large size, increases in output would generally be accompanied by declining costs and increasing returns. Decreasing returns gradually were dismissed as being of little importance in the real world, confined largely to extractive fields, although even the use of coal mines as an example was questioned after the introduction of mechanized mining methods. Constant returns were dismissed as simply an abstraction, without counterpart in the real world. In the words of J. H. Clapham:

> Constant returns, it may be observed in passing, must always remain a mathematical point. . . . It is inconceivable that a method can ever be devised for so measuring these real but infinitely subtle tendencies toward diminishing and increasing returns that someone will be able to say, Lo, here a perfect balance. If this is so, constant returns industries may be relegated finally to the limbo of the categories, in company for the present with such still disembodied phantoms as the "commodity whose elasticity of demand is unity." [48]

The technical impossibility of precise measurement aside, the type of relationship between output and profitability evidenced by these 5 leaders is certainly not that anticipated by Clapham or any other theorist. They can surely be forgiven, however, for not having anticipated either a method of pricing which takes as its starting point a predetermined, constant rate of return, or a control of the market which makes such pricing possible, even in the short run.

Deviations from the target rate

Throughout the entire 16-year interval, noteworthy deviations from target occurred on only a few occasions. Most of the significant deviations above target took place in the mid-1950's. An unexpected sharp increase in automobile production, which saw production reaching a then all-time high of 7.2 million cars in 1955, imparted a strong stimulus to the entire economy. Both the steel and oil industries were benefiting from a series of substantial price increases that began shortly after World War II. Largely as the result of the development of new uses, processes, and products, the aluminum and chemical industries were enjoying unusually marked increases in demand. But this era of exceptionally high profit rates proved to be short-lived, coming to an end in

[48] J. H. Clapham, "On Empty Economic Boxes," *Economic Journal,* Sept., 1922, p. 310.

the recession year of 1958. From that time on these 5 leaders have recorded only one instance of conspicuous above-target performance; this was the achievement by General Motors of a profit rate of 26.8 percent in 1965, when automobile production reached a new all-time high of 9.3 million cars. Aside from this one instance, the significant deviations since 1958 have consisted of below-target performances, i.e., by U.S. Steel in 1962, by Alcoa in the late 1950's, Standard Oil in 1958–59, and by Du Pont in the late 1960's.

Despite a 6.6-percent gain in output over the previous year, U.S. Steel's profit rate in 1962 fell to only 4.9 percent—the lowest since World War II and little more than half the company's target. The famous confrontation between President Kennedy and the steel industry, resulting in a rollback of a substantial steel price increase, took place in the spring of 1962.[49]

The explanation for the below-target performance of Alcoa is to be found in the entry of competitive foreign sources of supply into the U.S. market. During the late 1950's and early 1960's nonintegrated aluminum fabricators were able to secure their raw materials from foreign producers, notably the Norwegian firm Ardal and the French concern Pechiney.[50] Ardal, as well as other Norwegian producers, cut prices below those of the principal domestic producers who follow Alcoa's price leadership, selling at discounts up to 10 percent. The competition in prices intensified when, after making technological advances around 1960, Pechiney began to cut prices in the United States, though not, interestingly enough, in West Germany. According to Heinrich Kronstein, Germany "was assigned to Alcan, Alusuisse, Kaiser and the German Vereinigte Aluminum-Werke. Pechiney refrained from supplying the German market in spite of the fact that Germany and France, as members of the Common Market, have no tariffs between them." Largely as a result of the price cutting, aluminum markets, particularly in the United States and Great Britain, became unstable. The price fell in September, 1961, from 26 to 24 cents and in December to 22.5 cents per pound: "In a market famous for its stability . . . such a change indicated serious problems from the point of view of planned market regulation."

Thereupon two important changes were made in the industry's structure. Alcan Aluminium Ltd. of Canada acquired 50 percent of Ardal's stock from the Norwegian government, while Pechiney became part owner of a new joint venture: the Intalco Aluminum Company, with 50-percent participation by American Metal Climax and 25-percent participation each by Pechiney and Howmet Corporation. Both the Norwegian and French firms had gained an interest in a stable U.S. market and thereafter ceased to be sources of instability. According to Kronstein, "after the participation of Pechiney in the American market, the French no longer engaged in price cutting . . . after the acquisition of Ardal by Alcan, Ardal and the other Norwegian firms no longer undersold the domestic producers in the U.S. and in West Germany. As a matter of fact, the full completion of vertical integration in the United States and Europe would have been enough to reestablish a stable market. . . ." Beginning in 1962 Alcoa's profit rate began to improve, and throughout the late 1960's the company closely approached or exceeded its target return of 10 percent.

[49] For a further discussion see Ch. 23.
[50] This account of postwar developments in the aluminum industry is taken from testimony by Heinrich Kronstein in *Hearings on Economic Concentration*, Pt. 7, pp. 3654–70.

Although Standard Oil of New Jersey has had greater success in achieving its target than any of the other leaders, it did experience 2 years of conspicuous failure. From 1953 to 1957 its earnings had been well above its target (12 percent), averaging 15.8 percent. But in 1958 its profit rate fell to 9.4 percent, rising only slightly in the following year to 9.7 percent. As in the case of aluminum, the explanation is to be found in the importation of low-cost foreign supplies, which were able to penetrate domestic markets as far west as Ohio, despite a "voluntary" oil import quota plan.

Efforts by the federal government to limit petroleum imports began in 1956 through "hold-the-line" exhortations by the director of the Office of Civilian and Defense Management. With the first Suez crisis this phase passed into limbo, to be replaced on July 1, 1957, with a more formal program under which importers "voluntarily" agreed to accept quotas established by the Oil Import Administration of the Department of Commerce. Anyone without a quota was required to apply for permission to import at least 6 months in advance. While the program proved to be effective in limiting imports of *crude oil*, it broke down in 1958 primarily because of loopholes permitting the importation of oil in a partly processed form ("unfinished" oils) or as finished products (gasoline, fuel oil, and the like). By mid-1958 imports of unfinished oil had risen more than a hundred fold, reaching a level of more than 150,000 barrels a day. This, combined with imports of finished products, which had risen to approximately the same level, made a shambles of the voluntary program. As a result it was replaced the following year with a mandatory import program, under which the power of the federal government was invoked to prohibit the importation of oil in any form above a specified quota. Although formally instituted on March 11, 1959, the new program took some time to become fully effective, as the means of administration had to be perfected and previously accumulated inventories worked off. As can be seen from Figure 18-3, Standard Oil's profit rate began a gradual improvement in 1960, reached its target 2 years later, where it has since remained.

After surpassing its 20-percent target every year since World War II, Du Pont's profit rate turned sharply downward in the late 1960's. The decline in earnings, which affected most of the other producers of industrial chemicals, was the result of declining concentration, intensifying competition, and a general weakening in the control over markets. Between 1963 and 1967 the share of the 4 largest producers declined from 51 percent to 45 percent in organic chemicals, from 31 percent to 27 percent in inorganic chemicals, from 35 percent to 27 percent in plastics materials and resins, from 94 percent to 84 percent in organic fibers, and from 53 percent to 45 percent in cyclic intermediates and crudes. In addition, the chemical companies have been suffering a peculiarly difficult form of competition at the hands of the major oil companies, which have been expanding rapidly into the chemical industry. On some types of chemicals, such as nitrogeneous fertilizer materials, the oil companies appear to be selling at a loss, subsidizing their operations with after-tax profits made in oil production. In endeavoring to compete with the oil companies, the chemical firms face another formidable obstacle; under the oil import quota system they have been forced to pay a substantial premium for "tickets" giving them the right to import additional quantities of petroleum feedstocks needed to meet the rising demand for petrochemicals.

The sustainability of target return pricing

In the case of at least some of the leaders, a continuation into the future of the growth rates recorded annually during the 1960's raises a question of the sustainability of target return pricing—at least at its historical levels. The question at issue is the leaders' ability to match the growth in their size (as reflected in net worth) with increases in actual net income sufficient to attain the target objectives. The question seems to be particularly relevant to the 2 largest leaders, General Motors and Standard Oil of New Jersey. Throughout most of the 1960's they steadily increased their size, as can be seen from Figure 18-4, which shows the amount of net income required to meet the target objectives and the net income actually earned. From 1962 on, the size of General Motors, as reflected by its net worth, increased by the remarkably constant increment of $500 million per year; for Standard Oil the increase averaged $400 million per year.[51] The Figure also makes it clear that over the 16-year period the aggregate excess during the years in which the actual income exceeded the required target income was greater than the deficits during the years when the reverse was true.

But what is of particular interest here is the failure of GM to earn its required net income in 1967 and 1968. At an annual increase of $500 million in its net worth, General Motors, to meet its 20-percent target, must increase its after-taxes income by $100 million per year. In 1964 GM's net income was $1.735 billion, which gave it an above-target return of 23.5 percent on a net worth of $7.381 billion. Four years later its net income was virtually the same—$1.732 billion. But because its net worth had risen to $9.503 billion, its rate of return fell to 18.2 percent. To have attained its target objective in 1968, the company would have had to achieve an income of $1.900 billion after taxes (or nearly $4 billion before taxes!). As will be brought out in the next chapter, there do exist some constraints on General Motors' pricing power, particularly competition from imports and a demand that is elastic with respect to both price and income. The question arises whether GM has now so far exceeded optimal size that even its impressive share of the market and pricing power, in the face of these constraints, will prevent it from meeting its 20-percent target with a growth rate in net assets of a half-billion dollars per year.

Unlike General Motors, Standard Oil has been successful even during the late 1960's in meeting its target. Admittedly, the task is somewhat easier in view of its lower target (12 percent) and the somewhat lesser annual increase made in its net worth ($400 million). Nonetheless, the company will still not be without its problems. In order to find uses for its huge cash flow ($2.126 billion in 1968), it has expanded into a variety of industries, some of which (e.g., coal mining and fertilizer materials) have historically yielded profit rates well below Standard Oil's own target return. While increasing the company's size (and thus its net worth), such expansions tend to make it more difficult for the company to achieve its overall target objective. This depressing effect can be offset by increasing the profitability of operations in its traditional field, which Standard Oil attempted to do by increasing the prices of gasoline and other petroleum products in both 1969 and 1970. It can be offset also by increasing the profitability of operations in its new industries, which in the case of coal Standard Oil endeavored to do by creating the fiction, with the helpful coopera-

---

[51] Annual averages between 1962 and 1968 were $501 million for GM and $398 million for Standard Oil.

tion of the federal government, that the nation is confronted with an emerging "energy crisis."

This general problem has been recognized by at least one of the 5 leaders. Since 1965 U.S. Steel has lessened the difficulty of achieving its target rate by actually reducing its size. Between 1965 and 1968 the company reduced its net worth by $330 million. In the latter year its reported earnings of $253.7 million gave it a profit rate of 7.7 percent, only slightly below its target objective of 8 percent. If instead of reducing its net worth, U.S. Steel had continued to enlarge it by the same annual increase of the 3 preceding years ($80 million per year), its actual earnings in 1968 would have yielded a profit rate of only 6.6 percent.

Other pricing standards

Although they comprise a distinct minority of oligopolistic industries, there are fields in which the market shares held by the largest firms are about the same. In such symmetrical oligopolies the different oligopolists may use different standards of pricing, or one company may have become recognized by custom as the traditional price leader, even though it does not hold a clearly dominant position in the industry. For example, the Brookings study found that in the metal can industry, "American Can, whose percentage [like U.S. Steel's] has . . . been reduced, can revise prices only twice a year, as long as Continental Can adopts the same tactics, and the small can companies are

Figure 18-4

COMPARISON OF TARGET WITH
ACTUAL NET INCOME, 1953–1968
General Motors and Standard Oil (New Jersey)

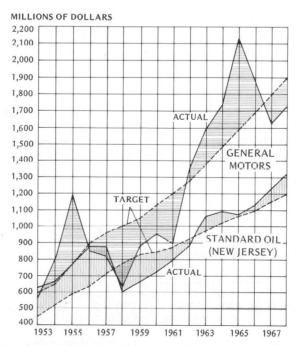

Source: Federal Trade Commission, special tabulation

willing to minimize their undercutting." [52] In such cases the accepted price leader may employ the same pricing standards as the dominant firm in an asymmetrical oligopoly, although it must give greater weight to the possibility of independent action on the part of the other oligopolists. Where there is no such tradition, price changes, up or down, may be initiated by any of the oligopolists; whether or not they "stick" will depend on whether all the other oligopolists elect to make corresponding revisions in their prices in order to "meet competition."

While advanced principally by the price followers in asymmetrical oligopolies,[53] the "meeting competition" standard, curiously enough, is also employed in symmetrical oligopolies in pricing new products. Thus, referring to American Can, the Brookings study found, "Meeting competition—or using the cost of a substitute product to determine the price it charges—has also been the company's policy in marketing paper milk containers." [54] This use of the "meeting competition" standard can best be illustrated by the pricing behavior of the ethical-drug industry. Because it is not an asymmetrical oligopoly, the structure of the drug industry does not lend itself to target return pricing; there is no price leader for the industry as a whole. Positions of leadership among the various important classes of drugs—antibiotics, corticosteroids, tranquilizers, antidiabetic drugs, and the like—shift among a dozen major pharmaceutical manufacturers in accordance with their success in developing patentable specialties and persuading physicians to prescribe them under their brand names.

The broad-spectrum antibiotics provide a case in point. On September 27, 1951, Pfizer adopted a price of $5.10 for Terramycin; 4 days later both American Cyanamid and Parke, Davis announced the same price for Aureomycin and Chloromycetin, respectively. A little more than 2 years later American Cyanamid became the first company to introduce the new broad-spectrum, tetracycline; the price it adopted was the same as that of the earlier broad-spectrums, $5.10. Shortly thereafter the 4 other sellers of tetracycline put their products on the market at the same price.[55] The use of this standard thus provided a means of achieving price identity on new but competing products and in addition eliminated price differences among the different sellers of a given product.

Similarly, the first wide-selling corticosteroids were prednisone and prednisolone, introduced by Schering under the trade names Meticorten and Meticortelone. They were followed by the introduction of methylprednisolone by Upjohn under the trade name Medrol and of triamcinolone by Squibb and Lederle under the trade names Kenacort and Aristocort. Each of these successive products was introduced at the price charged by Schering for Meticorten and Meticortelone, 18 cents per tablet to the druggist.[56] This price had been established when the manufacture of corticosteroids was an expensive and complex process involving the use of oxbile, which required hundreds of slaughtered animals to yield a few grams of steroids. In its place Upjohn introduced a microbiological process, involving the use of a vegetable source, Mexican yams. In addition to replacing a scarce and costly source of supply with an abundant and inexpensive source, the new process reduced greatly the steps

[52] Kaplan, Dirlam, Lanzillotti, *op. cit.,* p. 287.
[53] See Ch. 19.
[54] Kaplan, Dirlam, Lanzillotti, *op. cit.,* p. 211.
[55] Federal Trade Commission, *Economic Report on Antibiotics Manufacture,* 1958, p. 192. The prices are for 16 capsules, 250 mg.
[56] *Administered Prices: Report on Drugs,* pp. 98–99.

involved in production. In a letter to the head of another drug company, E. Gifford Upjohn referred to the new method as constituting "the most economical and versatile steroid processes presently available anywhere in the world today." In contrast, Upjohn described the older process in these words: "Now oxbile is not a readily available commodity on the market in large quantities. It was scarce. It was expensive. The process . . . had some 40 steps or more. It was an extremely complicated chemical synthesis, as you have said. The costs of the material were very high." [57] Yet the prices charged by Upjohn for its new corticosteroid, produced by the low-cost microbiological process, were the same as the prices charged for the older steroids made by the high-cost oxbile method.

The replacement of older, higher-cost products with newer, low-cost items sold at approximately the same price is a common occurrence in the drug industry. The drug traditionally used for the treatment of diabetes, insulin, is a relatively high-cost product made from animal pancreas. For many patients, it has been replaced by tolbulamide (Orinase) and other oral antidiabetic drugs, which are synthetically produced, low-cost products. The chief counsel of the Senate Antitrust Subcommittee, Paul Rand Dixon, outlined to E. Gifford Upjohn, president of the Upjohn Company, his understanding of the manner in which the price of Orinase had been arrived at:

> MR. DIXON: Figuring this out on a dosage formula, we understand that a diabetic who can shift from insulin to an oral drug normally is one who must take 30 units of insulin daily, usually 10 units shortly before each meal. Regular insulin is sold in 10 cubic centimeter vials containing 40 units per cubic centimeter or a total of 400 units per bottle. According to the Blue Book, the price to the consumer is $1.40 and, as I stated, I believe that price has been unchanged since 1947. Thus, every time the patient gives himself an injection of 10 units of insulin, the cost of the drug to him for such injection is about 14 cents. This is the same price also for an Orinase tablet, I believe.
>
> *　　*　　*
>
> SENATOR KEFAUVER: Apparently you priced it just about the same as the injectable insulin, as I understand your testimony. Maybe it is a little different, but just about the same.
>
> DR. UPJOHN: Senator, that would be a very difficult thing to say one way or another because there are so many variables.
>
> SENATOR KEFAUVER: The point is, isn't insulin in injectable form a much more expensive product to manufacture than a tablet of oral insulin? I understood the injectable insulin had to be made out of animal pancreas of which there is a shortage, and it is a very difficult process, whereas Orinase is a chemical combination which is comparatively much cheaper and much easier to make.
>
> DR. UPJOHN: I haven't any information about that at all. I don't know anything about the production costs of insulin. We do not manufacture insulin.
>
> *　　*　　*
>
> SENATOR KEFAUVER: My question was, Why didn't you set Orinase at a lower price? Why did you just set it the same as insulin which was already on the market?
>
> DR. UPJOHN: That was our competition, Senator.[58]

[57] *Hearings on Administered Prices*, Pt. 14, pp. 8291–92.
[58] *Ibid.*, Pt. 20, pp. 11037–39.

CONSTRAINTS ON OLIGOPOLISTIC PRICING

It should not be thought that the price-setting discretion of oligopolists is absolute. Even the most dominant corporation with the largest market share is subject to constraints upon its pricing power that it can ignore only at its peril. Principal among these constraints is price competition. While oligopolists usually follow the leader's price changes and confine their rivalry to the various forms of nonprice competition, they may on occasion become dissatisfied with their share of the market and embark on a course of independent price behavior. Competition in price may also stem from the industry's small producers and from importers. Yet even where price competition is quiescent there are constraints on pricing power. These include the effect of price increases in reducing sales (the elasticity of demand), the bargaining power of large buyers (monopsony and oligopsony), and the existence of substitute products (the cross-elasticity of supply).[1]

Before the various constraints on price-making discretion are examined, attention should be directed to the *customary* behavior of oligopolists with respect to each other. Although there are exceptions, concern over nonacceptance by the other oligopolists seldom deters a dominant producer from making such price changes as he regards necessary to meet his target return. If it were otherwise, the leaders examined in the previous chapter would have been far less successful in meeting their target objectives, particularly in the short run.

Price followership: a nonconstraint

Where lesser oligopolists have long accepted the dominant firm as the price leader, they usually have no internal standards of price determination of their own. In a colloquy with Theodore Yntema, vice president of Ford Motor Company, Senator O'Mahoney brought out that Ford, unlike General Motors, does not price in terms of a target rate objective; its objective is to "meet competition":

> MR. YNTEMA: . . . in our own particular company, we do not have a simple cost-plus formula. We do not have any simple way in which you go just from cost to price.
> We have to look at our competitive situation. Ordinarily, what we find is this: We have very little leeway.

*   *   *

[1] For a discussion of substitute products see Ch. 6.

SENATOR O'MAHONEY: Do you have a goal of a certain profit or invested capital or net worth?

MR. YNTEMA: We are not in the fortunate position—we would like to do better than we are doing. . . . Sometimes we get more than 15 percent. It just depends upon the competitive situation. I mean we do not just have costs and add a profit margin and arrive at a price. We are in this tough, rough business of trying to get business from General Motors and Chrysler and they are trying to get it from us.[2]

Senator O'Mahoney pointed out that General Motors' officials had previously testified that their pricing objective was to earn 15 to 20 percent on net worth. He inquired: "Now, is that your concept of it?" The answer came: "No; we do not have a goal of that kind. We just like to do better than we are doing. I mean the objective judgment in the market place is we ought to do better than we are doing. We are just interested in improving ourselves. Sometimes we have to price at a loss. We cannot help ourselves. It is the only way we can sell our product."[3]

The president of Chrysler made a similar acknowledgment. Senator Kefauver inquired whether Chrysler, like General Motors, had a "definite profit figure" in mind in arriving at prices. L. L. Colbert replied, "We do not have a definite profit figure. All we know is our profits in recent years have been far too low and we are trying to improve them."[4]

The Brookings study included two corporations that are lesser oligopolists in industries dominated by a leader: Gulf Oil and National Steel. In neither was pricing to achieve a target return found to be the company's principal, or even a collateral, pricing goal. With respect to Gulf the Brookings study stated that "in general the pricing policy of the company is to keep its prices on the same level as their competitors'. They never lead in price changes and are not considered a 'reference seller' in the industry, as is Standard Oil of New Jersey."[5] National Steel followed a "few brief pricing rules" enunciated by its long-time head, Ernest Weir:

> 1. Follow the lead of the price leader, which is U.S. Steel, while sweetening the base price a little when, as in Detroit, the company has a considerable freight advantage.
> 2. Absorb freight if necessary on a single order, but watch closely the annual bills.
> 3. Never manipulate extras to get an order; reduce the base price if necessary to meet a competitive cut.
> 4. Price is never built on cost; pressure is backward on cost.[6]

In most of the nation's major oligopolistic industries price leadership has been observed for so long as to have assumed the character of an institution. Originally through the famous "Gary dinners" and later through price leadership, the prices of U.S. Steel have been the prices of the steel industry for nearly three-quarters of a century. Except in some geographic markets, Standard Oil of New Jersey has been the "reference seller," as it is termed in the petroleum industry, for about as long. International Harvester has played the same role in

[2] *Hearings on Administered Prices,* Pt. 6, p. 2683.
[3] *Ibid.,* p. 2679.
[4] *Ibid.,* p. 2825.
[5] A. D. H. Kaplan, Joel B. Dirlam, Robert F. Lanzillotti, *Pricing in Big Business,* Brookings Institution, 1955, p. 206.
[6] *Ibid.,* p. 205.

farm machinery for a half-century. General Motors' span of effective leadership has lasted over 40 years. The new integrated producers of aluminum have usually followed Alcoa's changes with monotonous regularity. The leader's price changes are followed partly because that is the way the industry has behaved in the past. While an independent course of action may appear tempting, there must be good and sufficient reason for avoiding it, otherwise independent pricing would have been pursued more frequently in the past. Moreover, lesser oligopolists may have followed the leaders for so long that they are simply not equipped to establish prices on their own, which would require additional cost data, market surveys, the formulation of pricing standards, and so on.

The role of U.S. Steel as unquestioned leader in the steel industry has been brought out on numerous occasions. In 1936 Senator Wheeler, chairman of the Senate Committee on Interstate Commerce, engaged in an exchange with William A. Irvin, president of U.S. Steel:

> THE CHAIRMAN: All the witnesses thus far give the impression that their prices were set only to meet competition. In other words, they indicate that they only follow the bellwether. Somebody, somewhere, must set the original price. During the era of the "Gary dinners" we knew how the prices were set. They were set because, when they got together in these dinners, they set the price. In earlier days they got together and sat down and agreed in writing what the prices should be, but at the present time it seems to be extremely difficult to find out who the bellwether is and who fixes the price originally that they follow to meet that competition.
>
> MR. IRVIN: I would say we generally make the prices.
>
> THE CHAIRMAN: You generally make the prices?
>
> MR. IRVIN: Yes, sir, we generally make the prices, unless some of the other members of the industry think that that price may be too high, and they make the price.
>
> THE CHAIRMAN: You lead off, then, with a price change, either up or down, at Gary, is that correct?
>
> MR. IRVIN: Yes.[7]

Again in 1939 Eugene C. Grace, president of Bethlehem, was questioned by A. H. Feller, special assistant to the U.S. Attorney General, during hearings before the Temporary National Economic Committee:

> MR. FELLER: Mr. Grace, do you recall any occasions on which your company took the initiative in announcing a lower price on any steel commodity?
>
> MR. GRACE: I can't recall whether we have or whether we haven't. I know, generally, we haven't.
>
> MR. FELLER: Then I take it—
>
> MR. GRACE (interposing): I know—I am telling you what the general practice is from our company standpoint. Whether we have ever initiated any, I just couldn't say, but in the main we would normally await the schedules as published by the steel corporation.
>
> MR. HENDERSON: That went back as far as you can remember the policy of Bethlehem?
>
> MR. GRACE: Yes.

* * *

[7] 74th Cong., 2nd Sess., Senate Committee on Interstate Commerce, *Hearings on S. 4055,* 1936, p. 596.

MR. FELLER: . . . you remember there were two price increases in 1936, and when the steel corporation published a new price list in the early part of 1936, and another one in the latter part of 1936, your policy was also to announce prices as high as those which had been announced.

MR. GRACE: That is right. It was very encouraging to find them doing that.

MR. FELLER: Then you follow them up and you follow them down?

MR. GRACE: I would follow them up in that instance.

MR. FELLER: Do you remember any instance where you didn't follow them up?

MR. GRACE: No; and I certainly remember no instance when we didn't follow them down.[8]

That the prices announced by U.S. Steel are indeed the prices of the industry was again brought out in 1957 hearings by the Senate Antitrust Subcommittee. Roger Blough, chairman of the board of U.S. Steel, at one point contradicted Senator Kefauver's observation that "You fixed your price and generally the other companies went up about the same amount." [9] The Senator then challenged Blough to cite instances where this had not happened, requesting that he "take some time where the small companies were not strikebound, or when they were strikebound and you were not, or when it was not a seller's market." [10]

As a result of discussions held by the Subcommittee's staff with the company's officials it was agreed that the substance of the request could be met if the company would supply instances of price changes initiated by competitors during the year 1954—a period in which there was no strike and in which demand for steel was relatively slack. In response, U.S. Steel on October 16, 1957, submitted a listing of such price actions, entitled "Examples of Price Changes Made by Competitors of United States Steel and Action Taken by United States Steel, Year 1954." There are 19 instances in the listing of price changes initiated by competitors that are set forth in dollar terms. A comparison of the "new" price of the competitor (i.e., the price after the change had been made) with the "old" price of U.S. Steel (i.e., the corporation's price at the time that the competitor made his change and before U.S. Steel had made any adjustments thereto) reveals that, with one exception, the price changes initiated by competitors consisted of merely a narrowing or elimination of a *premium* which had been charged above U.S. Steel's price. After the change the competitor's new price was equal to or even still above U.S. Steel's price.[11]

On the face of it, the price uniformity that exists in steel is hardly to be expected in automobiles. While a given steel shape is a homogeneous product made to the same exacting specifications by each producer, there is no complete identity of product among automobile manufacturers. Whereas steel is a pro-

---

[8] 76th Cong., 1st Sess., Temporary National Economic Committee, *Hearings,* 1939, Pt. 19, pp. 10601–03.

[9] *Hearings on Administered Prices,* Pt. 2, p. 231.

[10] *Ibid.,* p. 312.

[11] The one exception relates to galvanized sheets. From the date shown on the listing, the sequence of events appears to be as follows: on July 3, 1954, U.S. Steel increased its price by $3.50 per ton, bringing it to a level of $120 per ton. Four days later Republic increased its price, but the amount of its increase, which was only 50 cents, brought its price to $117. In the face of this lower price of Republic's, U.S. Steel retained the $120 price for about a month, but on August 5, 1954, lowered it to the $117 level of Republic (see *ibid.,* Pt. 3, p. 956).

ducer good purchased by skilled procurement experts, the average car buyer is far less able to make interproduct comparisons. In steel slight variations in the price may make the difference between profit and loss to the buyer; in contrast minor variations in the price of an automobile would not be expected to be determinative of the final choice of the purchaser. It is therefore surprising that examinations of their prices, both before and after the addition of optional equipment, have revealed a striking uniformity of price for comparable models among the 3 major car manufacturers.[12] In some cases prices have been found to be identical to the last dollar; in the majority of instances the companies have been within a few dollars of each other, except that Chrysler's products have traditionally been priced slightly above the comparable models of its competitors.

As in steel, the effective leader in the automobile industry is not always the first to announce. In seeking to create the impression of an intensely competitive industry, General Motors sometimes considers it expedient for the initial announcement to be made by one of its rivals. As long as the general direction is upward, the risk is exceedingly small. When Ford and Chrysler act as initiators, the issue facing them is whether their increases are about what would be called for under GM's target return formula. When no subsequent revisions are required, their judgment has been accurate. If the announced increases are more than what is called for by the formula, GM will theoretically announce smaller increases, and Ford and Chrysler will be forced to adjust their prices downward; this incidentally has rarely, if ever, occurred. But if their advances are too small and GM goes higher, they can revise their quotations upward "to meet competition." For example, in introducing the 1957 automobile models Ford was the first of the Big Three to make public its prices, which showed an average increase of 2.9 percent. Some two weeks later Chevrolet's prices were announced, but they represented an average increase of over 6.1 percent. Shortly thereafter Ford revised its prices upward, bringing them almost exactly into line with Chevrolet's higher prices.

Where the lesser oligopolists are less efficient than the leader, observance of the latter's price increases is understandable, since it is the leader who would presumably emerge victorious in any price war. Realizing this, the lesser oligopolists could be expected to be content to operate under the leader's "price umbrella." If they did not follow him up, he could retaliate with price reductions, which, because of his greater efficiency, they could not match. This represents the most widely advanced rationale for the behavior of lesser oligopolists in concentrated industries. But it is applicable to only a minority of oligopolies, since, as has been brought out earlier, the leader in most concentrated industries is usually less efficient than the other large producers.[13] Where such is the case the reasons why lesser but more efficient oligopolists would exactly match the leader's price increases are more obscure. The smaller producers are, in effect, permitting the leader to operate under *their* umbrella. During the hearings by the Senate Antitrust Subcommittee on the steel industry, this was the subject of a line of inquiry

---

[12] See *Administered Prices: Report on Automobiles,* pp. 61–74.

[13] See Ch. 8. Even in automobiles, where the leader is widely assumed to be the most efficient producer, Ford's net profit per car resulting from automotive operations between 1954 and 1957 would not have been substantially below that of GM had Ford been able to secure the same average revenue as GM through more effective coverage of the price range above the low-price field and had it not incurred the unusual expenses of reviving the Continental line in 1955 and introducing the Edsel in 1957.

directed by Senator Kefauver to the heads of 2 long-term price followers, Beth lehem and National. The Senator began his interrogation by addressing a series of questions to A. B. Homer, president of Bethlehem Steel Corporation:

> SENATOR KEFAUVER: Mr. Homer, as one who always thought competition set prices, I can understand why you would follow them [U.S. Steel] down in order to carry on your part of the business. But I cannot understand why you would follow them up in order to meet competition. It would seem to me you would be making more competition if you perhaps went up some but not quite all the way. Then you would be attracting more customers and getting more business.[14]

Since the industry was not operating at capacity, Homer's reply was somewhat surprising: "we did not feel, as I stated yesterday, that the reduction in price or a non-increase in price would create any more business for us or make us any more through increased volume." [15]

Citing a specific example, the Senator then noted that on the product, hot-rolled bars, U.S. Steel had raised the price $7 or 6.9 percent to $108.50:

> SENATOR KEFAUVER: Would you not be engaging in competing more if, instead of raising your price $7 and coming out with exactly the same price of $108.50, you would raise your price $6 or $5?
>
> MR. HOMER: . . . we felt that a reduction below the competitive level would not bring us any more business and, of course, would mean reduced profit.
>
> SENATOR KEFAUVER: Mr. Homer, you say at that point reducing below the competitive level would not bring you any more business. How can you explain that? You would be a dollar below your competitive price, and a lot of buyers would be coming your way.
>
> MR. HOMER: I explained that yesterday.
>
> SENATOR KEFAUVER: Mr. Homer, as Mr. Grace has said, you always follow them up, and you always follow them down. How do you know that you would not get more business if you were a dollar below United States Steel?
>
> MR. HOMER: How do we know whether or not we would get more business?
>
> SENATOR KEFAUVER: Yes, sir.
>
> MR. HOMER: Well, I think I pointed that out to you yesterday and I will go back to that, and I would be glad to read it again.[16]

Mr. Homer's "explanation" of the day before had been to the effect that because of a wage increase the industry as a whole needed a price increase.

Senator Kefauver then introduced an exhibit showing that Bethlehem was the nation's largest producer, outranking even U.S. Steel, in 7 steel products, including such important items as structural shapes and universal plates. He said, "You are the production leader in these items, but you did not take the initiative in setting their price. You waited until United States Steel set the price. How does that happen?" [17] Homer's response was that the question was "meaningless." The Senator then introduced into the record statistical data showing that over a long period of time Bethlehem had averaged higher profit rates than U.S. Steel and apparently had been a more efficient company.

[14] *Hearings on Administered Prices*, Pt. 2, p. 619.
[15] *Ibid.*
[16] *Ibid.*, pp. 620–21.
[17] *Ibid.*, p. 624.

SENATOR KEFAUVER: So my question is, Mr. Homer, in view of the fact that your profit rate has generally been better than that of United States Steel, why do you have to charge the same prices? Why can you not give the customer the benefit of your apparent greater efficiency as indicated by your higher profit rate?

MR. HOMER: Well, we sell at the competitive price, Senator, and if that results in our making a better performance than our competitor, that pleases us very much and pleases our stockholders, and makes a much better situation.[18]

Here, as elsewhere in his testimony, Homer, in using the term "competitive price," was referring to U.S. Steel's price. Thus, a meaningful translation would be that selling at U.S. Steel's price levels, Bethlehem with its lower costs made a better performance than U.S. Steel, which "pleases us very much and pleases our stockholders, and makes a much better situation."

SENATOR KEFAUVER: Mr. Homer, you could make the same profit rate as United States Steel with a lower price. Why do you not give the customer the benefit of that lower rate?

MR. HOMER: Well, I doubt if your statement is correct, because if we should lower our price, then it would be met by our competitors, and that would drop their profit so that we would still be right back to the same price, relatively, because our efficiencies were different.

SENATOR KEFAUVER: Would that not be good competition? Would that not be in the public interest?

MR. HOMER: Then you can carry it on to the point where you would not be making any money, if you do embark on this process.

SENATOR KEFAUVER: Nobody is talking about that.

MR. HOMER: If you embark on that process, step by step, you will end up without making any money at all. That certainly would not be in anybody's interest.

SENATOR KEFAUVER: I am not advocating that.[19]

Homer's argument implies that the more efficient company cannot charge a lower price because if it were to do so the higher-cost company would simply meet it—a process that would continue until not only the higher-cost but the lower-cost company as well would "end up without making any money at all." Homer did not enlighten the Subcommittee as to how in a price war a higher-cost company could drive a lower-cost company out of business.

Commenting on the efficiency of National Steel, the Brookings study observed: "The pricing policy of National Steel is one of matching the market. It has assumed that it is at least as efficient in its field as any of its competitors." [20] Its efficiency is in part the result of its specialization on a few products, notably cold-rolled sheets and tin plate. Representing National Steel before the Subcommittee was its chairman, George M. Humphrey, former Secretary of the Treasury. After pointing out that National had an outstanding earnings record and also that it had the largest capacity for cold-rolled sheets in both the nation as a whole and in the northeastern area, Senator Kefauver asked: "In this product in which you are the leader and in the part of the country in which you operate, you have 18.9% as compared to [17.2%] for United States Steel. Yet you let

[18] *Ibid.,* p. 631.
[19] *Ibid.,* p. 632.
[20] Kaplan, Dirlam, Lanzillotti, *op. cit.,* p. 204.

United States Steel set your price. Why do you do that?" Humphrey responded as if the question were why National Steel had not raised its price *more* than U.S. Steel: "We cannot fix it higher if they want to put this price in. There is no way we can sell our commodity and get business if they will sell theirs and take less. . . ."

Stressing the difference between meeting a price reduction and matching a price increase, the Senator continued:

> SENATOR KEFAUVER: I can understand you going down to meet the lower price of United States Steel.
>
> MR. HUMPHREY: That is what we did this time.
>
> SENATOR KEFAUVER (continuing): to be competitive. But I do not understand this going up to be competitive.
>
> MR. HUMPHREY: As I said to you yesterday, it is possible that we might have gone higher if we had been doing it all by ourselves.
>
> SENATOR KEFAUVER: If you had gone higher, you think you would not have gotten any business, but if you had not gone quite so high would you have been more competitive, Mr. Humphrey?
>
> MR. HUMPHREY: I do not know.
>
> SENATOR KEFAUVER: Why do you not try it sometime? [21]

In an industry of relatively high fixed costs, routine upward price matching by lesser oligopolists during an economic downturn means that they are forgoing an immediate opportunity to increase earnings by attracting new buyers (until and unless their lower price is met) and by spreading their overhead costs over a greater number of units. In reference to the question of whether his company would not have been more competitive "if you had raised your price $6 a ton on hot-rolled bars instead of $7," Homer replied by saying, "Well, we did not need the business, Senator." [22] This answer would hardly be applicable to 1958, 1961, and 1970, when Bethlehem had about one-third of its capacity unutilized but still consistently and uniformly matched U.S. Steel's increases.

During the hearings the rationale for National's upward price matching came to light. National could not sell at a higher price than U.S. Steel, and if it did not get as much as U.S. Steel, Humphrey would be personally embarrassed: "I would be ashamed of myself if I could not get the price that was justified, that conditions justified, yes sir; that other people could get." [23] In a seller's market, with demand exceeding supply, Humphrey might be excused his sense of personal mortification at his product's failure to command as high a price as his competitor's. But what of the situation where demand was falling and a substantial amount of unused capacity had developed? Referring to the decline in National's operating rate from 98 percent of capacity in the first quarter of 1957 to 80 percent in the second quarter, Senator Kefauver commented: "I would think that getting down from 98% to 80% ought to be coming somewhere close to putting into application your formula here for getting more business by reducing your price increase from $6 to $5." And Humphrey replied: "Not at the present time." [24]

---

[21] *Hearings on Administered Prices,* Pt. 3, pp. 824–25, 866–67.
[22] *Ibid.,* Pt. 2, p. 621.
[23] *Ibid.,* Pt. 3, p. 868.
[24] *Ibid.,* p. 872.

Stressing that he was not referring to an increase in the "total demand" for steel resulting from an industry-wide price reduction but rather to the gain to Humphrey's particular firm from a smaller price increase, the Senator went on:

> SENATOR KEFAUVER: I cannot understand, not speaking of the steel industry as a whole, but why a reduction in the price increase to $5 which you are talking about here would not give you more business. Would not this help National? Would not more buyers come to National to get their steel?
>
> MR. HUMPHREY: All I can tell you, Senator, is perhaps if you had some experience in the steel business you would understand it better.[25]

Humphrey did not completely rule out the possibility of independent price action, stating that "if you can get $6 for your steel, I am just a little ashamed of myself if I cannot sell equally with you and not get $6, but if I cannot, rather than shut down I will take $5 and take some business, and that is the way it works." [26] However, neither in the recession of 1958 nor in the downturns of 1960 and 1970 was Humphrey's company willing to make a lesser increase "and take some business."

A persuasive explanation for upward price matching is that if the lesser oligopolists do not participate in the price rise, the leader will rescind his increase. In this event the follower will have gained nothing in the way of increased sales volume and will have forgone the added revenue from the price increase. With his price met, would the follower want to take the next step of cutting prices? Because what he would then be considering is an actual price reduction, the logic of imperfect competition would come into play. Presumably, he would abstain from lowering his price since his output, by definition, is large enough to affect the market and since he would assume that any price reduction on his part would be promptly met.

Yet under certain circumstances the underlying assumption in this line of reasoning—i.e., that the leader will rescind his price increase—may not be valid. Where the lesser oligopolist's capacity is sufficient to supply only a relatively small proportion of the total demand and where he cannot quickly expand his capacity, the leader may conclude that the revenue lost on the specific orders going to the lower-price firm is less than the amount he would lose on all orders by reducing his price. Moreover, there is the possibility of a time lag. The leader may not rescind his increase until the lesser oligopolist has enjoyed the benefit of a payout period in which the revenue lost by failure to raise the price is more than offset by an increase in sales volume.

Another opportunity for nonconformity arises when the leader labors under a cost burden not borne by the followers. An opportunity of this type has been available to Ford and Chrysler in those years in which they have escaped the very considerable expenses incurred by General Motors in making complete model changes. The 1958 Plymouth was virtually indistinguishable from the 1957 model; the 1958 Ford had, not a complete model change, but only a "face lift"; only Chevrolet of the Big Three underwent a complete model change. The opportunity was thus presented to both Ford and Plymouth of making gains in sales at the expense of Chevrolet by holding their prices unchanged. Had Chevrolet then endeavored to match these lower prices, its profits per car would have been reduced very materially. That Chevrolet under these circumstances

[25] *Ibid.,* p. 872.
[26] Quoted in *ibid.*

would have rescinded its increase is something less than self-evident. It might well have contented itself that year in relying on its established consumer acceptance and perhaps intensifying its selling and advertising efforts. Yet, while the opportunity presented itself, neither Ford nor Plymouth availed themselves of it but instead matched the Chevrolet price increases.

One possible explanation for price followership, generally, may lie in the possession by the leader of such substantial monopoly power that it can discipline the lesser oligopolists, even though they are sizable producers and may indeed be more efficient than the leader. Typically, the dominant oligopolist produces a wider range of products and is engaged in more industries than are its lesser rivals. It is often in the possession of substantial monopoly power which it can bring to bear through various forms of "leverage" against any nonconformist producer. If, following a price increase by a multiproduct leader on all of its products, a single-product firm making one of those products were to hold its price constant (or make a smaller advance), the rescission by the leader of its price increase *on that product* would lose for it the added revenue on only part of its output, whereas the single-product firm would have forgone the added revenue on its entire output. As between a single-product and a multiproduct company a price reduction on the product made by each will always result in a greater relative loss of revenues to the former than to the latter. This can be illustrated by the example shown in Table 19-1, in which the smaller firm makes successive price reductions on product A, each costing $1 million in revenues, which are matched by the larger firm at a similar cost, while at the same time the revenues of the larger firm on product B remain unchanged. The single-product firm would realize that the disparity in the revenues of the 2 companies would inevitably widen if it were to engage in a price war, assuming its larger rival were to match its price reductions, while holding prices unchanged on its other products. Accordingly, even if it were the more efficient producer, the single-product firm would for this reason abstain from engaging in a price war with a large multiproduct rival.

In the steel industry the largest company is the leading producer of a majority of all steel products, which are sold in discrete markets to different buyers for different uses. In most of these markets its share is sufficient to give it substantial monopoly power. Among steel products with an industry-wide capacity of more than a half-million tons, Bethlehem is the leading producer of 4, Republic of 2, and National of one. But U.S. Steel is the leading producer of 22, including

Table 19-1

ILLUSTRATION OF EFFECT OF PRICE REDUCTION
ON REVENUES

Single- versus multiproduct firms
($ Millions)

Single-Product Firm	Multiproduct Firm		Single-Product Firm's Revenues as Percentage of Multiproduct Firm's
Product A	Product A	Product B	
$10	$10	$10	50%
8	8	10	44
6	6	10	37
4	4	10	28

such diverse, large-tonnage items as rails, hot-rolled sheets and strips, galvanized sheets, hot-rolled bars, most forms of pipe and tubing, most wire products, and tin mill products. For 15 of the products U.S. Steel alone accounts for more than 30 percent of the industry's capacity.

Any steel company contemplating not matching an increase by U.S. Steel would be not only inviting a probable rescission by the leader of its increase but risking the possibility of a price war. It would be aware that the rescission and possible war would in all probability be limited to the one or few products of which it is a significant producer. And it would also realize that such selective and limited retaliation, while probably disastrous to it, would pose no great financial hardship to U.S. Steel. It is because of their awareness of U.S. Steel's power of reprisal that other steel companies privately refer, without affection, to U.S. Steel as "Big Brother." [27]

What is true of the largest company in steel is also true, to a greater or lesser extent, of the leaders in most of the other asymmetrical oligopolistic industries. In addition to its dominance of *all* price ranges in the automobile industry, General Motors has monopolized the locomotive and bus industries; it is a leading producer of trucks and household appliances; and it derives substantial revenues from a finance company subsidiary, General Motors Acceptance Corporation. Alcoa has in the past used its power over the price of primary aluminum to impose a price "squeeze" on small, nonintegrated manufacturers engaged in the fabrication of products out of aluminum—an area in which Alcoa is also the leading producer.[28] Standard Oil of New Jersey not only is the largest oil company but ranks among the two or three leading factors, both at home and abroad, at each stage of the oil industry—production, transportation, refining, and marketing. What is most important is its outstanding position in the derivation of after-tax revenues as an oil producer. In any given field in which any of these leaders operates, the cost of a period of price rivalry, relative to total income, would be less for it than for any nonconformist rival—a fact of which the latter cannot help but be aware.

Price competition

Although competitive rivalry in concentrated industries customarily is limited to following the leader's price and engaging in the various forms of nonprice competition, competition in price may spring from a variety of sources. In even the most well-mannered industry competition may break out among the oligopolists themselves. When not prevented by patents, price discrimination, or other artificial restraints, small and medium-size producers can be an important source of price competition. And when not prevented by quotas and tariffs, supplies offered by foreign sellers can be a further constraint.

[27] A small steel producer, according to a story attributed to Thurman Arnold, testified that he followed the price leadership of U.S. Steel because it had a better management, a wider outlook, and greater experience at its disposal. During a recess Arnold is said to have asked the producer to comment privately on what would happen if he were not to respect the prices of U.S. Steel. The businessman is said to have replied, "This, sir, I hope never to experience." (Cited and quoted by Kurt H. Biedenkopf in *Hearings on Economic Concentration,* Pt. 7A, p. 4058.)

[28] See Ch. 2.

Competition among oligopolists

While the lesser steel producers have generally displayed exemplary behavior in following U.S. Steel's leadership, price cutting has occasionally made its appearance. According to a study of pricing by steel companies during the NRA Code period, National Steel, under the direction of the aggressive Ernest Weir, followed an independent pricing policy:

> At least in the pricing of the products studied, the National Steel Corporation appears to have played an independent role during the Code period, a part which . . . was contrary to the pricing policies of other important firms. It became an exponent of lower steel prices in a most effective way for it initiated price declines and refused to conform to price increases initiated by others at the most important basing points—Pittsburgh, Chicago, Gary and Cleveland. Other companies might qualify for similar mention, but the data at hand will not permit their designation in so unambiguous a manner.[29]

Long one of the economy's most concentrated sectors, the chemical industry is undergoing a rapid transformation. Concentration has been declining, the profit rate has been falling, and both new and substitute products are continually being introduced. In past years patents had been an effective means of establishing control of the market. But in this industry the effectiveness of patents as a protection against competition has diminished as all the large manufacturers of chemicals have developed the research capability of developing their own patented variants. Not infrequently these closely related substitutes are put on the market at substantially reduced prices. The Du Pont company, for example, found that its sales of an acrylic fiber, which it had priced at $1.75 per pound, were threatened by a new fiber introduced by a rival chemical company at $1.40 per pound: "opinions in du Pont on effective countermoves ranged from a strict holding of the line at du Pont's higher price, with continuing emphasis on du Pont quality, to a direct meeting of price at the expense of profit margin. . . . How far could awareness of the superiority of the du Pont product be carried over into consumer willingness to accept a spread between the prices of the du Pont and the competing fiber?"[30] Implying little confidence in the enduring allegiance of consumers, the company jettisoned the established price, reducing it from 25 percent to only 7 percent above that of its competitor.

The introduction by Du Pont of two of its most recent developments, Corfam and Delrin, was followed shortly by the appearance of alternative products developed by its rivals:

> it is said that du Pont had by 1964 invested over $25 million in the development and marketing of Corfam, a substitute for leather, doubtless hoping that they would be far ahead of competitors. But a rival product was quickly put on the market by Goodrich. When du Pont introduced their plastic, Delrin, they must have believed that they had something new; but Celanese shortly afterwards introduced a competitive plastic. As C. B. McCoy, the president of du Pont put it, "the more discoveries we make, the more rapidly our competitors move in against us."[31]

[29] C. R. Daugherty, M. G. de Chazeau, S. S. Stratton, *The Economics of the Iron and Steel Industry*, McGraw-Hill, 1937, Vol. II, p. 670.
[30] Kaplan, Dirlam, Lanzillotti, *op. cit.*, p. 277n.
[31] John Jewkes, David Sawers, Richard Stillerman, *The Sources of Invention*, rev. ed., Macmillan, 1969, pp. 213, 216.

Competition from small producers

One possible source of price competition in an oligopolistic industry is its small producers. Yet there has been a tendency among economists to discount the potential importance of this source because of the widespread (and generally erroneous) assumption that efficiency is related directly to size. What small concern wishes to precipitate a price war with a competitor who is both larger *and* more efficient? The reluctance of the small producer to cut prices may, however, be due to factors that have nothing whatever to do with efficiency. He may be prohibited effectively from competing by patents or regulations of some government agency. Or he may have good reason to fear a reprisal directed specifically against him in the form of price discrimination, cross-subsidization, or other predatory practices. Nonetheless, in certain markets small producers have been an important source of price competition.

This is true, for example, of those drug products that are nonpatented or, if patented, are licensed to small as well as large firms. While until recently the broad-spectrum antibiotics were sold only by the large companies, small firms for some time have offered vigorous price competition for the older forms of penicillin, which are not patented, and for streptomycin, which is produced by a number of firms as licensees under the patent held by Rutgers University. Figure 19-1 contrasts their price movements with those of the patented broad-spectrum antibiotics. As will be seen, the prices of penicillin and streptomycin fell about 90 percent between 1951 and 1960—from $2.50 to 21 cents and from $3.24 to 36 cents, respectively. In contrast, what appears to be a straight

Figure 19-1

ANTIBIOTIC PRICES
Broad versus narrow spectrum, 1951–60

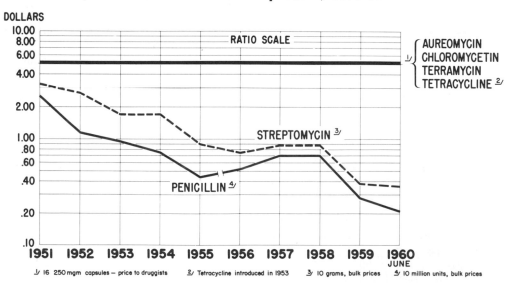

Source: *Administered Prices: Report on Drugs*, Chart 10

black line near the top of the chart is the price trend of the broad-spectrum antibiotics during this 10-year period. In this case the difference in price trends can be attributed neither to differences in costs, as the manufacturing costs of all antibiotics are about the same; nor to differences in quality, as each batch of these antibiotics had to be certified by the Food and Drug Administration; nor to a shortage of supply, as idle capacity existed for the production of all antibiotics.

A similar contrast appears in Figure 19-2, in a comparison of one of the newer patented forms of penicillin (V-Cillin), sold by only one drug company, with the trends in the older, nonpatented forms, sold by small as well as large companies. Since its introduction in 1956 the price of V-Cillin, like the prices of the broad-spectrum antibiotics, is represented by a straight line. During the same period the price charged by the same company for the older penicillin in tablet form declined by 14 percent, while the bulk price dropped by 60 percent.

Figure 19-2

PENICILLIN—LILLY
Bulk prices compared with prices to druggists
1948–60

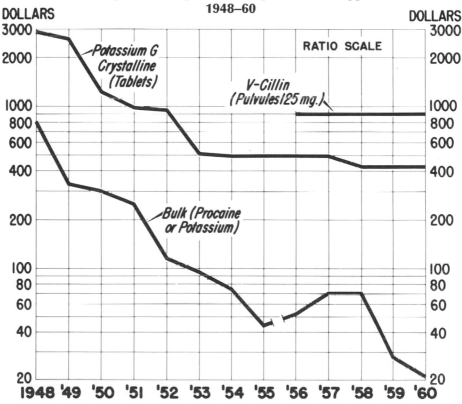

Source: *Administered Prices: Report on Drugs*, Chart 11

Because of a lengthy patent fight over prednisone and its companion product, prednisolone, during which time no patent was issued, a bulk market developed for these antiarthritic drugs somewhat similar to that for the unpatented penicillins. This market was supplied by small producers, by foreign concerns, and by some of the major companies. The availability of these competitive sources made it possible for small manufacturers to sell those drugs in package form to drugstores and institutional buyers under their generic names. As can be seen from Figure 19-3, substantial differences existed between the prices of the small and the large companies (the overall size of the companies is shown along the horizontal scale). Three major companies—Schering, Upjohn, and Merck—charged the same price, $17.90. With total annual sales in the $1- to $5-million range, Physicians' Drug & Supply had the lowest price, $4.85. Two even smaller firms—Bryant and Penhurst—offered prednisone for $6.75 and $6.95, respectively.

In addition to sales through drugstores, drugs are sold to institutional buyers —private nonprofit hospitals, state and local government hospitals, clinics and dispensaries, and federal agencies. To help hold down costs, it has become a common practice for institutional buyers to use generic formularies and to purchase from large and small suppliers on a price basis. The largest institutional buyer is the Department of Defense, which purchases drugs through its procurement arm for medical supplies, the Military Medical Supply Agency (MMSA). Its experience in buying drugs is illustrated in Figure 19-4, which was prepared from data for 44 products purchased in significant quantities during 1959 and early 1960. In each case the lowest price at which MMSA was able to buy during the period is expressed as a percentage of the price to the retail druggist for the same product sold under the brand names of the large

Figure 19-3

PREDNISONE
Wholesale prices by size of company, 1959 [a]

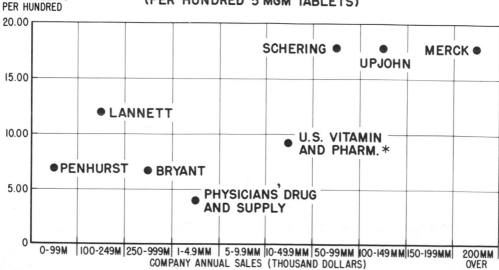

Source: *Administered Prices: Report on Drugs*, Chart 13

CONSTRAINTS ON OLIGOPOLISTIC PRICING

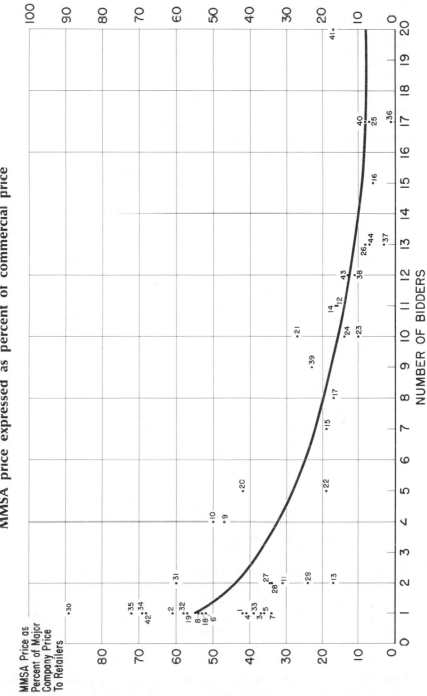

Figure 19-4

MMSA DRUG PROCUREMENT [a]

Relationship of number of bidders to

MMSA price expressed as percent of commercial price

Source: *Administered Prices: Report on Drugs*, Chart 16

companies. Inasmuch as the average sale is substantially larger and advertising and selling costs are considerably less on sales to MMSA, it is to be expected that prices to the government will be at a substantial discount below prices to the retail druggist. What is of interest here is the difference in the discount among products with differing numbers of bidders.

The scatter reveals clearly the existence of an inverse relationship between MMSA prices and the number of bidders; the greater the number of available suppliers, the larger the discount.[32] A free-hand curve, fitted to the plotted points to show the approximate relationship between MMSA prices and the number of bidders, tends to fall sharply as the number of sellers rises. When its sources of supply are limited to a single firm or a very few companies, MMSA pays prices far closer to the price paid by the retail druggist than when, say, 10 firms are competing for the agency's contracts. There were 15 products in which 10 or more companies sought the agency's business. On more than two-thirds of these products MMSA was able to secure discounts of 85 percent or more below the prices charged to the commercial trade for principal brands. At the other end of the chart were 24 products for which there were only one to 4 bidders. On none of these concentrated 24 products did MMSA obtain a discount of this magnitude, and on more than half its discount was less than 50 percent. All of the products of which MMSA received a discount of more than 90 percent had more than 12 bidders; all of the products on which its discount was less than 40 percent had only one bidder.

The effect of small producers on price is evident also from the experience of some large firms which have ventured outside their traditional oligopolistic industry into a highly competitive, atomistic field. Not infrequently they have found it impossible to cope with the intense price competition that is the normal way of life in such industries. The experiences of the Aluminum Company of America in aluminum cable and of International Harvester in electric refrigerators are cases in point:

> For several years after the war . . . Alcoa realized its target return or better on cable. By 1954, however, the capacity of the available aluminum stranding equipment in the United States surpassed the demand for cable, and price cutting broke out in the market. In order to obtain business, Alcoa was forced to bid on contracts at firm prices with no provision for escalation to compensate for increasing costs over the longer terms. This situation has persisted since mid-1954, in the face of increased base metal and labor costs, and Alcoa has fallen far short of its target. Company officers stated in 1956 that rigorous price competition on cable prevailed, especially from the eight non-integrated fabricators. The company has found it difficult to make a recent increase of around 5 per cent stick in the market.[33]

The experience of International Harvester in trying to sell electric refrigerators, priced on the basis of its target formula, was similar. The company had entered the refrigerator industry as a logical extension from home freezers, for which it enjoyed at one time about half the national market. Its venture into the refrigerator field, however, fell far short of anticipations: "It is clear that the company was not able to price refrigerators in terms of the general target, but found it necessary to accept the industry price structure and concentrate on production

---

[32] The number of "available suppliers" has been considered to be the number of firms that actually entered bids for MMSA contracts during the period covered by the tabulation.
[33] Kaplan, Dirlam, Lanzillotti, *op. cit.,* p. 134.

costs." [34] Finally, it abandoned the whole effort, selling its refrigerator plant to Whirlpool-Seeger: "The withdrawal of International Harvester from the refrigeration field may have resulted in part from the inflexibility of its standard cost pricing in a market where products are priced at a conventional figure, and cost is tailored accordingly." [35]

Import competition

The unsettling influence of foreign competition has already been illustrated by the experiences of the petroleum industry between 1958 and 1959 and of the aluminum industry during the early 1960's. Foreign supplies have also filled an important gap in the demand for automobiles. The U.S. demand for low-priced foreign cars tends to reach a peak about every 10 years. To meet this competition the American manufacturers then put on the market "compact" or "low-price economy" makes. But because profit per car tends to rise as the size of the vehicle increases, there is a natural tendency for the dimensions, weight, accouterments, and price to be upgraded with the passage of time. Yesteryear's compacts become the medium-price models of today. The logical consequence is of course an increase in imports, which in turn impels the domestic manufacturers to offer still newer "subcompacts," thus starting the cycle all over again. As had been true 10 years earlier, imports by the late 1960's had reached sizable proportions, which undoubtedly contributed to GM's below-target earnings in 1967 and 1968. In the steel industry imports have also been a source of growing concern which, though limited largely to low-profit products (e.g., reinforcing bars and wire products), have nonetheless made it necessary for the steel companies to spread their fixed costs over a smaller volume of production.

In some cases the loss of U.S. markets to foreign imports seems almost self-induced. In the early 1950's the U.S. steel industry appears to have made a conscious decision to abandon any effort to compete in world markets. The reason for this decision remains obscure, for up to that time the United States had been a net exporter of steel. Aided by various forms of government assistance the U.S. industry had emerged from World War II with some of the most efficient steel-making plants in the world. Of the three roughly coequal elements in steel-making costs—coking coal, iron ore, and labor—it enjoyed a great advantage over the rest of the world in the first and a moderate advantage in the second. When allowance is made for the greater productivity of its mills, the effect on its costs of higher wage rates could not possibly have offset its advantage in materials costs.

But whatever the reason, the U.S. industry's export prices by the later 1950's had begun to move independently of world export prices. As can be seen in the accompanying chart (Figure 19-5), presented to the Senate Antitrust Subcommittee by Egon Sohmen, the export price of the European steel industry declined during the 1957–58 recession, dropping further in the following year, whereas the U.S. industry's export price moved steadily upward.[36] In 1955 the U.S. price had been well below the European figure ($103 versus $122 per ton), but by 1958 they were about on a par ($125 versus $129). Thereafter, except in 1960 when a strike-induced shortage in the U.S. industry caused world prices to shoot up, the U.S. price has been above the European price. During the early

[34] *Ibid.,* p. 140.
[35] *Ibid.*
[36] *Hearings on Economic Concentration,* Pt. 7, pp. 3444–46, testimony of Egon Sohmen.

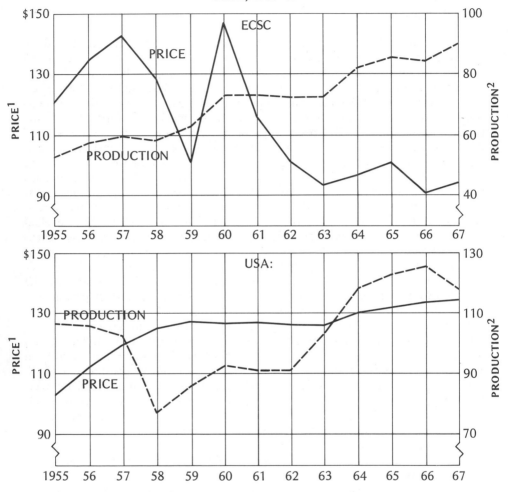

Figure 19-5

STEEL EXPORT PRICES AND PRODUCTION

European Coal and Steel Community and United
States, 1955–67

[1]Average export prices, open–hearth grade, beginning of year, per metric ton.

[2]Millions of metric tons.

Source: 88th Cong., 1st Sess., Joint Economic Committee, *Hearings on Economic Concentration*, "Steel Prices, Unit Costs, Profits, and Foreign Competition," pp. 186, 339

1960's the European price fell sharply, declining from $117 in 1961 to $96 in 1964, whereas the U.S. price moved moderately upward from $127 to $130. During the next 3 years the European price fluctuated within a narrow range, reaching a level of $94 in 1967, while the U.S. price continued its advance, rising to $134. For the 12-year period as a whole the U.S. price had thus changed from 15 percent below to 42 percent above the European price.

As the chart also brings out, the declining trend of the European price was accompanied by a generally rising level of output. Indeed, the trend of European steel production bears a striking resemblance to the price trend of the U.S. industry. In the United States the trend of production was downward from 1955 to 1958, relatively stable during 1959–63; noticeably upward during the next 3 years, and downward again during 1966–67. For the 12-year period, the increase in European steel production was 70 percent as compared to only 11 percent in the United States. Between 1955 and 1967 European steel production rose from exactly half to more than three-fourths of U.S. output.

The consequences of the withdrawal from world trade not only on the steel industry but on the entire U.S. economy can hardly be exaggerated. As Sohmen put it:

> Had the industry worked at capacity during the early sixties, and had it exported the additional steel at world market prices, the additional export revenue (taking into account the fact that steel prices on the world market would have been somewhat lower as a consequence) would have eliminated the U.S. balance-of-payments deficits during these years. One need hardly go into details of what the United States would have been spared in this event.
>
> This comparison is, if anything, likely to understate the contribution of high steel prices to the U.S. balance-of-payments troubles. If steel prices in the United States had uniformly been at the lower world market levels, many important American industries using steel (the automobile or the machinery industries to name only a few), could have reduced their prices. This would have entailed a rise of exports of these industries and a fall of competing imports, further improving the U.S. trade balance.

Sohmen discounted the importance of cost differentials as an explanation for the difference in prices:

> While imports must necessarily exceed exports for certain commodities in order to carry on fruitful international exchange, steel appears to be a particularly unlikely candidate for this ever to have happened in the United States. Steel is produced in a highly capital-intensive industry, and the country most abundantly equipped with capital relative to labor ought to enjoy a definite comparative advantage in its production. Coal, one of the principal raw materials for steel, is substantially cheaper in the United States than in Western Europe, while iron ore is at least not more expensive than elsewhere.
>
> High wages, the factor usually blamed by American steelmen for uncompetitive steel prices, have not prevented other American industries, many of them considerably more labor-intensive than the steel industry, from enjoying a competitive advantage on the world markets.

In Sohmen's view the real explanation was the absence of "competitive behavior" in the United States and its presence in Europe, at least during the period in question:

> By contrast, and in sharp contrast also to its behavior before the war, the West European steel industry has exhibited highly competitive behavior until very recently. A number of possible reasons come to mind. Most important among them was undoubtedly the gradual elimination of steel tariffs between the six member countries of the European Coal and Steel Community after 1952 which sharply reduced the market power of individual steel producers in the enlarged market. There was no single overpowering giant comparable to the United States Steel Corp. in the Ameri-

can market. This result was materially helped by the postwar deconcentration measures of the Allied occupation authorities in Germany. Among other things, these measures involved the dissolution of the Vereingte Stahlwerke, by far the largest steel producer in prewar Europe.

The elasticity of demand

In addition to the force of competition, the price-making discretion of oligopolists is restricted by the adverse effect of price increases on sales. Sir Dennis Robertson is authority for the observation that businessmen in his long experience almost invariably, and usually erroneously, regarded the demand for their industry's products as inelastic with respect to price. This appraisal is certainly in accord with the position taken, indeed emphasized, by representatives of large enterprises before congressional committees and elsewhere. If the management of a dominant oligopolist believes demand for its industry to be inelastic (i.e., that a given percentage increase in price will result in a smaller percentage decrease in sales) and if, for whatever cause, the realized profit rate has fallen below the target, what course of action to ensure the attainment of the target would seem more logical than an increase in price? If, however, demand were elastic, the price increase would compound the problem, since it would lead to a proportionately greater decline in sales, for the correction of which an additional price increase might be regarded as the logical remedy, and so on *ad infinitum*.

Spokesmen for the steel industry have long taken the position that demand for their products is inelastic. The demand for steel is "derived," reaching the consumer through products made from steel. Since steel is only one of the cost elements, it would take a very sizable reduction in steel prices, the argument runs, to bring about any reduction in *their* prices. Statistical support for this position was provided in an elaborate study of the elasticity of demand for steel, prepared by Theodore Yntema for the U.S. Steel Corporation and submitted to the Temporary National Economic Committee:

> The statistical analysis indicates, although not entirely conclusively, that the demand for steel is very inelastic, i.e. that changes in the levels of steel prices (other conditions of steel demand remaining the same) cause much smaller percentage changes in the opposite direction in the quantity of steel sold. The best estimate of the elasticity of demand for steel indicated by this analysis is approximately 0.3 or 0.4.
>
> This means that very large reductions in price would be necessary to effect significant increases in the volume of sales.[37]

The conclusion that the demand for steel is "very inelastic" should not, however, be accepted without reservation. As is true of any product for which the demand is derived, to know the elasticity of demand for steel it is necessary to know the aggregate elasticity of demand for the various consumer products in which it is ultimately incorporated. Such a body of knowledge does not exist. And it is virtually impossible to determine the relationship of the *total* cost of steel to the price of a finished consumer product. While crude estimates can be made, based upon such factors as the amount of steel in a finished product, they ignore the amount of steel used by manufacturers of parts and components sold to the consuming industry; they ignore the amount of steel lost in the process of

[37] TNEC Hearings, *op. cit.*, Pt. 26, p. 13914.

fabrication; they ignore the indirect costs of steel affecting the product's prices —i.e., the cost of steel that enters into machines and equipment, into buildings, into transportation, and so on.

Price increases in steel serve to delimit the ability of the consuming industries, some of which may have relatively high elasticities of demand, to lower *their* prices. To the producers of finished goods, the constantly rising prices for steel exert an upward pressure on costs that may make it difficult for them to reduce prices, even if they are so inclined. It is conceivable that were they able to reduce their prices, their sales might increase to such an extent as to generate a significant increase in the demand for steel. But whether this might in fact prove to be the reality is something that is not likely to be known as long as the price of the basic material rarely declines.

Finally, a distinction must be made between the short run and the long run. Confronted with a recession, the steel industry probably could do little, by itself, to reverse a decline in demand for its products. But the long-range effect of a continuing upward trend in its price is to spur its users into finding ways of using cheaper, alternative materials. Each increase in the price of steel gives a further impetus to the demand for plastics, fiberglass, prestressed concrete, cement, and other substitute materials. The process of substition is of course accelerated if, as has been true of most of these materials, the prices of substitutes have been declining while the price of steel has been moving upward.[38] As has been pointed out by Frank J. Kottke:

> Decisions on prices have been made on a wrong conception of the nature of demand. Steel company officials who appeared before this committee seemed to believe that the amount of steel the American economy will absorb is affected very little by price changes of $5 to $10 a ton. While this probably is so in the short run, over a period of 2 or 3 years consumers respond to a price rise by cutting back on their use of steel. Between the 3-year period ending with 1949 and the 3-year period ending with 1961, our gross national output—in dollars of constant purchasing power—increased 52 percent, while steel production grew only 16 percent. Steel exports fell by over half. The output of cement rose 63 percent; the output of polystyrene, 520 percent; and the apparent consumption of aluminum, about 175 percent. Steel consumption has grown far less rapidly than steel-making capacity, and part-time operations result in substantially higher unit costs. Thus the industry is in danger of being trapped in a vicious circle, with increases in unit costs leading to higher prices, which lead to lower plant utilization, which in turn would lead to still higher unit costs, and to still higher prices.[39]

Between 1955 and 1968—both years of high economic activity—industrial production rose by 71 percent. But the increase in the available domestic supply of steel products (domestic shipments plus imports minus exports) was only 32 percent. Obviously, most of the expansion in the industrial economy must have been based on the use of materials other than steel.

In contrast to steel the demand for automobiles has been found to be elastic. Most studies of the subject are in agreement that a one-percent increase in price will be accompanied by a decline in new car purchases ranging from 1.2 to 1.5 percent. Demand with respect to income has been found to be even more elastic, a one-percent decrease in income being accompanied by a decline in new-car pur-

[38] See Ch. 6.
[39] *Hearings on Administered Prices*, Pt. 29, pp. 18043–44.

chases ranging from 2.5 to 4.2 percent. Using conservative estimates of elasticities of −1.2 for price and 3.0 for income, the combined effect on automobile sales of given percentage changes in per capita income and relative price is shown in Table 19-2.[40] If income were to remain unchanged, the automobile companies could increase sales 6 percent by reducing prices 5 percent. A price decrease of this magnitude would offset a 2-percent reduction in income. But a 5-percent increase in price would mean a 6-percent decrease in annual purchases. If, in addition, real per capita income fell by 4 percent, a 5-percent price increase would mean a decline of 18 percent in purchases, which, considering the pivotal importance of the automobile industry, would have a serious depressing effect on the entire economy; the combination of a 10-percent increase in price and a 6-percent decrease in income would produce the calamitous result of a 30-percent decrease in new-car purchases.

In industries with elastic demand the maintenance of relatively stable prices during periods of rapid economic expansion contributes to the meeting of the target objective, since the stimulus to sales resulting from higher incomes is not offset by the depressing effects on demand of an increase in price. But in times of recession the attempt to offset the decline in revenues by raising prices may make a bad situation worse. Depending on how elastic demand is and how rapidly unit fixed costs rise with declining output, a policy of raising prices, coupled with the decline taking place in income, may make the target rate unattainable. Under such circumstances the type of price behavior customarily followed in downswings by concentrated industries would be self-defeating.

Monopsony and oligopsony

The area of discretion available to oligopolistic price makers is limited also by the bargaining power of large buyers, which, where effective, represents a true case of J. Kenneth Galbraith's "countervailing power." For products sold mainly to a few large buyers, even the possibility that they may take their business elsewhere or, worse, establish their own sources of supply injects a strong note of moderation in the price-making process. This is a consideration that even the most powerful supplier must bear in mind. In the words of the Brookings study, "the net effect of the bargaining position of tin plate users like American Can and Continental will, of course, impose limitations on the ability of the corporation [U.S. Steel] to extract high profits in this market." [41] The can manufacturers must in turn concern themselves with the possibility that *their* customers may enter into the can-making business:

> The fact that the largest canners may undertake their own manufacture of containers must mean that American and Continental have to keep the price of the can and the servicing of customers under the "roll your own" costs of canners in manufacturing. It is not certain that other large customers will not emulate such large can users as Campbell's Soup, Heinz, Pet Milk, Carnation, Sherwin Williams and Texas Company, which are manufacturing their own cans in whole or in part.[42]

[40] See *Administered Prices: Report on Automobiles,* pp. 130–51, esp. App. A, pp. 184–94 by Marc Nerlove; *Hearings on Administered Prices,* Pt. 6, Sen. Paul Douglas, pp. 3281–317.
[41] Kaplan, Dirlam, Lanzillotti, *op. cit.,* p. 173.
[42] *Ibid.,* p. 210.

Table 19-2

PERCENTAGE CHANGES IN ANNUAL PURCHASE
OF AUTOMOBILES PER CAPITA

As related to percentage changes in income per capita and to
percentage changes in relative price of automobiles

Percent Change In Relative Price	Percent Change in Income (Per Capita in Constant Dollars)						
	−8	−6	−4	−2	0	+2	+4
+10	−36	−30	−24	−18	−12	−6	0
+5	−30	−24	−18	−12	−6	0	6
0	−24	−18	−12	−6	0	6	12
−5	−18	−12	−6	0	6	12	18
−10	−12	−6	0	6	12	18	24
−15	−6	0	6	12	18	24	30
−20	0	6	12	18	24	30	36

Source: *Administered Prices: Report on Automobiles,* Table 28, p. 145

Although theirs is a highly concentrated industry, the large tire makers are confronted with strong buyers in both the original equipment and the replacement markets: "In the original equipment market, the powerful automobile manufacturers, capitalizing in part on the advertising provided by the selection of a tire as original equipment, have been able, by negotiating with a few firms, to force prices to levels well (perhaps 50 per cent) below those charged to any customer for replacement purposes." [43] In the replacement market the tire makers are also confronted with large buyers—mail order houses, oil companies, auto supply chains—who market tires under their own private brands: "The private brands have undercut the factory brands and necessitated a continuous procession of sales and special discounts, allowances and so on. . . ." [44]

One way by which a supplier may meet the reality of monopsony and still retain the principle of target return pricing is to establish a relatively low target for products purchased by large buyers. Thus, in the case of Union Carbide, the dominant firm for certain chemicals, "the target return for gas products is normally lower than for chemicals. The major fraction of the Linde gas output is taken by large customers like du Pont and Detroit Steel—a situation also found in some chemicals and alloys." [45] More simply, in instituting a general price increase a supplier may make an exemption of those particular products that are purchased by large buyers. After the wage settlement of August, 1971, U.S. Steel and other leading steel producers announced an across-the-board price increase of 8 percent, the largest advance since the mid-1950's. Shortly thereafter, however, Bethlehem announced that it would not apply the increase—to have become effective on December 1—to the industry's most important product, cold-rolled sheets. Accounting for nearly one-fifth of the industry's output (and a higher proportion of its earnings), cold-rolled sheets are used principally in the manufacture of automobiles and other consumer durable goods. The *New York Times* reported that under an agreement between the steel producers and

[43] *Ibid.*, p. 202.
[44] *Ibid.*, p. 203.
[45] *Ibid.*, p. 162.

the automobile manufacturers, an exemption was to have been made for cold-rolled sheets produced before December 1, even though actual shipment was not made until after that date.[46] In anticipation of a steel strike, which did not materialize, the automakers had stockpiled sizable steel inventories, and the steel mills were starved for orders. Bethlehem refused to go along with this understanding, electing instead to make a public announcement. According to the *Times,* an "automobile executive added . . . that Bethlehem's motives might not have been entirely public-spirited. 'They don't have as much warehouse capacity as some of the other major steel companies and possibly couldn't have taken on this make-and-hold proposition,' he said." [47]

[46] *New York Times,* Aug. 13, 1971.
[47] *Ibid.*

THE ECONOMIC EFFECTS
OF OLIGOPOLY

Under classical theory the criticism of monopoly was that it prevents an optimal allocation of resources. That concentration prevents not only an optimal allocation but an optimal use of resources can be shown from an empirical examination of its specific effects. Although interacting with one another, these effects can be classified under a number of groupings.

There is, first, what may be termed the *efficiency* effect, which happens also to be a cause of structural change. Because they have customarily been treated as causes, this type of effect was examined in Part II of this work. Under today's conditions one of the effects of concentration, as compared to a more competitive, or polyopolistic, economy, would appear to be higher costs, particularly those arising from managerial diseconomies. A corollary effect would appear to be a slower rate of invention, and possibly also, a slower rate of innovation.

Another grouping is what might be referred to as the *price behavioral* effects. In Part IV it was found that rising concentration was accompanied by decreasing depression price flexibility; that prices of concentrated industries declined less than those of unconcentrated industries during the 1929–32 depression; that in the recessions of 1953–54 and 1957–58 prices of concentrated industries tended to behave perversely by rising; that in upturns they have regularly risen less rapidly than prices in unconcentrated industries; but that in the postwar era their long-term increase has been considerably greater than that of unconcentrated industries.

A further result concerns the distribution of income—the *income* effect. This effect can be examined through an analysis of the relationship of concentration to margins (above direct costs) and to profits.

Concentration can also have an adverse effect on the rate of *production* (and thus employment), particularly if during a downswing it makes possible the clearing of the market by a greater curtailment in output and a lesser reduction in price than would obtain under competition.

Finally, the perverse price flexibility of concentrated industries during recessions not only frustrates efforts to arrest inflation by a *policy* of monetary and fiscal restrictions but makes a bad situation worse, leading inexorably to the direct control of prices by the state.

This chapter will be concerned with the *income, production,* and *policy* effects of concentration.

The income effect

If concentration makes for prices which, in relation to costs, remain for extended periods significantly above the level that would prevail under competition, the result will tend to be a redistribution of income favoring recipients with higher savings and lower consumption patterns of income use.

The overhead-plus-profits margin

The difference between price and the inescapable materials and labor costs of production has been referred to variously as "overhead plus profits," "indirect costs plus profits," or the "margin above direct costs," and includes, in addition to profits, all of the various forms of indirect costs such as insurance, taxes, interest, research and development expenses, costs of maintenance and repair, depreciation, and advertising and other selling costs. If concentration tends to result in margins higher than would prevail under competition, a greater proportion of income will go to interest and monopoly profits as well as to other forms of monopoly gains.[1] George J. Stigler has called attention to the existence of monopoly gains in payments to factors of production other than capital: "the magnitude of monopoly elements in wages, executive compensation, royalties and rents is possibly quite large." [2] All but the first is part of the overhead-plus-profits margin.

For different reasons three of the principal components of the margin—depreciation, advertising and selling costs, and profits—tend to be greater in concentrated than in unconcentrated industries. Thus, it has long been assumed that, in general, concentrated industries tend to be more capital-intensive and will accordingly incur higher depreciation charges. Similarly, as industries become concentrated, price competition tends to be replaced by the various forms of nonprice competition, with a resulting increase in expenditures on the latter. And, whether the objective is profit maximization or a target rate of return, the profit objective will be higher, and the probability of achieving it greater, under oligopoly than under competition.[3]

The analysis of the overhead-plus-profits margin is facilitated by a prosaic but not unimportant attribute: the margin can be derived from Census data for each of the 400-odd manufacturing industries. And, as is *not* the case of analyses based on profit data, the different types of data involved are available on an unconsolidated basis (i.e., only that portion of a firm's total margin which is applicable to a given industry relates to that industry).

The procedure of computing the gross margin involves a series of subtractions. The starting point is the Census Bureau's measure of total output—i.e., value of shipments—from which the Bureau derives value added by manufacture by subtracting the cost of materials, supplies and containers, fuel, purchased electric energy, and contract work. From value added, wages or wages and salaries (total payroll) can then be subtracted, yielding the difference between price and direct

---

[1] See K. W. Rothschild's comment on Kenneth Boulding's "In Defense of Monopoly," *Quarterly Journal of Economics,* Aug., 1946, pp. 615–18.

[2] George J. Stigler, "The Statistics of Monopoly and Merger," *Journal of Political Economy,* Feb., 1956, p. 35.

[3] For a further discussion of the reasons why profit rates may be expected to be higher in concentrated industries, see pp. 532–36.

Table 20-1

AVERAGE GROSS MARGINS FOR 417 MANUFACTURING INDUSTRIES, 1963

Concentration Ratio	Number of Industries	Average Gross Margins
50% and over	114	30.5%
21% to 49%	204	24.0
Under 21%	99	22.5
Total	417	24.9

Source: Norman R. Collins and Lee E. Preston, "Price-Cost Margins and Industry Structure," *Review of Economics and Statistics*, Aug., 1969, p. 272

costs.[4] To translate it into relative terms this residual is then divided by a measure of the industry's output.[5]

For manufacturing as a whole a study by Norman R. Collins and Lee E. Preston reveals the percentage gross margin, in relation to value of shipments, to be considerably greater in concentrated than in unconcentrated industries; in industries of moderate concentration the margin is between the two extremes. In their words, "For industries with four-firm concentration less than 50 percent, average margins are less than 25%. . . . By contrast, average margins for industries with more than 50 percent concentration tend to be substantially higher."[6] (See Table 20-1.)

[4] Norman R. Collins and Lee E. Preston have narrowed the margin further by deriving from special Census studies estimates for maintenance and repair, insurance premiums, rental payments, property taxes, and supplemental employee costs, which, in addition to payrolls, were subtracted from value added (Norman R. Collins and Lee E. Preston, *Concentration and Price Cost Margins in Manufacturing Industries,* University of California Press, 1968, p. 56).

[5] The preferred measure would be one of physical quantities produced. Except for simple industries with homogeneous products (e.g., cement) such measures are available only in the form of indexes over time. And studies of the change in margins over time have generally been made on this basis (i.e., in terms of margins per unit of output). But to determine the actual margin as of a given year, the only measure available for any large number of industries is value of shipments. For this purpose, however, its use results in a bias. If the hypothesis being tested is that indirect costs and profits tend to be above average in concentrated industries, those above-average costs and profits will be included not only in the margin of the concentrated industries (the numerator) but in their value of shipments as well (the denominator). The result of course is a tendency to understate the margin in the concentrated industries.

[6] Norman R. Collins and Lee E. Preston, "Price Cost Margins and Industry Structure," *Review of Economics and Statistics,* Aug., 1969. In the summary table the figures shown are unweighted averages for 3 groups of the gross margins shown for 10 by Collins and Preston. The average margins in terms of deciles are as follows:

Concentration Ratio Decile	Number of Industries	Average Gross Margins	Concentration Ratio Decile	Number of Industries	Average Gross Margins
1–10	20	23.3%	51–60	41	26.7%
11–20	79	21.8	61–70	32	28.5
21–30	76	24.0	71–80	18	29.0
31–40	79	24.2	81–90	11	38.0
41–50	49	23.8	91–100	12	30.2

(*Ibid.,* p. 272.)

Figure 20-1

COMPARISON OF CONCENTRATION RATIOS, 1963

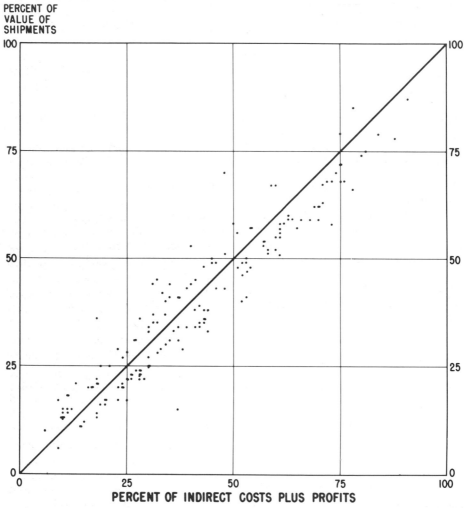

PERCENT OF
VALUE OF
SHIPMENTS

PERCENT OF INDIRECT COSTS PLUS PROFITS

Source: *Concentration Ratios in Manufacturing Industry, 1963, 1966.*

That the association of higher margins with concentration does not stem merely from the influence of a few large-scale industries is indicated by a comparison for individual industries of the concentration of output with the concentration of the margin. In Figure 20-1, the vertical scale shows for each of 164 industries the share of its shipments made by its 4 leading firms, the horizontal scale their share of the overhead-plus-profits margin.[7] Industries with identical ratios for the two measures would fall on the line of equal proportions, drawn diagonally from the lower left-hand to the upper right-hand corners of the chart. In the case of indus-

---

[7] To simplify graphic exposition small industries, defined as those with shipments of less than $250 million, were excluded, as were those in which the difference between the two measures was less than 3 percentage points.

tries falling below the line the proportion of the margin accounted for by the largest companies is greater than their share of the industry's output. For example, an observation near the upper right corner of the chart reveals that for this industry (household laundry equipment) the 4 largest companies accounted for 74 percent of the shipments but 80 percent of the margin. Conversely, for those industries falling above the line the largest companies accounted for a smaller share of the margin than of shipments.

For the entire range of concentration the industries are about equally distributed above and below the line of equal proportions. But in nearly four-fifths of the concentrated industries (39 of 50) the 4 leading firms accounted for a greater share of the margin than of output. In other words, relative to total output the 4 largest companies in these industries made greater profits and/or incurred greater indirect costs than their smaller competitors.

Collins and Preston also examined the effect on margins of differences in the types of market: "In general, we would expect that producer goods markets might be characterized by greater specifications and other 'objective' purchasing criteria, and lesser emphasis on product differentiation by source and brand than consumer goods markets." Their expectation was confirmed: "the regression coefficient for concentration is much higher for consumer than for producer goods industries. Concentration alone explains 26 percent of the variation in margins in the former, compared with only 4 percent in the latter." [8] This conclusion is of course consistent with the findings, shown earlier, that increases in concentration have predominated among consumer goods industries and decreases among producer goods industries. Within consumer goods, however, Collins and Preston found no difference in the effect of concentration on margins in industries with undifferentiated products as contrasted to those whose products are differentiated by brand or trade names: "no clear difference in the concentration-margins relationship between less-differentiated and more-differentiated consumer products industries emerges." [9] And this is not inconsistent with the conclusion that among consumer goods industries the critical factor associated with increasing concentration is not whether the products are differentiated but whether they are promoted extensively through TV advertising.[10]

With respect to the trend of margins over time Alfred C. Neal found during the Depression "some correlation between concentration and changes in the overhead-plus-profit margin per unit . . . concentration did have a small but significant influence upon the decline in the difference between unit price and unit direct cost . . . the overhead-plus-profit margin. This margin tended to decline least where the concentration was high; most where it was low. The relationship is not clear-cut but it is consistent with theoretical presumptions." [11] Neal was able to obtain continuous margin data from 1929 to 1937 for 67 industries, which he grouped into three classes—industries of low, medium, and high concentration (see Table 20-2). Between 1929 and 1933 the unit margins in industries of low concentration fell by nearly one-third. Although suffering a greater decline in physical production (−26 percent versus −15 percent), the industries of high concentration registered a margin decrease of only −15 percent. For industries of moderate concentration the decline in margins was between these extremes.

[8] Collins and Preston, *op. cit.*
[9] *Ibid.*
[10] See Ch. 13.
[11] Alfred C. Neal, *Industrial Concentration and Price Inflexibility,* American Council on Public Affairs, 1942, pp. 137, 165–66.

Table 20-2

INDEXES OF UNIT OVERHEAD-PLUS-PROFITS MARGIN AND PRODUCTION, 1929–1937

Year	Low Concentration		Medium Concentration		High Concentration	
	Margin	Production	Margin	Production	Margin	Production
1929	100.0	100.0	100.0	100.0	100.0	100.0
1931	76.8	83.7	84.4	80.1	92.0	77.4
1933	68.3	85.0	75.1	73.5	85.7	74.4
1935	70.2	99.5	76.0	89.0	78.3	88.1
1937	72.0	109.7	78.4	109.5	80.9	107.9

Source: Alfred C. Neal, *Industrial Concentration and Price Inflexibility,* Council of Public Affairs, 1942, p. 137

Table 20-3

DISTRIBUTION OF CHANGES IN UNIT OVERHEAD-PLUS-PROFITS MARGIN, 1929–1931[a]

42 manufacturing industries

Concentration Ratio	Total	Change in Margin			
		−20% and Over	−10% to −19%	0% to −9%	Increase
50% and over	22	4	3	10	5
25% to 49%	11	3	4	3	1
Under 25%	9	5	2	2	
Total	42	12	9	15	6

[a]Of the Census years Ross regarded 1931 as preferable to 1933, owing to the stimulus imparted to the economy by recovery measures taken in the latter year.

Source: Howard Norman Ross, *The Theory and Evidence of Price Flexibility,* doctoral dissertation, Columbia University, 1964, p. 181

Similar findings for the Depression were reached by Howard Norman Ross, who examined the change in unit gross margins in 42 industries.[12] As will be seen from Table 20-3, in more than two-thirds of the 22 concentrated industries the unit gross margin declined by less than 10 percent or actually increased. In contrast, more than half of the unconcentrated industries registered margin decreases of 20 percent or more.

Earlier it was shown that during the early 1930's prices in concentrated industries fell less than prices in unconcentrated industries. The findings of Neal and Ross make it clear that during the Depression prices fell less in concentrated than in unconcentrated industries *in relation to the decreases in their materials and labor costs.*

In the years following World War II changes in unit margins can be derived only for those Census years for which comparable indexes of production are available, to date only 1954, 1958, and 1963. A comparison between 1954 and

[12] Howard Norman Ross, *The Theory and Evidence of Price Flexibility,* doctoral dissertation, Columbia University, 1964.

Table 20-4

CHANGE IN UNIT OVERHEAD-PLUS-PROFITS MARGIN

Concentration Ratio	1954–58		1954–63	
	Number of Industries	Change in Margin	Number of Industries	Change in Margin
50% and over	42	24.0%	42	29.7%
25% to 49%	37	18.8	37	26.7
Under 25%	29	13.5	29	19.2
Total	108	19.4	108	28.1

Source: Howard Norman Ross, "Relative Prices and Margins," article to be published

1958 involves 2 recession years; a comparison between 1954 and 1963 involves a recession year and one of a considerably higher (though not rapidly rising) rate of economic activity. For the former there is no particular reason to assume any differential change in the margin of concentrated as against unconcentrated industries. For the latter, the expectation would be for a greater margin increase in unconcentrated industries, since it has been well established that during an interval of rising economic activity their prices tend to rise more rapidly than prices of concentrated industries. Unit overhead-plus-profits margins have been computed by Ross for both intervals, covering over 100 industries. The comparison between the recession years is shown in Table 20-4.[13]

Between 1954 and 1958 the margin increase of 13.5 percent for the unconcentrated industries was well exceeded by the increase of 24 percent for the concentrated industries. Despite the expectation to the contrary, margins in concentrated industries also showed a greater increase between the recession year of 1954 and the more prosperous year of 1963. In 9 years the difference between labor and material costs and price widened in the case of concentrated industries by nearly 30 percent, as compared to less than 20 percent in unconcentrated industries. In both periods margins for industries with concentration ratios of between 25 and 49 percent rose less than margins in concentrated industries but more than those in unconcentrated industries.

The influence of concentration can be seen more clearly if one compares the percent change in unit margins of those industries in which concentration registered a marked increase (of over 5 percentage points) with those in which it recorded a corresponding decline (see Table 20-5). In those industries where concentration rose by more than 10 percentage points, the increase in margins (42 percent) can only be regarded as extraordinary. And those whose concentration increased from 5 to 10 percentage points also enjoyed a substantial margin gain (28 percent). But where concentration registered a marked decline (more than 5 percentage points), margins remained almost unchanged, rising less than 4 percent. An equally arresting showing is the distribution, by change in margin, of industries with increasing and decreasing concentration. Of the 22 industries with concentration increases of more than 5 percentage points, margins widened

[13] The sample of 108 industries was chosen on the basis of the consistency of Census and concentration data between 1954 and 1963 and the availability of production indexes. Numerous industry redefinitions in 1958 limited the sample, as did the following exclusions: industries not elsewhere classified, industries with local and regional markets, and industries where value of shipments data included sizable duplications due to interplant transfers.

Table 20-5

CHANGE IN CONCENTRATION RATIO AND
UNIT OVERHEAD-PLUS-PROFITS MARGIN, 1954–1963

(8-Companies)

Change in 8-Company Concentration Ratio	Change in Margin					
	Average Change		Number of Industries			
		Total	Over 10% Pts.	.1 to 10% Pts.	−.1 to −10% Pts.	Over −10% Pts.
Over 10% Pts.	41.6%	9	9	—	—	—
5.1 to 10% Pts.	27.7	13	10	2	1	—
−5.1 to −10% Pts.	3.7	12	5	1	3	3
Over −10% Pts.	3.9	3	1	—	1	1

Source: Howard Norman Ross "Relative Prices and Margins," article to be published

in all but one; and in 19 of the 22 the margin increase was more than 10 percent. Conversely, in the majority of industries with declining concentration (8 of 15), margins also decreased.

Earlier it was pointed out that two of the centripetal forces making for greater concentration are mergers and TV advertising. Reflecting the frequency of horizontal acquisitions, the textile industry was cited as an outstanding example of the former,[14] while examples of the latter are provided by virtually the whole spectrum of extensively advertised, differentiated consumer goods. Of the 22 industries in Ross's sample with concentration increases of more than 5 percentage points, 12 were of these two types (see Table 20-6).[15]

All but 2 of these 12 industries registered margin increases of more than 10 percent, and in only one, corsets and allied garments, did the margin decline. In the TV-advertised industries the increase in gross margins undoubtedly reflects the growing importance of advertising and selling costs—and possibly of widening profit margins as well. But in textiles advertising and selling costs are of distinctly minor importance, while no unusual advances appear to have taken place in the other forms of indirect costs. Consequently, the increase in the margin above direct costs strongly suggests a noticeable widening of textile profit margins —a remarkable achievement for an area widely regarded as in a "distressed" condition.

The 8 industries characterized by both declining concentration and narrowing margins were also widely scattered: one each in textiles (coated fabrics not rubberized); paper (pressed and molded pulp goods); chemicals (plastic materials and resins); rubber (rubber footwear); stone, clay, and glass (glass containers); fabricated metal products (fabricated pipe and fittings); machinery (commercial laundry equipment); and electrical machinery (transformers). About the only characteristic they share is that all but one (rubber footwear) are producer goods industries and are thus subject to the pressures of oligopsony and informed buyers. The narrowing of margins may also be associated in the case of glass containers with increasing competition from other types of containers, in the case

[14] See Chs. 1, 11.

[15] The remaining 10 industries with marked increases in concentration (and widening margins) appear to share no common characteristics—except for the increase in concentration: 3 were in stone, clay, and glass; 2 each in machinery and miscellaneous products; and one each in apparel, furniture, and petroleum.

Table 20-6

CHANGES IN CONCENTRATION RATIO AND
UNIT OVERHEAD-PLUS-PROFITS MARGIN, 1954–1963
2 groups of industries
(8-Companies)

Industry	Change in 8-Company Concentration Ratio	Change in Margin
Textile mill products		
Weaving mills, cotton	17% pts.	34.8%
Knit-underwear mills	12	62.2
Weaving mills, synthetics	9	11.6
Narrow-fabric mills	9	34.5
Thread mills	7	52.1
Knit-outerwear mills	6	5.0
TV-advertised products		
Cutlery (including razor blades)	15	60.6
Sporting and athletic goods	13	20.8
Toilet preparations	12	24.1
Household laundry equipment	10	34.5
Corsets and allied garments	7	– 4.1
Flavoring extracts and syrups[a]	7	15.7

[a]Includes beverage bases and soft drink syrups (e.g., cola syrups) manufactured for sale to local bottlers.

Source: Howard Norman Ross, "Relative Prices and Margins," article to be published

of plastics with the spectacular growth and increased competitiveness of the industry,[16] and in the case of transformers with the termination of a price fixing conspiracy.[17]

But no explanation suggests itself for the 7 anomalies in which declining concentration was accompanied by widening margins. Three were in furniture (metal office furniture, metal household furniture, and public-building furniture), and one each was in textiles (cordage and twine); stone, clay, glass (vitreous plumbing fixtures); and miscellaneous products (needles, pins, and fasteners).

The significant finding, however, is that in nearly four-fifths of the industries with a substantial change in concentration (more than 5 percentage points), increasing concentration was associated with widening margins and declining concentration with narrowing margins.

Earlier, data were presented pointing to the development during the last quarter of a century of a widening divergence in price trends between concentrated as compared to unconcentrated industries.[18] Between 1947 and 1966 the difference in these price trends is certainly consistent with the behavior of margins as shown above. During the interval for which margin data are available (1954 to 1963), products registering only one price change per year rose 5.6 percent, and those averaging 2 changes increased 11.3 percent. In contrast, those averaging 8 or more changes *fell* 14.0 percent. With the comparison limited to durable goods (to avoid the effect on the flexible group of distressed farm products), a pronounced divergence is also evident. Durable goods with one change per year

[16] See Ch. 6.
[17] See Ch. 21.
[18] See Ch. 17.

rose 20.7 percent, those with 2 changes 24.0 percent. But durable goods averaging 8 or more changes registered an increase of only 7.4 percent.

According to one widely accepted point of view, it is in the concentrated, inflexible-price industries that labor unions are strongest and increases in unit labor costs greatest. But the pronounced widening of the overhead-plus-profits margin in the concentrated industries makes it clear that the upward trend of their prices cannot be explained fully in terms of "cost-push" inflation, at least insofar as labor and material costs are concerned. The explanation must be found, in part, in the increasing relative importance of profits and/or indirect costs in concentrated industries.

Profits

While other consequences of concentration may be of equal or greater importance, it is the effect on profits that has received the greatest attention from economists. As Fritz Machlup has put it, "profits have long been regarded as the monopoly index *par excellence*. . . Of all the possible effects of monopoly, high profits of the firms in monopolistic industries are probably the most notorious." [19] Although the measurement of profits has become something of an arcane art, particularly as practiced by conglomerate corporations bent on improving their price-earnings ratios, the basic concept is what remains after all costs. In the words of William A. Paton:

> The periodic net earnings of a corporation . . . are measured by the excess of the revenues of the period over all applicable expenses, losses and taxes. There are two "net" figures of significance that emerge: (1) the amount earned on all the resources made available by all furnishers of funds, including the short-term and long-term creditors and the senior or preferred stockholders, if any; (2) the earnings applicable to the equity of the common stockholders, the furnishers of the junior or risk capital. This second balance is computed by deducting interest and other senior claims from (1), and it is to this balance that the term "profits" may most reasonably be attached.[20]

There are several grounds for assuming that the "earnings applicable to the equity of the comon stockholders" will be higher in concentrated than in unconcentrated industries. According to one line of argument, the goal of profit maximation will be more attainable under high concentration because of the greater ease of collusion, explicit or implied. Industries which are so unconcentrated that collusion is impossible will yield only opportunity costs. But above this point behavior will differ depending on the feasibility of collusion. As set forth by Joe S. Bain:

> Moderate concentration, it may be argued, should tend to give rise to quasi-competitive market behavior—imperfect collusion, kinked demand curve conformations, and the sporadic appearance of chaotic competition —whereas high concentration should provide an environment conducive to effective collusion or its equivalent. This hypothesis essentially rests on the premise and argument that, given the incentive to joint profit maximization, the impediments to express or tacit agreement increase, while the restraint of recognized interdependence on independent price cutting

[19] Fritz Machlup, *The Political Economy of Monopoly,* Johns Hopkins Press, 1952, pp. 474, 490.
[20] William A. Paton, *Corporate Profits,* Irwin, 1965, p. 60.

should decrease (with ordinary frictions and imperfections) as concentration decreases, and at such a rate that a shift in competitive pattern results over a certain concentration zone within oligopoly.[21]

In asymmetrical oligopolies observance of the leader's prices may stem not so much from collusion as from fear of reprisal by a firm with considerably greater monopoly profits and other resources. In such industries the profit rate will be higher than in unconcentrated industries if the leader's target rate of return is higher; if the leader is usually successful in meeting its target objective; if the other producers (at least the other oligopolists) match the leader's price changes, upward as well as downward; and if the profitability of the industry's other producers is not so far below the leader's as to bring the industry average down to (or below) the level that would prevail under competition.

Whatever the reason, the evidence seems clear that profit rates tend to be higher—and substantially higher—in concentrated than in unconcentrated industries. Figure 20-2 brings together the findings of four studies—by Bain,[22] Sherman,[23] Collins and Preston,[24] and Levinson.[25] In each grid of the chart, the horizontal scale reflects the level of concentration, and the vertical scale represents the measure of profitability, which in the first three cases is the rate of return on net worth (i.e., stockholders' equity).[26] In the Levinson study the measure used is "cash flow" (profits plus depreciation and depletion), which reflects the total amount of funds internally available to the firm for expansion and modernization as well as for dividends. The time periods range from 1936–40 (Bain), to 1954 (Sherman), to 1952–56 (Levinson), and to 1956–60 (Collins-Preston).

In each of the studies the profit rate was found to be significantly higher among the more concentrated industries. Summarizing his findings Bain states, "The positive conclusion which does emerge is that there is a rather distinct break in average profit-rate showing at the 70 percent concentration line (8-firm), and that there is a significant difference in the average of industry average profit rates above and below this line." [27] He also reported that the effect of concentration could not be explained by firm size, percentage overhead, capital-output ratios, product durability, or type of buyer. Collins and Preston found an increase of 10 percentage points in the weighted average concentration index to be associated with an increase in the profit rate of nearly 2 percent. The greater profitability of the more concentrated industries found in the Levinson and Sherman studies is self-evident.

These are by no means the only studies that have been made of the subject. In a study covering 40 quarters Weiss found a high correlation between the concentration of the major industry groups (based on the weighted average of their product concentration ratios) and their quarterly average rate of return (after

[21] Joe S. Bain, "Workable Competition in Oligopoly: Theoretical Considerations and Some Empirical Evidence," *American Economic Review,* May, 1950, p. 44.

[22] Joe S. Bain, "Relation of Profit Rate to Industry Concentration: American Manufacturing, 1936–1940," *Quarterly Journal of Economics,* Aug., 1951, pp. 293–324.

[23] Howard H. Sherman, *Macrodynamic Economics,* Appleton-Century-Crofts, 1964, Ch. 8.

[24] Norman R. Collins and Lee E. Preston, *Concentration and Price-Cost Margins in Manufacturing Industries,* University of California Press, 1968, pp. 57–62.

[25] 86th Cong., 2nd Sess., Joint Economic Committee, Study Paper No. 21, Harold M. Levinson, *Postwar Movement of Prices and Wages in Manufacturing Industries,* 1960.

[26] For the Bain study the measure shown is based on profits after taxes; for the Sherman and Collins-Preston studies it is based on profits before taxes.

[27] Bain, *op. cit.,* p. 314.

Figure 20-2

RELATIONSHIP OF CONCENTRATION TO PROFIT RATES
Four studies

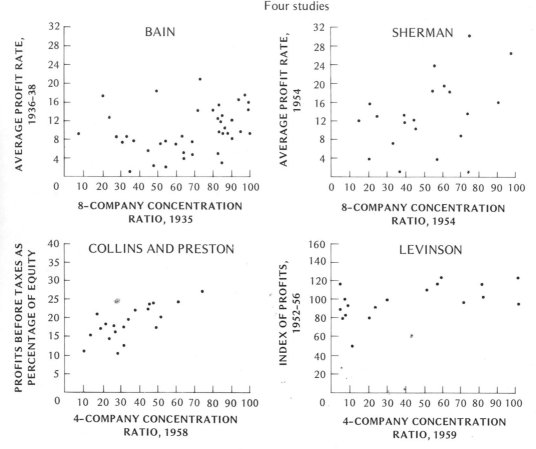

Source: Norman R. Collins and Lee E. Preston, *Concentration and Price-Cost Margins in Manufacturing Industries,*
University of California Press. 1968, Figures 1, 3, 6, 8

taxes) on net worth.[28] In an analysis of leading firms in 28 narrowly defined industries, K. D. George found the average 1950–60 pretax rate of return on net assets to be closely correlated with a composite of concentration, entrance barriers, and a growth factor.[29] Listing them in order of appearance Weiss noted, "There have been at least thirty-two tests of some form of the classic profit-determination hypothesis over the last 18 years, and the number seems to be accelerating if anything." [30]

[28] Leonard W. Weiss, "Average Concentration Ratios and Industrial Performance," *Journal of Industrial Economics,* July, 1963, pp. 237–54.
[29] K. D. George, "Concentration Barriers to Entry and Rates of Return," *Review of Economics and Statistics,* May, 1968, pp. 273–75.
[30] Leonard W. Weiss, "Econometric Studies of Industrial Organization," in M. Intraligator, ed., *Frontiers of Quantitative Economics,* Holland, 1971, p. 364. The one exception to the general run of findings was a study by George J. Stigler (*Capital and Rates of Return in Manufacturing Industries,* Princeton University Press, 1963, Ch. 4). For profit data he used the 3-digit industry groups of the Internal Revenue Service. Weighted average concentration ratios were then derived based on 4- and 5-digit product classes. Industries were

The only problem is that as the methods of analysis have become more complex and sophisticated, as simple correlations have been replaced with multi-
variate analyses employing refined mathematical tests of "significance," the
underlying financial data on which they are based have become less and less
usable for the purpose. The wave of conglomerate mergers during the mid- and
late 1960's profoundly altered the structure of many, if not most, of the largest
industrial corporations.[31] Relating concentration to profitability for a given industry obviously makes little sense if the major source of earnings for the industry's
leading firms lies elsewhere. For a substantial number (perhaps as many as half)
of the 200 largest industrial corporations, findings of profit relationships based
on the assignment of all of the corporation's earnings to a single 4-digit, or
even 3-digit, industry has come to have little value. Attempts to by-pass the
dilemma by using the broader 2-digit major industry groups will be futile not
only because conglomeration has extended beyond the major groups but also
because the scope of these groups usually encompasses such a variety of unrelated markets as to make concentration ratios for such groups virtually meaningless.[32] Except for studies based on specialized firms in narrowly defined industries, further light on the relationship of concentration to profitability will
probably have to await the institution of a meaningful program of divisional
financial reports utilizing standard and uniform industry definitions.[33]

Although generally in agreement that profitability is higher among the more
concentrated industries, the investigators differ as to whether the relationship is
linear or dichotomous. Do profit rates tend to rise more or less continuously with
increasing concentration, or is there a "distinct break" between higher and lower
profit rates around some level of concentration? Bain regarded the results of his
analysis as indicating the latter:

> There is no conclusive indication of any closely observed linear relation-
> ship of industry concentration to profit rates. The general showing is that
> of a fairly high average level of profit rates down to the 70 percent con-
> centration line, a much lower average level down to the 30 percent line,
> and (based on a very small sample) a higher level again below the 30
> percent line. . . . The positive conclusion which does emerge is that there

classified as "concentrated" (those with national markets and a 4-firm ratio of more than
60%), "unconcentrated" (those with national markets and a ratio of less than 50% or
with regional markets and a ratio of less than 50%), and an "ambiguous" group (i.e., all
others). Because part of their salaries should properly be regarded as profits, an adjustment
was made for withdrawals by officers of small corporations. This adjustment caused what
had been at best a weak relationship to "almost vanish."

Several reasons have been advanced to explain, in Weiss's words, "the difference between
Stigler and the rest of us." By eliminating small firms completely (and thus the need of an
adjustment for entrepeneurial withdrawals), Kilpatrick on reworking Stigler's data found
a strong positive relationship in 1956 and 1963 (B. W. Kilpatrick, "Stigler on the Relationship Between Industry Profit Rates and Market Concentration," *Journal of Political Economy*, May-June 1968, pp. 479–88). Weiss's own "guess" is that the difference is "more a
matter of timing than technique." Citing a recent unpublished work by Gambeles, he notes
that the concentration-profits hypothesis does not hold up well in years of open inflation or
price controls, observing that "every period examined by Stigler except the last (1953–6)
contained a preponderance of such years." (Weiss, *op. cit.*, p. 366.) Finally, note can be
taken of the fact that the upper limit of Stigler's "unconcentrated" category, a 4-firm ratio
of up to 50% for industries with national markets, is far higher than that usually associated
with the definition of an "unconcentrated" industry (see Ch. 1).

[31] See Chs. 11, 12.

[32] See Ch. 1.

[33] See Ch. 22.

is a rather distinct break in average profit-rate showing at the 70 percent concentration line (8-firm) and that there is a significant difference in the average of industry average profit rates above and below this line.[34]

On this point the "distinct break" hypothesis gained indirect support from a study of 17 *concentrated* industries by Stigler, who found that "there is no relationship between profitability and concentration if . . . the share of the 4 largest firms is less than about 80 percent." [35] But, employing tests involving the use of margin data, Collins and Preston reached the opposite conclusion: "We are . . . led to conclude that the association between concentration and price-cost margins revealed in this data may be described as continuous rather than discrete." [36]

Reference to Figure 20-2 reveals the relationship to be clearly dichotomous in the case of the Bain and Levinson studies. In the case of the Sherman and Collins-Preston studies much of the impression of linearity derives from the observations at the extremes (apparel and motor vehicles in the former and lumber and tobacco products in the latter). If these observations were removed, the relationship could just as readily be interpreted as being discrete, with the "distinct break" appearing at a concentration ratio of around 60 percent in the Sherman study (8-firm) and around 50 percent in the Collins-Preston analysis (4-firm).

As has been pointed out earlier, a theoretical basis exists for the presumption that price behavior will differ between oligopolistic and competitive industries, but not for the presumption that it will differ among industries that differ only in the degree to which they are oligopolistic.[37] The appearance of the distinct break in the profit studies suggests that the type of price behavior expected of oligopolies (and confirmed by the evidence) is reflected in a profit performance clearly superior to that of competitive industries.

The production effect

In competitive industries the theoretical expectation will be for production to be maximized, as each seller finds it profitable to expand his production until the cost of further units of output exceeds the selling price. Referring to the competitive producer "who feels he can do nothing about the price but that he can sell any quantity he cares to at that price," Machlup writes:

> If a seller of this type wants to make as much money as his business can bring, he will push his production up to a volume where the expense of a *further* increase in output would exceed the selling price. Since he expects that he *can* sell at the given price any quantity he cares to sell, he *will* care to produce and to sell any quantities whose additional costs of production and handling would be below the price.
>
> The accepted technical language for this situation is that the marginal revenue equals the selling price (because total proceeds are increased by

[34] Bain, *op. cit.*

[35] George J. Stigler, "A Theory of Oligopoly," *Journal of Political Economy,* Feb., 1964, p. 58.

[36] Collins and Preston, *op. cit.,* pp. 105–06.

[37] See Ch. 16.

an amount equal to the selling price of the additional unit of output); and since the highest possible profit is obtained at the volume of output where marginal cost is equal to marginal revenue (because at smaller output volumes additional cost would still be below additional revenue, and profit, therefore, not yet maximized), the firm seeking to maximize profit will push its output up to the point where marginal cost is equal to selling price (or below it by the smallest possible margin).[38]

Oligopolists will be influenced, however, by an additional consideration. They will be acutely aware of the need *not* to expand their own production to the point where the supply is great enough to result inevitably in a reduction in price, with all of its adverse consequences. Consequently their output will fall short of the point where "marginal revenue equals marginal cost." The result will be unused productive resources. In Machlup's words:

> Sellers can set prices so high as to restrict the purchase of products to an output level at which additional production would cause an addition to total cost of production that would still be more than covered by the prices at which the added output would sell. The productive resources which remain unused for the industry concerned as a result of its smaller output would either remain unemployed or they might find employment for uses less desired than the one from which they were excluded.[39]

For an economy made up partly of competitive and partly of oligopolistic industries the logical product of these contrasting patterns of adjustment during an economic downturn should be an inverse relationship between price and production declines. The existence of such a relationship was first noted by Gardiner C. Means in 1935:

> One can make the broad generalization, having of course many exceptions, that for industries in which prices dropped most during the depression production tended to drop least, while for those in which prices were maintained, the drop in production was usually greatest. Indeed, the whole depression might be described as a general dropping of prices at the flexible end of the price scale and a dropping of production at the rigid end with intermediate effects between.[40]

This conclusion was based on data showing the price and production behavior of some 10 rather broadly defined industry groups. As presented in a later and more refined form, the data are as shown in Table 20-7.[41]

On this issue Means's conclusions were corroborated by the findings of other investigators. Thus Thorp and Crowder came to speak of the association between price and production changes as "the *usual* inverse relationship," which they found existed in products of both "low" and "high" concentration.[42] They

---

[38] Fritz Machlup, *The Economics of Seller's Competition,* Johns Hopkins Press, 1952, pp. 138–39. Emphasis in original.

[39] Machlup, *The Political Economy of Monopoly,* p. 31.

[40] 74th Cong., 1st Sess., S. Doc. 13, Gardiner C. Means, *Industrial Prices and Their Relative Inflexibility,* 1935, p. 8.

[41] Three of the 4 product groupings with price declines of 16% or less had production losses of more than 70%.

[42] Willard L. Thorp and Walter Crowder, *The Structure of Industry,* Monograph No. 27, Temporary National Economic Committee (TNEC), 1941, p. 370.

Table 20-7

COMPARISON OF PRICE AND PRODUCTION CHANGES

10 major industries, 1929–1932

Industry Group	Percentage Decline	
	Price	Production
Motor vehicles	12	74
Agricultural implements	14	84
Cement	16	55
Iron and steel	16	76
Automobile tires	25	42
Leather and products	33	18
Petroleum products	36	17
Textile products	39	28
Food products	39	10
Agricultural commodities	54	1

Source: National Resources Committee, *The Structure of the American Economy*,
1939, Pt. 1, p. 386, prepared under the direction of Gardiner C. Means

observed that "a definite pattern is evident . . . within broad limits in both sections," adding that in the "low" concentrated products, the pattern "is more pronounced." [43] Similarly, on the basis of an examination of the 1929–33 changes in price and production of 85 manufacturing industries, Alfred C. Neal found that "a tendency toward inverse association is apparent, thus confirming the findings of Thorp and Crowder for individual commodities and of Means for selected industries." [44]

On this issue the only point of criticism was raised by Jules Backman, who questioned Means's findings on the grounds that some of his product groupings were excessively broad and lacked consistency in definition: "In some cases the data represented composites of many commodities with diverse characteristics (e.g. textile products) while in others the data referred to an individual commodity (e.g. cement)." [45] Means replied, in effect, that data for a small number of broad industry groups may well be more meaningful than information for a larger number of individual products.[46] But on the basis of his own empirical evidence, consisting of data on price (BLS) and production changes for 264 individual commodities, Backman acknowledged, "Within very broad limits there is evidently some tendency for inflexible price products to be accompanied by greater decreases in production than those which were more responsive to

[43] Both the Thorp-Crowder and the Neal analyses use for their price data the Census realization figures. Because of the excessive breadth of their definition such prices during a downswing tend to overstate the true price decline as shifts occur within the product definitions toward a greater relative importance of lower-priced items. If the distortion is greater among products with large price declines, it contributes to the appearance of an inverse relationship by overstating the price reductions of products with small production declines. But if the reverse is true, it operates against the appearance of the relationship by overstating the price reductions of products with large production declines. For a hypothesis as to why the latter should be true see John M. Blair, "Means, Thorp and Neal on Price Inflexibility," *Review of Economic Statistics*, Nov., 1956, p. 433.

[44] Neal, *op. cit.*, p. 114.

[45] Jules Backman, "Price Flexibility and Changes in Production," *Conference Board Bulletin*, Feb. 20, 1939, pp. 45–54.

[46] National Resources Committee, *op. cit.*, p. 141n.

THE ECONOMIC EFFECTS OF OLIGOPOLY

outside forces." And, "There is some tendency for the data to swing downward to the right." But, he went on to add, "this movement is within such a broad range that generalizations such as those made by Dr. Means do not have much practical value." [47]

The inverse relationship appears more clearly from Backman's data in a table prepared by H. Gregg Lewis and used in an article by Ernest Doblin (see Table 20-8).[48] In this table Backman's 264 products were distributed between durable and nondurable goods and, within each, into finished and unfinished goods. The price ratios were arrayed in order of increasing magnitude and distributed among a number of class intervals according to degree of price change. Averages were then formed of the price and production changes for each class interval. In each separate subgroup of products—durable finished, durable unfinished, nondurable finished, and nondurable unfinished—the inverse relationship is clearly evident.[49] Thus, among finished durable goods, products that averaged a price reduction of only 2 percent suffered a 78 percent decrease in output, whereas those whose price fell 32 percent had a decrease in output of only 59 percent. For unfinished durable goods a 12 percent decline in price was accompanied by a 69 percent decrease in production, but a 57 percent fall in price by a 54 percent decline in output. Among finished nondurable goods, products that averaged an 18 percent price reduction suffered a 20 percent decrease in output, whereas those whose price fell by 72 percent had a production decrease of only 4 percent. For unfinished nondurable goods a 2 percent decline in price was accompanied by a 34 percent decrease in production, but a 73 percent fall in price by only a 10 percent decline in output.

It has been argued that the general inverse relationship that is evident for the economy as a whole represents nothing more than the sum total of the different types of behavior of products with different demand and cost characteristics. Thus, owing to the ease with which the purchases of producer goods can be postponed, their production would tend to be curtailed, thereby lessening the pressure of excessive output on price. Conversely, owing to the perishability of farm products, the inability of the farmer to produce for inventory, and his constant tendency to plant the same or a greater acreage regardless of price, production of agricultural products would tend to be sustained, with the adjustment falling largely on price. But an explanation of the inverse relationship in

[47] Backman, op. cit.
[48] Ernest Doblin, "Some Aspects of Price Flexibility," *Review of Economic Statistics,* Nov., 1940, p. 188.
[49] Using a different statistical approach, Means also came to this conclusion—i.e., if anything, the Backman study tended to reinforce rather than refute his findings: "The evidence presented in the [Backman] study shows that even for *individual commodities* there is a clearly marked tendency, with of course many exceptions, for a drop in production between 1929 and 1933 to be associated with a smaller drop in prices and a large drop in prices to be associated with a small drop in production. This tendency is clearly indicated in the attached table which was compiled directly from the bulletin.

Number of Items Listed in NICB Bulletin Falling Into Different Categories of Price and Production Changes Between 1929 and 1933.

| | With Production Drop of | | |
	More than 50%	25% to 50%	Less than 25%
Items with price drop of less than 25%	40	25	18
Items with price drop of 25% to 50%	23	26	19
Items with price drop of more than 50%	11	24	68

(National Resources Committee, *op. cit.,* p. 140n.)

Table 20-8

PRICE AND PRODUCTION CHANGES BY TYPE OF COMMODITY, 1929–1933

Goods	Type	Average price change	Average production change	Number of items in group
Durable Goods	Finished and Unfinished	− 4.6%	−72.6%	19
		−18.4	−68.3	18
		−29.0	−64.8	19
		−52.5	−57.1	19
	Finished	− 1.9%	−78.3%	8
		−12.5	−74.7	7
		−20.6	−62.7	7
		−32.4	−59.3	8
	Unfinished	−11.8%	−69.4%	12
		−24.9	−60.3	11
		−42.5	−63.3	11
		−56.7	−53.6	11
Nondurable Goods	Finished and Unfinished	− 5.5%	−29.5%	31
		−28.2	−30.2	32
		−44.4	−23.0	32
		−54.6	−25.4	31
		−66.8	+ 3.2	32
		−73.6	−10.1	31
	Finished	−18.0%	−20.1%	14
		−39.9	−15.7	14
		−51.2	−10.4	14
		−60.1	+ 4.9	14
		−72.3	− 3.7	14
	Unfinished	− 2.1%	−34.2%	24
		−29.0	−36.4	24
		−48.1	−28.1	24
		−65.9	− 4.0	24
		−73.0	− 9.9	23

Source: H. Gregg Lewis, "Some Aspects of Price Inflexibility," *Review of Economic Statistics*, Nov., 1940, p. 188

Table 20-9

RELATION BETWEEN CHANGES IN REALIZED PRICES AND PRODUCTION, 1957–1958

38 manufacturing industries

Industries with Price Changes of	Total	Industries with Production Changes of			
		Over −5%	−1 to −5%	1% to 5%	Over 5%
Over 5%	13	4	7	1	1
1% to 5%	13	6	2	1	4
−1% to −5%	5	1	2	1	1
Over −5%	7	3	1	1	2
Total	38	14	12	4	8

Source: Special tabulation from Bureau of the Census 1968

terms of the characteristics of the products ignores the fact that the relationship was found to recur *within* individual groups of products possessing generally similar characteristics.[50]

Because of their limited severity, it is difficult to make this type of analysis for the post-World War II recessions. For the most severe of the recessions, that of 1957–58, realized prices and physical output data were obtained from the Census Bureau for a sample of 38 4-digit industries. Only 14 had an output decline of over 5 percent, and even fewer (12) had a price decline of that magnitude. Nearly three-fourths of the industries (26) registered an actual increase in price. With respect to the relationship of changes in price to changes in production, about all that can be said is that among the industries with an increase in price, only a little more than one-fourth also had increases in output, whereas of those with decreases in price, output rose in nearly half (see Table 20-9).

The theoretical implications of the inverse relationship have long been recognized as far-reaching. Recalling the impact of Means's "administered price" thesis on economic thinking during the 1930's, George J. Stigler has observed: "The previously relatively unnoticed phenomenon of price rigidity was forcibly impressed on everyone and the persistent economic malaise made everyone receptive to suggestions of deficiencies in the price system. If true, Means's suggestion—it was no more—that rigid prices led to large decreases in output and employment, whereas industries with flexible prices underwent small (if any) reductions in output, was of the highest importance." [51]

The prevailing point of view among economists was well expressed at the time by Henry C. Simon: "The existence of extreme inflexibility in large areas of the price structure is one of the primary factors in the phenomenon of severe depression. Thus inflexibility increases the economic loss and human misery

[50] Thorp and Crowder, *op. cit.*, pp. 379–95; Backman, *op. cit.*, pp. 45–51.
[51] George J. Stigler, "Administered Prices and Oligopolistic Inflation," *Journal of Business*, Jan., 1962, p. 1. Stigler, however, dismissed the idea of the inverse relationship, stating, "Unfortunately, the facts did not support this conclusion." The source of the "facts" cited by Stigler is Thorp and Crowder, *op. cit.* As has been brought out above, on this issue Thorp and Crowder were in full agreement with Means. Apparently what happened is that Stigler confused the issue of whether a direct relationship existed between concentration and price rigidity (on which the TNEC monograph did not support Means) with the separate issue of whether an inverse relationship existed between price and production declines.

accompanying a given deflation, and it causes deflation itself to proceed much farther than it otherwise would." [52]

The inverse relationship should certainly put to rest the idea, put forward by Alvin Hansen, that price rigidity during a downswing is a positive good.[53] Hansen's objection to flexible prices centered around their effect on expectations. Once the opportunities for investment have been exhausted and economic activity begins to decline, the expectation that *further* decreases in prices may take place will result in a withholding of investment and purchases and thus "accelerate" the downswing. The expectation by business and consumers that prices will fall farther thus tends to intensify a downswing by generating a cumulative decline in expenditures and investment.[54] Hansen's reasoning assumed that the relationship between price and production changes is direct. If prices do not decline, businessmen will not withhold their purchases and production will be maintained; if prices do decline, purchases will be withheld (in anticipation of a greater decline) and production will fall. Yet if in the flexible-price areas of the economy businessmen, confronted with falling prices, hold off their purchases in the expectation of further price decreases, how does it happen that production in such areas remains high? Similarly, if in the rigid-price areas businessmen are stimulated to go ahead with their purchases by the knowledge that price reductions will not be forthcoming, how does it happen that production in such areas drops sharply? Clearly, Hansen's argument cannot be reconciled with the empirical evidence of an inverse relationship between price and production declines.

But the most important implication of the inverse relationship concerns the elasticity of demand with respect to price. This implication derives not so much from the existence of the relationship within the economy as a whole as from its prevalence within individual groups of products possessing much the same characteristics. That a substantial reduction in price for, say, a food product was accompanied by only a limited drop in its production does not necessarily imply that the curtailment in output of, say, a metal product would have been less severe had there been a greater reduction in its price. But the existence of the relationship *within* food products, constitutes a basis for the assumption that the consumption of those food products whose prices remained relatively rigid would have been better maintained had their prices been more flexible. And even if their consumption did not increase, their availability at a lower price would have made it possible for consumers to increase their purchases of other products.

In point of fact, the inverse relationship was found to have existed within such diverse fields as foods and metals, as well as within many other product groups. With respect to food products Thorp and Crowder observed, "Among agricultural products there appears to be a marked tendency for relatively large price changes to be associated with small quantity changes (many of the products

---

[52] Henry C. Simon, *A Positive Program for Laissez-Faire,* University of Chicago Press, 1934, p. 14.

[53] Hansen was referring only to cyclical flexibility, as distinct from secular, or what he termed "structural" flexibility: "There is, as far as I am aware, no disagreement among economists with respect to the desirability of structural price flexibility. Without structural price flexibility it is quite impossible for the community to obtain the full fruits of economic progress. Arbitrary interferences which obstruct structural price flexibility necessarily result in an uneconomic utilization of resources." (Alvin Hansen, *Fiscal Policy and Business Cycles,* Norton, 1941, p. 314.)

[54] Alvin Hansen, *Fiscal Policy and Business Cycles,* Norton, 1941, p. 319.

actually experienced increases in quantity output in the downswing . . .) and small price changes to be associated with large quantity changes as represented by the usual regression line sloping downward to the right." [55] Although based on a different type of price data, Backman's finding with respect to foods was to the same effect: "The larger declines in price were generally accompanied by either small decreases or actual increases in production." [56]

Thorp and Crowder found the inverse relationship to exist within both semi-finished and finished goods: "The conformation of the product points reflecting the behavior of both semi-manufactured and finished goods . . . indicates a rather clearly marked inverse relation between changes in price and changes in quantity for the products in these categories. The scatter in the case of finished goods is somewhat wider owing to the larger changes in quantity experienced by these items. But the evidence of relationship is unmistakable." [57] It also obtained within consumer goods: "For those products ultimately used by consumers . . . , there is a fairly well marked tendency, as reflected in the conformation of the product points, for small price decreases to be associated with relatively large contractions in output and for sizeable price decreases to be associated with relatively small contractions in quantity produced." [58] Among nondurable goods the relationship was clear: "the conformation of product points in the 'nondurable' sections reflects a rather obvious inverse relation between changes in price and changes in quantity for products in that category." [59] The relationship was also evident in products sold in a national market and in those sold in a regional market: "for products in both categories the usual inverse relationship between changes in quantity and price is apparent. It is somewhat closer, however, for those products in the regional than for those in the national category." [60] Among producers' supplies the relationship was also to be found: "the usual inverse relation between changes in price and quantity is quite evident among those products classified as producers supplies." [61]

When Backman organized his data into groups of products he found, like Thorp and Crowder, that in most cases the relationship obtained. Speaking of semifinished goods, he wrote that there is revealed "a clear tendency for reduced prices to be accompanied by better sustained volume, and for maintained prices to be paralleled by a substantial reduction in output." [62] Concerning metals he stated, "There is a clearly-defined trend indicating that large production declines occurred for metals and metal products with inflexible prices, while the more flexibly-priced products recorded smaller declines in output." [63] In the case of finished goods he found that the relationship existed "within very broad limits." [64]

The recurrence of the inverse relationship in so many different product groups does not mean that demand is more elastic with respect to price than with respect to income; indeed, most studies of demand elasticity indicate the opposite.

[55] Thorp and Crowder, *op. cit.,* p. 395.
[56] Backman *op. cit.,* p. 51.
[57] Thorp and Crowder, *op. cit.,* p. 389.
[58] *Ibid.,* p. 379.
[59] *Ibid.,* pp. 388–89.
[60] *Ibid.,* p. 394.
[61] *Ibid.,* p. 395. Product groups in which the relationship was not found to exist were producer goods and construction materials (*ibid.,* pp. 379, 395).
[62] Backman, *op. cit.,* p. 48.
[63] *Ibid.,* p. 50.
[64] *Ibid.,* p. 45. No relationships were apparent among building materials or chemicals and drugs.

But it does imply that production would be better maintained with a greater reduction in price. If so, the curtailment of output during a downturn will be greater under oligopolistic than under competitive conditions. In competitive industries, each producer, realizing that nothing he can do will influence the price and anxious to offset the loss in income stemming from the falling price, will endeavor to maintain (or even increase) his output. Conversely, since it takes an ever smaller volume of output to avoid weakening the price, oligopolists wishing to avoid price cuts (and the expected retaliation) will progressively reduce their production. If demand with respect to price were inelastic, the natural tendency of oligopolists to avoid reducing the prices of their products would of course have no direct effect on their level of output. But if, as the inverse relationship implies, a greater fall in price would be accompanied by a lesser decline in output, the natural behavior of oligopolists will tend to reduce output below the levels that would prevail under competition.

The policy effect

In addition to its effects on margins, profitability, and production, concentration through "perverse" recession price behavior may lead to the inducement or aggravation of a downswing, resulting in needless unemployment and substantial underutilization of resources. This comes about as government officials, assuming a competitive industry structure (or at least one that responds in more or less the same general way to expansions and contractions in demand) attempt to check an upward movement in prices by reducing the general level of demand through the application of restrictive macroeconomic policies. To this end either fiscal or monetary policy, or both, may be employed. Under the former, taxes may be increased and government expenditures curtailed; under the latter, the growth in the money supply may be reduced and interest rates increased. While disagreeing strongly (and at times acrimoniously) over the efficacy of the two approaches, the proponents of both have shared the common assumption that, given a reduction in demand, prices will respond by declining or at least not rising. True, there will be frictions and lags (of unspecified duration), which may delay the impact of the restrictive policies. But nowhere in the fiscalists' or monetarists' models (which in their more elaborate forms embrace hundreds of variables) is there any variable representing an acceleration of the rate of price increase for a substantial segment of the economy accompanying a reduction in demand.

Beginning in 1969 the Administration began to attempt to bring inflation "under control" by a combination of fiscal and monetary restraints. Tax concessions (e.g., the investment credit) were ended; a whole series of congressional enactments calling for greater government spending were vetoed by the President; a drastic slowdown of the growth in the money supply was imposed; interest rates climbed to all-time highs. Insofar as the rate of economic activity is concerned, these measures had their planned effect, producing what by December, 1970, had been officially designated by the National Bureau of Economic Research as a "recession." As compared to a year earlier, industrial production in manufacturing had by that time fallen 5.8 percent; capacity utilization in manufacturing had dropped from 81.7 percent to 72.4 percent; and the unemployment rate had risen from 3.6 percent to 6.2 percent. But, instead of slowing down, the rate of inflation actually accelerated. For the year 1970 the increase in the wholesale price level was 3.7 percent, as compared to 2.5 percent in 1968. When it continued to rise at an annual rate of 5.9 percent in the first 6 months of 1971 (with no reduction in the unemployment rate), the attempt to restrain inflation by macroeconomic policies was finally jettisoned by President Nixon's action on August 15, 1971, in imposing a mandatory freeze on prices and wages.

When one examines the behavior of individual prices, particularly those of concentrated industries, the reasons for the failure are not difficult to ascertain. Essential to such an examination has been the work of the Bureau of Labor Statistics in reclassifying its own product designations to achieve comparability with the industry and product class designations of the Standard Industrial Classification, thereby permitting comparisons with other variables. Comparability has thus far been achieved for over 300 5-digit product classes, making possible direct comparisons between the price series and the Census concentration ratios. The price changes between December, 1969, and December, 1970—the officially designated beginning and trough of the 1970 recession—are shown in Table 20-10 for 325 industrial product classes, plus 19 farm product classes and 3 classes of scrap materials.[65] While it includes products representing more than half of the value of manufacturing output, this body of data is not designed to be a representative sample. The job of reclassifying and reorganizing its own price series to match the SIC classifications is carried on intermittently by the Bureau of Labor Statistics as resources permit. A visual inspection suggests that the Bureau has made the greatest progress in the basic, mass-production industries (which tend to be concentrated areas) and least progress in small-scale specialty fields (which tend to be areas of low concentration).

Nonetheless, even allowing for this underrepresentation of the unconcentrated industries, it is interesting to note that only slightly more than one-seventh (52) of the 347 product classes reacted to the planned recession by declining in price. A slightly greater number (65) remained relatively stable, changing by less than 2 percent. But two-thirds of the product classes (230) registered increases, of which 132 recorded advances of 5 percent or more. When account is taken of the underrepresentation of unconcentrated areas, it would appear that about one-half of the price structure exhibited perverse flexibility. This proportion, it might be observed, is about the same as would be inferred from past recession price behavior of the BLS quintiles.[66]

Further examination of the table reveals that the great majority of decreases which did take place were in industries of low and moderate concentration (with ratios of under 25 percent and 25 to 49 percent, respectively), each accounting for approximately two-fifths of the decreases. In contrast only one-sixth of the declines were in concentrated industries (those with ratios of 50 percent or more). While more than half of the unconcentrated products showed increases in price, one-third of these products recorded decreases. In contrast, more than

---

[65] Wholesale price indexes are available for 24 product classes of the Wholesale Price Index major grouping farm products. Five are for products that have been deliberately insulated from the effect of declining demand by various price support programs—raw cotton, milk, coffee, and tobacco. It has been assumed that, were they available, the concentration ratios for the remaining 19 farm products would be below (and probably well below) 25%. Indexes are also available for scrap iron and steel, nonferrous scrap, and wastepaper—all of which are also assumed to have concentration ratios below 25%.

[66] See Ch. 17.

Table 20-10

CONCENTRATION RATIO AND PERCENTAGE PRICE CHANGE OF 347 PRODUCT CLASSES

December, 1969, to December, 1970

Industry Grouping	Total	Increases 5.0% and Over	2.0% to 4.9%	Changes of Less than +2.0% or −2.0%	Decreases −2.0% to −4.9%	−5.0% and Over
Farm, food and tobacco						
50% and over	21	12	5	3	1	—
25% to 49%	32	12	7	3	3	7
Under 25%[a]	29	12	2	1	1	13
Total	82	36	14	7	5	20
Textiles, apparel, and leather						
50% and over	9	1	2	3	—	3
25% to 49%	14	1	1	7	3	2
Under 25%	11	1	6	3	1	—
Total	34	3	9	13	4	5
Lumber, furniture, and paper						
50% and over	6	3	3	—	—	—
25% to 49%	15	3	3	6	1	2
Under 25%	13	—	5	3	4	1
Total	34	6	11	9	5	3
Chemicals and petroleum						
50% and over	12	—	2	8	2	—
25% to 49%	15	8	5	2	—	—
Under 25%[b]	1	—	1	—	—	—
Total	28	8	8	10	2	0
Stone, clay, and glass						
50% and over	10	4	3	3	—	—
25% to 49%	5	2	3	—	—	—
Under 25%	3	3	—	—	—	—
Total	18	9	6	3	0	0
Primary metals						
50% and over	26	12	5	6	2	1
25% to 49%	12	6	4	0	—	2
Under 25%[c]	2	1	—	—	1	—
Total	40	19	10	5	3	3

Machinery and fabricated metal products						
50% and over	21	10	9	2	—	—
25% to 49%	27	14	11	2	—	—
Under 25%	8	5	2	1	—	—
Total	56	29	22	5	0	0
Electrical machinery						
50% and over	19	6	8	5	—	—
25% to 49%	14	9	2	1	1	1
Under 25%	2	1	1	—	—	—
Total	35	16	11	6	1	1
Transportation equipment						
50% and over	3	3	—	—	—	—
25% to 49%	1	—	—	1	—	—
Under 25%	—	—	—	—	—	—
Total	4	3	0	1	0	0
Miscellaneous						
50% and over	7	2	1	4	—	—
25% to 49%	5	—	4	1	—	—
Under 25%	4	1	3	—	—	—
Total	16	3	8	5	0	0
All product classes						
50% and over	134	53	38	34	5	4
25% to 49%	140	55	40	23	8	14
Under 25%	73	24	20	8	7	14
Total	347	132	98	65	20	32

a Includes 19 farm product classes.
b Includes one product class, wastepaper.
c Includes 2 product classes of scrap metal.

Source: Prices: Bureau of Labor Statistics, Department of Labor, Wholesale Price Index; Concentration Ratios. Concentration Ratios in Manufacturing Industry, 1963, 1966, Pt. 1, Table 4

Table 20-11

CONCENTRATED FOOD AND TOBACCO PRODUCTS WITH PRICE INCREASES OF 5 PERCENT AND OVER

December, 1969, to December, 1970

Product Class	Concentration Ratio	Price Increase
Chewing gum	86%	14.6%
Concentrated coffee	81	7.9
Biscuits, crackers, and pretzels	71	6.8
Refined cottonseed oil	68	9.2
Beet sugar	66	8.2
Cane sugar refining	62	5.4
Canned vegetable juices	55	6.5
Chewing and smoking tobacco	53	9.7
Other dry bakery products	52	6.9
Shortening and cooking oils	51	10.4
Margarine	50	12.5
Cigarettes	n.a.[a]	7.0

[a]Not available.

Source: Prices: Bureau of Labor Statistics, Department of Labor, Wholesale Price Index; Concentration ratios: *Concentration Ratios in Manufacturing Industry*, 1963, 1966, Pt. 1, Table 4

two-thirds (69 percent) of the concentrated products registered increases, while decreases occurred in less than 7 percent. As compared to the concentrated products, a slightly smaller proportion of the intermediate group (67 percent) registered increases and a considerably larger share (nearly a fifth) showed decreases.

More light can be shed on the differences in price behavior through an examination of the 10 broad groupings into which the 347 products have been combined.[67] Of the 21 concentrated farm, food, and tobacco products, only one (fresh and frozen lamb and mutton) declined in price, while 17 rose—12 by 5 percent or more. But among the unconcentrated products in this grouping the distribution was equal, and decreases would have been in the majority had it not been for episodic occurrences affecting the output of individual farm products —the corn blight, which raised grain prices, and poor weather, which increased prices for fresh fruits. The 12 concentrated products in this grouping with price increases of 5 percent or more were as shown in Table 20-11.

Textiles, apparel, and leather products made up the only grouping in which products with price increases were in the minority. And aside from the farm and food and lumber and furniture groupings, it has the lowest ratio of concentrated to total products. In contrast to the upward trend of prices in general, 13 products in this grouping remained unchanged, while 9 registered decreases. The pattern was much the same in lumber, furniture, and paper products, although products with price increases constituted one-half of the total. Of the 17 increases, 6 were in concentrated products, increases of 5 percent or more being recorded by sanitary napkins and tampons, sanitary-tissue health products, and paperboard and other fiber drums. In contrast, reacting to the sharp curtailment in construction activity caused by the tight monetary policy, 6 of the 8 lumber products declined in price, the other 2 remaining relatively stable. Five of the lumber products are unconcentrated, 3 are moderately concentrated.

[67] The use of these broader groupings was necessitated by the inadequate coverage for some of the 2-digit major industry groups.

In chemicals and petroleum products increases were more pronounced, 8 of the 28 products registering advances of 5 percent or more. As has been noted earlier, the oil import quota has the effect of raising the effective control of the market for petroleum products above the levels indicated by their national concentration ratios (usually between 25 and 49 percent). Without the quota the increases in their prices during the 1970 recession would probably have been replaced, as in the 1958 prequota recession, by price decreases. Sizable increases also predominated in stone, clay, and glass, occurring in 9 of the 18 products. The national concentration ratios of the 3 unconcentrated industries in this grouping with price increases of 5 percent or more (glazed brick, concrete block, and ready-mix concrete) greatly understate the actual control existing in local markets.

In primary metals three-fourths of the products, including all of the shapes and forms of steel, rose in price. In contrast, reflecting the historical sensitivity of nonferrous metals to world market conditions, decreases were recorded in copper (3 products), lead (one product), and zinc (one product). It is interesting to note that secondary copper made from scrap by nonintegrated producers declined by 19.2 percent, while primary copper made by the integrated companies dropped by only 9.9 percent. Increases in price also predominated in the 2 broad groupings of machinery and fabricated metal products and electrical machinery, nine-tenths of the former and three-fourths of the latter registering advances. The 2 decreases in electrical machinery took place in industries of moderate concentration that have been characterized by intense price competition—solid-state semiconductor devices and resistors for electronic applications.

In transportation equipment sizable increases were registered by passenger cars, trucks, and motor coaches. Again the exception is of particular interest. Little change was shown in the price of motorcycles and bicycles, an industry of moderate concentration that has been affected strongly by import competition. Among miscellaneous products the 2 concentrated items showing price increases of 5 percent or more were matches and organs; the unconcentrated product was wood caskets and coffins.

In short, this body of data suggests that the chances of a product's reacting to a recession by declining in price or at least remaining stable are close to even in the unconcentrated areas, one out of 3 in the moderately concentrated fields, and only slightly better than one out of 4 in the concentrated industries. Commenting on the failure of restrictive monetary and fiscal policies to arrest the upward movement in prices, it is not surprising that in testimony before the Joint Economic Committee in August, 1971, Chairman Arthur F. Burns of the Federal Reserve Board observed, "Prices no longer behave as they used to." [68]

Their failure to behave "as they used to" made the imposition of direct controls over price by government as certain as anything can be in a political democracy.

Relevance to overall economic activity

The starting points of macro- and microeconomic analyses are at the opposite extremes of the economic process. Macroeconomic analysis starts with some

[68] 92nd Cong., 1st Sess., Joint Economic Committee, *Hearings,* 1971. To be published. That more than 12 years earlier many prices were not behaving "as they used to" is evident from an examination of price behavior during the 1958 recession (see, e.g., *Hearings on Administered Prices,* Pt. 8).

measure of overall economic activity, usually gross national product (GNP). Changes in this *aggregate* can with reasonable accuracy be predicted on the basis of assumed changes in its *components*—consumer income (less consumer savings), business income (less business savings), and government expenditures (less taxes). A further influencing factor is the change in the money supply (and, through it, in the rate of interest). True, some uncertainty still surrounds the effect on GNP of changes in some of these variables, notably the "multiplier" effect of changes in expenditures on new plant and equipment and the effect of varying rates of increase in the money supply. But these are matters of extent. The real problem is that changes in the components are not known but have to be assumed. In the case of those components that are directly subject to government policy (government expenditures, taxes, the money supply), the actual change can, at least in theory, be made to accord with an *a priori* assumption. For the other components the basis for the expected change is usually the experience of the recent past, adjusted for expected minor differences in the near future. The problem with such projections is not only the uncertainty which inevitably surrounds volatile components (e.g., plant and equipment outlays) but the episodic and seemingly inexplicable changes which from time to time take place in even relatively stable components (e.g., the increase in the rate of consumer savings in 1970–71). The fact of the matter is that in the private sector not too much of a definitive character is known concerning the causes of changes in the underlying *determinants* of the *components* of GNP. For example, *to what extent* would consumer expenditures be affected by changes in price, or savings by changes in margins, or capital formation by changes in profit rates, or production by rigid or perverse price behavior?

The starting point of microeconomic analysis is at the other end of the spectrum—i.e., with prices and costs (and factors related thereto) in individual markets. Where demand with respect to price is elastic, a price higher than would obtain under competition directly reduces consumption. Where margins and profits are enlarged by changes in price-cost relationships, the result will tend to be a redistribution of income toward savings and away from consumption. Where the market during a downswing is cleared by a reduction in output rather than price, the result will be a reduction not only in demand (because of the higher price) but in employment and capital formation (because of the lower level of output).

Thus far, the effect on total income, savings, and expenditures of these and other forms of market behavior has never been quantified. A gap in knowledge exists between the determinants of GNP's components on the one hand and the macroeconomic effects of changing price-cost relationship on the other. If this gap could be closed, it is certainly within the realm of possibility that the latter would be found to exert a very real effect on the components and thus on the general level of economic activity.

Concentration and Public Policy

FIVE

What should public policy be toward the reality of concentration? It is simply wishful thinking to assume that concentration is of *de minimis* proportions;[1] or that it is a problem of declining importance which, if left to "natural forces," will tend gradually to disappear;[2] or that in their behavior concentrated industries do not differ significantly from competitive industries.[3] It is also wishful thinking to assume that, as a general proposition, managers of large corporations are restrained in their exercise of power by what Adolf A. Berle referred to as "the public consensus," a set of beliefs held generally by society that certain uses of economic power are improper. These beliefs, which, he felt, are part of the "corporate conscience" of management,[4] would induce managers to exercise moderation in their pricing and other policies. But, as the Senate Antitrust Subcommittee observed after its exhaustive investigation of the prescription drug industry:

[1] See Part I.
[2] See Parts I, III.
[3] See Part IV.
[4] "The first sanction enforcing limitation imposed by the public consensus is a lively appreciation of that consensus by corporate managements. This is the reality of the 'corporate conscience.' Violation leads to loss of prestige, public standing and popular esteem for the men in the organization itself as loyalty to it is undermined. Deprivation of prestige is one of the very ancient methods by which a society enforces its value systems upon individuals and groups within it. And if loss of privilege does not produce results more acceptable to the community, other and more forceful means of imposing the ideas embodied in the public consensus of community commonly appear." (Adolf A. Berle, *Power Without Property*, Harcourt Brace Jovanovich, 1958, p. 91.)

> Surely if enlightened management could be relied upon in any industry to adopt pricing policies which reasonably reconcile management's drive for profit with the public interest, it would presumably be drug manufacturing, owing to its crucial relationship to the public health. If in this industry the "public consensus" has been rather ostentatiously ignored, as might logically be inferred from the data on profits and margins . . . this constraint would appear to be a slender reed on which to rely for the protection of the public interest in administered price industries generally.[5]

Regardless of whether the ownership of productive facilities is in private or public hands or whether they are directed by private or public management, the performance of any economic system should be measured in terms of its ability to achieve an optimal use of resources. In an industrial economy this means that: (a) prices should be at the level needed to bring forth the production necessary to supply the given level of demand (i.e., price should equal marginal cost); (b) costs should be responsive to technological advances and other improvements that make cost reductions possible (i.e., there should be a constant downward pressure on costs); (c) invention and innovation should proceed at the maximum possible rate with the results thereof rapidly being accepted and transformed into commercial realities (i.e., there should be a constant stimulus to and use of the processes of discovery and development); and (d) resources should readily be transferred from industries in which they are no longer needed to those in which they are (i.e., there should be an optimal allocation of resources).

Broadly speaking, there are three basic approaches to public policy—the competitive approach, the regulatory approach, and the ownership approach. Under the first the ownership of the means of production is in private hands, and the public interest is assumed to be protected by the free play of competitive forces. Under the second ownership remains in private hands but in one way or another the state restrains the exercise of private economic power. And under the third the state not only owns but manages and operates the productive facilities.

In what follows each of these approaches will be examined in terms of its relevance to the problem of economic concentration. Specifically, the means of implementing the competitive approach—the antitrust laws—will be examined in Chapters 21 and 22. The former will be concerned with the application of the remedies of traditional antitrust policy; the latter will offer a positive program of promoting competition by restraining the centripetal forces and stimulating the centrifugal forces. Occupying a middle area between the competitive and the regulatory approaches is voluntary suasion, also referred to variously as "jawboning," "focusing the spotlight of publicity," seeking voluntary compliance with "price and wage guidelines," and so on; it will be examined in Chapter 23. More direct forms of government control will be examined in Chapter 24, which will be concerned with price

---

[5] *Administered Prices: Report on Drugs*, p. 5.

freezes, utility-type regulation and proposals designed to improve the social performance of corporations. The final chapter will be addressed to the ownership approach, as revealed particularly by the experience of the U.S.S.R. and Czechoslovakia.

THE COMPETITIVE APPROACH:
TRADITIONAL ANTITRUST

Although generally thought of as an indigenous institution, the antitrust laws of the United States are no more than a logical extension of prohibitions against interferences with competitive markets that go back for centuries into British common law. To interfere with the flow of goods to any "faire or market" by "forestalling," "regrating," or "engrossing" was a crime, the punishment for which became more severe with successive transgressions. Among the practices prohibited was the mentioning "by word, letter, message or otherwise to any person or persons for the enhancing of the price, or deerer selling of any of the things above mentioned. . . ." A forestaller was not fit for the company of decent men: "no forestaller should be suffered to dwell in any towne, for he is a manifest oppressor of the poore, a publike enemie of the countery, and whole Commonwealth." [1]

[1] "Forestalling," "regrating," and "engrossing" are defined and the punishments therefor set forth in a compendium collected by Fernando Pulton and published in 1617, entitled, *A Kalender, or Table Comprehending the Effect of all the Statutes That Have Been Made and Put in Print, beginning with Magna Charta,* printed for the "Companie of Stationers," London.

"Whosoever doth buy or cause to be bought any merchandise, victual or other thing coming by land or water, towards any faire or market, to be sold in the same, or coming toward any citie, port, haven, creeke or rode of this realm or Wayles, from any part beyond the sea, to be sold, or make any bargain, contract, or promise, for the having or buying of the same, or any part thereof . . . before the said merchandise, victuals or other thing that be in the market, faire, citie, port, haven, creeke or rode, ready to be sold, or shall make any mention by word, letter, message, or otherwise, to any person or persons for the enhancing of the price, or deerer selling of any of the things above mentioned, or else dissuade, move, or stir any person coming to the market or faire to forbear to bring any of the things above mentioned to any market, citie to be sold as in aforsaid shall be adjudged a forestaller. It was enacted that no forestaller should be suffered to dwell in any towne, for he is a manifest opressor of the poore, a publike enemie of the Countery, and whole Commonwealth.

"Whosoever shall regrate or get into his possession in any faire or market any foodstuffs that shall be brought to any faire or market within this realm or Wayles to be sold, and doth sell the same againe in any faire or market, holden in the same place, or in any other faire or market within four miles thereof shall be reputed a regrator.

"Whosoever doth ingrosse, or get into his hands by buying, contracting or promise taking . . . any corne growing in the field (or other foodstuffs) within England, to the intent to sell the same again shall be taken an unlawful ingrosser.

"Whosoever offendeth in any of the things before rehearsed, and being thereof duly convicted or attainted . . . that for his first offense suffer imprisonment by the space of 2 months, without baile or mainprise, and forfeit the value of the goods, chattel, and victual sold by him bought or had: and being thereof once lawfully convicted or attainted, shall for his second offense . . . suffer imprisonment for the space of one halfe yeare, without baile or mainprise, and shall lose the double value of the goods; and being twice convicted

Concern over interferences with competition existed in other countries as well. Antitrust laws were enacted not only in the United States but in most of the major industrialized countries. What is unique about the U.S. experience is that the laws did not disappear.

At the time Adam Smith wrote his *Wealth of Nations,* England was becoming the workshop of the world. The great inventors—Hargreaves, Arkwright, Crompton, Cartwright, Watt, and others—were beginning to set the Industrial Revolution in motion. The factory system was being introduced with its large buildings, expensive machines, bands of workers, employers, and overseers. The old guild monopolies were in the process of disintegrating, and the doctrine of free competition was making great headway, even among the business classes. Some of Smith's immediate pupils were so convinced of the unconditional value of competition as to contend that the individual desire for gain would sooner or later break down every monopolistic combination, "even if it operated to the common advantage of the interests concerned." [2] In his authoritative history of English industry William Cunningham wrote:

> It is at least conceivable that the cotton manufacturers of the early part of the nineteenth century should have endeavoured to retain for a time a monopoly of industrial power, and have forced other peoples to pay such prices as would have enabled them to remodel the conditions of production in a satisfactory fashion. . . . *But the spirit of keen competition had caught hold of the employing classes;* they were of the opinion, and in all probability their judgment on this point was perfectly sound, that it was only by a continued exercise of the activity by which they had found their way into foreign markets that they could hope to retain them.[3]

But Smith himself was less sanguine. On this issue he is most noted for his observation, "people of the same trade seldom meet together, even for merriment or diversion, but the conversation ends in a conspiracy against the public or in some contrivance to raise prices." [4] Smith was concerned not only with conspiracies but with what he referred to as "enlarged monopolies":

> The exclusive privileges of corporations, statutes of apprenticeship, and all those laws which restrain, in particular employments, the competition to a smaller number than might otherwise go into them, have the same tendency, though in a less degree. They are a sort of enlarged monopolies, and may frequently, for ages together and in whole classes of employments, keep up the market price of particular commodities above the natural price. . . ." [5]

Later Alfred Marshall recognized that the appearance of large corporations destroyed his famous analogy in which industry was likened to a forest of individual trees, sprouting, growing to maturity, and finally dying, the old

---

of any of the said offenses . . . for his third offense that he be set on the pillorie in the citie, towne or place where he shall dwell, and shall forfeit all his goods and chattel which he hath to his owne self, and that he be committed to prison. . . ." (*Ibid.,* p. 242.) For a chronology of "antimonopoly policy" dating back 3,500 years, see Fritz Machlup, *The Political Economy of Monopoly,* Johns Hopkins Press, 1952, pp. 185–93.

[2] Herman Levy, *Monopolies, Cartels and Trusts in British Industry,* Macmillan, 1927, p. 18.

[3] William Cunningham, *The Growth of English Industry and Commerce in Modern Times,* Cambridge University Press, 1929, pp. 619–20. Emphasis added.

[4] Adam Smith, *Wealth of Nations,* Random House, 1937, p. 128.

[5] *Ibid.,* p. 61.

trees constantly being replaced by the new entrants. In its sixth edition, 20 years after his *Principles of Economics* was first published, Marshall changed the tree analogy to read, "As with the growth of trees, so it was with the growth of business as a general rule before the recent development of vast joint stock companies."

By the early part of this century the common-law prohibitions and other restraints on interferences with competition had fallen into disuse or been repealed. By 1927 Robert Liefman, writing approvingly of cartels, was able to say of Great Britain, "In recent years . . . the courts have shown a preception of the fact that free competition is not necessarily in the interests of the community, and that, on the contrary, competition may be accompanied by or followed by serious disadvantages. There has consequently been a tendency for the law relating to combinations to be stated with modifications." [6] By the 1930's the condition of much of British industry had been transformed from competition to cartelization. As described by Ben W. Lewis:

> Today, as a member in good standing of a "rationalized" industry he [the British industrialist] is allotted a specific percentage of the total business which his industry has decided to handle during the year (and he will pay into a "pool" if he exceeds his quota and will be compensated if he is "short"); he will consult the industry schedule before pricing his goods and will not deviate therefrom without permission; he will submit his sales contracts to the officials of his industrial association for advance approval and will throw open his books for industry inspection; he will pay a levy to be used by the industry to purchase and destroy "redundant" capacity; and he will deposit with the officers of his association a substantial amount to be forfeited if he is found guilty of noncompliance. British industrialists have ceased their warfare, and now, far behind the battle lines, are "negotiating" for the riches which once lured them into open combat.[7]

In France, the penal code of 1870 specifically declared any concerted action for the purpose of influencing prices to be a criminal offense. Here, again, was a manifestation of the popular sentiment against the most common and well-known practice of monopoly. But, as in the case of other nations, "This provision was . . . given a liberal interpretation by the courts." [8] To remove any lingering doubts, the French government in 1926 passed a supplementary law declaring combinations to be lawful if intended to secure only "normal profits" to their members.[9]

In Germany public resentment against monopolistic agreements following World War I led to the German Cartel Decree of 1923, issued by the Stresemann Cabinet, which permitted the Minister of Economics to order all members of a cartel or monopolistic agreement to withdraw from it, to demand that all cartel measures be submitted to him before becoming effective, and to petition a special Cartel Court to declare cartel agreements null and void. The decree also provided that cartels had to obtain permission of the Court before declaring boycotts or "penalties of like nature" and that all cartel agreements

---

[6] Robert Liefman, *International Cartels, Combines and Trusts,* Europa, 1927, p. 147.
[7] Ben W. Lewis, *Price and Production Control in British Industry,* University of Chicago Press, 1937, pp. 1–2.
[8] Library of Congress, Legislative Reference Service, Public Affairs Bulletin No. 32, *Cartels and International Patent Agreements,* 1944, p. 11.
[9] *Ibid.*

should be in writing.[10] The repeal of this decree was one of the Hitler government's first orders of business.

The keystone of the American antitrust laws, once termed by Chief Justice Hughes a "charter of freedom" for American industry,[11] is the Sherman Act. Passed in 1890, the Sherman Act was a reflection of the temper of the times. But determining the intent of Congress from its legislative history is complicated by the fact that "the bill which was arduously debated was never passed, and . . . the bill which was passed was never really discussed."[12] The Sherman Act contained two types of prohibitions: one made it illegal for anyone to "monopolize" or "attempt to monopolize"; the other proscribed "restraints of trade." The former was intended to give the government the power to break up monopolies or trusts; the latter was directed primarily against conspiracies among independent firms to fix prices, divide up markets, restrict production, and the like. These two types of prohibition are the warp and woof of traditional American antitrust policy.

Monopoly

Broadly speaking, enforcement of the Sherman Act's proscription of monopoly began with a little more than a decade of quiet neglect, followed by vigorous application up to 1911, only to be followed by nearly a half-century of quiet judicial interment, then by a little-noted rebirth in the late 1940's and early 1950's, and finally by a second interment—this time at the hands of the enforcing agency.

The initial decisions

After some first uncertain decisions, the courts settled down in the opening decade of this century to enforce the antimonopoly feature of the law—and enforce it vigorously. Monopoly had been condemned by the people and by their representatives in Congress. Congress had passed what the circuit court in the *American Tobacco* case called a "drastic statute." Accordingly, the courts developed far-reaching standards, which caused what was generally described as "great unrest" in the business community. Through a series of decisions, including especially the *Trans-Missouri Freight* case, the *Northern Securities* case, and the circuit court opinions in the *Standard Oil* and *American Tobacco* cases, two drastic standards were laid down: (a) consolidations and mergers *between previously competing firms* were illegal since they would necessarily destroy previously existing competition; and (b) "*every* contract, combination . . . or conspiracy in restraint of trade" was illegal. In addition, it was the government's contention that great size and power resulting from consolidation were illegal.

In the celebrated *Northern Securities* case the Supreme Court in 1904 emphasized the first standard—the effects on competition of mergers between previously competing firms—stating that the Sherman Act was violated by com-

---

[10] William M. Kessler, "German Cartel Regulations under the Decree of 1923," *Quarterly Journal of Economics,* August, 1936, p. 680.

[11] *Appalachian Coals* v. *United States,* 280 U.S. 344 at 359.

[12] Temporary National Economic Committee, Monograph No. 16, *Antitrust in Action,* by Walton Hamilton, 1941, p. 11.

bining and forming "a distinct corporation to hold the stock of the constituent corporation and by destroying competition between them. . . ." [13] With considerable understatement Myron W. Watkins commented, "Evidently, according to this view, it did not require very extensive consolidation to 'restrain trade.' " [14] In the *American Tobacco* case the circuit court spelled out in explicit terms its preoccupation with the elimination of competition between formerly competing firms:

> What benefits may have come from this combination . . . it is not material to inquire, nor need subsequent business methods be considered. . . . The record in this case does not indicate that there has been any increase in the price of tobacco products to the consumer. There is an absence of persuasive evidence that by unfair competition or improper practices independent dealers have been dragooned into giving up their individual enterprises and selling out to the principal defendant. During the existence of the American Tobacco Company new enterprises have been started, some with small capital, in competition with it and have thrived. *But all this is immaterial.* Each one of these purchases of existing concerns, complained of in the petition, was a contract and combination in restraint of a competition existing when it was entered into, and that is sufficient to bring it within the ban of this drastic statute.[15]

The illegality of *every* restraint of trade was set forth most explicitly in the *Trans-Missouri Freight* case.[16] The Supreme Court took great pains to emphasize the apparently obvious fact that Congress, in putting the word "every" into the law, had meant exactly what it had said and that the Court was not free to regard some restraints as permissible and invoke the law only against those which, in its own judgment, were "unreasonable":

> The language of the Act includes every contract, combination . . . or conspiracy in restraint of trade. So far as the very terms of the statute go, they apply to any contract of the nature described. It is now with much amplification of argument urged that the statute, in declaring illegal every combination . . . or conspiracy in restraint of trade or commerce, does not mean what the language used therein plainly imports, but that it only means to declare illegal any such contract which is in unreasonable restraint of trade, while leaving all others unaffected by the provisions of the act. . . . [But] the plain and ordinary meaning of such language is not limited to that kind of contract alone which is in unreasonable restraint of trade, but all contracts are included in such language, and no exception or limitation can be added without placing in the act that which has been omitted by Congress.[17]

Furthermore, the government contended that great size and power brought about by consolidation was also illegal. The Attorney General in arguing the *Standard Oil* case pointed to the Court's previous decision in the *Northern Securities* case and to other precedents, contending that "the power of suppression of competition, and therefore of restraint of trade exercised or which could be

---

[12] *United States* v. *Northern Securities Co.,* 193 U.S. 338 (1904).

[14] Myron W. Watkins, *Mergers and the Law,* National Industrial Conference Board, 1929, p. 38.

[15] *United States* v. *American Tobacco Co.,* 164 Fed. 700 (C.C.N.Y. 1908), 702–03. Emphasis added.

[16] *United States* v. *Trans-Missouri Freight Assn.,* 166 U.S. 290 (1897).

[17] *Ibid.,* at 312, 327–28.

exercised by reason of stock ownership and control of the various corporations, was as much in violation of the antitrust act as direct restraint by contract." [18]

The Attorney General raised the question of why Congress had passed Section 2 of the Sherman Act at all if it had not intended to prohibit those "attempts to monopolize" that did *not* involve any "restraints of trade." Presumably all attempts that did involve restraints would be caught by Section 1 of the Act. In the words of the Attorney General, "The two sections of the Act were manifestly not intended to cover the same thing; otherwise the second section would be useless." [19]

The "Rule of Reason"

Not only did the Court soon overturn these early and stringent standards, but it replaced them with standards that made the Sherman Act prohibition against monopoly practically unenforceable. The vehicle by which this reversal was accomplished was the celebrated "Rule of Reason," introduced, ironically, in the very cases that made the Court famous for "trust busting." In the *Standard Oil* and *American Tobacco* cases the Supreme Court concurred with the opinions of the lower courts that the trusts should be broken up. However, it did so for entirely different reasons, holding that Congress had intended to legislate only against those restraints of trade that were "unreasonable." [20]

In a bitter dissent, Justice Harlan called attention to the fact that the Court had previously been urged to adopt the Rule of Reason: "As we have twice already deliberately and earnestly considered the same arguments which are now for a third time pressed upon our attention, it could hardly be expected that our opinion should now change from that already expressed." [21] Previously, Congress had repeatedly been importuned to accept the Rule of Reason and just as repeatedly had refused to do so. In a report on one such bill, Senator Nelson in 1909 on behalf of the Senate Judiciary Committee had said that

> the injection of the rule of reasonableness or unreasonableness would lead to the greatest variableness and uncertainty in the enforcement of the law. The defense of reasonable restraint would be made in every case and there would be as many different rules of reasonableness as cases, courts and juries. . . . A court or jury in Ohio might find a given agreement or combination reasonable, while a court and jury in Wisconsin might find the same agreement and combination unreasonable. . . . To amend the Antitrust Act, as suggested by this bill, would be to entirely emasculate it, and for all practical purposes render it nugatory as a remedial statute.[22]

Justice Harlan went on to excoriate the majority for accepting a doctrine the Court had already specifically rejected: "But my brethren, in their wisdom, have deemed it best to pursue a different course. They have now said to those

[18] *Standard Oil Co. of New Jersey, et al.,* v. *United States,* 221 U.S. (1911), at 22.
[19] *Ibid.* at 24.
[20] "Thus not specifying but indubitably contemplating and requiring a standard, it follows that it was intended that the *standard of reason* which had been applied at the common law and in this country in dealing with subjects of the character embraced by the statute, was intended to be the measure used for the purpose of determining whether in a given case a particular act had or had not brought about the wrong against which the statute provided." (*Ibid.* at 60.) Emphasis added.
[21] 221 U.S. 1 (1911) at 94.
[22] Cited and quoted in *ibid.,* 96, 97–98, 102.

who condemn our former decisions and who object to all legislative prohibitions of contracts, combinations and trusts in restraint of interstate commerce, 'You may now restrain such commerce, provided you are reasonable about it; only take care that the restraint is not undue.' " [23] Under this doctrine the law was violated only if consolidations and mergers between previously competing companies "unreasonably" restrained trade, if restraints of trade were "unreasonable," or if great size and power were acquired or used "unreasonably." Hence it is not surprising to find that although the *Standard Oil* and *American Tobacco* decisions ordered dissolution of the trusts, they "were received with a great sense of relief in the business world." [24]

To determine what was unreasonable the new decisions laid down the standard that the law was violated if the company had demonstrated an "intent to monopolize." [25] But how was the government to determine intent; how was it to establish what was really "in the back of the minds" of those who, for example, promoted a consolidation? And how was the intent to be proved, since the intent to exclude others or oppress the public might be only one of a number of motives at work? "To isolate from the complex of impulses playing upon a host of persons a particular motive or to make one impulse to action dominant and the others recessive is to indulge sheer fiction." [26] Moreover, the Court gradually weakened even this nebulous standard of intent by holding that consolidations might be permissible, even though they resulted from an intent to monopolize, as long as the consolidation resulted in greater efficiency and thus, by implication, in greater savings to consumers. In upholding the consolidation in the *International Shoe Company* case, the Court stated: "On the face of it, the combination was simply an effort after greater efficiency." [27] Moreover, the Court was impressed by the lessening use of predatory practices once a monopolistic position had been achieved. After the U.S. Steel Corporation and the International Harvester Company had gained control over more than half of their respective industries, their need to use the practices by which they had secured their dominant positions naturally tended to diminish. To the Court this meant that they had corrected their evil ways and should "go and sin no more." [28] In arguing the *Standard Oil* case in 1911 the Attorney General, George W. Wickersham, had pointed to this probable development. Replying to the company's argument

---

[23] 221 U.S. 1 (1911) at 102.

[24] Watkins, *op. cit.*, p. 40.

[25] "The element which is most stressed in the [*Standard Oil*] opinion is the defendants' intent to monopolize the industry and to maintain their monopoly through the exclusion of competitors." And in the *American Tobacco* case the Court "rested its decision essentially upon the ground that the intent and purpose of this long series of combinations was to monopolize the tobacco industry and to stamp out competition." (Milton Handler, *A Study of the Construction and Enforcement of the Federal Antitrust Laws*, Monograph No. 38. Temporary National Economic Committee [TNEC], 1941, pp. 51, 53.)

[26] Hamilton and Till, *op. cit.*, p. 5.

[27] *United States* v. *Winslow*, 227 U.S. 202 (1913), at 217. See also cases cited by Watkins, *op. cit.*, the Armour-Morris merger, 1923; the Bethlehem-Lackawanna merger, 1923; the *War Food Products* case, 1925; and the Standard Oil merger, 1926.

[28] "It may be definitely stated that whatever may have been the original intent in the formation of a business merger, and though an illegal intent might be established by other circumstances, this question does not by itself determine the legal status of the consolidation. In order that a remedial or penal decree may be obtained, it is necessary for the Government to prove, in addition, that exclusive business policies which evidenced a continuation of an original, unlawful intent have been pursued up to the time of the institution of corrective proceedings." (Watkins, *op. cit.*, p. 82.)

that the Sherman Act was directed only against "unlawful means used to acquire a monopoly," the Attorney General said:

> If such be the true interpretation, the result would be that one could combine all the separate manufactures in a given branch of industry in this country by use of unlawful means such as discriminatory freight rates, but, if not attacked by the Government, before it had obtained complete control of the business, its very size, with its ramifications through all the States, would make it impossible for anyone else to compete, and it could control the price of products . . . and yet the Government would be powerless to destroy the monopoly because the unlawful means had been abandoned.[29]

As time passed, the determination and proof of intent became increasingly difficult. The activities of the oil and tobacco trusts in gaining control had been so glaring than an intent to monopolize was almost self-evident. But as industry became more sophisticated, relying more on mutual understanding than on threats, intimidation, and force, the tangible evidences of intent tended to disappear. The effect of introducing the standard of intent was, in Milton Handler's words, "to open the door to metaphysical distinctions, evasions, and further uncertainty." [30]

As evidence of an unlawful intent to monopolize, the Court had placed great emphasis on predatory practices, such as the exclusion of competitors, discrimination, the cutting of prices below costs to force competitors out of business, artificial restrictions on potential competition, and the general abuse of power. The industrial empire builders who had been busily engaged in creating the oil and tobacco trusts had not hesitated to use whatever competitive devices, fair or unfair, were at hand. In the *Standard Oil* case the Court listed the unfair practices:

> Rebates, preferences and other discriminatory practices in favor of the combination by railroad companies; restraint and monopolization by control of pipe lines, and unfair practices against competing pipe lines; contracts with competitors in restraint of trade; unfair methods of competition, such as local price cutting at the points where necessary to suppress competition; espionage of the business of competitors, the operation of bogus independent companies, and payment of rebates on oil, with the like intent; the division of the United States into districts and the limiting of the operations of the various subsidiary corporations as to such districts so that competition in the sale of petroleum products between such corporations had been entirely eliminated and destroyed. . . .[31]

The emphasis given by the Court to the widespread use of predatory practices by the oil and tobacco trusts—which it dissolved—coupled with its emphasis on their lesser frequency on the part of the Steel and Harvester corporations—which it did *not* dissolve—led to the popular distinction between "good" and "bad" trusts. It also helped inter dissolution proceedings for over a quarter of a century. From 1920 (when in the *U.S. Steel* case the Supreme Court rendered its famous ruling that "the law does not make mere size an offense, or

---

[29] 221 U.S. 1 (1911), 28–29.
[30] Milton Handler, *A Study of the Construction and Enforcement of the Federal Antitrust Laws,* Monograph No. 38, Temporary National Economic Committee (TNEC), 1941, p. 78.
[31] 221 U.S. 22 (1911), 42, 43.

the existence of unexerted power an offense"[32]) until the mid-1940's all was quiet, or nearly so, on the dissolution front. Size and power, no matter how great, if not achieved by a demonstrable "intent to monopolize" and not accompanied by "unlawful practices," remained inviolate. The doctrine was firmly nailed down in 1927 by the decision in the *International Harvester* case, in which the Court left no room for doubt, stating, "The law . . . does not make the mere size of a corporation, however impressive, or the existence of an unexerted power on its part, an offense, when unaccompanied by unlawful conduct in the exercise of its power."[33] Contending that it was the "effective power . . . to control and restrain competition and freedom of trade" that Congress intended to limit and control, Justice Day, joined by two other members of the Court, objected: "That the exercise of the power may be withheld, or exerted with forbearing benevolence, does not place combinations beyond the authority of the statute which was intended to prohibit their formation, and when formed to deprive them of the power unlawfully attained."[34]

The results of dissolution

Any dissolution case presents the problem of determining the precise way in which the breaking up of the enterprise is to be carried out. Hence, it should be instructive to analyze briefly the more important of the early cases in order to determine just how this job of "busting the trusts" was done and how effective these actions actually were.

The breakup of the Standard Oil combination in 1911 went farther than any other dissolution and thus should serve as the best available example of the manner in which dissolution was carried out and of its effectiveness. But, while it is perhaps the best, it is not a particularly good example of what can be accomplished by dissolution, since the decree unfortunately left the ultimate economic power in the hands of those who possessed it before the dissolution. The assets of the parent corporation were distributed to its own stockholders— the assets consisting of the stock of operating companies, which were spread over production, transportation, refining, and marketing. The result of leaving the ownership of the operating companies in the hands of those who had owned the old parent corporation was, specifically, to leave the dominant ownership with the Rockefeller interests. In a subsequent investigation of the Standard Oil companies, the Federal Trade Commission suggested a law to prohibit the common ownership of stock of companies that had been members of a combination dissolved under the Sherman Act, the Commission noting, "There is, as is generally known, an interlocking stock ownership in the different organizations [of the Standard Oil group] which has perpetuated the very monopolistic control which the Court sought to terminate."[35] In addition, the separated companies had each been dominant in its own market, with the result that monopoly power in the market was left largely undisturbed by the decree.[36]

In dissolving the American Tobacco trust, the Court adopted a "three-way

---

[32] *United States* v. *United States Steel Corp.,* 251 U.S. 417 (1920), at 451.
[33] *United States* v. *International Harvester Co.,* 274 U.S. 693 (1927), at 708.
[34] 251 U.S. 417 (1920) at 464.
[35] Federal Trade Commission, *Report on the Petroleum Trade in Wyoming and Montana,* 1922, p. 3.
[36] Joel B. Dirlam and Alfred E. Kahn, *Fair Competition; the Law and Economics of Antitrust Policy,* Cornell University Press, 1954, Ch. 5.

principle" whereby monopoly was conceived to be eliminated and competition restored by the division of a trust into three roughly equal parts. As the reason for selecting this figure and not some other, such as 60 (as was proposed by Louis Brandeis, then a private attorney for the smaller tobacco interests) the Court stated: "This whole line of argument deals with the economics of the tobacco business. No doubt the novel problem presented to this Court is connected with questions of economics as well as with questions of law. But this is a court of law, not a commerce commission, and the legal side of the proposition would seem to be the controlling one." [37] Under the decree there were to be 3 large "full-line" companies producing most of the tobacco products, and at least 2 companies in each of the specialty lines. The largest company was permitted to control about 39 percent of the national business. In comparison, the trust had controlled in 1910 some 76 percent of the smoking tobacco, 80 percent of the fine-cut tobacco, 85 percent of the black tobacco, and 96 percent of the snuff. The effect of the dissolution was thus to put into the hands of 3 corporations the control that formerly had been exercised by one.

By comparison with the oil and tobacco actions, the dissolutions in powder (explosives) and photographic equipment were relatively minor affairs. In dissolving the powder combination, the Court again followed the three-way principle, dividing up the Du Pont monopoly among Du Pont, Atlas, and Hercules. That the Eastman Kodak Company was the victim of a dissolution suit generally comes as a matter of some surprise, owing to the continuing preeminent position of the company in the photographic-equipment field. The company was ordered to dispose of certain brands of plates, plants, and so on. But according to George E. Hale, "the corporation sustained the losses in magnificent fashion, for it still does an enormous percentage of the national (and world) business in photographic supplies." [38]

Despite these limitations the results achieved through dissolution have not been altogether unimpressive. Had the old Standard Oil trust not been dissolved in 1911, it is not unlikely that the present level of concentration in the petroleum industry would be even higher. Surveying the long-term effects of the dissolution, Hale, in his authoritative study of dissolution, states: "In general . . . it seems that the Standard interests as a whole have lost ground to their competitors—a result which may be partly attributed to the decree. . . ." [39] Similarly, had the Court not broken up the old American Tobacco trust, it is not unlikely that the industry's present symmetrical oligopoly would have been replaced by an extremely asymmetrical one. As in the case of the *Standard Oil* decision, the *American Tobacco* decision made possible the entrance of newcomers—including the companies which, during the Depression, introduced low-priced ("10-cent") brands.

Another impressive example of divestiture was the result of a little-known action by the Federal Trade Commission preventing the nation's largest automobile producer and its largest steel company from being bound together through stock ownership with its largest chemical company. Following its purchase of 22.9 percent of the stock of General Motors, E. I. du Pont de Nemours & Company announced on July 27, 1927, that it had purchased 114,000 shares

[37] *United States* v. *American Tobacco Co., et al.,* (C.C. S.D. N.Y., Nov., 15, 1911) 191 Fed., 371 at 376.
[38] George E. Hale, "Trust Dissolution," *Columbia Law Review,* April, 1940, pp. 615–32.
[39] *Ibid*.

of the common stock of U.S. Steel Corporation, for which it paid some $14 million. Alarmed over the vertical relationships that might develop among the 3 companies as well as over the establishment of such a "community of interests," the FTC two days later initiated a general investigation. Six months later Du Pont announced that it had sold its entire holdings of U.S. Steel.

Had it not been for far-reaching dissolution actions brought under another statute, the Public Utility Holding Company Act, it is not unlikely that all public utility services in the nation would today be furnished by operating companies owned and controlled by a handful of gigantic utility-holding companies. And had it not been for the establishment of new competitors through the disposal of government-owned facilities, the innovations in new uses and forms of aluminum pioneered by Reynolds and Kaiser might still be waiting their development and introduction.

Dissolution since World War II

Shortly after World War II decisions in two important cases gave rise to the belief that the courts were in the process of forging the Sherman Act into an effective instrument against monopoly power. This point of view has been set forth persuasively by Eugene V. Rostow: "The Supreme Court is on the threshold of recognizing what the economists call monopolistic competition as the offense of monopoly. . . ." [40] Placing his faith primarily in the monopoly section, he argued, "The idea of monopoly under Section 2 of the statute has the great advantage of neglect. It has been considered separately from Section 1 in very few cases, none of which would stand in the way of a redefinition of the term in the light of our present view of the monopoly problem." [41]

The cases that gave rise to this resurgence of faith were the *Alcoa* and *American Tobacco* decisions.[42] In the *Alcoa* case the Supreme Court withdrew itself on the grounds that several of its members had been officials of the Department of Justice at the time the case was in process, and a decision was therefore rendered by a special court of last resort headed by Judge Learned Hand. According to Rostow,

> In the Aluminum case Judge Hand finally interred and reversed the old dictum that size is not an offense under the Sherman Act. Size, he concluded was not only evidence of violation, or a potential offense, as in Justice Cardozo's conciliatory formula of the Swift case: it was the essence of the offense. Size, meaning market control, was what competition and monopoly were about. All other aspects of the case were subordinated to the central and decisive fact that the Aluminum Company of America, many years after its patents had expired, made, and then fabricated or sold, over 90 percent of the virgin aluminum and therefore had monopoly power. "The producer of so large a proportion of the supply has complete control within certain limits." [43]

Acknowledging that for all its potential import the decision was not without its limitations, Rostow noted, "The line of the opinion is marred by dicta which

[40] Eugene V. Rostow, *A National Program for the Petroleum Industry,* Yale University Press, 1948, p. 126.
[41] *Ibid.,* p. 24.
[42] *United States* v. *Aluminum Co. of America,* 148 F. 2d 416 (C.C.A. 2, 1945); *American Tobacco Co.* v. *United States,* 328 U.S. 781 (1946).
[43] Rostow, *op. cit.,* pp. 126–27.

somewhat confuse its import. The control of 90 percent of supply, Judge Hand said, is enough to constitute a monopoly; it is doubtful whether sixty or sixty-four percent would be enough; and certainly thirty-three percent is not." But the interjection of these dicta, which stem from the old *International Harvester* case, was, in Rostow's view, a matter of relative unimportance: "Judge Hand's opinion is a practical and feasible restatement of the conception of monopoly, giving the law new and far-reaching scope." [44]

In the *American Tobacco* case, a criminal proceeding, the defendants were the 3 major companies that account for some three-fourths of all cigarettes sold in the United States. Because it was a criminal action brought under both Sections 1 and 2 of the Sherman Act, it is impossible to draw from the decision a specific interpretation that is clearly applicable only to the problem of monopoly power. Nonetheless, because of its emphasis on the power to discourage potential competition, the decision is not without its implications for dissolution proceedings. It is a short step from establishing the point at which the possession of power becomes sufficient "to deter or discourage potential competition" to determining the point at which monopoly power becomes unlawful per se. Moreover, the Court stated that it welcomed the opportunity to endorse the statement in the *Alcoa* opinion that a monopoly cannot be dissociated from its exercise.[45]

With this encouragement, the Department of Justice launched a new program aimed at achieving "divestiture, divorcement and dissolution." Appearing before a Senate subcommittee on May 31, 1946, Attorney General Clark stated: "the times require that it [competition] be restored by the seldom used processes of divestiture, divorcement, and dissolution. The use of all of these weapons of enforcement will establish complete and independent units of enterprise which can and will in fact compete one with the other. This is the only way to maintain free enterprise." [46] Similarly, in his annual report for the fiscal year ending June 30, 1947, the Attorney General again called attention to the importance of dissolution actions, stating:

> In regard to monopolies, I have encouraged the application of the remedies of divestiture and divorcement in civil suits brought under Section 2 of the Sherman Act, as the most expeditious means of eradicating this economic evil. The ramifications of monopoly are myriad and, when allowed to develop unchecked, have an effect upon every aspect of the economic scene. Nowhere is this effect more apparent than in the fields of production and pricing and upon no one is the impact of monopolistic policies more severe than upon the small businessman.[47]

---

[44] *Ibid.,* p. 129. If these percentage figures were regarded as general statements of law rather than dicta, their application, in themselves, would have had only a limited effect on industry generally. Of 1,807 Census products, there were only 97 of which the leading producer in 1937 accounted for over 65% of the nation's output (and they represented only 5.3% of the total number and 2.3% of the total value of all products surveyed); the leading producer accounted for over 60% of the output of only 152 products (only 8.1% of the total number and 3.3% of the total value). See Willard L. Thorp and Walter Crowder, *The Structure of Industry,* Monograph No. 27, Temporary National Economic Committee (TNEC), 1941, p. 292.

[45] *American Tobacco Co.,* v. *United States,* 328 U.S. 781 (1946) at 813, 814.

[46] Annual Report of the Attorney General of the United States for the fiscal year ended June 30, 1947, p. 8.

[47] Annual Report of the Attorney General of the United States for the fiscal year ended June 30, 1947, p. 8.

In *United States* v. *Pullman Co.*, the Court found that the Sherman Act had been violated in both the manufacture and operation of sleeping cars. The Court required the Pullman Company to dispose of either the business of operating Pullman cars or the manufacture of sleeping cars, the company electing to sell the operating business. Although the Department objected to the manner in which the operating business was to be disposed of, the case did break up what had long been one of the most conspicuous examples of monopoly in the American economy.

On January 19, 1949, an opinion was rendered in the District Court of New Jersey holding that General Electric Company had monopolized the incandescent-lamp industry, the court finding that General Electric's market control was made up of its own production of approximately 55 percent of the lamps sold and manufactured in the United States and the production of its licensees, which General Electric effectively controlled, comprising 30 percent of the lamps made and sold in the United States. But the court did not order dissolution, requiring only that GE's patents and know-how be opened up to competitors.

On September 15, 1948, the Department filed a complaint against the 4 major meat-packing companies alleging that the large meat packers, by market sharing of livestock purchases and identical buying and selling policies and practices, had suppressed competition. The Department asked that these practices be terminated and that the 4 defendants be divided into 14 separate and competing companies. The case was lost in the District Court and not appealed by the Department.

On December 15, 1947, the Department filed a complaint against the United Shoe Machinery Corporation charging monopoly in the manufacture of shoe machinery, shoe machinery parts, shoe factory supplies, and tanning machinery. The Government sought to compel the defendant to sell all plants used in the manufacture of shoe factory supplies and some of the plants engaged in the manufacture of shoe machinery and tanning machinery, to offer to sell (rather than merely lease) its machinery to shoe manufacturers, and to make available to its competitors all patents and know-how relating to shoe machinery. While the government won a decisive victory in the lower court, the form of relief ordered by Judge Wyzanski stopped short of dissolution.

On January 14, 1949, the Department filed a complaint against the Western Electric Company and the American Telephone and Telegraph Company, charging that AT&T bought substantially all of its telephone equipment from Western Electric, its wholly owned subsidiary. The complaint also alleged that the absence of effective competition resulted in higher prices paid for telephone equipment, which in turn tended to raise subscriber rates to consumers, since the higher prices for telephone equipment increased the "rate base" used by regulatory commissions in establishing rates. As part of the relief sought, the suit asked for a separation of Western Electric from AT&T and a dissolution of Western Electric into 3 competing manufacturing concerns. But the case was settled by a consent order, which again did not require divestiture.

On June 30, 1949, the Department announced the filing of a suit charging the Du Pont Company, General Motors Corporation, and United States Rubber Company with combining and conspiring to violate the Sherman Act and Section 7 of the Clayton Act. The suit sought the following relief: the sale by Du Pont of all its stock in General Motors; the sale by the members of the Du Pont family of all their stock in United States Rubber Company; the sale by Du Pont of its business of making tetraethyl lead, ethyl fluid, and ethyl chloride; the sale by General Motors of its 50 percent stock interest in the Ethyl Corporation; the sale by Du Pont and General Motors of their respective interests in Kinetic Corporation, a manufacturer of refrigerants; and the cancellation of all existing contracts between Du Pont, General Motors, and United States Rubber relating to the sale of products, the granting of licenses, agreements to license under patents, and agreements providing for the exchange of know-how. Stressing the Clayton Act charge and virtually ignoring the alleged violations of the Sherman Act, the Supreme Court held that the original Section 7 had always applied to vertical acquisitions and ordered the Du Pont interests to dispose of their stock holdings in General Motors.

An examination of the outcome of these six cases brought under Attorney General Clark's program suggests that much can be accomplished under the present law in the way of divorce, divestiture, and dissolution. The *Alcoa* decision's 60–64 percent "doubtful" test applies, it will be recalled, to share of the market per se. But, as the actual evidence in these cases illustrates, a dominant position in the real world is seldom achieved or even retained without the abuse of power. Therefore, the point of illegality under the Sherman Act might well be regarded as a market share of considerably below 60–64 percent if accompanied by evidence of abuse of power. Not only would such an interpretation be consistent with past decisions; it would make the Sherman Act, as it is, applicable to the most common structure of concentrated industries—the asymmetrical oligopoly.

Of the six cases, the decision went against the Department of Justice in only one—the meat-packing case. And this was a district court decision that was *not* appealed. Moreover, the action against the leading meat packers was the most sophisticated case of the group. The Department was seeking to break up an oligopoly by showing through circumstantial or "economic" evidence the existence of a collusive agreement. Had the decision of the lower court been appealed and reversed by the Supreme Court, a milestone of enormous import would have been reached. In the two cases that did reach the Supreme Court, *Pullman* and *Du Pont-General Motors,* not only was the government sustained, but effective relief was ordered. In two others, *General Electric* and *United Shoe Machinery,* the decisions also were in favor of the government. Although these were decisions of district courts, they were not appealed by the defendants. Insofar as the restoration of competition is concerned, the deficiency was not in the decisions but in the form of relief ordered. In both, the district courts, it has developed, were overly optimistic that competition would be injected into the industry by the simple act of opening up patents and know-how. The persistence of high levels of concentration indicates that they were not sufficiently aware of the defendants' other sources of monopoly power. In the final case, *Western Electric-AT&T,* no decision was rendered, the defendant agreeing to a consent order, worked out and accepted at the highest level of government, which fell far short of the type of relief—divestiture—originally sought by the government.

An argument that dissolution not only of "persistent monopolies" but of oligopolies, or "shared monopolies," can be achieved under Section 2 of the Sherman Act has recently been advanced by Donald F. Turner.[48] Insofar as "persistent monopolies" are concerned, Turner expresses the belief that, under the law as it is, the courts would order dissolution even in the absence of exclu-

[48] Donald F. Turner, "The Scope of Antitrust and Other Economic Regulatory Policies," *Harvard Law Review,* April, 1969, pp. 1207–44.

sionary practices if the monopoly were "persistently maintained over a substantial period of time." There would, however, be two defenses: dissolution could not be expected where the persistent monopoly power is "based solely on economies of scale or where it arose out of and still depends upon valid unexpired patents." [49]

Contending that the decision in *United Shoe Machinery* would have been the same had the substantial monopoly power in the industry (some 80 percent of sales) been held not by one firm but by 2 or 3 companies, Turner argues that "the law on shared monopoly may be brought virtually in line with the law on individual monopoly, and divestiture where feasible invoked as a remedy. . . ." [50]

> Where oligopolists sharing monopoly power have engaged in restrictive conduct lacking any substantial justification, they may appropriately be said to have unlawfully attempted to monopolize. Where it appears that their decisions to carry on particular exclusionary practices are interdependent, where one would not have carried on the practice unless the others had gone along, they may also be charged with a conspiracy or combination to monopolize. Finally, where each of the companies effectively sharing monopoly power has engaged in possibly justifiable conduct that nevertheless has unnecessary exclusionary effects, it seems logical and appropriate to me to charge each with having individually "monopolized" in violation of section 2. Each has obtained and maintained monopoly power—real, though shared—to which factors other than skill, foresight, industry, and the like have contributed. [51]

Turner does not regard the "efficiency" and the "valid patent" defenses as constituting a much more serious barrier in oligopoly than in monopoly cases: "I doubt that the feasibility of divestiture is generally less in oligopoly than in monopoly, since feasibility depends on the absolute size of the firm in relation to economies of scale rather than on market structure." [52]

But conceding that much can be accomplished under the present law one good and sufficient reason for the enactment of new legislation is the tortuous, time-consuming legal labyrinth through which dissolution cases now have to pass before final relief is obtained. The typical dissolution case involves an interminable series of legal steps, each of which can consume months or even years, depending on the size and complexity of the case. A case in point is *United States* v. *Hartford-Empire Glass Co.*—an action that involved the leading producer in an important industry and, in view of the issues, was handled rather expeditiously. The investigation by the Department of Justice was initiated on December 12, 1939; the trial was started in March, 1941, and ended in January, 1942; the opinion of the district court was rendered in August, 1942; the final judgment of the district court was issued in September, 1942; the case was argued before the Supreme Court on November 17, 1943; it was set down for a rehearing in October, 1944; it was decided by the Supreme Court on January 8, 1945, the judgment of the district court being affirmed in part and modified in part; it was then sent back for a second hearing on relief before a Master, appointed by the district court, the proceeding starting in November, 1946. Some 6 months later, all the parties involved decided they had enough of litigation, and on May

[49] *Ibid.*
[50] *Ibid.*
[51] *Ibid.*
[52] *Ibid.*

23, 1947, precisely 7 years, 5 months, and 11 days after the original initiation, the case was settled in an order agreed to by both the Department and Hartford-Empire.

Legislative proposals for dissolution

Not surprisingly, the delays and uncertainties under the Sherman Act have given rise to proposals for new legislation on dissolution. William Fellner has suggested that the test of law applicable to mergers be extended to the fruits thereof: "There is not much logic in the position that socially unjustified mergers should be prevented but that the results of past mergers should be regarded as untouchable." [53] The same proposal was made to the Antitrust Subcommittee in 1958 by Victor R. Hansen, assistant attorney general in charge of the Antitrust Division: "One thought that has been running through my mind and some members of our staff, is there some means whereby Section 2 of the Sherman Act could be amended to give us a similar type of tool that we have in the Clayton Act in the case of mergers? . . . could we have some amendment to Section 2 that would give us some sort of provision that we have in Section 7?" [54] Several bills embodying this line of thought have been introduced in Congress; an example is H.R. 11872, introduced on May 23, 1962, by Chairman Celler of the House Judiciary Committee, which would amend Section 2 of the Sherman Act by providing that: "No person or group of persons shall exercise power to monopolize or *to substantially lessen competition in any line of commerce.* The exercise of such power shall be ground for injunction, divestiture, dissolution, or other appropriate relief. . . ." [55] To be completely correlative with the amended Section 7, the bill would have to make unlawful the possession, in any line of commerce in any section of the United States, of a share of the market such that the result may be to substantially lessen competition or tend to create a monopoly.

Other proposals for dissolution have been put forward by Walter Adams, by the Federal Trade Commission, by Carl Kaysen and Donald Turner, and by the Neal Task Force. Adams proposed applying the principles of the Public Utility Holding Company Act of 1935 to industry generally: "This was the kind of question noted under the act. Why should a gas company and an electric company be owned by the same outfit? Is there any benefit to efficiency? Is there any benefit to the public interest? Or if there is an electric company in New England, should that electric company be owned by the same group that owns another electric company out in the Pacific Northwest?" [56]

---

[53] 88th Cong., 1st Sess., Senate Subcommittee on Antitrust and Monopoly, Senate Committee on the Judiciary, *Administered Prices: A Compendium on Public Policy,* 1963, p. 136.

[54] *Hearings on Administered Prices,* Pt. 8, p. 4408.

[55] 87th Cong., 2nd Sess., H.R. 11872, 1962. Emphasis added.

[56] *Hearings on Administered Prices,* Pt. 9, pp. 1793 *et seq.* (see also p. 4852). The same type of proposal has been put forward by Howard J. Triemens. He concluded, "Recent experiences under the Utility Act as well as in the 1905–1915 Sherman Act cases does indicate that large scale readjustment of the structure of an industry in the public interest can be accomplished." He went on to note that there is "considerable similarity" between the Utility Act and the Sherman Act that can be utilized in future cases or legislation dealing with the problems presented by undue concentration of economic power." ("The Utility Act as a Solution to Sherman Act Problems," *Northwestern Illinois Law Review,* July–Aug., 1949, p. 339.)

Contained in a little-noted report submitted in 1950,[57] the FTC's recommendations were founded on an industry-by-industry analysis of the varying "patterns of divergence—the difference between concentration on a plant versus a company basis." [58] The distinctive feature of the report is the tailoring of policy recommendations to the degree of divergence as well as to the level of concentration. The report found that the levels of plant and company concentration were largely a function, respectively, of the nature of technological requirements (reflected in the average size of plant) and the extent of centralized ownership of separate plants (reflected in the average number of plants per company):

> The conclusion may tentatively be drawn, subject to many limitations and exceptions, that the larger the average size of plant (and the smaller the number of large plants), the higher tends to be the level of plant concentration. Similarly, the greater the extent of multiple-plant operations (and the greater the centralization of such operations within the industry's leading concerns), the higher tends to be the level of company concentration.[59]

Dissolution is most feasible where company concentration is high (reflecting extensive multiplant operations) and plant concentration is low (reflecting relatively small plants). It is also feasible where plant concentration is moderately high but is still well below the level of company concentration. It is manifestly not possible in industries where company concentration is only slightly above plant concentration, specifically in industries where the position of the leading firms is based on their operation of one or a few large plants. Where dissolution is feasible, the Commission recommended: "Among those industries with high company concentration and high divergences, there is need to guard against not merely collusive agreement but also monopoly; and if monopoly should be found to exist, the available remedies include the possibility of reducing the size of the largest business concerns." [60] But, where it is not feasible, the logical alternative is some form of regulation: "Finally, in those industries with high company concentration and low divergence, monopolistic concentration cannot readily be corrected by dissolution of monopolistic business firms but must be remedied instead by appropriate correction, or, if necessary, by regulation of business behavior." [61]

As the basis for their legislative proposals, Kaysen and Turner emphasized the existing shortcomings of the law, noting that under present interpretations the Sherman Act does not proscribe large relative size unless: "(1) it is associated with predatory conduct; or (2) in an oligopoly situation it becomes the basis of a conspiracy charge . . . or (3) large size, along with some kind of conduct, shows that the single large firm is monopolizing or has monopo-

---

[57] Federal Trade Commission, *The Divergence Between Plant and Company Concentration,* 1950. Unlike legislative proposals on concentration contained in later reports (e.g., *Economic Report on Corporate Mergers,* 1969) these proposals were made by the Commission itself and not merely by its staff.

[58] See Ch. 5.

[59] FTC, *op. cit.,* p. 29.

[60] *Ibid.,* p. 35.

[61] *Ibid.* The Commission also noted that in those industries with low company and low plant concentration "the task of protecting the public interest appears to be that of preventing collusive agreements and arresting any such increase in company concentration as may tend to lessen competition." (*Ibid.*)

lized. . . ." [62] Since monopolization by one company is uncommon in American industry, the heart of the concentration issue is the problem of oligopoly: "The principal defect of present antitrust law is its inability to cope with market power created by jointly acting oligopolists." [63] Relief should be secured by a movement "toward less concentrated markets in which there are more sellers with smaller shares." To this end they suggest a new statute directed against unreasonable market power, defined as the persistent ability "to restrict output or determine prices without losing a substantial share of the market, or without losing substantial profits or incurring heavier losses, because of the increased output or lower prices of rivals." Among the types of behavior that may be held to constitute evidence of such power are persistent rigidity of prices in the face of either substantial excess capacity or substantial declines in demand or costs, persistence of abnormally high profits, and comparative lack of newcomers during a period of strong demand and high profits.[64]

But market power could also be inferred from a structural test "where, for five years or more, one company has accounted for 50 percent or more of annual sales in the market, or four or fewer companies have accounted for 80 percent of sales." [65] Dissolution would not be required, however, if the defendant companies could show that their possession of the excessive share of the market was a result of any one of three "justifications": (a) "economies" dependent on size in relation to the market, (b) ownership of valid patents, or (c) a general "superior performance" catchall—"low prices or superior products attributable to the introduction of new processes, product improvements, or marketing methods, or to extraordinary efficiency of a single firm in comparison with that of other firms having a substantial share of the market." [66]

What would be the effect of the Kaysen-Turner proposals if they were actually implemented? To arrive at any type of empirical answer one would have to determine in some way the scope of the various "defenses." This is manifestly impossible in the case of the "patent" defense and the "superior performance" defense. On the other hand, Kaysen and Turner limit the scope of the "efficiency" defense by excluding economies resulting from superior management abilities.[67]

---

[62] Carl Kaysen and Donald F. Turner, *Antitrust Policy—an Economic and Legal Analysis,* Harvard University Press, 1959, p. 106.

[63] *Ibid.,* p. 110.

[64] *Ibid.,* p. 266.

[65] *Ibid.,* p. 267.

[66] *Ibid.,* p. 268.

[67] "We reject completely the argument—sometimes implicit and sometimes explicit in discussions of size and efficiency—that the only really scarce resource is managerial talent. The argument is that large firms exist because of the superior talents of their managers, and that any obstacles placed in the way of their continued expansion will only lead to the substitution of inferior for superior management, with the consequent waste of resources. The argument has no support in any evidence. If the advantages of the 'superior' management are cost advantages in production and distribution, there is no evidence to support their widespread existence. That some firms are more efficient than others is clear; but that these differences are large and relatively permanent does not seem to be the case. If the advantages are to be seen in 'superior' decisions with regard to market strategy, rather than in more efficiency in day-to-day operations, the whole argument takes on a question-begging character. Market power is justified on the grounds of the superior ability of the dominant firm to exercise its market power to its own advantage. In other words, antitrust policy should aim to punish those firms holding market power who do not use it to the full advantage of their stockholders. But once a market departs substantially from competitive conditions, the test of management wisdom in terms of 'results' from the stockholders' viewpoint is hardly a test of economic efficiency." (*Ibid.,* p. 117.)

Some impression of the effect of excluding those industries to which the efficiency test on a plant basis would apply can be gathered from an examination of the divergences between plant and company concentration. It can be taken as a certainty that dissolution could not be effected in those industries in which the share held by the 8 largest companies exceeded that of the largest plants by fewer than 10 percentage points, and it is quite probable that the same would be true of industries with a divergence of fewer than 20 percentage points.[68]

In 1963 there were 27 industries whose national concentration ratios exceeded Kaysen and Turner's 80 percent standard; they accounted for 12 percent of the value of shipments of all manufacturing industries. Of these, 7 had divergences of fewer than 10 percentage points and an additional 4 had divergences of from 10 to 19 percentage points. The effect of excluding these 11 industries would be to reduce the number remaining above the Kaysen-Turner standard from 27 to 16 and the proportion of manufacturing output represented by their shipments from 12 to 11 percent. If account were taken of their "patent" and "superior performance" defenses, less than 10 percent of the output of the industrial economy would probably be affected by their dissolution program.

On July 5, 1968, Phil C. Neal, dean of the University of Chicago Law School, presented to President Johnson a report of the Task Force on Antitrust Policy.[69] Among their major recommendations the most important related to "oligopolies or highly concentrated industries." As the basis for their recommendations for dissolution, the Task Force noted that highly concentrated industries represent "a significant segment of the American economy" and that a high degree of concentration "precludes effective market competition and interferes with the optimum use of economic resources." Market behavior can be improved by a reduction in concentration, which, in the absence of dissolution, "is not likely to decline significantly." Moreover, the chances of achieving significant deconcentration under the Sherman Act appear remote: "While new legal approaches might be developed to reduce concentration under existing law—a result which should be encouraged—the history of antitrust enforcement and judicial interpretations do not justify primary reliance on this possibility."

To reduce the concentration of oligopolistic industries the Task Force recommends the enactment of a Concentrated Industries Act. Industries to be subjected to dissolution are defined as those in which (a) the 4 largest firms had an aggregate market share of 70 percent or more during at least 7 of the 10 and 4 of the most recent 5 base years; (b) the share of those *same* companies during a preceding 5-year base period was at least 80 percent of that of the most recent 5-year period; and (c) total industry sales had not fallen by more than 20 percent between the preceding and the most recent base period. These standards are intended to limit the law's application to industries in which concentration is not only very high but stable and in which output is not declining. An oligopoly firm is defined as one whose market share of an oligopoly industry exceeds 15 percent.

The objective would be to bring the 4-firm market share of such industries below 50 percent and the market shares of individual firms below 12 percent. Formal dissolution need not be the only means utilized to achieve this objective: "The decree may use a variety of techniques short of divestiture if they

---

[68] These would be the industries of, respectively, "narrow" and "moderate" divergence, in contrast to industries of "wide" and "extreme" divergence (see Ch. 5).

[69] Included in *Hearings on Economic Concentration*, Pt. 8, pp. 5053–82.

promise to bring about the desired reduction in market share. These steps would include the removal of such barriers to entry as contractual arrangements and patents." Like the recommendations of the Federal Trade Commission and of Kaysen and Turner, the Task Force recommendation contains an "efficiency" defense: "A decree cannot require a firm to take steps which would result in substantial loss of economies of scale. This provision would, for example, preclude divestiture reducing a firm below minimum efficient size or creating new entities below minimum efficient size."

On the issue of managerial efficiencies the Neal Task Force report is not altogether clear. On the one hand it states, "Net loss of economies of scale beyond the plant level might be established directly or by considering the minimum size of viable competitors in an industry. Thus the Court would not ordinarily divide an oligopoly firm into firms smaller than that indicated by experience to be necessary to survival in the industry. *We are not unaware* of efficiencies other than economies of scale. . . ." [70] On the other hand, it recognizes the difference between economic efficiency and economic rent: "other efficiencies (i.e., beyond the plant level) will generally reflect scarce resources such as unique management talent. These resources may be transferred pursuant to a deconcentration decree without significant loss."

It is impossible to determine the proportion of the industrial economy for which dissolution would be required under the Neal Task Force's recommendations, since knowledge concerning one of its standards—the shares of the same companies over a 10-year period—could presumably be obtained only through direct access to Census Bureau files. On the one hand the proportion would be greater than under Kaysen-Turner because of the use of a lower standard of illegality (70 percent versus 80 percent). On the other hand it would be smaller because of the "stability" requirement and the exclusion of declining industries. But the principal drawback to both proposals is that neither goes far enough. For reasons set forth earlier, there are theoretical and empirical bases for the assumption that economic behavior will be significantly different under oligopoly than under polyopoly, but none for the assumption that behavior will differ among industries which differ only in the degree to which they are oligopolistic. If the achievement of a more competitive behavior is the objective, the evidence suggests the need for restructuring industries with concentration ratios of more than 50%, not just those with ratios of more than 70–80%. This objective could be achieved more readily by the application to existing concentration of the standards of law developed under the Celler-Kefauver antimerger statute. [71]

There is one further aspect to the problem of monopoly power per se; this is its enhancement by the control of 2 or more competing enterprises by banks or other financial interests. As was shown in Chapter 4, Morgan Guarantee Trust Company has common stock holdings in 3 competing airlines—8.2% for United Airlines, 7.5% for American Airlines, and 7.4% for Trans World Airlines. Similarly, the Cleveland Trust Company was shown to have significant shareholdings in 6 competing manufacturers of machine tools, ranging from 52.4% in the case of Cleveland Twist Drill Company to 9.1% for Warner and Swasey Company. Such common shareholdings potentially inhibit management from making competitive moves which would adversely affect competitors subject to

[70] Emphasis added.
[71] See Ch. 22.

the same common ownership. While the danger to competition is obvious, any proposal to simply prohibit financial institutions from owning the common stock of competing firms would immediately run into the probably insurmountable objection that it would prevent purchases of securities merely for investment purposes, thereby depressing security values. One way of meeting the problem while avoiding the objection would be to prohibit any financial institution (or its nominees) from voting the stock (either directly, by proxy, or otherwise) which it holds (for itself or for others) in 2 or more competing firms. Objections to such a proposal from the financial community would certainly invite the suspicion that the suppression of competition is among the objectives of stock ownership in competing companies.

Collusion

The second thrust of the traditional antitrust approach is directed against collusion and other "restraints of trade." When competitors enter into an agreement, arrangement, or understanding to fix the price of goods or services they sell or purchase, they are violating Section 1 of the Sherman Act. Since the courts have held that any unlawful conspiracy is also an "unfair method of competition," they are also violating Section 5 of the Federal Trade Commission Act. Although only a few such cases have been brought, it is equally illegal for producers to conspire to control output. Likewise, the courts have struck down any sharing of the market through such means as allocating percentages of the business to each producer, dividing sales territories on a geographical basis, allotting customers to each seller, or distributing business through a common sales agency that apportions orders, imposes production or sales quotas on its members, or limits their competitive behavior in any predetermined way.

The Supreme Court categorically condemned price fixing during the first 10 years of the Sherman Act[72] and has reaffirmed its position in almost every subsequent decade. In *United States* v. *Trenton Potteries Co.*, the Court in 1927 held:

> The aim and result of every price-fixing agreement, if effective, is the elimination of one form of competition. The power to fix prices, whether reasonably exercised or not, involves power to control the market and to fix arbitrary and unreasonable prices. The reasonable price fixed today may through economic and business changes become the unreasonable price of tomorrow. Once established, it may be maintained unchanged because of the absence of competition secured by the agreement for a price reasonable when fixed. Agreements which create such potential power may well be held to be in themselves unreasonable or unlawful restraints, without the necessity of minute inquiry whether a particular price is reasonable or unreasonable as fixed and without placing on the Government in enforcing the Sherman Law the burden of ascertaining from day to day whether it has become unreasonable through the mere variation of economic conditions. Moreover, in the absence of express legislation requiring it, we should hesitate to adopt a construction making the difference between legal and illegal conduct in the field of business relations depend upon so uncertain a test as whether prices are reasonable—a determination which can be satisfactorily made only after a complete

[72] *United States* v. *Trans-Missouri Freight Assn.*, 166 U.S. 290 (1897); *United States* v. *Joint Traffic Assn.*, 171 U.S. 505 (1889); *Addyston Pipe and Steel Co.* v. *United States*, 175 U.S. 211 (1899).

survey of our economic organization and a choice between rival philosophies.[73]

In *United States* v. *Socony Vacuum Oil Co.*, the Court in 1940 stated that it was endeavoring earnestly "to plug every hole that may have existed or might be driven through the doctrine of that [the *Trenton Potteries*] case." [74] The Court restated the rule in the following words: "Thus for over 40 years this Court has consistently and without deviation adhered to the principle that price-fixing agreements are unlawful *per se* under the Sherman Act and that no showing of so-called competitive abuses or evils with which those agreements were designed to eliminate or alleviate may be interposed as a defense." [75] And in order to eliminate all possibility of confusion the Court specified: "Under the Sherman Act a combination formed for the purpose and with the effect of raising, depressing, fixing, pegging, or stabilizing the price of a commodity in interstate or foreign commerce is illegal *per se*." [76]

To illustrate different types of collusion, attention will be directed here to probably the two most important sets of cases of this type since World War II —the actions brought by the Department of Justice against the manufacturers of heavy electrical equipment and those brought by the Federal Trade Commission against producers in a number of industries using the basing-point system and other methods of equalizing delivered prices. The former represented the highest degree and most explicit form of collusion; the latter ranked considerably lower in both degree and formality and higher in sophistication and complexity. In addition attention will be focused on another group of cases which have been somewhat neglected but might be of far-reaching importance from an economic point of view—cases against the concerted restriction of production.

The electrical-equipment cases

In 1960 the Department of Justice brought actions against General Electric, Westinghouse, and virtually all other producers of heavy electrical equipment.[77] The cases had their origins in a statement by the Tennessee Valley Authority that it was forced to invite bids from foreign electrical manufacturers because prices charged by U.S. firms showed essentially no variation from producer to producer and since 1951 had increased over 50 percent, while the average wholesale price of all commodities had risen only about 5 percent. The TVA statement said that on invitations for a 500,000-kilowatt turbogenerator it had received a bid from an English firm that was $6 million under GE and Westinghouse, whose bids were substantially equal. In September, 1959, the Senate Antitrust Subcommittee held hearings at which voluminous evidence of identical bidding compiled by the TVA was introduced into the record. Witnesses included purchasing agents of the TVA and of 5 municipal utilities. A transcript of the hearings was promptly transmitted to the Attorney General.

Shortly after the announcement of these hearings, the Antitrust Division stepped up what had been a routine investigation by its Philadelphia field office to a headquarters investigation and obtained the empanelment of a grand jury. In view of this criminal investigation, the Subcommittee suspended further hear-

---

[73] 273 U.S. 392 (1927) at 397.
[74] Handler, *op. cit.*, p. 12.
[75] *United States* v. *Socony Vacuum Oil Co.*, 310 U.S. 150 (1940) at 218.
[76] *Ibid.*
[77] For a fuller exposition see John Herling, *The Great Price Conspiracy*, Luce, 1962.

ings after having made all its information available to the Department of Justice. On February 14, 1960, the first six indictments were returned, and by October 20, 1960, twenty indictments had been brought by the United States against 29 corporations and 45 individuals, alleging violation of Section 1 of the Sherman Act for price fixing of electrical machinery and equipment, ranging from two-dollar insulators to multi-million-dollar turbine generators. All defendants pleaded guilty or *nolo contendere*. The Court levied a total of $1,924,500 in fines and sent seven men to jail for 30 days each. Twenty-five other managers and executives received 30-day suspended sentences, and each was placed on probation for 5 years. The 2 largest corporate defendants, GE and Westinghouse, were fined a total of $810,000. In addition, a number of the officials involved in these conspiracies were forced to resign or retire from their jobs or were demoted with substantial reductions in salary, and multi-million-dollar civil damage suits were lodged against the companies.

In his statement prior to the sentencing of defendants in Philadelphia on February 6, 1961, Chief Judge Ganey stated:

> This is a shocking indictment of a vast section of our economy, for what is really at stake here is the survival of the kind of economy under which America has grown to greatness, the free enterprise system. The conduct of the corporate and individual defendants alike . . . have flagrantly mocked the image of the economic system of free enterprise which we profess to the country and destroyed the model which we offer today as a free world alternative to state control and eventual dictatorship. . . .[78]

Although one effect of the defendants' pleas of guilty or *nolo contendere* was to keep the evidence secured by the government from being introduced into a trial record, some impression of the nature of their meetings and agreements can be obtained from the indictments and the arraignment hearings before Judge Ganey and from the testimony of company officials before the Senate Antitrust Subcommittee.[79] The principal product lines involved in the agreements apparently were switchgear and control apparatus, transformers, and turbines. Concerned in the switchgear conspiracies were several different categories of product—notably oil circuit breakers, power switching equipment, and power switchgear assemblies. With respect to the first, it appears from the indictment and the hearings that meetings were held from 1951 to 1957 for the purposes of allocating sealed bids to government agencies on the basis of 45 percent to GE, 35 percent to Westinghouse, 10 percent to Allis-Chalmers, and 10 percent to Federal Pacific. Executives of these companies allegedly exchanged weekly inter company memos dealing with sales to private utilities and including a list of the jobs coming up for the week, the price each company was to bid, comments on the general price structure, and other essential information. In 1957 the price stabilization plan had begun to fall apart, and representatives of the 4 companies allegedly met some seven times, arriving at an agreement to hold to GE's catalog prices on nongovernment sales.

The sealed-bid part of this business was apparently divided by agreement

---

[78] Transcript of *United States* v. *Westinghouse Electric Corp., et al.,* United States District Court, Eastern District of Pennsylvania, Criminal No. 20361, p. 502.

[79] *United States* v. *General Electric Co., et al.,* United States District Court, Eastern District of Pennsylvania, Criminal No. 20,399, filed June 20, 1960; *Hearings on Administered Prices,* Pts. 27, 28.

among the companies during a meeting of the National Electrical Manufacturer's Association (NEMA) at the Traymore Hotel in Atlantic City in November and at subsequent (non-NEMA) meetings in Philadelphia, New York, Chicago, and other cities. The following procedure was stated to have been carried out: a list of the sealed-bid business would be circulated and relative standings of the defendants would be compared; there would then be discussions as to who would make the low bid on new business; if the designated low bidder had not yet computed his bid, the defendant representatives would be notified through coded conversations on the telephone; the low bidder usually quoted the "book" price, and the other defendants quoted higher prices; on small transactions defendants would all agree to quote "book" prices.

On power-switching equipment it was alleged that on November 11, 1958, at the Haddon Hall Hotel in Atlantic City, representatives of the defendant companies agreed to adhere to new catalog prices, which would be announced by I-T-E Circuit Breaker. Apparently, in accordance with this agreement, I-T-E published and made effective a schedule of discounts to be applied to existing prices, and these were adopted and used by defendants in selling to the private utilities. In addition, the indictment asserted that on November 27, 1958, defendants met at the Warwick Hotel in Philadelphia and agreed to allocate government sealed bids by dividing the United States into four "quadrants," within each of which a designated defendant was to act as chairman for the purpose of administering the bids. During the period November, 1958, to August, 1959, numerous meetings were said to have been held to discuss the effect of the new discounts and the operation of the quadrant system.

The pricing arrangement allegedly followed in power switchgear assemblies bore the distinctive designation of the "phase of the moon" plan. According to the indictment, at some twenty-five meetings starting in November, 1958, a scheme for quoting nearly identical prices to private electrical-utility companies, private industrial corporations, and contractors was developed, consisting of a periodic rotation of bid positions (high, medium, and low) for each of the defendants in line with the phases of the moon. The spread of prices was said to have been calculated to be so narrow as to eliminate actual price competition among defendants but wide enough to give the appearance of competition. The system necessitated the keeping of detailed records showing which companies had received what percentage of sales and required meetings every week or two to administer the agreement; the officers of I-T-E testified that the record keeping was done by GE.

In addition to effecting this pricing scheme for private business, the producers were said to have met periodically to allocate bids to federal, state, and local governments, giving approximately 39 percent of the market to GE, 35 percent to Westinghouse, 11 percent to I-T-E, 8 percent to Allis-Chalmers, and 7 percent to Federal Pacific. It was alleged that at these meetings a cumulative list of all sealed-bid business was circulated; standings in accordance with agreed-upon percentages were compared; future bid invitations were discussed; and defendants designated which corporation should submit the lowest bid, the amount of such bid, and the amounts of the bids to be submitted by the others.

In the indictments handed down with respect to power transformers and distribution transformers, the defendants were alleged to have met since at least 1956 and to have agreed to allocate the sealed-bid business as follows: Westinghouse and GE, 30 percent each; Allis-Chalmers, 15 percent; Moloney Electric, 10 percent; McGraw-Edison, 8 percent; and Wagner, 5 percent. Lists, it was charged, were kept by the defendants to determine what percentages they had obtained. It was alleged also that during the early part of 1958 prices were well below list and that later in the year a meeting was held at which agreement was secured to quote sealed bids at list price. During this period the defendants agreed to change the list prices they would use for negotiated sales. In early 1959 another meeting allegedly was held at which it was agreed to raise prices by about 5 percent by quoting at 10 percent below list prices rather than 15 percent, as had been quoted previously on negotiated private sales. On distribution transformers the indictment stated that each company agreed to study its volume of sales and submit to General Electric statistical data, which it in turn would tabulate and distribute to the conspirators; that GE, using these data as a basis for discussion, would then issue revised price sheets in accordance with the agreement; and that at other times agreements were reached upon uniform terms and conditions of sale.

Turbogenerators are an extreme example of "tailor-made" machinery—costly items made to order with few unit sales per year. Sales range from only 6 to 75 turbine generators per year, with the price varying from $2 million to about $19 million per machine. Since it was virtually impossible to derive an "automatic" price-matching system for individual machines with varying specifications, the mechanics of the conspiracy appear to have been unusually complex, requiring three types of agreement: high-level meetings at which market price levels were fixed, specific price agreements, and the allocation of individual jobs. In the meetings it allegedly was determined who would have "position"—i.e., would submit the lowest bid on both sealed bids and negotiated transactions. While agreement could usually be reached, on at least one occasion "position" was held to have been determined by drawing lots.

With respect to condensers, which are used in connection with steam turbine generators, 7 companies were indicted. It was charged that between 1956 and 1959 there were about twenty-five meetings, one every six to eight weeks except during the summer. Under the method used in this group the "position" of each company on sealed bids was allegedly determined by the drawing of numbered slips out of a container, each slip containing a different price, which that company would then bid. On commercial sales there were said to have been general agreements that list prices would be quoted on all jobs not discussed specifically, the companies simply agreeing in 1956 and 1957 to quote all jobs at 5 percent off list price and in July, 1957, to increase prices by 5 percent.

That the corporate officials were well aware of the illegal nature of their activities is suggested by the lengths to which they apparently went in order to avoid detection. Most of the indictments recite that the defendants had employed one or more of a variety of specific procedures, including the use of public-telephone pay stations and telephone communications to the homes rather than the offices of company representatives, the use of plain envelopes addressed to the homes of such representatives without the use of return addresses or other means of identification of the senders, the destruction of such written communications shortly after receipt, the practice of leaving no notepapers in hotel rooms where meetings were held, the shunning of social contacts in the hotels while meetings were being held, and the use of code numbers identifying defendant corporations.

Although differing here and there in detail, the operations of the other conspiracies were generally similar to the methods and procedures summarized above. Broadly speaking, the less uniform and more "tailor-made" the product, the greater the detail and complexity of the collusive arrangement, while the more standardized and homogeneous the product, the simpler the arrangement and the greater the attention devoted to simply raising the price level.

The question of evidentiary requirements

In the electrical-equipment cases the government was fortunate enough to come upon informants who were willing to describe the time, place, participants, and purposes of numerous meetings at which the price fixing was worked out, implemented, and modified. But what of situations where meetings took place but no such informants and no telltale documents indicating agreement can be found? And what of situations where no meetings are even required, but where the results of price fixing are achieved through the observance by all producers of some automatic price-matching formula, such as the basing-point system? It must be remembered that much of the heavy electrical machinery consisted of extremely expensive equipment "tailored" to the requirements of a particular customer. For such individualized orders the only practical way of securing uniformity of bidding was through meetings and overt agreements.

The essential question thus concerns not the uncertainty of the law but the evidentiary requirements: What are the types and amounts of evidence required to establish unlawful collusion? Where, as in electrical machinery, evidence can be adduced that competitors entered into a formal agreement, met, exchanged minutes or correspondence, or in other overt ways agreed to fix prices, a violation of the law has been established, and criminal penalties can be imposed. But the courts have long recognized that it is not necessary to have express proof of agreement to establish a violation of Section 1 of the Sherman Act, to say nothing of Section 5 of the Federal Trade Commission Act.[80] In the well-known *Interstate Circuit* case the Supreme Court held: "Acceptance by competitors, without previous agreement, of an invitation to participate in a plan, the necessary consequences of which, if carried out, is restraint of interstate commerce, is sufficient to establish an unlawful conspiracy under the Sherman Act." [81] The doctrine was reiterated in *American Tobacco Co.* v. *United States,* in which, without direct evidence of meetings or agreements, the Court found a conspiracy from the parallel business behavior of 3 major cigarette manufacturers: "No formal agreement is necessary to constitute an unlawful conspiracy. . . . Where the circumstances are such as to warrant a jury in finding that the conspirators had a unity of purpose or a common design and understanding, or a meeting of the minds in an unlawful arrangement, the conclusion that a conspiracy is established is justified." [82]

One of the clearest statements of the law is to be found in a decision by Judge Parker of the Fourth Circuit Court of Appeals in a case brought by the Federal Trade Commission against Armstrong Cork Company and the Crown Manufacturers of America involving crown bottle caps—the closures for bottles used by the brewing and bottling industry:

> There is no proof of any express agreement to charge uniform base prices; but the evidence shows that since 1938 the prices of all the manu-

---

[80] Early cases include *American Column & Lumber Co.* v. *United States,* 257 U.S. 377 (1921), and *United States* v. *American Linseed Oil Co.,* 262 U.S. 371 (1923).
[81] *Interstate Circuit, Inc.* v. *United States,* 306 U.S. 208 (1939), at 222.
[82] 328 U.S. 781 (1945) at 809.

facturing petitioners have been the same. Prior to 1938, there were but few changes, the same price, with minor variations, was charged by all, and, when changes in prices were made, they were made by all at about the same time.

* * *

As in the case of most conspiracies to restrain trade and destroy competition, there is no direct evidence of any express agreement to do what the law forbids; but no such evidence is required, nor is the Commission required to accept the denials of those charged with the conspiracy merely because there is no direct evidence to establish it, for it is well settled that "The essential combination or conspiracy may be found in a course of dealings or other circumstances as well as in any exchange of words." *Fort Howard Paper Co. v. Federal Trade Com'n.* 7 Cir. 156 F. 2d. 899, 905. Where, as here, the evidence is sufficient to support the findings of the Commission, it is for that body, and not the courts, to say what conclusions are to be drawn from it. *Federal Trade Com'n. v. Standard Education Society* 302 U.S. 112, 117; *Federal Trade Com'n. v. Algoma Lumber Co.* 291 U.S. 67, 71 [83]

Were it not for the ability to infer collusion from the economic evidence of its operation and effects, we would be back at the turn of the century, when the value of a new invention known as the telephone was being extolled as a means of evading the antitrust laws. In 1901 the report of the Industrial Commission on Transportation contained the following exchange relating to an increase in the price of coal made simultaneously by different producers. Mr. Conger of the Commission was questioning Mr. Saward, editor of the *Coal Trade Journal*:

MR. CONGER: Is it or is it not a fact that on a certain day all of these producers raise their prices to the wholesalers and to the jobbers? . . . How can you explain this uniform action. Is there no agreement?

MR. SAWARD: Oh, I don't know. It is the advance in civilization, I guess. Possibly it is the hypnotism that prevails—the unity of minds; all think alike. I do not know but there is a telephone that might be used by somebody to ask, "What are you going to ask for coal? I have my circulars all at the printer's, and I am ready to send them out. I am going to ask so-and-so." "All right," might be the response; "I will ask the same."

* * *

MR. CONGER: This communication by telephone or wireless telegraphy, whatever you might call it, answers the same purpose as the combination would, does it not?

MR. SAWARD: It seems to be a wonderful invention; it beats writing on a piece of paper and putting a signature to it.

MR. CONGER: In what way does it beat it?

MR. SAWARD: No record kept.

MR. CONGER: In other words, if there were a record kept, would it be an illegal combination, conspiracy, or something of that kind?

MR. SAWARD: So construed by a good many lawyers in Congress, you know.

MR. CONGER: It might be conspiracy in restraint of trade?

MR. SAWARD: It might be.

[83] *Bond Crown & Cork Co.* v. *Federal Trade Commission,* 176 F. 2d 974 (C.C.A. 4, 1949), at 978.

MR. CONGER: But if it is done by telephone or wireless telegraphy, it is not? That is the advantage, I suppose.

(No reply by the witness.) [84]

As Machlup has pointed out, there are degrees of collusion, ranging from "the most tender forms of understanding without contact or communication to the most formal and elaborate compacts or treaties." [85] As an example of a low degree of collusion he cites the case where "a seller has reason to trust his competitors not to initiate a price cut independently unless their volume falls below a subsistence minimum." Another low degree of collusion is where "a seller has reason to trust his competitors not to start selling without provocation in the territory (or to the customer group) which he considers his own market unless their business volume falls below a subsistence minimum. . . ." [86] It is a somewhat higher degree of collusion if there is a continuation of forbearance even during periods of very bad business. An example of an even higher degree is the case where "a seller has reason to trust his competitors to announce a list of the prices they are going to quote to any potential buyer or to specific groups of buyers, and not to recede from these prices without giving him advance notice in some form, provided he adheres to the same code of behavior." And it is collusion of a very high degree "if a seller has reason to trust his competitors to announce a list of their prices, not to recede from these prices without advance notice, and to report all sales and selling prices to the statistical service of their trade association." [87]

Drawing a distinction between the "degrees" and the "forms" of collusion, Machlup notes that "collusion of a relatively high degree may be most informal, based on nothing but tacit understanding. On the other hand, a rather elaborate apparatus is sometimes established to accomplish collusion of a relatively low degree." [88] The simplest forms of collusion are those that require neither direct nor indirect communication among the participants—e.g., the use of the same sales agent. Among those based on explicit agreement there is a greater variation in the degree of formality:

> The least formal is the gentlemen's agreement, purely oral, with no minutes, no correspondence, no record whatever. Then there are the gentlemen's agreements with minutes of meetings, however cryptic, or with memoranda on some complicated points. Written agreements come next, first those concluded by each producer "separately" with a central agency or trade association, then those among the producers themselves, either in the form of simple correspondence or in the form of formal contracts. In countries with antitrust laws contracts must take the form of patent license agreements. In other countries they may be "straight" cartel contracts. They may provide sanctions for contravention, penalties for sales above quota, etc. And, in a still tighter form, they sometimes provide for the deposition of collateral as security for the payment of fines assessed in the case of violations. The "highest" of all forms of collusion may be seen in governmental orders and in private contracts with governmental stipulations for sanctions in the event of contravention.[89]

[84] Quoted in *Hearings on Administered Prices,* Pt. 8, pp. 4413–14.
[85] Fritz Machlup, *The Economics of Seller's Competition,* Johns Hopkins Press, 1952, p. 434.
[86] *Ibid.,* p. 437.
[87] *Ibid.,* p. 438.
[88] *Ibid.,* p. 440.
[89] *Ibid.,* pp. 441–42.

If cases against collusion are to be limited to those of the higher degrees and tighter forms, the law inevitably will be directed away from the more serious restraints of trade and toward the unconcentrated small-business industries, whose unsophisticated members, untutored and unguided in the law by high-priced New York and Washington law firms, have taken what to them seems the obvious, simple, and direct route of meeting together and agreeing on prices.

The freight equalization cases

The greatest progress in keeping the law on business conduct *au courant* with the realities of modern business has been made by the Federal Trade Commission in its cases against freight equalization systems. Under these systems producers have been able to achieve delivered prices identical to the fourth decimal point. Historically, this result has been attained by the action of each producer in applying to the industry's products a formula under which, no matter where he himself is located, he quotes a delivered price to a customer at any given point of destination by aggregating (a) the base price at the basing point nearest the customer, (b) freight charges based on rail freight from that point to the customer, and, where appropriate, (c) so-called extra charges applicable to the particular specification ordered.

In the *Cement Institute* case, decided by the Supreme Court in 1948, the Federal Trade Commission charged, first, that the cement manufacturers had conspired to use the basing-point system to eliminate price competition among themselves in violation of Section 5 of the Federal Trade Commission Act and, second, that this had resulted in price discrimination that substantially lessened competition among the sellers of cement. The Federal Trade Commission's record in this case 50,000 pages of testimony and 50,000 pages of exhibits— reveals concerted action among cement manufacturers, extending intermittently over almost a half-century, designed to eliminate competition in the sale of cement. Under the system, cement manufacturers persistently offered in secret bids to supply cement at prices identical to the fourth decimal place. An example was cited by Senator Paul Douglas, who noted that the Illinois Department of Highways in January, 1947, asked for bids for 50,000 barrels of cement delivered inside each of the 102 counties in the state. Eight firms presented such sealed bids. While these differed between counties, as would be expected from the manner in which the basing-point system operates, *within* each of the 102 counties all of the eight bids were absolutely identical. Senator Douglas then asked C. O. Oakley, chairman of the Department of Mathematics at Haverford College, what was the chance that this identity of bids was purely accidental. The answer was one out of 8 followed by 214 zeros, or less than that of picking at random a single predetermined electron in the universe. In reversing the lower court's decision, the Supreme Court affirmed the Commission's orders to the cement manufacturers that they cease and desist from perpetuating the use of the basing-point system through any planned common course of action.

This case rested not only upon indirect evidence of the pricing system's operations and effects but also upon direct or overt evidence, an example of which was the so-called Treanor letter. On May 17, 1937, John Treanor, former president of the Riverside Cement Company, and one-time trustee of the Cement Institute, wrote to B. H. Rader of the National Recovery Administration Code Authority:

Do you think any of the arguments for the basing point system which we have thus far advanced will arouse anything but derision in and out of the government. I have read them all recently. Some of them are very clever and ingenious. They amount to this however: that we price this way in order to discourage monopolistic practices and to preserve free competition, etc. The truth is of course—and there can be no serious, respectable discussion of our case unless it is acknowledged—that ours is an industry above all others that cannot stand free competition, that must systematically restrain competition or be ruined.[90]

Most of the more noted examples of direct evidence, such as the Treanor letter, originated during periods when enforcement of the antitrust laws had for years been conspicuous by its rarity. Such documents turn up much less frequently when the antitrust laws are being vigorously applied. At such times the point of diminishing returns sets in very quickly. In order to find one scrap of direct evidence, investigators must examine hundreds and perhaps thousands of file cases, interview witnesses by the score, and plow through letters, minutes, and records by the ream. Moreover, opportunities for the destruction of evidence abound:

> Investigators are regretfully informed that files which are "now no more than ancient history" are miles away in an old warehouse. Or that, as "no longer useful," they have been destroyed. If they are in existence, it may be some weeks before subordinates of the company can be freed for the necessary search. It sometimes happens, through the inadvertence inseparable from such a matter, that a file under critical scrutiny reveals obvious gaps—apparently as surprising to the officials of the corporation as to the investigator. . . .
>
> Always some time elapses between the first appearance of Antitrust investigators and the granting or withholding of material. The initial call is an event which officials may turn to the advantage of their corporation. It is, in effect, an announcement of an impending antitrust suit and a warning to the company to regiment its activities for defense. In the interval marked by "deliberation," files may be rifled, entombed in some unlikely spot, mysteriously disappear for all time.[91]

The high-water mark in the effort to keep the law abreast of changing business conditions was the upholding of the order by the Federal Trade Commission in the *Rigid Steel Conduit* case. Fourteen manufacturers of rigid-steel conduit were charged with engaging in unfair methods of competition in violation of Section 5 of the Federal Trade Commission Act. Specifically, the Commission's complaint charged violation of the law on two counts—count 1, that the respondents had *conspired* to use a delivered-price system of pricing and, count 2, that the respondents had *independently* followed a common course of conduct, each with the knowledge that the others did likewise. Under the latter the Commission held that for any seller individually to quote prices under a price-matching system with the knowledge that his rivals were doing the same and with the result that such practices eliminated competition among them is itself an unfair method of competition in violation of Section 5 of the Federal Trade Commission Act. Rival producers independently observing formula methods that systematically eliminate competition among them cannot be assumed to be sleepwalkers. If they know where they are going, Congress, having outlawed their goal, has said their journey is illegal. The Supreme Court split four to four on

[90] Docket 3167, in the matter of Cement Institute, et al., 37 F.T.C. 87 at 126.
[91] Hamilton and Till, *op. cit.*, pp. 50–51.

the issue, thus sustaining the decision of the Seventh Circuit Court of Appeals on May 12, 1948, upholding the Commission. Yet, inexplicably, the FTC has made no use of this potentially momentous breakthrough to reduce the burden of evidentiary requirements not only on freight equalization cases but on other types of parallel-pricing cases as well.

At some point, collusion, as it is implemented in its various forms, meshes with what is regarded as unlawful conduct. As long as the law consists of general prohibitions rather than a code of highly detailed and specific prohibited activities, the locus of this point will be determined by the courts. The courts have manifested no inability to find illegality from evidence concerning the operations and effects of common behavior. The real problem is that the courts have been given so few opportunities to do just this.

It has been held by some that in its decision in the *Theatre Enterprises* case the Supreme Court reversed its long-sustained line of thought on the issue of evidentiary requirements. In that case, which was a private, triple-damage action, the Court in a decision by Justice Clark held that "this court has never held that proof of parallel business behavior conclusively establishes agreement, or, phrased differently, that such behavior itself constitutes a Sherman Act offense. Circumstantial evidence of consciously parallel behavior may have made heavy inroads into the traditional judicial attitude toward conspiracy, but 'conscious parallelism' has not yet read conspiracy out of the Sherman Act entirely." [92]

What was at issue in *Theatre Enterprises* was not whether conspiracy can be inferred by indirect evidence stopping short of proof of meetings and agreements but whether the complainant, a private litigant, had made an adequate showing in terms of such evidence. Moreover, "conscious parallelism" is a term originally and usually applied to actions brought under the Federal Trade Commission Act. Hence, in stating that "conscious parallelism" has not yet read conspiracy out of the Sherman Act entirely, the Court was merely saying that rulings under the Federal Trade Commission Act have not read out of the Sherman Act the responsibility for establishing conspiracy. And conspiracy under that act can continue to be proven by the types of evidence employed in the past. According to Eugene V. Rostow, *Theatre Enterprises* "in no way weakens the authority of *Interstate Circuit, Cement Institute, Paramount Pictures* or *American Tobacco*." [93] In *Cement Institute* the court had said that "individual conduct, or concerted conduct, which falls short of being a Sherman Act violation may as a matter of law constitute 'an unfair method of competition' prohibited by the Trade Commission Act. A major purpose of the Act, as we have frequently said, was to enable the Commission to restrain practices as 'unfair' which, although not yet having grown into Sherman Act dimensions would, most likely, do so if left unrestrained." [94]

The concerted restriction of production

In a competitive industry a decline in demand results in the loss of output from those producers whose costs are above the price required to call forth the needed supply to meet the lower level of demand. Not surprisingly those high-cost producers (who would be eliminated) as well as the lower-cost producers (whose

[92] *Theatre Enterprises, Inc.* v. *Paramount Film Distributing Corp., et al.*, 346 U.S. 537 (1954), at 541.
[93] *Report of the Attorney General's National Committee to Study the Antitrust Laws*, 1955, p. 40.
[94] *Federal Trade Commission* v. *Cement Institute, et al.*, 333 U.S. 683 (1948), 708.

margin would be reduced) endeavor to resist this natural adjustment process. The logical form of the resistance is to seek to maintain the price by restricting production below the levels that would have obtained had the price been permitted to decline with the falling off of demand. The objective is to "stabilize" the market, by preventing "excessive" production, retiring "redundant" capacity, avoiding the installation of "unnecessary" new facilities, and so on. Such restrictions of output tend to aggravate an economic downswing in a number of ways. On the demand side there is no increase in real money incomes since there is no decline in prices. On the supply side the loss of their jobs by workers in plants where production is curtailed will tend to lower demand, while the reduction in purchases of materials and supplies will reduce production and employment in the supplying industries, thereby further depleting demand, inducing additional curtailments of output, and so on.

As in the case of price fixing itself, concerted efforts to restrict production are unlawful per se. Milton Handler observed, "It is indeed curious that on a problem of such paramount importance there should be such a paucity of authoritative rulings." Nonetheless, the law appears clear: "Such decisions as there are indicate quite clearly that any concerted effort to regulate production contravenes the antitrust laws." [95] As early as 1902, the Ninth Circuit Court of Appeals in *Gibbs* v. *McNeeley* held illegal a program designed to fix prices for red-cedar shingles by shutting down mills and otherwise curtailing output whenever supply exceeded demand. The court stated: "The combination in the case before the court is more than a combination to regulate prices; it is a combination to control the production of a manufactured article more than four-fifths of which is made for interstate trade, and to diminish competition in its production, as well as to advance its price. These features, we think, determine its object, and bring it under the condemnation of the law." [96] Similarly, in 1921 the Supreme Court in *American Column & Lumber Co.* v. *United States* held illegal a scheme to control output and discourage "over-production" in the hardwood lumber industry, which had been carried out through an elaborate program of trade statistics and involved suggestions and exhortations by the statistical manager of the trade association to limit the production of its members.[97] In Handler's words:

> Private output control is inconsistent with the maintenance of competition, and like price-fixing, cannot be tolerated in any economy dedicated to free competition. The economic effects of private regulation of output are the same as price-fixing. . . . That excess capacity and the tendency of many industries to over-produce raise serious economic problems cannot be denied. But a solution of such problems is not to be found in any industrial policy which destroys competition and vests dictatorial control of vital industrial processes in the hands of a limited number of business managers.[98]

The prolonged lower levels of outputs during and following the Depression gave rise to a series of actions by the antitrust agencies against concerted restrictions of production. For example, an order to cease and desist from price fixing and attempting to limit production of vitrified pipe was issued to members of

---

[95] Handler, *op. cit.*, pp. 14–15.
[96] 118 Fed. 120 (C.C.A. 9, 1902) at 127.
[97] 257 U.S. 377 (1921).
[98] TNEC Monograph No. 38, *op. cit.*, p. 16.

that industry by the Federal Trade Commission.[99] Lumbermen's associations have frequently been prosecuted for their attempts to maintain prices by limiting production. In addition to the *American Column & Lumber* case, the Department of Justice has proceeded on these grounds against an association of southern pine producers,[1] a group of western pine lumbermen,[2] and an association of lumbermen operating in the Northwest states.[3] Still another case, also charging price fixing and restrictions on production, was brought by Justice against a national lumbermen's association.[4] A successful action for price fixing and attempts to limit output was prosecuted by the FTC against a group of veneer package manufacturers representing 75 percent of the industry's output.[5] The FTC broke up a conspiracy among manufacturers of liquid-tight paper containers to maintain prices by limiting production.[6]

Although, like price-fixing cases in general, actions against concerted restrictions of production have been directed principally against small-business industries, a number of such cases have been brought against large firms in concentrated industries. For example, the Department of Justice proceeded against a cartel of magnesium producers, which operated not only through agreements to limit output and fix prices but also through the use of patent pools to exclude newcomers from trying to manufacture. The members of the cartel were the German firm I. G. Farben, the Aluminum Company of America, the Dow Chemical Company (at that time the only American producer of magnesium), and the American Magnesium Corporation (the largest fabricator of magnesium products).[7] Similarly, an action against price fixing and limiting the production of certain types of cans was brought by the Department of Justice against American Can Company and Continental Continental Can Company, which reputedly produced about 85 percent of all tin cans manufactured in the United States. Pleading *nolo contendere,* they were fined in January, 1947.[8]

Here again, the central issue concerns evidentiary requirements. Where, as is the case of unsophisticated, small-business industries, the restriction of production is the result of agreements or is implemented by any of a variety of overt activities, the courts have had little difficulty in finding a violation of law. But what of the sophisticated, concentrated industry, whose members adjust to a decline in demand in precisely the same way but without the need for agreement or overt activity of any kind? How does it happen that in the face of a decline in the industry's demand, the reduction in output by *each* of the large producers is sufficient to preclude the existence of an excessive aggregate sup-

---

[99] F.T.C. Order No. 3868, May 31, 1940, in the matter of Southern Vitrified Pipe Assn., 30 F.T.C. 1349.

[1] *United States* v. *Southern Pine Assn., et al.,* United States District Court, District of Louisiana (CCH-56,007), 1940–43 Trade Cases, 8th Ed., Vol. 3, Par. 25,394.

[2] *United States* v. *Western Pine Assn.,* United States District Court, District of California (CCH-56,107), 1940–43 Trade Cases, Par. 52,548.

[3] *United States* v. *West Coast Lumbermen's Assn.,* United States District Court, District of California (CCH-56,122), 1941–43 Trade Cases, Par. 52,588.

[4] *United States* v. *National Lumber Manufacturer's Assn.,* United States District Court, District Court of the District of Columbia (CCH-56,123), 1941–43 Trade Cases, Par. 52,593.

[5] F.T.C. Order No. 3556, May 15, 1940, in the matter of American Veneer Packaging Assn., 40 F.T.C. 665.

[6] F.T.C. Order No. 4675, May 29, 1945, in the matter of Liquid Tight Paper Container Assn., 40 F.T.C. 630.

[7] *United States* v. *Aluminum Company of America, et al.,* CCH Trade Reg. Rpts., 8th Ed., Vol. 3, Par. 15,125 (1941).

[8] *United States* v. *American Can Company, et al.,* CCH Ct. Decs. 1944–47, Par. 54,121.

ply that would overhang the market, causing the price structure to break down? Price leadership, which is presumed to be lawful, depends for its success in a period of declining demand on the willingness of the different producers to reduce supply to a level that can be sold at the prevailing price. In so doing they must accept an increase in their unit fixed costs and forgo the opportunity of increasing sales by pursuing an independent course of action. On the question of whether such concerted reductions in output might constitute evidence of unlawful collusion the courts have had no opportunity to rule. Yet the former chief economist of the Antitrust Division, George P. Comer, observed:

> Normally in industries where price leadership is prevalent inventories overhanging the market are minimized because the production schedule of each of the few large producers is geared directly to the price level. Each producer would deny that "following the leader" on prices involves control of production for the industry as a whole, *but his policy of producing and selling only the amount of goods which can be marketed at prevailing prices is production control in an obvious and practical form.* Control of production by the followers of the leader is a necessary corollary of their acceptance of his price leadership.[9]

The practice takes on a new dimension when, in the face of substantial unused capacity, the amount by which each of the producers restricts his output is sufficient not merely to support the existing level of prices but to make a price increase "stick." The existence of some type of understanding or agreement, express or implied, seems even more probable if the restrictions in output to support a higher price are made under the circumstances that (a) demand is not only well below capacity but falling, (b) the industry is one of high overhead costs and (c) efficient producers whose costs are well below the leader's participate in the advance.

The steel price increase during the 1958 recession occurred in the presence of all of these circumstances. In August U.S. Steel "met" Republic's advance of $4.25, which was then promptly matched by the remainder of the industry. At the time the industry was operating at 48 percent of capacity and demand was continuing to fall. All of the producers ignored the opportunity of spreading their considerable fixed costs over a larger volume of output by not participating in the increase or at least by making a smaller advance. Among the firms joining in the increase were such efficient producers as Bethlehem, Inland, and National, whose costs, judging from their profit showings, appear to have been well below those of U.S. Steel. Because of their cost advantage as well as their sizable resources, they could probably weather for some time any retaliatory attack by the leader.[10] Again in the recession of 1971 each of the steel producers restricted production—in the face of "distressed" market conditions and sizable accumulated steel inventories—by an amount sufficient to make effective the largest across-the-board price increase in 15 years, raising their prices at virtually the same time, by the same amount, to the same level.

From the evidence presented earlier concerning the widespread incidence of "perverse" price flexibility during recessions,[11] it would not appear that industry-wide restrictions of production to support price increases, under the circum-

---

[9] George P. Comer, "Price Leadership," *Law and Contemporary Problems,* School of Law, Duke University, Winter, 1940, p. 68. Emphasis added.
[10] See *Hearings on Administered Prices,* Pt. 8.
[11] See Chs. 17, 20.

stances delineated above, are limited to the steel industry. The question is whether such conduct under such circumstances would be interpreted by the Supreme Court as constituting sufficient circumstantial evidence to warrant a finding of "implied conspiracy" in violation of the Sherman Act or of "planned common course of action" in violation of the Federal Trade Commission Act. The Court has never been given an opportunity to rule on such a case. But if it were given the opportunity and did find the conduct, under the specified circumstances, to be in violation of the law, the government would be provided with a powerful weapon to use against one source of contemporary price inflation.

THE COMPETITIVE APPROACH: PREVENTING FURTHER CONCENTRATION

Traditional antitrust as embodied in the Sherman Act, is oriented toward the past. Through dissolution it seeks to break up monopolies which have developed over the years. Through other actions (including criminal citations) it endeavors to put an end to price-fixing agreements, meetings, understandings and other restraints of trade. It is therapeutic, not prophylactic.

The need to reinforce the Sherman Act with measures oriented toward the future was first recognized in 1914, when Congress passed the Clayton Act. The action by the Supreme Court 3 years earlier in breaking up the Standard Oil and American Tobacco trusts had made it clear that the government was already armed with the power to break up existing monopolies, at least where they had acted "unreasonably." But instead of waiting until a monopoly had been formed and then trying to dissolve it, why not prevent it from developing in the first place; why not "nip it in the bud"? In a report dated July 22, 1914, accompanying the Clayton Act, the Senate Judiciary Committee said: "Broadly stated, the bill, in its treatment of unlawful restraints and monopolies, seeks to prohibit and make unlawful certain trade practices which, as a rule, singly and in themselves, are not covered by the Act of July 2, 1890 (the Sherman Act) or other existing antitrust acts and thus, by making these practices illegal, to *arrest the creation of trusts, conspiracies, and monopolies in their incipiency and before consummation.*" [1] Similarly, in discussing the pending Clayton Act on the Senate floor, Senator Walsh stated, "It was intended to reach the practices that were not the practices of things that have developed into trusts and monopolies, but are practices of trade *which, if persevered in and continued and developed would eventually result in the creation of a monopoly or trust.*" [2]

At the time, Congress was legislating against those actions and practices with which it was most familiar—mergers, price discrimination, exclusive dealing and tie-in contracts, and interlocking directorates. When account is taken of supplementary remedial legislation to close up loopholes in the sections relating to mergers and price discrimination, much has been accomplished under the Clayton Act approach.

[1] 63rd Cong., 2nd Sess., Senate Committee on the Judiciary, Senate Report No. 698 (to accompany H.R. 15657), 1914, p. 1. Emphasis added.
[2] 83rd Cong., 2nd Sess., *Congressional Record,* Sept. 28, 1914, Vol. 51, p. 15820. Emphasis added.

Restraining the centripetal forces

But, as Congress recognized in 1914, when it comes to devising new and more ingenious ways of suppressing competition, "there is no end to the inventiveness of the mind of man." After the passage of more than 60 years, it is therefore high time to update the approach followed in the Clayton Act by identifying and acting against the principal forces making for greater concentration in our present-day economy. These would appear to be the centripetal forces examined in this work—mergers and acquisitions, TV advertising, predation, and government intervention in the market.

What would distinguish the new approach from that followed in 1914 would be an explicit recognition that there are also forces working in the opposite direction—the centrifugal forces. Unlike the centripetal forces, which may be thought of as "man-made," readily lending themselves to restraints imposed by the state, the centrifugal forces are "machine-made," inherent in the nature of things. They may be given greater force and effect, however, by measures designed to stimulate the development of new decentralizing technologies and to remove barriers confronting independent inventors and smaller innovative firms. By simultaneously restraining the centripetal forces and stimulating the centrifugal forces such an approach may not only arrest but actually reverse the upward trend in concentration.

Mergers and acquisitions

In 1950 Congress enacted the Celler-Kefauver amendment to Section 7 of the Clayton Act, which, among other things, made it abundantly clear that the law applied to all mergers that "may . . . substantially . . . lessen competition or to tend to create a monopoly." [3] Yet in 1969 merger activity, made up largely of conglomerate mergers, reached an all-time high. To gain an understanding of this apparent anomaly, it is necessary to have some understanding of the history of the law.

In framing the original Section 7, Congress used as its model tests that, prior to the "Rule of Reason" decisions, had been developing in the *Northern Securities* case, the *Trans-Missouri Freight* case, and the circuit court opinions in the *Standard Oil* and *American Tobacco* cases. The prohibition of consolidations and mergers *between* previously competing firms on the grounds that they would necessarily destroy previously existing competition was incorporated into Section 7 almost without change. In addition to outlawing mergers between directly competing firms, the law also forbade those which injured competition generally, a test which incidentally provided the Supreme Court with a basis for its decision in the DuPont-General Motors case that Section 7 had always applied to vertical mergers. Preserving the symmetry of the Sherman Act which, in addition to proscribing restraints of trade also outlawed monopolization, the new law, while forbidding mergers that injured competition, also prohibited those that "may tend to create a monopoly." This prohibition, which traced to the Attorney General's argument in the Standard Oil case,[4] plus those relating to competition, constituted standards of illegality which added up to a potentially forbidding measure.

---

[3] 81st Cong., Public Law 899, amending Sec. 7 of the Clayton Act.
[4] See Ch. 21.

Unhappily, the wording of the law related only to acquisitions of stock; it said nothing about a company's assets—i.e., its physical plant, inventories, and so on. If the acquiring company purchased the assets entirely, not bothering with stock, it was free from any action by the Federal Trade Commission. However, in some cases acquisition of assets was not feasible unless the stock could be purchased first. What was the legal status where a firm bought up the stock first and then used it to obtain the assets? The Federal Trade Commission argued that those who broke the law should not gain immunity by subsequently using the fruits of their unlawful action to make another type of acquisition. Yet in a five-to-four decision, with Justices Brandeis, Taft, Holmes, and Stone dissenting, the Court held in 1926 that where a corporation had acquired the stock first the Commission was powerless to take effective action against its use to absorb assets.[5]

The question has often been raised as to why Congress, in acting against mergers effected through the purchase of stock, did not also include under the law absorptions of assets. The answer is to be found in the nature of the great consolidation movement that began early in the last decade of the nineteenth century and extended through 1907. As has been described earlier, the great consolidations of the day were usually effected through the purchase of stock. In bringing together different companies under one corporate roof, promoters typically followed the method of forming a holding company, which would issue under its own name vast amounts of stock, part of which could then be used to pay off the owners of the separate companies absorbed in the consolidation. That acquisitions of stock were, indeed, the customary and prevailing method of absorbing competitors was brought out by Justice Stone, who, in a dissenting opinion in a merger case, said that corporate mergers were "commonly" effected through stock acquisitions, that "only in rare instances" would a merger be successful without advance acquisition of working stock control, that such control was "the normal first step toward consolidation," that it was by this process that most consolidations had been brought about, that this was "the first and usual step," and that the statute therefore reached the evil of corporate mergers "in its most usual form by forbidding the first step." [6]

When Congress in 1950 enacted the Celler-Kefauver amendment, closing up the "assets" loophole, it modified the law in a number of other respects. The "between the acquiring and acquired company" test was deleted on the grounds that, taken literally, it would prohibit all horizontal mergers and the very stringency of the test might provoke the courts into introducing a "Rule of Reason" type of interpretation. Each of the two remaining tests—the effect on competition and the tendency to create a monopoly—would be contravened if a merger had such an effect in "any line of commerce" and in "any section of the country." The accompanying committee reports also made clear that under the new law it is not necessary to show predatory practices; that it is not necessary to show the possession of monopolistic power to destroy competitors or fix prices; that the law's intent is to reach "far beyond the Sherman Act"; that its central purpose is to prevent further increases in concentration; and that all mergers are within the scope of the law—horizontal, vertical, and conglomerate.

By 1958 the Department of Justice had won a signal victory in a district court

[5] *Federal Trade Commission* v. *Western Meat Co., Thatcher Manufacturing Co.* v. *Federal Trade Commission, Swift & Co.* v. *Federal Trade Commission,* 272 U.S. 554 (1926).
[6] *Arrowhart and Hegeman Company* v. *Federal Trade Commission,* 291 U.S. 587 (1934) at 601.

against horizontal mergers by preventing the merger of the Bethlehem and Youngstown steel companies. In 1962 the Supreme Court in the *Brown Shoe* case ruled against a predominantly vertical merger. By 1965 the then assistant attorney general in charge of the Antitrust Division, William H. Orrick, Jr., voiced the opinion that the new law had proved to be "adequate to deal with the problem of merger-created concentration in particular markets."

> Our experience with amended section 7 suggests that the statute is adequate to deal with the problem of merger-created concentration in particular markets, at least where one or the other of the merging firms is a major factor in the market. . . . In many cases, however, litigation proved unnecessary; the prospect of a successful government challenge was enough. And, I am sure, in numerous other instances, the advice of private counsel dissuaded the merging parties.
> Visible antitrust enforcement in terms of its impact in preventing anticompetitive mergers is therefore very much like an iceberg. Indeed, probably the most substantial tribute which can be paid to the effectiveness of the antimerger statutes and the enforcement efforts of the Federal Trade Commission and the Antitrust Division, is that there are not more major mergers attempted today.

· · ·

> Mergers of major competitors were rampant in the late 19th and early 20th centuries. Today, however, after the recent Supreme Court decisions in *Brown Shoe*,[7] *Philadelphia Bank*,[8] *Lexington Bank*,[9] *Continental Can*,[10] *Alcoa-Rome*,[11] and *El Paso*,[12] and our district court successes in *Bethlehem Steel*,[13] *Kennecott*,[14] *Chrysler-Mack*,[15] *Alcoa-Cupples*,[16] and now, *Manufacturers-Hanover*,[17] the amalgamation of major competitive factors in a particular industry would be highly unlikely. Therefore, I feel reasonably confident in asserting that the 1950 amendments to section 7 are proving effective in dealing with one aspect of the concentration problem with which Congress was concerned, that is, concentration in particular markets and industries.[18]

While effective against horizontal and vertical mergers, the law has been applied only sporadically against conglomerate acquisitions. Yet, as was brought out in Chapter 3, there is no shortage of theories on how market competition can be lessened by conglomerate mergers. To recapitulate briefly: competition may be affected adversely if smaller competitors of the acquired company are destroyed by cross-subsidization; or if, out of fear of retaliation by a large conglomerate, smaller single-line producers abstain from making competitive moves they would otherwise initiate; or if, because of reciprocal buying and selling arrangements, smaller competitors are denied access to important suppliers or markets; or if rival conglomerates, encountering each other in a number of

[7] *Brown Shoe Co.* v. *United States*, 370 U.S. 294, 316, 333 (1962).
[8] *United States* v. *Philadelphia National Bank*, 374 U.S. 321 (1963).
[9] *United States* v. *First National Bank & Trust Co. of Lexington*, 376 U.S. 665 (1964).
[10] *United States* v. *Continental Can Co.*, 378 U.S. 441 (1964).
[11] *United States* v. *Aluminum Co. of America*, 377 U.S. 271 (1964).
[12] *United States* v. *El Paso Natural Gas Co.*, 376 U.S. 651 (1964).
[13] *United States* v. *Bethlehem Steel Corp.*, 168 F. Supp. 576 (S.D.N.Y. 1958).
[14] *United States* v. *Kennecott Copper Corp.*, 231 F. Supp. 95 (S.D.N.Y. 1964).
[15] *United States* v. *Chrysler Corp.*, 232 F. Supp. 651 (D.N.J. 1964).
[16] *United States* v. *Aluminum Co. of America*, 233 F. Supp. 718 (E.D. Mo. 1964).
[17] *United States* v. *Manufacturers Hanover Trust Co.*, 240 F. Supp. 367 (S.D.N.Y. 1965).
[18] *Hearings on Economic Concentration*, Pt. 2, pp. 811–12.

different industries, forbear from launching a competitive attack on each other in any one of them out of fear of retaliation in others. And potential competition may be lessened if a company with the resources and ability required for internal expansion makes its entrance into an industry by acquisition rather than by building new plant capacity.[19]

Although a number of these theories of the case have been tested successfully in the courts, up to 1969 fewer than a half-dozen such cases had been brought by the Federal Trade Commission and the Department of Justice. While other factors have been present, including the continuing problem of inadequate appropriations, the principal reasons for this relative inactivity are conceptual. Thus, there was a state of disbelief among key antitrust officials that conglomerates actually engage in cross-subsidization or other forms of predation, coupled with a belief that any adverse effect on competition should be weighed against possible improvements in efficiency. Also impeding enforcement has been the implicit assumption that the second test of the law is a redundancy— that mergers tending to create a monopoly are prohibited only if they also have a demonstrable adverse effect on competition. The leading proponent of these concepts has been Donald F. Turner, who developed them at considerable length in a 1965 law review article,[20] continued to articulate them while head of the Antitrust Division during 1965–68, and reiterated them in early 1970 before the Senate Antitrust Subcommittee. In the 1970 hearings, Turner stated: "Nor do I believe, any more than I did when I wrote on the subject in 1965, that predatory pricing, disciplinary price cutting, or other invidious forms of cross-subsidization are a sufficiently probable consequence of conglomerate organizations to warrant serious consideration in the formulation of conglomerate merger rules."[21] And of course if the practice is non-existent, single-line producers are not dissuaded by the fear of cross-subsidization from making competitive moves which they would otherwise initiate.

During the hearings the subsequent colloquy brought out the underlying basis for this point of view as well as the arguments against it. Such practices, Turner argued, must be engaged in only infrequently because evidence of their use appears so rarely. The number of instances on which there is evidence "is extremely small in terms of the large numbers, vast numbers, of conglomerate firms

[19] In addition, during early 1970 what might be referred to as a "loss-of-viability theory" was suggested by the Antitrust Subcommittee's chief economist in a colloquy with Richard W. McLaren, assistant attorney general in charge of the Antitrust Division:

> DR. BLAIR: Another possible theory of the case relates to the possible loss of viability by the acquired firm as a competitive factor in the market. I have in mind the situation in which a long-established, well-known company, after acquisition is so mismanaged by the acquiring conglomerate that it loses sales, profits decline, and it ceases to be an important factor in the market. If it thus loses its ability to compete, is there not a substantial lessening of competition?
>
> MR. MCLAREN: Yes. We have considered that theory in certain cases, but I think all of the cases we have filed have been on the theory that it advantaged the parties in the competitive picture rather than disadvantaged one of them.

(*Hearings on Economic Concentration,* Pt. 8, p. 4813.)

[20] Donald F. Turner, "Conglomerate Mergers and Section 7 of the Clayton Act," *Harvard Law Review,* May, 1965.

[21] *Hearings on Economic Concentration,* Pt. 8, p. 4758.

that we have and the vast time span that is involved, and what I describe, therefore, as the countless opportunities for engaging in this." [22]

In rebuttal the Subcommittee's chief economist argued that the scarcity of cases does not signify an absence of the practices but only the fact that "the type of data needed to establish the incidence of cross-subsidization is jealousy guarded by corporate management." [23] Referring to breakdowns of profit data showing a particular division to be losing money, he observed, "I know of no other type of data that is harder to get at, with the possible exception of unit cost." [24] As an example, he pointed out that, even using its mandatory powers, after over a year the Federal Trade Commission had been able to secure reports containing divisional profit data from only 4 of 9 leading conglomerates, and 2 of the 4 had requested that the Commission keep the data confidential.[25] Commenting that "the very difficulty of obtaining the needed data is one of the reasons why this type of case is not initiated in the first place," Blair called attention to another source of information: "The congressional committees are the recipients of complaints from independent, smaller producers who insist that they are as efficient as the large conglomerate, yet the price which the conglomerate is charging is less than their costs." [26] Recognizing that complaints are something less than proof, he pointed out that subsequent investigation appeared to confirm the substance of the complaints in such important fields as trucks, fertilizer materials, and household appliances.

A further inhibiting factor has been the assumption, which Turner reiterated during the 1970 hearings, that any gains in competition from actions against conglomerate mergers may be offset by the failure to realize gains in efficiency.[27] Quite apart from whether this position derives support from the available empirical evidence,[28] the issue had been resolved by Congress in the enactment of the Celler-Kefauver amendment. The legislative history affirms the opinion of Justice Douglas in the *Procter & Gamble-Clorox* case: "Possible economies cannot be used as a defense to illegality. Congress was aware that some mergers which lessen competition may also result in economies but it struck the balance in favor of protecting competition." [29] The original bills to amend Section 7 of the Clayton Act, as introduced in February, 1945, by Senator O'Mahoney and Representative Kefauver, prohibited acquisitions involving property with a value of more than a specified amount unless the Federal Trade Commission found the acquisition "to be consistent with the public interest"; and the FTC was not to find the acquisition to be "consistent" unless it also found, among other things, "that the acquisition will not be incompatible with greater efficiency and economy of production, distribution and management." [30] These bills

[22] *Ibid.,* p. 4768.
[23] *Ibid.*
[24] *Ibid.*
[25] *Ibid.*
[26] *Ibid.,* pp. 4768–69.
[27] *Ibid.,* pp. 4764–65.
[28] See Ch. 8.
[29] *Federal Trade Commission* v. *Procter & Gamble Co.,* 386 U.S. 568 (1966), at 580.
[30] 79th Cong., 1st Sess., S. 615, H.R. 2357, 1945. The other points on which an affirmative finding had to be made by the FTC were as follows:
"1. The acquisition will not substantially lessen competition, restrain trade, or tend to create a monopoly (either in a single section of the country or in the country as a whole) in the trade, industry, or line of commerce in which the corporations are engaged.
"2. The size of the acquiring corporation after acquisition will be compatible with the

had been modeled on the recommendation of the Temporary National Economic Committee, which had included a more stringent standard: the FTC had to find that the acquisition would be promotive of greater efficiency and economy of production, distribution, and management. In response to inquiries as to the reason for the change, Representative Kefauver wrote:

> There is a substantial difference between an administrative affirmative finding that a proposed merger will promote greater efficiency and economy and a finding that it will not be incompatible with that result. I can well understand why an administrative agency would hesitate to make such an affirmative finding in any but the most obvious circumstances and this would tend to block a large proportion of all mergers on that score alone. By contrast under the provisions of H.R. 2357, while mergers found to be incompatible with greater efficiency and economy could not meet the required standard, mergers found to be compatible and those found to be not incompatible with that standard could be approved, provided all the other requirements were met.[31]

Partly because of the obvious administrative difficulties inherent in any efficiency test and partly because of the inability of the bill's opponents over a 5-year period to produce evidence, or even examples, indicating that mergers do result in gains in efficiency, the efficiency requirement was dropped. During the floor debate on the measure Representative Boggs of Louisiana summarized the evidence:

> In all of the hearings before the House and Senate Judiciary Subcommittees on this bill, going back to 1945, officials of a number of large corporations have been asked specifically whether the recent mergers made by their companies had resulted in increased efficiency. It is rather interesting to note that, universally, these representatives of big business did not know whether efficiency had been increased; they were unable to present any evidence whatever showing that mergers have brought about greater efficiency; and this is not surprising when it is remembered that the Temporary National Economic Committee Monograph No. 13 found that there was no definite relationship between size and efficiency.[32]

From the studies summarized in Chapter 8 it is clear that 20 years later the proposition that mergers are generally promotive of efficiency is still without an empirical foundation.

Thus far the second test of the Celler-Kefauver amendment has suffered the same fate as befell Section 2 of the Sherman Act for so many years—the fate of redundancy. The tendency-toward-monopoly test has not been interpreted by the enforcing agencies as prohibiting mergers that were *not* unlawful under the injury-to-competition test.[33] Yet Congress in 1950 wanted to proscribe

---

existence and maintenance of effective competition in the trade, industry, or line of commerce in which it is engaged.

"3. The acquisition will not so reduce the number of competing companies in the trade, industry, or line of commerce affected as materially to lessen the effectiveness of competition therein.

"4. The acquiring company has not indulged in unlawful methods of competition in order to induce the acquisition—or otherwise violated the FTC Act." (*Ibid.*)

[31] Estes Kefauver, unpublished letter dated Dec. 8, 1947, to Charles Alan Wright, *Yale Law Journal.*

[32] 81st Cong., 1st Sess., *Congressional Record,* Aug. 15, 1949, Vol. 95, p. 11725, remarks by Representative Boggs.

[33] Congress was fully aware that it was incorporating two distinct and separate tests into the

mergers without a demonstrable adverse effect on competition for the same reason that it had included the identical test in the 1914 law.[34] Congress was again evidencing its concern with monopoly-promoting mergers even though they could not be shown to transgress the injury-to-competition test in a particular case. Quite apart from sociopolitical considerations, the tendency-to-monopoly test rests firmly on a strong congressional preference for an economy of many sellers. The view was widely shared and expressed in the floor debate that an economy in which opportunity was unrestricted was apt to be more responsive to new ideas, more flexible in its adjustments, and better able to make the best use of the talents, skills, and creativeness of its citizens.

Under Turner's successor, Richard W. McLaren the Antitrust Division in 1969 brought actions against 5 important conglomerate mergers, challenging the acquisitions by Ling-Temco-Vought of the Jones & Laughlin Steel Corporation, by Northwest Industries of B. F. Goodrich Company, and by International Telephone and Telegraph Corporation of Canteen Corporation, Hartford Fire Insurance Company, and Grinnell Corporation. In describing these actions McLaren emphasized their anticompetitive effects, observing that "our complaint in these five cases dealt with such matters as the elimination of potential competition; the creation of power to engage in systematic reciprocity on a large scale; the entrenchment of leading firms in concentrated markets; and the contribution to, and proliferation of, a merger trend." [35]

When a problem arises for which relief might possibly be secured under an existing statute (whose scope, however, is uncertain), the question for public policy is always whether to press for new legislation or to endeavor to cope with the problem under the existing law. In this case—the wave of conglomerate mergers—is it better to emphasize the need for a further strengthening amendment or to try to reach conglomerate mergers under the Celler-Kefauver amendment to Section 7? In practice the two approaches tend to be mutually exclusive. If primary reliance is placed on obtaining new legislation, few cases are likely to be brought under the existing law, since any successes in the courts tend to cut the ground out from under the argument that a new statute is needed. Indeed, the very bringing of cases under existing law makes it difficult to persuade the legislature of the need for a new law—until and unless the cases are lost. And, on the other side, any argument made to the legislature that the present law is inadequate would jeopardize the cases in the courts. Another consideration is that in opening up an existing law for amendment, one opens it up not only for strengthening but for weakening amendments; on this issue it is by no means a certainty that the former would prevail.

During the late 1960's however, the very dimensions of the conglomerate merger movement persuaded even members of the business community to urge

---

law, as is clear from the law's legislative history. The accompanying report of the Senate Judiciary Committee states:

Thus, the phrase, 'in many sections of the country' was made applicable to *both* the lessening of competition and the tendency to create a monopoly. As the bill originally stood, it applied only to the former. Similarly the phrase 'in any line of commerce' was made applicable to *both* as above. As the bill originally stood, the phrase applied only to the tendency to create a monopoly.

(81st Cong., 2nd Sess., Senate Report No. 1775, 1950, p. 5.) Emphasis added.

[34] See Walton Hamilton and Irene Till, *Antitrust in Action,* Monograph No. 16, Temporary National Economic Committee (TNEC), 1941, p. 5.

[35] See *Hearings on Economic Concentration,* Pt. 8, pp. 4800–02, testimony of Richard W. McLaren.

new and stronger legislation. This viewpoint was expressed by A. C. Hoffman of the Kraft Foods Company:

> The time seems to have come for a complete rethinking of the problem of concentration of control in the American economy and of public policy with respect to it. I have been led to this conclusion because I can see nothing on the horizon to stop the avalanche of mergers and acquisitions, short of positive government legislation to prohibit them under certain stipulated conditions. I would not have thought this ten years ago, or even five, but I think it now.[36]

The need for a stronger law has also been stressed by Donald Turner[37] and the "Task Force" headed by Dean Philip Neal of the University of Chicago law school. In proposing a new bill the Neal Task Force emphasized the need to eliminate uncertainty in the business community. Referring to cases that have been brought against conglomerate mergers under the existing law, the group stated that

> such attacks have been predicated primarily on the likelihood of reciprocal dealing and on the law of potential competition. While the members of the Task Force differ in their appraisal of these doctrines, they agree that in their more extended applications, they introduce many elements of uncertainty and unpredictability into the law. The result is that many lawful mergers with potentially beneficial effects on competition may be discouraged, and that many unlawful mergers with adverse effects on competition may be consummated without attack because the lack of clear and precise standards places an excessive strain on enforcement resources and discourages voluntary compliance.[38]

The recommendation of the Task Force was for a prohibition that would combine size with market share: no "large" firms (those with sales of over $500 million or assets of over $250 million) could merge with or acquire a "leading" firm (one with more than 10 percent of a market in which the 4 largest firms had more than 50 percent) or vice versa.[39] As in the case of its proposal for dissolution, what the Task Force's recommendation offers in clarity might well be more than offset by the restrictive scope of its standards. There are slightly more than 100 industries in which the 4-company concentration ratio exceeds 50 percent. Reflecting the prevailing asymmetrical structure of oligopolies, none but the largest, or at most the second largest, firm in most of these industries probably has a market share of over 10 percent. In only a very few industries has the largest, or even the second largest, firm in an industry been absorbed

---

[36] A. C. Hoffman, "The Economic Rationale for Conglomerate Growth from a Management Perspective," in L. Garoian, ed., *Economics of Conglomerate Growth,* Recorder-Sunset, 1969, p. 62.

[37] See 90th Cong., 1st Sess., Hearings before a subcommittee of the Senate Select Committee on Small Business, "Planning, Regulation and Competition," 1967, p. 32.

[38] White House Task Force, "Report on Antitrust Policy," *Antitrust & Trade Regulation Report,* May 27, 1969, Pt. 2, Special Supplement, pp. 1–28. Included in *Hearings on Economic Concentration,* Pt. 8, pp. 5053–82.

[39] The reverse test, which prohibits a "leading" company from acquiring a "large" company, would have little applicability. Between 1948 and 1968 there were only 22 acquisitions of manufacturing companies with assets of over $250 million, or a little over 2 per year, and some of these were acquired by "nonleading" firms—e.g., petroleum companies (see *Hearings on Economic Concentration,* Pt. 8A, p. 670).

during recent years in a merger.[40] When firms of substantial size are absorbed, they are almost invariably of considerably lower rank. Furthermore, under the proposed bill, acquisitions can be made of *part* of the assets of even the largest companies if they are "not sufficient to constitute a large firm" (i.e., if sales are less than $500 million or assets less than $250 million). Finally, there is the troublesome question of the effect of the proposal on enforcement policy against those horizontal acquisitions that are clearly prohibited by the present law but could not be reached under the Task Force's standards. True, the Task Force report states, "The Act supplements and does not replace section 7 of the Clayton Act and sections 1 and 2 of the Sherman Act as applied to mergers. . . ."[41] But would the deliberate action by Congress in not bringing them under the prohibition of the new law be given no weight by the courts in deciding cases under the existing law or by the enforcement agencies in their allocation of inadequate resources? For all these reasons, the question arises as to how far, if at all, the committee's proposal would actually go beyond the present law.[42]

All legislative proposals, however, have been of only academic interest and are likely to remain so until and unless Congress is persuaded that a deficiency exists in the law itself and this will probably continue to be the case as long as there is a manifest inability of the Department of Justice and the Federal Trade Commission to attribute their failure to halt conglomerate mergers to any shortcoming in the statute. It is true that the Supreme Court has handed down very few decisions on conglomerate mergers. But it is also true that not only has the Court been presented with very few occasions on which to render judgments, but its opinions thus far have hardly been a setback to enforcement. Indeed, the victory achieved by the FTC in the *Procter & Gamble-Clorox* case must be regarded as epochal. Yet, as was true of its potentially far-reaching victory against parallel pricing in the *Rigid Steel Conduit* cases, the Commission, as if aghast at its own temerity, has failed to follow up with subsequent actions based on the same theory of the case. During the late 1940's one of the principal roadblocks to the passage of the Celler-Kefauver amendment was the argument that new legislation was unnecessary since mergers destructive of competition could be prevented under the Sherman Act. Not until this argument was laid to rest by the Court's decision in the *Columbia Steel* case[43] did the Celler-Kefauver amendment have any real chance of passage. Similarly, not until *Procter & Gamble-Clorox* is overturned or narrowly circumscribed is Congress likely to be persuaded that the problem of conglomerate mergers can be met only by new legislation.

[40] Although no distributions of acquisitions in terms of market shares are available, it is known that during 1948–68 there were 1,206 acquisitions of manufacturing firms with assets of $10 million or more. Of these, 975, or 81%, had less than $50 million in assets, and 138, or 11%, had from $50 to $100 million. It is unlikely that there are many of the former, or even of the latter, in which the acquired firm had a market share of more than 10% *and* the industry's 4-firm concentration ratio exceeded 50% (see *Hearings on Economic Concentration*, Pt. 8A, p. 670).
[41] White House Task Force, *op. cit.*
[42] The definition given by the Neal Task Force to the term "market"—i.e., "a relevant economic market, appropriately defined with reference to geographic area . . . and product or service" (*ibid.*) does not appear to go beyond the interpretation given by the courts to the phrases in the present law—"in any line of commerce" and "in any section of the country."
[43] *United States* v. *Columbia Steel Co.*, 334 U.S. 495, 534 (1948).

If the objective is to stop conglomerate mergers, the proper approach is simply to ban them outright, or perhaps to prohibit *all* mergers by the largest companies (e.g., the 500 largest).[44]

TV advertising

If weights could be assigned according to importance, TV advertising would rank high among the centripetal forces. The frequency with which concentration has increased among products promoted heavily through this medium attests to the claims of its own salesmen; its success in promoting the sales of sponsors' products *vis-à-vis* those of competitors has been remarkable. Since the airways are owned by the public and the TV stations receive their licenses from a federal agency, the means of correction is at hand. But the question of how to proceed is a thorny one.

One solution would be to ban, or greatly reduce, the incidence of TV commercials. Although viewers might find it possible to bear such a change with considerable equanimity, the solution implies that the costs of TV would be borne by some other source. If they are to be borne by the state, the question arises as to how a government in power can be restrained from using its influence to have programs slanted in its favor—particularly news broadcasts, commentaries, discussion programs, and the like. Those who feel that the problem can be resolved point to the British Broadcasting System, but the experience of France is hardly reassuring. Another possible line of approach was discussed in a colloquy before the Senate Antitrust Subcommittee:

> MR. COULTER.[45] Mr. Chairman, if I might make this comment, in the political field where two groups—Republicans and Democrats, have achieved a level of concentration in excess of 99 percent of the total market, total number of votes, Congress has found it necessary to enact what is commonly called equal time legislation dealing with television. I don't suppose the witness would be prepared to pass judgment at this time whether he would want equal time legislation in advertising for these various industries.
>
> DR. BLAIR: Perhaps the term of "equal time" goes too far, but I think something in that direction is certainly worth contemplating. Some such approach must be followed if we are not going to have a virtual monopolization of consumer goods industries.
>
> SENATOR DODD: Well, certainly we ought to find some remedy, because if the big can get bigger, just because they are big, the small fellow will go out pretty fast, won't he, and this will have a bad effect.[46]

Before such an approach could be put into effect, it would be necessary to resolve a number of practical difficulties. How many commercials, of what duration, and at what times would be set aside for smaller firms? On what basis would the products to be advertised be selected? Under even the most generous set-asides the number of producers of any consumer good would well exceed those for

[44] As a condition for making an acquisition it has been proposed that a large firm be required to divest itself of an equivalent amount of assets. The implied assumption is that the assets to be acquired and those to be sold are of equivalent value. But this is hardly likely to be the case since most large firms have unprofitable operations—"cats and dogs"—that they would be happy to get rid of as a condition for acquiring a valuable new property.

[45] Kirkley Coulter, economist for the minority of the Senate Subcommittee on Antitrust and Monopoly.

[46] *Hearings on Economic Concentration,* Pt. 5, pp. 1911–12.

which equal time could possibly be granted. Of course, if a state subsidy is to be avoided, the beneficiaries would have to be large enough to pay the cost of the commercials, which however should not be greater than the rate for a similar time slot currently charged the lowest-cost advertiser of a competitive product. Since the number able to pay the cost would probably still exceed the number of available time slots, some further equitable method of selecting the program's beneficiaries, perhaps a lottery, would have to be employed.

Predation

As has been noted, investigations conducted by the Industrial Commission and the Bureau of Corporations, as well as knowledge gained in enforcing the Sherman Act, had convinced Congress by 1914 of the need to place restraints on certain forms of predation, e.g., price discrimination, and exclusive dealing contracts. To invoke the prohibitions of the law the antitrust agencies were required to show only that these practices "may" be injurious to competition.

Since their enactment no particular problem has arisen concerning either the law or its enforcement with respect to exclusive dealing and tie-in contracts. As has been set forth in Chapter 4, the present prohibition on interlocking directorates, Section 8 of the Clayton Act, appears to be effective in preventing direct interlocks between competitors; how much of a stimulus to competition would result from broadening its provisions to encompass indirect interlocks is open to question.

The effectiveness of the restraint on price discrimination has come to revolve largely around what is technically known as the "good faith" defense. To gain an understanding of its meaning and significance one should review briefly the congressional enactments against discrimination in business. Their history can be traced back to the passage in 1887 of the Interstate Commerce Act, which sharply limited the extent to which railroads through preferential freight rates could favor one shipper over a competitor, one industry over another, one community over another, or one region over another. The growth of industry during this period was also accompanied by abuses of power that led to the passage of the Sherman Act 3 years later. Again the exercise of power through discriminatory pricing was one of the elements contributing to the passage of the legislation. When Congress in 1914 passed the Clayton Act, a central purpose was to curb the destruction of competition through discrimination. As set forth in H.Rept. 627 of the Sixty-third Congress, the prohibition against price discrimination was directed at the practice of large concerns

> to lower prices of their commodities, oftentimes below the cost of production in certain communities and sections where they had competition, with the intent to destroy and make unprofitable the business of their competitors, and with the ultimate purpose in view of thereby acquiring a monopoly in a particular locality or section in which the discriminating price is made. Every concern that engages in this evil practice must, of necessity, recoup its losses in the particular communities or sections where their commodities are sold below cost or without a fair profit by raising the price of the same class of commodities above their fair market value in other sections or communities.[47]

The prohibition, however, was accompanied by what was known as the good-faith defense, which permitted price discriminations to be made in good faith to

[47] 63rd Cong., 2nd Sess., H.Rept. 627, pp. 8–9, 1914.

meet competition. Partly as a result of this loophole the law became ineffective. An exhaustive chain store investigation by the Federal Trade Commission completed in 1934, as well as investigations by congressional committees, showed that large chains frequently were receiving discounts, allowances, and other advantages greatly in excess of those granted to competing retailers and occasionally even to wholesalers. Thus, the Federal Trade Commission in its final report on the chain store investigation stated:

> Variation in price between different branches of a chain would seem to be a discrimination, the effect of which "may be" to produce the forbidden results. It is one thing, however, to reach such a broad conclusion on the results of this practice by chains in general and quite another to prevent by legal means its use by some particular chain. The reason is that the Clayton Act itself specifically permits price discrimination "in the same or different communities made in good faith to meet competition." The commission has no evidence which would establish that price discrimination by chain stores has not been in good faith to meet competition and there is good ground to conclude that in many cases it has been for that purpose.[48]

To eliminate this loophole and strengthen the law in other respects, Congress in 1936 passed the Robinson-Patman amendment to the Clayton Act. Section 2 was amended to make good faith a procedural rather than a complete defense to a charge of discrimination. The amendment introduced a new subsection, 2(b), which provided that the seller could show that his lower price was made in good faith to meet the equally low price of a competitor merely for the purpose of rebutting a preliminary or *prima facie* case. Referring to the old exemption incorporated in the Senate bill, the report of the House conferees stated: "This language is found in existing law, and in the opinion of the conferees is one of the obstacles to enforcement of the present Clayton Act. The Senate receded and the language is stricken. A provision relating to the question of meeting competition, intended to operate only as a rule of evidence in a proceeding before the Federal Trade Commission, is included in subsection b. . . ."[49] Yet in 1951 the Supreme Court held the defense of discriminating in price to meet a lawful (that is, nondiscriminatory) price in good faith overrode a showing of substantial injury to competition.[50] Once again the difficult and often impossible burden was placed on the FTC of tracing back the history of a discrimination and showing that it had been instigated by the company charged or, if not so instigated, had not been made in "good faith."

Following the handing down of this decision Senator Kefauver and Representative Patman introduced bills—S. 11 and H.R. 11—to eliminate the good-faith

[48] 74th Cong., 1st Sess., S. Doc. 4, "Chain Stores: Final Report on the Chain-store Investigation," 1935, p. 51.
[49] 74th Cong., 2nd Sess., House Report No. 2951, pp. 6, 7. Speaking of the new language, a report submitted by the chairman of the House conferees stated: "It is to be noted, however, that this does not set up the meeting of competition as an absolute bar to a charge of discrimination under the bill. It merely permits it to be shown in evidence. This provision is entirely procedural. It does not determine substantive rights, liabilities, and duties. They are fixed in the other provisions of the bill. . . . If this proviso were construed to permit the showing of a competing offer as an absolute bar to liability for discrimination, then it would nullify the act entirely at the very inception of its enforcement. . . ." (74th Cong., 2nd Sess., *Congressional Record,* June 15, 1936, Vol. 80, p. 9418.)
[50] *Standard Oil of Indiana* v. *Federal Trade Commission,* 340 U.S. 231 (1950).

defense where the effect of the discrimination was of such dimensions as to result in a probable injury to competition generally; under these bills good faith would remain a complete defense where the effect was limited to injury to an individual competitor. The arguments on behalf of the measures were to the effect that under the good-faith defense the difficulty of enforcement had made the law against price discrimination a nullity; that without an effective law large firms would, by virtue of their size and power, be enabled to destroy or intimidate their smaller competitors and thus affect competition adversely; that selective price concessions made to large buyers do not "erode" into general across-the-board price cuts; that knowing of the difficulty good faith injects into the enforcement process the large firm is given a strong inducement to offer price discriminations it would not otherwise make; that it is always easy to "arrange" for the existence of a lower price which would constitute the justification for a discrimination; and that good faith as a complete defense creates the ironic situation that a initial "lawful" or nondiscriminatory, price cut by a firm too small to have any appreciable effect on competition makes permissible a retaliatory attack by a rival whose operations are of such magnitude that they cannot help but injure competition.

Although passed by the House of Representatives and the Senate Judiciary Committee in 1958,[51] the measures died at the end of the 85th Congress and have never been revived. Thus since 1951 the enactment of legislation to limit the scope of the good-faith defense has remained one of the more important pieces of unfinished business on the antitrust calendar.

Another form of discrimination is inherent in the reporting of financial statements only on a consolidated basis—i.e., for the company as a whole—which works against the single-line company and in favor of its conglomerate rivals. As David Solomons, a professor of accounting, has observed, "The fact is, of course, that a grave inequity is perpetrated by *not* requiring the reporting of segmental results, for companies making a narrow line of products may feel at a disadvantage compared with more diversified companies." Citing as an example the Maytag Company, a single-line firm specializing in home laundry equipment, he pointed out, "Its principal competitors are no more than subdivisions of the major appliance division of companies like General Electric, Westinghouse and the Frigidaire Division of General Motors. Maytag's results are of considerable interest to the home laundry subdivisions of these companies, whereas Maytag can learn little from its competitor's accounts." [52]

Moreover, without divisional reporting (also referred to with minor differences in meaning as "product-line" or "segmental" reporting) knowledge of the extent to which cross-subsidization is practiced will continue to be virtually nonexistent. In interpreting this information it will of course have to be recognized that a large multiproduct firm will normally have differing profit rates in the different industries in which it is engaged.[53] Losses may also be due to nothing more than inefficiency, a not unlikely possibility in view of the evidence on the inverse relationship between conglomeration and profitability.[54] At some point the con-

[51] See 85th Cong., 2nd Sess., Senate Judiciary Committee, Senate Report No. 2010, *Strengthening the Robinson-Patman Act and Amending the Antitrust Law Prohibiting Price Discrimination,* 1958.
[52] David Solomons in A. Rappaport, P. Firmin, S. Zeff, eds., *Public Reporting by Conglomerates,* Prentice-Hall, 1968, pp. 93–94.
[53] See Carl Kaysen, *United States* v. *United Shoe Machinery Corporation,* Harvard University Press, 1956, p. 127.
[54] See Ch. 8.

glomerate that is doing poorly in a new field may decide to cut its losses and withdraw from the industry.[55] From a broad economic point of view the most important justification of divisional reporting concerns the allocation of resources, specifically the flow of capital away from industries where it is redundant and into those where it is needed.

Just as a competitive economy implies free product markets, so also does it presuppose the supplying of capital by a large number of individual investors who, in deciding where to make their investments, are able to arrive at informed judgments based on objective facts concerning individual industries. If, because of rapidly growing demand, monopolistic restraints, or other factors, profits in a given industry are high, the expected reaction of investors should be to provide an influx of capital. As a result, supply would be increased, thereby promoting the socially desirable objectives of lower prices and elimination of monopoly profits.

But this sequence of events cannot even begin if investors are not able to determine the profitability of different industries. And such is the case where conglomerate corporations have come to account for a substantial share of an industry's output. In such circumstances investment becomes less a matter of rational decision making by an informed investment community than one of simple trust in the business acumen of rival corporate managements. The benefit of widely dispersed decision making is lost. It is management, not investors, who decide whether to withdraw capital from industries in which it has become redundant and place it in industries where it is needed. Yet since managerial compensation has been found to be associated more with size and growth than with profitability,[56] there is reason to question whether such reallocations of capital will meet the economic objectives that would be served by informed investors, if indeed they are met at all.

The need for divisional reporting has been recognized increasingly by investors themselves.[57] A senior partner of Price, Waterhouse and Company, Herman W. Bevis, has remarked, "A very few [corporations] report in general or specific terms about net incomes of one or more of these lines. Any information of this type is highly useful to the stockholder. . . . This reporting of meaningful data about major separable segments of the entire enterprise deserves careful consideration by all corporate managements." [58] Similarly, according to Yura Arkus-Duntov, then investment officer of the Dreyfus Fund:

> The stockholder, who is entitled to know how his company is being managed, has the choice of either extrapolating past performance, obviously a purely mechanical and unsatisfactory procedure, or to rely on "anecdotal" information. "Anecdotal" information would include information based on hearsay, rumor, conjecture, or—and this, unfortunately, may be the most well-founded source—information obtained from inside sources not available to the general public. The latter may well involve a violation of ethical standards of conduct, SEC rules and regulations, or ordinary corporate law.[59]

Opposition to divisional reporting has centered around the accounting problems that would be involved, principally those relating to the allocation of common costs and shared assets and the treatment to be accorded to interdivisional

---

[55] See *Hearings on Economic Concentration,* Pt. 6, p. 3275.
[56] See Ch. 8.
[57] W. David MacCallan in *Public Reporting by Conglomerates, op. cit.,* p. 47.
[58] Quoted in *ibid.,* p. 4.
[59] *Hearings on Economic Concentration,* Pt. 4, pp. 1706–07.

transfers. While such problems exist, their importance should not be exaggerated. For one thing, the more disparate a company's divisions, the fewer are the costs and assets they will share. It is precisely in the wide-ranging "true" conglomerate that the problem of allocating joint costs and assets is minimal. Moreover, in the general run of businesses, central research and administrative expenditures are not of overriding dimensions. As Solomons has pointed out, "Most discussion of the difficulties of segmental reporting has centered on this question of the allocation of corporate expenses, without much regard to their quantitative importance. In fact, they do not often represent more than 5 percent of a company's total expenditures. . . ." [60] Much the same is true of interdivisional transfers. In Solomons' words, "It is worth adding that, in the majority of diversified companies, inter-divisional transfers are small in amount when compared with sales to outside customers, and it is easy to exaggerate the difficulty which they put in the way of measuring divisional performance. There are many companies in which the whole question could be forgotten without any serious distortion of the accounting results.   " [61]

To the argument that divisional reporting would require the use of arbitrary, nonobjective rules, Solomons' response was that accounting today is shot full of arbitrary requirements (e.g., depreciation schedules): "If some of the . . . figures (e.g., some expense allocations) are not completely objective, this is no reason for denying the usefulness of the results. The trade-off between objectivity and relevance in accounting is going on all the time, and there is nothing unusual in the discovery that to increase the relevance of reported company results there has to be some sacrifice of objectivity." [62] Moreover, as was pointed out by George E. Brandow, executive director of the National Commission on Food Marketing, the different bases customarily employed for the allocation of common costs yield about the same results: "I think in a general case it would not make much difference which of various alternative methods, all of them acceptable and widely used, were used." [63] Citing the experience of the National Commission on Food Marketing, he stated: "Furthermore, in the Food Commission's work we did get large, diversified firms to split out certain fields of operations, and it was our general impression in looking at the reports which came to us that this had been well done and we had a good deal of confidence in the statistical results they presented to us."

That divisional reporting is well within the area of the possible has been attested to by the ability of even extremely diversified companies to make such breakdowns when they have considered it in their interest to do so. Beginning in 1961 Martin Marietta Company began to make certain divisional data public and by 1965 was issuing a detailed divisional breakdown, which, as presented by its president, George M. Bunker, is summarized in Table 22-1. In explaining the reasons for publicizing the company's operation in such detail, Bunker referred to the patience displayed by the stockholders during a lengthy period of "substantial change" in the company's operations. Moreover, "we also recognized that the company was competing for investor attention with many other major corporations with diverse activities, most of which have a much longer corporate history than our own. . . ." [64] For the corporation as a whole and for 3 of its

[60] Solomons, *op. cit.*, p. 99.
[61] *Ibid.*, p. 101.
[62] *Ibid.*, pp. 92–93.
[63] *Hearings on Economic Concentration,* Pt. 5, pp. 1961–63, testimony of George E. Brandow.
[64] *Ibid.*, p. 1969.

Table 22-1

DIVISIONAL PROFIT STATEMENT OF MARTIN MARIETTA, 1965

Division	Net Profits (000)	Return on Sales		Return on Stockholders' Equity	
		Martin Marietta	Competing Companies	Martin Marietta	Competing Companies
Aerospace (Martin)	$13,057	3.7%	2.9%	17.7%	14.7%
Cement and lime	12,500	11.3	8.7	9.1	8.5
Chemical	7,300	8.9	n.a.[a]	16.2	15.0
Rock products	5,400	10.0	7.9	11.3	12.9
Electronic (Bunker-Ramo)	-7,800	n.a.[a]	n.a.[a]	n.a.[a]	n.a.[a]
Total	$30,514	5.0	4.4	12.6	10.5

[a]Not available.

Source: Compiled from *Hearings on Economic Concentration*, Pt. 5, pp. 1971–74

principal divisions, he was able to point out that the profit rates were superior to the performance of what he regarded as "comparable" groups of companies. Revealing the actual performance of the electronics division also served to allay rumors that had ascribed to it even greater losses.

Another case when management publicized its operations, and in detail, was cited by Abraham J. Briloff.[65] It occurred when Ling-Temco-Vought broke up the Wilson Company, which it had previously acquired, into 3 component parts —one for meat products, one for sporting goods, and one for pharmaceutical and chemical products:

> When, in 1967, LTV determined to deploy old Wilson into the three little Wilsons they prepared separate and complete prospectuses for each of these three companies; each of these prospectuses included statements of income for each of these three entities showing what their separate sales, expenses, taxes and net incomes would have been—right down to the bottom line for each of the 5 years preceding the takeover and subsequent step-down. And to prove that these statements were all properly presented, each prospectus had its own "Opinion of Independent Auditors" addressed to the board of directors of the particular company. The certificate doesn't quibble—it says very explicitly that these pro forma income statements, for each of the 5 years there presented, were "in conformity with generally accepted accounting principles consistently applied."

But the process did not end there, as LTV then decided to make a further breakdown of Wilson's meat-packing component. In Briloff's words,

> when it turned out just a few months ago to be even more in accord with LTV's objectives to subdeploy the assets and operations of the new Wilson "meat ball" into four little sausages—the one to slaughter and

[65] *Ibid.*, Pt. 8, pp. 4783–84, testimony of Abraham J. Briloff.

sell livestock in the East and Midwest; another, in the Midwest and West; a third, to slaughter and sell lambs and cattle; and the fourth, poultry; lo! The same auditors were capable of preparing new pro forma statements of income for each of the new four subsidiary entities—again reaching back into the dead coals of 5 years past. And the auditors (judging from their certificate given last December) were entirely capable of asserting that: "In our opinion the pro forma net income [of the four new companies] have been properly compiled to reflect the assumptions described in the notes to the respective pro forma statements and summaries of the [new entities]."

All one needs to do is to review what the Wilson, sub-Wilson, and sub-sub-Wilson auditors were capable of doing in this single, most complex, situation and we have an immediate and effective response to almost all of the arguments heretofore advanced in objection to the demands from investors, government, the business community, labor, for segmented reporting by diversified industries.[66]

Concerted efforts to secure divisional reporting began with a recommendation by a professor of economics. Appearing before the Senate Antitrust Subcommittee on April 15, 1965, Joel B. Dirlam urged, "The relative profitability of different divisions and product lines should be brought out in order to appraise the competitive tactics utilizing diversification. We are operating in almost complete ignorance in this area where we do not know even the sales of many of the major firms in different lines, let alone the profitability or losses incurred in these lines." In addition to the light that would be shed on "competitive tactics" Dirlam also stressed the importance of divisional reporting for the allocation of capital. "I would speak also on behalf of the average investor who does not know what he is buying into when he purchases one of these large diversified firms. He has only the overall statement to go by. He judges then not the industry but the behavior of the firm itself, and he stakes his money on the management with a minimum of information." [67]

The recommendation was transmitted to the Securities and Exchange Commission for comment. Given the agency's long-standing preoccupation with matters of far less moment (often approaching trivia), its initial reaction was predictably adverse. On June 4, 1965, Chairman Manuel F. Cohen sent a memorandum to the Subcommittee, which, while conceding that the agency possesses the necessary legal powers, set forth five reasons against instituting such a program. He expressed concern over its "cost," over the problems of "allocation of overhead, research and development, taxes, etc.," over the possible injury to a reporting company's "competitive position," over the "problems of rulemaking," and over the "liabilities which would be faced by registrants and accountants in furnishing such information." Furthermore, if things were just let alone, according to the memorandum, the problem would solve itself; some companies, it was pointed out, were already furnishing such information voluntarily, "a trend which we believe should be encouraged." [68]

A year later, however, the SEC had changed its mind. Appearing before the Antitrust Subcommittee on September 20, 1966, Chairman Cohen acknowledged that "changes have been occurring recently which have made it necessary for us to reconsider our requirements in this area despite the difficulties we will have

[66] Ibid., Pt. 8, pp. 4783–4.
[67] Ibid., Pt. 2, pp. 769–70.
[68] Ibid., pp. 1069–71.

to face." [69] The "changes" referred to were the alterations in corporate structures resulting from the wave of conglomerate mergers.

Since that time divisional reporting has suffered the fate that seems increasingly to befall reform proposals of any kind—interminable delay finally followed by adoption in form but not in substance. The proposal was studied and restudied— by the Financial Executives Institute,[70] by the Securities and Exchange Commission, by the Bureau of the Budget, by the Federal Trade Commission, and most recently by the White House. Finally, in 1970 the SEC required registered firms to report separate profit data for product lines representing more than 10 percent of the company's sales. This percentage standard had the obviously inequitable effect of requiring reports from relatively small divisions of medium-size concerns but of not requiring them from larger competitive divisions of much larger corporations. Moreover, the program suffers from a deficiency that has made the resultant reports of very little use to anyone for any purpose. In making their reports the companies are *not* required to use a standard system of classification such as that employed by the Internal Revenue Service[71] or the company-industry categories of the Census Bureau. The result, a tribute to public-relations imagery, has been a mélange of intriguingly named corporate segments, which conceal more than they reveal. They vary so greatly from company to company as to make it impossible to compare the performance of similar product lines in different companies or to derive statistical aggregates of any kind. That such would inescapably prove to be the case had been predicted in 1966 by Brandow:

> It would seem best to define the fields by which firms should report rather than to accept companies' own divisional organization. Some firms' divisions are freakish because of historical accidents or the like, *and equally freakish divisions could be contrived for reporting if a purpose was to be served by it.* Moreover, valuable statistical information about the economy will be lost unless reports by fields can be aggregated in a meaningful way.
>
> Again for statistical reasons, it would be desirable to mesh definitions of fields with the Standard Industrial Classification of the Bureau of the Census. Probably three-digit categories are at about the right level of aggregation for fields but closely related categories might be combined in some instances.[72]

An FTC staff study of 19 "line-of-business" reports submitted to the SEC is reported to have found that "large conglomerates included in the sample tend to define their lines-of-business so broadly that the profit information for the category is valueless." The report noted as an indication of their excessive breadth, that "the average number of lines-of-business per company was 5, while the average number of corporate divisions was 31." [73]

---

[69] *Ibid.,* Pt. 5, p. 1983.

[70] Robert K. Maitz, professor of accounting at the University of Illinois, was retained by the Financial Executives Institute through its foundation to prepare a comprehensive study of the problem. For the results of his study of the conceptual problems involved see *Financial Executive,* July, Sept., Nov., 1967.

[71] See *Hearings on Economic Concentration,* Pt. 5, pp. 2150–52.

[72] Emphasis added.

[73] Quoted in the *Washington Star,* April 25, 1971. As an example of the way in which the use of the percentage standard favors very large concerns, the report is quoted as citing the manufacture of refrigerators by General Motors: " 'General Motors' profits in refrigerators, for example, would go unreported even though it produces Frigidaire, one of the industry's leading brands. . . . Its sales of refrigerators would have to exceed $2.3 billion (10 percent of GM's total sales of about $23 billion in 1968) before it

The Role of Government

For the competitive approach to have any real chance of success the government must cease or alter those of its activities that lead to greater concentration and the suppression of competition. It need only stop doing some of the things it is now doing and do others in a different manner.

First, the government should cease trying to protect American industries from foreign competition, particularly those that have long outlived their "infant industry" status. Likewise, the independent regulatory agencies should stop trying to protect established companies in industries under their jurisdiction. An end should be put to those activities of the Interstate Commerce Commission that protect the railroads from the trucks; of the Civil Aeronautics Board that protect the large airlines from the smaller carriers; of the Federal Communications Commission that protect AT&T, the licensed TV stations, and the TV networks from new communications technologies; of the Oil Import Administration that protect the major oil companies from the small oil importers; of the Food and Drug Administration that protect the large drug companies from smaller drug manufacturers; and so on.

If new technologies, particularly those of a capital-saving, decentralizing character, continue to proliferate, pressures will be strong to use the instrument of government as a barrier against their acceptance. In retrospect, the acceptance of the automobile might well have proceeded much more slowly had there been in existence a government agency regulating stagecoaches and other commercial horse-drawn vehicles. In addition to restraining what appears to be a natural impulse to intervene, government could give a powerful stimulus to competition by changing its current ways of doing things. In some cases making the change would be the essence of simplicity. For example, simply by altering its regulations the Department of the Interior could replace the current "cash bonus" system for offshore oil leases with a system of royalties spread over the life of the lease. Not only would this open up the bidding to smaller companies and even individuals, but in the long run it would probably result in greater revenues accruing to the government.

In other areas—e.g., procurement and patents—such a reversal would require coming to grips with issues of considerably greater complexity. No significant change in the impact of government procurement on industry structure is likely to take place until and unless the Defense Department comes to realize that the present highly centralized system is working against the best interests of national security. Most of the major items of military hardware are currently procured through a "weapons systems" approach, under which the starting point is the end product. The functions of drawing up the proposals for the new product, of serving as the prime contractor, and indeed of doing much of the subcontracting work are generally carried on by about a dozen large companies. The justification for such centralization is their reputation for specialized expertise and ability to perform, which in some cases is well deserved. But the very same type of "top-down" hierarchical system in which the military services are themselves organized has thus been imposed on the private sector engaged in defense production.

The drawbacks of the system arise not so much from deficiencies on the part of the companies—spectacular though they occasionally may be—as from the na-

---

would be required to make a report.'" In this connection it should be pointed out that according to the 1967 Census of Manufactures the total value of shipments of the entire household refrigerator and freezer industry was only $1.8 billion.

ture of the system itself. Instead of starting with an end product which assumes a given technology, the determining variable should be not what the military thinks it wants but what technology can deliver. A new technology may appear anywhere in the stream of production from raw materials (e.g., carbon and boron composites) to sophisticated motors (e.g., the fuel cell). Moreover, the appearance of a new technology is an episodic occurrence, lending itself neither to prediction nor to planning.

Under the systems approach, the end product must not be so different from existing weapons as to make "do-ability" appear impossible, but it must seem sufficiently new and different as to warrant large expenditures of funds. It thus achieves the worst of two possible worlds. Because their "do-ability" seems completely out of the question, the truly radical forms of weaponry are excluded, as indeed are all new technologies that cannot be integrated into a given system. On the other hand, without a certain modicum of "newness," the product would be only a replica of existing weapons, lacking the novelty required to justify sizable appropriations for a "new" weapons system. The exclusion of far-reaching, revolutionary ideas is virtually automatic. As Donald Schon has pointed out, "There are the stories of Prof. Robert H. Goddard who tried in the 1930's, for the most part unsuccessfully, to interest the U.S. military in rocketry; or George Christie, inventor of the [torsion bar] suspension system for tanks—rejected by the U.S. Army, later adopted successfully by the Russians; and of Nicholas C. Christofilos 'the crazy Greek' who turned up with project Astron." Unless they can be fitted into an approved system innovations of any kind suffer the same fate. In Schon's words, "A military technical administrator operating within such a system cannot easily shift his attention to radical technical ideas not obviously related to his requirements. . . ." [74]

The losses incurred by what it excludes are only one of the present system's principal liabilities; the other consists of the costs of trying to force from a given technology a performance it cannot deliver. The implicit assumption is that a new weapon's requirement for a minimal advance in performance can be met by improvements in, or better applications of, or more complex gadgetry involving *existing technologies*. Just as there is a tendency for procurement officials to discount the new and unfamiliar, so do they often exaggerate what can be accomplished with what is old and proven. But where the existing technology cannot meet what is demanded of it, as in the case of titanium for the F-111 (formerly the TFX) or of electronic fire control systems for the Sheridan tank, the result is disaster.

What is required is a complete reversal of approach. The starting point of procurement should be the appearance of a new technology, around which new end products can be designed and produced and, incidentally, tested at each step in the production process. "Do-ability" should be demonstrated before there is a large-scale commitment of funds to any end product. Not only would such an approach result in impressive savings in appropriations, but it would provide military planners with better weapons than could possibly have been supplied with existing technologies. Fitting the end product to technology rather than trying to fit technology to the end product is the only way of eliminating staggering cost overruns, intolerable delays in delivery, and dismaying failures in performance. Given the decentralizing character of modern technology, it should also lead to a marked decentralization of defense production.

The granting by the government of monopolies through patents also readily

[74] *Hearings on Economic Concentration,* Pt. 3, p. 1212.

lends itself to correction. The form of the correction—compulsory licensing—has been continuously urged since it was recommended by an international patent congress held in 1873. The reasons behind the compromise have been described by Fritz Machlup:

> The friends of the patent system saw if they would provide or accept a compromise solution which would reduce the monopoly character of the patent grant, they could save the patent system.
>
> The idea was that if patents could be open to anyone who wanted to use them, if these inventions became open for everyone paying a reasonable royalty, then the monopoly character of the patent law would no longer be prevalent, technology would be used more widely, and the opposition to the patent system would withdraw.
>
> The people who were opposed to the patent system felt that with compulsory licensing it was tolerable.[75]

Nearly a century later compulsory licensing still appears to be the best compromise between the conflicting objectives of protecting the public from monopoly and providing an adequate incentive to the inventor. In the interim compulsory licensing has been widely adopted by different countries throughout the world.[76] In 1949, for example, the British government, in making drugs patentable, imposed compulsory licensing on such patents and shifted the burden of proof from the applicant for license to the patentee. In commenting on the record of compulsory licensing, Machlup observed, "The effectiveness of compulsory licensing provisions cannot be measured by the amount of litigation about licensees . . . The realization that compulsory license may be issued under the law would induce patentees to make their inventions voluntarily available against reasonable royalties."[77] The principal arguments against compulsory licensing have been that it eliminates incentives, thus destroying the patent system, and that it is ineffective. As Machlup noted, these arguments are contradictory: "If compulsory licensing destroys the patent system, it must be effective, and if it is ineffective, it cannot destroy the patent system."[78]

Before compulsory licensing could be adopted, it would be necessary to determine the circumstances under which licenses would have to be awarded (e.g., an "excessive" price, restricted production or capacity, non-use); the products to which the requirement would apply (e.g., all, or—as in some countries—foods, drugs, chemical products); whether it would apply to processes as well as products; the time period after a patent's issuance before it could be involved (e.g., 3 years); the amount of the "reasonable" royalty; and the like. Inasmuch as entrée to the large corporations is often dependent upon the possession of a patent, the individual inventor or small company might be exempted from the requirement; in other words, compulsory licensing would be required of patents assigned to, or obtained by employees of, say, the 200 or 500 largest companies. The devising of

---

[75] 87th Cong., 1st Sess., Senate Subcommittee on Antitrust and Monopoly, Senate Committee on the Judiciary, *Hearings on S. 1552,* "To Amend and Supplement the Antitrust Laws, with Respect to the Manufacture and Distribution of Drugs," 1962, Pt. 3, p. 1367.

[76] See 86th Cong., 1st Sess., Senate Subcommittee on Patents, Trademarks and Copyrights, Senate Committee on the Judiciary, Study No. 19, *Compulsory Licensing of Patents Under Some Non-American Systems,* 1959.

[77] Senate Subcommittee on Antitrust and Monopoly, *op. cit.,* p. 1369.

[78] *Ibid.*

acceptable solutions to these and related questions should not be beyond the mind of man.

Stimulating the centrifugal forces

Under the new approach outlined here, restraining the centripetal forces would represent one side of the coin; the other would involve policies designed to promote the operation of the centrifugal forces. If introduced within a given industry, a new technology can lower company concentration by reducing the capital entrance requirements, thereby making possible the entry of newcomers and an expansion of smaller producers at a rate impossible with the older technology. Cases in point are the rapid growth of such medium-size steel producers as McLouth and Kaiser, facilitated by their early installation of oxygen conversion, and the subsequent and even more rapid growth of small producers using electric furnaces and continuous casting. If introduced outside any given industry, a new technology can not only lessen the importance of concentrated industries in the economy as a whole but may provide a stimulus to market competition in the form of a substitute product. Again, the steel industry is illustrative: the introduction of prestressed concrete is depriving the steel industry of several hundred million dollars a year in sales of structural steel and concrete reinforcing bars. Where, as in this case, the inroads are being made by an unconcentrated industry at the expense of a more concentrated field, concentration in the performance of a given function is lessened, even though concentration in the respective individual industries may remain the same. If technology is in fact working toward decentralization, it follows that reducing the barriers confronting the small innovative company[79] would accelerate the rate of development of new decentralizing technologies.

First and foremost among the problems of such small companies is the lack of adequate sources of financing. There has long been an "institutional gap" in the sources of financial aid available to small business, and this is particularly true where the nature of its product is new, untried, and untested. Venture capital is hard to come by, owing partly to the reluctance of underwriters to handle the offerings of small firms. Even where their securities can be issued, the cost to the small firms in underwriters' fees is far higher than the cost to their large competitors. Long-term bank loans are also something of a rarity, and when they can be secured the interest costs are, again, far higher than the costs to the large firm.

In a study prepared for the Panel on Invention and Innovation of the Department of Commerce and summarized before the Antitrust Subcommittee, Daniel V. DeSimone, Director of Invention and Innovation of the National Bureau of Standards, identified the several stages in its life history when the typical small innovative concern must secure financing or perish.[80] The first stage is the idea: "The inventor who has conceived the idea firmly believes in the value of his invention and is totally committed to it. He has to be, for what lies between him and the marketplace is a tortuous obstacle course, bristling with hazards and disappointments." To be in business innovators need capital: "As a rule they

<hr/>

[79] The term "small innovative company" is used here to encompass the enterprises variously referred to by such terms as "the technological entrepreneur," "the scientific enterprise," and "the small, research-oriented company."

[80] *Hearings on Economic Concentration,* Pt. 6, pp. 2921–32, testimony of Daniel V. DeSimone.

have none, and nothing will happen to their idea until they get some financial backing. It is not just any kind of money they are seeking. What they require is startup, or 'seed,' venture capital, and they must know something about the intricacies of venture capital acquisition or enlist the aid of somebody who does." To get their initial venture capital they have to pay a high price: "Venture capital is very-high-risk money, especially when the investment is in a mere idea. High-risk money requires high potential return. This is a fundamental principle, for there must be opportunities for large gains from a few successful ventures in order to offset the risk of losses from the many failures." Assuming that the fledgling enterprise is successful in obtaining the initial capital, "It is now in business, but it is losing money. Let us put some rough dimensions on the firm at this stage. It is small, lean, proud, hard working. It is quartered in very modest facilities. During this garage stage, as we call it, it is typically less than 5 years old, has less than 100 employees, and less than $1 million in capital." Offsetting the diseconomics resulting from its small size are certain important advantages. "This kind of company has a fast reaction time; it is quick on its feet, so to speak. It has to be: the distance from the front to the back of the garage or from smooth sailing to bankruptcy is very short, indeed. Each adversity is a major crisis for a fledgling enterprise. It has limited marketing problems, because it typically has only a few customers."

At this stage the company must find some way of attracting competent management and marketing talent: "The typical inventor lacks managerial skills. The firm needs these skills, but how is it to get them? The salaries, pensions, and other fringe benefits used by successful firms to lure and hold key people cannot be offered by a struggling small company which is fighting for its survival. Other incentives must be found." But, to provide the incentives and keep the company growing, a new type of financing is required: "The earlier risks and uncertainties have been reduced and, therefore, obtaining secondary financing is usually easier than the acquisition of start-up capital. This time the company can look to the more conventional sources of capital—public stock offerings, for example." With the secondary financing the firm must improve product quality, lower manufacturing costs, expand its research, development, and marketing activities, and in general complete the metamorphosis from an "idea" into an "operating" company: "Let us assume, however, that the company solves all of these problems— that in its wisdom, persistence, and good fortune, it has become a successful growth business. Because the company has become successful, it has attracted other companies to its field, and the competition intensifies. Technological innovation and vigorous, healthy competition go hand in hand."

Perhaps the simplest way of meeting these problems would be through changes in the tax laws, designed to help the small innovative company over the formidable barriers to its early growth. Thus, fast write-offs might be permitted on investments in small innovative companies—the nature of which would of course have to be defined. Investors who back such enterprises might be permitted to write off their investments in only a very few years. Also, small innovative companies which lose money during the research and testing stage of an invention could be permitted to carry forward the loss, so that income received when an invention finally does "pay off" could be spread over the prior and unprofitable years of its creation. Another possibility would be to treat the amounts expended on research by small firms (which would have to be defined arbitrarily in some way) as a tax credit—i.e., a dollar-for-dollar offset against income. Since 1954 it has been permissible to treat research expenditures as a "deferred expense" to be amortized in 5 years or more, but with the amortization period beginning only *after* income resulting from the research is realized. Along the same line small firms could be granted a tax credit on research expenditures against income resulting therefrom. That is to say, on that portion of a small firm's income resulting from research it conducted (or contracted for) it would pay no tax until the amount of such income exceeded the amount expended on the research.[81]

Like any other offset or deduction under the tax laws, such a credit could be subject to abuse. The major potential loophole would be an unduly broad definition of what constitutes "research." Specifically excluded should be work on modifying or finding new uses or applications for existing products and processes.[82] But it is certainly easier to justify the use of the principle of the tax credit for this limited and obviously desirable purpose than for certain other uses to which it has been put (e.g., the subsidization of the major oil companies through the foreign tax credit).

In addition to changes in the tax laws Arkus-Duntov urged that steps be taken to make inventors and investors more aware of each other:

> The basic problem is that those who have the funds usually do not know the inventors and those who have the creative ideas do not know the potential financiers. Developing ways and means of closing this gap is a project which lends itself to the attention of your subcommittee.
>
> For instance, the Department of Commerce should be able, with modern computers, to provide much better information to the investing community as to which inventors are working on what projects. The Securities and Exchange Commission should establish a separate category for something like "radical new inventions." For such issues it would be recognized and indeed emphasized in the registration statements, prospectuses, and all other informational material that security is a very secondary consideration. This is a class of securities from which widows, orphans, and small investors generally would be advised to stay away, since the chances of losing your total investment would indeed be very good. But those who are willing and able to play this admittedly dangerous game, should not be encumbered by the restraints devised to protect those whose principal interest is security.[83]

The competitive approach: an evaluation

At least in theory the advantages of the competitive approach are impressive. It prevents prices from rising above the level necessary to bring forth the supply needed to meet the given demand. It exerts a continuous downward pressure on costs. The producer whose costs at the existing level of demand are above the market price must lower them by making a more economic use of his materials, labor, and capital or go out of business. The producer who through a new technology or other means is able to lower his costs below the existing market price will try to enlarge his sales by cutting the price, forcing his competitors to make a similar improvement or fall by the wayside. In the meantime his innovation will bring him the reward of increased sales and profits. Thus, through competition the benefits of technological advance are passed on rapidly to the consumer

[81] See *ibid.*, p. 2782.
[82] Step 4 of David Novick's classification (see Ch. 9).
[83] *Hearings on Economic Concentration,* Pt. 6, pp. 2781–82.

in the form of lower prices. At the same time producers must be responsive to the changing desires of consumers. When consumers want less of a product, the resultant decline in price forces its high-cost producers out of business. The resources released from its production then flow into other industries where demand is rising, a process that continues until the increase in supply is sufficient to satisfy the demand. Each seller's efforts to maximize his own gain thus serve the ends of society by bringing about an optimal use of resources. And the whole process, guided by the "unseen hand" of competition, takes place without direction by government.

These benefits could be realized much more fully by a national program for competition, which would be directed partly toward the objectives of traditional antitrust policy—achieving dissolution and preventing collusion; and the application to existing concentration of law on mergers. In view of the well-established position of the Court, all that needs to be done on collusion is to enforce the law.

In its orientation toward the future, a program for competition should seek to employ J. Kenneth Galbraith's principle of countervailing power by restraining those forces that experience has shown are bringing about higher concentration—mergers, TV advertising, predatory practices, and government intervention—while at the same time stimulating and promoting the forces operating in the opposite direction.

Some of the elements of such a program would require new legislation; many would not. In the case of still others, notably dissolution and mergers, new and stronger legislation would certainly be desirable, but there is a real potentiality for accomplishment under the present law. In such cases, neither the consideration of new legislation nor the initiating of actions based on existing statutes should wait upon the other. The principal elements of a national program for competition, each of which has been discussed above in greater detail, are summarized in Table 22-2.

In retrospect, it is somewhat surprising to note how many of the needed steps are *not* dependent on new legislation. Changes in the law are essential to open up TV time to smaller companies, to narrow "good faith" as a complete defense in price discrimination cases, to require compulsory licensing under patents, and to ease the financial problems of small, innovative companies. They are desirable in the case of dissolutions and mergers. But no legislation is required to arrest many conglomerate mergers, to make the enforcement of the law against collusion accord with the realities of modern business behavior, to institute a meaningful program of divisional reporting, to reorient procurement policy, to change agency regulations with respect to the lease of government-owned property, to eliminate import quotas and make significant reductions in tariffs, to cease protecting from competition the industries under the jurisdiction of the regulatory agencies, and to establish a clearinghouse between inventors and investors.

None of these proposals lies beyond the realm of the politically possible. While each would strengthen the others, they are not interdependent. To be effective they do not have to be put into effect *en masse;* if, as, and when adopted, each can make its own individual contribution to a more competitive economy.

A note on enforcement

Neither the competitive nor any other type of approach can be successful if the laws designed to implement it are poorly enforced. While it may be idle to expect

Table 22-2

A NATIONAL PROGRAM FOR COMPETITION

Element	Legislation Needed	Potentialities Under Present Law
1. Dissolution	Reduction of market share of 4 largest companies below 50%; prohibition of financial institutions from voting shareholdings in competing companies	a. Cases against one-company dominance based on possession and use of substantial monopoly power b. Cases against oligopolies as "shared monopolies"
2. Collusion		a. Cases, based on economic or circumstantial evidence, against "implied conspiracies" or "planned common course of action," including particularly cases against reductions of production accompanying price increases made in the face of falling demand. b. Cases against "planned common course of action" based on Count II of *Rigid Steel Conduit*
3. Mergers	Prohibition of all acquisitions by largest companies	Cases against conglomerate mergers based on: a. *Procter & Gamble—Clorox* b. Other "lessening-of-competition" theories c. "Tendency-to-monopoly" test
4. TV Advertising	"Equal time" amendment to Federal Communication Act opening up greater TV time for smaller companies	

5. Predation	
a. Price discrimination	Elimination of "good faith" as complete defense in cases involving probable substantial injury to competition
b. Cross-subsidization	Institution by SEC or FTC of divisional reporting program using a standard industry classification
6. Government Intervention	
a. Procurement	New technologies, not end products, made the starting point of procurement
b. Lease	Change of regulations to provide greater participation by smaller firms
c. Protectionism	Elimination of all quotas (particularly oil import quota) and lower tariffs
d. Patents	Requirement of compulsory licensing
e. Regulatory agencies	End to activities that protect industries under their jurisdiction from competition
7. Centrifugal Forces	Amendment of tax laws to attract capital to small, innovative companies
	Establishment of clearing house to make inventors and investors more aware of each other

any law to be well and properly enforced, there are degrees of imperfect enforcement, ranging from the tolerable down to the utterly hopeless. As the experience of the Federal Trade Commission attests, one way of *not* achieving even tolerable success is by constantly subjecting the agency to reorganization. An article of faith among every incoming administration seems to be that whatever is wrong with an agency can be cured by a new reorganization chart, complete with lines of authority progressing neatly downward from the agency head through middle-level bureaus and divisions to a multitude of sections and units at the bottom. Recasting the organizational structure may, on occasion, produce economies, though they will be marginal at best as long as pretty much the same people are doing the same work with the same resources and under the same legislative authority. At the same time it always yields diseconomies, since time is required for the personnel to adjust to the new lines of authority, to accommodate themselves to their new superiors or subordinates, and in other ways to get used to new relationships and procedures. In the case of the Federal Trade Commission, any failure in enforcement cannot be attributed to improper organization, since every conceivable form of organization has been tried without any noticeable effect on the agency's performance.

Rather, the authorities who have studied the Commission are in substantial agreement that the besetting sin of the agency's law-enforcement work has been its persistent and dedicated preoccupation with trivia. Although the Commission has displayed occasional flashes of brilliance—as in its cases involving delivered-prices and conglomerate mergers—it has devoted itself with such thoroughness to the mundane and trivial that it has had little resources available for anything else.

The Hoover Committee Task Force *Report on Regulatory Commissions* concluded:

> As the years have progressed, the Commission has become immersed in a multitude of petty problems; it has not probed into new areas of anti-competitive practices; it has become increasingly bogged down with cumbersome procedures and inordinate delays in disposition of cases. Its economic work—instead of being the backbone of its activities—has been allowed to dwindle almost to none. The Commission has largely become a passive judicial agency, waiting for cases to come up on the docket, under routinized procedures, without active responsibility for achieving the statutory objectives.[84]

A similar conclusion had already been reached in a report submitted by then Representative Estes Kefauver of the House Small Business Committee. Analyzing the extent to which the FTC had brought proceedings involving the most highly concentrated products in the economy (products with annual shipments of more than $10 million in which the leading 4 producers accounted for more than 75 percent of the output), this report found that between 1932 and 1947 fewer than one-third of the 121 products were covered by FTC antitrust actions. In another test the report matched the FTC case record against the names of the largest manufacturers and discovered that of the 107 largest industrial corporations, action had been taken against only 15.[85]

[84] Committee on Independent Regulatory Commissions, U.S. Commission on Organization of the Executive Branch, Report 125 (Hoover Commission. Task Force Rept. App. N, 1949).

[85] Staff of Monopoly Subcommittee, House Committee on Small Business, 79th Cong., *United States Versus Economic Concentration and Monopoly,* pp. 21–22 (Comm. Print 1946).

The reasons for the Commission's long-standing emphasis on matters of little consequence are many. For one thing, there is the continuing pressure to present to the Budget Bureau and the Appropriations Committee a respectable record of case work; unfortunately each case, no matter how significant, tends to count as one. While the informed examiner of the Budget Bureau may readily concede that one *Cement* case may be more important to the public interest than hundreds of small advertising cases, there seems to be an almost inescapable tendency to fall back on the "headcount" of cases as the final measure of performance. A second factor is the comparative immunity from attack to be gained by concentrating upon practices that are obviously illegal and, preferably, outrageous. Nothing tempers the wrath of an indignant critic like the explanation that the Commission's action is merely in response to a complaint from a businessman, particularly a reputable one. The agonies that the Commission went through in trying to justify its attack upon the basing-point system—whose harmful effects were exceeded only by its difficulty of description—left a scar which has long remained.

A further problem that has become increasingly serious in recent years has been the shortage of trained personnel competent to handle the "big cases." When, as was true in the *Cement* case, three Commission attorneys and one economist were pitted against 41 law firms and an expenditure by the respondents in excess of \$5 million, the Commission's staff must be exceedingly able—as they were. Insofar as money is an inducement, the Commission under present pay scales is simply unable to offer the type of compensation necessary to attract and keep professional personnel of such competence.

But the most important factor is the *point of departure* used by the Commission in instituting legal actions. Except for its merger activities, the point of departure is usually a complaint originating with an aggrieved competitor. This is a singularly undesirable *modus operandi,* since the higher the level of concentration, the less the probability of the Commission's receiving complaints. A complete monopoly can hardly be accused of engaging in unfair practices by rivals who do not exist. And in oligopolistic industries, the small firms are understandably hesitant about lodging complaints against their more powerful rivals, while the oligopolists themselves are frequently tolerant of their unimportant rivals and able to forgive the use by other oligopolists of practices no different from their own. By contrast, in highly competitive industries, there is usually an abundance of producers all too eager to complain of a rival's slightest transgression. Hence reliance upon complaints as the initiating factor has the unhappy but inescapable effect of putting last things first.

Except for its work on mergers, the Commission (the Antitrust Division as well) largely dispenses with the exercise of economic expertise in the initial and crucial first step of instituting an investigation, which may result in the issuance of a formal complaint, which may then be the subject of hearings before a trial examiner and the Commission itself, which may subsequently lead to the issuance of a cease and desist order, which may in turn be argued before the court of appeals and the Supreme Court.

What is it that sets in motion these ponderous wheels of justice which grind so exceedingly fine and so exceedingly slow? "The inescapable conclusion from a review of the Federal Trade Commission antitrust case record is that there is little attempt to give first attention to the most serious areas of concentration. Why is this? The answer is quite simple. It is because the Federal Trade Commission operates as a kind of court handling complaints big and little, as they come to them, and processes them as they are received." [86] Like the oyster, it waits for what the tide brings in.

In virtually any form of organized contest, ranging from wars to football games, planning is recognized as the indispensable means by which resources are effectively mobilized, strategically deployed, and brought into action in the right way to achieve the crucial objectives. If the competitive approach is to have any degree of success, the FTC and the Antitrust Division must mobilize their resources to have the greatest strategic effect on what is happening in the more concentrated industries and on what is being done by the largest corporations with substantial monopoly power. To the extent that they succeed in planning for competition, the need for planning the economy will diminish.

[86] Staff of Monopoly Subcommittee, *op. cit.,* p. 22.

Contrary to a widespread impression, which dates the use of "jawboning," "suasion," and "voluntary controls" to the 1962 *Economic Report of the President,* this country has had a long tradition of placing reliance on an informed public to prevent the abuse of concentrated economic power. The approach is rooted in the view that corporate management can be induced by the force of an informed and enlightened public opinion to follow policies that accord with the public interest.

The history of voluntary suasion

On February 10, 1902, the United States Industrial Commission, after an extensive study of the industrial economy, recommended that a federal agency be established to supervise corporations engaged in interstate commerce: "Theodore Roosevelt and his friends were deeply convinced that publicity on corporate organizations' activities, expressly on technological deficiencies in production or in distribution, would be a sufficient method of business policing." [1] Accordingly, a Bureau of Corporations was created on February 14, 1903, with the "power and authority . . . to make . . . diligent investigations into the organization, conduct and management of the business of any corporation, joint stock company, or corporate combination engaged in commerce." [2] In the view of the Commissioner of Corporations, his objective was to bring about better corporate behavior through the collection and publication of strategic economic facts. Thus, in December, 1904, he stressed the importance of continued fact finding and reporting, stating: "In addition to the value to Congress of such information, the publication of facts, the dissemination of knowledge, will bring into existence the influence of an enlightened public opinion which, properly applied, will go far to develop the sense of public trust involved in the control of private wealth and the sense of personal responsibility on the part of officers and managers of corporations." [3]

The Bureau conducted extensive investigations of steel, coal, petroleum, timber, cotton, and other industries. In 1906, for example, the Commissioner re-

---

[1] Heinrich Kronstein, "Reporting of Corporate Activities," *University of Detroit Law Journal,* June, 1961, pp. 589–99. Included in *Hearings on Economic Concentration,* Pt. 7, pp. 3824–30.

[2] 57th Cong., Public Law 87.

[3] *Annual Report of the Commissioner of Corporations,* 1904, p. 47.

ported that as a result of its investigation into the transportation of petroleum, "the railroads cancelled substantially all secret rebates, illegal or improper discrimination, and in many cases discrimination in open rates." [4] Two years later he recommended that a federal agency undertake a continuing study of financial conditions, business organizations, and corporate transactions of large interstate corporations, with the agency to have access at all reasonable times to the records and accounts of such corporations. The important facts and tendencies were to be disclosed to the public.[5] In 1914 the Federal Trade Commission was established, and the Bureau's investigatory powers were enlarged and transferred to the new agency. Thus the power of the Federal Trade Commission to make general economic investigations antedates its power to institute formal legal proceedings.

At its founding, the Commission's "principal purpose . . . was to strengthen and extend the work of the Bureau of Corporations." [6] To carry out its economic fact-finding function, the newly created agency was given in Section 6 of its organic act the sweeping investigatory power: "To gather and compile information concerning, and to investigate from time to time the organization, business, conduct, practices, and management of any corporation engaged in commerce excepting banks and common carriers . . . and its relation to other corporations and to individuals, associations and partnerships." [7] An examination of the legislative history reveals that the compiling and disseminating of economic information was intended to be the Commission's principal function, far transcending the enforcement of the law against "unfair" and "monopolistic" business practices and activities, which over the years has come to preempt all but a small share of the agency's manpower and resources. In Kronstein's words:

> When Congress, on the suggestion of Brandeis and La Follette, undertook drafting an act organizing the Federal Trade Commission, all draftsmen approached their task with the assumption that the principal duty of this Commission would be to improve upon the reporting job started by the Bureau. A Commission, independent from the three governmental branches, once entrusted with such a task, was expected to do a more forceful and penetrating job.
>
> While the Bureau had only 120 employees, it was intended to allow the Federal Trade Commission a substantially larger staff for its reporting job. Analysis of the history of the Federal Trade Commission Act and of the Commission's first period of operation shows that section 5 of the act authorizing the Commission to issue cease-and-desist orders for unfair competitive practices was included in the draft only in the latter stages of its preparation. The purpose of this inclusion was to authorize the Commission to act, itself, if in exceptional cases such action appeared to be necessary to correct abuses brought to light as a result of continuous observation of and reporting on industrial and corporate structure.[8]

Commenting on the legislative history William Z. Ripley urged a vigorous use of the fact-finding power:

[4] *Annual Report of the Commissioner of Corporations,* 1906, p. 5.
[5] *Annual Report of the Commissioner of Corporations,* 1906, p. 5.
[6] Kronstein, *op. cit.*
[7] Federal Trade Commission Act (1914), Sec. 6(a).
[8] Kronstein, *op. cit.*

This statute . . . contains in section 6, a positive delegation of authority to this body which is entirely adequate to the performance of the service so greatly needed at the present time. . . . The record of debate upon the subject makes it clear that Congress intended this work to constitute one of its chief activities. . . . Here then we have plainly indicated the most obvious, the simplest, the most effective remedy of all. . . . No legislation is necessary. There is nothing revolutionary about it—nothing paternalistic . . . let the word go forth that the Federal Trade Commission is henceforward to address itself vigorously to the matter of adequate and intelligent corporate publicity, and, taken in conjunction with the helpful agencies already at work, the thing is as good as done.[9]

Economic investigations carried out under these fact-finding powers are most noted for their role in contributing to the enactment of legislation. The passage of the Packers and Stockyards Act of 1921 stemmed in large part from the Commission's general investigation of the meat-packing industry, the Grain Futures Act of 1922 from the Commission's grain trade report; the Securities Act of 1933, the Federal Power Act of 1935, and the Public Utility Holding Act of 1935 from the Commission's public utility investigation; the Robinson-Patman Anti-Price Discrimination Act in 1936 from the Commission's chain store investigation; and the Celler-Kefauver antimerger amendment of 1950 from the Commission's reports and evidence on mergers.

Less well known are the direct effects of its inquiries on prices. The Commission's 1920 *Report on the Causes of High Prices of Farm Implements* disclosed a scheme to control and maintain prices under the guise of cost studies carried on by the National Implement and Vehicle Association. When the facts were made public the scheme was abandoned, competition was restored, and prices fell. A similar device operated by the furniture industry was likewise abandoned shortly after the Commission published the facts in 1923. Again competition set in and prices were reduced. One of the most interesting episodes in the Commission's history had its origins in August, 1919, when a subcommittee of the House Committee on Appropriations invited the Commission to suggest what might be done to reduce the high cost of living. The Commission recommended the collection and publication of current figures on costs and prices in important industries. Upon receiving an appropriation of $150,000 specifically for this purpose, the Commission called for monthly reports, beginning in January, 1920, from bituminous- and anthracite-coal operators, iron and steel companies, and coke producers; moreover, plans for similar projects were outlined for lumber, textiles, and other industries. In a bizarre decision a lower court held that the information demanded by the Commission had to do with "production" and was therefore not subject to the Commission's jurisdiction, which was limited to matters affecting "commerce." [10] Although the decision was ultimately reversed, during the interim the program suffered a gradual demise.

Through other investigations, however, the Commission continued to exert a real and direct influence on pricing policy. For instance, price reductions representing savings to farmers of $40 million, or over twenty times the Com-

[9] William Z. Ripley, *Main Street and Wall Street,* Little, Brown, 1927, pp. 222, 227.
[10] *Maynard Coal Co.* v. *Federal Trade Commission,* 22 F. 2d 873 (C.A.D.C. 1927). *Federal Trade Commission* v. *Claire Furnace Co.,* 274 U.S. 160 (1927).

mission's budget, followed the publication in 1938 of its *Report on the Agricultural Implement and Machinery Industry.* Under the price leadership of a dominant firm prices of farm machinery were shown to have had smaller decreases during the Depression and greater subsequent increases than either the prices of farm products or the prices of a number of comparable consumer products in which there was lower concentration and a greater degree of price competition.

Another often overlooked example of the effectiveness of the fact-finding approach was provided by the price stabilization efforts of the federal government between August, 1939, and February, 1942.[11] During this period all of the price-restraining efforts by the government were on a purely voluntary basis. By the time the Price Control Act was passed in early 1942 the prices of most basic industrial commodities, including steel, had already been stabilized successfully by voluntary action, despite the fact that demand for these products had been increasing rapidly. The success of the voluntary efforts is attested by comparisons of price increases between August, 1939, and December, 1941, with the increases during the comparable period before World War I—July, 1914, to November, 1916:

> Thus, prices of metals and metal products rose 54 percent from July 1914 to November 1916, as compared with 11 percent from August 1939 to December 1941. List prices of iron and steel rose 103 percent in the first 28 months of World War I and only 2 percent in the same interval of World War II. For nonferrous metals the increase in the earlier period was 114 percent, and in the later period, 14 percent; for building materials, the increases were 34 percent and 20 percent; for chemicals and allied products, 93 percent and 23 percent; and for fertilizer materials, 176 percent and 19 percent.[12]

It is noteworthy that effective restraints were almost wholly absent during the earlier period: "Prices were not controlled at all in the first world conflict until a considerable time after our entrance, and even then efforts at stabilization were subjected to prolonged resistance and objection by many industries, notably the steel industry."[13] As Bernard M. Baruch put it, "In 1917, the principle that a sound mobilization program must adapt the law of supply and demand to the needs of the war was considered revolutionary. Because we ignored this principle, we floundered during the first year of the war while shortages developed, production lagged, prices rose and many profiteered."[14]

In contrast, upon the invasion of Poland in September, 1939, President Roosevelt called on Senator O'Mahoney, as chairman of the Temporary National Economic Committee, to keep a watchful eye on prices and investigate any increases that appeared unwarranted. In May of the following year the National Defense Advisory Commission was established, with price stabilization and

---

[11] The argument has been advanced that this experience was peculiar to wartime conditions and constitutes no basis for appraising the possible effect of the approach during peacetime, when appeals to patriotism fall on less responsive ears. While there is some substance to this contention, it should nevertheless be remembered that the United States was at war only during the last 3 months of this 28-month period, that most of the voluntary measures had already gone into effect, and that prior to Pearl Harbor this country was far from united in support of the Allied governments.

[12] Bureau of Labor Statistics, Department of Labor, John M. Blair and Melville J. Ulmer, *Wartime Prices,* 1944, Pt. 1, p. 8.

[13] *Ibid.,* p. 10.

[14] Bernard M. Baruch, *The Public Years,* Holt, Rinehart & Winston, 1960, p. 54.

consumer protection divisions to watch the impact of the defense program on the price structure. It in turn was replaced by the Office of Price Administration and Civilian Supply, which carried on a wide variety of price stabilization efforts, including the issuance of public statements and even the imposition of price control orders whose only sanction was public opinion. Some 50 formal price schedules were issued up to December, 1941, and another 58 appeared between the attack on Pearl Harbor on December 7, 1941, and the passage of the Price Control Act on January 30, 1942. The public statements and voluntary price ceilings generally were backed up by economic analyses of the industry's prices in relation to their past behavior, profits, costs, and so on. Even when these analyses were not issued, the mere threat of their publication usually exerted a restraining effect on prices.

The 2 industry groups most dramatically affected during the "defense period" were metals and metal products and industrial chemicals. Despite a great increase in demand, stemming originally from buying by the British Purchasing Mission, then from Lend-Lease procurement, and finally from direct U.S. war preparations, the average price of the metals and metal products group rose only 11 percent between August, 1939, and December, 1941. Maximum prices on steel were established as early as April, 1941. In the case of nonferrous metals, "price advances were effectively limited by the prompt establishment of Government controls and the cooperation received from many producers." [15] These price actions were taken in the face of increases in direct costs: "Unit labor costs between 1939 and 1941 rose from 11 to 12 percent in steel works and rolling mills, in blast furnaces and in nonferrous primary smelters and refiners. For imported products such as chrome ore and tin, there were higher costs of transportation. For commodities such as quicksilver and zinc, there were expenses of operating mines formerly considered too costly to work in order to expand production." [16] Hence, if the government's price policy had been based only on changes in direct costs, as was later the case with the 1962 "guideposts," actions that actually stabilized prices would have been few and far between. But the increases in direct costs were more than offset by decreases in unit fixed costs, as "greater utilization of existing productive capacity reduced overhead costs substantially . . . although some price increases did take place, they tended to be moderate and infrequent. It was primarily because of their greater volume of business that profits in the industries producing metals and metal products rose on a broad scale." [17]

In industrial chemicals the pattern was much the same: "Consumption of industrial chemicals increased as the defense program developed. . . . At one time or another, scarcity was reported in markets for almost all chemicals and related products." [18] Nonetheless, prices remained remarkably stable, prices for industrial chemicals as a group rising only 6 percent between August, 1939, and December, 1941. Price ceilings during this period were issued for most of the major industrial chemicals, while informal agreements to stabilize prices

[15] Bureau of Labor Statistics, *op. cit.*, pp. 195–96. There were in addition some indirect price increases—particularly in steel, as producers who had been operating far below capacity in the summer of 1939 withdrew concessions, required buyers to shift to higher-priced sources, and in other ways increased their net realized price. According to a special survey of the BLS, however, these indirect increases ranged from only .5% for cold-finished bars to at most 15% for hot-rolled strip (see *ibid.*, p. 210).

[16] *Ibid.*, p. 197.

[17] *Ibid.*, p. 199.

[18] *Ibid.*, p. 141.

were reached with producers of others. As in metals, total unit costs showed little change: "In almost all cases, higher expenses for labor and materials were significantly offset by lower unit costs for overhead." [19]

Since World War II the voluntary approach has been pursued through the use of general exhortations, "guideposts" in wages and prices, and the focusing of "the spotlight of publicity" on specific industries.

Exhortations

Entreaties to labor and management for moderation in their wage and price actions have been made by every President since Truman. Indeed, in pressing for price stabilization both Truman and Eisenhower advocated the very principle later formalized in the "guideposts" issued under Kennedy; "as early as 1952, President Truman's Council [of Economic Advisers] held that wage increases should be limited by the gain in productivity, which was then considered to be in the range of 2 to 3 per cent. During President Eisenhower's administration, the Council repeatedly endorsed this proposition in general terms." [20] Alarmed over the balance-of-payments "problem" and concerned that a decline in the unemployment rate to 4 percent(!) indicated an overheating of the economy, the Eisenhower Administration became almost evangelical in the cause of stabilization.[21] Typical was a public statement by President Eisenhower on June 26, 1957: "Frankly, I believe that boards of directors of business, of business organizations, should take under the most serious consideration any thought of a price rise and should approve it only when they can see that it is absolutely necessary in order to continue to get the kind of money they need for the expansion demanded in this country." [22]

The case against generalized exhortations on the grounds that they are neither a proper nor an effective public policy has been summarized by Ben W. Lewis. Contending that businessmen cannot logically be asked to subordinate the acquisitive urge to social ends, he stated, "Creeping admonitionism is wholly foreign to our economic way of life" in which profit seeking is the purpose of business undertakings. If the market is performing its task with any efficiency, "admonitions marinated in goodness would be as pointless as in any event they are bound to be ineffective." He went on to inquire:

> Does it, then indicate confusion to admonish business and labor leaders and the rest of us to ignore market warnings and considerations of self-interest, and to take off on courses which for each of us as individuals can lead only to economic disaster, in the hope that, if each moves toward disaster, all will be saved? Does it suggest confusion to admonish us as individuals voluntarily to forego economic satisfaction in order that all may be more fully satisfied? [23]

[19] *Ibid.*, pp. 141–42.
[20] A. M. Ross in G. Schultz and R. Aliber, eds., *Guidelines, Informal Controls, and the Market Place*, U. of Chicago Press, 1966, p. 119 (hereafter referred to as *Guidelines*).
[21] *Ibid.*, p. 98.
[22] Office of the Federal Register, "Public Papers of the Presidents. Dwight D. Eisenhower, 1957," pp. 501–02.
[23] *Hearings on Administered Prices*, Pt. 9, p. 4713.

The guideposts of 1962

The attainment of a stable price level through stability in unit labor costs was formalized into an objective of government by the 1962 Report of the Council of Economic Advisers:

> The general guide for noninflationary wage behavior is that the rate of increase in wage rates (including fringe benefits) in each industry be equal to the trend rate of overall productivity increase. General acceptance of this guide would maintain stability of labor cost per unit of output for the economy as a whole—though not of course for individual industries. The general guide for noninflationary price behavior calls for price reduction if the industry's rate of productivity increase exceeds the overall rate—for this would mean declining unit labor costs; it calls for an appropriate increase in price if the opposite situation prevails. . . .[24]

The general purpose of the guideposts, in the words of John T. Dunlop, was "to prevent sectors with strong market power from dissipating expansionary measures into wage and price increases while the system as a whole operated with considerable slack." Or, as Robert M. Solow put it, "The logic of a guidepost policy is, I suppose, something like this. In our imperfect world there are important areas where market power is sufficiently concentrated that price and wage decisions are made with a significant amount of discretion. When times are reasonably good, that discretion may be exercised in ways that contribute to premature inflation." [25]

Plaguing the Kennedy Administration had been the continuing problem of how to reduce the persistent unemployment level of around 6 percent without touching off an unacceptable rate of inflation. According to then recent macroeconomic studies, achieving a 4-percent unemployment rate would involve annual increases in wages of around 5 percent[26] and in prices of 6 percent or more.[27] The "trade-off" for achieving a higher level of economic activity through the stimulus of expansionistic fiscal and monetary policies thus appeared to be an intolerable rate of inflation. It was in this setting that the guideposts were promulgated as a means of utilizing the existing discretionary power over markets to restrain the advances in wages and prices which would otherwise occur. Their background has been described by Gardner Ackley:

> Beginning about 1955, the American economy began to develop an increasing shortfall of employment and output. By the Council's measurements, the shortfall of output was at an annual rate in excess of $25 billion at the business cycle peak in 1960, and in excess of $50 billion in early 1961. This shortfall did not disappear until the end of

[24] *Annual Report of the Council of Economic Advisers, 1962,* 1963, p. 189. The report uses the term "guideposts" for wages and prices; later programs relating to business investment and the extension of bank credit abroad used the term "guidelines."

[25] Gardner Ackley in *Guidelines,* pp. 82, 44. Although using different terms—"considerable slack" and "times [that] are reasonably good"—both Dunlop and Solow appear to be referring to the same general state of economic activity—below that of full employment and above that of recession. There seems to be a general consensus that during the former guideposts would be ineffective and during the latter unnecessary.

[26] 86th Cong., 1st Sess., Joint Economic Committee, Charles L. Schultze, *Recent Inflation in the United States,* 1959, pp. 61–62.

[27] Paul A. Samuelson and Robert M. Solow, "Analytical Aspects of Anti-Inflation Policy," *American Economic Review,* May, 1960, pp. 177–94.

1965. . . . By our calculation the total shortfall of output over the years 1958–63 exceeds $200 billion. The average unemployment rate during the six-year period was 6 percent; it was still 5.5 percent at the end of 1963.[28]

Inasmuch as the problem to which they were addressed was an expected consequence of macroeconomic fiscal and monetary policies, it is not surprising that the guideposts were framed in terms of the economy as a whole. Thus, changes in wages were to be related, not to productivity changes in particular industries, but to the annual rate of productivity increase in the private economy as a whole, which for the preceding 5 years had averaged 3.2 percent. Owing to differences in productivity changes among different industries, some prices, it was recognized, would show greater (and others lesser) increases than the average change in unit labor costs. Moreover, certain modifications were allowed for to adapt the guideposts "to the circumstances of particular industries." [29] Specific wage rate increases would exceed the general productivity increase where an industry "would otherwise be unable to attract sufficient labor," where wage rates "are exceptionally low," or where the bargaining position of workers "has been weak." Conversely, wage rate increases would fall short of the general guide rate where an industry "could not provide jobs for its entire labor force even in times of generally full employment" or where wage rates "are exceptionally high . . . because the bargaining position of workers has been especially strong." Specific "modifications" were also outlined for price changes. Thus, as compared to changes in average unit labor costs, prices "would rise more rapidly, or fall more slowly," where the level of profits "was insufficient to attract the capital required to finance a needed expansion in capacity" or where nonlabor costs "had risen." Similarly, prices "would rise more slowly or fall more rapidly" where an industry suffered an excess of capacity at full employment demand, where nonlabor costs "have fallen," or where excessive market power "has resulted in rates of profit substantially higher than those earned elsewhere on investments of comparable risk." [30]

As to precisely how these laudable economic objectives were to be accomplished, the report was silent. It suggested no means of implementation to bring about a type of behavior quite different from that which would otherwise prevail. How are wage rate increases to be held below the general rise in productivity where "the bargaining position of workers has been especially strong"? How are increases in price to be held below the general rise in unit labor costs in industries with excessive market power? Except for declining industries, the argument could always be made that a price increase is needed "to attract the capital required to finance a needed expansion in capacity." And where supplies are purchased from competitive sources an exception would be justified when demand was rising because "costs other than labor costs had risen."

In restraining increases in wages there is, however, impressive evidence of accomplishment. For a 12-year period (1948–60) preceding the issuance of the guideposts, George L. Perry found that the percentage change in hourly wages in manufacturing from one quarter to the same quarter of the next year

[28] Ackley in *Guidelines,* pp. 69–70.
[29] *Annual Report of the Council of Economic Advisers, 1962,* 1963, p. 189.
[30] *Ibid.*

appeared to be explained largely by four determinants—the unemployment rate, the change in the Consumer Price Index, the rate of profit in manufacturing, and the change in the rate of profit.[31] During the first half of the 1960's the actual increase in wages was less than would have been expected on the basis of these variables. As summarized by Robert Solow:

> In 1961 and the first half of 1962, wages rose faster than the theory would expect. Beginning with the third quarter of 1962, and without exception for the next fourteen quarters to the end of 1965, wages rose more slowly than the theory would expect. Runs in the residuals are not uncommon but this run is uncommonly long. Moreover, although the overestimation of wage changes was initially small, it became substantial in 1964 and 1965. In 1965, the annual increase in wage rates was about 1.7 percent lower than the 1948–60 expansion would lead one to expect.[32]

The very fact that conformity with the guideposts could readily be determined for wages contributed not only to their observance in the wage sphere but to a growing disenchantment of organized labor with the whole approach. Among the objections to the guideposts stressed in 1966 by the AFL-CIO Executive Council was that while wage increases could readily be compared with the 3.2-percent productivity yardstick, there was no comparable quantitative standard for profits and dividends. The AFL-CIO also objected on the grounds that the average increase in wages would necessarily tend to be less than the average productivity increases, since wage increases by strong unions would be held down to 3.2 percent, whereas wage gains of this magnitude were beyond the reach of unorganized labor and weak unions. The argument was also made that failure to incorporate changes in living costs into the formula subjected labor to the very real danger of a decline in real purchasing power, even though the guideposts were fully observed. But on this point Arthur M. Ross, former Commissioner of Labor Statistics, has demurred: "Attaching a cost-of-living escalator clause to the guideposts, under circumstances like those of the present, would not only contribute to a wage-price spiral but also yield a target figure beyond the reach of all but the most powerful unions. Guideposts of 6 percent or more would hardly be a stabilizing device in today's economy." [33]

That the guideposts exerted a definite restraining effect on wage increases seems clear from the statistical evidence—as well as from the protests of organized labor. Concerning their effect on prices, economists associated with the guideposts are convinced of their efficacy. Drawing on his experience as former chairman of the Council of Economic Advisers, Gardner Ackley has stated: "I know of many instances in which prices have not been raised, or were raised less, or were raised on a smaller range of products." [34] In an effort to

---

[31] George L. Perry, "Wages and the Guideposts," *American Economic Review,* Sept., 1967, pp. 897–904.

[32] Solow in *Guidelines,* p. 46. An examination of wage and price movements between 1962 and 1966 led Gardiner C. Means to the same conclusion (see 91st Cong., 1st Sess., Joint Economic Committee, *Hearings: 1970 Mid-Year Review,* pp. 226–44).

[33] Ross in *Guidelines,* p. 119. The AFL-CIO objected also to a technical change in the method of computing the annual average of increase in productivity. The original method, a 5-year moving average, would have permitted a slightly greater increase in wages, but it was dropped in 1966. (*Ibid.,* p. 295.)

[34] Ackley in *Guidelines,* p. 73.

appraise the general effects of the 1962 guideposts, Arthur M. Okun, also a former member of the Council, compared the price change during the year 1969 with the change during preceding years for 22 "responsive" products—i.e., those which in Okun's judgment had been "directly responsive to administration persuasion in one or more specific instances during the 1966 to 1968 periods." [35] The significance of 1969 stems from a change in government policy: "In January, 1969, President Nixon made clear his intention not to attempt to influence particular price (and wage) decisions in the private economy. . . . The distinct shift in White House posture produced a situation about as close to a controlled experiment as we are ever likely to find in observing the inherently complex relationship between private decisions on prices and the attitudes of Government officials." [36]

Nearly all of the "responsive" group are products of concentrated industries. Since most of the large-volume concentrated products are included in this group, the average level of concentration for "all other industries," used for comparative purposes, must be considerably lower. The price movements of both the "responsive" and the "all other" groups conform closely to the behavior expected of concentrated and unconcentrated products generally, as shown in Chapter 17. This was true of the years of economic stability (1961–65) as well as of the years of rapid growth (1966–68): "From 1961 to 1965, prices of the responsive group were especially stable. Between December, 1960, and December, 1965, the index for the responsive group rose only 0.1 percent a year, on average, while the index for all other (i.e. nonlisted) industrials crept up at an average annual rate of 0.5 percent." [37] And during the ensuing period of rapid expansion the actual movements of the two types of price again corresponded closely with their expected behavior: "During the inflation of the next three years, 1966 to 1968, the price index of the responsive group rose at an annual rate of 1.7 percent; meanwhile all other industrials advanced at an annual rate of 2.3 percent." [38] Because other factors were at work it is difficult to ascertain the influence of the guideposts: "Again, the over-all differential cannot be reliably attributed to Government appeals for restraint, although several specific rollbacks and reversals of announced price increases provided evidence of some stabilizing import." [39]

It was the experience of 1969 that, in Okun's view, dramatically demonstrated the effectiveness of the guideposts: "In light of the three—indeed eight —previous years of experience, anyone who believed that the responsive prices, as a group, had not been influenced by White House persuasion should have expected them to rise no more rapidly than other industrials in 1969." [40] Yet the very opposite proved to be the case. During that year the responsive group advanced on the average 6.0 percent, while all other industrials rose only 1.2 percent: "And the pattern of marked acceleration was widespread, extending to petroleum, steel, copper, aluminum, passenger cars, glass containers, cigarettes, newsprint, photographic supplies, and paperboard. The exceptions were

[35] Arthur M. Okun, *Inflation: The Problems and Prospects Before Us,* Brookings Institution, 1970, p. 43. The change is from December of the previous year.
[36] *Ibid.,* pp. 43, 47.
[37] *Ibid.,* p. 46.
[38] *Ibid.,* p. 47.
[39] *Ibid.*
[40] *Ibid.*

sulfur products, tires, tin cans, and laundry equipment. There were exceedingly few new wage settlements that could have accounted for any acceleration." [41] The explanation appears obvious: "I conclude that the shift in Government policy is central and crucial to the explanation of the especially large speed-up of the responsive prices during 1969." [42]

On the other hand, the effectiveness of the guideposts has been questioned by John T. Dunlop. Regarding them as a type of formalized "macro-preach-ment," he feels that they rarely fit the specific issues and problems facing decision makers in particular industries. Based on his long experience as a negotiator between labor and management, Dunlop observes:

> The wage and price guideposts are not expressed in criteria that are meaningful to private decision makers. The "trend rate of overall productivity increase" and the relative rate of an industry's increase in productivity compared to the average are scarcely standards which are meaningful to decision makers on wages and prices. The concepts are not congenial or directly applicable in their operating experience. Wage decisions are typically argued in terms of comparative wages, living costs, competitive conditions, labor shortages, ability to pay, specific productivity, job content and bargaining power. Negotiators and their constituents understand these concepts. Pricing decisions are considered in terms of specific competitive prices, quality, advertising, market prospects, responses to changes in other prices, costs and the like. The diffuse structure of collective bargaining and pricing makes the standards of the guideposts appear remote and unrealistic. The guideposts simply "do not come through." The macro-standards not only have no simple application to specific wage or price decisions, they do not appear relevant, controlling or decisive to micro-decision makers. *You cannot effectively prescribe micro-decisions with macro-precepts.*[43]

But the difference between Dunlop on the one hand and Ackley and Okun on the other appears to be largely a matter of semantics. In stating that guideposts designed for the economy as a whole do not "come through" to private decision makers, Dunlop is not questioning the effectiveness of government suasion when focused on particular industries. Similarly, when Ackley refers to "instances in which prices have not been raised," he undoubtedly has in mind the results achieved by those government actions that have been aimed at particular industries. And the subject of Okun's survey was not the private economy as a whole but specific products that were "*directly responsive* to administration persuasion." From this point of view the question is not whether the behavior of the private economy accords with the guideposts; it is whether effective results can be achieved by sharply focusing the spotlight of publicity on identifiable holders of power. Where it has been so focused, neither corporate officials nor union leaders have been able to take refuge in the comfortable assumption that official norms of desirable performance, while applicable to others, certainly do not apply to them. Here, the governmental standards, to use Dunlop's words, are indeed made "relevant, controlling [and] decisive to micro-decision makers."

[41] *Ibid.,* p. 48.
[42] *Ibid.,* p. 49.
[43] John T. Dunlop in *Guidelines,* p. 86. Emphasis added.

Microsuasion: the case of steel

Although the government has from time to time focused its attention on other fields, the industry most frequently subjected to what might be referred to as "microsuasion" is steel. Since World War II four Presidents have felt it necessary to importune the steel industry not to raise prices. Although their emphases and methods of approach have differed, Presidents Eisenhower, Kennedy, Johnson, and Nixon (in 1971) have been of one mind in regarding the price of steel as no longer a matter of purely private concern. The industry has come to be regarded as affected with a public interest because, as the underpinning of the economy, any increase in the price of steel tends to "pyramid." By the time it reaches the ultimate consumer an increase in the price of steel will have grown until it is a significant multiple of the steel price increase itself. This comes about as steel users at each successive step of manufacturing raise their prices by an amount sufficient not only to cover the higher cost to them but also to preserve their customary percentage margins. As a result of pyramiding, a $5-per-ton rise in the price of steel was reported in *Iron Age* to have been transformed into a $50 increase in the cost of an automobile.[44] Since an automobile contains on an average only about one and a half tons of steel, the increase in direct costs attributable to the price increase of steel itself would have been only some $7.50.[45] Similarly, a $6-per-ton increase in the price of steel was reported in the *Wall Street Journal* to have been transformed into a $75 increase in the price of a tractor.[46] Since the average tractor probably contains no more steel than an automobile, the increase in direct costs from the steel price rise would have been only around $9.[47]

In addition, there is a psychological effect. A price increase in steel will be viewed by producers in other industries, anxious to raise their own prices, as a sign that the time is propitious. Resistance by buyers and concern by the government is likely to be at a minimum if "everything is going up." For steel users a higher price for their raw material, in itself, provides at least a partial justification for their own price advances. Failure of the government to act against anything so basic as steel is thus interpreted as indifference to price increases in less important industries.

The history of governmental efforts to influence steel pricing divides into three stages. In the first, which lasted from the middle of 1957 to the spring of 1962, the initiative was taken by the legislative branch, specifically by the Senate Antitrust Subcommittee; the second stage was the bitter encounter between President Kennedy and the industry in April, 1962; in the third, efforts to restrain price advances stemmed almost exclusively from the White House and the Council of Economic Advisers.

The Kefauver hearings

On August 8, 1957, the Senate Antitrust Subcommittee began hearings on "administered prices in the steel industry." The chairman was Senator Kefauver, and the

[44] *Iron Age,* April 25, 1963.
[45] *Hearings on Administered Prices,* Pt. 7, p. 3596.
[46] *Wall Street Journal,* June 23, 1958. Included in *Hearings on Administered Prices,* Pt. 8, p. 4471.
[47] *Hearings on Administered Prices,* Pt. 7, p. 3596.

first witness was Roger Blough, chairman of the board of the U.S. Steel Corporation. During the hearings, which were concluded on November 5, 1957, other witnesses included officials of the Bethlehem Steel Corporation and the National Steel Corporation, as well as representatives of the United Steel Workers of America and technical experts.[48]

The hearings had been authorized by a Senate resolution empowering the Subcommittee to make "a complete, comprehensive and continuing study and investigation of the antitrust and monopoly laws of the United States and their administration, interpretation, operation, enforcement and effect."[49] In its subsequent report the Subcommittee was at pains to point out that the steel hearings had properly been within its legislative jurisdiction, since they had been directed to the "No. 1 weakness of the antitrust laws today . . . their inadequacy as a means of coping with . . . the problem of the concentration of economic power."[50] The Subcommittee noted that the antitrust statutes represented a body of law which, properly interpreted, could be regarded as "reasonably adequate" to protect the country from one company monopolies, from conspiracies to fix prices, and from some of the individual practices by which competition is suppressed. There remained, however, the problem exemplified by the steel industry—control by the few: "At the same time authorities on the subject are in general agreement that there does not exist anything approaching an adequate body of law against the control of the market by a few large enterprises which may behave in such a manner as to yield exactly the same results as would be produced by a complete one-company monopoly or by outright conspiracy."[51]

The selection of the steel industry as the subject for hearings was "dictated" by its importance: "Beginning with the elementary necessities of life and extending through all modes of transportation to a myriad of goods involved in our complex industrial system, this industry above all others is basic in our modern economy."[52] The immediate occasion for the hearings was the announcement of a higher price for steel effective July 1, 1957. Together with a previous advance in April, this increase was estimated to have added over a half-billion dollars a year to the direct cost of steel. Alluding to the "pyramiding" effect, the Subcommittee stated, "This figure represents only the direct increases to the immediate buyers of steel mill products; it does not include the indirect increases in the form of higher prices for machinery, equipment, plants, etc. in which steel is a component."[53]

The hearings and subsequent report focused on concentration in the various steel products, the "stairstep" pattern of price increases, their cost to buyers, the identity of the increases, the role of U.S. Steel as the price leader, the "upward price followership" by the other major producers, the effect of price changes on demand, and an economic anomaly—"the behavior of prices during periods of contracting markets." Referring to years of declining steel demand, specifically 1949, 1951, 1953–54, and 1956–57, the report stated:

> In theory, the softening state of the market should have been reflected
> in price reductions. The presumption would be that individual com-

[48] See *ibid.*, Pts. 2, 3, 4.
[49] 85th Cong., 1st Sess., S. Res. 57, 1957.
[50] *Administered Prices: Report on Steel*, p. 2.
[51] *Ibid.*
[52] *Ibid.*, p. 1.
[53] *Ibid.*

panies would have at least attempted to maintain operations at or near capacity by price cutting and an aggressive search for new business. Not only did this fail to occur, but prices did not even remain stable. Instead when the demand for steel has fallen (as when it has risen) the price leader, followed perfectly by every other large firm in the industry, has raised prices. The market has been "cleared" (if the term may properly be used in this context) by reducing output throughout the industry to any level necessary to maintain the price increase.[54]

The issue of greatest interest here is the Subcommittee's examination of the cost justification. Blough placed primary responsibility for the $6-per-ton price rise on a new contract with the United Steel Workers, which, he estimated, raised U.S. Steel's employment cost by $3.50 to $4 per ton. But this estimate, it developed, was based not only on the increase granted to 161,500 members of the union but to increases received at the same time by 47,600 other employees. The latter averaged 37 percent more than increases called for under the union contract. In the Subcommittee's words, "This may be excellent personnel policy, but there is some question as to the propriety of charging the cost of such a policy to the union agreement." [55] For reasons set forth in its report, the Subcommittee also regarded as excessive the company's estimates for Sunday and holiday premium pay and for pension and Social Security costs.[56] After appropriate adjustments for these upward biases, the resultant rise in hourly compensation was multiplied by the number of man-hours required per ton of steel, which, according to the industry's own figures, averaged 15.2 hours per ton for the first half of 1957. The Subcommittee concluded: "A reasonable guess as to the magnitude of increased labor costs which have arisen from the July 1957 adjustments in wages and other benefits, would fall somewhere between $2.50 and $3 per ton of finished steel. The margin between such a figure and the $6 per ton increase in steel prices would be between $3 and $3.50 per ton. This would be available to cover increases in costs other than employment costs." [57]

In steel making two of the major "other costs"—iron ore and coking coal—merely reflect the arbitrary values at which these supplies are transferred by the major steel companies from their own vertically integrated mines. There is, however, another important direct cost—steel scrap—which is purchased in a competitive market. It happens that in 1957 the price of scrap was declining. From the 2 largest steel producers the Subcommittee was able to obtain figures on the consumption and prices actually paid for purchased scrap. This information showed that the cost of scrap *per ton of finished steel* had fallen from $12.56 in 1956 to $8.69 in September, 1957. In its report the Subcommittee stated, "In other words, the estimated reduction in the cost of purchased scrap ($3.87 per ton of finished steel) from 1956 to September 1957 had been more than enough to offset even a generous estimate of the increased labor costs incurred through the July 1 wage adjustments." [58] In short, it appeared that the 1957 steel price increase was without a cost justification of any kind.

What effect did these revelations have on the industry's pricing policy? Certainly they were not successful in bringing about a rollback of the 1957 increase.

[54] *Ibid.*, pp. 27–28.
[55] *Ibid.*, p. 39.
[56] *Ibid.*, pp. 39–40.
[57] *Ibid.*, p. 41.
[58] *Ibid.*, p. 44.

Moreover, this advance was followed a year later by a further increase of $4.50 per ton, instituted at a time when the industry was operating at less than 50 percent of capacity. Again, the Subcommittee held hearings, but this time the witnesses were the heads of the Antitrust Division and the Federal Trade Commission.[59] The subject was the possibly collusive nature of identical price advances made by supposedly competitive producers with admittedly different costs at a time of substantial unused capacity.[60] No antitrust action was taken, and again the price increase "stuck."

On the other hand, there is good reason to believe that the hearings did exert a very definite restraining effect on the industry's pricing policies. In sharp contrast to its increase of 27 percent between 1954 and 1958, the index of steel mill prices actually declined .5 percent during the 3 years following the hearings. It is true that 1959–61 was a period of general economic stability, but it is also true that during the earlier period prices had been raised regardless of the level of economic activity—whether relatively stable (1956), rapidly expanding (1955), or sharply contracting (1958).

Moreover, from the industry's point of view conditions for a price increase were propitious, particularly following a steel strike in 1959. Wage rates had been increased under a new union contract, while the strike had depleted steel inventories. Predictions of demand were optimistic. Some metal-using companies, according to the trade press, were looking forward to a steel price increase as "a good peg" on which to hang higher price tags that would recoup even more than any additional steel costs. But the Antitrust Subcommittee had made it clear that if steel prices were increased, it would resume hearings to compare, among other things, the price advance with the costs of the wage increase. For their part the steel producers were very much aware of the Subcommittee's interest. Thus the trade journal *Steel* reported that the trend toward "progressively smaller price hikes will probably continue," partly because "Government leaders from President Eisenhower to Senator Estes Kefauver have put them on the spot in the battle against inflation." [61] Similarly, it was reported, "One of the most ticklish things about raising steel prices is that it lately seems to arouse the ire . . . of Senators like Estes Kefauver of Tennessee. . . ." [62]

The Kennedy-Blough imbroglio

This record of virtual stability appeared at an end with the announcement by U.S. Steel in the spring of 1962 of a $6.00-per-ton across-the-board increase. The first general increase since mid-1958, this action touched off the most dramatic confrontation in history between a President and corporate management. In a visit to the White House on Tuesday, April 10, 1962, Roger Blough, chairman of the board of U.S. Steel, informed President Kennedy of the steel price increase as a *falt accompli*. Secretary of Labor Goldberg had labored long and hard in persuading the United Steel Workers (of which he had formerly been general counsel) to agree to a "noninflationary" wage increase—one not exceeding the increase in productivity. In exchange, the industry had informally committed itself, so the Administration believed, to refrain from increasing prices. To labor leaders, a price increase would be proof of the uselessness of

[59] See *Hearings on Administered Prices,* Pt. 8.
[60] See Ch. 22.
[61] *Steel,* May 4, 1959.
[62] *Christian Science Monitor,* May 16, 1960.

cooperating with government; to business it would serve as an enlightening example of how government could be "used"; and to the general public it would be evidence of impotence, if not hypocrisy, at the highest level. It is therefore not surprising that President Kennedy's reaction was a mixture of incredulity and outrage. In his study of the episode Grant McConnell describes the Administration's reaction:

> There is no doubt whatsoever that the President was exceedingly angry. . . . What had occurred was a betrayal, a double cross. The Administration had gone out of its way to indicate that the White House would use its influence with labor in return for the exercise of forbearance by the steel industry on prices. A low-cost labor settlement had been obtained and it had been achieved early and without a strike. Now the implicit agreement had been repudiated.[63]

In the next few days Cabinet members denounced the increase at press conferences. Demands were made for congressional investigations. The Senate devoted an entire day to speeches attacking the increase. FBI agents were sent out by the Department of Justice to seek evidence of collusion. The Solicitor General drafted new legislation to deal with the steel crisis. Bills to break up excessive concentration of economic power were introduced. An important and generally overlooked action was the issuance shortly after the price rise of subpoenas by Chairman Kefauver of the Senate Antitrust Subcommittee, calling upon the 12 major steel producers to produce their unit cost data in great detail —by product, by mill, and by type of expense. In its 1957 hearings the Subcommittee had learned that this was a type of data the steel companies were most reluctant to divulge. If, as was anticipated, the information demonstrated widespread differences in unit costs, the companies would have been faced with the necessity, in a period of substantial unused capacity, of justifying price increases that brought their prices to identical levels. Moreover, cost information would have permitted a definitive determination of the precise extent by which the price increase may have exceeded the higher costs resulting from the wage settlement.

Another important action was an announcement by Secretary McNamara that the Defense Department would henceforth require firms doing business with it to buy their steel from producers who had not increased their prices. To underscore his words the Department awarded a $5-million contract to a small steel producer, Lukens, which had not yet raised its prices. To add insult to injury, the contract was for a type of steel originally developed by U.S. Steel. In addition, 5 medium-size steel companies were still "studying" the matter. Yet it is unlikely that their failure to raise prices, by itself, would have forced U.S. Steel to rescind its across-the-board increase, although prices might have been "adjusted" on particular products and freight absorbed into particular areas. As compared to Big Steel each of the 5 produced a limited line of products and served relatively insulated market areas.

Bethlehem, however, was a different matter, with more than half the output of U.S. Steel and with sizable works in both the East and Midwest. A withdrawal by Bethlehem would have forced Big Steel to retreat. Bethlehem, it happens, is also one of the nation's biggest shipbuilders and, as such, was acutely sensitive to changes in government procurement policy. Whether because of McNamara's warning or other considerations, Bethlehem withdrew its

[63] Grant McConnell, *Steel and the Presidency,* Norton, 1962, p. 8.

increase on the morning of Friday, April 13. U.S. Steel's capitulation, something of an anticlimax, followed in a matter of hours.

In assessing the reasons for the dramatic reversal McConnell states that "consideration of the market largely determined the ending of the steel crisis." President Kennedy prevailed but in McConnell's view only because of a happy coincidence:

> The President did oppose the price increase announced by United States Steel, and the price increase was rescinded. The sequence, however, did not represent cause and effect. For this one time at least, the frequent contention of steel industry leaders that strong competitive market forces were at work in the industry was correct. These forces were much more important in bringing about abandonment of the price increase than the actions of the President. Those actions showed weakness, not power.[64]

Inasmuch as his study has come to be cited in support of the proposition that voluntary controls "never work," it is important to examine the basis for McConnell's conclusion. His reasoning hangs on the slender thread of one of three "reasons" offered by the head of Inland Steel, Joseph Block, in explaining his observation that a price increase "at this time was not in the national interest." According to McConnell, Block's "reasons were, first, that the time was too close to the labor settlement, second that most of the smaller companies were still negotiating with the union, and third that 'the order book was disappearing.' "[65] McConnell added that, "of the three reasons, the third in his eyes was by far the most important; it is the worst possible time to increase prices when orders are running out."[66]

While possibly true for Inland, it is most unlikely that demand in the industry as a whole was "disappearing," since steel production turned out actually to be higher in 1962 than in the previous year. In essence, McConnell is arguing that the April 2 increase and subsequent withdrawal were merely the result of an overly optimistic estimate of demand, which was promptly corrected by the deus ex machina of the market. Aside from the improbability that such a correction in this industry would have been made in only 11 days, McConnell's argument ignores the experience of the past. Market forces did not correct the price increases made during the recession years of 1954 and 1958, when demand for steel *was* disappearing.[67] While perhaps comforting to believers in the all-pervasive influence of competition—even in oligopolistic industries—this effort to discount the influence of government has little relevance to the events of 1962 or to the industry's past or subsequent behavior.

"Jawboning" under Johnson

Following the withdrawal of the April, 1962, increase, the steel industry all but abandoned across-the-board raises in favor of "selective" increases, limited to one or a few closely related products. And during the next 6 years most of

[64] *Ibid.*, p. 114.
[65] *Ibid.*, p. 94.
[66] *Ibid.* That demand at the time the price rise was announced appeared to be strong enough to support the increase is suggested by Block's comment that "probably Inland would have gone along with the price increase if the government had done nothing." (*Ibid.*)
[67] Nor, despite press speculation that it would act to the contrary, did Inland abstain from participating in the price increase made during the recession year of 1971.

these increases also met with opposition from the administration in office. In a study of governmental policy on steel prices during this period Edward Knight commented: "Generally it [the government] has adhered to the view that selective moderate price increases are justified if affected products are in short supply relative to demand. Policy makers are quick to add, however, that such adjustments should be paralleled by downward adjustments in prices for products which are in excess supply, and particularly in instances where production facilities are operating with considerable excess capacity." [68]

Although far from numerous, there were in fact a number of instances in which increases on some products were accompanied by decreases on others. When, on October 12, 1965, U.S. Steel raised the price of electrolytic tinplate, it also announced a decrease for a newly developed type of tin-free steel, which, it was hoped, would make steel containers more competitive with aluminum, plastic, and glass containers. Similarly when, on February 28, 1966, the corporation made known its intention to raise the price of wideplate steel and heavy sheets, it announced the immediate availability of new very-heavy-gauge hot-rolled sheet steel in coils, which it believed could offer customers a savings of from $2 to $25 per ton under previous plate prices. And when, on May 20, 1966, Republic Steel raised prices on some types of steel bars and billets, it made reductions on others: "In making these selective price adjustments, the industry followed the same price strategy it had resorted to earlier in the year in making certain price changes more palatable to the White House. This involved the mixing of selective increases with certain price reductions to achieve a small net gain in steel prices generally." [69]

Less palatable to the government was a two-step procedure that the steel industry over the years has refined to a high art. It begins with the announcement by some producer, other than U.S. Steel, of a large price increase, which is promptly denounced by government spokesmen as unwarranted, inflationary, and sometimes unpatriotic. After private but well-publicized conferences between its officers and government officials, U.S. Steel then announces a lesser increase, which, the corporation points out, is absolutely necessary to cover recent cost increases and in no way breaches the government's anti-inflation policy. The company that had made the original announcement is then forced to retreat to the leader's lower figure. Both the government and U.S. Steel share modestly in the resultant era of good feeling—the former for having averted a still greater increase, the latter for its manifest willingness to cooperate in the fight against inflation.

A case in point was the announcement by Bethlehem Steel of a $5-per-ton increase, effective January 1, 1966, on structural shapes. Denouncing the action, Gardner Ackley, then chairman of the Council of Economic Advisers, expressed the hope that it "will be withdrawn and that other producers will refrain from raising their prices." After its officers had made the customary pilgrimage to Washington, U.S. Steel announced 3 days later a price increase of $2.75 per ton. Whereas Chairman Ackley had termed the $5.00 increase "unjustified and inflationary," he regarded the effect of the $2.75 advance as "inconsequential—about as close to absolute stability as you could get." [70] A

[68] Library of Congress, Legislative Reference Service, Edward Knight, *Steel Price Increases and Government Policy*, 1968, p. 31.
[69] *Ibid.*, p. 12.
[70] Quoted in *ibid.*, pp. 6–7. In addition, U.S. Steel announced a decrease in the price of cold-rolled sheets made in a California plant.

similar course of conduct was followed upon the announcement on July 31, 1968, of the first across-the-board increase since April, 1962. In posting a 5-percent increase Bethlehem attributed the action to the need for revenues "to offset" increases in labor costs resulting from a new wage contract. President Johnson immediately denounced the increase on the grounds that it would cost the American consumer over a half-billion dollars and would set back efforts to reverse the prevailing inflationary trend. After several meetings with government officials, U.S. Steel announced a week later an increase of about 2.5 percent to apply to about 70 percent of the industry's volume. According to a spokesman for the White House President Johnson "welcomes the substantial improvement from the general inflationary threat that was posed last week." Speaking on behalf of the Administration Chairman Ackley said, "It is gratifying that the U.S. Steel action significantly reduces the threat of a large and general inflation in steel prices." [71] But after U.S. Steel's action, to which Bethlehem of course retreated, the index of the Bureau of Labor Statistics for steel mill products rose 2.3 percent—the largest single increase in a decade.

From the government's point of view the most unsatisfactory response is of course the complete rebuff. The rejection of its entreaties dramatizes the principal weakness of voluntary controls—their lack of sanctions. Of even greater import, rejection places the government in the ignominious position of being a bargainer among equals with private parties—and an unsuccessful one at that. It is for this reason that, with a few conspicuous exceptions, Presidents have very infrequently committed the prestige of their high office to a direct confrontation with industry, usually delegating the task to subordinates.

On August 2, 1966, a $3-per-ton increase in the prices of sheet and strip was announced by Inland Steel. Making up 30 percent of total steel shipments, these products have a direct and immediate effect on the costs of important consumer goods industries such as automobiles and appliances. Telegrams were sent by Chairman Ackley directly to 12 major steel producers, requesting that they meet with the Council of Economic Advisers before following suit. Only one company, Bethlehem, availed itself of the opportunity. When it had become clear by August 4 that even his request for a meeting was being ignored, Ackley remarked bitterly, "This is not an hour in which this business leadership of America can take pride" and that refusal "to hear and understand the Government's position . . . is deliberately to flout the public interest in cost-price stability at a critical time in our economic affairs." By comparison the public posture of President Johnson was one of aloofness from the fray. After calling attention to the President's "very well known" position on the desirability of restraint, a White House spokesman went on to say, "But no one can force them to do what they may not want to do. . . . [The President] feels that one of the prices you pay for the kind of free society we have is that, from time to time, a decision by business and labor is made that is not in accord with the national interest as the Government sees it." [72]

A year later the government was subjected to a similarly humiliating experience. On August 31, 1967, Republic Steel announced a price increase of 1.8 percent on steel bars. Characterizing the action as "distressing," Chairman Ackley made it clear that his concern extended beyond this one product: "With the addition of bars . . . the increases since last November (1966) can no longer be regarded as isolated and selective price adjustments. Rather,

---

[71] Quoted in Knight, *op. cit.*, p. 29.
[72] Quoted in *ibid.*, pp. 12–15.

they must be viewed as a consistent pattern that has resulted in higher prices for nearly half the steel tonnage produced in this country." In going along with Republic's increase, U.S. Steel stated, "Very thoughtful attention was given to Mr. Ackley's comments. . . ." Nonetheless, "inflationary pressures" made the increase necessary: "after the long period of relative price stability in steel, notwithstanding rising costs and shrinking profits, these modest price changes cannot be considered either unwarranted or inflation-inducing." Once again President Johnson abstained from direct involvement; in the words of a White House spokesman, "Mr. Ackley spoke for the Administration. . . ." [73]

Despite the occasional rebuffs, the industry's record during the 1960's was one of remarkable price stability. Between 1959 and 1968 the price of iron and steel rose at an average annual rate of only .4 percent, or less than one-tenth its annual rate of 5.3 percent in 1954–59. Its average annual rate of increase during 1959–68 was only half the increase registered by both the all-commodities and all-industrials indexes; during 1954–59 its annual increase had averaged nearly three and one-half times the rise in all commodities and nearly two and one-half times the advance in all industrials.

Inasmuch as there were other forces at work tending to increase the supply and decrease the demand for steel, this remarkable record of stability can be attributed only in part to government suasion. By 1968 imports had come to account for nearly one-third of the domestic supply. At the same time serious inroads on demand were being made by such competitive materials as plastics, fiberglass, cement, and prestressed concrete. And these forces received a fresh impetus with every increase in steel prices.

Nevertheless there are good reasons to conclude that suasion, in and of it-self, made an important contribution to stability. To argue otherwise is to as-sume that steel company officials had no reluctance to risk another high-level confrontation similar to the one with President Kennedy or to undergo a session of hearings similar to those conducted by Senator Kefauver. It is also to ignore the obvious manifestations of cooperation evidenced by the industry, particularly its virtual abandonment of across-the-board increases and its matching of in-creases with decreases. For those familiar with the actual relationship between government and the industry, such assumptions strain credulity beyond the breaking point.

Further evidence of the effectiveness of suasion is provided by changes that took place in the leader's profit rate. The Brookings study of pricing objectives, published in 1955, found that U.S. Steel's "target" was an after-tax rate of return on investment of 8 percent.[74] There is reason to believe that during the mid- and late 1950's the corporation was endeavoring to raise its target but abandoned the effort following the Kefauver hearings and the confrontation with President Kennedy.

Figure 23-1 shows the relationship between U.S. Steel's rate of return on net worth and its operating rate. Three regression lines are shown: the first, or historical, line shows the relationship between 1920 and 1954 (excluding the war years of 1941–46 and 1951–52); the second shows the relationship pre-vailing during the mid- and late 1950's (1955–60); and the third shows the relationship during the 1960's (1961–67). (Data for the years 1953–68 are

<hr>

[73] Quoted in *ibid.*, pp. 19–20.
[74] A. D. H. Kaplan, Joel B. Dirlam, and R. F. Lanzillotti, "Pricing in Big Business," The Brookings Institution, 1958, p. 171.

Figure 23-1

U.S. STEEL

Relationship between percentage of capacity operated and
rate of return on stockholders' investment after taxes

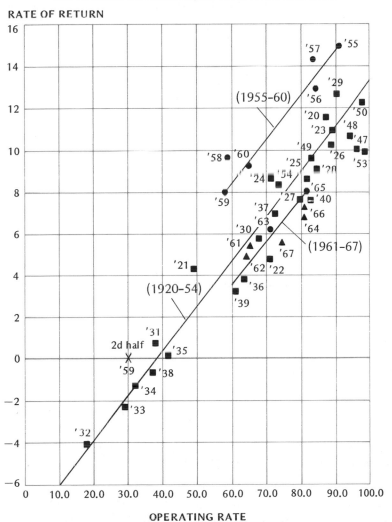

RATE OF RETURN

OPERATING RATE

Source: Rate of return: Federal Trade Commission, *Report on Rates of Return
in Selected Manufacturing Industries*, 1940–67, and special tabulation
for earlier years; *Moody's Industrial Manual*; operating rate: U.S.
Steel Corp., *Basic Facts About U.S. Steel*; U.S. Steel Corp.,
Financial Reports; *Moody's Industrial Manual*; *Hearings on Economic
Concentration*, Pt. 7, p. 3811

given in Table 23-1.) The observations for the 1920–54 period are indicated
by squares; for 1955–67 by triangles.

At any given operating level the profit rate under the relationship of the
1950's was nearly 4 percentage points above that of the historical relationship.
Under the old relationship the company's target return of 8 percent was at-

Table 23-1

RELATIONSHIP BETWEEN PROFIT RATE AND OPERATING RATE

Year	U.S. Steel Return on Net Worth	Steel Industry Operating Rate
1968	7.7%	n.a.[a]
1967	5.3	76%
1966	7.2	82
1965	7.6	81
1964	6.8	81
1963	6.0	71
1962	4.9	64
1961	5.7	65
1960	9.2	67
1959	8.0	63
1958	9.7	61
1957	14.3	85
1956	12.8	90
1955	14.8	93
1954	8.3	n.a.[a]
1953	9.9	n.a.[a]

[a]Not available.

Source: Federal Trade Commission, *Report on Rates of Return in Selected Manufacturing Industries, 1953–69; Hearings on Economic Concentration*, Pt. 7, p. 3811

tained with an operating rate of approximately 75 percent; under the relationship of the 1950's it could be attained with an operating rate of 60 percent. The operating rate that yielded an 8-percent profit rate under the historical relationship yielded a return of approximately 11.5 percent during the late 1950's. Operating at 90 percent of capacity the company enjoyed a profit rate of 11 percent under the former but more than 14 percent under the latter. Operating at 60 percent the company enjoyed an increase in profit rate of from slightly below 5 percent to above 8 percent. Clearly the effect of the stairstep increases of $7.35 per ton in 1955, $8.50 in 1956, $6.00 in 1957, and $4.50 in 1958 (plus "interim adjustments") well exceeded any increases in costs, thus widening the profit margin and raising the return on investment.[75]

But it would appear from the third line that during the 1960's this gain was more than lost. At any given operating level the profit rate under the 1961–69 relationship was more than 4 percentage points below that of 1955–60 and about one percentage point below the historical 1920–54 relationship.[76]

[75] Incidentally, it will be noted that in the second half of 1959 the corporation "broke even" while operating at only 30% of capacity. Although steel production was greatly curtailed by a strike, the corporation still managed to show a slight profit while operating at less than one-third of capacity.

[76] Following the Kefauver hearings the American Iron and Steel Institute discontinued the publication of company operating-rate figures. Accordingly, the figures for 1961–67 refer to the industry as a whole (see *Hearings on Economic Concentration*, Pt. 7, p. 3811). During the 1950's the difference was negligible. From 1953 through the first half of 1957 the average operating rate for the steel industry was 88.6%; for U.S. Steel it was 88.0%. For the fourth quarter of 1956 U.S. Steel's operating rate was 3.4 percentage points below the industry average; for the first quarter of 1957 it was .3% below the industry average; and for the second quarter of 1957 it was 2.3 percentage points above (see *Administered Prices: Report on Steel*, pp. 47–48, 27).

At the 75 percent operating rate that had yielded the company's 8 percent target during 1920–54, the profit rate during the 1960's was slightly below 7 percent. Moreover, during the 1960's the company had not been able to achieve its historical target return even during years of increasing steel production:

	Increase in Steel Production[77]	Profit Rate of U.S. Steel
1968	5.9%	7.7%
1965	4.8	7.6
1964	16.0	6.8
1963	6.9	6.0

The principal effect of the rise in imports and the growing use of substitute materials would have been to reduce volume, not to lower the rate of profit earned at a given volume. Rather, the explanation for the loss of the ability of the corporation to pass on more than the cost of wage and other cost increases, so evident during the mid- and late 1950's, currently must be sought elsewhere. As long as wage increases could readily be absorbed—and indeed used as the pretext for still greater price increases—the company could well afford to be generous in its wage settlements. Moreover, its ability to raise prices contributed to an indifference toward the need for efficiency; hence its 10-year neglect of oxygen conversion and its delay in adopting continuous casting. During the 1960's the union continued its demands for substantial wage increases while the company suffered from the mounting fixed costs of expensive and increasingly obsolescent equipment. If, as a result of government suasion, increases in costs could no longer be passed on in the form of higher prices, the logical expectation would have been an abandonment of the effort to raise the target return and a retreat to the lower historical return. And this, it would appear, is exactly what took place, except that the company was not able to achieve even the historical objective.

Price notification

To put government suasion on a systematic basis, the proposal has from time to time been made that legislation be enacted requiring any large firm in a concentrated industry to notify some designated government agency of its intention to make a price increase, which it would then have to justify in public hearings. While the agency would lack any legal authority to prevent the increase, the disclosure of relevant data on profits, costs, and the like would, it is hoped, serve as a powerful restraining influence on prices. The need for such legislation was set forth in 1957 by J. Kenneth Galbraith in hearings before the Senate Antitrust Subcommittee:

> Under present procedures—the case of oil last autumn and now of steel are cases in point—the industry announces the price advance. Then if a wage settlement is involved, the relevant union leader points out that the increase is excessive.
>
> At the same time the administration states its regret that the advance has occurred, coupled with a strong disclaimer of any knowledge of the specific issues.

[77] Increase from previous year.

> Thereafter a Congressional Committee holds hearings, the increase is denounced and the matter is then forgotten.
>
> While it will be agreed that this ritual has an impressive solemnity, it can scarcely be satisfactory to the public which pays.[78]

He proposed that "where major movements in prices and wages are in prospect, we might have a requirement of notice and the public discussion before, rather than after, the fact. Firms, and also unions, would then proceed in light of a full knowledge of public reaction to their policies." [79] In later hearings he suggested some of the specific procedures that might be employed. Thus, for example, there should be

> some kind of official finding each year as to the wage advances that can be afforded within the framework of stable prices [which] . . . of course, should be after full hearings and full discussion. Perhaps then, since the situation in each industry would be different, there might be tripartite committees representing labor, management, and the public to deal in decentralized fashion with the application of the standards to particular industries. . . . Were it claimed that a price increase were required in steel, machinery, automobiles, or elsewhere, this claim would come before the committee for investigation and finding of fact. Certainly in the beginning the sanctions for noncompliance should be mild and with reliance on the force of public opinion. However, we should always have in mind that too easy acceptance of noncooperation is discrimination against the man who does cooperate.[80]

Emphasizing that his recommendation was occasioned by the existence of monopoly power, Galbraith stated: "These proposals do not interfere with free markets. Rather they bring the public interest to bear on what is now private price fixing. It is obvious that if private discretion over prices did not exist, the problem that we are here talking about would not arise. Where that private discretion does not exist, as say in agriculture, the problem does not arise." [81]

Two years later the Antitrust Subcommittee held hearings on a bill introduced by Senator O'Mahoney requiring any corporation in a concentrated industry (i.e., with a 4-company concentration ratio of 50 percent or higher) with shipments in such an industry of over $100 million to notify a designated government agency of its intention to raise prices. Within a specified period after receiving such notice, the agency would be obliged to call a public hearing at which it would examine the company "with respect to the reasons for and justifiability of the proposed increase." [82] It would then submit a report to Congress summarizing the arguments and would make its own findings of fact. To obtain the information necessary for intelligent findings, the agency would be granted broad fact-gathering powers.[83]

---

[78] *Hearings on Administered Prices,* Pt. 1, p. 50.
[79] *Ibid.*
[80] *Hearings on Administered Prices,* Pt. 10, p. 4932.
[81] *Ibid.,* pp. 4932–33.
[82] 86th Cong., 1st Sess., S. 215, 1959. In addition Senator Clark and Representative Reuss introduced a measure that would have authorized the Council of Economic Advisers to hold hearings on price increases.
[83] During the hearings on the bill spokesmen for the brass industry pointed out that their discretion over price was limited sharply by the importance of their materials costs. Accordingly, an amendment was drafted exempting industries whose cost of materials represented more than two-thirds of their value of shipments.

Summarizing the arguments in favor of the O'Mahoney bill, Colston E. Warne pointed out that its passage would constitute a recognition of the fact that "no longer are the key prices of large corporations, in the field covered, to be established arbitrarily and privately, without notice to the public"; that it would impose a mandate upon government "to bring out the facts concerning increases in such administered prices"; that it would provide a mechanism "by which the protective force of public opinion would actually be accorded to companies unjustly accused of profiteering"; and that it would "give consumers information to offset the smoke screen of competing propaganda which has hitherto surrounded administered pricing." [84]

Voluntary suasion: an evaluation

Despite the criticism that it "never works," suasion by government has an impressive record of accomplishment. Over a long period of years substantial savings for consumers have resulted from economic investigations by the Federal Trade Commission. During the early years of World War II prices of most of the concentrated industries were stabilized in the face of rapidly rising demand. Wage increases were moderated by the guideposts of 1962. A sharp upward movement in steel prices was checked first by congressional hearings, then by the strenuous efforts of a President, and finally by continuous surveillance on the part of the Council of Economic Advisers. The Council's efforts also have served to restrain the price advances in a number of other concentrated industries.[85]

As compared to more formal types of public control, the voluntary approach has several important advantages. It can be put into effect quickly, without the delay of hearings, legal opinions, findings, appeals, and so on. Because the private parties involved are free to ignore the government's entreaties, there is no possibility of "confiscation" and thus no need to determine what constitutes "a fair return on investment." The staffing requirements can be extremely modest. The economic data introduced into the record of the Senate Antitrust Subcommittee throughout its lengthy hearings on administered prices were developed by a staff ranging from three to four economists.

Under the voluntary approach the government enjoys considerable discretion in the selection of industries with which it can choose to be concerned. As has been noted, the selection of the steel industry was dictated primarily by the "pyramiding" effect of its price increases, along with its egregious noncompetitive behavior. To these considerations was added the Kennedy Administration's bitter opposition to the 1962 price rise, aroused by its own strenuous efforts in persuading the union to accept a moderate wage increase. Concern with automobile prices has stemmed from that industry's overriding importance as a source of employment, the extraordinary profitability of its leader, and the latter's method of pricing. The selection of ethical drugs for congressional hearings was prompted by their unique role in averting illness and death, by the industry's continuing record as the most profitable in the nation, and by its extraordinary margins between direct costs and prices.

The government also enjoys wide discretion in the selection of standards against which to appraise the "reasonableness" of price. Among those employed

[84] *Hearings on Administered Prices*, Pt. 11, p. 5497.
[85] See Okun, *op. cit.*, pp. 48, 49.

have been comparisons of price trends in concentrated versus competitive sectors, intra-industry comparisons of profits and similar data showing rising prices in the face of declining demand, evidence of price leadership and price followership, showings of relatively low "breakeven" points, and comparisons of prices to costs—particularly unit labor costs.

But it is in connection with such analyses that one of the principal weaknesses of voluntary restraints is revealed—the frequent inadequacy of data. If their propriety is to be a matter of public concern, prices must be compared with something; by themselves they are meaningless. The current price of a product can be compared with its price in the past, with its prices in other markets, with prices of other products, with profits, and with costs. The problems of comparing prices with prices, while often troublesome, are not insurmountable. Where profits are used to evaluate prices, a problem arises in that published profit figures are usually available only on a "consolidated" basis—i.e., for the corporation as a whole. But, as has been noted, for the large corporation that makes many products in different industries, the company's overall profit rate will probably be nothing more than a statistical accident, representing an average of high profits made in some industries and low (or nonexistent) profits made in others. In such cases changes in the profit rate for the company as a whole bear little or no relationship to price changes for any one of its products.

If an effort is made to obtain profits on an "unconsolidated" basis (i.e., broken down by each of the industries in which the corporation is engaged) or if figures on unit costs are to be sought, two conceptual problems must be dealt with: (a) what should properly be included in costs and (b) how are indirect or overhead costs to be allocated among different divisions or products? If, as in drugs, the vast expense of supporting armies of detail men and carrying on other promotional and selling activity (much of it unnecessary), or, as in automobiles, the enormous expense involved in model changes (much of it pure waste) are included in costs, the contrast of price to costs no longer provides a comparison of what is charged for the product with the inescapable expenses of offering it on the market. Instead, it becomes a comparison of price with the sum of (a) those necessary costs plus (b) other expenses of nonprice competition, which the seller is able to incur because of his possession of substantial monopoly power and which he elects to incur as an alternative to price competition.

The problem of allocating overhead costs is one that all large diversified corporations have to meet in order to have some idea of the profitability of their own various divisions or products. The customary procedure is for the corporation to distribute its total overhead expenses in terms of some arbitrary standard, such as sales. In order to assure comparability all companies reporting profits on a divisional basis to any government agency would have to be required to employ the same standard.

The difficulties faced by the body politic in judging the propriety of a price will be infinitely compounded by the good offices of public-relations agencies. By the time they have finished with their ministrations the confusion in the public mind will have been magnified into a significant multiple of the legitimate differences in interpretation. Some of the more-or-less standard ploys to be expected are: the two-step procedure followed in steel pricing, in which the actual increase is preceded by an announcement of a still greater rise; the reference to profits in terms of the lower and less meaningful measure of percentage of sales rather than of investment; attacks on the meaningfulness of "quoted" or "list" prices coupled with refusal to supply the "real" prices; dismissal of profit rates as failing to reflect "adequate" depreciation charges combined with refusal to acknowledge generous depreciation allowances; protestations over the "inadequacy" of earnings without mention of the size and significance of cash flow (earnings plus depreciation); pleas of the necessity of "meeting" the higher profit rate of some other corporation or industry in order to attract capital even though most capital requirements are financed out of earnings, and so on. Whether the American people would have the economic sophistication to see through these and similar artful stratagems remains to be seen.

Even granted a reasonably sophisticated audience, the government faces the very real problem of actually getting the substance of its findings and analyses through to the public. If the message does not get through, the public does not become informed, and the whole basis of restraining the exercise of monopoly power through an enlightened public opinion disappears. There is, of course, no problem in obtaining adequate press and TV coverage where what is involved is of a dramatic, "newsworthy" nature—e.g., the acrid steel price confrontation of 1962. But for a President to become involved personally in such a controversy is, necessarily, something of a rarity. In the eyes of the Washington editors, newsmen, columnists, and TV commentators who decide which legislative hearings and administrative activities shall be covered, economic arguments concerning the propriety of an industry's prices have a low dramatic or "newsworthy" content, rating a very low priority for space and time.

Important as these other problems may be, the most serious weakness of voluntary suasion is the possibility that it will be ignored. The steel industry ignored entreaties of the Council of Economic Advisers in both 1966 and 1967. Following the 1962 price rise 4 steel companies—Bethlehem, Republic, National, and Armco—refused to respond to a subpoena issued by Senator Kefauver calling for unit cost data, even though U.S. Steel and 7 other major producers agreed to supply most of the needed information.[86] The data had been sought immediately after the 1962 price rise to determine how much of the increase was actually traceable to higher wage costs. When the parent Senate Judiciary Committee refused to support its own Subcommittee and recommend a citation for contempt of Congress, the whole effort to obtain the information collapsed. It is not just a coincidence that since that time no hearings on the steel industry have been held by the Antitrust Subcommittee.

As a general proposition, the frequency with which voluntary suasion is ignored will be greater the lower the ranking of the agency in the hierarchy of government. At least since World War II no President has ever had his direct request to a specific industry refused; requests by the Council of Economic Advisers have occasionally been ignored; rebuffs to lower-ranking agencies range from the frequent to the routine.

[86] See 87th Cong., 2nd Sess., Senate Judiciary Committee, *Hearings on Refusal of Certain Steel Companies to Respond to Subpoenas,* 1962.

CH 24 THE REGULATION OF PRICES

Reliance on competition as the automatic regulator of the economy has long been supplemented by mandatory regulation of prices and profits for those industries regarded as "natural monopolies." Where, because of technological or other barriers, there can be only one source of supply, competition obviously can provide little protection to the consuming public. The first recognition that the federal government has a responsibility to protect the public interest from "inherent monopoly" was the enactment in 1880 of the Interstate Commerce Commission Act. This was followed by direct regulation at the federal level in such diverse areas as trucking, airlines, natural gas, and long-distance telephone service. In addition, rates for electricity, gas, local telephone service, and transit fares are under direct regulation by most of the individual states. The only feature most (though not all) of these disparate areas have in common is that service in any given market cannot feasibly be supplied by more than one or at the most a very few suppliers and that anything approaching the protection afforded by the competition of many rival enterprises is inherently absent.

The rationale of price regulation

The argument has been advanced that just as we accept the inevitability of mandatory regulation of "natural monopolies," we should not cavil at the imposition of similar controls over those industries in which competition is absent for other reasons. The argument runs that many industries are so concentrated as to all but preclude the possibility of price competition; that because of considerations of mutual self-interest, the industry's few producers will tend to refrain from competing in price with one another; that because of technological barriers or for other reasons it is wishful thinking to assume that competition in such industries can be restored by antitrust action; and that it is only logical, therefore, to apply to such fields the same type of regulation that has long been imposed on the natural monopolies. A corollary argument is that where subjected to state control, the regulated industry must be "protected" from competition; thus the extension of regulation from railroads to trucks.[1]

To some authorities the coming of direct regulation is merely a matter of time. In the words of Ben W. Lewis:

[1] For a comprehensive discussion of the latter argument, see Alfred E. Kahn, *Economics of Regulation,* John Wiley, Vol. II, 1971, Ch. 1.

My own prediction—and I stress that I am predicting, not prescrib ing—is that the years ahead will see a great increase in conscious, collective governmental controls and of governmental enterprise; and that bigness will be a major focal point of the development. . . . Our giant firms are sitting like fat, delectable ducks, virtually inviting the Government to open fire with something more effective than antitrust. The invitation will be accepted. One cannot even guess at the occasions which will prompt the firing or the pattern which the firing will take. . . . But the conviction that great power over the economy must reside only in a government of the people will be acted on relentlessly, bluntly, and with force. Events will count more heavily than fine logic in determining the action; but events will surely occur, and public action to repossess the power to economize will surely follow.[2]

The heart of the problem, in Lewis's words, "is whether the presence in our markets of giant concentrates leaves enough natural, self-generating, unchecked and uncheckable drive in market competition to enable it to discharge to our satisfaction the compelling, coercive, directive, regulatory, economizing task which the logic of free enterprise requires it to carry." Since it cannot be broken up, bigness, it follows, is here to stay:

> Tutored by its attorneys, bathed, barbered and cosmeticized by Madison Avenue, nourished and sanctified by war and cold war, and enthroned by public opinion which sees only goodness in bigness that is well-mannered and well behaved, bigness exhibits the supreme confidence and gracious assurance that bespeak stature, status and a clear conscience. Bigness was once the bad boy in Sunday School; now it sits on the vestry. It may not yet have acquired a full-sized soul, but the contract has been let and the press has been alerted.

The reasoning of J. Kenneth Galbraith in *The New Industrial State* proceeds along much the same lines.[3] The free market of classical economic theory, with its many sellers, has been replaced by an economy dominated by a few great corporations, which for all practical purposes are free from any outside force or influence. Their size frees them from the constraints of the market, while their ability to raise capital from retained earnings frees them from the influence of investors. Producing their own raw materials, they are free of concern over supplies. And, through modern advertising and other forms of nonprice competition, they can "manage" their demand, freeing themselves from the vagaries of unpredictable changes in consumer preferences. In this "revised sequence" the consumer is no longer king; the new sovereign is the corporation, which by managing its demand determines what and how much will be produced and, through the artful use of the means of communication, can induce the consumer to like what is proffered.

To rely on antitrust would be to forgo the efficiencies the large corporation has made possible: "It would require that we have simple products made with simple equipment from readily available materials by unspecialized labor."[4] Because concentration is too pervasive and efficiency too dependent on size, the choice is clear: an essential element of the planning structure of the industrial system will be "maximum levels established by the State for wages and prices."[5] In addition, there should be applied to many public sectors the kind

[2] *Hearings on Administered Prices,* Pt. 9, pp. 4714–19, testimony of Ben W. Lewis.
[3] J. Kenneth Galbraith, *The New Industrial State,* Houghton Mifflin, 1967.
[4] *Ibid.,* p. 33.
[5] *Ibid.,* p. 260.

of overall planning that AT&T has brought to the telephone system.[6] These rationales have been immeasurably strengthened by the growing importance of what has been referred to as "cost-push" inflation. The ability of strong labor unions to exact continuing increases in wage and other benefits, it is argued, makes inflation inescapable. In concentrated industries the cost of the wage increase is at least passed on in the form of a higher price; in what amounts to a "coalescing" rather than "countervailing" power, it is frequently used as a pretext for a still greater increase in price. In competitive industries the effect of higher wage costs, in the absence of an increase in demand, would be to reduce supply by eliminating high-cost producers, thereby shoring up a new and higher level of price.

Price freezes

The simplest form of price regulation is the freeze order, which may be applied across the board or selectively. Until August 15, 1971 across-the-board freezes were employed only in periods of general inflation, as in wartime national emergencies, when demand has exceeded supply. Indeed, it is difficult to conceive how an attempt to keep all, or most, prices unchanged for any length of time in the face of changes that are bound to take place in costs and demand could be viewed as a desirable instrument of public policy. Any general order freezing prices at levels prevailing in some designated base period will inevitably favor some producers and discriminate against others, since at any given time the prices of some products will be relatively high and those of others relatively low. If prices are frozen during a recession, the flexible prices will always be depressed; if during a period of high-level economic activity, they will always be inflated. When prices began to be frozen early in World War II, prices of some products were low relative to others, leaving the Office of Price Administration with a legacy of difficult "adjustment" problems to cope with. A related problem is that posed by monopolistic industries—e.g., motor vehicles and drugs—whose prices would probably be high by any standard, regardless of the base period employed, and would be legitimized by a government freeze. If wages were also frozen, the familiar problem would be presented of effecting a distribution of productivity gains.

Then there are the problems of administration and enforcement, which in the case of across-the-board freezes are horrendous. Although they are at their maximum during periods of general demand-pull inflation, evasions even during normal times are endless. Virtually impossible to stop are adulterations of quality and similar forms of hidden price increases. "Old" products with established price ceilings are replaced by only slightly dissimilar "new" products with no, or higher, ceilings. Tie-in contracts flourish, with the sale of an article with a low ceiling conditioned upon the purchase of an unwanted item with a high ceiling. Buyers are charged for "extras" and services formerly included in the price, and the like.

The problems occasioned by selective freezes would of course diminish the more selective they became. But selective freezes, or indeed any similar form of control, will encounter two types of problem—one economic, and the other legal. Industries whose prices are controlled may well find themselves in a squeeze,

[6] *Ibid.*, p. 76.

caught between fixed prices for the products they sell and rising prices for the uncontrolled materials, components, and parts they buy. For the government merely to authorize upward price adjustments commensurate with cost increases (if they could be ascertained) would not necessarily meet the legal problem. The Fourteenth Amendment has long been interpreted as requiring that a balance be struck between protecting the consumer from monopoly and guarding the investor from confiscation. In the oft-cited words of Justice Holmes:

> On the one side, if the franchise is taken to mean that the most profitable return that could be got, free from competition, is protected by the Fourteenth Amendment, then the power to regulate is null. On the other hand, if the power to regulate withdraws the protection of the Amendment altogether, then the property is nought. This is not a matter of economic theory, but of fair interpretation of a bargain. Neither extreme can have been meant. A midway between them must be hit.[7]

The very need for adjustments makes it clear that selective controls are not an alternative but merely a way station en route to a more systematic form of regulation which would have to be based on a "fair return" on investment. This brings one face to face with the very issues that have developed during nearly a century of utility regulation.

Utility-type regulation

Aside from short-term emergency "freezes," the control of prices in this country has been limited to the form of regulation imposed on privately-owned public utilities. The question to be examined here is not whether the regulation of utilities has been successful, which is itself a matter of considerable dispute; rather it is whether the principles and procedures developed for such regulation can be applied to concentrated manufacturing industries. For this to be done, it would be necessary to overcome serious additional difficulties stemming from inherent differences in industry structure, the nature of market control, the elasticity of demand, the volatility of consumer preferences, the rate of technological progress, and so on. In some cases the effect of the differences would be to magnify problems already present in the regulation of utilities; in others it would be to introduce entirely new problems. As Dudley Pegrum has pointed out, utility companies are for the most part "isolated and insulated monopolies" and, as such, lend themselves admirably to regulation:

> the shortcomings [of utility regulation] are obvious; many of these are inherent in any type of control designed to secure the results of competitive efficiency when competition is absent. The task is unavoidable, because monopoly is unavoidable in public utilities. Public ownership faces the same type of problem, simply because it cannot eliminate the monopoly. The experience of public utility regulation should give pause to those who wish to extend this form of control to other areas of economic activity. Thorough-going regulation is difficult enough when applied to single monopolies; it is literally impossible when competition intrudes to any appreciable extent.[8]

[7] *Cedar Rapids Gas Light Co.* v. *Cedar Rapids*, 223 U.S. 655 (1912), 669–70.
[8] Dudley Pegrum, *Public Regulation of Business,* Irwin, 1959, pp. 651–52.

Determining "fair value"

In striking the bargain between protection of the consumer on the one hand and the rights of the investor on the other, the courts over many years have evolved the principle that prices must be low enough to be "just and reasonable" but high enough to cover operating expenses, depreciation, and taxes and also a "fair return" on the "fair value" of the capital invested in the business. Since the larger the capital investment, or "rate base," the greater the permissible earnings, an interminable controversy has revolved around the method of its determination. The heart of the controversy is whether the value of the capital investment should be measured on the basis of how much it would cost in terms of current dollars to reproduce facilities built many years earlier ("reproduction cost") or, alternatively, how much actually has been invested on the facilities ("original cost" or "prudent investment").[9] Depending on which would yield higher profits, the utilities have been strong partisans of both bases, though at different times. As recounted by Charles F. Phillips, Jr.:

> The State of Nebraska in 1893 passed a law which established a Board of Transportation. Among other things, the board was given the authority to determine the rates charged for hauling freight. One of the first orders, setting maximum rates, was challenged by the railroads on the basis that rates were confiscatory. The roads contended that much of their property had been constructed during and after the Civil War when prices were high, and that they were entitled to a return on their original cost. The State, represented by William Jennings Bryan, based its measure of reasonable earnings on the lower reproduction costs. The property valuation problems thus came to the front.
>
> *　　*　　*
>
> Before World War I, regulated companies generally based their valuation estimates on original cost, while commissions based theirs on reproduction cost. But during the war, construction costs soared, and reproduction cost became higher than original cost. Consequently, the two parties changed sides. The companies now began to demand consideration of reproduction cost; the commissions started to urge original cost.[10]

Assuming a continuation of inflation, the utilities would logically continue to press for reproduction cost, since it would yield valuations higher than those based on original cost. But, as Phillips observes, "if the price level should fall sharply, many present supporters of reproduction cost valuations and price level depreciation would become advocates of original cost measures." [11]

It should be taken as granted that the capital investment of industrial oligopolies cannot possibly be measured in terms of reproduction cost. For one thing it would be necessary to settle certain conceptual questions, which after nearly a century of utility regulation are still unresolved. As summarized by Clair Wilcox, they include:

> (1) What is it that is being reproduced: a modern replacement for an old plant, the old plant in its original condition, or the old plant as it stands today? . . .

[9] "Prudent investment" is the same as "original cost" after the elimination of any costs found to result from "speculation and fraud" and not the result of the exercise of "good judgment."

[10] Charles F. Phillips, Jr., *The Economics of Regulation,* Irwin, 1969, pp. 219–21.

[11] *Ibid.,* p. 240.

(2) Under what conditions is reproduction cost to occur: those originally existing or those existing at the present time? . . .

(3) What methods of reproduction are to be assumed: simultaneous rebuilding of the whole plant involving large-scale operations and employing modern techniques, or piecemeal reconstruction with techniques no longer in use? [12]

To determine what it would cost today to duplicate a plant built many years ago requires a type of price information that does not exist. Overall price series, such as the Wholesale Price and Consumer Price Indexes, are wholly unsuited, since they are influenced strongly by farm products, food products, textiles, apparel, and other products whose price trends differ markedly from those of industrial plant and equipment. Even "construction cost" indexes may not reflect the prices charged for the specialized plant and equipment used in specific industries, particularly where much of the equipment is "tailored" to unique requirements.

Because of these conceptual ambiguities and difficulties of application, widely differing estimates are almost inevitable. In a case cited by Justice Frankfurter six estimates were made of the cost of reproducing telephone facilities in New York: the majority of the Commission, $367 million; a federal court, $397 million; the minority of the Commission, $405.5 million; the court-appointed "master," $518 million; and two independent appraisals, $529 million and $615 million.[13] In other words, the highest exceeded the lowest by more than two-thirds.

The shortcomings of the reproduction cost approach have been summarized by Pegrum as follows:

> The public is scarcely likely to sanction profits on modern equipment not in existence when the prices necessary to yield those profits may be coming from inferior property and services from which the prices may be obtained because of the presence of monopoly.
>
> Apart from these considerations, cost of reproduction is impractible. In other words, it fails to meet the test of expediency. It can be obtained only by extensive engineering appraisals, which are costly and time-consuming. They require years to complete in the case of large properties and lead to marked differences of opinion on amounts, because of the imponderables which must be evaluated. As a practical matter, they cannot be kept up to date; a new evaluation is needed every time an adjustment of the general level of rates is in order; but the process of making it is so slow that it would literally be out of date every time it is used.[14]

The original cost basis possesses all of the attributes reproduction cost lacks. It is the product of actual records and not of a form of "imaginary costing." Theoretically, price regulation based on original costs should be a matter of relative simplicity, involving nothing more than applying a predetermined "fair return" percentage rate to the sum of actual capital investments plus actual costs of acquisitions minus depreciation charges and write-offs of retired property. But, while simple enough in principle, it can be difficult in practice. One problem is the absence of adequate cost records: "The basing of rates on costs

[12] Clair Wilcox, *Public Policies Toward Business,* 3rd ed., Irwin, 1966, p. 530.
[13] Phillips, *op. cit.,* p. 235.
[14] Pegrum, *op. cit.,* p. 629.

proceeds on the assumption that costs are readily and almost unequivocably ascertainable; whereas in fact this is not so." [15] An essential requirement of regulation based on original costs is strict control over accounting, involving uniform procedures and detailed reports. Uniform records are rarely available when the investment antedates the regulation. Referring to utilities, Pegrum notes, "Because a good deal of utility investment was made before adequate regulation and control of accounting took place, it was necessary to make physical appraisals to determine the investment at the time of valuation." [16] Even for utility commissions whose jurisdiction is limited to a single state, this has proved to be a laborious, time-consuming, and expensive undertaking. If similar appraisals were to be required for facilities owned by giant industrial corporations, operating in every state in the nation, the magnitude of the task would be almost inconceivable. Moreover, once industrial enterprises were brought under regulation, they would have a strong incentive to overstate the value of their capital investment. And the older the facilities, the less the availability of cost records, and thus the more difficult the task. According to a McGraw-Hill survey, nearly one-quarter (24 percent) of the manufacturing capacity in 1966 was more than 16 years old, while nearly half (43 percent) was more than 10 years old.[17]

In recent years the principal objection to original cost has been that during a long-term period of price inflation, returns to investors are in dollars of constantly declining purchasing power. As one of the nation's leading authorities on public-utility regulation, James C. Bonbright has put it:

> A close reading of the literature written in recent years in support of the fair value rule revealed two greatly different asserted objections to an actual cost rate base. According to one objection, which is in line with the older legal tradition of property rights, investors are entitled to a reasonable return on the value of their property and not on its cost, not even on its replacement cost except to the extent to which the latter cost may happen to serve as a measure or clue to the real value of the property. But according to the other objection, which now is receiving much greater emphasis in this postwar period of price inflation, what makes the original cost standard of rate making so deficient in the opinion of those who object to it is not any failure to reflect value rather than cost, but rather its failure to reflect original cost itself when restated in terms of current dollars.[18]

This latter argument can be rebutted on the grounds that investors must have been aware of the general upward trend in prices; that they took this trend into account in deciding to invest in utilities, which happen to offer certain other advantages for investors even during an inflationary period; and that they accordingly have no right to expect payment in dollars of constant purchasing power.

But even if the argument is accepted, the protection of investors could be accomplished far more readily by raising the permissible rate of return than by re-evaluating the rate base; increasing the permissible rate from, say, 6 to 8

[15] *Ibid.*, p. 623.
[16] *Ibid.*, p. 631.
[17] *Business Week*, Nov. 26, 1966.
[18] James C. Bonbright, "The Ill-Defined Meaning of a Fair Value Rate Base," May, 1962. Mimeograph. Quoted in Phillips, *op. cit.*, pp. 258–59.

percent would provide investors with the same benefits as a 33-percent increase in the evaluation of the rate base. To the early proponents of original cost, this seemed the proper way of coping with changing conditions. Regulatory authorities have been most reluctant, however, to vary the permissible rate, preferring instead to adjust for the rising price level by incorporating reproduction cost values into the rate base. The result is that rate bases have increasingly come to be irrational amalgams, subjectively arrived at, of original cost and reproduction cost values. In a study of the various concepts of "value" found in state statutes, Joseph R. Rose found:

> The Illinois Commission has assigned one-quarter weight to reproduction cost and three-quarters to original cost; Alabama has assigned one-third to reproduction cost and two-thirds to original cost; Minnesota, Delaware, Pennsylvania and Arizona have given approximately equal weight to each element. North Carolina and Indiana have also attributed equal weight to each in some proceedings, but in others have given greater weight to original cost. New Mexico, Maryland and New Jersey have used original cost as the principal factor and have added an increment to compensate for reproduction cost, while Missouri has given "greater weight" to original cost than to reproduction cost.[19]

Not only have commissions varied the composition of the rate base; they have also varied the rate of return with the nature of the base. Independent studies have shown that when commissions adopt either reproduction cost or fair value rate bases, they offset the effect of the larger base by allowing a lower percentage rate of return.[20] Thus, in the case of telephone companies, the average rate of return was found to be only 5.93 percent where the rate base was determined by reproduction cost but 7.98 percent, or 35 percent higher, where it was based on original cost.

These findings also provide support for a conclusion reached by Bonbright:

> In the opinions that accompany their rate orders, commissions seldom attempt to disclose the reasons why they find, say, 5.85 percent fair in one case and 6.2 percent fair in another. Especially in fair value jurisdictions some of the decisions lead one to suspect that the commissions have first reached a conclusion as to reasonable revenue requirements in terms of dollars per annum and then have proceeded to translate these requirements into whatever combination of a rate base and a percentage rate of return will be likely to pass muster with the appellate courts or with public sentiment.[21]

If Bonbright is correct and the experience of public utilities were carried over to the regulation of industry generally, the regulated companies would be permitted to make such aggregate profits as the regulatory bodies subjectively deemed appropriate—a decision that would then be rationalized on some more systematic basis.

[19] Joseph R. Rose, "Confusions in Valuation for Public Utility Rate-Making," *Minnesota Law Review,* Nov., 1962, pp. 19–20.
[20] See David K. Eiteman, "Interdependence of Utility Rate-Base Type, Permitted Rate of Return, and Utility Earnings," *Journal of Finance,* March, 1962; Frederic Stuart, "Rate Base vs. Rate of Return," *Public Utility Fortnightly,* Sept. 27, 1962.
[21] James C. Bonbright, *Principles of Public Utility Rates,* Columbia University Press, 1961, p. 281.

Establishing a "fair return"

Compared to determining the rate base, the task of establishing the allowable rate of return has been a matter of comparative simplicity. The rate must be low enough to prevent the exploitation of consumers but high enough to enable the utility to maintain its credit standing, operate efficiently, and attract needed capital: "The concept of a fair rate of return, therefore, represents a range or zone of reasonableness." [22]

But within this zone there has been considerable room for variation: "The Supreme Court has clearly indicated that no single rate of return is always fair. Rather, a fair return varies with investment opportunities, the location of a company, the nature of the business, and general economic conditions." [23] Rates have tended to be higher for utilities with poor credit ratings, for those in fast-growing areas, and for those under the jurisdiction of lenient commissions. They have also tended to be higher during prosperous times than during recession. Some idea of the variation can be gathered from the fact that in 1967 the rate of return was 5.99 percent or below for 11.6 percent of the privately owned electric utilities but 9.0 percent or above for 13.2 percent of the companies. [24]

This variation, it should be emphasized, occurs within just one industry and relates to companies that for the most part are "isolated and insulated monopolies." If the same principles apply, the variation would be greater the larger the number of industries and the greater the number of firms brought under regulation. Although tending to be higher than in unconcentrated fields, rates of return on stockholders' investment in oligopolistic industries vary widely, ranging in 1968 from 7.0 percent for cement to 18.8 percent for drugs and medicines. [25] If industrial oligopolies are to be brought under price regulation a first question would be whether the allowable profit rate is to be the same or is to vary from industry to industry.

Each alternative has its drawbacks. If a uniform return were employed, the function of allocating capital among the various industries would no longer be performed at all by the market but would have to be assumed by the government. Capital could not possibly flow automatically away from industries in which it was no longer needed and into those with rapidly expanding demand. The probabilities are that capacity would continue for long periods to be redundant in the former and inadequate in the latter. Moreover, price reductions in industries whose profit rates had been above the permissible level might well be offset by price increases in industries with profit rates below the allowable return. This would be the case if, as so often happens, the regulatory body took steps to suppress competition in the regulated industries, with the result that the maximum would also tend to become the minimum.

If the returns were to vary, however, the government would have to develop standards to govern the variation. Here great care would have to be exercised to avoid disastrous economic consequences. The existence of high profit rates may reflect an excess of demand over supply; it may also result from substantial

---

[22] Phillips, *op. cit.*, p. 260.
[23] *Ibid.*, p. 266.
[24] Federal Power Commission, *Statistics of Privately-Owned Electric Utilities in the United States*, 1968, p. 651.
[25] Federal Trade Commission, *Rates of Return in Selected Manufacturing Industries*, 1959–68.

monopoly power. The existence of low returns may reflect an excess of capacity in relation to demand; it may also be simply the result of inefficiency. Unless some way were developed to ascertain the importance of these different determinants, the use of existing profit rates as a guide in establishing the permissible return could easily perpetuate monopoly power in high-profit fields and inefficiency in low-profit ones.

The problem of plural firms

A further difficulty would be applying regulation to a number of firms within a given industry. In regulating utilities, state bodies generally need concern themselves with establishing rates that are "just and reasonable" for only one electric company, one gas company, and so on. But in manufacturing, the need for regulation arises not from monopoly but from oligopoly. No particular problem occurs where, as in petroleum, all of the leading firms regularly show about the same profit rate. But in most oligopolistic industries there is a distinct variation of profit rates with size among the oligopolists themselves.[26] And the character of the regulatory problem will depend upon the nature of this relationship.

Where the relationship between size and profitability is direct, as in motor vehicles, a regulatory action reducing the profit rate of the largest producer may well spell bankruptcy for the smaller firms. Where the relationship is inverse, as in steel, an allowable return high enough to be "fair and equitable" for the largest company will permit exploitation of consumers by the lesser and more efficient oligopolists. Yet to reduce the allowable return of the smaller firms might well create a shortage of supply by making it impossible for the industry's largest and less efficient producer to operate or expand.

The problem of multiple products

The typical concentrated manufacturing industry differs from a public utility in still another respect—the number of products per firm. Under utility-type regulation the standard of performance (the allowable profit rate) relates to a company; the means of its implementation (maximum prices or rates) relate to its products (or services). Although a utility may charge different rates to different classes of customer (e.g., residential as against industrial), the task of regulation is simplified greatly by the fact that most utilities are single-product (or single-service) enterprises. The regulatory body can thus determine with a fair degree of precision the relationship between profits earned and prices charged. But the greater the diversification, the less is the contribution made by any given product to a company's overall earnings, and the greater is the difficulty of establishing the relationship between product prices and company earnings. The multiple-product structures of most large corporations thus present a formidable problem, which, incidentally, has received little attention in the literature on public regulation. The problem would of course be most extreme in the case of conglomerate corporations. But even major steel producers, which are generally regarded as essentially single-industry enterprises, turn out a score or more of different shapes and forms (e.g., bars, sheets, plates, structural shapes, tinplate, wire products); with the addition of "extras" for particular specifications, these shapes and forms are transformed into thousands of individual products.

[26] See Ch. 8.

Assuming a rate of return to have been established applicable to a multi-product industrial firm, how is that profit rate to be translated into prices for its individual products? If the prices are to be based on costs, it will be necessary, first, to secure the costs (which can prove to be a rather difficult undertaking) and, second, to devise a workable solution for the always troublesome problem of allocating the company's overhead costs among its various individual products. There is also the question of whether certain types of expenditure should properly be included in costs. Such questionable expenditures as the cost of annual model changes in the automobile industry and of detail men in the ethical-drug industry have already been cited.[27] In utility regulation a controversy has developed over whether certain forms of institutional advertising, particularly those stressing the virtues of private over public ownership, should be included in costs and, as such, passed on to the consumer.

On the other hand, if costs are to be ignored, the chances are good that prices will be exorbitant for some products and below cost for others. Consumers of the former not only will be exploited but will be subsidizing buyers of the latter. Without information on costs the regulatory agency will have no defense against complaints that its price ceilings, unless they are promptly revised upward, will force a corporation to abandon important lines of production. And this type of complaint will usually be supported enthusiastically by organized labor and received sympathetically by members of Congress.

As a practical matter, the product diversification of most large industrial enterprises makes it impossible to translate an approved, predetermined profit rate for the corporation as a whole into ceiling prices for individual products. And, conversely, neither can ceiling prices for hundreds or even scores of individual products be set, maintained, and changed in such a way as to yield a specified profit rate. Increased diversification may force the abandonment of the widely shared view that competition will ultimately give way to regulation; ironically, regulation as an alternative to antitrust has been rendered inoperable by the failure to restrain conglomerate mergers through antitrust.[28]

The elasticity of demand

Another critical difference between utilities and most manufacturing industries lies in the nature of demand. Changes in price and even in income have relatively little effect on the demand for electricity, gas, or telephone service. The task of regulatory bodies is thus greatly simplified, since they can take as given one of the important determinants of costs and profits—the rate of production. With few exceptions, no such certainty is possible for manufacturing industries. Where demand is elastic, price increases approved to yield an authorized profit rate will result in a reduction in sales, a consequent increase in unit fixed costs, a decline in labor productivity, a rise in total unit costs, and a decrease in profits. Regulatory bodies governing transit systems have for some years been confronted with exactly this endless cycle. To enable the transit company to attain an authorized rate of return an increase in its fares is approved, as a result of which traffic falls off, unit costs rise, and earnings decline, providing a justification for a further increase in fares, which the regulatory body feels obligated to approve, and so on *ad infinitum*.

This is also the sequence that in 1970 confronted an industry subject to

[27] See Ch. 23.
[28] See Ch. 22.

federal price regulation. Fundamentally the troubles of the airline industry are traceable to an assumption held by all of the parties involved—airline management, the Civil Aeronautics Board, and surprisingly enough, the industry's bankers. This is the assumption that the rapid growth rate of the middle and later 1960's was a permanent fixture of the industry. During the 5-year period 1963–68, revenue passenger miles in domestic scheduled service of trunk airlines had increased by the unbelievable rate of 17.7 percent a year.[29] In 1969 the figure fell to 8.8 percent, while in 1970 the industry experienced virtually a zero growth rate. Although revenue passenger miles rose by 6.7 percent between 1969 and 1970, the industry's available seat miles, reflecting decisions made in earlier years, rose by 9.8 percent. As a result, the "actual passenger load factor" declined to only 50 percent of capacity.

The predictable effect on unit fixed costs was aggravated by the huge indebtedness incurred by the airline companies in financing their roseate expansion plans. Between 1964 and 1969 annual interest costs of the 12 major airlines had tripled, rising from $89 million to $262 million. According to one industry observer,

> airline financing has produced interest charges of such magnitude as to dwarf any profits that exist. An ATA "overview" notes that, "as a result of the general strain on credit sources and the industry's low earnings record, debt placements by trunk airlines have been extremely costly, particularly within the last year." They have had to pay interest rates of up to 11% for public debt issues and private bank loans.
>
> *　　*　　*
>
> It is worthy of note that the two most consistently profitable airlines in the nation—Northwest and Delta—have capital structures in which their equity is greater than their long-term debt. They are the only two trunk carriers that carry no convertible debt. They are the only two trunk carriers that do not lease any aircraft. They are, in short, two airlines that have surrendered the least to suppliers of debt capital.
>
> In the front offices of most other airlines, few decisions are made independently of the money lenders. Quite naturally, bankers are happy when the airlines are going good and paying their bills—and unhappy when the reverse occurs. But, like labor unions, they are exacting a toll of such proportions that industry survival is now being questioned.[30]

The other predictable effect on costs of a decline in demand also took its toll. As compared to the same quarter of the previous year, labor productivity, as measured by route-ton-miles (RTM) per employee, had risen 9.6 percent and 5.5 percent in the first quarters of 1967 and 1968, respectively; in the first quarter of 1970 it dropped by 4.5 percent. In the two earlier periods productivity gains had been sufficient to offset increases in wages and other employee compensation; in fact, labor cost per RTM actually declined by 4.4 percent in the 1967 quarter, rising only slightly in the 1968 interval. But in the first quarter of 1970 unit labor costs rose by 12.7 percent.[31]

With traffic falling well below expected levels, unit fixed costs rising, and wage increases exceeding productivity gains, profits fell disastrously. Accord-

[29] Civil Aeronautics Board, *Forecast for 1970 for the Trunk Airlines and Pan American of Scheduled Domestic Passenger Traffic*, 1970.
[30] William V. Henzey, "Is Nationalization Inevitable?" *Airline Management,* Jan., 1971, pp. 20–23.
[31] Civil Aeronautics Board, *Trends of Productivity and Employment Costs in the Trunk Airline Industry, 1967–First Quarter 1970*, 1970, p. 24.

ing to the Air Transport Administration the airline industry lost $66.2 million in the year ending September 30, 1970. Only 4 of the 12 major carriers—Continental, Delta, Eastern, and Northwest—were reported to have made profits. Even greater deficits were predicted for 1971. Confronted with declining demand, the association called for the type of solution that has become customary in concentrated industries; an overall 20-percent increase of fares was urged to eliminate the losses and enable the carriers to earn a "reasonable" rate of return.[32] In addition, flights were to be reduced and other services curtailed. But even from the industry's point of view such a restrictionist policy presented serious drawbacks: "In searching for answers, it is significant to note that industry's reaction has been in the form of pleas for higher prices coupled with retrenchment in service personnel and general expenditures. Coming at a time when traffic is poor—declining in many cases—these moves, logical as they may be, serve to depress traffic further. We are in the midst of a scaling down for air transport that could assume drastic proportions." [33]

The demand for higher fares placed the Civil Aeronautics Board in a dilemma partly of its own making. In a medieval effort to arrive at a "just" price, the Board had followed the usual government procedure of seeking a solution to an economic problem from its legal staff. In true lawyerlike fashion a CAB examiner held numerous days of hearings, examined thousands of documents, heard testimony from hundreds of witnesses, and amassed a transcript of thousands of pages. The product of this ceremonial exercise was a judgment that the airline industry be permitted to earn a rate of return of 10.5 percent on its investment.[34] Formally accepted by the Civil Aeronautics Board in 1960, this rate has been achieved by the airline industry in only one year, 1966. In 1969 the industry's actual profit rate, according to the Air Transport Association, was only 3.6 percent, and in 1970 it dropped further to 2.3 percent. Widening still more the breach between legal truth and economic reality, a CAB examiner in the latter year recommended, again after a "full and complete" hearing, that the "reasonable" return be raised to 11 percent.

According to the Association, the attainment of the 10.5-percent "approved" return would require fare increases in 1971 averaging 20 percent. The airlines were granted an actual increase of 6 percent. For the industry to be helped by such increases, the gains in revenues would have to exceed the losses resulting from a resulting decrease in traffic. If, as a result of fare increases, demand declined, the Board would have contributed to further disuse of the industry's facilities while easing only slightly, if at all, the financial plight of the companies. With half of the industry's capacity currently idle while more than four-fifths of the nation's populace have never used its services, the record of public regulation in the airline industry has little to commend it for application to industry generally.

Procedural delay

For public utilities, delay in the rate-making process, while troublesome, is seldom a serious threat to earnings. Changes in utilities' demand and supply usually take place at a gradual pace and can be planned for well in advance. Demand is inelastic with respect to both prices and income and is usually a

---

[32] *New York Times,* Jan. 6, 1971.
[33] Henzey, *op. cit.*
[34] *New York Times,* Jan. 6, 1971.

function of population and area growth, which can be forecast with considerable accuracy. Likewise, changes in technology and other factors affecting supply are introduced slowly, partly to avoid disruptions in service and partly because of inhibitions imposed by the regulatory agency itself. Moreover, being a monopoly, a utility need not concern itself with the prospect that while its own proposal is under consideration by the regulatory body, a similar proposal by a competitor will be approved.

In manufacturing, however, delay can prove fatal. Surprisingly rapid changes can and do occur in consumer preferences, technology, and the nature of the product itself. It is the very nature of competitive rivalry that one firm precedes its rivals in introducing a demand-expanding or cost-reducing innovation. If a request for approval of the change (or a price modification based thereon) is handled in the manner customary to regulatory bodies, the pioneering company and the consuming public will benefit only after an interminable delay—for delay is endemic to the regulatory process.

According to the Landis report on regulatory agencies,[35] 35 percent of 464 proceedings pending on June 30, 1959, before the Civil Aeronautics Board had been pending for more than 3 years. With its existing staff it would take the Federal Power Commission 13 years to clear up 2,313 producer rate cases pending as of July 1, 1960. In the case of the Interstate Commerce Commission contested proceedings were found to run from 18 to 36 months, while numerous proceedings before the Federal Communications Commission and the Maritime Board had been pending for more than 3 years. The report went on to say, "Numerous similar statistics can be gathered from other agencies, including individual instances when even 10 to 14 years have elapsed before a final determination has been made. They all corroborate the fact of interminable delay." [36]

The root of delay is the difficulty of resolving issues that are economic in character by a procedure originally designed to protect the rights of an individual citizen against a criminal charge. In most regulatory proceedings two assumptions are accepted implicitly: first, that a corporation, which may be of immense size, has the same rights as a natural person and, second, that answers to complex economic questions can be arrived at through adversary proceedings. There is something manifestly absurd in the spectacle of a lawyer representing a multi-million-dollar utility claiming for his client rights similar to those properly accorded a defendant in a murder trial. There is also something manifestly absurd in the idea that through the process of argument and counter-argument by opposing lawyers, a third lawyer (or group thereof) can arrive at sound economic judgments.

The ability of federal regulatory agencies "to get on with the job" suffered a serious setback with the passage in 1946 of the Administrative Procedures Act. The history of this important, and often overlooked, piece of legislation is described in the Landis report:

> At the outset, spurred on by an antagonism to the very powers exercised by the regulatory agencies, the bar as a whole sought to impose the strait-jackets of traditional judicial procedure on the agencies. They were countered by other forces which sought to retain the value of the administrative process but still advocated reforms that would assure fairness in the exercise of powers delegated to those agencies.

[35] James M. Landis, *Report on Regulatory Agencies to the President-Elect,* 1960.
[36] *Ibid.,* pp. 5–6.

Some eight years thereafter a compromise between these two opposing views was effected by the Administrative Procedures Act of 1946. That Act, however one may evaluate it, is far from a definitive solution of the problems with which it dealt. It has achieved some uniformity of procedure, some assurance of the application of fairer standards, *but with its emphasis on "judicialization" has made for delay in the handling of many matters before these agencies.*[37]

Confronted with the conflict between its duty to protect the legal and Constitutional requirements of due process on the one hand and the need for promptness and efficiency in carrying out statutory responsibilities on the other, Congress in passing the Act opted for the former. The results have been the overtrial of cases; the taking of repetitive testimony from endless processions of witnesses; the admission of vast bodies of irrelevant and redundant evidence; the presentation of voluminous exhibits; interminable quarrels over minor points of law; constant objections, arguments, and decisions on procedural matters; attempts at character assassination of government witnesses; wordy and cliché-ridden documents of all kinds expressed in the semantics peculiar to the particular agency involved—briefs, complaints, findings of fact, decisions, opinions, and the like—all absorbing numerous days of hearings and terminating in a transcript record of thousands of pages, which those outside the agency and the lawyers practicing before it rarely read and seldom understand. As Justice Black said of a decision by the Interstate Commerce Commission, "I am compelled to say that the Commission could have informed me just as well if it had written its so-called findings in ancient Sanskrit." [38]

Another heritage of the judicial process is the practice of excluding from consideration all matters not in the formal record of hearings. Inasmuch as the typical hearing record is made up almost exclusively of presentations by private interests with a monetary stake in the particular case at hand, questions of broader public interest are automatically excluded from consideration. The nature of the problem can be illustrated by proceedings involving railroad merger proposals before the Interstate Commerce Commission. There, decisions affecting directly the economic growth of communities, the adequacy of freight and passenger transit, and other issues of direct concern to the consumer are made solely on the basis of what evidence may find its way into a court-type record. Railroads petitioning for approval to merge are represented by highly paid, skilled lawyers, who pour into the cases thousands of pages of complicated testimony and exhibits. This evidence remains largely untested because other railroads capable of challenging the petitioners' cases either fail to appear or give only token opposition for fear of upsetting their own merger plans or disrupting the industry as a whole. Other participants, such as rail labor, states and municipalities, stockholders, and smaller railroads, have struggled to fill the void in these records, but their funds and manpower have been so limited and their efforts so disorganized that their presentations generally have not been effective. As a result, a special staff group from the Interstate Commerce Commission was moved to state in an official report that "no voice speaks before the Commission for the public as a whole in rail consolidation cases. Thus the question arises as to whether the Commission receives all of the evidence it

[37] *Ibid.*, p. 16. Emphasis added.
[38] *Chicago and Eastern Illinois Railroad Co., et al.* v. *United States, et al.*, 373 U.S. 150 (1963), at 154.

requires respecting the over-all public interest as differentiated from the various private interests." [39]

Faced with voluminous records but virtually no effective "public interest" presentation, the Commission at the last minute called into a few cases its enforcement lawyers. Largely unschooled in economics and merger issues, these counsel generally have remained silent during cross-examination and have presented little significant evidence. Although recognizing the problem, neither the ICC nor any of the other regulatory agencies has devised a workable means of injecting into its proceedings pointed and telling evidence concerning the probable effects of its own actions on the consuming public.

Industry orientation

Whatever influence is exerted on state regulatory commissions by utilities would be exceeded many times over by the pressures brought to bear on any federal agency saddled with the responsibility of controlling prices in large-scale industries such as steel, petroleum, or motor vehicles. Influence over existing federal regulatory bodies has at times been so conspicuous as to give rise to an intriguing theoretical explanation for the changes that take place in an agency's vigor and independence.[40] In its early days an agency, it is held, will tend to be aggressive and crusading. The act it was set up to enforce was probably passed as a result of arresting disclosures—usually by a congressional committee —which had excited the public's interest. Gradually, however, the agency matures. It becomes occupied more with form than with substance, turns more legalistic than dynamic, and grows to be concerned more with observing than with changing precedents. The support it had formerly enjoyed from Congress and the public erodes. Preservation of the agency—its staff, laws, and jurisdiction—and protection of the industry from change become its principal objectives. Gradually the power of the industry being regulated comes to be greater than the power of the regulatory agency; the regulated becomes the regulator.

The theory does not want for supporting case examples—nor for conspicuous exceptions. Some of the newer agencies, such as the Civil Aeronautics Board and the Oil Import Administration, have been industry-oriented from their very inception. Others, such as the Federal Power Commission and the Federal Communications Commission, enjoyed only a very short span of independence. In contrast, an old agency, the Federal Trade Commission, displayed remarkable rebirths of vigorous activity 15 and again 35 years after its creation.[41] Strong protectionist influences have periodically been rebuffed by another old agency, the U.S. Tariff Commission.

Industry orientation is due partly to a complex of rather prosaic occurrences—poor presidential appointments, inadequate funding (for which the Bureau of the Budget, *not* Congress, must bear primary responsibility), and the

---

[39] Bureau of Transport Economics and Statistics, Interstate Commerce Commission, *Railroad Consolidations and the Public Interest,* 1962, p. 1.

[40] See, e.g., Marver H. Bernstein, *Regulating Business by Independent Commission,* Princeton University Press, 1955, Ch. 3.

[41] The former witnessed the Commission's landmark investigations of the public-utility industry and chain stores, agricultural machinery, and motor vehicles; the latter, under the chairmanship of Robert E. Freer, witnessed the Commission's broad-scale attack on basing-point pricing systems, its investigations of cartels, particularly in the petroleum industry, and its reports on mergers and concentration.

pervasive influence, both in and on the agency, of skilled lobbyists and Washington law and public-relations firms. Nonetheless, evisceration appears to be inherent in the regulatory process itself. With regard to appointments, no President, besieged by foreign and domestic issues that he considers of far greater moment, is particularly anxious to send up for confirmation a nominee who is sure to "run into trouble" on Capitol Hill. Yet there is nothing that so destroys the vitality and dedication of an agency staff as a constant procession of appointees who are at worst industry apologists and at best mediocre and therefore uncontroversial. When an agency does finally draw the line on an issue, its chances for success are not too promising; the contest has become too unequal. On the one side are a few overworked lawyers and economists for the agency, unsupported by an indifferent and largely uninformed public; on the other are all the immense resources that regulated industry can bring to bear. Retained by the industry is a veritable army of lawyers, accounting firms, and economic consultants. Public-relations firms are engaged to drum up "grass-roots" campaigns and "condition" the public mind by planting propaganda in the form of slanted news stories, articles, and TV interviews. Lobbyists, whose cost can be deducted from corporate income taxes as a business expense, go about earning their compensation in myriad ways. Even where coercive tactics fail on a particular issue, the agency is not likely to forget its experience when contemplating a controversial action in the future.

In contrast, where the agency is "reasonable" in its approach the industry can be a powerful ally in getting appropriations, securing the passage of "helpful" legislation, and warding off the depredations of other expansion-minded government agencies. As the regulated and the regulator coalesce, the agency comes to look upon itself as the protector of the industry, suppressing new forms of competition, freezing obsolete methods of doing business, excluding new entrants, and perpetuating high-cost suppliers.[42] Through this symbiotic process the industry and the agency come to merge into one institutional complex.

The tendency of concentrated industries to use the agencies of government to protect themselves from "destructive competition" has become so endemic as to give rise to the question of whether some general principle may not be at work. Inasmuch as regulation usually brings immunity from the pressures of normal intraindustry competition, the resourcefulness and vigor of a regulated industry tend to atrophy. Therefore, confronted with some unexpected threat, such as competition from a new technology or a lower-cost source of supply, the industry obviously finds it easier to call upon its friendly government agency for protection than to try to compete in the market.

To deal with this problem of influence over the regulatory authority, two opposing approaches have been proposed. The first is to place the task of regulation in an "independent" body or commission. Independence is to be achieved by appointing commissioners for designated terms during which they cannot be removed by the President, by staggering the terms, and by maintaining among the commissioners some kind of settled balance between the two political parties. Certainly the commissions have displayed a greater degree of independence than would have been the case had the regulatory activities been carried out directly by administrators in the executive branch of government. At the same time, however, anything approaching true independence remains more

[42] See Ch. 15.

THE REGULATION OF PRICES

of an aspiration than a reality, owing to indirect controls maintained by the executive.

The most obvious form of control over the independent regulatory commissions is through the power of appointment—and, of equal importance, the power of reappointment. Either because he is interested in the agency's work, likes the job (and its not insubstantial salary), or is apprehensive about his chances in the uncertain world of private practice, it is a rare commissioner who ignores the probable reaction of the administration to his decisions and other activities. A less obvious but extremely effective form of indirect influence is control over funds. The amount of money the agency will receive is determined in the first instance by the Estimates Division of the Bureau of the Budget. Though often reduced, their recommendations are rarely exceeded by Congress. This control over purse strings is particularly effective with the truly dedicated commissioner who regards the agency's resources as hopelessly inadequate to the task at hand and who is consequently most reluctant to alienate those who control its funds. Through the Federal Reports Act the administration keeps control over the ability of the commission to obtain information necessary to carry out its duties. Through the control exercised by the Solicitor-General's Office the administration is able to control which adverse decisions by the lower courts shall be appealed to the Supreme Court and which shall be left standing. Because of these and other indirect controls, the shortcomings attributed by students of government to the independent commissions are due in good part to the fact that they have not been permitted to be independent enough.

The alternative approach is to place control over regulation high within the hierarchy of government. The higher the level, the greater the potentiality for reform, but also the shorter the route for influence, as was brought out in a colloquy between a political scientist, Robert Engler, and the Antitrust Subcommittee's chief economist. The issue was whether placing control over the oil industry in some high international body would make it even easier for the industry to gain control over government.

> DR. BLAIR: . . . You are urging "the setting up of an integrated policy for coordinating and planning energy and natural resource development." In point 6 you would create a "public planning agency." You would in point 9 "move toward world planning through international agreements on oil and, ultimately, international public agencies which will attempt to formulate international definitions of the public interest."
>
> Here it seems is something of an inconsistency. You are urging, as a remedy for the evils of excessive centralization, a still greater degree of centralization. What is your basis for even hoping that these larger public bodies, even these international bodies, will be immune from the very pressures and influences that you have so extensively delineated in your statement?
>
> DR. ENGLER: . . . I agree completely that, given my portrait of the present society and the neutralization of public government in this society, to talk about internationalism would merely give an official public blessing to this private government that I am describing. But it seems to me, if people are to tackle this industry and this problem of private power with something more than collecting trading stamps from the gas stations, they are going to have to respond to some alternative public policy.

I think you are in for a hell of a fight but it seems to me there is no fight until you formulate an alternative policy, and as I see oil, I think you have to formulate an international policy. I think this is true of all natural resources. I think it is increasingly true of the nature of industrial society.

DR. BLAIR: . . . The great problem when you are in the public service and dealing with an industry of the power and size of oil, is that whatever you try to do may well be overridden, frustrated, negated by some higher body. And, as a general principle, the higher the body, the greater the ease with which it can be influenced by the very interests that you at a lower level are striving to control.

Thus, it seems to me that what you are doing is proposing the setting up of a pyramid of supranational international bodies, which can lend themselves very readily to captive control and influence by the very forces you are decrying here.[43]

Improving corporate performance

As an alternative to the virtually insurmountable difficulties of utility-type regulation, proposals have from time to time been advanced that public policy be directed toward improving the economic performance of large enterprises. Implicit in such proposals is the acceptance of the large corporation as an economic fact of life, which is here to stay at least for the foreseeable future. But, while abandoning any thought of establishing formal controls over day-to-day corporate behavior, the state, it is held, could nonetheless establish socially desirable standards of corporate performance and promote their attainment through systems of rewards and penalties.

The first and only effort to apply standards of "social performance" to different industries was a study by Theodore J. Kreps published in 1940.[44] Its underlying economic thesis was that a corporation's justification should be found not in profit maximization but in contribution to the public good: "Any practice that restricts production, keeps up prices to consumers or keeps down wages and other forms of mass income is contrary to the charter under which business receives public protection and approval. The acid test of business is not the profit-and-loss statement but the social audit." [45] Kreps's "social audit" was based on a variety of statistical series. Indexes of industrial production "measure to a certain extent the amount of restraint on production." Price series reveal "the relative strength of industrial prices and the social cost or benefit of industrial price policies." Figures on value added by manufacture "measure the stream of funds available for apportionment (to labor and to the proprietorship account)." Series on dividend and interest payments "indicate in a general way the nature of business policies vis-à-vis stockholders and bondholders." [46]

Applying these and other statistical series to 22 industries for the period 1919–38, Kreps found widely different "patterns" of performance. Thus, there was what he referred to as the pattern of full employment: "It is one in which

[43] 91st Cong., 1st Sess., Senate Subcommittee on Antitrust and Monopoly, Senate Committee on the Judiciary, *Hearings on Governmental Intervention in the Market Mechanism: The Petroleum Industry,* 1969, Pt. 1, pp. 379–80.
[44] Theodore J. Kreps, *Measurement of the Social Performance of Business,* Monograph No. 7, Temporary National Economic Committee [TNEC], 1940.
[45] *Ibid.,* p. 2.
[46] *Ibid.,* p. 5.

production increases steadily; employment also increases but at a relatively lower rate, while consumer effort (the ratio of the industry's price series to the general price level) rises at a still lower rate or shows a gradual tendency downward." In contrast was the pattern of unemployment: "It is one in which the amount of consumer effort commanded rises steadily in relation to production while employment declines, not only relatively but in an absolute sense." Under a third pattern the payroll dollar becomes a steadily increasing percentage of the consumer dollar: "Industries with this pattern . . . increase the share of their disbursements going to labor. This contributes to the maintenance of a mass market and mass purchasing power." But in the fourth pattern dividends and interest rise while "the flow of funds going into payrolls dwindles relative to that collected from consumers' pocketbooks." [47]

What is significant about this work is not so much its findings or even its methodology (which is based on far more primitive data than are currently available) but rather its basic concepts: that the social performance of different industries differ widely and that the more desirable types of performance should be promoted. Either explicitly or implicitly this assumption has underlain the more specific performance proposals that have been put forward.

Federal incorporation

The idea that businesses engaged in interstate commerce—or at least the nation's largest corporations—should receive their charters from the federal government has been strongly advocated for many years, originally by Justice Brandeis and later by the chairman of the Temporary National Economic Committee, Senator O'Mahoney.[48] Indeed, this was the first recommendation of the TNEC, which in its *Final Report and Recommendations* stated:

> The principal instrument of the concentration of economic power and wealth has been the corporate charter with unlimited power—charters which afforded a detour around every principle of fiduciary responsibility: charters which permitted promoters and managers to use the property of others for their own enrichment to the detriment of the real owners; charters which made possible the violation of law without personal liability; charters which omitted every safeguard of individual and public welfare which common sense and experience alike have taught are necessary.[49]

The argument for federal incorporation rests upon the simple logic that the power of granting a firm the right to do business is lodged in the state; that any firm desiring to do business must secure that right in the form of a charter, franchise, or license; and that firms whose business operations far transcend the boundaries of a particular state should receive that right from the level of government having jurisdiction over interstate commerce. As a condition of granting the right, the federal government would require the enterprise to conform to certain requirements and standards. The principle that in granting a privilege society may impose the conditions on which it may be exercised is rooted in the common law and has been affirmed repeatedly by the courts. As Justice Bradley stated in

---

[47] *Ibid.*, pp. 109–11.
[48] See, e.g., 81st Cong., 1st Sess., S. 10, 1949. Bills to require federal incorporation, perennially introduced by Senator O'Mahoney, regularly bore the designation S. 10.
[49] 77th Cong., 1st Sess., S. Doc. 35, Temporary National Economic Committee, *Final Report and Recommendations*, 1941, p. 28.

the *Central Pacific* case: "A franchise is a right, privilege or power of public concern which ought not to be exercised by private individuals at their mere will or pleasure, but should be reserved for public control and administration, either by the government directly or by public agents acting under such conditions and regulations as the government may impose in the public interest and for the public security." [50] Yet because corporations are permitted to operate under extraordinarily permissive state charters, society has in effect granted a privilege without imposing any substantive conditions under which it may be exercised.

The chain of events that led to the transformation of the common-law safeguards into the unrecognizable stepchild of state incorporation acts began in 1846 with the passage of a law granting to corporations the right of limited liability. The next step was the legalization in 1890 of the holding company, which had been proscribed by the common law as well as by the early state statutes. New Jersey led the way by changing its laws to permit the holding by one corporation of the stock of other corporations. In 1899 Delaware revamped its corporation laws along similar lines. Since corporate charters, through filing fees and annual franchise payments, were a lucrative source of state revenue, other states soon followed suit.

The Delaware corporation laws have been described as "plentifully supplied with provisions which depart radically from the more straitlaced provisions of earlier State laws." [51] Any kind of stock may be issued, which may or may not carry voting powers. The stockholders need not receive the right to subscribe to similar new stock issues before they are offered to others. There is no transfer tax on the resale of securities. It is not necessary to own stock in a company to qualify as one of its directors. Charters may be approved which allow directors to issue new stock, change the terms of stock that has been authorized but not sold, retire preferred stock, and change the company's bylaws without obtaining the stockholders' consent.

The small state of Delaware thus creates and projects into national and international commerce giant corporations whose size far exceeds that of most of the states. Calling attention to this paradox, Senator O'Mahoney observed:

> The anomaly in our system is that we permit the States to create corporations which actually do things forbidden to the States by the Federal constitution. Then we have allowed ourselves to become so involved in legal metaphysics, that we listen with straight faces while brilliant lawyers and judges say that though Congress has the constitutional power to regulate interstate commerce and the States have no such power and indeed cannot constitutionally delay, hinder or impede such commerce, it would be unconstitutional for Congress to impose licenses upon the corporate agencies of the States which operate in the field assigned by the Constitution to the Federal government.[52]

It is true that each of the states has the legal power to regulate the activity within its borders of corporations incorporated in other states. But noting the operation of a sort of Gresham's Law in state regulatory activities, the Temporary National Economic Committee observed, "The right exists but has seldom been exercised. Indeed, in the nature of things it cannot be successfully exercised because so much business is essentially national in scope and the economic power

[50] *California* v. *Central Pacific Railroad Co.,* 127 U.S. 1 (1888), at 40.
[51] Harry L. Purdy, Martin L. Lindahl, William A. Carter, *Corporate Concentration and Public Policy,* Prentice-Hall, 1942, p. 48.
[52] Speech given over the Columbia Broadcasting System, Dec. 9, 1936.

of the corporations which carry it on is so great that individual States fear to place themselves at a possible disadvantage by imposing requirements which other States would not lay down." [53]

There is no lack of precedent for the issuance by the federal government of charters to private enterprise. In 1781 the Bank of the United States was given a charter by Congress. In 1816 the second Bank of the United States was incorporated by Congress. In 1819 the Supreme Court, under Chief Justice Marshall, upheld the validity of this charter as a proper exercise of the power of Congress to pass any law "necessary and proper" to carry out its powers. In 1864 Congress passed the National Bank Act, under which thousands of private banking corporations have been created. While these actions were taken under the power to control money, Congress in 1922 passed an act drafted by Senator Walsh for the incorporation of companies to engage in the China trade, which was passed in furtherance of the power to regulate foreign commerce—a power that is contained in the same clause of the Constitution as the authority to regulate interstate commerce. To the argument that a federal incorporation law would infringe upon rights reserved to the states, Senator O'Mahoney's prediction of 35 years ago would appear to have even greater force today: "Let Congress asserting its responsibility to the people, define commerce among the States in a Federal incorporation and licensing bill and I venture the prediction that the Supreme Court will not be found to be an obstacle to the march of social justice." [54]

By itself, federal incorporation is merely a legal instrument. The requirements imposed by the federal government as conditions for obtaining a charter could be as generous as those of the state of Delaware. The Temporary National Economic Committee recommended that among the possible conditions might be restrictions that would prohibit interlocking directorships, make corporation directors trustees in fact as well as in law, prevent business dealings by corporation officers and directors for their own personal profit with the corporations they manage, make corporation officers and directors civilly liable personally for violations of the antitrust laws that they themselves conceive and direct, clearly define the scope of subsidiary corporations, and standardize intercorporate financing.[55] But the TNEC also recognized that "other necessary reforms could be effected by a national charter law" which could certainly include obligations to conform to designated standards of economic performance relating to profitability, price behavior, rate of production, and so on. It is this possibility which, probably more than anything else, explains why this eminently reasonable proposal, though advocated for nearly three-quarters of a century, has never received any serious consideration in Congress.

Reorienting managerial incentives

Gardiner C. Means has recommended a recasting of the incentives motivating top management that would involve financial rewards for operating their corporations in accordance with certain standards of desirable economic performance.[56] The first step would be to repeal stock options. No longer would a principal induce-

---

[53] TNEC, *op. cit.*, p. 28.
[54] Speech, Dec. 9, 1936.
[55] TNEC, *op. cit.*, p. 29.
[56] 88th Cong., 1st Sess., Senate Subcommittee on Antitrust and Monopoly, Senate Committee on the Judiciary, *Administered Prices: A Compendium on Public Policy,* 1963, pp. 232–37. For a fuller exposition see Gardiner C. Means, *Pricing Power and the Public Interest,* Harper, 1962, Ch. 18.

ment for corporate managers be the enhancement of the company's stock value or even its overall profit rate; instead their rewards would be in accordance with their corporation's performance in the public interest. Specifically, Means would establish for tax purposes a new category of manufacturing enterprises "whose pricing power is found to be vested with substantial public interest." [57] These might be corporations with assets of, say, over a half-billion dollars. A corporation so designated would then have three options: (a) to remove itself from the category by breaking itself into smaller enterprises, no one of which would have substantial pricing power; (b) to stay in the new category but pay a heavy excess profits tax; or (c) to adopt a new pricing policy and performance bonus plan. Managers who adopted the third alternative would, as individuals, receive bonuses on which they would be granted "especially favorable income tax treatment." [58] In order to receive such treatment, they would have to adopt pricing policies yielding an average rate of return on capital commensurate with the competitive cost of capital. This would result in substantially lowering the profit rates of most of the large corporations subject to the act. The bonuses would be made for such purposes as "reducing costs, improving products and a variety of other items which now go into performance bonuses for management below the top level." [59] An economic-performance bonus system must meet canons of practice in measuring economic performance that would be developed by accountants, engineers, and economists. The task of translating these general canons into a performance bonus system for a particular company would be left to the management-engineering profession.

Obviously, the plan can be applied only to corporations in which there exists a clear-cut separation between ownership and control. Where ownership and financial groups are able to exert direct or indirect influence over management, managers will not long remain managers by sacrificing owners' dividends to their own rewards for desirable corporate performance.

While there is an elementary logic in seeking to improve corporate performance by rewarding those who determine what that performance will be, Means's proposal, as thus far developed, suffers from a lack of specificity as to both the nature of the general canons of performance and the means by which they would be translated into plans for individual companies. It is true, as Means points out, that bonus systems regularly are developed for the lower levels of management in which achievement is measured in terms of specific performance. But the achievement is usually one that would be debarred by the very nature of Means's proposal. Under most of the bonus systems currently in effect, lower-level officials are rewarded in accordance with their performance in carrying out functions that increase the profitability of their organizational unit. If the corporation's overall profit rate is held down to something approaching the competitive cost of capital, bonus systems based on increased profitability would of course be out of place.

Inducing higher production

A somewhat different bonus system was suggested by Frank J. Kottke, under which bonuses would go directly to the corporation itself, to be paid in accordance with the degree to which its production exceeded a specific rate of capacity:

[57] *Ibid.*, p. 232.
[58] *Ibid.*
[59] *Ibid.*, p. 233.

"Assume, for example, that with present price and promotional policies, estimated steel consumption will permit operations averaging 70% of capacity. The Government might pay each producer a bonus of $3 for every ton of steel ingot produced during a given year in excess of 70% of the company's rated capacity. For production in excess of 72% of the company's capacity, it would pay an additional bonus of $3, and so on . . . ." [60]

The bonuses would have to be high enough to induce at least some of the major producers to expand their output above what the market would absorb at the existing price. This they could do only by reducing prices, thereby breaking down uniform price structures: "the immediate objective . . . is to insure that suppliers would make higher profits by operating near capacity, even though it is necessary for them to reduce their prices to attract a large volume. The more basic objective is to make competition work . . . ." [61] The plan rests fundamentally upon the assumption that, granted adequate bonuses, at least some of the companies would pursue an independent course of action, sacrificing the interests of the industry as a whole to their own immediate gain. In addition to gaining the bonuses themselves, lower-cost producers in industries such as steel could increase their sales and income by simply refusing to go along with the leader's price increases.

As Kottke recognizes, his proposal inherently gives rise to a number of difficult technical problems. There is, for example, the perennial problem of measuring "capacity." Moreover, pegging the bonus payments to the operating rate means that payments would result not only from an increase in production but also from a decrease in capacity. If the operating rate at which bonus payments would begin were established during years of general economic stagnation, it would probably be set at a relatively low level; this in turn would yield excessive payments in a subsequent period of high economic activity. To meet this contingency, Kottke suggests raising the rate at which payment begins. But making the rate flexible would inevitably introduce into the plan the very pressures and influences that it seeks to avoid.

Inducing competitive pricing through regulation

Under a proposal advanced by Abba Lerner regulation would be used to impose on concentrated industries the price behavior of competitive industries. Drawing a distinction between what he refers to as "price control" and "price regulation," Lerner emphatically rejects the former, "i.e., a price so low that the amount available is insufficient to satisfy fully the demand by all the would-be buyers. At the controlled price there is therefore excess demand." [62] Incidentally, Lerner does not make it clear whether he would exempt from his criticism controls imposed during times of war or similar emergencies, when no matter how high the price, demand remains strong and supply cannot expand to "clear the market" because it is diverted to other objectives. In any event the establishment of a price below that which clears the market brings in its wake a host of undesirable consequences:

> This results in disorganized supply, waiting in line, tyranny of sellers over housewives and other buyers, selling under the counter, gray markets

[60] *Ibid.*, p. 190.
[61] *Ibid.*, p. 191.
[62] *Ibid.*, p. 209.

and black markets, evasion of and disrespect for the law, corruption and gangsterism, and finally, as a lesser evil, the installation of rationing with all its administrative burden, economic inefficiency and public inconvenience. The original sin from which all the evils stem and to which all the objections apply is the setting of a price below that which clears the market and the consequent creation of excess demand.

*   *   *

In fact price regulation is more properly seen as the opposite of price control. The function of a price is to clear the market. Price control is bad because it interferes with this function by attempting to establish a different and lower price which does not clear the market. Price regulation restores the function of price by adjusting the price so that it does clear the market at the optimum output. It interferes only with interferences, preventing the monopolists from fixing a price above that which would clear the market at the potential supply, which is the socially most desirable supply.[63]

Under Lerner's proposal wages, as a general principle, would be permitted to rise at a rate corresponding to the average rate of increase in national productivity.[64] The consideration governing price changes would be the operating rate, production as a percentage of capacity. When the operating rate is high, prices would be permitted to rise—both decreasing demand and increasing supply. Such price increases are to be permitted even though profits are already high. Conversely, when the operating rate is low, the government would require decreases in price until demand and thus production had risen to a high proportion of capacity. Such price reduction would be required even in the face of low or nonexistent profits:

> The full utilization of existing capacity may sometimes lead to inadequate profits, or even to losses, but that is the nature of the competitive profits and loss system. . . . The low profits or the losses are then performing their proper function of discouraging further investment in such industries.
> In other cases the prices that clear the market at full capacity output will yield very large profits. These large profits are then performing their proper function of encouraging further investment in such industries . . . just as the low profits form no excuse for monopolistic restriction of output so the high profits are no excuse for enforcing price reductions below the level which clears the market.[65]

Lerner recognizes that even though his proposal attempts to by-pass the issue of a "fair return" on investment, it is still not without problems. For one thing there is the matter of developing "generally acceptable criteria of capacity of different firms and industries";[66] this is a problem, incidentally, that has become increasingly important with the growth of product substitution and the increasing use of multipurpose facilities. Then there is the problem of "dealing with possible attempts by monopolistic industries to restrict the installation of capacity if they are prevented from restricting the utilization of existing capacity."[67] Another difficulty arises from the fact that the plan could provide buyers with a positive inducement to withhold purchases during periods of falling demand. During the

---

[63] *Ibid.*, pp. 209–10.
[64] Greater-than-average wage increases would be permitted wherever the labor market is tight, while less-than-average increases would be allowed wherever it is slack (*ibid.*, p. 208).
[65] Senate Subcommittee on Antitrust and Monopoly, *op. cit.*, p. 211.
[66] *Ibid.*, p. 209.
[67] *Ibid.*

Depression Alvin Hansen advanced the argument that price flexibility tends to aggravate an economic downswing, since buyers tend to withhold purchases in anticipation of still further price reductions. While the validity of this argument has never been established,[68] it would obviously become an important consideration if buyers knew as a fact that withholding their purchases (and thereby lowering the supplying industry's operating rate) would *automatically* bring about a further reduction in price as a result of government order. At what point would the process of deliberate withholding and successive government-ordered price reductions come to an end?

A further formidable objection is the Constitutional prohibition against confiscation, which would of course be most acute in industries with inelastic demand, such as steel. By the time the price had been reduced sufficiently to provide a stimulus to demand for those products of which steel is only one component, the steel producers could well be operating in the red. Complaints to the courts that such a requirement is unconstitutional would assuredly not be long in forthcoming. In the light of past judicial constructions, the complaints would undoubtedly be upheld, if indeed appropriate revisions in the law had not already been made by Congress.

Inducing competitive pricing through tax policy

A precedent for preempting those corporate profits that by some designated standard are deemed to be "excessive" is provided by the excess-profits tax of World War II. Earnings above a specified return on investment or greater than those earned during a base period had to be returned to the Treasury. The purpose of the excess-profits tax was to prevent corporations from profiteering through high prices made possible by war-induced excessive demand and by excessive prices on war contracts. The same principle can be applied to prevent corporations from profiteering through high prices made possible by the possession of substantial monopoly power.

While there can be no question of its workability, such a policy would, in itself, benefit the consumer only by lightening his tax burden. Its scope, however, could be broadened through a "forgiveness" feature under which the tax owed would be forgiven *to the extent that price reductions were made.* With such a feature the objective of the tax would be to return monopoly profits to the public either through tax revenue or lower prices at the corporation's discretion. Any corporation involved could obtain "forgiveness" of all or any part of the tax owed by the simple means of reducing the prices of its products in the following year. That is to say, if a corporation's proposed price reductions in the following year, as applied to its physical output in the taxable year, represented an amount equal to all of its monopoly profits tax, it would owe no tax and pay no tax. If its proposed price reductions, as applied to the physical output in the taxable year, represented an amount equal to part of its tax, its tax would be reduced by that amount. The corporation would have full discretion in determining whether it simply wanted to pay the tax or whether it wanted to obtain "forgiveness" through price reductions on all or any part of its output.

The monopoly profits net income on which the tax would be applied would be similar to the excess profits net income computed under the federal excess-profits

---

[68] Indeed, its validity is put into serious question by the existence of the inverse relationship during depressions between price and production declines. If the theory were valid, the least declines in production would not be found in industries with the greatest decreases in price (see Ch. 20).

Table 24-1

ILLUSTRATION OF OPERATION OF MONOPOLY PROFITS TAX

Product	1970 Units	1970 Price	1970 Sales	1971 Units	1971 Price	1971 Sales	Difference Due to Price Reductions, 1970–71
Product A	500,000	$10	$ 5,000,000	500,000	$ 9.50	$ 4,750,000	$250,000
Product B	300,000	15	4,500,000	300,000	14.50	4,350,000	150,000
Product C	200,000	20	4,000,000	200,000	19.50	3,900,000	100,000
Total	1,000,000		$13,500,000	1,000,000		$13,000,000	$500,000

tax of World War II, which was repealed by the Revenue Act of 1945. Against this net income there might be allowed (a) a specific exemption of $500,000 and (b) a credit of, say, 10 percent of the invested capital. To illustrate the manner in which the granting of "forgiveness" might operate, assume that a corporation had a monopoly profits tax in 1970 of $500,000 and sales of $12 million, which, let it be further assumed, represented the sale of a million units at $12 each. In computing the amount to be forgiven, it would be assumed that in 1971 the corporation would sell the same number of units as in 1970. Whether it actually sells a larger or a smaller number of units is immaterial, since the computation only determines the amount of "forgiveness" of a tax on income *that has already been earned.* In this example, the corporation can obtain complete "forgiveness" of its 1970 tax of $500,000 by reducing the prices of its products in 1971 by 50 cents per unit. A more complicated example, in which a corporation produces 3 different products and owes a monopoly profits tax for 1970 of $500,000, is illustrated in Table 24-1. In this case the corporation, by reducing the price in 1971 on each of its products by 50 cents, would achieve a savings, based on the number of units sold in 1970, of $500,000, or the entire amount of the monopoly profits tax due for 1970. Or it could achieve the same result by reducing the price of its $10 product by $1 or by any one of an almost infinite number of other combinations of price reductions. The same wide latitude of choices would be available if the corporation desired to obtain "forgiveness" on only part, rather than all, of its monopoly profits tax.

Such a monopoly profits tax would not only stimulate actual *reductions* in prices but help to break up noncompetitive pricing structures. The latter would flow from the uncertainties that the tax would inject into the minds of rival oligopolists. Without an agreement or understanding (which would remain unlawful under the antitrust laws), no oligopolist could have any assurance as to the option that would be elected by his rivals. The oligopolist who did not lower his prices but elected to pay the "excessive profits" to the government should have good cause for concern that one or more of his large competitors might *not* do likewise. Alternatively, if he assumed that they would elect the other option, to what extent would they reduce their prices and how would the reductions be distributed among their various products? Thus, from uncertainty would spring price competition, which in turn would impel the oligopolists to economize or lose out in the competitive struggle.

The administration of the tax could be made practically automatic, requiring no determination by the Internal Revenue Service as to what is a "reasonable" or "unreasonable" tax, profit, or price. The bases of determining the monopoly profits to which the tax applies should be explicitly set forth in the law itself. In enforcing the law, the only administrative functions to be performed by Internal Revenue would be those of (a) collecting the tax from those corporations that decided to pay it; (b) checking the arithmetic of those corporations that decided to take advantage of the price reduction "forgiveness" feature (i.e., checking the accuracy of the corporation's estimate of the amount to be yielded by its proposed price reductions as applied to its physical output in the taxable year); and (c) determining whether or not price reductions proposed in order to secure the "forgiveness" of the tax are actually put into effect.

The same objectives could be achieved by applying the "forgiveness" feature to a portion of the tax owed under the present corporate income tax—e.g., companies could obtain forgiveness through price reductions applied against output in the taxable year on that amount of tax owed that was represented by the difference between the current corporate tax rate of 50 percent and, say, a rate of 40 percent.[60] Such a proposal could readily be integrated into the present tax structure and also would obviate the necessity of determining the invested capital. The advantage of the excess-profits tax form is that it could more readily be limited to specified corporations—e.g., those above a certain size and/or primarily engaged in concentrated industries.

But like all forms of social control the tax forgiveness proposal is not without its drawbacks. Corporations would be provided with a powerful incentive, in the form of an excess-profits tax, to inflate their capital investment. In World War II corporations were given the alternative of using as their base their earnings during a specified past period, but the use of base periods inherently creates inequities among companies in different industries with different growth rates. The use of the excess-profits form would reduce greatly the administrative problems by confining its application to a few hundred corporations. If invested capital were used as the base, the Internal Revenue Service, moreover, could use as a benchmark the figures on capital investment filed by the affected corporations before the plan went into effect.

Another drawback is that the large conglomerate corporations would be furnished with a further means of destroying their smaller single-line competitors. Suppose it were assumed that the hypothetical company in the previous example had enjoyed substantial monopoly profits on products B and C but had encountered vigorous competition on product A. It could obtain complete forgiveness of its proposed tax by reducing the price of product A by 10 percent. Such a price reduction might bring the price level below the cost of production and thus force the single-line producers out of business. Various limitations could be put on the extent to which the tax "forgiveness" could be applied to a particular product or industry, while further restraints might be devised if profit figures were obtained on a divisional basis. But the greater the restraints upon the manufacturer's flexibility, the less automatic would be the plan's administration, and the more susceptible it would be to manipulation and arbitrary changes in the restraints themselves.

The regulation of prices: an evaluation

The disadvantages of the various forms of price regulation vary directly with the extent, stringency, and formality of the control involved. Any extended across-

[60] The author is indebted to Alfred E. Kahn for pointing this out.

the-board price (and presumably wage) freeze during peacetime would deprive the economy of a most useful instrument in bringing about better adjustments between supply and demand and a higher utilization of capacity; it would also be administratively unworkable. The necessity of making adjustments to selective controls would make them merely a transitory stage on the way to a more systematic form of regulation. For a more systematic form to be effective, workable solutions would have to be evolved for problems relating to both the level and trend of costs. Involved in the former are such questions as the propriety of including in an authorized price the costs of economic waste (e.g., annual model changes, excessive selling expenses, and so forth). With respect to trend, the problem is one of evolving methods of restraining cost increases, particularly the upward movement of labor costs.

These problems are in addition to those peculiar to utility-type regulation, which, if applied to manufacturing would range from the difficult to the insuperable. Determining capital investment would be difficult even on the basis of original costs, to say nothing of reproduction costs. Equally difficult would be securing agreement on a rate of return appropriate for industries with a lesser degree of monopoly protection and a greater degree of risk than the typical utility—a problem that would be aggravated by the differences in profit rate among industries and among oligopolists in the same industry. The existence of diversified product structures would make it impossible as a practical matter to translate an approved profit rate for the corporation into ceiling prices for its individual products. Where demand is elastic, the regulatory agency would be confronted with the very real possibility that the approval of a requested price increase might not only be self-defeating but contribute to an even greater lack of use of resources. The already serious problem of procedural delay would be magnified many times over, at a cost intolerable not only to the public but to the regulated companies themselves. And the problems of political influence and industry orientation would achieve entirely new dimensions if any serious effort were made to control the prices and profits of the real giants of the industrial economy.

As compared to price freezes and utility-type regulation, some of the proposals to improve corporate performance, discussed above, are at least not unworkable on their face. This is a type of approach that has received comparatively little attention in the past and should certainly be given the benefit of further study. If, like death, war, and taxes, regulation proves to be inevitable, the advantage of the performance approach over other forms of regulation is that it does not suffer from *all* of their disadvantages. Nonetheless, no form of regulation, even if it narrows the margin between costs and price, approaches a competitive free market in performing the additional functions of exerting a downward pressure on costs, stimulating invention and innovation, and allocating resources among industries. The desirability of any form of regulation can be said to be directly proportionate to its ability to emulate competition in achieving these other objectives.

The last and ultimate stage of governmental intervention in the economy is represented by government ownership of the means of production. The placing of industrial resources under state ownership has come about under a variety of circumstances. Most common is government ownership of an organization providing a function that, by its very nature, is both essential and unprofitable (e.g., postal service, railroads). Increasingly widespread among underdeveloped countries is the expropriation of a valuable natural resource (e.g., oil by Mexico or copper by Chile). Reflecting socialist ideology, "basic" industries in highly developed countries have been nationalized (e.g., the British steel industry). Finally, and most important, is government ownership of industry in the Communist world.

As Clair Wilcox has pointed out, there has been an "air of unreality" about discussions of the merits and demerits of state ownership: "In the writings of socialists, in the past, much was said concerning the shortcomings of private enterprise, but little or nothing concerning those of public enterprise. In the writings of socialism's critics, on the other hand, the inevitable failures of public enterprise were asserted, but little was offered in the way of proof." [1] Little is to be learned of course from the experience of subsidized exceptions, such as postal services. Nor is much to be learned from the history of expropriated natural resources; usually a state agency merely replaces the former private owners as a full-fledged (and often particularly avaricious) member of an existing international cartel. Something, of course, can be learned from the performance of nationalized industries in Western countries. But the broadest area for study is represented by the Communist countries, in which government ownership is not the exception but the ubiquitous rule.

Nationalized industries in Western countries

In the Western world the state may own and operate an enterprise directly or through a public corporation. Or through stock ownership, either a majority or substantial minority, the state may in effect be a "silent partner"—e.g., in petroleum in Great Britain, in automobiles in West Germany, in petroleum and aviation in France.

Inherent in state ownership are certain potential economies notably rationalization and lower capital costs: "When the [U.S.] government operated the rail-

[1] Clair Wilcox, *Public Policies Toward Business,* 3rd ed., Irwin, 1966, p. 555.

roads, during World War I, it eliminated competing trains and circuitous routes, pooled locomotives and cars, and required the common use of terminals and shops." With respect to capital costs, bonds issued by the government bear lower interest rates because the risks are underwritten by the taxpayer. Nonetheless, as Wilcox notes, this advantage is not without its limitations: "The capitalization of a public enterprise will be exclusively in bonds. As a result, its payments to its creditors must be as large in bad years as in good. Its capital cost, though low, will be inflexible. Its legal obligation, during a depression, may be heavier than that of a private firm." [2]

On the other hand, state ownership not only removes the downward pressure on costs that prevails under competition but presents opportunities for unnecessary cost enhancement not present even under monopoly capitalism. Government-owned enterprise may be called on by the party in power to assist with labor problems. In Wilcox's words: "They may be compelled to take in workers as a means of relieving unemployment. They may be required by the demands of political patronage, to discharge workers who are competent and well-trained in order to make room for those who are incompetent and untrained." [3] In purchasing their materials and supplies, government agencies are faced with restraints not encountered by any private buyer; an example is the Buy American Act, under which federal agencies are required to buy goods from domestic sources until their price exceeds that of imports plus tariff by more than a specified percentage. Political pressures may interfere with cost reductions in still other ways: "Removal of uneconomic locations or abandonment of unprofitable services are likely to be forestalled by pressure politics . . . . Public enterprises, being public, may often be governed by policies that do not make for economy." [4]

A fundamental problem peculiar to state ownership is how these and other diseconomies are ever to be eliminated. Removed is the discipline of bankruptcy, which imposes some measure of restraint on even the most firmly entrenched private monopoly. The new self-perpetuating managerial class, or "technocracy," that runs the state-owned enterprises seldom criticizes itself. Outsiders, such as members of legislative bodies, usually lack the technical expertise on which to base meaningful questions. Turning aside the uninformed critic is one of the easiest tasks of any well-trained bureaucrat. As *The Economist* observed, "Britain's industrial structure is now composed of a large number of private industries over which the state has considerable powers of control and a small number of public industries over which it has no control whatsoever." [5] Moreover, with the competitive market eliminated, against what yardstick or benchmark can the performance of a nationalized industry be evaluated? As Wilcox has put it, "With nationalization the yardstick of competition is abandoned and the market rendered ineffective as an arbiter of cost and price. There are no agreed criteria by which to judge success or failure, no way to tell how well an enterprise has done or how much better it might have done." [6]

Upon gaining power after World War II the Labor Party in Great Britain between 1946 and 1948 nationalized the gas and electrical utilities, railroads and trucking, the largest airline, the coal mines, the steel mills, as well as the Bank of England and radio. The steel industry was then denationalized by the succeeding Conservative government, only to be renationalized in 1964 when the Labor

[2] *Ibid.,* p. 558.
[3] *Ibid.*
[4] *Ibid.,* p. 559.
[5] *Economist,* May 19, 1956. Quoted in Wilcox, *op. cit.,* p. 573.
[6] Wilcox, *op. cit.,* p. 574.

Party returned to power. As Wilcox stresses, it is difficult to assess the effect of bringing these sectors under state ownership because so many other factors are at work: "There is no basis, in the evidence available, for asserting that greater efficiency is always to be attained by private versus public enterprise. Examples can be adduced to support a case for either side of the argument." Nonetheless, he goes on to state, "Observers of the performance of the nationalized industries in Britain, for instance, are inclined to agree that gas, electricity and road haulage have been well run and that railroads and coal mines have not. But this judgement would doubtless be passed on the performance of the same industries, under private enterprise, in the United States." [7]

In France the postwar nationalization program added to the industries already under state ownership (railroads and telephone) those gas and electric utilities still in private hands, the coal mines, an automobile manufacturer (Renault), and an airplane engine company. The government also increased its stock ownership of mixed companies in petroleum, chemicals, aviation, shipbuilding, and various communication media. In addition, it absorbed the Bank of France, the four largest commercial banks, and the 34 largest insurance companies. Nationalization was seen by its proponents as a means of transferring economic power from the capitalists to the workers, of promoting postwar economic reconstruction and, as in the case of Renault, of punishing wartime collaborators. Commenting on the performance of the nationalized sectors, John Sheahan observes:

> Nationalization and public ownership . . . turned out to be helpful in some cases and not in others, but in general to have much more modest consequences than anticipated. The managers of the new corporations owned by the government quickly began to act much like those of private corporations, trying to get rid of unprofitable activities, to insist on the need of adequate prices and profits for investment, and above all to resist governmental intrusion in their operations. They demonstrated fairly well that orientation toward profit remains an essential aspect of rational management even when there are no capitalists in the picture.[8]

As in Great Britain, the performance of the coal industry has been disappointing, but this is largely traceable to its high costs and the loss of markets to petroleum. Substantial subsidies have been required for electricity, gas, and the railroads, but this has been due to the refusal of the Ministry of Finance to permit rate increases in the interest of stabilizing the price level. According to Sheahan, "The railroad system runs much better than ours, which is perhaps faint praise but worth noting. On the other hand, the telephone system, under government ownership from its inception, works very poorly. . . . In the oil industry, the government firms have participated whole-heartedly in domestic cartel-type selling arrangements." [9] Renault has been a technologically progressive firm, pioneering the application of automatic transfer methods in French industry, but, in terms of profits, " Renault has not done as well as Peugeot." In general, public ownership in French industry "has been less revolutionary than one might expect. It has done some good; precisely the kind of good that more dynamic private industry could have done itself, but which French private industry sometimes did not do." [10]

[7] *Ibid.*, p. 557.
[8] John Sheahan, *An Introduction to the French Economy,* Charles E. Merrill, 1969, p. 26.
[9] *Ibid.*, pp. 27, 28.
[10] *Ibid.*, pp. 28, 29.

The size mystique in socialist ideology

In the Communist countries the economic performance of state-owned industry has been seriously injured by an almost religious adherence to Marx's beliefs concerning the nature of the relationship between size and efficiency. On this point he was explicit:

> The cheapness of commodities depends, *ceteris paribus,* on the productiveness of labor, and this again on the *scale of production.* Therefore the larger capitals beat the smaller.
>
>   *   *   *
>
> The *increased volume of industrial establishments* forms everywhere the point of departure for a more comprehensive organization of the cooperative labor of many, for a wider development of their material powers, that is, for the progressive transformation of isolated processes of production carried on in accustomed ways into socially combined and scientifically managed processes of production.[11]

Writing in 1916 Lenin elaborated on the theme of the progressive stages of capitalism. Citing statistical evidence from Germany and the United States, he observed, "The enormous growth of industry and the remarkably rapid process of concentration of production in ever larger enterprises represent one of the most characteristic features of capitalism." [12] As a result of the trend toward concentration, competition is replaced by understandings and agreements, so that

> at a certain stage of its development, concentration leads, so to speak, very close to monopoly. For a score or so of giant enterprises can easily arrive at an agreement, while on the other hand, the difficulties of competition and the tendency toward monopoly arise precisely from the large size of the enterprises. This transformation of competition into monopoly is one of the most important—if not the most important—phenomena of the newest capitalist economy . . . .[13]

But the result of the replacement of competition by monopoly capitalism is to be welcomed. "Competition is transformed into monopoly. The result is an immense progress toward the socialization of production. The production of technical invention and improvement, in particular, is becoming socialized." [14]

Convinced that concentration was the "highest" and most efficient form of economic organization, Lenin, upon achieving power, set about applying it to the Russian economy. Under a decree issued on August 9, 1921, enterprises engaged in the same "branch of production" were to be "concentrated" in what were known at that time as "unions" and later as "trusts." In the words of the late Leon M. Herman, senior specialist in Soviet economics of the Legislative Reference Service of the Library of Congress, "The formation of 'trusts' . . . proceeded apace in the major industries of the country. The enterprises of heavy industry, located largely in the south of Russia—coal, oil, steel—soon became 'the most thoroughly trustified and concentrated' branches of production. By the

[11] Karl Marx, *Capital,* Kerr, 1906, Vol. I, pp. 685–89. Emphasis added.
[12] V. I. Lenin, *Imperialism: The Highest Stage of Capitalism,* International Publishers, 1933, p. 17.
[13] *Ibid.,* p. 18.
[14] *Ibid.,* p. 24.

middle of 1922, the trust-building process was completed, pulling together a total of 421 trusts throughout the country's industry." [15]

Under Stalin, belief in the superiority of size degenerated into megalomania. The crucial decision on the projected capacity of the Magnitogorsk steel mill—a decision that is said to have set giantism in motion in other industries as well—was made, according to one of Stalin's closest associates, in the following manner: "Comrade Stalin asked us what is the size of the (latest) American plants, and was answered that large works in the U.S.A. produce 2.5 million tons of pig iron a year. Comrade Stalin said that such a plant must be constructed here, at first with a capacity of 2–2.5 million tons, which will then be expanded to four million tons. The party and the country decided to erect such a plant." [16]

With little consideration of their economic inefficiency or their bottleneck effects officials then began to vie with one another for the prestige of having the "world's largest projects." The result, in Herman's words, was an "unmanageable proliferation of giant industrial projects, an experience that forced them to recognize some of the diseconomies of scale. There were, for example, such 'super-giant' projects as 10 million-ton coal mines, which had to be quietly dropped." Growing political tensions between the U.S.S.R. and Germany during the mid-1930's produced "a visible degree of frustration among the leaders in Moscow who had been waiting in vain for the output of some of the ambitiously conceived industrial enterprises." These serious delays resulted in a decree, dated February 26, 1938, which ordered a "fight against gigantomania." Overambitious projects were denounced as leading to a needless prolongation of building schedules and the waste of critically scarce transportation facilities and building materials. Although the party leadership began to place specific ceilings on the scale of new projects, the effect of the new policy, according to Herman, was minimal; the imposition of ceilings "was ordered not so much in recognition of the existence of inefficiencies in these huge enterprises, but rather in response to acute immediate pressures for speeding up existing construction schedules in order to help prepare for the gathering storms of war."

After the war the situation, in Herman's words, "returned to normal." With the death of Stalin, however, Khrushchev endeavored to check the drive toward bigness for bigness' sake. As the principal speaker at ceremonies marking the completion of the gigantic new Kuibyshev power station on August 10, 1958, Khrushchev criticized the time and capital involved in building projects of such a scale: this was not the way, he declared, to meet the Soviet goal of "overtaking the United States in terms of over-all industrial output per capita within the shortest period of time." [17] In such a race, he reminded his audience, the important thing is to gain time and capital. He offered his own calculation that several smaller thermal stations with the same aggregate capacity could be built in a much shorter period of time, and with less capital outlay, than one hydroelectric station of equal capacity. If such smaller stations were built instead, he concluded, the state would benefit from having more capital for other industries as well as more power for use during the 7 years it took to build what Khrushchev called "the world's largest hydroelectric power station." [18]

[15] *Hearings on Economic Concentration*, Pt. 7A, Leon M. Herman, "The Cult of Bigness in Soviet Economic Planning," pp. 4346–48.

[16] G. K. Ordzhonikidze, *Selected Articles and Speeches* (in Russian), Moscow, 1945, pp. 276–77. Quoted by Herman in *Hearings on Economic Concentration*, Pt. 7A, p. 4350.

[17] Quoted by Herman in *Hearings on Economic Concentration*, Pt. 7A, p. 4351.

[18] Quoted in *ibid.*, p. 4351.

Table 25-1

AVERAGE SIZE OF INDUSTRIAL ENTERPRISE, BY COUNTRY

(Number of employees per enterprise)

Country	Industry as a Whole[a]	Machine Building and Metalworking	Clothing, Shoes, and Furs
U.S.S.R. (1963)	565	2,608	872
United States (1958)	48	74	45
Britain (1961)	45	193	83[b]
Federal Republic of Germany	83	139	56
France (1962)	18	23	10
Japan (1963)	17	69	35[b]

[a]All industry except powerplants.
[b]Enterprises with fewer than 10 employees excepted.

Source: Ya. Kvasha, "Concentration of Production and Small Scale Industry," *Voprosy ekonomiki*, May, 1967, pp. 26–31. Translated in *Hearings on Economic Concentration*, Pt. 7A, pp. 4358–62

Despite these reservations, however, still larger hydroelectric power stations were soon to follow: the station at Stalingrad, completed in 1961, had a capacity of 2.5 million kilowatts. In Herman's words, "The old penchant for extra-size industrial establishments remained in full force." Moreover, there appears to be no end in sight. Writing in 1967, Herman observed, "Soviet planners have recently approved new steel mills of 6 and 12 million ton capacity, and are now busy on a project advertised as 'the enterprise of the future,' namely a 24-million ton steel plant. Designers have also been busy working on cement works of 2.5 million ton capacity. The two latest power dams built in Siberia (at Bratsk and Krasnoyarsk) will have an installed capacity of 4.5 and 5.0 million kilowatts, respectively."

Nor, it would seem, did Stalin's search for economies of scale in agriculture yield better results. He was known to be especially attached to the "state farm" type of organization. With an average land area in 1966 of over 120,000 acres, these farms were much larger than the more prevalent collective farms. Here, too, the addiction to bigness on the part of Soviet officialdom could not be cured by negative practical experience. The state farms remained the preferred model of agricultural organization, not only for Stalin but for his successors as well, the number having risen, according to Herman, from 4,988 in 1950 to 12,196 in 1966.

Concentration under Communism

In carrying out the maxims of Marx and Lenin on size, the Soviet government has displayed a dedication verging on fanaticism, with the result that the Soviet economy has become the most concentrated in the world. The Soviet economist Ya. Kvasha compared the average size of industrial enterprise (in terms of average number of employees) in the Soviet Union with the average size in 5 other industrialized countries (see Table 25-1).[19] The size of the typical Soviet enterprise exceeds that of any other industrialized economy by many orders of mag-

[19] Ya. Kvasha, "Concentration of Production and Small Scale Industry," *Voprosy ekonomiki*, May, 1967, pp. 26–31. Translated in *Hearings on Economic Concentration*, Pt. 7A, pp. 4358–62.

Table 25-2

DISTRIBUTION OF INDUSTRIAL ENTERPRISES BY NUMBER OF EMPLOYEES IN U.S.S.R. AND CAPITALIST COUNTRIES

Enterprises and Employees	U.S.S.R.[a] 1963	United States[b] 1958	Britain[c] 1961	Federal Republic of Germany[b] 1963	France[d] 1962	Japan[e] 1963
Number of enterprises	41,226	334,400	195,161	102,162	272,944	563,327
Includes number of enterprises with payrolls (in percentage of total) of—						
Up to 10	4.1	54.3	71.8	43.4	80.4	73.9
11 to 50	11.3	30.4	12.0	32.6	13.9	21.1
51 to 100	14.4	6.9	8.5	10.1	2.6	2.8
101 to 500	45.8	7.0	6.2	11.2	2.6	1.9
501 to 1,000	12.7	.8	.9	1.6	0.3	.2
over 1,000	11.7	.6	.6	1.1	0.2	.1
Number of employees	23,302,000	16,126,000	8,738,000	8,450,000	5,112,000	9,728,000
Includes enterprises with payrolls (in percentage of total) of—						
Up to 10	.1	3.9	6.4	2.0	11.1	16.7
11 to 50	.7	14.1	7.2	9.4	17.5	26.1
51 to 100	1.9	9.9	11.6	8.6	10.0	11.2
101 to 500	19.8	30.2	29.2	28.2	28.4	21.7
501 to 1,000	15.7	12.2	13.3	13.0	11.0	7.8
over 1,000	61.8	29.7	32.3	38.8	22.0	16.5

[a]All industry except powerplants. The first group includes enterprises with payrolls of up to 16, the second of 16 to 50.
[b]Extracting and processing industries.
[c]Processing industry; the number employed in the groups of enterprises with payrolls of up to 10 and 11 to 50 has been calculated by the author.
[d]Extracting and processing industry. 230,735 enterprises without hired personnel were excluded.
[e]Processing industry.

Source: Ya. Kvasha, "Concentration of Production and Small Scale Industry," *Voprosy ekonomiki*, May, 1967, pp. 26–31. Translated in *Hearings on Economic Concentration*, Pt. 7A, pp. 4358–62

nitude. In Kvasha's words, "The average size, in terms of number of employees, of an industrial enterprise in the U.S.S.R. is 35 times greater than in the U.S.A. In the garment, leather footwear and fur industries it is nearly 20 times greater." [20]

In another table (Table 25-2) Kvasha presents for the same countries size distributions of the number of enterprises[21] and their payrolls. In the Soviet

[20] *Ibid.*
[21] The meaning of the term "enterprise," as used by Kvasha, is not clear. Apparently he is referring to what the Census Bureau in the United States refers to as "establishments." The total number of enterprises he cites for the United States is 334,300, which is stated to encompass "extracting and processing industry." In 1958 the total number of manufacturing establishments was just under 300,000 (298,182). An allowance for

Union, the largest size group (those with over 1,000 employees) accounted for 61.8 percent of the payrolls; in the other countries the proportions ranged from a high of 38.8 percent in West Germany to a low of 16.5 percent in Japan. In the U.S.S.R. the share held by the largest enterprises was more than twice that in the United States.[22]

On the basis of this same table Kvasha also discovered what he termed a general "rule of concentration": "With an increase in the size of enterprise, their number decreases." [23] In the United States, for example, enterprises with over 1,000 employees, representing .6 percent of the total number of enterprises, accounted for 29.7 percent of the payrolls. Thereafter, as the size decreases, the number rises; more than half the number of enterprises have 10 or fewer employees. But, he noted, the Soviet Union is an exception: after a medium-size category, the number of enterprises declines with decreasing size, the smallest size group accounting for less than 5 percent of the number of enterprises.

Moreover, concentration under Communism appears to be in the process of reaching even further heights. Russian enterprises with a gross product of over 10 million rubles increased their share of total industrial employees from one-third in 1960 to more than half in 1964 and their share of fixed capital from 51 percent to almost 60 percent.[24] Similarly, while industrial employment in Czechoslovakia increased from 2.268 million in 1960 to 2.476 million in 1965, the number of national enterprises declined from 1,509 to 1,236. During the same period the number of enterprises employing more than 2,500 workers grew steadily.[25]

As the signs of lagging economic performance have multiplied, Soviet economists have been permitted to inquire into some of the possible causes, one of which has been the possibility of excessive concentration.

> Ordained economic ideas are not easily modified or discarded in an authoritarian society like the Soviet Union. They neither die nor do they fade away. This is especially true in the case of ideas containing some kernel of validity such as, in this instance, the economies of scale in modern industrial production. However, in the present comprehensive effort being made in the USSR to discover the sources of inefficiencies in the domestic production system, Soviet economists have been granted a measure of freedom to criticize established practices.[26]

---

whatever he includes for "extracting" activity would raise the total to somewhere within the vicinity of Kvasha's total.

[22] Kvasha advances the hypothesis that this comparison understates the importance of small-scale production in Russia: "It is difficult to find any large enterprise, or institution, be it a metallurgy plant, confectionary factory or administrative institution that does not have a number of auxiliary, subsidiary and collateral production lines." (Kvasha, *op. cit.*) But insofar as the United States is concerned these secondary activities would not appear to vitiate the comparison, since such secondary activities are carried on by establishments that the Census Bureau classifies by the size of their major activity.

[23] Kvasha, *op. cit.*

[24] I. Pogosov, "Questions of the Economic Effectiveness in Concentrating Industrial Production," *Voprosy ekonomiki,* Jan., 1968, pp. 12–23. Translated in *Hearings on Economic Concentration,* Pt. 7A, pp. 4395–4404.

[25] *Hearings on Economic Concentration,* Pt. 7, pp. 3670–80, testimony of George Staller.

[26] Some of the results of this "measure of freedom" in the form of papers and articles by Soviet economists were obtained by the staff of the Senate Antitrust Subcommittee and translated by the Legislative Reference Service of the Library of Congress. Along with similar writings on concentration in countries outside the United States, they were published in an appendix volume, Pt. 7A, of the *Hearings on Economic Concentration.* Although the volume contains articles on concentration in additional Communist countries,

Size and efficiency

Studies of the relationship between size and efficiency in the U.S.S.R. tend to be biased in favor of the largest units since, being in the nature of chosen instruments, they have been deliberately equipped with newly designed and better manufactured machinery and staffed with more capable managers and engineers. Nonetheless, studies of several major Soviet industries by Western economists had shown that during the 1930's average unit costs increased directly with the size of plant.[27] According to a recent study by the Soviet economist I. S. Sachko, the equipping of smaller textile plants with better machinery results in a lower cost of production and an increase in labor productivity, but additions to scale, as such, appeared to make little difference: "Even a ten-fold increase in the scale of production (in light industry) tends to result in a reduction of only 2–3 percent in the cost of production." [28]

In February, 1967, the Institute of Economics of the U.S.S.R.'s Academy of Sciences held a conference on optimal sizes for enterprises.[29] R. S. Livshits reported that "in certain branches [of industry] (above all, in machine building) the largest enterprises have worse technical and economic indices than the smaller ones. This was established with calculations made on the basis of indices for labor productivity and capital yield which were measured by prime cost and the cost of processing, that is, by means of indices which are more precise than those which are customary in statistics . . . ." [30] In reporting on the conference N. Lelyukhina commented upon "shortcomings which are caused by excessive consolidation: the capacities of certain newly built or expanded enterprises do not correspond to the sizes of their raw material bases, to the manpower resources on hand, and to the demand for the output of these enterprises in their efficient marketing zones. In addition, difficulties frequently arise in mastering and operating very large enterprises and units, difficulties which are most often caused by the fact that the real conditions of their work do not correspond to the planned conditions." [31]

Somewhat belatedly, Soviet economists have come to recognize the decentralizing potential of modern technology: thus, L. Ya. Berri pointed out, "The development of technology brings about an appreciable change in the power base of industry . . . . For example, in contrast to steam engines, electric engines not only do not compel production concentration, but, on the contrary, create a technical base for the economically efficient work of smaller enterprises, etc." [32] In a later article, I. Pogosov has shown that although the large plants are better equipped, they make poorer use of their equipment than small plants.[33]

---

the analysis presented in this chapter is based largely on the writings of Soviet economists and of the Czechoslovakian economists associated with the Dubchek regime, as well as on the testimony of Western economists specializing on Communist economies (Joel B. Dirlam, Norton Dodge, John Montias, and George Staller).

[27] Leon Smolinski, "The Scale of Soviet Industrial Establishments," *American Economic Review,* May, 1962, pp. 138–48.

[28] I. S. Sachko, *Concentration of Production in Industry* (in Russian), Moscow, 1968, p. 90. Quoted by Herman in *Hearings on Economic Concentration,* Pt. 7A, p. 4355.

[29] N. Lelyukhina, "Optimal Sizes for Enterprises," *Voprosy ekonomiki,* June, 1967, pp. 149–52. Translated in *Hearings on Economic Concentration,* Pt. 7A, pp. 4362–66.

[30] Cited in *ibid.*

[31] Lelyukhina, *op. cit.*

[32] Cited in *ibid.*

[33] Pogosov, *op. cit.*

Table 25-3

OUTPUT PER RUBLE OF FIXED CAPITAL
INVESTMENT IN U.S.S.R.

By size of enterprise[a]

Value of Fixed Industrial Productive Capital in Thousands of Rubles	All Industry	Machine Building
100 and less	100%	100
101 to 200	80	100
201 to 500	60	100
501 to 3,000	40	90
3,001 to 10,000	30	80
10,001 to 50,000	20	60
Above 50,000	10	53
All enterprises	30	63

[a]Smallest size group equals 100.

Source: I. Pogosov, "Questions of the Economic Effectiveness in Concentrating Industrial Production," *Voprosy ekonomiki*, Jan., 1968, pp. 12–23. Translated in *Hearing on Economic Concentration*, Pt. 7A, pp. 4395–4404

Electricity available to labor in the largest enterprises was found to be over twice that of industry as a whole; for the smallest size groups it was only one-fifth the industry average. The amount of capital available to labor in the largest enterprises, as shown in Table 25-3, was nearly one and one-half times that of the industry average; for the smallest size groups it was below the industry average: "The data given show the higher technical equipping of labor at the large enterprises." [34] The efficiency of the use of equipment is measured by "gross product" per ruble of "fixed industrial-productive capital." Size distributions are shown both for all industries and for machine building. For industry as a whole, as well as for machine building, output in terms of amount of invested resources was found to be "significantly less" for larger than for smaller size groups. Pogosov warns against the use of conventional comparisons based on monetary measures of output: "At the technically fully outfitted enterprises, costs, as a rule, are high and respectively prices are higher and this creates the illusion of higher labor and equipment productivity." [35]

At the same time that Communist economists have been discovering the diseconomies of size, they have also become aware of the positive advantages of small enterprise. Kvasha has been quite outspoken:

> It is a mistake to assume that small enterprises are an unavoidable evil or alien appendages of the socialist economy. Such an appraisal of small- or even medium-sized enterprises would in practice degenerate into megalomania, which would lead to extremely unfavorable consequences for the development of the national economy and the progress of technology. Moreover, small and medium enterprises, with their simpler equipment and organization, with the shorter periods required for their construction and their smaller fixed assets, play an indispensable role

[34] *Ibid.*
[35] *Ibid.*

in the national economy. . . . The fact that the equipment of small enterprises is fundamentally different from that of large ones does not mean that it is necessarily stagnant and archaic. Here electrification has transformed the methods of production.[36]

In a paper written shortly before the Soviet occupation of his country, Ota Sik, the chief architect of Czechoslovakia's short-lived economic reforms, sharply criticized the preceding regime for its virtually complete rejection of small enterprise: "We have always tried to be more Catholic than the Pope. We had to nationalize everything, down to the last cobbler: only then did we feel really socialist." [37] But under the new economic reforms the growth of "small and medium-size enterprises" would be encouraged: "If for example ten people decide to get together and they have a good idea of how to fill a certain gap in our output, or how to reach certain objectives, it is our duty to subsidize their incentive, to give them easy credit, to allow for tax deductions, etc. In other words, we have to do precisely the opposite of what has been the practice up to now." [38]

None of the Soviet economists suggested that the determination of plant size be left to impersonal market forces. There is no inference that the force of competition should be permitted to eliminate those enterprises which, either because they are too small or too large, have costs above the price necessary to call forth the supply needed to meet the demand. Instead the emphasis is on merely correcting an error in planning. Thus, at the 1967 conference a permanently operating commission was established at the Institute of Economics to work on "methods for determining optimal enterprise sizes in USSR industry that take account of branch and regional characteristics." [39] That the economists have not been completely successful in correcting the error is suggested by an announcement in 1971 that Russia planned to construct the biggest truck plant in the world. In 1968 I. S. Sachko observed that "most designers of projects for the future perceive the new enterprises as giant-factories with an output capacity running tens of times greater than present-day large enterprises." [40]

Sources of diseconomies

Although the measure of freedom granted the Soviet economists has extended to identifying specific sources of diseconomies, they refer only obliquely to what must certainly be one of the principal sources—the stifling effects of an over-inflated bureaucracy. Yet there is no logical reason why the inefficiencies inherent in all hierarchies[41] should not also be present in the organizational structures of the Soviet Union. Certainly Ota Sik left no room for doubt concerning the importance of this factor in Czechoslovakia:

> Ministries are the highest management organs of their production sectors for which they are responsible. Therefore, their interest lies in defending and promoting their narrow production goals, attaining the

[36] Kvasha, op. cit.
[37] Hearings on Economic Concentration, Pt. 7A, Ota Sik, "On the Economic Problems in Czechoslovakia," pp. 4509–30.
[38] Ibid.
[39] Lelyukhina, op. cit.
[40] Sachko, op. cit., p. 181. Quoted by Herman in Hearings on Economic Concentration, Pt. 7A, p. 4356.
[41] See Ch. 7.

highest possible investments, manpower, the lowest possible delivery quotas, highest economic premiums, surcharges, and possibly even prices. It acts therefore as the worst possible monopolist. This is not a problem of individuals, or of changes in operating methods within these ministries, it is the question of liquidating these ministries. . . . We believe, that we do not need production ministries at all. . . . The problem is to liquidate the enormous and over-inflated administrative apparatus.[42]

Associated with both the size of projects and the time-consuming nature of organizational processing have been the diseconomies resulting from delays in completion. The Western economist Leon Smolinski pointed out that during the 1930's 10 small 100,000-ton coal mines could be built in 15 months; a large million-ton mine took 10 years to construct and required an additional "shake-down" period of several years: "These unexpectedly long gestation delays ran contrary to the planners' time preference and to their very concept of industrialization which was conceived as a battle against time, on the premise of an imminent armed conflict with the capitalist world." [43] That the situation has not materially improved is suggested by a tabulation presented by Pogosov: "of the 500 installations completed prior to 1 January 1965 and which had not reached designed capacity in 1965, there were 177 installations which were completed even before 1963." [44]

In addition to occasioning interminable delays, the addiction to giantism also created bottlenecks whose effects "rippled out" to other areas. According to Smolinski, "The new large plants raised demand per unit of output for factors that were in desperately short supply: capital in general and imported capital goods in particular; skilled and highly skilled labor; top-notch management; highly processed and regularly supplied raw materials; social overhead; and, last but not least, transportation." [45]

In a country of the geographic dimensions of the U.S.S.R., transport costs frequently constitute an important proportion of the delivered price. In the words of one Soviet economist, "In no country in the world is there such a constant battle with space." [46] Yet, as Leon Herman observed, "By following their ideological bias in favor of giant plants, Soviet planners have managed to make the outcome of this battle more uncertain." As expressed by L. Ya. Berri, the reason is in the nature of a principle:

optimalness cannot be determined by means of the usual methods of calculating the relative economic efficiency of capital investments, since with these methods the amounts of production are taken as given and output costs are determined at the place of production without consideration of the transport expenditures involved in delivering output to consumers. *Yet, as enterprises are enlarged, these expenditures increase as a consequence of an expansion of the radius for the sale of their output.*[47]

When, as, and if it embarks on large-scale automobile production, the Soviet Union, like the elder Henry Ford in the 1920's, will be confronted with a "mo-

[42] Sik, *op. cit.*
[43] Smolinski, *op. cit.*
[44] Pogosov, *op. cit.*
[45] Smolinski, *op. cit.*
[46] A. B. Markin, *Soviet Electric Power: Development and Prospects* (in Russian), Moscow, 1956, p. 67. Quoted by Herman in *Hearings on Economic Concentration*, Pt. 7A, p. 4356.
[47] Cited in Lelyukhina, *op. cit.*

ment of truth." Demand for automobiles from such remote areas as eastern Siberia and the Far East is expected to reach 270,000 cars per year. The Soviet government, in Herman's words, will then "have to face up to the need of deconcentrating the giant auto- and truck-producing enterprises that have been built up over the years in the center of the land." Even before the completion of River Rouge, then the world's largest plant, Ford had begun to recognize the savings inherent in decentralization and had started to construct branch assembly plants throughout the country.[48]

In Part II of this work the point was made that large corporations do not appear to be a particularly fertile source for the creation, or even the development, of new products and processes. If this is true in the United States, it should be even more true of the even more concentrated economy of the U.S.S.R. And, according to an unpublished report of the Organization for Economic Cooperation and Development, such appears to be the case.[49] Although the 750-page report was not issued to the public, its general nature and principal findings have been summarized by *The Economist*.[50]

Russia's relatively poor technological performance (outside a few fields such as space exploration) is not to be explained by a shortage of trained manpower. In the words of *The Economist*, "The Russians are, after all, training a quite staggering number of scientists and engineers; half of the students coming out of the universities have qualified as either the one or the other, making the number of young qualified graduates coming out each year substantially higher than it is in the United States . . . . Whatever else they lack, those Soviet scientists are not short of money." Yet, training and money, by themselves, do not appear to be enough: "The Russians themselves estimate that the productivity of their researchers is only about half the Americans' and that innovations take two or three times as long to put into effect." [51] Among the areas of lagging technological progress, the OECD report cites electronics, engineering, atomic energy, computer-controlled machine tools, and iron and steel. But the biggest failures appear to have been the lag in the development of a modern chemical industry, energy policies that for many years "tied the country to coal rather than oil," and transportation policies "that were based on steam locomotives rather than diesels." [52] In each case the problem seems to have been the reluctance of Soviet planners to scrap an old technology, with which they were familiar, in favor of a new technology, of which they were largely ignorant. In the absence of market forces compelling their adoption, these new technologies were not accepted until long after they had been adopted in the West.

A similar reluctance to venture into the unknown was present in Czechoslovakia. According to Sik, "We failed to create many needed modern industries which are now, in the world, the basis for the realization of the scientific-technological revolution. These are, especially, the areas of chemistry, electronics, instrument technology, etc., in which our country is far behind. This is understandable, because we used all our investments and labor force in heavy industry, heavy metallurgy, heavy machinery, etc." [53]

---

[48] See Ch. 5.
[49] Paris, Organization for Economic Cooperation and Development (OECD), *Science Policy in the U.S.S.R.*
[50] *Economist*, Feb. 8, 1969. The article, entitled "The Technological Gap—in Russia," is included in *Hearings on Economic Concentration*, Pt. 7A, pp. 4507–09.
[51] *Economist*, Feb. 8, 1969.
[52] *Ibid.*
[53] Sik, *op. cit.*

The OECD report, according to *The Economist,* stresses the absence of incentives for innovation: "If a factory manager's success is measured by his volume of output, and if his worker's wage bonuses depend on exceeding a certain rate of output, he is going to object to any form of re-tooling that is going to interfere with production." [54] The same point is made by R. W. Davies in his historical study, "Science and the Soviet Economy":

> if any major change were made in the pattern of output or in the production process it would disrupt the flow of production and endanger the success of the plan on which the earnings of the workers and the bonuses and promotion projects of the managerial staff depended. Consequently, factory managements naturally tended to resent innovations proposed by research organizations, and hoped not to be entrusted with developing industrial prototypes for design bureaux or with bringing industrial prototypes into batch production: the dissemination of developed innovations in industry at large was also inhibited. . . . According to Academician Kapitsa just before the war, the Soviet economic cabinet instructed a factory to develop his process for producing liquid oxygen, but in spite of this powerful backing, and in spite of the interest shown by the engineers at the factory and even by its management, the work did not progress:
>
> "They recognized the value and interest of the new process, but could not find time for it. They were tied up with routine work and above all with carrying out the basic plan of the factory. Our apparatus required a lot of effort and interfered with carrying out the plan; but production was on a small scale and hardly appeared in the annual record of the factory." [55]

From these and other writings the picture thus emerges of a more than sufficient supply of adequately trained scientists and engineers who spend their time in autonomous research institutes, with little chance that their innovative ideas will be adopted by unsympathetic managers. Their plight is not entirely unlike that of inventors—whether independently engaged or employed by large firms—in Western countries. There are, however, three important differences. In the West the number of possible users is likely to be larger; freedom to approach them is unquestionably greater; and, as Davies has pointed out, the chances are better that the inventor will find support from allies within the enterprise: "in Western firms working for the market the application of innovations in production is often assisted by pressure from the marketing department, which cooperates with the research department to overcome the resistance of the production manager." [56]

The Communist planners have made an important contribution to inefficiency in still another way: they have contrived to channel resources into industries in which capacity is already excessive and away from those in which demand exceeds supply. Like the addiction to bigness, this remarkable achievement is the result of another *idée fixe* stemming from nineteenth-century technology—the belief in the overriding importance of "heavy industry." Decrying the fact that Czechoslovakia has been putting as much as "65 percent of . . . investments in heavy industry," Sik observed:

[54] *Economist,* Feb, 8, 1969.
[55] R. W. Davies, "Science and the Soviet Economy," Lecture given at the University of Birmingham, England, Jan. 18, 1967. Included in *Hearings on Economic Concentration,* Pt. 7A, pp. 4332–45.
[56] *Ibid.*

STATE OWNERSHIP

What Lenin mentioned as a theoretical possibility has, alas, been realized under Socialism. Indeed, we created a production for production's sake.

We had the idea that, first of all, we must secure the growth of heavy industry, especially machine industry. Yet the more we expanded big machine-manufacturing enterprises, especially of heavy machinery, the more we felt the need for metallurgical production. Therefore, we built iron works and opened new mines. In turn, we needed more heavy machinery for these branches of industry and had to expand their production. Heavy machinery, again, required additional metal works which we had to further expand. In this way, machine industry and metal works mutually added to their output.

Balance-wise everything was in order. On the balance sheet we simply balanced the growing demand against growing resources. Growing resources caused the growth of the demand. Thus everything was balanced. However, there was a shortage of the necessary final products, or the required quantity of consumer's goods and services. Thus the true objective of our production was not achieved.[57]

The overemphasis on traditional industries has led to the neglect not only of the newer, science-based industries (e.g., chemicals, plastics, synthetic fabrics, electronics) but to other fields in which, paradoxically, Czechoslovakia has a "raw material basis":

Industrial branches producing commodities for which the demand in the world was growing much faster than for others, were declining. This pertains especially to china, glass, wood-working, and other industries. Many consumer goods industries are now in real disastrous conditions. We failed to build with the purpose of increasing the capacity of our wood-working industry. The result of it was that, today, there exist in Europe only two countries which export lumber. They are the Soviet Union and Czechoslavakia. At the same time, all other capitalist countries and many other countries much richer in timber than Czechoslavakia are taking it from us. It pays for them to manufacture cellulose, paper, furniture, etc. while our country does not have adequate manufacturing capacity to utilize our own timber treasures.[58]

The improper allocation of resources has extended to human labor. On the one hand, the predilection in the U.S.S.R. for a few big plants has naturally led to the centralization of output in a few major industrial centers. It is in these cities that the problems of overcrowding, housing shortages, and the like are acute. At the same time a considerable proportion of the urban populace residing in small towns is simply unused. Because of the planners' antipathy to small plants, they have no place in which to work; because of overcrowding in the large metropolitan centers, they are forbidden to migrate. In Herman's words:

Soviet figures show that *about half of the urban population* continues to live in cities of less than 100,000 inhabitants. There are about 1600 of these towns in number, out of a total of 1800 urban communities. Yet, they seem to have been virtually by-passed by the dynamics of the industrialization process in the USSR. The large cities are getting steadily larger, despite all official efforts to limit their size, while the small and medium towns are becoming relatively smaller as well as more backward. Employment opportunities in these communities are extremely

[57] Sik, *op. cit.*
[58] *Ibid.*

limited, with the result that a high percentage of the able-bodied population is compelled to engage in two of the most despised occupations in the Soviet economic lexicon, namely housework and private plot cultivation. Apart from the lack of jobs, however, living conditions in these towns are described as quite pleasant, sanitary facilities are favorable, and above all, the cost of providing the necessary housing for new industrial workers is regarded as minimal.[59]

Extensive versus intensive growth

The argument can be made that the overconcentration of production is not inherent in state ownership but, as it developed in Russia and eastern Europe, was more or less in the nature of an historical accident. Had Marx and Lenin not been so convinced of the superiority of size (of which nineteenth-century technology provided many examples), and had later Communist leaders not been so determined "to be more Catholic than the Pope," the structure of Communist industry would be far less concentrated and the shortcomings of state ownership less apparent. But even in the absence of what has proved to be a remarkable case of "ideological determinism," there are still grounds for questioning whether state ownership can operate with any real measure of success, at least after a country emerges from the stage of "extensive growth" into that of "intensive growth." The former has been characterized by John Montias as "a rapid expansion of industrial output accomplished by dint of massive injections of labor and capital, using mainly established techniques," whereas the latter is based on "technical progress, improved organization, product development and new combinations of inputs capable of yielding increases in output with only moderate net additions to total input." [60] The less the industrialization of a country, the longer will be the period of extensive growth. In a country such as China it may be expected to last for many years. In Czechoslovakia, which has long had a strong industrial base, its duration was short. In Sik's words:

> During the early years, our national income grew fast because, as we know, we were in a position to expand the production with very simple, so-called extensive, means. It sufficed to reach for the accumulated resources or even remissions of all the existing enterprises and, out of these resources, build new plants. There we could employ new labor forces. Each new factory contributed to the growth of production and during the early years to the fast growth of the consumption by the citizens.
>
> Very soon, the extensive sources of the growth of our national economy were exhausted. Nearly all young people left farming. At a certain period even labor reserves among women in households became very low. And among the nations of the world, we belong to those with the greatest employment of women. As we exhausted the reserves of the simple extensive expansion of the production, other sources of the production growth were found not adequately prepared. We did not create preconditions required for continuous modernization of the factories, and for the reconstruction of the production process. As time went on,

---

[59] Emphasis added.
[60] *Hearings on Economic Concentration*, Pt. 7, pp. 3785–92, testimony of John Montias.

the production went on more and more within a structural setup that was quite unsuitable and ineffective.[61]

The central purpose of the economic reforms under the Dubchek regime was to achieve a better articulation of supply with a more complex pattern of demand. Although with the Soviet invasion the reforms died aborning, the same underlying conditions that gave rise to them had also been developing in the U.S.S.R. and the other Communist countries. As the Soviet Union moved from extensive to intensive growth the techniques of planning and control developed during the former were found to be not only unworkable but counterproductive. Their shortcomings have been described by Norton Dodge:

> Following the reconstruction period after World War II, the Soviet Union entered a more complex phase of development. By the late 1950's, the larger number of enterprises, the wider assortment of products, and the greater sophistication of consumer tastes and technology greatly increased the intricacy of the interrelationships among enterprises and consequently the difficulties of planning The old methods of highly centralized economic planning and administrative control were found to be increasingly clumsy and inefficient in meeting the requirements of the new circumstances. Primitive methods of planning which placed heavy reliance on crude physical indicators and irrational prices were poorly adapted for sophisticated decisionmaking and resulted in poor articulation of supply and demand. Such difficulties were further compounded by political interference at all levels and the persistence of a dogmatic approach in dealing with matters such as pricing. Furthermore, it became apparent that the system of incentives motivating managers and specialists was failing to produce the required results. At a time of rapidly shifting technology and consumer tastes the old incentives often discouraged rather than encouraged improvements in quality and design, the introduction of new products, and technological advance generally.
>
> The problem of impaired or misplaced incentives became particularly evident in the consumer sector. With more discretionary spending available in recent years, consumers began to pick and choose rather than to purchase anything found on the shelves regardless of quality or style. Inventories of unwanted consumer goods began piling up in embarrassing quantities.[62]

Unpredictability in supply and demand

In any type of controlled economy the essential problem faced by planners is the unpredictability of technology on the supply side and of consumer preferences on the demand side. If there is one lesson to be learned from the history of invention, it is that the course of technological progress is episodic, volatile, and unpredictable.[63] That the U.S.S.R. is so far behind in such areas as chemicals, plastics, synthetics, photocopying, and electronics is traceable largely to the fact that its planners did not, and could not, anticipate the discoveries and breakthroughs that unleashed their explosive growth. Even after a discovery has been

[61] Sik, *op. cit.*
[62] *Hearings on Economic Concentration*, Pt. 7, pp. 3739–57, testimony of Norton Dodge.
[63] See Chs. 9, 10.

made, it would be a daring planner who risked any substantial investment on a new product or process in which serious "bugs" might later develop. For the planner the incentives are all with sticking to what is tried and true and avoiding what is novel and unproven. As is true for his Western counterpart, the manager of a large corporation, the planner will bear the responsibility for failure, while any credit for success will probably attach to his superiors.

On the demand side unpredictability stems from the impossibility of either predicting or measuring consumer preferences. Long stressed by marginal-utility theorists, the law of diminishing utility can safely be ignored during the stage of external growth. As long as the central objective is simply to provide minimal levels of the absolute essentials, demand can be forecast with tolerable accuracy (the per capita requirements for food, clothing, housing, and other essentials times the expected population). It is after the economic system has been able to meet those minimal needs and provide in addition some discretionary income that demand tends to become unpredictable. In Emil Kauder's words,

> As Socialist economies begin to offer something more than a subsistence standard of living, as the consumer not only has a coat but a choice of coats and indeed discretion as to whether he wants a second coat or a radio or indeed prefers to put that money into saving toward the purchase of a TV set or an automobile, consumer wants can no longer be ignored. Centralized planning can no longer be concerned almost exclusively with costs and output.[64]

To illustrate the point that "utilities can be scaled, not quantified," Kauder drew an analogy between the scaling of utilities and the scientific method of determining hardness: "Moh's scale indicates the hardness of a mineral in comparison with other minerals. We can measure neither hardness nor utility, but only weight, distances and volumes. Scaling is only possible because equal units of the same good bring generally a decreasing amount of satisfaction." The fact that successive units of any given product provide progressively less satisfaction is of little value to planners as long as the consumption of a certain number of units of one product cannot be said to be equivalent to that of a certain number of units of another product. The problem is compounded by the fact that the declining scale of preferences for successive units of a given product does not proceed in a smooth, progressive manner. As Kauder has observed, "The line of advance toward the lower ranks of utility is unequally pushed forward on account of the discontinuous character of many needs; for instance the unit of needs for living quarters is one room. The need for the first room is separated from the need for the second and third room by wide distances in which the scale of needs does not register an urge for more housing."

Given the existence of discretionary income, the question confronting planners is what priorities will be set by different consumers in satisfying their wants for the different available classes of goods. What additional satisfactions for a given class of products will they seek to meet before obtaining the satisfactions provided by the consumption of successive items of another class? Thus, how many consumers will use their additional income to enrich their diet, how many to expand their wardrobe, how many to secure better living quarters? How many will keep their consumption of essentials as is and use their additional income to purchase a consumer durable good; and of those who follow this course how many will purchase a refrigerator, how many a TV set? And how many will save

[64] *Hearings on Economic Concentration,* Pt. 7, pp. 3793–3807, testimony of Emil Kauder.

the discretionary income toward the purchase of an automobile or simply against a rainy day?

Failure to find a method of measuring utility has not been for want of trying. In Kauder's words,

> If utility could be measured, the job of selling for the merchant in the capitalist world and the distribution for the respective agency in communism would be considerably simplified. The corporation or ministry would still not know what concrete form of utility should be delivered to each person, whether or not the income receiver should get more food and less clothing, or vice versa, but he would know that each one gets the same amount of measured utilities.

Although numerous "solutions" have been put forward by mathematicians, the problem remains unresolved. As Kauder has put it, "During the last 260 years ingenious attempts have been made to construct a yardstick of utility. It has been to no avail. It is the frustrating story of the philosopher's stone all over again."[65]

This is not to imply that nothing can be learned about consumers' wants. By studying their actual expenditure patterns, one can "reveal" the "preferences" of consumers for one set of commodities over another. But, as Kauder points out,

> while a valuable tool for planning, there is one essential drawback to revealed preferences. By the preparation of her budget the housewife distinguishes between the bulk of goods which she buys following the tradition of her social surrounding and the new goods which she selects by trial and error. The old standby goods are not selected with each new period: they are accepted. For the new goods no standard preference during the period of experiments is worked out. The pattern of preference may change time and again.

Market surveys can be conducted in an effort to ascertain consumers' probable response to a proposed new product. Such surveys tend to have a built-in negative bias, as consumers are naturally wary of the untried and skeptical of its purported attributes. If a new product does have important utilities, these tend to be discovered only through use. A market survey, it will be recalled, found little potential demand for xerography.[66] Market surveys also cannot forecast consumers' reactions to what in the future will be the "fad." If a market survey had been conducted shortly before the miniskirt became the rage, it would undoubtedly have found the overwhelming majority of the female populace to be shocked at the very idea. Moreover, to get any real insight into where a new item would rank among consumer preferences, the market survey would have to provide some approximation of its price. But until the item is in production and its costs are known, such approximations will be only abstractions.

While their attention has been centered on the supply side, Communist economists have not been wholly unmindful of the problem of consumer preferences. If there is a Communist theory on this issue, it is the "trial-and-error" approach

---

[65] For further discussions of the efforts to derive a measure of utility see Emil Kauder, *A History of Marginal Utility Theory*, Princeton University Press, 1965, Chs. 19, 20; William J. Baumol, *Economic Theory and Operations Analysis*, 2nd ed., Prentice-Hall, 1965, pp. 210 *et seq.*

[66] See Ch. 10.

put forward by Oskar Lange. Under this theory supply and demand for each commodity are at the outset assumed to be in equilibrium:

> Any price different from the equilibrium price would show at the end of the accounting period a surplus or a shortage of the commodity in question. Thus the accounting prices in a socialist economy, far from being arbitrary, have quite the same objective character as the market prices in a regime of competition. Any mistake made by the Central Planning Board in fixing prices would announce itself in a very objective way—by a physical shortage or surplus of the quantity of the commodity or resources in question—and would have to be corrected in order to keep production running smoothly. As there is generally only one set of prices which satisfies the objective equilibrium condition, both the prices of products and costs are uniquely determined.
>
> Our study of the determination of equilibrium prices in a socialist economy has shown that the process of price determination is quite analogous to that in a competitive market. The Central Planning Board performs the functions of the market. It establishes the rules for combining factors of production and choosing the scale of output of a plant; for determining the output of an industry, for the allocation of resources and for the parametric use of prices in accounting. Finally, it fixes the prices so as to balance the quantity supplied and demanded of each commodity. It follows that the substitution of planning for the functions of the market is quite possible and workable.[67]

In practice, prices under Communism have almost invariably been based on costs—or what are presumed to be costs—either for the enterprise or for the industry as a whole. A heritage of the past, the assumption has been that demand is excessive and can therefore be taken as given. If prices have been set initially at equilibrium levels, it has been by accident. Nor has there been anything approaching a reasonably current appraisal to determine whether, in Lange's words, there is "a surplus or a shortage of the commodity in question." According to Montias, "revisions in wholesale price levels were made only every three to five years." Moreover, "The prices of goods traded among socialized enterprises, far from equating supply and demand and from expressing the relative scarcities of the goods to which they were attached, diverged significantly from production costs for reasons that had more to do with administrative inertia than with the state of their demand."

That in the Communist countries the prices so poorly reflect the changing conditions of demand is due partly to the human problems involved in the administrative processes of planning. But it is also due to immutable problems. In addition to the impossibility of measuring demand, there is the problem of the mutual interaction of prices on each other. In the words of Ota Sik:

> The old system of central management lacks entirely an economic focus. It is a system of production ministries, which were justified at the time of the directive management, when central plans, on their way down to lower components, were broken down into appropriate details. This system, of course, has no capability of providing economic man-

---

[67] Oskar Lange and Fred M. Taylor, *On the Economic Theory of Socialism*, University of Minnesota, 1938, pp. 82–83. This work represents an effort to reply to arguments advanced by Ludwig von Mises and F. A. von Hayek (see Ludwig von Mises, "Economic Calculations in the Socialist Commonwealth," and F. A. von Hayek, "The Nature and History of a Problem," in F. A. von Hayek, ed., *Collectivist Economic Planning*, Routledge, 1935).

agement. These ministries, even if they wanted to, are unable to manage the economy, since sound economic management requires management with the help of a thorough knowledge of prices, wages, credits, foreign trade mark-ups or discounts, etc., i.e. by means of economic instruments. *No ministry is capable of using these tools, because there is a horizontal relationship between them. All prices are interconnected. It is impossible to change prices in one sector without considering how the change will affect prices in other sectors. All economic tools are mutually conditioned.* It is impossible to contemplate changes in prices or taxes, without considering their mutual relationship, or their relationship to interest, credit, etc. This is why we cannot accuse individual ministers of ignorance, ineptitude, etc. In a system of central management, even the best expert could not act differently than the present ministers or ministries are acting.[68]

The economic reforms

As they entered into the stage of intensive growth, the Communist countries were confronted increasingly with two formidable obstacles to centralized planning. In the first place, the plant managers were inundated by a never-ending torrent of highly detailed orders, directives, quotas, regulations, targets, and requirements of all kinds flowing down from the ministries. Approval to deviate had to be laboriously requested and obtained from higher authority for countless decisions that should have been made on the spot. The overriding norm was quantity; anything that might interfere with its attainment—improvements in quality, a wider range of products, or even reductions in costs—was discouraged. Moreover, for the reasons cited above, there was—and is—no practicable way of measuring changing consumer preferences and incorporating them into the planning mechanism. As a result of both factors, Sik noted, "We produce a great deal of unnecessary goods. They either remain unsold or we sell them with great difficulty. The consumers are forced to buy them because they don't get anything else." [69]

This was the background against which the "economic reforms" in the U.S.S.R. and the eastern European countries were formulated. Associated with the name of the Soviet economist Yevsei Liberman, guidelines for the reforms were first presented by Premier Kosygin on September 27, 1965. As described by Liberman in 1967, their objectives were: "increasing the independence of enterprises; appraising their work by the criterion of profitability; introducing payment for production assets; raising the material incentives for personnel, in ratio to the enterprise's performance, out of profits; increasing the enterprises' direct contracting with one another for the supply of goods; and establishing economically based, as opposed to arbitrarily set, prices." [70]

In their testimony before the Senate Antitrust Subcommittee the economic specialists in the area were in agreement that the reforms have succeeded in granting the managers a greater degree of freedom from the ministries. But, as Liberman himself has acknowledged, even here accomplishment has lagged well behind intention:

[68] Sik, *op. cit.* Emphasis added.
[69] *Ibid.*
[70] Yevsei Liberman, "The Soviet Economic Reform," *Foreign Affairs*, Oct., 1967, pp. 53–63. Included in *Hearings on Economic Concentration*, Pt. 7A, pp. 4366–71.

Due to lack of experience, sometimes the same old sharply criticized targets were simply made the new ones . . . the superior agencies frequently have been incapable of freeing themselves fast enough from old habits and from superfluous regimentation of the work of plants and factories. The inertia of thought, views, and ideas which was so characteristic of some executive agencies over a long period has proved more persistent than had been expected. . . . The enlargement of the rights of enterprises is an important condition of the reform. In many cases, however, the superior agencies have proved insufficiently prepared for this development. Sometimes this has taken the form of the old bureaucratic ills—inflexibility, irresponsibility and lack of initiative, reliance on the formality of issuing orders instead of working out economic as opposed to administrative methods of influencing production.[71]

With respect to the second objective of the reforms—establishing "economically based, as opposed to arbitrarily set prices"—the consensus among the authorities appears to be that little, if anything, has been accomplished. In the U.S.S.R., according to Norton Dodge, "The price reform introduced on July 1, 1967 merely updated prices in a hurried and makeshift fashion. Price theory and pricing methodology was not improved." [72] In Czechoslovakia, according to George Staller, "The overhaul of wholesale prices was a central feature of the reform. The new wholesale prices were centrally calculated and were based on average costs, as submitted by sectors, and supplemented by percentage surcharges. These synthetic prices were to be subsequently adjusted by the forces of supply and demand. . . . However, unexpected inflationary pressures were generated after the new model came into operation, and consequently almost all wholesale prices were frozen." [73] On the basis of his analysis of the reforms in 5 eastern European countries, John Montias found,

> In only two countries (Czechoslovakia and Hungary) will enterprises and associations be allowed to set prices for any significant proportion of output for standardized producer goods. . . . To the extent that most prices, even where the reforms are most far-reaching, will be linked to past production costs reflecting an inefficient state of affairs, they will not offer a reliable guide to determine which production lines should be curbed and which developed, which factories should be closed down and which expanded.[74]

As long as prices are not allowed to find their own levels in free markets, they will of course reflect arbitrary values and judgments. In the case of the Communist countries these judgments have been based in theory on costs but in practice on costs plus or minus subsidies, turnover taxes, premiums, incentive allowances, and so on. These increments and deductions have become em-

---

[71] *Ibid.*

[72] *Hearings on Economic Concentration*, Pt. 7, pp. 3739–57.

[73] *Ibid.*, pp. 3670–80. The reform differed conceptually from Lange's prescription in that the initial prices were to be based only on costs but conformed in that the reviews were to be based on supply *and* demand. The fate of the price reform after the Soviet occupation is unknown, but presumably, like other reforms of the Dubchek regime, it has been abandoned.

[74] *Hearings on Economic Concentration,* Pt. 7, pp. 3785–92. Montias' survey antedated the Soviet occupation of Czechoslovakia.

bedded so deeply into the cost-price structure that, according to Sik, "No one can prove whether or not a certain product could be sold for $1,200 instead of $1,000." [75] The need of the Communist countries for objectively determined prices was stressed by Montias:

> The paramount importance of prices correctly reflecting relative scarcities—or at least coming closer to this norm than pre-reform prices—is that this will make it possible to calculate meaningful costs and returns and thus provide an *impersonal measure of efficiency*, which had so far been absent. Anyone today may, with some justice, deny that an enterprise should be wound up or a product line discontinued because none of the indicators at hand provide totally convincing evidence of the inefficiency of these operations. Costs are so distorted by subsidized raw-material prices, by deviations from opportunity cost in foreign trade and by the absence or the inadequate levels of capital charges that no firm conclusions about the inefficiency of a given operation can be inferred from them. An incontrovertible measure of efficiency would equip "rationalizers" of production with a weapon that, while it might not be proof against political lobbying by threatened interests, would permit them to offer a good deal more resistance against arbitrary interference than in the recent past.

The lack of objectively determined costs and prices breeds protection of inefficiency. As long as it is impossible to establish objectively that a plant is operating inefficiently, it will be permitted to exist with—and indeed be subsidized by—efficient plants. As Sik has put it,

> every enterprise in Czechoslovakia, no matter how efficient, has been protected. We protect our enterprises by subsidies, grants, and allocations, foreign trade mark-ups and premiums, and price policy. This situation enabled even the most inefficiently working enterprises, the obsolete ones and those lacking in initiative, to survive to the detriment of the good and efficiently working ones. We take the profit of the efficient enterprises and give support to inefficient plants, taking the means either from the budget or from within the production branch itself.
>
> This is an enormous, complicated, and unclear system of permanent redistribution. By now it is so widespread that it is impossible to discern which enterprise is working efficiently and which is inefficient because even the worst enterprise shows no difficulties and often lives quietly in a much better situation than the efficient one, from which the profit is being taken in such a way that often no resources are left for its further economic development.
>
> Naturally, the obsolete enterprises lacking in initiative develop under this protection a feeling of satisfaction and a strong belief that this situation will last forever and cannot change. The efficient enterprises, on the other hand, reconcile themselves with the idea that "the more profit they make, the more will be taken away," and this idea undercuts their initiative.
>
> Obviously, this situation cannot be changed overnight because in such a case many, *perhaps half, of the enterprises, would be reduced to bankruptcy by not being able to pay their workers' wages.* [76]

[75] Sik, *op. cit.*
[76] *Ibid.* Emphasis added.

Oligopoly, cartels, and the reforms

An inescapable result of the long-term drive for greater concentration in the Communist countries has been the monopolization of individual markets. A corollary restrictive development has been the official policy of inducing, and even forcing, the formation of cartels among separate enterprises. Justified as a means of securing the economies of rationalization, cartels have conveyed important benefits to the large enterprises and to the government ministries. If the data presented earlier on size and efficiency have any validity, the large enterprises have much to fear from smaller and more efficient competitors. For ministerial officials, the existence of cartels immeasurably simplifies their work, since nothing in government is more difficult than seeking to regulate a large number of competing enterprises.

In the Soviet Union the number of enterprises with "economic independence" has been reduced greatly over the years. The Soviet economist Pogosov notes: "According to the data of a survey on the structure and production activity of the firms on 1 April 1964 carried out by the USSR TsSU [U.S.S.R. Central Statistical Administration], of the 1,900 enterprises comprising the production associations, 1,200 enterprises had been deprived of economic independence. Thus concentration and centralization in production lead to an increase in the average size of enterprise." [77] A parallel development, according to Staller, took place in Czechoslovakia: "The intention of the reformers was to create a decentralized competitive industry regulated by the state through direct and indirect means. The outcome so far has been the creation of a horizontally integrated, cartelized industrial structure which could be described as 'decentralized centralization.'"

To the Czechoslovakian economists associated with the reform movement the trusts and cartels made it extremely difficult, in Sik's words, "to step from the present administrative prices to real market prices." [78] According to Montias:

> The Czech and Slovak writers who have given a good deal of attention of late to issues of market organization have thrown up a number of objections to the "monopolistic management" of production sectors. First and foremost, those among them who favor the creation of a full-fledged socialist market economy deplore the elimination of competition. They argue that initiative and drive, which were stifled under the old system, can only be recaptured in a competitive climate. A second point that is often made is that the monopoly management of a production sector (corresponding to a given range of goods) tends to perpetuate the old bureaucratic procedures for allocating materials and capital goods—especially the mechanical distribution of the quotas of rationed materials available to the sector on the basis of "standard" shares for each region and for every enterprise within a region, thereby "embalming" the negative features of the old system. Third, the monopoly position of an enterprise or of a group of enterprises distorts the nature and direction of technical progress, especially if the prices of the outputs are set by a centralized agency. For it has been observed, at least under present Czechoslovak conditions, that R and D efforts are biased toward innovations capable of raising output and cutting costs in preference to those that might improve the quality of the product or the

[77] Pogosov, *op. cit.*
[78] Sik, *op. cit.*

range of choice open to consumers. Finally, and most obvious of all, a sales monopoly in a line of products invites open price increases wherever prices are free to move and covert increases where they are not.

Despite these arguments, the principal effect of the reforms thus far seems to have been the transfer of a considerable latitude for decision making from the ministries either directly to the plants, which, as oligopolists, have substantial control over the market, or to an intermediate level represented by cartels. Although their purpose would call for greater competitiveness, the course of actual developments, according to Dodge, has been in the opposite direction: "rather than the present reforms spawning more independent, small-scale enterprises . . . the combination of many existing enterprises into trusts, combines or 'firms,' as the Soviets call them, seems a more likely prospect. Those who have a stake in the operation of the central organs are making a strong case that an enterprise cannot use its new-found independence wisely because it cannot see the entire picture." Referring to "market socialism" as a "distant prospect," Dodge went on to say that "the devolution of decision-making power from the center will of necessity be limited. Rather than the enterprise acquiring the bulk of the shifted powers, an industry-level cartel or association may become the major recipient and the dominant form of industrial organization." The strictures of their economists notwithstanding, the transfer of power in Czechoslovakia appears to have been proceeding along similar lines, even before the Soviet occupation. After noting the prevalence of oligopoly and cartels, Staller observed: "In such a situation one would not expect perfect competition, but rather a behavior similar to that in Western imperfect markets, including output restriction and price manipulations."

That what has taken place under the reforms represents in no way "a step from . . . administrative prices to real market prices" but only a shift in the locus of price administration was suggested in an article by S. Vacha appearing in the May, 1967, issue of *New Trends in Czechoslovakian Economics*:

> With the transition to the new system of management, contradictions have been revealed in our economy which the former administrative system of management easily "solved" and concealed. The suppliers among whom the process of concentration and centralization took place under the old system of management, discovered that monopoly producers are thoroughly protected on the territory of Czechoslovakia against foreign competition by a barrier of foreign trade, not dissimilar from the medieval protectionist methods. . . .
>
> If we compare this monopolistic position of our producers and its consequences with monopolies under capitalism, we immediately notice a striking difference. Our monopolies are not interested in exploiting the potential demand. They do not wipe out the competitors in order to seize the entire market for themselves, it looks more as if they disregarded the market which is offered to them for exploitation. They behave unnaturally even as monopolies. This can only be explained by the survival of the indifference which has become a habit, to the possibility of satisfying economic interests, to the possibility of improving the economic effect of their operation. It would therefore be desirable that our monopolies should at least sell like capitalist monopolies. Why even an expansion of production without technical improvements would, under these monopolistic conditions, raise the gross income of the producers. Our monopolies are not expansive.[79]

[79] Quoted in *Hearings on Economic Concentration*, Pt. 7, p. 3804.

Market socialism in Yugoslavia

Yugoslavia has progressed so much farther toward free markets than the other Communist countries as to be in a class by itself. Immediately after World War II Yugoslavia adopted a highly centralized, "command" form of economic organization, patterned after the Soviet model and even employing its terminology. But in 1950–51, some 15 years before the adoption of economic reforms by the other Communist countries, it abandoned centralized decision making by national ministries on prices, output, and investment. Based upon an intensive analysis of the Yugoslav economy, Joel B. Dirlam described the nature of the Yugoslav business firm in the following words:

> The key concept that describes the Yugoslav business firm, its powers, and relations with other firms and the Government, is "self-management." Its property is not owned by the state, but is held in trust by the firm for society. Only businesses with less than five employees are in the private sector, where private ownership of assets is allowed. The enterprise is not run by either local or Federal Government but by managers selected by workers in the firm. A workers' council, selected by the employees, in turn chooses a management committee, which roughly corresponds to the executive committee of a board of directors in a U.S. corporation. The general director, or manager of the firm, is chosen by a nominating committee, and the choice must be ratified by the workers' council. A representative of the local government sits on the committee to choose the general director. With this exception there is no provision for state intervention into the affairs of a solvent firm, although its financial reports go to the local government. The local authorities are required to take over management when the firm is insolvent. If a firm under receivership cannot be restored to profitability it must liquidate.[80]

The firm must plan its own output, buy its own materials, arrange for its own distribution, pay interest on its loans, and—if its product is not under price control—set its own prices. Anyone can start a firm. Dirlam cites the example of two engineers who with $100 started a construction and design firm in Belgrade in 1962; 4 years later they were earning over $2 million and in the fall of 1967 caused something of a sensation by offering, with bank cooperation, to lend $5 million on a competitive basis to firms wanting to modernize or expand.

To implement its policy of economic independence Yugoslavia has its own antitrust laws, described by Dirlam as follows:

> Article 30 of the Constitution prohibits mergers or associations aimed at preventing free commerce of goods and services for the purpose of material advantages not based on work, or promoting other relations of inequality in business. The basic Law on Commodity Trade, adopted in 1967, in Article 52 forbids agreements among business enterprises which achieve a monopoly or other discriminatory (favored) situation in the market.
>
> Prohibited agreements specifically include market sharing, price fixing on internal markets, production limitation or use of capacity, or other business activities resulting in limitation or prevention of free rivalry. Article 53 forbids speculation or activities resulting in shortages of goods on the market. Unfair ("nelojalna") competition is prohibited in Article 54. No precise definition of the term is given; it includes, generally, anything that damages other firms, consumers, or the economy.

[80] *Hearings on Economic Concentration,* Pt. 7, pp. 3758–84, testimony of Joel B. Dirlam.

Deceptive labeling, packaging, or advertising practices are outlawed when they involve quality, quantity, or origin of a commodity or service.

A further means of implementation has been import policy. Though the exceptions are many, the general trend of import policy has been toward greater liberalization. By 1967 the completely free list, which included raw materials, foodstuffs, spare parts, and some consumer goods, accounted for about 25 percent of total imports. Moreover, according to Dirlam, "The authorities apparently attempt to coordinate liberalization of imports with freeing domestic prices from controls."

Lest an impression be created that the free-enterprise millennium has arrived in a Communist state, note should be taken of a number of offsetting considerations. As in the West, the existence of antitrust laws is one thing; their enforcement, which in Yugoslavia is in the hands of "courts of honor," is another. Dirlam reports, "How the decisions of the 'court of honor' are to be enforced is not clear, nor do I know what penalties can be enforced for violation." Moreover, "I have come across no instance of an attack by the authorities on a monopoly under Article 52." Firms are permitted to join together in "business associations," some of which allocate detailed production requirements to their members. The associations are not supposed to limit output or capacity, exclude competitors, share markets, or fix domestic prices. But, according to Dirlam, "There have been no serious attempts that I am aware of, to examine the behavior of the business associations to determine whether they actually conform to this provision of the basic statute."

The stimulus to competition resulting from trade liberalization, particularly the tariff reductions of 1965, has also been partly negated. In a move reminiscent of giant oil companies under capitalism, the worker-owned Yugoslav oil refinery urged that tariffs on petroleum products be increased. Going beyond the voluntary import quotas enjoyed by the U.S. steel industry, Yugoslav steel producers in 1968 secured higher steel tariffs, with differential rates depending on whether imports were in excess of a quota. In March, 1968, tariffs were increased on 20 groups of products, including typewriters, of which there were only 2 manufacturers: "Opinion," notes Dirlam, "was not unanimously favorable to the increase." Strong protectionist pressures have come also from other highly concentrated Yugoslav industries, notably automobiles, tires, tractors, railroad equipment, and electrical equipment. It would appear that, as in capitalist countries, the absence of competition in the domestic market renders an industry ill-equipped to meet competition from abroad. By way of contrast, Dirlam cites a report of the reaction to import competition of a plant director in a highly competitive industry, women's stockings: " 'He said he was not troubled; his quality was better than the imports which lasted no more than a month.' Nor did he use the occasion of the interview to complain publicly about unfavorable circumstances, high taxes, dumping, et cetera. 'He says clearly . . . the plant has lowered the price of stockings.' " [81]

But important as they are in particular industries, neither the business "associations" nor the tariff increases were regarded by Dirlam as representing any fundamental reversal of government policy:

> There is no indication that in their policies the authorities have surrendered to the narrow market interests of the enterprises, or that the firms themselves have really pressed for a general retreat from the prin-

[81] Quoted by Dirlam in *ibid.*, p. 3772.

ciples laid down in the July 1965 reforms. While growth has been sacrificed—industrial production in 1967 stagnated—there is general recognition that the rapid rates of expansion in earlier years had been achieved at the expense of both rational allocation of investment resources and the international reserve position of the country. It has required time for the enterprises to adapt themselves to a regime of financial rationality; in the long run a more flexible pricing policy will prevent the accumulation of excess inventories, and achieve closer adoption of quality to market needs.

*　　*　　*

Yugoslav businessmen seem to be fairly independent, agreements may be breached, may not be observed, there are often powerful firms that remain outside of the associations, and there is no requirement that they join, so that, while there may be moves toward cartel-like price agreements, I am not convinced that they are yet a serious threat.

As far as the import limitations are concerned, the Government is still disposed to try to move for complete trade and exchange liberalization.

There remains, however, one formidable barrier to the attainment of market socialism—the highly concentrated structure of Yugoslav industry itself. Partly because of its limited markets and partly because of the deliberate efforts to centralize production during the immediate postwar years, concentration, both aggregate and market, is higher in Yugoslavia than in the United States. In Yugoslavia the 200 largest enterprises in 1965 accounted for 60 percent of the total assets of industrial firms (excluding handicrafts); in the United States the corresponding proportion was 56 percent. In Yugoslavia industries with 4-company concentration ratios of 50 percent or more accounted for 58.2 percent of the value added; in the United States the corresponding figure (after a minimal upward adjustment for "regional market" industries) was 39.6 percent.[82]

Whether the benefits of market control accrue to stockholders as dividends or to workers as their share of operating income apparently makes little difference in the behavior of the enterprise. Referring to the rapid increases in enterprise income devoted to earnings,[83] Dirlam observed:

> Given these characteristics of the Yugoslav business firm, issuing from the perspectives and motivations of the participants in it, there is no reason to believe it will price in a significantly different manner from a capitalist counterpart. In a market that is starved for goods, it will take advantage of inelastic demand to raise prices, and increase net incomes— whether they are paid out or reinvested. If the firm has what amounts to a national monopoly, like JAT (the only scheduled airline), or a regional monopoly like Jukepetrol, or INA, gasoline distribution, it clearly will have an incentive to restrict output so that the worker-participants enjoy larger incomes. There is much evidence to show that industries with a sufficient number of firms so that oligopolistic practices are unlikely, suffer from lower prices and lower incomes to workers, although disagreement among a few dominant firms on profits-maximizing oligopolistic policies is not unknown.

[82] The figures for Yugoslavia are those of the Yugoslav economist I. Drutter, as cited by Dirlam; the figures for the United States are from Ch. 4 and Ch. 1, respectively.

[83] Between 1958 and 1966 the increase in personal income was 570%, as compared to increases of only 61% in production and 110% in funds engaged in production. (*Hearings on Economic Concentration*, Pt. 7A, p. 4504.)

State ownership: an evaluation

Although a popularity poll is not an appropriate way to evaluate economic policy, the absence of any general popular support for further nationalization in the West does tell us something about its accomplishments. Referring to the Labour government's renationalization in 1964 of the British steel industry, which had been nationalized shortly after World War II and then denationalized under the ensuing Conservative government, Clair Wilcox observed, "The proposal had little relevance to Britain's problems at the time. It evoked little excitement in the country as a whole." [84] Since that time the industry has been particularly conspicuous for its continuing demands for further price increases, the rationalizations for which bear a striking resemblance to those periodically put forward by the U.S. Steel Corporation. In Great Britain and in Western Europe generally, Wilcox finds little support for further nationalization: "The high hopes held out at the end of the war have failed of fulfillment. Consumers, workers, and politicians alike have been disillusioned. There has been a widespread loss of faith in the benefits of public enterprise. As a result, the proponents of nationalization have come to regard the process as completed and have ceased to urge its extension to other fields." [85] Sheahan's conclusion concerning France is to the same effect: "As most private industries have become a good deal more dynamic since the war, serious political support for further nationalization has greatly weakened. None of the postwar nationalization has been undone, but no new ones have been carried out since 1946." [86]

With respect to the Communist countries, it can be said without much question that under state ownership industrialization was achieved, and probably (though this is less certain) at a faster pace than would have taken place under private ownership. But the centralization of control, the rigid hierarchical organizations and the highly concentrated industrial structures of the extensive-growth stage have proved to be incapable of meeting the problems of intensive growth. While based on the experience of his own country, a summary of the deficiencies of the command economy by the Yugoslav economist Stevan Kuboleca would appear to be applicable to the Communist countries generally:

> (1) Failures in selecting the products to be manufactured resulting in increased inventories of goods which nobody wanted to buy in spite of big shortages of many other kinds of goods immediately after the war. Planning procedure was too stiff and too inelastic to take in consideration the desires and inclinations of individual consumers.
> (2) The workers had no interest in the increase of productivity, because they received fixed salaries. Even later when the salaries of the individual workers were functionally related to their individual productivity measured by standard times, it did not have remarkable influence on the average productivity because of difference between the productivity realized on individual operations and that on the final products.
> (3) Of the same character was the lack of worker interest in the reduction of material costs. From the socio-economic point of view, spoilage of means of production caused by this indifference was of even

[84] Wilcox, *op. cit.*, p. 576.
[85] *Ibid.*, p. 486.
[86] Sheahan, *op. cit.*, p. 29.

greater importance than inefficiency in productivity because of shortage of means of production of any kind.

(4) Allocation of resources and funds for increased production was far from satisfactory. This caused two kinds of disturbances: in the short run, organizational troubles generating a tendency towards increasing bureaucracy; and in the long run, unsuccessful investments and plant locations, diminishing the efficiency of the productive powers of the country.

(5) In addition to these, slow turnover of capital, lack of interest in innovation, difficulties in organizing scientific research for technical development as well as in coordinating the development of scientific theory with application of its results in technical and economic practice.[87]

It would appear that the economic reforms designed to meet these deficiencies have succeeded in giving the plant managers greater flexibility but have accomplished little in the way of bringing about a better articulation of supply with changing consumer preferences. The latter requires a free market, which in turn requires a far greater degree of decentralization than exists in any of the Communist countries. The nature of the problem is recognized by Communist economists themselves.

Aside from such exogenous occurrences as intervention by Soviet armed forces, progress toward a more decentralized model has been impeded by cartels, which appear to have taken over many of the functions formerly carried out by the ministries under the old "inefficient" command system. But, even in the absence of this obstacle, the question remains as to how much progress toward free markets can be made in economies that are, for the most part, highly concentrated. In the Communist countries, as in the capitalist world, oligopoly stands as the principal barrier to the achievement of better economic performance:

Plus ça change, plus c'est la même chose.

[87] *Hearings on Economic Concentration,* Pt. 7A, Stevan Kuboleca, "Review of Movements in Yugoslav Economy Towards Decentralization," pp. 4495–96.

APPENDIX

APPENDIX

APPENDIX 1

Selected Hearings Before and Reports of the
Subcommittee on Antitrust and Monopoly,
Committee on the Judiciary, U.S. Senate
(1957–1971)

Administered Prices   Hearings

85th Cong., 1st Sess., part 1: "Opening Phase—Economists' Views" (1957)

part 2: "Steel" (1957)

part 3: "Steel (and Appendix A)" (1957)

part 4: "Steel (Appendix B)" (1957)

2nd Sess., part 5: "Asphalt Roofing" (1958)

part 6: "Automobiles" (1958)

part 7: "Automobiles (Appendix)" (1958)

part 8: "1958 Steel Price Increase" (1958)

86th Cong., 1st Sess., part 9: "Administered Price Inflation: Alternative Public Policies" (1959)

part 10: "Administered Price Inflation: Alternative Public Policies (continued)" (1959)

part 11: "Administered Prices: Price Notification Legislation" (on S. 215) (1959)

part 12: "Study of Administered Prices in the Bread Industry" (1959)

part 13: "Administered Prices: Identical Bidding (TVA)" (1959)

part 14: "Administered Prices in the Drug Industry (Corticosteroids)" (1959)

part 15: "Administered Prices in the Drug Industry (Corticosteroids—Appendix)" (1959)

2nd Sess., part 16: "Administered Prices in the Drug Industry (Tranquilizers)" (1960)

part 17: "Administered Prices in the Drug Industry (Tranquilizers—Appendix)" (1960)

part 18: "Administered Prices in the Drug Industry (General: Physicians and Other Professional Authorities)" (1960)

part 19: "Administered Prices in the Drug Industry (General: Pharmaceutical Manufacturers Association)" (1960)

part 20: "Administered Prices in the Drug Industry (Oral Antidiabetic Drugs)" (1960)

part 21: "Administered Prices in the Drug Industry (General: Generic and Brand Names)" (1960)

part 22: "Administered Prices in the Drug Industry (The Food and Drug Administration: Dr. Henry Welch)" (1960)

part 23: "Administered Prices in the Drug Industry (The Food and Drug Administration: Dr. Henry Welch—Appendix)" (1960)

86th Cong., 2nd Sess., part 24: "Administered Prices in the Drug Industry (Antibiotics)" (1960)

part 25: "Administered Prices in the Drug Industry (Antibiotics—Appendix A)" (1960)

part 26: "Administered Prices in the Drug Industry (Antibiotics—Appendix B)" (1960)

87th Cong., 1st Sess., part 27: "Price Fixing and Bid Rigging in the Electrical Manufacturing Industry" (1961)

part 28: "Price Fixing and Bid Rigging in the Electrical Manufacturing Industry" (1961)

88th Cong., 1st Sess., part 29: "Public Policy on Administered Prices" (1963)

Reports, etc.

85th Cong., 2nd Sess., S. Rept. #1387: "Administered Prices: Steel" (1958)

Committee print: "Administered Prices: Automobiles" (1958)

Committee print: "Administered Prices: Asphalt Roofing" (1958)
86th Cong., 2nd Sess., S. Rept. #1923: "Administered Prices: Bread" (1960)
87th Cong., 1st Sess., S. Rept. #448: "Administered Prices: Drugs" (1961)
88th Cong., 1st Sess., Committee print: "Administered Prices: A Compendium on Public Policy" (1963)

Drug Industry Antitrust Act (S. 1552)   Hearings

87th Cong., 1st Sess., part 1: "A.M.A. and Medical Authorities" (1961)
part 2: "A.M.A. and Medical Authorities (Appendix)" (1961)
part 3: "Patent Provisions" (1961)
part 4: "Pharmaceutical Manufacturers Association" (1961)
part 5: "Government Agencies and Organizations" (1961)
2nd Sess., part 6: "Advertising Provisions" (1962)
part 7: "Advertising Provisions (Appendix)" (1962)

Report

87th Cong., 2nd Sess., S. Rept. #1744: "Drug Industry Act of 1962" (to accompany S. 1552) (1962)

Economic Concentration   Hearings

88th Cong., 2nd Sess., part 1: "Overall and Conglomerate Aspects" (1964)
89th Cong., 1st Sess., part 2: "Mergers and Other Factors Affecting Industry Concentration" (1965)
part 3: "Concentration, Invention and Innovation" (1965)
part 4: "Concentration and Efficiency" (1965)
2nd Sess., part 5: "Concentration and Divisional Reporting" (1966)
part 5A: "Concentration and Divisional Reporting—Appendix: The *Fortune* Directory of the 500 Largest U.S. Industrial Corporations, 1954–1965" (1966)
90th Cong., 1st Sess., part 6: "New Technologies and Concentration" (1967)
2nd Sess., part 7: "Concentration Outside the United States" (1968)
part 7A: "Concentration Outside the United States—Appendix: A Compendium of Supplementary Material" (1968)
91st Cong., 2nd Sess., part 8: "The Conglomerate Merger Problem" (1970)
1st Sess., part 8A: "The Conglomerate Merger Problem—Appendix: Staff Report of the Federal Trade Commission, 'Economic Report on Corporate Mergers' " (1969)

Governmental Intervention in the Market Mechanism: The Petroleum Industry
Hearings

91st Cong., 1st Sess., part 1: "Economists' Views" (1969)
part 2: "Industry Views" (1969)
part 3: "Complainants' Views" (1969)
2nd Sess., part 4: "The Cabinet Task Force on Oil Import Control: Majority and Minority Recommendations" (1970)
part 5: "Federally-Owned Oil and Gas Lands on the Outer Continental Shelf" (1970)

Concentration Ratios

87th Cong., 2nd Sess., Committee print: "Concentration Ratios in Manufacturing Industry, 1958" (prepared by the Bureau of the Census for the Subcommittee on Antitrust and Monopoly) (1962)

89th Cong., 2nd Sess., Committee print: "Concentration Ratios in Manufacturing Industry, 1963," part 1 (prepared by the Bureau of the Census for the Subcommittee on Antitrust and Monopoly) (1966)

90th Cong., 1st Sess., Committee print: "Concentration Ratios in Manufacturing Industry, 1963," part 2 (prepared by the Bureau of the Census for the Subcommittee on Antitrust and Monopoly) (1967)

APPENDIX 2

Economist Witnesses Before the Senate Subcommittee
on Antitrust and Monopoly, 1957–1970

Hearings on Administered Prices; Administered Prices: A Compendium on Public Policy; Hearings on S. 1552; Hearings on Economic Concentration; Hearings on Governmental Intervention in the Market Mechanism

Note: Academic affiliations are as of time of testimony. Page numbers indicate beginning of each witness's testimony.

Adams, Walter (Michigan State): *Administered Prices*, Pt. 9, p. 4780; Pt. 29, p. 18032; *Compendium*, p. 5; *Economic Concentration*, Pt. 1, p. 248; *Governmental Intervention*, Pt. 1, p. 304.

Adelman, M. A. (M.I.T.): *Compendium*, p. 22; *Economic Concentration*, Pt. 1, p. 223; *Governmental Intervention*, Pt. 1, p. 6.

Allvine, Fred C. (Northwestern): *Governmental Intervention*, Pt. 3, p. 1285.

Arndt, H. (Free U. of Berlin [Germany]): *Economic Concentration*, Pt. 7, p. 3486.

Arnould, Richard F. (Illinois): *Economic Concentration*, Pt. 8, 4679

Backman, Jules (N.Y.U.): *Administered Prices*, Pt. 29, p. 17978; *Compendium*, p. 25; *Economic Concentration*, Pt. 2, p. 560; Pt. 8, p. 4713.

Barnes, Irston (Columbia): *Administered Prices*, Pt. 29, p. 17982; *Compendium*, p. 44.

Bernini, Giorgio (Padua [Italy]): *Economic Concentration*, Pt. 7, p. 3552.

Bjorksten, Johan (economic consultant): *Economic Concentration*, Pt. 5, p. 1940.

Bradley, Paul G. (British Columbia): *Governmental Intervention*, Pt. 1, p. 284.

Brandow, George (Penn State): *Economic Concentration*, Pt. 5, p. 1967.

Brubaker, Otis (United Steelworkers): *Administered Prices*, Pt. 2, p. 418.

Chow, Gregory (M.I.T.): *Administered Prices*, Pt. 6, p. 3167.

Clark, John M. (Columbia): *Compendium*, p. 86.

Collins, Norman R. (California [Berkeley]): *Economic Concentration*, Pt. 2, p. 711.

Cooper, Arnold C. (Purdue): *Economic Concentration*, Pt. 3, p. 1293.

Dean, Joel (economic consultant): *Administered Prices*, Pt. 11, p. 5582; *Economic Concentration*, Pt. 4, p. 1687.

deJong, H. W. (Leyden [Holland]): *Economic Concentration*, Pt. 7, p. 3608.

DeSimone, Daniel V. (Bureau of Standards): *Economic Concentration*, Pt. 3, p. 1093; Pt. 6, p. 2921.

Dirlam, Joel B. (Rhode Island): *Administered Prices*, Pt. 29, p. 18068; *Compendium*, p. 97; *Economic Concentration*, Pt. 2, p. 745; Pt. 7, p. 3758; *Governmental Intervention*, Pt. 1, p. 249.

Dixon, Robert L. (Michigan): *Economic Concentration*, Pt. 4, p. 1668.

Dodge, Norton (Maryland): *Economic Concentration*, Pt. 7, p. 3739.

Edwards, Corwin D. (Oregon): *Administered Prices*, Pt. 9, p. 4803; *Economic Concentration*, Pt. 1, p. 36; Pt. 7, p. 3636.

Eslick, Donald F. (Loyola): *Economic Concentration*, Pt. 8, p. 4702.

Fackler, Walter D. (Chamber of Commerce): *Administered Prices*, Pt. 11, p. 5221.

Fellner, William (Yale): *Compendium*, p. 134.

Florence, P. Sargant (Birmingham [England]): *Economic Concentration*, Pt. 7, p. 3571.

Frank, Helmut J. (Arizona): *Governmental Intervention*, Pt. 1, p. 339.

Frankel, Paul H. (economic consultant): *Governmental Intervention*, Pt. 1, p. 197.

Frucht, P. J. (Chamber of Commerce): *Administered Prices*, Pt. 11, p 5221.

Galbraith, J. Kenneth (Harvard): *Administered Prices*, Pt. 1, p. 32; Pt. 10, p. 4726.

Gardner, Fred V. (economic consultant): *Administered Prices*, Pt. 3, p. 713; Pt. 11, p. 5533.

Garoian, Leon (Oregon State): *Economic Concentration*, Pt. 8, p. 4657.

Gort, Michael (S. U.N.Y. [Buffalo]): *Economic Concentration*, Pt. 2, p. 673.

Graham, Earl (economic consultant): *Administered Prices*, Pt. 11, p. 5560.

Gray, Horace M. (Illinois): *Administered Prices*, Pt. 29, p. 18064; *Compendium*, p 140; *Economic Concentration*, Pt. 3, p. 1555.

Hadley, Eleanor (Tariff Commission): *Economic Concentration*, Pt. 7, p. 3508.

Hamberg, Daniel (S. U.N.Y. [Buffalo]): *Economic Concentration*, Pt. 3, p. 1281.

Havas, Eugene (economic consultant): *Administered Prices*, Pt. 10, p. 5076.

Heflebower, Richard B. (Northwestern): *Economic Concentration*, Pt. 2, p. 777.

Hogarty, Thomas F. (Northern Illinois): *Economic Concentration*, Pt. 8, p. 4647.

Homan, Paul T. (S.M.U.): *Governmental Intervention,* Pt. 1, p. 103.
Houghton, Harrison F. (FTC): *Compendium,* p. 152; *Economic Concentration,* Pt. 1, p. 155.
Houssiaux, J. (Nancy [France]): *Economic Concentration,* Pt. 7, p. 3583.
Johnson, William Summers (City of Honolulu): *Governmental Intervention,* Pt. 1, p. 233.
Kahn, Alfred E. (Cornell): *Administered Prices,* Pt. 29, p. 18036; *Compendium,* p. 166; *Economic Concentration,* Pt. 2, p. 591.
Katona, George (Michigan): *Administered Prices,* Pt. 6, p. 3112.
Kauder, Emil (Florida Presbyterian): *Economic Concentration,* Pt. 7, p. 3793.
Kaysen, Carl (Harvard): *Economic Concentration,* Pt. 2, p. 540.
Kelly, Eamon M. (Ford Foundation): *Economic Concentration,* Pt. 8, p. 4632.
Kottke, Frank J. (Washington State): *Administered Prices,* Pt. 29, p. 18041; *Compendium,* p. 182; *Economic Concentration,* Pt. 2, p. 622.
Lanzillotti, Robert F. (Michigan State): *Administered Prices,* Pt. 29, p. 18028; *Compendium,* p. 5.
Leeman, Wayne A. (Missouri): *Governmental Intervention,* Pt. 1, p. 268.
Lerner, Abba P. (Michigan State): *Compendium,* p. 196.
Lewis, Ben W. (Oberlin): *Administered Prices,* Pt. 9, p. 4708.
Lichtblau, John H. (Petroleum Industry Research Foundation): *Governmental Intervention,* Pt. 1, p. 317.
Loescher, Samuel M. (Indiana): *Economic Concentration,* Pt. 2, p. 830.
Lorie, James H. (Chicago): *Economic Concentration,* Pt. 8, p. 4745.
Machlup, Fritz (Johns Hopkins): *Administered Prices,* Pt. 10, p. 4950.
Malone, John R. (economic consultant): *Economic Concentration,* Pt. 4, p. 1609.
Mannis, Richard (A. D. Little, Inc.): *S. 1552,* Pt. 4, p. 2090.
Markham, Jesse W. (Princeton): *S. 1552,* Pt. 4, p. 2086; *Economic Concentration,* Pt. 3, p. 1269.
Martin, David D. (Indiana): *Economic Concentration,* Pt. 2, p. 687.
Mead, Walter J. (California [Santa Barbara]): *Economic Concentration,* Pt. 4, p. 1630; *Governmental Intervention,* Pt. 1, p. 77.
Means, Gardiner C. (economic consultant): *Administered Prices,* Pt. 1, p. 74; Pt. 9, p. 4746; Pt. 10, p. 4897; Pt. 29, p. 17972; *Compendium,* p. 213; *Economic Concentration,* Pt. 1, p. 8.
Montias, John (Yale): *Economic Concentration,* Pt. 7, p. 3785.
Moore, John R. (Tennessee): *Administered Prices,* Pt. 1, p. 164.
Mueller, Willard (FTC): *Economic Concentration,* Pt. 1, p. 109; Pt. 2, p. 501; Pt. 5, p. 1864; Pt. 8, p. 4544.
Nakamura, T. (Nanzan [Japan]): *Economic Concentration,* Pt. 7, p. 3534.
Nelson, Ralph L. (Queens): *Economic Concentration,* Pt. 1, p. 263.
Nelson, Richard (Rand Corp.): *Economic Concentration,* Pt. 3, p. 1135.
Newton, Walter L. (economic consultant): *Governmental Intervention,* Pt. 1, p. 41.
Norris, Ruby Turner (Connecticut): *Administered Prices,* Pt. 6, p. 2434.
Nourse, Edwin G. (Brookings Institution): *Administered Prices,* Pt. 1, p. 8; Pt. 9, p. 4701; Pt. 29, p. 17969; *Compendium,* p. 245.
Novick, David (Rand Corp.): *Administered Prices,* Pt. 18, p. 10510; *Economic Concentration,* Pt. 3, p. 1241.
Orr, Lloyd (Indiana): *Economic Concentration,* Pt. 6, p. 2786.
Oxenfeldt, Alfred R. (Columbia): *Economic Concentration,* Pt. 4, p. 1583.
Patterson, James M. (Indiana): *Governmental Intervention,* Pt. 3, p. 1285.
Penrose, Edith (London [England]): *Governmental Intervention,* Pt. 1, p. 156.
Prakash, V. (Government of India): *Economic Concentration,* Pt. 7, p. 3724.
Preston, Lee E. (California [Berkeley]): *Economic Concentration,* Pt. 1, p. 56.
Quinn, T. K. (economic consultant): *Administered Prices,* Pt. 10, p. 4973.
Reid, Samuel Richardson (Illinois): *Economic Concentration,* Pt. 5, p. 1914; Pt. 8, p. 4603
Rieber, Michael (Missouri): *Governmental Intervention,* Pt. 1, p. 181.
Ross, Howard Norman (C.U.N.Y.): *Economic Concentration,* Pt. 7, p. 3706.
Ruggles, Richard (Yale): *Administered Prices,* Pt. 1, p. 128.
Scherer, Frederic M. (Princeton): *Economic Concentration,* Pt. 3, p. 1188.
Schlaifer, Robert (Harvard): *Economic Concentration,* Pt. 3, p. 1230.
Schmookler, Jacob (Minnesota): *Economic Concentration,* Pt. 3, p. 1257.
Schon, Donald (economic consultant): *Economic Concentration,* Pt. 3, p. 1206; Pt. 6, p. 2725.

Shepherd, William G. (Michigan): *Economic Concentration*, Pt. 2, p. 636; Pt. 7, p. 3682.
Shultz, George P. (Department of Labor): *Governmental Intervention*, Pt. 4, p. 1694.
Smith, Bradford (U.S. Steel Corp.): *Administered Prices*, Pt. 2, p. 467.
Smith, Spencer M. (economic consultant): *Economic Concentration*, Pt. 3, p. 1333.
Sohmen, E. (the Saar [Germany]): *Economic Concentration*, Pt. 7, p. 3441.
Staller, George (Cornell): *Economic Concentration*, Pt. 7, p. 3670.
Steele, Henry (Houston): *Governmental Intervention*, Pt. 1, p. 208.
Steinberg, David J. (Committee for National Trade Policy): *Governmental Intervention*, Pt. 3, p. 1329.
Stelzer, Irwin M. (economic consultant): *Economic Concentration*, Pt. 1, p. 181.
Suits, Daniel B. (Michigan): *Administered Prices*, Pt. 6, p. 3195.
Symonds, Edward (First National Bank, N.Y.): *Governmental Intervention*, Pt. 2, p. 835.
Thompson, Earl A. (California [Los Angeles]): *Governmental Intervention*, Pt. 2, p. 868.
Warne, Colston (Amherst): *Administered Prices*, Pt. 11, p. 5492; *S. 1552*, Pt. 3, p. 1391.
Weiss, Leonard W. (Wisconsin): *Economic Concentration*, Pt. 2, p. 728.
Weston, J. Fred (California [Los Angeles]): *Economic Concentration*, Pt. 1, p. 135; Pt. 8, p. 4735.
Whitney, Simon N. (FTC): *Administered Prices*, Pt. 10, p. 5014.
Wilcox, W. W. (Department of Agriculture): *Economic Concentration*, Pt. 6, p. 2802.
Young, Ralph A. (Federal Reserve Board): *Administered Prices*, Pt. 10, p. 4839.

Index

Bell Aircraft Co., 273
Bell Telephone Co., 244
Bell Telephone Laboratories (Bell Laboratories), 253
Benada Aluminum Co., 273
Bendix Aviation Corp., 231
Bendix Corp., 237
Bendix washers, 272
Ben Hogan Co., 273
Bennett Mfg. Co., 33
Berger, Frank M., 217
Berglund, Abraham, 414
Berkeley-Stanford area, research units in, 252
Berle, Adolf A., 67n., 75, 78, 186, 265n., 267n., 551
Berle-Means thesis, in aggregate concentration, 79–80
Bernstein, Marver H., 662n.
Berri, L. Ya., 685, 688
Berst-Forster-Dixfield Co., 413
Bertrand, J. L., 5
Bethlehem-Lackawanna merger, 561n.
Bethlehem Steel Corp., 33, 130, 181, 265, 269, 376, 381, 383, 500, 503, 505, 507, 521, 588, 593, 633, 636–39, 647; see also Steel industry
Betz, Albert, 220
Bevis, Herman W., 604
Biddle, Francis, 382
Biedenkopf, Kurt H., 508n.
Bigelow-Sanford Co., 125
Bigness: "creative backwardness" of, 228–54; as industrial goal, 87–88; planning ability and, 650; profitability and, 657; in steel industry, 89–90
Blair, John M., 82–83, 90n., 159n., 207, 232, 348–51, 404n., 432n., 459, 462n., 594, 600, 624n., 665
Blank, David M., 320n.
Blaw-Knox Co., 290
Bliss, E. W., Co., 287
Blitzkrieg, 246–47
Block, Joseph, 637
Blough, Roger, 501, 633–37
BLS Wholesale Price Index, see Bureau of Labor Statistics; see also Wholesale Price Index
Bluhdorn, Charles G., 300–01, 305
Blythe & Co., 269
Boggs, Hale, 596
Bolt, Beranek, and Newman, Inc., 252
Bonbright, James C., 654–55
Bonus plan, pricing policy and, 670
Book shareholdings, stock ownership and, 79
Borden Corp., 56, 184, 260, 266, 270, 279
Borg-Warner Corp., 117, 273, 326–27
Boron composites, 127
Boslet, Robert, 313, 319
Bossons, John, 186n.
Boulding, Kenneth E., 309, 467n., 524n.

Boycotts, effectiveness of, 370
Bradley, Albert, 470
Bradley, Joseph P., 667–68
Brandeis, Louis D., 262, 564, 622
Brand names, concentration and, 527
Brandow, George E., 605
Braniff Airways, 287
Brassert, J. E., 233
Brassert, H. H., & Co., 233
Brattain, Walter, 210
Bread industry, price discrimination in, 348–49
Bread manufacture, continuous mix process in, 226–27
Breck, John H., Co., 272
Breweries: concentration ratios in, 324; size of, 179–80
Bridgeport Brass Co., 270
Briley, John M., 120, 123, 125
Briloff, Abraham J., 292–93, 294n., 295, 304n., 606
Bristol-Myers Co., 314, 320, 326
British Admiralty, officials in, 162
British Broadcasting System, 600
British common law, 555
British Labour party, 705
British Match Corps, Ltd., 214
British Petroleum, Ltd., 283–84
British Purchasing Mission, 625
British Standing Committee on Prices, 96–97
British steel industry, nationalization of, 705
Brookings Institution, 475, 495, 499, 504, 520, 640
Brooks, Robert C., Jr., 340, 341n.
Brown, Donaldson, 470–72, 474
Brown Co., 287
Browne, E. Wayles, 386
Brown Forman & Co., 182
Brown Shoe case, 593
Brunswick Corp., 125, 273
Bryan, William Jennings, 652
Bryant & May, Ltd., 413
Buchdahl, Rolf, 126n.
Buda Co., 272
Budget Bureau, see Bureau of the Budget
Building materials, price behavior in, 549
Bulk purchasing, economies of, 154–55
Bunker, George M., 605
Bureaucracy: in Communist countries, 687; as impediment, 162–63
Bureau of the Budget, 608, 618, 663, 665
Bureau of the Census, see Census Bureau
Bureau of Corporations, 601, 621
Bureau of Labor Statistics (BLS), 410, 424–37, 440, 461–62, 464, 545; production changes and, 538; "quintile" study by, 438–48; vs. National Bureau price index, 462–63; steel price index of, 639; Wholesale Price Index of, see Wholesale Price Index
Bureau of Mines, 433

Classical theory, macroeconomics and, 1
Clausewitz, Karl von, 467
Clayton Antitrust Act, 77n., 260, 341, 368–69, 567, 570; Celler-Kefauver amendment to, 591–92, 595–96; "future" orientation of, 590; loophole in, 591; Neal Task Force and, 598–99; predation and, 601; Robinson-Patman amendment to, 602
Clemens, Eli, 41n.
Cleveland Trust Co., 81, 91n., 409n., 574
Cleveland Twist Drill Co., 81n., 574
Clock regulator, 237–38
Clorox Co., 46
Coal prices, changes in, 417
Coal Trade Journal, 581
Coca-Cola Co., 270, 317, 323–24
Cohen, Manuel F., 607
Colbert, L. L., 337, 499
Colgate-Palmolive Co., 314, 320
Collins, Norman R., 19, 63, 65, 525, 527, 533, 536
Collusion: antitrust approach and, 575–89; concentration and, 532; conspiracy and, 585; "degrees" and "forms" of, 582; electrical-equipment cases in, 576–80; evidentiary requirements in, 580–83; freight equalization cases in, 583–85; production restriction and, 585–89
Colonial Mills, Inc., 269
Colorado Fuel & Iron Corp., 355, 383
Colorado Milling Co., 269
Color television, 209
Columbia Broadcasting System, 209
Columbia Steel case, 599
Columbia University Hospital, 391
Combe, Ivan, 320
Combe Chemical Co., 317, 320
Comer, George P., 588
Commander-Larabee Milling Co., 269
Commercial Credit Corp., 268
Commercial Investment Trust Corp., 268
Commissioner of Corporations, 621
Committee, inefficiency of, 244
Committee meeting, "status" of, 172–73
Communism: concentration under, 682–84; "free enterprise" under, 702–03; industrial employment under, 684; oligopoly under, 706; price behavior and, 696–97
Communities of interest, in aggregate concentration, 60
Compact cars, import competition in, 515; see also Automobile industry
Company concentration, vs. plant, 102–04
Compazine, 242, 389
Competition: centripetal forces in, 591–612; conglomerate and, 47–48; destructive, 664; foreign, 515, 609; government and, 372–401; law enforcement and, 615–20; Marx on, 110; monopoly power and, 177, 556; naive ideas about, 112; national program for, 615; nonprice, 5, 308–38, 467; oligopoly and, 4–5; patents and, 386–91;

perfect, 153; "potential injury" doctrine in, 47; price regulation and, 664, 671–73; "protection" from, 648; shelf space and, 323; from small producers, 510–15; among suppliers, 281; suppression of, 78; in Yugoslavia, 703; see also Competitive approach; Competitive pricing
Competitor, aggressive, 370
Competitive approach: concentration prevention and, 590–620; evaluation of, 614–20; traditional antitrust as, 555–89
Competitive macroeconomic theory, 3
Competitive pricing: price regulation and, 671–72; tax policy and, 673–75
Compulsory licensing, government and, 610–12
Computer: age of, 145; conglomerates and, 158; cost of, 147; programming of, 147–48; for small businesses, 149
Concentrated industries, 4; "extreme" to "narrow" divergence ratings in, 103–05; importance of, 11–14; invention in, 213–15; market control by, 14; oligopoly in, 12; price guidelines and, 630; principles governing, 2; shifts in, 13–14; value of shipments by, 18
Concentrated Industries Act, 573
Concentration: advertising and, 256, 311, 527, 530, 615; advertising/sales ratio and, 332–34; aggregate, see Aggregate concentration; brand or trade names and, 527; centripetal forces in, 255–56, 591–612; collusion and, 532; under Communism, 682–84; competitive approach to, 614–20; conglomerate, see Conglomerate concentration; consolidation, mergers and acquisitions in, 257–84; cross-subsidization and, 362; declining, 530–31; dimensions of, 1–2; diminishing returns in, 92–95; "distinct profit break" hypothesis in, 536; economic behavior and, 403–04; economic thinking and, 107–13; further prevention of, 590–620; government disposal policy and, 381; growth and, 195–98, 534; industrial, 85–113; within industry groups, 15–18; "law" of, 111; legislation against, 615; market, see Market concentration; market control in, 14; Marx on, 111; merger-created, 593; and number of plants, 196; oligopoly and, 572; overstatement of, 11; price behavior and, 406–19; price-cost factors in, 526–27; price rigidity and, 424–37; production and, 537; profitability and, 535; profit margin and, 527; public policy and, 551–53; single-plant vs. multiplant operations in, 101–02; in Soviet Union, 682–84; specialization factor in, 8–9; steam power development and, 87–88; in steel industry, 9, 74, 78–79; technology and, 87–113; transaction prices and, 461–66; TV advertising and, 256, 311, 321–31, 530, 615; understating of, 9–10; unit mar-

Concentration (*cont.*)
gins and, 527–29; vertical, *see* Vertical concentration; widening price margins and, 531; *see also* Aggregate concentration; Market concentration

Concentration ratios, 7–11; advertising/sales ratio and, 332; flexible-price products and, 449; for four companies, 323; market area and, 10; price changes and, 459, 465; product pairs and, 448; substitutability and, 8; trend in, 19–20; TV advertising and, 324–29; value of shipments and, 12

Confiscation, U.S. Constitution and, 673

Conglomerate(s): accounting methods of, 290–92; computer and, 158; concentration and, 307 (*see also* Conglomerate concentration); cross-subsidization and, 42; growth of, 285–91; merger diseconomies and, 173–74; mutual forbearance among, 53; new, 285; of 1920's, 265; output of, 57; "partial" and "pure" types, 57; "potential injury to competition" theory and, 47–48; price structure and, 46; "synergistic" quality and, 294; since World War II, 270

Conglomerate concentration, 41–59; in appliance industry, 55–56; competition and, 47–48; defined, 41; industry output and, 57; largest companies in, 53–54; market behavior and, 41–50; mutual forbearance in, 48–50; "outside" leadership in, 55–58; tobacco industry and, 53; trend in, 58–59; vs. vertical concentration, 56

Conglomerate expansion: Gulf & Western case history in, 300–07; high P/E ratios in, 292–95; liquidity in, 298–300; P/E ratios in, 292–300; low profitability and, 296; three stages of, 292–300

Conglomerate structure, theories of, 50–52

Console, A. Dale, 242–43

Consolidated Cigar Co., 268, 287, 325, 330

Consolidated Coal Corp., 80

Consolidated Vultee Corp., 273

Consolidation movement, 65, 257–84

Consumer, changing desires of, 614–15

Consumer Price Index, 629, 653

Container Corp., 181

Container industry, acquisitions and mergers in, 272

Continental Airlines, Inc., 660

Continental Baking Co., 227, 348–50

Continental Can Co., Inc., 520, 587; pricing standards of, 495

Continental Oil Co., 279, 281

Continuous casting, in steelmaking, 235

"Continuous mix" process, in bread industry, 225–26

Control center, special problems of, 170–73

Control threshold, in aggregate concentration, 80

Conversion deals, 27

Cook, N. A., 139

Cooper, Arnold C., 211

Cooperage industry, vertical concentration in, 31–34

Copper-mining companies, mergers in, 265

Cordiner, Ralph, 171

Corfam, 211, 509

Corning Glass Co., 70*n*.

Corn Products Refining Co., 257–60, 269

Corporate income tax, price regulation through, 674–75

Corporate performance: federal incorporation and, 667–69; higher production and, 670–01; marginal incentives in, 669; price regulation and, 666–75

Corporate research, alternatives to, 250–54

Corporate stock, holding of by other companies, 668

Corporation: control of, in larger firms, 75–80; vs. inventor, 251–52; responsibility for direction of, 75

Corporation laws, 668–69

Corrosion, prestressed concrete and, 132

Corticosteroids, 216

Cortisone, 216

Cost: captive supplier and, 35–36; "creep factors" in, 37; fixed vs. variable, 37, 470; full, 470–74, 477; general administration and, 36; "imaginary," 653; overhead, 36; "super-overhead," 37; vertical integration and, 25–26

Coty, Inc., 272

Coulter, Kirkley, 600

Council of Economic Advisers, 461, 627, 629, 638–39, 645, 647

Cournot, Antoine Augustin, 4

Courtalds, Ltd., 128

Crane Co., 183

Creep factors, costs and, 37

Creomulsion Co., 315–16, 321

Crompton, Samuel, 556

Croning, Johannes, 214

Cross-elasticity of demand, 8

Cross-freight saving, 154

Cross-subsidization: conglomerate and, 42; in fertilizer industry, 363–64; on geographic basis, 366; as predatory practice, 358–67, 594; in shoe machinery industry, 43; in unconcentrated industries, 51

Crowder, Walter, 59*n*., 99*n*., 158, 263*n*., 293*n*., 414*n*., 430*n*., 432*n*., 537–38, 541*n*., 542–43, 566*n*.

Crown Manufacturers of America, 580–81

Crucible Steel Corp. (Colt Industries, Inc.), 78, 174

Cruse, William T., 116, 118

Cunningham, William, 556

Curtice, Harlow, 472, 475–77

Curtiss Aeroplane & Motor Co., 222

Curtis-Wright Corp., 143

Czechoslovakia: bureaucracy in, 687; economic growth in, 692–93; economic reforms in, 687; industrial employment in,

684; inefficiency in, 690 91; price behavior in, 696–99; raw materials export
from, 691; trusts and cartels in, 700–01

Dairy products industry, mergers in, 264–
65
Data processing, 145–48
Daugherty, C. R., 509n.
David and Goliath, military lesson from,
245
Davies, R. W., 690
Davis, Francis, 236
Day, William Rufus, 563
DCF (discounted-cash flow) analysis, 158
DDT, 209
Dean, Joel, 158, 173–74, 296, 469
Decentralization: committee meeting and,
172–73; electrification and, 96; rivalry
and, 172; transportation and, 97 98
Decentralizing technologies, 95–98, 115–51;
electronics and, 144–51; energy as, 133–
44; high-performance composites and,
125–29; prestressed concrete and, 129–
32
Decision errors, decentralization and, 171–
72
Decision making: capital sources and, 157;
divisional reporting and, 604
Decline of Competition, The (Burns), 112
De Domenico, Paul, 318
Defense Department, U.S.: drug purchases
by, 512; government protection and, 609;
size and, 99–100
De Forest, Lee, 229
Delaware corporation laws, 668–69
Delrin plastic, 211, 509
Delta Airlines, Inc., 659–60
Demand: advertising and, 309; cross-elastic-
ity of, 8; elasticity of, 518–20, 542, 658–
60; price regulation and, 658–60; under-
estimation of, 236–38
Depletion allowance tax savings, 69
De Podwin, Horace J., 459
Depreciation, target return costs and, 472
Depression: mergers and, 264; prices in,
411; see also Great Depression
Design and model changes, automobile in-
dustry, 334–38
Desilu Productions, 287
De Simone, Daniel V., 224n., 225, 236n.,
238, 612
Detail men, in drug industry, 658
Detroit Steel Co., 521
Dever, Henry, 145
Dewing, Arthur S., 185
Diamond Match Co., 231, 413
Diamond-T Truck Co., 273
Di Benedetto, Anthony T., 118–19
Diesel fuel, 141
Diesel locomotives, 378
Dietz, Albert G. H., 125
Digitalis, 242

Dillon, Read & Co., 268–69
Diminishing returns, concentration and, 92–
93
Director, Aaron, 420n.
Directorates, interlocking, 76–77
Dirlam, Joel B., 173n., 234 35, 298, 339,
341n., 343, 346, 475n., 495n., 499n., 514n.,
520n., 563n., 607, 685n., 702–04
Discounted-cash flow, 158
Discrimination: financial statement and, 603;
good-faith clause and, 602–03; see also
Price discrimination
Diseconomies: management, see Manage-
ment diseconomies; in state ownership,
687–92
Disposal policy, concentration and, 381
Dissolution: feasibility of, 571; "justification"
against, 572; monopoly and, 563–65
Distillers, TV advertising by, 324–25
Distillers Corporation–Seagrams, 324
Distribution, in multiproduct firm, 156
Divergence, between company and plant con-
centration, 103–05
Diversification, mergers and, 189
Divisional reporting, 603–04, 607–08
Dixie Cup Co., 272
Dixon, Paul Rand, 349n., 496
Dixon, Robert L., 35–39
Doblin, Ernest, 424n., 539
Dodd, Thomas, 600
Dodge, Norton, 685n., 693, 698, 701
Dodge Brothers, 265
Doman, C. T., 365n.
Dooley, Peter C., 76–78
Douglas, Paul H., 401, 420n., 520n., 583
Douglas, William O., 595
Douglas Co., 412
Dow Chemical Co., 125, 587
Dowdey, Clifford, 392n.
Drexe, Anthony J., 262n.
Drexel & Co., 262n.
Dreyfus Fund, 604
Drug industry: patent protection in, 388;
price competition in, 510–13; pricing
standards in, 496–97
Drugs and drug products: average prices of,
389–90; British patenting of, 611; dis-
covery of by class, 391; price rigidity in,
409
Drutter, I., 704n.
Dry cell, mercury, 225
Dual-power automobile, 135n.
Dubchek, Alexander, 693, 698n.
Duchaine, Joseph P., 226–27
Dudinster, Vladimir, 244n.
Duerrer, Robert, 234
Dunlop, John T., 627, 631
Duopoly, 5n.
du Pont, Irenée, 58
du Pont de Nemours, E. I., & Co., Inc., 30,
58, 66, 118, 211, 224, 259–60, 263, 376,
521; General Motors stock ownership by,

General Telephone & Electronics Co., 272–73

General Theory of Employment, Interest, and Money, The (Keynes), 1

General Time Corp., 238

Gentlemen's agreement, collusion and, 582

George, K. D., 534

George Washington University, 205

Georgia Institute of Technology, 129

German Cartel Decree, 557

Germany: aerodynamic progress in, 220; blitzkrieg and, 246; monopoly in, 557; rocketry in, 222–23; steelmaking advances in, 234

Gibbs v. *McNeeley,* 586

Gillette Co., 326, 330

Glass fiber, plastics and, 120

Glass industry: aggregate concentration and, 74; indifference to technology in, 235–36; other concentration in, 116; paperboard containers and, 272; price changes in, 417, 466; revolution in, 89; selling pool and, 418; tapered integration in, 33

Goddard, Robert H., 210, 222, 224, 247–48, 610

Goldberg, Arthur J., 635

Goldbricks, hierarchy and, 162–63

Golden Grain Macaroni Co., 318

Golf clubs, manufacture of, 231

"Good-faith" defense, in price discrimination cases, 601–03, 615

Goodyear Aircraft Co., 125

Goodrich, B. F., Co., 265, 370, 509, 597

Gordon, Robert Aaron, 79, 481

Gort, Michael, 18

Göttingen University, 220

Government: as centripetal force, 609–12; competition and, 372; disposals by, 380–85; foreign competition and, 609–10; infant industry protection by, 394; intervention by, 372–73; leasing by, 385–86; licensing by, 611–12; monopolies granted by, 610–11; new technologies and, 609–10; price "reasonableness" standards and, 645; procurement by, 375–80; regulatory actions of, 373, 395–96; role of, 372–401; steel prices and, 632–41; tariffs and quotas in, 392–95

Government guidelines, price behavior and, 626–31

Government patents, 386–91

Government suasion, in price behavior, 626–45; *see also* Voluntary suasion

Graber, Dean E., 293n.

Grace, Eugene C., 500

Graf, George, 227

Grain Futures Act (1922), 623

Grainmill products industry, 75

Grant, I. F., 96n.

Gray, Horace M., 341n., 373–74

Gray market, oligopoly and, 7

Greatamerica Holding Co., 287

Great American Insurance Co., 300

Great Britain: high-performance composites in, 127–29; monopoly in, 557; Napoleonic Code in, 395–96; postwar nationalization in, 678–79

Great Depression, 266, 527; automobile production in, 336; coal prices in, 417–18; concentration in, 431; economic behavior in, 419; farm machinery prices in, 624; low production during, 586; prices and, 406, 420, 528; price theory and, 469

Greenspan, Alan, 116

Gresham's law, 668

Griliches, Zvi, 308

Grinnell Corp., 183, 286, 597

Griswold, A. Whitney, 244

Groner, John V., 234

Gross national product, oligopoly and, 550

Growth, concentration and, 87–92, 195–98

Guggenheim Foundation, 222

Guideposts, price behavior and, 626–31

Gulick, Charles A., Jr., 260n.

Gulf & Western Industries, Inc., 287, 291, 294, 297, 299, 300–06

Gulf Oil Co., 279, 281, 499

Hadley, Eleanor, 82

Haglund, Philip E., 93n.

Hale, George E., 156n., 564

Hall, R. L., 469–70

Hallmark Co., 326, 330

Haloid Co., 224

Hamberg, Daniel, 201n., 208n., 215

Hamilton, Walton, 597n.

Hamilton Paper Co., 271

Hamilton Watch Co., 328

Hand, Learned, 565–66

Handler, Milton, 561n., 562n., 586

Hannah Pickett Mill, 269

Hansen, Alvin, 542, 673

Hansen, Victor R., 570

Harding, Ralph L., Jr., 115

Hardy, Charles O., 405n.

Hargreaves, James, 556

Harkins, Kenneth R., 300–03

Harkness family, 79

Harlan, John Marshall, 560

Harrison, Benjamin, 392n.

Harrod, Roy, 5

Hart, Liddell, 164n.

Hartford-Empire Glass Co., 231, 569–70

Hartford family, 79

Hartford Insurance Co., 299, 597

Harvard Business School, 206

Haverford College, 583

Hayek, F. A. von, 696n.

Heal, William E., 236

Heat cycle, energy and, 133

Heflebower, Richard B., 341n., 469–70

Heinz, H. J., Co., 270, 520

Helene Curtis Industries, 320

International Telephone & Telegraph Co., 269, 286, 294, 299–300, 597
Interstate Circuit case, 580
Interstate Commerce Commission, 373, 396, 398, 601, 609, 648, 661–63
Invention and innovation, 199–227; in aircraft field, 291–92; company size and, 211–12; in concentrated industries, 213–15; corporate research and, 251–54; corporation vs. individual inventor in, 251; historical research in, 207–10; individual research and, 208–09; internal communication and, 212–13; list of inventions, 208; organization vs. creativity in, 242–44; and protection of older technology, 229–32; recent, 215–27; research and development in relation to, 200–04, 210–13; and resistance to change, 228–29; in rocketry, 222–24; statistical studies and, 200–07; time lapse before innovation in, 228; trade restraints and, 231–32; and underestimation of demand for product, 236–38; weapons systems and, 245–51; wonder drugs as, 216–19
Inventive-patents, number of firms holding, 205
Inventor: financing of, 240; greater emphasis needed on, 251–52; hostile attitude toward, 240–41; market research and, 241; neglect of, 238–41
Investment-banking houses, merger financing by, 267–69
Investment performance index, 190
Iowa Beef Packers Corp., 183
Iron Age, 28, 33, 462n., 632
Irvin, William A., 500
Island Creek Coal Co., 278, 290
I-T-E Circuit Breaker Co., 578

Jackson, P. H., 131
Japan: concentration in, 113; control of industry by Zaibatsu in, 81–82; industrial size in, 684
Jasinski, Raymond, 136–39
Jawboning, with steel industry, 621, 637–41
Jay, Antony, 159, 160n., 165, 167n.
Jefferson Electric Co., 291
Jerome, Harry, 89, 96n.
Jet engine, 221–22
Jewkes, John, 142n., 208, 209n., 235n., 236n., 241n., 243n., 244n., 509n.
Jewkes study, in invention and research, 208–10, 215, 242–43
Joffre, Marshal Joseph Jacques, 164
Johnson, Lyndon B., 573, 632; steel industry and, 637–43
Johnson, S. C., 328
Joint Economic Committee, 549
Jones, Eliot, 418n.
Jones, F. D., 407–08
Jones & Laughlin Steel Corp., 78, 287, 298
Ju Chin Chu, 138

Junghaus, Siegfried, 235
Justice Department, U.S., 30, 283, 341, 363, 383–84, 418, 594; antitrust suit against investment bankers by, 268; collusion and, 576–80, 587; conglomerate mergers and, 599; on horizontal mergers, 592–93; ITT and, 286; monopoly and, 566, 568; in price-fixing cases, 576–77; in steel wage increase case, 636

Kahn, Alfred E., 339, 343, 344n., 346, 373–74, 563n., 648n., 675
Kahn, R. F., 5
Kaiser, Henry J., Co., 34
Kaiser Aluminum Co., 565
Kaiser Steel Co., 612
Kaldor, Nicholas, 309–12, 334
Kaplan, A. D. H., 359, 475n., 495n., 499n., 514n., 520n.
Karyla, S. N., 364n.
Kauder, Emil, 694–95
Kaysen, Carl, 11, 27, 42–44, 308, 570–74, 603n.
Kaysen-Turner analysis, of concentrated industries, 11–12, 615
Kefauver, Estes, 497, 503–05, 595–96, 602, 618, 632–36, 640, 647
Kefauver hearings, steel prices and, 632–35
Kefauver-Harris amendment, 399
Kellogg Co., 324, 330
Kelly, Eamon, 191–92
Kennecott Copper Corp., 265
Kennedy, John F., 486, 492, 626, 632, 637, 640
Kennedy Administration, steel price rise and, 635–37, 645
Kern County Land Co., 287
Kerr-McGee Co., 278–79
Kerry, T. W., 475n.
Keynes, John Maynard, 1, 420, 436–37
Khrushchev, Nikita S., 681
Kieckhefer Containers Co., 271–72
Kilpatrick, B. W., 535n.
Kimberly-Clark Corp., 271, 326
Kindahl, James K., 419n. 461–63
Kinetic Corp., 568
Kiwi Polish Co., 328
Klein, Burton, 250
Knight, Edward, 638, 639n.
Kodachrome process, 209–10
Koldweld process, 214
Korean War, prices and, 405
Kosygin, Alexei, 697
Kottke, Frank J., 10, 12, 14, 519, 670
Kraft Foods Co. (Kraftco Corp.), 598
Kreps, Theodore J., 666
Kress family, 79
Krilium, 209
Kronstein, Heinrich, 492n., 621–22
Kuboleca, Stevan, 173n., 705, 706n.
Kuhn, Loeb & Co., 76n., 269
Kvasha, Ya., 682–86

Mamluks, warfare of, 246
Management control, of nonfinancial corporation, 79
Managerial diseconomies, 159–75; decentralization as, 170–71; forms and procedures in, 162–64; incompetence as, 168–69; line/staff conflict and, 164–66; mergers as, 173–75; resistance to change as, 169–70; success and, 170
Managerial economies: capital source and, 157–58; defined, 152–53; economic thinking and, 198; engineering estimates and, 176–77; evidence of, 176–98; financial controls and staff services in, 158–59; mergers and profitability as, 184–95; rationales of, 152–75; size vs. profitability in, 177–85
Manufacturing industries, value of shipments in, 12; *see also* Industry
Marathon Corp., 272
Marchant calculator, 272
Marconi, Guglielmo, 229
Maritime Board, 661
Market, substitutability in, 8
Market area concentration ratios, 10
Market behavior: aggregate concentration and, 60–61; conglomerate concentration and, 41–50; market concentration and, 3–6; vertical concentration and, 25–30
Market concentration, 3–24; defined, 2; within industry groups, 19–22; market behavior and, 3–6; monopoly power and, 41; summary of industry changes and, 22–24; turnover and mobility in relation to, 18–19; *see also* Concentrated industries; Concentration
Market control, concentration and, 14
Market-determined macroeconomic theory, 3
Market power, vertical integration and, 27
Market preemption, vertical concentration and, 30–31
Market research, inventor and, 241; *see also* Research; Research and development
Market share, of oligopolist, 6
Market socialism, in Yugoslavia, 702–04
Market surveys, state ownership and, 695
Markham, Jesse W., 341n.
Marshall, Alfred, 19, 110, 159, 198, 387, 470, 556–57
Marshall, John, 669
Martha Mills, 265
Martin Marietta Corp., 270, 273, 605; divisional profit statement of, 606
Marx, Karl, 373, 680, 682, 692; on competition, 110; on "law of concentration," 111
Maser, 215
Mason, Edward S., 408, 422n., 444n.
Massachusetts Institute of Technology, 252
Materials, new technologies and, 114–33
Materials Research Laboratory, 126
Materials Service Co., 273

Maximized returns, pricing and, 481–82
May, Elizabeth S., 416n.
Mayo Clinic, Rochester, Minn., 391
Maytag Co., 56, 603
Mead, Walter J., 296n., 297, 299
Means, Gardiner C., 63, 65, 67n., 75, 78, 186, 265n., 267n., 404, 419–20, 422–23, 425–27, 429–30, 436, 444, 459, 461, 463, 468–69, 537–39, 541, 629n., 669
Measday, Walter S., 281
Meat packing industry, size vs. professionalism in, 182–83
Medina, Harold R., 368
Medium Shell Program, World War II, 377
Mees, C. E. K., 241
Meleney, Frank, 391
Mellon family, 75, 79
Mentholatum Co., 312, 314, 317, 319–20
Mephenesin, 217
Meprobomate, 217
Mercedes automobile, 143
Merck & Co., Inc., 216, 218, 512
Mercury battery, 225
Mercury Media (agency), 312, 314, 316
Mergers: "acquirers" in, 186–87; aggregate concentration and, 266–67; as centripetal force, 591–600; competition avoidance through, 261; consolidations and acquisitions in relation to, 257–84; continuing absorption process and, 269–84; defined, 257; as external expansion, 257; financing of, 267–69; as management diseconomy, 173–75; monopoly power and, 266; in 1920's, 264–69; profitability and, 184–95; "purge" in, 174–75; quantitative importance of, 274–75; recent activity in, 286; stock ownership and, 66; stock-price changes and, 263; success in, 190–91; at turn of century, 257–59; vertical, 2; since World War II, 269–70
Merrill, Charles E., 679n.
Metal barrels industry, vertical concentration in, 34
Metal firms, mergers of, 265
Metal foil industry, vertical concentration in, 33–34
Metal prices, rigidity in, 409; *see also* Steel industry
Metals industry: concentration in, 15, 20; flexible-price products in, 449; price behavior in, 416, 549; size vs. profitability in, 181; *see also* Steel industry
Michigan Salt Association, 412n.
Microwave transmission, 244
Middle Ages, warfare in, 125
Midvale Steel Co., 265
Midwest Refining Co., 265
Miles, John, 234
Military-industrial complex, 248
Military Medical Supply Agency, 512–14
Military organizations: resistance to change in, 245 50; science and, 249

Navy Department, U.S., 222
Neal, Alfred C., 422n., 527–28, 538
Neal, Philip C., 573, 598
Neal Task Force, 572–74, 598, 615
Nelson, Ralph L., 65, 69n., 101, 197, 257, 259, 261, 263
Nelson, Saul, 443n., 560
Nerlove, Marc, 520n.
Nevins, Allan, 92n., 335
New Britain Machine Co., 291
New Deal, pricing in, 420
New Drug Application, 399–401
New Industrial State, The (Galbraith), 649
New Jersey Zinc Co., 293, 300–04
Newport News Shipbuilding Co., 287
New technologies, government as barrier to, 609; see also Technology
New York Central Railroad, 78
New York State Sheet Metal Roofing and Air Conditioning Contractors Association, 370
New York Times, 521–22
Neyland, T. H., 302
Nichol, A. J., 426n.
Nicholls, William H., 340n.
Nickel-cadmium battery, 137
Nicks, Jess, 312, 316
Nixon, Richard M., 339, 545, 630, 632
Nollard, Ralph E., 268
Nonelectrical machinery industries, concentration in, 22
Nonferrous metals industry, price behavior in, 416–17
Nonfinancial corporations: interlocking directorates in, 76; largest, 62; nonfinancial control of, 79
Nonprice competition, 5, 308–38; price rigidity and, 467
North American Rockwell Corp., 254
Northern Metal Products Co., 36
Northern Regional Research Laboratory, 218–19
Northern Securities case, 558, 591
Northern Trust Co., 78
Northwest Airlines, Inc., 659–60
Norwich Pharmacal Co., 313, 319
Nourse, Edwin G., 374, 421n.
Novick, David, 201–04, 207, 614n.
NRA Code, 509
NSU (German automobile mfr.), 142–43
Nutter, G. Warren, 63, 65
Nylon: development of, 211; reinforced, 119

Oakley, C. O., 583
Occidental Petroleum Co., 278, 290
Office of Civilian and Defense Management, 493
Office of Price Administration, 625, 650
Offshore oil leases, 609
Oil and chemicals group, successful mergers in, 193

Oil companies: communities of interest and, 283; depletion tax savings by, 69; fertilizers and, 282; mergers of, 275–84
Oil Import Administration, 493, 609, 663
Oil Insurance Association, 93
Oil spillage, 95
Oil tankers, destruction of, 95
Okonite Co., 287
Okun, Arthur M., 630–31
Old Age and Survivors Insurance, Bureau of, 376n.
Old Ben Coal Company, 278
Oligopolist(s): in business cycle, 6; competition among, 509; market share and, 6; rivalry among, 4–5; in seller's market, 7; turnover and mobility of, 18–19
Oligopolistic industry, 4
Oligopolistic price behavior, 438–66; concentrated vs. unconcentrated products and, 458; correlation analyses and, 458–60; in iron and steel industry, 450–52; pairs of products in, 448–58; in petroleum industry, 452–53; quintile study in, 438–48
Oligopolistic price determination and pricing, 467–97; competition and, 495; constraints in, 498–522; and elasticity of demand, 518–20; full-cost pricing and, 469–70; history of, 405–37; import competition and, 515–18; leadership and, 495; monopsony and oligopsony in, 520–22; price competition and, 508–18; price followership and, 498–508; "principal pricing goal" in, 475; productivity and, 477–78; target or maximized returns in, 481–95; since World War II, 469
Oligopoly: asymmetrical, 439, 533, 568; in Communist countries, 700–01; competition under, 4; concentration and, 572; conglomerate and, 41, 45; economic effects of, 523–50; overhead-plus-profits margin and, 524–32; policy effect of, 544–49; price behavioral effects of, 523 (see also Oligopolistic price determination and pricing); price competition and, 153; production effect of, 536–44; in steel industry, 26
Oligopsony, 520–22
Olin Chemical Co., 139n.
Olin Mathieson Corp., 272
Oliver Corp., 273
O'Mahoney, Joseph C., 380, 499, 595, 624, 644, 667–68
Opel, John R., 146, 150
Open-hearth process, 234
Operating rate, of United States Steel Corp., 641–43
Operations, rationalization of, 153–55
Orders, pooling of, 153
Ordnance Department, U.S. Army, 66, 378
Ordzhonikidze, G. K., 681n.
Organization: conflict with creativity in,

242–44; coordination in, 172; decentralization of, 170–73

Organizational structures, hierarchical or pyramidal, 159

Organization for Economic Cooperation and Development, 689–90

Original cost, price regulation and, 654–55

Orr, Lloyd, 134, 139

Orrick, William H., Jr., 593

Osborn Mfg. Co., 81n.

Oscar Mayer Corp., 183

Otto, Nikolaus August, 134

Outboard Marine Corp., 143

Output increase, efficiency and, 195

"Outside leadership," in conglomerate concentration, 54–58

Overall concentration, 2; see also Aggregate concentration

Overcapacity, "illness" of, 36

Overhead costs, 36, 646; see also Cost

Overhead-plus-profits margin, oligopoly and, 524–32

Owens-Corning Fiberglas Corp., 70n., 120, 125

Owens-Illinois Glass Co., 70n.

Owens Yacht Co., 273

Oxenfeldt, Alfred R., 35, 37, 39, 469

Oxford University, 217

Oxygen steelmaking, 215, 234, 612

Oxytetracycline, 219

Pabst, William R., Jr., 419n.

Pabst Brewing Co., 179

Pacific American Fisheries, 411

Pacific-American Steel & Iron Corp., 383

Pacific Mills Co., 270

Pacific Oil Co., 265

Pacific Packing & Navigation Co., 411

Pacific Petroleum Co., 265

"Packaged" TV commercials, 313; see also TV advertising

Packaging Corporation of America, 287

Packaging materials, oligopolistic price behavior in, 453–54

Packers and Stockyards Act (1921), 623

Pan American Petroleum & Transportation Co., 265

Pan American World Airways, 305

Panel on Invention and Innovation, 612

Paper industry: acquisitions and mergers in, 271; conglomerates in, 49

Paramount Pictures (Gulf & Western Industries, Inc.), 287, 303–04

Paris, University of, 216

Parke, Davis & Co., 496

Parker-Hannifin Corp., 184

Parkinson, C. Northcote, 159–62

Parkinson's Law, 159

Pashigian, P., 18n.

Patent Foundation, George Washington University, 205

Patent Office, U.S., 400

Patents: competition and, 386–91; compulsory licensing and, 611; in drug industry, 388–90; government control and, 386–91; government protection in, 609; monopoly granted through, 610–11; U.S. firms holding, 205

Patent statistics, meaning of, 206–07

Patent system, compulsory licensing and, 611

Patman, Wright, 81, 602n.

Paton, William A., 35, 532

Patterson, James M., 281

Patton, Arch, 482n.

Paulucci, Jeno F., 313–14

Peale, Gordon, 253

Pechiney Corp., 492

Peck, Merton J., 214–15

Pegrum, Dudley, 397, 651–64

Penicillin, 218

Pennick & Ford Co., 412

Penrose, Edith, 171n.

P/E ratio, see Price-earnings ratio

Permanente Metals Corp., 384

Permian Corp., 290

Perry, George L., 628

Peter, Laurence J., 159, 168–69

Peter Principle, 169, 171

Pet Milk Co., 520

Petroleum industry: concentration in, 14, 21; mergers in, 275–84; oligopolistic price behavior in, 453; price behavior in, 549; profit rate in, 489–93

Pew family, 79n.

Pfizer, Charles, & Co., Inc., 242, 272, 320, 496

Phalanx, in warfare, 245–46

Pharmaceuticals, TV advertising of, 329; see also Drug industry; Drugs and drug products

Phelps-Dodge Corp., 181, 265

Philco Corp., 272–73

Philip Morris, Inc., 193

Phillips, Almarin, 341n.

Phillips, Charles F., Jr., 652

Phillips curve, 1

Phillips Oil Co., 279

Photographic equipment industry, concentration in, 21

Pig iron industry, price behavior in, 451–52

Pig iron manufacturers, steel production by, 28

Pigou, A. C., 5, 109n., 110n.

Pilkington, Alastair, 235

Pilkington Bros., Ltd., 235

Pitcairn family, 79

Pittsburgh Plate Glass Co., 157, 236

Planning: "bigness" factor in, 650; in Soviet Russia, 111

Plant, Arnold, 387

Plant capacity, full-cost pricing and, 474

Plant concentration, vs. company concentration, 102–06, 196–97

Plant efficiency, 152
Planters Co., 270
Plant facilities, government disposals of, 383–84
Plant operation: diseconomies of, 152; rationalization of, 153–55; single vs. multiplant, 101–02
Plant size: Census Bureau on, 99; vs. profitability, 177–85; relative importance of, 98; transportation and, 99; and value of shipments, 101
Plastic boats, 121
Plastics: cost of, 117–19; decentralizing technology and, 114–20; future of, 115, 120; inventions in, 208–09
Plastics industry, history of, 117
Plastics Technology, 116
Plate glass industry, revolution in, 89
Plax Corp., 271
Pogosov, I., 684*n.,* 685, 688, 700
Polaroid Corp., 252, 330
Policy effect, oligopoly and, 544–49
Polyacrylonitrile, 127
Polyoply, defined, 3
Polystyrene, 118
Polyurethane, 118
Pope, Alexander, 401*n.*
Postal Telegraph Co., 229, 269
Potash Company of America, 47–48
Power-creating technologies, 133
Power Jets, Ltd., 221
Power steering, 236
Prandtl, Ludwig, 220
Pratt & Whitney Co., 139
Predatory practices (predation), 339–70; as centripetal force, 591; chain store buying and, 343–46; cross-subsidization and, 358–67; exclusive dealing and tie-in contracts as, 367–69; existence of, 339–58; price discrimination and, 342–58; primary-line discrimination and, 346–57; restriction in, 601–08; Robinson-Patman Act and, 602
President's Task Force on Antitrust Policy, 572–74
Preston, Lee E., 19, 63, 65, 341*n.,* 525, 527, 533, 536
Prestressed concrete, 572–74
Prestressed Concrete Institute, 129
Price(s): administered, 461 (*see also* Administered prices); Administration-dominated, 464; elasticity of demand and, 542; entry-limiting, 468; long-term trend in, 405–06; transaction, 461–66; vertical integration and, 25; *see also* Price behavior; Price determination; Pricing
Price, Waterhouse and Co., 604
Price behavior: under Communism, 696–99; concentration and, 406–19; concentration ratio and, 459; following World War II, 404, 528–29, 541; general changes and, 407–09; in Great Depression, 528–29;

guideposts of, 626–31; history of, 405; individual product changes and, 409–19; oligopolistic, 438–66, 523; overhead costs and, 646; "upswings" and "downswings" in, 444; voluntary suasion in, *see* Voluntary suasion; White House influence on, 630
Price changes: concentration ratios and, 465; frequency vs. amplitude in, 421; inflation and, 545
Price competition: aggregate concentration and, 61; import competition and, 515–18; marginal economies and, 153; in oligopolistic pricing, 508–18; in steel industry, 625; *see also* Price regulation
Price Control Act (1942), 625
Price-cost margins, industry structure and, 525*n.*
Price cutting, conglomerate and, 46; *see also* Price behavior; Pricing
Price data, empirical studies in, 430–32
Price determination, oligopolistic, *see* Oligopolistic price determination
Price discrimination: basing-point system and, 353–57; in bread industry, 348–50; concentration and, 351; erosion theory in, 342; financial statement and, 603; good-faith clause and, 602–03; as predatory practice, 342–58; primary-line type, 346–57; secondary-line type, 347, 357–58
Price-earnings ratio: conglomerate expansion and, 292–95; low, 294–98, 300
Price fixing: in electrical industry, 576–80; by General Electric Co., 363; Supreme Court and, 575; *see also* Collusion
Price followership, oligopolistic pricing and, 498–508
Price freezes, 650–51
Price indexes, BLS vs. NB, 461–63
Price inflexibility: concentration and, 424–37; theoretical refutations of, 427–30
Price leadership: collusion and, 588; monopoly and, 47
Price margins: concentration and, 529–31; for durable goods, 531–32; *see also* Pricing
Price notification, government suasion and, 643–45
Price "reasonableness," 645–46
Price-reduction campaigns, 467
Price regulation, 648–76; competitive pricing and, 671–73; corporate performance and, 666–75; elasticity of demand and, 658–60; evaluation of, 676; "fair return" in, 652–57; industry orientation and, 663–66; managerial incentives and, 669–70; multiple products and, 657–58; original cost and, 654–55; plural firms and, 657; price freeze and, 650–51; procedural delay and, 660–63; production volume and, 670–71; for public utilities, 660–62; rationale of, 648–50; reproduction cost and, 652, 655; utility-type, 651–66

Price rigidity: concentration and, 422; and nonprice competition, 467; production volume and, 541

Price squeeze, vertical concentration and, 28–30, 39

Price theory, Great Depression and, 469

Pricing: administered-price controversy and, 419–23; bonus plan and, 670; competition and, 495, 671–72; full-cost, 469–70, 473–74; labor unions and, 479–80; oligopolistic, see Oligopolistic pricing; production and, 486–89, 537; productivity and, 477; target return, 470–75; wage advances and, 479–80

Prime time, nonavailability of in TV advertising, 313–16

Prince family, 80

Principles of Economics (Marshall), 557

Printing and publishing industry, concentration in, 22

Private-label brands, 329

Prochlorperazine, 389

Procter & Gamble Co., 46, 271, 314, 319, 324, 326

Proctor & Gamble–Clorox case, 595, 599

Procurement, government and, 375–80

Product changes, price behavior in, 409–19

Product classes, concentration ratios and, 7–8

Product differentiation, TV advertising and, 331–32

Product group, SIC classification and, 8*n*.

Production: concentration and, 537; concerted restriction of, 585–89; "excessive," 586; pricing and, 537

Production effect, oligopoly and, 536–44

Productivity: target return pricing and, 477–78; wage increases and, 672

Product line broadening, economies of, 156–57

Product-line reporting, 603

Products, substitutable, 8, 11

Profit: "distinct break" hypothesis and, 535–36; unconsolidated, 646; see also Profit margin

Profitability: concentration and, 535; firm size and, 657; mergers and, 184–95; plant size and, 177–84

Profit allowance, vertical concentration and, 37

Profit margin: concentration and, 527, 535; income effect and, 531–36; target return pricing and, 474–75; for United States Steel Corp., 640–42

Profits squeeze, pricing and, 480

Profit statement, divisional, 603–08

Programming, computer and, 147

Prohibition, repeal of, 411

Project Astron, 610

Promotion: diseconomies of, 167; frustration and, 168

Property disposal, 381–85

Providence Washington Insurance, 287, 299

Proxmire, William, 249

Public policy, concentration and, 551–53

Public relations activities, as management diseconomy, 165–66

Public utilities: price regulation in, 660–61; state regulatory commissions and, 663

Public Utility Holding Company Act (1933), 565, 570, 623

Pujo Committee, 262

Pullman, George M., 262

Pullman Company, 262, 567–68

Pulp and paper industry, size vs. profitability in, 181; see also Paper industry

Punched card systems, 144

Purdy, Harry L., 668*n*.

Pure Oil Co., 193

Pyramid structure, organization as, 159

Quaker Oats Co., 330, 344

Quality Bakers of America, 226

Quinn, T. K., 362

"Quintile" study, 438–48, 545; cyclic changes in, 444–48; secular changes in, 440–44; strengths and weaknesses of, 448

Quotas, tariffs and, 392–95

Rabinow, Jacob, 237

Rader, B. H., 583–84

Radio Corporation of America, 263, 266; see also RCA Corp.

Radio transmission, early days of, 229–30

Railroads, transaction prices by, 463

Ralston-Purina Co., 270, 320

Rand Corporation, 201, 251

R&D expenditures, see Research and development

Rappaport, A., 603

Raskob, John J., 66

Rate discrimination, in TV advertising, 318–31

Rate of return, for multiproduct firm, 658

Rauwolfia, 217

Raw materials, vertical concentration and, 35

RCA Corp., 116, 272, 327, 330; see also Radio Corporation of America

RCA-Victor trade name, 266

Recessions, following World War II, 541

Red Springs Mill, 269

Red tape, as impediment, 162–63

Refrigerators, TV advertising of, 326–27

Regrating, crime of, 555

Regulatory actions, by federal government, 395–401; see also Government; Price regulation; Voluntary suasion

Regulatory commissions, Hoover report and, 618

Reid, Samuel Richardson, 185–87, 194

Reinforced plastics, 118–20

Reliance Insurance Co., 300

Renault Co., 679

Reo Motors, Inc., 273
Reproduction cost, price regulation and, 653–55
Republic Steel Corp., 235, 381, 383, 507, 638–39, 647
Research: alternatives to corporate form of, 251–54; as "deferred expense," 613–14; misdirection of, 241–54
Research and development: applied research and, 203; vs. basic research, 203; as empirical evidence, 200; inventions and, 209–10; meaning of, 201–04; patents and, 205
Research and development expenditures, 210–13; Internal Revenue Code and, 202; statistical studies in, 200–04
Research director, responsibilities of, 244–45
Research laboratories, private or individual, 251
Research rationale, 200
Reserpine, 217
Restraints of trade: antitrust approach and, 575; invention and, 231
Retailing Daily, 361
Retired officers, employment of in industry, 249
Revenue Act (1945), 674
Revere Camera Co., 273
Revlon, Inc., 192–93
Revolutionary War, 392
Reynolds, R. J., Co., 260
Reynolds Aluminum Co., 384, 565
Reynolds family, 79
Rheem Manufacturing Co., 269
Rhesus halmalytic disease, 215
Rhone-Poulenc Co., 216
Richfield Oil Co., 278
Rigid Steel Conduit case, 584, 599
Riley, Herschel Ernest, 438n.
Ripley, William Z., 623n.
Rivalry, among oligopolists, 5; decentralization and, 172
River Rouge Plant, Ford Motor Co., 92–93
Rivers, W. K., 315, 321
Robbins, Lionel, 109n., 387, 388n.
Robbins Mill, 269
Robertson, D. H., 107, 109, 110n., 198
Robertson, Sir Dennis, 518
Robinson, Austin, 152–53, 159, 171
Robinson, H. S., 93–94
Robinson, Joan, 5, 34, 35n., 41
Robinson-Patman Act, 155, 602, 623
Rockefeller family, 75, 79
Rockefeller Foundation, 218
Rocketry: inventions in, 222–24; military use of, 247; U.S. rejection of, 610
Rodney Metals Co., 290
Roerig, J. B., Co., 272
Rolling mill, continuous, 233
Roman legion, warfare and, 246
Romney, George, 155, 334

Roosevelt, Franklin Delano, 269, 624
Roosevelt, Theodore, 248, 621
Rose, Joseph R., 655
Ross, Arthur M., 629
Ross, Howard Norman, 468, 528, 529, 530
Rostow, Eugene V., 565–66, 585
Rotary engines, 140–44
Rothschild, K. W., 467, 524n.
Route-ton-miles, airlines prices and, 659–60
Royal Aircraft Establishment, 128
Royal Air Force, 221
Royal Dutch Shell Co., 283
Royal McBee Co., 291
Royal Navy, number of officials in, 162
Ruben, Samuel, 225
Ruggles, Richard, 460
"Rule of reason," in antitrust legislation, 560–63, 591–92
Russia, *see* Soviet Union
Rutgers University, 219, 391
Ryan Aeronautical Co., 290

Sachko, I. S., 685
St. Regis Paper Co., 271
Salk polio vaccine, 391
Salt industry, pools in, 412
Samuelson, Paul A., 627n.
Sanders, Barkev S., 206n.
Sanitary paper products, TV advertising of, 326
Sawmill industry, acquisitions and mergers in, 270
Sawyers, David, 142n., 208, 219–21, 235n., 236n., 241n., 243n., 244n., 509n.
Saxton, C. C., 469
Say, Jean-Baptiste, 420n.
Schenley Industries, Inc., 182, 324
Scherer, Frederic M., 201n., 205
Schering Drug Co., 496, 512
Schlaifer, Robert, 221–22
Schmookler, Jacob, 205, 207
Schon, Donald, 232, 250–51, 253, 610
Schultz, Charles L., 627n.
Schumpeter, Joseph, 199
Schwarz, C. V., 234
Science, military and, 249
Science stocks, 202
Scientist, vs. inventor, 239
Scitovsky, Tibor, 422n.
SCM Corp., 272
Scott & Williams Co., 290
Scott Paper Co., 271, 326
Scoville, Warren, 417n.
Seagar, Henry R., 260n.
Seagram, Joseph E. Sons, Inc., 182
Sears, Roebuck & Co., 80
Secondary-line discrimination, 357–58
Secrecy, perfect competition and, 343
Securities and Exchange Act, 76, 623
Securities and Exchange Commission, 78–79, 178, 604, 607–08, 614
Seeley, Joseph, 343

"Segmental" reporting, 603; *see also* Divisional reporting
Selden, Richard P., 459
Self-interest, price regulation and, 648
Seller's market, oligopoly and, 7
Semiconductor industry, 144, 253
Senate Antitrust Committee, *see* Senate Subcommittee on Antitrust and Monopoly
Senate Committee on Interstate and Foreign Commerce, 356, 500
Senate Judiciary Committee, 560, 603, 647
Senate Select Committee on Small Business, 397, 399
Senate Small Business Committee, 399
Senate Subcommittee on Antitrust and Monopoly, 35–36, 82, 126, 134, 141, 146, 150, 202, 210–11, 215–16, 232, 238, 251, 256, 309, 312, 316, 319, 322, 334, 336, 340, 343, 347, 373, 388, 421, 444, 470, 476, 496, 501–02, 515, 551, 570, 577, 594, 600, 607, 632–35, 665, 697
Seversky, Alexander de, 247
Shakespeare Co., 123
Shaped charge, 247
Shaw, Robert, 47–48
Sheahan, John, 679, 705
Shelf space, as bottleneck, 323
Shell molding, 214
Shell Oil Co., 279
Shell Research, Ltd., 139
Shepherd, William G., 99, 197, 459–60
Shepherd-Niles Crane & Hoist Co., 272
Sherman, Howard H., 533, 536, 572
Sherman Antitrust Act, 30, 262*n.*, 341, 558, 562*n.*, 563, 565–68, 570, 589, 601; collusion and, 575, 580; conspiracy and, 585; "past" orientation of, 590; shortcomings of, 571
Sherwin-Williams Co., 520
Shipbuilding, vertical control in, 34
Shipments: by concentrated industries, 18; concentration ratios and, 12; value of related to plant size, 101
Shockley, William, 253
Shoe machinery industry: monopoly in, 42–43; restraints used in, 231
Shove, G. F., 109*n.*, 110*n.*, 198*n.*
SIC classifications, *see* Standard Industrial Classifications
Sik, Ota, 687, 689, 693*n.*, 696–99
Silver Campaign Depression, 409*n.*
Simon, Henry C., 541
Simon, Norton, 174, 298
Sinclair Oil Co., 305
Singer Co., 272
"Sister" plants, 102
Size: efficiency and, 177, 657, 685–87; in socialist ideology, 680–82; in Soviet Union, 682–84; *see also* Plant size
Skelton, Alex, 416*n.*
"Small business," 75, 397, 399; financial aid

to, 612; relative efficiency of, 371; tax laws and, 613; venture capital and, 613; weaknesses and strengths of, 149
Small Business Administration, 372, 377
Smaller War Plants Corporation, 376, 378
Small producers, competition from, 510–15
Smith, Adam, 34, 386, 392, 556
Smith, Edward B., and Co., 269
Smith-Corona Corp., 272
Smith Douglas Co., 279
Smithsonian Institution, 223
Smolinski, Leon, 688
Smyth, Henry D., 201
Socialist ideology, size mystique in, 680–82
"Social performance," of industries, 666
Society of the Plastics Industries, 115–16, 118
Socony Mobil Co. (Mobil Oil Corp.), 265, 279, 281, 283
Sohmen, Egon, 515*n.*, 517
Solomons, David, 603, 605
Solow, Robert M., 627, 629
Sources of Invention, The (Jewkes et al.), 208
Soviet Union: automobiles in, 689; bureaucracy in, 170; Central Statistical Administration in, 700; concentration in, 682–84; diseconomies in, 687; economic reforms in, 697–99; exports from, 691; industrial employment in, 684; inefficiencies in, 687; Institute of Economics of, 685; planning in, 111; size mystique in, 680–84; size vs. efficiency in, 685–87; supply/demand unpredictability in, 693–97; transport costs in, 688; *see also* Communism; State ownership
Space capsules, fuel cells for, 137
Specialist suppliers, 34–39
Special Senate Committee on Atomic Energy, 248
Specialization, 8–9; economies of, 153–54; perfect competition and, 153; transportation costs and, 154; *see also* Specialist suppliers
Speed Queen washers, 272
Spencer Chemical Co., 279, 281
Spencer Kellogg Co., 273
Sputnik, 222
Squibb, E. R. & Sons, Inc., 218, 242, 272
Sraffa, Piero, 109*n.*, 110*n.*, 198*n.*
Staff/line conflicts, 164–66
Stalin, Joseph, 681, 684*n.*, 685*n.*, 698
Standard & Poor's index, 299
Standard Brands, Inc., 270, 358
Standard Industrial Classification (SIC), 7–8, 11, 31, 178, 545
Standard Oil Co. case, 339, 558, 560, 561*n.*, 562–64, 590–91
Standard Oil Co. of California, 265, 277–78, 368–69
Standard Oil Co. of Indiana, 265, 343, 346
Standard Oil Co. of Kentucky, 278

Target return pricing, 470–75; extent of, 475–76; implementation of, 476–80; profit margin and, 474–75; sustainability of, 494–95; wage increases and, 479–80

Target returns: attainment of, 482–91; long-term performance and, 482–83; year-to-year changes in, 483–91

Taxes: excess profits, 673; income, 674–75

Tax "forgiveness," 674–75

Tax laws, small business and, 613

Tax policy, competitive pricing and, 673–74

Taylor, Fred M., 696n.

Taylor, George, 405n.

Technical development, scientist and, 199

Technocracy, state ownership and, 678

Technological advance, indifference to, 232–36

Technological entrepreneur, 251

Technology: concentration and, 87–113; decentralizing, 95–98, 114–51; diminishing returns and, 92–95; economic thinking and, 107–13; inventions and, 208, 229–32; and military-industrial complex, 249–50; new materials and, 114–33; organization vs. creativity in, 242–44; protection of, vs. invention, 229–32; single-plant vs. multiplant operations and, 101–02; as "spectre," 112; weapons systems approach to, 609–10

Teledyne, Inc., 174, 286, 290, 294, 300

Telser, Lester G., 308–09, 332–33

Temporary National Economic Committee (TNEC), 78, 79n., 430, 500, 518, 596, 624, 667–69

Tenneco, Inc., 287

Tennessee Coal & Iron Co., 154

Tennessee Corp., 279, 281

Tennessee Gas & Transmission Co., 287

Tennessee Valley Authority, 576

Terramycin, 219

Terylene, 209

Texaco, Inc. (Texas Corp.), 265, 282, 520

Texas Instruments, Inc., 202, 253–54

Textiles industry: concentration in, 20; mergers in, 270–71; price behavior in, 548

Textron, Inc., 125, 270, 273, 299

Theatre Enterprises case, 585

Thermoplastics, 118–19

Thiokol Corp., 202

Thomson Houston Electric Co., 262

Thorazine, 216, 242

Thorp, Willard L., 66n., 99n., 158, 263, 266, 293, 414n., 422n., 430–33, 537–38, 541n., 542–43, 566n.

Thorp Finance Co., 300

Tidewater Oil Co., 279

Tie-in contracts, 367–69

Till, Irene, 597n.

Timken Roller Bearing Co., 81n., 184, 194

Tintner, Gerhard, 419, 422n.

Tire industry: secondary-line discrimination in, 357–58; vertical concentration in, 31–32

TNEC, *see* Temporary National Economic Committee

Tobacco industry: concentration in, 21, 74; conglomerates in, 49, 53; dissolutions in, 563–64

Toilet preparations, TV advertising of, 326

Townes, Charles H., 210

Townsend, Robert, 159–60, 165–66, 170

Toynbee, Arnold, 245–46

Toyo Nogyo, Japanese auto firm, 142

Trade names, concentration and, 527

Trane Co., 81

Tranquilizers, 216–17

Transaction prices, concentration and, 461–66

Transistors, 210, 253

Transition Electronics Co., 254

Trans-Missouri Freight case, 558–61

Transportation: decentralizing technology and, 97; plant size and, 99; revolution in, 88–89

Transportation costs, economies of specialization and, 154

Transportation equipment: concentration in, 21; price behavior in, 549

Trans World Airlines, Inc., 574

Treanor, John, 583–84

Treanor letter, in collusion case, 583

Trench warfare, 246

Triemens, Howard J., 570n.

Triumph-Adler Co., 291

Trucking industry, government regulation in, 396–97

Trucks, large-scale operations and, 114

True Temper Corp., 231

Truman, Harry S, 626

Tsai, Stephen, 126–28, 133

Tucker, Rufus, 408, 427–30

Tunnel diode, 215

Turbine engine, 140

Turbogenerators, price fixing and collusion in, 579

Turbojet engine, 221–22, 247

Turner, Donald F., 11, 27, 311, 339, 568, 570–72, 594–95, 598

Turnover, market concentration and, 18–19

Tuve, Merle A., 201

TV advertising: by car manufacturers, 327–28; as centripetal force, 591, 600–01; by cereal manufacturers, 324; by cigar manufacturers, 325; by cigarette manufacturers, 329; concentration and, 256, 311, 357, 530, 615; expenditures on, 321–22; favoritism toward larger companies in, 314–15; of food, 328–29; concentration ratios in, 323–24, 328–29; of household appliances, 326–27; of insecticides, 328; monopolistic character of, 311–13; "Net TV" vs. "Spot TV" in, 330; network control of, 314–18; networks as form of con-

A 2
B 3
C 4
D 5
E 6
F 7
G 8
H 9
I 0
J 1